CLASSIC
NORTH AMERICAN
STEAM

CLASSIC
NORTH AMERICAN
STEAM

NILS HUXTABLE

MetroBooks

MetroBooks

An Imprint of the Michael Friedman Publishing Group, Inc.

This edition published by the Michael Friedman Publishing Group, Inc., by arrangement with World Publications Group, Inc. and Barnes & Noble, Inc.

Library of Congress Cataloging-in-Publication Data available upon request.

ISBN 1-58663-205-1

Printed in China by Leefung Asco Printers, Ltd

10 9 8 7 6 5 4 3 2 1

For bulk purchases and special sales, please contact:
Friedman/Fairfax Publishers
Attention: Sales Department
15 West 26th Street
New York, NY 10010
212/685-6610   FAX 212/685-3916

Visit our website:
www.metrobooks.com

Page 1: No 19 of the Oregon, Pacific & Eastern leads an excursion past Dorena Lake in Oregon. *Pages 2-3:* Bound for Summit, Wisconsin, Western Coal & Coke No 1 doubleheads with Saginaw Timber No 2. *These pages:* Leaving a billow of smoke behind it, Union Pacific's 4-6-6-4 Challenger No 3985 charges across the gently rolling foothills of the West.

All photos by Nils Huxtable unless otherwise noted.

Contents

INTRODUCTION

An era ended in 1960, when the major railroads in the United States and Canada dieselized. Having served the continent for more than a century, North America's most visible symbol of industrial supremacy was obsolete. In railroad yards everywhere, thousands of steam engines stood gathering rust or waiting silently in their roundhouse stalls for an emergency call to service. Reinstatement, even a temporary one, never came: a recession, the accompanying decrease in traffic and an abundance of new diesel power made sure of that.

Indeed, the commitment to advanced technology was so complete that the management of most railroads wanted nothing to do with nostalgia, and most of the surviving steam locomotives—some of them recently rolled out—were sold for a fraction of their true value and unceremoniously cut up for scrap. A few were donated to parks and museums, but, even so, such historically significant classes as the New York Central's Niagaras met the torch. Some railroads—for whom profit was far more important than preservation and the past something to be obliterated rather than cherished—could not be bothered to save even one steam locomotive for posterity. Certain railfan extremists may be justified in holding the view that such companies, whose names have since been lost to mergers over the years, are hardly worth remembering.

Still, rather than mourn what is gone, it is better to appreciate what remains. We can be grateful that a handful of railroads went out of their way not only to preserve part of their heritage but to continue operating steam locomotives long after the cost of overhauling and maintenance had become an extravagance. Tribute is owed to such railroads as the Union Pacific and the Southern (now Norfolk Southern), who felt a steam locomotive was a more effective public relations tool at the head of a train than behind a chain link fence. The author well remembers his first steam excursion: a trip from Denver to Laramie behind 4-8-4 No 8444—the only steam locomotive in North America never to be officially retired. That was 30 years ago. These days, the UP and Norfolk Southern are still in the forefront of main line steam operation, and other railroads—among them Conrail and Southern Pacific—are eager to join the club.

The increase in the number of main line steam excursions in recent years has been paralleled by a flourishing of tourist railroads and museums. On a few miles of track, smaller steam locomotives—2-6-0s, 2-8-0s, Ten-wheelers—and geared engines

are put through their paces, providing passengers with an earful of bells and whistles for a nominal charge. In California, for example, where main line steam after 1958 was anathema to the principal railroads serving the state, the Sierra Railway became a shrine for enthusiasts in need of a whiff of smoke, hot steam and lubricating oil. Everything remains in its original condition, and steam trains are once again whistling their way through the foothills of the Mother Lode.

In certain instances, however, restoration of steam locomotives has been less than satisfying, especially for those who remember them in regular service. Alas, some tourist lines hold the philosophy that the real thing is just not good enough. Gaudy paint schemes, 'old time' smokestacks, headlights, cowcatchers and, more recently, plates and plaques advertising the locomotive's sponsorship have been added in what can be termed the 'Petticoat Junction' approach to preserving railroad history, or what noted railroad authority Ron Zeil has labeled 'Tasteless, Tedious and Tortured.'

Fortunately, these eyesores are the exceptions. Among preservationists and the general public alike, there is an increasing awareness that a steam locomotive need only be itself to arouse fascination and draw a crowd. With a degree of selectivity, an album such as this can show many examples of accurate restoration that illustrate the development of steam locomotives while evoking the mood of this exciting period in North American history. Thus, worthy organizations such as the Mid-Continent Railway Museum at North Freedom, Wisconsin, which have resisted the temptation of crass commercialism, are given extensive coverage. The author still recalls his first glimpse of the museum's Chicago & Northwestern 4-6-0 charging through the autumn foliage of Wisconsin. It captured the feeling of branch line railroading as it once was, free from fakery or tomfoolery. Here, then, are a few glimpses of the North American steam scene as it is today. The dedication and enthusiasm of those involved in steam preservation—many of them volunteers—have helped to make these photographs possible. May Jamestown and North Freedom and the steam programs of Union Pacific and Norfolk Southern live on as a legacy to future generations.

Opposite: No 28 of the Sierra Railway serves as a reminder of the glorious days of steam.

The 4-4-0 American

For fifty years, the American, or Eight-wheeler, enjoyed widespread popularity as the predominant locomotive on the North American continent. The swivel four-wheel leading truck made the 4-4-0 well-suited to the steep grades, severe curvature and primitive roadbed of railroads in the mid-nineteenth century. With widely spaced wheels, the American was easy to maintain and repair, but a narrow firebox limited its hauling capacity and the increasingly heavy trains of the 1900s required larger locomotives, such as the 4-6-2 Pacific. By 1900, construction of new 4-4-0s had almost ceased, but not before a grand total of 25,000 had been turned out by such manufacturers as Rogers, Baldwin, Cooke and Mason.

On the *opposite page* is the famous *Inyo*, built in 1875 by Burnham, Parry, Williams and Company (later Baldwin) for the Virginia & Truckee Railroad. Used by Paramount Pictures in many movies between 1938 and 1968, the *Inyo* now resides at the Nevada State Railroad Museum in Carson City.

One of the oldest operating 4-4-0s in Canada is former Canadian Pacific Railway No 22, supplied by Dubs and Company of Scotland in 1882. Sold in 1918 to City of Winnipeg Hydro to become their No 3, the 4-4-0 remained in regular service until the early 1960s. During the summer months, the engine hauls tourist trains for the Prairie Dog Central. Both the No 3, owned by the Vintage Locomotive Society, and the *Inyo* are seen *below*, side by side at Vancouver's Steamexpo.

Among the last 4-4-0s built was Pennsylvania Railroad No 1223 *(right)*, which emerged from the Pennsy's own Juniata Shops in 1905. Donated to the Railroad Museum of Pennsylvania in 1979, the 1223 is a regular performer on the Strasburg Railroad.

The 4-4-2 Atlantic

A 4-4-2 built in 1896 for the Atlantic City Railroad gave the wheel arrangement its name. The two-wheel trailing truck supported a larger firebox, resulting in a passenger locomotive that was powerful as well as fast. The most remarkable Atlantics of all were those built by Alco for the Milwaukee Road's *Hiawatha* in 1935. Fitted with air-smooth shrouds, these streamlined speedsters could top 100 miles per hour with ease. Unfortunately, none were preserved.

An Atlantic that still sees occasional use, however, is the Railroad Museum of Pennsylvania's No 8063. This locomotive carries the identity of a more famous classmate, No 7002—which in 1905 was credited with a maximum speed of 127.1 miles per hour. The original was scrapped, and the 8063 is its stand-in. Doublehead-ing with 4-4-0 No 1223, the replacement 7002 *(below)* represents the classic turn-of-the-century 4-4-2. Longer trains of heavy-weight steel cars were beyond their hauling capacity, and the more powerful Pacifics relegated most Atlantics to suburban service.

Also on display at the Railroad Museum of Pennsylvania is one of the Pennsy's large-boilered E6 Class Atlantics: No 460 *(opposite)*, built in 1914. This engine hauled a two-coach 'Flyer' from Washington to New York, carrying news footage of aviator Charles Lindbergh's return from Paris in 1927.

Eighty E6s were built, making a grand total of 573 Pennsylvania Railroad 4-4-2s. Later employed on New Jersey commuter trains, No 460 and other E6s lasted into the 1950s.

The 0-6-0 Switcher

The 0-6-0 type was more widespread in Europe than in North America, where it was generally limited to switching duties. Even so, large numbers were built in the United States and Canada, and the very last steam locomotives constructed for a US railroad were 0-6-0 switchers that emerged from the Norfolk & Western Railroad's Roanoke factory in 1953. Small driving wheels and a small firebox and boiler characterized most of these engines.

Coal-fired 4466 (*these pages*) is one of the 'Harriman Standard' designs adopted by both the Union Pacific and Southern Pacific railroads. Built by Lima, the 4466 was among the last in a series of similar engines delivered to the UP in 1920. After working in Cheyenne, Wyoming, and Grand Island, Nebraska, for most of its career, the powerful switcher was donated to the California State Railroad Museum in Sacramento.

Although the 4466 usually hauls a train of passenger cars, museum staff kindly consented to the photographer's request for a 'caboose hop'. The resulting picture shows the 0-6-0 in a more authentic pose, reminiscent of the days when the 4466 was still earning its keep for the mighty UP.

One of the smaller 'goats' that once switched yards and factories across the continent is Northern Pacific E-9 Class 0-6-0 No 1070 *(below)*, built by Alco in 1907. Taken out of service in 1959, this was the NP's last active steamer. Today, the 1070 belongs to the Culp family and operates on their Lake Whatcom Railway, near Wickersham, Washington.

Saddle- and side-tank 0-6-0s were also built. Typical of the group is Great Western's 0-6-0 ST No 3 *(below)*, a 1928 Porter that was used to position hoppers of sugar beets at the company's plant in Billings, Montana. No 3 was one of the few steam locomotives to see revenue service in North America in the 1980s. The two principal Canadian railroads—the Canadian Pacific Railway and Canadian National—acquired large numbers of 0-6-0s. Former CNR No 7312 was built by Baldwin for the Grand Trunk Railway in 1908. After various renumberings, the locomotive became a member of Class 0-9a and survived until the end of steam in Canada. It is now on the Strasburg Railroad's roster as their No 31 *(opposite)*.

The 2-6-0 Mogul

The first 2-6-0, or Mogul, appeared in France in 1841, but it was not until the 1860s, when North American builders began turning out 2-6-0s en masse, that the type came into its own in the United States and Canada as a general service locomotive. Between 1860 and 1910, no fewer than 11,000 Moguls were built. In practice, 2-6-0s were assigned to freights, but despite their relatively small driving wheels, they could exceed their accepted maximum speed limit of 50 miles per hour when used on light passenger trains. The Moguls became useful branch line engines when larger, more powerful locomotives of the 2-8-0 Consolidation type ousted them from main line duties.

Dardanelle & Russellville No 9 (below) was built by Baldwin for the Cincinnati, New Orleans & Texas Railroad Company. The diminutive 2-6-0, now part of the Mid-Continent Railroad Museum's meticulously restored collection at North Freedom, Wisconsin, is seen heading a train along the branch to Quartzite.

In the picture opposite, No 9 takes water from the wooden water tank in the North Freedom yard. Such scenes were once commonplace in rural areas of North America, where the country branch line served as an important link with the outside world. Though the D & R itself is now history, No 9's cab and tender still carry the initials of that backwoods Arkansas railroad.

D & R No 9 *(opposite)*—doubleheading with Chicago & North-western Ten-wheeler No 1385—looks puny by comparison, yet it puts on an impressive show while helping the 4-6-0 pull a passenger train of heavyweight equipment upgrade near Summit, Wisconsin.

A much larger Mogul and another Baldwin graduate is Southern Pacific Class M-6 No 1744 *(below)*, one of the numerous 2-6-0s saved by the railroad and donated to cities along its route as the steam era came to a close. On display at Corrine, Utah from 1959 until 1981, the 1744 now leads a more useful existence: hauling passengers on the Heber Creeper, located at Heber City, Utah.

Southern Pacific owned 355 Moguls, some of which transferred their lines south of the Rio Grande; these engines remained in Mexico City after 1951 when the Mexican government assumed control of SP's operations there.

Another view of the 1744 *(these pages)* shows the engine nearing the end of its run at Charleston, Utah. Projects to restore at least two more Southern Pacific Moguls have been considered.

More recent steamings of No 25 have included movie work (*Stand By Me*) and snow trains. Near the wooden water tank in Bartle, California, No 25 *(below)* makes a run-by for photographers.

The 4-6-0 Ten-Wheeler

Indisputably the best general service type of all was the 4-6-0, or Ten-wheeler. Beginning in 1850, approximately 16,000 4-6-0s were constructed. They were used in fast passenger service, on commuter trains and on slow freights. Equally comfortable on main or branch lines, the Ten-wheeler survived into the last decade of steam operation in the United States and Canada. Many 4-6-0s escaped the scrapper's torch, and a few have been restored to active duty by museum groups.

The Chicago & Northwestern Railroad employed many of its Ten-wheelers—including No 1385 (Alco 1907)—on commuter trains. These days the locomotive *(these pages)* seems quite at home on the Mid-Continent Railway at North Freedom, Wisconsin. Those former Lackawanna commuter cars may seem a bit out of place on this rural branch line, but minor details are perhaps best overlooked when the desired effect of railroading as it used to be has been achieved.

Ten-wheelers also served the narrow gauge. Looking as though it just arrived with the thrice-weekly freight from Owenyo, Southern Pacific's *Slim Princess* No 9 *(opposite)* waits at Laws, California, as it has done since 1960, when the last segment of the old Carson & Colorado closed. Built by Baldwin in 1909 for the Nevada-California-Oregon Railway, No 9 became SP's last steam locomotive to operate in regular service.

Undoubtedly the most-photographed locomotive in the world is Sierra Railway No 3 *(below)*, which has been featured in many television shows and Westerns, including the classic *High Noon*. Built as a coal-burner in 1981 by Rogers Locomotive Works for the Prescott & Arizona Central Railway, the 4-6-0 continues 'to act naturally' for the cameras of the rail buff and Hollywood director alike.

To celebrate the 1988 resumption of steam excursions on the Sierra Railway, No 3 doubleheaded with 2-8-0 No 28 *(these pages)* on the grade up Montezuma Hill, between Chinese Camp and Jamestown, California. Based at the Railtown 1897 roundhouse, both engines are favorites with railway enthusiasts, particularly those in California, where the Sierra continued to operate steam locomotives long after other railroads had dispensed with theirs.

There is no mistaking the Baldwin lineage of Nevada Northern No 40, shown *below* at East Ely, Nevada. Built in 1910, the Ten-wheeler returned to active duty in 1987, after a quarter century of storage inside the East Ely locomotive shops. Occasionally, the engine is fired up to take two wooden clerestory-roof cars over the tracks of this once bustling copper-hauling short line.

Another Baldwin, No 25 *(below)* of the Virginia & Truckee Railroad, served its owner from 1905 until 1947, when the engine was sold to RKO Radio Pictures. Now housed at the Nevada State Railroad Museum in Carson City, Nevada, No 25 is one of the many pieces of V & T equipment keeping the memory of that lost, lamented railroad alive. On selected weekends, the comely Ten-wheeler hauls three restored V & T cars around a mile-long loop of museum trackage.

Northern Pacific Class S-10 No 328 *(opposite)* was intended, not for the branch lines of Minnesota, but for the main lines of South Manchuria in China. Alco built the engine in 1905, and NP acquired it in 1907, using it primarily on branch freight and mixed train duties, for which those 57-inch diameter driving wheels were ideal. Donated to the city of Stillwater, Minnesota, in 1955, this maid-of-all-work is currently operated by the Minnesota Transport Museum.

Western Coal & Coke No 1, another Canadian in exile, was built by Montreal Locomotive Works in 1913 for a coal mining concern in Alberta. Nowadays, No 1 hauls passengers on the Mid-Continent Railway, where its duties sometimes include pulling a snow train. *Below* we see the 4-6-0 piloting a 2-8-2 through the February snow near Devil's Chair, Wisconsin.

The 4-6-2 Pacific

Mystery surrounds the origin of the name 'Pacific.' One theory holds that the 4-6-2 earned the name Pacific when some locomotives of this wheel arrangement were shipped across the Pacific to New Zealand. Another theory suggests that the source is the Missouri Pacific, following delivery of a batch of 4-6-2s to that railroad in 1902. Whatever the origin of the name, the advantages of the Pacific over the Atlantic were its longer boiler and greater horsepower.

Between 1900 and 1930, roughly 6000 4-6-2s were constructed. Many of the engines built for the Harriman-controlled railroads eventually received boosters and larger cylinders, with a resulting increase in tractive power. Though considered pas-

senger locomotives, some Pacifics were pressed into freight service, particularly during the motive power shortages of World War II. Under the United States Railway Association (USRA), formed during World War I to relieve locomotive shortages, a number of standard designs—including light and heavy versions of the Pacific—were constructed for US Railroads.

The Kentucky Railroad Museum's 4-6-2 No 152 is one of the few surviving Louisville & Nashville steam locomotives. Built by Rogers in 1905, the K-1 Class engine now gleams with years of restoration work by museum volunteers. On *these pages*, we see the graceful 4-6-2 traveling the tracks of the 'Old Reliable' once more, with a fantrip from Louisville to Corbin, Kentucky.

Savannah & Atlanta No 750 *(these pages)* originally belonged to the Florida East Coast Railroad. Donated to the National Railroad Historical Society, Atlanta Chapter in 1962, the 1910 Alco became a familiar sight on excursions during the 1960s and 1970s as the Southern Railway steam program gained momentum. Today, the 750 is operated out of Atlanta on specials for the New Georgia Railroad.

The Pacific type was a favorite with both Canadian transcontinentals, particularly the CPR, and hundreds of them were added to that railroad's roster over the years. CPR Pacific G-3 No 2317 *(below)*, wearing the traditional CPR passenger paint scheme of Tuscan red with gold lining, black and gunmetal grey, was built by the Montreal Locomotive Works in 1923. Purchased by the late Nelson Blount in 1965, it was restored to working order in 1978. Today, No 2317 forms part of the Steamtown collection in Pennsylvania, where it has been repainted black with gold lining and lettering.

The last steam locomotive constructed at the CPR's own Angus shops was G-5a No 1201 *(opposite)*, shown here at Taft, British Columbia, during the Last Spike celebrations of 1985. Normally, the engine resides at the National Museum of Science and Technology in Ottawa. The 1201 powers excursions over a branch line to Wakefield, Quebec, and appears at special rail events in other parts of eastern Canada.

The 4-6-4 Hudson

In Europe, the 4-6-4 was called a Baltic. In the United States, however, the New York Central bestowed the name 'Hudson' in honor of the river that paralleled the railroad's 'water level route.' The 4-6-4 was basically an extended 4-6-2, but the Hudson's four-wheel trailing truck and larger firebox enabled the engine to produce more steam and attain higher speeds than the average Pacific. Over 500 Hudsons saw service in the United States, and 70 in Canada.

The most famous 4-6-4 in the United States was the New York Central's fabulous J3a, a later Alco design of 1937. Some of these engines were given futuristic streamlining and assigned to such premier trains as the *Empire State Express*. Alas, none of the Central's Hudsons were preserved.

In Canada, the CPR used its 65 Hudsons as general service locomotives, and 45 of them were semi-streamlines and named Royal Hudsons after two 4-6-4s hauled King George VI across the country in 1939. Embossed crowns were later fitted to the side skirting. While the restoration of H-le Class Royal Hudson No 2860 under provincial sponsorship in 1974 was a welcome development, authenticity was largely ignored. As a result, the only operating Royal Hudson in Canada was redecorated with plates, plaques and crests. The flaws in 2860's appearance are obvious when one compares the photograph on the *opposite page*, taken near Britannia, with the pre-restoration scene from 1974 *(below)*. No frills or frippery here; just the genuine article. A view from the vestibule *(right)* shows the 4-6-4 climbing through the West Vancouver.

Close to the water's edge, No 2860 *(these pages)* passes Porteau Cove, on the southbound run from Squamish to North Vancouver. CPR enthusiasts can only hope that one day the locomotive will be returned to its original condition and regain some of its lost glory. Perfection, after all, cannot be improved upon.

The 2-8-0 Consolidation

The first radially turning two-wheel truck was invented in 1866. The feature made the 2-6-0 and the 2-8-0 Consolidation among the most useful of early steam designs. So-named because the arrival of the first 2-8-0 on the Lehigh Valley coincided with that railroad's consolidation with the Lehigh & Mahoning, the type became the principal freight hauler on most main lines. More than 23,000 2-8-0s were built for domestic use and about 12,000 for export, but a relatively small firebox and driving wheels no larger than 63 inches limited both steaming capacity and speed. Large-boilered 2-8-0s were home-built by such railroads as the Pennsy, the Western Maryland and the Reading. The most powerful Consolidations were three experimental compounds constructed by Alco for the Delaware & Hudson, but by 1930, the effectiveness of the 2-8-0 as a heavy freight engine was already being challenged by the 2-8-2, or Mikado.

Two Baldwin Consolidations appear on these pages; both exemplify short line motive power of the early 1900s. Former Longview, Portland & Northern No 680 (*opposite*) began its tour of duty in 1916 with the Louisiana & Pacific Railway. Carrying the name of the Virginia & Truckee Railroad and the number 29, the 2-8-0 is seen climbing the grade into Virginia City with a special photographer's freight train.

In contrast, the 68-year life of Sierra Railway No 28 (*below*) has been relatively uncomplicated. The Jamestown, California roundhouse has always been its home, and apart from roles in movies, it has always worn the hallowed name 'Sierra' on its tender.

Heading a special freight jointly sponsored by Steamscenes, Trains Unlimited Tours and the Whistle Stop Hobby Shop of Sacramento, No 28 *(these pages)* turns back the clock. With a plume of smoke that would make an environmentalist shudder, the sprightly 2-8-0 makes yet another movie run-by for the appreciative cameramen.

Dedicated enthusiasts will go to great lengths to recreate the past: Baldwin-built 2-8-0 No 77 *(these pages)* of 1920, a former Frisco engine, mirrored in the water below, crosses the Mississippian Railway trackage that was relocated to make way for the Tombigbee Waterway. The MR was one of a handful of short lines using steam power on a regular basis during the 1960s. This freight, organized by noted photographer and author John Craft, effectively recaptures the atmosphere of a bygone era.

A full frontal view of No 77 (*opposite*) shows preserved steam as it should be—authentically restored, unspoiled by the bright paint and ornamentation many tourist railroads are convinced will attract the public.

In Mexico, main line steam lingered until 1967, although it was not until recently that Mexico's now dieselized National Railways began to understand the appeal of the steam locomotive. One of the fortunate few to be spared the scrapper's torch is 2-8-0 No 1150 (*below*), shown here with diesel assistance on an excursion from Mexico City to Tula. Most of Mexico's steam power came over from the United States and No 1150, a 1921 Alco, is no exception.

On the narrow gauge, too, the Consolidation proved to be a reliable workhorse. The Colorado Railroad Museum's Denver & Rio Grande Western C-19 Class 2-8-0 *(these pages)* was 102 years old when this picture was taken in 1983. Sold to a junkyard in 1948, the engine was saved through the efforts of Bob Richardson, the museum curator, who has managed to assemble an impressive collection of steam locomotives, both narrow and standard gauge.

Some Mikados were custom-built for logging railroads. Porter No 5 *(opposite)* went to the Flora Logging Company at Carlton, Oregon, in 1924. The engine had three more owners before being donated to the Western Washington Forest Industries Museum. These days it powers excursions on the Mount Rainier Scenic Railroad at Elbe, Washington.

Another 2-8-2 logger with a varied career is No 2 *(below)*, a Baldwin of 1912 shown switching the Mid-Continent Railway's yard at North Freedom, Wisconsin, prior to heading a snow train. The locomotive is lettered for the company it first served: Saginaw Timber of Keniston, Washington. Subsequent owners included Rayonier, the last logging company in that state to operate conventional rod engines.

So successful was the Mikado type that the USRA designated both light and heavy versions as part of its standardization program. One of the 1266 lightweights used by more than 50 railroads is Nickel Plate Road No 587, shown here getting underway from Frankfort, Indiana, with an excursion returning from Logansport to Indianapolis. Restored by volunteers of the Indiana Transportation Museum, the H-61 was making its first fantrip since retirement in 1955.

Few logging railroads remain today. And though the tracks of Rayonier, a company that relied upon steam locomotives into the 1960s, have been torn up in favor of trucks, No 70 (Baldwin 1922) has found a new home on the Puget Sound & Snoqualmie Valley Railroad, located just east of Seattle. The handsome 2-8-8 is shown *below*, approaching a grade crossing near the Snoqualmie depot.

On the slim-gauge tracks of the Rio Grande, the Mikado staged a last stand in the history of the steam locomotive in North America. Though the real show ended in 1968, the whistles of outside-frame 2-8-2s continue to echo in Cumbres Pass and through the canyon of the Animas River. With aspen leaves turning gold in the crisp autumn air, two K-28s (*opposite*) combine forces near Elk Park, Colorado.

At work on both the Durango & Silverton and the Cumbres & Toltec Scenic Railroads are the newer and heavier Mikes of Class K-36. No 481 (*below*), fitted with a snowplow, waits for an assignment at the Durango roundhouse. Two K-36s (*left*), silhouetted against the night sky, are ready to roar away from Chama's leading water tower.

Under Rio Grande ownership, the K-36s never appeared on the Silverton branch. However, they did visit Durango on freights from Antonito. The K-28 Class was constructed by Alco in 1923, the K-36 by Baldwin in 1925.

In what writer Lucius Beebe would have described as 'railroading in the grand manner,' the two K-36 Mikados pictured on the previous page blacken the skies near Dalton, on the climb to Cumbres Pass with a photographer's freight. The practice of positioning a helper engine in the middle of the train was made necessary by weight restrictions on the Lobato trestle.

The 2-8-4 Berkshire and the 2-10-4 Texas

The 2-8-4 Berkshire and 2-10-4 Texas types have much in common: they were the first 'superpower' designs developed by the Lima Locomotive Factory. Employing the first four-wheel trailing truck to accommodate a huge firebox, the Berkshires and Texas types could outpull any 2-8-2 or 2-10-2. The locomotive that ushered in the modern superpower steam era in North America was the 2-8-4 Lima built for the Boston & Albany Railroad: the A-1. The A-1 proved that a steam locomotive could combine both power and speed. The Berkshires were named for a mountain range in Massachusetts, where they first entered service on the B & A.

The Nickel Plate Road and fast freight were synonymous. To roll the cars at speed, the railroad ordered 65 S-Class Berkshires between 1942 and 1948. Many NKP 2-8-4s remained at work until 1958, and a number have been preserved, including No 765 *(opposite and right)*, restored by Fort Wayne Historical Society volunteers. Almost identical to the NKP engines were the 2-8-4s of the Chesapeake & Ohio. No 2716 was overhauled by the Norfolk Southern for steam excursions; the Berk *(below)* received its finishing touches at the NS Irondale, Alabama shops. (Photo by Thomas R Schultz.)

Superpower personified: 2-10-4 No 610 was one of Lima's second batch of Texas engines delivered to the Texas & Pacific Railroad in 1927. A beauty this Texan is not, but the huge boiler and firebox, jutting feedwater heater and maze of pipework indicate pure muscle, augmented by a booster for extra power on starting. After accumulating a million miles in freight service between Texarkana and El Paso, the mighty 2-10-4 was donated to the city of Fort Worth. Restored for the Freedom Train in 1976, the 610 spent its next four years as the Southern Railway's most powerful excursion engine. Little of its 98,000 pounds of tractive effort is needed to roll this twenty-car excursion train into Chattanooga's Citico Yard *(these pages)*, but the sight is impressive nevertheless. Five hundred Texas locomotives and 750 Berkshires were produced.

In the 1940s, the FEFs, or 800s, were assigned all over the Union Pacific, frequenting Portland and Los Angeles, Denver, Omaha and Kansas City. Nowadays, the railroad's only active 4-8-4 visits part of the system where Northerns were seldom, if ever, seen during the 'real' days of steam. Pictured *below* is the 4-8-4 on a run-by near Draper, Utah, on the line from Salt Lake City to Provo.

Constructed at the Norfolk & Western's own shop at Roanoke, Virginia, the streamlined J Class 4-8-4s were powerful, fast and efficient. With driving wheels of 70 inches, they could haul heavy passenger trains unassisted through the Allegheny and Blue Ridge mountains. At the same time, lightweight rods and roller bearings made possible speeds of 100 miles per hour on the straightaway. The J8s air-smooth look—streamlined pilot, bullet nose, skyline casing and running board skirts—made it one of the most aesthetically pleasing modern steam designs. A close-up of sole survivor No 611 (opposite) shows its sleek lines to good advantage. At speed near Appomattox, Virginia (below), the engine is seen making its first excursion run for Norfolk Southern. The 611 belongs to the City of Roanoke, Virginia, and operates under a lease agreement.

Even though the Js were at their best when hauling such name trains as the *Powhatan Arrow*, the *Pocahontas* and the *Tennessean*, they were pressed into freight service during their last years. Even today, the 611 occasionally appears on a freight today. Making light work of a short train coupled behind it to aid in braking, the J *(these pages)* roars away from Anniston, Alabama.

The 2-6-6-2 Articulated

In 1888, the first articulated locomotive appeared, consisting of two engines hinged together and supporting one boiler. This was a Mallet compound built in France. Its high- and low-pressure cylinders provided increased tractive power at slow speeds. Articulated locomotives had two distinct advantages over conventional types, particularly those with ten or more coupled driving wheels: two sets of drivers could carry a larger boiler around sharp curves, and two sets of cylinders required side rods of lighter weight.

The first American articulateds were 0-6-6-0 Mallets built for the Baltimore & Ohio by Alco in 1904. Two years later, Baldwin built the first American Mallet with leading and trailing wheels: a Great Northern 2-6-6-2. This wheel arrangement became widely popular; in fact, the last locomotive constructed by Baldwin for the US market was a 2-6-6-2 for the Chesapeake & Ohio.

Smaller engines of this type were also produced, usually equipped with water tanks, for the logging railroads of the West. US Plywood No 11 (Baldwin 1926), like many other logging locomotives, had more than one owner. The 11 was renumbered twice and modified. A major alteration was the removal of the saddle tanks with which the engine had originally been provided in favor of a water tender. The scenes on *these pages* show No 11 powering Santa trains on the Puget Sound & Snoqualmie Valley Railway in western Washington.

Before surgery, No 11 looked like No 4 of the Clover Valley Lumber Company. Remaining in the Feather River region for most of its working life, the 2-6-6-2T was finally donated to the Pacific Locomotive Association, which now operates trains on the Niles Canyon Railway near Fremont, California. *Here* we see No 4, a Balwin graduate of 1924, passing a California Western 'Skunk' railcar at Molate Beach, formerly the preservation group's operating center.

The Climax

The cylinders on the Climax were mounted high, one on each side of the smokebox. Slanting downward, they were connected to a lateral shaft which drove a main shaft running longitudinally, as on the Heisler.

Ex-Hillcrest Lumber No 10 is also on the Mount Rainier Scenic Railroad's roster. These two views of the 62-year-old engine show it with a train of skeleton log cars near Mineral, Washington *(opposite)* and at the head of a passenger consist on the Nisqually River Bridge *(below)*.

The No 10 was one of the last steam engines to see service on Vancouver Island, British Columbia, where it was used by Hillcrest Lumber until 1969. In 1981, the 10 had the distinction of being the only geared locomotive to appear at the Sacramento Railfair.

COPYRIGHT © 1998 By FOUNDATION PRESS

11 Penn Plaza, Tenth Floor
New York, NY 10001
Phone (212) 760–8700
Fax (212) 760–8705

Library of Congress Cataloging-in-Publication Data

Teeter, Dwight L.
    Law of mass communications : freedom and control of print and
broadcast media / by Dwight L. Teeter, Jr., Don R. Le Duc, Bill
Loving. — 9th ed.
        p.   cm.
    Includes index.
    ISBN 1–56662–602–1
    1. Press law—United States.   2. Mass media—Law and legislation—
United States.   I. Le Duc, Don R.   II. Loving, Bill.   III. Title.
KF2750.N4 1998
343.7309'98—dc21   98–7518

*TEXT IS PRINTED ON 10% POST
CONSUMER RECYCLED PAPER*

LAW

OF

MASS COMMUNICATIONS

FREEDOM AND CONTROL OF PRINT AND BROADCAST MEDIA

By

DWIGHT L. TEETER, JR., Ph.D.
Professor and Dean, College of Communications
University of Tennessee, Knoxville

DON R. LE DUC, J.D., Ph.D.
Professor Emeritus, Department of Mass Communication
University of Wisconsin—Milwaukee

BILL LOVING, J.D.
Associate Professor, H.H. Herbert School of Journalism
and Mass Communication, University of Oklahoma

NINTH EDITION

New York, New York
FOUNDATION PRESS
1998

FOR TISH, ALICE AND JODY

*

PREFACE TO THE NINTH EDITION

Students in media law classes frequently ask, "Can they do that?" The answer is, "Apparently so, they did it and it seems they could." Now was it legal? And if so, was it ethical? All too often, students and practitioners return a blank stare when such questions confront them.

They will learn—through taking a first course in communications law that this textbook serves—that no law class or law text can give the right answer for every question that comes up. Each occurrence rests on its own unique facts that will govern its outcome. New issues arise as media evolve. Because of this, Law of Mass Communications presents governing principles along with case illustrations.

This textbook is not intended to turn students of mass communications into legal experts. It is intended to point out pitfalls involved in professional communication and to lay out compelling reasons for preserving free expression, openness in government, and the rights of the individual.

The book continues to serve four purposes for students of mediated communication:

First, gaining added appreciation for (or dismay over) the workings of the legal process.

Second, surveying areas of law essential for the mass communication practitioners who hope to "stay out of legal trouble," areas including libel, invasion of privacy, and copyright.

Third, discussing and suggesting ways of coping with problems of getting access to government records and meetings.

Fourth, acquainting students with some of the emerging contours of the rapidly evolving information environment from government regulation of new communication technology to regulation of old and familiar systems.

As this Ninth Edition of Law of Mass Communications reflects change in the law, it also reflects changing authorship of this long-lived textbook.

Dr. Harold L. Nelson, founding co-author of this book, died in 1996, although much of his scholarship remains in this book. A brief statement of tribute to Bud Nelson appears in the front-matter of this edition.

Dr. Don R. Le Duc, Ph.D., J.D., Emeritus Professor of Mass Communication, University of Wisconsin-Milwaukee, provided his expertise in electronic communication, new technologies, and entertainment law in the Sixth (1989), Seventh (1992), and Eighth (1995) Editions. His contributions also remain, and form the backbone of those chapters dealing with regulation of electronic and emerging media and media ownership. Although he took no active part in preparing this edition, his contributions—in both substance and friendship—continue.

Bill Loving, J.D., Associate Professor of Journalism, and Adjunct Professor of Law at the University of Oklahoma, terms himself an occasional First Amendment litigator and consultant on libel, privacy, copyright, and access lawsuits. In 1997, he won a freedom of information award from the Oklahoma Society of Professional Journalists.

The authors thank those who have helped us in the preparation of this Ninth Edition. We gratefully acknowledge the American Society of Newspaper Editors and the Society of Professional Journalists for permission to reproduce their codes of ethics in Appendix E. Special thanks go to the librarians at the University of Wisconsin-Milwaukee, to Professor Steven M. Barkan of the Marquette University Law Library, to William J. Beintema, Director, and to Jean E. Moore, Instructor, both of the University of Tennessee Law Library. Special mention goes to Dean Richard S. Wirtz and to Peggy Goodman, Assistant to the Dean, University of Tennessee College of Law.

Particularly helpful to Dwight Teeter were Tennessee colleagues, Professor Dorothy A. Bowles, Daniel J. Foley, Herbert H. Howard, Barbara A. Moore, and Dean Emeritus Kelly Leiter. Noted also are the contributions of Knoxville attorney Richard L. Hollow, a distinguished advocate for the First Amendment.

Bill Loving's thanks go to Professor David Dary, Director of the University of Oklahoma's H.H. Herbert School of Journalism and Mass Communication and to Professor Wilma Wirt of Virginia Commonwealth University.

DWIGHT L. TEETER, JR.
BILL LOVING

TRIBUTE TO HAROLD L. NELSON
(1917–1996)

With sadness, we note the passing of the founding author of this book, Dr. Harold L. (Bud) Nelson, Professor Emeritus of the University of Wisconsin-Madison. He died February 8, 1996, at the age of 78. A native of Fergus Falls, MN, he received a B.A. in Journalism from the University of Minnesota before enlisting in the Navy on December 8, 1941, the day after the attack on Pearl Harbor. He served in the Navy until 1946. He worked for United Press before returning to the University of Minnesota to complete M.A. and Ph.D. degrees.

He arrived in Madison in 1955, after teaching at Texas Tech University, the University of Iowa, and at the University of California, Berkeley. In Madison, he taught media law and history to generations of mass communication students. His teaching was fueled by his distinguished scholarship, for which he won the Deutschmann Award, the signal honor of the Association for Education in Journalism and Mass Communication (AEJMC) for significant contributions to Journalism research. His path-breaking scholarship in the legal history of early America and in communication law was widely known and admired. His books included Law of Mass Communications: Freedom and Control of Print and Broadcast Media, which he led for five editions and provided the impetus for the sixth. His other books were Libel in News of Congressional Investigating Committees, and Freedom of the Press from Hamilton to the Warren Court. He also served the AEJMC as president and won the Alumni Distinguished Service Award of the University of Minnesota.

As his obituary said, "Bud Nelson was known for his love of poetry and music, his sense of humor, his dedication to the University of Wisconsin, his integrity in all matters, his love of family." He is survived by his wife of 54 years, Ann Sullivan Nelson, by his children, Susan Goldsmith and Eric Nelson, and by six grand-children.

We count ourselves blessed to have known and worked with Bud Nelson, as his students, his colleagues, and as his fond and admiring friends. We're still his students.

DWIGHT L. TEETER, JR.
DON R. LE DUC

*

SUMMARY OF CONTENTS

TABLE OF CONTENTS

APPENDICES

TABLE OF CONTENTS

*

LAW

OF

MASS COMMUNICATIONS

FREEDOM AND CONTROL OF PRINT AND BROADCAST MEDIA

*

Part I

PHILOSOPHICAL AND CONSTITU-TIONAL FOUNDATIONS OF FREE EXPRESSION

Chapter 1

FOUNDATIONS FOR FREEDOM

Sec.
1. The Worth of Freedom.
2. The Constitutional Guarantees.
3. "The Intent of the Framers."

A major test of a nation's freedom is the degree of liberty its people have in speaking, writing, and publishing. The hand of authority rests lightly on speech and press at some places and times, heavily at others. But its presence is felt everywhere, including the nations of the Western World which generally consider themselves the most freedom-loving of all.

Throughout history, some degree of legal control over expression has been in force even in the freest societies. Although values of free speech and press may be considered paramount and exalted, there are circumstances where other values may take priority and win in a conflict over rights. For example, the individual's right to a good reputation limits verbal attacks through the law of civil libel. In wartime, assertions of national security may take precedence over press freedom. Multitudes of laws regulating business, industry and trade apply fully to the commercial press, to advertising, to public relations, and to broadcasting and to newer communication technologies.

The goal of this textbook is to serve students in a first or survey course in communication law. A major reason for this book is to help communicators try to "stay out of trouble," to learn something about the pitfalls of libel and slander, invasion of privacy, and copyright infringement. Perhaps the examples and discussion offered here can serve, as legal historian James Willard Hurst has suggested of his field, like training for wrestlers: to help keep their balance, to avoid being upset by sudden and unexpected onslaughts.[1] And on many occasions, of course, trying to behave ethically will prevent legal questions from arising at all.

[1] James Willard Hurst, Introductory Lecture, course on Legal History, University of Wisconsin–Madison, Spring, 1961.

This book will provide students with some "how to" information, especially in chapters dealing with access to information.[2] It also tries to give students some understanding of the legal systems of the United States, especially as they interact with the sweeping field vaguely called "communication law." The law of mass communications can *not* be taught as if it is some compartmentalized area marked off by logical boundaries. Of necessity, this book cuts across most areas covered in a law school curriculum:

Constitutional Law deals with the basic governmental framework, as with a state constitution or the federal Constitution. The federal Constitution—the highest law of the land—divides government powers into the legislative, executive, and judicial branches. Powers of government are apportioned among those branches, and the document also lists, in the First Ten Amendments, powers that the U.S. government may *not* bring to bear on its citizens.

The federal Constitution is one of many constitutions in the United States. There are, after all, fifty-one legal systems: the federal system plus fifty state systems. In addition, there are charters governing the organization and operation of cities and counties. Keep in mind that the federal Constitution is the highest law of the land: state constitutional provisions in conflict with it are not enforceable.

By their nature, as basic or "organic" law, written constitutions are not easily changed. As spelled out in the federal Constitution, it takes the vote of three-fourths of the states (via states' legislatures or called constitutional conventions) to amend the Constitution.

If a state or lower federal court decision conflicts with the federal Constitution, that law or decision may be found unconstitutional and thus null and void. Constitutional law involving the First Amendment guarantee of free speech and press is central to this book.

Most of the nation's law is *statutory:* made by legislatures, from Congress to state legislatures to county boards and city councils. If the meaning of a statute is at issue in a legal case or controversy, the meaning of the statute can be interpreted by courts. This search for meaning, called *statutory construction,* tries to define vague terms in the statute, often by digging back into the statute's *legislative history.* What did the legislature intend to do when it passed the measure?

There are plentiful examples of statutes directly affecting the communication media. Consider, for example, the basic federal anti-

[2] See Chapters 8 and 9.

obscenity law, 18 U.S.C.A. § 1461 [Title or Volume 18, United States Code, at Section 1461.] That statute, passed more than a century ago, forbids sending obscene material through the mails or in interstate commerce. But what is obscene? The statute is unclear. As discussed in Chapter 3, U.S. courts have devoted much energy trying to define "the obscene."

Statutory law was not always the most important branch of law in the United States. Well into the nineteenth century, *common law* was the most important point of growth. *Common law* was law that was "found" or "discovered" by judges, based on the way particular disputes or transgressions were handled by prior judges or courts. It was a tradition of the law. *Common law* is distinct from *civil law*[3]. As Winston Churchill explained in his A History of the English Speaking Peoples, "The law was already there, in the customs of the land, and it was only a matter of discovering it by diligent study and comparison of recorded decisions in earlier cases, and applying it to the particular dispute before the court."[4]

The United States bases its legal system on the *common law* system derived from the English tradition and well into the Nineteenth Century, *common law* was the most important point of growth. Actual judge-made law-making involving an entire area has been rare during the past century. It has been suggested that because of the rarity of common-law creation in this century, there has grown up considerable scholarly fascination with the law of privacy. Privacy law is largely common-law, made by courts instead of legislatures.

Equity is an area which originated in England centuries ago. The Chancellor devised a court—called a Court of Chancery or a Court of Equity (based on what was fair or equitable)—to decide disputes which did not fit into the ordinary framework of the regular or "law" courts. Courts in the United States have combined the functions, and now are said to "sit in both law and equity." Pieces of "equity" remain and are sometimes in the news. For example, in some situations the monetary award remedy available by winning a lawsuit would not be appropriate. Sometimes, what is "equitable" is to have a court order someone to do something (as in a writ of "mandamus," which is Latin for "we demand"), or not to do something (as by a court granting an injunction or "cease and desist" order).

---

[3] *Civil law* also is the term applied to civil lawsuits where one party sues another party to protect private rights. It can be confusing but for all intents and purposes, when you are dealing with law in the United States, the term *civil law* will refer to civil lawsuits. The exception is Louisiana which continued its *civil law* tradition from its French legal antecedents.

[4] Winston S. Churchill, A History of the English Speaking Peoples (New York: Barnes & Noble, 1993), p. 224.

One of the most famous First Amendment cases featured in this book—the "Pentagon Papers" to be discussed in Chapter 2—involved the Supreme Court's overturning a lower court's injunction forbidding *The New York Times* from publishing a series of secret documents on the Viet Nam conflict.

Administrative law has grown rapidly in the past century. As the nation grew more complex, Congress found itself overmatched by commercial and industrial growth involved in the industrial revolution and the nation's westward expansion. Beginning in 1890 with the Interstate Commerce Commission (to regulate railroads), Congress delegated some of its power to an agency. Similar agencies followed; two having particular applicability to the mass media are the sometime regulator of advertising, the Federal Trade Commission (FTC), established in 1914, and the Federal Communications Commission (FCC, established in 1934 but actually following a pattern set by the Federal Radio Commission Act of 1927).

Additionally, the federal Executive branch has the power to make a kind of law through *executive orders*. For example, the "Confidential," "Secret" and "Top Secret" document classifications were established in 1951 by a Presidential executive order by Harry S Truman, and remain in effect today.

Another way of classifying legal actions is as *criminal* and *civil* actions. *Black's Law Dictionary* (Rev. Fifth Ed.) defines a crime as an offense against the state. A crime can be accomplished by *omission,* failing to perform a legally commanded duty (e.g. failure to register for the draft) or *commission* (e.g. killing someone on purpose with a blunt instrument). The latter example could lead to a charge of murder, or wrongful taking of another's life. Crimes are variously classified as *misdemeanors* (minor crimes, usually carrying a jail term of less than a year) and *felonies* (major crimes, generally defined as carrying a jail term of more than a year).

Crimes to be taken up in this book include obscenity, seditious libel, and some aspects of copyright infringement.

Civil Law includes personal damage actions ("lawsuits") in which a person asks for "the establishment, recovery, or redress of private and civil rights." If a publication hurts your reputation by printing a false and harmful statement about you, you could bring a legal action ("sue"), asking for "damages" (see "money"). Much of this book is taken up with discussion of damage actions in the areas of libel, invasion of privacy, and copyright infringement.

Another term which is a staple area in law school curricula is *tort*. It is a French word meaning "wrong," and the law assumes that if persons have serious wrongs done to them, they ought to be able to sue for compensation. Libel is a tort. Invasion of privacy is a tort.

For a further exposure to legal terminology, please see Appendices B and C of this book.

SEC. 1.   THE WORTH OF FREEDOM

Major values underlying free speech and press include society's need for maximum flow of information and opinion, and the individual's right to fulfillment.

Freedom to speak, to write, to travel—and to criticize governments and government officials—now seems as natural as breathing to most residents of the United States. Late in the Twentieth Century, North Americans generally take for granted systems of representative self-government, with legislative and executive officials—and some judges as well—selected at regular intervals via secret ballots.

Taking freedoms for granted can be the world's most dangerous complacency. Particular concern should be directed at official efforts to discourage dissent or to push for some particular orthodoxy. If dissenters' freedoms are not protected, then all freedoms are in danger. Sometimes, individuals will find that they hold views that are widely despised, and will take risks in speaking out, especially in times of great social or political tension. And if there is no dissent, the results may be disastrous. Consider the words of Martin Niemoeller, haunted by the millions of Jews killed in Hitler's Holocaust:[5]

> First they came for the socialists, and I did not speak out—because I was not a socialist. Then they came for the trade unionists, and I did not speak out—because was not a trade unionist. Then they came for the Jews, and I did not speak out—because I was not a Jew. Then they came for me—and there was no one left to speak for me.

Challenges to free expression reach every conceivable topic of discussion and actual and symbolic speech. Laws have been passed and enforced protecting particular religions,[6] flags of both individual states and the United States[7] and even foods.[8]

---

[5] Martin Niemoeller, Exile in the Fatherland, ed. by H.G. Locke (Grand Rapids, MI: Eerdmans, 1986), p. viii.

[6] New York once had a statute denying motion picture exhibitors the ability to show their films if a part of the movie was "immoral, inhuman" or "sacrilegious." Similarly, Tennessee had a statute making it a crime for persons to engage in disorderly conduct which was defined to include the use of "blasphemous" language.

[7] Examples include a Massachusetts statute that made it a crime punishable by fine and imprisonment for "Whoever publicly mutilates, tramples upon, defaces or treats contemptuously the flag of the United States or of Massachusetts ..." and an Arizona Law that declared that "a person who publicly mutilates, defaces, defiles, tramples upon, or by word or act casts contempt upon a flag is guilty of a misdemeanor." "Flag" was defined as including "any flag, standard, color, ensign or

---

8.   See note 8 on page 6.

One crucial test of freedom is the ability to go unpunished after venting severe criticism of those holding political power. And, if a government official can check over what you've written and deny you the right to publish it, that's pre-publication censorship. More than 350 years ago, the now-legendary poet John Milton argued in his *Areopagitica* against pre-publication censorship by church authorities, who then had power inseparable from government. Writing in 1644, Milton declared that because religious truth was so essential to the fate of mankind the authorities should open up the arena for debate. Truth was the only safe basis for a society's life, he wrote in 1644:[9]

> And though all the winds of doctrine were let loose to play upon the earth, so truth be in the field, we do injuriously, by licensing and prohibiting, to misdoubt her strength. Let her and falsehood grapple; who ever knew Truth put to the worse, in a free and open encounter?

Those words from John Milton—expressing what is often called the "diversity principle"—still resound in key American court decisions on the scope of freedom.[10]

Legal scholars generally look to four philosophical bases for freedom of expression.

    I.   *Marketplace of Ideas*

    II.   *Individual Fulfillment*

    III. *Safety Valve*

    IV. *Self–Governance*

    I. Marketplace of Ideas—This philosophy generally is tied to John Milton. Strictly speaking, however, the "marketplace" phrasing should be thought of as a twentieth-century re-wording of

---

shield, or any copy, picture or representation thereof, made of any substance or of any size, purporting to be the flag, standard, color, ensign or shield of the United States or of this state."

    [8] Talk show host Oprah Winfrey was sued under a Texas food disparagement law for more than $1 million after she broadcast a program in which she declared, after learning about bovine spongiform encephalopathy or "mad cow" disease, "It has just stopped me cold from eating another burger." More than a dozen states have enacted laws allowing suits over comments critical of particular foods. See Marianne Lavelle, "Food Abuse: Basis for Suits," The National Law Journal, May 5, 1997, p. A1.

    [9] John Milton, Areopagitica (Chicago, 1953). See Thomas I. Emerson, The System of Freedom of Expression (New York: Random House, 1970), Chap. 1, for discussion of social and individual values of free expression. See also Vincent Blasi, "The Checking Value in First Amendment Theory," 1977 Am.Bar Found.Res.J. 523.

    [10] See, e.g., the dissent by Justice O.W. Holmes, Jr., in Abrams v. United States, 250 U.S. 616, 40 S.Ct. 17 (1919) and Justice Hugo L. Black's opinion for the Court in Associated Press v. United States, 326 U.S. 1, 65 S.Ct. 1416 (1945). See also discussion in Zechariah Chafee, Jr., Free Speech in the United States (Cambridge, Mass., 1964 [6th printing of 1941 ed.]), pp. 3, 29, 298, 316, 325, 559–561.

Milton's arguments from seventeenth-century England re-cast to make a judicial argument in twentieth century America. The "marketplace of ideas" locution came from a passionate dissent by Justice Oliver Wendell Holmes, Jr., denouncing the World War I-era conviction of Jacob Abrams for violating the Espionage Act of 1917 and its 1918 "sedition" amendment. [The case of Abrams v. U.S. (1918) is discussed in more detail at page 19 of this chapter.] In his dissent in *Abrams*, Justice Holmes declared that "the best test of truth is the power of the thought to get itself accepted in the competition of the market ..."[11] So even though "marketplace of ideas" is not precisely in Milton's terminology, his words echo in the history of the Supreme Court. And in some cases, a majority of the Supreme Court of the United States has adopted Milton's belief that a clash of ideas is needed to produce truth.[12]

Milton wrote Areopagitica in response to an act of the English Parliament giving exclusive permission to the Stationers' Company. The Stationers' Company was a guild of government-approved printers who operated essentially in London, where censors could keep close watch on what was being printed. It should be noted that although Milton argued that truth was more likely to emerge from open discussion than from repression, Milton had his own limits. He opposed giving Roman Catholics religious freedom, and even served for a time as a censor under Oliver Cromwell.

Whatever Milton's context, his ideas continued to be important late into the twentieth century. In 1988, for example, New York Times columnist Anthony Lewis quoted from a Miltonian-sounding expression of the diversity principle written by Supreme Court Justice Robert H. Jackson in 1943: After referring to the United States as a country of "individualism and rich cultural diversities," Justice Jackson wrote for the Court in support of a freedom to differ.[13]

> If there is any fixed star in our constitutional constellation, it is that no official, high or petty, can prescribe what shall be orthodox in politics, nationalism, religion or other matters of opinion ...

[11] Abrams v. United States, 250 U.S. 616, 629, 40 S.Ct. 17, 22 (1919).

[12] See, e.g., Associated Press v. United States, 326 U.S. 1, 28, 65 S.Ct. 1416, 1428 (1945), quoting Judge Learned Hand, United States v. Associated Press, 52 F.Supp. 362, 372 (1943). The Supreme Court approvingly quoted Judge Hand's declaration that the First Amendment " ' ... presupposes that right conclusions are more likely to be gathered out of a multitude of tongues than through any kind of authoritative selection.' " That language bears great similarity to John Milton's arguments against licensing and pre-publication censorship made three centuries earlier.

[13] West Virginia State Board of Education v. Barnette, 319 U.S. 624, 63 S.Ct. 1178 (1943). Justice Jackson wrote for the Court in a 7–2 decision that children of Jehovah's Witnesses could not be compelled to salute the flag because this ceremony conflicted with their religious beliefs.

Justice Jackson's words amounted to an extension of the "marketplace of ideas" philosophy. This extension was very much in line with the ideas of the nineteenth century British philosopher John Stuart Mill. In *On Liberty*, Mill wrote that members of society needed access to many kinds of ideas, false as well as true, to discern the truth. Mill declared that government had no legitimate power to suppress opinions:[14]

> If all mankind minus one were of one opinion, and only one person were of the contrary opinion, mankind would be no more justified in silencing that one person, than he, if he had the power, would be justified in silencing mankind.

It is not always easy to separate society's need from the individual's right as the reason for freedom of expression. If the individual's right is thoroughly protected, the social good in the confrontation of ideas presumably follows. The English writer John Locke, often called the philosophical father of the American Revolution, argued persuasively late in the Seventeenth Century in favor of the individual's rights. In words which later echoed in the Declaration of Independence, Locke wrote of the "natural right" of every person to life, liberty, and property. His ideological descendants included speech and press as among those liberties, equally applicable to all men in all times and situations.[15]

In the Twentieth Century, social good arguments have been more compelling than natural rights as a basis for freedom of expression. Society's stake in free speech and press is plain in the structure and functioning of a self-governing people. Only through a "clash of ideas in the open marketplace"[16] can working truths be reached. The social good argument runs that the widest diversity of opinion and information must flow through channels of debate and discussion to arrive at worthwhile solutions to problems adding up to sound public policy. Although Milton's pleas for freer debate were couched in terms of seeking religious truth, Twentieth Century theorists and judges have found the confrontation of idea against idea and fact against fact essential to all kinds of "truth," whether in social relations, politics, economics or art.

II. Individual Fulfillment—A great free press theorist—the late Thomas I. Emerson—argued that the proper goal for a persons is to realize their character and potential as human beings. To do that, minds must be free. Therefore, if any ideas, opinions or beliefs are suppressed, that is negating human nature. So free expression

---

[14] John Stuart Mill, On Liberty (New York: Appleton–Century, 1947), p. 16.

[15] John Locke, Second Treatise of Government, ed. Thomas P. Peardon (N.Y., 1952); Leo Strauss, Natural Right and History (Chicago, 1953).

[16] Cf. Holmes, supra note 5.

is an essential part of a good society that would maximize the goals of its members. Part of Professor Emerson's formulation for freedom was expressed in this way:[17]

> The root purpose of the First Amendment is to assure an effective system of freedom of expression in a democratic society. * * * [F]reedom of expression can flourish, and the goals of the system can be realized only if expression receives full protection...against governmental curtailment at all points.

Another aspect of the Individual Fulfillment basis for free expression comes from Professor C. Edwin Baker who wrote that allowing people to engage in free expression is a way of letting them define themselves. An example can be found in what happened during Operation Desert Storm. Some groups protested against the war, while others demonstrated in favor of the action. During those protests, if you talked with a protester from either group, she would admit that she didn't expect the war to end or Saddam Hussein to abdicate because she is carrying a sign and parading up and down the street. That protester is participating to *define* herself publicly. This is what would be, in Professor Baker's terms, self-realization or self-fulfillment through expression.[18]

III. Safety Valve—A third contention for free expression is the *Safety Valve* argument. That is, if you allow free speech such as in the demonstration against Desert Storm it allows people to make their statements, to vent pressure that might otherwise be diverted into violence such as bombing of ROTC buildings. One of the dangers even of peaceful protest, of course, is that it can reap violence. That is what happened, for example, on a spring day in 1970 at Kent State University, when the National Guard fired on students protesting the Vietnam conflict, killing four and wounding nine. Perhaps the lesson here is that freedom is a risk, and that even a "safety valve" isn't absolutely safe. The risk of freedom, however, however, carries great rewards with it. As legal historian James Willard Hurst has noted, freedom releases creative energies and makes for a productive and livable society.[19]

The importance of freedom to the individual and to society often is challenged. Freedom is always a risk, and in any society, many persons hate and fear the expression of ideas contrary to their own. Is it permissible to denigrate races, nationalities or religions? Should pornographers be allowed to "subordinate" wom-

---

[17] Thomas I. Emerson, The System of Freedom of Expression (New York: Random House, 1970), p. 17.

[18] C. Edwin Baker, Human Liberty & Freedom of Speech (New York: Oxford University Press, 1989), 48–52.

[19] James Willard Hurst, Law and Conditions of Freedom, passim.

en in demeaning or violent depictions? Should a socialist newspaper be allowed to publish in times of threat from "alien ideologies?" Even today, after more than two centuries under the First Amendment to the Constitution proclaiming freedom of speech and press, many Americans would answer that *true freedom* protects only virtuous or responsible communication. But who is to say what is responsible?

There is also the related view that true "liberation" of societies is not possible as long as toleration of aggression in national policies is practiced, or if racial, religious, or class hatred may be stirred up. Following this position, some ideas and policies must be forbidden, for to permit them to be expressed is to tolerate conditions that perpetuate servitude and misery.[20]

Ironically, the right to challenge the very principle of free expression is an indicator of the extent of freedom in a society. In John B. Wolfe's words, " * * * Man can *seem* to be free in any society, no matter how authoritarian, as long as he accepts the postulates of the society, but he can only *be* free in a society that is willing to allow its basic postulates to be questioned."[21]

Selective views of freedom seem insipid when one considers great words by the great Justice Louis D. Brandeis from Whitney v. California.[22] Whitney involved the conviction of a society woman on charges of "syndicalism," that she had participated in the founding of the California Chapter of the Communist Party, a crime worth years in prison.

In a concurring opinion, Justice Brandeis said the Founding Fathers recognized the hazards of discouraging " ...thought, hope and imagination; that fear breeds repression; that repression breeds hate; that hate menaces stable government; that the path of safety lies in the opportunity to discuss freely supposed grievances and proposed remedies, and that the fitting remedy for evil counsels is good ones ..." And fear is a devil. "Men feared witches and burnt women."[23]

IV. Self–Governance—The guarantee of free expression under this theory put forth by constitutional law scholar Alexander Meiklejohn is that speech must be absolutely protected when it deals with issues with which voters will have to deal. If it has to do with public issues, it should be protected. Testifying before a Senate committee in 1955, when rabid anti-Communism known as

[20] Robert P. Wolff, Barrington Moore, Jr., and Herbert Marcuse, A Critique of Pure Tolerance (Boston, 1965), pp. 87ff.

[21] John B. Wolfe, in Wilbur Schramm, Responsibility in Mass Communication (New York, 1957), p. 106.

[22] Whitney v. People of the State of California, 274 U.S. 357, 47 S.Ct. 641 (1927).

[23] 274 U.S. at 375–376, 47 S.Ct. at 648.

McCarthyism caught few if any Communists but smeared the reputations of many loyal Americans, Meiklejohn declared:[24]

> The First Amendment * * * admits of no exceptions. It tells us that the Congress, and by implication, all other agencies of Government are denied any authority whatever to limit the political freedom of the citizens of the United States.

On the other hand, does expression have to be about public issues—about government or politics—to be valuable and protected? Who decides what is public and what is private? What standards will courts and legislatures and prosecutors apply? What about poetry or art? Such expression can inspire, can uplift, and can cause shocked efforts to suppress art or words which energize censors to "do their thing." Under the Meiklejohn self-governance approach, political speech is protected and nonpolitical or commercial speech is in a "second tier:" it may or may not find constitutional protection.

At the dawning of the Twenty-First Century, it seems that self-governance has the greatest support of the four bases for expression discussed above.

SEC. 2. THE CONSTITUTIONAL GUARANTEES

Federal and State Constitutions all guarantee freedom of expression but some State Constitutions declare that citizens are responsible for the abuse of that right.

Protection for the dissenters as well as the advocates of the status quo is part of the basic, organic law of the United States. The Federal and State constitutions unanimously give free expression a position of prime value.

The Americans who wrote and in 1791 adopted the Bill of Rights of the United States Constitution followed a theme in Anglo–American liberty. Those Americans who had seen the breaking of the ties connecting them to Britain in 1776 with the Declaration of Independence drew on a long history of struggle against arbitrary power. With their lively knowledge of their past, they knew of the Englishmen who in 1215 forced King John to sign the Magna Charta—the "large charter" of rights promising lawful rule by duly constituted authority and trial by jury. They knew also of the Englishmen who passed the Habeas Corpus Act in 1679 saying that persons could not be imprisoned except by lawful

---

[24] Alexander Meiklejohn, Testimony of November 14, 1955, U.S. Senate Committee on the Judiciary, Sub–Committee on Constitutional Rights, "Security and Constitutional Rights," pp. 14–15.

authority, and of the English Bill of Rights of 1689.[25]

This sense of history doubtless impelled Americans, after the War for Independence, to set down frameworks of government—first of the emerging states after the Declaration of Independence, and later the Articles of Confederation and Constitution—*in writing*. Government's powers were to be made explicit.[26]

The Constitution of 1787, adopted after weeks of meetings *in secret* by the Constitutional Convention in Philadelphia, proposed much more centralization of power in the national government than did the nation's first constitution, the Articles of Confederation. Although the Constitution of 1787 is much revered today, and was elevated virtually to the level of Divine inspiration by the 1987 Bicentennial Celebration, it should be kept in mind that the Constitution was—and is—a practical political "frame of government" document.[27]

Although much rhetoric has flowed over the Bill of Rights and the First Amendment, the practical political fact remains that the Bill of Rights—and the First Amendment—were political afterthoughts, compromises. Strong Antifederalist opposition led supporters of the Constitution to conclude that the required nine (of thirteen) states would never ratify the Constitution as written.[28] The Antifederalists pushed a boisterous campaign to prevent adoption of the Constitution, claiming it would create a tyrannical, monolithic national government that would trample liberties then enjoyed by the people under the Articles of Confederation. Supporters of the Constitution defused their opposition enough to secure ratification in the states by pledging to add a Bill of Rights to place explicit limits on the national government, providing a list of rights that the United States could not infringe.[29]

After initial reluctance to see a Bill of Rights added, James Madison—as a representative to the First Congress from Virginia—served as a major draftsman and the prime mover in getting the Bill of Rights passed for submission to the states. Madison, although staunchly for civil liberties, had questioned whether a national Bill of Rights would be effective. Later, evidently seeing both substance and political usefulness, Madison finally managed—after several months—to get Congress to consider drafting proposed amendments. Such delay suggests that Congress found other mat-

---

[25] Winston Churchill, The Birth of Britain (New York, 1956), pp. 252–254; Leonard W. Levy, Emergence of a Free Press (Oxford, 1985), Chs. 1 and 2.

[26] Sanford Levinson, Constitutional Faith (Princeton, N.J., 1988) pp. 30–31.

[27] Jackson Turner Main, The Antifederalists: Critics of the Constitution (Chapel Hill, 1961), *passim.*

[28] Ibid., 158–161.

[29] Ibid.

ters more pressing than the promised Bill of Rights. (Although some boosterish renditions of journalism history of the after-dinner speech variety claim the First Amendment was listed first because it was considered most important, it clearly became the first merely because a couple of early draft amendments were edited out.) On December 15, 1791, state ratification of the Bill of Rights gave force to these words making up the First Amendment:[30]

> Congress shall make no law respecting an establishment of religion, or prohibiting the free exercise thereof; or abridging the freedom of speech, or of the press; or the right of the people peaceably to assemble, and to petition the Government for a redress of grievances.

The meaning of the First Amendment was by no means clear. The noted constitutional historian Leonard Levy once contended that a long and bitter civil war—called by Americans the War for Independence—was hardly a good time for the birth or nurturing of civil liberties. In an inspired phrase, Levy asserted in 1960: "There is even reason to believe that the Bill of Rights was more the chance product of political expediency on all sides than of principled commitment to personal liberties."[31]

In the late eighteenth century, and even today, "freedom of speech and press" was an ill-defined and much-debated phrase. But however unsettled the nation's founders were about expanding the reach of free expression beyond that in England, they stated a broad principle in firmly protective terms, and left it to future generations to interpret.[32]

The states adopted their own constitutions, some beginning as early as 1776 and then revising those documents over the years. Freedoms of speech and press evidently were not seen as "absolutes;" this was recognized, over time, by most states' constitutions. Nearly all agreed that freedom of expression could be "abused," although that "abuse" was not defined. Typically, the sentence in the state constitution that started with the guarantee of free expression ended with a qualification. The Constitution of Pennsylvania of 1790 said: "The free communication of thoughts and opinions is one of the invaluable rights of man, and every citizen may freely speak, write and print on any subject, being responsible for the abuse of that liberty."[33]

As the Federal Constitution's First Amendment left the "freedom of speech and press" to future interpretation, the state constitutions tended to leave "abuse" to later definition. The principle

---

[30] U.S. Constitution, Amendment 1.

[31] Levy, Legacy of Suppression (Cambridge, Mass., 1960), pp. vii–viii.

[32] Levy, Emergence, pp. 348–349.

[33] Constitution of Pennsylvania, Art. 1, § 7.

resembled that expressed by Sir William Blackstone, prestigious English legal authority whose famed *Commentaries,* published in 1765–1769, amounted to a kind of legal Bible for the lawyers of the emerging United States. Blackstone's definition of press freedom declared:[34]

> The liberty of the press is indeed essential to the nature of a free state: but this consists in laying no *previous* restraints upon publications, and not in freedom from censure for criminal matter when published. Every freeman has an undoubted right to lay what sentiments he pleases before the public: to forbid this, is to destroy the freedom of the press: but if he publishes what is improper, mischievous, or illegal, he must take the consequences of his own temerity.

Blackstone's formulation had great force as state legal systems emerged. In times before law schools, when would-be lawyers "read law" as assistants to experienced lawyers, a law practice would often be started with two books: the Bible and a copy of Blackstone. Note that Blackstone's definition of freedom guaranteed little beyond no pre-publication censorship. As will be discussed in later sections, criticism of government which Blackstone likely would have considered illegal "abuse" of press freedom now is fully protected as courts interpret the Constitution.

Gitlow v. New York (1925)

Each state's power to define what it considered abuse of free expression long went unchallenged before the Federal courts. But in 1925, the United States Supreme Court in effect *nationalized* the First Amendment.[35]

A hapless radical, Benjamin Gitlow, had been charged with violating the criminal anarchy law of the state of New York. That statute defined criminal anarchy as the doctrine " ' . . . that organized government should be overthrown by force or violence, or by assassination of the executive head or of any of the officials of government, or by any other means.' " The state's statute also made it a crime to advocate, advise or teach such a doctrine. Gitlow and friends had circulated "The Left Wing Manifesto," which advocated "revolutionary mass action" to establish Communist Socialism.[36]

Ironically, even though the Supreme Court of the United States found that a New York jury was warranted in finding Gitlow guilty of advocating governmental overthrow, it also held that the

34 4 Blackstone Commentaries 151, 152.

35 Gitlow v. New York, 268 U.S. 652, 666, 45 S.Ct. 625, 630 (1925).

36 Chafee, op. cit., pp. 318–325.

protections of the First Amendment were applicable to the states through the Fourteenth Amendment, which had been adopted in 1868 to protect the rights of slaves freed by the Civil War. The Fourteenth Amendment declares that *no state* shall "deprive any person of life, liberty or property, without due process of law * * *."[37] In the Gitlow case, the Supreme Court broadened the "liberty" mentioned in the Fourteenth Amendment. Until Gitlow v. New York (1925), state courts' rulings on freedom of expression cases were allowed to stand without review by the U.S. Supreme Court. In the Gitlow decision, however, Justice Sanford wrote for the seven-man majority of the Court that:[38]

> * * * we may and do assume that freedom of speech and of the press—which are protected by the First Amendment from abridgment by Congress—are among the fundamental rights and "liberties" protected by the due process clause of the Fourteenth Amendment from impairment by the States.

These words did not help Ben Gitlow; since the Supreme Court had upheld his conviction, he went to jail. But two members of the Supreme Court—Justices Oliver Wendell Holmes and Louis D. Brandeis—dissented, saying that the "Manifesto" posed little threat of doing harm, let alone a "clear and present danger"[39] from the small minority who shared Gitlow's views. In later years, when the Supreme Court of the United States tended to be more tolerant and supportive of expression than many state courts, the 1925 decision in Gitlow v. New York proved to be the case which opened the door to the Supreme Court review of state courts' actions involving speech and press. After the Gitlow case the Fourteenth Amendment took its place with the First Amendment as a major protection for expression. By helping to "bring the First Amendment home to the states," the Gitlow decision made possible the landmark case limiting pre-publication censorship, Near v. Minnesota ex rel. Olson (1931),[40] and the famous decision protecting the news media against libel suits by public officials, New York Times Co. v. Sullivan (1964).[41]

The Fifth Amendment

One other amendment to the Federal Constitution also applies to expression. This is the Fifth Amendment, which has language similar to part of the Fourteenth Amendment.[42] The Fifth Amend-

[37] U.S. Constitution, Amendment 14.

[38] 268 U.S. 652, 672, 45 S.Ct. 625, 630 (1925).

[39] 268 U.S. 652, 672, 45 S.Ct. 625, 632 (1925).

[40] 283 U.S. 697, 51 S.Ct. 625 (1931).

[41] 376 U.S. 254, 84 S.Ct. 710 (1964).

[42] U.S. Constitution, Amendment 14.

ment says "No person shall be compelled in any criminal case to be a witness against himself, nor be deprived of life, liberty, or property, without due process of law."[43]

When those words are taken together with the First Amendment's command protecting "the freedom of speech, or of the press," the Fifth Amendment may be read as helping guarantee the liberty to speak or write. The Fifth Amendment also provides protection for a witness against self-incrimination. The right against self-incrimination stems from a revolting practice, common in England until the Seventeenth Century, of forcing people—often through torturing them—to testify against themselves. Again, knowledge of history by the men who wrote and adopted the Bill of Rights no doubt come into play. One person who became a symbol to that generation was "Freeborn John" Lilburne, one of the most contentious figures in the history of England's freedoms. Brought before the secret Court of the Star Chamber in 1641 for his alleged importation of anti-government and heretical books, Lilburne was whipped and pilloried because he refused to take an oath to testify against himself. He then petitioned Parliament for compensation for the wrongs he had suffered. Parliament declared Lilburne's sentence "illegal and against the liberty of the subject," and voted him an indemnity of £3,000. Lilburne had won the day for the "right not to accuse oneself," a right given constitutional status in the U.S. when the Fifth Amendment was ratified 150 years later, in 1791.[44]

Think again about the wording of the First, Fifth and Fourteenth Amendments to the Constitution as discussed in the preceding pages. The First Amendment says, with no limiting words that "Congress shall make no law ... abridging the freedom of speech, or of the press.... " On the other hand, both the Fifth and the Fourteenth Amendments, say that persons *can* be deprived of life, liberty, or property through due process of law. Further, many State constitutions state that although there is freedom of speech and press, those freedoms can be abused, and the abusers of those freedoms held responsible. Even in a Constitution granting freedoms, certain boundaries for speech and press were suggested.

Boundaries For Freedom

As the final authority on what the Constitution means, it has fallen to the Supreme Court of the United States to say what expression is protected—or "constitutional" and what is not protected. Although the First Amendment says "Congress shall make no law * * * abridging freedom of speech, or of the press * * *,"

---

[43] Ibid., Amendment 5.

[44] Erwin N. Griswold, The First Amendment Today (Cambridge, 1955) pp. 3, 4.

the nation's courts have been unable to draw an exact, ruler-straight line between the permissible and the punishable. American theorists, courts, legislatures, and laymen have stated the boundaries of expression in various ways. If a scale could be made with "freedom" at one end and "restraint" at the other, many Americans would cluster toward "freedom."

Of all American spokesmen, the late Justice Hugo L. Black most flatly stated the position for a right of unlimited expression, interpreting the First Amendment as an "absolute" command forbidding any restraint on speech and press:[45]

> I believe when our Founding Fathers * * * wrote this [First] Amendment they * * * knew what history was behind them and they wanted to ordain in this country that Congress * * * should not tell the people what religion they should have or what they should believe or say or publish, and that is about it. It [the First Amendment] says "no law," and that is what I believe it means.

> * * *

> I have no doubt myself that the provision, as written and adopted, intended that there should be no libel or defamation law in the United States.

Although such ringing statements made Justice Black a hero to many journalists and civil libertarians, such words might also cause consternation among legal historians. Many legal scholars, writing before and after Justice Black, have contended that such historical assertions were flawed by one-sidedness, ignoring abundant contrary evidence of libel actions brought by the generation that adopted the First Amendment.[46]

Such "absolute" positions, however, although theoretically appealing to some, have never found official acceptance or support in the United States. Ever since John Milton wrote *Areopagitica* in 1644, the case for freedom of expression has been qualified and limited in various ways as efforts are made to define the boundaries of legal control.

Written about 1765, Sir William Blackstone's vastly influential commentaries expounded the doctrine that government shall lay no restraint on writers *before* publication, but may punish them *after* publication of anything violating the law. (The problem here, of

---

[45] Edmond N. Cahn, "Justice Black and First Amendment 'Absolutes': A Public Interview," 37 N.Y.U.L.Rev. 548 (1962).

[46] See, e.g., Paul Murphy, "Time to Reclaim: The Current Challenge of American Constitutional History," 69 Amer.Hist.Rev. 64–654 (1963); Dwight L. Teeter and MaryAnn Yodelis Smith, "Mr. Justice Black's Absolutism: Notes on His Use of History to Support Free Expression," in Everette Dennis, et al., eds., Justice Hugo Black and the First Amendment (Ames, Iowa, 1978).

course, is that if it is against the law to criticize government, going to jail or being executed after publication is likely to discourage other dissident speakers or writers.)

Briefly, here are some other concepts to keep in mind as you consider efforts to define freedom of expression:

Liberty v. License: This often heard old distinction rolls easily off the tongue but contains little operational content. It is said, "Liberty is not the same as licentiousness." (Beyond personal predilections, it is impossible to say where one notion begins and the other leaves off.)

Bad Tendency: Under this theory supporting restrictions on expression, the utterance of a bad idea will bring about a bad occurrence: "If you say it, people will do it."

The Bush Administration became embroiled in a controversy over its approach to public health, specifically sex and safe sex education. In 1992, National Public Radio reported on criticism of the Administration over its decision to delete a chapter from a book on children's health problems because the chapter dealt with contraception and the use of contraceptives to prevent sexually transmitted diseases and teen pregnancies. Critics also cited the Administration's reluctance to use the word condom in AIDS prevention advertising. The National Centers for Disease Control and Prevention had, at the time, some 92 different television ads dealing with AIDS. Only four of them dealt with condoms. Only one of the agency's 75 radio ads mentioned them. National Public Radio's Morning Edition reported that Bush Administration officials were afraid that emphasis on condoms and other safe sex techniques could encourage young people to have sex and make the problem worse.[47] A few years later the New York City school system found itself embroiled in a controversy over the mandatory teaching of condom use to teens in a required AIDS and H.I.V. curriculum.[48]

Bad Tendency has been used to justify the suppression of speech and to punish speech that threatened orthodox views. One requirement of most criminal laws is that the defendant must have intended to commit the illegal act. In theft cases, the defendant must have intended to deprive the lawful owner of the property in question. In prosecutions using the *bad tendency* theory, governments had to come up with a way to tie the expression of an idea to the encouragement of the bad result. The solution was the creation of "presumed intent," in which the courts would presume that the defendant speaker had intended to bring about the bad act that

[47] Michael Skoler, "Bush Evades Sex Issues Say Critics," National Public Radio Morning Edition, April 16, 1992.

[48] Maria Newman, "Schools Chancellor is Proposing Limits to Condom Lessons," The New York Times, Dec. 9, 1995, Sec. 1, p. l.

would result from uttering a bad idea. That would make the speaker responsible for anyone else's subsequent action.

For example, individuals accused of opposing or disrupting the United States war effort during World War I often were convicted and jailed for words which in more recent years would be regarded as innocent expression.

Consider the case of Jacob Abrams. He and some other Russian immigrants were convicted of violating the Espionage Act of 1917, as amended in 1918. The 1918 amendment, since repealed, made punishable (among other things) any false statements harmful to the war effort. The statute went further, forbidding[49]

> " ... any disloyal, profane, scurrilous or abusive language about the form of government of the United States, or the Constitution ... or the military or naval forces of the United States, or the flag ... or the uniform of the United States ... "

Jacob Abrams and his friends were convicted of violating that statute by throwing leaflets out of a manufacturing building in New York. One leaflet, headlined "THE HYPOCRISY OF THE UNITED STATES AND HER ALLIES" did not criticize the war efforts of the U.S. against Germany. Instead, it protested United States taking part with other nations in sending an expeditionary force into Russia, calling for workers in munitions factories to strike so bullets made by them would not strike down Russians.[50] There was no proof that such pamphleteering had any harmful effect or caused one less bullet to be made in a munitions factory. But World War I was a time of war hysteria and freedoms taken for granted in peacetime were cast aside. The pamphlet's fervent language, denouncing President Woodrow Wilson and "the plutocratic gang in Washington" was then enough to convince a jury to convict Abrams and three others.[51]

The U.S. Supreme Court upheld the conviction, basing its decision not on any demonstrable harm from the pamphlets, but on their "bad tendency." Writing for the Court, Justice Clarke declared that[52]

> It will not do to say, as is now argued, that the only intent of these defendants was to prevent injury to the Russian cause. Men must be held to have intended, and to

---

[49] U.S. Stats. at Large, vol. XL, p. 553ff.

[50] Abrams v. United States, 250 U.S. 616, 40 S.Ct. 17 (1919); see also Zechariah Chafee, Jr., Free Speech in the United States (Cambridge, 1941 ed.) 114ff.

[51] Chafee, p. 109ff.

[52] 250 U.S. 616, 621, 40 S.Ct. 17, 19 (1919).

be accountable for, the effects their acts were likely to produce.

That prosecutor's delight, the "bad tendency" test, was enough for a majority of the Supreme Court to uphold Abrams' conviction. In dissent, Justice Oliver Wendell Holmes presented a moving expression of the "marketplace of ideas" philosophy, declaring:[53]

> In this case sentences of twenty years imprisonment have been imposed for the publishing of two leaflets that I believe the defendants had as much right to publish as the Government has to publish the Constitution now vainly invoked by them.
>
> * * *
>
> Persecution for the expression of opinions seems to me perfectly logical. If you have no doubt of your premises or your power and want a certain result with all your heart you naturally express your wishes in law and sweep away all opposition. * * * But when men have realized that time has upset many fighting faiths, they may come to believe even more than they believe the very foundations of their own beliefs that the ultimate good desired is better reached by free trade in ideas—that the best test of truth is the power of the thought to get itself accepted in the competition of the market, and that truth is the only ground upon which their wishes safely can be carried out. That at any rate is the theory of our constitution. It is an experiment, as all life is an experiment. Every year if not every day we have to wager our salvation upon some prophecy based upon imperfect knowledge.

Expression v. Action—In 1919, shortly before the *Abrams* case, Justice Holmes wrote for the Court's majority in Schenck v. United States. Schenck and his co-defendants had mailed circulars in violation of the Espionage Act of 1917, urging men who had been called to military service to resist the draft. Writing for a unanimous Court, Holmes created some famous, flashing phrases which seemed to offer promise to protect some kinds of anti-government expression, even in wartime. Justice Holmes then stated the famous *clear and present danger test.*[54]

> We admit that in many places and in ordinary times the defendants in saying all that was said in the circular would have been within their constitutional rights. But the character of every act depends upon the circumstances in which it is done. The most stringent protection of free

---

[53] 250 U.S. 616, 629, 40 S.Ct. 17, 22 (1919).
[54] 249 U.S. 47, 52, 39 S.Ct. 247, 249 (1919).

speech would not protect a man in falsely shouting fire in a theatre and causing a panic. * * * The question in every case is whether the words used are used in such circumstances and are of such a nature as to create a clear and present danger that they will bring about the substantive evils that Congress has a right to prevent. It is a question of proximity and degree. When a nation is at war many things that might be said in time of peace are such a hindrance to the effort that their utterance will not be endured ...

The clear and present danger test did not free Schenck, nor was it to be used by Supreme Court majorities in support of free expression for two decades to come.[55] Although this helped few defendants at the time, its development by Justices Holmes and Brandeis in later dissents—as in Abrams v. United States (1919)— served as a rallying point for libertarians for years.[56]

The clear and present danger test asked judges to assess the *likelihood* that dissident speech would be transmitted into illegal action. At what point, however, does "expression" become so dangerous that it creates a "clear and present danger?"

A major formulation by Thomas I. Emerson, one of the nation's foremost First Amendment scholars, was expressed this way in 1970:[57]

> The central idea of a system of freedom of expression is that a fundamental distinction must be drawn between conduct which consists of "expression" and conduct which consists of "action." "Expression" must be freely encouraged. "Action" can be controlled.

SEC. 3.   "THE INTENT OF THE FRAMERS"

"Law office history"—assertions by judges, lawyers and politicians that they know the "intent of the Framers"—sometimes makes law affecting First Amendment rights.

Statements continue to be heard about the "intent of the Founding Fathers" or the "Framers" on the true meaning of the national constitutional provision on freedom of the press. This is a cautionary note for readers of court decisions or legal arguments which purport to offer *the* meaning of The First Amendment or

[55] See Bridges v. California, 314 U.S. 252, 62 S.Ct. 190 (1941), for use of that test in a contempt case.

[56] See Chafee, *passim.*

[57] Emerson, The System of Freedom of Expression, p. 17.

some other facet of the Constitution of the United States. If you believe such legal arguments, the authors of this book have some real estate and a bridge they'd like to sell you.[58]

First, there's what might be called the journalistic fallacy, talking about the First Amendment as if it contained only guarantees for freedom of speech and press. But read again what that Amendment says: it is a group of rights protecting religion, speech, press, assembly, and petition ... mentioned in that order, for whatever order of mention is worth. The exact words say:

AMENDMENT I

Congress shall make no Law respecting an establishment of religion, or prohibiting the free exercise thereof; or abridging the freedom of speech, or of the press; or the right of the people peaceably to assemble, and to petition the Government for a redress of grievances.

Obviously, the First Amendment is not just about speech and press. As civil libertarians frequently observe, it is a bundle of rights, and whatever affects one part of that Amendment almost certainly will have repercussions for the other rights it lists.

When you hear a politician assert that "all history proves," brace yourself for a whopper. And be similarly skeptical about lawyers' and judges' use of history-as-argument or history-as-precedent. The legal process in this nation, after all, is an adversary system, and selective perception of evidence—especially historical evidence—is not infrequent in the judicial system.[59]

Many of the following pages will contain assertions made by judges, lawyers, and journalists about the intent underlying the First Amendment as it applies—to name just a few examples—to criticism of government, or prior restraint, access to information, defamation, or invasion of privacy.

If communicators, lawyers, judges or scholars talk about "the First Amendment intent of the Framers," regard their words skeptically. Face it, the Framers were the men who met in secret, behind closed doors—so much for their intent concerning access to information?—in Philadelphia during the spring and summer of 1787. If someone insisted that their true intent on free speech or press or religion could be found in that document, then what? The body of the Constitution mentioned nothing at all about the rights guaranteed by the First Amendment. Members of the Constitutional Convention signed the document they produced in 1787. Al-

---

[58] See, Levy, Original Intent and the Framers' Constitution (New York: 1988) pp. xii–xiii, 377.

[59] Charles Miller, The Supreme Court and the Uses of History (Cambridge, Mass. Belknap Press, 1969).

though the Constitution was ratified by the necessary nine states in 1788, and although the new government began in the spring of 1789 the Bill of Rights was not adopted by the states until the end of 1791.

It has been said that the War for Independence and the troubled early years of the struggling new United States of America, instead of securing rights for speech and press, came close to eradicating them.[60] The Bill of Rights, indeed, was created to overcome the objections of the Antifederalists who were seeking another constitutional convention to undo the draft Constitution of 1787 aiming toward a centralized, truly national government. Under that analysis, the Bill of Rights was drafted out of pragmatism, to overcome Antifederalist charges that freedom of speech, press, assembly, and religion would be taken away under a monolithic new government. Other charges included taking away of right to trial by jury and that a heartless national government would torture people until they confessed to crimes they had not committed. Pay specific attention to the language of the First Amendment: it does *not* say that freedoms of speech and press shall not be abridged. It says that Congress (not the states) "shall make no law." True, the Federalists argued that the various states had their own free speech and press guarantees, but the Antifederalists anti-ratification arguments dealt with what the new national government *might* do. As John Adams said so well, "the Constitution was 'a game at leapfrog.' "[61]

Anthony Lewis has written that a meaningful understanding of "original intent" would have to include posthumous reading of the minds of the different groups of men who drafted the Constitution, and the men who were voting in the ratifying conventions of each state. The intent behind the Bill of Rights is even harder to discern: there is hardly any record of the legislative history of what members of the First Congress meant in offering the Amendments in 1789.[62]

It took some time and there is virtually no record of how the First Amendment developed. James Madison wrote a version and then the House select committee wrote a version and incorporated Madison's clauses about right of assembly and petition and freedom of speech and press. The Senate prepared its own version, rejecting a proposal to protect free speech based on common law principles.

[60] Levy, Legacy of Suppression (Cambridge: Belknap/Harvard, 1960) p. 182; Jackson Turner Main, op. cit., pp. 160–161.

[61] John Adams quoted in Merrill Jensen, review of Legacy of Suppression, 75 Harvard Law Rev. No. 1 (Dec.1961) at p. 458.

[62] Anthony Lewis, review of Leonard W. Levy's Original Intent and the Framers' Constitution (New York: Macmillan, 1989), New York Times Book Review, Nov. 6, 1988, p. 11.

The Senate version included the first five words,"Congress shall make no law." Considering the politics of the time, this phrasing evidently was aimed at defusing Antifederalist fears of a too-powerful central government. The House and Senate versions went to conference committee where differences were hammered out, including deleting a Senate clause prohibiting establishment of "articles of faith, or a mode of worship."[63]

Some journalism teachers used to say that the First Amendment was the First Amendment because Congress wanted to make it the most important amendment. In fact, the First Amendment started out as the Third Amendment. The first two amendments dealt with the manner of electing congressmen and how they were to be paid.

The Constitution and the Bill of Rights have not remained frozen in time. It is likely that this nation was able to celebrate 200 years under its Constitution because it is a brief, broadly stated "frame of government." And it may be asserted with safety that the First Amendment has been changed, over time, as courts— however haltingly or imperfectly—interpreted new meanings into the document. And the Framers' intent? As David A. Anderson has argued, " ... [M]ost of the Framers perceived, however dimly, naively, or incompletely, that freedom of the press was inextricably related to the new republican form of government and would have to be protected if their vision of government by the people was to succeed."[64]

[63] See, e.g., Jackson Turner Main, The Antifederalists: Critics of the Constitution (Chapel Hill: University of North Carolina, 1961), pp. 158–161; Merrill Jensen, The Making of the Constitution (New York: Van Nostrand, 1964), pp.147–150, and Irving Brant, The Bill of Rights: Its Origin and Meaning (Indianapolis: Bobbs Merrill, 1967) pp. 48–52, 58–74.

[64] David A. Anderson, "The Origins of the Press Clause," 30 UCLA L.Rev No. 3 (February, 1983), p. 537.

Chapter 2

THE FIRST AMENDMENT: HISTORICAL BACKGROUND AND TODAY'S LAW

Sec.
4. Seditious Libel: Ancient Enemy of Freedom.
5. Prior Restraint.
6. Prior Restraint: Licensing.
7. Forcing Communication to Occur.
8. Criminal Libel.
9. Taxation.
10. The Contempt Power and Criticizing Courts.

It has been said that the present is only the cutting edge of the past. This is especially true in law, with courts for the most part looking to earlier decisions, "following precedent." In studying struggles for freedom of expression, it is easy to wonder if there is much that is new. Old patterns of control—ancient enemies of freedom—may be traced to authoritarian philosophies hundreds and hundreds of years old. Major controls over the press well known in Seventeenth and Eighteenth Century England and America set the pattern for battles for freedom of expression which will continue into the first decades of the Twenty–First Century.[1] Patterns of control continue, and so do the fights against them.

SEC. 4. SEDITIOUS LIBEL: ANCIENT ENEMY OF FREEDOM

Sedition—defined roughly as expression attacking government's form, laws, institutions, or officers—is a criminal charge many centuries old. In the United States of the Twentieth Century the crime has been restricted by court rulings.

The crime of seditious libel or "sedition" has a long and bloody history. Generally, sedition has been defined as attacking government (its form, laws, institutions) or government officers (including, in Seventeenth Century England, members of the Royal family).

---

[1] Fredrick S. Siebert, Freedom of the Press in England, 1476–1776 (Urbana: Univ. of Illinois Press, 1952). This is the classic treatment of the instruments of control. See also Norman L. Rosenberg, Protecting the Best Men: An Interpretive History of the Law of Libel (Chapel Hill: Univ. of North Carolina Press, 1986), and Leonard W. Levy, Emergence of a Free Press (New York: Oxford, 1985).

Consider the case of William Prynn, a prude who advocated strict Puritanism. In his book, *Histrio–Mastix*, he denounced such popular pastimes as dancing, hunting, Christmas-keeping, and play-going. How did this attack government? The attack was inferred from Prynn's assertion that lewd women and whores acted in plays: It seems the Queen of England had taken part in a pastoral play at Somerset House. Prynn was fined £10,000 and given life imprisonment. In addition, he was pilloried (made to "stand in the stocks," held in a frame in a public square where passers-by could taunt him) and had his ears cropped off.[2] A year later, in 1637, Dr. John Bastwick and Henry Burton were treated similarly by the infamous Court of the Star Chamber for their attacks on the Pope. Mob demonstrations against authority followed Prynn's sentencing. He was released from prisons by the Long Parliament in 1641 after Puritan forces had gained ascendancy in England and after the abolition of the Court of the Star Chamber.[3]

Today, treason is thought of as betraying a nation to an enemy and conjures up visions of spying or sabotage or of the notorious "Tokyo Rose" who made pro-Japanese broadcasts to American military forces during World War II. Treason is a crime punishable by death. It had been defined very broadly in England since 1352, in the time of Edward III. Treason then meant not only making war against the King or giving aid and comfort to enemies, it also included "compassing the death of the king," or imagining his death. (Put this concept into today's language: How many times have citizens heard and read comments "imagining the death of the President of the United States?" What about comments about candidates for Vice President of whom it is asked, "Do you want this person only a heartbeat away from the Presidency?")

Consider the case of John Twyn, who printed a book called *A Treatise on the Execution of Justice*. Writing was included in "compassing the death of the king," and at a 1663 session of the Old Bailey court in London Twyn was indicted for treason. The book contended that a ruler is accountable to the people, and that the people may take up arms against and even kill a king who refuses accountability. Although Twyn had not written the book, he refused to say who did. And as the printer, he then received the full weight of the law's brutality. The judge pronounced the sentence of guilty:[4]

> ... "that you be ... drawn upon a hurdle [sledge] to the place of execution; and there you shall be hanged by the neck, and being alive, shall be cut down, and your privy-

[2] 3 Howell's State Trials 561 (1632–3).

[3] Siebert, pp. 123–125.

[4] Howell's State Trials 513 (1663).

members shall be cut off, your entrails shall be taken out of your body, and you living, the same to be burnt before your eyes; your head to be cut off, your body to be divided into four quarters.... And the Lord have mercy upon your soul."

Martyrs to the principle of free expression had their impact as spokesmen for a new philosophy such as John Milton and John Locke had theirs. But the legal principle of seditious libel remained in force: if people criticized government, they did so at their peril. Seditious libel soon was transported to the English colonies in America, although punishments for the crime never descended to the level of cruelty inflicted on the drawn-and-quartered John Twyn.

Sedition in America: The Zenger Trial

At least four colonial Americans faced sedition prosecutions for printed words before the most celebrated criminal trial of the colonial period took place in 1735. The outcome of that famous trial—involving *New York Weekly Journal* printer John Peter Zenger—still symbolizes press struggles for freedom to criticize government, even late in the Twentieth Century.

Zenger became a hero of press freedom by getting into the middle of a bitter factional dispute in New York colony politics. New York Governor William Cosby, a greedy and autocratic man, was opposed by lawyer James Alexander, a leader of the powerful Lewis Morris faction. Alexander wrote anonymous attacks labeling Governor Cosby a tyrant and oppressor of the colony. Those attacks were published in John Peter Zenger's *New York Weekly Journal*.[5]

The colony's attorney general tried, unsuccessfully, to get a grand jury to indict the printer. Thwarted in that direction the attorney general brought charges of sedition on his own, filing an "information" with the New York court. Zenger was jailed, and remained there for eight months awaiting trial for seditious libel. While Zenger sat in jail, Alexander—as the behind-the-scenes political agitator—kept the *Journal* printing and the campaign against Governor Cosby simmering. Wearing his lawyer's hat, Alexander prepared to defend Zenger. He was unable to do so, however, because Chief Justice De Lancey, who had been appointed by Cosby, disbarred Alexander from practicing law. Alexander then turned to Andrew Hamilton of Philadelphia to plead Zenger's case.

The original "Philadelphia lawyer," Hamilton had built a reputation as the ablest attorney in the colonies. His bold advocacy that

---

[5] Stanley Nider Katz, A Brief Narrative of the Case and Trial of John Peter Zenger (Cambridge: Harvard, 1963); Harold L. Nelson, "Seditious Libel in Colonial America," 3 Am.Jour.Legal History 160 (1959).

the court discard old patterns of thinking about sedition came to bear in an irresistible way with jurors already sympathetic to Zenger's cause. The law of sedition then held that the defendant was not to be permitted to plead that his offending words against government were true. The truth, it was held, only aggravated the offense, for it was more likely than falsehood to cause the target to seek violent revenge and breach the community's peace. Furthermore, a jury then had only a minor role in a sedition trial: its job was to decide whether the accused had, indeed, published the words. It was up to the court to decide whether they were illegal words.

Jockeying with Chief Justice De Lancey, Hamilton urged the jury to recognize truth as a defense for Zenger, and argued that the jury should decide "the law"—whether the words were libelous—as well as the fact of printing. Blocked by the judge from expanding on these points, he shifted argument to the importance of permitting men to criticize their governments:[6]

> Men who injure and oppress the people under their administration provoke them to cry out and complain, and then make that very complaint the foundation for new oppressions and prosecutions. * * * [T]he question before the Court and you, gentlemen of the jury, is not of small or private concern; it is not the cause of a poor printer, nor of New York alone, which you are trying. No! it may, in its consequences, affect every freeman that lives under a British government, on the main of America. It is the best cause; it is the cause of liberty; and I make no doubt but your upright conduct, this day, will not only entitle you to the love and esteem of your fellow citizens, but every man who prefers freedom to a life of slavery, will bless and honor you as men who have baffled the attempts of tyranny; and by an impartial and uncorrupt verdict, have laid a noble foundation for securing to ourselves, our posterity, and our neighbors, that to which nature and the laws of our country have given us a right—the liberty—both of exposing and opposing arbitrary power in these parts of the world at least, by speaking and writing truth.

Hamilton ended his plea in an emotion-charged courtroom; De Lancey delivered a confusing charge to the jury, which retired to deliberate. In a short time the jury emerged with a "not guilty" verdict. There were celebrations in the streets that night; there were printings and re-printings of the Hamilton plea for years to come, more even in England than in the colonies. The court trial for seditious libel was finished for the colonial period in America as

---

6 Stanley Katz (ed.), A Brief Narrative . . . pp. 2–9.

an instrument for control of the press. Not for 40 years or more would seditious libel be used again in America by a court.[7]

It was the elected Assembly, or lower house of the colonial legislature, that was the most successful and most active force in official control of Eighteenth Century colonial printers. Jealous of its powers under the view that it was Parliament in miniature, and unwilling to have its acts criticized, this agency of government disciplined printer after printer. Even as it emerged as the main check on the powers of the Crown's governors, even as it showed itself as the seat of government support for the movement for independence, the Assembly demonstrated its aversion to popular criticism. Its instrument for control was the citation for contempt ("breach of privilege"), and it haled a long line of printers before it for their "seditious" attacks on its performance. The legislative contempt citation was a legislative sedition action.

Historian Leonard Levy has demonstrated the relative power and activity of the Assemblies in respect to the press. Up and down the seaboard, printers were brought to the legislative bar and there were forced to kneel and beg the pardon of the stern law-makers, swear that they meant no harm by their writings, and accept rebuke or imprisonment. Printer James Franklin's irony put him in jail in 1722; he had speculated that the Massachusetts government might get around to outfitting a ship to pursue a pirate "sometime this month, wind and weather permitting." New Yorkers James Parker and William Weyman were jailed for an article on the poverty of Orange and Ulster counties; the Assembly construed it as a reflection upon its stewardship. These were only a few actions among many, and they continued to the eve of the Revolutionary War in some colonies.[8]

The great article of faith that heads America's commitment to free expression was adopted in 1791 by men who had not yet thought through all that "free speech and press" implies. The First Amendment to the Constitution states that "Congress shall make no law * * * abridging freedom of speech, or of the press * * *." Although some then argued over precisely what they meant by the words, none spoke doubts about the importance of the principle. They were deeply aware of the lasting symbolic power of the

[7] Harold L. Nelson, "Seditious Libel in Colonial America," 3 Am.Journ.Legal History 160 (1959).

[8] Levy, Emergence of a Free Press, 71–84. No other historian has stimulated others to study 18th-Century American press freedom as has Levy, whose thesis that the First Amendment was not intended by the Framers to end the British common law of seditious libel in America has aroused many to dissent. Revising his earlier, provocative Legacy of Suppression (1960) in Emergence of a Free Press (1985), and conceding some errors and misinterpretations in Legacy, he responds directly to many of the protestors but concedes nothing central to his main thesis. See Emergence of a Free Press, passim, for many of the confrontations.

courageous Zenger in accepting prison in the cause of free press. They knew well the spirited, soaring arguments for free press by England's famed "Cato," whose essays were printed and re-printed in the little colonial newspapers. Behind them lay the great pamphleteering and newspapering that had raised sedition to an art in bringing the colonies to revolt against the Mother country, printed words indispensable in bringing down the most powerful nation on earth.

Yet in the searing newspaper debates of the nation's first years, with Federalists and anti-Federalists indulging in heated political speech seen by many as seditious and thus criminal, the axioms of centuries were with them. It still seemed to many that no government could stand if it could not at some point punish its critics, if their new government was meant to last. Some words surely were illegal. Not, perhaps, in the realm of religion, where James Madison, among others, argued an unlimited freedom to speak and write; but could sedition be given such scope? It was the party of Thomas Jefferson that gave an answer, in the debates over and sequel to the Alien and Sedition Acts of 1798–1800.

The Alien and Sedition Acts, 1798–1800

In the complex story about the reluctant retreat of the crime of sedition through more than 150 years of American history, no episode stands out more than the controversy of 1798–1800 over the Alien and Sedition Acts. It was only seven years after the adoption of the Bill of Rights and its First Amendment that the Acts were written, at a time of high public and official alarm. With France and England in conflict through the 1790s, America had been pulled by both toward war. The Republicans—Jefferson's party—had favored France, while the Federalists sided with England. Angered at Jay's Treaty of 1794 with England, which France believed placed America on the side of her enemy, France had undertaken the raiding of American shipping. America's envoys, sent to France to negotiate a settlement, were faced with a demand for an American war loan to France, and a bribe of a quarter-million dollars. This unofficial demand as a price for negotiations was revealed to Americans as the notorious "X, Y, Z Affair." Now most of America was incensed; President John Adams called for war preparation, which his Federalist Congress set about in 1797.[9]

The Republicans, although they suffered heavy political losses because of the nation's war fever, did not abandon their support of France. Stigmatized in the refusal to do so, associated by the Federalists with the recent French Revolution and its Terror, and beleaguered on all sides for their continued opposition to Britain,

[9] James M. Smith, Freedom's Fetters (Ithaca: Cornell Univ.Press, 1956), Chap. 2. This is the leading work on the Alien and Sedition Acts.

the Republicans were in deep trouble. And in this context, the Federalist Congress passed the Alien and Sedition Acts as measures to control opposition to America's war policy and to the Federalist majority party.

It was the Sedition Act that struck most lethally at opposition and at the Republicans. The Act made it a crime to publish or utter false, scandalous, and malicious criticism of the President, Congress, or the government with the intent to defame them or bring them into disrepute.[10]

Fourteen indictments were brought under the Act, all against Republican newspapermen and publicists, and all 14 resulted in convictions.[11] The first action put Rep. Matthew Lyon in jail for four months and cost him a fine of $1,000. He had claimed that under President Adams, the Executive Branch showed "an unbounded thirst for ridiculous pomp, foolish adulation, and selfish avarice," and that the public welfare was "swallowed up in a continual grasp for power." Anthony Haswell, Republican editor of the (Bennington) *Vermont Gazette,* came to Lyon's defense while the latter was in prison. He wrote that Lyon was held by "the oppressive hand of usurped power," and said that the federal marshal who held him had subjected him to indignities that might be expected of a "hard-hearted savage." Haswell's fine was $200 and his term in federal prison two months.[12]

Its back to the wall under the attempt of the Federalists to outlaw it as a party of disloyalty and subversion, the Republican Party found spokesmen who declared that the idea of sedition betrayed a self-governing society, and denied that the federal government had any kind of power over the press. The Acts, the Jeffersonian Republicans said, were unconstitutional in making it a crime to criticize the President and government. No matter that the Acts permitted the defenses for which Andrew Hamilton had argued in defending Zenger: truth was of little use in defending opinions (how to prove the truth of an opinion?), and jury power to find the law could be circumvented by judges in various ways. A people, they argued, cannot call itself free unless it is superior to its government, unless it can have unrestricted right of discussion. No natural right of the individual, they contended in Philosopher John Locke's framework, can be more important than free expression. The Jeffersonians rested their case on their belief in reason as the central characteristic of men, and on the people's position of ascendancy over government.[13] The radical Thomas Cooper demol-

[10] Ibid., Chap. 6.

[11] Ibid., p. 185.

[12] Each trial is treated in Smith, Chaps. 11–17.

[13] Levy, Chap. 10. And see Chap. 9 for evidence that several Jeffersonians had no objection to a sedition power in *state* governments.

ished one by one the arguments for permitting a sedition power in government.[14] Calmly and systematically, lawyer Tunis Wortman worked out philosophical ground for freedom in the fullest statement of his era.[15] James Madison, St. George Tucker, and others drove home the arguments for free expression.

The unpopularity of the Alien and Sedition Acts and outrage at the prosecutions of Republican printers helped defeat the Federalist Party and President John Adams in 1800. President Jefferson was committed to letting the Acts lapse, and they died in early 1801. The nation would see no federal peacetime sedition act again for 140 years. Furthermore, the alternative route of using the common law as a basis for federal sedition actions was closed to the government only a few years later. The Supreme Court ruled in cases of 1812 and 1816 that federal courts had been given no authority over common-law crimes by the Constitution, and that whatever question there had been about the matter had been settled by public opposition to such jurisdiction.[16]

The fear and hatred of French revolutionary doctrine had been real factors in the passage of the Alien and Sedition Acts. Different fears, different hatreds led to suppressive laws in the South about a generation later, when states began passing laws to silence Abolitionists. The anti-slavery drive, coupled with incidents such as Nat Turner's slave rebellion, caused convulsions of fear among Southerners that their "peculiar institution" and the shape of society and government would be subverted and destroyed. Laws were passed—sedition laws, though not labeled as such in statute books—making it a crime to advocate the abolition of slavery or to argue that owners "have no property" in slaves, and denying abolitionist literature access to the mails.[17] The suppression of anti-slavery argument became almost total in most of the South by 1850.

Sedition in World War I

Sedition actions surfaced again in the early Twentieth Century when both state and federal lawmakers acted to halt criticism of government in response to alarm at the rise of socio-political protest. Prosecutions to punish verbal attacks on the form of government, on laws, and on government's conduct, found new life at the federal level some 100 years after they had been discredited by the Alien and Sedition Act prosecutions of 1798–1800. The

14 Political Essays (Phila.: Printed for R. Campbell, 1800), pp. 71–88.

15 Treatise Concerning Political Enquiry, and the Liberty of the Press (New York: Printed by George Forman, 1800).

16 United States v. Hudson and Goodwin, 11 U.S. (7 Cranch.) 32 (1812); United States v. Coolidge, 14 U.S. (1 Wheat.) 415 (1816).

17 Three Virginia laws passed between 1832 and 1848 are in Harold L. Nelson, Freedom of the Press from Hamilton to the Warren Court, pp. 173–178.

actions focused on a new radicalism, flourishing in the poverty and sweat-shop conditions of industrial cities and in the lumber and mining camps of the West. Whether seeking an improved life for the deprived, driving for power, or fostering revolution, socialists, anarchists, and syndicalists advocated drastic change in the economic and political system. Laws and criminal prosecutions rose to check their words.[18]

World War I brought a wave of legislation across the states to make criminal the advocacy of violent overthrow of government. Yet it was the federal government's Espionage Act of 1917 and its amendment of 1918 to include sedition that put most muscle into prosecution for criminal words. Foremost among forbidden and prosecuted statements were those that were construed to cause insubordination or disloyalty in the armed forces, or to obstruct enlistment or recruiting.[19] Some 1,900 persons were prosecuted for speech, and possibly 100 newspapers and periodicals were barred from the mails.[20] Polemics in pamphlet form, as well as books, also were the cause of prosecutions.

The best-known of the Socialist newspapers prosecuted under the Espionage Act were the *New York Call,* the *Masses,* also of New York, and the *Milwaukee Leader.* In the last of these, editor Victor Berger had denounced the war, the United States government, and munitions makers. Postmaster General Albert Burleson considered this the kind of opposition to the war forbidden by the Espionage Act, and excluded it from the mails as the Act provided. Further, he said, the repeated attacks on the war effort in the Leader were evidence that it would continue doing the same in the future, and on these grounds, the Leader's second-class mail permit should be revoked. He was upheld in his revocation of the permit by the United States Supreme Court, and the Leader was thus denied the low-rate mailing privilege from 1917 until after the war.[21]

Pamphleteers of the left were convicted under the Espionage Act and under state anarchy and sedition acts. The famous case of Schenck v. United States, led to the articulation of the famous "clear and present danger" test discussed at page 21 of Chapter 1.[22]

The Smith Act of 1940

Immediately after World War I, the thrust of revolutionary communism had spurred the Attorney General of the United States

[18] William Preston, Jr., Aliens and Dissenters, Federal Suppression of Radicals, 1903–1933 (Cambridge: Harvard Univ.Press, 1963).

[19] 40 U.S. Statutes 217. For state laws, see Zechariah Chafee, Jr., Free Speech in the United States (Boston, 1941), pp. 575–597.

[20] Chafee, p. 52.

[21] United States ex rel. Milwaukee Social Democratic Pub. Co. v. Burleson, 255 U.S. 407, 41 S.Ct. 352 (1921).

[22] 249 U.S. 47, 39 S.Ct. 247 (1919).

to urge the passage of a federal peacetime sedition act. His call for such a peacetime measure (the Espionage Act of 1917 had applied only to war) was defeated although widespread deportation of Russians and other aliens for their ideas and words was accomplished. But 20 years later, similar fears accompanied the coming of World War II and the activity of domestic communists brought passage of a similar bill. This was the Alien Registration Act of 1940, known as the Smith Act for Rep. Howard W. Smith of Virginia who introduced it.[23] For the first time since the Alien and Sedition Acts of 1798, America had a federal peacetime sedition law. The heart of its provisions, under Section 2, made it a crime to advocate forcible or violent overthrow of government, or to publish or distribute material advocating violence with the intent to overthrow government.

The Act was to have little or no impact upon the mass media of general circulation. Media advocated the *status quo,* not radical change or revolution. But for speakers, teachers, and pamphleteers of the Communist Party, the Smith Act came to mean a great deal. Fewer than 20 persons had been punished under the Alien and Sedition Acts of 1798–1801; it is estimated that approximately 100 persons were fined or imprisoned under the Smith Act between 1940 and 1960.[24] In one sense, however, the Smith Act was less suppressive than its ancestor: The Alien and Sedition Acts had punished criticism of government officials, Congress, and the laws, an everyday exercise of the press, but the Smith Act limited the ban to advocating violent overthrow of government.

The government made its first move in 1943. Leaders of a revolutionary splinter group, the Socialist Workers Party which followed Russia's banished Trotsky, were the target. They were brought to trial in Minneapolis and convicted for the advocacy of violent overthrow in their printed polemics. The Court of Appeals sustained the conviction, and the United States Supreme Court refused to review the case.[25]

But the Communist Party was much more the target of government prosecution than the little group of Trotskyites. In the context of the cold war between the United States and the U.S.S.R. following World War II, almost 10 years of prosecution took place. The first case, Dennis v. United States, brought major figures in the Communist Party to trial and convicted 11 of them.[26] The charges in *Dennis* were that the defendants had reconstituted the

[23] 54 U.S. Statutes 670.

[24] Don R. Pember, The Smith Act as a Restraint of the Press, Journalism Monographs #10, May 1969; Zechariah Chafee, Jr., The Blessings of Liberty (Phila., N.Y.: J.B. Lippincott Co., 1954), p. 22.

[25] Dunne v. United States, 138 F.2d 137 (8th Cir.1943).

[26] 341 U.S. 494, 71 S.Ct. 857 (1951).

American Communist Party in 1945, and conspired to advocate violent overthrow of the government.

For almost nine months the trial went on in federal district court under Judge Harold Medina. The nation was fascinated and bored in turn as the defense introduced complex legal challenges to the trial and the prosecution introduced exhibit after exhibit. Newspapers, pamphlets, and books were employed as evidence of the defendants' intent, from the *Daily Worker* to *The Communist Manifesto*. Scores of pages were read into the record, as the government sought to show conspiracy by publishing and circulating the literature of revolutionary force. Judge Medina followed the doctrine of the *Gitlow* case in instructing the jury that advocacy or teaching of violent overthrow of the government was not illegal if it were only "abstract doctrine." What the law forbade was teaching or advocating "action" to overthrow the government.[27] The jury found that the 11 did, indeed, conspire to advocate forcible overthrow. The Court of Appeals upheld the conviction and the case was accepted for review by the Supreme Court of the United States.

The justices wrote five opinions, three opinions concurring in conviction and two dissenting. Chief Justice Vinson wrote the opinion that carried the most names (three besides his). He said that free expression is not an unlimited or unqualified right, and that "the societal value of speech must, on occasion, be subordinated to other values and considerations."[28] But a conviction for violation of a statute limiting speech, he said, must rest on the showing that the words created a "clear and present danger" that a crime would be attempted or accomplished. Thus he went to the famous Holmes rule first expressed in the *Schenck* case in 1919, and interpreted it as follows:[29]

> In this case we are squarely presented with the application of the "clear and present danger" test ... * * * Overthrow of the Government by force and violence is certainly a substantial enough interest for the Government to limit speech. Indeed, this is the ultimate value of any society, for if a society cannot protect its very structure from armed internal attack, it must follow that no subordinate value can be protected. * * * Certainly an attempt to overthrow the Government by force, even though doomed from the outset because of inadequate numbers or power of the revolutionists, is a sufficient evil for Congress to prevent.

[27] United States v. Foster, 80 F.Supp. 479 (S.D.N.Y.1948). Upon appeal, this case became United States v. Dennis et al., 183 F.2d 201 (2d Cir.1950).

[28] Dennis v. United States, 341 U.S. 494, 71 S.Ct. 857 (1951).

[29] Ibid., at 508–509, 71 S.Ct. at 867.

The *Dennis* court thus rejected the position that likelihood of success in committing a criminal act is the criterion for restricting speech, Chief Justice Vinson adopted the statement of the Court of Appeals in interpreting the clear and present danger test. Chief Judge Hand had written: "In each case [courts] must ask whether the gravity of the 'evil,' discounted by its improbability justifies such invasion of free speech as is necessary to avoid the danger."[30] Vinson was arguing that the danger need not be immediate when the interest (here, self-preservation of government) is important enough.

Deep disagreements split the Court over such limiting of free expression, as seen in the dissents of Justices Black and Douglas. Douglas could see no clear and present danger to the government and state in the words and papers of the 11 Communists, writing:[31]

> Communists in this country have never made a respectable or serious showing in any election * * *. Communism has been so thoroughly exposed in this country that it has been crippled as a political force. Free speech has destroyed it as an effective political party. It is inconceivable that those who went up and down this country preaching the doctrine of revolution which petitioners espouse would have any success.
>
> * * *
>
> * * * Free speech—the glory of our system of government—should not be sacrificed on anything less than plain and objective proof of danger that the evil advocated is imminent.

Through most of the 1950's, cases under the Smith Act continued to move through the courts. But in the wake of the decision in Yates v. United States in 1957, prosecutions dwindled and died out. In this case, the Supreme Court reversed the conviction of 14 Communist Party leaders under the Smith Act. Its decision turned in large part on the difference between teaching the need for violent overthrow as an abstract theory or doctrine, and teaching it as a spur to action.[32] Since the trial court had not required the jury which found the defendant guilty to make the distinction, the conviction was reversed. There was no reference to the famous clear and present danger doctrine.

The Warren Court—so called for chief Justice Earl Warren who had been appointed in 1953—had grown less and less willing to uphold convictions under the Smith Act, and with the *Yates* deci-

---

[30] Ibid., at 510, 71 S.Ct. at 868, from 183 F.2d at 212.

[31] Dennis v. United States, 341 U.S. 494, 588, 71 S.Ct. 857, 906–907 (1951).

[32] Yates v. United States, 354 U.S. 298, 77 S.Ct. 1064 (1957).

sion, charges against many other defendants in pending cases were dismissed in lower courts. The Smith Act soon lapsed into disuse, and in the several versions of a bill for the broad reform of the federal Criminal Code that labored toward adoption by Congress beginning in 1977, the Act was omitted and thus scheduled for repeal.[33]

Yates had found that the trial judge's instructions had allowed conviction for mere advocacy without reference to its tendency to bring about forcible action, and overturned the convictions.

Brandenburg v. Ohio (1969)

In 1969, the Supreme Court was presented with the appeal of a Ku Klux Klan leader who had been convicted under the Ohio Criminal Syndicalism statute for advocating the duty or necessity of crime, violence or unlawful methods of terrorism to accomplish political reform. The leader, Brandenburg, had been televised as he made a speech in which he said the Klan was "not a revengent [sic] organization, but if our President, our Congress, our Supreme Court, continues to suppress the white, Caucasian race, it's possible that there might have to be some revengeance [sic] taken." He added that "We are marching on Congress * * * four hundred thousand strong."

The Supreme Court reversed the conviction. Citing precedent since *Dennis,* it said:[34]

> These later decisions have fashioned the principle that the constitutional guarantees of free speech and free press do not permit a State to forbid ... advocacy of the use of force or of law violation except where such advocacy is directed to inciting or producing imminent lawless action and is likely to incite or produce such action. * * * A statute which fails to draw this distinction impermissibly intrudes upon the freedoms guaranteed by the First and Fourteenth Amendments.

The "inciting" or producing imminent lawless action clause has been called merely a version of the "clear and present danger" test.[35] It has continued to serve a protective role. Words challenging the authority of the state have brought criminal conviction at trial, but under the test have continued to find protection upon appeal to

[33] For other controls on news media embraced by the Act (S.1437), see Reporters Committee for Freedom of the Press, News Media Alert, Aug. 1977, pp. 4–5.

[34] Brandenburg v. Ohio, 395 U.S. 444, 89 S.Ct. 1827 (1969).

[35] Gerald Gunther, Cases and Materials on Constitutional Law, 9th ed., Mineola, N.Y.1975, p. 1128; Thomas I. Emerson, "First Amendment Doctrine and the Burger Court," 68 Univ. of Calif.L.Rev. 422, 445–46, wrote that the "incitement" test is subject to "serious objections," including its permitting government to interfere with expression "at too early a state."

the Supreme Court.[36] Less than an absolute barrier to government's control of expression, the *Brandenburg* test nevertheless was a strong element in crippling sedition actions.[37]

Symbolic Speech: U.S. v. O'Brien (1968) as a "Gift" to Communications Law

"Mass communications law" is not an island unto itself. It often is affected—and buffeted—by winds of change touching other parts of American law and society. Take the example of a 1968 conviction of a young man who violated federal law by burning his draft card. Daniel James O'Brien claimed that his act was "symbolic speech" to protest the Vietnam War and thus was protected by the First Amendment. Seeking a rationale for upholding O'Brien's conviction, the Supreme Court of the United States hit upon a rather complicated formula which has showed up as pivotal to the reasoning in cases far removed from draft cards on fire.

In particular, this decision has been used by courts in cases upholding regulation of advertising[38] and of cable television.[39] The crucial terminology in United States v. O'Brien was found in Chief Justice Earl Warren's opinion for the Court:[40]

> This court has held that when "speech" and "nonspeech" elements are combined in the same course of conduct, a sufficiently important governmental interest in regulating the non-speech elements can justify incidental limitations on First Amendment freedoms. * * * [W]e think it clear that a government regulation is sufficiently justified if it is within the constitutional power of the government; if it furthers an important or substantial governmental interest; if the governmental interest is unrelated to the suppression of free expression; and if the restriction on alleged First Amendment freedom is no greater than is essential to the furtherance of that interest.

[36] Hess v. Indiana, 414 U.S. 105, 94 S.Ct. 326 (1973); Healy v. James, 408 U.S. 169, 92 S.Ct. 2338 (1972).

[37] See Harry Kalven, "The New York Times Case: a Note on The Central Meaning of the First Amendment", 1964 Sup.Ct.Rev. 191.

[38] See, e.g., Chapter 14's treatment of the four-part test in Central Hudson Gas & Electric Corp. v. Public Service Comm'n., 447 U.S. 557, 100 S.Ct. 2343 (1980); Posadas de Puerto Rico v. Tourism Co., 478 U.S. 328, 340, 106 S.Ct. 2968, 2976 (1986), and Board of Trustees of the State University of New York v. Fox, 492 U.S. 469, 109 S.Ct. 3028 (1989).

[39] See, e.g. Chapter 12's discussion of key cable TV regulation decisions, including Home Box Office v. FCC, 567 F.2d 9 (D.C.Cir.1977); Quincy Cable TV, Inc. v. FCC, 768 F.2d 1434 (D.C.Cir.1985); Century Communications Corp. v. FCC, 835 F.2d 292 (D.C.Cir.1987); Turner Broadcasting v. FCC, 810 F.Supp. 1308 (D.C.D.C.1992); Turner Broadcasting v. FCC, 512 U.S. 622, 114 S.Ct. 2445 (1994), 22 Med.L.Rptr. 1865.

[40] United States v. O'Brien, 391 U.S. 367, 376, 88 S.Ct. 1673, 1678–1679 (1968).

Those factors listed in United States v. O'Brien have been turned to repeatedly as the Supreme Court has tried to craft constitutionally acceptable rationales for regulating both cable TV (see Chapter 12) and advertising/commercial speech (see Chapter 14).

SEC. 5. PRIOR RESTRAINT

Despite authoritative statements that the chief purpose of the First Amendment guarantee is to prevent previous restraints upon publication, prior restraints have continued to be exerted into the late Twentieth Century.

In perhaps the most influential First Amendment decision by the Supreme Court of the United States, Chief Justice Charles Evans Hughes wrote that it is generally considered " ... that it is the chief purpose of the [First Amendment] guarantee to prevent previous restraint on publication."[41] Journalists and civil libertarians have long counted pre-publication censorship as the most despised of all controls. Prior restraint's origins may be traced back virtually as long as there has been printing. It was tied in Sixteenth and Seventeenth Century England to requiring printers to get permission or license from government to publish. And then censors often pored over every word, to make sure that nothing harmful to those in authority would be printed.

Obviously, if government can stop publication before it occurs, that is the ultimate in repressiveness. Although it is true that a person may be deterred from publishing by the threat of post-publication punishment (as in the case of libel, invasion of privacy, or obscenity), that is not the issue here. As the U.S. Supreme Court has said: "If it can be said that a threat of criminal or civil sanctions after publication 'chills' speech, prior restraint 'freezes' it ... "[42]

Government attempts to use prior restraint have taken place, with almost predictable regularity, when some form of crisis occurs. During pre-Civil War days when Abolitionists' agitating threatened "the peculiar institution" of slavery, the South often used prior restraint as a weapon. Postmasters regularly refused to deliver mailings from Northern anti-slavery societies. And during the Civil War, Northern generals would occasionally shut down pro-South ("Copperhead") publishers. President Abraham Lincoln himself ordered the closing of newspapers on one occasion.[43] Later in the

---

[41] Near v. Minnesota ex rel. Olson, 283 U.S. 697, 713, 51 S.Ct. 625, 630 (1931).

[42] Nebraska Press Ass'n v. Stuart, 427 U.S. 539, 559, 96 S.Ct. 2791, 2803 (1976), 1 Med.L.Rptr. 1064.

[43] Russel Blaine Nye, Fettered Freedom (East Lansing: Michigan State, 1951).

Nineteenth Century, heavy restrictions on publishing and distributing of materials discussing sex were extensively used, and prior restraint was part of the control. Postal and customs officials' use of prior restraint, in peacetime to control materials labeled "obscene" and in wartime to stop "sedition," was vigorous and frequent through the first third of the Twentieth Century.[44]

The area of prior restraint expanded in the Twentieth Century in matters not related to governmental acts of self-protection. As discussed in Chapter 12, there still is the governmental licensing of all broadcasters to regulate who has access to the airwaves. There are also many areas in which courts can issue injunctions against speaking, publishing, or distributing words or symbols—and those are prior restraints. For example, the Federal Trade Commission can issue "cease and desist" orders against anticompetitive or deceptive ads, and can order advertisers to publish corrective statements.[45] Copyright law provides for court-issued injunctions to restrain illegal use of copyrighted materials.[46]

In 1984, the U.S. Supreme Court allowed a trial court to forbid newspaper publication of material from pre-trial "discovery" proceedings.[47] This echoed the 1970s, when a striking extension of prior restraint burst out as courts across the nation forbade publishing of accounts of part or all of the records in pre-trial hearings and even in trials. (See Chapter 9).

Later chapters will detail additional aspects of prior restraint. In this chapter, the special concern goes to government's claims to suppress, on its own behalf, attacks on its personnel and structure, or words constituting danger to national security.

Near v. Minnesota

Mr. Chief Justice Hughes' majority opinion in Near v. Minnesota, a case of 1931, established groundwork that may be seen as a watershed which turned United States Supreme Court majorities in the direction of expanded press freedom.[48]

That decision grew out of scruffy origins. Howard Guilford and J.M. Near were publishing partners in producing *The Saturday Press,* a Minneapolis "smear sheet" which charged that gangsters

[44] Vincent Blasi, Toward a Theory of Prior Restraint, 66 Minn.L.Rev. 11, 14–15 (Nov.1981).

[45] Anon., The FTC's Injunctive Authority Against False Advertising of Food and Drugs, 75 Mich.L.Rev. 745 (March 1977).

[46] 17 U.S.C.A. §§ 502, 503.

[47] E.g. Seattle Times Co. v. Rhinehart, 467 U.S. 20, 104 S.Ct. 2199 (1984), 10 Med.L.Rptr. 1705.

[48] Near v. Minnesota ex rel. Olson, 283 U.S. 697, 51 S.Ct. 625 (1931); Paul L. Murphy, Near v. Minnesota in the Context of Historical Developments, 66 Minn. L.Rev. 95 (Nov.1981); Fred W. Friendly, Minnesota Rag (N.Y., 1981).

were in control of Minneapolis gambling, bootlegging and racke-
teering, and that the city law enforcement and government agencies and officers were derelict in their duties. It vilified Jews and
Catholics. And it published the articles that eventually required the
Supreme Court of the United States to make one of its most
notable descriptions of the extent of freedom of the press in
America.

Publication of *The Saturday Press* was halted when a Minnesota statute authorizing prior restraint of "nuisance" or "undesirable" publications was invoked. That statute declared that any
person publishing a "malicious, scandalous and defamatory newspaper, magazine or other periodical" could be found guilty of
creating a nuisance and could be enjoined from future wrongdoing.[49] Near and Guilford were indeed brought into court after a
temporary injunction ordered cessation of all activity by their
paper. After the hearing, the injunction was made permanent by a
judge, but with the provision that *The Saturday Press* could resume
publication if the publishers could persuade the court that they
would run a newspaper without objectionable content described in
the Minnesota "gag law" statute.[50]

Near and Guilford appealed to the Supreme Court, which
found in their favor by the margin of five votes to four. Speaking
for the Court, Chief Justice Charles Evans Hughes noted the
importance of this case: "This statute, for the suppression as a
public nuisance of a newspaper or periodical, is unusual, if not
unique, and raises questions of grave importance transcending the
local interest involved in the particular action." Hughes declared of
this prior restraint, "This is the essence of censorship."[51]

Hughes then turned to history-as-precedent to answer the
question of whether a statute authorizing such proceedings in
restraint of publication was consistent with the concept of liberty of
the press, declaring here that the chief purpose of the constitutional guaranty is to prevent previous restraints.

He embarked upon a two-fold modification of the old English
authority, Blackstone. Blackstone would have had *no prior restraint,* period. The Chief Justice, however, conceded that such a
prohibition against all prior restraint might be "stated too broadly," and said that " * * * the protection even as to previous
restraint is not absolutely unlimited." In a few exceptional cases,

---

[49] Chapter 285, Minn.Sess.Laws 1925, in Mason's Minn.Stats., 1927, Secs. 10123–1
to 10123–3.

[50] Near v. Minnesota ex rel. Olson, 283 U.S. 697, 702–707, 51 S.Ct. 625, 628
(1931).

[51] Ibid., at 707, 713, 51 S.Ct. at 627, 630.

limitation of the principle of "no prior restraint" could be recognized:[52]

> No one would question but that a government might prevent actual obstruction to its recruiting service or the publication of sailing dates of transports or the number and location of troops. On similar grounds, the primary requirements of decency may be enforced against obscene publications. The security of the community life may be protected against incitements to acts of violence and the overthrow by force of orderly government. The constitutional guaranty of free speech does not "protect a man from an injunction against uttering words that may have all the effect of force."

Although Blackstone's "no prior restraint" was thus modified, another aspect of Blackstone was liberalized. Blackstone had approved punishing the publication of criticisms of government or government officials. But Hughes said that the press had a right— and perhaps even a duty—to discuss and debate the character and conduct of public officers.[53]

> ... [T]he administration of government has become more complex, the opportunities for malfeasance and corruption have multiplied, crime has grown to most serious proportions, and the danger of its protection by unfaithful officials and of the impairment of the fundamental security of life and property by criminal alliances and official neglect, emphasizes the primary need of a vigilant and courageous press, especially in great cities.

> The fact that the liberty of the press may be abused by miscreant purveyors of scandal does not make any the less necessary the immunity of the press from previous restraint in dealing with official misconduct. Subsequent punishment for such abuses as may exist is the appropriate remedy, consistent with constitutional privilege.

Despite the four dissenting votes, Near v. Minnesota has stood since 1931 as one of the most important decisions of the Supreme Court. *Near* was the first case involving newspapers in which the Court applied the provisions of the First Amendment against states through the language of the Fourteenth Amendment.[54] And it was to serve as important precedent for protecting the press against government's demands for suppression.

[52] Ibid., at 716, 51 S.Ct. at 631.

[53] Ibid., at 719–720, 51 S.Ct. at 632–633.

[54] William A. Hachten, The Supreme Court on Freedom of the Press: Decisions and Dissents (Ames, Ia.: Iowa State Univ. Press, 1968), p. 43.

The "Pentagon Papers" Case: New York Times Co. v. U.S. (1971)

It was 40 years before the press again collided with government bent on protecting its own interest and functions through prior restraint. On June 30, 1971, the United States Supreme court cleared the confrontation with a decision hailed by many news media with such headlines as "VICTORY FOR THE PRESS" and "The Press Wins and the Presses Roll."[55] These triumphant headlines were tied to the "Pentagon Papers" case. Early in 1971, *New York Times* reporter Neil Sheehan was given photocopies of a 47–volume study of the United States involvement in Vietnam titled *History of the United States Decision–Making Process on Vietnam Policy.* On Sunday, June 13, 1971, the *New York Times*—after a team of reporters had worked with the documents for three months—published a story headlined: "Vietnam Archive: Pentagon Study Traces 3 Decades of Growing U.S. Involvement." Within 48 hours after publication, Attorney General John Mitchell sent a telegram to the Times, urging that no more articles based on the documents be published, charging that the series would bring about "irreparable injury to the defense interests of the United States."[56] The Times chose to ignore Attorney General Mitchell's plea, and columnist James Reston angrily wrote: "For the first time in the history of the Republic, the Attorney General of the United States has tried to suppress documents he hasn't read about a war that hasn't been declared."[57]

After the Times' refusal to stop the series of articles, the Department of Justice asked U.S. District Court Judge Murray I. Gurfein to halt publication of the stories. Judge Gurfein, who was serving his first day as a federal judge, issued a temporary injunction on June 15, putting a stop to the Times' publication of the articles. But silencing the Times did not halt all publication of the "Pentagon Papers." *The Washington Post*—and a number of other major journals—also weighed in with excerpts from the secret report. The Justice Department likewise applied for—and was granted—a temporary restraining order against *The Washington Post.*[58]

After two weeks of uncertainty, the decision by the Supreme Court of the United States cleared the papers for publication. *New York Times* Managing Editor A.M. Rosenthal was jubilant: "This is

---

[55] Newsweek, Time, July 12, 1971.

[56] Don R. Pember, "The Pentagon Papers Decision: More Questions Than Answers," Journalism Quarterly 48:3 (Autumn, 1971) p. 404; New York Times, June 15, 1971, p. 1.

[57] New York Times, June 16, 1971, p. 1.

[58] For a clear account of the cases' journeys through the courts, see Pember, pp. 404–405.

a joyous day for the press—and for American society." *Time* added, "Certainly the Justice Department was slapped down in its efforts to ask the courts to enjoin newspapers, and will not likely take that route again."[59] Despite such optimism, some observers within the press were disturbed by the outcome of the *"Pentagon Papers"* case. Not only were there three dissents against lifting the injunction among the nine justices, there was also deep reluctance to do so on the part of two of the majority justices. Furthermore, federal court injunctions had now, for the first time in American history, been employed to impose prior restraint upon newspapers, and the courts had preserved those injunctions intact for two weeks.

The Court's decision was short. It refused to leave in effect the injunctions which the Justice Department had secured against the Times and the Post, and quoted Bantam Books v. Sullivan:[60]

> "Any system of prior restraints of expression comes to this Court bearing a heavy presumption against its constitutional validity." Bantam Books, Inc. v. Sullivan, 372 U.S. 58, 83 S.Ct. 631 * * * (1963); see also Near v. Minnesota ex rel. Olson, 283 U.S. 697, 51 S.Ct. 625 * * * (1931). The Government "thus carries a heavy burden of showing justification for the imposition of such a restraint." Organization for a Better Austin v. Keefe, 402 U.S. 415, 91 S.Ct. 1575, 1578 (1971).

With those words, a six-member majority of the Court ruled that the government had not shown sufficient reason to impose prior restraint. Of the six, four found nothing in the facts of the case to qualify their positions. Justices Hugo L. Black and William O. Douglas expressed abhorrence for prior restraint, Douglas saying "uninhibited, robust and wide-open debate" on public questions was essential, and "The stays in these cases that have been in effect for more than a week constitute a flouting of the principles of the First Amendment as interpreted in Near v. Minnesota * * *."[61]

Justice William J. Brennan, Jr., although not subscribing to an absolutist position about prior restraint, nevertheless declared that it was permissible in only a "single, extremely narrow" class of cases, as when the nation was at war or when troop movements might be endangered. For all the government's alarms as to possible dangers of nuclear holocaust if secrecy were breached, it had not presented a case that publication of the Pentagon Papers would cause such an event. Therefore:[62]

[59] Time, July 12, 1971, p. 10.

[60] New York Times Co. v. United States, 403 U.S. 713, 714, 91 S.Ct. 2140, 2141 (1971).

[61] Ibid., at 724, 91 S.Ct. at 2146.

[62] Ibid., at 727, 91 S.Ct. at 2148.

     * * * every restraint issued in this case, whatever its form, has violated the First Amendment—and none the less so because the restraint was justified as necessary to examine the claim more thoroughly.

With reluctance, Justices Byron White and Potter Stewart joined the majority. Stewart approved secrecy in some contexts, and said he was convinced that the Executive branch of government was correct in attempting to suppress publication of some of the documents here. But he voted with the majority, he said, because he could not say that disclosure of any of the Pentagon Papers "will surely result in direct, immediate, or irreparable damage to our Nation * * *."[63] White said that if any of the published material proved, after publication, to be punishable under the Espionage Act of 1917, the newspapers now stood warned: "I would have no difficulty in sustaining convictions under [the Espionage Act] on facts that would not justify * * * the imposition of a prior restraint."[64]

Justice Marshall declared that Congress had twice rejected proposed legislation that would have given the President war-time powers to prohibit some kinds of publication. And, he said, it would be inconsistent within the concept of separation of powers for the Court to use its contempt power to prevent behavior that Congress had specifically declined to prohibit.[65]

Dissenting, Justice Harlan wrote that disputes about matters so grave as the alleged contempt and publication of the Pentagon Papers needed more time to resolve, and he voted to support the injunctions.[66] He found that the Court had been almost "irresponsibly feverish in dealing with these cases" of such high national importance in only a few days' time. Justice Blackmun agreed with Harlan, and added a shrill indictment of the press:[67]

     If, however, damage has been done, and if, with the Court's action today, these newspapers proceed to publish the critical documents and there results therefrom "the death of soldiers, the destruction of alliances, the greatly increased difficulty of negotiation with our enemies, the inability of our diplomats to negotiate," to which list I might add the factors of prolongation of the war and of further delay in the freeing of United States prisoners,

[63] Ibid., at 730, 91 S.Ct. at 2149.

[64] Ibid., at 735–738, 91 S.Ct. at 2152–2154.

[65] Ibid., at 746, 91 S.Ct. at 2157.

[66] Ibid., at 753, 91 S.Ct. at 2161.

[67] Ibid., at 763, 91 S.Ct. at 2165. Blackmun was quoting the dissent of Judge Wilkey in the Pentagon Papers case involving the Washington Post in the Court of Appeals for the Second Circuit, United States v. Washington Post Co., 446 F.2d 1327 (D.C.Cir.1971).

then the Nation's people will know where the responsibility for these sad consequences rests.

It should be recognized that no new legal course was charted by the *Pentagon Papers* case. After a delay of two weeks—a prior restraint imposed by lower federal courts at the insistence of the Department of Justice—the Supreme Court allowed the press to resume publication of the documents. By a 6-to-3 margin, the Supreme Court adhered to Near v. Minnesota, that classic case which, by a 5-to-4 margin, forbade prior restraint except in time of war, or when the materials involved were obscene, or when there was incitement to violence or to the overthrow of the Government.

The *Pentagon Papers* case underlines the important truth that no freedom is ever won, once and for all.

Doom for national security had been forecast by officials of the State Department as they testified against permitting the Times to continue publishing the Pentagon Papers, one of them declaring that further publication would "irreparably harm the United States." But, as Times columnist Anthony Lewis remarked some five years later, "the Republic still stands," and "Today, hardly anyone can remember a single item of the papers that caused all the fuss."[68]

United States v. Progressive, Inc. (1979)

A multi-volume history of policy-making in the Vietnam War was not the publication at issue, however, when at the end of the decade the federal government learned that *The Progressive,* a magazine of Madison, Wis., was about to print an article titled "The H-Bomb Secret: How We Got It, Why We're Telling It." The manuscript, the U.S. Attorney charged, carried the deepest of technical secrets relating to the security of our weapons. Publication would endanger national security and that of the world, and in the process would violate the U.S. Atomic Energy Act of 1954 by making public "restricted data" about thermonuclear weapons. The government sought and got a temporary injunction against publication of the article by journalist Howard Morland.[69]

Morland swore that everything in the article was in the public domain, that he had in no way been forced to secret sources for the information; the government denied that this was the case. While the trial was in mid-course, it also came to light that similar information had been available to the public by accident, for a time,

---

[68] "Congress Shall Make No Law," New York Times, Sept. 16, 1976, p. 39.

[69] United States v. Progressive, Inc., 467 F.Supp. 990 (W.D.Wis.1979), 4 Med. L.Rptr. 2377. Major prior restraint cases are discussed by U.S. Circuit Judge J.L. Oakes in "The Doctrine of Prior Restraint Since the Pentagon Papers," 15 U.Mich. Journ.L. Reform 497 (Spring, 1982).

in a government science laboratory.[70] Federal District Judge Robert Warren was fully aware of the Supreme Court's rule that "any prior restraint on publication comes into court under a heavy presumption against its constitutional validity." Warren found the revelation of secret technical details about the H-bomb quite different, however, from revealing a secret history of war-policy making. He found that publication offered the possibility of "grave, direct, immediate and irreparable harm to the United States," and said:[71]

> * * * because the government has met its heavy burden of showing justification for the imposition of a prior restraint on publication of the objected-to technical portions of the Morland article ... the Court finds that the objected-to portions of the article fall within the narrow area recognized by the Court in Near v. Minnesota in which a prior restraint on publication is appropriate.

Yet Warren's deep concern at the possible outcome of publication ("I'd want to think a long, hard time before I'd give a hydrogen bomb to [dictator] Idi Amin.") was questioned in the national debate and discussion which surged over the case. The government, it was asserted, had not shown that publication would result in "direct, immediate, or irreparable damage to the Nation" that the Pentagon Papers decision had insisted was necessary to justify prior restraint. The field of journalism was divided in its support.[72]

The Progressive and Morland, seizing on implications of the Atomic Energy Act that conceivably rendered even innocent conversations about nuclear weapons subject to classification ("classified at birth") insisted that no real secrets had been told. They appealed, and prior restraint held through six months of court process. Suddenly intruding into the matter was the publication on Sept. 16, 1979, of a long letter in the Madison, Wis. *Press Connection,* a daily of 11,000 circulation, from an amateur student of the nuclear bomb. A copy of a letter from computer programmer Charles Hansen to Sen. Charles Percy of Illinois, it included a diagram and list of key components of an H–bomb. Other newspapers which had received copies had not yet published it when, on the following day, the government moved to drop its court action to bar publication of the Morland article. A U.S. Justice Department spokesman said

[70] United States v. Progressive, Inc., 486 F.Supp. 5 (W.D.Wis.1979), 5 Med.L.Rptr. 2441.

[71] United States v. Progressive, Inc., 467 F.Supp. 990 (W.D.Wis.1979), 4 Med. L.Rptr. 2377, 2380.

[72] Civil Liberties, No. 328, June 1979, p. 1; Ben Bagdikian, "A Most Insidious Case," Quill, 67:6, June 1979, pp. 21, 22; "Editors and Lawyers Share Mixed Views on Story Ban," Editor & Publisher, March 17, 1979, p. 13.

that the Hansen letter had exposed three "crucial concepts" that the government was trying to protect from publication.

Morland's article was published. *The Progressive* set about trying to raise $200,000 from the public, which was the cost, it said, of defending. No prosecution of the *Press Connection* or other newspapers that published the Hansen letter materialized. Judge Warren dismissed the case against *The Progressive* on Sept. 4, 1980.[73]

Not only the security of the United States' war effort and the provisions of the Atomic Energy Act have made a groundwork for the government's demand for prior restraint. Rules of administrative agencies can furnish the same.[74] The CIA is experienced in the matter. Its employee Victor L. Marchetti resigned from the agency and, with John Marks, wrote *The CIA and the Cult of Intelligence*. This, the CIA charged upon learning of its existence in manuscript form, violated the secrecy contract Marchetti had signed when first employed, promising not to divulge any classified information without specific permission from the CIA.[75] It obtained an injunction in federal district court, the judge ordering Marchetti to submit all writings about the CIA or intelligence work to the Agency for review as to whether it contained classified information that had not been released to the public. As the case proceeded (the Supreme Court of the United States denied certiorari),[76] the CIA's scrutiny of the manuscript resulted in its demand that 339 deletions be performed. "It was the Devil's work we did that day," said Marchetti's attorney, Melvin L. Wulf, after he and the authors spent hours literally cutting out passages of the manuscript—perhaps as much as 20 per cent.[77] Resisting all the way, Marchetti finally won agreement from the court that all but 27 of the 339 deletions would be restored.[78] The book was finally published with blank spaces and the prominent, repeated boldface notation: **DELETED**.

Snepp v. United States (1980)

Frank Snepp, strategy analyst for the CIA in Vietnam, succeeded in getting his case against the CIA to the Supreme Court. He, too, had resigned from the agency and written a book—*Decent*

---

[73] Milwaukee Journal, Sept. 4, 1980, Part 2, pp. 1, 10.

[74] Ithiel de Sola Pool, "Prior Restraint," New York Times, Dec. 16, 1979, p. E19, portrays unintended prior restraint on research publication through elaborate funding rules of the U.S. Dept. of Health, Education, and Welfare—"a nightmare of bureaucracy run wild, producing results that no one intended."

[75] United States v. Marchetti, 466 F.2d 1309 (4th Cir.1972).

[76] Marchetti v. United States, 409 U.S. 1063, 93 S.Ct. 553 (1972).

[77] Melvin D. Wulf, Introduction to Victor Marchetti and John D. Marks, The CIA and the Cult of Intelligence (New York: Alfred A. Knopf, 1974), p. xxv.

[78] Ibid., p. xxiv.

Interval—about his experiences. He, too, had signed an agreement not to publish without first submitting the manuscript to the CIA, and the agency brought legal action. The Supreme Court, by a 6–3 vote, ruled that Snepp had broken his contract, approved an injunction requiring Snepp to submit future writings for publication review, and ruled that he must give all profits from the sale of the book to the CIA through a "constructive trust" imposed on him by the court.[79] He had a fiduciary obligation to the CIA and had breached his trust by publishing.

The government had not alleged that classified or confidential information was revealed by the Snepp book. Rather, it alleged "irreparable harm" in his failure to clear the material with the CIA, and the Supreme Court approved the lower courts' finding that publication of unreviewed material "can be detrimental to vital national interests even if the published information is unclassified."[80]

If the agent published unreviewed material in violation of his fiduciary and contractual obligation, said the court, the constructive trust remedy simply "required him to disgorge the benefits of his faithlessness * * *." Snepp "disgorged" about $138,000, the proceeds from *Decent Interval*.[81]

Non-disclosure agreements similar to those Snepp and Marchetti had signed so appealed to President Ronald Reagan that in 1983, he issued a directive requiring them of all persons who had access to classified government information, numbering—declared protesting media—more than 100,000 employees. The President withdrew the directive in the face of congressional and media protests.[82]

If the emergence of non-disclosure agreements in the decade beginning with Marchetti appeared as one more example of government creativity in devising prior restraints in the name of national security, predictably enough that newly minted instrument was not the end of invention in prior restraint. In 1982, the Secretary of State's denial of a passport to former CIA agent Philip Agee was upheld by the United States Supreme Court: Agee had asserted his purpose of exposing CIA agents abroad, driving them out of the countries where they operated, and obstructing the operations and recruitment efforts of the CIA, and had taken measures to do so. These statements and actions, the Court said, were no more pro-

[79] Snepp v. United States, 444 U.S. 507, 100 S.Ct. 763 (1980), 5 Med.L.Rptr. 2409.

[80] Ibid., 2411.

[81] Herbert Mitgang, "Royalties to the Treasury," New York Times Book Review, Aug. 31, 1980.

[82] Directive on Safeguarding National Security Information, 9 Med.L.Rptr. 1759 (1983).

tected by the First Amendment than those prohibited in Near v. Minnesota half a century earlier.[83] By 1982, Congress and the President put into effect a law making it a crime for news media to make public the names of secret U.S. intelligence agents or their sources.[84]

Procter & Gamble v. Bankers Trust Co. (6th Cir.1996)

When Business Week magazine was hit with a prior restraint order in 1995, it seemed as if U.S. District Judge John Feikens was oblivious to the precedent set in Near v. Minnesota (1931). Business Week, trying to report on manufacturing giant Procter & Gamble's (P & G's) take-no-prisoners lawsuit against Banker's Trust, a huge financial institution P & G was suing for millions of dollars in losses supposedly caused by bad investments. Judge Feikens put a restraining order on Business Week, ordering it not to reveal the contents of court-sealed documents involved in the P & G–Bankers Trust litigation.[85]

After three weeks passed—and after several hearings were held, Judge Feikens finally ended the restraining order he had issued against Business Week. Even so, the judge held that his prior restraint order against Business Week was constitutionally defensible.

The dispute arose in mid–1995 when a P & G public relations representative tipped Business Week that a newsworthy filing would soon be made when P & G amended its lawsuit against Bankers Trust. Although the motion to amend was not sealed, the supporting documents—having to do with RICO allegations were filed and immediately sealed by a broad "protective order." The RICO [Racketeer Influenced Corrupt Organizations] filing was irresistably newsworthy, for it meant that industrial giant Procter & Gamble was claiming fraud against financial giant Bankers Life. Also, a RICO civil lawsuit, in addition to carrying the "Racketeer Influenced" stigma, could have resulted in *treble damages*, a $3 return for every $1 awarded. Because P & G claimed a loss of more than $100 million, the stakes were enormous.

[83] Haig v. Agee, 453 U.S. 280, 101 S.Ct. 2766 (1981), 7 Med.L.Rptr. 1545.

[84] News Media and the Law, Sept./Oct. 1982, 39.

[85] Procter & Gamble v. Bankers Trust Co. and The McGraw–Hill Companies, 78 F.3d 219 (6th Cir.1996), 24 Med.L.Rptr. 1385, overturning U.S. District Court ruling reported at 900 F.Supp. 186 (D.S.D.Ohio1995), 23 Med.L.Rptr. 2505. Note that Judge Feikens inherited this complex litigation from a terminally ill judge who had allowed the parties virtually free rein in sealing documents, which allowed the parties to keep many of their allegations and much of their evidence away from public view. After the death of the first judge, Judge Feikens " ...inherited this unusual protective order and the voluminous set of documents already filed under the seal of secrecy." 78 F.3d at 222.

Business Week quickly asked that the order sealing documents be set aside. Attorneys representing McGraw–Hill, publishers of Business Week magazine, were unable to reach Judge Feikens in Cincinnati. They then found Sixth Circuit Judge Danny J. Boggs at his home in Kentucky, but he refused to delay enforcement of the prior restraint order.[86] Three Sixth Circuit Court of Appeals judges held an expedited hearing on September 18, 1995, but concluded that because the prior restraint order was *temporary*, the appeals court had no jurisdiction. Only permanent injunctions are "immediately appealable to this court." Supreme Court Justice John Paul Stevens, Jr., assigned to supervise the Sixth Federal Circuit, also refused to review the injunction, saying that the district court should hold a fact-finding hearing on how the magazine got the sealed documents.[87]

Business Week said that it had received the documents from a lawyer, who had sent them to reporter Linda Himelstein on September 12, 1995, using a courier service. This was hardly secretive behavior. Business Week staffers later said that they noticed a statement stamped on the documents, "Filed Under Seal Pursuant to Court Order." Business Week's efforts to publish on Sept. 13, 1995, were cut short by the arrival of Judge Feikens faxed temporary restraining order. That order was renewed three times, staying in effect for a total of three weeks.

Finally, on October 3, 1995, Judge Feikens approved Procter & Gamble's motion to add a RICO complaint to its lawsuit, and proceeded to unseal the documents. Anyone was then free to read or publish them. However, in a symbolic gesture to uphold the power of his court, Judge Feikens declared that his temporary injunction against *the* copy of the documents already in the magazine's possession was made permanent. Of course, Business Week— like any other citizen or journalistic organization—then had access to the identical words at the federal courthouse in Cincinnati. Judge Feikens' anger at the magazine was evident: "I cannot permit Business Week to snub its nose at court orders."[88]

Business Week's Sixth Circuit Victory

On appeal, Sixth Circuit Chief Judge Richard Gilbert S. Merritt declared that release of the documents did not end the matter or make it moot. He termed restraining orders as "capable of repeti-

---

[86] Keith H. Hammonds and Catherine Yang, "Business Week vs. the Judge," Business Week cover story for Oct. 16, 1995.

[87] Procter & Gamble v. Bankers Trust Co., 23 Med.L.Rptr. 2535, 2536 (6th Cir. 1995); Hammons and Yang, op. cit. For Justice Stevens' order, see McGraw-Hill Cos. v. Procter & Gamble, 23 Med.L.Rptr. 2247, 2249 (S.Ct. of U.S., Sept. 21, 1995).

[88] 900 F.Supp. 186, 193 (S.D.Ohio 1995).

tion, yet evading review," adding: "The doctrine of mootness is not to be used as a spoof on appellate courts."[89]

In overturning the district court's temporary restraining order (TRO), Chief Justice Merritt turned to some of the Supreme Court's most persuasive language against prior restraint:[90]

> It has long been established that a prior restraint comes to a court "with a heavy presumption against its constitutional validity." Bantam Books v. Sullivan, 372 U.S. 58, 70, 83 S.Ct. 631 (1963). In this case ...Business Week obtained information from a confidential source and prepared a story on a matter of public concern. Following standard journalistic protocol, Business Week sought comment from the parties and proceeded to take its story to print. Instead, the magazine received a facsimile transmission from a Federal District Court prohibiting publication ...and citing "irreparable harm" as the reason.
>
> * * *
>
> ...[P]rohibiting the publication a news story ...is the essence of censorship and is allowed only under exceptional circumstances.

Chief Judge Merritt's understanding of—and denunciation of—prior restraint was applauded by civil libertarians. That he had to craft such a decision is a reminder that hard-won freedoms cannot be taken for granted.

Technology and Prior Restraint: The Oklahoma City Bombing Trial (1997)

The law of prior restraint was changed radically on February 28, 1997, and again on March 11, 1997. On February 28, The Dallas Morning News published an exclusive story on its Web site detailing Timothy McVeigh's purported admission to the 1995 Oklahoma City bombing that killed 168 persons and injured hundreds more. On March 11, Playboy magazine published an on-line story by freelance reporter Ben Fenwick providing more details from McVeigh defense team documents.

McVeigh defense attorney Stephen Jones blasted both stories and both periodicals, at first claiming that the documents underlying the stories were stolen, and later, fraudulent. Even so, federal investigators used some of the details from the Playboy Web site story to look for significant new evidence in the bombing case

---

[89] Procter & Gamble v. Bankers Trust, 78 F.3d 219, 223, 224 (6th Cir.1996), citing Nebraska Press Association v. Stuart, 427 U.S. 539, 546, 96 S.Ct. 2791 (1976).

[90] 78 F.3d 219, 224, 225 (6th Cir.1996).

involving the purchase of nitro-methane fuel by McVeigh at a Texas raceway.[91]

Although the Dallas Morning News broke its story first, Playboy's Fenwick had been working on the story for many months. The documents Fenwick received purported to be a chronology of the bombing and a detailing of the development of McVeigh's ideology, both written by members of McVeigh's defense team. Even as he worked to confirm details in the documents and to flesh out the story, Fenwick faced what seemed to be an insurmountable problem: how to publish his story.

Fenwick knew about the case of United States v. Cable News Network, 865 F.Supp. 1549 (S.D.Fla.1994), in which CNN was found guilty of criminal contempt of court for broadcasting secretly recorded tapes of telephone calls between deposed Panamanian dictator Manuel Noriega and his attorney. As discussed in Sec. 61, Chap. 9 of this edition of Law of Mass Communications, after CNN announced that it had the tapes, presiding judge William Hoeveler concluded that the broadcast would harm Noriega's rights by violating his attorney-client privilege and also by revealing information that could harm his defense.

After the Eleventh Circuit Court of Appeals upheld the injunction, but before the U.S. Supreme Court ruled on the case, CNN broadcast one of the taped conversations, this one between a legal secretary and Noriega. Eventually, CNN was charged with and convicted of contempt by Judge Hoeveler.[92]

In Fenwick's case, the documents clearly fell within the attorney-client privilege and were damning to the defense. In chilling detail, they laid out the plans for bombing the Murrah Federal Building, the arrangement for the getaway car and McVeigh's touching off the fuse. One of the McVeigh defense documents said:

> He pulled [the Ryder rental truck] carrying the explosives back into the street and at the light at Harvey and NW 5th Street he lit the fuse. When the light turned, he pulled into the parking spot in front of the Murrah Building. Possibly two vehicles passed the Ryder truck as he was parking it. One woman looked at Tim as she was headed down the steps to walk into the Murrah Building. She was a white woman, dirty blonde hair, probably mid thirties. He still had on his hat.

[91] Pete Slover, "McVeigh admitted bombing, memo says," The Dallas Morning News Web site, March 1, 1997. See also Martha T. Moore and Tony Mauro, "Can both sides be right and wrong simultaneously?", USA Today, March 5, 1997; Jo Thomas, "Bomb Suspect's 'Confession' Is Called Ploy by the Defense," The New York Times, March 6, 1997, and Gordon Witkin, "A Disputed Story Threatens a Trial," U.S. News & World Report, March 17, 1997, p. 36.

[92] U.S. v. CNN, 865 F.Supp. 1549 (S.D.Fla.1994).

Fenwick and Playboy kept the CNN case in mind as they worked on the story. One idea they considered was holding the story until the jury was picked. They anticipated that presiding judge Richard Matsch would sequester the jury and that publication at that point would cause little or no harm to McVeigh's defense. But Judge Matsch decided that he would not sequester the jury.

That left Fenwick and Playboy with no safe time to publish. Any announcement of the story, any leak likely would draw an immediate injunction against Playboy, keeping the magazine from being distributed and keeping the story away from the public.

The Dallas Morning News, however, beat Playboy to the punch. The newspaper broke the story on its Web site on February 28, 1997. The story was out. There was no compelling reason to prevent its publication in paper form. It was like the case of The Progressive, trying to show the easy availability of nuclear bomb-building information. The Progressive planned to publish a recipe for building a hydrogen bomb. After The Progressive publicized its intentions, the U.S. government obtained a federal court injunction to prevent publication, arguing that it was a crime to publish secret information about thermonuclear weapons. During the appeal of the injunction, a letter containing H-bomb information appeared in a short-lived publication, The Press Connection, published in Madison, Wis. during an American Newspaper Guild strike. Once the information was made public, the government dropped its injunction, thus permitting publication of information in The Progressive.[93]

Playboy prepared to release a one-thousand word excerpt of the story on the Internet. Editors delayed the release in favor of publication of the complete full-length story on the McVeigh documents and Fenwick's reporting on the defense papers and on the bombing itself.

With the story in the hands of the public and no effective means of preventing further distribution, neither the prosecution nor the defense sought to prevent further publication of the articles. McVeigh subsequently was convicted and sentenced to death.

Use of the Internet to publish at a moment's notice has made the imposition of prior restraint ineffective and unlikely. Unless a party can learn of a story before it reaches the Internet, there is no real means of permitting its publication. Judges still will have contempt power to person persons or entities interfering with the orderly administration of justice, but that will come only after the news has been delivered.[94]

[93] United States v. The Progressive, Inc., 486 F.Supp. 5 (W.D.Wis.1979) is discussed earlier in this Chapter, at page 46.

[94] Evan Ramstad, "Putting News on Internet First Seen Protective," The Wall Street Journal, March 5, 1997, p. B6.

Prior Restraint and the High School Press

As was evident from the discussion of Near v. Minnesota (1931), the key case on prior restraint, not all pre-publication censorship is unconstitutional. Early in 1988, in Hazelwood School District v. Kuhlmeier,[95] the U.S. Supreme Court held that public school officials have the power to impose pre-publication censorship on student newspapers. The newspaper involved in this case, *Spectrum,* was published at Hazelwood High School near St. Louis, Mo.

The newspaper was to be six pages long in its 1983 school-year-end edition as produced by the school's Journalism II class. On May 10, 1983, Principal Robert Reynolds was shown proofs for the edition due to appear on May 13. The proofs were taken to the principal by an interim newspaper adviser; the regular Journalism II instructor had left Hazelwood East for another job just 12 days earlier.

After Principal Reynolds was shown page proofs, he objected to publication of two stories. One described three Hazelwood East students' experiences with pregnancies; the other discussed the effect of divorce on students at the school. Although the pregnancy story used fictitious names to mask identities, the principal decided that the masking was insufficient. Evidently he also thought that the article's references to sex and birth control were not appropriate for some of the younger students in the school. Finally, he was concerned that a student was identified by name in the divorce story, and that the student's parents had not been given the opportunity to respond.

Apparently believing that there was no time for redoing the stories—and that the paper could not appear at all at school year's end if delays occurred—Principal Reynolds deleted two entire pages containing the stories he found offensive. The deleted pages contained other articles—on teen marriages, runaways, juvenile delinquency, and a general article on teenage pregnancy. Principal Reynolds later testified that he had no objection to those articles; they were deleted only because they were on the same pages with the articles that troubled him.[96]

Cathy Kuhlmeier and two other former Hazelwood East students who had been newspaper staffers claimed Reynolds' action violated their First Amendment rights, and sought injunctive relief and monetary damages in a Federal district court.

The trial court upheld the principal's actions. Deletion of the divorce article on invasion-of-privacy grounds was held reasonable, as was the principal's desire to avoid younger students' exposure to

[95] 484 U.S. 260, 108 S.Ct. 562 (1988), 14 Med.L.Rptr. 2081.

[96] 484 U.S. at 264, 108 S.Ct. at 566 n., 14 Med.L.Rptr. at 2082–2083, 2083 n.

"unsuitable material." Further, the district court concluded that the principal was justified in having a " 'serious doubt that the article complied with the rules of fairness which are standard in the field of journalism and which were covered in the textbook used in the Journalism II class.' "[97]

The Eighth Circuit Court of Appeals, however, reversed the district court, holding that the newspaper was both a part of the school's curriculum *and* a public forum, " 'intended to be operated as a conduit for student viewpoints.' " Since the newspaper was a public forum, the appeals court held, school officials could not censor its contents except when necessary " ' . . . to avoid material and substantial interference with school work or discipline . . . or with the rights of others.' "[98]

The Court of Appeals thus found no evidence in the trial court's record to indicate that the principal could have predicted reasonably that the articles would be disruptive or cause disorder. Also, the court added that the articles could have caused no tort liability for libel or privacy, and concluded that school officials had violated the students' First Amendment rights.

The U.S. Supreme Court granted certiorari and reversed the Court of Appeals, thus upholding the principal's prior restraint of the newspaper. Justice White wrote for the majority in this 5–3 decision. He outlined circumscribed freedoms available to students in public high schools. Although quoting from the famous language of the Vietnam war armband protest case—Tinker v. Des Moines Independent Community School District[99]—public school students do not " 'shed their constitutional rights at the schoolhouse gate' "—Justice White then took a restrictive tack. He declared that "the First Amendment rights of students in the public schools 'are not automatically co-extensive with the rights of adults in other settings.' "[1]

Student rights must be applied " 'in the light of special charac- teristics of the school environment.' "Quoting Bethel School Dis- trict No. 403 v. Fraser (1986), he wrote that a school need not tolerate speech that is inconsistent with its educational mission, even though government could not censor such speech outside the school. (The Bethel case involved disciplining a student who had made a campaign speech in behalf of a student politician; the speech was replete with sexual double entendres.)[2]

---

[97] Hazelwood School Dist. v. Kuhlmeier, 484 U.S. 260, 265, 108 S.Ct. 562, 566 (1988), 14 Med.L.Rptr. 2081, 2083.

[98] Ibid., at 265, 108 S.Ct. at 567, 14 Med.L.Rptr. at 2083.

[99] See Tinker, 393 U.S. 503, 511, 89 S.Ct. at 739, quoted in Ibid.

[1] Ibid.

[2] 478 U.S. 675, 106 S.Ct. 3159 (1986).

Justice White's majority opinion declared that the *Spectrum* was not a forum for public expression: It was a part of the school's curriculum, a regular educational activity. He also interpreted the school board's policy statement supporting free expression for school-sponsored publications as suggesting "at most that the administration will not interfere with the students' exercise of those First Amendment rights that attend the publication of a school-sponsored newspaper. It does not reflect an intent to extend those rights by converting a curricular newspaper into a public forum."[3]

The majority opinion also said that a school in its capacity of publisher may " 'disassociate itself' " from speech which is disruptive, or which sets a bad example in terms of speech that is "ungrammatical, poorly written, inadequately researched, biased or prejudiced, vulgar or profane, or unsuitable for immature audiences."

This meant, the Court said, that educators

... do not offend the First Amendment by exercising editorial control over the style and content of student speech in school-sponsored expressive activities so long as their actions are reasonably related to legitimate pedagogical concerns.

In dissent, Justice William J. Brennan, Jr., joined by Justices Marshall and Blackmun, said that when the students enrolled in that Journalism II course, they expected a civics lesson. They argued that only substantially disruptive speech should be censored, conceding that poor grammar, writing or research would disrupt or subvert the school's curricular purpose.[4]

The same cannot be said of official censorship designed to shield the *audience* or dissociate the *sponsor* from the expression. Censorship so motivated ... in no way furthers the curricular purpose of a student *newspaper,* unless one believes that the purpose of the school newspaper is to teach students that the press ought never to report bad news, express unpopular views, or print a thought that might upset its sponsors.

* * *

The young men and women of Hazelwood East expected a civics lesson, but not the one the Court teaches them today.

At least two kinds of fallout can now be seen from the bombburst unleashed by *Hazelwood.* On the one hand, censorship of high

---

[3] 484 U.S. at 270, 108 S.Ct. at 569, 14 Med.L.Rptr. at 2085, 2086.

[4] 484 U.S. at 290, 108 S.Ct. at 580, 14 Med.L.Rptr. at 2091, 2094.

school (and some college) papers increased dramatically after that decision. Director Mark Goodman of the Student Press Law Center (SPLC) reported that as the 1988 *Hazelwood* decision began to be put to use, calls to the SPLC (mostly about threatened or actual censorship) doubled in the first half of 1990.[5] On the other hand, all was not bleak. By the fall of 1994, five states—California, Colorado, Iowa, Kansas and Massachusetts—had passed statutes providing student journalists with protection for free expression, and adoption in New Jersey was expected. Efforts to pass similar legislation continue in a number of other states.

State-by-state action now seems the student journalists' best chance to overcome *Hazelwood*. As Justice Brennan and others have suggested, the more expansive among state constitutions may offer help. That is, some state charters may provide leverage to overcome mechanical application of the *Hazelwood* rule that if high school journalism is embedded in a class setting, it is not a First Amendment-protected public forum.

Carefully drawn legislation treating high school students with respect as thinking individuals who need to work with ideas to prepare themselves for life in a self-governing society can provide some hope.

For example, the section of the Colorado Revised Statutes (C.R.S.) on student freedom of speech and press declares:[6]

> (1) The general assembly declares that students of the public schools shall have the right to exercise freedom of speech and of the press, and no expression contained in a student publication, whether or not such a publication is school-sponsored, shall be subject to prior restraint except for the types of expression described in section (3) ... [below] This section shall not prevent the advisor from encouraging expression which is consistent with high standards of English and journalism.
>
> (2) If a publication written substantially by students is generally available throughout a public school, it shall be a public forum for students of such school.
>
> (3) Nothing in this section shall be interpreted to authorize the publication or distribution by students of the following:
>
> > (a) Expression which is obscene;
> >
> > (b) Expression which is libelous, slanderous, or defamatory under state law;

[5] Student Press Law Center Report, Fall, 1990, p. 3.

[6] Colorado Rev. Stat. § 22–1–120.

(c) Expression which is false as to any person who is not a public figure or involved in a matter of public concern; or

(d) Expression which creates a clear and present danger of the commission of unlawful acts, the violation of lawful school regulations, or the material and substantial disruption of the orderly operation of the school or which violates the rights of others to privacy.

(4) The board of education of each school district shall adopt a written publications code, which shall be consistent with the terms of this section 22–1–120 C.R.S., and shall include reasonable provisions for the time, place, and manner of conducting free expression within the school district's jurisdiction. Said publications code shall be distributed, posted, or otherwise made available to all students and teachers at the beginning of the 1991–1992 school year and at the beginning of each school year thereafter.

(5)(a) Student editors of school-sponsored student publications shall be responsible for determining the news, opinion, and advertising content of their publications subject to the limitations of this section. It shall be the responsibility of the publications advisor of school-sponsored publications within each school to supervise the production of such publications and to teach and encourage free and responsible expression and professional standards for English and journalism.

(b) For the purposes of this section, "publications advisor" means a person whose duties include the supervision of school sponsored student publications.

(6) If participation in a school-sponsored publication is part of a school class or activity for which grades or school credits are given, the provisions of this section shall not be interpreted to interfere with the authority of the publications advisor for such school-sponsored publications to establish or limit writing assignments for the students working with the publication and to otherwise direct or control the learning experience that the publication is intended to provide.

(7) No expression made by students in the exercise of freedom of speech or freedom of the press shall be deemed to be an expression of school policy, and no school district or employee, or parent, or legal guardian, or official of such school district shall be held liable in any civil or criminal action for any expression made or published by students.

(8) Nothing in this section shall be construed to limit the promulgation or enforcement of lawful school regulations de-

signed to control gangs. For purposes of this section, the definition of "gang" shall be the definition found in section 19–2–111(2)(d)II, C.R.S.

Where favorable legislation like that in Colorado is not available, some high school students have chosen to avoid prior restraint allowed by Hazelwood by going off-campus to create "underground newspapers." Such newspapers, of course, do not offer the substantial educational benefits of guidance in writing and editing from a professional adviser, but can offer students freedom to publish their views on matters they believe to be important. Such freedom, given the chilling effect of Hazelwood, is important in itself.[7]

Prior Censorship in High Schools After Hazelwood: The "Forum" Question

As attorney Mark Goodman of the Student Press Law Center (SPLC) has pointed out, not all censorship of official school newspapers is automatically constitutional. If censorship is not " 'reasonably related to pedagogical concerns,' " it may be overturned. Goodman also noted that if a newspaper had been "opened as a forum for student expression where student editors had been given control over content," a court could rule against school officials' censorship.[8]

The "forum" question is of great importance in determining whether or not an official school publication has full First Amendment protection. For example, in Planned Parenthood of Nevada v. Clark County School District, the United States Court of Appeals (9th Cir.) upheld a school's decision to exclude advertising relating to birth control and pregnancy from a school publication. Crucial to the decision, the court said, was " ... whether the school newspapers, yearbooks, and athletic programs are forums for public expression." The court held that under school policy, officials had substantial discretion to reject advertising, and that the school publications involved never had been opened to public forum status. The school's restrictions on advertising, based on the school's desire to appear neutral on controversial issues, was upheld as conforming to the reasoning of the *Hazelwood* decision discussed above.[9]

---

[7] Mark Goodman, Law of the Student Press (Washington, D.C.: SPLC, 1995), pp. 76-79.

[8] Goodman, p. 38, citing Hazelwood School District v. Kuhlmeier, pp. 273, 267. As Mr. Goodman noted, before Hazelwood, the rule on student freedom of expression came from Tinker v. Des Moines Independent Community School Dist., 393 U.S. 503, 511, 89 S.Ct. 733, 739 (1969), where the U.S. Supreme Court declared that if school officials can "reasonably" predict that student expression would cause "material disruption" or interference with the rights of other students, then censorship could be justified.

[9] Planned Parenthood of Southern Nevada v. Clark County School District, 887 F.2d 935 (9th Cir.1989), affirmed en banc 941 F.2d 817 (1991).

Distribution on High School Grounds

Related to the forum question are issues involved in on-campus distribution. People with causes—including young people—want to publicize their views. Consider Hemry by Hemry v. School Board (1991), involving a group of Christian students who believed it their religious duty to distribute a religious newspaper to other students. This collided with school district policy forbidding distribution of any material that would interfere with normal educational activities at a school. The court held that hallways of a school are not a public forum, and that the distribution regulations—because they were not content-based and did not take away other avenues for distributing the religious newspaper—were appropriate under the First Amendment.[10]

On the other hand, if school's policy restricting distribution can be characterized as content-based, that may overturn the regulation. In Johnston–Loehner v. O'Brien (1994), a federal district court knocked down a school's policy requiring students to get permission from the school superintendent before distributing materials. The court declared this to be a "content-based prior restraint" and therefore invalid. Furthermore, the school had not made a determination that distribution of particular religious materials would "materially and substantially interfere" with the rights of students or with normal school activities.[11]

Meanwhile, Justice Brennan's warning about the dangerous "civics lesson" offered by *Hazelwood* in permitting school authorities to habituate students to accepting governmental prior restraint is worrisome to civil libertarians.[12] If, indeed, secondary schools are primary training grounds for citizens who will be expected to take their place in a democracy, freedom from stultifying censorship is not too much to ask. Unfortunately, high schools and school boards, in their quest to be presented in a good light, too often have shown themselves willing to censor student expression, even expression that had no chance of causing a disruption or causing harm.

One example—both funny and somewhat tragic—involved the "Death by Cheeseburger" incident in 1971 at Vance High School in Henderson, N.C. A school newspaper was shut down because of just three articles. One, titled "Death by Cheeseburger," was a satire that will strike a familiar chord (or gag reflex) in most persons who have survived the fare offered up in most high school cafeterias.[13]

[10] Hemry by Hemry v. School Board, 760 F.Supp. 856 (D.Colo. 1991).

[11] Johnston–Loehner v. O'Brien, 859 F.Supp. 575 (M.D.Fla.1994).

[12] See the quotation from Justice Brennan's dissent in *Hazelwood*, discussed at footnote 4, above.

[13] Death by Cheeseburger: High School Journalism in the 1990s and Beyond (Freedom Forum, 1994), frontispiece.

Hazelwood and Freedom of the Collegiate Press

Attorney and student press law expert Mark Goodman has written that despite the many problems caused by *Hazelwood* for high school publications, "college student press freedom is a much more certain matter." **[Note: This discussion deals only with censorship and post-publication punishment matters. Real, continuing problems of access to what should be public information on public campuses, including access to meaningful police/crime news, is discussed in Sec. 54 of Chapter 8.]** For example, when Troy State University editor Gary Dickey was ordered by officials not to publish an editorial deemed controversial by the university president, his newspaper then published blank space with the label **"censored."** Editor Dickey was suspended from school but reinstated after U.S. Court of Appeals found that high school students have full First Amendment rights of free expression unless the expression " 'materially and substantially interfere[s] with requirements of appropriate discipline in the operation of the school.' "[14]

The U.S. Supreme Court enunciated a "material and substantial disruption" standard in Tinker v. Des Moines Independent Community School District.[15] In Papish v. Board of Curators of the University of Missouri (1973), the Supreme Court said that a graduate journalism student expelled from school for distributing an underground newspaper must be reinstated. The court declared that despite the tastelessness of the paper—which had a front page cartoon showing the Statue of Liberty being raped by a policeman— was not the point. " 'Conventions of decency' " were not enough to allow a state university to close down the distribution of ideas.[16] For college-level public institutions, the key First Amendment interpretation was expressed by the Supreme Court of the United States in Healy v. James (1972). There, the Court declared: "[I]n the absence of any disruption of campus order or interference with the rights of others, the sole issue was whether a state university could proscribe this form of expression."[17]

As Mark Goodman of the Student Press Law Center has written, *Hazelwood* (1988), dealing with high schools, on its face had no direct implications for the college press. It remains to be seen, however, whether in the long run—given the appropriate case

[14] Suggested by Goodman, p. 52, discussing Dickey v. Alabama State Board of Education, 273 F.Supp. 613, 618 (M.D.Ala.1967), vacated in Troy State University v. Dickey, 402 F.2d 515 (5th Cir.1968).

[15] Tinker v. Des Moines Independent Community School District, 393 U.S. 503, 511, 89 S.Ct. 733, 739 (1969).

[16] Papish v. Board of Curators of the University of Missouri, 410 U.S. 667, 93 S.Ct. 1197 (1973).

[17] Healy v. James, 408 U.S. 169, 189, 92 S.Ct. 2338 (1972).

to decide—the U.S. Supreme Court will finally hold,as did a U.S. Court of Appeals, that "First Amendment rights 'on college campuses are coextensive with those in the community at are coextensive with those in the community at large.' "[18]

Other Forms of Prior Restraint

Government pre-publication censorship continues to be discouraged by courts, but—as discussed earlier—it can occur. In addition, prior restraint may occur in other contexts, cropping up in connection with topics covered in following chapters of this book. Courts are petitioned for prior restraint orders—injunctions against publication—in areas of law including defamation,[19] privacy,[20] copyright,[21] obscenity,[22] access to government information,[23] and advertising/commercial speech.[24] Although courts, in general, grant prior restraint orders grudgingly, the issue lives on. In libel, for example, courts usually will not halt defamatory publications via injunction. In copyright law and other areas dealing with business relationships, pre-publication injunctions may be found frequently enough that they are not aberrations. Prior restraint assumes so many guises that it can not safely be said that battles against pre-publication controls are ever won, once and for all time.

SEC. 6.   PRIOR RESTRAINT: LICENSING

When licensing power over expression amounts to prior censorship, it is constitutionally forbidden. Broadcasting, however, has long been a special case, outside some protections of the print media.

[18] Goodman, p. 54, quoting Thonen v. Jenkins, 491 F.2d 722 (4th Cir.1973).

[19] For an annotated listing of prior restraint cases in general, see Floyd Abrams, "Prior Restraints," in James C. Goodale, chairman, Communications Law 1993 (New York: Practising Law Institute, 1993), Vol.3, pp. 799–1079. See Chs. 4 and 5, below, on defamation. Libel decisions refusing to grant injunctions to plaintiffs include Dworkin v. Hustler Magazine, Inc., 634 F.Supp. 727 (D.Wyo.1986), and Lothschuetz v. Carpenter, 898 F.2d 1200 (6th Cir.1990).

[20] Similarly to defamation, courts have been reluctant to issue injunctions to plaintiffs in privacy cases. See Abrams, op. cit., p. 484. See Organization for a Better Austin v. Keefe, 402 U.S. 415, 91 S.Ct. 1575 (1971).

[21] See Ch. 13, above, and Abrams, op. cit., pp. 515–531. Injunctions occur more frequently in trademark disputes, although they are occasionally granted—temporarily—in copyright cases. See, e.g., Rosemont Enterprises, Inc. v. Random House, Inc., 256 F.Supp. 55 (S.D.N.Y.1966), reversed at 366 F.2d 303 (2d Cir.1966).

[22] The seminal prior restraint case, Near v. Minnesota, specifically listed obscenity—along with information of aid to an enemy in wartime and expression inciting to violence/governmental overthrow—as kinds of expression subject to prior restraint. 283 U.S. 697, 51 S.Ct. 625 (1931).

[23] See Ch. 8, above.

[24] See Ch. 14, above. See especially Posadas de Puerto Rico Associates v. Tourism Co., 478 U.S. 328, 106 S.Ct. 2968 (1986).

Licensing is one aspect of prior restraint. And, where broadcast regulation is concerned, licensing is still alive and well in the United States: a government license is required to operate a broadcast station.

Past forms of licensing, as in England in the Sixteenth and Seventeenth Centuries, meant that only licensed printers who had government's approval were allowed to print. At the end of the Twentieth Century, licensed broadcast stations have the freedom to criticize government, knowing full well that broadcast re-licensing by the Federal Communications Commission has become largely a routine matter.

If licensing broadcasting stations seems a benign form of that ancient control, other kinds of official prior permission raise sharper-edged issues. Consider the American Nazis decision to march, displaying swastikas, through a mostly Jewish neighborhood in Skokie, Illinois, in 1977. Nazi leader Frank Collin asked a number of Chicago suburbs for permits (licenses) for demonstrations in their parks or on their streets. Skokie officials responded that the Nazis would have to post an insurance bond of $350,000 as a hedge against property damage.[25]

The American Civil Liberties Union, which lost much of its membership over this issue, was cast in the ironic role of defending Nazis' right to demonstrate. The Illinois Supreme Court supported the ACLU's position, striking down the Village of Skokie's licensing attempt. The court said that however offensive displaying the swastika would be, it was symbolic political speech. "It does not," the court said, "...fall within the doctrine of 'fighting words,' and that doctrine cannot be used here to overcome the heavy presumption against the constitutional validity of prior restraint."[26]

Major weapons against licensing in the Twentieth Century were hammered out by repeated battles by Jehovah's Witnesses. Repeatedly, they fought their cases all the way to the U.S. Supreme Court and ultimately won. This religious group endured great suffering. As Professor William A. Hachten noted, "The ACLU reported ...that in one six-month period of 1940, 1,488 men, women and children in the sect were victims of mob violence in 355 communities in 14 states."[27] The Witnesses made themselves unpopular with their refusal to salute the American flag and by their disdain for other religions, particularly the Catholic Church. And,

[25] See Areyeh Neier, Defending My Enemy: American Nazis, the Skokie case, and the Risks of Freedom (New York: E.P. Dutton, 1979).

[26] Village of Skokie v. National Socialist Party of America, 69 Ill.2d 605, 14 Ill.Dec. 890, 373 N.E.2d 21 (1978).

[27] William A. Hachten, The Supreme Court on Freedom of the Press (Ames, Iowa: Iowa State University Press, 1968), p. 73.

their persistent street sales of literature and doorbell-ringing for their beliefs often irritated non-believers.[28]

The Jehovah's Witness cases are useful reminders that freedom of expression belongs to the people, not merely to media corporations. Furthermore, a landmark case won by the Witnesses—Lovell v. City of Griffin, Georgia—is crucially important because it explicitly sets out constitutional protection for *distribution* of information as well as to publication.

Alma Lovell, a Jehovah's Witness, was convicted in municipal court in Griffin, Ga., and sentenced to 50 days in jail when she refused to pay a $50 fine. Her crime? She had not received advance permission from the City Manager of Griffin to hand out literature, as required by a municipal ordinance.

Alma Lovell simply could not be bothered with such technicalities. She saw herself as a messenger sent by Jehovah and believed that applying to the City Manager for permission would have been " 'an act of disobedience to His commandments.' " The Supreme Court, however, regarded the ordinance as far more than a technicality. Speaking for a unanimous Court, Chief Justice Charles Evans Hughes denounced the ordinance:[29]

> We think that the ordinance is invalid on its face. Whatever the motive which induced its adoption, its character is such that it strikes at the very foundation of the freedom of the press by subjecting it to license and censorship.

> The liberty of the press is not confined to newspapers and periodicals. It necessarily embraces pamphlets and leaflets. These indeed have been historic weapons in the defense of liberty, as the pamphlets of Thomas Paine and others in our own history abundantly attest. * * *

> The ordinance cannot be saved because it relates to distribution and not to publication. "Liberty of circulation is as essential to that freedom as liberty of publishing; indeed, without circulation, the publication would be of little value." Ex parte Jackson, 96 U.S. 727, 733, 24 L.Ed. 877.

Because the ordinance of the City of Griffin was not limited to " 'literature' that is obscene or offensive to public morals or that advocates unlawful conduct," the ordinance could not be upheld. In Schneider v. Town of Irvington, New Jersey, the Supreme Court reviewed four cities' anti-littering ordinances. Three of these ordinances in effect punished distributors if the recipient of a leaflet

[28] Ibid., p. 74; Lovell v. City of Griffin, Georgia, 303 U.S. 444, 58 S.Ct. 666 (1938).

[29] Lovell v. City of Griffin, 303 U.S. 444, 451–452, 58 S.Ct. 666, 669 (1938).

threw it to the ground. The Supreme Court held such ordinances unconstitutional.[30]

"Time, Place and Manner"

Such cases, of course, do not mean that advocates can distribute anything they want at at any time or place. What the courts call "time, place and manner" restrictions may be upheld as lawful if they are administratively even-handed and do not favor some kinds of content over others. A city, in other words, may set reasonable hours when canvassing may be done.[31]

Jehovah's Witnesses were to have many other days in court, defending freedoms of religion, speech and press guaranteed by the First Amendment and protected from state encroachment by the Fourteenth Amendment. The persistence of the religious group has resulted in some of the Supreme Court's most sweeping language in support of the First Amendment.[32]

In Jones v. City of Opelika (1942), writing words used to decide a city ordinance unconstitutional, Justice Harlan Fiske Stone asserted a favored position for the First Amendment. Justice Stone's "preferred position" view—generally out of judicial favor late in the Twentieth Century—showed a principled belief in expression. Justice Stone wrote:[33]

> The First Amendment is not confined to safeguarding freedom of speech and freedom of religion against discriminatory attempts to wipe them out. On the contrary, the Constitution, by virtue of the First and Fourteenth Amendments, has put those freedoms in a preferred position.

Cincinnati v. Discovery Network, Inc. (1993)

A city has an interest in keeping litter off its streets, but can it limit distribution of free-circulation publications that get taken from newsracks and thrown about?

Discovery Network, Inc., had permission from Cincinnati to place its newsracks on public property to distribute free-circulation magazines consisting mostly of advertising. In 1990, because of littering around the newsracks, the city revoked permission, declar-

---

[30] Schneider v. Town of Irvington, New Jersey, 308 U.S. 147, 60 S.Ct. 146 (1939).

[31] Ibid.

[32] Other Jehovah's Witness cases include Jones v. Opelika, 316 U.S. 584, 62 S.Ct. 1231 (1942); Martin v. Struthers, 319 U.S. 141, 63 S.Ct. 862 (1943); Douglas v. Jeannette, 319 U.S. 157, 63 S.Ct. 877 (1943); Murdock v. Pennsylvania, 319 U.S. 105, 63 S.Ct. 870 (1943).

[33] Jones v. City of Opelika, Ibid.

ing that the magazines were "commercial handbills." A pre-existing Cincinnati ordinance forbade distribution of commercial handbills.[34]

A U.S. District Court held that although the city may regulate newsracks for safety and esthetics, its regulations must be "narrowly tailored to achieve the desired objective."[35] A government entity regulating commercial speech bears the burden of establishing a "reasonable fit" between the ends and the means chosen to achieve those ends.[36]

When this case reached the U.S. Supreme Court, Justice Stevens declared for a 6–3 majority that although the city's interest in protecting against litter had some validity, it was not a sufficient reason to discriminate against the free circulation of magazines that were predominantly advertising. Justice Stevens wrote:[37]

> In our view, the city's argument attaches more importance to the distinction between commercial and noncommercial speech than our cases warrant and seriously underestimates the value of commercial speech.

Dissenting, Chief Justice Rehnquist—joined by Justices Byron White and Clarence Thomas—complained that the Cincinnati newsracks decision will "unduly hamper our cities' efforts to come to grips with the unique problems posed by the dissemination of commercial speech."[38]

SEC. 7. FORCING COMMUNICATION TO OCCUR

The other side of prior restraint (preventing communication in the first place) is forcing communication to occur. Except for the broadcast media, forcing communication to occur generally is forbidden.

Forcing communication to take place is closely connected with—is often the "flip side" of—a system of prior restraint. As Fredrick Siebert showed in his pathbreaking study of the development of freedom of expression in England from 1476 to 1776, printers who did not publish what they were told to print by government often put themselves in real peril.[39] Similarly, in the

[34] Cincinnati v. Discovery Network, Inc., 507 U.S. 410, 113 S.Ct. 1505 (1993); 21 Med.L.Rptr. 1161, 1163.

[35] The District Court cited Board of Trustees of State University of New York v. Fox, 492 U.S. 469, 109 S.Ct. 3028 (1989).

[36] Cincinnati v. Discovery Network, Inc., 507 U.S. 410, 113 S.Ct. 1505 (1993), 21 Med.L.Rptr. 1161, 1163.

[37] Ibid., 1165.

[38] Ibid., p. 1173.

[39] Siebert, Freedom of the Press in England, 1476–1776; Clyde A. Duniway, The Development of Freedom of the Press in Massachusetts (Cambridge: Harvard Univ. Press, 1906), pp. 104–05.

early years of Britain's American colonies, printers—who needed
government subsidies to survive—had to display "Published by
Authority" on their newspapers. Such printers often learned that
they dared not deviate from printing only the official accounts—
edited for public consumption—of the meetings (held in secret) of
colonial legislatures of Governor's councils.[40]

After the War for Independence and the creation of the United
States, the development of strongly competing political factions—
and later, political parties—helped distribute "official printing"
business while criticizing government raucously.[41] Later, in the
first four decades of the Nineteenth Century, the rise of mass
circulation newspapers supported primarily by advertising helped
free the press from government.[42]

Over time, the libertarian ideas borrowed from England
evolved, with arguments taken from John Milton from the Seventeenth Century and from "Country Whig" philosophers of the
Eighteenth Century.[43] Those ideas developed in the crucible of
American politics into the ideas that government should keep
hands off the press, allowing criticism of government through a
"free marketplace of ideas," assuming that truth would win over
falsehood in the process of argumentation.

This "marketplace of ideas" philosophy became a kind of
received truth, cited with the force of binding precedent by the
Supreme Court of the United States in important Twentieth Century decisions.[44] But when major riots occurred after the assassination of Martin Luther King, law professor Jerome Barron articulated a troubling and persistent viewpoint. He argued that lack of
access to media of communication by disadvantaged minorities
showed that government should intervene to give the voiceless a
voice. Otherwise, people left voiceless were going to "take it to the
streets," violently.[45]

In an age of mass communication, Barron asserted, the members of the public must have access to the columns and airwaves of
the mass media. Barron elaborated the position that for many

[40] Jean Folkerts and Dwight L. Teeter, Jr., Voices of a Nation (New York:
Macmillan, 1989), pp. 18–23.

[41] See, e.g., Jackson Turner Main, The Antifederalists: Critics of the Constitution
(Chapel Hill: Univ. of North Carolina Press, 1961); Teeter, "Press Freedom and the
Public Printing: Pennsylvania, 1775–1783," Journalism Quarterly XLV (Autumn,
1968), p. 445.

[42] Folkerts & Teeter, op. cit., pp. 129–149.

[43] See Chapter 1, Sec. 1; see also Norman L. Rosenberg, Protecting the Best Men
(Chapel Hill: Univ. of North Carolina Press, 1985).

[44] See, e.g., the classic newspaper antitrust case of Associated Press v. United
States, 326 U.S. 1, 28, 65 S.Ct. 1416, 1418 (1945).

[45] Jerome A. Barron, "Access to the Press—a New First Amendment Right," 80
Harv.L.Rev. 1641 (1967).

decades the high cost of ownership had barred countless voices from a part in the "marketplace of ideas." The media—giant in size and cost, relatively few in number, and owned by largely like-minded entrepreneurs devoted to the economic and political *status quo*—have the power to deny citizens the right to have their message communicated widely.

The media themselves, in Professor Barron's view, are crucial barriers to a diversity of opinion and fact in the marketplace. "At the very minimum," Barron wrote, "the creation of two remedies is essential—(1) a nondiscriminatory right to purchase editorial advertisements in daily newspapers, and (2) a right of reply for public figures and public officials defamed in newspapers."[46]

Professor Barron's "right of access to the press" ideas were tested—and found wanting—in a famed 1974 decision by the U.S. Supreme Court. In Miami Herald v. Tornillo, the Supreme Court took on a case that had arisen in Florida under that state's "right of reply" statute. The Miami Herald had refused to print a reply by a political candidate, Pat L. Tornillo, Jr., to a Herald editorial criticizing his candidacy for the Florida legislature. When Tornillo asked for his right of reply in the columns of the newspaper, he was refused access, so he sued.

The Florida Supreme Court upheld Tornillo's arguments, and said he should have a right of reply to the print media similar to the right granted under the equal opportunities and fairness doctrines to persons attacked by broadcast media and cable. (See Chapter 12.) At this writing the "equal opportunities" ["equal time"] law for political candidates is still in force, as is the "personal attack" portion of the Federal Communications Commission's fairness doctrine. Other portions of that doctrine, however were repealed by the FCC in 1987. The First Amendment, said the Florida Court, "is not for the benefit of the press so much as for the benefit of us all," and added:[47]

> The right of the public to know all sides of a controversy and from such information to be able to make an enlightened choice is being jeopardized by the growing concentration of the ownership of the mass media into fewer and fewer hands, resulting ultimately in a form of private censorship.

The Supreme Court of the United States, however, reversed the Florida court.[48]

[46] Barron, Freedom of the Press for Whom? (Bloomington: Indiana Univ. Press, 1973), p. 6.

[47] Tornillo v. Miami Herald Pub. Co., 287 So.2d 78 (Fla.1973).

[48] Miami Herald Pub. Co. v. Tornillo, 418 U.S. 241, 94 S.Ct. 2831 (1974).

In so doing, the nation's highest court conceded the dangers of concentration of media ownership, cross-channel ownership and chains and syndicates all of which focused great power to inform and to influence public opinion in the hands of a few. However valid those arguments, the Court said, government coercion by a remedy such as a right of reply "brings about a confrontation with the express provisions of the First Amendment."

Chief Justice Warren Burger wrote for a unanimous court in rejecting the arguments advanced by Pat Tornillo and Jerome Barron. Reviewing past decisions of the Court, the Chief Justice declared:[49]

> The clear implication has been that any such compulsion to publish that which " 'reason' tells them [editors] should not be published" is unconstitutional. A responsible press is an undoubtedly desirable goal, but press responsibility is not mandated by the Constitution and like many other virtues it cannot be legislated.

The Florida statute, the Court said, penalized on the basis of the content of a newspaper. The penalty is increased cost of production, and taking up space that could go to other material the paper may have preferred to print. Infinite expansion of its size to accommodate replies that a statute might require is not to be expected of a newspaper.

But cost aside, the Florida statute failed "to clear the barriers of the First Amendment because of its intrusion into the function of editors." The functions of choosing content, determining size of the paper and treatment of public issues, may be fair or unfair, said the Chief Justice. He added that "[i]t has yet to be demonstrated how governmental regulation of this crucial process can be exercised consistent with First Amendment guarantees of a free press . . ."

The Tornillo decision developed no reasoning as to why newspapers were exempt, but broadcasting need not be, from the requirements of furnishing opportunities to reply. Once again, as in other circumstances, the First Amendment's shield proved stronger for printed journalism than for broadcasting.[50]

SEC. 8.   CRIMINAL LIBEL

Control of words critical of officials and other citizens was provided by criminal libel law in the states the nation's early years, almost disappearing in the years after World War II.

[49] Ibid. Quotes and paraphrases following are from Chief Justice Burger's majority opinion at 2838–2840.

[50] See Chapter 12, Sec. 73.

Like the vampire legend, criminal libel never quite seems to die out. Even though it was conventional wisdom late in the Twentieth Century to assert that criminal libel is dead in the United States, it showed up in Kansas as recently as 1995.

In 1991, Mr. Fitts won a measure of vindication, when a U.S. District Court held that South Carolina's criminal libel statute unconstitutional. The statute was declared overbroad in that it did not stipulate that the publisher had to know information published to be false or published with reckless disregard for truth.[51]

In origins, criminal libel overlaps the old crime of sedition: laws making verbal attacks on government applied also to words that assailed government officials. That may be seen earlier in this chapter in Section 4's discussion of the Alien and Sedition Acts of 1798. After the death of the Alien and Sedition Acts in 1801, statutes making libel a crime began to proliferate in the states.

Keep the phrase *criminal libel* in mind, distinguishing it from *civil libel*. A *criminal* charge or case is brought by an official or agency of government; if a defendant is convicted at trial he or she is subject to imprisonment, payment of a fine, or possibly both. *Civil* libel—dealing with publications (including broadcasts) which are false and which harm a person's *reputation*—do not involve criminal penalties. The person winning a civil libel case can receive "damages" (money) for reputational damage caused by the defendant.

The Jeffersonians who successfully ended the Federalists' Alien and Sedition Acts had a limited sense of freedom themselves. The Jeffersonians, hating the *national* sedition law when brought to bear on their newspapers and editors, nevertheless accepted the power to punish political speech when it was held by the states.[52] Supposedly, citizens could control their local-state affairs and check tendencies toward oppression close to home more easily than they could check a remote, centralized national government.

Laws of the new states provided that libel could be a crime whether it was aimed at plain citizens or government men. That the laws went under the name "criminal libel" laws instead of under the hated term "seditious libel" made them no less effective as tools for prosecution of those who attacked officials.

Under the British common law tradition for criminal libel, truth was not a defense. The old reasoning was that the truer the disparaging words, the more likely the insulted person to seek violent revenge, breaching the peace. Thus the legal aphorism of

---

[51] Fitts v. Kolb, 779 F.Supp. 1502 (D.S.C.1991), 20 Med.L.Rptr. 1033, 1045–1046.

[52] Levy, Emergence of a Free Press, Chaps. 9 and 10; Berns, pp. 89–119.

the Eighteenth Century: "the greater the truth, the greater the libel."

The states drew up safeguards against some of the harshest features of the old English law of libel. The principles that Andrew Hamilton pleaded for in defending Zenger emerged as important ones early in the Nineteenth Century as states embarked upon prosecutions. Truth slowly was established as a defense in criminal libel actions, and juries were permitted to "find the law" (rule whether the words were defamatory) under growing numbers of state constitutions and statutes as the century progressed.

A celebrated early case in New York encouraged the spread. It stemmed from a paragraph reprinted by Federalist editor Harry Croswell from the *New York Evening Post* attacking President Thomas Jefferson:[53]

> Jefferson paid Callender [a Republican editor] for calling Washington a traitor, a robber, and a perjurer; for calling Adams a hoary-headed old incendiary, and for most grossly slandering the private characters of men who he well knew to be virtuous.

The great Federalist leader, Alexander Hamilton, in 1804 took the case after Croswell had been convicted of criminal libel in a jury trial in which he had not been permitted to show the truth of his charge. Hamilton argued that "the liberty of the press consists of the right to publish with impunity truth with good motives for justifiable ends though reflecting on government, magistracy, or individuals." This, of course, made the intent of the publisher crucial. He also urged that the jury be allowed to find both the law and the facts of the case. He lost, the appeals court being evenly divided. The result, however, was so repugnant to people and lawmakers that the New York Legislature in 1805 passed a law embracing the principles that Hamilton urged.[54]

Other states adopted Hamilton's formula, and a few, indeed, made truth a defense no matter what the intent of the writer. But the death of the vicious "the greater the truth the greater the libel" doctrine was slow and reluctant.

Nineteenth Century American courts were reluctant to give truth a protected position in the law, even though statutes seemed to endorse the position that the public needs to know the truth. As legislatures adopted truth as a defense in libel statutes during the Nineteenth Century, courts nevertheless clung tenaciously to the old idea that if the truth produced a breach of the peace, it could be

---

[53] People v. Croswell, 3 Johns.Cas. 337 (N.Y.1804).

[54] An Act Concerning Libels, Laws of the State of New York, Albany, 1805.

punished.[55] Although few statutes or constitutions retained words' "tendency to breach the peace" as a basis for criminality in libel in the Twentieth Century, judges who wanted to employ it found it readily accessible in common law principles.

Criminal libel actions were few through most of the Nineteenth Century. They surged in number in the 1880s and held at some 100 reported cases per decade for 30 years or more. Not all, by any means, were brought for defamation of public officials in the pattern of seditious libel actions.[56] But criticism of police, governors, mayors, judges, prosecutors, sheriffs, and other government officials was the offense in scores of criminal libel cases.

For whatever reasons, criminal libel actions dropped after World War I from about 100 per decade to much smaller numbers.[57] Courts increasingly held that civil libel suits to recover damages were much to be preferred to criminal libel prosecutions, which more and more seemed inappropriate to personal squabbles between citizens. Duelling, that extreme breach of the peace, was out of favor as a means of settling personal differences or avenging verbal insults, as in centuries past. Also, the defamed person ordinarily had more to gain through a civil judgment for money damages than through a criminal conviction.

Criminal Libel of Officials

In 1966, the U.S. Supreme Court focused on the concept of breach of the peace from common law criminal libel, finding that it did not square with the First Amendment. Merely to say that words which tend to cause breach of the peace are criminal is too indefinite to be understandable, the Court said. The case, Ashton v. Kentucky, involved a pamphlet in which Ashton charged, among other things, that a police chief had acted lawlessly during a strike of miners. Ashton was convicted under a judge's definition of criminal libel as "any writing calculated to create disturbances of the peace." The Supreme Court said that without more specificity, that was too vague an offense to be constitutionally permissible.[58]

Garrison v. Louisiana (1966)

In a second 1966 criminal libel decision, Garrison v. Louisiana, the Supreme Court reached back to its 1964 ruling in the civil libel

---

[55] Elizabeth Goepel, "The Breach of the Peace Provision in Nineteenth Century Criminal Libel Law," (Univ. of Wis.1981), unpublished Master's thesis.

[56] John D. Stevens, et al., Criminal Libel as Seditious Libel, 43 Journalism Quar. 110 (1966); Robert A. Leflar, The Social Utility of the Criminal Law of Defamation, 34 Texas L.Rev. 984 (1956). Stevens et al. found that about one-fifth (31) of the 148 criminal libel cases reported in the half-century after World War I grew out of charges made against officials.

[57] Stevens, op. cit.

[58] Ashton v. Kentucky, 384 U.S. 195, 198, 86 S.Ct. 1407, 1409–1411.

case, New York Times v. Sullivan. Applying the logic of *Sullivan* to a criminal libel case involving criticism of public officials had a heavy impact on the law. The *Sullivan* decision said that critical words must be used with actual malice if they were to be the object of a civil libel action against officials. In Garrison v. Louisiana (1966), the Court transferred the same rule into the field of criminal libel. There "Big Jim" Garrison, a flamboyant prosecuting attorney for the State of Louisiana, gave out a statement at a press conference saying several judges of his parish (county) were lazy and inattentive to their official duties. Garrison was convicted of criminal libel, and his case ultimately reached the Supreme Court.

The Court cited the *Sullivan* rule defining actual malice: a public official might recover damages for civil libel—or now, sustain a prosecution for criminal libel—only if it could be shown that there was knowing falsity or reckless disregard for the truth. The Court said:[59]

> The reasons which led us so to hold [in *Sullivan*] * * * apply with no less force merely because the remedy is criminal.* * * Truth may not be the subject of either civil or criminal sanctions where discussion of public affairs is concerned. And since " * * * erroneous statement is inevitable in free debate * * * "only those false statements made with a high degree of their probable falsity demanded by New York Times may be the subject of either civil or criminal sanctions. For speech concerning public affairs is more than self-expression; it is the essence of self-government.

In the late 1990s, criminal libel seemed to have little in the way of constitutional support, but there are occasional signs that criminal libel is not yet buried. As Robert Sack has noted, a 1991 Colorado Supreme Court decision held that state's criminal libel statute invalid "only insofar as it reaches constitutionally protected statements about public officials or public figures on matters of public concern." The Colorado Supreme Court found that "where one private individual has disparaged the reputation of another private individual," the Colorado statute remains valid.[60]

So the good news is that criminal libel cases are rare. The bad news is that criminal libel won't quite go away. The Kansas case of

---

[59] Garrison v. Louisiana, 379 U.S. 64, 85 S.Ct. 209 (1964); Harry Kalven, "The New York times Case: A Note on the Central Meaning of the First Amendment," 1965 Supreme Court Review 191.

[60] People v. Ryan, 806 P.2d 935 (1991), 19 Med.L.Rptr. 1074, 1078, cited in Sack, op. cit., at p. 174n. This case involved a fake "wanted poster" distributed to several bars and businesses in Fort Collins, Colo., by a disgruntled former date, falsely accusing a woman of being wanted for a number of crimes and falsely warning that she had sexually transmitted diseases.

Phelps v. Hamilton (1995) is a reminder that criminal libel law slumbers in most states and may wake up and cause trouble. In this unusual case, the Tenth Circuit interpreted a 1988 Kansas statute in order to make it constitutional. That is, the court ruled that because the statute was enacted after Garrison v. Louisiana (1966), the Kansas legislature must have meant to include *Garrison's* twin pronouncements, (1) that truth must be allowed as a defense to criminal libel, and (2) that proof of actual malice is required to make a criminal libel conviction stick.[61]

The Libel Defense Resource Center's valuable 50–State Survey reported in 1995 that a number of states—including Alaska, Arizona, California, Hawaii, Indiana, Nebraska, Oregon, Vermont, and Wyoming—had repealed their criminal libel statutes. Most of these repeals came in the 1970s and 1980s, and Pennsylvania's criminal libel statute was declared unconstitutional in 1972.[62]

Criminal Libel of Groups

Perhaps adding tenacity to the shrinking offense of criminal libel was a highly unusual case of 1952 that claimed the attention of much of the world of civil liberties. It involved a special and rarely employed version of the ancient criminal libel law—that under some circumstances, *groups* could be libeled and the state could bring criminal action against the libeler. Beauharnais v. Illinois was decided in 1952 with a finding of "guilty."[63] It involved a leaflet attack on the African Americans in Chicago, at a time when the memory of Hitler Germany's mass killing of Jews was fresh in the minds of the nation. Migration of blacks from the south into northern cities was swelling. Beauharnais, president of the White Circle League, had organized his group to distribute the leaflets, and they did so in downtown Chicago. Among other things the leaflet called for city officials to stop "the further encroachment, harassment, and invasion of the white people * * * by the Negro * * * ", and predicted that "rapes, robberies, knives, guns, and marijuana of the negro" surely would unite Chicago whites against blacks.

Beauharnais was prosecuted and convicted under an Illinois law making it unlawful to exhibit a publication which "portrays depravity, criminality, unchastity, or lack of virtue of a class of citizens, of any race, color, creed or religion which said publication * * * exposes the citizens of any race, color, creed or religion to

---

[61] Phelps v. Hamilton, 59 F.3d 1058 (10th Cir.1995), 23 Med.L.Rptr. 2121.

[62] Libel Defense Resource Center, op. cit., passim.

[63] 343 U.S. 250, 72 S.Ct. 725 (1952). See also People v. Spielman, 318 Ill. 482, 149 N.E. 466 (1925). Also "Knights of Columbus" cases: People v. Turner, 28 Cal.App. 766, 154 P. 34 (1914); People v. Gordan, 63 Cal.App. 627, 219 P. 486 (1923); Crane v. State, 14 Okl.Crim. 30, 166 P. 1110 (1917); Alumbaugh v. State, 39 Ga.App. 559, 147 S.E. 714 (1929). And see Joseph Tannehaus, "Group Libel," 35 Cornell L.Q. 261 (1950).

contempt, derision, or obloquy or which is productive of breach of the peace or riots."[64]

The charges against Negroes, said the Court, were unquestionably libelous; and the central question became whether the "liberty" of the Fourteenth Amendment prevents a state from punishing such libels when they are directed not at an individual, but at "designated collectivities." The Court said that only if the law were a "willful and purposeless restriction unrelated to the peace and well-being of the State," could the Court deny a state power to punish utterances directed at a defined group.

Justice Frankfurter found that for more than a century, Illinois had been "the scene of exacerbated tension between races, often flaring into violence and destruction." He cited the murder of abolitionist Elijah Lovejoy in 1837, the "first northern race riot"— in Chicago in 1908—in which six persons were killed, and subsequent violence in the state of Illinois down to the Cicero, Ill. race riot of 1951. He concluded that "In the face of this history and its frequent obligato of extreme racial and religious propaganda, we would deny experience to say that the Illinois legislature was without reason in seeking ways to curb false or malicious defamation of racial and religious groups."[65]

Four members of the court delivered strong dissents to the majority opinion that sustained Beauharnais' conviction. Justice Hugo Black stated much of the case against the concept of group libel as an offense acceptable to American freedom. Calling the law a "state censorship" instrument, Black said that permitting states to experiment in curbing freedom of expression "is a startling and frightening doctrine in a country dedicated to self-government by its people."[66]

By 1992, hate-crime legislation was adopted in most states: All but four states—Alaska, Nebraska, New Mexico and Wyoming—had hate crime statutes. Thirty-one states' laws closely followed a model of the Anti–Defamation League of B'nai B'rith calling for both criminal sanctions and civil penalties. But in 1992, the U.S. Supreme Court was decided R.A.V. v. St. Paul, a test of a city ordinance's application to a 17–year-old accused of cross-burning in a black family's fenced yard.[67]

The 17–year-old—identified as R.A.V.—was accused of violating a St. Paul, Minnesota, "Bias–Motivated Crime Ordinance." That

---

[64] Beauharnais v. Illinois, 343 U.S. 250, 251, 72 S.Ct. 725, 728 (1952).

[65] Ibid., at 258–261, 72 S.Ct. at 731–733. Illinois dropped this statute in 1961, but later enacted a hate-crime law.

[66] Ibid., at 270, 272, 273, 72 S.Ct. at 737, 738, 739.

[67] Mary Deibel, "Hate Crimes," Scripps–Howard News Service, Knoxville News–Sentinel, Dec. 1, 1991, p. F–1, and see Hadley Arkes, "Civility and Restriction of Speech: Rediscovering the Defamation of Groups," 1974 Sup.Ct.Rev. 281–335; City of Chicago v. Lambert, 47 Ill.App.2d 151, 197 N.E.2d 448 (1964).

ordinance made it misdemeanor disorderly conduct for anyone to place, on public or private property, any symbol, object or graffiti "including, but not limited to, burning a cross or placing a Nazi swastika, which one knows . . . arouses anger, alarm, or resentment in others on the basis of race, color, creed, religion or gender. . . . "[68] The Minnesota Supreme Court upheld the ordinance, saying it merely made illegal speech of the "fighting words" variety, words long held to be beyond constitutional protection.[69]

Writing for five members of the Court, Justice Antonin Scalia declared the ordinance unconstitutional because "it prohibits otherwise permitted speech solely on the basis of the subject it addresses." He wrote:[70]

> [B]urning a cross in someone's yard is reprehensible. But St. Paul has sufficient means at its disposal to control such behavior without adding the First Amendment to the fire.

Although the other four members of the Court concurred, they took aim on the majority's reasoning. For example, Justice White argued that by equating fighting words with political expression, the Court's majority showed disrespect for the latter:[71]

> Fighting words are not a means of exchanging views, rallying supporters, or registering a protest: they are directed against individuals to provoke violence or to inflict injury. Therefore, a ban on all fighting words or on a subset of the fighting words category would restrict only the social evil of hate speech, without creating the danger of driving viewpoints from the marketplace.

> * * *

> Indeed, by characterizing fighting words as a form of "debate," the majority legitimizes hate speech as a form of public discussion.

Effects on Campus Hate Speech Codes?

Trying to curtail racist or ethnic hate speech, a number of colleges and universities have ladled good intentions into their student conduct codes. However, as Tim England wrote in 1992, speech codes of universities have been found unconstitutional when subject to court challenges.[72]

[68] R.A.V. v. St. Paul, 505 U.S. 377, 112 S.Ct. 2538, 2541 (1992).

[69] Ibid., citing Chaplinsky v. New Hampshire, 315 U.S. 568, 62 S.Ct. 766 (1942).

[70] 505 U.S. 377, 112 S.Ct. 2538, 2550 (1992).

[71] Ibid., p. 2554.

[72] Tim England, "Racist Speech: A First Amendment Issue on College Campuses," Southwest Colloquium of the Association for Education in Journalism and Mass Communication, 1992.

William Celis 3d reported in The New York Times that the R.A.V. case appeared to weaken if not invalidate some speech codes. He pointed out in 1992 that this was no small matter because perhaps as many as 100 universities had instituted codes to punish discriminatory or intimidating name-calling or symbolic acts based on racism or other prejudices: ethnic, religious, sex, sexual orientation, national origin, or handicap.[73]

Such codes collide with traditional ideas of free expression on campus. For example, if a sociology class discussed racial slurs, might that not violate a hate speech regulation? Because of such "overbreadth," codes at the University of Michigan and the University of Wisconsin–Milwaukee were found unconstitutional.[74]

William Celis found that such constitutional concerns have caused some university officials and lawyers to take another tack: looking toward language prohibiting one-on-one incidents of violence or intimidation. He wrote that such an approaches "are considered more likely to survive legal challenge because they closely follow state and Federal anti-discrimination laws."[75]

Criminal libel continues to be rare, but the impulse behind such laws—to punish dissidents, to silence criticism, by no means is gone.[76] As Norman L. Rosenberg has noted, although the means for suppression or intimidation may vary, the end remains the same.[77] Over time in the United States, when those in power could no longer use seditious or criminal libel effectively to muzzle or to punish dissent, they switched to lawsuits for civil libel.[78] The key question, then, revolves around the concept of *political* libel, regardless of the label the particular legal action may carry.[79]

SEC. 9. TAXATION

The mass media are constitutionally protected from discriminatory or punitive taxation.

Taxation has long been a fighting word to the press. Taxes on the press instituted in England were called "taxes on knowledge"

---

[73] William Celis 3d, "Universities Reconsidering Bans on Hate Speech," The New York Times, June 24, 1992, p. A11.

[74] England, op. cit. Cases discussed by him included Doe v. University of Michigan, 721 F.Supp. 852 (E.D.Mich.1989) and The UWM Post v. Board of Regents, University of Wisconsin System, 774 F.Supp. 1163 (E.D.Wis.1991).

[75] Celis, op. cit.

[76] Eberle v. Municipal Court, Los Angeles Judicial District, 55 Cal.App.3d 423, 127 Cal.Rptr. 594, 600 (1976). For a suggestion that criminal libel may not be dead, see Keeton v. Hustler Magazine, 465 U.S. 770, 104 S.Ct. 1473 n. 6 (1984), 10 Med. L.Rptr. 1405.

[77] See Norman L. Rosenberg, Protecting the Best Men: An Interpretive History of Libel (Chapel Hill: University of North Carolina Press), p. 6.

[78] Ibid., Chapters 4 and 5.

[79] Ibid., p. 7.

because they raised the purchase price of pamphlets and other printed materials beyond the means of most persons. Taxation also came to be a hated symbol of control and oppression in American history. The British Stamp Act of 1765 imposed great hardships on printers in colonial America, taxing newspapers, advertisements, pamphlets and many legal documents and became a great rallying cry for colonists who resisted British authority.[80] A huge storm of protest arose in the colonies, reflected in angry writings in newspapers and pamphlets and, ultimately, in mobs which forced British stamp agents to resign. Faced with such furious opposition, Parliament repealed the Stamp Taxes as they affected printer-editors.

If American colonists hated the Stamp Act taxes and argued against them in terms of "freedom of the press," American memories also were very short. In 1785, only two years after the War of Independence officially ended, the state of Massachusetts passed a newspaper stamp tax.

Protests echoing the Stamp Act disturbances soon resounded from the Massachusetts newspapers.[81] Such protests quickly led the to the repeal of the Massachusetts stamp tax on newspapers later in 1785, although the state's legislature soon enacted a tax on newspaper ads.[82] The advertising tax was repealed in 1788.[83]

Newspapers and other units of the mass media of communications are businesses. As such, the media are not immune from taxation just like other business enterprises, as long as the taxes fall with a more or less even hand upon the press as well as other businesses. *Discriminatory* or *punitive* taxation, however, raises quite different issues. The classic case in United States constitutional law occurred during the 1930s and involved the flamboyant Huey "Kingfish" Long, the political boss and governor of Louisiana who entertained dreams of someday becoming President. The Supreme Court decision in Grosjean, Supervisor of Accounts of Louisiana v. American Press Co., Inc.[84] effectively halted a Huey Long-instigated attempt to use a punitive tax to injure newspapers which opposed Long's political regime.

During the 1930s, Louisiana's larger daily newspapers were increasingly expressing opposition to Long's political machine. Lou-

[80] Arthur M. Schlesinger, Prelude to Independence: The Newspaper War on Britain, 1763–1776 (New York: Knopf, 1958), p. 68.

[81] Massachusetts Centinel, May 28, 1785.

[82] Ibid., July 6, July 30, 1785.

[83] Clyde Augustus Duniway, Freedom of the Press in Massachusetts (New York, 1906), p. 137.

[84] 297 U.S. 233, 56 S.Ct. 444 (1936).

isiana's larger newspapers' sniping at Governor Long's dictatorial posturings soon brought about retaliation. The Louisiana legislature passed a special two per cent license tax on the gross receipts of all newspapers, magazines, or periodicals having a circulation of more than 20,000 copies per week.[85] Of Louisiana's 163 newspapers, only 13 had circulations of more than 20,000 per week. Of these 13 newspapers to which the tax applied, 12 were opponents of Long's political machine.[86] This transparent attempt to silence newspaper critics was challenged in the courts by nine Louisiana newspaper publishers who produced the 13 newspapers then appearing in the state which had circulations of more than 20,000 copies a week.

In declaring the Louisiana tax unconstitutional, a noted conservative—Justice George Sutherland—spoke for a unanimous Supreme Court. Justice Sutherland, a man not revered for his felicity of expression, may indeed have had some able assistance in writing what has come to be known as "Sutherland's great opinion in *Grosjean.*" It has been asserted that Sutherland's opinion included a proposed concurring opinion which had been drafted by the famed liberal Justice Benjamin Nathan Cardozo, and which the Court wished to add into Justice Sutherland's opinion.[87]

Whether assisted by Cardozo or not, the Sutherland opinion in Grosjean remains noteworthy. Justice Sutherland began with a historical overview of government-imposed dangers to freedom of expression, including reference to John Milton's 1644 "Appeal for the Liberty of Unlicensed Printing" and to the end of the licensing of the press in England in 1695. As Sutherland noted, "mere exemption from previous censorship was soon recognized as too narrow a view of the liberty of the press." Sutherland wrote that taxes in Eighteenth Century England were quite commonly characterized as "taxes on knowledge."[88]

Justice Sutherland asserted that if taxes had been the only issue, many of England's best men would not have risked their careers and their lives to fight against them. The issue in England for many years, however, involved discriminatory taxation designed to control the press and silence criticism of government. The *Grosjean* opinion added:[89]

[85] Grosjean v. American Press Co., 297 U.S. 233, 240, 56 S.Ct. 444, 445 (1936).

[86] J. Edward Gerald, The Press and the Constitution 1931–1947 (Minneapolis, University of Minnesota Press, 1948) p. 100; William A. Hachten, The Supreme Court on Freedom of the Press: Decisions and Dissents (Ames, Iowa: Iowa State University Press 1968) p. 77; Grosjean v. American Press Co., 297 U.S. 233, 56 S.Ct. 444, 445 (1936).

[87] Irving Brant, The Bill of Rights: Its Origin and Meaning (New York: Bobbs–Merrill, 1965) pp. 403–404.

[88] Grosjean v. American Press Co., 297 U.S. 233, 249, 56 S.Ct. 444, 449 (1936).

[89] Grosjean v. American Press Co., 297 U.S. 233, 247–248, 56 S.Ct. 444, 448 (1936).

The framers of the First Amendment were familiar with the English struggle, which had then continued for nearly eighty years and was destined to go on for another sixty-five years, at the end of which time it culminated in a lasting abandonment of the obnoxious taxes. The framers were likewise familiar with the then recent [1785–1788] Massachusetts [stamp tax] episode . . .

Justice Sutherland rejected the State of Louisiana's argument that the English common law in force when the Constitution was adopted forbade only prior restraints on the press and said nothing about forbidding taxation.[90] In reply, Sutherland's opinion quoted from a great 19th century American constitutional scholar, Judge Thomas Cooley, and declared that Cooley had laid down the test to be applied.[91]

The evils to be prevented were not the censorship of the press merely, but any action of the government by means of which it might prevent such free and general discussion of public matters as seems absolutely essential to prepare the people for an intelligent exercise of their rights as citizens.

Application of this test led Justice Sutherland to rule that the Louisiana gross receipts tax on its larger newspapers was an unconstitutional abridgement of the First and Fourth Amendments. Sutherland declared:[92]

It is not intended by anything we have said to suggest that the owners of newspapers are immune from any of the ordinary forms of taxation for support of the government. But this is not an ordinary form of tax, but one single in kind, with a long history of hostile misuse against the freedom of the press.

* * *

The tax here involved is bad not because it takes money from the pockets of the appellees. If that were all, a wholly different question would be presented. It is bad because, in the light of its history and of its present setting, it is seen to be a deliberate and calculated device in

---

[90] Grosjean v. American Press Co., 297 U.S. 233, 249, 56 S.Ct. 444, 449 (1936).

[91] Grosjean v. American Press Co., 297 U.S. 233, 249, 56 S.Ct. 444, 449 (1936), quoting 2 Cooley's Constitutional Limitations (8th ed.) p. 886.

[92] Grosjean v. American Press Co., 297 U.S. 233, 250–251, 56 S.Ct. 444, 449 (1936). Accord: See City of Baltimore v. A.S. Abell Co., 218 Md. 273, 145 A.2d 111, 119 (1958). It was held that Baltimore city ordinances imposing taxes on advertising media were unconstitutional in that they discriminatorily taxed newspapers and radio and television stations. About 90 per cent of the impact of the taxes was on those businesses.

the guise of a tax to limit the circulation of information to which the public is entitled in virtue of the constitutional guaranties. A free press stands as one of the great interpreters between the government and the people. To allow it to be fettered is to fetter ourselves.

Despite these ringing words, it should be noted again that the communications media are not exempt from paying non-discriminatory general business taxes. A case in point involved *The Corona Daily Independent,* a California newspaper which challenged a $32–a–year business license tax imposed by the City of Corona. The newspaper, which had paid the tax in a number of previous years, in 1951 refused to pay the tax. The newspaper went to court, arguing that the tax violated freedom of the press as guaranteed by the First and Fourteenth Amendments. However, the California Appellate Court ruled:[93]

> There is ample authority to the effect that newspapers and the business of newspaper publication are not made exempt from the ordinary forms of taxes for the support of local government by the provisions of the First and Fourteenth Amendments.

Grosjean v. American Press Co. remains the leading case for the proposition that the mass media are constitutionally protected from discriminatory or punitive taxation. The *Grosjean* case, as seen on earlier pages, dealt with a garish fact situation, a transparent attempt by Louisiana Governor Huey "Kingfish" Long and his allies to silence newspaper critics.

Unlike the *Grosjean* situation, the State of Minnesota was operating out of more defensible motives during the 1970s when it enacted a "use tax" on paper and ink consumed applicable to newspapers. This apparently was only a revenue measure, not an attempt to control or to punish the press. Even so, the Supreme Court of the United States voided the tax by an 8–1 margin. The tax was held unconstitutional because it singled out the press for special treatment.

"Use taxes" are imposed by states to discourage their citizens from purchasing items in other states which have lower sales taxes. Minnesota's newspapers were exempted from use taxes until 1971, when the state began taxing the cost of paper and ink used in producing a publication.[94] In 1974, another change in the tax law

---

[93] City of Corona v. Corona Daily Independent, 115 Cal.App.2d 382, 252 P.2d 56 (1953), certiorari denied 346 U.S. 833, 74 S.Ct. 2 (1953). See also Giragi v. Moore, 49 Ariz. 74, 64 P.2d 819 (1937) (general sales tax law placing a one per cent tax upon businesses' sales or gross income not unconstitutional as applied to newspapers); Arizona Publishing Co. v. O'Neil, 22 F.Supp. 117 (D.Ariz.1938), affirmed 304 U.S. 543, 58 S.Ct. 950 (1938).

[94] Minn.Stat.Ann. §§ 297A.14, 287A.25i.

exempted a publication's first $100,000 of ink and paper consumed from the 4% use tax.[95]

The $100,000 exemption meant that only the largest of Minnesota's publishers were liable to pay the tax. Only 11 publishers, producing 14 of the state's 388 paid-circulation newspapers, had to pay the tax in 1974. The Minneapolis Star and Tribune Company was the major revenue source from the tax. Of $893,355 collected in 1974, $608,634 was paid by the Star and Tribune.[96]

The Star and Tribune Company sued, asking a refund of the use taxes paid from January 1, 1974, to May 31, 1975. The company contended that the use tax violated freedom of the press and equal protection of the laws as guaranteed by the First and Fourteenth Amendments.[97] The Minnesota Supreme Court ruled the use tax constitutional,[98] and the Supreme Court of the United States then noted probable jurisdiction.[99]

Justice Sandra Day O'Connor wrote for an 8–1 Supreme Court in declaring the Minnesota tax unconstitutional on its face because it singled out publications for unique treatment under the state's law. She declared that there is evidence that differential taxation of the press would have troubled the Framers of the First Amendment. "A power to tax differentially, as opposed to a power to tax generally, gives government a powerful weapon against the taxpayer selected."[1] Her opinion also suggested the threat of burdensome taxes might operate as a form of censorship, making the press wary of publishing the critical comments which often allow it to serve as an important restraint on government.

Even though the media are protected from discriminatory or punitive taxation by the First Amendment, a 1987 Ad Tax dispute in Florida was a sign of things to come. In 1987, Florida passed a 5% business service sales tax which included taxes on mass media advertising. That tax on services cast a wide net: other services declared taxable included accounting, legal services, and pest control.[2]

[95] Minn.Stat.Ann. § 297A.14.

[96] Minneapolis Star and Tribune Co. v. Minnesota Commissioner of Revenue, 460 U.S. 575, 103 S.Ct. 1365, 1368 (1983), 9 Med.L.Rptr. 1369.

[97] Ibid.

[98] Minneapolis Star and Tribune Co. v. Commissioner of Revenue, 314 N.W.2d 201 (Minn.1981).

[99] Minneapolis Star and Tribune Co. v. Minnesota Commissioner of Revenue, 457 U.S. 1130, 102 S.Ct. 2955 (1982).

[1] Ibid., at 586, 103 S.Ct. at 1372. Justice—later Chief Justice William H. Rehnquist was the sole dissenter.

[2] Marilyn Marks, "Florida Ends Tax on Services ...", Governing, January, 1988, p. 57; "Governor Acts to End Florida Tax," The New York Times, Sept. 19, 1987, p. 21.

Although that clumsily designed tax on services quickly fell under its own weight and a barrage of media complaints, that Florida episode symbolizes federal and state governments' ceaseless hunt for new revenues. Because governments are exhausting traditional sources of money, various aspects of the media industry present inviting possibilities for taxation which could well be held to be constitutional.

Small wonder that Florida's legislature repealed that tax within a matter of months. USA Today gave examples of the unwieldiness of the Florida tax as it would have applied to advertising:[3]

> IBM might pay $200,000 for a 30–second commercial during NBC's St. Elsewhere. If Floridians are 5% of the nationwide TV audience, IBM theoretically would pay $10,000 to reach them. So IBM's tax liability for that commercial would be 5% of $10,000, or $500.

Although that services tax died in Florida in 1987, it was evident in the 1990s that legislatures all over the nation were in hot pursuit of new sales revenues. The New York Times and Presstime magazine reported in 1992 that a tax on circulation was under consideration in California, and that other states might soon follow that approach. In addition, as of 1992, there were 14 states, including California, taxing newspaper sales, with sales taxes proposed in seven other states.[4]

In Leathers v. Medlock, the Supreme Court took up the kind of issue that could make it the High Court of Taxation for some years. In *Leathers,* the Court framed to the issue as "whether the First Amendment prevents a State from imposing its sales tax on only selected segments of the media." This case involved a complaint by Arkansas cable TV operators that a state sales tax applied to cable TV but excluded or exempted newspapers, magazines and satellite broadcast services.

The U.S. Supreme Court held that cable operators' rights were not violated because the Arkansas tax did not apply just to the media but was a tax generally applicable to businesses. Furthermore, unlike the Minnesota use tax on print and ink, applying to only 16 of 374 newspapers in that state, the Arkansas tax applied to all 100 cable TV operations in the state.[5]

[3] James Cox, "Big advertisers balk at new Florida sales tax," USA TODAY, p. B1, June 23, 1987.

[4] Alex S. Jones, "Newspapers See A Threat of Spreading Sales Taxes," The New York Times, Sept. 19, 1991, p. C6, using a graphic from Presstime magazine. States shown with sales taxes on newspapers: Alabama, Arizona, California, Delaware, Florida, Hawaii, Georgia.

[5] 499 U.S. 439, 111 S.Ct. 1438, 1443 (1991), 18 Med.L.Rptr. 1953, 1956.

In California, Sacramento Cable Television (SCT) and a cable subscriber challenged a city ordinance including cable TV under a city utility user's tax along with gas, electric, and telephone services. The California Court of Appeals, Third Circuit, agreed with the prevailing view that cable TV is speech protected by the First Amendment. Even so, that appellate court held it constitutional for Sacramento to tax cable TV because cable logically could be categorized along with other utilities.[6]

What of a tax applied to newspapers but not magazines? In Florida Department of Revenue v. Magazine Publishers of America (1992), the Florida Supreme Court ruled that a state sales tax imposed upon magazines but not upon newspapers did not pass muster under the First Amendment.

The Florida Supreme Court found that the state's sales tax was not "content neutral" in exempting newspapers. Although some of the requirements publications had to meet to be termed "newspapers" were content-neutral (usually published weekly or daily, intended for general circulation to the public), one requirement was a problem. One provision called for the Department of Revenue to determine whether publications—to be "newspapers" and thus exempt from the sales tax—contain " 'reports of current events and matters of general interest which appeal to a wide spectrum of the general public.' "[7] That criterion added up to an impermissible content-based judgment which invalidated the Florida tax exemption of newspapers under the First Amendment.

The magazine publishers—which hoped to join newspaper publishers in Florida in a tax exemption—were disappointed. Ironically, instead of invalidating the tax on magazines, the Florida Supreme Court invalidated the newspapers' exemption. If misery loves company, it now has more of it.

The basic rule remains: the press may not be singled out for "differential treatment" when being taxed. That does not mean the press will pay less in taxes than other kinds of businesses.

SEC. 10.　THE CONTEMPT POWER AND CRITICIZING COURTS

Criticism of judges while cases were pending was long considered an interference with justice, and was punishable as contempt of court.

The offense known as "constructive contempt of court"—notably, contempt shown toward judges in newspaper criticism—

---

[6] Sacramento Cable Television v. Sacramento, 234 Cal.App.3d 232, 286 Cal.Rptr. 470 (1991), 19 Med.L.Rptr. 1532, 1533, 1536. See also Cox Cable Hampton Roads Inc. v. Norfolk, 242 Va. 394, 410 S.E.2d 652 (1991), 19 Med.L.Rptr. 1656, holding that although cable TV may be taxed as a utility, the case should be returned to the trial court to consider Cox Cable's equal protection claim.

[7] Department of Revenue v. Magazine Publishers of America, 604 So.2d 459 (Fla.1992), 20 Med.L.Rptr. 1502, 1503.

had a long and 1sometimes troublesome life in the United States. This nation had been in existence almost 150 years before the U.S. Supreme Court issued decisions virtually demolishing that word crime.

Judges had—and still have—power to control what goes on in their courtrooms, or to punish persons who are under their jurisdiction and disobey court orders. That is the "direct contempt" power. If a person stands up in a courtroom and screams obscenities at a judge, the judge can use his or her "summary" power—can declare that person in contempt of court, and can sentence that individual *on the spot* to pay a fine, serve a jail term, or both. And journalists, as discussed in Chapter 10, sometimes run afoul of the contempt power when they defy court orders to reveal sources for stories or information gathered in the course of reporting.

The constructive contempt control over the press lay in the power of judges to punish their critics while cases were pending in court. Even though English precedent for such a power was weak, the American judiciary took this power unto itself and extended it.[8]

Judges taking such power upon themselves proved upsetting, and Pennsylvania and New York both passed statutes early in the Nineteenth Century to curb judges' power over published criticism. And in 1831, Congress passed a similar law. The reason for the Congressional action came from an attorney, Luke Lawless, who had been found in contempt by Federal Judge James H. Peck. Lawless, who had published newspaper articles critical of the judge's handling of land claims, had sought the impeachment of Judge Peck. Judge Peck retaliated by finding the lawyer in contempt and suspending him from the practice of law for eighteen months.

The House of Representatives ultimately impeached (brought charges) against Judge Peck, but the Senate ultimately found Peck not guilty by the narrowest of margins.[9]

But Congress wanted no more punishment for criticism of judges in the press. Only a month after the impeachment proceedings against Judge Peck, Congress passed an act in 1831 saying that federal judges might punish only misbehavior taking place "in the presence of the courts * * * or so near thereto as to obstruct the administration of justice."[10]

---

[8] Walter Nelles and Carol Weiss King, Contempt by Publication in the U.S., 28 Col.L.Rev. 401–431, 525–562 (1928).

[9] Arthur J. Stansbury, Report of the Trial of James H. Peck (Boston: Hilliard Gray & Co., 1833).

[10] Nelles and King, op. cit. at p. 430, citing Act of Mar. 2, 1831, c. 98, 4 Stat. 487.

Many states' judges, however, were not ready to permit criticism. The main line of cases from the mid-Nineteenth Century until 1941 found judges asserting their "immemorial power": to cite and punish for newspaper criticism taking place far from their courtrooms.[11]

Two rules emerged: "pendency" and "reasonable tendency." The pendency rule meant that criticism of courts and judges could not be published while a case was still pending. That included attempts to influence judges or participants in cases or publishing false or inaccurate reports of trials. "When a case is finished," said Justice Oliver Wendell Holmes, Jr., in a federal case in 1907, "courts are subject to the same criticism as other people ..." Published criticism could then be labeled as interference with the judicial process and punished as contempt.

The "reasonable tendency" judicial concept meant that there did not have to be any proof of harm to the judicial process from published criticism. A "tendency" to create such harm would be enough to cite for contempt, the U.S. Supreme Court said in a 1918 decision.[12]

Note that Justice Holmes, who wrote for the majority in the 1907 Patterson v. Colorado decision involving criticism of pending cases, valued the role of a free press more when he dissented from a 1919 decision involving "reasonable tendency." He declared that the Court's majority erred in upholding a contempt citation against a Toledo newspaper. His dissent invoked the 1831 federal statute, so long forgotten. Holmes wrote, "so near thereto" means so near as actually to obstruct justice, and misbehavior means more than unfavorable comment or disrespect.[13]

Then in a series of decisions in the 1940s, the Supreme Court yielded up its long-standing power, telling the entire judicial branch to do the same. In Bridges v. California,[14] Justice Hugo Black's majority opinion shredded both the pending case rule and the reasonable tendency test. In *Bridges*, trial-court judges had convicted Californians for contempt by publication for admonishing courts about pending cases. Black said that such contempt orders silence discussion when public interest would be at its height, and that any moratorium on public discussion—which could last for years during a case's "pendency" was not an insignificant abridgement of freedom of expression. Black also said that neither a reasonable tenden-

---

[11] Ronald L. Goldfarb, The Contempt Power (New York, 1963).

[12] Toledo Newspaper Co. v. United States, 247 U.S. 402, 421, 38 S.Ct. 560, 564 (1918).

[13] Ibid., at 422, 38 S.Ct. at 565. See Abrams v. U.S. (1919), discussed above at p. 20.

[14] 314 U.S. 252, 62 S.Ct. 190 (1941).

cy nor an "inherent tendency" of words to interfere with courts was enough to support a contempt order. A "clear and present danger" to the administration of justice had to be shown.

The clear and present danger rule was used in other cases to overturn contempt by publication convictions. The rare contempt conviction for criticizing courts now is almost certain to be overturned on appeal.[15]

[15] 314 U.S. at 268–269, 62 S.Ct. at 196–197. See also Pennekamp v. Florida, 328 U.S. 331, 66 S.Ct. 1029 (1946); Craig v. Harney, 331 U.S. 367, 67 S.Ct. 1249 (1947); Wood v. Georgia, 370 U.S. 375, 82 S.Ct. 1364 (962), and Cooper v. Rockford Newspapers, 34 Ill.App.3d 645, 339 N.E.2d 477 (1975).

Chapter 3

TESTING THE BOUNDARIES OF CONSTITU-TIONAL PROTECTION: FIGHTING WORDS, INCITEMENT/OUTRAGE AND OBSCENITY

They're not people from polite society, and you probably wouldn't invite them to have lunch with you. That said, let's consider some of the men and women who have made law with words that courts in the United States have ruled may be forbidden or punished. Examples considered in this chapter include two troublesome (and often hard to define) categories of words:

    (1) Fighting Words and Incitement

    (2) Obscenity

SEC. 11. FIGHTING WORDS AND INCITEMENT

In Chaplinsky v. New Hampshire (1942), the Supreme Court of the United States decided a classic case holding that some words are so hateful that saying them or publishing them may lead to punishment. Walter Chaplinsky's anger at a town marshal led to name-calling; the marshal was termed a "God-damned racketeer and a damned fascist." The Supreme Court of the United States upheld Chaplinsky's conviction for "offensive language," reasoning that these were "fighting words" which could be expected to cause violence. In a famous statement the Court outlined the kind of words which are not protected by the First Amendment:[1]

> There are certain well-defined and narrowly limited classes of speech, the prevention and punishment of which have never been thought to raise any Constitutional problems. These include the lewd and obscene, the profane, the

---

[1] Chaplinsky v. New Hampshire, 315 U.S. 568, 62 S.Ct. 766 (1942).

libelous and insulting or "fighting" words—those which by
their very utterance inflict injury or tend to incite an
immediate breach of the peace. * * * [Such words] are of
such slight social value that any benefit that may be
derived from them is clearly outweighed by the social
interest in order and morality.

However, as discussed at pages 74–77 of the preceding chapter,
courts in the United States have been slow to uphold statutes
forbidding hate speech or racist speech, evidently because the laws
cast such a wide net in forbidding some kinds of expression that
they also caught categories of speech protected under the First
Amendment.[2] Similarly, see Brandenburg v. Ohio (1969), discussed
at pages 37–38, above. Ku Klux Klan leader Brandenburg's rambling televised call for "revengeance" [sic] against the President,
Congress, and the Supreme Court was held not to be a direct
incitement likely to produce lawless action. As a result, Ohio's
conviction of Brandenburg under the state's Criminal Syndicalism
Act was overturned by the U.S. Supreme Court.[3]

"Incitement" and Soldier of Fortune

A recent and potentially expansive area of media liability is
termed "incitement." Where the media are concerned, that means
bringing a lawsuit against the makers of a publication or movie or
video tape or disc, blaming the media product for some harmful
outcome.

One of the more lurid examples of this emerging area is
Eimann v. Soldier of Fortune Magazine, Inc., where a 1988 jury
award of $9.4 million ($7.2 million in punitive damages) was made
against this macho magazine. A jury ordered the civil damage
award, evidently believing that Soldier of Fortune had published an
advertisement offering the services of a hired killer. The classified
ad by John Wayne Hearn offered his services as a Vietnam veteran,
a weapons specialist who knew jungle warfare, to perform "high
risk assignments." Hearn, indeed, is serving several life terms for
shooting Sandra Black to death in her home in Bryan, Texas. Her
husband, Robert Black, who hired Hearn for $10,000, was sen-
tenced to death.

This case's outcome led Editor & Publisher, a trade journal for
the newspaper industry, to call for a reversal of the huge civil
damage verdict. "The Texas decision," Editor & Publisher said,
"would mean that a reader with a grudge against a publication
could bring suit claiming damages for ads believed to be untruthful
or misleading unless the publisher investigated every advertising

---

[2] See R.A.V. v. St. Paul, 505 U.S. 377, 112 S.Ct. 2539 (1992).

[3] Brandenburg v. Ohio, 395 U.S. 444, 89 S.Ct. 1827 (1969).

claim."[4] Soldier of Fortune escaped liability in this case, because the U.S. Court of Appeals (5th Cir.) concluded that this advertisement was innocuously worded and that the magazine, therefore, had no duty to refuse to publish such a classified ad.[5]

Braun v. Soldier of Fortune Magazine (1991)

In a 1991 decision, however, an Alabama federal court found Soldier of Fortune liable for damages of totaling $4,375,000 in an incitement case. In Braun v. Soldier of Fortune, brothers Michael and Ian Braun sued for wrongful death and personal injury, claiming that their father had been killed by the person who placed the following ad:[6]

> GUN FOR HIRE: 37–year-old professional mercenary desires jobs. Vietnam Veteran. Discreet and very private. Body guard, courier, and other special skills. All jobs considered Phone (615) * * * or write * * * Gatlinburg, TN 37738.

That advertisement was placed by Richard Savage. A business associate of Mr. Richard Braun saw the ad and negotiated with Savage. Savage hired Sean Trevor Doutre as a contract killer, with these results: On an August day in 1985, as Richard Braun and his 16–year-old son Michael drove out of their suburban Atlanta home, Doutre stepped in front of the car and fired several shots with an MAC–11 automatic pistol. Father and son rolled out of the car on opposite sides. The father died when Doutre fired two shots into the father's head. Doutre then pointed the pistol at 16–year-old Michael Braun, but did not fire. Instead, Doutre put his finger over his lips, signaling Michael to be quiet, and ran into the woods.

The Braun court distinguished Savage's Soldier of Fortune ad from the classified ad involved in the Eimann case discussed above, refusing to grant the magazine a summary judgment, holding that the advertisement carrying phrases such as "Gun for Hire" and "All jobs considered" was far more explicit than the "innocuous" language of the ad in the Eimann case. The court held that the Soldier of Fortune ad had harmed the Braun family.[7]

The U.S. Court of Appeals, 11th Circuit, allowed the jury verdict to stand, voting 2–1 that a standard of legal duty may be set for publishers. Advertisements should not be published that expose the public to a substantial danger of harm.[8]

---

[4] Editor & Publisher, "Responsibility for ad content," March 12, 1988.

[5] Eimann v. Soldier of Fortune Magazine, Inc., 880 F.2d 830 (5th Cir.1989), 16 Med.L.Rptr. 2148, 2152.

[6] Braun v. Soldier of Fortune Magazine, 757 F.Supp. 1325 (M.D.Ala.1991), 18 Med.L.Rptr. 1732, 1733.

[7] Ibid., at 1729.

[8] Braun v. Soldier of Fortune Magazine, 968 F.2d 1110, 1121 (11th Cir.1992), 20 Med.L.Rptr. 1777, 1786. The Supreme Court denied certiorari. "See High Court Shuns Two Free Speech Cases," The New York Times, Jan. 12, 1993, p. A9.

We agree with the district court that "the language of this advertisement is such that, even though couched in terms not explicitly offering criminal services, the publisher could recognize the offer of criminal activity as readily as its readers obviously did." * * *

For the most part, however, outcomes of incitement cases against the media favor defendants, as did the Maryland case of Rice v. Paladin Enterprises (1996).

Hit Man Manuals' Publisher Not Liable in Wrongful Death Suit: Rice v. Paladin Enterprises (1996)

James Perry did some research. He purchased two books published by Paladin Enterprises (*Hit Man: A Technical Manual for Independent Contractors* and *How to Make a Disposable Silencer*) before performing killings-for-hire. He killed Mildred Horn, her 8–year-old quadriplegic son, Trevor, and the boy's nurse, Janice Sanders. Perry was hired by Lawrence Horn, who—like Perry—was convicted of murder and sentenced to life imprisonment without parole.

In 1992, Lawrence Horn plotted with Perry to carry out the killings of his ex-wife and son. While planning the killings, Perry ordered the two books, modified an AR–7 rifle according to instructions in the books, even using a home-made silencer on the rifle while killing Mildred Horn and Janice Sanders.[9]

District Court Judge Williams expressed loathing toward the books involved, finding that Paladin engaged in a marketing strategy to assist criminals. Even so, he found that First Amendment principles commanded granting a summary judgment to Paladin Enterprises.

The judge noted that several classes of speech receive limited or no protection under the First Amendment. He listed obscenity, fighting words, libel, commercial speech, and "words likely to incite imminent lawless action." The court ruled that the books published by Paladin Enterprises did not fit these categories and, further, that they were not actionable incitement to unlawful activity.[10]

Another "incitement" case which received substantial publicity was Herceg v. Hustler, in which a teenage boy died experimenting with "autoerotic asphyxiation" after he read about it in Hustler magazine. The U.S. Court of Appeals, 5th Circuit, in 1987 reversed

[9] Rice v. Paladin Enterprises, Inc., 940 F.Supp. 836 (D.Md.1996), 24 Med.L.Rptr. 2185.

[10] Ibid., pp. 844–848, 2187–2189, citing key cases discussed elsewhere in this chapter of Law of Mass Communications, 9th ed.: Miller v. California (obscenity), 413 U.S. 15, 93 S.Ct. 2607 (1973) and Brandenburg v. Ohio, 395 U.S. 444, 89 S.Ct. 1827 (1969) (incitement to imminent lawbreaking).

a damage award of nearly $200,000 against Hustler. There, the court said:[11]

> The constitutional protection accorded to the freedom of speech and of the press is not based on the naive belief that speech can do no harm but on the confidence that the benefits society reaps from the free flow and exchange of ideas outweighs the costs society endures by receiving reprehensible and dangerous ideas.

Incitement and Rockers Ozzy Osbourne and Judas Priest

Rock star Ozzy Osbourne was sued by surviving family members of an adolescent who committed suicide. The grieving relatives, however, were unable to collect damages from Osbourne because his lyrics in his song "Suicide Solution" were held to be entertainment. In any event, the survivors could not prove that Osbourne's music had been intended to cause suicide.[12]

In an even stranger and more pathetic case, a Nevada judge ruled in Vance v. Judas Priest (1989) that subliminal messages do not have First Amendment protection. This case involved a lawsuit by anguished survivors of Raymond Belknap, 18, who committed suicide with a 12–gauge shotgun aimed under his chin, and James Vance, 20, grievously injured in a suicide attempt with the same shotgun. Vance, horribly disfigured, died three years later in the psychiatric unit of a hospital.

The self-inflicted shootings occurred after Belknap and Vance had spent an afternoon drinking beer, smoking marijuana, and listening to Judas Priest albums. Arguments for the plaintiffs included assertions that subliminal messages urging self-destruction were present in the albums along with overt heavy-metal themes of death, destruction, and violent sex.

A Nevada court held that subliminal messages are outside free-speech theories and are not protected by the First Amendment.[13] Finding that testimony linking the deaths to the music of Judas Priest was not "inherently incredible," the Nevada district court (2d District) ordered that the case go to trial. At trial, however, it was held that there was insufficient proof that the defendants put subliminal messages in the songs or that the lyrics caused the suicides.[14]

[11] Herceg v. Hustler Magazine, 814 F.2d 1017, 1019 (5th Cir.1987), 13 Med.L.Rptr. 2345. The quoted passage was used by the court in deciding the case discussed above, Rice v. Paladin Enterprises, 940 F.Supp. 836 (D.Md.1996), 24 Med.L.Rptr. 2185, 2195.

[12] McCollum v. CBS, Inc., 202 Cal.App.3d 989, 249 Cal.Rptr. 187 (1988), 15 Med.L.Rptr. 2001.

[13] Vance v. Judas Priest, 16 Med.L.Rptr. 2241, 2257 (Nev.1989).

[14] Outcome cited in Victor A. Kovner, Harriette K. Dorsen, and Suzanne Telsey, "Recent Developments . . . ," in James C. Goodale, chairman, Communications Law

SEC. 12.   OBSCENITY AND AMERICAN LAW

Obscene expression has never been considered worthy of constitutional protection, but the growth of the hard-core pornography industry during the 1950s prompted the Supreme Court to create standards to establish what could legally be classified as obscene.

Obscenity was not considered a significant legal issue during the first 170 years of this nation's history. In fact, the Supreme Court did not decide to review the constitutionality of existing obscenity laws until 115 years after the first federal anti-obscenity law had been enacted.[15]

The main reason for this long era of judicial neglect was the limited scope of pornographic business in the United States prior to the 1950s. Before this time those who engaged in the sale of sexually explicit materials tended to be small-time operators, specializing in procuring a few erotic books or batches of grainy French postcards for a very select and secretive clientele.[16]

During the 1950s, however, as organized crime began to move into the field, its operation became much more efficient and profitable, employing mass mailings for the first time to promote the sale of slickly produced erotic magazines to a much broader segment of the population.[17] By 1960, annual revenues from the sale of sexually explicit materials were estimated to be in excess of $500 million, earnings that at the time rivaled those of both the American

1991, Vol. 2, at p. 105, discussing a New York Times story dealing with Priest v. Belknap Records, Aug. 25, 1990, p. 11.

[15] The first federal anti-obscenity law was contained in the Tariff Act of 1842, U.S. Public Statutes at Large, Vol. 5, Ch. 270, forbidding the, "importation of all indecent and obscene paintings, lithographs, engravings and transparencies." In 1957, the United States Supreme Court ruled on the constitutionality of such anti-obscenity laws for the first time in Roth v. United States, 354 U.S. 476, 77 S.Ct. 1304 (1957). In this regard it is informative to note that the word "pornography" itself did not exist in the English language until sometime during the early 1850s, and that it originally referred only to the scientific (or pseudo-scientific) study of prostitutes. See Walter Kendrick, The Secret Museum, New York, Viking Press, 1987.

[16] See the Gathings Committee: Us Congress, House, Select Committee on Current Pornographic Materials, Hearings Before Select Committee, and Report of Select Committee to the House, 83rd Cong. 2d Sess. 1952.H. Rept. 2510 and the Kefauver Committee: U.S. Congress, Senate, Committee on the Judiciary, Obscene and Pornographic Materials, 84th Cong., 2d Sess. 1956, H. Rept. 2381.

[17] Federal Bureau of Investigation: Report Regarding the Extent of Organized Crimes Involvement in Pornography (1978). Also see, Attorney General's Commission on Pornography: Final Report (1986), pp. 291–301. Although an earlier government study, the Report of the President's Commission on Obscenity and Pornography (1970), found insufficient evidence to document the extent of mob involvement in this field, (pp. 142–143), its efforts to establish such a connection were admittedly quite limited.

television and motion picture industries.[18]

Prior to this time obscenity always had been assumed to be an illegal form of expression, denied any First Amendment protection. As Justice Holmes had declared in Frohwerk v. United States[19]

> The First Amendment ... cannot have been, and obviously was not, intended to give immunity for every possible use of language.

But in 1957, just as hard-core pornography was emerging as a major industry throughout the nation, the Supreme Court decided to intervene in this field of law for the first time. Concerned that overly broad anti-obscenity statutes might be improperly infringing on protected free speech, the Court acted to impose its own federal guidelines on these laws, requiring them to conform to one uniform standard in determining what could legally be classified as "obscene."[20] Unfortunately, this decision of the Court to assume ultimate authority over obscenity law in the United States was made on the eve of the "sexual revolution," a frenzied era that would soon cast the nine Justices adrift in a flood of obscenity appeals, foundering aimlessly for a time upon its surging waves of controversy.

SEC. 13.   THE COMMON LAW ORIGINS

British common law principles drawn from an era of soapbox orators and humble printers could offer only limited guidance to American courts facing the need to develop a legal definition of obscenity for a modern society.

Although nineteenth century America was never a hot-bed of erotic literature, the moral and religious fervor that swept the nation during the 1870s launched crusades to seek out every kind of depravity or vice, wherever it might be found. In 1873, Anthony

---

[18] The Granahan Committee: U.S. Congress, House, Committee on the Post Office and Civil Service, Subcommittee on Post Operations, Hearings before Subcommittee and Report of Subcommittee to Committee, 86th Congress, 2d sess. 1960. Although both the Kefauver and the Granahan Committee reports acknowledged the difficulty of accurately estimating the revenues generated by an illegal industry whose major operators were not likely to disclose this information on their tax forms, the figures were considered to be rather conservative projections of actual earnings. For comparative purposes, the total revenues earned by all TV stations in the United States in 1960 was $962 million, while the total domestic box office receipts for all films shown in the U.S. that year was $710 million. Christopher H. Sterling and Timothy R. Haight, The Mass Media: Aspen Institute Guide to Communication Industry Trends. New York, Praeger Publishers, 1976. Table 380–A, p. 207 and Table 340–B, p. 182.

[19] 249 U.S. 204, 206, 39 S.Ct. 249, 250 (1919).

[20] Roth v. United States, 354 U.S. 476, 77 S.Ct. 1304 (1957).

Comstock, a sexually fixated religious crusader whose slogan was "Morals! Not Art or Literature," was able to convince Congress to adopt federal legislation making it a crime to use the mail to distribute obscene materials. During the next few years several State legislatures also responded to the demands of Comstock and his followers by passing their own anti-obscenity laws.

After these laws had been enacted, it was then up to each State court to decide how the term "obscene" should be defined. In the absence of any precedents from earlier American case law, these courts were forced to seek guidance from English common law where a number of judges eventually discovered and applied the standard an English court had established in 1868 in the case of Regina v. Hicklin.

The Hicklin Rule

In *Hicklin,* Lord Chief Justice Cockburn ruled that an anti-Catholic pamphlet, The Confessional Unmasked, was obscene. Lord Cockburn set down this test for obscenity:[21]

> Whether the tendency of the matter charged as obscene is to deprave and corrupt those whose minds are open to such immoral influences and into whose hands a publication of this sort might fall.

In States that followed the "Hicklin rule" it was not necessary to prove that any publication under review was likely to harm or offend a normal adult.[22] All the rule required was proof that the work in question could have a damaging effect on children or abnormal adults—"those whose minds are open to such immoral influences"—in order to satisfy its standard. In time some State courts added the so-called "partly obscene" test to the *Hicklin* rule. If a publication contained one or more obscene passages, the entire work could be classified as obscene.[23]

Perhaps the most troublesome portion of the *Hicklin* rule, though, was the concept that a book could be classified as obscene if it suggested "thoughts of a most impure and libidinous character."[24] In the law of obscenity, no harm or even likelihood of harm to readers need be shown in order to suppress a book.[25]

[21] L.R. 3 Q.B. 360, 370 (1868).

[22] See United States v. Bennett, 24 Fed.Cas. 1093, 1103–1104, No. 14,571 (C.C.S.D.N.Y.1879); Commonwealth v. Friede, 271 Mass. 318, 320, 171 N.E. 472, 473 (1930).

[23] Lockhart & McClure, op. cit., p. 343.

[24] Ibid.

[25] See Roth v. United States, 354 U.S. 476, 490, 77 S.Ct. 1304, 1312 (1957); see also dictum by Mr. Justice Frankfurter, Beauharnais v. Illinois, 343 U.S. 250, 266, 72 S.Ct. 725, 735 (1952).

In 1913, Judge Learned Hand wrote an often quoted protest against the *Hicklin* rule, which he termed "mid-Victorian precedent." Although Judge Hand felt compelled to uphold the condemnation as obscene of Daniel Goodman's novel *Hagar Revelley,* the judge wrote:[26]

> I question whether in the end men will regard that as obscene which is honestly relevant to the adequate expression of innocent ideas, and whether they will not believe that truth and beauty are too precious to be mutilated in the interests of those most likely to pervert them to base uses. * * *

Despite his protest, the *Hicklin* rule remained the leading test of obscenity in America until the 1930s.[27]

The Ulysses Decision

About this time, however, other American courts began to relax enforcement of the *Hicklin* rule to some extent. A mother who wrote a book to help her children learn about sex—and who later published the book at the suggestion of friends—successfully defended herself against charges that the book *(Sex Side of Life)* was obscene.[28] And in 1933, James Joyce's famed stream-of-consciousness novel *Ulysses,* now an acknowledged classic, was the target of an obscenity prosecution under the Tariff Act of 1930.[29]

Customs officers had prevented an actress from bringing *Ulysses* into this country. When *Ulysses* reached trial, Judge John Woolsey decided that a literary work deserved be judged in its entirety, rather then by the contents of a few selected passages. On this basis he attacked the *Hicklin* test head-on and ruled that *Ulysses* was art, not obscenity.

His decision has become one of the most noted in the law of criminal words, even though it by no means brought the end of the *Hicklin* rule, which continued to applied in the decisions of other courts.[30] Overrated or not, the *Ulysses* decision represents an often-cited step toward nullifying some of the most restrictive aspects of the old *Hicklin* standard.

The *Ulysses* decision provided a new definition of obscenity for

[26] United States v. Kennerley, 209 Fed. 119 (S.D.N.Y.1913).

[27] See, e.g., Commonwealth v. Friede, 271 Mass. 318, 320, 171 N.E. 472, 473 (1930).

[28] United States v. Dennett, 39 F.2d 564, 76 A.L.R. 1092 (2d Cir.1930).

[29] United States v. One Book Called "Ulysses," 5 F.Supp. 182 (S.D.N.Y.1933); Paul and Schwartz, op. cit., p. 66.

[30] See e.g., United States v. Two Obscene Books, 99 F.Supp. 760 (N.D.Cal.1951), affirmed as Besig v. United States, 208 F.2d 142 (9th Cir.1953).

other courts to consider: that a book is obscene if it[31]

> tends to stir the sex impulses or to lead to sexually impure and lustful thoughts. Whether a particular book would tend to excite such impulses must be the test by the court's opinion as to its effect (when judged as a whole) on a person with average sex instincts.

Only one portion of the old *Hicklin* rule appeared in Judge Woolsey's *Ulysses* opinion: the emphasis on thoughts produced by a book as an indicator of a book's obscene effect on a reader. This judicial preoccupation with thoughts—and the tests outlined by Judge Woolsey in 1933—are markedly similar to rules for judging obscenity laid down in the Supreme Court's landmark decision in the 1957 case of Roth v. United States.[32]

SEC. 14. THE ROTH LANDMARK

In Roth v. United States, the Supreme Court held that obscenity is not constitutionally protected expression and set down its most influential standard for judging what is—or is not—obscene.

In 1957 the Supreme Court acted to establish one uniform set of national standards to define what could properly be categorized by American law as obscene. In the case of Roth v. United States, the Court, while accepting the premise that obscene speech enjoyed no constitutional protection, insisted that all anti-obscenity laws contain specific safeguards to limit their application solely to those forms of expression that could properly be classified as obscene.[33]

Although this decision is usually referred to as the *Roth* case, it actually involved two different appeals. The Court simultaneously decided a case under the federal obscenity statute[34] (*Roth*) and under a state statute[35] (*People v. Alberts*). Taken together, the *Roth* and *Alberts* cases thus raised the question of the constitutionality of both federal and state anti-obscenity laws.

In the federal prosecution, Roth was convicted of violating the statute by mailing various pamphlets plus a book, *American Aphrodite*. He was sentenced to what was then the maximum sentence: a $5,000 fine plus a five-year penitentiary term. His conviction was affirmed by the United States Court of Appeals, Second Circuit,

[31] United States v. One Book Called "Ulysses," 5 F.Supp. 182, 184 (S.D.N.Y.1933).

[32] 354 U.S. 476, 77 S.Ct. 1304 (1957).

[33] Ibid.

[34] United States v. Roth, 237 F.2d 796 (2d Cir.1956).

[35] West's Ann.Cal.Pen.Code § 311; People v. Alberts, 138 Cal.App.2d Supp. 909, 292 P.2d 90 (1955).

although the noted jurist Judge Jerome M. Frank questioned the constitutionality of obscenity laws in a powerful concurring opinion.

In words which have been called the beginning of the modern law of obscenity, Judge Frank declared that obscenity laws are unconstitutionally vague.[36]

* * *

The troublesome aspect of the federal obscenity statute * * * is that (a) no one can now show that with any reasonable probability obscene publications tend to have any effects on the behavior of normal, average adults, and (b) that under the [federal] statute * * * punishment is apparently inflicted for provoking, in such adults, undesirable sexual thoughts, feelings or desire—not overt dangerous or anti-social conduct, either actual or probable.

Despite Judge Frank's denunciation of the "exquisite vagueness" of obscenity laws, Roth's conviction was upheld. The Supreme Court then granted certiorari in order to review the case.[37]

In jointly considering the *Roth* and *Alberts* cases, the Court did not rule on whether the books sold by the two men were in fact obscene. The only issue reviewed in each case was the validity of an obscenity law on its face.[38]

Alberts argued that this mail-order business could not be punished under California law because a state cannot regulate an area pre-empted by the federal obscenity laws. The majority opinion replied that the federal statute deals only with actual mailing and does not prevent a state from punishing the advertising or keeping for sale of obscene literature.[39]

Roth contended, on the other hand, that the power to punish speech and press offensive to morality belongs to the states alone under the powers of the First, Ninth, and Tenth Amendments to the Constitution. The majority opinion discarded this argument, saying that obscenity is not speech or expression protected by the First Amendment.[40] Justice Brennan added, in language which was to greatly affect later decisions in the law of obscenity:[41]

All ideas having even the slightest redeeming social importance—unorthodox ideas, controversial ideas, even

[36] 237 F.2d 796, 802 (2d Cir.1956). See Stanley Fleishman, "Witchcraft and Obscenity: Twin Superstitions," Wilson Library Bulletin, April, 1965, p. 4.

[37] 352 U.S. 964, 77 S.Ct. 361 (1957).

[38] 354 U.S. 476, 77 S.Ct. 1304, 1307 (1957).

[39] 354 U.S. 476, 493–494, 77 S.Ct. 1304, 1314 (1957).

[40] 354 U.S. 476, 492, 77 S.Ct. 1304, 1313 (1957).

[41] 354 U.S. 476, 484, 77 S.Ct. 1304, 1309 (1957).

ideas hateful to the prevailing climate of opinion—have the full protection of the guaranties [of free speech and press], unless excludable because they encroach upon the limited area of more important interests. But implicit in the history of the First Amendment is the rejection of obscenity as utterly without redeeming social importance.

Justice Brennan's majority opinion set the stage for obscenity law developments in two ways. First, he affirmed the prevailing common law view that obscenity laws might be used to punish *thoughts*. Overt sexual actions are not needed to bring a conviction.[42] Second—and more significantly—he affirmed the common law position that obscenity is *not* legally protected expression.[43]

Those are the two main strands in the law of obscenity. Other strands found in by concurring and dissenting Justices in Roth v. United States foreshadowed major and minor themes for the next 40 years in the complex fabric of obscenity law.[44]

The Roth Test

Writing for the Court, Justice Brennan offered this definition of obscenity: "Obscene material is material which deals with sex in a manner appealing to prurient interest."[45] "Prurient interest," refers to sexually oriented thoughts. Brennan then articulated "the Roth test" for judging whether or not material is obscene:[46]

> * * * whether to the average person, applying contemporary community standards, the dominant theme of the material taken as a whole appeals to prurient interest.

Subsequent decisions have returned for guidance to these words again and again. This *"Roth* test" repudiated some features of the American rendition of the *Hicklin* rule. The practice of judging books by the presumed effect of isolated passages upon the most susceptible persons was rejected because it "might well encompass material legitimately dealing with sex."[47]

[42] 354 U.S. 476, 486–487, 77 S.Ct. 1304, 1309–1310 (1957).

[43] 354 U.S. 476, 482, 77 S.Ct. 1304, 1307 (1957).

[44] For example, Chief Justice Earl Warren's concurrence in Roth argued that the conduct of a defendant was the key point in an obscenity prosecution. For a case which turned on the defendant's conduct, see Ginzburg v. United States, 383 U.S. 463, 86 S.Ct. 942 (1966).

[45] 354 U.S. 476, 486–487, 77 S.Ct. 1304, 1310 (1957). The terms used in the three "tests" approved in Roth—"lustful desire," "lustful thoughts," and "appeal to prurient interest"—all imply that if a book can be assumed to cause or induce "improper" sexual thoughts, that book can be "banned." The "appeal to prurient interest" test was drawn from the American Law Institute's Model Penal Code, Tentative Draft No. 6 (Philadelphia, American Law Institute, May 6, 1957).

[46] 354 U.S. 476, 489, 77 S.Ct. 1304, 1311 (1957).

[47] 354 U.S. 476, 489, 77 S.Ct. 1304, 1311 (1957).

However, Justice Brennan's words were obviously not wholly libertarian. Under *Roth,* a book could be declared obscene if it could be assumed that it might induce obscene thoughts in an hypothetical average person.[48] There was no need for the prosecution to prove that there is a "clear and present danger"[49] or even a "clear and possible danger"[50] that the reading of the book in question would lead to antisocial conduct.

Roth: Concurrences and Dissents

Chief Justice Earl Warren was evidently puzzled by the idea that *books* rather than persons were defendants in obscenity prosecutions. His brief concurring opinion in *Roth* proved to be remarkably predictive of future issues in the law. Chief Justice Warren stated that in an obscenity trial, the conduct of the defendant rather than the obscenity of a book should be the central issue.[51] He concluded that both Roth and Alberts had engaged in "the commercial exploitation of the morbid and shameful craving for materials with prurient effect" and said that the state and federal governments could constitutionally punish such conduct.[52]

Justice Brennan's majority opinion in *Roth* has influenced the course of the law of obscenity. So has Chief Justice Warren's concurring opinion, which insisted that the behavior of the defendant, rather than the nature of the book itself, was the "central issue" in an obscenity case.[53]

Justice William O. Douglas was joined by Justice Hugo L. Black in a scathing attack on obscenity laws and obscenity prosecutions. This dissent foreshadowed arguments these Justices would advance in obscenity cases which subsequently followed *Roth* to the Supreme Court. Douglas wrote that Roth and Alberts were punished "for thoughts provoked, not for overt acts nor antisocial conduct." He was unimpressed by the possibility that the books involved might produce sexual thoughts: "The arousing of sexual thoughts and desires happens every day in normal life in dozens of ways."[54]

Problems involving freedom of speech and press, it was argued, must not be solved by "weighing against the values of free expression, the judgment of a court that a particular form of expression

48 354 U.S. 476, 486, 77 S.Ct. 1304, 1310 (1957).

49 354 U.S. 476, 486, 77 S.Ct. 1304, 1310 (1957).

50 354 U.S. 476, 77 S.Ct. 1304, 1310 (1957), citing Dennis v. United States, 341 U.S. 494, 71 S.Ct. 857 (1951).

51 354 U.S. 476, 495, 77 S.Ct. 1304, 1314 (1957).

52 354 U.S. 476, 496, 77 S.Ct. 1304, 1315 (1957).

53 354 U.S. 476, 495, 77 S.Ct. 1304, 1314–1315 (1957).

54 354 U.S. 476, 509, 77 S.Ct. 1304, 1321 (1957).

has 'no redeeming social importance.' " Justice Douglas declared:[55]

> [T]he test that suppresses a cheap tract today can suppress a literary gem tomorrow. All it need do is incite a lascivious thought or arouse a lustful desire. The list of books that judges or juries can place in that category is endless.

SEC. 15. MONITORING COMPLIANCE: THE FEDERAL REVIEW ERA

Once the federal court system had asserted its right to review the constitutionality of all State obscenity laws, it found itself overwhelmed not only by the case-load it assumed, but also by the difficulty of defining obscenity in any uniform or clearly consistent way.

Although *Roth* remains the leading decision on obscenity and said much, later court decisions showed that it actually settled very little. Five years after *Roth* the Supreme Court attempted to refine its definition of obscenity in Manual Enterprises, Inc. v. Day, Postmaster General of the United States. In writing for the Court, Justice Harlan termed *MANual* [sic], *Trim,* and *Grecian Pictorial* "dismally unpleasant, uncouth and tawdry" magazines which were published "primarily, if not exclusively, for homosexuals."[56]

Despite this, a majority of the Supreme Court held that these magazines which presented pictures of nude males were not obscene and unmailable because they were not "patently offensive." Harlan wrote:[57]

> Obscenity under the federal statute * * * requires proof of two distinct elements: (1) patent offensiveness; and (2) "prurient interest" appeal.

In 1966, the Supreme Court again tackled the tough problem of defining obscenity as decisions were announced in three cases, the "Fanny Hill" case,[58] Mishkin v. New York,[59] and Ginzburg v. United States.[60]

First announced was the decision in the *Fanny Hill* case. *Fanny Hill,* or more accurately, *Memoirs of a Woman of Pleasure,* was written in England about 1749 by John Cleland. The book was well known in the American colonies and was first published in the

[55] 354 U.S. 476, 514, 77 S.Ct. 1304, 1324 (1957).

[56] 370 U.S. 478, 481, 82 S.Ct. 1432, 1434 (1962).

[57] 370 U.S. 478, 487, 82 S.Ct. 1432, 1437 (1962).

[58] A Book Named John Cleland's Memoirs of a Woman of Pleasure v. Attorney General, 383 U.S. 413, 86 S.Ct. 975 (1966).

[59] 383 U.S. 502, 86 S.Ct. 958 (1966).

[60] 383 U.S. 463, 86 S.Ct. 942 (1966).

United States around 1800. *Fanny Hill,* was also one of the first books in America to be the subject of an obscenity trial; in Massachusetts in the year 1821.[61] More than 140 years later, Fanny Hill was back in the courts of Massachusetts, as well as in New York, New Jersey and Illinois.

In Fanny Hill, there is not one of the "four letter words" which have so often brought modern literature before the courts. But although the language was quite sanitary, author Cleland's descriptions of Fanny's sexual gyrations left little to the imagination. Even so, some experts—including poet and critic Louis Untermeyer—testified that Fanny Hill was a work of art and was not pornographic. The experts, however, were asked by a cross-examining prosecuting attorney if they realized that the book contained "20 acts of sexual intercourse, four of them in the presence of others; four acts of lesbianism, two acts of male homosexuality, two acts of flagellation and one of female masturbation."[62]

Fanny Hill, then, is a frankly erotic novel. Justice Brennan summed up the tests for obscenity which the highest court had approved:[63]

> We defined obscenity in *Roth* in the following terms: "[W]hether to the average person, applying contemporary community standards, the dominant theme of the material taken as a whole appeals to prurient interest." 354 U.S. at 489, 77 S.Ct. at 1311. Under this definition, as elaborated in subsequent cases, three elements must coalesce: it must be established that (a) the dominant theme of the materials taken as a whole appeals to a prurient interest in sex; (b) the material is patently offensive because it affronts contemporary community standards relating to the description or representation of sexual matters; and (c) the material is utterly without redeeming social value.

The Supreme Court ruled that the Massachusetts courts had erred in believing that a book could be deemed obscene even though not "unqualifiedly worthless." Justice Brennan, writing for the Court, stated that a book "can not be proscribed unless it is found to be *utterly* without redeeming social value."[64]

Justice Brennan then announced the Court's decision in the *Mishkin* case. Edward Mishkin, who operated a bookstore near New York City's Times Square, was appealing a sentence of three years and $12,500 in fines. Mishkin's publishing specialty was

---

[61] Commonwealth v. Peter Holmes, 17 Mass. 336 (1821).

[62] Cf. the outraged dissent by Justice Tom C. Clark, 383 U.S. 413, 441–445, 86 S.Ct. 975, 989–996 (1966).

[63] 383 U.S. 413, 418, 86 S.Ct. 975, 977 (1966).

[64] 383 U.S. 413, 419, 86 S.Ct. 975, 978 (1966).

sadism and masochism, and he had been found guilty by New York courts of producing and selling more than 50 different paperbacks. Titles involved included *Dance With the Dominant Whip, and Mrs. Tyrant's Finishing School.*[65]

Mishkin's defense was based on the notion that the books he published and sold did not appeal to the prurient interest of an average person. The average person, it was argued, would be disgusted and sickened by such books. Justice Brennan's majority opinion, however, dismissed Mishkin's argument, concluding that the Mishkin's books were aimed at members of a "clearly defined deviant subgroup" to appeal to their prurient interest.[66]

After upholding Mishkin's conviction, Mr. Justice Brennan then turned to the *Ginzburg* case. With this opinion, the Supreme Court brought another element to the adjudication of obscenity disputes: the manner in which the matter charged with obscenity was sold.[67]

The *Ginzburg* case involved three publications: "EROS, a hard-cover magazine of expensive format; Liaison, a bi-weekly newsletter; and The Housewife's Handbook on Selective Promiscuity, * * * a short book." Justice Brennan took notice of abundant evidence from Ralph Ginzburg's federal district court trial "that each of the accused publications was originated or sold as stock in trade of the sordid business of pandering—the business of purveying textual or graphic matter openly advertised to appeal to the erotic interest of their customers."[68]

Included as evidence of this "pandering" were EROS magazine's attempts to get mailing privileges from the whimsically named hamlets of Intercourse and Blue Ball, Pa. Mailing privileges were finally obtained in Middlesex, N.J.[69] Also, Justice Brennan found "the leer of the sensualist" permeating the advertising for the three publications. *Liaison,* for example, was extolled as "Cupid's Chronicle," and the advertising circulars asked, "Are you a member of the sexual elite?"[70]

The Court split severely over the *Ginzburg* case, however, with Justices Black, Douglas, Harlan and Stewart all registering bitter dissents. Justice Black set the tone for his dissenting brethren, declaring:[71]

[65] 383 U.S. 502, 514–515, 86 S.Ct. 958, 966–968 (1966).

[66] Mishkin v. New York, 383 U.S. 502, 508–509, 86 S.Ct. 958, 963–964 (1966).

[67] 383 U.S. 463, 465–466, 86 S.Ct. 942, 944–945 (1966).

[68] 383 U.S. 463, 467, 86 S.Ct. 942, 945 (1966).

[69] 383 U.S. 463, 467, 86 S.Ct. 942, 945 (1966).

[70] 383 U.S. 463, 469n, 86 S.Ct. 942, 946 (1966).

[71] 383 U.S. 463, 476, 86 S.Ct. 942, 950 (1966).

* * * Ginzburg * * * is now finally and authoritatively condemned to serve five years in prison for distributing printed matter about sex which neither Ginzburg nor anyone else could possibly have known to be criminal.

Justice Harlan accused the court's majority of rewriting the federal obscenity statute in order to convict Ginzburg, and called the new "pandering" test unconstitutionally vague.[72] And Justice Stewart asserted in his dissent that Ginzburg was not charged with "commercial exploitation," with "pandering," or with "titillation," and to allow him to be convicted on such grounds was to deny him due process of law.[73]

Justice Douglas added his denunciation of the condemnation of materials as obscene not because of their content, but because of the way they were advertised.[74]

Protecting the Young: The Ginsberg Case and the "Variable Obscenity" Concept

As if to confound careless spellers, it happens that one of the most important cases after the Ralph *Ginzburg* case involved a man named *Ginsberg*: Sam Ginsberg. In the 1968 *Ginsberg* case, the Supreme Court held by a 6–3 vote that a New York statute which defined obscenity on the basis of its appeal to minors under 17 was not unconstitutionally vague.

Sam Ginsberg and his wife operated "Sam's Stationery and Luncheonette" in Bellmore, Long Island. In 1965, a mother sent her 16–year-old son to the luncheonette to buy some "girlie" magazines. The boy purchased two magazines—apparently *Sir* and *Gent* or similar publications—and walked out of the luncheonette.

On the basis of this sale, Sam Ginsberg was convicted of violation of a New York law making it a misdemeanor "knowingly to sell * * * to a minor under 17 any picture * * * which depicts nudity * * * and which is harmful to minors" and "any * * * magazine * * * which contains * * * [such pictures] and which, taken as a whole, is harmful to minors."[75]

It should be noted that magazines such as the 16–year-old boy purchased from Sam Ginsberg's luncheonette in 1965 had been held *not* obscene for adults by the Supreme Court.[76] However the judge at Sam Ginsberg's obscenity trial found pictures in the two magazines which depicted nudity in a manner that was in violation

---

[72] 383 U.S. 463, 495, 86 S.Ct. 942, 955 (1966).

[73] 383 U.S. 463, 497, 86 S.Ct. 942, 956 (1966).

[74] 383 U.S. 463, 494, 497, 86 S.Ct. 942, 954, 956 (1966).

[75] Ginsberg v. New York, 390 U.S. 629, 633, 88 S.Ct. 1274, 1276 (1968). The statute is Article 484–H of the New York Penal Law, McKinney's Consol. Laws c. 40.

[76] Redrup v. New York, 386 U.S. 767, 87 S.Ct. 1414 (1967).

of the New York statute. The trial judge found that the pictures were harmful to minors under the terms of the New York statute.

In affirming Ginsberg's conviction, Justice Brennan approved the concept of "variable obscenity."[77] Brennan acknowledged that the magazines involved in the *Ginsberg* case were not obscene for sale to adults, However, he upheld the right of a State to accord to minors under the age of 17 a more restricted right of access than assured to adults to judge and determine for themselves what sex material they may read or see.[78]

In the case that resulted in the fining and jailing of *Eros* publisher Ralph Ginzburg, the Supreme Court served notice that not only *what* was sold but *how* it was sold would be taken into account.[79] The *how* of selling or distributing literature can include a legitimate public concern over the materials which minor children see. In essence, *Ginsberg* established the concept of "variable obscenity", holding that materials not obscene for adults can be found to be obscene if children are allowed access to them.[80]

Indecisiveness: *Redrup* and *Stanley*

In 1967, the Supreme Court of the United States openly admitted its confusion over obscenity law in a case known as Redrup v. New York.[81] This decision did not *look* important: it took up only six pages in United States Reports and only about four pages were devoted to its unsigned *per curiam* ["by the court"] majority opinion. The other two pages were given over to a dissent by Justice John Marshall Harlan, with whom Justice Tom C. Clark joined.

Redrup was a significant case simply because the Court said that a majority of its members could not agree on a standard which could declare so-called "girlie magazines" and similar publications to be obscene. *Redrup* seemed for a time to be the most important obscenity case since Roth v. United States because it was used by both state and federal courts for several years to avoid many of the complexities of judging whether works of art or literature are obscene.

On June 12, 1967, the date the Court's term ended that year and less than two months after *Redrup* was decided, the Court reversed 11 obscenity convictions by merely referring to Redrup v.

---

[77] Ginsberg v. New York, 390 U.S. 629, 635 n., 88 S.Ct. 1274, 1278 n. (1968), quoting Lockhart and McClure, "Censorship of Obscenity: The Developing Constitutional Standards," 45 Minnesota Law Review 5, 85 (1960).

[78] Ginsberg v. New York, 390 U.S. 629, 635, 88 S.Ct. 1274, 1277–1278 (1968); see Butler v. Michigan, 352 U.S. 380, 77 S.Ct. 524 (1957); Roth v. United States, 354 U.S. 476, 77 S.Ct. 1304, 1309 (1957).

[79] Ginzburg v. United States, 383 U.S. 463, 86 S.Ct. 942 (1966).

[80] Ginsberg v. New York, 390 U.S. 629, 88 S.Ct. 1274 (1968).

[81] 386 U.S. 767, 87 S.Ct. 1414 (1967).

New York.[82] Another dozen state or federal obscenity convictions were reversed during the next year, with *Redrup* being listed as an important factor in each reversal.[83]

The majority opinion in *Redrup* placed significant reliance upon the Court's 1966 decision in Ginzburg v. United States. In *Ginzburg,* discussed earlier in this chapter, it will be recalled that the Court took special notice of the *manner* in which magazines or books were sold.[84] *Redrup* echoed this concern, but also took into account the *recipients* of materials charged with obscenity. The Court suggested that convictions for selling or mailing obscenity should be upheld in three kinds of situations:

(1) Where there is evidence of "pandering" sales as in Ginzburg v. United States.

(2) Where there is a statute reflecting "a specific and limited state concern for juveniles."[85]

(3) Where there is "an assault upon individual privacy by publication in a manner so obtrusive as to make it impossible for the unwilling individual to avoid exposure to it."[86]

Beyond these kinds of forbidden conduct *Redrup* gave little guidance. Perhaps, however, it could be assumed that *Redrup* meant this: If the *conduct* of the seller did not fit the three kinds of prohibited actions listed above, and if the *contents* were not so wretched that they would be held to be "hardcore pornography,"[87] then the materials involved were constitutionally protected.[88]

Stanley v. Georgia (1969)

In 1969, there was hope that the Supreme Court—clearly frustrated by its growing caseload of obscenity appeals-would find

[82] Dwight L. Teeter, Jr., and Don R. Pember, "The Retreat from Obscenity: Redrup v. New York," Hastings Law Journal Vol. 21 (Nov., 1969) pp. 175–189.

[83] 386 U.S. 767, 770–771, 87 S.Ct. 1414, 1415–1416 (1967).

[84] 383 U.S. 463, 86 S.Ct. 942 (1966).

[85] Redrup v. New York, 386 U.S. 767, 769, 87 S.Ct. 1414, 1415 (1967). Note that (2) above, announced in Redrup on May 8, 1967, forecast with considerable precision the Court's decision in Ginsberg v. New York, 390 U.S. 629, 88 S.Ct. 1274 (1968).

[86] Ibid., citing Breard v. Alexandria, La., 341 U.S. 622, 71 S.Ct. 920 (1951), and Public Utilities Commission of Dist. of Columbia v. Pollak, 343 U.S. 451, 72 S.Ct. 813 (1952).

[87] 386 U.S. 767, 771n, 87 S.Ct. 1414, 1416n, referring to Justice Potter Stewart's quotation, in his dissent in Ginzburg v. United States, of this definition of hardcore pornography, including writings and "photographs, both still and motion picture, with no pretense of artistic value, graphically depicting acts of sexual intercourse, including various acts of sodomy and sadism, and sometimes involving several participants in scenes of orgy-like character. * * * verbally describing such activities in a bizarre manner with no attempt whatsoever to afford portrayals of character or situation and with no pretense to literary value." See Ginzburg v. United States, 383 U.S. 463, 499n, 86 S.Ct. 942, 956n (1966).

[88] 386 U.S. 767, 87 S.Ct. 1414, 1416 (1967).

some way to bring order to this complex and troublesome area of law. The Court's resolution of Stanley v. Georgia added to this hope.[89]

The *Stanley* case arose when a Georgia state investigator and three federal agents, operating under a federal search warrant, searched the home of Robert E. Stanley, looking for bookmaking records. Evidence of bookmaking was not found, but the searchers found three reels of 8 millimeter film and a projector. They treated themselves to a showing and decided—as did the court-that the films were obscene. When Stanley's appeal reached the Supreme Court, Mr. Justice Thurgood Marshall—writing for a unanimous Court—overturned the conviction, naming two constitutional rights.[90]

> (1) A right growing out of the First Amendment, a "right to receive information and ideas, regardless of their social worth."[91]

> (2) A constitutional right to privacy against government intrusions interfering with receiving information and ideas in the privacy of one's home:[92]

Additionally, Justice Marshall wrote that "States retain broad power to regulate obscenity; that power simply does not extend to mere possession by the individual in the privacy of his own home."[93]

Taken together, Redrup and Stanley indicated to some judges that prohibitions on obscenity had been loosened by the Supreme Court. Redrup suggested that the Court wouldn't define anything but hard-core pornography as obscene. For example, in a case involving distribution of sexual material, a U.S. District Court ignored both Roth and the express limitation on the reach of the Stanley decision. The District Court judge in Reidel v. United States reasoned that " 'if a person has the right to receive and possess this material, then someone must have the right to deliver it to him.' " He concluded that § 1461 of the United States Code could not be validly applied unless obscene material is directed at children or unwilling adults.[94]

[89] Stanley v. Georgia, 394 U.S. 557, 89 S.Ct. 1243 (1969).

[90] Black, J., concurred in the decision.

[91] 394 U.S. 557, 564, 89 S.Ct. 1243, 1247 (1969), citing Winters v. New York, 333 U.S. 507, 510, 68 S.Ct. 665 (1948).

[92] 394 U.S. 557, 564–564, 89 S.Ct. 1243, 1247–1248 (1969).

[93] 394 U.S. 557, 564, 89 S.Ct. 1243, 1247–1248 (1969).

[94] Quoted in United States v. Reidel, 402 U.S. 351, 355, 91 S.Ct. 1410, 1412–1413 (1971).

However, The Supreme Court in United States v. Reidel (1971) held that the District Court judge had misread Stanley: [95]

> The District Court gave Stanley too wide a sweep. * * * Whatever the scope of the "right to receive" referred to in Stanley, it is not so broad as to immunize the dealing in obscenity in which Reidel engaged here—dealings that Roth held unprotected by the First Amendment.

Also, in Byrne v. Karalexis (1971), [96] the U.S. Supreme Court upheld the prosecution of a theater owner for showing the Swedish film, "I Am Curious (Yellow)." This mentioned a U.S. district court reading of Stanley saying that people ought to be able to watch sexy movies in the relative privacy of a theater's darkness. The Supreme Court, however, voted to allow a State to prosecute theater owners exhibiting this film.[97]

SEC. 16.   CREATING A NEW CONSENSUS: THE MILLER STANDARD

In 1973, Chief Justice Burger succeeded in developing a new set of obscenity standards that a majority of the Court could accept.

Miller v. California

The most important of the five obscenity cases decided by the Supreme Court on June 21, 1973—and indeed the most important such case since Roth v. United States (1957)—was Miller v. California. In that case, as in the four others decided that same day, the Court split 5–4, revealing a new coalition among the Justices where obscenity and pornography were concerned.[98]

Miller v. California arose when Marvin Miller mailed five unsolicited—and graphic—brochures to a restaurant in Newport Beach. The envelope was opened by the restaurant's manager, with his mother looking on, and they complained to police. The brochures advertised four books, Intercourse, Man–Woman, Sex Orgies Illustrated, and An Illustrated History of Pornography, plus a film

---

[95] United States v. Reidel, 402 U.S. 351, 355–346, 91 S.Ct. 1410, 1412–1413 (1971).

[96] Byrne v. Karalexis, 401 U.S. 216, 91 S.Ct. 777 (1971).

[97] Ibid., overturning 306 F.Supp. 1363 (D.Mass. 1969).

[98] Paris Adult Theatre I v. Slaton, 413 U.S. 49, 93 S.Ct. 2628 (1973); United States v. Orito, 413 U.S. 139, 93 S.Ct. 2674 (1973); Kaplan v. California, 413 U.S. 115, 93 S.Ct. 2680 (1973), and U.S. v. Twelve 200–ft. Reels of Super 8 mm Film, 413 U.S. 123, 93 S.Ct. 2665 (1973). That coalition included Justice Byron R. White (appointed by President Kennedy) plus four justices appointed by President Nixon: Chief Justice Warren Burger, plus Justices Harry Blackman, William H. Rehnquist, and Lewis Powell. Dissenting in *Miller* plus the four cases listed were Justices Thurgood Marshall, Potter Stewart, William O. Douglas, and the author of the Roth test of 1957 and of many obscenity decisions thereafter, Justice William J. Brennan, Jr.

titled Marital Intercourse. After a jury trial, Miller was convicted of a misdemeanor under the California Penal Code.[99]

Writing for the majority in *Miller,* Chief Justice Burger ruled that California could punish such conduct. He noted that the case involved "a situation in which sexually explicit materials have been thrust by aggressive sales action upon unwilling recipients or juveniles."

Endeavoring to formulate a new standard, Chief Justice Burger first returned to *Roth's* declaration that obscene materials were not protected by the First Amendment.[1] Then, he denounced the test of obscenity outlined in the Fanny Hill (*Memoirs of a Woman of Pleasure*) case in 1960, nine years after *Roth.* In that case, three justices, in a plurality opinion, held that material could not be judged obscene unless it were proven to be "utterly without redeeming social importance." Burger wrote that such a standard forced prosecutors to "prove a negative," which he termed a "burden virtually impossible to discharge under our criminal standards of proof."[2]

The Chief Justice wrote that since the 1957 decision in *Roth,* the Court had not been able to muster a majority to agree to a standard of what constitutes "obscene, pornographic material subject to regulation under the States' police power."[3] In 1973, however, Burger found himself in substantial agreement with four other Justices. He made the most of it, setting out general rules on what States could regulate ("hard-core pornography") and re-wording the *Roth* and *Memoirs* tests into a standard reducing the States' burden of proof necessary to convict persons for distribution or possession of sexually explicit materials.[4]

[99] Miller v. California, 413 U.S. 15, 93 S.Ct. 2607 (1973). West's Ann. California Pen. Code § 312.2(a) makes it a misdemeanor to knowingly distribute obscene matter. After the jury trial, the Appellate Department, Superior Court of California, Orange County, summarily affirmed the conviction without offering an opinion.

[1] 413 U.S. 15, 20, 93 S.Ct. 2607, 2613 (1973), citing Roth v. United States, 354 U.S. 476, 77 S.Ct. 1304 (1957).

[2] 413 U.S. 15, 22, 93 S.Ct. 2607, 2613–2614 (1973), citing Memoirs of a Woman of Pleasure v. Massachusetts, 383 U.S. 413, 86 S.Ct. 975 (1966). Emphasis the Court's.

[3] 413 U.S. 15, 22, 93 S.Ct. 2607, 2614 (1973).

[4] 413 U.S. 15, 23–24, 93 S.Ct. 2607, 2614, 2615 (1973). Emphasis the Court's. Chief Justice Burger wrote that a State could, through statute, forbid:

"(a) Patently offensive representations or descriptions of ultimate sexual acts, normal or perverted, actual or simulated.

(b) Patently offensive representations or descriptions of masturbation, excretory functions, and lewd exhibition of the genitals."

Burger also stated that, "Sex and nudity may not be exploited without limit by films or pictures exhibited or sold in places of public accommodation any more than live sex and nudity can be exhibited or sold without limit in such public places. At a minimum, prurient, patently offensive depiction or description of sexual conduct

* * * [W]e now confine the permissible scope of such regulation to works which depict or describe sexual conduct. That conduct must be specifically defined by the applicable state law, as written or authoritatively construed. A state offense must also be limited to works which, taken as whole, appeal to the prurient interest in sex, which portray sexual conduct in a patently offensive way, and which, taken as a whole, do not have serious literary, artistic, political, or scientific value.

The basic guidelines for the trier of fact must be: (a) whether "the average person, applying contemporary community standards" would find that the work, taken as a whole, appeals to the prurient interest * * * (b) whether the work depicts or describes, in a patently offensive way, sexual conduct specifically defined by the applicable state law, and (c) whether the work, taken as a whole, lacks serious literary, artistic, political or scientific value. We do not adopt as a constitutional standard the *"utterly* without redeeming social value" test of Memoirs v. Massachusetts * * *: that concept has never commanded the adherence of more than three Justices at one time.

The majority opinion also declared that it would be unwise to attempt to formulate a uniform national standard to determine what appeals to "prurient interest" or what is "patently offensive." "[O]ur nation is simply too big and diverse for this Court to reasonably expect that such standards could be articulated for all 50 States in a single formulation * * *"[5] The First Amendment, Burger said, did not force citizens in Maine or Mississippi to accept all depictions of sexual conduct that might be tolerated in Las Vegas or New York City.

This new recognition "community standards" in the area of obscenity law also appeared to furnish the Court the justification it had been seeking to reduce its obscenity appeal workload: let obscenity be defined on a state-by-state basis. That way, the Court might not have to review the contents of each allegedly obscene book or film that had been banned in order to decide whether it actually was obscene under federal law.[6] Because *Miller* permitted "community standards" to be a factor evaluated in determining what was obscene, the Supreme Court could now defer in those matters to the lower courts, pointing out that local judges and

must have serious literary, artistic, political or scientific value to merit First Amendment protection."

[5] 413 U.S. 15, 30, 93 S.Ct. 2607, 2618 (1973).

[6] Although the *Roth* decision did not specifically require that a single uniform federal standard be applied in all obscenity cases, Justice Brennan interpreted it that way in Jacobellis v. Ohio, 378 U.S. 184, 84 S.Ct. 1676 (1964).

juries were much better situated than Supreme Court Justices to interpret and apply local sexual standards. Unfortunately, once again, those who hoped for this result had underestimated the inherent capacity of obscenity law to confound the judicial system.

Justice Brennan's opposition to these decisions founded in on his growing belief that no matter what set of standards were used, obscenity statutes would always be unconstitutionally vague. That is, there are *"scienter"* problems: obscenity laws are by their nature so formless that defendants can not have fair notice as to whether publications or films they distribute or exhibit are obscene. Without fair notice, there will be a "chilling effect" upon protected speech.

Brennan wrote:[7]

> I am convinced that the approach initiated 15 years ago in Roth v. United States * * * culminating in the Court's decision today, cannot bring stability to this area of the law without jeopardizing First Amendment values, and I have concluded that the time has come to make a significant departure from that approach.

> * * *

> Our experience with the *Roth* approach has certainly taught us that the outright suppression of obscenity cannot be reconciled with the fundamental principles of the First and Fourteenth Amendments. * * * [W]e have failed to formulate a standard that sharply distinguishes protected from unprotected speech....

> * * *

> I would hold, therefore, that at least in the absence of distribution to juveniles or obtrusive exposure to unconsenting adults, the First and Fourteenth Amendments prohibit the state and federal governments from attempting wholly to suppress sexually oriented materials on the basis of their allegedly "obscene" contents. Nothing in this approach precludes those governments from taking action to serve what may be strong and legitimate interests through regulation of the manner of distribution of sexually oriented material.

From the *Miller* decision of 1973 well into the 1980s, the Court split 5–4 in many of the obscenity cases it has decided. The majority followed *Miller,* and favored stringent regulation of sexually explicit material. Time and time again, including many *per curiam* deci-

---

[7] Brennan dissent in Paris Adult Theatre I v. Slaton, 413 U.S. 49, 73–74, 83, 93 S.Ct. 2628, 2642, 2647, 2662 (1973), which concentrated, however, on the reasoning in *Miller*. This dissent relied on the Court's conclusion in Redrup v. New York, 386 U.S. 767, 87 S.Ct. 1414 (1967).

sions in which the Court upheld obscenity prosecutions without an explanatory opinion, Brennan dissented, constantly contending that obscenity can not be described with sufficient clarity to give defendants fair notice.[8]

The Meanings of *Miller*: Defining "Community Standards"

If the Supreme Court Justices had expected that the new "contemporary community standards" test introduced by the *Miller* case would significantly reduce their obscenity caseload, they were soon to be disappointed.

Jenkins v. Georgia

Take a Georgia case involving Mike Nichols' serious and much-praised film, *Carnal Knowledge*, a film containing no frontal nudity or explicit depictions of sex acts. Nevertheless, in Jenkins v. Georgia, theater manager Billy Jenkins was convicted under a Georgia statute forbidding distribution of obscene material. This State action was so ludicrous that the Supreme Court of the United States was compelled to intervene by granting certiorari. Writing for the Court, Justice William H. Rehnquist declared that the film was not patently offensive and therefore not obscene because it contained none of the actions listed in Miller v. California:[9]

> "representations or descriptions of ultimate sexual acts, normal or perverted, actual or simulated," and "representations or descriptions of masturbation, excretory functions, and lewd exhibition of the genitals."

In essence, the Court was saying that although it was now willing to accept the fact that "contemporary community standards" regarding sexual matters might vary to some extent from region to region, there could be no finding of obscenity anywhere in the United States unless the material in question could reasonably be considered to be obscene.

Hamling v. United States

William Hamling and several co-defendants were convicted on 12 counts of using the mails to deliver obscene advertisements in 1971, two years *before* the *Miller* decision recognized the relevance of local community standards in determining whether the average person could reasonably find that a work appealed to prurient interest.

[8] See, e.g., Trinkler v. Alabama, 414 U.S. 955, 94 S.Ct. 265 (1973); Raymond Roth v. New Jersey, 414 U.S. 962, 94 S.Ct. 271 (1973); Sharp v. Texas, 414 U.S. 1118, 94 S.Ct. 854 (1974); J–R Distributors, Inc. v. Washington, 418 U.S. 949, 94 S.Ct. 3217 (1974). See also Hamling v. United States, 418 U.S. 87, 140–152, 94 S.Ct. 2887, 2919–2924 (1974).

[9] Jenkins v. Georgia, 418 U.S. 153, 160, 94 S.Ct. 2750, 2755 (1974).

Hamling and friends were attempting to sell an illustrated version of the government's own *Presidential Report of the Commission on Obscenity and Pornography*, offering in their promotional mailer a wide assortment of graphic photographs illustrating those lurid and obscene sexual activities the government report had simply described.

During the trial, conducted in San Diego, California, the judge had refused to allow the defense to introduce the results of a survey of 718 San Diego residents suggesting that a majority of those surveyed felt this brochure should be made available to the public.

When the Supreme Court reviewed the case in 1974, Justice Rehnquist, writing for the majority, concluded that the refusal of the trial judge to admit evidence of community standards did not prejudice the rights of the defendants because the advertisements themselves were clearly obscene.[10]

Justice Brennan, joined by Justices Stewart and Marshall, dissented vigorously. He asserted that material should not be suppressed unless there is distribution to juveniles or obtrusive exposure to non-consenting adults.[11] He also criticized the concept of "community standards" itself, pointing out that national distributors, facing "variegated standards * * * impossible to discern," will be forced to abide by the most repressive standard when distributing sexually oriented materials.[12]

Pope v. Illinois

One example of the difficulties lower courts have had in knowing exactly how the "community standards" test should be applied is illustrated by Pope v. Illinois.[13] Here the question was whether the artistic value of a work was to be determined by the typical citizen in the community where the case was being tried.

It should be recalled that Miller v. California set out a three-part test:[14]

(1) Does the material, when viewed by an average person applying contemporary community standards, appeal to prurient interest?

[10] Hamling v. United States, 418 U.S. 87, 94 S.Ct. 2887 (1974).

[11] 418 U.S. 87, 141–142, 94 S.Ct. 2887, 2919 (1974).

[12] 418 U.S. 87, 144, 94 S.Ct. 2887, 2921 (1974).

[13] Pope v. Illinois, 481 U.S. 497, 107 S.Ct. 1918 (1987). For other examples of the type of problems lower courts have encountered in attempting to apply this standard see Pinkus v. United States, 436 U.S. 293, 98 S.Ct. 1808 (1978)-children not to be included in considering community standards-and Smith v. United States, 431 U.S. 291, 97 S.Ct. 1756 (1977)-jury can find material obscene under federal law even if State in which offense occurs has no anti-obscenity law.

[14] 413 U.S. 15, 23–24, 93 S.Ct. 2607, 2614–1615 (1973).

(2) If so, then is the appeal "patently offensive?"

(3) Then, even though the material does appeal to prurient interest in a patently offensive manner, does it deserve free speech protection despite such qualities because of having serious literary, artistic, political or scientific value?

In this case—involving sales of magazines to undercover agents in a Rockford, Illinois adult bookstore—the constitutionality of judge's instructions to the jury were challenged. At their trials, the defendants argued that the literary or artistic value of a work should be based on a uniform national standard.[15] The judge rejected this argument, instructing the jury instead to consider its value in terms of, "how it would be viewed by ordinary adults in the whole state of Illinois." Writing for the majority, Justice White stated:

> There is no suggestion in our cases that the opinion of the value of an allegedly obscene work is to be determined by reference to community standards. Indeed, Smith v. United States, 431 U.S. 291, 97 S.Ct. 1756 (1977) held that, in a federal prosecution for mailing obscene materials, the first and second prongs of the *Miller* test—appeal to prurient interest and patent offensiveness—are issues of fact for the jury to determine applying contemporary community standards. The Court then observed that unlike prurient appeal or patent offensiveness, "[L]iterary, artistic, political, or scientific value ... is not discussed in *Miller* in terms of contemporary community standards."

White maintained that "artistic value" was not a relative term that each community could be permitted to establish for itself.

> Just as the ideas a work represents need not obtain majority approval to merit protection, neither, insofar as the First Amendment is concerned, does the value of a work vary from community to community based on the degree of local acceptance it has won. The proper inquiry is ... whether a reasonable person would find such value in the material, taken as a whole.

Other Obscenity Issues

To what extent can federal enforcement officials involve themselves in the process of distributing obscene materials without being found to have improperly enticed a defendant into committing a crime?

[15] This has come to be known as the "SLAPS" test; does the material have *S*erious *L*iterary, *A*rtistic, *P*olitical or *S*cientific value that protects it from being classified as obscene.

In United States v. Kuennen,[16] the Supreme Court refused to review the conviction of an individual whose shipment of obscene materials from Denmark was first intercepted by U.S. Customs officials and then re-mailed to him by that agency. Kuennen claimed that he had not violated federal postal laws because the law simply prohibited "causing" obscene materials to be sent through the mail and in this case it was the federal agency that "caused" these materials to be mailed to him. The federal court was unmoved by his argument, finding that although a Customs official may have mailed the package to Kuennen, it was the defendant himself who "caused" the mailing of these materials when he ordered them from his foreign supplier.

However, in Jacobson v. United States[17], in a 5–4 decision, the Supreme Court held that a government enforcement agency could not actively solicit customers for obscene materials and then charge them criminally for having responded to the solicitation. In this case an organization secretly sponsored by the government was sending promotional materials offering a wide assortment of explicit child pornography books and magazines to individuals it suspected were already purchasing these materials from other sources.

Keith Jacobson, an elderly Nebraska farmer, received such advertisements for more than two years before he finally ordered a pornographic magazine, *Boys Who Love Boys*, from the organization. On the basis of his order, Jacobson was convicted of violating a federal mail statute by knowingly receiving materials showing minors engaged in sexually explicit activities.

Justice White, writing for the majority, held that while government agents might be permitted to offer citizens an opportunity to commit crimes they are already predisposed to commit, it was illegal entrapment for them to engage in such an elaborate subterfuge to induce an innocent person to commit a crime.

Computer Sex

Efforts by enforcement agencies to prevent the sale of sexually explicit and child pornography films has been made even more difficult by recent technological advances that simplify the process of shipping high-quality video images to home computers.[18] In Oklahoma and Texas a number of individuals have been charged with offering to sell obscene CD–ROM images to computer bulletin board members while a New Jersey man has been arrested for

---

16 901 F.2d 103 (8th Cir.1990), cert. denied 498 U.S. 958, 111 S.Ct. 385 (1990).

17 503 U.S. 540, 112 S.Ct. 1535 (1992).

18 See, for example, Andrea Gerlin, "Electronic Smut vs. Drawing Fire of Prosecutors, Raising Questions" New York Times, June 27, 1994, p. B3.

possessing digitized pictures depicting sexually explicit images of minor-aged girls.

Are such computer networks personal channels of communication, protected by privacy law from government intrusion? Probably not. And even if such a defense should fail, do current federal and State anti-obscenity laws extend to the sale of sexually explicit digitized CD–ROM images? Probably not. The only thing that seems certain at this point is that this complex area of law is not likely to become any less complicated in the immediate future.

Yet, while it is too soon to predict how technological advances may affect the field of obscenity law in the future, the *Mapplethorpe* and *2 Live Crew* cases suggest that at least for the moment freedom of expression is not being unduly hampered by the existence of such laws.

The Mapplethorpe Exhibit Case

Concern that mid-American juries lacked the sophistication to distinguish between "art" and "smut" lessened to some extent in October 1990 after a Cincinnati, Ohio jury acquitted a local museum director charged with displaying obscene works.[19] Dennis Barrie, director of Cincinnati's Contemporary Arts Center, had scheduled an exhibition of pictures by Robert Mapplethorpe, a nationally recognized photographer who died of AIDS in 1989.

The exhibition included five photos of nude men in sadomasochistic poses and two of children with their genitals exposed. The exhibit had attracted little attention in its previous showings in Philadelphia and Chicago, but at its opening in Cincinnati, Barrie and the Museum were charged with pandering obscenity, and unlawfully displaying pictures of nude children, both misdemeanor offenses carrying maximum sentences of one year in jail, and a fine of $5,000.

To simplify the issue, the State called just one witness to testify as to the artistic merit of the exhibit, a self-styled communications "specialist" whose only claimed expertise as an art critic involved writing songs for the "Captain Kangaroo" television show. In contrast, the defense called more than a dozen expert witnesses, including directors from some of the nation's leading art museums who were unanimous in their assessment of Mapplethorpe as a serious and important artist.

If the prosecution believed the photos themselves would be enough to shock the mostly working class, church-going jury of four men and four women into returning a guilty verdict, they clearly

---

[19] Contemporary Arts Center v. Ney, 735 F.Supp. 743 (S.D.Ohio 1990). Also see "Jury Finds Merit in Mapplethorpe Exhibit with Verdict of Not Guilty" Milwaukee Journal, October 7, 1990, p. A1.

underestimated the intelligence of the panel. After the trial had ended, several jurors admitted being personally offended by these pictures they felt were "lewd", "grotesque" and "disgusting".[20] But even though they felt that these photos did appeal to prurient interests and were patently offensive, they accepted the judgment of art experts who believed these works also had artistic merit, and therefore could not be classified as being obscene.

Reacting in part to public criticism of the federal funding Mapplethorpe had received, Congress amended the statute governing awards made by National Endowment for the Arts, requiring the NEA to consider "general standards of decency" in deciding who might qualify for funding from the organization. Applying this new standard, NEA denied requests for government funds from several artists who applied for grants, including one who planned theatrical performances of simulated masturbation and another who intended to smear her body with excrement to portray the debasement of women. When these individuals were unable to obtain taxpayer funding they sought, they challenged the new "decency" standard in court.

A California federal district court upheld their challenge, finding the term "decency" to be unconstitutionally vague and overbroad because it prevented applicants from fully understanding what was required of them in order to qualify for federal financial support.[21]

2 Live Crew Case

In June 1990, a U.S. District Court in Fort Lauderdale, Florida had entered a decree forbidding the sale or distribution of a music video "Nasty As They Wanna Be" by rap group *2 Live Crew* anywhere within the jurisdiction of the Court. District Judge Jose A. Gonzales conducted extensive hearings before deciding that the music video was in fact obscene, and therefore could be prevented from being sold.[22]

---

[20] Isabel Wilkerson, "Obscenity Jurors Were Pulled 2 Ways But Deferred to Art" New York Times October 10, 1990, p. B1. Five of the eight jurors had never visited an art museum.

[21] Finley v. National Endowment for the Arts, 795 F.Supp. 1457 (C.D.Cal.1992).

[22] Skyywalker Records, Inc. v. Navarro, 739 F.Supp. 578 (S.D.Fla.1990), 17 Med. L.Rptr. 2073. According to testimony presented at the hearings, this single music video contained more than a dozen references urging violent sex, some 200 descriptions of women as either "bitches" or "ho" (whores), 115 explicit terms for male or female genitalia, 87 descriptions of oral sex, 9 descriptions of male ejaculation, 4 extensive descriptions of group sex, all within a general theme glorifying the debasement and humiliation of women. The declaratory judgement of obscenity entered by the District Judge was later vacated on appeal. The reviewing court pointed out that the judge who had tried the case had not demonstrated that he possessed either the artistic or literary background necessary to find that the work

A local music store owner, Charles Freeman, sold a copy of the music video to an undercover police officer a few days after the decree had been entered and was convicted of violating this ban. Shortly after Freeman's arrest, *2 Live Crew* performed selections from the music video during an all-adult concert in Fort Lauderdale. The three members of the group were each charged with one misdemeanor count of disseminating obscene material, and were tried in October 1991, soon after Freeman's conviction.

The defense maintained that white jurors on the 6 member jury panel would be incapable of understanding this unique form of black artistic expression, but the jury voted unanimously for acquittal, finding that the performance was not obscene.[23] Once again, the verdict turned on the "artistic merit" issue, for the jury accepted the judgment of a black English professor that "rapping" represented a serious black cultural art form, whose words were not to be taken at their face value but to be understood in the historical context of black culture.[24]

In both of these censorship cases, those who had been predicting that a new wave of artistic censorship would sweep across the nation could take some comfort in the verdicts of two predominately white, working-class juries who respected their obligations as jurors to decide these emotion-packed obscenity issues impartially and objectively. Perhaps, then, there is reason to believe that the time-honored American trial by jury system deserves more respect than its erudite critics have sometimes been willing to accord it.

"The Tin Drum" Meets the Tin Badge

On the other hand, the June, 1997, seizure of the 1979 Oscar-winning film, *The Tin Drum* in Oklahoma City illustrates some problems encountered in the protection of speech and press. That movie, which won a Golden Palm in the Cannes Film Festival and was honored as Best Foreign Film by the Academy of Motion Picture Arts and Sciences, is the filmic version of the acclaimed book of the same title by Gunter Grass.

It tells the story of Oskar, born in the 1920s into a world that he rejects for the sins and hypocrisies of adults. Coaxed from the womb by a promise of a tin drum on his third birthday, Oskar sees with painful clarity what adulthood has to offer. He decides to stop growing and does so. "[A]rmed with his little tin drum, which he

lacked "serious artistic, scientific, literary or political value." Luke Records v. Navarro, 960 F.2d 134 (11th Cir.1992).

[23] "Rap Members Found Not Guilty in Obscenity Trial," New York Times, October 21, 1990, p. 1.

[24] Another factor that may have aided the defense is that the vocals the prosecution recorded at the concert were virtually unintelligible to the jury, providing very little basis for the jury to find the lyrics to be obscene.

beats to drown out the sounds of nonsense, and with a glass-shattering scream that is his ultimate weapon, Oskar chooses to bear witness to the folly and evil deeds of adults."[25]

The first complaint about the movie came in Minnesota in 1996 where a former student of Bethel College, a Christian seminary near Minneapolis–St. Paul, sued the college claiming she had been forced to watch pornography. She complained about three films, *The Tin Drum*, *Like Water for Chocolate*, and *Do The Right Thing*. The court dismissed her suit, but the complaint was widely reported. The head of a special interest group in Oklahoma heard about the suit on the radio. He found a copy of *The Tin Drum* in the Oklahoma City public library. He checked out the movie and also rented a copy at an Oklahoma City video store. Armed with the two copies, he turned them over to a police officer with whom he had prior dealings.

After viewing the films, police officers took the tapes to District Court Judge Richard Freeman. At this point the story becomes muddled as Freeman told local reporters that he had viewed either a few minutes of the film or the film in its entirety. However much he saw, Freeman spoke with one of the officers the next day and *said* that he thought that the movie was obscene. Based on that spoken opinion about the movie, police officers visited a half-dozen video stores and three private homes in Oklahoma County. They seized the movie from the stores and the homes, including the home of Michael Camfield, a staff member of the American Civil Liberties Union of Oklahoma. Camfield said he rented the movie when he heard the complaints about it.

The seizure sparked at least two lawsuits against the Oklahoma City Police Department. At issue is the constitutionality of the seizures. At no time did police have an opinion of the court that the film was obscene. Requests to Judge Freeman for a copy of his opinion were met with the declaration that none existed, that he was offering an advisory opinion, and that he was expression his own opinion about the movie. First Amendment practice requires that due process be followed even when dealing with works that are adult in nature.

In Fort Wayne Books, Inc. v. Indiana,[26] the Court made abundantly clear that constitutional due process attaches even to obscene materials. Justice White's opinion lays out the need for a prior judicial determination before the state moves against what it considers to be obscenity. "[B]ooks or films may not be taken out of circulation completely until there has been a determination of

---

[25] Richard Schickel, "Dream Work," Time, April 28, 1980, p. 76.

[26] Fort Wayne Books, Inc. v. Indiana, 489 U.S. 46, 109 S.Ct. 916 (1989).

obscenity after an adversary hearing."[27] The Court referred to *Heller v. New York*,[28] which dealt with the wholesale seizure of materials to block their distribution. "[W]e concluded that until there was a 'judicial determination of the obscenity issue in an adversary proceeding,' exhibition of a film could not be restrained by seizing all the available copies of it."[29]

The controversy surrounding *The Tin Drum* involves conflicting claims from both sides. Judge Freeman told one reporter that he saw a scene which involved "a young boy about six or seven, and he was having sex with a girl who was about 16 in a bath house."[30] But the character in the movie is 16 years old as is the girl in the scene. Critics charge the scene depicts the boy performing oral sex on the girl, but repeated viewings of the film failed to turn up a scene in which sex takes place. The film does not show genitalia or penetration of any sort. The ages of consent in German and Poland are 16 and 15 respectively. The actor who plays Oskar was 12 during the production but director Volker Schlondorff said that the two scenes implying sexual intercourse were simulated through creative editing.[31] One scene shows Oskar and the 16–year-old housekeeper in bed. Both are covered with sheets. The others scene shows Oskar's widowed father in intercourse with the housekeeper. Both are partially clothed and there are no views, explicit or otherwise, of their private parts. "All of this seems to come from the dirty minds of the would-be censors," Schlondorff said.[32]

Even so, the debate in Oklahoma focused on the "oral sex scene." That was carried into the regional, national and international media, demonstrating the difficulties in trying rationally to resolve the issues where sex is involved or thought to be involved. A benefit of the attention was to bring a new audience to *The Tin Drum*. The movie was included in a number of film programs and sent sales climbing. A representative of Kino International, distributor of the movie, said that monthly sales averaged 100 copies but in the three months since the controversy erupted, Kino had received more than 1,000 orders.[33]

[27] Ibid., at 48, 920.

[28] Heller v. New York, 413 U.S. 483, 93 S.Ct. 2789 (1973).

[29] Fort Wayne Books, Inc. v. Indiana, at 62, 927, citing *Heller* at 492–493, 2794–2795. See also Bantam Books, Inc. v. Sullivan, 372 U.S. 58, 83 S.Ct. 631 (1963).

[30] Holly Bailey, "Busted: How The Tin Drum Was Declared a Dirty Movie—and What Happened Afterward," The Oklahoma Gazette, Oct. 16, 1997, p. 16.

[31] Ibid., at p. 20.

[32] Ibid.

[33] Joe Holleman, "Webster Series Picks Up Controversial 'Tin Drum,'" St. Louis Post–Dispatch, Oct. 16, 1997.

SEC. 17. BALANCING CONFLICTING SOCIETAL INTERESTS

As private industry content standards continue to become more permissive, pressure is mounting for laws to protect society from mass culture messages that demean certain groups, or erode fundamental tenets of decency.

Motion Picture Industry Standards

Until the late 1940s, five major film companies dominated the motion picture business in the United States. Paramount, MGM, Warner Brothers, Twentieth Century Fox and RKO owned more than 3000 of the nation's first-run motion picture theaters and controlled film industry production, distribution and exhibition by following a policy of trade-offs and cross-preferences with other studio-owned theaters to deny some 15,000 independently owned theaters access to these feature films until their box office appeal had diminished.

This concentration of control within the film industry also allowed the major studios to cooperate in adopting and enforcing a code of industry standards to ensure that no feature film would contain themes or scenes that might be offensive to certain segments of the film audience.[34] Independent film producers had no choice but to conform to these standards of decency, because without the industry's "Production Code Seal of Authority" they would be denied access to those essential first-run theaters owned by the major studios.[35]

Then, in 1948, the Justice Department was able to force the major film studios to enter into a Consent Decree in which they agreed to rid themselves of their motion picture theaters.[36]

Losing control of these major first-run theaters also meant that these studios lost the capacity to impose industry standards on feature film content. As television viewing increased during the 1950s, film attendance plunged downward from 90 million a week

[34] The Motion Picture Producers and Distributors of American (MPPDFA) established a film review office in 1922, largely as a public relations gesture to reduce the bad image resulting from a rash of personal scandals in Hollywood. Known as the "Hay's Office", because of its first director, Will Hays, its role in reviewing film content did not become significant until the major studios adopted a much more stringent set of standards, known as the Production Code, in the mid 1930s.

[35] In many ways this private content supervisory system closely resembled that employed by National Association of Broadcasters. In both cases, a small group of studios or networks were able to avoid offending audiences by exerting their control over the main channels of distribution, and this power that gave them to deny distribution to material they believed was in bad taste. In television as in film, the later fragmentation of that power diminished their ability to continue to perform that function.

[36] United States v. Paramount Pictures, 334 U.S. 131, 68 S.Ct. 915 (1948). The studios were actually given the option of divesting themselves of either their role as film distributors or film exhibitors, but sensing the threat that television would soon pose for film theaters, they chose to retain their more profitable distribution role.

in 1948 to less than 40 million a week only a decade later.[37] To lure audiences back to the film theaters, their new owners needed motion pictures promising special attractions television couldn't provide. One technique was to use technology to expand the screen, surround the viewer with sound, and portray action on a massive scale.

Another was to show sexier or more provocative dramas than television offered the public. Freed of the constraints of the Hollywood Production Code, theater chains began turning to European producers for daring, far more explicit motion pictures than American audiences had ever seen in the past.

At this point a number of local film boards originally formed in the early 1900s, but then dormant for decades as Hollywood closely supervised motion picture content, suddenly came to life as these new independent films began appearing in their communities. Now as such boards, operating under State authority, began trying to fill that void left by the collapse of industry controls, the issue soon arose about their legal right as government agencies to impose conditions on the local exhibition of feature films.

The first of these cases to challenge the authority of a State to control film content was Burstyn v. Wilson, a 1952 Supreme Court decision involving Roberto Rossellini's film, *"The Miracle."*[38]

This was a story about a simple-minded goatherd who had been raped by a bearded stranger whom she believed to be St. Joseph. The film was accused not of obscenity but of "sacrilege." The New York Education Department had issued a license to allow showing of "The Miracle," but the Education Department's governing body, the New York Regents, ordered the license withdrawn after the regents had received protests that the film was "sacrilegious." Burstyn appealed the license's withdrawal to the New York Courts, claiming that the state's licensing statute was unconstitutional. New York's courts, however, rejected that argument.

The Supreme Court of the United States ultimately ruled unanimously that the New York statute and the term "sacrilegious" were both so vague that they abridged freedom of expres-

[37] Christopher Sterling and Timothy Haight, eds. The Mass Media: Aspen Institute Guide to Communication Industry Trends (New York: Praeger, 1978) pp. 34–35.

[38] Joseph Burstyn, Inc. v. Wilson, 343 U.S. 495, 72 S.Ct. 777 (1952). Some film historians claim that Mutual Film Corp. v. Industrial Commission of Ohio, 236 U.S. 230, 35 S.Ct. 387 (1915) was the first test of film's free speech rights, a test in which a federal court held that a State law could restrict film distribution because film was not a form of protected expression, but rather only a business. What these historians overlook is that it was not until 1927 that the Supreme Court finally recognized the power of federal courts to overturn State laws restricting free speech, so that in this case, determining whether or not film was a protected form of free speech was really irrelevant to the actual decision, and therefore not a precedent controlling future federal court decisions in this field.

sion. Although the Court said in *dicta* that a clearly drawn obscenity statute to regulate motion pictures might be upheld, the main
thrust of the *Burstyn* decision was toward greater freedom. Not
only were films given protection under the First and Fourteenth
Amendments, movies which offended a particular religious group
need not, for that reason alone, be banned. Thus "sacrilege" can no
longer be a ground for censoring movies.

Seven years after the *Burstyn* decision, the Supreme Court—in
Kingsley International Pictures Corp. v. New York—again upheld
the concept that films are within the protection of the First
Amendment. In *Kingsley*, however, the Court specifically refused to
decide whether "the controls which a State may impose upon this
medium of expression are precisely co-extensive with those allowable for newspapers, books, or individual speech."[39]

In 1961 Times Film Corporation paid the City of Chicago the
customary license fee to exhibit the film *"Don Juan"* but then
refused to submit the film as required by local ordinance to Chicago's Film Review Board for pre-screening and a license. Instead, in
Times Film Company v. City of Chicago, it challenged the city's
authority to impose these conditions on the exhibition of a motion
picture, contending that the ordinance constituted an unconstitutional prior restraint on free speech.

The Supreme Court upheld the city's right to impose these
conditions on its local film exhibitors by a 5–4 vote. The majority
denied that there was complete freedom to exhibit any motion
picture and added, "Nor has it been suggested that all previous
restraints are invalid."[40]

Four years later, in Freedman v. Maryland (1965), the Supreme Court invalidated a state prior restraint system. This time,
unlike the *Times Film* case, *all* prior restraint was not challenged
as unconstitutional. Instead, the Maryland Film Review Board was
challenged because it could arbitrarily halt the showing of a film
until the exhibitor was able to complete a time-consuming appeal
procedure through the State court system. The Maryland review
process was held invalid because of insufficient procedural safeguards for the protection of the film exhibitor. But even Justice
Brennan—the legendary First Amendment supporter—suggested
that an orderly, speedy procedure for prescreening films could be
constitutional.[41]

[39] 360 U.S. 684, 689, 79 S.Ct. 1362, 1366 (1959).

[40] Times Film Corp. v. Chicago, 365 U.S. 43, 47, 81 S.Ct. 391, 393 (1961), citing
Near v. State of Minnesota ex rel. Olson, 283 U.S. 697, 51 S.Ct. 625 (1931).

[41] Freedman v. Maryland, 380 U.S. 51, 85 S.Ct. 734 (1965). For a similar result,
see Interstate Circuit, Inc. v. Dallas, 390 U.S. 676, 88 S.Ct. 1298 (1968).

In fact, a later Maryland-based film review system was upheld by an affirming vote of the Supreme Court—in Star v. Preller (1974)—demonstrating that a reasonably structured process was constitutional. The provisions of the new statute, cited with approval by the Court[42]

— Granted the Review Board only five days in which to review and license a film.

— Required, if a license is denied, that the Review Board begin review proceedings within 3 days before the Baltimore City Circuit Court.

— Required that a court make a prompt determination of obscenity (or lack of it) in an adversary hearing before the Review Board can make final denial of the license.

— Required the Board to bear the burden of proof at all stages of the proceeding.

At this time, then, prior restraint of film is still constitutional, but only when strict procedural safeguards are followed. These film industry decisions reflect the difficult role the Supreme Court has had to play when attempting to balance the free speech rights of a film distributor against the inherent right of each State to protect the welfare of its citizens.

In 1968 the major film studios began a new effort to enhance the image of the industry. Unable any longer to enforce standards of good taste, the studios instead established a rating system designed to inform audiences in advance what type of content each film contained. In the original rating system, a "G" designated films suitable for all audiences; "PG" meant parents were cautioned that some material might not be suitable for children; "R" indicated that children under 17 would not be admitted unless accompanied by a parent or guardian; and "X" meant no one under 17 would be admitted.

The rating system had at least two unintended effects. One was to destroy the appeal of the "G" rated film, as children began refusing to attend those films that adults thought were good for them. In 1968, 32 percent of the films released by major studios had a "G" rating, but by 1990, only 4 percent were rated "G".[43]

In contrast, "R" rated films rose from 22 percent of all major releases in 1968 to 48 percent in 1990, as average age of the film audience dropped from 22 to 16, and "R" became virtually synony-

---

[42] Al Star v. Preller, 419 U.S. 956, 95 S.Ct. 217 (1974), affirming 375 F.Supp. 1093 (D.Md.1974).

[43] "MPAA Film Ratings 1968–90" Variety November 8, 1991, p. 26. One example of this film industry fear of the dreaded "G" rating was the John Wayne, Katharine Hepburn film, "Rooster Cogburn" where the producers insisted that one violent scene be inserted to guarantee a "PG" rather than "G" rating.

mous with this age group's favorite film genre; violent, action packed adventures laced with suitable amounts of mayhem and gore.

The other was to make it virtually impossible to successfully market an "X" rated film. Soon after the code was adopted, a number of major newspaper chains established the policy of refusing to accept display ads for "X" rated films, and several television groups began following the same policy a few years later. In addition, most major video rental organizations refused to handle "X" rated films. In view of these severe constraints an "X" rating imposed on the earnings potential of a picture, Hollywood producers generally insisted on contractual agreements that allowed them to re-edit any feature film rated as "X" to delete any scenes that prevented it from receiving a "R" rating.[44]

Because of the bitter controversies these agreements created between producers-investors and directors attempting to make serious but extremely graphic films such as "Henry and June" or "Tie Me Up! Tie Me Down," the film code was revised in 1990. Then, NC–17 (No One Under 17 Admitted) replaced the X rating. Jack Valenti of the MPAA said that over time, the "X" had "taken on a surly meaning."

Unfortunately for the film industry, several States, as well as most newspapers, television stations and video rental organizations, were unimpressed by this distinction drawn by the rating group, continuing to treat the "NC–17" rating as nothing more than an artsy "X."[45]

Although the film industry's rating system is far from perfect, it has at least been designed to perform a public service by notifying audiences in advance what type of content they can expect from each film the industry releases.

Recent efforts to persuade the music industry to adopt a similar code system have been far less successful to date. After agreeing in principle in 1985 to label all violently pornographic or sexually explicit record and music video releases, several years passed before six major music distributors finally declared their willingness in 1990 to begin on a voluntary basis to establish standards for applying notification stickers on all musical cassettes and albums containing obscene or otherwise patently offensive material.

[44] "Taking the Hex Out of X" Time, October 8, 1990, p. 79. See Jack Valenti, The Voluntary Movie Rating System, MPAA Website (rev'd. Dec. 1996) at <http:www.mpaa.org/ratings.html>.

[45] "NC–17 X'd Out at Blockbuster; Wildmon, AFA Boycott" Variety January 21, 1991, p. 27.

Unfortunately, as soon as this agreement was reached, several States began consideration of legislation that would prevent anyone under the age of 18 from purchasing any record or cassette bearing such a label. The music industry immediately went on the offensive, declaring that they would abandon this labelling effort if any State passed such a law abridging their right of free speech.[46]

While this concern for freedom of expression is certainly praiseworthy, another factor that might have some effect on the attitude of these music distributors is that purchasers under the age of 18 not only accounted for 32 percent of all revenues earned by the music industry in 1988, but also represented the largest age segment of buyers for "heavy metal" and "black/urban" music, the two types of music most likely to be affected by any labeling law.[47]

Rights of Women and Children

To this point we have been focusing primarily on the legal rights of those who create, finance and distribute sexually oriented magazines, books, films or music. We have seen that the marketing of these items cannot be restricted unless a State decides to enact a statute prohibiting their dissemination, and that statute conforms in all respects to those protections accorded these corporate entities or individuals by the Constitution.[48]

But what about those in our society who are *victimized* by these materials? Does media free speech carry with it the privilege to ridicule or insult any group with impunity, secure in the knowledge that they have neither the legal right nor the media connections needed to respond to such attacks? In this era of "PC", there is a heightened awareness of the sensitivity of various racial and ethnic groups to comments or depictions that would have been considered perfectly appropriate only a decade ago, but one group in our society still does not appear to have benefitted from this change of attitude.

Today as in the past, certain "sexually oriented" magazines, films and music continue to stereotype women either as mindless sex objects constantly seeking gratification, or as subhuman victims to be subjugated and used. Unfortunately, efforts by militant feminists to ban beauty pageants or bar the viewing of even the most innocent of pin-up pictures have tended to obscure differences

---

[46] Kevin Zimmerman, "Music Biz Rising to Free–Speech Challenge" Variety, July 25, 1990, p. 53.

[47] Charles Fleming, "Stickers for Minors a Major Headache" Variety, July 25, 1990, p. 1.

[48] These protections, as defined in California v. Miller, require that there be reasonable findings, based on acceptable evidence, that the material in question does appeal to prurient interests in a patently offensive way, and does not have any serious literary, artistic, political or scientific value.

between images which glamorize or revere and those that degrade. Clearly, it is one thing for an artist to strive to convey the beauty of the female form to an admiring public and quite another for a hard-core pornographer to display the body of a nude woman in a sordid depiction of sexual debasement merely to gratify the urges of those eager to savor such abuse.[49]

During the 1980s, women's groups in the United States mounted two different types of legal attacks on pornographic materials that dehumanize women. One involved sponsoring a local ordinance that would allow a woman to sue a pornographic dealer for damages sustained as a result of the sale of such materials. The other sought a local law to suppress pornographic material in order to protect the civil rights of women.

The Minneapolis Experiment

In Minneapolis, a group of women opposing pornography thought it unwise to involve government in their efforts to prevent the dissemination of such material. As Wendy Kaminer, one of the group's leaders, wrote, "Feminists need not and should not advocate censorship, but we have every right to organize politically and to protest material that is degrading and dangerous to women."[50]

Her solution, as that of Andrea Dworkin and Catharine McKinnon—driving forces behind the Minneapolis ordinance—was to sue for violation of their personal rights as women. Since they believed that pornography was sex-based discrimination—"the sexually explicit subordination of women, graphically depicted"—then persons offended by such materials should have the right to sue for damages.[51] However, this approach was eventually abandoned when its supporters failed on two separate occasions to override the veto of Minneapolis Mayor Fraser.

[49] The Supreme Court also seems to have had its own difficulties through the years in distinguishing art from exploitation. In 1972, in California v. LaRue, 409 U.S. 109, 93 S.Ct. 390, the Court held that nude female dancers performing in a bar were engaged in a form of constitutionally protected expression. However, more recently in Barnes v. Glen Theatre, Inc., 501 U.S. 560, 111 S.Ct. 2456 (1991) a divided Court upheld by a 5–4 vote an Indiana statute requiring female dancers in a barroom setting to be covered by pasties and a G-string, declaring that although a nude dancer in a bar might be conveying a message, the State's interests in safeguarding societal order and public morality would outweigh such free speech considerations.

[50] Wendy Kaminer, "Pornography and the First Amendment: Prior Restraint and Private Action" in Take Back the Night, p. 241.

[51] See Attorney General's Commission on Pornography Final Report (1986). This report has been disputed by leading researchers including Edward Donnerstein who question "the purported causal link" between sexually explicit materials and sexual violence. See Nadine Strossen, *Defending Pornography: Free Speech, Sex, and the Fight for Women's Rights* (New York: Scribner, 1995), p. 252.

The Indianapolis Ordinance: Prior Restraint

In the spring of 1984, the Indianapolis–Marion County City–County Council passed and then amended an ordinance to define, prevent, and prohibit "all discriminatory practices of sexual subordination or inequality through pornography." Mayor Richard Hudnut signed them into law. The ordinance said, in part:[52]

16. "Pornography" is defined in the Ordinance as follows:

"(q) Pornography shall mean the graphic sex—sexually explicit subordination of women, whether in pictures or in words, that also includes one or more of the following:

(1) Women who are presented as sexual objects or who enjoy pain or humiliation; or

(2) Women are presented as sexual objects who experience sexual pleasure in being raped; or

(3) Women are presented as sexual objects tied up or cut or mutilated or bruised or physically hurt, or as dismembered or truncated or fragmented or severed into body parts. . . .

In response, the American Booksellers Association—plus other groups and individuals including the Association of American Publishers and the Freedom to Read Foundation of the American Library Association—challenged the constitutionality of the ordinance. It was contended that the ordinance "severely restricts the availability, display and distribution of constitutionally protected, non-obscene materials in violation of the First and Fourteenth Amendments."

District Judge Barker's lengthy opinion found major defects in the ordinance. The expression it sought to control might not meet the obscenity test specified in Miller v. California and the language of the ordinance was, in Judge Barker's view, "impermissibly vague."

On appeal, a three-judge panel of the U.S. Court of Appeals, Seventh Circuit, affirmed the district court's judgment that the Indianapolis anti-pornography ordinance was unconstitutional.

Even though the appeals court conceded that the subordinate status of women had led to "lower pay at work, insult and injury at home, and battery and rape," it concluded that the definition of illegal pornography contained in this ordinance improperly infringed upon constitutionally protected free speech.[53]

---

[52] 598 F.Supp. at 1320 (S.D.Ind.1984), 11 Med.L.Rptr. at 1106, quoting Indianapolis ordinance.

[53] American Booksellers Association, Inc. v. Hudnut, 771 F.2d 323 (7th Cir.1985); see also, Tamar Lewin, "Canada Court Says Pornography Harms Women and Can Be Banned," The New York Times, Feb. 28, 1992, p. 41.

Feminist Voices Against Censorship

In a book bearing the combative title of Defending Pornography (1995), American Civil Liberties Union president Nadine Strossen took issue with the drastic efforts to combat sexism with censorship, the "MacDworkinite" proposals of Andrea Dworkin and Catherine MacKinnon discussed on the preceding pages. Ms. Strossen wrote tellingly of an "unholy alliance" between the Religious Right and a hard-edged faction of feminists who characterized any sexual writings they would like to a suppress with the pejorative term "pornography." In Ms. Strossen's words: [54]

> An increasingly vocal cadre of feminist women who are dedicated to securing equal rights for women and to combating women's continuing second-class citizenship in our society strongly opposes any effort to censor sexual expression. * * * [W]e believe that suppressing sexual words and images will not advance ... [the] crucial goals of eradicating violence and discrimination against women.

Child Pornography

Although American law has been unsympathetic to the pleas of women to stop the flood of pornographic materials in the United States, child pornography has been treated in an entirely different fashion. Legislation has been created to outlaw using minors to perform or act in the creation of films, books, or magazine articles or other items depicting the sexual exploitation of children.[55]

The measure was designed to put a stop to magazines which could be purchased in 1977 such as "Chicken Delight," "Lust for Children," "Lollitots," and "Child Discipline" that were then being sold. Dr. Judianne Densen–Gerber, president of the Odyssey Institute, made this outraged statement to the Subcommittee on Crime of Congress' Committee on the Judiciary:[56]

> There comes a point where we can no longer defend by intellectualization or forensic debate. We must simply say "I know the difference between right and wrong and I am not afraid to say 'no' or demand that limits be imposed."

> Common sense and maternal instinct tell me that this [child pornography that she found in New York, Philadelphia, Boston, Washington, New Orleans, Chicago, San

[54] Nadine Strossen, Defending Pornography: Free Speech, Sex, and the Fight for Women's Rights (New York: Scribner, 1995), p. 14.

[55] Senate Bill 1585, 95th Congress, 1st Session, No. 95–438, "Protection of Children Against Sexual Exploitation Act of 1977;" Report of the Committee on the Judiciary, United States Senate, on S. 1585.

[56] Prepared Statement of Judianne Densen–Gerber, J.D., M.D., F.C.L.M., President, Odyssey Institute, for submission to The U.S. House of Representatives, Committee on the Judiciary, Subcommittee on Crime, May 23, 1977.

Francisco, and Los Angeles] goes way beyond free speech. Such conduct mutilates children's spirits; they aren't consenting adults, they're victims. The First Amendment isn't absolute.

This legislation, signed into law in 1978 by President Carter, was formally called the "Protection of Children Against Sexual Exploitation Act of 1977." This legislation, in the words of U.S. Senators John C. Culver of Iowa and Charles McC. Mathias of Maryland, was intended to do the following:[57]

— Make it a Federal crime to use children in the production of pornographic materials.

— Prohibit the interstate transportation of children for the purpose of engaging in prostitution, and

— Increase the penalty provisions of the current Federal obscenity laws if the materials adjudged obscene involve the use of children engaging in sexually explicit conduct.

This measure tried to correct loopholes in federal obscenity statutes. Before this law was passed, there was no federal statute prohibiting use of children in production of materials that depict explicit sexual conduct. This statute defined "minor" as any person under the age of 16 years. Penalties for violation of this statutory provision are two–ten years imprisonment and/or a fine of up to $10,000 on first offense, or five–fifteen years imprisonment and/or a fine of up to $15,000 for subsequent offenses.[58]

Committees of the U.S. Senate and House of Representatives found a close connection between child pornography and the use of young children as prostitutes. For example, a 17–year-old Chicago youth who had sold himself on the streets for two years, could often earn close to $500 a week in 1977—the equivalent of perhaps $2,000 a week in 1997—by selling himself two or three times a night to perform various sex acts with "chicken hawks" or pose for pornographic pictures or both.[59]

Kidporn and New York v. Ferber (1982)

In 1982, the Supreme Court of the United States made one thing clear about the murky law of obscenity: it will uphold state

[57] Form letter sent to the author by Senators Culver and Mathias, circa September 1977; letter to the author of October 19, 1977, by Rep. John Conyers, Jr. of Michigan's First District. See Public Law 95–225.

[58] 18 U.S.C.A. § 2251, Chapter 110—Sexual Exploitation of Children. The Mann Act, 18 U.S.C.A. § 2423, prohibits the interstate transportation of minor females for purposes of prostitution and did not include young males until amended in 1977.

[59] Report of the Committee on the Judiciary, United States Senate on S.1585, Protection of Children Against Sexual Exploitation Act of 1977 (Washington, D.C., 1977), p. 7. See also Robin Lloyd, For Money or Love: Boy Prostitution in America (New York: Vanguard Press, 1976).

efforts to punish individuals for the production or sale of "kid-porn."

In New York v. Ferber, the Court declared valid a New York criminal statute prohibiting persons from knowingly authorizing or inducing a child less than 16 years old to engage in a sexual performance.[60] "Sexual performance" was defined by the New York statute as, "any performance or part thereof which includes sexual performance or part thereof which includes sexual conduct by a child less than sixteen years of age."

The case began when Paul Ira Ferber, proprietor of a Manhattan bookstore specializing in sexually oriented materials, sold two films to undercover police officers. The two films dealt almost exclusively with depictions of boys masturbating. A jury trial convicted Ferber of two counts of promoting a sexual performance and Ferber was sentenced to 45 days in prison.

Ferber's convictions were upheld on first appeal, but the New York Court of Appeals said that the statute section under which Ferber was convicted was too sweeping, that it might be used to punish sale or promotion of material protected by the First Amendment, including "medical books and educational sources, which deal with adolescent sex in a realistic but nonobscene manner."[61]

The Supreme Court of the United States granted certiorari and overturned the New York Court of Appeals. Writing for the Court, Justice Byron White said:

> Like obscenity statutes, laws directed at the dissemination of child pornography run the risk of suppressing protected expression by allowing the hand of the censor to become unduly heavy. For the following reasons, however, we are persuaded that the States are entitled to greater leeway in the regulation of pornographic depictions of children.
>
> *First.* It is evident beyond the need for elaboration that a state's interest in "safeguarding the physical and psychological well being of a minor" is "compelling." Globe Newspaper Co. v. Superior Court, 457 U.S. 596, 607, 102 S.Ct. 2613, 2620 (1982), 8 Med.L.Rptr. 1689.
>
> * * *
>
> *Second.* The distribution of photographs and films depicting sexual activity by juveniles is intrinsically related to the sexual abuse of children in at least two ways. First, the materials produced are a permanent record of the children's participation and the harm to the child is exac-

---

[60] 458 U.S. 747, 752–753, 102 S.Ct. 3348 (1982), 8 Med.L.Rptr. 1809.

[61] 458 U.S. 747, 102 S.Ct. 3348, 3352 (1982).

erbated by their circulation. Second, the distribution network for child pornography must be closed if the production of material which requires the sexual exploitation of children is to be effectively controlled.

Justice White noted the economic motive involved in the production of such materials. "It rarely has been suggested that the constitutional freedom for speech and press extends immunity to speech or writing used as an integral part of conduct in violation of a valid criminal statute."[62] Further, classifying child pornography as a category outside protection of the First Amendment is compatible with the Supreme Court's earlier rulings.

Courts Extend Protection Against "Kidporn"

Two 1994 federal court decisions illustrate how far courts will extend the "Protection of Children Against Sexual Exploitation Act of 1977." Government efforts continue to discourage traffic in forms of sexually suggestive depiction of minors.

In United States v. Knox (1994), a U.S. Court of Appeals affirmed the conviction of a man charged with man who obtained films through the mails of minors engaging in "lascivious exhibition of the genitals or pubic area." These convictions were affirmed even though all of the under-age females in the films wore some form of clothing covering their private parts. The court held that these films, featuring young girls dancing provocatively or spreading their legs as cameras focused on their pubic areas, were clearly intended to produce images "sexually arousing to pedophiles."[63]

Then, in United States v. X–Citement Video Inc., the U.S. Supreme Court affirmed the conviction of an X-rated film distributor for selling one of the first films featuring porn star Traci Lords, produced when she was 15 years old. The Court held that even though Ms. Lords might have sought such roles eagerly as an adult, she could not consent retrospectively to having appeared in films made when she was still a minor. Because the distributor knew that Ms. Lords was under-age when this film was made, the Court upheld the defendant's conviction for knowingly distributing pornography involving minors.[64]

Electronic Media Standards

For broadcasters, transmission of obscene programming is a federal criminal offense, and also grounds for FCC revocation of a broadcast license.[65] In addition, however, the Commission has been

[62] Quoting Giboney v. Empire Storage & Ice Co., 336 U.S. 490, 69 S.Ct. 684 (1949).

[63] United States v. Knox, 32 F.3d 733 (3d Cir.1994).

[64] United States v. X–Citement Video, Inc., 513 U.S. 64, 115 S.Ct. 464 (1994).

[65] For radio and television, this prohibition against the transmission of obscene content is contained in the criminal provisions of 18 U.S.C.A. § 1464. A similar

attempting to establish more rigorous standards for sexually oriented broadcast programs, prohibiting "indecent" content, which the
agency has defined in general terms as being patently offensive
descriptions of sexual or excretory activities.[66]

The public appears to expect a far higher standard of good
taste from broadcasters, and particularly from television networks,
than from other media simply because even in an era when these
networks attract perhaps 50 percent of the nation's primetime
viewers, they still remain the most powerful and pervasive force in
American mass culture. On a typical evening, any modestly popular
situation comedy scheduled by one of the major television networks
will be viewed by more Americans than will read any best selling
novel or attend any single feature film that entire year. In other
words, virtually every network television series producer has a
greater opportunity to influence public sentiments, beliefs and
values than even the most popular of novelists or film makers.

Until the early 1980s, all broadcast programming was regulated by the federal government. Although the amount of supervisory
control the FCC actually exerted over television network program
policies was minimal, the fact that a federal agency was authorized
by law to make television responsive to the concerns of the public
was in itself sufficient to satisfy most citizens.

The deregulation of broadcasting closed this one channel of
legal influence that had been open to the average citizen, at a time
when the industry was dismantling its own private system of
program content standards and looking for ways to attract a
younger, more affluent and less traditional group of listeners and
viewers.[67]

Competition from the Fox Network and a wide array of cable
services forced the three major television networks to become
slightly more venturesome during the 1980s, as both series and
made-for-TV movies began treating topics that would have been
summarily rejected only a decade before. Although very little that
was broadcast during this era could have been classified as "indecent," much less obscene, American audiences were not accustomed
to even mildly risqué programs from a medium readily accessible to
children in the home.

prohibition against the carriage of obscene cable TV programming is contained in
the Cable Policy Act, 47 U.S.C.A. § 559.

[66] The FCC's indecency activities are discussed in the following chapter.

[67] Although the FCC's current crusade against "indecent" programs as described
in Chapter 7 may deserve criticism for attempting to repress constitutionally
protected expression, it is at least an effort by the FCC to demonstrate to the more
than 6,000 individuals who write to the agency each year to complain about such
programs that the federal government is still trying to be responsive to public
concerns about the quality of broadcast service. See, for example, "Defining the Line
Between Regulation and Censorship" Broadcasting April 15, 1991, p. 74.

Even so, because of widespread concern caused by broadcasting being released from virtually all of its "public interest" obligations, one of the major results of broadcast deregulation has been to popularize the forming of countless local and national private pressure groups, ranging from religious right to radical left, from Gay and Lesbian League to the AFL–CIO, to fight for each group's own perceived interests in broadcast programming. Using a broad range of economic, legal and political threats, these groups have already forced a number of stations to modify their programming policies in response to their demands.

SEC. 18.   OBSCENITY LAW AND THE INTERNET

In an early battle over sexually explicit materials on the Internet, Reno v. ACLU (1997) invalidated the Communications Decency Act of 1996.

In 1997, the Supreme Court of the United States pondered the nature of the Internet and World Wide Web following a challenge to the Communications Decency Act (CDA) by a group of business, library, and non-commercial organizations led by the American Civil Liberties Union. The CDA, part of the Telecommunications Act of 1996, made it a crime to send "indecent" or "patently offensive" communications to persons under 18 years of age.[68]

The CDA also made it a crime to transmit information about abortions. Specifically, § 223(a)(1)(B) provided for fines and imprisonment for any person convicted of making or soliciting and transmitting "any comment, request, suggestion, proposal, image or other communication which is obscene or indecent knowing that the recipient is under 18 years of age."

In a trial before a three-judge panel in Philadelphia, the plaintiffs argued that the CDA violated the First Amendment, and that terms "indecent" and "patently offensive" were so vague that they violated the free speech and due process clauses of the Constitution and the Bill of Rights.

After studying computers, the Internet, and the uses people make of electronic communication, the three-judge panel concluded that freedom should win out in this new medium. In the end, the panel concluded that the CDA was unconstitutional. These judges declared that "With the possible except of e-mail to a known

---

[68] The Court noted: that the major part of The Telecommunications Act of 1996, Pub. L. 104–104, 110 Stat. 56, was an unusually important legislative enactment. Its first 103 pages deal with reducing regulation and hastening " 'the rapid deployment of new telecommunications technologies.' " Whereas the bulk of The Telecommunications Act of 1996 was the product of extensive committee hearings, the CDA and its challenged portions were added either after the hearings were ended or during floor debate on legislation. See 25 Med.L.Rptr. at 1839.

recipient, most content providers cannot determine the identity and age of every user accessing their material."[69] At issue was a section of the CDA which declared the "knowing" transmission of obscene and indecent messages to any recipients under 18 years old to be a crime.[70]

Reno v. ACLU in the U.S. Supreme Court

Unusually lengthy oral arguments occurred before the Supreme Court of the United States, dealing with technology and the with reach of the CDA. Justice John Paul Stevens, who later wrote the Court's decision, asked about the liability of a library which might put sexually explicit materials on-line where children as well as adults might view them. Deputy Solicitor General Seth P. Waxman answered for the government that in such a situation, sexual materials could not be sent. And what, then, of an adult who indicated that he would let his 16–year-old son see such materials. Again, that would violate the CDA. Justice Scalia broke in at that point: "You're saying that any adult has a heckler's veto on the whole operation by simply saying, 'I'm going to let my son watch it.' "[71]

Justice John Paul Stevens wrote for the seven-Justice majority:[72]

Notwithstanding the legitimacy and importance of the congressional goal of protecting children from harmful material, we agree with the three-judge federal court that the statute abridges "the freedom of speech" protected by the First Amendment.

True, communication over the Internet via the World Wide Web makes enormous amounts of information available to an explosively growing list of users expected to reach 200 million by 1999. " 'Once a provider posts its content on the Internet, it cannot prevent that content' "—including sexually explicit language or images—" 'from entering any community.' "[73]

Justice Stevens then endeavored to distinguish the Internet from radio and television:[74]

[69] ACLU v. Reno, 929 F.Supp. 824, 853 (E.D.Pa.1996).

[70] Title U.S.C.A. § 223(a)(1)(B)(ii) (Supp. 1997). Section 223(d) approached defining obscenity and indecency with this language about sending persons under 18 years old any message "that, in context, depicts or describes, in terms patently offensive as measured by contemporary community standards, sexual or excretory activities or organs."

[71] 1997 WL 136253 (U.S.Oral.Arg.).

[72] Reno v. American Civil Liberties Union, ___ U.S. ___, ___, 117 S.Ct. 2329, 2334 (1997), 25 Med.L.Rptr. 1833, 1835.

[73] ___ U.S. at ___, 117 S.Ct. at 2335, Ibid., p. 1837.

[74] ___ U.S. at ___, 117 S.Ct. at 2335, 2336, Ibid., pp. 1837–1838, citing Findings 88 and 89, from 929 F.Supp. at 844–845.

Though [sexually explicit] material is widely available, users seldom encounter such content accidentally. * * * Almost all sexually explicit images are preceded by warnings as to the content. For that reason, " 'odds are slim' that a user would enter a sexually explicit site by accident." Unlike communications received by radio and television, "the receipt of information on the Internet requires a series of affirmative steps more deliberate and directed than merely turning a dial. A child requires some sophistication and some ability to retrieve material and thereby to use the Internet unattended."

The Supreme Court noted, however, that the U.S. District Court decision it upheld " 'expressly preserves the Government's right to investigate and prosecute the obscenity and child pornography.' "[75] The Government, however, was ordered not to enforce Internet communication prohibitions as they related to "indecent" content. "Indecency," which may be prohibited from radio and television broadcasts, nevertheless has been held to have some First Amendment protection. "Obscenity," on the other hand, is not protected expression.[76]

Justice Stevens' opinion declared that ambiguities in the language of the CDA "...render it problematic for purposes of the First Amendment."[77]

For example, each of the two parts of the CDA uses a different linguistic form. The first uses the word "indecent," 47 U.S.C.A. § 223(a) (Supp. 1997), while the second speaks of material that "in context, depicts or describes, in terms patently offensive as measured by contemporary community standards, sexual or excretory activities or organs," § 223(d). Given the absence of a definition of either term, this difference will provoke uncertainty among speakers about how the two standards relate to each other and just what they mean. Could a speaker confidently assert that a serious discussion about birth control practices, homosexuality, * * * or the consequences of prison rape would not violate the CDA?

* * *

We are persuaded that the CDA lacks the precision that the First Amendment requires when a statute regulates the

---

[75] __ U.S. at __, __, 117 S.Ct. at 2335, 2340, 25 Med.L.Rptr. at 1841–1842 (1997), noting that the District Court's judgment "enjoined the Government from enforcing the prohibitions in § 223(a)(1)(B) insofar as they relate to 'indecent' communications, but expressly preserves the Government's right to investigate and prosecute the obscenity and child pornography activities prohibited therein."

[76] See FCC v. Pacifica Foundation, 438 U.S. 726, 98 S.Ct. 3026 (1978), discussed in Chapter 11, at p. 624.

[77] __ U.S. at __, __, 117 S.Ct. at 2339, 2334, 25 Med.L.Rptr., at 1845, 1846 (1997).

content of speech. In order to deny minors access to potentially harmful speech, the CDA effectively suppresses a large amount of speech that adults have a right to receive and to address to one another. That burden on adult speech is unacceptable if less restrictive alternatives would be at least as effective in achieving the legitimate purpose that the statute was enacted to serve.

In evaluating the free speech rights of adults, we have made it perfectly clear that "[s]exual expression which is indecent but not obscene is protected by the First Amendment." *Sable*, 492 U.S., at 126. See also *Carey v. Population Services Int'l*, 431 U.S. 678, 701, 97 S.Ct. 2010 (1977).

The Court stated that "parental control software" could help to restrict access to sexually explicit materials.[78] Parental control is one thing; blanket control by the Government is another. Justice Stevens wrote that "the CDA is a content-based blanket restriction on speech, and, as such, cannot be 'properly analyzed as a form of time, place and manner regulation.' "[79]

* * *

...[S]ome of our cases have recognized special justifications for regulation of the broadcast media that are not applicable to other speakers, see *Red Lion Broadcasting Co. v. FCC*, 395 U.S. 367 [1 Med.L.Rptr. 2053] (1969); *FCC v. Pacifica Foundation*, 438 U.S. 726 (1978) [3 Med.L.Rptr. 2553] (1978). In these cases, the Court relied on the history of extensive government regulation of the broadcast medium * * * the scarcity of available frequencies at its inception, see, e.g., *Turner Broadcasting System, Inc. v. FCC*, 512 U.S. 622, 637–638 [22 Med.L.Rptr. 1865] (1994); * * * and its "invasive" nature, see *Sable Communications of Cal., Inc. v. FCC*, 492 U.S. 115, 128 [16 Med. L.Rptr. 1961] (1989).

These factors are not present in cyberspace. Neither before nor after the enactment of the CDA have the vast democratic fora of the Internet been subject to the type of government supervision and regulation that has attended the broadcast industry. Moreover, as the Internet is not as "invasive" as radio or television. The District Court specifically found that "[c]ommunications over the Internet do not 'invade' an individual's home or appear on one's computer screen unbidden. Users seldom encounter content 'by accident.' " 929 F.Supp., at 844 (finding 88). It also found that " '[a]lmost all sexually

[78] ___ U.S. at ___, ___, 117 S.Ct. at 2335, 2336, 25 Med.L.Rptr. at 1837.

[79] ___ U.S. at ___, ___, 117 S.Ct. at 2335, 2336, 25 Med.L.Rptr. at 1843, 1844 (1997).

explicit images are preceded by warnings as to the content,' "
and cited testimony that "odds are slim" that a user would
come across a sexually explicit sight by accident. *Ibid.*

In any event, the Supreme Court of the United States did not
demolish all government weapons against transmitting obscenity
and child pornography. However transmitted, whether via the
Internet or by other means, obscenity and child pornography already were illegal under federal law.[80]

Most significant, the Court emphasized that the Internet is
something new, that it is not to be controlled as rigidly as broadcasting under its licensing model. It is likely that many more
legislative and court battles will be fought over content on the
Internet. But Round One—the decision in *Reno v. ACLU*—saw the
Supreme Court of the United States viewing the First Amendment
through a Twenty–First Century legal prism. In this decision, at
least, the Court emphasized freedom for the Internet more than its
control.

[80] 25 Med.L.Rptr. at 1848, n. 44 (1997), citing 18 U.S.C. §§ 1464–1465 (criminalizing obscenity), and § 2251 (criminalizing child pornography).

Part II

DEFAMATION, PRIVACY AND NEWSGATHERING TORTS

Chapter 4

DEFAMATION: LIBEL AND SLANDER

SEC. 19. DEFAMATION DEFINED

Defamation is communication which exposes persons to hatred, ridicule, or contempt, lowers them in the esteem of others, causes them to be shunned, or injures them in their business or calling. Its categories are libel—broadly, printed, written or broadcast material—and slander—broadly, spoken words of limited reach.

We have long been concerned with our reputations in the communities in which we live. The words of the children's rhyme: "sticks and stones may break my bones, but words will never hurt me" do not apply in the field of mass communications. Words can injure and under the civil law, the victims of hurtful words have a right to sue for the damage they cause.

Juries have no problem delivering damage awards in the millions of dollars for the sting of words. In the spring of 1997, a jury in Houston, Texas, came back with a $222.7 million award against the publisher of the *Wall Street Journal* over an article which defamed a Texas securities company[1]. That award, subsequently

---

[1] Iver Peterson, "Firm Awarded $222.7 Million in a Libel Suit Vs. Dow Jones," New York Times, March 21, 1997, C–1. The court later tossed out $200 million in

appealed, topped the previous record libel award of $58 million awarded to a Texas district attorney over statements made about him in a television station's investigative reports into ticket fixing.[2]

Although more attention to fair play and ethical considerations might well stave off many of the libel suits now brought against the media, a free society by its nature is going to allow communication which harms many reputations. Freedom, after all, is a risk. Although society has a strong interest in the free flow of information, there is also a societal stake in allowing protection of one's good name.

Protection of reputations is not a new concept and neither is punishment for people who defame. The Law of the 12 Tables, compiled about 300 years after the founding of Rome declared that anyone who slandered another and injured his reputation would be beaten with a club. We can recall the Biblical injunction against bearing "false witness against thy neighbor."

In ancient Britain at the time of Alfred in the ninth century, slander was either painful or expensive, depending on the slanderer's social standing. "The penalty for slander was the tearing out of tongue."[3] The only way to avoid mutilation was to pay the "wergild," the price set for each social class. According to a set and firmly fixed system of social worth, a prince was worth 1500 shillings, a nobleman 300, a farmer 100 and an agricultural serf between 40 and 80. That reflected a social view of the worth of the person and his words. A prince's words were dear while a serf's were insignificant (that is unless you were a serf trying to raise up to 80 shillings to keep a civil tongue in your head).[4]

The English church court had jurisdiction over slander cases in connection with its jurisdiction over the conduct and morality of its members (church courts could prosecute sins). Harmful statements about a person were enough to subject him to the jurisdiction of the church courts. Such a defendant was referred to as a *diffamatus* one whose reputation was bad enough to justify bringing him to trial.[5] In those cases where the reputation was determined to be unfounded, the church court then had to deal with the people who spread the now-proven-false statements about the defendant. The slanderers had therefore committed a crime in the eyes of the

punitive damages, leaving $22.7 million in actual damages and a punitive award of $20,000 against the reporter who wrote the story.

[2] The parties later agreed to a settlement of about $16 million while the case was being appealed.

[3] Winston S. Churchill, A History of the English Speaking Peoples, The Birth of Britain (New York: Barnes & Noble, 1993) p.67.

[4] The shilling of the time was the price of a cow or sheep.

[5] Theodore F.T. Plucknett, A Concise History of the Common Law, (London: Butterworth, 1948), p. 455 (Chap. 5).

church and faced punishment as provided for in the Langston constitution of 1222, "furthermore, we excommunicate all those who for lucre, hate, favour, or any other cause maliciously impute a crime whereby anyone is defamed among good and grave persons in such wise that he has been put to his purgation at least, or otherwise aggrieved."[6]

More modernly, Supreme Court Justice Potter Stewart addressed the issue of reputation in the 1966 Supreme Court case of Rosenblatt v. Baer which we will discuss later in this chapter: [7]

> The right of a man to the protection of his own reputation from unjustified invasion and wrongful hurt reflects no more than our basic concept of the essential dignity and worth of every human being—a concept at the root of any decent system of ordered liberty.

But the protection of reputation as a legal concept within the structure of secular government arose more than 700 years ago with the creation of *De Scandalis Magnatum*, an act of the English crown in 1275 which made it a crime to slander the leading men of England—the king and his magnates. Its re-enactment in 1378 made clear the purpose of the protection of those men declaring that false statements regarding the character, conduct and reputations of the leaders of the nation, now extended to peers, prelates, justices and specifically named officials, threatened peril and mischief "to all the realm, and quick subversion and destruction of the said realm."[8] The penalties for such statements were severe, the loss of the ears for spoken words and the loss of the right hand where the statements were in writing. These acts and their punishments were intended to preserve the political power of the government, an aim that has lain at the heart of much of defamation law and which became of paramount importance in preserving the freedom of the press and public in the United States.

The Star Chamber became the forum for many of these cases where defamatory statements carried criminal penalties as breaches of the peace, seditious libel or criminal libel. In large measure, the Star Chamber took jurisdiction because it was considered more reliable (more likely to render the "right" decision) than local courts when dealing with political criminals. While there were legislative acts that could provide justification for the defamation prosecutions, the Star Chamber relied on the "absolute power" of

---

[6] Ibid.

[7] Rosenblatt v. Baer, 383 U.S. 75, 92, 86 S.Ct. 669, 679 (1966).

[8] Norman L. Rosenberg, Protecting the Best Men: An Interpretive History of the Law of Libel, (Chapel Hill: University of North Carolina Press, 1986), p. 4 (Introduction).

the realm as well as the "law of God."[9] That was invoked in the case *De Libellis Famosis*.

But in the 16th century, local and church courts in England began to hear cases regarding spoken attacks on personal and business reputations. The rise of the merchant class made reputation a valuable property and the courts began awarding monetary damages for injuries to both personal reputation and reputations affecting business relationships with others. From a legal point, the evolution of monetary damages came about under a doctrine that held that where a statute created a punishment for conduct that harmed others, then the person harmed could sue for damages even where the statute did not mention the possibility of a civil suit. Plaintiffs then applied the *scandalum magnatum* in the civil courts, supplementing the body of common law regarding defamation.

English colonists brought many legal traditions to America and with them, attitudes about defamation. But these colonial suits were unlike the multimillion dollar cases we see played out in the courts these days. For one thing, the purpose of the defamation suit was to repair the damage to the plaintiff's reputation. Damage awards were often small and often the losing defendant was forced to acknowledge the falsity of his statement either in court or at some public place where the retraction would quickly be spread and the reputation of the plaintiff rehabilitated. To help restore the status quo, the courts would sometimes offer the losing defendant the choice of paying a large damage award or making his public apology and retraction.

There also was concern about the effect of slanderous words on the community and government and several colonies passed laws against making false or vilifying statements against others. A Pennsylvania statute called for punishment of "Spreaders of False News." A Connecticut law made it a crime to knowingly tell lies about people and made the penalties more severe for each subsequent offense. All told, defamation cases made up about 17 percent of the criminal cases of colonial courts. The *Zenger* case had a symbolic impact on the treatment of seditious libel in the courts, but the prosecution of speech attacking the established power structure continued in the colonial assemblies. The assemblies held that they were protected from any and all criticisms under their power to prohibit "breaches of parliamentary privileges." In his *Freedom of the Press from Zenger to Jefferson*, Leonard Levy noted that prosecutions in these assemblies probably ran into the hundreds. As we will see in the next chapter, the practice of using the

---

[9] Theodore F.T. Plucknett, A Concise History of the Common Law, (London: Butterworth, 1948), p. 458 (Chap. 5).

courts to stifle criticism of public officials is a major concern in the law of defamation.

Following the excesses of the Sedition Act of 1798, defamation law evolved with public officials turning more often to purely civil libel suits rather than criminal libel actions to deter criticism against them. It was not just public officials, either. The novelist and political essayist James Fenimore Cooper carried on a series of libel suits against newspapers. Cooper was initially angered by the treatment of his literary works in the popular press and more outraged by the press coverage of a dispute surrounding a controversy over property owned by the Cooper family. In many ways similar to current criticisms of the media, Cooper was concerned that the popular press was inflaming the masses and threatening to replace reasoned government with the tyranny of public opinion. As Norman Rosenberg wrote in his Protecting the Best Men: [10]

> Cooper could still hope that the republic's descent into tyranny might be halted if, among other things, the landed gentry—Cooper's version of the best men—regained political power; this could only happen, he believed, if strict defamation laws prevented the press from destroying the characters and reputations of these worthy citizens.

Opinion leaders and the political and social elite still sue to advance or protect their own agendas, but more often media defendants face libel suits over published statements that have tarnished reputations. While many defamation suits arise from stories about the powerful and famous, many others come about from the "routine" and "everyday" stories and communications generated in the modern media.

The average cost of defending a libel suit may run as high as $100,000 or even $150,000, and that refers only to legal costs and not to money paid out as part of a judgment. And those costs could include the expenses run up by the winning plaintiff. Clint Eastwood won $150,000 in damages against the *National Enquirer* in 1996. The court ordered the *Enquirer* to pay an additional $653,000 to Eastwood to cover the costs of his lawsuit. Litigation that might sting a large newspaper or radio station or its insurance company could ruin a small media outfit.

In one extraordinary case in 1985, costs to *Time* magazine were estimated as $3 million for its successful defense; and in Westmoreland v. CBS—arguably one of the most-publicized libel case in the nation's history—one estimate was $8 million in legal costs for both sides, although the plaintiff dropped his suit before it reached the

---

[10] Norman L. Rosenberg, Protecting the Best Men: An Interpretive History of the Law of Libel, (Chapel Hill: University of North Carolina Press, 1986), p. 138 (Chap. 6).

jury. Such prospects may lead media to avoid the huge costs of defending a drawn-out trial by settling out of court—for $800,000 in case of a 1984 agreement by the *Wall Street Journal*.[11]

Insurance, which is not required and not always available, does not eliminate the expenses of defamation litigation. As with car or homeowner insurance, libel insurance comes with a deductible, the amount the policy holder must pay to cover the first part of the costs and award. In one libel case in which one of the authors was involved in a consulting capacity, the deductible was $100,000 and that is what the defendant television station had to pay first before its insurance carrier opened its checkbook.

It is not just the newspaper, television or radio station that needs to be wary of defamation suits. Press releases and advertising copy can give rise to a costly defamation suit. Novels and short stories have resulted in courtroom cases and multimedia presentations and Internet communications are a new and fertile field for litigation. This chapter will then discuss the elements of defamation with an eye toward incorporating the liabilities involved in every form of mass communication.

It will be a sometimes confusing excursion. The late William L. Prosser, long considered America's leading torts scholar, assessed this area of the law in this way:[12]

> It must be confessed ... that there is a great deal of the law of defamation which makes no sense. It contains anomalies and absurdities for which no legal writer ever has had a kind word, and it is a curious compound of a strict liability imposed upon innocent defendants ... with a blind and almost perverse refusal to compensate the plaintiff for real and very serious harm.

As a distinguished study asserted in 1987, the law of libel aims at one thing and hits another. This study, entitled Libel Law and the Press: Myth and Reality, noted that the law assumes that by suing, plaintiffs whose reputations have been injured can somehow be made whole by receiving money. That study found, however, that plaintiffs tend to be more interested in correction of falsity and in "setting the record straight."[13]

Moreover, many defamation cases are filed because of the treatment that the subjects of these publications receive once they bring the matter to the attention of the publisher. In many of the

---

[11] Sharon v. Time, Inc., Time, Feb. 4, 1985, 64; Westmoreland v. CBS, New York Times, Feb. 19, 1985, 1, Feb. 20, 1985, 13; 10 Med.L.Rptr. #25, 6/19/84, News Notes, citing LDRC Report of July 29, 1984.

[12] Prosser, Law of Torts, 4th ed. (1971), at p. 737.

[13] Randall P. Bezanson, Gilbert Cranberg, and John Soloski, Libel Law and the Press: Myth and Reality (New York: The Free Press, 1987).

suits, the plaintiffs reported that they would have been willing to listen to an explanation for the harmful words from the defendant.[14] But, more often than not, the reaction they got was a harsh and abrupt, "we stand by our story." Adding insult to injury was the critical factor in bringing about the lawsuit. All publishers, managers and administrators will develop their own policies to deal with complaints about stories, but a key factor in avoiding costly and risky litigation is a willingness to hear the aggrieved person out. It is unnecessary and improvident to apologize or accept responsibility for what one person claims are errors or misstatements about him, but it is possible and very helpful to take a complaint seriously and relay the matter to the appropriate supervisor.

SEC. 20.   THE FIVE ELEMENTS OF LIBEL

The plaintiff in a libel suit must plead that there was Publication, Identification, Defamation, Fault and Injury.

Potential libel suit defendants—and that includes all of us—need to know (as do lawyers filing libel suits) that five conditions must be present before a suit can hope to succeed. This discussion assumes that the action for defamation will have been filed in a timely fashion to conform to the deadline set by the state where the suit is filed: the *statute of limitations*. In 26 states and the District of Columbia, the statute of limitations for libel is one year after publication. Among the rest, 19 states set their statute of limitations at two years and five give the plaintiff three years to file suit.[15] As you can see from the range of statutes of limitations, the 50 states and the District of Columbia have developed the law of

---

[14] Although the case comes from England, printed in The Mirror newspaper on Aug. 1, 1997, the story offers food for thought for all professional communicators:

"One little word was all that was needed to save four and a half years of courtroom agony for Poinsias de Rossa.

The word was "sorry" but it was not a part of the vocabulary of write Eamon Dunphy and his bosses at the Sunday Independent.

A simple apology could have saved the newspaper group an estimated pounds million in damages and costs. The former minister said last night he'd never have sued if the paper had printed the apology he sought.

'They failed to do the decent thing,' he said."

(The pound was worth about $1.68 at the time of the story.)

[15] States with two-year statutes include Alabama, Alaska, Connecticut, Delaware, Florida, Hawaii, Idaho, Indiana, Iowa, Maine, Minnesota, Missouri, Montana, Nevada, North Dakota, South Carolina, South Dakota, Washington, and Wisconsin. Arkansas, Massachusetts, New Hampshire, New Mexico and Vermont's limitations are three years. Although Tennessee gives plaintiffs a year to sue for libel, it provides only a six month statute of limitations for slander. (See LDRC 50–State Survey 1995–1996).

defamation in their own ways. There are general principles, but each state is free to follow its own judicial philosophies, subject to the requirements of the First Amendment and the Constitution.

The five necessary conditions for suit are:

1. Publication
2. Identification
3. Defamation
4. Injury
5. Fault

SEC. 21. PUBLICATION

There is an old saying: "They can't shoot you for what you think." The same holds true for defamation suits. You can think all the nasty things you want to about people, organizations and corporations. It is not until you publish the statement that we start down the painful path of litigation. Publication means that someone other than the publisher and the subject of the statement receives the communication. You may speak harshly to someone or write about them or paint pictures, but until some other person perceives the message you have little to fear from defamation. But as soon as someone else sees or hears, you are in for a bumpy ride. Even when we broadcast or record our defamatory statement, we still call it publication, a term of art in defamation.

The reason for the publication requirement is easy to understand when we keep in mind that defamation arises over damage to reputations, the esteem in which we are held by others. In professional communication we think of defamatory stories appearing in newspapers with hundreds of thousands of readers, seen or heard by millions in broadcast audiences or accessible by the millions hooked into the World Wide Web. But in defamation law, it takes only one person to make up an audience for purposes of publication. In one case, a man dictated a letter to his secretary accusing the addressee of grand larceny. The secretary typed the letter and it was sent through the mail. The letter's recipient brought a successful libel suit: the court held that publication took place at the time the stenographic notes were read and transcribed.[16]

Litigation Note: *Even if you are in a jurisdiction where intra-company communication is not considered publication, those memos*

---

[16] Ostrowe v. Lee, 256 N.Y. 36, 175 N.E. 505 (1931). See also Arvey Corp. v. Peterson, 178 F.Supp. 132 (E.D.Pa.1959). This is the majority position although there is a significant minority of jurisdictions which hold that communication between employees of a company does not create publication because it is akin to talking to one's self. Remember though, that the odds are that you will be in a jurisdiction where you incur liability.

can create significant legal problems. In a defamation suit, a good plaintiff's attorney will seek to develop evidence to show the defendant's bad motives. To that end, the plaintiff's attorney will demand that the defendant produce all notes, memos and even e-mail that have relevance to the suit. And discovery, as you recall from your earlier chapters, is intended to bring out any materials arguably related to the case, it can be far reaching. The National Law Journal has reported on the growing use of discovery for e-mail and its potential for damage to clients. "Think of e-mail as a corporate CB radio," one litigation support firm said of electronic discovery. "It is full of corporate gossip, and derogatory or indiscreet remarks. It paints a very down-to-earth picture of corporate knowledge and behavior. And it is meticulously transcribed and stored."[17] An e-mail message in which a reporter or editor crows that, "we are going to get that #%*&@$" or which speaks unflatteringly about the subject of a story can significantly increase the risk of losing a defamation suit and adding to the size of a damage award. Such statements help to turn juries against media defendants and provide fuel for the plaintiff's attorney who will seek to inflame the passions and prejudices of the jurors against the "mean spirited, arrogant and willful" media defendants.

One significant question that arises in defamation is the extent of liability from a published defamatory statement. If your newspaper or magazine has a circulation of 250,000, how many libel suits can be brought? Similarly, what is the extent of liability for a broadcast that has 500,000 viewers, a home page on the Internet that can be accessed by millions of persons or the 20,000 copies of a novel? The answer comes in two parts. The first is liability for each of the copies of the single edition of the newspaper, book, generation of the home page or broadcast seen or heard in each of the homes. Those are considered to be a single publication and would create liability for only defamation lawsuit. The second question arises when that edition, home page or broadcast crosses state lines. Can a plaintiff sue in each and every state in which the defamatory statement was published? In 27 states and the District of Columbia, either case law or statute say that the single edition can give the plaintiff a single lawsuit.[18] In 20 other states it is either unclear from a reading of the statutes or case law whether a plaintiff could bring multiple lawsuits over a single edition. Three

[17] Martha Middleton, "A Discovery: There May Be Gold in E–Mail," The National Law Journal, Sept. 20, 1993, A–1.

[18] The rule is laid out in the Restatement (Second) of Torts § 577A(4) (1977) "As to any single publication, (a) only one action for damages can be maintained; (b) all damages suffered in all jurisdictions can be recovered in the one action; and (c) a judgment for or against the plaintiff upon the merits of the action for damages bars any other action for damages between the same parties in all jurisdictions."

states appear to allow for multiple lawsuits for a single publication.[19]

The single-publication rule also applies to the statute of limitations. The statute of limitations, already mentioned above, is the time in which a plaintiff has to commence the suit. This limitation on the time in which a plaintiff can start a suit is based on the idea that potential defendants should not have to look over their shoulders for potential plaintiffs for their whole lives. It also means that plaintiffs will bring their suits in a timely fashion when evidence and witnesses are more likely to be reliable. In the majority of states, the statute of limitations is a year. That means that a plaintiff who waits a year and a day to commence suit will be barred from proceeding and a defendant who may well have defamed will be free from liability. It may seem counterintuitive for this to happen but texts on civil procedure have numerous such cases.

Because deadlines are so important,[20] one consideration in defamation is when the statute begins to run. For newspapers or other daily publications it is simple enough—the day the publication comes out. For magazines, the question becomes more complicated. In Tocco v. Time, Inc., it was held that the publication takes place at the time a magazine is mailed to subscribers, or put in the hands of those who will ship the edition to wholesale distributors.[21] That approach, however, is not universally accepted. To the contrary, Osmers v. Parade Publications, Inc., held that a publication date is when the libel was "substantially and effectively communicated to a meaningful mass of readers—the public for which the publication was intended, not some small segment of it."[22] For the Internet and World Wide Web publishers, the more reasonable rule would appear to be when the statement became available.

[19] Arizona, Arkansas, California, Colorado, Connecticut, Florida, Georgia, Idaho, Illinois, Kansas, Minnesota, Mississippi, Missouri, Nebraska, New Hampshire, New Jersey, New Mexico, New York, North Dakota, Ohio (in federal cases at least), Oklahoma, Oregon, Pennsylvania, Tennessee, Texas, Virginia, Washington and the District of Columbia apply the single publication rule by case law or statute. The rule is unclear in Alabama, Delaware, Indiana, Kentucky, Maine, Massachusetts, Michigan, Nevada, Rhode Island, South Carolina, South Dakota, Utah, Vermont, Wisconsin and Wyoming because the issue has not come up in a defamation case. Alaska has declined to adopt either the single-or multiple-publication rule, West Virginia case law suggests it might lean toward the multiple-publication rule and the issue is unsettled in North Carolina. Iowa and Montana appear to support the multiple-publication rule, a Maryland case adopted the multiple-publication rule, the issue is not clear from recent cases in Hawaii and it is not definite in Louisiana (See LDRC 50–State Survey 1995–1996.).

[20] Civil procedure texts provide many examples of cases where plaintiffs (through their attorneys) failed to comply with the rules and so lost their cases or the right to bring their cases.

[21] Tocco v. Time, Inc., 195 F.Supp. 410 (E.D.Mich.1961).

[22] Osmers v. Parade Publications, Inc., 234 F.Supp. 924, 927 (S.D.N.Y.1964).

But even when the beginning of the statute of limitations can be identified, the question remains which statute to apply. If the statute of limitations has expired in one jurisdiction, can a plaintiff still sue in another state where the statute of limitations is longer? In Keeton v. Hustler,[23] the United States Supreme Court allowed the plaintiff to sue *Hustler* magazine in New Hampshire, the only state where the statute of limitations had not expired.[24] The key to the case was the fact that *Hustler* magazine had circulation in New Hampshire. Having taken advantage of doing business in the state, the magazine had to accept the jurisdiction of the state. The magazine pointed out that it sold only between 10,000 and 15,000 copies in New Hampshire out of its entire circulation but the Supreme Court found that to be sufficient to confer jurisdiction.

While publication limits liability by applying a specific statute of limitations, publishers (including station management and those on the Internet) need to understand the limitations on the single-publication rule. It does not apply when a defamatory statement is republished. This can be a tricky issue. If a defamatory statement is published on Feb. 1, the publisher has a year to worry about. On Feb. 2 of the next year, the statute of limitation will have tolled (in the majority of jurisdictions) and the plaintiff will be barred from bringing suit. It does not matter if the newspaper or magazine sells a back issue on the following Feb. 3. The initial publication is the controlling date for purposes of the statute of limitation.

The problem arises when the publisher republishes the defamatory statement. If a newspaper republishes, in a later edition, a story it published earlier, the newspaper faces the possibility of a new defamation suit with a newly begun statute of limitations. This can be a significant problem for those media entities that create "remember when" or "10 years ago today" features. The reprinting of those articles from 10, 20 or 50 years earlier creates a new publication and lawsuit. The same applies to book publishers who may issue a subsequent edition of a book. In Rinaldi v. Viking Penguin,[25] a New York court of appeals ruled that although the allegedly defamatory statements in a hard-cover book were protected from suit by the statute of limitations, a paperback edition of the same book started a new statute of limitations. For newspapers, subsequent editions of the same day's newspaper can be considered new publication of defamatory materials. The same holds true for rebroadcasts. The key in these cases is the choice the publishers made to publish again and the opportunity, whether they took advantage of it, to correct the statement.

[23] Keeton v. Hustler, 465 U.S. 770, 104 S.Ct. 1473 (1984).

[24] At the time New Hampshire's statute of limitation was six years.

[25] Rinaldi v. Viking Penguin, 52 N.Y.2d 422, 438 N.Y.S.2d 496, 420 N.E.2d 377 (1981).

This can be a particular problem when periodicals reprint investigative series in book or other form. In Warford v. Lexington Herald–Leader Co., the 1986 republication of a 1985 series charging an assistant basketball coach with recruiting violations brought a lawsuit. The Kentucky Supreme Court noted that a basketball player who was a source for damaging information published by the newspaper about assistant coach Reggie Warford had promptly denied and retracted his statements, and his denial was published by the *Herald–Leader.*

The series, which won a Pulitzer Prize, was then republished in 1986, retitled "1985: A Year of Crisis in College Athletics." The 1986 publication, which omitted the athlete's denial, was sent to "the president, athletic director, faculty representative, and head football and basketball coaches at each [NCAA] member university, as well as 100 major newspapers. . . . "[26] Assistant Coach Warford, who asserted that the series had damaged his employment chances, won his lawsuit against the newspaper.

Republication does not necessarily apply to the independent parties who distribute defamatory publications. The courts have said that it would be unreasonable to hold a newsstand operator liable for the contents of all the publications sold at the newsstand. Before a court will hold a distributor liable, it must first determine that the distributor knew of the defamatory content. The Minnesota Supreme Court applied this to a libel suit brought by the Church of Scientology against the Minnesota State Medical Association Foundation: "Those who merely deliver or transmit defamatory material previously published by another will be considered to have published the material only if they knew, or had reason to know, that the material was false and defamatory."[27] This also can protect broadcasters who carry network programs containing defamatory statements as well as newspapers republishing defamatory wire service reports. It is a significant issue for Internet operators. There has been a split of authority as to whether service providers are liable for what appears on their systems. In the first case to be decided on this issue, Cubby, Inc. v. CompuServe, Inc.,[28] a federal judge held that Compuserve was a distributor and not a publisher. But in another case brought in 1995, Stratton Oakmont, Inc. v. Prodigy,[29] a court in New York said that Prodigy's conduct and declaration that it was "an online service that exercised editorial control over the content of messages posted on its computer bulle-

[26] Warford v. Lexington Herald–Leader Co., 789 S.W.2d 758, 759–760 (Ky.1990).

[27] Church of Scientology v. Minnesota State Medical Ass'n. Found., 264 N.W.2d 152, 156 (Minn.1978), 3 Med.L.Rptr. 2177.

[28] 776 F.Supp. 135 (S.D.N.Y.1991).

[29] (N.Y.Sup.1995), 23 Med.L.Rptr. 1794.

tin boards,"[30] made it a publisher. Although the parties resolved their differences, the presiding court rejected an attempt to drop its conclusions and avoid a troubling precedent.

The Congress specifically overruled *Stratton Oakmont* in the Communications Decency Act. "No provider or user of interactive computer services shall be treated as the publisher or speaker of information provided by another information content provider."[31] The ruling by the Supreme Court that the Communications Decency Act was unconstitutional may mean that this area of the law will remain unsettled until Congress acts again.

The republication issue also is a major concern because in most cases, the defamation suit is brought because the defendant has quoted someone else's statement about the plaintiff. Both students and professionals (who ought to know better) have claimed the "defense" of merely quoting another person's defamation. That is not a defense. "The common law of libel has long held that one who republishes a defamatory statement 'adopts' it as his own and is liable [for false, defamatory statements] in equal measure to the original defamer."[32] Modern defamation law holds that the original speaker also can be held liable if he knew it would be republished or reasonably could foresee the statement being repeated.

In a case that illustrates the problems of relying on others and points out just how unwise it is to rely on anonymous sources, a television reporter in Florida wound up in court for reporting a story in which he did not know who the sources for his story were.

In Holter v. WLCY T.V., Inc.,[33] reporter Mike Halloran received three anonymous calls suggesting that state officials were investigating corruption in two communities, Redington Shores and Redington Beach and that the mayor of Redington Beach was going to resign over his involvement in embezzlement and extortion. The calls came in two-hour period. Halloran said that he dismissed the first caller because the caller didn't seem very reliable. Halloran testified that he got a second call about an hour later. "Halloran testified that this 'older, very stable voice led me to believe that he was somebody in government.' He testified that the voice even sounded like it possibly might be a county commissioner." Halloran told the court he did not ask the anonymous caller if he were a county commissioner and he did not offer the name of the county commission it might be at trial. Halloran related the essence of the call:

[30] Ibid.

[31] 47 U.S.C.A. § 509 230(c)(1).

[32] Liberty Lobby, Inc. v. Dow Jones & Co., 838 F.2d 1287, 1298 (D.C.Cir.1988), 14 Med.L.Rptr. 2249 .

[33] Holter v. WLCY T.V., Inc., 366 So.2d 445 (Fla.Dist.Ct.App.1978).

(This) person called me and said, "I have some news to relate to you concerning beach communities" that (an investigation) was taking place. I asked the person to disclose who he was. (The) person said, "I cannot disclose who I am because I am involved in the investigation." I asked him, "Well, what is the nature of this investigation?" Source said that, "Auditor General's investigation currently going on here in the beach communities of Redington Shores and Redington Beach." And he said that, "Some people will have to leave office because of the probe into their activities," and he related that Mayor Holter, along with another commissioner, would step down, would resign from their office.[34]

Halloran received his third anonymous phone about 45 minutes later and testified that the caller said what the first caller had told him. Caller number three simply said that she was a resident of the beach communities and declined to give her name. Halloran made two telephone calls to the local State Attorney's office and the Auditor General. He testified that no one in authority in either place and that he was not able to confirm even whether or not an investigation was under way. Halloran had a secretary place a call to the mayor's office and she got the mayor to tell her the correct spelling of his name, his marital status, how long he had served in office and whether he was resigning. Holter testified that the secretary gave no explanation as to why she was making her inquiry. After these attempts at verification Halloran typed up the story and made a sound-on-film recordation for the 5:30 p.m. news telecast that day:

A very hush hush undercover probe by the State Attorney General's office into the current operation of local government in Reddington [sic] Beach and it's [sic] sister community Reddington [sic] Shore's [sic] has uncovered possible serious irregularities with officials who are running those government's [sic]. According to reliable sources who refused to be identified the mayor of Reddington [sic] Beach, Charles E. Holter, who's been in office five years, has reportedly resigned effective January first of 1974 under strong suspecision [sic] that he's been implicated in embasselment [sic] and extortion of monies from private contractor's [sic] who wanted to build in the area ... but this has not been confirmed ... I've also been told that one of the three commissioner's [sic] in Reddington [sic] Beach will also step down pending the outcome of the corruption probe. People who live in Reddington [sic] also disclosed to me that a full team of undercover men are

34 Ibid. At 446.

looking in to [sic] the practice's [sic] of all local government's [sic] within the beach communities here in Pinellas County because of those extreme irregularities.[35] . . .

Mayor Charles Holter sued. The trial court granted the defendants a directed verdict on the grounds that the story did not reflect the required level of fault. The Florida court of appeals reversed, leaving reporter Halloran and his station with a renewed libel suit and others with a cautionary tale about repeating the unsubstantiated words of anonymous sources.

Defamation "Live!"

This issue of responsibility for republishing the statements of another is of particular importance to broadcasters, especially with the increasing ability to go "live" to the scene of news stories and also for radio stations that feature the call-in talk show. We begin our analysis by looking at one of the first cases of "live" defamation encountered by the courts and the resolution applied there.

In Summit Hotel Co. v. National Broadcasting Co.[36], the Pennsylvania Supreme Court was faced with a new legal issue, how to assign liability in a case of an extemporaneous remark made in the course of a live radio broadcast. NBC had sold air time to an advertising company which put together a radio series featuring Al Jolson, the comedian. The advertising company hired all the performers and provided the scripts which were reviewed and approved by NBC in advance. In the June 15, 1935 show, Jolson was to interview the winner of a golf tournament. During that interview, Jolson made his extemporaneous remark:

Jolson: But tell me, Sam, what did you do after you got out of college?

Sam: I turned golf professional and in 1932 I got a job at the Summit Golf Club in Uniontown, Pennsylvania.

Jolson: That's a rotten hotel.

The Summit Hotel was not amused and sued NBC, winning $15,000. NBC appealed and the Pennsylvania Supreme Court had to figure out what to do with this new medium which had little legal history surrounding it. The justices rejected the approach of treating broadcasts just like newspapers. Unlike newspapers which are written ahead of time and subjected to the scrutiny of the copy desk, broadcasts were live and changes made in previously reviewed scripts or ad libs might not be foreseen. The justices noted that Jolson had been employed by the advertising company and that the script, previously reviewed and approved, had nothing offensive in

[35] Ibid. At 446.

[36] Summit Hotel Co. v. National Broadcasting Co., 336 Pa. 182, 8 A.2d 302 (1939).

it. Further, there was no means by which NBC could have prevented the spontaneous remark. The Pennsylvania court reversed the judgment.

But the court did not grant NBC, or any other broadcasters for that matter, absolute immunity from liability in live broadcast, either its own or those who bought air time. It placed strict limits on the protections it gave to NBC in the Summit Hotel case.

> We therefore conclude that a broadcasting company that leases its time and facilities to another, whose agents carry on the program, is not liable for an interjected defamatory remark where it appears that it exercised due care in the selection of the lessee, and, having inspected and edited the script, had no reason to believe an extemporaneous defamatory remark would be made. Where the broadcasting station's employee or agent makes the defamatory remark, it is liable, unless the remarks are privileged[37] [e.g. as part of a public record]. . . .

And so, broadcasters may have a means of avoiding liability, if they exercise proper care in the manner of their live broadcasts. It is not automatic. The broadcaster must have taken adequate steps to try to prevent any spontaneous defamation. A good example of what happens when a broadcast simply throws open the microphone to anyone comes from the Louisiana case of Snowden v. Pearl River Broadcasting Corp.[38]

In Snowden, radio station WBOX in Bogalusa, La., had created a radio call-in program in early 1968. It was called "Call and Comment" and ran from January or February of 1968 until April 3, 1968, when the station broadcast the program that cost it a libel judgment of $11,500 (of course that was in addition to the costs of the suit). On April 3, 1968, the station opened up its microphones to any topic, except segregation, integration and religion. Drug use was in the news. The previous day, the moderator had read a wire service story about drug addiction and suggested drugs as a topic for the April 3 program.

The station had chosen not to purchase equipment that would have allowed it to delay callers comments and allow the moderator to block statements. The station manager said that he did not think the station could afford the device. The only controls the station placed on callers was the request that, "in fairness to all people and jobs unless you are willing to identify yourself and to tell us who is

---

[37] Ibid. At 204, 312.

[38] Snowden v. Pearl River Broadcasting Corp., 251 So.2d 405 (La.App.1971), appeal denied, 259 La. 887, 253 So.2d 217 (La.1971).

calling, we would rather you would not use specific names or places."[39]

In the course of the program, callers talked about drug use and drug sales in Bogalusa. The names of three residents and one business were linked to drug sales:

Unidentified Caller: I've been listening to your program every day for two or three weeks here.

Announcer: Yes, sir.

Unidentified Caller: And I've been noticing that its very evidence that there is proof being narcotics been going around here in town at these certain places. The police know about it but the facts that I've heard over at the station and you all know about it. It looks like they could to down there and they could do something to the Pizza Shanty and stop this stuff.

Announcer: Sir.

Unidentified Caller: It's obvious that Doctor Newman is writing those prescriptions and Guerry Snowden is filling them and they are selling them down there.

Announcer: Who's calling please?

* * *

Unidentified Caller: Well I didn't hear anybody else say who they were.

Announcer: Okay.[40]

Snowden, Newman and the owners of the Pizza Shanty sued and were awarded, respectively, $4,000, $5,000 and $2,500. The station appealed, and in upholding the judgments, the Louisiana Appeals Court explained in detail why the station's behavior was indefensible:

The question here presented is whether a radio station, having invited the public to speak freely through its facilities on a matter of public interest, is impressed with the duty of preventing such persons from making defamatory statements over the air. We would have no difficulty in finding a station liable, if it received defamatory material from an anonymous source, and broadcast the report without attempting verification. The direct broadcast of such anonymous defamatory material, without the use of

[39] Ibid. At 407.
[40] Ibid. At 408.

any monitoring or delay device, is no less reprehensible in our judgment.[41]

The Wyoming Supreme Court reached the opposite conclusion in the case of Adams v. Frontier Broadcasting.[42] Here a caller to a talk-show charged falsely that businessman Adams (a former state official) "had been discharged as Insurance Commissioner for dishonesty," and Adams sued. The trial court ruled that he did not have a suit, because the station did not have "reckless disregard" for truth or falsity in failing to use a delay device to cut dangerous words off the air. Adams appealed, and the Wyoming Supreme Court upheld the trial court. It said that requiring stations to use the delay system would mean that[43]

> * * * broadcasters, to protect themselves from judgments for damages, would feel compelled to adopt and regularly use one of the tools of censorship, an electronic delay system. While using such a system a broadcaster would be charged with the responsibility of concluding that some comments should be edited or not broadcast at all. Furthermore, we must recognize the possibility that the requirement for the use of such equipment might, on occasion, tempt the broadcaster to screen out the comments of those with whom the broadcaster * * * did not agree and then broadcast only the comments of those with whom the broadcaster did agree.

The court said that uninhibited, robust, wide-open debate "must, in the balance, outweigh the * * * right of an * * * official or public figure to be free from defamatory remarks." Reports such as the call-ins, the court added, are a modern version of the town meeting, and give every citizen a chance to speak his mind on issues. The *Adams* case turns on the fault requirement for defamation, one of the five elements required for a defamation suit. It does not stand for the proposition that anonymous, live calls are automatically protected.

We can apply both cases to live news. If a station goes live to a scene and broadcasts defamatory statements from field, it may have liability as in the *Snowden* case. There will, of course be significant differences. The field crew will have the opportunity to see the person or persons they are going to put on the air. They will have the ability to judge for themselves whether or not the subjects are credible. They will, more likely than not, have had the chance to at least introduce themselves and get an idea of what the source is

[41] Ibid. At 410.

[42] Adams v. Frontier Broadcasting, 555 P.2d 556, 565 (Wyo.1976), 2 Med.L.Rptr. 1166.

[43] Ibid., 564–567, 2 Med.L.Rptr. at 1173–75.

going to say. If that source appears to be unreliable, the remote crew would be better served by avoiding the live interview. To put someone on the air live just because the technology makes it possible, puts the station at risk because it will have adopted the statement. The analysis will then turn on what the field crew observed about the source, how they assessed the source's credibility and whether it was reasonable for the station to rely on the source's being able to provide information without defaming.

If the Wyoming decision just discussed on the preceding page is followed, then broadcasters could relax to some extent about the dangers inherent in using ENG equipment. The Wyoming decision valued free discussion over a system of taped delays that might justify broadcasters in airing only those views agreeable to them.[44]

In either case, part of that analysis will turn on the need for going live. A routine story that could have been reported with taped interviews and edited before the newscast will lose some of the protections afforded. Of course, stations rely on live stories to generate excitement and give their stories weight that they would not otherwise have so newscasters will continue to rely heavily on them despite the risks of litigation.

A final, but significant issue in publication is the question of where a plaintiff can bring suit. It is easy enough to see that a periodical's circulation area or the limits of a broadcaster's signal carve out an area where plaintiffs can show publication took place. For publishers on the Web, the question of jurisdiction is more of a problem. Anyone, anywhere in the world with a computer and modem can open up a page. Traditional analysis for jurisdiction have turned on the contacts that a party has had in the place where the lawsuit is brought. That means that if someone went to a neighboring state to sell merchandise, that conduct would create jurisdiction in that state, that state's courts could exercise power over the merchant. So far, conduct analysis has helped resolve some questions of jurisdiction. A trademark case brought by a nightclub named the Blue Note in New York against another nightclub by the same name in Missouri was resolved by a federal district court in New York which ruled that because the Missouri nightclub did not seek customers in New York, it did not have jurisdiction.[45] But where Internet entities carry out business with businesses in other states, jurisdiction has been found. That is based on the intentional entry into the state and the conducting of business.

---

[44] Ibid. See also Teeter, "ENG and the Law: An Introduction," chapter in Richard D. Yoakam, Charles F. Cremer and Phillip O. Keirstead, ENG: Television News and the New Technology, 3rd ed. (New York: Random House, 1995).

[45] Geanne Rosenberg, "Trying to Resolve Jurisdictional Rules on the Internet," New York Times, April 14, 1997, C-1.

What about defamation, though? A newspaper case decided in 1996 provides a good deal of guidance. Berry Gordy, famous as the founder of Motown Records, sued the *New York Daily News* over an article it published about him.[46] Gordy was a resident of California and the paper was published on the opposite side of the country. More than 99 percent of the copies of the newspaper published by the *Daily News* were circulated within 300 miles of the New York area. Only 13 copies of the daily *Daily News* and 18 copies of the *Sunday Daily News* were circulated in California but that was enough to create jurisdiction in California. The Ninth Circuit said that the actions of the defendants were aimed at Gordy, a California resident, that the *Daily News* had distributed the 13 to 18 copies of its paper in California, and that Gordy had suffered the damage to his reputation in California. All of these together created jurisdiction. The question for Internet publishers is how their activities will be analyzed in a distant state or country.

A federal judge ruled in 1995 in favor of U.S. defendants when plaintiffs sought to enforce a libel judgment they won in England, where the laws favor plaintiffs. Judge Ricardo Urbina said that a "repugnant" foreign judgment could not be enforced in the U.S. Judge Urbina's decision made the denial of enforcement mandatory. A previous case in the New York courts said that U.S. judges could exercise discretion in enforcing foreign libel judgments.[47] Neither ruling would affect the enforcement of a libel judgment in the nation where the case was tried. That means that people and businesses with assets in those foreign countries could still lose their property.

Litigation Note: *The issue of jurisdiction plays into what is known as "forum shopping," looking for a jurisdiction where a party will have an undue advantage. In some instances it will be a tendency for juries to find for plaintiffs or a jurisdiction with higher-than-average awards. In the Keeton v. Hustler case it was a matter of finding the one jurisdiction where the statute of limitations had not expired. While this should not drive circulation and distribution decisions, it should be kept in mind as a litigation issue. There are special rules that can come into play with forum choice but those are best left to the attorneys who have already endured Civil Procedure class.*

SEC. 22.   IDENTIFICATION

To bring a successful libel action—once publication has been established—a plaintiff must also demonstrate that he or she was

[46] Gordy v. Daily News, 95 F.3d 829 (9th Cir.1996), 24 Med.L.Rptr. 2301.

[47] Andrew Blum, "U.S. Libel Defendants, Sued Abroad, Gain a Shield," The National Law Journal, Feb. 20, 1995, A–12. The case is Matusevich v. Telnikoff, 94–1151 (D.D.C.).

identified in the alleged libel. Plaintiffs must show that the statement complained about refers to them. In legal terms this is known as the requirement that the publication be "of and concerning" the plaintiff.

Most of the time, the identification is obvious. A plaintiff's name or picture is used, right along with the statements claimed to be defamatory. But sometimes identification may occur in a less direct way: in one case, a camera shop answered a competitor's ads with these words:

> USE COMMON SENSE * * *
> You Get NOTHING for NOTHING!
> WE WILL NOT

1. Inflate the prices of your developing to give you a new roll free!

2. Print the blurred negatives to inflate the price of your snapshots!

The Cosgrove Studio sued for libel, claiming that ad implied Cosgrove used dishonest business practices. In upholding a damage award for Cosgrove, a Pennsylvania appeals court made an important point: Identification of the defamed need not be by name. "A party need not be specifically named, if pointed to by description or circumstances tending to identify him," the court held.[48]

In the majority of the states, the rule generally is that the recipient of the communication understand it to refer to the plaintiff. This rule means that statements that refer to subjects generally may pose as much or more of a problem than a specific reference to a particular person. For example, in Eyal v. Helen Broadcasting,[49] a radio station broadcast the following: "The owner of a Brookline [d]elicatessen and seven other people are arrested in connection with an international cocaine ring." Haim Eyal, the owner of Haim's Delicatessen in Brookline, Mass., brought suit claiming that the broadcast defamed him and his business. The Massachusetts Supreme Court said that the broadcast could support a claim of defamation and could have identified Eyal and his business. The court said: "If the defendant intends to refer to a particular person, the communication will be deemed 'of and concerning' that person, if it is so understood by the recipient of the communication, no matter how bizarre or extraordinary it is that the communication was in fact so understood."[50]

---

[48] Cosgrove Studio & Camera Shop, Inc. v. Pane, 408 Pa. 314, 182 A.2d 751 (1962). See also Grove v. Dun & Bradstreet, Inc., 438 F.2d 433 (3d Cir.1971), and Dictaphone Corp. v. Sloves (N.Y.Sup.1980), 6 Med.L.Rptr. 1114.

[49] Eyal v. Helen Broadcasting, 411 Mass. 426, 583 N.E.2d 228 (1991).

[50] Ibid. citing New England Tractor–Trailer Training of Conn., Inc. v. Globe Newspaper Co., 395 Mass. 471, 483, 480 N.E.2d 1005, 1012 (1985).

Photographs create ready identification. The composition of a photograph, caption or context within an article or advertisement can create liability. Although defamatory content comes later in this chapter, the case of Holmes v. Curtis Publishing[51] provides a warning. James Holmes was depicted in one of two photographs that appeared in the *Saturday Evening Post* to illustrate the story, "The Mafia: Shadow of Evil on an Island in the Sun." The photograph in question showed a group of four tourists, including Holmes, playing blackjack. The photo caption referred to "High–Rollers at the Monte Carlo club," and said that the club's casino grossed $20 million a year with a third "skimmed off for American Mafia 'families'." Holmes, the focal point of the picture and a man in no way connected with Mafia, said that he was identified as a participant in organized crime activities.

Surprising as it may seem, the intent of the defendant does not determine the final outcome. But, if one considers the heart of defamation is the standing in which the plaintiff is held by the community, then the intent of the defendant cannot decide the case. Courts have found identification even when defendants have truthfully claimed that they were referring to someone other than the plaintiff. In Washington Post Co. v. Kennedy,[52] the *Washington Post* reported on the arrest of Harry P.L. Kennedy, an attorney, in Michigan. Kennedy was brought back to Washington, D.C. to face charges. The *Post* reported on the arrest and ran the following headline and story:

Attorney Held as Forger

Harry Kennedy Brought Back from Detroit to Face Charge.

Harry Kennedy, an attorney, 40 years old, was brought back to Washington from Detroit yesterday to face a charge of forgery.

According to Headquarters Detective Vermillion, who trailed Kennedy to Detroit, the man forged the name of a client for $900.

Harry Kennedy, 37, and the only Harry Kennedy known as an attorney in the District of Columbia, brought suit. The D.C. Circuit found that Harry Kennedy had been identified, saying: "Unless the true intent of the publisher of libelous matter is to be gathered from the contents of the article, rather than from what the writer subsequently says was in his mind, innocent parties may suffer without redress."[53]

[51] Holmes v. Curtis Pub. Co., 303 F.Supp. 522 (D.S.C.1969).
[52] Washington Post Co. v. Kennedy, 3 F.2d 207 (D.C.Cir.1925).
[53] Ibid.

And in an old case from English courts that has been quoted and followed by U.S. courts, including the D.C. Circuit in the Kennedy case, a completely fictional character cost a newspaper substantial damages. The *Manchester (England) Sunday Chronicle* published a humorous article about the adventures of one Artemus Jones. Jones was a churchwarden (a lay officer of the Anglican Church) who led a quiet and respectable life at home, but who engaged in wild orgies across the English Channel in France. It so happened that there was a lawyer by the name of Artemus Jones and he complained that other members of the bar were giving him a hard time about "his" exploits. Even though the *Chronicle* said it was a completely fictitious Artemus Jones and even published a story to that effect, a jury took only 15 minutes to award the real-life Jones £1,750.[54] The lesson to be drawn from this is to be aware of the risks of using fictitious names, or, more likely to occur, granting anonymity to subjects of stories in return for their cooperation or to protect them. The false identity or name given to a subject or source may open the door to a successful claim by someone who bears the name in reality.

The World Wide Web has resulted in an astronomical increase in the number of potential plaintiffs who can claim identification. Those entities that have begun to put their pages and broadcasts on the Internet need to be aware of the increased danger. Those who communicate directly through e-mail or on their home pages should take notice of one recent case of mistaken identity involving an Alabama judge and a New Mexico State University engineer. The Alabama circuit judge, Roy S. Moore, gained notoriety for fighting to keep a hand-carved set of the Ten Commandments in his courtroom. The New Mexico engineer has been receiving e-mail in support of the judge's position and has not been pleased. "I had gotten very tired of writing telling people that I had no clue what they were talking about, especially since I do not agree with them," Moore told the Associated Press. Moore's home page features a Viking proverb, "Praise not beer, till it is drunk." The Judge Moore does not have e-mail or a home page.[55] The judge's position on beer is not known.

The identification issue becomes more difficult for the plaintiff when dealing with works of pure fiction. But even then, plaintiffs have won cases, though far less often than with nonfiction. The disclaimer that, "the work is purely fictional and does not depict any persons living or dead," can help to build a defense that the

[54] Robert H. Phelps and E. Douglas Hamilton, Libel: Rights, Risks, Responsibilities, New York: Macmillan Co., (1966), p. 31, quoting from E. Hulton & Co. v. Jones, 2 K.B.D. 444 (1910).

[55] In Flux, "Moore of the Same is Keeping a New Mexico Man in E–Mail," The National Law Journal, May 5, 1997, A–23.

allegedly defamatory statement is not "of and concerning" the plaintiff but it is not the end to the case. Fiction based on real-life occurrences carry greater risk as in Bindrim v. Mitchell.[56] A best-selling author, Gwen Davis Mitchell, was working on a project about women in the leisure class. She tried to join Bindrim's therapy group that incorporated nudity in group therapy. Bindrim refused to allow Mitchell to join the group if she were to write about it. Mitchell denied any intention to write about the experience and even signed an agreement not to disclose what occurred in the sessions.

Two months after joining the therapy group, Mitchell signed a book deal with Doubleday for a novel and got an advance royalty payment of $150,000. After the book came out, Bindrim sued Mitchell and Doubleday. The defendants said that Bindrim had not been identified in the book, which dealt with a nude therapy session and its leader. The California appellate court analyzed the issue in this way, "In the case at bar, the only differences between plaintiff and the Herford character in 'Touching' were physical appearance and that Herford was a psychiatrist rather than psychologist. Otherwise, the character Simon Herford was very similar to the actual plaintiff. We cannot say, as did the court in Wheeler, that no one who knew plaintiff Bindrim could reasonably identify him with the fictional character."[57]

Litigation Note: *Discovery also can help play a part in determining who the fictional character really was. In Bindrim, the plaintiff introduced tape recordings that the defendant made at the therapy sessions to show that the novel was based on the actual sessions and that Bindrim was the lead character. Notes, character bibles and correspondence can help to establish that the plaintiff was the one written about. Such evidence can be helpful in establishing that the defendant did not intend to write about the plaintiff but, as explained above, that may not resolve the case.*[58]

[56] Bindrim v. Mitchell, 92 Cal.App.3d 61, 155 Cal.Rptr. 29 (1979).

[57] Ibid. At 37, 76.

[58] In his reference work Law of Defamation, Prof. Rodney Smolla offers 11 factors to establish identity in works of fiction:

1.   Whether the plaintiff's name, or a very similar name, is used;

2.   whether there are physical similarities between the plaintiff and the character;

3.   whether the ages of the plaintiff and the character are close;

4.   whether there are similarities in geographic location and setting;

5.   whether there are similarities in occupation or career progress;

6.   whether there are similarities in relationships and personality characteristics;

7.   whether the work as a whole is clearly presented as fiction;

8.   whether a disclaimer labeling the work as fiction and similarities as "coincidental" is employed;

Identification cannot be established by a person who says that an attack on a large heterogeneous group libels her because she happens to belong to it. To suggest some examples, derogatory statements about a political party, an international labor union, the Presbyterian Church, or the Rotary Club do not identify individuals so as to allow them to bring a libel action. The only exception comes in the case law of the individual states. In Arkansas, for example, a plaintiff who is part of a large group must prove that the statement applied to him personally.

More generally speaking, such defamation cases arise when the defamatory statement is made about a small sub-group of an organization, that's quite different. Suppose a defamatory attack is made on the directors of the Smithjones County Democratic Party, on the officers of a labor union (whether it be a national or local unit), or the presiding elders of a church, or on the civic club's officers. Then, each individual member of the attacked sub-group may be able to establish identification—even though his or her name was not used—and bring suit.

A sleazy book—*U.S.A. Confidential*—resulted in the often cited—and often misinterpreted—case known as Neiman–Marcus Co. v. Lait. That case set down these guidelines:

(1) Where the group or class libeled is large, none can sue even though the language used is inclusive.

(2) When the group or class libeled is small, and each and every member of the group or class is referred to, then any individual member can sue.

(3) That while there is a conflict in authorities where the publication complained of libeled some or less than all of a designated small group, the federal court ruling in the Neiman–Marcus case said it would allow such an action.

Those guidelines were drawn from a garish fact situation. Authors Jack Lait and Lee Mortimer claimed in *U.S.A. Confidential* that swingers looking for a "good time" need look no further in Dallas than that city's famed department store, Neiman–Marcus. The book's chapter on Dallas asserted that all of the store's models (there were nine) were prostitutes, the highest-paid in town. The book also said that the "nucleus of the Dallas fairy colony" was in the Neiman–Marcus men's store (which had 25 salesmen). Finally,

9.   whether there are similarities between the plot of the fictional work and real events in the plaintiff's life;

10.   whether the use of the plaintiff's name or the fictional character allegedly representing the plaintiff play prominent roles in the fictional work or have only "fleeting and incidental" significance; and,

11.   whether the events that take place in the fictional work are so fantastical or bizarre that no reasonable reader would treat them as realistic depictions.

these fearless authors declared that the store's "salesgirls" (there were 382) were prostitutes too, cheaper and more fun than the models.[59]

In applying these rules to the facts, the court dismissed the lawsuits of the saleswomen (382 was simply too large a group to have identification take place), but allowed the suits of the models and the salesmen.

But please note what the *Neiman–Marcus* case did NOT say. It did not say that if a group is larger than 25, you can publish anything you want about that group. In point of cold legal fact, identification has been held to take place when an unnamed person was a member of a large group. In Fawcett Publishing v. Morris[60], the Oklahoma Supreme Court held that a member of the University of Oklahoma football team made up of 60 to 70 players had been identified in an article that referred to the OU football team and was defamatory.

Fawcett was the publisher of *True Magazine* which had printed a story in 1958 about, amphetamine use by athletes under the headline, "The Pill That Can Kill Sports." The story contained the following passages:

> The amphetamines are administered to athletes by hypodermic injection, nasal spray, or in tablets or capsules, but pills are the most common form, at least according to those athletic figures who are willing to talk.

> There is, however, one statistic which is available, and which strongly indicates that consumption is rapidly increasing. Recently I was able to buy 30 cc.'s of dextroamphetamine sulphate for 95 cents. This amount— enough to hop up an entire football team—cost three times this much a few years ago. Also, I was able to buy a thousand amphetamine pills for $1.40 less than a third of the 1954 price. When sales go up, prices go down.

> Speaking of football teams, during the 1956 season, while Oklahoma was increasing its sensational victory streak, several physicians observed Oklahoma players being sprayed in the nostrils with an atomizer. And during a televised game, a close-up showed Oklahoma spray jobs to the nation. "Ten years ago," Dr. Howe observed acidly, "when that was done to a horse, the case went to court. Medically, there is no reason for such treatment. If players need therapy, they shouldn't be on the field."[61]

[59] Neiman–Marcus v. Lait, 107 F.Supp. 96 (S.D.N.Y.1952); 13 F.R.D. 311 (1952).

[60] Fawcett Publications, Inc. v. Morris, 377 P.2d 42 (Okl.1962), cert. denied, 376 U.S. 513, 84 S.Ct. 964 (1964)

[61] Ibid. At 47.

Dennit Morris, the plaintiff, was a fullback on the alternate squad of the 1956 football team that went to and won in the Orange Bowl. He also played in 1957 and 1958. Morris brought evidence at the trial conducted in Oklahoma that it was spirits of peppermint that was administered to the football team. Spirits of peppermint was used for the relief of "cotton mouth," or dryness of mouth, resulting from prolonged or extreme physical exertion. Morris also presented evidence that he did not use amphetamines or any other drugs. Morris won his case and $75,000.

Fawcett appealed and one of the bases for that appeal was it contention that because Morris had not been individually named, that it was just the team, consisting of 60 to 70 players, that he was not identified sufficiently to have been libeled. But the Oklahoma Supreme Court was not persuaded. It agreed that there was a substantial precedent for the proposition that a member of a large group could not recover unless he was referred to personally. But in this case, the court said, Morris was not just some anonymous member of a large group. He was a readily identifiable member of a group that had been defamed by the article and that:

> the article libels every member of the team, including the plaintiff, although he was not specifically named therein; that the average lay reader who was familiar with the team, and its members would necessarily believe that the regular players, including the plaintiff, were using an amphetamine spray as set forth in the article; that the article strongly suggests that the use of amphetamine was criminal; and that plaintiff has sufficiently established his identity as one of those libeled by the publication.

> In reaching the conclusion that plaintiff has established his identity in the mind of the average lay reader as one of those libeled, we are mindful that a full-back on the alternate squad of a university team who has played in nine out of eleven all victorious games in one season will not be overlooked by those who were familiar with the team, and the contribution made by its regular players.[62]

Apart from *Fawcett*, other courts have held that groups made up of as many as 53 still permit individual members to bring their suits.[63] The number will depend on both precedent within the

[62] Ibid. At 52.

[63] See Brady v. Ottaway Newspapers, Inc., 84 A.D.2d 226, 445 N.Y.S.2d 786 (1981), 8 Med.L.Rptr. 1671, where a plaintiff policeman who was a member of a group of 53 unnamed policemen was not barred from bring a libel suit. Courts also have held that members of a jury can be defamed [Byers v. Martin, 2 Colo. 605 (1875)]; all four officers of a labor union [De Witte v. Kearney & Trecker Corp., 265 Wis. 132, 60 N.W.2d 748 (1953)]. Another court, however, has held that a libel action would not work against a magazine which attacked all distributors of the controver-

jurisdiction and the facts of the case. There is no magic number, above which publishers are safe.

A final note on identification deals with who can be the plaintiff in a defamation suit. Defamation is a tort that is personal to the person harmed. That means that only the person identified can bring the suit. Husbands cannot file defamation suits for statements made about their wives. Wives cannot sue when their husbands were the subjects of the defamatory statements. Friends, acquaintances and business associates have no standing to sue.

The question of defamation of the dead has generally been settled in that dead people have no reputations to be harmed. Although Louisiana had a criminal defamation statute that made defaming the memory of the dead, that state's supreme court rejected any civil actions for defamation of the dead saying dead people have no reputations.[64] A Rhode Island statute provides for a slander or libel suit based on a person's obituary[65]

The other issue dealing with death and the defamation suit is the question of the effect of the plaintiff's death on the suit. Twenty-one states say that the defamation suit dies with the plaintiff. Another five states and the District of Columbia say the suit ends with the death of either the plaintiff or the defendant. Fourteen states say that the case continues. In the remaining 10 states there are either no cases or the only cases are so old as to have limited weight in current case law.[66]

SEC. 23. DEFAMATION

Is the publication or broadcast defamatory? The third necessary part of the defamation suit is that the published statement that identified the plaintiff did indeed defame. That says in effect that the words injured reputation, or, in some circumstances, caused emotional distress. Plaintiffs must assert that defamation occurred and prove the same at trial. What can constitute defamation? Noted libel experts Robert Sack and Sandra Baron summed it up in their reference work on libel when they said: " ... what is defamatory shares with hard-core pornography the characteristic that, whatever its precise definition, judges and jurors think they

---

sial anti-cancer drug laetrile [Schuster v. U.S. News & World Report, Inc., 602 F.2d 850 (8th Cir.1979), 5 Med.L.Rptr. 1773.] Also, a newspaper was ruled not to have identified individuals when 21 individuals of a town police department sued following publication of a printed rumor about one unidentified officer. Arcand v. Evening Call Pub. Co., 567 F.2d 1163 (1st Cir.1977).

[64] Gugliuzza v. K.C.M.C., Inc., 606 So.2d 790 (La.1992), 20 Med.L.Rptr. 1866.

[65] Rhode Island General Laws § 10–7.1–1.

[66] Libel Defense Resource Center, 50–State Survey 1995–96, Current Developments in Media Libel Law, (New York, LDRC, 1995).

'know it when [they] see it.' "[67]

Generally, what judges and juries will not find to be defamatory are words that merely annoy, embarrass or hurt the feelings of the plaintiff. The words or other communication must affect the plaintiff's reputation in the community or some portion of the community. The plaintiff does not need to prove that the entire community would change its opinion of him or that "all the right-thinking people" now think less of him.

This approach differs from the English approach, which American courts followed until the early part of the 20th Century. Under the English approach, defamation would be determined by seeing how the "right-thinking Englishman" would view the statement. The difficulties in using this approach are illustrated in the case of Mawe v. Piggott[68] in which an Irish priest was accused of informing on Catholic insurgents. Even though such an accusation would strongly damage anyone's reputation in Ireland, the courts ruled that the statement was not defamatory. The reason given by the court was that no reasonable person would think less of a person for telling the authorities about law breakers. "The very circumstances which will make a person be regarded with disfavour by the criminal classes will raise his character in the estimation of right-thinking men," the court said.[69] Under this English approach, defamation would depend on orthodoxy rather than the effect of words on reputations.

The case that turned American defamation law away from the English approach was Peck v. Tribune.[70] Elizabeth Peck, a resident of Chicago, discovered an advertisement in the *Chicago Sunday Tribune* which featured her picture and a testimonial for a brand of whisky. The name attached to the ad was that of a Mrs. A. Schuman who was identified as a nurse who both consumed Duffy's Pure Malt Whisky and gave it to her patients as part of her treatment of them. Peck was not a nurse and she was a teetotaler (she did not drink any alcohol). Peck sued, but her case was tossed out by the trial court because, the trial court concluded, there was no general disapproval of drinking whisky and therefore the statement could not harm Peck's reputation.

The Seventh Circuit Court of Appeals had ruled that the publication was not libelous. "It was pointed out that there was no general consensus of opinion that to drink whisky is wrong,"

---

[67] Quoting Justice Potter Stewart's concurrence in Jacobellis v. Ohio, 378 U.S. 184, 197, 84 S.Ct. 1676 (1964). Robert Sack and Sandra Baron, Libel Slander, and Related Problems, (Michie and Practising Law Institute, New York, 1996).

[68] Mawe v. Piggott, 4 Ir. R.—C.L. 54 (1869).

[69] Ibid. At p. 62.

[70] Peck v. Tribune, 214 U.S. 185, 29 S.Ct. 554 (1909).

Justice Oliver Wendell Holmes said of the circuit decision. But Justice Holmes disagreed with that approach. "If the advertisement obviously would hurt the plaintiff in the estimation of an important and respectable part of the community, liability is not a question of a majority vote."[71] Justice Holmes' reference to a "respectable part of the community" places some limitations on how defamation is determined.

Courts will not support a conclusion that a statement is defamatory if the finding would go against public policy or be so far out of step with the community as to constitute a greater harm. Before the 1954 decision in Brown v. Board of Education,[72] some courts ruled that making the statement that a white person was black was defamatory. The Supreme Court and society's demand that people be treated equally regardless of race meant that after *Brown* no court could support a finding that a white person's being described as black was defamatory. Similarly, a statement that a person was a law-abiding member of the community would not be considered defamatory even if a group of anarchists or criminals found the statement to be repugnant.

The problem for the media professional is knowing how to "know it when they see it," or, more importantly when they write, broadcast or post it. Words will have different meanings in different contexts including the social, temporal and regional settings where the statements appear. Perhaps the best way to avoid defaming is to look at the legal analysis that statements are subjected to.

Defamation *per se* and *per quod*

Defamatory statements fall into two analytical categories: defamation *per se* and defamation *per quod*. Defamation *per se* is libel on its face and the courts will presume that such defamatory statements automatically damage reputations. The list below provides the categories of words that are defamatory *per se*. Defamation *per quod* is libel arising from the context of the words. Here, the courts (and juries) must determine whether the statement did, in fact, damage the plaintiff's reputation. Unlike defamation *per se*, under defamation *per quod* plaintiffs must plead and prove special damages.[73] The *per se* and *per quod* distinction is a part of the legacy of slander, spoken defamation.

Understanding the nature of people and the process of communication, the English courts divided slanderous statements into two categories—slander *per se* and *per quod*. Slander *per se* consisted of

---

[71] Ibid., at 190, 556.

[72] Brown v. Board of Education, 347 U.S. 483, 74 S.Ct. 686 (1954).

[73] Special damages are treated under the harm section, but generally, special damages means that the plaintiff suffered an actual pecuniary (measurable in actual dollars) loss as the result of the defamatory statement.

those categories of spoken statements that would, by their very speaking, cause harm to the plaintiff. The four categories were:

1.   Words that impute to the plaintiff a crime for which he can be made to suffer corporally by way of punishment;

2.   Words that impute to the plaintiff a contagious or infectious disease;

3.   Words that impute adultery or unchastity to a plaintiff who is a woman or a girl (based on the Slander of Women Act of 1891); and,[74]

4.   Words that, when spoken of the plaintiff in relation to his office, profession, or trade, would tend to injure his reputation therein.

These slanders were considered to be serious enough to merit treatment based on their presumed damage to the plaintiff's reputation. But if a plaintiff complained of slander that fell outside these categories, he would have to prove that the words, in fact, damaged his reputation. This meant that words that were simply annoying or personally troublesome would not justify the awarding of damages. This approach was carried by English colonists to America and applied to American cases. The distinction still applies as illustrated by he case of Wardlaw v. Peck.[75]

Robert Newton Peck, an author of children's books, was to speak at the convocation at Erskine College in South Carolina. Mary Jo Wardlaw, an Erskine student, was to meet Peck at an airport, about an hour away, and drive him to the college. Wardlaw did not show up and Peck, angry and complaining about the treatment, took a cab to the college which paid the fare. Despite receiving additional apologies for Wardlaw's mistake, Peck remained angry and said he would "deal with Mary Jo the next day in convocation."[76]

During his speech, Peck began referring to Wardlaw as "Mary Jo Warthog" and "Warthog." Peck said that he hated her because she was late in picking him up at the airport. Peck likened Wardlaw to "Janice," a character in one of his books, a person "built like a garbage truck" who was the "bully of his childhood." He said that both the character and Wardlaw had an ape-like walk, which he demonstrated before the convocation audience. Peck said that the walk had made Wardlaw late. At some point in the speech, Peck said that he had a recurring nightmare that Wardlaw and another Erskine student "were breeding under his sink."

[74] Generally, Clement Gatley, Law and Practice of Libel and Slander, (London: Sweet & Maxwell Ltd., 1929), at 45.

[75] Wardlaw v. Peck, 282 S.C. 199, 318 S.E.2d 270 (App.1984).

[76] Ibid. at 200, 272.

Wardlaw sued, alleging that Peck had slandered her, causing her great emotional distress and forcing her to remain secluded in her room the day after the convocation and making it impossible for her to face people in public. She also sued based on Peck's statement regarding her "breeding under his sink." Peck's statements about Wardlaw, calling her "Warthog" and comparing her to the character in one of his books, did not fall into any of the four categories of speech that are slander *per se*. They were slander *per quod* and in order to prove that the words were defamatory, Wardlaw had to show that she suffered damages, for if she was not damaged, then the statement was not damaging or defamatory.

The trial court dismissed the first part of her suit because Wardlaw had not shown that the words were damaging to her reputation. The South Carolina Court of Appeals affirmed and explained its ruling on the *per quod* claim saying:

> We do not view Wardlaw's hurt feelings, however genuine, as special damage making Peck's words actionable per quod. The gist of defamation lies not in the hurt to the defamed person's feelings, but in the injury caused his reputation ... Where special damage is necessary to maintain an action, that special damage must consist of some provable material loss to the plaintiff as a result of the injury to his reputation.[77]

The trial court allowed the portion of Wardlaw's suit over the charge of unchastity, a slander *per se* statement, to go forward. Wardlaw won her case on that claim and was awarded $4,000 in actual damages and $20,000 in punitive damages. Peck appealed the judgment making an argument that the slander *per se* category of imputing unchastity or adultery to a woman was unconstitutional because it was gender based and denied equal treatment to men. The South Carolina appellate court disposed of Peck's argument simply, by saying that it could find no cases that prevented men from pursuing lawsuits when they were charged with unchastity.

This slander analysis is important in those jurisdictions that treat broadcast defamation as slander, rather than libel. The requirement that the plaintiff plead and prove special damages makes lawsuits more difficult and give broadcasters an edge in defamation cases. California and South Carolina treat broadcast defamation as slander as a matter of law. Case law suggests that broadcasts would be treated as slander in Nevada and Arizona. Depending on circumstances, Hawaii will treat broadcasts as either slander or libel. In Tennessee, the distinction between slander and libel is based on how the defamatory statement is created. Scripted broadcast defamation is libel while extemporaneous broadcasts are slander. Twen-

[77] Ibid. at 205, 274–275.

ty other states and the District of Columbia treat broadcast defamation as libel, while the rest of the states have either not addressed the issue conclusively or are not clear on the issue. [78]

As literacy grew and the greater impact of the printed word was recognized, the courts created the category of libel. The distinctions between *per se* and *per quod* accompanied the growth of libel law. Today, libel *per se* is classified as a statement whose defamatory meaning is apparent on its face. Libel *per quod* is a statement whose defamatory meaning is based on the extrinsic knowledge of the recipient. This distinction applies to an essential element of the defamation case—damages. In the majority of jurisdictions, libel *per se* carries a presumption of damage. That is because of the apparent damage to reputation from the statement on its face. For cases of libel *per quod*, where the reputational damage must rely on outside fact, the plaintiff must plead and prove actual damage. The significance of this becomes apparent in the damage section below.

Per se should be fairly easy to see in many cases. The categories follow those laid out in slander *per se*. In short, any published statement that on its face would injure a person's reputation in the community or hinder him or her in a chosen occupation or trade falls under libel *per se*.

1. Imputing Crime

Publishing falsely that a person is held in jail on a forgery charge,[79] or to say incorrectly that one has illicitly sold or distributed narcotics,[80] is libelous on its face. To say without legal excuse that one made "shakedown attempts" on elected officers,[81] or committed bigamy,[82] perjury,[83] or murder[84] is libelous. Some "crimes" are so minor that courts will not find them libelous *per se*. But some allegations, while not charging that the plaintiff committed a specific crime may still be considered libelous *per se*. In *Clemente v. Espinosa*,[85] a claim that an attorney had an association

---

[78] Libel Defense Resource Center, 50–State Survey 1995–96, Current Developments in Media Libel Law, (New York, LDRC, 1995).

[79] Oklahoma Pub. Co. v. Givens, 67 F.2d 62 (10th Cir.1933); Barnett v. Schumacher, 453 S.W.2d 934 (Mo.1970).

[80] Snowden v. Pearl River Broadcasting Corp., 251 So.2d 405 (La.App.1971).

[81] Bianco v. Palm Beach Newspapers, Inc., 381 So.2d 371 (Fla.App.1980), 6 Med.L.Rptr. 1484.

[82] Taylor v. Tribune Pub. Co., 67 Fla. 361, 65 So. 3 (1914); Pitts v. Spokane Chronicle Co., 63 Wash.2d 763, 388 P.2d 976 (1964).

[83] Milan v. Long, 78 W.Va. 102, 88 S.E. 618 (1916); Riss v. Anderson, 304 F.2d 188 (8th Cir.1962).

[84] Shiell v. Metropolis Co., 102 Fla. 794, 136 So. 537 (1931); Frechette v. Special Magazines, 285 App.Div. 174, 136 N.Y.S.2d 448 (1954).

[85] Clemente v. Espinosa, 749 F.Supp. 672, 679 (E.D.Pa.1990).

with the Mafia was sufficient as an accusation of criminality.[86]

But some *per se* statements may not seem so obvious. Robert Sack and Sandra Barron give this example to show how libel *per se* may crop up, even in a case that appears to be one of libel *per quod:*

> If, for example, a Mr. Johnson were falsely reported by a newspaper to have withdrawn funds kept in the bank account of the firm of Johnson, Smith, and Jones, but in fact, as members of the community knew, Johnson had been thrown out of the firm a month before, in a per se/per quod jurisdiction, Johnson might or might not have a cause of action without proving "special damages." The analysis is as follows: the statement's defamatory meaning can be understood only by reference to an extrinsic fact, that Johnson is no longer with the firm. It is thus libel per quod. Special damages must therefore be proven. In some per se/per quod jurisdictions, however, the further question must be asked: Does the statement fall within one of the slander per se categories? It does, because the charge is the crime of theft. In those jurisdictions, the necessity to plead and prove special damages would first arise because the statement is libelous per quod and then would be removed because it falls within one of the slander per se categories.[87]

2. Imputing Unchastity

It should be obvious that one should beware of publishing words imputing sexual acts either outside the bounds of a marital relationship or outside prevailing moral codes. Courts have found that charging without foundation that a woman is immoral as actionable libel. The charge of indiscretion need not be pronounced; any statement fairly imputing immoral conduct is actionable.[88]

Pat Montandon, author of *How To Be a Party Girl*, was to discuss her book on the Pat Michaels "Discussion" show. *TV Guide* received the show producer's advance release, which said that Montandon and a masked, anonymous prostitute would discuss "From Party–Girl to Call–Girl?" and "How far can the 'party-girl' go until she becomes a 'call-girl'." *TV Guide* ineptly edited the release, deleting reference to the prostitute and publishing this: "10:30 Pat Michaels—*Discussion* 'From Party Girl to Call Girl.' Scheduled guest: TV Personality Pat Montandon and author of

---

[86] Ibid. at 679.

[87] Robert Sack and Sandra Baron, Libel Slander, and Related Problems, (Michie and Practising Law Institute, New York, 1996).

[88] Baird v. Dun & Bradstreet, 446 Pa. 266, 285 A.2d 166 (1971); Wildstein v. New York Post Corp., 40 Misc.2d 586, 243 N.Y.S.2d 386 (1963); Youssoupoff v. Metro–Goldwyn–Mayer, 50 Times L.R. 581, 99 A.L.R. 964 (1934).

'How to Be a Party Girl'." Montandon sued for libel and won $150,000 in damages.[89]

On the other hand, a woman who posed in the nude for a film maker but later got his agreement not to show the film, was unsuccessful in a libel action following his breaking of the agreement. She charged that his showing of the film to people who knew her caused her shame, disgrace and embarrassment. But the court said that "a film strip which includes a scene of plaintiff posing in the nude does not necessarily impute unchastity", and that it was not libel *per se.*[90]

Under the strict interpretation of the unchastity category, the sexual conduct need not violate law regulating sexual conduct but rather requires only a statement that the plaintiff had engaged in intimate relations. There has been a movement to loosen the tight constraints of the category, especially in light of changing mores. However, the rule still remains and poses risks for the publisher. Of special concern is the publication of defamatory statements on the Internet. Statements regarding sexual activity which might not raise a single eyebrow in some places might constitute the gravest defamation in a foreign jurisdiction.

3. Imputing Loathsome Disease

The law has long held that diseases which may be termed "loathsome, infectious, or contagious" may be libelous when falsely attributed to an individual. This category of *per se* defamation is a holdover from English law and prejudices that date back centuries. It comes from misunderstandings and ignorance of the disease process that meant that the sick were shunned. Professor Rod Smolla reports that there have been relatively few American cases regarding this category.[91] Those diseases that have been found to be loathsome generally have been venereal diseases such as gonorrhea and syphilis. Leprosy also is counted among the loathsome diseases, probably because of the ancient fear of the disease.

Perhaps because of its linkage with sex, AIDS has been treated as a loathsome disease in a number of cases. The authors have not found any cases where the inclusion of AIDS as a loathsome disease was disputed. In a case which represents a more enlightened approach to the disease category, *Chuy v. Philadelphia Eagles*

---

[89] Montandon v. Triangle Publications, Inc., 45 Cal.App.3d 938, 120 Cal.Rptr. 186 (1975).

[90] McGraw v. Watkins, 49 A.D.2d 958, 373 N.Y.S.2d 663 (1975). But contra, see Clifford v. Hollander (N.Y.Civ.1980), 6 Med.L.Rptr. 2201, where a photo of a nude woman, identified falsely as that of a woman journalist, was held libelous.

[91] Rodney A. Smolla, Law of Defamation, (Clark, Boardman Callaghan, New York, 1995), p. 7–11.

Football Club,[92] the Third Circuit held that the false statement that the plaintiff had cancer was not defamatory, because cancer is not a "loathsome disease" and the public reaction to it "is usually one of sympathy rather than scorn, support and not rejection."[93] Publication of a statement that a person is an alcoholic falls into the *per se* category.[94]

An incorrect assignment of mental impairment or of mental illness to a person is libel on its face.[95] The magazine *Fact* published in its September–October issue of 1964, an article billed as "The Unconscious of a Conservative: A Special Issue on the Mind of Barry Goldwater." Goldwater was the Republican Party's candidate for president and a senator from Arizona at the time. He was portrayed in one of two articles as "paranoid," his attacks on other politicians stemming from a conviction that "everybody hates him, and it is better to attack them first." A *Fact* poll of psychiatrists, asked to judge whether Goldwater was psychologically fit to serve as president, also was reported on. A jury found libel and awarded Goldwater $1.00 in compensatory damages and $75,000 in punitive damages

4. Imputing Incompetence or Lack of Skill in Trade, Occupation or Profession

So long as one follows a calling that is lawful, he has a claim not to be defamed unfairly in the performance of it. The possibilities are rich for damaging one through words that impugn honesty, skill, fitness, ethical standards, or financial capacity in his chosen work, whether it be banking or basket-weaving. Observe some of the possibilities: that a University was a "degree mill;"[96] that a contractor engaged in unethical trade;[97] that a clergyman was "an interloper, a meddler, a spreader of distrust;"[98] that a schoolmaster kept girls after school so that he could court them;[99] that a jockey

[92] Chuy v. Philadelphia Eagles Football Club, 595 F.2d 1265, 1281–82 (3d Cir. 1979), 4 Med.L.Rptr. 2537 (en banc).

[93] Ibid. At 1281–82. Readers should note that in this case the plaintiff was able to recover damages on a theory of intentional infliction of emotional harm so the defendant did not avoid responsibility.

[94] Hedrick v. Center for Comprehensive Alcoholism Treatment, 7 Ohio App.3d 211, 454 N.E.2d 1343 (1982).

[95] Cowper v. Vannier, 20 Ill.App.2d 499, 156 N.E.2d 761 (1959); Kenney v. Hatfield, 351 Mich. 498, 88 N.W.2d 535 (1958). But not in Virginia: Mills v. Kingsport Times–News, 475 F.Supp. 1005 (W.D.Va.1979), 5 Med.L.Rptr. 2288.

[96] Laurence University v. State, 68 Misc.2d 408, 326 N.Y.S.2d 617 (1971). Reversed on grounds that State official's words were absolutely privileged, 41 A.D.2d 463, 344 N.Y.S.2d 183 (1973).

[97] Greenbelt Co-op. Pub. Ass'n v. Bresler, 253 Md. 324, 252 A.2d 755 (1969), reversed on other grounds 398 U.S. 6, 90 S.Ct. 1537 (1970).

[98] Van Lonkhuyzen v. Daily News Co., 195 Mich. 283, 161 N.W. 979 (1917).

[99] Spears v. McCoy, 155 Ky. 1, 159 S.W. 610 (1913).

rode horses unfairly and dishonestly;[100] that an attorney was incompetent,[1] and that a corporation director embezzled.[2]

By no means every statement to which a businessman, tradesman or professional takes exception, however, is libelous. Thus Frederick D. Washington, a church bishop, sued the *New York Daily News* and columnist Robert Sylvester for his printed statement that Washington had attended a nightclub performance at which a choir member of his church sang. The bishop argued that his church did not approve of its spiritual leaders' attending nightclubs, and that he had been damaged. The court said the account was not, on its face, an attack on the plaintiff's integrity, and called the item a "warm human interest story" in which there was general interest. This was not libel on its face and the court upheld dismissal of Bishop Washington's complaint.[3]

Nor did David Brown convince the court that there was libel in a pamphlet that opposed his attempt to get a zoning change from the City Council of Knoxville, Tenn. The pamphlet attacked a change that would have permitted Brown to build apartments in a residential district, and asked the question: "Have the 'Skids Been Greased' at City Council?" Brown sued for libel, arguing that the question suggested he had bribed the City Council and that it had accepted the bribe. But the court held that the question did not suggest bribery in its reasonable and obvious meaning; but rather, that pressure in the form of political influence had been brought to bear on certain Council members to expedite matters. This was not libel. Had the pamphlet said that "palms are greased at the City Council," that would have been libel on its face and actionable.[4]

A margin of protection also exists in the occasional finding by a court that mistakenly attributing a single instance of clumsiness or error to a professional man is not enough to damage him. Rather, such cases have held, there must be a suggestion of more general incompetency or lack of quality before a libel charge will hold. One court said:[5]

---

[100] Wood v. Earl of Durham, 21 Q.B. 501 (1888).

[1] Hahn v. Andrello, 44 A.D.2d 501, 355 N.Y.S.2d 850 (1974).

[2] Weenig v. Wood, 169 Ind.App. 413, 349 N.E.2d 235 (1976).

[3] Washington v. New York News Inc., 37 A.D.2d 557, 322 N.Y.S.2d 896 (1971).

[4] Brown v. Newman, 224 Tenn. 297, 454 S.W.2d 120 (1970). An official who resigned from a "financially troubled bank" was not libeled: Bordoni v. New York Times Co., Inc., 400 F.Supp. 1223 (S.D.N.Y.1975).

[5] Blende v. Hearst Publications, 200 Wash. 426, 93 P.2d 733 (1939); November v. Time Inc., 13 N.Y.2d 175, 244 N.Y.S.2d 309, 194 N.E.2d 126 (1963); Holder Const. Co. v. Ed Smith & Sons, Inc., 124 Ga.App. 89, 182 S.E.2d 919 (1971). But see Cohn v. Am–Law, Inc. (N.Y.Sup.Ct.1980), 5 Med.L.Rptr. 2367, where defamation was found in a magazine story saying an attorney went "unprepared" to a single hearing.

To charge a professional man with negligence or unskillfulness in the management or treatment of an individual case, is no more than to impute to him the mistakes and errors incident to fallible human nature. The most eminent and skillful physician or surgeon may mistake the symptoms of a particular case without detracting from his general professional skill or learning. To say of him, therefore, that he was mistaken in that case would not be calculated to impair the confidence of the community in his general professional competency.

This also applies to the reputations of corporations, the artificial legal entities created to carry on business. It is possible to damage the reputation of a corporation or partnership by defamation that reflects on the conduct, management, or financial condition of the corporation.[6] To say falsely that a company is in shaky financial condition, or that it cannot pay its debts, would be libelous, as would the imputation that it has engaged in dishonest practices. While a corporation is an entity quite different from the individuals that head it or staff it, there is no doubt that it has a reputation, an "image" to protect.

Publishing or broadcasting casual statements that a business or corporation is "broke" or "going bankrupt" or "has a rotten credit rating" can be risky business indeed unless you are prepared to prove the truth of such statements in court. When Dun & Bradstreet—which is in the business of giving credit ratings—published erroneous information indicating falsely that a Greenmoss Builders had filed for bankruptcy, that was held to be defamatory. Both the Vermont courts and the United States Supreme Court agreed that a $350,000 award should be paid to the building firm.[7]

Charging dishonest or unethical behavior by a firm can also result in a successful defamation suit. In a case that may be difficult to understand in light of the damaging revelations and admissions by tobacco companies in 1996 and 1997, the Chicago TV station WBBM—owned by the CBS Network—found in 1988 that such a firm could still be libeled. The Supreme Court denied *certiorari*, leaving intact a $3 million damage award in the case of Brown & Williamson Tobacco Corp. v. Jacobson and CBS, Inc.

Back in 1981, Walter Jacobson had delivered a "Perspective" report denouncing the makers of Viceroy cigarettes for hiring

[6] Dupont Engineering Co. v. Nashville Banner Pub. Co., 13 F.2d 186 (M.D.Tenn. 1925); Electric Furnace Corp. v. Deering Milliken Research Corp., 325 F.2d 761 (6th Cir.1963); Golden Palace, Inc. v. National Broadcasting Co., Inc., 386 F.Supp. 107 (D.D.C.1974).

[7] Dun & Bradstreet, Inc. v. Greenmoss Builders, Inc., 472 U.S. 749, 105 S.Ct. 2939 (1985).

advertising "slicksters" to create an advertising strategy to "hook" the young. The strategy used by Brown & Williamson, Jacobson said, was taken from a report recommending that smoking be portrayed to youth as a kind of rite of passage involving wearing a bra or shaving, or drinking wine or beer. The broadcast added up to an accusation of unethical youth-oriented advertising by Brown & Williamson for its Viceroy cigarettes, thus endangering the health of the impressionable young.[8] But in the case, the cigarette maker was able to show that it had not put the plan into effect. It even presented evidence that it had fired the advertising agency that developed the advertising strategy. (We will have more on the case, including the cautionary tale about destroying evidence, later.)[9]

5. Other Statements Damaging Reputation

Esteem and social standing can be lowered in the eyes of others by statements concerning political belief and conduct other than that grouped under crime and under sexual immorality in the preceding pages. To take political belief first, many important cases since the late 1940's have largely involved false charges of "Communist" or "Red" or some variant of these words indicating that one subscribes to a generally hated political doctrine. But before these, a line of cases since the 1890's produced libel convictions against those who had labeled others as anarchists, socialists, or fascists.

In the days of Emma Goldman and Big Bill Haywood, it was laid down by the courts that to call one an "anarchist" falsely was libelous;[10] when socialism protested capitalism and America's involvement in World War I, "red-tinted agitator" and "Socialist" were words for which a wronged citizen could recover;[11] In the revulsion against Nazi Germany and Japan during World War II, false accusations of "Fascist" and "pro-Jap" brought libel judgments.[12]

[8] Certiorari denied 485 U.S. 993, 108 S.Ct. 1302 (1988), upholding the judgment of the United States Court of Appeals, Seventh Circuit. See 827 F.2d 1119 (7th Cir.1987) 14 Med.L.Rptr. 1497.

[9] Years too late for Walter Jacobson, Liggett Group acknowledged that tobacco companies aimed sales pitches at 14–to 18–year-olds. That admission came in March of 1997, more than a decade after the libel verdict against him and his Chicago television station. "I smiled inwardly, yes," Jacobson was quoted in Electronic Media. "I dug out a wonderful picture taken a few years ago when the tobacco executives testified before Congress and said, 'Look what they're saying now.' "Jeff Borden, "Jacobson buoyed by new tobacco headlines," Electronic Media, April 28, 1997, p. 9.

[10] Cerveny v. Chicago Daily News Co., 139 Ill. 345, 28 N.E. 692 (1891); Wilkes v. Shields, 62 Minn. 426, 64 N.W. 921 (1895).

[11] Wells v. Times Printing Co., 77 Wash. 171, 137 P. 457 (1913); Ogren v. Rockford Star Printing Co., 288 Ill. 405, 123 N.E. 587 (1919).

[12] Hartley v. Newark Morning Ledger Co., 134 N.J.L. 217, 46 A.2d 777 (1946); Hryhorijiv v. Winchell, 180 Misc. 574, 45 N.Y.S.2d 31 (1943).

Magazines, columnists, newspapers, and corporations have paid for carelessness indulged in by charging others as "Communist" or "representative for the Communist Party." The "basis for reproach is a belief that such political affiliations constitute a threat to our institutions * * *."[13]

In the famous case of Gertz v. Robert Welch, Inc.,[14] the trial court found that the publication of the John Birch Society had libeled Chicago Attorney Elmer Gertz in charging falsely that he was a "Leninist," a "Communist-fronter," and a member of the "Marxist League for Industrial Democracy." Gertz was awarded $400,000. In another case, where one organization called another "communist dominated" and failed to prove the charge in court, $25,000 was awarded to the plaintiff organization.[15]

Not every insinuation that a person is less than American, however, is libelous. Goodman, a selectman of Ware, Mass., phoned a call-in radio talk-show of the Central Broadcasting Corp. station, WARE, to explain his opposition to a proposed contract for the local police union, at issue in the town prior to a citizen vote on the matter. During his extended and agitated discussion, he said that " * * * if we do not get together and stop the inroad of communism, something will happen." A libel suit was brought by the police local's parent union against Central Broadcasting, and the Massachusetts Supreme Judicial Court held that this fragment of Goodman's statement was "mere pejorative rhetoric," and an "unamiable but nonlibelous utterance."[16]

Finally, there are many words among those lowering esteem or social standing that defy classifying. Appellations that may be common enough in the excited conversation of neighborhood gossips can turn to actionable libel when reduced to print or writing. It has been held actionable on its face to print and publish that one is "a liar,"[17] "a skunk,"[18] or "a scandalmonger";[19] "a drunkard,"[20] "a

---

[13] Anon., "Supplement," 171 A.L.R. 709, 712 (1947). Grant v. Reader's Digest Ass'n, Inc., 151 F.2d 733 (2d Cir.1945). And see Wright v. Farm Journal, 158 F.2d 976 (2d Cir.1947); Spanel v. Pegler, 160 F.2d 619 (7th Cir.1947); MacLeod v. Tribune Pub. Co., 52 Cal.2d 536, 343 P.2d 36 (1959).

[14] 306 F.Supp. 310 (N.D.Ill.1969); 418 U.S. 323, 94 S.Ct. 2997 (1974).

[15] Utah State Farm Bureau Federation v. National Farmers Union Service Corp., 198 F.2d 20 (10th Cir.1952). See also Cahill v. Hawaiian Paradise Park Corp., 56 Haw. 522, 543 P.2d 1356 (1975).

[16] National Ass'n of Government Employees, Inc. v. Central Broadcasting Corp., 379 Mass. 220, 396 N.E.2d 996 (1979). Also McAuliffe v. Local Union No. 3, 29 N.Y.S.2d 963 (Sup.1941); McGaw v. Webster, 79 N.M. 104, 440 P.2d 296 (1968); "pro-Castro," Menendez v. Key West Newspaper Corp., 293 So.2d 751 (Fla.App. 1974).

[17] Melton v. Bow, 241 Ga. 629, 247 S.E.2d 100 (1978); Paxton v. Woodward, 31 Mont. 195, 78 P. 215 (1904); Smith v. Lyons, 142 La. 975, 77 So. 896 (1917); contra, Bennett v. Transamerican Press, 298 F.Supp. 1013 (S.D.Iowa 1969); Calloway v. Central Charge Service, 142 U.S.App.D.C. 259, 440 F.2d 287 (1971).

18.–20. See notes, 18–20 on page 180.

hypocrite,"[21] or "a hog";[22] or to call one heartless and neglectful of his family.[23] Other actionable epithets include linking a person to a swastika symbol,[24] or calling one a "despicable human being,"[25] or a "bitch" (implying a woman is a prostitute).[26] Name-calling where private citizens are concerned is occasionally the kind of news that makes a lively paragraph, but the alert and responsible reporter recognizes it for what it is and decides whether to use it on better grounds than its titillation value.

Ridicule also falls into this general category. It is pointless to try to draw a narrow line to separate words that ridicule from those that lower esteem and social standing. That which ridicules may at times have the effect of damaging social standing. Yet that which attempts to satirize, or which makes an individual appear uncommonly foolish, or makes fun of misfortune has a quality distinct enough to serve as its own warning signal.

Ridicule must be more than a simple joke at another's expense, for life cannot be so grim that the thin-skinned, the solemn, and the self-important may demand to go entirely unharried. A number of courts have specifically included ridicule in the laundry list of definitions of defamation. In New York, defamation is defined picturesquely as, "words which tend to expose one to public hatred, shame, obloquy, contumely, odium, contempt, ridicule, aversion, ostracism, degradation or disgrace ..."[27] When the jocular barb penetrates too deeply or carries too sharp a sting, or when a picture can be interpreted in a deeply derogatory manner, ridicule amounting to actionable libel may have occurred.

To sensationalize the poverty of a woman so as to bring her into ridicule and contempt, and to make a joke out of the desertion of a bride on her wedding day[28] have been held libelous. A famed case arose from a photo in an advertisement that accidentally gave

---

[18] Massuere v. Dickens, 70 Wis. 83, 35 N.W. 349 (1887).

[19] Patton v. Cruce, 72 Ark. 421, 81 S.W. 380 (1904).

[20] Giles v. State, 6 Ga. 276 (1848); cf. Smith v. Fielden, 205 Tenn. 313, 326 S.W.2d 476 (1959).

[21] Overstreet v. New Nonpareil Co., 184 Iowa 485, 167 N.W. 669 (1918).

[22] Solverson v. Peterson, 64 Wis. 198, 25 N.W. 14 (1885).

[23] Brown v. Du Frey, 1 N.Y.2d 190, 151 N.Y.S.2d 649, 134 N.E.2d 469 (1956).

[24] Mullenmeister v. Snap–On Tools, 587 F.Supp. 868 (S.D.N.Y.1984).

[25] Smith v. McMullen, 589 F.Supp. 642 (S.D.Tex.1984).

[26] Stone v. Brooks, 253 Ga. 565, 322 S.E.2d 728 (1984).

[27] Kimmerle v. New York Evening Journal, 262 N.Y. 99, 102, 186 N.E. 217 (1933).

[28] Moffatt v. Cauldwell, 3 Hun. 26, 5 Thomp. & C. 256 (N.Y.1874), but "poverty" and "unemployment" have been held not actionable words: Sousa v. Davenport, 3 Mass.App.Ct. 715, 323 N.E.2d 910 (1975); Kirman v. Sun Printing & Pub. Ass'n, 99 App.Div. 367, 91 N.Y.S. 193 (1904).

the illusion of a "fantastic and lewd deformity" of a steeplechaser holding a riding crop and his saddle.[29]

Yet there is room for satire and exaggeration. *Boston Magazine* published a page titled "Best and Worst Sports," including the categories "sports announcer," "local ski slopes," and "sexy athlete," some categories plainly waggish, some straightforward and complimentary. Under "sports announcer," the best was named and given kudos; and then appeared: "*Worst:* Jimmy Myers, Channel 4. The only newscaster in town who is enrolled in a course for remedial speaking." Myers sued, lost at trial for failure to establish defamation, and appealed.[30]

The Massachusetts Supreme Judicial Court described the appearance of the magazine's page, with its title, lampooning cartoons, and a mood of rough humor in the words, including "one-liners" and preposterous propositions under such titles as "Sports Groupie." It ruled that the statement about Myers made on such a page would not reasonably be understood by a reader to be an assertion of fact. "Taken in context, it can reasonably be considered to suggest that Myers should have been so enrolled," even though the words read "is enrolled." The words stated "a critical judgment, an opinion." And since Myers was himself available to the critic's audience, being often on view, his performances were in line with the rule that facts underlying opinions could be assumed—the performances "furnished the assumed facts from which the critic fashioned his barb." The court said that words such as these are meant to "sting and be quickly forgotten". Although for the plaintiff who "is the victim of ridicule, the forgetting may not be easy," the law refuses to find a statement of fact where none has been uttered. This was opinion, and if such "is based on assumed, nondefamatory facts, the First Amendment forbids the law of libel from redressing the injury."[31]

Perhaps the case that best illustrates the fine line that the courts draw between actionable statements and the price one pays for public recognition came in the case of the Rev. Jerry Falwell v. Larry Flynt, the publisher of Hustler magazine. Falwell and Flynt have been described as the opposite ends of the moral spectrum. Each man had singled out the other as an example of the odium of modern society. In 1988, Flynt published a cartoon parody ad which asserted that, among other things, that Falwell had lost his virginity to his mother in a drunken state in an outhouse. Falwell sued Flynt for libel, invasion of privacy and intentional infliction of

---

[29] Burton v. Crowell Pub. Co., 82 F.2d 154 (2d Cir.1936).

[30] Myers v. Boston Magazine Co., Inc., 380 Mass. 336, 403 N.E.2d 376 (Mass.Sup. Jud.Ct.1980), 6 Med.L.Rptr. 1241.

[31] Ibid., 1243, 1245.

emotional distress. The libel and privacy claims were eliminated at the trial level. The jury found for Falwell on the emotional distress claim. The Fourth Circuit affirmed and the case went to the Supreme Court where the justices by an 8–0 vote reversed the lower court. Chief Justice Rehnquist, writing the decision, concluded that the nature of the publication, a commentary on a public figure, deserved the utmost protection of the First Amendment.[32] Falwell had not made his case sufficient to overcome that protection.

While a living man whose obituary has mistakenly been printed may feel annoyed and injured, and may attract unusual attention and perhaps a rough joke or two as he walks into his office the next morning, he has not been libeled. As one court said, death "is looked for in the history of every man," and where there is notice of a death that has not occurred, "Prematurity is the sole peculiarity."[33] Yet an erroneous report of death has been held to be the cause of an action for "negligent infliction of emotional distress"— an injury closely related to defamation.[34]

The court decides whether a publication is libelous *per se* (by itself). But when the words complained of can have two meanings— one innocent and the other damaging—it is for the jury to decide in what sense the words were understood by the audience. Both judge and jury, in their interpretation of the statement claimed to be defamatory, should give language its common and ordinary meaning.[35]

Defamation in Different Form

Defamation comes in as many forms as there are means of communication. Defamation can be expressed by the broadcast or printed word. It can come in the form of gesture. For example, publishing a picture or video of someone being stopped by a security guard and frisked could amount to defamation. Pictures in and of themselves can be defamatory if they convey false impressions about the conduct and character of those depicted. That is a particular concern with the current ability to digitally manipulate pictures. Photographs may be scanned into a computer or taken with a digital camera. The elements can be rearranged or new elements introduced with the click of a mouse button. Plaintiffs can

---

[32] The nature of the First Amendment defense is taken up in the next chapter on defenses to libel claims.

[33] Cohen v. New York Times Co., 153 App.Div. 242, 138 N.Y.S. 206 (1912); Cardiff v. Brooklyn Eagle, Inc., 190 Misc. 730, 75 N.Y.S.2d 222 (1947).

[34] Rubinstein v. New York Post Corp. (N.Y.Sup.Ct.1983), 9 Med.L.Rptr. 1581. Emotional distress is treated in Sec. 20, below.

[35] Peck v. Coos Bay Times Pub. Co., 122 Or. 408, 259 P. 307, 311 (1927); Prosser, 4th ed., p. 746.

find themselves with a cause of action after being digitally imposed into a defamatory picture. While they are not defamation cases, Mira Sorvino and Dustin Hoffman have taken legal action in connection with digitalization. Sorvino complained of the alteration of her picture to make her look like Joan Crawford for Allure magazine. Hoffman sued Los Angeles Magazine for taking a picture of him as "Tootsie" and putting it in a Richard Tyler outfit.[36]

But almost invariably in the mass media, illustration is accompanied by words, and it is almost always the combination that carries the damaging impact. In an issue of *Tan,* a story titled "Man Hungry" was accompanied by a picture taken several years earlier in connection with a woman's work as a professional model for a dress designer. With it were the words "She had a good man— but he wasn't enough. So she picked a bad one!" On the cover of the magazine was the title, "Shameless Love."

The woman sued for libel, and the court granted her claim for $3,000. "There is no doubt in this court's mind that the publication libeled plaintiff," the judge wrote. "A publication must be considered in its entirety, both the picture and the story which it illustrates."[37]

During a program broadcast in Albuquerque, N.M. over station KGGM–TV, the secretary of a Better Business Bureau was speaking about dishonest television repairmen. He held up to the camera a newspaper advertisement of the Day and Night Television Service Company.... The speaker said that some television servicemen were cheating the public:

> This is what has been referred to in the trade as the ransom. Ransom, the ransom racket. The technique of taking up the stuff after first assuring the set owner that the charges would only be nominal, and then holding the set for ransom....

The New Mexico Supreme Court pointed up the effect of combining the picture and the words: "Standing alone, neither the advertisement nor the words used ... could be construed as libel. But the two combined impute fraud and dishonesty to the company and its operators."[38]

[36] Amy Spindler, "Making the Camera Lie, Digitally and Often," The New York Times, June 17, 1997, p. B8.

[37] Martin v. Johnson Pub. Co., 157 N.Y.S.2d 409, 411 (1956). See also Farrington v. Star Co., 244 N.Y. 585, 155 N.E. 906 (1927) (wrong picture); Wasserman v. Time, Inc., 138 U.S.App.D.C. 7, 424 F.2d 920 (1970), certiorari denied 398 U.S. 940, 90 S.Ct. 1844 (1970).

[38] Young v. New Mexico Broadcasting Co., 60 N.M. 475, 292 P.2d 776 (1956); Central Arizona Light & Power Co. v. Akers, 45 Ariz. 526, 46 P.2d 126 (1935).

In a few states, headlines may be libelous even though modified or negated by the story that follows. A 1956 decision explains how headlines and closing "tag-lines" of a news story can be libelous (even though in this case the newspaper defended itself successfully). One story in a series published by the *Las Vegas Sun* brought a libel suit because of its headline and closing tag-line advertising the next article in the series. The headline read "Babies for Sale. Franklin Black Market Trade of Child Told." The tag-line promoting the story to appear the next day read "Tomorrow–Blackmail by Franklin." The body of the story told factually the way in which attorney Franklin had obtained a mother's release of her child for adoption. Franklin sued for libel and won. But the *Sun* appealed, claiming among other things that the trial judge had erred in instructing the jury that the words were libelous. The *Sun* said that the language was ambiguous, and susceptible of more than one interpretation.

But the Nevada Supreme Court[39] said that the headline and tag-line were indeed libelous. Under any reasonable definition, it said, "black market sale" and "blackmail" "would tend to lower the subject in the estimation of the community and to excite derogatory opinions against him and hold him up to contempt."

But in the majority of jurisdictions, headlines and cutlines must be read in the context of the entire article and a headline that defames may be rehabilitated by explanatory or correcting copy. Does this mean that a publisher can defame with impunity in a headline as long as she explains away the defamatory statement somewhere in the body of the story? The West Virginia Supreme Court, faced a case involving outsize headlines that were clearly defamatory but not necessarily supported by the text of the stories they ran with. In Sprouse v. Clay Communication, Inc.,[40] an unsuccessful candidate for governor of West Virginia sued over a series that suggested that he had used a dummy corporation to make substantial profits in real estate. Included in the headlines were: "Pendleton Realty Bonanza By Jim Sprouse Disclosed," "More Asks Federal Probe in Sprouse's Land Grab," and "Dummy Firm Seen Proving Corruption."

The court noted the extraordinary size of the headlines in deciding the issue of whether the headlines should be judged by themselves or should be taken as a whole with the texts of the stories:

> Generally, where the headline is of normal size and does not lead to conclusion totally unsupported by the

[39] Las Vegas Sun, Inc. v. Franklin, 74 Nev. 282, 329 P.2d 867 (1958). The *Sun* won the appeal on other grounds.

[40] Sprouse v. Clay Communication, Inc., 158 W.Va. 427, 211 S.E.2d 674 (1975).

body of the story, both headlines and story should be considered together for their total impression. However where outsized headlines are published which reasonably lead the average reader to an entirely different conclusion than the facts recited in the story, and where the plaintiff can demonstrate that it was the intent of the publisher to use such misleading headlines to create a false impression on the normal reader, the headlines may be considered separately with regard to whether a known falsehood was published.[41]

In terms of Internet publishing, the lessons to be learned from this section are especially important. Because the Internet appears anywhere a user accesses a page, newsgroup or e-mail, it can be easy for a plaintiff to find that she has been defamed in a jurisdiction that allows consideration only of headlines. Further, the type of "headline" used in the Internet communication may have the same effect as the oversize and clearly defamatory headlines found in Sprouse.

Broadcasters also must take care in preparing teases and promos. Promos, in and of themselves, may be considered to constitute a separate publication from the actual newscast or story. Therefore, a sexy promo which hypes a story that later proves to be more conservative may have the effect of landing the broadcaster in court. Teases, which precede the story and are separated by introductions of other stories and commercial breaks, can be problematic as well. Prof. Rod Smolla notes in his work, The Law of Defamation, that the tease in a 60 Minutes report on U.S. involvement in Vietnam was one of the strongest negative statements at issue. In the tease, reporter Mike Wallace told the viewing audience that CBS would present evidence of what it had come to believe was a "conspiracy" of U.S. military intelligence to conceal the strength of enemy troops in Vietnam.

SEC. 24. ACTUAL INJURY

The fourth element that needs to be pleaded by a plaintiff in a libel suit: "actual injury." The private-person plaintiff must demonstrate loss or reputational injury of some kind. Actual injury may include a showing in court of out-of-pocket money loss, of impairment of reputation and standing in the community, of personal humiliation, and of mental anguish and suffering, as the Supreme Court of the United States said in Gertz v. Robert Welch, Inc.[42]

Before publishing, broadcasting, making movies, writing novels or going online, students need to realize how many zeroes juries

---

[41] Ibid. At 441, 686.

[42] Gertz v. Robert Welch, Inc., 418 U.S. 323, 348–350, 94 S.Ct. 2997, 3011–3012 (1974).

can put in a damage award. The Wall Street Journal was hit with a libel award of $222.7 million, the largest libel award on record. Dow Jones, the publisher of the Journal, appealed the award and the court reduced it by $200 million, roughly the amount of the punitive damages. That still left $22.7 million in actual damages and a personal punitive damage award of $20,000 against a Wall Street Journal reporter. Barricade Books, a New York publisher, faced closure after losing a defamation suit that carried a $3 million award. Barricade published a biography of casino owner Steve Wynn, "Running Scared: The Life and Treacherous Times of Las Vegas Casino King Steve Wynn." Barricade had published a catalog and the description of the book included a reference to a "why a confidential Scotland Yard report calls Wynn a front man for the Genovese crime family." Barricade could not post an appeal bond in order to challenge the decision. The publisher chose not to obtain libel insurance because of the cost, estimated by Barricade owner Lyle Stuart to range from $25,000 to $100,000.[43]

Courts and statutes are not entirely consistent in their labeling of the kinds of damages that may be awarded to a person who is libeled. Generally, however, three bases exist for compensating the injured person.

The first is that injuring reputation or causing humiliation ought to be recognized as real injury, even though it is impossible to make a scale of values and fix exact amounts due the injured for various kinds of slurs. If such injury is proved, "general" or "compensatory" damages are awarded.

There is also harm of a more definable kind—actual pecuniary loss that a person may suffer as a result of a libel. It may be the loss of a contract or of a job, and if it can be shown that the loss is associated with the libel, the defamed may recover "special" damages—the cost to him. It is plain, however, that some states use the term "actual damages" to cover both pecuniary loss and damaged reputations. Thus it was held in Miami Herald Pub. Co. v. Brown:[44]

> Actual damages are compensatory damages and include (1) pecuniary loss, direct or indirect, or special damages; (2) damages for physical pain and inconvenience; (3) damages for proven mental suffering; and (4) damages for injury to reputation.

[43] Doreen Carvajal, "Defamation Suit Leaves Small Publisher Near Extinction," New York Times, Oct. 8, 1997, C1.

[44] Miami Herald Pub. Co. v. Brown, 66 So.2d 679, 680 (Fla.1953). See, also, Ellis v. Brockton Pub. Co., 198 Mass. 538, 84 N.E. 1018 (1908); Osborn v. Leach, 135 N.C. 628, 47 S.E. 811 (1904).

The third basis for awarding damages is public policy—that persons who maliciously libel others ought to be punished for the harm they cause. Damages above and beyond general and actual damages may be awarded in this case, and are called punitive or exemplary damages. Some states deny punitive damages, having decided long ago that they are not justified.[45] For more than a century, Massachusetts, for example, has rejected punitive damages, under a statement by the famed Oliver Wendell Holmes, Jr., then judge of the Massachusetts high court: "The damages are measured in all cases by the injury caused. Vindictive or punitive damages are never allowed in this State. Therefore, any amount of malevolence on the defendant's part in and of itself would not enhance the amount the plaintiff recovered by a penny * * *."[46]

The Supreme Court has laid down some rules regarding punitive damages. In Gertz v. Robert Welch, Inc.,[47] the Court acknowledged that the states have a "strong and legitimate * * * interest in compensating private individuals for injury to reputation," but compensation may not be limitless. A private plaintiff proving negligence can collect only "compensation for actual injury," otherwise known as "compensatory" or "general" damages.[48] To collect punitive damages, private persons (like public officials or public figures) have to prove "actual malice" rather than mere negligence. It found that awarding presumed damages ("compensatory" or "general" damages) or punitive damages where there is no demonstrated loss, "unnecessarily compounds the potential of any system of liability for defamatory falsehood to inhibit the vigorous exercise of First Amendment freedoms."[49]

Precisely what the Court meant by the permitted "compensation for actual injury" was not spelled out, but Justice Powell made it plain that he was not speaking strictly of compensation for proved dollar losses flowing from false defamation:[50]

> We need not define "actual injury," as trial courts have wide experience in framing appropriate jury instructions in tort action. Suffice it to say that actual injury is not limited to out-of-pocket loss. Indeed, the more customary types of actual harm inflicted by defamatory falsehood include impairment of reputation and standing in the community, personal humiliation, and mental anguish and

[45] In addition to Massachusetts, the Oregon Supreme Court has held that punitive damages are not permitted. Damages are limited to compensation for damage to reputation. Michigan has reached a similar conclusion.

[46] Burt v. Advertiser Newspaper Co., 154 Mass. 238, 245, 28 N.E. 1, 5 (1891).

[47] Gertz v. Robert Welch, Inc., 418 U.S. 323, 348, 94 S.Ct. 2997, 3011 (1974).

[48] Ibid.

[49] Ibid. At 348–351, 3011–3012.

[50] Ibid.

suffering. * * * all awards must be supported by competent evidence concerning the injury, although there need be no evidence which assigns an actual dollar value to the injury.[51]

Huge amounts of damage are often claimed, and sometimes awarded although juries' judgments in the multimillion dollar range are most often reduced by trial judges or by appeals courts. A California court jury in 1981 awarded $1.6 million to comedienne, Carol Burnett, who was falsely portrayed by the *National Enquirer,* said the judge in the case, as "drunk, rude, uncaring and abusive" in the Rive Gauche restaurant, Los Angeles.[52] The judge disagreed with the jury only in the amount of damages, which he cut in half to $50,000 compensatory plus $750,000 punitive, and the punitive total was cut to $150,000 by the California Court of Appeal more than two years after the jury trial.[53]

"Miss Wyoming" of 1978, Kimerli Jayne Pring, won a jury award of $25 million in punitive damages plus $1.5 million in compensatory damages from *Penthouse* magazine in 1981. She alleged that a *Penthouse* story falsely implied that she was sexually promiscuous and immoral. The staggering punitive award was quickly halved by Federal District Court Judge Clarence C. Brimmer, *Penthouse* appealed the enormous remainder, and after another year received the judgment clearing it of liability: the article could be reasonably understood by readers as only a "pure fantasy," not as defamation of Pring.[54] That meant the magazine would only have to deal with the costs of defending itself and appealing the case.

But even when reduced, as with the Wall Street Journal case, a damage award of $22.7 million is significant. Even an award of a million dollars is still a million dollars that a company or its insurance carrier must pay. In at least one case, a libel judgment drove one family from the newspaper business. The *Alton Telegraph* lost a $9.2 million judgment in 1980 in an Illinois court over a memo sent by two reporters to a Justice Department task force on crime. The memo dealt with a realtor who learned of the memo some time later. The paper filed for bankruptcy protection (the judgment exceeded the net worth of the paper) pending the conclusion of the appeals process. During the appeal, the paper and the plaintiff settled the case for a reported $1.4 million. After that the family that had owned the paper sold it to a media chain.

[51] Ibid. at 349–350, 94 S.Ct. at 3011, 3012.

[52] Burnett v. National Enquirer (Cal.Super.Ct.1981), 7 Med.L.Rptr. 1321, 1323.

[53] Burnett v. National Enquirer Inc., 144 Cal.App.3d 991, 193 Cal.Rptr. 206 (1983), 9 Med.L.Rptr. 1921, appeal dismissed 465 U.S. 1014, 104 S.Ct. 1260 (1984).

[54] Pring v. Penthouse Intern., Ltd., 695 F.2d 438 (10th Cir.1982), 8 Med.L.Rptr. 2409.

As with just about everything else, defamation has grown more expensive with time. Libel awards rose in 1996 to an average of $2.8 million. That was substantially higher than the $620,000 average in 1995.[55] Those awards come from juries, people from the community who are called upon to, first determine whether the media defendant did anything wrong that would support the payment of damages, and then decide how much those damages should be. Observers say that juries are at least unsympathetic to the media and at worst openly hostile. In those cases that actually went to trial, and it should be noted that most defamation cases never make it to the courtroom, the media lost 70 percent in 1996.

What are some of the things that give rise to these staggering libel awards? Studies point to three significant factors: (1) a sympathetic plaintiff; (2) an unsympathetic defendant; and, (3) jurors' perceptions about the nature of big media entities.

A 1992 study of libel cases written by Thomas B. Kelley for the Practising Law Institute considered these and other factors in which juries awarded large amounts to plaintiffs, amounts that appeared to be disproportionate to the evidence regarding the plaintiff's actual injuries. The plaintiff was a significant factor. In the cases studied, the plaintiffs were people who had enjoyed the respect of the community and whose career was based on public trust. Juries could categorize the plaintiff as a person of integrity who stood for the truth and justice. Because the nature of news means that so many stories involve persons in public office or who occupy positions of public trust, professional communicators need to exercise due care.

While juries were finding the plaintiff to be deserving of their sympathy, the media defendants were found to be the opposite. Juries saw media defendants as smug, arrogant and incompetent. In his analysis of about First Amendment cases for the Practising Law Institute, James J. Brosnahan wrote "Many jurors probably have a healthy skepticism about the accuracy of what is published and may have a fixed opinion about the defendant newspaper." Other commentators have pointed to behaviors that jurors find disturbing and that help them reach overly large damage awards. Included in the laundry list are the use of leading questions during interviews, an apparent attempt to get a source to make damaging statements, a failure to contact obvious and available sources, the emotional involvement of the reporter in the story or regarding the plaintiff, and reliance on sources who are clearly not credible or bear a grudge against the plaintiff.

[55] Keith J. Kelly, "A Familiar Wring to Libel Suits," New York Daily News, April 7, 1997, p. 47.

The Houston Chronicle interviewed jurors in the original $222.7 million libel award against the Wall Street Journal over its reporting on the activities of MMAR, a Houston securities firm. The newspaper talked with three of the seven members of the jury. They told the newspaper that the damage figure was based on the worth of the Journal's parent company, Dow Jones. Evidence at the trial set Dow Jones' worth at between $2 billion to $3 billion. The jurors said that a damage award that amounted to 10 percent of the company's worth would be a warning but not cripple the company.

The Journal reported that Money Management Analytical Research Group was reckless with clients' money, had acted in a fraudulent manner on some occasions and was living high on the hog. MMAR was a firm that had grown by dealing in securities that traditional Wall Street bond firms avoided. Jurors said that they started the case with substantial confidence in the Journal. They also said that they valued the role that the media play. "We depend on the media as our protectors of the First Amendment," juror Mike Johnson was quoted by the Chronicle. But the jury found that the Journal's reporting included eight false and defamatory statements. Sources for the story testified that the Journal reporter misquoted them. A juror recalled that one source for the Journal article denied ever talking to the reporter. The evidence showed that the reporter also failed to read some key documents that would have shown that one of the most damaging statements in the story was not true. The Journal reported that "We wanted to punish them for betraying a trust," Johnson was quoted as saying.[56]

Getting to the particulars of damage awards, Judge Posner of the 7th Circuit said in Douglass v. Hustler Magazine, "[w]e have repeatedly emphasized—and take this opportunity to emphasize again—that we will not allow plaintiffs to throw themselves on the generosity of the jury; if they want damages they must prove them."[57]

But not in all cases. In a number of jurisdictions the courts will permit presumed damages. Presumed damages are compensatory damages for which the plaintiff need not give evidence. It is part of a doctrine of compensation that assumes that in many cases it is not possible to show the extent of the harm from a defamatory publication. The Supreme Court said in Dun & Bradstreet v. Greenmoss Builders[58] that " 'proof of actual damage will be impossible in a great many cases where, from the character of the defama-

---

[56] Deborah Tedford, "Jurors Hope Libel Award Will Scream a Message," The Houston Chronicle, March 27, 1997, p. A–25.

[57] Douglass v. Hustler Magazine, Inc., 769 F.2d 1128, 1144 (7th Cir.1985), 11 Med.L.Rptr. 2264 (Posner, J.), cert. denied, 475 U.S. 1094, 106 S.Ct. 1489 (1986).

[58] Dun & Bradstreet, Inc. v. Greenmoss Builders, Inc., 472 U.S. 749, 105 S.Ct. 2939 (1985).

tory words and the circumstances of the publication, it is all but certain that serious harm has resulted in fact.' "[59] In those jurisdictions where the presumed harm doctrine is applied, the jury is told that it may presume that the plaintiff was injured as a result of the publication of the defamation. That does not mean that the plaintiff will not offer evidence of damage, only that the plaintiff can rely on the jury to assess the impact of the defamatory statement if she so chooses.

In other jurisdictions, the plaintiff must plead and prove special damages, actual pecuniary losses. This is a significant burden and many cases are disposed of early on when the plaintiff has not met his burden. Special damages apply in defamation per quod cases, those cases where the defamation is not apparent on its face, those cases which rely on extrinsic facts to make the defamatory meaning apparent. Special damages are actual economic losses. These may include the loss of employment, contracts, customers, credit, and being denied accommodation at restaurants and other public houses. Social losses, including the loss of friends, is not considered a pecuniary loss unless those social losses can be tied to some monetary loss. Mental distress in and of itself is not considered sufficient as proof of pecuniary loss.

When a plaintiff comes to court, she may introduce any number of elements to show the jury the extent of the damage her reputation has suffered and which the jury will use to compute its damage award. The jury will consider a number of things, including the nature of the publication, the extent to which the defamation was believed, and her prior good reputation. Here, less credible media outlets have an advantage. That advantage may turn into a liability later, but in this area less credibility can help.

The tabloid Sun, published by Globe International, ran a story about Nellie Mitchell, a resident of Mountain Home, Arkansas. Mitchell had run a newsstand and delivered newspapers for 50 years. She gained notoriety for her long service and was featured in a number of stories in 1980. On Oct. 2, 1990, the Sun ran Mitchell's photograph in connection with a story that appeared under the headline, "Pregnancy Forces Granny to Quit Work at Age 101." A second photograph of Mitchell appeared with a story about an Australian woman named Audrey Wiles. According to the Sun, Wiles, who was 101, had to quit her paper route after a millionaire customer made her pregnant. Mitchell sued. Globe International built part of its defense on the claim that no one believed what it ran in the pages of the Sun. Although Mitchell did not recover on her libel claim, she did receive an award of $650,000 in compensatory damages and $850,000 in punitive damages on a related claim.

---

[59] Ibid. at 760, 105 S.Ct. at 2946.

The Eighth Circuit Court of Appeals reduced the damage award saying it was excessive under the facts of the case.

The defendant, on the other hand, may introduce evidence to show the jury that the damages suffered by the plaintiff were not so serious. That will include evidence that the plaintiff had a bad reputation to begin with, the defendant's reason for publishing the defamatory statement and the plaintiff's ability to respond to the statement. The defendant also may introduce evidence of retraction or correction. A number of states have passed retraction statutes that require that a plaintiff first notify the media defendant of the defamation and allow the defendant to retract the statement. If the defendant does publish a retraction, the statutes will limit the damages the plaintiff can recover.

SEC. 25. FAULT

The final element of libel that the aggrieved person must allege and persuasively demonstrate is "fault" on the part of the publisher or broadcaster.

Before recovery, the plaintiff must prove that the defendant was at fault in publishing the defamatory statement. There are two general levels of fault in defamation cases: negligence and actual malice. Actual malice is a term of art and means that the publisher published the defamatory statement either with knowledge that it was false or with reckless disregard of its probably falsity. Actual malice does not mean, as most people commonly understand it, that the publisher published with ill will or bad motives. It should be evident that the actual malice standard gives the press a very large benefit of the doubt; it is difficult for a public person to prove that the news organization knew something was false, for example.

Private persons—that is, people who are not classed as public officials or public figures by a court—often have to meet a lesser, easier standard of proof. They have to prove only that the defamation complained of was negligently published, or published without the "due care" that would be used by an "average person of ordinary sensibilities."[60] Some states have decided to apply a negligence standard based on the conduct of the reasonable professional in the same industry.[61] This means that the defendant will bring evidence that his conduct conformed to the general standards of others in the profession. It can work to the advantage of the

[60] See Gertz v. Robert Welch, Inc., 418 U.S. 323, 94 S.Ct. 2997 (1974); see also Black's Law Dictionary.

[61] Robert Sack reports that Arizona, Delaware, Georgia, Iowa, Maryland, Massachusetts, Michigan, Minnesota, Kansas, Oklahoma, and Utah have adopted the reasonable professional standard. Robert Sack and Sandra Barron, Libel Slander, and Related Problems, (Michie and Practising Law Institute, New York, 1996).

defendant who will not have his conduct gauged by the common sense of the juror, but rather by standards set in the industry and which fellow professionals and academics will testify to. One can argue that the reasonable professional standard in fact allows sloppy practices in an industry to protect the poor reporting of individual defendants.

This split approach has resulted from the Supreme Court case of Gertz v. Robert Welch, Inc.[62] The Court told private people they would not have to meet the constitutional demand of proving actual malice against publishers in bringing libel suits. What, then, would be required of them? Justice Powell wrote for the majority that the states might set their own standards of liability for private people to prove, except that the Constitution would not permit states to impose "liability without fault." Powell was saying that state standards could not include an ancient rule in libel *per se*—that for those words which are damaging on their face, the law presumes injury to reputation and liability for libel by the publisher; the only question is the amount of damages that may be recovered.[63] This was the long-standing rule of "strict liability" in libel, and the Court was saying that the media must be shielded from strict liability. The standard of fault for private people to prove, Powell said, need be no more than "negligence," instead of the "actual malice" of *Sullivan*. The Powell opinion significantly returned to the states much of the jurisdiction in libel cases that had been lost to them through the sweep of *Sullivan*, even as it made it plain that there must not be a return to "automatic" liability for defamation.

And so, *Gertz*, put the burden of defining the standard of fault to be used onto the state courts: "We hold that, so long as they do not impose liability without fault, the States may define for themselves the appropriate standard of liability for a publisher or broadcaster of defamatory falsehood injurious to a private individual."[64] The result, unsurprisingly, has been to encourage lack of uniformity in libel law among the states. Note, also, that the majority in Gertz v. Welch—by not spelling out a lesser standard of fault—by indirection invited the states to fall back to the familiar (if squishy) concept of negligence. The dissent by Justice William O. Douglas made that point:[65]

> The standard announced today leaves the States free to "define for themselves the appropriate standard of

[62] Gertz v. Robert Welch, Inc., 418 U.S. 323, 94 S.Ct. 2997 (1974).

[63] Gertz v. Robert Welch, Inc., 418 U.S. 323, 346, 94 S.Ct. 2997, 3010 (1974); Prosser, 780–781.

[64] Ibid., at 346, 94 S.Ct. at 3010.

[65] Douglas dissent, 418 U.S. 323, 360, 94 S.Ct. 2997, 3017 (1974).

liability for a publisher or broadcaster" in the circumstances of this case. This of course leaves the simple negligence standard as an option with the jury free to impose damages upon a finding that the publisher failed to act as "a reasonable man." With such continued erosion of First Amendment protection, I fear that it may well be the reasonable man who refrains from speaking.[66]

Robert D. Sack and Sandra S. Baron have found that at least two-thirds of the states–34 in 1994–have adopted the negligence standard in private figure defamation lawsuits.[67]

But states were not restricted to the "negligence" which Justice Powell implied in *Gertz*. Some states have chosen other standards which are more difficult for plaintiffs to prove against media defendants. Consider New York, important because of the amount of libel litigation in that state. New York has fashioned a standard known by the shorthand label of "gross irresponsibility by the news medium," to be applied when a private figure lawsuit falls "arguably within the sphere of legitimate public concern."[68]

John B. McCrory and colleagues have listed four states— Alaska, Colorado, Indiana, and New Jersey—as using an "actual malice" standard, at least as applied to private individuals involved in a matter of public interest. In addition, four states—Connecticut, Louisiana, and Montana, and New Hampshire—were "undecided" on a standard of fault in private figure defamation cases.[69]

Which Guideline? "Reasonable Journalist" or "Reasonable Person?"

As John B. McCrory, Robert D. Sack, and others have noted, the question arises whether the standard of conduct is going to be the traditional "reasonable man" or "reasonable person" standard of general negligence law, or whether a standard of conduct set by the media industry will be the guidepost.[70]

---

[66] Ibid. At 360, 94 S.Ct. at 3017.

[67] Robert D. Sack and Sandra S. Baron, Libel, Slander and Related Problems, 2d ed. (New York: Practising Law Institute, 1994), p. 340.

[68] Chapadeau v. Utica Observer–Dispatch, Inc., 38 N.Y.2d 196, 379 N.Y.S.2d 61, 341 N.E.2d 569 (1975). The similarity to Justice John Marshall Harlan's standard for public figures to meet in Curtis Pub. Co. v. Butts, 388 U.S. 130, 157, 87 S.Ct. 1975, 1992 (1967) has been commented upon by several observers, including Sack and Baron, op. cit., at p. 350.

[69] John B. McCrory, Robert C. Bernius, Robert D. Sack, et al., "Constitutional Privilege in Libel Law" in James C. Goodale, chairman, Communications Law 1993, Vol. 2, pp. 321–322.

[70] John B. McCrory, Robert C. Bernius, Robert D. Sack, et al., "Constitutional Privilege in Libel Law" in James C. Goodale, chairman, Communications Law 1993, Vol. 2, pp. 322–327; Sack and Baron, op. cit., p. 344.

Both kinds of standards pose problems for media defendants. With the reasonable person standard, the non-journalists sitting on juries seem to have an inborn belief that by definition, journalists are not reasonable persons: journalists are intrusive and tell things that shouldn't be told. And if an industry standard is used—such as Justice Harlan's formulation, "standards of investigation and reporting ordinarily adhered to by responsible publishers,"[71] then expert witnesses for a lawsuits two sides will no doubt disagree over what those standards properly should be. And once again, non-journalists—jurors and judges—will sit in a position to second-guess reporters, editors, and broadcasters.

Courts and Setting of Journalistic Standards

In no part of journalism law have the courts more clearly and consistently entered the realm of setting journalistic standards than where they judge the level of "fault"—whether the fault of actual malice or the fault of negligence or gross irresponsibility. Courts examine carefully the reporting and writing process at least as much when a plaintiff is private as when he is public.

In Tennessee, the state Supreme Court decided that it was up to the jury to say whether there had been negligence in a reporter's reliance on a single police record to suggest mistakenly that a woman was an adulterer. Using the "arrest report" of the Memphis police, a Press–Scimitar reporter wrote a story saying that Mrs. Nichols had been shot. The suspect, said the story, was a woman who went to the Nichols home and found her own husband there with Mrs. Nichols. The story used "police said" and "police reported" in attribution, the reporter testifying that these were common terms used to indicate that a source was either a written police record or a policeman's spoken words.

Had the reporter gone to the police record called the "offense report," he would have learned that not only was Mrs. Nichols with the suspect's husband (named Newton), but also Mr. Nichols and two neighbors. There would thus have been no suggestion that Mrs. Nichols was having an adulterous affair and had been "caught" by Mrs. Newton. Almost a month later, the newspaper printed a story correcting the implication of the first story. But Mrs. Nichols sued for libel, and testified at trial that the article had torn up her home, children, and reputation, that the family had had to move, that she had had telephone calls asking how much it cost to get the newspaper to run the correcting account. A friend testified that after the initial story, people gossiped about Mrs. Nichols and "said that she was a whore." Before the case went to the jury for decision, the trial court granted the newspaper a directed verdict:

[71] Curtis Pub. Co. v. Butts, 388 U.S. 130, 87 S.Ct. 1975 (1967).

While "no fault had been shown" on the part of the reporter, the trial court said, it did note its uncertainty as to what standard of fault was required on the basis of *Gertz*. The Tennessee Court of Appeals, which reversed the trial court decision on several grounds, said that the standard of liability was "ordinary care." The case then went to the Tennessee Supreme Court, which in upholding the Court of Appeals and sending the case back for trial, laid down Tennessee's requirement upon private libel plaintiffs: negligence.[72]

> In determining the issue of liability the conduct of defendant is to be measured against what a reasonably prudent person would, or would not, have done under the same or similar circumstances. This is the ordinary negligence test that we adopt, not a "journalistic malpractice" test whereby liability is based upon a departure from supposed standards of care set by publishers themselves * * *.

In General Products v. Meredith, an article on wood stoves in *Better Homes and Gardens Home Plan Ideas Magazine* warned against fire danger with the use of triple-walled chimneys in certain stoves. The manufacturer (found to be "private") of one type, not subject to the hazards of creosote buildup, brought suit. The federal District Court denied part of the magazine's motion for summary judgment, saying that there was evidence of possible negligence by the reporter in his fact gathering:[73]

> * * * he relied on an earlier book and article and did not examine them directly, but drew on his general recall of their content. He did not contact the author of either source for an update, was not aware that the information in the magazine article had been repudiated by a subsequent article in another publication, and did not contact anyone in the industry on testing relevant to his subject.

A KARK–TV reporter who happened to be near the scene of police activity in a shopping center store was alerted to the fact, and a camera crew from the station was sent. The crew filmed the scene of police handcuffing two men and placing them in a squad car. Reporter Long questioned the police but got no comment, and interviewed a store clerk from whom she received vague responses. Her story accompanying the broadcast film called the event a "robbery attempt," and said that the two men "allegedly held a store clerk hostage." But the handcuffed men were never arrested, merely detained until police determined that the "tip" on which

---

[72] Memphis Pub. Co. v. Nichols, 569 S.W.2d 412, 418 (Tenn.1978), 4 Med.L.Rptr. 1573.

[73] General Products Co., Inc. v. Meredith Corp., 526 F.Supp. 546 (E.D.Va.1981), 7 Med.L.Rptr. 2257, 2261.

they acted was false and there had been no robbery attempt. On libel trial, each plaintiff was awarded $12,500.[74]

The Arkansas Supreme Court said there was enough evidence of reporting negligence for the trial court to send that issue to the jury: a news report relying completely on information from a police scanner, without any checking, an on an eye-witness account from a reporter who didn't know the context for what she observed, was not "found to be due care as a matter of law."[75]

If reports from a police "scanner" were suspect in that case, a news story about a gunshot death, based on a written report to media from a police "hot line" was not negligent. The line was started to lessen the need for interviews with police. The reporter, who had often used the "hot line" and found it reliable, accurately quoted the report's statement that the shooting occurred during a domestic argument. Later, the shooting was ruled accidental. The husband sued the newspaper for implying that he intentionally shot his wife, saying the reporter should have waited for a more "official" report. The Court found no negligence.[76] Nor, in another case, was there negligence in a reporter's failure to interview all eight persons arrested on drug charges, before publishing a story in which a father and son of the same name were confused. The court said that the reporter "undoubtedly could have taken additional steps to insure the accuracy of his facts." But he had talked with several officials, with an attorney, and with neighbors of the raided house, and had listened to a tape of a news conference about the event. His "procedures were well within the bounds of professionalism in the news gathering business." The court found no negligence.[77]

Illinois' Supreme Court adopted negligence as its standard, saying recovery might be had on proof that the defendant knew the statement to be false, or "believing it to be true, lacked reasonable grounds for that belief." It added that a journalist's "failure to make a reasonable investigation into the truth of the statement is obviously a relevant factor."[78] And it quoted the Kansas Supreme Court with approval as further elaboration of what "negligence" means: " * * * the lack of ordinary care either in the doing of an act or in the failure to do something. * * * The norm usually is the

---

[74] KARK–TV v. Simon, 280 Ark. 228, 656 S.W.2d 702 (1983), 10 Med.L.Rptr. 1049. The Arkansas Supreme Court reversed and remanded the case because of the trial court's error in permitting the jury to consider punitive damages, even though it granted none.

[75] Ibid., at 704, 10 Med.L.Rptr. at 1051.

[76] Phillips v. Washington Post (D.C.Sup.Ct.1982), 8 Med.L.Rptr. 1835.

[77] Horvath v. Telegraph (Ohio App.1982), 8 Med.L.Rptr. 1657, 1662.

[78] Troman v. Wood, 62 Ill.2d 184, 340 N.E.2d 292, 298–299 (1975).

conduct of the reasonably careful person under the circumstances."[79]

If it's any help to the reporter, it may be noted that the word "care" is used in various courts' discussions of negligence. It is simply the "care" of the reasonably prudent person in the Arizona and Tennessee cases discussed above. And in the Illinois and Kansas cases just mentioned, the guideline is "ordinary care," while it is "reasonable care" (Washington),[80] and "due care" (Ohio).[81]

One analyst found that the first decade's use of the negligence standard demonstrated high uncertainty and severe contradictions in results, plus a likelihood that it produces self-censorship by media. He wrote in 1984 that the *Gertz* approach has failed,[82] and the view from 1994 indicates that the term "negligence" continues to be excruciatingly vague.

"Gross Irresponsibility"

In New York, the fault of negligence is not serious enough for a private individual to maintain a libel suit. The New York Court of Appeals has specified that, where the subject matter is of public concern, recovery for the private individual depends on his establishing "that the publisher acted in a grossly irresponsible manner without due consideration for the standards of information gathering and dissemination ordinarily followed by responsible parties."[83] The Utica *Observer-Dispatch* had reported two different episodes involving drug-charge arrests in a single story. At one point, it incorrectly brought together school teacher Chapadeau and two other men at a drug-and-beer party, referring to "the trio." Chapadeau was not there, and he brought a libel action. The Court of Appeals noted the error but also pointed out that the story was written only after two authoritative agencies had been consulted, and that the story was checked by two desk hands at the newspaper. "This is hardly indicative of gross irresponsibility," said the court. "Rather it appears that the publisher exercised reasonable

[79] Ibid., 299; Gobin v. Globe Pub. Co., 216 Kan. 223, 531 P.2d 76 (1975).

[80] Taskett v. KING Broadcasting Co., 86 Wash.2d 439, 445, 546 P.2d 81, 85 (1976).

[81] Thomas H. Maloney and Sons, Inc. v. E.W. Scripps Co., 43 Ohio App.2d 105, 334 N.E.2d 494 (1974).

[82] Marc Franklin, "What Does Negligence Mean in Defamation Cases?", 6 Comm/ Ent 259, 276–281 (Winter, 1984), and see pp. 266–271 for an excellent analysis of journalistic practices as examined by courts under the negligence standard.

[83] Chapadeau v. Utica Observer–Dispatch, Inc., 38 N.Y.2d 196, 379 N.Y.S.2d 61, 64, 341 N.E.2d 569, 571 (1975). The similarity to U.S. Supreme Court Justice Harlan's recommended standard for public figures to meet, in Curtis Pub. Co. v. Butts, 388 U.S. 130, 87 S.Ct. 1975 (1967), above, p. 117, is too striking to avoid a connection.

methods to insure accuracy."[84] Summary judgment for the newspaper was upheld. It was denied, however, where a television reporter who had broadcast an account of fraudulent practices concerning burial expenses could recall little or nothing about his sources and how he obtained the information, and made little or no effort to authenticate his report. A jury, said the appeals court, would have to decide whether that was gross irresponsibility.[85]

Litigation Note: *If a case goes to trial, the plaintiff's attorney will focus on the conduct of the media defendant in allowing the defamatory statement to be published. They will ask the reporter the steps he took in gathering the information. No matter how careful the reporter, the plaintiff's attorney will point to "that one last call that would have let the reporter know that the story was wrong." The plaintiff's attorney will present witnesses who will testify that they would have told the reporter that vital piece of information, "if he had only asked." A good plaintiff's attorney will create a time line to show the jury that the reporter spent days or weeks working on his investigation, but called the defendant for a response only a day before publication. At each stage of the way, the plaintiff's attorney will be sending a message to the jury, asking in effect: "would you have done such a poor job and ruined my client's reputation?" The answer will be a "no." And since jurors will think of themselves as reasonably prudent people, the plaintiff's attorney will be building his case that the defendant failed to live up to that reasonable standard of conduct. In those jurisdictions that use the reasonable professional standard, the plaintiff's attorney will look for experts to lay out standards of conduct that the defendant did not meet in preparing the story. Under these circumstances, the defendant may wind up putting on a case to show the miserable state of the profession.*

SEC. 26. DISCOVERY

In the course of litigation, both sides have the opportunity to learn about the other side. This process, called discovery, is intended to avoid trial by ambush. More practically, it means that the parties will be able to get an idea of the strengths and weaknesses of the other side. The defendant can delve into the plaintiff's past in order to show that the plaintiff's reputation was far from pristine.

The plaintiff can go into the defendant's conduct in the course of preparing the story. That discovery can go into great detail.

---

[84] Ibid., at 65, 341 N.E.2d at 572. See also Goldman v. New York Post Corp., 58 A.D.2d 769, 396 N.Y.S.2d 399 (1977).

[85] Meadows v. Taft Broadcasting Co., Inc., 98 A.D.2d 959, 470 N.Y.S.2d 205 (1983), 10 Med.L.Rptr. 1363.

Every interview, every telephone call can and will be intensely scrutinized. The plaintiff's lawyer will even look to the editorial process and what the publisher was thinking while preparing to publish.

In one of the most celebrated media cases of the 1970s, Barry Lando and Mike Wallace of CBS' "60 Minutes" refused to answer questions in discovery proceedings that sought to probe their "state of mind" in preparing a segment on one Col. Anthony Herbert. Herbert, a public figure (the public figure issue comes up in Chapter 5), was suing for words in the broadcast which, he said, portrayed him as a liar in his accusations that his superiors covered up reports of Vietnam War crimes. He was seeking evidence of actual malice on the part of Lando and Wallace. Confronted in discovery proceedings that lasted a year and produced almost 3,000 pages of Lando's testimony alone, Lando refused to respond when it came to inquiries into his state of mind in editing and producing the program, and into the editorial process in general. He said this was a realm of journalistic work that must not be intruded upon for fear of its chilling effect on expression protected by the First Amendment.

While the Court of Appeals, Second District, held on a 2–1 vote that First Amendment interests warranted an absolute evidentiary privilege for Lando, the U.S. Supreme Court reversed, saying that the First Amendment does not prohibit plaintiffs from directly inquiring into the editorial processes of those whom they accuse of defamation.[86] Journalists in libel cases had been testifying as to their motives, discussions, and thoughts relating to their copy, for a century and more before Times v. Sullivan without objecting to the process, said Justice White in writing the majority opinion; and Times v. Sullivan "made it essential to proving liability that plaintiffs focus on the conduct and state of mind of the defendant." He elaborated:[87]

> To be liable, the alleged defamer of public officials or of public figures must know or have reason to suspect that his publication is false. In other cases proof of some kind of fault, negligence perhaps, is essential to recovery. Inevitably, unless liability is to be completely foreclosed, the thoughts and editorial processes of the alleged defamer would be open to examination.

A few newspaper editorials and media voices recognized that the *Herbert* decision had broken no new ground and presented no fresh menace to the First Amendment, but attacking of the Supreme Court was far more common as media took the view that the

---

[86] Herbert v. Lando, 441 U.S. 153, 99 S.Ct. 1635 (1979), 4 Med.L.Rptr. 2575.

[87] Ibid., at 160, 99 S.Ct. at 1641, 4 Med.L.Rptr. at 2578.

justices had violated the integrity of the "editorial process" and the First Amendment.[88] Alarmed reactions of shock over presumed new damage by the Court to the First Amendment were often without understanding that what the Court was finding was in line with what lower courts had found for decades or for a century. In general, press reactions spoke eloquently to journalists' superficial education in the history of press freedom, and to their necessary occupational fix upon the world's current "hot scoop," unalloyed by knowledge of the history in which their own First Amendment roots were embedded.

Discovery in libel had arrived to stay, the *Herbert* case confirming its applicability. Said one media attorney at the time:[89] "While there was an outcry from some representatives of the press at the time, it now seems unlikely that the opinion will have any dramatic effect. Before *Herbert* journalists had routinely testified about the editorial process in establishing their freedom from 'actual malice' or 'fault.' As a result of *Herbert,* they will continue to do so."

A federal judge opened up the discovery process even further in a 1997 libel case against Time Magazine.[90] Richard Ellis, a former Moscow photographer for Reuters sued Time, claiming that the magazine had gotten him fired for exposing faked photographs in the magazine. Ellis said that Time had a policy and practice of using false or doctored pictures and that Time had libeled him in a letter and story to keep him from exposing the practice.

The controversy arose over the publication of a number of pictures purporting to show prostitution in Moscow. Ellis suggested that the photos were faked because they showed crimes being committed in the light of day with the people pictured unconcerned about being photographed. Ellis contacted one of the people pictured, a Russian pimp, and talked about the photos. The pimp contacted Time and offered them a recording which allegedly contained a promise from Ellis to the pimp of money from Time if he were to say the photos were faked. Ellis finally posted a statement on Compuserve calling the photos fakes. Time published a letter to its readers accusing Ellis of trying to bribe the Russian pimp. It was on the basis of that letter that Ellis filed his suit. U.S. Magistrate Patrick Attridge ordered Time to comply with discovery and disclose the editors' states of mind in the publication of the Moscow prostitution pictures.

[88] Editorials on File, April 16–30, 1979, pp. 437–446.

[89] Robert D. Sack, "Special Discovery Problems in Media Cases," Communications Law 1980, I, 235, 242 (Practising Law Institute 1980).

[90] Iver Peterson, "Court Broadens Scrutiny in Time Libel Case," New York Times, April 28, 1997, p. C–8.

The inquiry did not end there. Judge Attridge's order also required that Time's editors also reveal the decisions that led to the publication of a computer-altered photograph of O.J. Simpson and a photograph of a frowning Bill Clinton where the photo used was not related to the headline on the cover. The order went so far as to include "instances of other deceptive photographs at Time involving one or all of the persons" in the Moscow pictures. The sweep of the discovery order went far beyond the traditional libel inquiry, which would normally go only to the editorial process involved in the allegedly libelous publication. In addition, the discovery covered publication decisions made at dates later than the first allegedly faked photos.

Because the discovery process can be so intrusive, sensible journalists (or public relations or advertising people who get involved in litigation) should always conduct themselves carefully. Self-protective reporters have long understood that their story notes (or tape recordings, or video out-takes) may be subpoenaed as part of the discovery process in litigation. If you and your newspaper are being sued for libel by a mayor, do you want to explain the doodles you've sketched on your note pad to a jury? What if you've drawn a passable likeness of the mayor but added fangs? But even if you have embarrassing materials in your notes or in video out takes, do *not* destroy any materials relating to litigation once "the papers have been filed" to start a legal action. Don't destroy such materials while there is still any possibility of an appeal or further proceedings. If you do, the court may assume that destruction of materials subject to discovery is evidence of actual malice, or may be punishable as contempt of court.

Remember the case of Brown & Williamson Tobacco Corp. v. Jacobson and CBS, Inc.[91]? In 1981, Jacobson had delivered a "Perspective" report denouncing the makers of Viceroy cigarettes for hiring advertising "slicksters" to create an advertising strategy to "hook" the young. The strategy used by Brown & Williamson, Jacobson said, was taken from a report recommending that smoking be portrayed to youth as a kind of rite of passage involving wearing a bra or shaving, or drinking wine or beer. The broadcast added up to an accusation of unethical youth-oriented advertising by Brown & Williamson for its Viceroy cigarettes, thus endangering the health of the impressionable young.[92]

The report was said to be based on a "confidential report in the files of the federal government." Such a report did exist in the files of the Federal Trade Commission (FTC); it had been prepared by a

---

[91] Brown & Williamson Tobacco Corp. v. Jacobson, 827 F.2d 1119 (7th Cir.1987).

[92] Certiorari denied 485 U.S. 993, 108 S.Ct. 1302 (1988), upholding the judgment of the United States Court of Appeals, Seventh Circuit. See 827 F.2d 1119 (7th Cir.1987) 14 Med.L.Rptr. 1497.

research firm working for Ted Bates & Co., an ad agency once employed by Viceroy Cigarettes' parent company, Brown & Williamson.

At one point, a *confidential* FTC report had assumed, evidently erroneously, that Viceroy had adopted a "hook the young" ad strategy. A researcher for the CBS station—Michael Radutzky— had learned of the FTC report from a newspaper article, and even received copies of some pages of that report. However, Radutzky couldn't persuade FTC staffers to send him copies of the confidential report; the staffers would only "confirm that the report and its findings were accurate."

The FTC's ambiguous response to Radutzky, however, was contradicted directly by a Thomas Humber, a spokesman for Brown & Williamson. Humber told Radutzky that Brown & Williamson had rejected the strategy suggested in documents submitted by the Ted Bates ad agency.[93]

> Humber stated [to Radutzky, according to Humber's notes] that the proposals referred to in the FTC report were similar to a proposed libelous story that a young inexperienced reporter might submit to his editors but that it was corrected by a news organization's editors and attorneys. Humber stated that in such a case no legitimate criticism could be leveled at the news organization.

In response to a request from Jacobson, researcher Radutzky had searched unsuccessfully for "pot, wine, beer and sex" ads for Viceroy cigarettes. Radutzky had made lengthy notes as he conducted interviews and read those pages of the FTC report provided to him by a newspaper reporter. Radutzky also made handwritten entries on the margins of the FTC report pages he had, and also developed an 18–page sample script.

The jury, however, never saw this work by Radutzky. Before the trial, Radutzky "destroyed all of his contemporaneous interview notes, five of the ten pages of the FTC report ... and fifteen of the original eighteen pages of the sample script."[94]

Radutzky testified that he had destroyed those materials while "housecleaning" after a district court had dismissed an original Brown & Williamson libel complaint. The lawsuit, however, was later reinstated and, as the Court of Appeals noted, the destruction of materials violated CBS policy. The Court of Appeals concluded that Brown & Williamson had proved "by clear and convincing evidence that the defendants either knew the Perspective [Jacob-

[93] Brown & Williamson Tobacco Corp. v. Jacobson, 827 F.2d 1119, 1123 (7th Cir.1987).

[94] Ibid.; see Stuart Taylor, Jr., "Justices Uphold $3 million Libel Award on CBS," The New York Times, April 4, 1988.

son's commentary] was false or in fact entertained serious doubts as to its truth," thus allowing the district court jury's verdict against the TV station to stand. Furthermore, "[t]he most compelling evidence of actual malice submitted to the jury was the intentional destruction of critical documents by Jacobson's researcher. . . . "[95]

An important lesson to be learned from this case is that publishers and broadcasters need to develop clear policies about preparation of news or commentary reports. In any event, once a legal proceeding has started—and until it has concluded, beyond possibility of re-filing or appeal—notes, memos, tapes, or videotapes may not be destroyed safely.

NBC's "Dateline" and the Pickup Fire Debacle

NBC discovered the hazards of diligent discovery and the effective use of public relations in litigation.

As media properties such as newspapers and television networks scramble to hang onto their revenue shares, big stories about ethical lapses by the "news media" are more undesirable than ever. Adding to general public dissatisfaction with "the media" was the revelation in 1993 that a November 17, 1992 "Dateline NBC" television program had rigged "sparking devices" to make sure that a General Motors pickup truck would burst into flames during a staged collision. GM full-size pickup trucks made with side-mounted gasoline tanks from 1973 to 1987 were blamed for a number of truck fires.

After the NBC broadcast showing the staged crashes, General Motors officials told NBC News the "Dateline NBC" segment was unfair, and asked to inspect the vehicles used in the crashes. The network responded that "the vehicles had been junked and were not available."[96]

In January, 1993, GM evidently was tipped off that the staged fiery crash was not all it seemed. On January 18, GM got an injunction against the Indianapolis-based Institute for Safety Analysis, which had conducted the crash tests for NBC, order the Institute from destroying the vehicles used in the crash tests. The vehicles later were retrieved from a junkyard by GM.[97]

In February, 1993, after asking NBC for a retraction, GM filed a libel suit against the network, claiming the rigged tests were blatantly deceptive and caused irreparable harm, GM charged that the "crash test" fires had been touched off by radio transmitters

[95] Ibid.

[96] Doron P. Levin, "In Suit, GM Accuses NBC of Rigging Crash Tests," The New York Times, Feb. 2, 1993, p. A11.

[97] Ibid.

which caused model rocket engines affixed to gasoline tanks to ignite.

Michael Gartner, then NBC News president, at first defended the Dateline NBC segment, comparing the sparking devices used in the crash tests to a heated headlight lamp filament, and declared the broadcast to be "fair and accurate."[98] Later, at Gartner's direction, NBC anchors Stone Phillips and Jane Pauley apologized on "Dateline NBC" for the rigged pickup crash tests. General Motors quickly dropped its lawsuit against NBC, and, on March 2, Gartner resigned from the presidency of NBC News, although no one had accused him of having personal knowledge of the deception.[99]

Although the lawsuit was dropped, the reputation of NBC News was not enhanced by the rigged pickup truck crash misadventure. Although this kind of credibility shortfall may lead to more jurors hostile to media in lawsuits, NBC's crash tests can be seen as disserving the public in another way. General Motors pickup trucks with side-mounted gas tanks were the subject of a National Highway Safety Administration (NHSA) study of whether the trucks should be recalled. Refitting nearly five million vehicles with new tanks would be a huge expense for GM. Late in 1994, GM reached agreement with the U.S. Department of Transportation to give $51 million to safety programs in exchange for not recalling the pickups.[100]

Slipshod journalism has its price. As pointed out by Paul McMasters, executive director of the Freedom Forum First Amendment Center at Vanderbilt University, this crash test flap enabled GM to divert attention from the real issue: Are those pickup trucks as safe as they should be?[1]

This case is fascinating in light of GM's record in hiding news about design problems with the placement of gas tanks in passenger cars, a topic taken up in the chapter on covering courts.

[98] Adler, op. cit.

[99] Ken Auletta, "Changing Channels," The New Yorker, March 15, 1993, p. 38.

[100] James Bennett, "U.S. and G.M. End Truck Case Without Recall," The New York Times, Dec. 3, 1994, p. A1.

[1] Remarks at Region 3 Society of Professional Journalists conference, Knoxville, TN, March 6, 1993.

Chapter 5

THE CONSTITUTIONAL DEFENSE
AGAINST LIBEL SUITS

SEC. 27.   THE PUBLIC PRINCIPLE

Media defend against libel suits on grounds of their service to the public interest.

Libel may be an old area of law, but its dangers are exceedingly real today. This chapter deals with defenses to libel both new and old. Sweeping changes in libel law since 1964 have changed not only the law of defamation but also have altered key interpretations of the Constitution of the United States.

The American Constitution was nearly two hundred years old before courts, attorneys, and journalists concluded that it ought to protect speech and press against libel actions. It was in 1964 that the Supreme Court of the United States ruled in New York Times Co. v. Sullivan that public officials who sued for libel would have to clear a First Amendment barrier rather than the long-used lesser barriers of state laws and precedents. The emergence of multiple suits claiming formerly unheard-of amounts of damages threatened losses so high as to turn "watchdog" media into sheep. The public interest in vigorous, unintimidated reporting of the news was endangered. Society could not accept self-censorship on the part of media "chilled" by fear of libel awards. The United States Constitution itself, through the First Amendment, would provide the shield for discussion of public matters that the narrow vagaries of many state libel laws denied and that the public welfare demanded.

Striking as the new application of the Constitution was, it really amounted to an expansion of the "public principle" inherent in centuries-old defenses against libel suits. Defenses had grown in the context of the need of an open society for information. Society needs full discussion in media if its citizens are to participate in decisions that affect their lives, are to have the opportunity to choose, are to maintain ultimate control over government. Those who claimed harm to their reputations might find their suits unavailing if certain public concerns and values were furthered by the publication: Where the hard words were the truth, or were privileged as in news of court proceedings, or were fair criticism of performances by artists and others, the public had a real stake in receiving those words.

The First Amendment protection raised by the Supreme Court in the 1964 *Sullivan* case told public officials they would have to accept more fully the verbal rough-and-tumble of political life. Most notably, they would have to show that the news medium published the offending words with *actual malice*—knowledge of falsity, or reckless disregard for falsity.

Libel suits remain at the forefront of media's legal encounters. Suits do not drop in number, jury awards to plaintiffs are often astronomical and are sometimes found by courts to reflect deep jury prejudice against media, defense attorneys' fees may reach six or seven figures, public hostility toward media is widespread and intense. The self-censorship and "chill" that the *Sullivan* decision was intended to avert nevertheless has penetrated some newsrooms, diluting investigative reporting. Journalists, legal scholars, the American Civil Liberties Union, and others have urged strengthening of the *Sullivan* doctrine.[1] They are of course opposed by some who feel that *Sullivan* has been too protective of media.[2]

SEC. 28.   DEFENSE AGAINST PUBLIC OFFICIALS' SUITS

Under the doctrine of New York Times Co. v. Sullivan, the First Amendment broadly protects the news media from judgments for defamation of public officials.

The Supreme Court of the United States handed down a decision in 1964 that added a great new dimension of protection to

[1] Anthony Lewis, "The Sullivan Case," The New Yorker, Nov. 5, 1984, 52; Marc Franklin, "Good Names and Bad Law: a Critique of Libel Law and a Proposal," 18 Univ.S.F.L.Rev. 1, Fall 1983; "Symposium, Defamation and the First Amendment: New Perspectives," 25 William & Mary L.Rev. 1983–1984, Special Issue; Michael Massing, "The Libel Chill: How Cold Is It Out There?," Columbia Journ. Rev., May/June, 1985, 31; Gilbert Cranberg, "ACLU Moves to Protect All Speech on Public Issues from Libel Suits," Civil Liberties, Feb. 1983, 2.

[2] Jan Greene, Libel Plaintiffs Organize Against Media, 1985 Report of Society of Professional Journalists, Sigma Delta Chi, Freedom of Information '84–'85, 4; Bruce E. Fein, "New York Times v. Sullivan: an Obstacle to Enlightened Public Discourse * * *," quoted in 11 Med.L.Rptr. #3, 12/18/84, News Notes.

news media in the field of libel. It said that news media are not liable for defamatory words about the public acts of public officials unless the words are published with "actual malice." This defined the word "malice" with a rigor and preciseness that had been lacking for centuries and in a way that gave broad protection to publication. Public officials, it said, must live with the risks of a political system in which there is "a profound national commitment to the principle that debate on public issues should be uninhibited, robust, and wide-open * * *." Even a factual error, it said, will not make one liable for libel in words about the public acts of public officials unless actual malice is present.

The case was New York Times Co. v. Sullivan.[3] It stemmed from an "editorial advertisement" in the Times, written and paid for by a group intensely involved in the struggle for equality and civil liberties for African Americans. Suit was brought by L. B. Sullivan, Commissioner of Public Affairs for the city of Montgomery, Ala., against the Times and four black clergymen who were among the 64 persons whose names were attached to the advertisement.[4]

The now-famous advertisement, titled "Heed Their Rising Voices," recounted the efforts of southern Negro students to affirm their rights at Alabama State College in Montgomery and told of a "wave of terror" that met them. It spoke of violence against the Reverend Martin Luther King, Jr. in his leadership of the civil rights movement:[5]

Heed Their Rising Voices

As the whole world knows by now, thousands of Southern Negro students are engaged in wide-spread, non-violent demonstrations in positive affirmation of the right to live in human dignity as guaranteed by the U.S. Constitution and the Bill of Rights. In their effort to uphold these guarantees, they are being met by an unprecedented wave of terror by those who would deny and negate that document which the whole world looks upon as setting the pattern for modern freedom * * *.

* * *

[3] New York Times Co. v. Sullivan, 376 U.S. 254, 84 S.Ct. 710 (1964).

[4] It should be noted that this protection for the media sprang from an advertisement rather than a news story. No matter what discipline, all professional communicators share in the risks of defamation and all rely on the First Amendment for protection of their rights of expression.

[5] Ibid., facing 292; see also Anthony Lewis, *Make No Law* (New York: Random House, 1991).

In Montgomery, Alabama, after students sang "My Country, 'Tis of Thee" on the State Capitol steps, their leaders were expelled from school, and truck-loads of police armed with shotguns and tear-gas ringed the Alabama State College Campus. When the entire student body protested to state authorities by refusing to re-register, their dining hall was padlocked in an attempt to starve them into submission.

* * *

Again and again the Southern violators have answered Dr. King's protests with intimidation and violence. They have bombed his home almost killing his wife and child. They have assaulted his person. They have arrested him seven times—for "speeding," "loitering" and similar "offenses." And now they have charged him with "perjury"— a *felony* under which they could imprison him for *ten years.* Obviously, their real purpose is to remove him physically as the leader to whom the students and millions of others—look for guidance and support, and thereby to intimidate *all* leaders who may rise in the South * * *. The defense of Martin Luther King, spiritual leader of the student sit-in movement, clearly, therefore, is an integral part of the total struggle for freedom in the South.

Sullivan, one of three elected Commissioners of the City of Montgomery was commissioner of Public Affairs. His duties included supervision of the police department, fire department, department of cemetery and department of scales. Sullivan was not named in the advertisement, but claimed that because he supervised the Montgomery Police Department, people would identify him as the person responsible for police action at the State College campus. He said also that actions against the Rev. King would be attributed to him by association.

It was asserted by Sullivan, and not disputed, that there were errors in the advertisement. Police had not "ringed" the campus although they had been there in large numbers. Students sang the National Anthem, not "My Country, 'Tis of Thee." The expulsion had not been protested by the entire student body, but by a large part of it. They had not refused to register, but had boycotted classes for a day. The campus dining hall was not padlocked. The manager of the Times Advertising Acceptability Department said that he had not checked the copy for accuracy because he had no cause to believe it false, and some of the signers were well-known persons whose reputation he had no reason to question.

Sullivan wrote to the Times complaining of the advertisement which, he said, imputed to him all of the actions taken by police

including the ringing of the campus, padlocking of the dining hall
and arresting the Rev. King seven times. In fact, three of the Rev.
King's arrest took place before Sullivan became commissioner.
Sullivan also wrote similar letters to four black ministers whose
names were appended to the advertisement. None of the ministers
responded because they had not consented to having their names
attached and so they did not consider that they had published
anything. The Times responded by asking Sullivan what his complaint was. The letter said, "we ... are somewhat puzzled as to
how you think the statements in any way reflect on you," and "you
might, if you desire, let us know in what respect you claim that the
statements in the advertisement reflect on you."[6]

Sullivan filed his suit without explaining his retraction demand. The Times ran a retraction of the advertisement for Ala-
bama Gov. John Patterson who also complained, saying that the
advertisement charged him with "grave misconduct and * * *
improper actions and omissions as Governor of Alabama and Ex-
Officio Chairman of the State Board of Education of Alabama." The
Times later explained that it had published the retraction for Gov.
Patterson because, "we didn't want anything that was published by
The Times to be a reflection on the State of Alabama and the
Governor was, as far as we could see, the embodiment of the State
of Alabama and the proper representative of the State and, further-
more, we had by that time learned more of the actual facts which
the ad purported to recite * * * "[7]

Even so, Gov. Patterson sued. So did three other current and
former Montgomery officials. Each suit sought $500,000 in dam-
ages. Each suit named the four ministers as co-defendants. The
inclusion of the four ministers guaranteed that the trial would be
held in Alabama. That was because the ministers were Alabamians.
If the suit had been limited to the Times, a New York corporation,
on one side and an Alabama plaintiff on the other, the case might
have been removed to federal court under rules created to ensure
that out-of-state parties get a fair shake. Realizing that parties
might be at a disadvantage when facing a plaintiff in his home
state, federal civil practice allows for removal to federal court which
are perceived as less vulnerable to state partisanship. But in order
to go to federal court, the parties must be "diverse," that is to say
that there can be no overlap of state citizenship. Each side must be
from a different state than the opposing side. By including the four
ministers, the plaintiffs destroyed diversity and kept the trial in a
friendly state court.

[6] New York Times Co. v. Sullivan, 376 U.S. 254, 261, 84 S.Ct. 710 (1964).
[7] Ibid. At 262.

The presiding judge's jury charge left little to the jury's discretion. The judge ruled that the advertisement was libel *per se*. Because it was libel *per se*, it was presumably false and Sullivan did not have to prove damages because damages were presumed. The trial jury ruled that Sullivan had been libeled and awarded him $500,000, the full amount of his claim. The Supreme Court of Alabama upheld the finding saying that the First Amendment did not protect libel.

The impact was profound, as Anthony Lewis notes in his book "Make No Law." Lewis wrote:

> Sullivan and Governor Patterson and the others were out to transform the traditional libel action, designed to repair the reputation of a private party, into a state political weapon to intimidate the press. The aim was to discourage not false but true accounts of life under a system of white supremacy: stories about men being lynched for trying to vote, about cynical judges using the law to suppress constitutional rights, about police chiefs turning attack dogs on men and women who wanted to drink a Coke at a department-store lunch counter. It was to scare the national press—newspapers, magazines, the television networks—off the civil rights story.[8]

The Times appealed to the Supreme Court of the United States. In addition to procedural issues, the Times argued that the First Amendment would not permit a public official like Sullivan to collect damages for presumed damages for statements critical of his performance in office. Such an approach would leave open the door for public officials and governments to silence their opponents by using the courts and the tool of the libel case.

In the oral argument before the Supreme Court, M. Roland Nachman, Jr., the attorney for Commissioner Sullivan, and Justice White took up the matter of how careful publishers would have to be in printing stories about public officials.

White: But if were held here that a newspaper could publish a falsehood which it thought to be true, that would still not save the Times here?

Nachman: You mean a reasonable belief in truth?

White: Yes.

Nachman: No, sir, not under Alabama law. It would have to be true.[9]

---

[8] Anthony Lewis, Make No Law, Random House, New York, 1991, p.35.

[9] Peter Irons, editor, "May It Please The Court The First Amendment," (New York, The New Press, 1997), at 176.

Alabama law, like that in most states, held publishers liable for defamatory statements. Truth could serve as a defense, but inaccuracies would take away that defense and leave publishers open to damage awards even when they published in good faith. That meant that, without a First Amendment defense, the *Times* would have to pay all the libel judgments. The effect would be to stop the *Times* and every other news organization covering the civil rights movement. Beyond that, every publisher would have to stop coverage of public officials for fear that some story would contain an error and result in a costly defamation suit.

The Supreme Court agreed and reversed the decision, holding that the Alabama rule of law was "constitutionally deficient for failure to provide the safeguards for freedom of speech and of the press that are required by the First and Fourteenth Amendments * * *."

One issue was the fact that the statement at issue came in an advertisement. Sullivan had argued that advertisements did not deserve the First Amendment protection sought by the Times. The Court disagreed, saying that the advertisement:[10]

> ... communicated information, expressed opinion, recited grievances, protested claimed abuses, and sought financial support on behalf of a movement whose existence and objectives are matters of the highest public concern * * *. That the Times was paid for publishing the advertisement is as immaterial in this connection as is the fact that newspapers and books are sold * * *. Any other conclusion would discourage newspapers from carrying "editorial advertisements" of this type, and so might shut off an important outlet for the promulgation of information and ideas by persons who do not themselves have access to publishing facilities—who wish to exercise their freedom of speech even though they are not members of the press. The effect would be to shackle the First Amendment * * *.

The Court said that the question about the advertisement was whether it forfeited constitutional protection "by the falsity of some of its factual statements and by its alleged defamation of respondent".

The Court rejected the position that the falsity of some of the factual statements in the advertisement destroyed constitutional protection for the Times and the clergymen. "[E]rroneous statement is inevitable in free debate, and * * * it must be protected if the freedoms of expression are to have the 'breathing space' that

---

10 Ibid., at 266, 84 S.Ct. at 718.

they need to survive, * * * "it ruled. Quoting the decision in Sweeney v. Patterson,[11] it added that " 'Cases which impose liability for erroneous reports of the political conduct of officials reflect the obsolete doctrine that the governed must not criticize their governors * * *. Whatever is added to the field of libel is taken from the field of free debate.' "

Elaborating the matter of truth and error, it said that it is not enough for a state to provide in its law that the defendant may plead the truth of his words, although that has long been considered a bulwark for protection of expression:[12]

> A rule compelling the critic of official conduct to guarantee the truth of all his factual assertions—and to do so on pain of libel judgments virtually unlimited in amount—leads to * * * "self-censorship." Allowance of the defense of truth, with the burden of proving it on the defendant, does not mean that only false speech will be deterred.

This was the end for Alabama's rule that "the defendant has no defense as to stated facts unless he can persuade the jury that they were true in all their particulars." But the decision reached much farther than to Alabama: Most states had similar rules under which public officials had successfully brought libel suits for decades. In holding that the Constitution protects even erroneous statements about public officials in their public acts, the Court was providing protection that only a minority of states had provided previously.

Having decided that the constitutional protection was not destroyed by the falsity of factual statements in the advertisement, the Court added that the protection was not lost through defamation of an official. "Criticism of their official conduct," the Court held, "does not lose its constitutional protection merely because it is effective criticism and hence diminishes their official reputations."[13]

Then Justice Brennan, who wrote the majority decision, stated the circumstances under which a public official could recover damages for false defamation: Only if actual malice were present in the publication:[14]

> The constitutional guarantees require, we think, a federal rule that prohibits a public official from recovering damages for a defamatory falsehood relating to his official

---

[11] Sweeney v. Patterson, 76 U.S.App.D.C. 23, 128 F.2d 457, 458 (1942).

[12] New York Times Co. v. Sullivan, 376 U.S. 254, 279, 84 S.Ct. 710, 725 (1964).

[13] Ibid., at 273, 84 S.Ct. at 722.

[14] Ibid., at 279–280, 84 S.Ct. 725–726.

conduct unless he proves that the statement was made with "actual malice"—that is, with knowledge that it was false or with reckless disregard of whether it was false or not.

Malice in the new context was no longer the vague, shifting concept of ancient convenience for judges who had been shocked or angered by words harshly critical of public officials. It was not the oft-used "evidence of ill-will" on the part of the publisher; it was not "hatred" of the publisher for the defamed; it was not "intent to harm" the defamed. Rather, the actual malice which the plaintiff would have to plead and prove lay in the publisher's knowledge that what he printed was false, or else disregard on the part of the publisher as to whether it was false or not.

The old, tort-based libel requirement that the publisher would have to prove the truth of his words disappeared in Brennan's formulation: No longer would the publisher carry the burden; instead, the plaintiff official would have to prove falsity. Further, it would not be enough for the plaintiff to prove knowing or reckless falsity by "the preponderance of evidence." Instead, he would have to prove it "with convincing clarity." Also, to learn whether the trial court had properly applied the law in this important case over how expression might be regulated, the appellate courts were to independently review the trial record itself to make sure that there had been no forbidden intrusion on free expression.[15]

As court interpretation and litigation proceeded after these drastic revisions of the libel law of centuries, New York Times Co. v. Sullivan came to be recognized as the most important First Amendment case for decades. Famed attorney Floyd Abrams termed the decision "majestic," and "one of the most far reaching, extraordinary, and beautiful decisions in American history."[16]

SEC. 29.   ACTUAL MALICE

Courts examine reporting procedures in testing for actual malice, and find reckless disregard for falsity much more often than knowledge of falsity.

If a libel plaintiff is found by the judge to be a public official or public figure, the plaintiff's next move is to try to show that the

[15] Ibid., at 285, 84 S.Ct. 728. Reaffirmed 20 years later by the Supreme Court in Bose Corp. v. Consumers Union, 466 U.S. 485, 104 S.Ct. 1949 (1984), 10 Med.L.Rptr. 1625, 1636–1639, this rule was held to govern all appellate courts in the determination of actual malice under *Sullivan,* rather than a lesser legal standard which provides that trial-court findings of fact are not to be set aside by appellate courts unless they are "clearly erroneous." Appeals courts have usually practiced independent review: LDRC Bulletin #13, Spring 1985, 2.

[16] 10 Med.L.Rptr. #17, 4/24/84, News Notes.

offending words were published with actual malice. This term, as we have seen, is defined by the Supreme Court as reckless disregard for falsity in the words, or as knowledge that the publication is false. The burden is on the plaintiff to prove falsity, although the defendant may well undertake to demonstrate truth—a complete privilege.

It is worth remembering that, as was said earlier, the actual malice of *Sullivan* is quite different from the concept "malice" as it is usually understood. The word ordinarily has to do with hostility, ill will, spite, intent to harm—as, indeed, it was defined in libel law for generations before *Sullivan,* and as it continues to be defined in its tort-related sense in state libel law where the constitutional standard does not apply. But old-style malice can play a part in determining the existence of constitutional malice. Evidence that the publisher harbored ill feelings toward the plaintiff may help the jury conclude that such hatred took the form of publishing knowing falsehoods or a willingness to publish with reckless disregard of the falsity.

The Supreme Court has said that "actual malice" is a "term of art, created to provide a convenient shorthand expression for the standard of liability that must be established"[17] where public persons bring libel suits. The court that is trying the libel issue must direct itself to the factual issue as to the defendant's subjective knowledge of actual falsity or his high degree of awareness of probable falsity before publishing.[18]

Very soon after *Sullivan* had established the new definition of actual malice, the Supreme Court began the process of defining "reckless disregard." In Garrison v. Louisiana, [19] a criminal libel action, it said that reckless disregard means a "high degree of awareness of probable falsity" of the publication. In a non-media civil libel case where one candidate for public office sued his opponent (St. Amant v. Thompson), the Supreme Court said that for reckless disregard to be found, "There must be sufficient evidence to permit the conclusion that the defendant in fact entertained serious doubts as to the truth of his publication."[20]

Garrison was convicted of criminal libel, and the Supreme Court of the United States reversed the conviction. It said that the fact that the case was a criminal case made no difference to the principles of the Times v. Sullivan rule, and that malice would have to be shown. And the "reckless disregard" of truth or falsity in malice, it said, lies in a "high degree of awareness of probable

---

[17] Cantrell v. Forest City Pub. Co., 419 U.S. 245, 95 S.Ct. 465 (1974).

[18] Orr v. Argus–Press Co., 586 F.2d 1108 (6th Cir.1978).

[19] Garrison v. Louisiana, 379 U.S. 64, 74, 85 S.Ct. 209, 216 (1964).

[20] St. Amant v. Thompson, 390 U.S. 727, 731, 88 S.Ct. 1323, 1325 (1968).

falsity" on the part of the publisher. Nothing indicated that Garrison had this awareness of falsity when he castigated the Louisiana judges.[21]

Since the first case providing the constitutional protection in libel, the courts have been at pains to distinguish between "reckless disregard of truth" and "negligence."[22] Negligence is not enough to sustain a finding of actual malice. In the leading case, the Court went to this point. Errors in the famous advertisement, "Heed Their Rising Voices," could have been discovered by the *New York Times* advertising staff had it taken an elevator up a floor to the morgue and checked earlier stories on file. Failure to make this check, the Supreme Court said, did not constitute "reckless disregard;" at the worst it was negligence, and negligence is not enough to indicate actual malice.[23]

In Washington Post v. Keogh, a Congressman sued the newspaper for a story by columnist Drew Pearson which the Post carried. The story accused the congressman of bribe-splitting. The Post did not check the accuracy of the columnist's charges. The Federal Court of Appeals held that the Post showed no reckless disregard in not verifying Pearson's charge, regardless of Pearson's shaky reputation for accuracy. The court held that to require such checking by the Post would be to burden it with greater responsibilities of verification than the Supreme Court required of the *New York Times* in the landmark case. It said:[24]

> Verification is * * * a costly process, and the newspaper business is one in which survival has become a major problem. * * * We should be hesitant to impose responsibilities upon newspapers which can be met only through costly procedures or through self-censorship designed to avoid risks of publishing controversial material.

[21] Garrison v. Louisiana, 379 U.S. 64, 85 S.Ct. 209 (1964). The case arose in a dispute between Garrison, who achieved national notoriety for his investigation of the John F. Kennedy assassination, and eight judges of the Criminal District Court. It began with a judge denying Garrison money from a fines and fees fund for office furnishings. Garrison obtained the money by going to a different judge and misrepresenting that the first judge had withdrawn his objection. The eight judges responded by requiring that at least five approve further disbursements to Garrison's office. Garrison then asked for money for undercover agents investigating vice in the Bourbon and Canal Street districts. The judges refused citing Louisiana constitutional concerns. The judge from the original controversy then criticized Garrison's conduct in office. Garrison replied with a press conference of his own in which he suggested that the judges had been influenced by racketeers and were lazy.

[22] Priestley v. Hastings & Sons Pub. Co. of Lynn, 360 Mass. 118, 271 N.E.2d 628 (1971); A.S. Abell Co. v. Barnes, 258 Md. 56, 265 A.2d 207 (1970).

[23] New York Times Co. v. Sullivan, 376 U.S. 254, 288, 84 S.Ct. 710, 730 (1964).

[24] Washington Post Co. v. Keogh, 125 U.S.App.D.C. 32, 365 F.2d 965, 972–973 (1966).

In the foregoing decisions in *Garrison* and *Keogh*, courts defined reckless disregard by saying what it is *not*. Defining reckless disregard can be difficult for practitioners and so it is a troubling issue for professional communicators. A more easily understandable, common sense analysis was offered in Dombey v. Phoenix Newspapers, Inc.,[25] where the Arizona Supreme Court said:

> The disregard must be more than "reckless"—conscious disregard would be a better description of the test.

> [R]eckless conduct is not measured by whether a reasonably prudent man would have published, or would have investigated before publishing. There must be sufficient evidence to permit the conclusion that the defendant in fact entertained serious doubts as to the truth of his publication. Publishing with such doubts shows reckless disregard for truth or falsity and demonstrates actual malice.[26]

The Arizona court acknowledged that its preference in analyzing reckless disregard would protect some less-than-admirable publishers, but that it was a cost of doing business under the First Amendment.

> It may be said that such a test puts a premium on ignorance, encourages the irresponsible publisher not to inquire, and permits the issue to be determined by the defendant's testimony that he published the statement in good faith and unaware of its probable falsity. Concededly the reckless disregard standard may permit recovery in fewer situations. . . . But to insure the ascertainment and publication of the truth about public affairs, it is essential that the First Amendment protect some erroneous publications as well as true ones.[27]

In the actual malice analysis we spend less time on knowledge of falsity than on reckless disregard. That is a matter of practicality. It is rare that a publisher will have admitted to publishing, knowing that the defamatory statement is false. Where such evidence exists, the fault issue will be a moot point. But there are some that come from time to time.

Knowing Falsity

One case involved a suit by State Sen. Richard Schermerhorn of New York. He was interviewed by reporter Ron Rosenberg of the Middletown *Times Herald Record* about the senator's proposal for

---

[25] Dombey v. Phoenix Newspapers, Inc., 150 Ariz. 476, 724 P.2d 562, 573 (1986), 13 Med.L.Rptr. 1282.

[26] Ibid. At 487.

[27] Ibid. Quoting St. Amant v. Thompson, 390 U.S. 727, 88 S.Ct. 1323 (1968).

the redevelopment plan (the NDDC) in Newburgh. They discussed a community controversy about whether minorities' chances for benefiting from NDDC were sufficient. Rosenberg wrote a story which was published under the headline SCHERMERHORN SAYS NDDC CAN DO WITHOUT BLACKS. There was no reference to this in the story. A storm of protest against the senator arose, and Senators Beatty and von Luther proposed a resolution of censure in the Senate against Schermerhorn. In a later story, Beatty was quoted as saying that he had access to tapes in which Schermerhorn made subtle anti-black and anti-Semitic statements.

Schermerhorn denied making the headline statement and told his Senate colleagues that if there were tapes showing he had made such statements, he would be unfit to serve in the Senate and would resign. He brought a libel suit, and charged knowing falsehood.[28] At trial, Rosenberg agreed that Schermerhorn had not told him what the headline reported, and that a copy editor—who was never produced at the trial—had written it. But both von Luther and Beatty testified, that, in telephone calls to them, Rosenberg had assured them that Schermerhorn had said that the NDDC could do without blacks, and von Luther added that Rosenberg volunteered that he had a tape in which Schermerhorn made racial and ethnic slurs. The tape was never produced, although both senators testified that they made repeated requests for it.

The jury was unconvinced that a copy editor who never showed up for Rosenberg's trial had written the headline, and in addition, the jury had von Luther's and Beatty's testimony that Rosenberg assured them the headline was accurate. The jury brought in a verdict of $36,000 in damages for Schermerhorn. The New York Supreme Court, Appellate Division, upheld the verdict on three of four counts saying "In our view, then, the evidence was sufficient to sustain the jury's determination that Rosenberg * * * had composed a defamatory headline with actual knowledge that the matter asserted therein was false."[29]

Rational Interpretation and Time Inc. v. Pape

In a case that tested the bounds of knowing falsity and helped expand the protections of media, the Supreme Court took up the case of the deputy chief of detectives of the Chicago Police Department against Time Magazine.[30]

---

[28] Schermerhorn v. Rosenberg, 73 A.D.2d 276, 426 N.Y.S.2d 274 (1980), 6 Med. L.Rptr. 1376.

[29] Ibid., 1381. See also Morgan v. Dun & Bradstreet, Inc., 421 F.2d 1241 (5th Cir.1970); Sprouse v. Clay Communication, Inc., 158 W.Va. 427, 211 S.E.2d 674 (1975).

[30] Time, Inc. v. Pape, 401 U.S. 279, 91 S.Ct. 633 (1971).

In November 1961, the United States Commission on Civil Rights issued the fifth volume of its Report for that year, a document entitled "Justice." A part of "Justice" was devoted to a study of "police brutality and related private violence," and contained the following paragraph:

"Search, seizure, and violence: Chicago, 1958.—The Supreme Court of the United States decided the case of Monroe v. Pape on February 20, 1961. Although this decision did not finally dispose of the case, it did permit the plaintiff to sue several Chicago police officers for violation of the Federal Civil Rights Acts on the basis of a complaint which *alleged* (emphasis supplied) that: '. . . On October 29, 1958, at 5:45 a. m., thirteen Chicago police officers led by Deputy Chief of Detectives Pape, broke through two doors of the Monroe apartment, woke the Monroe couple with flashlights, and forced them at gunpoint to leave their bed and stand naked in the center of the living room; that the officers roused the six Monroe children and herded them into the living room; that Detective Pape struck Mr. Monroe several times with his flashlight, calling him 'nigger' and 'black boy'; that another officer pushed Mrs. Monroe; that other officers hit and kicked several of the children and pushed them to the floor; that the police ransacked every room, throwing clothing from closets to the floor, dumping drawers, ripping mattress covers; that Mr. Monroe was then taken to the police station and detained on 'open' charges for ten hours, during which time he was interrogated about a murder and exhibited in lineups; that he was not brought before a magistrate, although numerous magistrate's courts were accessible; that he was not advised of his procedural rights; that he was not permitted to call his family or an attorney; that he was subsequently released without criminal charges having been filed against him.' "[31]

Time Magazine took up the issue, printing a report a week later. Time reported, "Justice carries a chilling text about police brutality in both the South and the North—and it stands as a grave indictment, since its facts were carefully investigated by field agents and it was signed by all six of the noted educators who comprise the commission."[32] Time quoted at length from Monroe's story. But Time failed to say that the allegations were Monroe's rather than the Commission's. Instead, the article made it appear that the statements were factual findings of the Commission.

Pape sued. He and other Chicago police officers testified that nothing like the complaint occurred at the Monroe residence. When the case reached the Supreme Court, the justices were faced with the question of whether Time's reporting, with the knowledge that

[31] Ibid. At 281.
[32] Ibid. At 282–283.

it had reported as fact what were allegations, constituted actual malice. Time did not claim mistake. The writer and the researcher acknowledged that the article was different from the wording of the report. But, they added, it was true to the essential meaning of what the Commission reported.

The Supreme Court decided that the Time report amounted to a report that was a "rational interpretation" of the Commission's report, which was itself subject to a number of interpretations. As such, Time's story did not rise to the level of actual malice. That does not mean that "alleged" will immunize defamatory statements. Calling someone an "alleged killer" still labels him killer.

With that warning we move on to those cases resting on the resolution of the reckless disregard issue.

Curtis Publishing Co. v. Butts & Associated Press v. Walker

And so, our cases focus on finding those factors that constitute reckless disregard. Curtis Publishing Co. v. Butts.[33] In that case, decided along with the case of Walker v. Associated Press, helped to establish what would and would not be considered reckless disregard. Wally Butts was the athletic director at the University of Georgia. He was the subject of an "investigative" story in the Saturday Evening Post that ran under the headline, "The Story of a College Football Fix."

The story ran with the following editor's note, "Not since the Chicago White Sox threw the 1919 World Series has there been a sports story as shocking as this one.... Before the University of Georgia played the University of Alabama ... Wally Butts ... gave [to its coach] ... Georgia's plays, defensive patterns, all the significant secrets Georgia's football team possessed."[34] The story began when Atlanta insurance salesman George Burnett stopped at a restaurant with a another man to make a telephone call. Through some crossed wires, Burnett overheard a conversation between Butts and Alabama football coach Paul "Bear" Bryant about a week before Georgia played Alabama.

Burnett took what he said he heard to the Saturday Evening Post. Burnett told the Post that he heard Butts giving Bryant Georgia's game plan and plays. The Post reported that, "the Georgia players, their moves analyzed and forecast like those of rats in a maze, took a frightful physical beating."[35] The Post reported on Alabama's victory and said that players and those on the sidelines knew of the betrayal. The magazine reported that

[33] Curtis Publishing Co. v. Butts, 388 U.S. 130, 87 S.Ct. 1975 (1967).

[34] Ibid. At 136.

[35] Ibid.

Burnett turned his notes of the telephone conversation over to Georgia's head coach, that Butts resigned his position for health and business reasons and what it expected the article would do to the former athletic director, "The chances are that Wally Butts will never help any football team again. * * * The investigation by university and Southeastern Conference officials is continuing; motion pictures of other games are being scrutinized; where it will end no one so far can say. But careers will be ruined, that is sure."[36]

Butts sued, claiming that while Burnett had overheard the conversation between him and Bryant, he gave no secrets away. He won $60,000 in actual damages and $3 million in punitive. The trial court reduced the total to $460,000.[37] He appealed and the Supreme Court considered his case along with that of Edwin Walker, a former Army general who was suing the Associated Press over a report of his involvement in a riot on the campus of the University of Mississippi. The Supreme Court held that Butts was a public figure because of the public interest in what he did. It then applied an actual malice analysis.

The evidence showed that the Butts story was in no sense "hot news" and the editors of the magazine recognized the need for a thorough investigation of the serious charges. Elementary precautions were, nevertheless, ignored. The Saturday Evening Post knew that Burnett had been placed on probation in connection with bad check charges, but proceeded to publish the story on the basis of his affidavit without substantial independent support. Burnett's notes were not even viewed by any of the magazine's personnel prior to publication. John Carmichael, who was supposed to have been with Burnett when the phone call was overheard, was not interviewed. No attempt was made to screen the films of the game to see if Burnett's information was accurate, and no attempt was made to find out whether Alabama had adjusted its plans after the alleged divulgence of information.

The Post writer assigned to the story was not a football expert and no attempt was made to check the story with someone knowledgeable in the sport. At trial such experts indicated that the information in the Burnett notes was either such that it would be evident to any opposing coach from game films regularly exchanged or valueless. * * * The Saturday Evening Post was anxious to change its image by instituting a policy of "sophisticated muckraking," and the pressure to produce a successful expose might have induced a stretching of standards. In short, the evidence is ample to support a finding of highly unreasonable conduct constituting an

[36] Ibid.

[37] Bryant filed his own suit but settled with Curtis Publishing.

extreme departure from the standards of investigation and reporting ordinarily adhered to by responsible publishers.[38]

The Court reached a different conclusion in *Walker*. Retired Maj. Gen. Edwin A. Walker, had resigned from the Army in 1961 after a storm of controversy over his troop-indoctrination program. Opposed to the integration of the University of Mississippi, he had in 1962 appeared on the scene there when James H. Meredith became the school's first black student. Dan Rather, covering the story for CBS, wrote in his autobiography, The Camera Never Blinks, about Walker's appearance on the campus where he lectured, "the students and rednecks who poured in." Rather described the scene, writing, "It struck me as rather comic, a former Army general standing under those hundred-year-old trees, rallying southern manhood against the threat of one lonely black freshman. But I quickly changed my mind. I could see what was coming like a storm at sea."[39] Thousands rioted. Two people were killed, including a foreign reporter, and hundreds injured. It took federal marshals and troops to restore order.

An Associated Press dispatch, circulated to member newspapers around the nation, said that Walker had taken command of a violent crowd and had personally led a charge against federal marshals. Further, it described Walker as encouraging rioters to use violence.

Walker's chain libel suits totaled $23,000,000 against the *Louisville Courier–Journal* and *Louisville Times* and their radio station; against *Atlanta Newspapers Inc.* and publisher Ralph McGill; against the Associated Press, the *Denver Post*, the *Fort Worth Star–Telegram* and its publisher, Amon G. Carter, Jr.; against *Newsweek*, the Pulitzer Publishing Co. (*St. Louis Post–Dispatch*), and against the *Delta* (Miss.) *Democrat-Times* and its editor, Hodding Carter.[40]

Walker had won $500,000 against the Associated Press in a suit he filed in Texas. The case made it to the U.S. Supreme Court. Justice Harlan looked to the facts brought out in the trial. Walker admitted he had gone to the campus and said that he had talked to a group of students. But he said, he "counseled restraint and peaceful protest, and exercised no control whatever over the crowd which had rejected his plea. He denied categorically taking part in any charge against the federal marshals."[41]

[38] Curtis Publishing Co. v. Butts, 388 U.S. 130, 157–158, 87 S.Ct. 1975 (1967).

[39] Dan Rather and Mickey Herskowitz, "The Camera Never Blinks," (William Morrow, New York, 1977), at 74.

[40] Editor & Publisher, Oct. 5, 1963, p. 10.

[41] Associated Press v. Walker, 388 U.S. 130, 141, 87 S.Ct. 1975 (1967).

There wasn't much about the reporting. The reporter, Van Savell, was at the scene and reported the story to the AP. The evidence showed a discrepancy between a call to the wire service and a written story, but it the sole difference was about whether Walker had spoken to the group before or after approaching the marshals. "No other showing of improper preparation was attempted, nor was there any evidence of personal prejudice or incompetency on the part of Savell or the Associated Press."[42] The trial court refused to find that assigning a young reporter constituted actual malice. The Court found, "nothing in this series of events gives the slightest hint of a severe departure from accepted publishing standards. We therefore conclude that General Walker should not be entitled to damages from the Associated Press."[43]

St. Amant v. Thompson

A year later, the Court took up the issue of reckless disregard and laid out a whole laundry list of things that could lead to a finding of reckless disregard. St. Amant v. Thompson[44] is yet another case that does not involve journalists. Instead, it arose over a radio broadcast by a political candidate St. Amant, a candidate for public office, made a televised speech in Baton Rouge, Louisiana. In the course of this speech, St. Amant read a series of questions which he had put to J. D. Albin, a member of a Teamsters Union local, and Albin's answers to those questions. The exchange concerned the allegedly nefarious activities of E. G. Partin, the president of the local, and the alleged relationship between Partin and St. Amant's political opponent. Albin said that Partin had stolen union funds and had decided to get rid of a safe containing union records. Albin also referred to Herman A. Thompson, an East Baton Rouge Parish deputy sheriff and the person who sued St. Amant:

> "Now, we knew that this safe was gonna be moved that night, but imagine our predicament, knowing of Ed's connections with the Sheriff's office through Herman Thompson, who made recent visits to the Hall to see Ed. We also knew of money that had passed hands between Ed and Herman Thompson ... from Ed to Herman. We also knew of his connections with State Trooper Lieutenant Joe Green. We knew we couldn't get any help from there and we didn't know how far that he was involved in the Sheriff's office or the State Police office through that, and it was out of the jurisdiction of the City Police."[45]

---

[42] Ibid.

[43] Ibid. at 160.

[44] St. Amant v. Thompson, 390 U.S. 727, 88 S.Ct. 1323 (1968).

[45] Ibid. At 729.

Thompson sued over the statement. The Louisiana trial court found that the statement was defamatory and that St. Amant had broadcast with actual malice. The Louisiana Supreme Court agreed and affirmed the trial court. The U.S. Supreme Court disagreed saying, that the test required proof of knowing falsity or serious doubts as to truth.[46] In St. Amant's case, he had known Albin for eight months. St. Amant had verified other parts of Albin's claims and collected affidavits from others. Albin also gave an affidavit to reporters and St. Amant believed that Albin was placing himself at personal risk by revealing details about the union's activities.

It is the subjective belief of the defendant that is the test for finding reckless disregard, the Court said. But that does not mean that defendants can slide off the hook simply by swearing that they published with belief in the truth of what they said.

> "Professions of good faith will be unlikely to prove persuasive, for example, where a story is fabricated by the defendant, is the product of his imagination, or is based wholly on an unverified anonymous telephone call. Nor will they be likely to prevail when the publisher's allegations are so inherently improbable that only a reckless man would have put them in circulation. Likewise, recklessness may be found where there are obvious reasons to doubt the veracity of the informant or the accuracy of his reports."[47]

Investigative Reporting and Tavoulareas v. Washington Post

It is good to keep in mind the public's perception of journalists and the comments of the Supreme Court in *Butts*, in which the Saturday Evening Post's conduct was criticized. Justice Harlan talked about the Post's new-found commitment to investigative journalism and the effect of that new emphasis on its reporting. To journalists, investigative reporting is a high calling, a valued enterprise. They don't mind when they are called "muckrakers" when they try to find and to expose societal ills or corporate or governmental wrongdoing. It came as a shock, therefore when for a time the Washington Post was on the losing end of a $2 million libel award, with its investigative aggressiveness being used against the paper as evidence of its "actual malice."

The feisty and aggressive Mobil Oil Co. president, William Tavoulareas, sued the Post for a story saying he had "set up" his son to head an international tanker fleet carrying petroleum, implying misuse of his corporate position. Tavoulareas, a public figure, sued the Post for $100 million, claiming actual malice (knowing

---

[46] Ibid. At 731.

[47] Ibid. At 732.

falsity or reckless disregard for the truth) by the newspaper.[48] The jury agreed and awarded him $250,000 compensatory and $1.8 million punitive damages. But after reviewing the facts at length, the judge threw out the jury award (rendered a "judgment n.o.v."). He said that while the story in question was far short of being a model of fair, unbiased investigative journalism, there was "no evidence in the record * * * to show that it contained knowing lies or statements made in reckless disregard of the truth," and no evidence to support the jury's verdict.[49]

The U.S. Court of Appeals, District of Columbia Circuit, reversed the trial judge on a 2–1 vote, and reinstated the jury verdict of $2.05 million.[50] The majority found clear and convincing evidence of reckless disregard under the rules of *Butts, St. Amant,* and *Garrison* and added these other indicators of fault in the story: (1) The story carried on its face the warning to the newspaper that it had high potential for harm to Tavoulareas' reputation; (2) the journalists "were motivated by a plan to 'get' the plaintiffs, and deliberately slanted, rejected and ignored evidence contrary to the false premise of the story;" (3) the reporter's interview notes "reflect exactly the opposite of what he was told by the interviewees;" (4) the newspaper refused to retract the story or to print Tavoulareas' letter to the paper.[51]

In elaborating, Judge George MacKinnon (joined by Judge, and later, Supreme Court Justice Antonin Scalia) raised alarm among journalists. The Post's policy of exposing wrongdoing in public life might be characterized as "hard hitting investigative journalism" or as "sophisticated muckraking," the Court said, and either "certainly is relevant to the inquiry of whether a newspaper employee acted in reckless disregard of whether a statement is false or not." The suggestion that a newspaper's devotion to these two honored traditions in journalism might be evidence of reckless disregard of falsity shocked the field.

Judge J. Skelly Wright, at almost total odds with the court majority, spoke for countless journalists in his wide-ranging dissent that rejected MacKinnon's analysis. Holding that a newspaper policy of investigative journalism and muckraking could be evidence

---

[48] Tavoulareas v. Washington Post Co., 567 F.Supp. 651 (D.D.C.1983), 9 Med. L.Rptr. 1553.

[49] Ibid., 1555, 1561.

[50] Tavoulareas v. Washington Post, 759 F.2d 90 (D.C.Cir.1985), 11 Med.L.Rptr. 1777. The same judges denied a petition of the Post to re-hear the case on another 2–1 vote, 763 F.2d 1472 (D.C.Cir.1985); but the 3–member panel's decision was vacated by the full Circuit Court (10 judges), which voted to hear the case *en banc*: Ibid., 1481.

[51] Ibid., 134–135, 1809–1810.

of reporters' acting in reckless disregard of falsity endangered the First Amendment, Wright declared:[52]

> It is a conclusion fraught with the potential to shrink the First Amendment's "majestic protection" * * *.

> Muckraking—a term developed when writers like Lincoln Steffens, Ida Tarbell, and Upton Sinclair relentlessly exposed pervasive corruption—may be seen to serve that high purpose even if it offends and startles * * *.

Wright found in the majority opinion "deep hostility to an aggressive press" that "is directly contrary to the mandates of the Supreme Court and the spirit of a free press," and concluded that "neither a newspaper's muckraking policy nor its hard-hitting investigative journalism should *ever* be considered probative of actual malice."

Ultimately, the Washington Post was rescued by a rehearing of the case by the full panel of the U.S. Court of Appeals for the District of Columbia. That court (with Supreme Court Justice–Designate Antonin Scalia not participating) voted 7–1 to throw out the jury's $2.05 million verdict. The court decided that actual malice had not been proven against the Washington Post. Further, a reputation for "sensational" or investigative reporting was *not* to be taken as evidence of actual malice.[53]

Court-determined indicators of "reckless disregard" (which amount to court-determined standards of news reporting) do not end with those at issue in *Tavoulareas*. They include: where a reporter did not make personal contact with anyone involved in the event before writing;[54] where a publication relied on an obviously biased source, was advised of the falsity of information, and published with no further investigation of the story;[55] where the publication printed although the story was inherently improbable.[56] Ill will of the reporter toward the subject of the story may in some cases contribute to a finding of reckless disregard.[57]

---

[52] Ibid., 154, 1798, 1821–1822. For coverage of similar reactions from journalists, see Peter Prichard, "Tavoulareas Case Returns—with Bite," Quill, May 1985, 25; "Anthony Lewis, Getting Even," New York Times, 4/11/85, A27; Anon., "Press Must Be Tough, but Fair," Milwaukee Journal, 4/12/85, 14.

[53] Tavoulareas v. Washington Post Co., 817 F.2d 762 (D.C.Cir.1987), cert. denied by the Supreme Court of the United States, 484 U.S. 870, 108 S.Ct. 200 (1987).

[54] Akins v. Altus Newspapers, Inc., 609 P.2d 1263 (Okl.1977).

[55] Stevens v. Sun Pub. Co., 270 S.C. 65, 240 S.E.2d 812 (1978).

[56] Hunt v. Liberty Lobby, 720 F.2d 631 (11th Cir.1983), 10 Med.L.Rptr. 1097, 1107.

[57] Cochran v. Indianapolis Newspapers, Inc., 175 Ind.App. 548, 372 N.E.2d 1211 (1978), 3 Med.L.Rptr. 2131; Tavoulareas v. Washington Post, 759 F.2d 90, 114 (D.C.Cir.1985), 11 Med.L.Rptr. 1777, 1820, vacated 763 F.2d 1472 (1985), affirmed 817 F.2d 762 (D.C.Cir.1987).

Defining Reckless Disregard: Harte–
Hanks v. Connaughton (1989)

The *Connaughton* decision of 1989 marked the first time in two decades that the U.S. Supreme Court held against the media in a public figure libel case.[58] (Keep in mind, however, that the media have lost some public figure libel cases over the years in lower courts. See, for example, the $3.05 million libel loss incurred in Brown & Williamson v. Jacobson in 1987.)[59]

Harte–Hanks Communications, Inc. v. Connaughton says that the media may be held responsible for defamation in reporting on a candidate for public office if a jury could reasonably find "actual malice" misconduct by news organizations. The key here turned on how "reckless disregard for the truth" was defined.

The case arose in 1983 because of judicial election reporting by the Hamilton, Ohio, Journal–News, owned by Harte–Hanks until 1986. The newspaper published a story about municipal judge candidate Daniel Connaughton. The newspaper, which had endorsed Connaughton's opponent, published assertions that Connaughton had promised a grand jury witness and her sister jobs and trips if they would provide testimony embarrassing to his opponent for the judgeship.[60] (It did not help appearances that the Journal–News was in a circulation battle with the Cincinnati Enquirer, a newspaper which endorsed Connaughton.)

Connaughton lost the election, and sued the Hamilton Journal–News for defamation. The newspaper tried to defend itself by asserting a "neutral reportage" (see discussion later in this chapter) privilege to present accurate and unbiased accounts of charges against a public figure/political candidate. The newspaper asked unsuccessfully for a summary judgment.[61]

Hindsight suggests that the Journal–News exposed itself to liability by failing to investigate thoroughly. When questioned by a reporter, Connaughton reportedly denied offering grand jury witnesses jobs or trips. Perhaps most damaging to the newspaper: It published its attack on Connaughton without interviewing key sources—who had been identified to the newspaper as such—whose denials could have put an end to the derogatory stories about Connaughton. Also, the newspaper decided not to listen to tape

[58] Harte–Hanks Communications, Inc. v. Connaughton, 491 U.S. 657, 109 S.Ct. 2678 (1989), 16 Med.L.Rptr. 1881; News Media & the Law, Summer, 1989, p. 16.

[59] Brown & Williamson Tobacco Corp. v. Jacobson, 827 F.2d 1119 (7th Cir.1987), 14 Med.L.Rptr. 1497, cert. denied 485 U.S. 993, 108 S.Ct. 1302 (1988).

[60] Harte–Hanks Communications, Inc. v. Connaughton, 491 U.S. 657, 660, 109 S.Ct. 2678, 2682 (1989), 16 Med.L.Rptr. at 1883.

[61] Ibid.

recordings available to it which could have provided additional information. As Justice John Paul Stevens wrote for the Court:[62]

> ... [D]iscrepancies in the testimony of Journal–News witnesses may have given the jury the impression that the failure to conduct a complete investigation involved a deliberate effort to avoid the truth.

And that adds up to actual malice. The key lesson for journalists is that they must not cut corners. They should always assume that non-journalists—such as members of a jury—may eventually be looking over their shoulders. The practical reporter's internal voice must keep asking: "If we publish this, will I be able to explain what I did to a jury?"

The jury in the Connaughton case did not believe the newspaper's explanations, and assessed damages totaling $200,000: $5,000 compensatory, and $195,000 punitive.[63] Upholding that outcome, Justice Stevens wrote:[64]

> ... [I]t is clear that the conclusion concerning the newspaper's departure from accepted standards and the evidence of motive were merely supportive of the court's ultimate conclusion that the record "demonstrated a reckless disregard as to the truth or falsity ... [of the largely unsupported allegations against Connaughton] ... and thus provided clear and convincing proof of 'actual malice' as found by the jury." 842 F.2d at 847. Although courts must be careful not to place too much reliance on such factors, a plaintiff is entitled to prove the defendant's state of mind through circumstantial evidence, see Herbert v. Lando, 441 U.S. 153, 99 S.Ct. 1635 (1979).

Prozeralik v. Capital Cities, Inc.

The case of Prozeralik v. Capital Cities, Inc.[65] provides a warning about the need to double check facts. *Prozeralik* began with a report of an abduction and beating in the Niagara Falls area of New York. The identity of the victim was not released, but the case was linked to organized crime and it was suggested that the victim was a local restaurateur. During a news meeting at a Capital Cities television and radio station, the news staff speculated about

---

[62] Ibid., 684–685, 2694, 1893.

[63] Damages are discussed in Sec. 24.

[64] Harte–Hanks Communications, Inc. v. Connaughton, 491 U.S. 657, 697, 109 S.Ct. 2678, 2701 (1989), 16 Med.L.Rptr. at 1886. Justice Stevens also emphasized judges' constitutional duty to " 'exercise independent judgment and determine whether the record establishes actual malice with convincing clarity,' "quoting Bose v. Consumers Union, 466 U.S. 485, 514, 104 S.Ct. 1949, 1967 (1984): See 10 Med.L.Rptr. 1625, 1682.

[65] Prozeralik v. Capital Cities, Inc., 222 A.D.2d 1020, 635 N.Y.S.2d 913 (1995).

the identity of the beating victim. John Prozeralik's name came up. It was pure speculation, based only on the fact that Prozeralik was a restaurateur in the area, the owner of John's Flaming Hearth Restaurant.

The station's noon news anchor took that name and contacted the FBI. What happened during that telephone call was hotly disputed. The anchor testified that she brought up Prozeralik's name and the FBI's media coordinator, an Agent Thurston, told her, "You can go with that unless I call you back."[66] Thurston hotly denied saying that. He told the trial court that he did not provide Prozeralik's name or confirm that he was the victim (The victim was one David Pasquantino and not Prozeralik). Thurston denied telling the anchor she could go with the name unless he called back. The evidence showed that such procedure was not Thurston's normal method of operation.

The stations ran several stories that identified Prozeralik as the victim. Prozeralik and his attorney called and denied any involvement. The station news director then called Thurston back and Thurston said he did not know the victim's identity when the anchor called nor did he confirm it was Prozeralik. The station then ran retractions that included the following: "Tonight, we have developments on two fronts in the abduction that ended yesterday in a Cheektowaga motel. First, the victim is not, and I repeat, is not, John Prozeralik, the operator of John's Flaming Hearth Restaurant. The FBI earlier today said and confirmed the victim was Prozeralik, but our independent investigation is revealing he was not involved * * * "[67]

As a practical matter, it probably did not advance the station's cause to publicly blame the FBI for the mistaken identity and further take credit for eliminating Prozeralik as the victim when Prozeralik himself called the station to deny being the beating victim. Additional problems arising in the case included the fact that a rival television station had correctly identified the victim the day before the defendant station broadcast its first story and the fact that the plaintiff's attorney could point to the pressures of the sweeps competition at the time. Professional communicators should keep in mind their relative positions in the public eye. A Harris poll reported in the National Law Journal placed journalists at the bottom of a list of 11 occupations. The poll asked more than a thousand adults which occupations had "very great prestige." It was a repetition of a similar poll of more than a thousand adults taken in 1977. In 1977, 17 percent of the public thought that

---

[66] Prozeralik v. Capital Cities Communications, Inc., 82 N.Y.2d 466, 471, 605 N.Y.S.2d 218, 220–221, 626 N.E.2d 34, 36–37 (1993), 21 Med. L. Rptr. 2257, 2258.

[67] Ibid.

journalists had "very great prestige." In 1997, it had dropped to 15 percent.[68] With that perception, putting the word of a broadcast journalist against that of an FBI agent becomes problematic.

Altered Quotes: Masson v. The New Yorker, Alfred A. Knopf, and Janet Malcolm (1991)

If a writer alters an interview subject's quotations materially, is that "knowing falsity?" That was a key issue in a decade-long defamation suit which resulted in a Supreme Court decision[69] and which finally seemed to have been resolved by a November, 1994, jury verdict. The case, described as a soap-opera for the highly literate, involved a defamation suit by a flamboyant psychiatrist against a gifted writer of biographical profiles whose work frequently appears in The New Yorker. Once the case reached Supreme Court, its ruling meant that the psychiatrist had overcome a lower court's summary judgment ruling against him and could force the author to trial on his libel suit.[70] So in the fall of 1994, the dispute was back where it had started in 1983, in a U.S. district court in San Francisco.[71]

In 1983, psychiatrist Jeffrey M. Masson sued for defamation based on a two-part article by Janet Malcolm, first appearing in The New Yorker, and later published in book form by Knopf. The article/book stemmed from Ms. Malcolm's extensive tape-recorded interviews with Dr. Masson and dealt with his dismissal from his post as projects director of the Sigmund Freud Archives.

In his lawsuit, Dr. Masson argued that Ms. Malcolm had " . . . fabricated words attributed to him with quotation marks, and misleadingly edited his statements to make him appear 'unscholarly, irresponsible, vain and lacking in personal honesty or moral integrity.' "[72] Masson contended that the magazine and Knopf knew of author Malcolm's misconduct before the book and the article were published.

All three defendants were granted summary judgments by a federal district court on the grounds that Dr. Masson had not established actual malice: " 'No clear and convincing evidence ex-

---

[68] Chris Klein, "Poll: Lawyers Not Liked," The National Law Journal, Aug. 25, 1997, p. A6. The story focused on the public's perception of lawyers, but it included journalists, who occupied the lowest ranking for both the 1977 and the 1997 polls.

[69] Masson v. New Yorker Magazine, Inc., 501 U.S. 496, 111 S.Ct. 2419 (1991), 18 Med.L.Rptr. 2241.

[70] Masson v. New Yorker Magazine, Inc., 881 F.2d 1452 (9th Cir.1989), 16 Med.L.Rptr. 2089.

[71] Seth Mydans, "New Libel Trial Opens With Blocks," The New York Times, Oct. 4, 1994, p. A13.

[72] Masson v. Malcolm, 881 F.2d at 1453, 16 Med.L.Rptr. at 2089–2090.

ists that would justify a holding that ... [the defendants] entertained serious doubts about the truth of the disputed passages.' "[73]

As a public figure, Dr. Masson was required by the Constitution to prove actual malice, and he had argued that a jury could find that standard of fault based on evidence of deliberately fabricated quotes that had been attributed to him. Dr. Masson presented evidence that several quotes ascribed to him did not appear on Ms. Malcolm's tape recordings, and contended that the writer herself had altered other quotes.

After the 1991 Supreme Court decision remanded the Masson case to the Ninth Circuit Court of Appeals, that court held the jury issue was whether Ms. Malcolm and the magazine abused the public trust by knowingly or recklessly published falsehoods.[74]

One of the disputed passages as published in Ms. Malcolm's writings involved her use of quotation marks around Dr. Masson's description of his plans to occupy Maresfield Gardens (home of the Freud Archives) after the elderly Anna Freud's death. Consider Justice Kennedy's repetition of that passage, and his comment upon it:[75]

> " 'It was a beautiful house, but it was dark and sombre and dead. * * * I would have renovated it, opened it up, brought it to life. Maresfield Gardens would have been a place of scholarship but also of sex, women, fun. It would have been like the change in The Wizard of Oz, from black-and-white into color.' " In the Freud Archives 33.

> [Justice Kennedy then commented:] The tape recordings contain a similar statement, but in place of the reference to "sex, women and fun," and the Wizard of Oz, petitioner [Masson] commented [in the tape recorded interview]:

> "[I]t is an incredible storehouse. I mean, the library, Freud's library alone is priceless in terms of what it contains; all his books with his annotations in them; the Schreber case annotated, that kind of thing. It's fascinating."

Even though the Supreme Court's 7–2 decision meant that Ms. Malcolm could not escape a libel trial via summary judgment,[76] the majority opinion was a great relief to lawyers for the news media.[77]

---

[73] Masson v. Malcolm, 881 F.2d at 1453, 16 Med.L.Rptr. at 2090.

[74] Masson v. The New Yorker, Alfred A. Knopf, and Janet Malcolm, 960 F.2d 896, 902–903 (9th Cir.1992), 20 Med.L.Rptr. 1009, 1014–1015.

[75] Masson v. New Yorker Magazine, Inc., 501 U.S. at 503, 111 S.Ct. at 2426 (1991), 18 Med.L.Rptr. at 2245.

[76] "Summary judgment" procedures terminate a lawsuit unless the plaintiff can make a good showing of having a strong case.

[77] Linda Greenhouse, "Justices Refuse to Open a Gate for Libel Cases," The New York Times, June 21, 1991, p. A1.

Justice Anthony M. Kennedy wrote that deliberate misquotation of a public figure cannot be libelous unless the wording changes the meaning of what really was said.[78]

Some excerpts from Justice Kennedy's opinion follow:[79]

In general, quotation marks around a passage indicate to the reader that the passage reproduces the speaker's words verbatim. They inform the reader that he or she is reading the statement of the speaker, not a paraphrase or other indirect interpretation by an author. By providing this information, quotations add authority to the statement and credibility to the author's work.

* * *

Second, regardless of the truth or falsity of the factual matters asserted within the quoted statement, the attribution may result in injury to reputation because the manner of expression or even the fact that the statement was made indicates a negative personal trait or an attitude the speaker does not hold.

* * *

Justice Kennedy noted that in some circumstances, as in a printed hypothetical conversation or in a work of fiction, a writer's use of quotation marks will not be understood be readers to mean the reproduction of actual conversations.[80]

* * *

In some sense, any alteration of a verbatim quotation is false. But writers and reporters by necessity alter what people say, at the very least to eliminate grammatical and syntactical infelicities.

(Among journalists, editing to "fix" an interviewee's syntax is by no means an agreed-upon procedure. For one thing, if a print journalist is reporting on words captured "live" in all their ungrammatical splendor, editorial splicing to make a flaming illiterate's words read as if they were spoken by George Will or Sam Donaldson will make the print media appear foolish. Also, what if the grammatical atrocities are spoken by, say, a State Higher Education Commissioner or a U.S. Department of Education offi-

[78] Masson v. New Yorker Magazine, Inc., 501 U.S. at 516, 111 S.Ct. at 2432 (1991), 18 Med.L.Rptr. at 2250–2251.

[79] Masson v. New Yorker Magazine, Inc., 501 U.S. at 511, 111 S.Ct. at 2430–2431 (1991), 18 Med.L.Rptr. at 2248.

[80] Masson v. New Yorker Magazine, Inc., 501 U.S. at 514, 111 S.Ct. at 2431 (1991), 18 Med.L.Rptr. at 2248.

cial? Can they be edited into proper English without truly deceiving the public?)

Justice Kennedy's decision spoke cautiously to the issues at hand, declaring:[81]

> If every alteration constituted the falsity required to prove actual malice, the practice of journalism, which the First Amendment standard is designed to protect, would require a radical change, one inconsistent with our precedents and First Amendment principles.

* * *

> We conclude that a deliberate alteration of the words uttered by a plaintiff does not equate with knowledge of falsity for purposes of *New York Times v. Sullivan* ... and *Gertz v. Robert Welch* ... unless the alteration results in a material change in the meaning conveyed by the statement. The use of quotations to attribute words not in fact spoken bears in a most important way on that inquiry, but it is not dispositive in every case.
>
> Deliberate or reckless falsification that comprises actual malice turns upon words and punctuation only because words and punctuation express meaning. Meaning is the life of language. And for the reasons we have given, quotations may be a devastating instrument for conveying false meaning. * * * [R]eaders of In the Freud Archives may have found Malcolm's portrait of petitioner especially damning because so much of it appeared to be a self-portrait, told by petitioner in his own words. And if the alterations of petitioner's words gave a different meaning to the statements ... then the device of quotations might well be critical in finding the words actionable.

The Supreme Court's majority thus overturned the summary judgment, ruling that defendants Janet Malcolm and the New Yorker magazine could be taken to trial on the issue of libel. (Later, the magazine was removed from the case, in part because of its reputation for accuracy in editing and in part because Ms. Malcolm was regarded as an independent contractor, not a New Yorker employee.) In a minority opinion, Justices White and Scalia argued that under New York Times v. Sullivan, reporting a known falsehood is sufficient proof of actual malice.[82]

---

[81] Masson v. New Yorker Magazine, Inc., 501 U.S. at 514, 517–518, 111 S.Ct. at 2431, 2433 (1991), 18 Med.L.Rptr. 2241, 2249, 2251.

[82] Masson v. New Yorker Magazine, Inc., 501 U.S. at 526, 111 S.Ct. at 2437–2438 (1991), 18 Med.L.Rptr. at 2255.

Journalists and legal commentators differed on the potential impact of Masson v. New Yorker. Jane Kirtley, director of the Reporters Committee for Freedom of the Press, said " '[a] lot more reporters are going to start using tape recorders in addition to notebooks—a kind of belt and suspenders protection.' "[83]The New York Times, however, said editorially that the Supreme Court had produced a measured decision meaning that[84]

> ... fallible journalists won't be held to stenographic exacti-
> tude for everything they put between quotation marks. Yet
> if a deliberately altered quote makes the speaker look like
> a self-confessed fool or rascal, the journalists had better be
> prepared to defend themselves in court.

Masson v. Malcolm: The Jury Returns (1994)

On November 2, 1994 a federal district court jury ruled in favor of Janet Malcolm. Its verdict said that her 1983 profile of Dr. Jeffrey Masson—although libelous in one passage—was not a product of the actual malice required for the psychiatrist to collect damages for defamation.[85]

This evidently meant the end of a 10–year-old battle in which Dr. Masson sought $7 million in damages. Ms. Malcolm continued to assert that her article was accurate, although she conceded that she had engaged in "compression," taking separate statements and molding them into a unified statement. In fact, the one quote the jury held to be libelous (even if not actionable defamation because of the absence of knowing falsity) was the product of compressing quotations.[86]

As published in Ms. Malcolm's article, these sentences were juxtaposed:

> " 'Because it is the honorable thing to do.' Well, he had the
> wrong man."[87]

However, the tapes of Malcolm's interviews with Dr. Masson revealed that there were 35 intervening words between the two sentences quoted above. In those words—present in the tapes but excluded from the article—Freud Archives director Kurt Eissler, who had dismissed Dr. Masson from his post as projects director—

---

[83] Tony Mauro, "Journalists may need taped evidence of quotes," USA Today, June 21, 1991, p. 8A.

[84] "Misquotations, Measured," The New York Times, June 21, 1991, p. A12.

[85] The Associated Press, "Jury clears writer, says falsehoods not deliberate, reckless," The Knoxville News–Sentinel, Nov. 3, 1994, p. A8.

[86] Edward Felsenthal, "New Yorker's Malcolm Is Cleared of Libel," The Wall Street Journal, Nov. 3, 1994, P. B12.

[87] David Margolick, "Psychoanalyst Loses Libel Suit Against a New Yorker Reporter," Nov. 3, 1994, pp. A1, A14.

was urging Masson to accept his firing quietly, to remain silent and then there might be the possibility of someday getting his job back. This silence was sought, evidently, in the context of Eissler urging Masson not to "poison" or upset the aged Anna Freud's last days. The second sentence quoted above—"Well, he had the wrong man"—this was Dr. Masson's saying he would not remain quiet, not—as the compressed quote may be read—that Dr. Masson was saying that he refused to do the honorable thing.[88]

First Amendment lawyer James C. Goodale told The Wall Street Journal that the verdict should " 'give reporters more confidence in reporting substantially what their sources say,' rather than being tied to someone's exact words."[89] It should also send the message that quotes are "massaged" or "compressed" at a writer's ethical if not legal peril.

But the number of cases in which juries find that professional communicators acted with reckless disregard is much less than the cases in which they or appellate courts have found that the professional communicator has acted with negligence, but not reached the level of actual malice.

Some decisions have held that "internal inconsistencies" in a reporter's story do not make reckless disregard;[90] nor does the possibility that the reporter harbored "animosity", or a "grudge" or "ill will" toward the plaintiff;[91] nor does a combination of a reporter's failure to investigate, his possession (but omission from the story) of material contradictory to the hard words, plus the fact that the material was not "hot news" and so could have been further checked.[92] And to repeat, reckless disregard is not carelessness or negligence, which are flaws found often enough in news stories but which must be accepted in news of public persons if freedom is to have the "breathing space" it requires to survive. The jury recognized this in the famous case of Ariel Sharon v. Time, Inc.: While it found *Time* magazine's story about public official Sharon to be false and defamatory, it said specifically that *Time* was negligent and careless, but not possessed of reckless disregard. *Time* had erred but not lied, and was not liable for any of the $50 million that Sharon sought.[93]

---

[88] Ibid., and Felsenthal, op. cit.

[89] Felsenthal, op. cit.

[90] Foster v. Upchurch, 624 S.W.2d 564 (Tex.1981), 7 Med.L.Rptr. 2533.

[91] Lancaster v. Daily Banner–News Pub. Co., Inc., 274 Ark. 145, 622 S.W.2d 671 (1981), 8 Med.L.Rptr. 1093; Curtis v. Southwestern Newspapers, 677 F.2d 115 (5th Cir.1982), 8 Med.L.Rptr. 1651.

[92] McNabb v. Oregonian Pub. Co., 69 Or.App. 136, 685 P.2d 458 (1984), 10 Med.L.Rptr. 2181.

[93] Time, Feb. 4, 1985, 64; 599 F.Supp. 538 (S.D.N.Y.1984).

The cases of public-person plaintiffs who must accept without compensation the negligent, the careless—indeed the "irresponsible" and the "unreasonable"[94]—sometimes warrant the journalist's reflection: Floyd Rood, a tireless worker and publicist in youth assistance efforts including drug rehabilitation, was said in a news story to have begun a money-raising project "to help solve his drug addiction problem." The word "his" was wrong; it had accidentally been changed from "the" in wire transmission. He lost his suit.[95] Alderwoman Glover, said erroneously by a newspaper to have had abortions, could not recover for libel, for the newspaper had been no more than negligent in its mistake.[96]

SEC. 30.   PUBLIC OFFICIALS AND FIGURES

Who bears the actual malice burden in defamation?

The United States Constitution's guarantee of freedom of speech and press—which of course rules in all states as well as in federal courts[97]—protects all that is said about public officials in their public conduct unless there is "actual malice." But did "public official" mean every person who is employed by government at any level? Justice Brennan foresaw that this question would arise, but said in a footnote in the *Sullivan* case: "It is enough for the present case that respondent's position as an elected city commissioner clearly made him a public official * * *."[98]

In 1966, Rosenblatt v. Baer helped the definition. Newspaper columnist Alfred D. Rosenblatt wrote in the *Laconia Evening Citizen* that a public ski area which in previous years had been a financially shaky operation, now was doing "hundreds of percent" better. He asked, "What happened to all the money last year? And every other year?" Baer, who had been dismissed from his county post as ski area supervisor the year before, brought a suit charging that the column libeled him. The New Hampshire court upheld his complaint and awarded him $31,500. But when the case reached the United States Supreme Court, it reversed and remanded the case. It said that Baer did indeed come within the "public official" category:[99]

---

[94] Lawrence v. Bauer Pub. & Printing Ltd., 89 N.J. 451, 446 A.2d 469 (1982), 8 Med.L.Rptr. 1536, 1543.

[95] Rood v. Finney, 418 So.2d 1 (La.App.1982), 8 Med.L.Rptr. 2047.

[96] Glover v. Herald Co., 549 S.W.2d 858 (Mo.1977), 2 Med.L.Rptr. 1846.

[97] Dodd v. Pearson, 277 F.Supp. 469 (D.D.C.1967); Beckley Newspapers Corp. v. Hanks, 389 U.S. 81, 88 S.Ct. 197 (1967).

[98] New York Times Co. v. Sullivan, 376 U.S. 254, 282 n. 23, 84 S.Ct. 710, 727 n. 23 (1964).

[99] Rosenblatt v. Baer, 383 U.S. 75, 86 S.Ct. 669 (1966).

Criticism of government is at the very center of the constitutionally protected area of free discussion. Criticism of those responsible for government operations must be free, lest criticism of government be penalized. It is clear, therefore, that the "public official" designation applies at the very least to those among the hierarchy of government employees who have, or appear to the public to have, substantial responsibility for or control over the conduct of governmental affairs.

The Court also said that the *Sullivan* rule may apply to a person who has left public office, as Baer had, where public interest in the matter at issue is still substantial.

Discussions of "who is a public official" (or "public figure") all too often come up after a publication or broadcast has been made that looks as if it may result in a defamation lawsuit. Some of the time, it will be apparent that the individual involved is a public official: the President of the United States, a governor, a state legislator. It would be simple if holding a government position automatically gave one the status of public official. But in the famous 1979 decision in Hutchinson v. Proxmire, the U.S. Supreme Court said in a footnote that "public official" is not synonymous with "public employee."[100]

Such uncertainty comes from the legal fact of life that every libel suit is tried on a case-by-case basis. Because, as has been said, courts move with adequate precedent if not with adequate grace, it is not surprising that courts sometimes reach inconsistent and even contradictory conclusions about who is and who is not a public official.

Consider these examples:

—A coach and athletic director at a 130–student Texas high school is a public official,[1] yet a wrestling coach known state-wide in Ohio was held to be a private figure.[2]

—As Robert D. Sack and Sandra S. Baron have noted, "authorities are sharply divided over whether a public school teacher . . . is a public official."[3]

[100] 443 U.S. 111, 119 n. 8, 99 S.Ct. 2675, 2680 n. 8 (1979). See David A. Elder, "The Supreme Court and Defamation: a Relaxation of Constitutional Standards," Kentucky Bench and Bar, Jan. 1980, pp. 38–39.

[1] Johnson v. Southwestern Newspapers Corp., 855 S.W.2d 182 (Tex.App.1993), 21 Med.L.Rptr. 1746.

[2] Milkovich v. News–Herald, 15 Ohio St.3d 292, 473 N.E.2d 1191 (1984), 11 Med.L.Rptr. 1598 (Ohio App. 1986).

[3] Robert D. Sack and Sandra S. Baron, Libel, Slander and Related Problems (New York: Practising Law Institute, 1994) p. 255, citing Basarich v. Rodeghero, 24 Ill.App.3d 889, 321 N.E.2d 739 (1974) (teacher is public figure) and Richmond

Cases that did not reach the United States Supreme Court have provided some guidance, starting soon after Times v. Sullivan was decided. During 1964, the Pennsylvania Supreme Court applied public figure status to a senator who was candidate for re-election.[4] Shortly, state legislators were included,[5] a former mayor,[6] a deputy sheriff,[7] a school board member,[8] an appointed city tax assessor,[9] and a police sergeant.[10] A state legislative clerk was ruled a public official, in his suit against a former state senator who accused the clerk of wiretapping when he was actually doing his clerk's duty in trying to identify a telephone caller of obscenities.[11]

In some cases, it has been held that one retains public-official status despite lapse of time: A former federal narcotics agent was designated "public official" in his libel suit for a story about his official misconduct, despite the fact that he had left office six years earlier.[12] And since 1971, the Supreme Court's rule has been that a charge of criminal conduct against a present official, no matter how remote in time or place the conduct was, is always "relevant to his fitness for office," and that he must prove actual malice in a libel suit.[13]

Although "public official" would seem to be readily identifiable, many questions remain. Courts and commentators have long taken the view that holding a government position almost automatically gives one the status of public official. There are others who are paid by government, but who are not government employees. Consultants and contractors who earn their entire livelihoods from government may escape the "public official" label.[14] In a Texas case, a county surveyor who brought a libel suit against a newspaper for its criticism of his work as an engineering consultant to a

Newspapers, Inc. v. Lipscomb, 234 Va. 277, 362 S.E.2d 32 (1987), 14 Med.L.Rptr. 1953, and others (teacher not public figure.)

[4] Clark v. Allen, 415 Pa. 484, 204 A.2d 42 (1964).

[5] Washington Post Co. v. Keogh, 125 U.S.App.D.C. 32, 365 F.2d 965 (1966); Rose v. Koch and Christian Research, Inc., 278 Minn. 235, 154 N.W.2d 409 (1967).

[6] Lundstrom v. Winnebago Newspapers, Inc., 58 Ill.App.2d 33, 206 N.E.2d 525 (1965).

[7] St. Amant v. Thompson, 390 U.S. 727, 88 S.Ct. 1323 (1968).

[8] Cabin v. Community Newspapers, Inc., 50 Misc.2d 574, 270 N.Y.S.2d 913 (1966).

[9] Eadie v. Pole, 91 N.J.Super. 504, 221 A.2d 547 (1966).

[10] Suchomel v. Suburban Life Newspapers, Inc., 84 Ill.App.2d 239, 228 N.E.2d 172 (1967).

[11] Martonik v. Durkan, 23 Wash.App. 47, 596 P.2d 1054 (1979), 5 Med.L.Rptr. 1266.

[12] Hart v. Playboy Enterprises (D.C.Kan.1979), 5 Med.L.Rptr. 1811.

[13] Monitor Patriot Co. v. Roy, 401 U.S. 265, 91 S.Ct. 621 (1971).

[14] Hutchinson v. Proxmire, 443 U.S. 111, 119 n. 8, 99 S.Ct. 2675, 2680 n. 8 (1979). See David A. Elder, "The Supreme Court and Defamation: a Relaxation of Constitutional Standards," Kentucky Bench and Bar, Jan. 1980, pp. 38–39.

municipality was ruled not to be a public official but a private person in his consultant's work.[15] And in a federal case of 1980, the Court of Appeals for the Fourth Circuit ruled that the Iroquois Research Institute, employed by the Fairfax County (Va.) Water Authority as a research consultant in a county project, was not a public official. Relying on the Rosenblatt v. Baer decision (discussed above), the court said that Iroquois was in the sole role of a scientific factfinder, merely reporting the facts it found to the Water Authority. It had no control over the conduct of government affairs, made no recommendations, was little known to the public, and exercised no discretion.[16] It was private.

Nine major media organizations unsuccessfully urged the United States Supreme Court to review the appeals court decision for Iroquois, asserting that the case "presents perhaps the most significant unresolved issue in the constitutional law of defamation * * *."[17] The Supreme Court denied review and the case went back to trial court with Iroquois confirmed for trial as a private agency.

John B. McCrory and Robert C. Bernius described a good analytical frame for determining when a person could be classed as a public official. If a person is in a position to make policy and has access to the press (presumably for self-defense), that can add up to classification as a public official.[18] That analysis—doubtless making too much sense to apply uniformly to defamation cases—cuts across whether an official is elected or appointed. Such an approach even meant that a receptionist in a public clinic was a public official, because she had sole responsibility for making appointments, making her job performance a matter of undeniable public interest.[19]

Extending the Public Official Status to Public Figures

The doctrine of New York Times Co. v. Sullivan extends the requirement of proving actual malice to public figures, such as non-official persons who involve themselves in the resolution of public questions.

In the *Rosenblatt* case treated above, Justice William O. Douglas of the Supreme Court wrote a separate concurring opinion. In it he raised the question of what persons and what issues might call

---

[15] Foster v. Laredo Newspapers Inc., 541 S.W.2d 809 (Tex.1976), certiorari denied 429 U.S. 1123, 97 S.Ct. 1160 (1977).

[16] Arctic Co., Ltd. v. Loudoun Times Mirror et al., 624 F.2d 518 (4th Cir.1980), 6 Med.L.Rptr. 1433, 1435.

[17] 6 Med.L.Rptr. #31 (Dec. 9, 1980), News Notes; John Consoli, "Consultants to Gov't. Aren't Public Figures," Editor & Publisher, Jan. 17, 1981, 9.

[18] 1993 edition of "Constitutional Privilege in Libel Law," by John B. McCrory and Robert C. Bernius, updated by Robert D. Sack et. al., in James C. Goodale, chairman, Communications Law 1993, Vol. II, p. 259.

[19] Ibid., p. 261, citing Auvil v. Times Journal Co. (E.D.Va.1984), 10 Med.L. Rptr. 2302.

for an extension of the *Sullivan* doctrine beyond "public officials."
He said:[20]

> * * * I see no way to draw lines that exclude the night
> watchman, the file clerk, the typist, or, for that matter,
> anyone on the public payroll. And how about those who
> contract to carry out governmental missions? Some of
> them are as much in the public domain as any so-called
> officeholder. * * *. [T]he question is whether a public
> *issue* not a public official, is involved.

Back in 1966, the decision in a suit brought by the noted
scientist and Nobel Prize winner, Dr. Linus Pauling, indeed said
that not only "public officials" would have to prove malice if they
were to succeed with libel suits.

Pauling sued the *St. Louis Globe–Democrat* claiming libel in an
editorial entitled "Glorification of Deceit." It referred to an appearance by Pauling before a subcommittee of the United States Senate,
in connection with Pauling's attempts to promote a nuclear test
ban treaty. It read in part: "Pauling contemptuously refused to
testify and was cited for contempt of Congress. He appealed to the
United States District Court to rid him of the contempt citation,
which that Court refused to do." Pauling said that he had not been
cited for contempt, that he had not appealed to any court to rid
himself of any contempt citation, and that no appeal was expected.

The federal court conceded that Pauling was not a "public
official" such as the plaintiff in New York Times Co. v. Sullivan.
But it added:[21]

> We feel, however, that the implications of the Supreme
> Court's majority opinions are clear. Professor Pauling, by
> his public statements and actions, was projecting himself
> into the arena of public controversy and into the very
> "vortex of the discussion of a question of pressing public
> concern". He was attempting to influence the resolution of
> an issue which was important, which was of profound
> effect, which was public and which was internationally
> controversial * * *.

* * *

Pauling took his case to the United States Supreme Court, but that
court denied certiorari, and the lower court's decision stood.[22]

[20] Rosenblatt v. Baer, 383 U.S. 75, 89, 86 S.Ct. 669, 678 (1966).

[21] Pauling v. Globe–Democrat Pub. Co., 362 F.2d 188, 195–196 (8th Cir.1966).

[22] Pauling v. National Review, Inc., 49 Misc.2d 975, 269 N.Y.S.2d 11 (1966).

Walker v. A.P. (1967)

While public figure Linus Pauling was thus being embraced within the *Sullivan* rules, another man who had formerly been a general in the United States Army was undertaking a set of "chain" libel suits. This was retired Maj. Gen. Edwin A. Walker, whose case appeared above. Walker had been involved in a controversy when he was forced to leave the service after it was disclosed that he was conducting political indoctrination of U.S. troops stationed in Germany.

Walker had opposed integration in the military and he continued to voice his opposition after he entered civilian life. Segregationists looked to him for leadership and Walker consented to the creation of a "Walker for president" political exploration committee. Walker was a "public figure," said Justice John Harlan in writing for four members of the Court, "by his purposeful activity amounting to a thrusting of his personality into the 'vortex' of an important public controversy." Agreeing, in writing for three members, Chief Justice Earl Warren said that "Under any reasoning, General Walker was a public man" in whose conduct society had a substantial interest. Warren said that giving a public figure, such as Walker, an easier burden to meet than a public official in recovering damages for libel[23]

> * * * has no basis in law, logic or First Amendment policy. Increasingly in this country, the distinction between governmental and private sectors are blurred * * *.
>
> Under any reasoning, General Walker was a public man in whose public conduct society and the press had a legitimate and substantial interest.

Harlan argued that the public figure should not have to meet as difficult a standard of proof as the public official. He articulated a lower barrier for the former:[24]

> We consider and would hold that a "public figure" who is not a public official may * * * recover damages for a defamatory falsehood whose substance makes substantial danger to reputation apparent, on a showing of highly unreasonable conduct constituting an extreme departure from the standards of investigation and reporting ordinarily adhered to by responsible publishers.

Rosenbloom v. Metromedia: Forget This Case

In 1971, the Supreme Court took up the case of Rosenbloom v. Metromedia, Inc.,[25]. George Rosenbloom, a distributor of nudist

---

[23] Ibid., at 163–165, 87 S.Ct. at 1995–1997.

[24] Ibid., at 155, 87 S.Ct. at 1991.

[25] Rosenbloom v. Metromedia, 403 U.S. 29, 91 S.Ct. 1811 (1971).

magazines in Philadelphia, was a private citizen arrested in a crackdown on obscenity. Metromedia radio station WIP had said Rosenbloom had been arrested on charges of possessing obscene literature, and linked him to the "smut literature rackets." Later acquitted of obscenity charges, Rosenbloom sued for libel in the WIP broadcasts, and won $275,000 in trial.

But the station took the case up to the Supreme Court. There was not majority opinion, but five justices agreed that Rosenbloom should not recover. The largest block, a plurality of three justices, approved extending the actual malice requirement in libel whenever the news was a "matter of public interest." It was a substantial extension of the protections for the media. The three justices endorsed the "matter of public interest" rationale, laid out by Justice William J. Brennan:[26]

> If a matter is a subject of public or general interest, it cannot suddenly become less so merely because a private individual is involved, or because in some sense the individual did not "voluntarily" choose to become involved. The public's primary interest is in the event * * *. We honor the commitment to robust debate on public issues, which is embodied in the First Amendment, by extending constitutional protection to all discussion and communication involving matters of public or general concern, without regard to whether the persons involved are famous or anonymous.

Lower courts accepted the plurality opinion as gospel. The sweep of "matter of public or general interest" was so powerful that few libel suits, whether by public or private persons were won. Commentators on press law predicted the disappearance of libel suits. But in mid–1974, hardly three years after *Rosenbloom,* the support of a three-justice plurality in that decision for the "matter of public interest" interpretation revealed itself as a shaky foundation. A five-man majority of the U.S. Supreme Court rejected it as a rule in Gertz v. Robert Welch, Inc.[27] Gertz would restore certainty to the process of deciding when professional communicators would have the protections of actual malice and when private persons would be able to recover after proving negligence. *Rosenbloom* is alive, sort of. See Bootstrapping below at page 256 for its renewed, but doomed to failure resurgence.

[26] Ibid., at 43, 91 S.Ct. at 1819.

[27] Gertz v. Robert Welch, Inc., 418 U.S. 323, 94 S.Ct. 2997 (1974). For the position that the "public interest" criterion should be the rule, see Anthony Lewis, New York Times v. Sullivan Reconsidered * * *, 83 Columbia L.Rev. 603 (1983).

SEC. 31.   DEFINING "PUBLIC FIGURE"

Distinguishing a public from a private person under *Gertz* rests on either of two bases—fame, notoriety, power or influence that render one a public figure for all purposes, or the status that makes one a public figure only for a limited range of issues. In either case, the person assumes special prominence in the resolution of public controversy.

Elmer Gertz, a Chicago lawyer, was retained by a family to bring a civil action against Policeman Nuccio who had shot and killed their son and had been convicted of second degree murder. *American Opinion,* a monthly publication given to the views of the John Birch Society, carried an article saying that Gertz was an architect of a "frame-up" of Nuccio, that he was part of a communist conspiracy to discredit local police, and that he was a Leninist and a "Communist-fronter." Gertz, who was none of these things, brought a libel suit and for six years battled the shifting uncertainties of the courts' attitudes toward "public official," "public figure," and "matter of public interest" for the purposes of libel. A jury found libel *per se* and awarded Gertz $50,000 in damages, disallowed by the trial judge and also by the Seventh Circuit Court of Appeals:[28] Because the *American Opinion* story concerned a matter of public interest, Gertz would have to show actual malice on its part, even though he might be a private citizen. Objecting, Gertz appealed to the U.S. Supreme Court.

Private Individuals Exempted From Actual Malice Rule

With four other justices agreeing, Justice Powell wrote for the majority.[29] The plurality opinion in Rosenbloom v. Metromedia, relied on by the Circuit Court, should not stand. Justice Powell had no quarrel with requiring public officials and public figures to prove actual malice in their libel suits. But he reasoned that the legitimate state interest in compensating injury to the reputation of private individuals—of whom, it was found, Gertz was one—requires that such persons be held to less demanding proof of fault by the offending news medium—only "negligence," rather than the stern actual malice standard. They are at a disadvantage, compared with public officials and public figures, where they are defamed:[30]

Public officials and public figures usually enjoy significantly greater access to the channels of effective communi-

[28] Gertz v. Robert Welch, Inc., 471 F.2d 801 (7th Cir.1972). A dozen years after Gertz brought his first action, a federal jury awarded him $400,000 upon re-trial, and the Seventh Circuit Court of Appeals upheld the award: Gertz v. Welch, Inc., 680 F.2d 527 (7th Cir.1982), 8 Med.L.Rptr. 1769.

[29] Gertz v. Robert Welch, Inc., 418 U.S. 323, 94 S.Ct. 2997 (1974).

[30] Ibid., at 344–346, 94 S.Ct. at 3009–3010.

cation and hence have a more realistic opportunity to counteract false statements than private individuals normally enjoy. Private individuals are therefore more vulnerable to injury, and the state interest in protecting them is correspondingly greater. * * *

An individual who decides to seek governmental office must accept certain necessary consequences of that involvement in public affairs. He runs the risk of closer public scrutiny than might otherwise be the case. * * *

Those classed as public figures stand in a similar position. Hypothetically, it may be possible for someone to become a public figure through no purposeful action of his own, but the instances of truly involuntary public figures must be exceedingly rare. For the most part those who attain this status have assumed roles of special prominence in the affairs of society.

* * * the communications media are entitled to act on the assumption that public officials and public figures have voluntarily exposed themselves to increased risk of injury from defamatory falsehoods concerning them. No such assumption is justified with respect to a private individual. He has not accepted public office nor assumed an "influential role in ordering society." * * *

Dissenting Justices Douglas and Brennan wanted to affirm the Court of Appeals finding that anyone—including Gertz—would have to prove actual malice in offending words from a story of general or public interest. Brennan argued that the *Gertz* decision damaged the protection which mass media ought to have under the First Amendment. Douglas repeated his view that the First Amendment would bar Congress from passing any libel law; and like Congress, "States are without power 'to use a civil libel law or any other law to impose damages for merely discussing public affairs'."[31]

Brennan, who had written the plurality opinion in *Rosenbloom,* reiterated his point there: "Matters of public or general interest do not 'suddenly become less so merely because a private individual is involved, or because in some sense the individual did not "voluntarily" choose to become involved.' "[32] He said it is unproved and highly improbable that the public figure will have better access to the media. The ability of all to get access will depend on the "same complex factor * * * : the unpredictable event of the media's continuing interest in the story." As to the assumption that private people deserve special treatment because they do not assume the

---

[31] Ibid., at 356, 94 S.Ct. at 3015.

[32] Ibid., at 362, 94 S.Ct. at 3018.

risk of defamation by freely entering the public arena, Brennan stated that " * * * voluntarily or not, we are all 'public' men to some degree."[33]

Gertz Is Not a "Public" Person

In Gertz v. Welch, the Supreme Court first brushed off the notion that he might be a public official.

He'd never had a paid government position and his only "office" had been as a member of mayor's housing committees years before. As for the suggestion that he was a "de facto public official" because he had appeared at the coroner's inquest into the murder (incidental to his representing the family in civil litigation). If that made him a "public official," the court said, all lawyers would become public officials in their status as "officers of the court," which would make little sense.

But the troublesome possibility that Gertz was a public *figure* remained. Because lower courts have so frequently relied on the Supreme Court's treatment of the matter in *Gertz,* detail is called for here.

To begin, the court said, persons in either of two cases "assume special prominence in the resolution of public questions."[34] Also, "they invite attention and comment."

> [A public figure] designation may rest on either of two alternative bases. In some instances an individual may achieve such pervasive fame or notoriety that he becomes a public figure for all purposes and contexts. More commonly, an individual voluntarily injects himself or is drawn into a particular public controversy and thereby becomes a public figure for a limited range of issues. In either case such persons assume special prominence in the resolution of public questions.

1. The first of the two—deemed a public figure for all purposes and in all contexts: One should not be deemed a public personality for all aspects of his life, "absent clear evidence of general fame or notoriety in the community and pervasive involvement in the affairs of society."

Gertz was not a public figure under this first category. He had, indeed, been active in community and professional affairs, serving as an officer of local civil groups and various legal agencies. He had published several works on law. Thus he was well-known in some circles. But he had "achieved no general fame or notoriety in the

[33] Ibid., at 364, 94 S.Ct. at 3019.

[34] Ibid., at 352, 94 S.Ct. at 3013. Succeeding definitions and procedures in determining "public figure" are taken from *Gertz,* pp. 343 and 351, 94 S.Ct. at 3009 and 3013.

community." No member of the jury panel, for example, had ever heard of him.

2. The second of the two—where "an individual voluntarily injects himself * * * into a particular public controversy and thereby becomes a public figure for a limited range of issues." Alternative wording used by the court was that "commonly, those classed as public figures have thrust themselves 'into the vortex' of particular public controversies in order to influence the resolution of the issues involved."[35]

In determining the status of this person who has no general fame or notoriety in the community, the court said the procedure should be one of "looking to the nature and extent of an individual's participation in the particular controversy giving rise to the defamation." In this statement, the Court was rejecting the trend under *Rosenbloom* to examine the *topic* of the news to determine whether the public principle held, and instead to examine the *individual* and his role in public life. Doing this for Attorney Gertz, the court found again that he was not a public figure: He had played only a minimal role at the coroner's inquest, and only as the representative of a private client; he had no part in the criminal prosecution of Officer Nuccio; he had never discussed the case with the press; and he "did not thrust himself into the vortex of this public issue * * * "nor "engage the public's attention in an attempt to influence its outcome." Gertz was not, by this second basis, a public figure, and he would not, consequently, have to prove that *American Opinion* libeled him with actual malice. The Supreme Court ordered a new trial.

The modification of *Sullivan* and *Rosenbloom* by *Gertz* was a damaging retreat in protection in the eyes of media commentators. Now, journalists suspected that although there were gains for the media under *Gertz*—in requiring plaintiffs to show fault and in limiting the reach of punitive damages—it was on the whole a great door-opener for libel suits by private plaintiffs who no longer had to prove actual malice.

David A. Anderson, legal scholar and former journalist, argued that even under the protection of the *Rosenbloom* interpretation, the self-censorship by the press which *Sullivan* had sought to minimize in establishing the malice rule and other safeguards, was real.[36] He wrote that the unconventional, non-established media,

---

[35] As a variant of the "limited range of issues" public figure, the Court identified the person who has not *voluntarily* entered a public controversy, but is *drawn* into it. Subsequent decisions have heavily vitiated this concept. See M.L. Rosen, "Media Lament: the Rise and Fall of Involuntary Public Figures," 54 St. John's L.Rev. 487, Spring 1980.

[36] David A. Anderson, "Libel and Press Self–Censorship," 53 Tex.L.Rev. 422 (1975); for an historic pattern supporting Anderson, see Norman L. Rosenberg, *Protecting the Best Men* (Chapel Hill: University of North Carolina Press, 1986).

sometimes known as the "alternative" press, and the world of magazines, are forced to self-censorship under *Gertz.* The people about whom the alternative press writes are frequently from spheres of life not much handled by the established newspaper media, and thus not established as "public figures." Often financially marginal, the unconventional media face a further problem in the high cost of legal defense. Anderson's worry over self-censorship, whether under *Gertz* or under Draconian jury awards even where the greater protection of *Sullivan* applies, runs strongly through the world of the media.[37]

Courts Determine the "Public" and the "Private" under *Gertz*

Whatever the level of press self-censorship under *Gertz* may be, subsequent cases show that media need to be discriminating. Sometimes, distinguishing the "public" from the "private" is not easy, even for the judge, who makes the decision before the case goes to the jury. One judge has said that the two concepts are "nebulous:" "Defining public figures is much like trying to nail a jellyfish to the wall."[38]

Recall that the Gertz decision set up two categories of public figures:

1) Persons (including organizations) who are "all purpose" or "pervasive" public figures because they have pervasive fame or influence, in their own communities if not regionally or nationally.

2) "Limited purpose" (sometimes called "vortex") public figures (including organizations), who voluntarily have injected themselves into a matter of public controversy, to help resolve that controversy.

"All-purpose" Public Figures

Sometimes it is easy to see that a person is an "all purpose" or "pervasive" public figure: entertainers Carol Burnett[39] and Johnny Carson,[40] famed evangelist Jerry Falwell, who comments constantly on politics and who has talked of running for President.[41]

But what about candidates, persons who want to be public officials. Should they enjoy the protections of private persons, subject only to their ability to win a majority of an every-shrinking electorate? Monitor Patriot Co. v. Roy[42] established that candidates

[37] 10 Med.L.Rptr. #13, 3/27/84, News Notes; 10 Med.L.Rptr. #34, 8/21/84, News Notes.

[38] Rosanova v. Playboy Enterprises, Inc., 411 F.Supp. 440, 443 (S.D.Ga.1976).

[39] Burnett v. National Enquirer (Cal.Super.1981), 7 Med.L.Rptr. 1321.

[40] Carson v. Allied News Co., 529 F.2d 206 (7th Cir.1976).

[41] Hustler v. Falwell, 485 U.S. 46, 108 S.Ct. 876 (1988).

[42] Monitor Patriot v. Roy, 401 U.S. 265, 91 S.Ct. 621 (1971).

are subject to the same requirements as office holders. The case began on September 10, 1960. It was three days before the New Hampshire Democratic Party's primary election of candidates for the United States Senate and the Concord Monitor, published a syndicated column discussing the forthcoming election. In the course of the column there appeared references to the criminal records of several of the candidates. The column said Alphonse Roy, one of the candidates, was a "former small-time bootlegger." Roy lost and he sued both the paper and the column's distributor.

The trial court concluded that Roy would have to meet the actual malice standard required of public officials. But the judge added that the actual malice standard would apply to official acts only and statements pertaining to private conduct, which might include bootlegging, would be tested by a different fault standard. The jury found for Roy and the case made its way eventually to the U.S. Supreme Court. There, the justices overturned the libel award saying that the *New York Times* rule would apply to candidates.

> "[I]t might be preferable to categorize a candidate as a 'public figure,' if for no other reason than to avoid straining the common meaning of words. But the question is of no importance so far as the standard of liability in this case is concerned, for it is abundantly clear that, whichever term is applied, publications concerning candidates must be accorded at least as much protection under the First and Fourteenth Amendments as those concerning occupants of public office."[43]

And the Court rejected the trial court's approach that made statements about public office activities different from private activities. In doing so, the Court drew from the case of *Garrison v. Louisiana*:

> Of course, any criticism of the manner in which a public official performs his duties will tend to affect his private, as well as his public, reputation. The New York Times rule is not rendered inapplicable merely because an official's private reputation, as well as his public reputation, is harmed. The public-official rule protects the paramount public interest in a free flow of information to the people concerning public officials, their servants. To this end, anything which might touch on an official's fitness for office is relevant. Few personal attributes are more germane to fitness for office than dishonesty, malfeasance, or improper motivation, even though these characteristics

---

[43] Ibid. at 271, 91 S.Ct. at 625.

may also affect the official's private character." 379 U.S., at 76–77.[44]

In seeming contradiction, however, a famous jet-setter with the household-word name of Firestone was held to be a private person.[45] This famous case is discussed later in this chapter.

For an example of a case with local or community involvement, consider the libel suit of attorney Myron Steere, who was labeled an all-purpose public figure. Steere had represented Nellie Schoonover in her homicide trial; she was convicted of first-degree murder. Later, an Associated Press story said the Kansas State Board of Law Examiners had recommended that the Kansas Supreme Court publicly censure Steere for his conduct of her defense. The examiners found that Steere had entered into a "contingency agreement" with Mrs. Schoonover to get all but $10,000 of her late husband's estate if she were acquitted.

Steere sued broadcasters and newspapers that had carried the AP account for defamation, claiming inaccuracies.[46] The trial court held that he would have to prove actual malice because—the Kansas Supreme Court said—"appellant was a public figure for all purposes by virtue of his general fame and notoriety in the community." Then it described the reach and breadth of Steere's involvement in the life of the community: He had practiced law in the county for 32 years and had been the county attorney for 8 of those years.[47]

> * * * He has achieved a position of some influence in local affairs capped by his representation of Nellie Schoonover in her well publicized, famous murder trial. We find the totality of his experience in Franklin County gave Myron Steere the requisite fame and notoriety in his community to be declared a public figure for all purposes.

Not only a *person* may be a "public figure." In Ithaca College v. Yale Daily News Pub. Co., Inc., the facts started with the publication of "The Insider's Guide to the Colleges 1978–79," 404 pages of material compiled and edited by the *Yale Daily News*. Through stringers, the editors obtained information on many colleges, and published of Ithaca College such statements as "Sex, drugs, and booze are the staples of life." Ithaca College sued for libel, charging falsity and damage to its business and academic reputation. While

---

[44] Ibid. at 274, 91 S.Ct. at 626.

[45] Time, Inc. v. Firestone, 424 U.S. 448, 96 S.Ct. 958 (1976).

[46] Steere v. Cupp, 226 Kan. 566, 602 P.2d 1267 (1979), 5 Med.L.Rptr. 2046. And see Sprouse v. Clay Communication, 158 W.Va. 427, 211 S.E.2d 674 (1975), 1 Med.L.Rptr. 1695, 1704.

[47] Ibid., 573–74, 1273–74, 2050–51. Note, "General Public Figures Since Gertz v. Welch," 58 St. John's L.Rev. 355 (Winter 1984).

Ithaca terms itself a "private" college, the New York Supreme Court said it could not be such in a libel suit.[48] The college assumes a role as a qualified educator of many students, serves the public good, is responsible for fair dealing with its students, the court ruled. It is recognized to be of "general fame or notoriety in the community [with] pervasive involvement in the affairs of society." The court decided that the college was a "public figure for all purposes." Similarly, corporations also may be classified as "public figures."[49]

Efforts to define public figures become especially troublesome where corporations are concerned.[50] For example, an insurance company, because of its power and influence, was held to be a public figure inviting attention and comment from the media.[51] On the other hand, the Supreme Court of the United States refused to hear an Oregon case holding that corporations—specifically banks—are not automatically public figures.[52] Note that this case was decided in 1985, several years before the savings and loan/banking crisis became big news, complete with U.S. senators' involvement in keeping regulators at bay in apparent exchange for campaign donations.

"Limited Purpose" Public Figures

Far more common than the person of general fame or notoriety who is a public figure for all purposes is the individual who is such for a "limited range of issues." Thus Dr. Frederick Exner for two decades and more had been "injecting" and "thrusting" himself into the fluoridation-of-water controversy through speeches, litigation, books, and articles. When he brought a libel suit for a magazine's criticism of his position, he was adjudged a public figure for "the limited issue of fluoridation" by having assumed leadership and by having attempted to influence the outcome of the issue. He had taken the role of "attempting to order society" in its concern with fluoridation.[53]

Harry Buchanan and his firm were retained to perform accounting services for the Finance Committee to Re-elect the President (CREEP) in 1971. Common Cause brought suit in 1972 to

[48] Ithaca College v. Yale Daily News Pub. Co., Inc., 105 Misc.2d 793, 433 N.Y.S.2d 530 (1980), 6 Med.L.Rptr. 2180.

[49] See WTSP–TV, Inc. v. Vick (Fla.Cir.Ct.1985), 11 Med.L.Rptr. 1543. But see Blue Ridge Bank v. Veribanc, Inc., 866 F.2d 681 (4th Cir.1989).

[50] Robert Drechsel and Deborah Moon, "Corporate Libel Plaintiffs and the News Media," 21 Am. Bus. L. Journ. 127 (Summer, 1983).

[51] American Benefit Life Ins. Co. v. McIntyre, 375 So.2d 239 (Ala.1979), 5 Med.L.Rptr. 1124.

[52] Bank of Oregon v. Independent News, Inc., 298 Or. 434, 693 P.2d 35 (1985), cert. denied 474 U.S. 826, 106 S.Ct. 84 (1985).

[53] Exner v. American Medical Ass'n, 12 Wash.App. 215, 529 P.2d 863 (1974).

force the Committee to report transactions, and Buchanan's deposition was taken in the matter. In reporting the suit, Associated Press compared matters involving Buchanan with the handling of money by convicted Watergate conspirator Bernard L. Barker. Buchanan sued AP for libel. Was he a public figure? The court said "yes." There was intense interest in campaign finances at the time Buchanan was working for CREEP. The system he helped set up for the committee and the cash transactions in which he took part were legitimate matters of public scrutiny and concern. Buchanan was a key person for attempts to investigate. He was an agent of the committee who voluntarily accepted his role, and as such a public figure.[54]

Other Examples of Limited Purpose Public Figures: The businessman-president of a state bail-bond underwriters' association attacked a Pennsylvania state commission's report on bail-bond abuses and attempted to have the commission dissolved; he had injected himself into controversy and was a public figure.[55] The United States Labor Party is a public political organization actively engaged in publishing articles, magazines, and books, and is a public figure "at least in regard to those areas of public controversy * * *in which [it has] participated."[56] The Church of Scientology seeks to play an influential role in ordering society, has thrust itself onto the public scene, and is a public figure.[57] So is a Roman Catholic priest who has actively involved himself in the debate over the independence of Northern Ireland, through radio, television, and speeches.[58]

If the above-listed persons and organizations strike you as plainly appropriate public figures in the contexts described, where does the problem arise? The fact is that there are hard cases disturbing to media people who are dismayed by courts' finding certain individuals to be private even though in the public eye. Consider that to be a problem caused by Gertz v. Robert Welch, Inc. (1974). Before that decision of the U.S. Supreme Court, the presumption was that government proceedings are public and almost inevitably made public figures out of participants. Thanks to the Gertz decision, such public figure presumptions need to be used with great caution. Take a notorious case attempting to draw a line

[54] Buchanan v. Associated Press, 398 F.Supp. 1196 (D.D.C.1975).

[55] Childs v. Sharon Herald (Pa.Ct.Com.Pl.1979), 5 Med.L.Rptr. 1679.

[56] United States Labor Party v. Anti–Defamation League (N.Y.Sup.Ct.1980), 6 Med.L.Rptr. 2209.

[57] Church of Scientology of California v. Siegelman, 475 F.Supp. 950 (S.D.N.Y. 1979), 5 Med.L.Rptr. 2021.

[58] McManus v. Doubleday & Co., Inc., 513 F.Supp. 1383 (S.D.N.Y.1981), 7 Med. L.Rptr. 1475.

between public figures and private persons, Time, Inc. v. Firestone (1974).

Time, Inc. v. Firestone (1976)

Mary Alice Firestone—wife of a prominent member of the wealthy industrial family and member of the "society" elite of Palm Beach, Fla. (the "sporting set," as U.S. Supreme Court Justice Marshall called it)—went to court to seek separate maintenance from her husband, Russell. He counterclaimed for divorce on grounds of adultery and extreme cruelty. The trial covered 17 months, both parties charging extramarital escapades ("that would curl Dr. Freud's hair," the trial judge said). Several times during the 17 months, Mrs. Firestone held press conferences. She subscribed to a clipping service. *Time* magazine reported the trial's outcome: Russell Firestone was granted a divorce on grounds of extreme cruelty and adultery, *Time* said. But the trial judge had not, technically, found adultery, and Mrs. Firestone sued *Time* for libel.[59] A jury awarded her $100,000 and *Time* appealed, arguing that Mrs. Firestone was a public figure and as such would have to prove actual malice in *Time's* story.

Justice Rehnquist, writing for the majority of five of the U.S. Supreme Court, said "no" to *Time's* appeal. He quoted various passages from the *Gertz* definition of "public figure" which he said did not fit Mrs. Firestone: "special prominence in the resolution of public questions," "pervasive power and influence," "thrust themselves to the forefront of particular public controversies in order to influence the resolution of the issues involved." The crux of the matter was that, for all the publicity involved:[60]

> Dissolution of marriage through judicial proceedings is not the sort of "public controversy" referred to in *Gertz,* even though the marital difficulties of extremely wealthy individuals may be of interest to some portion of the reading public.

In spite of her position in the "Palm Beach 400," her press conferences, and her clipping service, Mrs. Firestone was a "private" individual, and her "private" marital affairs did not "become public for the purposes of libel law solely because they are aired in a public forum."

Predictably, news media were outraged at the designation of Mrs. Firestone as "private." Accustomed to thinking of official proceedings including divorce trials as public matters which could be reported without fear of injuring the privacy of the participants, journalists had to make a conscious effort to think of Mrs. Fire-

---

[59] Time, Inc. v. Firestone, 424 U.S. 448, 96 S.Ct. 958 (1976).

[60] Ibid., at 454, 96 S.Ct. at 965.

stone as in some sense private. Their effort was made more difficult in that her position in society had for years before the divorce placed her among the "newsworthy" and in the public eye. And with her use of clipping services and press conferences during the drawn-out divorce trial, her "public" character had seemed confirmed. What might the decision mean for future cases?

Wolston v. Reader's Digest (1979)

Three years after *Firestone,* the Supreme Court took up another case whose background was also a public court proceeding. And again, the fact that a libel plaintiff's suit arose from his involvement in an official public matter did not destroy private status for his libel suit. Ilya Wolston had been summoned in 1958 to appear before a grand jury that was investigating espionage, but failed to appear. Later, he pleaded guilty to a charge of criminal contempt for failing to respond to the summons and accepted conviction. Sixteen years later, *Reader's Digest* published a book by John Barron on Soviet espionage in the U.S. The book said erroneously that the FBI had identified Wolston as a Soviet intelligence agent. Wolston sued for libel. He asserted that he had been out of the limelight for many years, and that if he had been a public figure during the investigations, he now deserved to be considered private. The lower courts disagreed, saying the long lapse of time was immaterial, that Soviet espionage of 1958 continued to be a subject of importance, and that Wolston thus remained a public figure.

He appealed to the Supreme Court, which by a vote of 8–1 reversed the lower courts and determined that Wolston was a private person who would not have to prove actual malice in his libel suit against the *Reader's Digest.* Justice Rehnquist wrote:[61]

> We do not agree with respondents and the lower courts that petitioner can be classed as such a limited-purpose public figure. First, the undisputed facts do not justify the conclusion of the District Court and the Court of Appeals that petitioner "voluntarily thrust" or "injected" himself into the forefront of the public controversy surrounding the investigation of Soviet espionage. * * * It would be more accurate to say that petitioner was dragged unwillingly into the controversy. The government pursued him in its investigation.

Hutchinson v. Proxmire (1979)

On the date of the *Wolston* decision, another Supreme Court ruling on the definition of public figure was handed down, and again the decision cast the public figure into a narrower light than

[61] Wolston v. Reader's Digest Ass'n, Inc., 443 U.S. 157, 99 S.Ct. 2701 (1979).

many journalists felt warranted. This time, the Court said that researcher Ronald Hutchinson, who had received some $500,000 in federal government grants for his experiments, including some on monkeys' response to aggravating stimuli, was a private figure.[62] He would not have to prove actual malice in his libel suit against Sen. William Proxmire of Wisconsin, who had labeled Hutchinson's work "monkey business" and had given a "Golden Fleece of the Month Award" to government funding agencies which he ridiculed for wasting public money on grants to Hutchinson. A Proxmire press release, a newsletter, and a television appearance were involved, all following Proxmire's announcement of the Award on the senate floor.

Concerned about the narrowing of the definition of "public figure," media attorney James C. Goodale had reasoned in advance of the decision that the lower courts' holding that Hutchinson was, indeed, a public figure deserved to be upheld in the Supreme Court. "Clearly information about how our government grants money and who gets it," he said, "should be the subject of unlimited comment by anyone—especially by a U.S. Senator."[63]

The Supreme Court, however, did not see it that way. It reversed the lower courts, saying that their conclusion that Hutchinson was a public figure was erroneously based upon two factors: one, his success in getting federal grants and newspaper reports about the grants, and two, his access to media as represented by news stories that reported his response to the Golden Fleece Award. But:[64]

> Hutchinson did not thrust himself or his views into public controversy to influence others. Respondents have not identified such a particular controversy; at most, they point to concern about general public expenditures. But that concern is shared by most and relates to most public expenditures; it is not sufficient to make Hutchinson a public figure. If it were, everyone who received or benefitted from the myriad public grants for research could be classified as a public figure.

"Subject-matter classifications"—such as general public expenditures—had been rejected in *Gertz* as the touchstone for deciding who would have to prove actual malice, the Court said: instead, the

[62] Hutchinson v. Proxmire, 443 U.S. 111, 99 S.Ct. 2675 (1979).

[63] "Court Again to Consider Who Is A Public Figure," National Law Journal, Feb. 8, 1979, 23.

[64] Hutchinson v. Proxmire, 443 U.S. 111, 134–135; 99 S.Ct. 2675, 2688 (1979). Proxmire was reported to have settled the suit out of court for $10,000, and the Senate was reported to have assumed his trial costs of more than $100,000. D.S. Greenberg, "Press Was a Co–Villain in Proxmire's Golden Gimmick," Chicago Tribune, April 17, 1980.

person and his activities must be the basis. And, finally, the Court said it could not agree that Hutchinson had such access to the media that he should be classified as a public figure; his access was limited to responding to the announcement of the Golden Fleece Award.

"Vortex" Public Figures Not Clearly Defined

Other circumstances complicate the defining of public figures. Justice Powell's definition in *Gertz* and various courts' since (as in *Firestone, Wolston,* and *Hutchinson*), make it crucial to decide whether the person has voluntarily injected himself into a matter of public controversy to help resolve that controversy. American courts, unfortunately, have not drawn clear or predictable lines to separate "public figures" from "private persons." Even so, it may be said that there are many public figures besides those who voluntarily "get involved" and try to influence the outcome of public issues. (Please note, as discussed later in Section 35, that older tort law, dating back long before New York Times v. Sullivan, has traditionally provided the defense of "fair comment" for media that are sued for their critiques of authors' works, restaurants, plays, celebrities and public entertainers.)[65]

If persons truly were not public figures before getting media coverage, the mere fact of that coverage will not make them public figures. At times however—although rarely—unwilling persons, through no fault of their own, can become "involuntary public figures."[66] For the most part, however, there are mainly two kinds of "public figures:" The person who, nationally or locally, has pervasive or all-purpose fame, and the "vortex" public figures who thrust themselves into public issues, particularly in an effort to influence the course of events in some significant way.

The safest generalization for journalists is not to generalize: Get legal advice on close calls whether a person is a "public figure" or a "private figure." At times, courts have ruled that some persons holding elective office—such as an elected but unsalaried county surveyor[67] or a justice of the peace[68]—are private persons.

---

[65] Prosser, 813–813.

[66] See, e.g., Wolston v. Reader's Digest Ass'n, Inc., 443 U.S. 157, 167, 99 S.Ct. 2701, 2707 (1979), and Waldbaum v. Fairchild Publications, Inc., 627 F.2d 1287, 1295 (D.C.Cir.1980), citing Gertz v. Robert Welch, Inc., 418 U.S. 323, 94 S.Ct. 2997 (1974), recognizing that—at least in theory—an involuntary public figure could exist.

[67] Foster v. Laredo Newspapers, Inc., 19 TX S.Ct.Jrnl. 390, 541 S.W.2d 809 (Tex.1976), cert. denied 429 U.S. 1123, 97 S.Ct. 1160 (1977).

[68] Guinn v. Texas Newspapers, Inc., 738 S.W.2d 303 (Tex.App.1987), 6 Med. L.Rptr. 1024, cert. denied 488 U.S. 1041, 109 S.Ct. 864 (1989). An error-filled article referred to "Guinn," not to Judge Guinn, asserting that Guinn had been convicted of a felony. (In point of fact, Guinn had been the attorney for the convicted thief.)

Bootstrapping

Bootstrapping refers to a physical and legal impossibility. It comes from a humorous story featuring a punch line in which the protagonist grasps his own bootstraps (pieces of leather that boot wearers use to help slip on their footwear) and lifts himself. It is used in defamation to refer to a process in which a defendant will try to take a private person plaintiff and turn him into a public figure in order to require the plaintiff to pass the actual malice hurdle. Some defense attorneys will try to apply *Rosenbloom*, suggesting to the trial court that the allegedly defamatory story is proof that the plaintiff is widely known in the community. The determination of public figure or private person status is a matter of law, that is to say, it is a decision by the court rather than any jury.

Sometimes, this attempt to bootstrap the plaintiff will take the form of offering up copies of the defendant's own stories, stories of other media outlets reporting on the defendant's stories and other stories laying out the progress of the defamation suit. Stories published subsequent to the initial, defamatory story will not make a private person a public figure. The public/private figure determination is made at that point in time when the initial and allegedly defamatory statement is published. The courts must look to the conduct of the plaintiff to see if she is an all-purpose public figure or a limited purpose public figure. Merely being caught up in an event that draws the attention of the media or a single media outlet does not necessarily make an otherwise private person a public figure. As the Supreme Court said in *Wolston*, to make people public figures just because they are caught up in a newsworthy event would reimpose the failed doctrine set forth in the plurality in *Rosenbloom*. "We repudiated this position in *Gertz* and in *Firestone*, however, and we reject it again today."[69]

SEC. 32.   SUMMARY JUDGMENT

Winning the libel suit without having to go to trial.

If a judge at the threshold of a libel trial finds that a plaintiff is a public figure or public official, the case moves at once to a second pretrial consideration, of great importance to the defending news medium and the plaintiff. The plaintiff alleges actual malice, and the defendant ordinarily denies it and moves that the judge dismiss the case in a "summary judgment" for the defendant. Winning such a motion avoids a trial.

Summary judgment is a way to maintain judicial efficiency. If a party cannot win a case, there is no need to go through the lengthy

---

[69] Wolston v. Reader's Digest Association, 443 U.S. 157, 99 S.Ct. 2701 (1979).

and costly process of trying a case. There can be two bases for coming to the conclusion that a party cannot win—either the facts won't support a case or the law will not let a party win. For example: John Doe makes a $1,000 bet with Jane Roe on the outcome of an election. Doe loses. Roe wants to collect but Doe refuses to pay. Roe sues in state court. Doe may be able to dispose of the case through summary judgment. Some states will not allow their courts to be used to enforce a gambling debt. There, the law will make it impossible for Roe to win and the case may be disposed of through summary judgment. On the other hand, if Doe is able to produce evidence that he has paid, such as a signed receipt from Roe, he can win on summary judgment based on the facts.

Avoiding trial is desirable for a number of reasons. First, to defend the average libel suit through a trial will cost an average of $175,000, according to a 1991 study by John Soloski.[70] Second, the extended distraction and emotional drain of a libel suit add up to a real threat to vigorous reporting. The importance of summary judgment to the media's defense and to the public need for robust, uninhibited, wide-open reporting was laid out in the decision in Washington Post Co. v. Keogh,[71] an early case that interpreted Times v. Sullivan:

> In the First Amendment area, summary procedures are * * * essential. For the stake here, if harassment succeeds, is free debate. One of the purposes of the *Times* principle, in addition to protecting persons from being cast in damages in libel suits filed by public officials, is to prevent persons from being discouraged in the full and free exercise of their First Amendment rights with respect to the conduct of their government.

In ruling on the motion for summary judgment by the defendant, the judge must make a decision: Is there a "genuine issue of material fact"—a substantial claim by the plaintiff supported by evidence—that there was knowing or reckless falsity in the publication?[72]

Chief Justice Warren Burger of the United States Supreme Court in 1979 wrote a famous footnote—number 9 in Hutchinson v. Proxmire—casting doubt on the appropriateness of summary judg-

[70] John Soloski, draft proposal for The Libel Law Reform Movement (with Randall Bezanson), published in 1992 by the Guilford Press of New York; "Libel Law and Journalistic Malpractice: A Preliminary Analysis of Fault in Libel Litigation," paper presented to the Law Division at the August, 1991, convention of the Association for Education in Journalism and Mass Communication.

[71] Washington Post v. Keogh, 125 U.S.App.D.C. 32, 365 F.2d 965, 968 (1966).

[72] Restatement, Second, Torts, Vol. 3, p. 220. Cerrito v. Time, Inc., 449 F.2d 306 (9th Cir.1971); Hayes v. Booth Newspapers, Inc., 97 Mich.App. 758, 295 N.W.2d 858 (1980), 97 Mich.App. 758, 295 N.W.2d 858, 6 Med.L.Rptr. 2319.

ment in libel cases. Lower courts take his admonition into account and sometimes have found it a basis for denial of summary judgment, but summary judgments seem to be granted defendants far more often in libel suits brought by public people than they are denied.[73] Despite the famed footnote, many defamation actions—perhaps as many as 75 per cent of those brought by public figures or officials in the last decade—have been ended by grants of summary judgments to media defendants.

In a decision helpful to the media, the Supreme Court ruled in Jack Anderson v. Liberty Lobby, Inc. (1986) that public official or public figure suits must be ended before trial by summary judgment unless libel can be shown with "convincing clarity." Anderson was sued after articles said to portray Willis Carto and Liberty Lobby as Neo–Nazi, racist, and fascist.

Plaintiffs Carto and Liberty Lobby argued against the summary judgment, saying that the researcher for the Jack Anderson column's articles had relied on several unreliable sources and because there were inaccuracies in the articles. Writing for the Supreme Court, Justice White wrote that trial judges must decide, based on pre-trial affidavits, whether a public plaintiff can meet the actual malice standard by "clear convincing evidence." If not, summary judgment should be granted.[74]

Police Chief Prease alleged in a suit that stories in the Akron, (O.) *Beacon Journal* libeled him. Assistant Managing Editor Timothy Smith said that all statements in the stories were made in good faith with no serious doubts about their accuracy, and the Chief did not refute Smith. Thus the judge found that there was no issue between them about actual malice—no "genuine issue of material fact" that would have to be argued before a jury for decision. He granted summary judgment for the newspaper.[75]

But the United States Court of Appeals, Fourth District, found such an issue in Fitzgerald v. Penthouse Intern., Ltd.,[76] and reversed a trial court's grant of summary judgment to *Penthouse.* Fitzgerald, a specialist in the use of dolphins as military weapons, sued *Penthouse* for an article about his work that might have been construed as an allegation of espionage—selling dolphins trained as

---

[73] Hutchinson v. Proxmire, 443 U.S. 111, 99 S.Ct. 2675 (1979). Yiamouyiannis v. Consumers Union of U.S., Inc., 619 F.2d 932 (2d Cir.1980), 6 Med.L.Rptr. 1065. Defendants' motions for summary judgment in the 1980s have been successful about 75% of the time, and Burger's "footnote 9" has been used rarely: Libel Defense Resource Center Bulletin #13, Spring 1985, 10.

[74] Anderson v. Liberty Lobby, Inc., 477 U.S. 242, 106 S.Ct. 2505 (1986), 12 Med.L.Rptr. 2297.

[75] Prease v. Poorman (Ohio Com.Pl.1981), 7 Med.L.Rptr. 2378.

[76] Fitzgerald v. Penthouse Intern., Ltd., 691 F.2d 666 (4th Cir.1982), 8 Med.L.Rptr. 2340.

"torpedoes" to other nations, for "fast bucks." The Court found that *Penthouse* relied almost exclusively for its story upon a questionable source, and detailed his "many bold assertions about the United States intelligence community" which in some cases "invite skepticism." It quoted St. Amant v. Thompson:[77] Recklessness may be found "where there are obvious reasons to doubt the veracity of the informant or the accuracy of his reports." Fitzgerald had presented a factual question about whether *Penthouse* had "obvious reasons to doubt" its source; *Penthouse* would have to go to trial on the matter of actual malice.

Litigation Note: *Experienced litigators will use summary judgment to throw a wrench into the plaintiff's case. Once the case is underway, the defendant's attorney will obtain affidavits from the publisher and other involved persons. Those affidavits will attest to the subjective belief of the affiants that they entertained no doubts as to the accuracy of the story and they surely did not publish with knowing falsity. The defense attorney will then move for summary judgment on the basis of those affidavits. The plaintiff will not have had time to complete discovery and so will have little evidence to present in opposing the motion. Some judges, willing to keep their dockets as clear as possible, will grant the motion. The plaintiff must then go through the appellate process to revive the case. The added time and expense will do much to discourage the plaintiff. The plaintiff's attorney, who most likely took the case on contingency, will have added expense. The attorney may wind up taking a bigger chunk of any ultimate recovery because of the extra steps in the lawsuit.*

Neutral Reportage

A sometimes useful—but not-to-be-trusted—defense against libel lawsuits goes under the name of "neutral reportage." The neutral reportage argument is one which lawyers sometimes use on behalf of media clients, but as of 1992, that defense had not attained the status of a reliable constitutional defense.

Back in 1977, Judge Irving Kaufman of the U.S. Court of Appeals, Second Circuit, pioneered the neutral reportage concept in Edwards v. National Audubon Society, Inc.[78] Judge Kaufman wrote for the court that the Constitution protects accurate, unbiased news reporting of accusations made against public figures regardless of the reporter's view of their truth. This concept is related to the long-standing common-law and statutory doctrine of qualified

---

[77] St. Amant v. Thompson, 390 U.S. 727, 732, 88 S.Ct. 1323, 1326 (1968).

[78] Edwards v. National Audubon Society, Inc., 556 F.2d 113 (2d Cir.1977). See Kathryn D. Sowle, "Defamation and the First Amendment: The Case for a Constitutional Privilege of Fair Report," 54 NYU Law Review 469 (June, 1969).

privilege immunity from successful libel suit for fair and accurate reports of official proceedings. (See Sec. 33.)

The case arose when The New York Times carried a story reporting accurately a National Audubon Society's written statement that some scientists were paid to lie about the effects of the pesticide DDT upon birds. This outraged scientists who were implicated, and they brought a libel suit against the Society and the Times. Overturning a jury verdict for the scientists, Judge Kaufman wrote for the Court of Appeals that "a libel judgment against the *Times,* in face of this finding of fact, is constitutionally impermissible." He reasoned:[79]

> At stake in this case is a fundamental principle. Succinctly stated, when a responsible, prominent organization like the National Audubon Society makes serious charges against a public figure, the First Amendment protects the accurate and disinterested reporting of those charges, regardless of the reporter's private views of their validity. * * * What is newsworthy about such accusations is that they were made. We do not believe that the press may be required under the First Amendment to suppress newsworthy statements merely because it has serious doubts regarding their truth.

Judge Kaufman applied this doctrine only to situations where the press was not taking sides or was deliberately distorting statements in order to launch a personal attack. But in this case, the judge said, reporter John Devlin of The Times wrote an accurate account, did not take the Audubon Society's side in his article. Further, Devlin's article included the scientists' indignant responses to the Audubon Society's charges. Judge Kaufman's opinion termed Devlin's work "an exemplar of fair and dispassionate reporting.... Accordingly, we hold that it was privileged under the First Amendment."[80]

Welcome as the "neutral reportage" concept was to the news media, it quickly was met by an opposing view from another U.S. Court of Appeals. Writing in Dickey v. CBS (1978), Judge Hunder ruled for his court that "no constitutional privilege of neutral reportage exists."[81] That case involved a libel action resulting from a television broadcast of a pretaped talk show in which a Pennsylvania Congressman accused a public figure of accepting payoffs. Although CBS won the case, it was not on "neutral reportage" grounds, which Judge Hunder said flew in the face of the much-

[79] Edwards v. National Audubon Society, Inc., 556 F.2d 113, 120 (2d Cir.1977).
[80] Ibid.
[81] Dickey v. CBS Inc., 583 F.2d 1221 (3d Cir.1978).

cited decision in St. Amant v. Thompson (1964)[82] (mentioned earlier at page 222.) Judge Hunder criticized the Audubon decision:[83]

> While the Second Circuit [in Edwards v. Audubon Society] found that there can be no liability despite the publisher's "serious doubts" as to truthfulness, *St. Amant* holds that for libel against a public figure to be proved, "[t]here must be sufficient evidence to permit the conclusion that the defendant in fact entertained *serious doubts* as to the truth of his publication. Publishing with such doubts shows reckless disregard for truth or falsity and demonstrates actual malice."

* * *

> We therefore conclude that a constitutional privilege of neutral reportage is not created * * * merely because an individual newspaper or television or radio station decides that a particular statement is newsworthy.

Since the Dickey case of 1978, the concept of neutral reportage has had an uneven and generally unpredictable history of acceptance and rejection, but it may be said that at times it has proven to be a useful defense for the media. A number of states have accepted the neutral reportage doctrine, including Florida and Ohio;[84] others have rejected it.[85] In Illinois in the 1980s, one Appellate Court adopted the neutral report privilege, another rejected it, and the state's Supreme Court refused to consider the issue.[86]

Efforts to use—and get wider recognition for—the defense of neutral reportage continued into the 1990s. When the defense has succeeded, it has been in situations where the plaintiff was a public figure and where the report involved was fair and accurate without the espousal of a point of view by the news medium.[87] For example, the defense failed in Cianci v. New Times Publishing Co. There,

---

[82] St. Amant v. Thompson, 390 U.S. 727, 731, 88 S.Ct. 1323, 1325 (1968).

[83] Dickey v. CBS, Inc., 583 F.2d 1221, 1225–1226 (3d Cir.1978).

[84] El Amin v. Miami Herald Pub. Co. (Fla.Cir.Ct.1983), 9 Med.L.Rptr. 1079; Horvath v. Telegraph (Ohio App.1982), 8 Med.L.Rptr. 1657. See especially John B. McCrory et al., "Constitutional Privilege in Libel Law," 1993 Revision by Robert D. Sack et.al., in James C. Goodale, Communications Law 1993, Vol. II (New York: Practising Law Institute, 1993), pp. 355–363.

[85] New York: Hogan v. Herald Co., 84 A.D.2d 470, 446 N.Y.S.2d 836 (1982), 8 Med.L.Rptr. 1137, affirmed 58 N.Y.2d 630, 458 N.Y.S.2d 538, 444 N.E.2d 1002 (1982), 8 Med.L.Rptr. 2567; Kentucky: McCall v. Courier–Journal and Louisville Times Co., 623 S.W.2d 882 (Ky.1981), 7 Med.L.Rptr. 2118; Michigan: Postill v. Booth Newspapers, Inc., 118 Mich.App. 608, 325 N.W.2d 511 (1982), 8 Med.L.Rptr. 2222.

[86] Fogus v. Capital Cities Media, Inc., 111 Ill.App.3d 1060, 67 Ill.Dec. 616, 444 N.E.2d 1100 (1982), 9 Med.L.Rptr. 1141, 1143.

[87] Goodale, loc. cit.

New Times was found by the Second Circuit (enunciator of the *Edwards* doctrine) to have violated many of the qualifications limiting the privilege. The publication was flatly denied the neutral reportage privilege for its story suggesting falsely that a mayor had been a rapist.[88]

In 1989, in a case setting (at least temporarily) a record for punitive damages against a newspaper in a case surviving the appeals process, the neutral reportage case was rejected as inapplicable. The Pittsburgh Post–Gazette paid (including $561,000 in interest) damages totaling $2.8 million. (Of that amount, a total of $2 million was in punitive damages.) In that case, DiSalle v. P.G. Publishing Co.[89], a Pennsylvania court held:

> ... [I]f neutral reportage is to be recognized as a constitutional privilege, it can offer protection irrespective of the publisher's belief in the truth or falsity of the charges only when a public official or public figure levels a false charge against a public official or figure.

On the other hand, as attorney Robert McGough said after representing the Pittsburgh–Post Gazette in this case, newspapers commonly report on accusations by private parties against public officials " 'without knowing or caring whether the accusation is true ... In Pennsylvania, it is now not enough to report the accusation accurately.' "[90]

Neutral reportage, then, is an unreliable defense. The policy decision to publish or broadcast a story involving defamatory charges in an unprivileged situation—even against a person or entity appearing to be a "public official" or a "public figure"— should be checked out not only by journalists but by their legal advisers before publication.

In a recent case that shows the continuing controversy over the doctrine, Khalid Khawar v. Globe International Inc.[91], the California Court of Appeals upheld a judgment against the Globe tabloid over a story that reported that a California farmer and former reporter was the "real assassin" of Sen. Robert F. Kennedy. The *Globe* ran a story about a book about the assassination. Author Robert Morrow published a book on the senator's murder, "The Senator Must Die: The Murder of Robert F. Kennedy," in which he claimed that Kennedy was killed by the Iranian secret police at the

---

[88] Cianci v. New Times Publishing Co., 639 F.2d 54 (2d Cir.1980), 6 Med.L.Rptr. 1625.

[89] Albert Scardino, "Pittsburgh Paper Pays $2.8 million Libel Award," The New York Times, July 12, 1989, p. 9; DiSalle v. P.G. Publishing Co., 375 Pa.Super. 510, 544 A.2d 1345, 1363 (1988), 15 Med.L.Rptr. 1873.

[90] Scardino, loc. cit.

[91] Khawar v. Globe International, 54 Cal.Rptr.2d 92, 24 Med. L. Rptr. 2345 (Cal.Ct.App.1996).

direction of the Mafia. Morrow, whose claims were not supported by any other investigators into the assassination, identified Khawar as the actual assassin and gave his name as Ali Ahmand, the name of Khawar's father.

Khawar sued and was awarded $1.1 million. The court found Khawar a private figure and said that neutral reportage would not apply. Further, the appellate court affirmed the jury's conclusion that the *Globe* published its article with actual malice. As with *Connaughton*, the jury concluded that the *Globe* had failed to contact sources who could have revealed the inaccuracy of the story. "The article is not merely false, but glaringly false—it makes assertions that on the surface seem extraordinarily improbable—a fact that certainly is circumstantial evidence that Globe's representatives had a very high degree of skepticism concerning the truthfulness of the charges."[92] The California Supreme Court accepted the case for consideration in the fall of 1996.[93]

SEC. 33. QUALIFIED PRIVILEGE AS A DEFENSE

News media may publish defamation from legislative, judicial or other public and official proceedings without fear of successful libel or slander action; fair and accurate reports of these statements are privileged.

Since long before the landmark year 1964 and the constitutional defense developed in and after New York Times Co. v. Sullivan, libel suits have been defended under statutory and common law provisions termed *qualified privilege, fair comment and criticism,* and *truth.* As noted earlier, the theory that free expression contributes to the public good in a self-governing society underlies the older defenses as well as the constitutional defense.

In some circumstances it is so important to society that people be allowed to speak without fear of a suit for defamation that their words are given immunity from a finding of libel or slander. The immunity is called privilege. For purposes of the mass media, it is applicable especially in connection with government activity.[94] The paramount importance of full freedom for participants in court, legislative or executive proceedings to say whatever bears on the matter, gives all the participants a full immunity from successful libel action. The immunity for the participant in official proceedings is called "absolute" privilege. No words relevant to the business of

---

[92] B.J. Palermo, "Who Killed RFK? Not This Guy," The National Law Journal, A–1, A–20, Aug. 25, 1997.

[93] Khawar v. Globe International, 57 Cal.Rptr.2d 277, 923 P.2d 766 (Cal.1996).

[94] For other circumstances where it applies, see Prosser, pp. 804–805; see also Robert Sack and Sandra Baron, op. cit., Chapter 6, pp. 361–408.

the proceeding will support a suit for defamation. If a person is defamed in these proceedings, he cannot recover damages.

Public policy also demands, in an open society, that people know to the fullest what goes on in the proceedings. For this reason, anyone who reports proceedings is given a limited or "qualified" immunity from successful suit for defamation. For the public at large, "anyone" ordinarily means the mass media. The protection is ordinarily more limited for the reporter of a proceeding than for the participant in the proceeding. It is thus called "qualified" (or "conditional") privilege.[95]

It may be argued that the mere fact of a person's participation in an official proceeding makes him a "public figure," and so puts him under the rigorous requirements of proving *Sullivan's* actual malice in a libel suit. The response, of course, is that neither Attorney Gertz nor Mrs. Firestone became a public figure through taking part in official court proceedings that resulted in news stories about them. As discussed in Chapter 5, both received damages for libel.

It has been held that any citizen has *absolute* immunity in any criticism he makes of government. The City of Chicago brought a libel suit against the *Chicago Tribune,* claiming damages of $10 million through the *Tribune's* campaign coverage in 1920. The stories had said that the city was broke, that its credit "is shot to pieces," that it "is hurrying on to bankruptcy and is threatened with a receivership for its revenue."

The court denied the city's claim. It said that in any libelous publication concerning a municipal corporation, the citizen and the newspaper possess absolute privilege.[96]

> Every citizen has a right to criticize an inefficient government without fear of civil as well as criminal prosecution. This absolute privilege is founded on the principle that it is advantageous for the public interest that the citizen should not be in any way fettered in his statements [97]
> . . .

Qualified privilege in reporting official proceedings is the heart of the concern here. The privilege arose in the law of England, the

---

[95] A few states give absolute privilege to press reports of official proceedings, e.g. Thompson's Laws of New York, 1939, Civ.P. § 337, Wis.Stats.1931, § 331.05(1). And as we have seen in Ch. 4, Sec. 22, broadcasters are immune from defamation suits brought for the words of politicians in campaign broadcasts: Farmers Educational & Coop. Union of America v. WDAY, Inc., 360 U.S. 525, 79 S.Ct. 1302 (1959).

[96] City of Chicago v. Tribune Co., 307 Ill. 595, 139 N.E. 86, 90 (1923).

[97] See also Grafton v. ABC, 70 Ohio App.2d 205, 435 N.E.2d 1131 (1980), 7 Med.L.Rptr. 1134, 1136, quoting Capital District Regional Off–Track Betting Corp. v. Northeastern Harness Horsemen's Ass'n, 92 Misc.2d 232, 399 N.Y.S.2d 597, 598 (1977).

basic rationale having been developed before the start of the nineteenth century in connection with newspaper reports of court proceedings.[98] While American courts relied on English decisions, America was ahead of England in expanding the protection for press reports. The immunity was broadened to cover the reporting of legislative and other public official proceedings by the New York legislature in 1854, 14 years before privilege for reporting legislative bodies was recognized in England.[99] Other states readily adopted the New York rule.

In America a famous figure in jurisprudence stated the heart of the rationale for qualified privilege in an early case that has been relied upon by American courts countless times since. Judge Oliver Wendell Holmes, Jr., then of the Massachusetts bench and later a Justice of the United States Supreme Court, wrote the words in Cowley v. Pulsifer (1884).[100] Publisher Royal Pulsifer's *Boston Herald* had printed the content of a petition seeking Charles Cowley's removal from the bar, and Cowley sued. Judge Holmes wrote that the public must have knowledge of judicial proceedings, not because one citizen's quarrels with another are important to public concern,

> * * * but because it is of the highest moment that those who administer justice should always act under the sense of public responsibility, and that every citizen should be able to satisfy himself with his own eyes as to the mode in which a public duty is performed.

The advantage to the nation in granting privilege to press reports, he stressed, is "the security which publicity gives for the proper administration of justice."[1]

The privilege is "qualified" in the sense that it must be fair and accurate. (For example, an accurate quote misleadingly published out of context may not be privileged if defamatory.) Also, in some jurisdictions, the privilege will not hold if the report of the proceeding is made with malice (in the sense of ill will). Fundamentally, however, if a news account is a fair and accurate summary of a public official proceeding or record, the citizen or reporter will be protected by the "reporter's privilege." Also, the story must be one of a "public and official proceeding," not a report of related material that emerges before, after, or in some way outside the proceeding.

---

[98] Curry v. Walter, 170 Eng.Rep. 419 (1796); King v. Wright, 101 Eng.Rep. 1396 (1799).

[99] New York Laws, 1854, Chap. 130; Wason v. Walter, L.R. 4 Q.B. 73 (1868).

[100] 137 Mass. 392, 394 (1884).

[1] Ibid.

Fair and Accurate Reports

Errors can destroy qualified privilege. Ponder the perils of careless note-taking, the constant danger of a misspelled name, the arcane and technical jargon and findings of law courts, and all the slip-ups of life that happen under tight deadlines. Further, if the report of an official proceeding is not fair to people involved in it, the reporter can be in trouble. We have seen in the previous chapter how Mrs. Firestone won a libel judgment for $100,000 from Time, Inc., for its error in reporting that her husband's divorce was granted on grounds of adultery.

In the case of Anthony Liquori of Agawam, Mass., a newspaper reporter made an error in an address after extracting other materials from a court record about a "breaking" case in which a man of the same name from Springfield pleaded guilty and was convicted. The reporter took an address from a phone book; the innocent Liquori was wrongly identified and sued the Republican Company, publisher of the Springfield papers which carried separate stories, both erroneous. The Republican defended with a plea of qualified privilege, arguing that the defense should hold "because the newspaper articles were a substantially accurate report of a judicial proceeding."[2] It asserted that since only the address of the accused was inaccurate, it had published an article which was "substantially true and accurate and entirely fair," and that no more was required. But citing several previous cases about fair and accurate press reports of official proceedings, the Massachusetts Appeals Court said:[3] " * * * an article which labels an innocent man as a criminal because it refers erroneously to his street address, which the reporter gained from a source outside the court records, is neither substantially accurate nor fair." It denied qualified privilege for the Republican. A wrong name, taken accurately from official police records, on the other hand, is privileged.[4]

Not every inaccuracy in reporting proceedings is fatal, however. Privilege did not fail in Mitchell v. Peoria Journal–Star, Inc.,[5] merely because the news story of a court action for liquor ordinance violation got the violators' place of arrest wrong. In Josephs v. News Syndicate Co., Inc.,[6] the newspaper did not lose privilege because somehow the reporter incorrectly slipped into his story of a

---

[2] Liquori v. Republican Co., 8 Mass.App.Ct. 671, 396 N.E.2d 726, 728 (1979), 5 Med.L.Rptr. 2180.

[3] Ibid., at 728–29, 5 Med.L.Rptr. at 2181.

[4] Biermann v. Pulitzer Pub. Co., 627 S.W.2d 87 (Mo.App.1981), 7 Med.L.Rptr. 2601. See also Murray v. Bailey, 613 F.Supp. 1276 (N.D.Cal.1985), 11 Med.L.Rptr. 1369. Report saying plaintiff arrested for drunk driving and assault and battery privileged as fair report when in fact plaintiff had been arrested for public intoxication and resisting arrest. Book author's later erroneous statement "convicted of drunken driving" held not privileged.

[5] Mitchell v. Peoria Journal–Star, Inc., 76 Ill.App.2d 154, 221 N.E.2d 516 (1966).

[6] Josephs v. News Syndicate Co., Inc., 5 Misc.2d 184, 159 N.Y.S.2d 537 (1957).

burglary arrest the statement that the accused had been found under a bed at the scene of the burglary.

Opinion and Extraneous Material

One way to destroy immunity for a news story is to add opinion or material extraneous to the proceeding. It is necessary for reporters to stick to the facts of what comes to light under officials' surveillance. Radio station KYW in Philadelphia broadcast a "documentary" on car-towing rackets, and Austin Purcell sued for defamation. The broadcast had used a judicial proceeding as a basis: a magistrate's hearing at which Purcell was convicted of violating the car-tow ordinance. (Purcell later was exonerated, on appeal.) But the producer of the documentary wove into his script some material he had gathered from other sources—the voices of a man and a woman claiming that they had been cheated and a conversation with detectives. Anonymous voices on the tape called Purcell a "thug" and a "racketeer." The producer added comment of his own to the effect that "the sentencing of a few racketeers is not enough." That was defamation, the court said, and it was not protected by qualified privilege. The documentary lost the protection of qualified privilege because it contained "exaggerated additions."[7]

"Old–Style Malice"

New York Times Co. v. Sullivan (1964) gave the term "actual malice" a restricted meaning where public officials and figures are concerned. Actual malice means that the publisher knew the words were false, or had reckless disregard for whether they were false or not. Malice before that decision was defined in many ways, including ill will toward another, hatred, intent to harm, bad motive, or lack of good faith. It used to be that people who claimed that news stories of government proceedings libeled them, often charged "malice" in the stories, in terms such as these. Such definitions of "old-style malice" are still alive for libel that does not proceed under the constitutional protection provided by New York Times v. Sullivan.

Consider a case in which the St. Paul Dispatch was accused of a malicious report based on a complaint filed in district court. The newspaper's story said that William and Frank Hurley had been accused of depleting almost all of the estate of an aged woman before her death. Some $200,000 was involved. The Hurleys sued for libel, saying that the report was malicious and therefore not privileged.

[7] Purcell v. Westinghouse Broadcasting Co., 411 Pa. 167, 191 A.2d 662, 666 (1963). Ibid., 668. See also Jones v. Pulitzer Pub. Co., 240 Mo. 200, 144 S.W. 441 (1912); Robinson v. Johnson, 152 C.C.A. 505, 239 Fed. 671 (1917); Embers Supper Club, Inc. v. Scripps–Howard Broadcasting Co., 9 Ohio St.3d 22, 457 N.E.2d 1164 (1984), 10 Med.L.Rptr. 1729.

The court did not agree, and in effect said the paper had showed neither "old style malice" (an inaccurate report " 'made solely for the purpose of causing harm to the person defamed' ") nor the harder to prove "actual malice" under the New York Times rule. The court ruled the Hurleys could not win their suit because they could produce no evidence of malice at the trial.[8]

Other courts have used old definitions of malice, where qualified privilege is pleaded, alongside knowing or reckless falsehood. Thus one says there is no malice in that which "the publisher reasonably believed to be true;" another speaks of malice as "intent to injure," and another of malice as "ill will."[9]

Official Proceedings

Reports of official activity outside the proceeding—the trial, the hearing, the legislative debate or committee—may not be protected. Some official activity has the color of official proceeding but not the reality.

To start with the courts: Any trial including that of a lesser court "not of record" such as a police magistrate's furnishes the basis for privilege.[10] The ex parte proceeding in which only one party to a legal controversy is represented affords privilege to reporting.[11] So does the grand jury report published in open court.[12]

In many states, the attorneys' "pleadings" filed with the clerk of court as the basic documents starting a lawsuit are *not* proceedings that furnish protection. In those states the judge must be involved; an early decision stated the rule that for the immunity to attach, the pleadings must have been submitted "to the judicial mind with a view to judicial action,"[13] even if only in pretrial hearings on motions.

A 1927 New York decision, as so often in defamation, led the way for several states' rejecting this position and granting protection to reports of pleadings. Newspapers had carried a story based on a complaint filed by Mrs. Elizabeth Nichols against Mrs. Anne Campbell, claiming the latter had defrauded her of $16,000. After the news stories had appeared, Mrs. Nichols withdrew her suit. Mrs. Campbell filed libel suit. Acknowledging that nearly all courts

---

[8] Hurley v. Northwest Publications, Inc., 273 F.Supp. 967, 972, 974 (D.Minn.1967).

[9] Bannach v. Field Enterprises, Inc., 5 Ill.App.3d 692, 284 N.E.2d 31, 32 (1972); and Brunn v. Weiss, 32 Mich.App. 428, 188 N.W.2d 904, 905 (1971). See, also, Orrison v. Vance, 262 Md. 285, 277 A.2d 573, 578 (1971), 3 Med.L.Rptr. 1170.

[10] McBee v. Fulton, 47 Md. 403 (1878); Flues v. New Nonpareil Co., 155 Iowa 290, 135 N.W. 1083 (1912); See also Sack, *loc. cit.*

[11] Metcalf v. Times Pub. Co., 20 R.I. 674, 40 A. 864 (1898).

[12] Sweet v. Post Pub. Co., 215 Mass. 450, 102 N.E. 660 (1913).

[13] Barber v. St. Louis Dispatch Co., 3 Mo.App. 377 (1877); Finnegan v. Eagle Printing Co., 173 Wis. 5, 179 N.W. 788 (1920).

had refused qualified privilege to stories based on pleadings not seen by a judge, the New York Court of Appeals said it would no longer follow this rule.

The New York high court conceded that it is easy for a malicious persons to file pleadings in order to vent hostility against others in news stories, and then withdraw the lawsuits. But it said that this can happen also after judges are in the proceeding; suits have been dropped before verdicts have been reached. It added that newspapers had so often printed stories about actions started before they reached a judge that "the public has learned that accusation is not proof and that such actions are at times brought in malice to result in failure."[14] The newspapers won.

That set up what is sometimes called the "Campbell Rule," which says that pleadings may be reported on, fairly and accurately, as soon as they are filed with a court and before a judge has acted upon them. Perhaps 20 states follow this rule today. That is, the filing of a pleading is a reportable public and official act appears to be a public and official act in the course of judicial proceedings in the District of Columbia and in a number of states, including Alabama, California, Georgia, Kentucky, Nevada, New York, Ohio, Pennsylvania, South Carolina, Tennessee, Texas, Washington and Wyoming.

The Campbell Rule, increasingly, seems to be "the modern rule," with more and more courts' language tending toward making the contents of pleadings starting a lawsuit a public record to be reported upon.[15] That is fortunate for reporters, editors and broadcast news directors, many who long have assumed that once a pleading is filed with a court clerk, it is fair game.

But other states have not chosen to follow this rule. Massachusetts specifically rejected it in 1945. *The Boston Herald–Traveler* had published a story based on pleadings filed in an alienation of affections case, had been sued for libel, and had lost. The state Supreme Court said:[16]

> * * * the publication of accusations made by one party against another is neither a legal nor a moral duty of newspapers. Enterprise in that matter ought to be at the risk of paying damages if the accusations prove false. To be safe, a newspaper has only to send its reporters to listen to

[14] Campbell v. New York Evening Post, 245 N.Y. 320, 327, 157 N.E. 153, 155 (1927).

[15] Henry R. Kaufman, ed., Libel Defense Resource Center (LDRC) 50–State Survey, 1991 (New York: LDRC, 1991).

[16] Sanford v. Boston Herald–Traveler Corp., 318 Mass. 156, 61 N.E.2d 5 (1945): But see Sibley v. Holyoke Transcript–Telegram Pub. Co., Inc., 391 Mass. 468, 461 N.E.2d 823 (1984), 10 Med.L.Rptr. 1557.

hearings rather than to search the files of cases not yet brought before the court.

Even in those jurisdictions where "pleadings" are privileged, careful adherence to basic rules of reporting is a must. That is, it should be made clear where the information is from: Attribution to the privileged document is good self-protection. The best rule, of course, is to play fair. Ethical reporters and editors will want to make sure that stories explicitly say that a pleading beginning a lawsuit tells only the plaintiff's side of the story. Reporters may wish to go further, phoning lawsuit defendants or the defendants' attorneys to give them an opportunity to comment. (It is likely that defendants may be unwilling to comment in the face of pending litigation, but it never hurts to ask and it will indicate reportorial fairness.)

Stories based on the following situations were outside "official proceedings" of courts and did not furnish news media the protection of qualified privilege: A newsman's interview of ("conversation with") a United States commissioner, concerning an earlier arraignment before the commissioner;[17] the words of a judge[18] and of an attorney[19] in courtrooms, just before trials were convened formally, and the taking by a judge of a deposition in his courtroom, where he was acting in a "ministerial capacity" only, not as a judge.[20] In Bufalino v. Associated Press,[21] the wire service did not actually demonstrate that it relied on FBI records, nor did it identify "officials" who were unnamed sources. So, the AP did not show that it was within the scope of privilege.[22] In a Louisiana case,[23] a newspaper reporter was held to be outside the privilege because he relied on another newspaper's story, even though the latter was based on a sheriff's press release.

Executive Officers and Privilege

Shift now to news stories about the executive and administrative branch of government. When government officials hold a hearing or issue a report or even a press release, absolute privilege usually protects them. And where absolute privilege leads, qualified privilege for press reports ordinarily follows. Yet while major and minor federal officials enjoy the privilege under federal decisions, state courts have not been unanimous in granting it.[24]

[17] Wood v. Constitution Pub. Co., 57 Ga.App. 123, 194 S.E. 760 (1937).

[18] Douglas v. Collins, 243 App.Div. 546, 276 N.Y.S. 87 (1934).

[19] Rogers v. Courier Post Co., 2 N.J. 393, 66 A.2d 869 (1949).

[20] Mannix v. Portland Telegram, 144 Or. 172, 23 P.2d 138 (1933).

[21] Bufalino v. Associated Press, 692 F.2d 266 (2d Cir.1982), 8 Med.L.Rptr. 2384.

[22] Ibid., 271–272, 2389.

[23] Melon v. Capital City Press, 407 So.2d 85 (La.App.1981), 8 Med.L.Rptr. at 1167.

[24] Barr v. Matteo, 360 U.S. 564, 79 S.Ct. 1335 (1959); Prosser, pp. 802–803; Kaufman, LDRC 50–State Survey.

The formal hearings of many administrative bodies have a quasi-judicial character, in which testimony is taken, interrogation is performed, deliberation is engaged in, and findings are reported in writing. The reporter can have confidence that such proceedings are "safe" to report. The minutes of a meeting and audits of a city water commission were the basis for a successful plea of privilege by a newspaper whose story reflected badly on an engineer.[25] The Federal Trade Commission investigated a firm and an account based on the investigation said that the firm had engaged in false branding and labeling; the account was privileged.[26] A news story reporting that an attorney had charged another with perjury was taken from a governor's extradition hearing, a quasi-judicial proceeding, and was privileged.[27]

Also, informal hearings or investigations carried out by executive-administrative officers, even those outside of hearing-chambers and without the banging of a gavel, usually furnish privilege. For example, a state tax commissioner audited a city's books and reported irregularities in the city council's handling of funds. A story based on the report caused a suit for libel, and the court held that the story was protected by privilege.[28]

Yet not every investigation provides a basis for the defense of qualified privilege; reporters and city editors especially need to know what the judicial precedent of their state is. In a Texas case, a district attorney investigated a plot to rob a bank and obtained confessions. He made the confessions available to the press. A successful libel suit brought was brought on the basis of the resulting news story. The confessions were held insufficient executive proceedings to provide the protection.[29]

Police reporters need to be especially alert to libel dangers. "Blotters" listing the records of arrests and charges made are sources for many news stories. Their status as a basis for a plea of privilege varies from state to state.[30] Police stations generally have a written record—now often kept on computer—which keeps track of incidents and activities around the clock. These reports vary in form and completeness; blotters usually are starting points in the reporting process, with additional checking—including interviewing

[25] Holway v. World Pub. Co., 171 Okl. 306, 44 P.2d 881 (1935).

[26] Mack, Miller Candle Co. v. Macmillan Co., 239 App.Div. 738, 269 N.Y.S. 33 (1934).

[27] Brown v. Globe Printing Co., 213 Mo. 611, 112 S.W. 462 (1908).

[28] Swearingen v. Parkersburg Sentinel Co., 125 W.Va. 731, 26 S.E.2d 209 (1943).

[29] Caller Times Pub.Co. v. Chandler, 134 Tex. 1, 130 S.W.2d 853 (1939). But see Woolbright v. Sun Communications, Inc., 480 S.W.2d 864 (Mo.1972).

[30] Sherwood v. Evening News Ass'n, 256 Mich. 318, 239 N.W. 305 (1931); M.J. Petrick, "The Press, the Police Blotter and Public Policy," 46 Journalism Quarterly 475, 1969.

of officials—needed to get reasonably complete information. As suggested earlier, larger departments often establish some form of police "hot line," which—for safety's sake—probably ought to be regarded as unprivileged.[31]

Oral reports of preliminary investigations by policemen do not support a plea of privilege in some states. The *Rutland Herald* published a story about two brothers arrested on charges of robbery, and included this paragraph:

> Arthur was arrested on information given to police by the younger brother, it is said. According to authorities, Floyd in his alleged confession stated that Arthur waited outside the window in the rear of the clothing store while Floyd climbed through a broken window the second time to destroy possible clues left behind.

A suit for libel was brought, and the court denied qualified privilege to the story. It reviewed other states' decisions on whether statements attributed to police were a basis for privilege in news, and held that "a preliminary police investigation" is not a proper basis.[32]

The State of New Jersey has provided by statute that "official statements issued by police department heads" protect news stories, and Georgia has a similar law.[33] In other states, courts have provided the protection through decisions in libel suits. In Kilgore v. Koen,[34] an Oregon case, privilege was granted to a story in which deputy sheriffs' statements about the evidence and arrest in a case involving a school principal were the newspaper's source.

Legislative Branch Reporting

As for the legislative branch, the third general sphere of government, state statutes have long declared that the immunity holds in stories from legislative settings. The legislative privilege is of paramount importance if the media are to fulfill their watchdog function.[35] For debates on the floor of Congress or of a state legislature, there has been no question that protection would apply to news stories. A few early cases indicated that stories of petty legislative bodies such as a town council[36] would not be privileged; but today's reporter need have little fear on this count.

---

[31] See note 30, above; see also Phillips v. Evening Star Newspaper Co., 424 A.2d 78 (D.C.App.1980), 6 Med.L.Rptr. 2191.

[32] Lancour v. Herald & Globe Ass'n, 111 Vt. 371, 17 A.2d 253 (1941); Burrows v. Pulitzer Pub. Co., 255 S.W. 925 (Mo.App.1923); Pittsburgh Courier Pub. Co. v. Lubore, 91 U.S.App.D.C. 311, 200 F.2d 355 (1952).

[33] Henry R. Kaufman, LDRC 50–State Survey 1990–91, pp. 249 and 263, citing O.G.C.A. § 51–5–7 and N.J.S.A. 2A:43–1.

[34] Kilgore v. Koen, 133 Or. 1, 288 P. 192 (1930).

[35] New York Laws, 1854, Chap. 130; Wason v. Walter, L.R. 4 Q.B. 73 (1868).

[36] Buckstaff v. Hicks, 94 Wis. 34, 68 N.W. 403 (1896).

In news stories about a New Jersey municipal council meeting, the city manager was quoted as saying that he was planning to bypass two policemen for promotion because they were insubordinate and "I should have fired them." There was some question as to whether the meeting was the regular one, or a session held in a conference room later. The New Jersey Supreme Court said that that didn't matter. It was not only an official but also a public meeting, at which motions were made by councilmen, heated discussion ensued, and the city manager was questioned by councilmen. Privilege held for the newspaper.[37]

One question about reporting legislatures was settled in a series of "chain" libel suits in the 1920s against several major newspapers. The "qualified privilege" immunity holds for news reports of committees of legislative bodies.[38] (Chain libel suits exist where one plaintiff sues a publisher in several states or jurisdictions on the basis of one allegedly defamatory report.)

Legislative committees have a long history of operating under loose procedural rules.[39] Irregular procedures raise the question whether committee activity always meets the requirements of a "legislative proceeding" which is the basis for immunity in news reports.[40] In reporting committee activity, the reporter may sense danger signals if the committee:

Holds hearings without a quorum;

Publishes material that its clerks have collected, without itself first investigating charges in the material;

Has not authorized the work of its subcommittees;

Has a chairman given to issuing "reports" or holding press conferences on matters that the committee itself has not investigated.

When state and congressional investigating committees relentlessly hunted "subversion" in the 1940s and 1950s, thousands of persons were tainted with the charge of "communist" during the committee proceedings. High procedural irregularity was common. Yet only one libel case growing out of these irregular proceedings

[37] Swede v. Passaic Daily News, 30 N.J. 320, 153 A.2d 36 (1959).

[38] Cresson v. Louisville Courier–Journal, 299 Fed. 487 (6th Cir.1924).

[39] Walter Gellhorn (ed.), The States and Subversion (Ithaca: Cornell Univ.Press, 1952); Ernst J. Eberling, Congressional Investigations (New York: Columbia Univ. Press, 1928); more recently, lax legislative evidence rules have resulted in dropping prosecutions against "Iran-contra" scandal defendants. (Because of such loose procedures, it was determined those defendants who testified before Congress on TV later could not get a fair trial.) See, e.g., David Johnston, "Judge in Iran–Contra Trial Drops Case Against North After Prosecutor Gives Up," The New York Times, Sept. 17, 1991, p. A1.

[40] H.L. Nelson, Libel in News of Congressional Investigating Committees (Minneapolis: Univ. of Minn.Press, 1961), Chs. 1, 2.

reached the highest court of a state, and the newspaper successfully defended with a plea of privilege.[41]

Again, there is much variation concerning privilege from jurisdiction to jurisdiction. It may be generalized that accurate and fair accounts of meetings which are both open to the public and deal with matters of public concern are privileged.[42] Matters get trickier when there is a newsworthy story which becomes available through confidential or secret reports dealing with charges of official misconduct.

The American Broadcasting Co. was sued after it telecast correspondent Bettina Gregory's five part series about scandals in the General Services Administration (GSA). From a confidential source, ABC received—and used as source material—some leaked GSA internal reports. Those reports led to broadcasting assertions that Excelon Security Co., which had been under GSA contract to provide security services, had provided guards who did not have security clearances.

The ABC broadcast added that unnamed top federal, county, and city officials said "the President of Excelon is alleged to have connection with organized crime."

Excelon president Salvatore J. Ingenere sued, arguing that the documents were erroneous and were not privileged because the GSA documents were internal memos not intended for publication. Ingenere lost his suit when the U.S. district court ruled that " ... the Massachusetts common law fair use report privilege extends to the fair and accurate reporting of confidential government reports that reveal possible government misconduct."[43]

Public Proceedings

The Restatement (Second) of Torts, that oft-quoted and influential summary of how law *ought* to be, says:[44]

> The publication of defamatory matter * * * in a report of an official action or proceeding or of a meeting open to the public that deals with a matter of public concern is privileged if the report is accurate and complete and a fair abridgement of the occurrence is reported.

Way back in 1854, the New York legislature enacted a statute saying something quite similar to the passage from the Restatement, dealing with a "fair and true report * * * of any judicial, legislative or public official proceeding."[45] Some 102 years later, in

---

[41] Coleman v. Newark Morning Ledger Co., 29 N.J. 357, 149 A.2d 193 (1959).

[42] Sack, in Goodale, ed., Communications Law 1991, Vol. I, p. 62.

[43] Ingenere v. ABC (D.Mass.1984), 11 Med.L.Rptr. 1227.

[44] Restatement (Second) of Torts, S 611 (1977).

[45] New York Laws, 1854, Chap. 130; Danziger v. Hearst Corp., 304 N.Y. 244, 107 N.E.2d 62 (1952).

1956, the New York legislature removed the word "public" from that statute. The change was made after editorial campaigning by New York City newspapers. The deletion of the word "public" made it possible to have immunity in publishing news of an official proceeding even though the proceeding was not public.[46]

In some cases, efforts to use the fair report privilege as a defense to libel suits growing out of coverage of secret government proceedings do not succeed. Despite the elimination of the word "public" from the New York statute, the state Court of Appeals ruled in 1970 that news stories of matrimonial proceedings—secret under New York law—are protected by qualified privilege.

That New York situation carries a message to all mass communicators: *Know the law of the state in which you work.* Outside of New York, journalists sometimes have lost immunity when they reported libelous stories after gaining access to secret governmental or quasi-governmental proceedings. In an old case, McCurdy v. Hughes, a newspaper reported on a secret meeting of a disciplinary board of a state bar association in which a complaint against an attorney was considered. The attorney brought a libel suit for derogatory statements in the story and won.[47]

Reporting gets tricky for the news media in those times where a meeting or record is not both *public* and *official.* Obviously, some government records do not have public status. If news media publish such non-public or secret materials containing defamatory information, the public interest in those materials needs to be compelling to afford the media protection from liability.

Take, for example, Time magazine's 1978 publication of an article about suspected criminal activities of a Congressman from Pennsylvania named Daniel J. Flood. The Medico v. Time, Inc. defamation suit resulted, beginning when the magazine—in an article tying the Congressman to the Mafia—published these words: "The suspected link, the Wilkes–Barre firm of Philip Medico and his brothers. The FBI discovered more than a decade ago that [Congressman Daniel] Flood steered Government business to the Medicos and often traveled in their company jet." Time's article was based on secret FBI files.[48]

In addition, the magazine story called Medico a member of an organized crime "family" and referred to him as a Mafia "capo" or chief. Time magazine, however, argued that the gist of its article

---

[46] Editor & Publisher, May 5, 1956, p. 52; See New York State Legislative Annual, 1956, pp. 494–495. Shiles v. News Syndicate Co., 27 N.Y.2d 9, 313 N.Y.S.2d 104, 107, 261 N.E.2d 251 (1970).

[47] McCurdy v. Hughes, 63 N.D. 435, 248 N.W. 512 (1933).

[48] Medico v. Time, Inc., 643 F.2d 134, 141 (3d Cir.1981), 6 Med.L.Rptr. 2529, 2535, cert. denied 454 U.S. 836, 102 S.Ct. 139 (1981).

was that the Federal Bureau of Investigation had recorded "Pennsylvania Rackets Boss" Russell Bufalino's description of Philip Medico.

The trial court refused to find that Time's article could be defended as true, but ultimately held that the article was protected under Pennsylvania's common law privilege to report official proceedings. The court recognized that Time had summarized secret FBI reports which had been given the magazine without authorization. But because Time's article was a fair and accurate report of the FBI documents, the trial judge ruled that publication was privileged. Recognizing the great public concern over allegations of wrongdoing by a member of Congress, it was held that secret FBI documents concerning Philip Medico were " 'a report of an official proceeding or meeting.' "[49]

Upholding the trial court, a U.S. Court of Appeals found that important "policies underlie the fair report privilege." First is an "agency theory," where one who reports on a public, official proceeding represents people who could not attend. But, said the appeals court, the agency rationale would not work for proceedings or reports not open to the public. A second policy—and the one the appeals court embraced—is a "theory of public supervision."[50]

> As public inspection of courtroom proceedings may further the just administration of the laws, public scrutiny of the records of criminal investigatory agencies may often have the equally salutary effect of fostering among those who enforce the laws "the sense of public responsibility." For example, exposing the content of agency records may, in some cases, help ensure impartial enforcement of the laws.

A final note about the word "public" in connection with qualified privilege: The immunity to lawsuit for reporting is clearest when the meeting or record is both *public* and *official*. Perhaps there is an emerging standard suggesting that even if a meeting or record is not both public and official, it is important for the community to know what is happening where matters of public welfare and concern are involved.[51] As for private gatherings of stockholders, directors, or members of an association or organization, they are no basis for privilege in news reports.

[49] Ibid., pp. 137–139.

[50] Ibid., p. 141, quoting Judge (later Mr. Justice Holmes) from Cowley v. Pulsifer, 137 Mass. 392, 394 (1884).

[51] See Robert D. Sack, op. cit., pp. 105–108, citing Kilgore v. Younger, 30 Cal.3d 770, 796, 180 Cal.Rtpr. 657, 673, 640 P.2d 793, 797 (1982), and Crane v. Arizona Republic, 729 F.Supp. 698 (C.D.Cal.1989).

SEC. 34.   TRUTH AS A DEFENSE

Most state laws provide that truth is a complete defense in libel cases, but some require that the publisher show "good motives and justifiable ends." The United States Supreme Court has not ruled on whether truth may ever be subjected to civil or criminal liability.

The defense of truth (often called "justification") in civil libel has ancient roots developed in the common law of England. It was taken up by American courts as they employed the common law in the colonial and early national periods, and was transferred from the common law to many state statutes. Its basis appeals to common sense and ordinary ideas of justice: Why, indeed, should an individual be awarded damages for harm to his reputation when the truth of the matter is that his record does not merit a good reputation? To print or broadcast the truth about persons is no more than they should expect. In addition the social good may be served by bringing to light the truth about people whose work involves them in the public interest.

It is held by some courts that truth alone is a complete defense, regardless of the motives behind its publication, and this squares with the libel statutes in most states. Some state laws continue to qualify, and provide that truth is a defense if it is published "with good motives and justifiable ends."[52] The qualifying term goes back to 1804, when Alexander Hamilton used it in his defense of newspaperman Harry Croswell in a celebrated New York criminal libel case.[53] So far as the comatose *criminal* libel offense is concerned, however, the United States Supreme Court has ruled that the Hamiltonian qualification is unconstitutional, and may not be required of a defendant.[54]

The Supreme Court has shied away from ruling that truth is always a defense. Justice White wrote in Cox Broadcasting Co. v. Cohn that the Court had not decided the question "whether truthful publications may ever be subjected to civil or criminal liability." Earlier cases, he said, had "carefully left open the question" whether the First Amendment requires "that truth be recognized as a defense in a defamation action brought by a private person * * * "[55]

[52] State statutes and constitutional provisions are collected in Angoff, op. cit. See also Note, 56 N.W.Univ.L.Rev. 547 (1961); Garrison v. Louisiana, 379 U.S. 64, 85 S.Ct. 209 (1964), footnote 7.

[53] 3 Johns.Cas. 337 (N.Y.1804).

[54] Garrison v. Louisiana, 379 U.S. 64, 85 S.Ct. 209 (1964).

[55] Cox Broadcasting v. Cohn, 420 U.S. 469, 490, 95 S.Ct. 1029, 1043–1044 (1975), a privacy decision. But see Restatement, Second, Torts, § 581A, p. 235, which says "There can be no recovery in defamation for a statement of fact that is true * * *."

The Burden of Proving Truth

Since the Supreme Court rules of *Sullivan* and *Gertz* have made it plain that some level of fault on the part of the media must be shown—from knowing falsity to negligence—the burden of pleading and showing falsity has largely been on the plaintiff where he is a public person. Yet the *Restatement of Torts (Second)* takes the position that it cannot yet be said that the burden is inescapably on the plaintiff:[56]

> Placing the burden on the party asserting the negative necessarily creates difficulties, and the problem is accentuated when the defamatory charge is not specific in its terms but quite general in nature. Suppose, for example, that a newspaper published a charge that a storekeeper short-changes his customers when he gets a chance. How is he expected to prove that he has not short-changed customers when no specific occasions are pointed to by the defendant?

Some courts have said that the burden of proof rests on the plaintiff to show defamation and to prove damages. It is clear that defendants in libel suits frequently have been at pains to prove that an alleged libel is true.[57] In 1986, however, in Philadelphia Newspapers v. Hepps, the U.S. Supreme Court held 5–4 that it is unconstitutional to put the burden of proving truth on a media defendant where the story involved deals with a matter of public concern.

The *Hepps* case was a close call, a 5–4 decision, but it nevertheless tilted the scales in favor of the media for expression "of a public concern." Justice Sandra Day O'Connor wrote for the majority that the old " * * * common-law presumption that defamatory speech is false cannot stand when a plaintiff seeks damages against a media defendant for speech of public concern."[58]

The news media, in other words, should not be punished for statements that *may* be true. This decision invalidated similar rules in eight other states, including New Jersey. Before the Hepps decision, a dozen or more other states—including New York and Connecticut—had already shifted the burden of proof concerning falsity to the plaintiffs.[59]

Not every detail of an allegedly libelous story must be proved accurate in order to rebut a charge of "falsity," but rather, that the

---

[56] Ibid., § 613, p. 310.

[57] See Memphis Pub. Co. v. Nichols, 569 S.W.2d 412 (Tenn.1978), 4 Med.L.Rptr. 1573.

[58] Philadelphia Newspapers, Inc. v. Hepps, 475 U.S. 767, 777, 106 S.Ct. 1558, 1564 (1986), 12 Med.L.Rptr. 1977, 1981.

[59] Stuart Taylor, Jr., Supreme Court Adds Protection for News Media in Libel Actions, The New York Times, April 22, 1986.

story is "substantially" true.[60] But no formula can measure just what inaccuracy will be tolerated by a particular court.

Late in 1995, the Ninth Circuit Court of Appeals upheld summary judgment for the popular CBS weekly news magazine, "60 Minutes." In 1989, the show broadcast a segment titled "A is for Apple," which made disparaging reference to Alar, a chemical growth regulator sprayed on apples. The story was based primarily on a National Defense Resources Council (NDRC) report titled, "Intolerable Risk: Pesticides in Our Children's Food."

The NDRC report used by CBS discussed the Environmental Protection Agency's (EPA) knowledge of the carcinogenic properties of the chemical daminozide, trade name Alar. In the "60 Minutes" story Ed Bradley said that the most powerful cancer-causing "agent in our food supply is a substance sprayed on apples to keep them on the trees longer and make them look better. That's the conclusion from a number of scientific experts." Bradley cited a number of sources to bolster the conclusion that the EPA, which could remove Alar from the market, hesitated to do so for fear of being sued by its manufacturer, Uniroyal.[61]

Grady and Lillie Auvil sued on behalf of themselves and other Washington state apple growers, claiming that the broadcast caused apple sales to drop markedly. The Auvils countered claims made in the course of the broadcast with statements that no scientific studies had yet shown that Alar caused cancer in people. The studies were limited to lab animals. The U.S. district court nonetheless granted CBS summary judgment on the grounds that the plaintiffs had failed to advance evidence to sustain a workable issue of fact as to the falsity of the broadcast.[62]

The Ninth Circuit cited a number of precedents in concluding that "animal studies are routinely relied on by the scientific community in assessing the carcinogenic effects of chemicals on humans."[63] That was enough for the Ninth Circuit to affirm the district court.

In an old but illustrative case, the *New York World–Telegram and Sun* tried to establish truth of the following statement from its pages, but failed:

> John Crane, former president of the UFA now under indictment, isn't waiting for his own legal developments.

---

[60] Hein v. Lacy, 228 Kan. 249, 616 P.2d 277, 282 (1980), 6 Med.L.Rptr. 1662, 1666; Prosser, 825.

[61] Auvil v. CBS "60 Minutes," 67 F.3d 816, 819 (9th Cir.1995), 23 Med. L. Rptr 2455, 2456.

[62] Auvil v. CBS, 836 F.Supp. 740, 21 Med. L. Rptr 2059 (E.D.Wash.1993).

[63] 67 F.3d 816, 821 (9th Cir.1995), 23 Med. L.Rptr. 2455, 2457.

Meanwhile, his lawyers are launching a $$$$$$ defamation suit.

Focusing on the word "indictment," Crane brought a libel suit against the newspaper and the columnist who wrote the item. He said that the defendant knew or could have learned the falsity of the charge by using reasonable care.

The defendants tried to dodge the libel action, arguing that the facts about John Crane already had been widely published and commented up by the press of the city. The lame argument that the phrase "under indictment" was used in a figurative, non-legal sense failed, and Crane won his suit against the newspaper. The court held that "under indictment" means a legal action by a grand jury to begin criminal charges, and that the use of the term to mean accusation by private persons is rare.[69] In any case, you cannot prove the truth of one charge against a person by showing he or she was suspected or guilty of another.[70]

The same term—"indictment"—was used by another newspaper in an incorrect way, but was held *not* to be libelous. The word appeared in connection with conflict-of-interest findings discussed in an editorial. A councilman was never truly indicted, but rather was charged by delivery of a summons, and convicted. The court held that "indictment" was substantially accurate, and although technically incorrect, did not constitute defamation.[71]

Thus loose usage of certain technical terms does not always destroy a plea of truth. This is what a court ruled when a Massachusetts newspaper said that a man named Joyce had been "committed" to a mental hospital when actually he had been "admitted" to the hospital at the request of a physician as the state law provided. The newspaper's words that caused the man to bring a libel suit were that the man "charges * * * that his constitutional rights were violated when he was committed to the hospital last November." In ruling for the newspaper which pleaded truth, the court said:[72]

> Strictly * * * "commitment" means a placing in the hospital by judicial order * * *. But the words [of the news story] are to be used in their "natural sense with the meaning which they could convey to mankind in general." This meaning of the word "commitment" was placing in

[69] Crane v. New York World Telegram Corp., 308 N.Y. 470, 126 N.E.2d 753 (1955); Friday v. Official Detective Stories, Inc., 233 F.Supp. 1021 (E.D.Pa.1964).

[70] Sun Printing and Pub. Ass'n v. Schenck, 40 C.C.A. 163, 98 Fed. 925 (1900); Kilian v. Doubleday & Co., 367 Pa. 117, 79 A.2d 657 (1951); Yarmove v. Retail Credit Co., 18 A.D.2d 790, 236 N.Y.S.2d 836 (1963).

[71] Schaefer v. Hearst Corp. (Md. Super.1979), 5 Med.L.Rptr. 1734.

[72] Joyce v. George W. Prescott Pub. Co., 348 Mass. 790, 205 N.E.2d 207 (1965).

the hospital pursuant to proceedings provided by law. In so stating as to the plaintiff * * * the defendant reported correctly.

Of course, writers or broadcasters who are highly attuned to nuances in word meanings may save their employers the expense and trouble of even successful libel defenses by avoiding gaffes such as confusing "commit" with "admit." While news media continue to be staffed in part by writers insensitive to shades of meaning, however, they may take some comfort in the law's willingness—however unpredictably—to bend on occasion.

Courts frequently hold that truth will not be destroyed by a story's minor inaccuracies. Thus truth succeeded although a newspaper had printed that the plaintiff was in police custody on August 16, whereas he had been released on August 15;[73] and it was not fatal to truth to report in a news story that an arrest, which in fact took place at the Shelly Tap tavern, occurred at the Men's Social Club.[74]

In accord with the maxim that "tale bearers are as bad as tale tellers," it is no defense for a news medium to argue that it reported accurately and truthfully someone else's false and defamatory statements. The broadcaster or newspaper reporter writes at the employer's peril and at his or her own peril, too. The words "it is reported by police" or "according to a reliable source" do not remove from the news medium faced with a libel suit the job of proving that the allegation or rumor itself is true.[75] Liability under the "republication" rule persists.[76]

Even though every fact in a story is truthful, an error of omission can result in libel. Recall, now, from Sec. 25, the *Memphis Press–Scimitar's* accurate facts about the shooting of Mrs. Nichols. A woman had gone to the home of Mrs. Nichols, and there, the newspaper said on the basis of a police arrest report, found her own husband (Newton) with Mrs. Nichols. The implication of an adulterous affair between the two was plain in the story, all of whose facts were accurate. Mrs. Nichols brought libel suits. The Press–Scimitar had omitted much from the story, as shown by a separate police document (the "offense report"): Not only were Mrs. Nichols and Mr. Newton at the home, but also Mr. Nichols and two other people. Had these facts been in the news story, there would have

73 Piracci v. Hearst Corp., 263 F.Supp. 511 (D.Md.1966), affirmed 371 F.2d 1016 (4th Cir.1967).

74 Mitchell v. Peoria Journal–Star, Inc., 76 Ill.App.2d 154, 221 N.E.2d 516 (1966).

75 Miller, Smith & Champagne v. Capital City Press, 142 So.2d 462 (La.App.1962); Dun & Bradstreet, Inc. v. Robinson, 233 Ark. 168, 345 S.W.2d 34 (1961).

76 Cianci v. New Times Pub. Co., 639 F.2d 54 (2d Cir.1980), 6 Med.L.Rptr. 1625, 1629–1630.

been no suggestion of an affair. The Press–Scimitar pleaded truth of its words, but the Tennessee Supreme Court said:[77]

> In our opinion, the defendant's reliance on the truth of the facts stated in the article in question is misplaced. The proper question is whether the *meaning* reasonably conveyed by the published words is defamatory * * *. The publication of the complete facts could not conceivably have led the reader to conclude that Mrs. Nichols and Mr. Newton had an adulterous relationship. The published statement, therefore, so distorted the truth as to make the entire article false and defamatory. It is no defense whatever that individual statements within the article were literally true.

Even ill will and an intent to harm will not affect truth where it is said of a public person; knowing or reckless falsehood must be shown.[78] As we have seen, however, against a *private* person's suit, some states provide that truth is a good defense only if made with good motives and for justifiable ends—that ill will (the "malice" of old tort law) may defeat the defense.[79] Belief in the truth of the charge may be useful in holding down damages, if it can be established to the satisfaction of the court. Showing honest belief indicates good faith and absence of malice, important to the mitigation of general damages and the denial or lessening of punitive damages to the successful suit-bringer in a libel case.

An article about a public official's criminal conviction failed to state that, upon retrial, the official was acquitted, and the defense of truth was denied the magazine.[80] Also, courts have refused to accept the plea of truth where news media would not identify anonymous sources upon whom defamatory stories were based.[81]

"Substantial Accuracy"

Mass communicators should keep in mind that "accuracy" and "truth" are not identical in law. Suppose that your source, a member of Congress, stops you on the street and says: "Your hometown banker, J.Q. Milquetoast, has embezzled thousands of dollars from three different banks."

If you quote your source exactly, that will be accurate.

---

[77] Memphis Pub. Co. v. Nichols, 569 S.W.2d 412, 420 (Tenn.1978), 4 Med.L.Rptr. 1573, 1579. See also for true facts but false implication, Dunlap v. Philadelphia Newspapers, Inc., 301 Pa.Super. 475, 448 A.2d 6 (1982), 8 Med.L.Rptr. 1974.

[78] Schaefer v. Lynch, 406 So.2d 185 (La.1981), 7 Med.L.Rptr. 2302.

[79] Sack, 130–131.

[80] Torres v. Playboy Enterprises (S.D.Tex.1980), 7 Med.L.Rptr. 1182.

[81] Dowd v. Calabrese, 577 F.Supp. 238 (D.D.C.1983), 10 Med.L.Rptr. 1208, 1213.

To prove truth, however you will have to prove that your source's statement about the banker is accurate too, and that Milquetoast indeed had embezzled thousands of dollars from banks.[82] Taking a cue from the common law, the courts today look to the published statement and its gist or sting. The determination lies in whether the published statement "would have had a different effect on the mind of the reader from that which the pleaded truth would have produced."

SEC. 35.   OPINION AND FAIR COMMENT AS DEFENSES

State statutes and the common law provide the doctrine of fair comment and criticism as a defense against libel suits brought by people and institutions who offer their work to the public for its approval or disapproval, or where matters of public interest are concerned. Despite assertions that the old fair comment defense was superseded by constitutional protections for opinion, its principles still are in use by media and courts. Furthermore, the effect of *Milkovich v. Lorain Journal* (1990) on the "opinion defense" stemming from expansive readings of *Gertz v. Robert Welch, Inc.* (1974) must be considered.

Fair Comment Under Common Law and State Statutes

Opinion embraces comment and criticism. The defense of fair comment was shaped to protect the public stake in the scrutinizing of important public matters. Comment and criticism have permeated news and editorial pages and broadcasts, explaining, drawing inferences, reacting, evaluating. The law protects even scathing criticism of the public work of persons and institutions who offer their work for public judgment: public officials and figures; those whose performance affects public taste in such realms as music, art, literature, theater, and sports; and institutions whose activities affect the public interest such as hospitals, schools, processors of food, public utilities, drug manufacturers. Under fair comment legal immunity against a defamation action is given for the honest expression of opinion on public persons and/or matters of public concern.[83]

Even the most public persons have some small sphere of private life. Although one's private character of course can deeply affect one's public acts, there are circumstances in which comment

---

[82] See, e.g., Rouch v. Enquirer & News, 440 Mich. 238, 487 N.W.2d 205 (1992), 20 Med.L.Rptr. 2265.

[83] Prosser, 812–816; Harper and James, Law of Torts (Boston, 1956). See also New York Times Co. v. Sullivan, 376 U.S. 254, 271, 84 S.Ct. 710, 721 (1964) quoting Cantwell v. Connecticut, 310 U.S. 296, 310, 60 S.Ct. 900, 906 (1940).

on private acts and personal character is not embraced by the protection of fair comment.[84] The wide sweep of *Sullivan,* it will be remembered, protects only statements about public persons' *public* acts; and courts continue to hold that public persons retain a private sphere.[85]

True and False Statements of "Fact"

States have varied in their fair comment rules. Most have said that the protection for comment does not extend to that which is falsely given out as "fact." This presents at the outset the often difficult problem of separating facts—which are susceptible of proof—from opinion—which cannot be proved true or false. As you will see, courts efforts to distinguish between statements of fact and of opinion have created one of the slipperiest slopes in all of American law. Beyond the problem of making that often cloudy distinction is the diversity of rules from state to state. The majority of states have insisted on the rule of "no protection for misstatement of fact." Oregon's Supreme Court, for example, held "it is one thing to comment upon or criticize * * * the acknowledged or proved act of a public man, and quite another to assert that he has been guilty of particular acts of misconduct."[86] Under this interpretation, "charges of specific criminal misconduct are not protected as 'opinions.' "[87]

But under common law, a minority of states provided protection for false statements of fact. One variation was illustrated by Snively v. Record Publishing Co., an old California decision.[88] The Los Angeles police chief brought suit against a newspaper for a cartoon which suggested he was receiving money secretly for illegal purposes. The California Supreme Court held that even if the charge of criminality were false, the cartoon was protected by fair comment. Political cartoons, indeed, do receive added "running room" from the courts. They are regarded as exaggerated statements which by their nature stretch facts to make a point.[89]

[84] Post Pub. Co. v. Moloney, 50 Ohio St. 71, 89, 33 N.E. 921, 926 (1893); Harper and James, 461.

[85] Zeck v. Spiro, 52 Misc.2d 629, 276 N.Y.S.2d 395 (1966); Stearn v. MacLean–Hunter Ltd., 46 F.R.D. 76 (S.D.N.Y.1969); Standke v. B.E. Darby & Sons, Inc., 291 Minn. 468, 193 N.W.2d 139, 144 (1971). Note, Fact and Opinion after Gertz v. Robert Welch, Inc., 34 Rutgers L.Rev. 81, 88–89 (Fall 1981).

[86] Marr v. Putnam, 196 Or. 1, 32, 246 P.2d 509, 523 (1952); Otero v. Ewing, 162 La. 453, 110 So. 648 (1926).

[87] Cianci v. New Times Pub. Co., 639 F.2d 54, 66 (2d Cir.1980), 6 Med.L.Rptr. 1625, 1635; Restatement (Second) of Torts, #571.

[88] Snively v. Record Pub. Co., 185 Cal. 565, 198 P. 1 (1921).

[89] See Keller v. Miami Herald Pub. Co., 778 F.2d 711 (11th Cir.1985), and Hustler Magazine v. Falwell, 485 U.S. 46, 108 S.Ct. 876 (1988), 14 Med.L.Rptr. 2281.

Substantial variation developed from state to state on the question of how directly and completely opinion had to be supported by accompanying implications or assertions of fact. In point is the case of private citizen Rollenhagen of Orange, Calif., an auto mechanic about whom CBS aired a television story. After one of his customers had complained to police about his charges for repairs, they arrested him for failure to give a written estimate in advance of auto repairs as required under California law, handcuffed him, and led him past a CBS camera crew. CBS interviewed auto mechanic Rollenhagen and the police, who said the customer had been victimized—and then ran the story. Rollenhagen sued for defamation, claiming the story was false, but a California Court of Appeal ruled that the story was protected by the state law of fair comment on matters of public interest. The court said that while Gertz v. Welch (1974) had recently permitted states to let private persons recover where there was negligence in a matter of public concern, California had not adopted that rule, but stayed with its half-century-old fair comment statute.[90]

A question of "fact" faces the writer under some states' rules of fair comment: the comment must be based on facts—facts stated with the comment, or facts that are known or readily available to the reader. The Fisher Galleries asked art critic Leslie Ahlander of the *Washington Post* to review an exhibition of paintings by artist Irving Amen. Later, Mrs. Ahlander's column carried this comment:

> [The Amen prints and paintings] are so badly hung among many commercial paintings that what quality they might have is completely destroyed. The Fisher Galleries should decide whether they are a fine arts gallery or a commercial outlet for genuine "hand-painted" pictures. The two do not mix.

Fisher sued for libel, and the *Post* defended on the grounds of fair comment and criticism. Fisher argued that in order for opinion to be protected by the fair comment doctrine, the facts upon which it is based must be stated or referred to so that the reader may draw his own conclusions. The court acknowledged that this is the rule in some jurisdictions.[91] But it instead took that view that the facts do not necessarily have to be stated in the article, but may be facts "known or readily available to the persons to whom the comment or criticism is addressed * * *."[92]

---

[90] Rollenhagen v. Orange, 116 Cal.App.3d 414, 172 Cal.Rptr. 49 (1981), 6 Med. L.Rptr. 2561, 2564. See Calif. Civil Code Sec. 47, sub.3, granting qualified privilege to all publications concerning a matter of legitimate public interest.

[91] A.S. Abell Co. v. Kirby, 227 Md. 267, 176 A.2d 340 (1961); Cohalan v. New York Tribune, 172 Misc. 20, 15 N.Y.S.2d 58 (1939).

[92] Fisher v. Washington Post Co., 212 A.2d 335, 338 (D.C.App.1965).

Besides the problem of "fact," the ancient question of what constituted "malice" entered the picture and had much to do with what was "fair." Malice would destroy the protection of fair comment; and malice for centuries before New York Times Co. v. Sullivan had been defined in various ways. Furthermore, various characteristics of "unfair" expression were sometimes treated as suggesting malice. Thus from state to state and jurisdiction to jurisdiction, malice could be pretty much what the court felt it ought to be: ill-will, enmity, spite, hatred, intent to harm; "excessive publication,"[93] vehemence,[94] words that were not the honest opinion of the writer,[95] words which there was no "probable cause to believe true,"[96] words showing reckless disregard for the rights of others, words which a reasonable man would not consider fair.[97] Malice still can be "adduced"[98] from such qualities of expression in some jurisdictions where qualified privilege or fair comment is at issue.

Thus the West Virginia Supreme Court held in denying fair comment's protection against the *Charleston Gazette* which had tongue-lashed several legislators who sued it for saying, among other things, that they had sold their votes. The court said that " ...if such comment is unfair or unreasonably violent or vehement, immunity from liability is denied."[99]

But in another state—Iowa—there was no suggestion in a Supreme Court decision that "matters of public interest must be discussed temperately." Journalists everywhere know the case of the Cherry sisters, one of the most famous in the annals of libel in America. The *Des Moines Leader* successfully defended itself in its libel suit, using the defense of fair comment. It started when the Leader printed this:

> Billy Hamilton, of the *Odebolt Chronicle* gives the Cherry Sisters the following graphic write-up on their late appearance in his town: "Effie is an old jade of 50 summers, Jessie a frisky-filly of 40, and Addie, the flower of the family, a capering monstrosity of 35. Their long skinny arms, equipped with talons at the extremities, swung mechanically, and anon waved frantically at the suffering audience. The mouths of their rancid features opened like caverns, and sounds like the wailing of damned souls

[93] Pulliam v. Bond, 406 S.W.2d 635, 643 (Mo.1966).

[94] England v. Daily Gazette Co., 143 W.Va. 700, 104 S.E.2d 306 (1958).

[95] Russell v. Geis, 251 Cal.App.2d 560, 59 Cal.Rptr. 569 (1967).

[96] Taylor v. Lewis, 132 Cal.App. 381, 22 P.2d 569 (1933).

[97] James v. Haymes, 160 Va. 253, 168 S.E. 333 (1933).

[98] Goldwater v. Ginzburg, 414 F.2d 324, 342 (2d Cir.1969).

[99] England v. Daily Gazette Co., 143 W.Va. 700, 718, 104 S.E.2d 306, 316 (1958).

issued therefrom. They pranced around the stage with a motion that suggested a cross between the *danse du ventre* and fox trot,—strange creatures with painted faces and hideous mien. Effie is spavined, Addie is stringhalt, and Jessie, the only one who showed her stockings, has legs and calves as classic in their outlines as the curves of a broom handle."

There was nothing moderate about Billy Hamilton's criticism of these Three Graces, but the Iowa Supreme Court said that that did not matter. What Hamilton wrote about the three sisters, and the Leader reprinted, was fair comment and criticism:[1]

One who goes upon the stage to exhibit himself to the public, or who gives any kind of a performance to which the public is invited, may be freely criticized. He may be held up to ridicule, and entire freedom of expression is guaranteed to dramatic critics, provided they are not actuated by malice or evil purpose in what they write. * * * Ridicule is often the strongest weapon in the hands of a public writer; and, if fairly used, the presumption of malice which would otherwise arise is rebutted * * *.

Opinion Under the Constitution

Opinion defenses against defamation, although remarkably useful, sometimes promise more than they deliver. True, as in the *Old Dominion* union dispute, the First Amendment was held to protect exaggerated, extravagant give-and-take in labor and political disputes. In such settings, deep feelings give rise to name-calling, to "rhetorical hyperbole" that is not to be construed literally.

Examples of epithets protected in labor or political disputes include:

—"Scabs" and "traitors" as used in a union publication against non-union workers.[2]

—"Blackmail" and "unethical trade" in a land-use dispute.[3]

—"Fellow traveler of the fascists" in a denunciation of a leader of a political fringe group.[4]

Such opinion was protected by courts, defined as immunized by *the context in which it occurred,* in labor or political disputes.[5]

[1] Cherry v. Des Moines Leader, 114 Iowa 298, 86 N.W. 323 (1901).

[2] Old Dominion Branch No. 496, Nat. Ass'n of Letter Carriers, AFL–CIO v. Austin, 418 U.S. 264, 94 S.Ct. 2770 (1974).

[3] Greenbelt Cooperative Pub. Ass'n v. Bresler, 398 U.S. 6, 90 S.Ct. 1537 (1970).

[4] Cianci v. New Times Pub. Co., 639 F.2d 54, 62 (2d Cir.1980), 6 Med.L.Rptr. 1625, 1631, quoting Buckley v. Littell, 539 F.2d 882 (2d Cir.1976).

[5] Sack, 157–58, 160–61.

With less than perfect consistency, courts distinguish hyperbole from specific charges of crime and wrongdoing. For example, charging one with a "SS [Nazi] background" and being associated with the Gestapo are not opinion or hyperbole, nor is "outright extortion" spoken of a councilman.[6]

In addition to such protection for rhetorical hyperbole, additional constitutional immunity was deduced by many courts from a dictum—a kind of judicial aside—written by U.S. Supreme Court Justice Lewis Powell in the majority opinion in Gertz v. Robert Welch, Inc.[7]

> Under the First Amendment there is no such thing as a
> false idea. However pernicious an idea may seem, we
> depend for its correction not on the conscience of judges
> and juries but on the competition of other ideas. But there
> is no constitutional value in false statements of fact.

Under this statement apparently giving an absolute protection for opinion, the Second Restatement of Torts (1977) said—prematurely, it has turned out—that common-law fair comment had been obliterated. It declared that only where a statement in the form of opinion implies the allegation of undisclosed defamatory facts as the basis is the statement actionable.[8]

Such a statement is "mixed" opinion, and not protected as "pure" opinion is. ("Mixed" opinion refers to an opinion expressed in such a way to appear to be based on facts, and where the opinion is expressed so as to imply there are undisclosed facts justifying the defamatory statement. "Pure" opinion, on the other hand, is based on provable facts which are explicitly stated as support for the opinion. [Restatement (Second) of Torts (1977), § 566, Comment b.])

After *Gertz,* many courts enthusiastically supported—and added to—the Supreme Court's statement that "there is no thing as a false idea." Under that slogan, constitutional support flourished, protecting expressions of opinion against defamation lawsuits. For example, the Massachusetts Supreme Judicial Court, using approaches from *Gertz,* from the Restatement of Torts, and from elements of rhetorical hyperbole. In doing so, it illustrated the horrendous difficulty in distinguishing between fact and opinion.

---

[6] Good Government Group of Seal Beach, Inc. v. Superior Court, 22 Cal.3d 672, 150 Cal.Rptr. 258, 586 P.2d 572 (1978).

[7] 418 U.S. 323, 339–340, 94 S.Ct. 2997, 3007 (1974). For a case boldly using *Gertz* to create an "opinion defense," see Miskovsky v. Oklahoma Publishing Co., 654 P.2d 587 (Okl.1982), cert. denied 459 U.S. 923, 103 S.Ct. 235 (1982), 8 Med.L.Rptr. 2302; see also discussion in Goodale, ch., Communications Law 1993, Vol. II, at p.153, including In re Yagman, 796 F.2d 1165, 1186 (9th Cir.1986): " ' "an opinion is simply not actionable defamation." ' "

[8] Restatement (Second) Torts (1977), S566, Comment b.

In that case, reporter Cole was fired from WBZ–TV for "reasons of misconduct and insubordination," an official statement from the general manager said. Newspapers reported the firing and the reasons, and added that station spokesman Konowitz elaborated by telephone to them that "unofficially" the firing also was based on "sloppy and irresponsible techniques". Cole sued for libel, seeking damages for those "unofficial words." In upholding the station's position, the court ruled that Konowitz's words could be viewed only as expressions of opinion regarding Cole's reporting abilities. It said:[9]

> Whether a reporter is sloppy and irresponsible with bad techniques is a matter of opinion. The meaning of these statements is imprecise and open to speculation. They cannot be characterized as assertions of fact. They cannot be proved false. "An assertion that cannot be proved false cannot be held libelous." Hotchner v. Castillo–Puche, 551 F.2d 910, 913 * * *.

It may puzzle journalists that one cannot prove such charges false. After all, the United States Supreme Court and other courts often have canvassed reporters' techniques, finding them acceptable at times despite angry charges by plaintiffs, flawed and faulty at other times, and on the basis of the latter sometimes have granted libel judgments.[10]

But the Massachusetts Court found precedent for its judgment: One writer, for example, had called a judge one of the ten worst judges in New York, said he had made a sufficient pattern of incompetent decisions and should be removed from office. The New York court denied recovery for these "opinions," saying that the defendants had simply expressed "their opinion of his judicial performance," and the judge could not recover "no matter how unreasonable, extreme or erroneous these opinions might be."[11] (The statement that the judge was "probably corrupt," on the other hand, was an accusation of crime that could be proved true or false.) In another case, "liar" merely expressed an opinion and could not be libelous however mistaken the opinion might be.[12] In

---

[9] Cole v. Westinghouse Broadcasting Co., Inc., 386 Mass. 303, 435 N.E.2d 1021 (1982), 8 Med.L.Rptr. 1828, 1832–1833. See also Marc A. Franklin, "The Plaintiff's Burden in Defamation * * *," 25 William and Mary L.Rev. 825, 868 (1983–1984), arguing that "goodness" and "badness" are evaluative statements, "simply not concepts that can be judicially characterized as being either true or false."

[10] Curtis Pub. Co. v. Butts, 388 U.S. 130, 87 S.Ct. 1975 (1967), finding the Associated Press reporter's techniques blameless and the Saturday Evening Post's constituting "reckless disregard." Where reckless disregard is found, it is commonly for bad reporting techniques.

[11] Citing Rinaldi v. Holt, Rinehart & Winston, Inc., 42 N.Y.2d 369, 376, 380–382, 397 N.Y.S.2d 943, 950–951, 366 N.E.2d 1299, 1306 (1977).

[12] Citing Edwards v. National Audubon Soc., Inc., 556 F.2d 113, 121 (2d Cir.1977).

another, "fascist" and fellow traveler of fascism were matters of opinion and protected ideas—but in this case,[13] the claim that the plaintiff had lied about people in his work as a journalist was ruled to be an assertion of fact.

The unsettled nature of the law as to opinion and comment under the Constitution was strikingly illustrated in Evans v. Ollman, a 1984 decision of the Court of Appeals, District of Columbia Circuit. Eleven judges sitting *en banc* delivered seven opinions. The majority found for two defendant newspaper columnists, and the U.S. Supreme Court refused to accept the plaintiff's appeal, in effect upholding the decision.[14] Bertell Ollman, a Marxist professor of political science at New York University under appointment procedures to head the department of government at the University of Maryland, sued syndicated newspaper columnists Evans and Novak. Their column stated that Ollman "is widely viewed in his profession as a political activist," whose "candid writings avow his desire to use the classroom as an instrument for preparing what he calls 'the revolution'." It also reported that an unnamed political scientist said that Ollman "has no status within the profession, but is a pure and simple activist."

Writing for himself and three others, Judge Kenneth W. Starr found this to be opinion protected under the First Amendment and the *Gertz* dictum. Judge Robert Bork, joined by three others, considered the statements in the column to be rhetorical hyperbole, and as such a category of words different from either "fact" or "opinion," but protected by the First Amendment. Judge (now Justice) Antonin Scalia, writing as one of five who dissented in part from the judgment, called the statement as to Ollman's status in the profession "a classic and cooly crafted libel," and treated it as an unprotected statement of fact.[15]

Judge Starr noted the difficulty and the "dilemma" that courts often face in distinguishing between fact and opinion. For doing so,

[13] Buckley v. Littell, 539 F.2d 882, 890–891 (2d Cir.1976). Decisions that have found indications of "undisclosed defamatory facts" and denied protection include: Braig v. Field Communications, 310 Pa.Super. 569, 456 A.2d 1366 (1983), 9 Med. L.Rptr. 1057, allegation that "Judge Braig is no friend of the Police Brutality Unit"; Nevada Independent Broadcasting Corp. v. Allen, 99 Nev. 404, 664 P.2d 337 (1983), 9 Med.L.Rptr. 1769, in a statement questioning whether a political candidate was "honorable"; Grass v. News Group Publications, Inc., 570 F.Supp. 178 (S.D.N.Y. 1983), 9 Med.L.Rptr. 2129, saying that Lew made the business a great success, while "Alex minded the store back home" and "was always in the shade when Lew was around."

[14] Ollman v. Evans, 750 F.2d 970 (D.C.Cir.1984), 11 Med.L.Rptr. 1433; appeal refused by Supreme Court, L. Greenhouse, "Supreme Court Roundup," New York Times, 5/29/85, 8.

[15] Ibid., at 1038, 11 Med.L.Rptr. at 1491.

he shaped a four-part test which periodically is used in decisions grappling with this perplexing realm of libel law:[16]

1. The inquiry must analyze the common usage or meaning of the words. Do they have a precise meaning such as a direct charge of crime, or are they only loosely definable?

2. Is the statement verifiable—"objectively capable of proof or disproof?"

3. What is the "linguistic" context in which the statement occurs? Here the article or column needs to be taken "as a whole": "The language of the entire column may signal that a specific statement which, standing alone, would appear to be factual, is in actuality a statement of opinion."

4. What is the "broader social context into which the statement fits?" Here there are signals to readers or listeners that what is being read or heard is likely to be opinion, not fact. An example would be the labor dispute of *Old Dominion* (at page 287), with its exaggerated rhetoric common in such circumstances. Another signal would be whether the article appeared on an editorial page— where opinion is expected—or in a front-page news story.

Despite the assertion in the Restatement (Second) of Torts in 1977, Gertz v. Robert Welch, Inc., did not obliterate the old libel defense of fair comment. Years later, some courts were still using common-law fair comment.[17]

For example, the Illinois Appellate Court, Fifth District, in 1982 held that repeated charges of "liar" against a county official in a newspaper editorial, and warning of two more years of his "lying leadership," were not protected opinion. For while a single charge of "liar" about a single event had been held not actionable in Illinois, the cumulative force of several such charges was "an actionable assault on the plaintiff's character in general, not mere criticism of his conduct in a particular instance."[18] The Court found that these were factual assertions, not expressions of opinion and not rhetorical hyperbole as argued by the defendant. Once more, the charge of "liar" had been found to be unprotected. It is unsafe, like accusations of criminal activity even in the form of "In my

---

[16] Ibid., at 979–983, 11 Med.L.Rptr. at 1440–1444.

[17] Sack, 178–82; Note, Fact and Opinion after Gertz v. Robert Welch, Inc., 34 Rutgers L.Rev. 81, 126 (Fall 1981); Jerry Chaney, "Opinion Dicta New Law of Libel?" 10 Med.Law Notes #2, 5 (Feb., 1983); 10 Med.L.Rptr. #15, 4/10/84, News Notes; Prosser & Keeton, Law of Torts, 5th ed. (1984), 831; Cianci v. New Times, 639 F.2d 54 (2d Cir.1980), 6 Med.L.Rptr. 1625, 1634. Goodrich v. Waterbury Republican–American, Inc., 188 Conn. 107, 448 A.2d 1317 (1982), 8 Med.L.Rptr. 2329; Orr v. Argus–Press Co., 586 F.2d 1108 (6th Cir.1978); Tawfik v. Loyd (N.D.Tex.1979), 5 Med.L.Rptr. 2067.

[18] Costello v. Capital Cities Media, Inc., 111 Ill.App.3d 1009, 67 Ill.Dec. 721, 445 N.E.2d 13 (1982), 9 Med.L.Rptr. 1434.

opinion, he is a rapist"[19] . . . a dangerous form of comment taken up in the 1990 U.S. Supreme Court decision discussed below.

Milkovich v. Lorain Journal Co. (1990)

As is evident from the preceding pages, Gertz v. Welch, Inc. (1974) generated numerous court decisions referred to under the general label of a "constitutional opinion defense." This defense was warmly welcomed by many commentators, adopted by many appellate courts, and rejected by some others.[20] When this defense was accepted, it meant that statements of opinion—variously defined—were held not to be actionable defamation. That opinion defense has been diluted, in substantial measure, by the U.S. Supreme Court decision in 1990 in a 15–year–old libel case, Milkovich v. Lorain Journal Co.[21]

Michael Milkovich, Jr., a retired high school wrestling coach whose teams won numerous state championships, taught the news media a practical lesson. Packaging attacks on individuals' reputations as "opinion" appears more risky after the Supreme Court's decision.

In 1974, Milkovich was coaching the Maple Heights (Ohio) High School wrestling team against Mentor High School when a fight broke out. Several persons were hurt. Later, Coach Milkovich was among those testifying in an investigation by the Ohio State High School Athletic Association (OSHAA). His Maple Heights team was put on probation and ruled ineligible for the 1975 state tournament, and Coach Milkovich was censured for his role in the fight. After OSHAA was sued by some Maple Heights parents and wrestlers, an Ohio Court of Common Pleas overturned the probation and ineligibility orders.[22]

The following day, a column by sportswriter J. Theodore Diadiun appeared in the News–Herald, a newspaper published by the Lorain Journal Co. The column's headline said: "Maple beat the law with the 'big lie.'" A headline on the jump page read, " * * * Diadiun says Maple told a lie." The column said, in part:[23]

"' * * * a lesson was learned (or relearned) yesterday by the student body of Maple Heights High School, and by

[19] Cianci v. New Times Pub. Co., 639 F.2d 54, 63 (2d Cir.1980), 6 Med.L.Rptr. 1625, 1631; Ollman v. Evans, 750 F.2d 970 (D.C.Cir.1984), 11 Med.L.Rptr. 1433, 1443.

[20] See discussion in David A. Anderson, "Is Libel Law Worth Reforming?", 140 *Pa.L.Rev.* (Dec.1991) pp. 505–510.

[21] Milkovich v. Lorain Journal Co., 497 U.S. 1, 110 S.Ct. 2695 (1990), 17 Med. L.Rptr. 2009.

[22] 497 U.S. at 4, 110 S.Ct. at 2698 (1990), 17 Med.L.Rptr. at 2010.

[23] 497 U.S. at 6, 110 S.Ct. at 2698 (1990), 17 Med.L.Rptr. at 2011.

anyone who attended the Maple–Mentor wrestling meet of last Feb. 8.

* * *

" 'It is simply this: If you get in a jam, lie your way out.

* * *

" 'The teachers responsible were mainly Maple wrestling coach, Mike Milkovich, and former superintendent of schools, H. Donald Scott.

* * *

" 'Anyone who attended the meet, whether he be from Maple Heights or Mentor, or impartial observer, knows in his heart that Milkovich and Scott lied at the hearing after each having given his solemn oath to tell the truth.

" 'But they got away with it.

" 'Is this the kind of lesson we want our young people learning from their high school administrators and coaches?

" 'I think not.' "

Milkovich sued for defamation, and 15 years later—in 1990–the U.S. Supreme Court granted certiorari "to consider the important questions raised by the Ohio courts' recognition of a constitutionally required 'opinion' exception to the application of its defamation laws."[24]

Writing for the Court, Chief Justice William H. Rehnquist summarized cases constitutionally limiting the application of state defamation laws, from New York Times v. Sullivan (1964) through *Gertz* and Philadelphia Newspapers v. Hepps. (See discussions of these cases at text, Secs. 28 and 34.) In addition, the Chief Justice cited Harte–Hanks v. Connaughton (1989) (discussed in Sec. 29): " 'The question whether the evidence in the record in a defamation case is sufficient to support a finding of actual malice is a question of law.' "[25]

The Chief Justice wrote:[26]

Respondents would have us recognize ... still another First Amendment-based protection for defamatory statements which are categorized as "opinion" as opposed to

[24] 497 U.S. at 10, 110 S.Ct. at 2701 (1990), 17 Med.L.Rptr. at 2013.
[25] 497 U.S. at 17, 110 S.Ct. at 2705 (1990), 17 Med.L.Rptr. at 2016.
[26] 497 U.S. at 17, 110 S.Ct. at 2705–2706, 17 Med.L.Rptr. at 2017.

"fact." For this proposition they rely on the following dictum from our opinion in *Gertz:*

"Under the First Amendment there is no such thing as a false idea. However pernicious an opinion may seem, we depend for its correction not on the conscience of judges and juries but on the competition of ideas. But there is no constitutional value in false statements of fact."

> Judge Friendly appropriately observed that this passage "has become the opening salvo in all arguments for protection from defamation actions on ground of opinion, even though the case did not remotely concern the question." Cianci v. New Times Publishing Co., 639 F.2d 54, 62 (C.A.2 1980). Read in context, though, the fair meaning of the passage was merely a reiteration of Justice Holmes' classic "marketplace of ideas" concept * * * [See Chapter 1, Sec. 2.]

> Thus we do not think this passage from *Gertz* was intended to create a wholesale defamation exemption for anything that might be labeled "opinion." * * * Not only would such an interpretation be contrary to the tenor and context of the passage, but it would also ignore the fact that expressions of "opinion" may often imply an assertion of objective fact.

> If a speaker says, "In my opinion John Jones is a liar," he implies a knowledge of facts which led to the conclusion that Jones told an untruth. Even if the speaker states the facts upon which he bases his opinion, if those facts are either incorrect or incomplete, or if his assessment of them is erroneous, the statement may still imply a false assertion of fact. Simply couching such statements in terms of opinion does not dispel these implications; and the statement, "In my opinion Jones is a liar," can cause as much damage to reputation as the statement "Jones is a liar."

Chief Justice Rehnquist wrote: "It is worthy of note that at common law, even the privilege of fair comment did not extend to 'a false statement of fact, whether it was expressly stated or implied from an expression of opinion.' *Restatement (Second) of Torts* * * * Sec. 566 Comment *a.*"[27]

The Chief Justice expressed a desire to avoid drawing lines between opinion and fact. " * * * [W]e think the 'breathing space' which 'freedoms of expression require' to survive *(Hepps,* 475 U.S. at 772, 106 S.Ct. at 1561, quoting *New York Times,* 376 U.S. at 272,

---

[27] 497 U.S. at 19, 110 S.Ct. at 2706 (1990), 17 Med.L.Rptr. at 2017.

84 S.Ct. at 721), is adequately secured by existing constitutional doctrine without the creation of an artificial dichotomy between 'opinion' and 'fact.' ''[28]

> Thus, unlike the statement, "In my opinion Mayor Jones is a liar," the statement "In my opinion, Mayor Jones shows his abysmal ignorance by accepting the teachings of Marx and Lenin" would not be actionable. *Hepps* ensures that a statement of opinion relating to matters of public concern which does not contain a provably false factual connotation will receive full constitutional protection.

It is to be doubted that the preceding paragraphs are going to settle legal squabbles over what is "fact," "opinion," or, as the Chief Justice stated earlier, an expression of opinion implying an "objective fact."[29]

Chief Justice Rehnquist listed several decisions limiting the severity of libel laws against defendants:[30]

—The *Bresler–Letter Carriers–Falwell* line of cases, protecting name-calling statements that cannot reasonably be interpreted as representing "actual facts" about a person.

—"The *New York Times, Butts,* and *Gertz* culpability requirements further ensure that debate over public issues remains 'uninhibited, robust and wide-open.' New York Times, 376 U.S., at 270 [1964]."

—Finally, the enhanced independent appellate review required by *Bose Corp.* provides assurance that determinations about libel will be made so as not to "constitute a forbidden intrusion into the field of free expression. *Bose,* 466 U.S. at 490 * * * "

Chief Justice Rehnquist concluded that the language the newspaper columnist used against Coach Milkovich was "loose, figurative or hyperbolic," and that the column's connotation that the coach had committed perjury was susceptible of being proved true or false.[31]

Dissenting, Justice Brennan—joined by Justice Marshall—seemingly agreed with the majority's rendition of the facts in the Milkovich case. Unlike the majority, however, Brennan characterized the columnist's words about the coach as "patently conjecture." Therefore, he disagreed with the finding that columnist Diadiun's statements were actionable because they implied an

---

[28] 497 U.S. at 20, 110 S.Ct. at 2706 (1990), 17 Med.L.Rptr. at 2017.

[29] 497 U.S. at 19, 110 S.Ct. at 2706 (1990), 17 Med.L.Rptr. at 2018.

[30] 497 U.S. at 20–22, 110 S.Ct. at 2706–2707 (1990), 17 Med.L.Rptr. at 2018.

[31] Ibid.

assertion of fact that the coach had perjured himself. Brennan countered:[32]

> Diadiun not only reveals the facts upon which he is relying but makes it clear at which point he runs out of facts and is simply guessing. Read in context, such statements simply cannot reasonably be interpreted as implying such an assertion of fact.

Brennan, in line with his years of supporting press freedom, suggested ways in which conjecture and opinion not grounded in verifiable fact could serve a very real public interest. Justice Brennan asked:[33]

> Did NASA officials ignore sound warnings that the Challenger Space Shuttle would explode? Did Cuban–American leaders arrange for John Fitzgerald Kennedy's assassination? Was Kurt Waldheim a Nazi officer? Such questions are matters of public concern long before all the facts are unearthed, if they ever are.

The *Milkovich* decision means that news organizations are well advised to look to their ethics. Reporters and their bosses had best repress the desire to clobber reputations—especially *private* reputations—with opinion statements if the underlying facts are squishy. The noted media attorney Bruce Sanford put it another way: He predicted that " 'our public debate will be more flannel-mouthed and more cautious' "because of self-censorship to avoid possible libel suits.[34] Caution may be indicated. The Lorain Journal Co. reportedly spent more than $500,000 in defending and losing the Milkovich libel suit.[35] And, the Milkovich decision does have its strange aspects. As Sanford noted, it is ironic that the more far-fetched " * * * or obviously absurd the commentary, the more constitutional protection it will have." Unsurprisingly, Sanford—along with a number of other lawyers who defend media clients—initially looked at this decision and predicted tough times ahead for the news media where defamation is concerned.[36]

Are Statements "Opinion" or Provable Fact?

Milkovich v. Lorain Journal (1990) proved perplexing for commentators, some who believed that the opinion defense based on a selective reading of Gertz v. Welch (1974) was all but defunct.

[32] 497 U.S. at 28, 110 S.Ct. at 2711 (1990), 17 Med.L.Rptr. at 2019.

[33] 497 U.S. at 34–35, 110 S.Ct. at 2714 (1990), 17 Med.L.Rptr. at 2021.

[34] Bruce Sanford, "Libel Defeat Is Troublesome For Broadcast News," *RadioWeek* July 16, 1990, p. 4.

[35] David Margolick, "How a '74 Fracas Led to a High Court Libel Case," The New York Times, April 20, 1990.

[36] Sanford, loc. cit.

Perhaps not. For, as Robert Sack and Sandra Baron have suggested, " ... most courts considering opinion since Milkovich have reached the results they likely would have reached before."[37]

Opinions, by their nature, are not objectively provable. Consider Unelko Corp. v. Rooney, a useful case making an effort find a fact/opinion distinction involving CBS curmudgeon Andy Rooney. "It didn't work," Rooney said during a broadcast about Rain–X, a windshield rain-repellent manufactured by Unelko. The Ninth Circuit Court of Appeals held this was an objectively supportable comment, a statement of fact not protected under *Milkovich*. The court expressed three tests for trying to draw a line between fact and opinion:[38]

1) Is figurative or hyperbolic language used of the kind not to be understood literally?

2) Was the general tenor of Rooney's broadcast commentary perceived as satirical or humorous?

3) Could the statement "It didn't work" be proved true or false?

Rooney and CBS actually defended successfully against this suit brought under California defamation law. Even though their case was undermined by the court's reading of Milkovich v. Lorain Journal (1990), the defendants won because Unelko did not show that Rooney's statement was false and because of public interest in whether products actually work as represented.

Moldea v. New York Times Co. (1994)

Litigation brought by an author against The New York Times Book Review may provide additional clues for what the Milkovich decision of 1990 (see above) means to protection of statements of opinion from libel suits. Dan Moldea wrote a book titled Interference: How Organized Crime Influences Professional Football. He asserted that an unfavorable review by Times sportswriter Gerald Eskenazi damaged the book's reception and injured Moldea's reputation and earning ability. The review said Moldea's book contained " 'too much sloppy journalism to trust the bulk of this book's 512 pages including its whopping 64 pages of footnotes' "and then listed some examples of what the reviewer saw as shortcomings.[39]

[37] Robert D. Sack and Sandra S. Baron, Libel, Slander and Related Problems, 2nd ed. (New York: Practising Law Institute, 1994), p. 214. Bryan Denham, a graduate student at Tennessee, reached a similar conclusion in his 1994 unpublished paper, "Legal Analyses of Milkovich: Consistencies and Contradictions."

[38] 912 F.2d 1049, 1051 (9th Cir.1990), 17 Med.L.Rptr. 2317, 2320–2321.

[39] Moldea v. New York Times Co., 22 F.3d 310 (D.C.Cir.1994), 22 Med.L.Rptr. 1673, 1674.

Moldea's defamation and false light invasion of privacy suit against The Times was at first unsuccessful, with a U.S. district court granting the newspaper summary judgment. That court ruled that the reviewer's statements could not be legally actionable as defamation because they were merely statements of opinion and thus unverifiable; no reasonable juror, this court said could find them to be true or false.[40]

In a 2–1 decision, however, a panel of the Court of Appeals, D.C. Circuit, at first found in favor of Moldea, ruling that some of the characterizations in Moldea's book were potentially actionable because they were verifiable, and could not be held to be true as a matter of law.[41]

But on rehearing, the Court of Appeals held that Gerald Eskenazi's review of Moldea's book was not defamatory. First, the genre of the writing and the context in which it appears must be taken into effect:[42]

> In contrast to the situation in *Milkovich*, the instant case involves a context, a book review, in which the allegedly libelous statements were evaluations quintessentially of a type readers expect to find in that genre. The challenged statements in the Times review consist solely of the reviewer's comments on a literary work and therefore must be judged with an eye toward readers' expectations and understandings of book reviews. * * *

> There is a long and rich history in our cultural and legal traditions of affording reviewers latitude to comment on literary and other works. The statements at issue in the instant case are assessments of a book, rather than direct assaults on Moldea's character, reputation, or competence as a journalist. * * * [W]hile a critic's latitude is not unlimited, he or she must be given the constitutional "breathing space" appropriate to the genre. New York Times v. Sullivan, 376 U.S. 254, 272 (1964).

The Times's petition for rehearing had real impact, for the court said in "Moldea (II):" "We believe that the Times has suggested the appropriate standard for evaluating critical reviews: 'The proper analysis would make commentary actionable only when the interpretations are unsupportable by reference to the written work.' "[43] The court declared that[44]

---

[40] Ibid., citing Moldea v. New York Times Co., 793 F.Supp. 335 (D.D.C.1992), 19 Med.L.Rptr. 1931.

[41] Ibid., p. 1673, citing Moldea (I), 15 F.3d at 1146–1148.

[42] Ibid., pp. 1676–1677.

[43] Ibid., p. 1677, quoting the Times's Petition for Rehearing (emphasis deleted).

[44] Ibid., p. 1677. The Court of Appeals found similar approaches to the "supportable interpretation" standard in Bose Corp. v. Consumers Union, 466 U.S. 485, 104

this "supportable interpretation" standard provides that a critic's interpretation must be rationally supportable by reference to the actual text he or she is evaluating, and thus would not immunize situations analogous to Milkovich in which a writer launches a personal attack, rather than interpreting a book.

The Court of Appeals decision in "Moldea (II)" meant that the district court's original grant of summary judgment to The Times was upheld, and thus halted Moldea's claims for both defamation and false light privacy.

Juries

If "actual malice" leaves journalists uncertain about the fine distinctions and contradictions among courts, it presents a broader problem for juries called upon to analyze and employ it in deciding libel suits.[45] Jurors' minds must be cleared of predispositions to consider that the ill will or spite associated in plain English with "malice" is not really at issue, but rather, knowing or reckless falsehood by the publisher. This may involve a difficult "turn-around" in jurors' thought processes, and possibly resentment at the idea that a writer/publisher who harbors spite, hatred, or ill will against the plaintiff nevertheless may be legally immune from a libel judgment. Justice Potter Stewart said, after 15 years' experience with the Times v. Sullivan actual malice, that he "came greatly to regret" the Court's employment of that term:[46]

> For the fact of the matter is that "malice" as used in the New York Times opinion simply does not mean malice as the word is commonly understood. In common understanding, malice means ill will or hostility * * *. As part of the * * * standard enunciated in the New York Times case, however, "actual malice" has nothing to do with hostility or ill will * * *.

And if a judge and attorneys in the case succeed in making the legal definition clear, there remains another problem for jurors enmeshed in libel law. Justice Goldberg of the United States Supreme Court warned of problems for juries in New York Times Co. v. Sullivan:[47] "The requirement of proving actual malice * * * may, in the mind of the jury, add little to the requirement of

S.Ct. 1949 (1984), and in Masson v. Malcolm, 501 U.S. 496, 518, 111 S.Ct. 2419, 2434, quoting Bose, 466 U.S. at 512, 513, concerning statements not so obviously false as to sustain a finding of "actual malice."

[45] Marc Franklin, "Good Government and Bad Law * * *," 18 Univ. S.F.L.Rev. 1, 8 (1983); 10 Med.L.Rptr. #12, 3/20/84, News Notes; 8 Ibid. #39, 11/30/82, News Notes; Randall P. Bezanson, Gilbert Cranberg, and John Soloski, Libel Law and the Press: Myth and Reality (New York: The Free Press, 1987), p. 237 and passim.

[46] Herbert v. Lando, 441 U.S. 153, 199, 99 S.Ct. 1635, 1661 (1979).

[47] 376 U.S. 254, 299, 84 S.Ct. 710, 736 (1964).

proving falsity, a requirement which the Court recognizes not to be an adequate standard.''

After trial Judge Oliver Gasch in *Tavoulareas* found the jury's verdict of some $2 million insupportable and disallowed it, Attorney Steven Brill interviewed five of the six jurors.[48] Brill found that they did not understand that falsity must be knowing or reckless to justify an award. They further believed that the *Post* was required to show the truth of its charges, whereas, of course, the rule actually was that Tavoulareas was required to show falsity.[49]

Brill asserted that the *Post* attorneys did not drum these points into the jury's minds, and talked to the jury of ordinary citizens in language appropriate to lawyers not laymen. As for Judge Gasch, his instructions to the jury consisted of almost two hours of review of legal points involved, bound to be difficult for jurors.[50]

A procedure widely praised as a clarification of the task for a jury was initiated in 1985 by Federal Judge Abraham Sofaer. Ariel Sharon, former defense minister of Israel, brought a libel suit for $50 million against *Time* magazine for its report that Sharon had discussed with Christian Phalangists of Lebanon the need for them to take revenge against assassins, just before the massacre of hundreds of Palestinians by Phalangists. In his instructions, Judge Sofaer had the jury take up three questions, one at a time, and report its finding on each before proceeding. First, he asked the jury, was the story defamatory? ("Yes," the jury found.) Next, was it false? ("Yes," the jury found.) Finally, was it done with actual malice? ("No," the jury found, and thus, *Time* was not liable for damages.)[51]

In the libel case brought by Gen. William C. Westmoreland against CBS in 1985—perhaps unequaled in the publicity attending it and costliness to the participants—[52] Judge Pierre Laval used another device to aid the jury: He simply barred the use of the confusing term "actual malice" during the trial, substituting the "state of mind" of the journalists as a clearer criterion.[53] Westmoreland, who sued for "CBS Reports" accusation that he engaged in a "conspiracy" to understate enemy troop strength when he was

---

[48] Steven Brill, "Inside the Jury Room at the Washington Post Libel Trial," American Lawyer, Nov. 1982, 1, 93, 94.

[49] Ibid., 1, 90.

[50] Ibid., 92. The Libel Defense Resource Center prepared a manual of jury instructions on libel: LDRC Bulletin #10, Spring 1984, 1–2. Proof of Actual Malice in Defamation Actions: an Unsolved Dilemma, 7 Hofstra L.Rev. 655, 701.

[51] Time, Feb. 4, 1985, 64, 66.

[52] The 18–week trial may have cost the parties well over $10 million in expenses, New York Times, Feb. 19, 1985, 10, 26; and see Ibid., from mid-October 8, 1984, to Feb. 19, 1985, for the extent of coverage.

[53] Washington Post National Weekly Edition, March 11, 1985, 28.

Commander of United States forces during the Vietnam War, withdrew his suit after 18 weeks of testimony. The jury was never put to the test of grappling with "actual malice" and "state of mind."

The troubling problem of legal technicalities confronting juries by no means ends the question of how media faced with libel suits need to cope with prejudice.[54] For example, widespread anti-media attitudes of recent decades are likely to be represented within the cross-section of people that often comprises a jury. A juror's support for media's rights to publish may be wiped out by resentment of and lack of trust in powerful institutions. Jurors react badly to perceived arrogance, inaccuracy, and invasion of privacy by newspapers, magazines, and broadcasters.

The many awards by juries of enormous judgments for libel—particularly punitive damages—suggest powerfully that jurors often are disposed to punish media. Jurors often, also, tend to sympathize with the individual whose reputation, feelings, and status among his friends seem tarnished by the rich media corporation, seen by the jury as callous and careless. Where unfairness in media stories is at issue in libel trials, such juror hostility may put a high price on freedom of expression.

[54] See James J. Brosnahan, First Amendment Jury Trials, 6 Litigation 4, 28 (Summer 1980); see Bezanson, et al., op. cit.

Chapter 6

THE LAW OF PRIVACY AND THE MEDIA

SEC. 36. DEVELOPMENT OF PRIVACY LAW

Privacy—"the right to be let alone"—is protected by evolving areas of tort law and is recognized as a constitutional right by the Supreme Court of the United States.

Privacy—roughly defined as "the right to be let alone"[1]—is one of the nation's hottest and most multifaceted issues at the turn of the 21st century. It is often said that the United States is "An Information Society." Increasingly, it is difficult for individuals to keep information about themselves from indiscriminate use by government agencies, from snooping businesses, or from predatory criminals who steal credit card numbers and infest the Internet. The worry of the 1970s—when privacy seen to be in peril—was the nightmare of the 1980s[2] and the reality of the 1990s.

The wonders of a nation and world interconnected by the Internet and cable or satellite television networks are now commonplace. The cornucopia of services offered by The Information Highway and cable and/or telephony is dazzling. But think, also, about the price in lost privacy being paid for such interconnectivity. Commercial interests thirst to know more and more about your buying habits, from supermarkets, from catalogs, or from Internet linkages replacing many catalogs. And know, for certain, that your E-mail is not secure from prying eyes.

[1] Thomas M. Cooley, A Treatise on the Law of Torts, 2nd ed. (Chicago: Callaghan and Co., 1888), p. 29.

[2] See, e.g., Arthur R. Miller, The Assault on Privacy (Ann Arbor: Univ. of Michigan Press, 1971); Don R. Pember, Privacy and the Press (Seattle: University of Washington Press, 1972); Alan Westin, Privacy and Freedom (New York: Atheneum, 1967); Warren Freedman, The Right to Privacy in the Computer Age (New York: Quorum Books, 1987), and George Orwell, 1984 (New York: Harcourt Brace Jovanovich, 1949).

So it is that the technology that serves us also ensnares us. Infrared telephoto lenses "see in the dark." Super-sensitive microphones hear across great distances. Computerized dossiers are compiled by credit agencies and by myriad government agencies. Back in 1964, Vance Packard wrote about dangers he then saw to privacy, calling his book The Naked Society.[3] Arthur Miller of the Harvard Law School published a prophetic 1971 study, The Assault on Privacy. Professor Miller investigated credit bureau abuses and systems (far less sophisticated than today) for data collection and information storage and retrieval. Acknowledging the helpful aspects of such technology, Miller then warned, "we must be concerned about the axiom ... that man must shape his tools lest they shape him."[4]

Privacy is worth fighting for, whether the fight is against governmental stupidity or arrogance, or against the prying of businesses or private individuals. Louis D. Brandeis, one of the Supreme Court's greatest Justices, wrote in 1928 that the makers of the American Constitution "sought to protect Americans in their beliefs, their thoughts, their emotions and their sensations. They [the Constitution-makers] conferred, as against the Government, the right to be let alone—the most comprehensive of rights and the right most valued by civilized man."[5]

Privacy is a problem for each citizen, a desired right to be fought for and passionately guarded. Privacy also is a communication media problem, one to be reported upon. Finally, privacy is a media problem in another sense because missteps by newspapers, magazines, broadcast stations, and Internet users have resulted in thousands of lawsuits.

Privacy as a Constitutional Right

Privacy is not mentioned in the Constitution, and its absence is understandable. In America during the Revolutionary generation, most people lived on farms. Urban residents made up not much more than 10 percent of the new nation's population. When the Constitution was ratified in 1788, Philadelphia, then the nation's largest city, had perhaps 40,000 residents. When people were out-of-doors, there was little real need for any legal or constitutional declarations about privacy. Indoors, lack of privacy often was a different matter. In 18th Century America, homes often had living, eating, and sleeping accommodations for an entire family in the same room. In public inns, travelers often had to share rooms—and beds—with wayfaring strangers.[6]

[3] Vance Packard, The Naked Society (New York: David McKay and Co.) 1964.

[4] Arthur Miller, The Assault on Privacy, op. cit., pp. 7–8.

[5] Olmstead v. United States, 277 U.S. 438, 48 S.Ct. 564 (1928).

[6] Pember, Privacy and the Press, p. 5.

Keep in mind that the Constitution guards the public against governmental excesses, not against misdeeds by fellow citizens. The remedy for harm done to an individual by another private person is a lawsuit for monetary damages, not a legal action invoking Constitutional law. Although privacy was not mentioned in the Constitution by name, its first eight amendments, plus the Fourteenth Amendment, include the right to be secure against unreasonable government searches and seizures of property, plus the underlying principle of due process of law. When those protections are taken together with the Declaration of Independence's demands for "life, liberty, and the pursuit of happiness," it can be seen that concerns were expressed early in this nation's life for something close to a "right to be let alone."

Even though privacy is nowhere to be found in the wording of the Constitution, since 1960 the Supreme Court of the United States has recognized privacy as a constitutional right. This recognition is rather narrow, but to some extent it protects individuals from unwarranted intrusions by government or by police agencies.[7]

Here, a useful distinction may be made between the *right* of privacy and the tort *law* of privacy. As James Willard Hurst of the University of Wisconsin Law School wrote, American legal history is full of concern for a broad *right* to privacy, represented by interests protected in the Constitution's Bill of Rights. (The Constitution, again, protects individuals only against *government* actions.) The narrower tort *law* of privacy as enunciated by judges and by legislatures deals with invasions of personal privacy by individuals or businesses, making possible civil lawsuits for monetary damages.[8]

The tort law of privacy, although older than the right first found by the Supreme Court in 1960, also is quite new. It has been traced to an 1890 Harvard Law Review article written by two young Boston law partners, Samuel D. Warren and Louis D. Brandeis. This article, often named as the best example of the influence of law journals on development of law, was titled (or perhaps mistitled) "The Right to Privacy." The article, in fact, did not argue for a new constitutional right, but did contend that a privacy tort could be constructed by taking pieces of existing law from a variety of areas, including defamation and trespass to property. Warren and Brandeis wrote:[9]

---

[7] See Mapp v. Ohio, 367 U.S. 643, 81 S.Ct. 1684 (1961) [search and seizure case], and Griswold v. Connecticut, 381 U.S. 479, 85 S.Ct. 1678 [overturned state law regulating birth control practices of married couples].

[8] James Willard Hurst, Law and Conditions of Freedom (Madison: University of Wisconsin Press, 1956), p. 8.

[9] Samuel Warren and Louis D. Brandeis, "The Right to Privacy," 4 Harvard Law Review (1890), p. 196. See also Munden v. Harris, 153 Mo.App. 652, 659–660, 134

The press is overstepping in every direction the obvious bounds of propriety and of decency. Gossip is no longer the resource of the idle and of the vicious, but has become a trade which is pursued with industry as well as effrontery. To satisfy a prurient taste the details of sexual relations are spread broadcast in the columns of the daily papers. To occupy the indolent, column upon column is filled with idle gossip, which can only be procured by intrusion upon the domestic circle. The intensity and complexity of life, upon advancing civilization, have rendered necessary some retreat from the world, and man, under the refining influence of culture, has become more sensitive to publicity, so that solitude and privacy have become more essential to the individual; but modern enterprise and invention have, through invasions upon his privacy, subjected him to mental pain and distress, far greater than could be inflicted by mere bodily injury.

The law of privacy, then, started from a theoretical beginning. In 1901, use of a woman's picture on a flour box led to an early—and famous—privacy case in New York: Roberson v. Rochester Folding Box Co. The judges of two New York courts evidently read the Harvard Law Review. They ruled that Abigail Roberson, who had sued for $15,000 because her likeness decorated posters advertising Franklin Mills flour without her consent, should be allowed to collect damages. But the New York Court of Appeals, the state's highest court, ruled that Miss Roberson could not collect because there was no precedent establishing "privacy."[10]

The state Court of Appeals decision, however, hinted that if the New York legislature wished to enact a law of privacy, it could. Public outcry and outraged newspaper editorials greeted the outcome of the Roberson case. The next year, in 1903, the New York legislature passed a statute making it both a misdemeanor and a tort to use the name, portrait, or picture of any person for advertising or "trade purposes" without that person's consent. Note that this was narrowly drawn legislation, limited to the kind of fact situation found in the Roberson case.[11]

In 1905, two years after the New York privacy statute was passed, the Georgia Supreme Court didn't wait for a legislative enactment to provide the first major judicial recognition of a law of privacy. An unauthorized photograph of Paolo Pavesich and a bogus testimonial attributed to him appeared in a newspaper adver-

S.W. 1076, 1078 (1911), where a state judge declared that the concept of privacy was not new: "Life, liberty, and the pursuit of happiness are rights of all men."

[10] Roberson v. Rochester Folding Box Co., 171 N.Y. 538, 64 N.E. 442, 447 (1902).

[11] New York Session Laws 1903, Ch. 132, §§ 1–2, now known as §§ 50–51, New York Civil Rights Law.

tisement for a life insurance company. Pavesich won a judgment when the Georgia court ruled that there is a law of privacy which prevents unauthorized use of pictures and testimonials for advertising purposes.[12]

Since the 1905 Pavesich decision, the tort law of privacy has grown mightily. The late William L. Prosser, for many years America's foremost torts scholar, outlined four kinds of torts under the broad label of "invasion of privacy."[13]

1. **Intrusion** on plaintiff's physical solitude. [This area will be discussed at length in the following chapter; it is now often referred to where the media are concerned as a "Newsgathering Tort."]

2. **False Light.** Dean Prosser wrote of putting plaintiff in a false position in the public eye, as by signing that person's name to a letter or petition, attributing views not held by that person. This is the area of privacy law most resembling defamation.

3. **Appropriation** of some element of plaintiff's personality—his or her name or likeness—for commercial use.

4. **Publication of Private Matters** violating the ordinary decencies.

It is emphasized that these categories are **not** mutually exclusive. More than one of these four kinds of privacy actions may be present in the same lawsuit.

The Spread and Nature of Privacy Torts

The law of privacy—or at least one of its four main sub-tort areas as listed above—now has been recognized by federal courts, in the District of Columbia, and—in one form or another—in about 45 states.[14] Court ("common law") recognition arrived first in the majority of states, with statutes recognizing at least some aspects of the law of privacy passed in others, including: California, Nebraska, New York, Oklahoma, Utah, Virginia, and Wisconsin. Even in those

[12] Pavesich v. New England Life Insurance Co., 122 Ga. 190, 50 S.E. 68, 79 (1905).

[13] Barbieri v. News–Journal Co., 56 Del. 67, 69–70, 189 A.2d 773, 774 (1963). The Delaware Supreme Court summarized Dean Prosser's analysis of the kinds of actions to be included by the law of privacy. For organizational purposes in this chapter and the next, the elements of privacy are presented in a different order. Dean Prosser had listed them in this sequence: (1) Intrusion; (2) Publication of Private Matters; (3) False Light, and (4) Appropriation. For an historically important treatment, see Prosser's much-quoted "Privacy," 48 California Law Review (1960), pp. 383–423. See also his Handbook of the Law of Torts, 4th ed. (St. Paul, Minn.: West Publishing Co., 1971), pp. 802–818.

[14] Robert D. Sack and Sandra S. Baron, Libel, Slander and Related Problems, 2nd ed. (New York: Practising Law Institute, 1994), pp. 557–560; Libel Defense Resource Center, LDRC 50–State Survey 1996–1997: Media Privacy and Related Law (New York: LDRC, 1996).

states which were slow to recognize the law of privacy, privacy interests were apt to be protected under other legal actions such as libel or trespass.[15]

Professor Prosser noted that an action for invasion of privacy is similar to the old concept *libel per se*: a plaintiff does not have to plead or prove actual monetary loss ("special damages") in order to have a cause of action. In addition, a court may award punitive damages. But while actions for defamation and for invasion of privacy have similarities, there also are differences. In a 1990 decision, the Arizona Supreme Court said that the fundamental difference between the two tort areas is freedom from emotional distress, while defamation's primary concern is reputation.[16]

That may be a distinction without a difference. It is difficult to imagine one having peace of mind if one's reputation has been unjustly harmed. In real life, the distinction between defamation and invasion of privacy is blurred. Privacy, it would seem, may often be regarded as a close cousin of defamation. Some publications, indeed, may be both defamatory and an invasion of privacy. Shrewd attorneys often sue for both libel and invasion of privacy on the basis of a single publication. Usually, however, courts do not allow a plaintiff to collect for both actions in one lawsuit.[17]

Privacy lawsuits also resemble defamation in that the right to sue, in general, belongs only to the injured person. As a rule, relatives or friends cannot sue because the privacy of someone else close to them is invaded, unless their only privacy also is invaded. In general, as with defamation, the right to sue for invasion of privacy dies with the individual.[18]

Keep two things in mind when considering privacy law:

[15] State privacy statutes include Calif. Civil Code, § 3444, which is similar to the New York privacy statute, New York Civil Civil Rights Law §§ 50–51. Wisconsin statutorily recognizes all privacy categories except false light. See Wis. Stat. Ann. §§ 895.50(2)(a) [intrusion]; 895.50(2)(b) [misappropriation of plaintiff's name or likeness], and 895.50(2)(c) [private facts].

[16] Godbehere v. Phoenix Newspapers, 162 Ariz. 335, 783 P.2d 781 (1989); see also Themo v. New England Newspaper Pub. Co., 306 Mass. 54, 27 N.E.2d 753, 755 (1940). Note that when Dean Prosser first categorized privacy torts in 1960, he could not have foreseen the U.S. Supreme Court decision in the libel case of Gertz v. Welch, 418 U.S. 323, 94 S.Ct. 2997 (1974), which demolished the old *libel per se* that if words were held defamatory, a plaintiff did not have to prove harm in order to collect damages.

[17] "Duplication of Damages: Invasion of Privacy and Defamation," 41 Washington Law Review (1966), pp. 360–377. See also Donald Elliott Brown, "The Invasion of Defamation by Privacy," 23 Stanford Law Review (Feb. 1971), pp. 547–568, and Sack and Baron, op. cit., pp. 562, 570–571.

[18] Bremmer v. Journal–Tribune Pub. Co., 247 Iowa 817, 76 N.W.2d 762 (1956). In at least one state, heirs can sue for false-light invasion of privacy. See the Utah intrusion statute, U.C.A. §§ 76–9–401–403, 406.

First, the law of privacy is not uniform. One judge once compared the state of the privacy law to a haystack in a hurricane, so there is great conflict of laws from state to state and jurisdiction to jurisdiction.

Second, when courts or legislatures become involved with privacy, they are attempting to balance interests. On one side of the scale are public interests in an open society, and in freedom of expression and the right to publish. On the other, you have the individual's desire to be protected by zones of privacy. Both sides of the scale contain worthy interests, but clumsy balancing can produce horrid results. See, for example, Professor Loving's discussion of the federal Department of Motor Vehicles secrecy act of 1997 in Chapter 8 of this textbook. Concern over privacy in that legislation, for example, could make it impossible for reporters to assemble lists of school bus drivers who have been convicted of drug offenses or of driving while intoxicated. What price "privacy?"

SEC. 37. "FALSE LIGHT:" COMMUNICATIONS INVADING PRIVACY

Elements of False Light Privacy

The area of privacy known as "putting plaintiff in a false light in the public eye" holds great dangers of lawsuits for communications media. It is privacy law's area of greatest similarity to defamation. Also, the first invasion of privacy case dealing with the mass media to be decided by the Supreme Court of the United States involved "false light."[19] Components of a false light lawsuit include:

(1) Publication and Identification. Like libel, false light requires distribution of an offending communication and identification of the plaintiff.

(2) The falsity must be substantial and it must be proven by the plaintiff.[20]

(3) The false light—as stated in the Restatement (Second) of Torts—must be "highly offensive to a reasonable person."

(4) The defendant must have "had knowledge of or acted in reckless disregard as to the truth or falsity of the publicized matter

---

[19] Time, Inc. v. Hill, 385 U.S. 374, 87 S.Ct. 534 (1967). Note that the "false light" area overlaps another area discussed elsewhere in this chapter, "appropriation of some element of plaintiff's personality for commercial use." This overlap is apparent in cases involving spurious testimonials in advertisements. See, e.g., Flake v. Greensboro News Co., 212 N.C. 780, 195 S.E. 55 (1938), where a woman's picture was placed, by mistake, in an advertisement, and Fairfield v. American Photocopy Equipment Co., 138 Cal.App.2d 82, 291 P.2d 194 (1955).

[20] Sack and Baron, op. cit., pp. 563–564.

and the false light in which the other would be placed."[21]

Lord Byron and Other "False Light" Plaintiffs

False-light privacy has roots going back to an outraged English poet, the flamboyant Lord Byron. Back in 1816, his Lordship sued successfully to prevent the publication of inferior poems dishonestly attributed to Lord Byron.[22] In more recent years, the media—or people who use the media—have misrepresented the views of other people at their peril.

Duncan v. WJLA–TV

The "false light" area of privacy law can be so close to libel that—with increasing frequency—people sue for both invasion of privacy and defamation. Take the case of Duncan v. WJLA–TV (1984), which illustrated that incautious picture captioning—or a video equivalent, the "voice-over"—can cause legal trouble. A young woman named Linda K. Duncan was standing on a street corner in Washington, D.C., perhaps waiting for a bus. Meanwhile, WJLA–TV was shooting a "journalist in the street" story featuring reporter Betsy Ashton.

WJLA broadcast two versions of a news story based on that videotaping of Ms. Duncan. For the 6 p.m. newscast, the camera was aimed down K Street and focused briefly on pedestrians on the corner behind reporter Betsy Ashton. The camera focused in on Linda Duncan as she faced the camera. Then, the camera shifted back to reporter Ashton, who reported a story (ostensibly related to a National Institutes of Health building nearby). The story was about a new treatment for genital herpes.

At the 11 p.m. newscast, a substantial amount of editing was done. Instead of the street scene including reporter Betsy Ashton in the foreground, reliance was placed on a "voice-over" by news anchor David Schoumacher. For the 11 p.m. version, Ms. Ashton was seen turning toward the camera, and then pausing. As she did so, Schoumacher intoned, "For the twenty million Americans who have herpes, it's not a cure." Then, the news video showed Mrs. Duncan turning away and walking off down the street.

A United States district court judge ruled that the 6 p.m. broadcast was neither defamatory nor a false light invasion of privacy. The early broadcast provided sufficient context for viewers not to associate the subject matter of the news story with Ms. Duncan. The court said, however, that the 11 p.m. newscast presented different questions and should be submitted to a jury for

---

[21] Restatement (Second) of Torts, § 652E.

[22] Lord Byron v. Johnson, 2 Mer. 29, 3 Eng.Rep. 851 (Chancery, 1816).

consideration.[23] Ms. Duncan won a small damage award from WJLA–TV.

Can Photographs Lie?

The cliché "photos don't lie" shouldn't be trusted. Photos—and especially their captions—must be watched carefully by editors. Pictures or videos which give, or are used so that they give a misleading impression about a person's character, are especially dangerous. Two old—and interrelated—cases make the point that if a picture—or photo caption—puts someone in a false light, don't use it. Two invasion of privacy lawsuits filed by Mr. and Mrs. John W. Gill, one successful and one not, are instructive.

Mr. and Mrs. Gill were seated on stools at a confectionery shop they operated at the Farmer's Market in Los Angeles, visible from a public walkway. Famed photographer Henri Cartier–Bresson took a photo of the Gills, with Mr. Gill's arm around his wife. The photograph was used in Harper's Bazaar magazine to illustrate a brief article on the theme that love makes the world go 'round. Although the Gills sued, they failed to collect from the magazine's publisher. The court held that the Gills had no right to collect because they took that voluntary pose in public and because there was nothing uncomplimentary about the photograph.[24]

In another false light lawsuit, however, Mr. and Mrs. Gill won damages from another magazine. Ladies Home Journal magazine had published the same photo taken at the Farmers Market but had made the photo an invasion of privacy by using a misleading caption. The Journal used the Gills' picture to illustrate an article tiled "Love." Underneath the picture was this caption: "Publicized as glamorous, desirable, 'love at first sight' is a bad risk." The story termed such love "100% sex attraction" and the "wrong" kind. The court held that the article implied that his husband and wife were "persons whose only interest in each other is sex, a characterization which may be said to impinge seriously upon their sensibilities."[25]

Context Providing a "False Light"

A 1984 Texas case suggests that the context in which something is published can cause lawsuits for defamation or for invasion of privacy. Jeannie Braun, trainer of "Ralph the Diving Pig" at Aquarena Springs Resort, San Marcos, Texas, took exception to publication of her photograph published in Chic, a Larry Flynt-

[23] Duncan v. WJLA–TV, Inc. 106 F.R.D. 4 (D.D.C.1984), 10 Med.L.Rptr. 1395, 1398.

[24] Gill v. Hearst Pub. Co., 40 Cal.2d 224, 253 P.2d 441 (1953).

[25] Gill v. Curtis Pub. Co., 38 Cal.2d 273, 239 P.2d 630 (1952).

published magazine specializing in female nudity and photos and cartoons of an overtly sexual nature.

Part of Mrs. Braun's job at Aquarena Springs was to tread water while holding out a baby bottle. Ralph the pig would then jump into the pool and feed from the bottle. The resort made pictures and postcards from a photo of an airborne Ralph jumping toward Mrs. Braun. She had signed a release saying the picture could be used for advertising and publicity so long as it was used in good taste, without embarrassment to her family.

Once the photo appeared in Chic—surrounded by pictures and cartoons with sexual content (captions on other items included "Lust Rock Rules" and "Chinese Organ Grinder")—Mrs. Braun sued for a total of $1.1 million for defamation and invasion of privacy. After ruling that Mrs. Braun was a private individual, the Fifth Circuit Court of Appeals held that Mrs. Braun could not receive damages for both defamation and privacy. Assessing damages only for false-light privacy invasion, the court awarded Mrs. Braun $65,000.[26]

Cher v. Forum International

Evidently the famed actress and entertainer "Cher" is determined to control as much of her performer's image as possible, and she has the resources and the willingness to sue. Cher said she consented to a taped interview with writer-talk show host Fred Robbins with the understanding that it would appear in US magazine, an innocuous people-celebrities feature publication. US did not publish the interview, but instead returned it to Robbins with a "kill" fee. Robbins then sold the interview to the sensational tabloid Star and to a pocket-sized magazine called Forum. That publication was owned by Forum International, of which Penthouse International owned 80 percent of the stock.

Cher's lawsuit did not claim that the interview was defamatory, nor that private facts had been published without her consent. Instead, claimed that publication in Star and Forum International put her in a false light, and further alleged breach of contact, unfair competition, and misappropriation of her name and likeness and of her right to publicity. Beyond the legal labels, Cher was complaining that she had consented to have her story appear in a much tamer kind of publication, US, only to have it appear in the juicy tabloid Star and the generally salacious Forum, creating misleading impressions.[27]

---

[26] Braun v. Flynt, 726 F.2d 245, 258 (5th Cir.1984), 10 Med.L.Rptr. 1497, 1498, 1499, 1507–1508.

[27] Cher v. Forum International, Ltd., et. al., 692 F.2d 634, 638 (9th Cir.1982), 8 Med.L.Rptr. 2484, 2485.

Cher accused the Star of having falsely represented that she had given that publication an "Exclusive Interview," degrading her as a celebrity given the nature of that publication. The Court of Appeals held, however, that The Star's promotional claim of exclusivity did not constitute knowing or reckless falsity under the doctrine of Time, Inc. v. Hill.[28] Therefore, the judgment against Star magazine was reversed.

Forum magazine, however, did not escape liability. The court held that Forum, although it identified Fred Robbins as the interviewer, made it appear that Forum itself was posing the questions put to Cher. The entertainer-actress complained that this created the false impression that she had given an interview directly to Forum. Further, Forum used Cher's name and likeness in promotional subscription "tear-out" ads saying: "There are certain things that Cher won't tell People and would never tell US. She tells Forum."[29]

The Court of Appeals ruled that publishers can use promotional ads or literature so long as there is no false claim that a celebrity endorsed a publication. Judge Goodwin wrote: "[T]he advertising staff [of Forum] engaged in the kind of knowing falsity that strips away the protection of the First Amendment." The Court of Appeals then cut the original damage award to Cher from the trial court amount of $600,000 to about $200,000.[30]

Fictionalization

One aspect of the false light privacy tort is sometimes termed putting plaintiff in a false but not necessarily defamatory light in the public eye. Out-and-out *fictionalization*, as the term is used by the courts, involves more than mere incidental falsity. Fictionalization appears to mean the deliberate or reckless addition of untrue material, perhaps for entertainment purposes or to exaggerate to "make a good story better." Although courts' rules for determining fictionalization are by no means crystal clear, communicators should be warned to look to their ethics and their accuracy. "Hyping" or "sensationalizing" a story by adding untrue material so that a false impression is created about an individual may well be actionable. For a plaintiff to collect damages, the fictionalization must be found to be *highly offensive*.

28 Time, Inc. v. Hill, 385 U.S. 374, 87 S.Ct. 534 (1967). This important case applying the libel defense of "actual malice" to the false-light area of privacy is discussed later in this chapter at p. 315.

29 692 F.2d 634, 638. The U.S. Court of Appeals, 9th Cir., found that Robbins did not participate in the publishing, advertising, or marketing of the articles, and the trial court judgment against him was vacated. Also, it was stipulated by the trial court that there was no contract between Cher and Robbins.

30 692 F.2d 634, 640 (9th Cir.1982), 8 Med. L.Rptr. 2484, 2487.

Cantrell v. Forest City Publishing Co. (1974)

Major fact errors—or large swatches of fictionalizing in something purporting to be a news story—can mean serious difficulty for the media. Mrs. Margaret Mae Cantrell and her son sued the Cleveland Plain Dealer newspaper ("Forest City Publishing") for an article published in 1968.

The underlying facts: Mrs. Cantrell's husband was killed, along with 43 others, when the Silver Bridge across the Ohio River at Point Pleasant, W.Va., collapsed. Cleveland Plain Dealer reporter Joseph Eszterhas (who later became wealthy as a Hollywood screen writer) covered the disaster and wrote a much-praised news feature on Mr. Cantrell's funeral. Five months later, Eszterhas and a photographer returned to Point Pleasant and visited the Cantrell residence. Mrs. Cantrell was not there, so the reporter talked to the Cantrell children and the photographer took 50 pictures. Eszterhas' story appeared as the lead article in the August 4, 1968, edition of the Plain Dealer's Sunday magazine.

The article emphasized the children's old clothes and the poor condition of the Cantrell home. Even though Mrs. Cantrell had not been home, Eszterhas wrote:[31]

> "Margaret Cantrell will talk neither about what happened nor about how they are doing. She wears the same mask of non-expression she wore at the funeral. She is a proud woman. She says that after it happened, the people in town offered to help them out with money and they refused to take it."

Ruling that Mrs. Cantrell should be allowed to collect the $60,000 awarded by a U.S. District Court jury, the Supreme Court said:[32]

> The District Judge was clearly correct in believing that the evidence introduced at trial was sufficient to support a jury finding that . . [Eszterhas and the publishing company] had published knowing and reckless falsehoods about the Cantrells. * * * In particular, his article plainly implied that Mrs. Cantrell had been present during his visit to her home and that Eszterhas had observed her "wearing the same mask of non-expression she wore at her husband's funeral."

Bindrim v. Mitchell (1979)

The flip side of a journalist lapsing into fiction is a person who purports to write a novel with a story line too closely paralleling actual persons and events. Take the case of Bindrim v. Mitchell.

---

[31] Cantrell v. Forest City Pub. Co., 419 U.S. 245, 248, 95 S.Ct. 465, 468 (1974), quoting Eszterhas, "Legacy of the Silver Bridge," The Plain Dealer Sunday Magazine , Aug. 4, 1968, p. 32, col. 1.

[32] 419 U.S. at 253, 95 S.Ct. at 470–471.

Although it was a libel action, the plaintiff—Paul Bindrim, Ph.D., a licensed clinical psychologist—could just as easily have sued for false light invasion of privacy. Dr. Bindrim used the so-called "Nude Marathon" in group therapy too help people shed their psychological inhibitions along with their clothes. And then novelist Gwen Davis Mitchell showed up and wanted to join his nude encounter group.

Ms. Mitchell had written a best-seller in 1969, and then set about writing a novel about women of the leisure class. When she asked to register in the therapy group, Dr. Bindrim told her she could not join the gathering if she was going to write about it. She asserted that she wanted to attend for therapeutic reasons and that she had no intention of writing about the group. Dr. Bindrim then presented her with a written contract including this language:[33]

> "The participant agrees that he will not take photographs, write articles, or in any manner disclose who has attended the workshop or what has transpired. If he fails to do so he releases all parties from this contract, but remains legally liable for damages sustained by the leaders and participants."

Ms. Mitchell reassured Dr. Bindrim that she would not write about the session, paid her money, signed the contract, and attended the nude marathon. Two months later, she entered into a contract with Doubleday publishers and was to receive $150,000 in advance royalties for her novel, which subsequently was published under the name "Touching." It depicted a nude encounter session in Southern California led by "Dr. Simon Herford." The fictional Dr. Herford was described as a "psychiatrist," not a clinical psychologist, " 'a fat Santa Claus type with long white hair, white sideburns, a cherubic rosy face and rosy forearms.' "

Dr. Bindrim, on the other hand, was clean shaven and had short hair. He alleged that he had been libeled because dialogue in the novel included some sexually explicit language which tapes of actual sessions run by Dr. Bindrim did not contain. As a therapist, the psychologist did not use vulgar language.[34]

Despite these differences—and probably because the author had attended the therapy group—it was held that there were sufficient similarities between the fictional Dr. Herford and the real Dr. Bindrim for identification to have occurred. Also, the author had to be offensive to the jury: she had signed a contract *not* to write about the sessions, and had then accepted money from a publisher to do just that. Doubleday and Ms. Mitchell were ordered to pay damages totaling $75,000.

[33] Bindrim v. Mitchell, 92 Cal.App.3d 61, 69, 155 Cal.Rptr. 29, 33 (1979), 5 Med.L.Rptr. 1113, cert. den. 444 U.S. 984, 100 S.Ct. 490 (1979).

[34] 92 Cal.App.3d 61, 70–71, 155 Cal.Rptr. 29, 34–35 (1979).

Defenses to False Light Privacy Lawsuits

(1) As in the law of defamation, *truth* is a defense to false light privacy. Note that false light is the only area of privacy where truth can be used as a defense.[35] (Also, of course, if the matter is covered by qualified privilege, the privilege will defeat false light litigation.)[36]

(2) In false light cases where public interest is involved, the plaintiff must meet a standard of fault borrowed from the constitutional defense to libel: *actual malice* (proof of publication with knowledge that it was false or with reckless disregard for the truth.)[37]

(3) *Consent*—as in all privacy tort areas—can serve as a defense if two conditions are present. First, the consent must be provable. Second, the consent must be broad enough to cover the situation complained of; consent to one thing is not consent to another.

Truth and the "Actual Malice" Constitutional Defense from Time, Inc. v. Hill (1967)

When the Supreme Court weighed the law of privacy against the First Amendment freedom to publish, the freedom to publish was given precedence. The key case, Time v. Hill (1967) was noteworthy because it was the first time that the Supreme Court decided a privacy case involving the mass media.[38]

In 1952, the James J. Hill family was living quietly in the upscale suburban Philadelphia town of Whitemarsh. The Hills' anonymity was shattered, however, when three escaped prisoners entered their lives, holding the Hills hostage in their own home for 19 hours. The family was not harmed, but the Hills—completely against their wishes—were thrust into the news. The story became even more sensational when two of the three convicts who had held them hostage were killed in a shoot-out with police.[39]

In 1953, Random House published Joseph Hayes' novel, The Desperate Hours, a tale of a family taken hostage by escaped

[35] See the discussion of truth as a defense in defamation cases in Sec. 34 of Chapter 4.

[36] See the discussion of the defense of qualified privilege in Chapter 5, Sec. 33.

[37] Time, Inc. v. Hill, 385 U.S. 374, 87 S.Ct. 534 (1967), which imported the "actual malice" standard of libel law into false light privacy. As discussed in Chapter 5, the landmark case on actual malice in defamation is New York Times v. Sullivan, 376 U.S. 254, 84 S.Ct. 710 (1964).

[38] This decision also was noteworthy because the Hill family's attorney was Richard M. Nixon, who later became President of the United States.

[39] 385 U.S. 374, 377, 87 S.Ct. 534, 536 (1967); Pember, Privacy and the Press, p. 210.

convicts. The novel later became a successful play and motion picture.

The publicity causing the Hills to sue for invasion of privacy was an article published in Life magazine in 1955 and titled "True Crime Inspires Tense Play," describing the ordeal suffered by the James Hill family of Whitemarsh, Pennsylvania. Life magazine used actors from the Philadelphia tryout version of play "The Desperate Hours," which was being readied for Broadway. Life's photographs showed actors posing in the Hills's home (the family had moved elsewhere), and included a depiction of the son being "roughed up" by one of the escaped convicts. This picture was captioned "brutish convict." Also, a picture titled "daring daughter" showed the daughter biting the hand of a convict, trying to make him drop a gun.[40]

The Joseph Hayes novel and play did not altogether match up with Life magazine's assertion that Hayes' writings were based on the Hill family's experience. The novelist named his family "Hilliard," not Hill. Also, the Hills had not been harmed by the escapees, while in the Hayes novel the father and son were beaten and the daughter "subjected to a verbal sexual insult."

The Hills asked damages for invasion of privacy claiming that the article falsely gave the impression that the play mirrored the family's experience, and that the magazine knew this was untrue. The magazine defended itself arguing that article was of legitimate news interest, " 'published in good faith without any malice whatsoever ...' "[41]

The Hills were awarded damages, but those damages were overturned by the Supreme Court of the United States.[42] Writing for the court, Justice Brennan focused on freedom of the press. First, Brennan asserted that it was "crystal clear ...that truth is a complete defense in actions under the [New York] statute based upon reports of newsworthy people or events." Thus, "[c]onstitutional questions which might arise if truth were not a defense are ...of no concern."[43]

Justice Brennan analyzed the issue of fictionalization. He noted that James Hill was a newsworthy person essentially without

[40] Life, Feb. 28, 1955; 385 U.S. 374, 377, 87 S.Ct. 534, 536–537 (1967).

[41] The Hills sued under §§ 50–51, New York Civil Rights Law, McKinney's Consol. Laws, Ch. 6; see 385 U.S. 374, 378, 87 S.Ct. 534, 537 (1967).

[42] A jury awarded $50,000 compensatory and $25,000 punitive damages. When a new trial was granted on the issue of damages, a jury was waived and the court awarded $30,000 in compensatory damages with no punitive damages. See Hill v. Hayes, 18 A.D.2d 485, 489, 240 N.Y.S.2d 286 (1963).

[43] Time, Inc. v. Hill, 385 U.S. 374, 383–384, 87 S.Ct. 534, 539–540 (1967). At the outset of his opinion, Justice Brennan relied heavily on Spahn v. Julian Messner, Inc., 18 N.Y.2d 324, 274 N.Y.S.2d 877, 221 N.E.2d 543 (1966).

privacy as he was involved in the hostage experience. He was entitled to sue to the extent that Life magazine "fictionalized" and exploited Hill for the magazine's benefit. Brennan turned for guidance to the libel decision he wrote in New York Times v. Sullivan:[44]

Material and substantial falsification is the test. However, it is not clear whether proof of knowledge of falsity or that the article was prepared with reckless disregard for the truth is also required.

* * *

We hold that the Constitutional protections for speech and press precluded the application of the New York statute to redress false reports of matters of public interest in the absence of proof that the defendant published the report with knowledge of its falsity or in reckless disregard of the truth.

Note that Justice Brennan's adaptation of the malice rule from the libel case of Times v. Sullivan to privacy applies only to instances involving falsity. Furthermore, the Court was badly split in Time v. Hill. A five-justice majority did vote in favor of the magazine, but only two justices—Potter Stewart and Byron White—agreed with Brennan's use of the "Sullivan rule."

To Justice Brennan, if innocent, nonmalicious error crept into a story, that was part of the risk of freedom, for which a publication should not be liable. Justice Brennan wrote:[45]

Erroneous statement is no less inevitable in * * * [a situation such as discussion of a new play] than in the case of comment upon public affairs, and in both, if innocent or merely negligent, * * * it must be protected if the freedoms of expression are to have the "breathing space" that they "need * * * to survive."

"Breathing space"—a phrase borrowed from New York Times v. Sullivan—indicated that the Court was giving the press a healthy benefit of the doubt. Press freedom, Brennan declared, is essential "to the maintenance of our political system and an open society." Yet this freedom could be dangerously invaded by lawsuits for libel or invasion of privacy. "We have no doubt," Brennan wrote, "that the subject of the *Life* article, the opening of a new play linked to an actual incident, is a matter of public interest. 'The line between informing and entertaining is too elusive for the protection of * * * [freedom of expression].' "[46]

---

[44] New York Times Co. v. Sullivan, 376 U.S. 254, 84 S.Ct. 710 (1964), used in Time, Inc. v. Hill, 385 U.S. 374, 386–388, 87 S.Ct. 534, 541–542 (1967).

[45] 385 U.S. 374, 388–389, 87 S.Ct. 534, 542–543 (1967).

[46] 385 U.S. 374, 388, 87 S.Ct. 534, 542 (1967), quoting Winters v. New York, 333 U.S. 507, 510, 68 S.Ct. 665, 667 (1948).

Time, Inc. v. Hill erected an important constitutional shield in false-light privacy cases. If persons caught up in the news are to recover damages for falsity, they must prove "actual malice." Making an important point, Robert Sack and Sandra Baron wrote that "[u]nder *Time, Inc. v. Hill*, whether [a privacy] plaintiff is a public official or public figure is immaterial. The pivotal question is whether the offending publication is about a matter of legitimate public interest."[47] As they pointed out, such a position distinguishes false-light privacy from the law of libel. In the 1974 defamation landmark, Gertz v. Welch, the Supreme Court rejected the rule that a private figure libel plaintiff caught up in a newsworthy event must prove actual malice.[48]

There are signs that Sack and Baron's nuanced optimism about public interest as pivotal to media defenses against private figure false-light privacy lawsuits could be overly hopeful. As noted in Chapter 5, developments in libel after Gertz v. Welch (1974) virtually annihilated the "involuntary public person" category, and that annihilation could be imported from defamation to false-light privacy.[49]

Consent as a Defense to False–Light Privacy Lawsuits

In addition to truth and the constitutional actual malice defense, consider *consent*. Logically, if persons have consented to have their privacy invaded, they should not be able to sue. As Warren and Brandeis wrote in their 1890 Harvard Law Review article, "The right to privacy ceases upon the publication by the individual or with his consent."[50]

The defense of consent, however, poses some difficulties. To make this defense stand up, it must be *pleaded* and *proved* by the defendant. An important rule here is that the consent must be as broad as the invasion. Consider the well-known New York case of Metzger v. Dell Publishing (1955). A young man had consented to have his picture taken in the doorway of a shop, supposedly discussing the World Series. The youth understandably was angered when Front Page Detective magazine used his photo to illustrate a story titled "Gang Boy." The Supreme Court of New York allowed the young man to recover damages, holding that consent to one thing is not consent to another. In other words,

---

[47] Sack and Baron, op. cit., p. 575.

[48] Gertz v. Welch, 418 U.S. 323, 94 S.Ct. 2997, overturning Rosenbloom v. Metromedia, 403 U.S. 29, 91 S.Ct. 1811.

[49] See Sack and Baron, op. cit., pp. 576–577, and cases listed pro and con on this point at 577n. See also Sallie Martin Sharp, "The Evolution of the Privacy Tort and Its Newsworthiness Defenses," Ph.D. dissertation, The University of Texas at Austin, 1981, and Don R. Pember and Dwight L. Teeter, Jr., "Privacy and the Press Since Time, Inc. v. Hill," 50 Washington Law Review (1974) at p. 77.

[50] Warren and Brandeis, op. cit., p. 218.

when a photograph is used for a purpose not intended by the person who consented, that person may be able to collect damages for false light.[51]

Consent as an Issue: Russell v. Marboro Books

A professional model was held to have a suit for invasion of privacy despite having signed a release. In states having privacy statutes, including California, New York, Oklahoma, Utah, Virginia and Wisconsin, prior consent in writing is required to use a person's name or likeness in advertising or "for purposes of trade." Miss Russell, at a picture-taking session, had signed a printed release form:[52]

Model Release

The undersigned hereby irrevocably consents to the unrestricted use by * * * [photographer's name], advertisers, customers, successors and assigns of my name, portrait, or picture, for advertising purposes or purposes of trade, and I waive the right to inspect approve such completed portraits, pictures or advertising matter used in connection therewith * * *.

Miss Russell maintained that her job as a model involved portraying "an intelligent, well-bred, pulchritudinous, ideal young wife and mother in ...socially approved situations." Her understanding was that the picture was to involve a wife in bed with her "husband"—also a model—in bed beside her, reading. Marboro books did use the pictures in an ad, with the caption "For People Who Take Their Reading Seriously." So far, there was nothing to which Miss Russell had not consented.

Marboro Books, however, sold the photograph to Springs Mills, Inc., a manufacturer of bedsheets with a reputation for publishing spicy ads. The photo of Miss Russell and the male model was retouched so that the title of the book she was reading appeared to be Clothes Make the Man, a book which had been prosecuted as pornographic. The advertisement suggested that the book should be consulted for suitable captions, including "Lost Weekend" and "Lost Between the Covers." The court held that Miss Russell had an action for invasion of privacy despite the unlimited release she had signed. Such a release, the court reasoned, would not stand up "if the picture were altered sufficiently in situation, emphasis, background or context * * *. [L]iability would accrue where the content of the picture had been so changed that it is substantially unlike the original."[53]

[51] Metzger v. Dell Pub. Co., 207 Misc. 182, 136 N.Y.S.2d 888 (1955).

[52] Russell v. Marboro Books, 18 Misc.2d 166, 183 N.Y.S.2d 8 (1959).

[53] Ibid.

Consent and Time–Lapse

Even if a signed release is in one's possession, it would be well to make sure that the release is still valid. In a Louisiana case, a man had taken a body-building course in a health studio. He agreed to have "before" and "after" photos taken of his physique, showing the plaintiff wearing trunks. Ten years later, the health studio again used the pictures in an ad. The court held that privacy had been invaded.[54]

A Bogus Consent: Wood v. Hustler Magazine (1984)

The topic of consent ought to make publishers wary. Hustler magazine was hoaxed by a snapshot and an un-neighborly neighbor, losing a $150,000 privacy judgment as a result. Billy and LaJuan Wood, husband and wife, had gone skinny-dipping in a secluded area in a state park. After swimming, they playfully took several photos of each other in the nude. Billy had the film developed by a business using a mechanical developing process, and they treated the snapshots as private, not showing them to others and keeping them out of sight in a drawer in their bedroom.

Steve Simpson, a neighbor living on the other side of the Woods' duplex, broke into the Woods' home and stole some of the photos. Simpson and Kelley Rhoades, who was then his wife, submitted a nude photo of LaJuan to Hustler magazine for publication in its "Beaver Hunt" section.

Simpson and Rhoades filled out a consent form requesting personal information. They gave some true information about LaJuan Wood (her identity, and her hobby of collecting arrow-heads) but also gave some false information such as her age and a lurid sex fantasy attributed to her. Ms. Rhoades forged LaJuan Wood's signature and the photography and consent form were mailed to Hustler in California. The faked consent form did not list a telephone number but gave Ms. Rhoades' address as the place where Hustler was to send the $50 it was to pay for each photo used in its "Beaver Hunt" section.

After Hustler selected LaJuan's photo, Kelley Rhoades received and answered a mailgram addressed to LaJuan Wood and phoned Hustler. A Hustler staff member then had about a two-minute conversation with Ms. Rhoades; that was the extent of the magazine's checking for consent.[55]

---

[54] McAndrews v. Roy, 131 So.2d 256 (La.App.1961).

[55] Wood v. Hustler Magazine, Inc., 736 F.2d 1084, 1085–1086 (5th Cir.1984), 10 Med.L.Rptr. 2113, 2114. The Woods had sued for both libel and invasion of privacy. The libel action was ruled out because of a one-year year statute of limitations on defamation actions in Texas., Tex. Civ. Stat. Ann. § 5524. However, a two-year statute of limitations period of § 5526 was held to apply to false-light privacy cases.

Hustler argued that it should not be held liable for placing LaJuan Wood in a false light because it did not publish in reckless disregard of the truth, having no serious doubts about the consent form.[56] However, the Court of Appeals, Fifth Circuit, held that since LaJuan Wood was a private figure she need prove only negligent behavior by Hustler in order to collect damages. Upholding the trial court damage award of $150,000, the appeals court said:[57]

> Hustler carelessly administered a slipshod procedure that allowed LaJuan to be placed in a false light in the pages of Hustler Magazine. The nature of material published in the Beaver Hunt section would obviously warn a reasonably prudent editor or publisher of the potential for defamation or privacy invasion if a consent form were forged.

Specificity of Consent: Raible v. Newsweek (1972)

If a privacy-invading defendants do not have consent, good intentions are not much of a defense. It may be pleaded that defendants believed they had consent, but this can do little more than mitigate punitive damages. Some consequences of a publication's not getting a specific consent for photographs may be seen in the case of Raible v. Newsweek. A Newsweek photographer visited Eugene Raible's home in 1969, asking to take a picture of Mr. Raible and his children in their yard for use in "a patriotic article." The October 6, 1969, issue of Newsweek featured an article which was headlined on the cover, "The Troubled American—A Special Report on the White Majority." Newsweek used Mr. Raible's photograph (with his children cropped out); he was shown wearing an open sport shirt and standing next to a large American flag mounted on a pole on his lawn. The article ran for many pages, with such captions as "You'd better watch out, the common man is standing up," and "Many think the blacks live by their own set of rules." Mr. Raible sued for libel and for invasion of privacy.

Although Raible's name was not used in the story, the court said it was understandable that his neighbors in Wilkinsburg, Pa., might consider him to be typical of the "square Americans" discussed in the article. Raible argued that his association with the article meant that he was portrayed as a " 'Troubled American,' a person considered 'angry, uncultured, crude, violence prone, hostile to both rich and poor, and racially prejudiced.' "[58]

Billy Wood's invasion of privacy lawsuit was disallowed because publication of the photo do not invade *his* privacy.

[56] 736 F.2d 1084, 1089 (5th Cir.1984), 10 Med.L.Rptr. 2113, 2116.

[57] 736 F.2d 1084, 1092 (5th Cir.1984), 10 Med.L.Rptr. 2113, 2116.

[58] Raible v. Newsweek, Inc., 341 F.Supp. 804, 805, 806, 809 (W.D.Pa.1972).

Raible's libel claims were dismissed via summary judgment, with Judge William W. Knox saying that if Raible was libeled, so was the white majority in the United States. Judge Knox, however, ruled that the privacy lawsuit should go to trial, saying that if Raible had consented to use of his photograph in connection with that particular article, he would have given up his right to sue for invasion of privacy. "However," the judge added, "it would appear ...that the burden of proof is upon the defendant [Newsweek] to show just what plaintiff consented to ...," and that such a factual issue would have to be resolved in a trial.[59]

Resistance to False–Light Privacy Law: Cain v. Hearst (Texas, 1994)

False-light privacy has been accepted by courts of most states, although growing resistance to this rather shapeless, defamation-like tort has been growing since 1980. In Cain v. Hearst (1994), the Texas Supreme Court renounced its earlier, if guarded, acceptance of the false light tort. Clyde Cain, a Texas prison inmate, had sued the Houston Chronicle, claiming the newspaper put him in a false light by calling him a burglar, thief, pimp, and killer. Cain's lawsuit objected to the newspaper's statement that he was "believed to have killed as many as eight people." Evidently, Mr. Cain had killed only three.

Rejecting false-light privacy by a 5–4 vote, the highest civil court in Texas said that false light "duplicates the tort of defamation while lacking many of its procedural limitations." The court listed eight other jurisdictions not accepting false-light privacy: Mississippi, Missouri, New York, North Carolina, Ohio, Virginia, Washington, and Wisconsin.[60]

---

[59] Ibid., p. 809.

[60] Cain v. Hearst Corp., 37 Tex.S.Ct.Jrnl. 1151, 878 S.W.2d 577 (Tex.1994), listing jurisdictions in addition to Texas not adopting false light privacy. These included (1) Mississippi, Mitchell v. Random House, 865 F.2d 664, 672 (5th Cir.1989); (2) Missouri, Sullivan v. Pulitzer Broacasting, 709 S.W.2d 475, 480 (Mo.1986); (3) New York, Arrington v. New York Times Co., 55 N.Y.2d 433, 449 N.Y.S.2d 941, 945, 434 N.E.2d 1319, 1323 (1982); (4) North Carolina, Renwick v. News & Observer Pub. Co., 310 N.C. 312, 312 S.E.2d 405, 410 (1984); (5) Ohio, Yeager v. Local Union 20, Teamsters, 6 Ohio St.3d 369, 453 N.E.2d 666, 660–670 (1983); (6) Virginia, Falwell v. Penthouse International, 521 F.Supp. 1204, 1205 (W.D.Va. 1981); (7) Hoppe v. Hearst Corp., 53 Wash.App. 668, 770 P.2d 203, 208, n. 5 (1989), and (8) Wisconsin, Zinda v. Louisiana Pacific Corp., 149 Wis.2d 913, 440 N.W.2d 548, 555 (1989), holding that Wisconsin's privacy statute did not provide a cause of action for putting a person in a false light in the public eye. In deciding Cain v. Hears, the Texas Supreme Court also cited Diane Lenheer Zimmerman, "False Light Invasion of Privacy: The Light that Failed," 64 N.Y.U. Law Rev. 364, 452 (1989).

SEC. 38. APPROPRIATION OF PLAINTIFF'S
NAME OR LIKENESS

The appropriation or "taking" of some element of a person's personality for commercial or other advantage has caused much litigation.

Often, careless use of a person's name or picture is a misstep resulting in a privacy action. The first widely known privacy cases—Roberson v. Rochester Folding Box Co.[61] and Pavesich v. New England Life Insurance Co.,[62] both discussed earlier in this chapter, turned on using a person's picture or name *without permission* for advertising purposes.

The use of a name, by itself, is not enough to bring about a successful appropriation lawsuit. A company could publish an advertisement for its breakfast cereal, saying that the cereal "gives Fred Brown his tennis-playing energy." There are, of course, many Fred Browns in the nation. However, should the cereal company— without explicit permission, identify a *particular* individual—that's trouble. For example, if a real-life person—we'll make up the name of "Olympic High Hurdle Champion Fred Brown"—get his name used without permission in an ad, he would have an action for invasion of privacy. So, a name can be used as long as a person's *identity* is not somehow appropriated.[63]

However, persons who use the media should develop a kind of self-protective pessimism: It might even be assumed that if something could go wrong, it *will* go wrong. Although this advice borders on paranoia, it can help avoid grief. Take, for example, the old case of Kerby v. Hal Roach Studios, where a simple failure to check as obvious a reference as a telephone directory led to losing a lawsuit. A publicity gimmick boosting one of the several *Topper* movies involved the studio's sending out 100 perfumed letters to me in the Los Angeles area. These gushy letters were signed: "Fondly, Your ectoplasmic playmate, Marion Kerby."

Marion Kerby was the name of one of the characters—a female ghost—portrayed in that series of movies. Unfortunately for Hal Roach Studios, there was a real-life Marion Kerby. After being annoyed by numerous impertinent phone calls and one personal

[61] Roberson v. Rochester Folding Box Co., 171 N.Y. 538, 64 N.E. 442 (1902), discussed at Note 10, above.

[62] Pavesich v. New England Life Insurance Co., 122 Ga. 190, 50 S.E. 68 (1905), discussed at Note 11, above.

[63] Joseph Angelo Maggio complained that use of the name "Angelo Maggio" in James Jones' best-selling novel, *From Here to Eternity* appropriated his name and thus invade his privacy. The court held that although the names were the same, his *identity* had not been taken; the fictional "Angelo Maggio" was not the same as the real-life Joseph Angelo Maggio. People on Complaint of Maggio v. Charles Scribner's Sons, 205 Misc. 818, 130 N.Y.S.2d 514 (1954).

visit, she sued for invasion of privacy and ultimately collected damages.[64]

Publications May Reproduce Own Pages in Promotional Materials: Montana v. San Jose Mercury News (1995) and Booth v. Curtis Publishing Co. (1962)

Football star Joe Montana sued the San Jose Mercury News because—to celebrate the San Francisco 49'ers winning the Super Bowl—the newspaper in 1990 distributed a "Souvenir Section" featuring an artist's depiction of the legendary quarterback. Pages of the section were made available as posters and either sold for $5 or given to charity.

Montana's suit against the newspaper failed on First Amendment grounds, with the California Court of Appeal, 6th Appellate District, concluding:[65]

> ...[T]he First Amendment protects the posters complained about for two reasons: first because the posters themselves report newsworthy items of public interest, and second, because a newspaper has a constitutionally protected right to promote itself by reproducing its originally protected articles or photographs. Our conclusion on the First Amendment makes it unnecessary to discuss ...the claim that the applicable statute of limitations bars recovery.

More than 30 years earlier, a New York court reached a similar outcome. With permission, a Holiday magazine took photograph of Academy Award-winning actress Shirley Booth. The picture was used in a Holiday magazine feature story about Jamaica's Round Hill resort. Several months later, without getting specific permission from Miss Booth, the same picture appeared in promotional advertisements for Holiday published in Advertising Age and New Yorker magazines.

Miss Booth sued Holiday's publisher, the Curtis Publishing Co., in New York, claiming that use of that picture in the magazine's advertising was impermissible. New York's privacy statute, after all, prohibits use of a person's name or likeness "for purposes of trade" unless consent has been given. Curtis Publishing retorted that promotional advertising of this kind was needed to sell magazines, thus supporting the public's interest in news. Although Miss Booth won $17,500 at trial, the award was reversed on appeal. New York Justice Charles D. Breitel termed the magazine's use of the

---

[64] Kerby v. Hal Roach Studios, 53 Cal.App.2d 207, 127 P.2d 577, 579 (1942).

[65] Montana v. San Jose Mercury News, Inc., 34 Cal.App.4th 790, 40 Cal.Rptr.2d 639 (6th Dist.1995), 23 Med.L.Rptr. 1920, 1924.

picture "incidental," and ruled that such use was not prohibited by New York's privacy statute.[66]

Arrington v. New York Times (1980)

A well-dressed young African–American's photograph was used on the cover of the New York Times Sunday magazine. His face was recognizable, although his name was not used. The newspaper had taken his picture walking in a public area along Wall Street to illustrate an article titled "The Black Middle Class: Making It." The newspaper argued that it had used his picture to illustrate upward mobility of blacks.

Use of Clarence Arrington's photograph in those circumstances was held not to violate New York Civil Rights Act, §§ 50–51, dealing with appropriation of a person's name or likeness for commercial purposes, meaning advertising. New York's highest court—the Court of Appeals—emphasized in its Arrington decision that the state's statute will be narrowly construed, limiting it to advertising and *not* interfering with publication of news stories.[67]

Appropriation and Celebrity Nudity

Playgirl magazine got overly playful in 1978 with an artist's representation—something "between representational art and a cartoon"—of a frontally nude black boxer, hands taped—sitting in the corner of a boxing ring. The facial features of the black male depicted resembled former heavyweight boxing champion Muhammad Ali. Ali's name was not used, but the drawing was accompanied by some doggerel referring to the figure as "the Greatest." Ali, of course, was known to call himself—and to be called by many others—"the Greatest" and came to be identified with that phrase to the public. Ali was granted a preliminary injunction to halt further circulation of the February, 1978, issue of Playgirl which contained the offensive artwork.[68]

Actress Ann–Margret and the Concept of Newsworthiness

The actress Ann–Margret's invasion of privacy action under Section 451 of the New York Civil Rights Law did not turn out to be "the greatest" for her. Her damage suit against High Society magazine and its spin-off publication, High Society Celebrity Skin,

---

[66] Booth v. Curtis Pub. Co., 15 A.D.2d 343, 223 N.Y.S.2d 737 (1962).

[67] Arrington v. New York Times Co., 55 N.Y.S.2d 433, 440, 449 N.Y.S.2d 941, 944, 434 N.E.2d 1319, 1322 (1982), 8 Med.L.Rptr. 1351. See also Estate of Hemingway v. Random House, Inc., where Mary Hemingway—widow of the Nobel laureate novelist Ernest Hemingway—sued to prevent publication of a biographical study by A.E. Hotchner. Mrs. Hemingway complained about references to her in Hotchner's book as an invasion of privacy, but the court held that with a biography of such a renowned figure, the public's interest in information outweighed privacy interests.

[68] Ali v. Playgirl, 447 F.Supp. 723 (S.D.N.Y.1978).

was unsuccessful. She contended that use of her photo in the "Celebrity Skin" publication, without her consent, was for purposes of trade and also invaded her right of publicity. In dismissing her lawsuit, a federal judge wrote that Celebrity Skin was not pornography, it was merely "tacky."

Judge Goettel indeed was sympathetic to Ann–Margret but said that the actress, "who has occupied the fantasies of Many movie-goers over the years," chose to perform unclad in one of her films; that was a matter of public interest. Judge Goettel then expressed a non-authoritarian view of newsworthiness as a defense generally useful defense in privacy actions, a defense which has lost favor in some other courts. He wrote:[69]

> And while such an event may not appear overly important, the scope of what constitutes a newsworthy event has been afforded a broad definition and held to include even matters of "entertainment and amusement, concerning interesting phases of human activity in general." Paulsen v. Personality Posters, Inc., * * * 113 F.2d 806 at 809. As has been noted, it is not for the courts to decide what matters are of interest to the general public. See Goelet v. Confidential, Inc. * * * 5 A.D.2d 226 at 229–230, 171 N.Y.S.2d 223 at 226.

SEC. 39.   APPROPRIATION'S COUSIN: "THE RIGHT OF PUBLICITY"

Courts have found property rights in performers' likenesses or personalities.

Zacchini v. Scripps–Howard Broadcasting (1977)

Hugo "The Human Cannonball" Zacchini catapulted into privacy law when he won a decision before the United States Supreme Court in 1977. The case arose when Zacchini was shot out of a cannon into a net 200 feet away at the Geauga County Fair in Burton, Ohio. This high-calibre entertainer, however, took exception to being filmed by a free-lancer working for Scripps-Howard Broadcasting. Zacchini spotted the free-lancer and asked him not to film his performance, which took place in a fenced area surrounded by grandstands.

Despite Zacchini's request, the television station broadcast film of the 15–second flight by Zacchini, with the newscaster calling the act a "thriller" and urging viewers to go to the fair: "[Y]ou really need to see it *in person* to appreciate it."

---

[69] Ann–Margret v. High Society Magazine, Inc., 498 F.Supp. 401, 403–404 (S.D.N.Y.1980), 6 Med.L.Rptr. 1774, 1775.

Zacchini sued for infringement of his "right of publicity," claiming that he was engaged in the entertainment business, following after his father, who had invented the act. He claimed that the television station had "showed and commercialized the film of his act without his consent," and that this was "an unlawful appropriation of plaintiff's professional property."

Although the Ohio Supreme Court rejected Zacchini's claims, the Supreme Court of the United States did not. The Supreme Court stated:[70]

Wherever the line . . . is to be drawn between media reports that are protected and those that are not, we are quite sure that the First and Fourteenth Amendments do not immunize the media when they broadcast a performer's entire act without his consent.

The Supreme Court declared that broadcasting a film of Zacchini's "entire act poses a substantial threat to the economic value of that performance." A five-member majority of the Court sent the Zacchini case back to the Ohio courts for a decision on whether the Human Cannonball could recover damages.

Property Rights in One's Name or Likeness

Celebrity athletes have led the way in trying to control the use of their images in commercial settings. Baseball "trading cards" have provided cases in point. Back in 1953, the famed Judge Jerome D. Frank wrote: "We think that in addition to an independent right of privacy * * * a man has a right in the publicity of his photograph, i.e., the right to grant the exclusive privilege of publishing his picture * * * . This right might be called a 'right of publicity.' "[71] Baseball outfielder Ted Uhlaender won an injunction against unauthorized use of his picture on trading cards (with associated advertising/promotional purposes). A court decided that a public figure such as a baseball player has a proprietary interest in his public personality, which includes name, likeness, or other personal characteristics.[72]

In dollar-driven American popular culture, athletes and other celebrities have the resources to bring lawsuits to protect against what they consider to be improper use of their identities. Basketball great Kareem Abdul–Jabbar (who changed his name from Lew Alcindor in 1970) had an actionable lawsuit against General Motors Corporation. In an advertisement for Oldsmobile, a GM ad broad-

---

[70] Zacchini v. Scripps–Howard Broadcasting Co., 433 U.S. 562, 574, 97 S.Ct. 2849, 2857 (1977).

[71] Haelan Laboratories, Inc. v. Topps Chewing Gum, Inc., 202 F.2d 866 (2d Cir.1953).

[72] Uhlaender v. Henricksen, 316 F.Supp. 1277, 1282 (D.Minn.1970); Cepeda v. Swift & Co., 415 F.2d 1205 (8th Cir.1969).

cast during the 1993 NCAA basketball tournament asked who had the record for being named Most Valuable Player most often in that tournament. The answer given in the advertisement: Lew Alcindor, with the voice-over asserting that Oldsmobile also was a definite first-round pick.[73]

Parodies in Name or Likeness

Efforts at social commentary through parody collided with celebrities efforts to control their images in Cardtoons v. Major League Baseball Players Association (1996). The association sued "Cardtoons," producer of satiric baseball playing cards, featuring pictures on one side and making fun of players on the other. San Francisco Giants' outfielder Barry Bonds—one of the game's highest-salaried players—was termed "Treasury Bonds" and, in reference to the nation's gold depository, was said to use a "Fort Knoxville Slugger" for his baseball bat. The U.S. Court of Appeals (10th Cir.) held that although the players' publicity rights were infringed, there was sufficient social commentary on the cards to entitle them to First Amendment protection.[74]

On the other hand, TV Celebrity Vanna White, famed for her role on the "Wheel of Fortune," was awarded $403,000 by a jury for a Samsung Electronics ad with featuring a quiz show with a robot resembling Ms. White. Vanna White's legal victory was upheld by a U.S. Court of Appeals, despite fiery dissents claiming that such parodies should be protected under the First Amendment.[75]

Strictly speaking, it may not have been a parody, but Ford Motor Company's use of a singer who sounded much like Bette Midler resulted in a $400,000 court victory for "the Divine Miss M." Ms. Midler had refused to sing a song her fans associate with her for a Ford Commercial, but Ford's ad agency—Young & Rubicam—hired a singer to perform the song. Ms. Midler collected even though the voice in the ad was not hers; it simply *sounded* like her.[76]

Can the Dead Sue for Invasion of Privacy?

As a general rule, the ability to sue for invasion of privacy dies with the individual. As tort scholar William L. Prosser noted, "there is no common law right of action concerning one who is

[73] Abdul–Jabbar v. General Motors, 85 F.3d 407 (9th Cir.1996).

[74] Cardtoons v. Major League Baseball Players Association, 95 F.3d 959, 962 (10th Cir.1996), 24 Med.L.Rptr. 2281, 2290–2291.

[75] White v. Samsung Electronics, 971 F.2d 1395 (9th Cir.1992), 20 Med.L.Rptr. 1457; rehearing denied, 989 F.2d 1512, 21 Med.L. Rptr. 1330; cert. den., 508 U.S. 951, 113 S.Ct. 2443 (1993).

[76] Midler v. Ford Motor Company, 849 F.2d 460 (9th Cir.1988), 15 Med.L.Rptr. 1620.

already dead." However, as with most general rules, there are exceptions. A workable lawsuit for invasion of privacy may exist after a person's death, "according to the survival rules of the particular state."[77]

Similarly, there is a general rule that relatives have no right of action for an invasion of the privacy of a deceased person. A satirical national television show, "That Was the Week that Was," included this statement in an NBC–TV broadcast: "Mrs. Katherine Young of Syracuse, New York, who died at 99 leaving five sons, five daughters, 67 grandchildren, 72 great-grandchildren, and 73 great-great grandchildren—gets our First Annual Booby Prize in the Birth Control Sweepstakes." Two of Mrs. Young's sons sued for invasion of privacy, but failed because their is no "relational" right to sue for invasion of the privacy of a deceased individual.[78]

"Descendibility" and the Famous Dead

What about the identities of dead celebrities, even about performers as wildly different as Bela Lugosi or Elvis Presley? Their likenesses, their personas, are still valuable commercial properties long after their deaths. (Presley was said to be making more money dead in 1997 than he had in life.)

Even though the legal ghost of the late horror-film star Bela Lugosi came back in courtrooms to haunt Universal Pictures Company, Universal eventually won its case after a series of long court battles. After Lugosi's death in 1956, Universal capitalized on his fame, entering into licensing agreements to allow manufacturing of items including shirts, cards, games, kites, bar accessories, and masks, all with the likeness of Count Dracula as portrayed by Bela Lugosi. The California Supreme Court, however, voted 4–3 that the exclusive right to profit from the actor's name and likeness did not survive his death. The California Supreme Court, before that state adopted a statute providing for "descendibility," adopted California Court of Appeal Presiding Justice Roth's opinion as its own.[79]

> "Such ' * * * a right of value' to create a business product or service of value is embraced in the law of privacy and is protectable during one's lifetime but it does not survive the death of Lugosi."

More has been heard, however, in the area of law involving profiting from celebrities names or likenesses after their deaths.

[77] Prosser, Handbook of the Law of Torts, 4th ed. (St. Paul: West Pub. Co., 1971), p. 815, citing the confusing decision in Reed v. Real Detective Pub. Co., 63 Ariz. 294, 162 P.2d 133 (1945).

[78] Young v. That Was the Week that Was, 423 F.2d 265 (6th Cir.1970).

[79] Lugosi v. Universal Pictures, 25 Cal.3d 813, 819, 160 Cal.Rptr. 323, 326, 603 P.2d 425, 428 (1979).

Courts—sometimes guided by state statutes—give different signals in different jurisdictions, although the scales seem to tip toward descendibility. Cases involving Elvis Presley are illustrative:

(1) In Factors, Etc., v. Pro Arts, Inc., the Court of Appeals for the Second Circuit held in 1978 that there *was* a property right in Presley's name that continued on for his heirs.

(2) On the other hand, the Court of Appeals for the Sixth Circuit concluded in Memphis Development Foundation v. Factors, Etc.(1980), that Presley's heirs could *not* assign exclusive rights to use Presley's name and likeness. So, the Memphis firm selling statuettes of Elvis was allowed to continue, leaving his heirs "All Shook Up."[80]

Ten years after Presley's June 5, 1974 death, Tennessee enacted the Personal Rights Protection Act of 1984—protecting a property right in name and likeness.[81]

SEC. 40.   PRIVATE FACTS

With the law of privacy, "truth can hurt." Unlike the law of defamation, truth is not necessarily a defense to an invasion of privacy lawsuit.

Poor Dorothy Barber. Stuck in a hospital with an ailment that caused her to lose weight while eating constantly, she clearly believed her medical problem was her private business. A sneaky photographer's picture taken in her hospital room wound up being published in Time magazine under the remarkably insensitive caption, "Starving Glutton." Mrs. Barber's lawsuit illustrates overlapping of privacy torts, for she clearly had legal actions because the magazine revealed private facts about her—publication of private matters violating the ordinary decencies. Also, as discussed at page 345 of the next chapter—Mrs. Barber had an action for intrusion for the unwanted entry into her hospital room and for photographing her despite her protests.[82]

In publishing details of private matters, the media may report accurately and yet—at least on some occasions—may be found

---

[80] Memphis Development Foundation v. Factors Etc., Inc., 616 F.2d 956 (6th Cir.1980).

[81] Victor Kovner, et. al., Communications Law 1993, Vol. I (New York: Practising Law Institute) p. 870, listed several states providing for a property right to publicity surviving death: California, Florida, Georgia, Nebraska, Oklahoma, Tennessee, and Virginia. See, e.g., California Civil Code § 990. The Tennessee statute, however, appears to limit heirs' use of a celebrity's personality to ten years after the death of the individual. See T.C.A. § 47–25–1104(b)(2).

[82] Barber v. Time, Inc., 348 Mo. 1199, 159 S.W.2d 291, 295 (1942). Mrs. Barber won $3,000 from the magazine.

liable for damages. Lawsuits for defamation will not stand where the media have accurately reported the truth, but the media nevertheless could lose an action for invasion of privacy based on similar fact situations. In such instances, the truth sometimes hurts.

In most cases, the existence of a public record usually has precluded recovery for invasion of privacy. Even if persons are embarrassed by publication of dates of a marriage or birth,[83] or other information from a public record,[84] publication accurately based on such records has been protected by qualified privilege and escaped successful lawsuits. This can be true even in some extreme fact situations, as when the Albuquerque Journal published a story—based on a public official record—that a 16–year-old boy had sexually assaulted his younger sister.[85]

Sipple v. Chronicle Publishing Co. (1984)

Much in the law of privacy is unpredictable, and the "private facts" area is no exception. Consider the lawsuits brought by ex-Marine Oliver Sipple, who saved President Gerald Ford's life in 1975 by disrupting the aim of pistol-packing would-be assassin Sarah Jane Moore. Two days after the incident, San Francisco Chronicle columnist Herb Caen wrote that the city's gay community was proud of Sipple and that his heroism might dispel stereotypes about homosexuals.[86]

Sipple objected that his sexual orientation had nothing to do with saving the President, and filed suit against The Chronicle, against columnist Caen, and against the Los Angeles Times and several other newspapers, seeking $15 million in damages. The Los Angeles Times countered that Sipple was a person "thrust into the vortex of publicity" of an event of worldwide importance, claiming that " ...many aspects of his life became matters of legitimate public interest." Sipple appealed the trial court's dismissal of his privacy lawsuit, but an appellate court held that Sipple was so newsworthy after saving President Ford's life that he could not collect damages. Sipple was involved in an event of international importance. But when the newsworthiness is less, the privacy protection for an individual can be correspondingly greater. Toni Ann Diaz, for example, had achieved a far more limited newsworthiness as the first woman student body president at a Northern California junior college, the College of Alameda.

[83] Meetze v. Associated Press, 230 S.C. 330, 95 S.E.2d 606 (1956).

[84] Stryker v. Republic Pictures Corp., 108 Cal.App.2d 191, 238 P.2d 670 (1951).

[85] Hubbard v. Journal Pub. Co., 69 N.M. 473, 474, 368 P.2d 147, 148 (1962).

[86] The News Media & The Law, Oct./Nov. 1980, p. 27.

Diaz v. Oakland Tribune

In 1978, Oakland Tribune columnist Sidney Jones published truthful—yet highly private—information about dealing with a sex change operation undergone by Ms. Diaz:[87]

> "More Education Stuff: The Students at the College of Alameda will be surprised to learn their student body president Toni Diaz is no lady, but is in fact a man whose real name is Antonio.

> "Now I realize, that in these times, such a matter is no big deal, but I suspect that his female classmates in P.E. 97 may wish to make other showering arrangements."

The trial court jury awarded Ms. Diaz a total of $775,000, finding that the information about the sex change surgery was not newsworthy and would be offensive to ordinary readers.[88] Later, an appellate court ordered a new trial, ruling that the trial judge had erred in not emphasizing to the jury that a newspaper has a right to publish newsworthy information. Also, the appeals court said that it was up to the plaintiff to show that the article she complained of was not newsworthy. The appeals court held that there was little evidence that the gender-corrective surgery was pat of the public record, refusing to consider Diaz's Puerto Rican birth certificate as relevant. Given Diaz's efforts to conceal the operation, and considering Diaz's needs for privacy and the publicity received as the first woman student body president at her college, the judge held that the question of the story's newsworthiness should have been left to a jury. The court added, however, that the Oakland Tribune's claim that the story was made newsworthy by the changing roles of women was not newsworthy.[89]

The appellate court then sent the case back to the trial level, but a second jury never heard this case. After the decision by the California Court of Appeal, First District, the case was reportedly settled out of court for between $200,000 and $300,000.

Howard v. Des Moines Register (1979)

Like so many other cases in privacy law, Howard v. Des Moines Register and Tribune Co. raised both ethical and legal concerns. Reporter Margaret Engel did an investigative story on a county home, publishing the name of a young woman who had undergone forced sterilization. The article included this passage: "He [Dr. Roy C. Sloan, the home's psychiatrist] said the decision to sterilize the resident Robin Woody was made by her parents and himself." The

[87] Diaz v. Oakland Tribune, Inc., 139 Cal.App.3d 118, 188 Cal.Rptr. 762, 766 (1983), 9 Med.L.Rptr. 1121, 1122.

[88] The News Media and the Law, Oct./Nov. 1980, p. 28.

[89] 139 Cal.App.3d 118, 188 Cal.Rptr. 762, 763 (1983), 9 Med.L.Rptr. 1121, 1127.

article, based on public records, also noted that the woman was 18 at the time of her sterilization in 1970, and was not mentally retarded but was an "impulsive, hair-triggered young girl," in the words of Dr. Sloan.

Years later, Ms. Woody had left the county home, and was living in Des Moines under her married name of Howard, holding a job, with her sad past unknown to neighbors. Even so, the Register defended itself successfully against the woman's private facts lawsuit, concluding that in context, use of the defendant's name was justifiable. The court held that use of Robin Woody Howard's name lent personal detail, specificity and credibility to a story on a newsworthy topic, care of residents in a county home.[90]

In at least six states, statutes prohibit publishing the identity of a rape victim. Those states are Alaska, Florida, Georgia, South Carolina, and New York.[91] A case based upon the South Carolina statute resulted in a federal district court ruling indicating that such statutes were valid. However, a 1975 Supreme Court of the United States decision held otherwise when publication of a rape victim's name was based accurately on a public record.[92]

Cox Broadcasting Corp. v. Cohn (1975)

In 1971, 17–year-old Cynthia Cohn was gang-raped and murdered, and six youths were indicted for the crimes against her. There was heavy coverage of the event, but the identity of the rape victim was not disclosed until one defendant's trial began. Five of the six youths entered pleas of guilty to rape or attempted rape after murder charges were dropped. Those guilty pleas were accepted, and the trial of the defendant who pleaded not guilty was set for a later date.[93]

A Georgia statute forbade publication of the identity of a rape victim. Despite this, a reporter employed by WSB–TV learned Cynthia Cohn's identity from indictments open to public inspection and broadcast her identity as part of his story. The report was repeated the next day.

Martin Cohn sued the TV station, claiming that the broadcasts identifying his daughter invaded his own privacy. After hearing the Cohn case twice, the Georgia Supreme Court ruled that the statute forbidding publication of the name of a rape victim was constitu-

[90] Howard v. Des Moines Register and Tribune Co., 283 N.W.2d 289, 302, 303 (Iowa 1979).

[91] Alaska Stat.

[92] Nappier v. Jefferson Standard Life Insurance Co., 213 F.Supp. 174 (D.S.C.1963); Cox Broadcasting Corp. v. Cohn, 420 U.S. 469, 95 S.Ct. 1029 (1975).

[93] Cox Broadcasting v. Cohn, 420 U.S. 469, 470–474, 95 S.Ct. 1029, 1034–1035 (1975).

tional, " 'a legitimate limitation on the right of freedom of expression contained in the First Amendment.' "[94]

The Supreme Court of the United States overturned the Georgia court by a vote of 8–1. Writing for the Court, Justice White said:[95]

> The version of the privacy tort now before us—termed in Georgia the "tort of public disclosure" * * * is that in which the plaintiff claims the right to be free from unwanted publicity about his private affairs, which, although wholly true, would be offensive to a person of ordinary sensibilities. * * * [I]t is here that claims of privacy most directly confront the constitutional freedoms of speech and press.

Justice White wrote that truth may not always be a defense in either defamation or privacy actions. First, concerning defamation, "The Court has * * * carefully left open the question whether the First and Fourteenth Amendments require that truth be recognized as a defense in a defamation action brought by a private person as distinguished from a public official or a public figure." Writing about privacy, he continued: "In similar fashion, Time v. Hill, supra, [385 U.S. 374, 383 n. 7, 87 S.Ct. 534, 539 (1967)] expressly saved [reserved] the question whether truthful publication of very private matters unrelated to public affairs could be constitutionally proscribed." Thus, the Supreme Court recognized—but backed away from—a troubling constitutional question: May a state ever define and protect an area of privacy free from unwanted *truthful* publicity in the press?

Having recognized this problem, Justice White then turned his majority opinion to narrower and safer ground. In Cox Broadcasting v. Cohn, the key question was whether Georgia might impose punishment for the accurate publication of the name of a rape victim, when that name was obtained from an official record open to public inspection. Justice White concluded that the news media could not be published from quoting accurately from such a record.[96] He wrote that the news media have a great responsibility to report fully and accurately the proceedings of government, "and official records and documents open to the public are the basic data of governmental operations."[97]

Smith v. Daily Mail (1979)

This was a case that cut across areas of constitutional limitations on prior restraint, privacy, and free press-fair trial consider-

[94] 420 U.S. at 475, 95 S.Ct. at 1036 (1975).

[95] 420 U.S. at 489, 95 S.Ct. at 1043 (1975).

[96] 420 U.S. 469, 490, 491, 95 S.Ct. 1029, 1044 (1975).

[97] 420 U.S. 469, 492, 95 S.Ct. 1029, 1044–1045 (1975), citing Sheppard v. Maxwell, 384 U.S. 333, 350, 86 S.Ct. 1507, 1515 (1966).

ations. A 14–year-old junior high school student in St. Albans, W.Va., shot and killed a 15–year-old fellow student. Reporters for the nearby Charleston newspapers learned the identity of the youth accused of the shooting by their routine monitoring of police radio. The Charleston Daily Gazette used the youth's name in violation of a West Virginia statute forbidding a newspaper's use of juveniles accused of crimes without a written court order.

The state of West Virginia argued that this was an allowable prior restraint because of the state's interest in protecting identities of juveniles caught up in the legal process. The U.S. Supreme Court, however, by a vote of 8–0, declared the West Virginia statute unconstitutional. Chief Justice Burger wrote: "At issue is simply the power of a state to punish the truthful publication of an alleged juvenile delinquent's name lawfully obtained by a newspaper. The asserted state interest cannot justify the state's imposition of criminal sanctions on this type of publication." [98]

The Florida Star v. B.J.F. (1989)

In 1989, the U.S. Supreme Court cautiously upheld the generalization that if material is part of a public record, it can be reported truthfully and accurately without legal penalty. A woman sued a Jacksonville weekly newspaper after it published an item identifying her and saying that she had been robbed and sexually assaulted. This information was made available in the sheriff's department, which had prepared a report using her full name and put it in the department's press room. Access to reports in this room was unrestricted.

A reporter-trainee for The Florida Star copied the report verbatim, and a reporter then wrote an accurate one-paragraph "Police Reports" item, which was published. This violated the newspaper's own policy against identifying rape victims; the newspaper had not done so previously. This mistake by the newspaper led to B.J.F.'s lawsuit under a Florida statute making it unlawful to publish or broadcast the name of a victim of a sexual offense.[99]

The U.S. Supreme Court overturned the directed verdict that awarded B.J.F. $100,000 in damages. By a 6–3 vote, the Court carefully confined itself to the specific fact situation. The Court again avoided deciding the tough constitutional issue of whether the press ever can have criminal responsibility or civil liability for publishing a privacy-invading news story. Note also that this deci-

---

[98] West Virginia Statute § 49–7–3; Smith v. Daily Mail Pub. Co., 443 U.S. 97, 105, 99 S.Ct. 2667, 2672 (1979). See also the key prior restraint cases discussed in Chapter 1, including Near v. Minnesota ex rel. Olson, 283 U.S. 697, 51 S.Ct. 625 (1931).

[99] Florida Stat. § 794.03.

sion did not declare unconstitutional the Florida statute making it a crime to publish a rape victim's name.[1]

Writing for the Court, Justice Thurgood Marshall turned to Smith v. Daily Mail (1979) for his rationale in The Florida Star case, carefully limiting this decision to the context of this case. The Smith v. Daily Mail principle, Justice Marshall wrote, protects only publication of information which a news medium has "lawfully obtained." "It is undisputed that the article describing the assault on B.J.F. was accurate ...[and] lawfully obtained ..." Some of Justice Marshall's words, however, suggested that the Court *might* look favorably upon punishment for publishing truthful information if the statute authorizing such punishment was precise and narrowly drawn. But where government did not "police itself in disseminating information," imposition of damages against the media cannot stand.[2]

Virgil v. Time, Inc. (1975): Questioning "Consent"

What about a situation where a news source freely gives information and then reneges on the permission to publish? That was one issue in the privacy lawsuit, Virgil v. Time, Inc. That litigation was based on a truthful article on body surfing published in 1968 in Sports Illustrated, a Time, Inc. publication. The article devoted much attention to Mike Virgil, a surfer well known at "The Wedge," a dangerous stretch of beach near Newport Beach, California. Sports Illustrated staff writer Curry Kirkpatrick interviewed Virgil at length, which obviously required a kind of consent from Virgil—and Virgil also had cooperated with the taking of pictures by a free-lance photographer hired by Kirkpatrick.

Before the article was published, another Sports Illustrated employee called Virgil's home to verify some of the information with his wife. At this point—evidently because Mrs. Virgil disapproved of the interview—Virgil "revoked all consent" for use of his name in the article and for use of the photographs. Judge Merrill wrote that Virgil had understood that the article was going to be limited to his prowess as a surfer at The Wedge, and that he did not know it would contain references to some "bizarre incidents" in his life not "directly related to surfing."

It can be objected that Judge Merrill was "playing editor." Should it be up to a judge to say whether some of the "bizarre incidents" in Virgil's life were not "directly relating to surfing?" If a person persists in body-surfing at a place known as one of the world's most dangerous beaches, might not some of his other

[1] Florida Star v. B.J.F., 491 U.S. 524, 538, 109 S.Ct. 2603, 2611 (1989), 16 Med.L. Rptr. 1801, 1803, 1805–1806.

[2] 491 U.S. at 536, 109 S.Ct. at 2611 (1989), 16 Med.L.Rtpr. at 1806.

actions be relevant? Wouldn't actions such as extinguishing a cigarette in his mouth, or diving down a flight of stairs because "there were all these chicks around" or eating spiders illustrate an unusually reckless (and therefore newsworthy) approach to life?[3]

Trial Coverage and a Rape Victim's Identity

Consider the case of Doe v. Sarasota–Bradenton Television. "Jane Doe" was raped, and agreed to testify against her assailant in his trial. It was important to her that her name and or countenance would not be revealed or photographed in connection with this trial.

In 1982, "Jane Doe" testified at the rape trial. A news team from Sarasota–Bradenton Television was present in the courtroom. (As noted in Chapter 9, Section 58, below, under Florida law, news cameras are allowed in that state's courtrooms.) That night, the TV station ran a videotape of the trial featuring "Jane Doe's" testimony. As the videotape ran, the newscaster identified "Jane Doe" to the viewing audience by her real name.[4]

"Jane Doe" sued the TV station, seeking damages under a Florida statute[5] and for common law invasion of privacy and for intentional infliction of emotional distress. However, both the trial court and a Florida Court of Appeal (Second District) agreed that the lawsuit must be dismissed, citing Cox Broadcasting v. Cohn, a case discussed a few pages earlier.[6] The Court of Appeal (Second District) conceded that in both the Cox Broadcasting and the "Jane Doe" cases, the broadcasts complained of contained completely accurate but pain-inflicting information. This Florida court had harsh words for the TV station:[7]

> We deplore the lack of sensitivity to the rights of others that is sometimes displayed by such an unfettered exercise of first amendment rights.

* * *

> The publication adds little or nothing to the sordid and unhappy story; yet, that brief little-or-nothing addition may well affect appellant's [Jane Doe's] well-being for years to come.

That court also chastised the prosecution—representatives of the State of Florida—"for not having sought a protective order

[3] Virgil v. Time, 527 F.2d 1122, 1125 n. (9th Cir.1975).

[4] Doe v. Sarasota–Bradenton Florida Television Co., Inc., 436 So.2d 328 (Fla. App.2d Dist. 1983), 9 Med.L.Rptr. 2074.

[5] Ibid., quoting Florida Statute § 794.03.

[6] 420 U.S. 469, 95 S.Ct. 1029 (1975).

[7] 436 So.2d 328, 329, 9 Med.L.Rptr. at 2075–2076.

regarding cameras in the courtroom or other proper steps to support its alleged assurance" to Jane Doe that she could testify in the rape trial without her name or picture being used. Recognizing frequent conflicts between freedom of the press and the right of privacy, the court urged "compassionate discretion" by the media in such situations.

Macon Telegraph v. Tatum (1993)

A similar result favoring the media was reached by the Georgia Supreme Court in Macon Telegraph v. Tatum (1993). The newspaper published two articles about a woman who shot and killed an intruder in her bedroom about 4 a.m. on a Saturday morning. Police ultimately cleared this incident as justifiable homicide. The articles identified Mrs. Tatum, mentioning the street where she lived, but did not mention that a rape or sexual assault had occurred. The newspaper's first article, however, was headlined "Woman Kills Attacker in Bedroom" and included the information that the intruder had his pants unzipped. The Georgia Rape Shield Statute forbids publication of names of sexual assault victims.[8]

At trial, facts in this case were in dispute, with the newspaper arguing that Mrs. Tatum's name and address already were available, and that the newspaper had not been aware that Mrs. Tatum had been the victim of a sexual assault. Police, on the other hand, testified that Mrs. Tatum's name had been released to the press only on condition that it not be published. Police contended it had been made clear that the incident was treated as a sexual assault, and that it was understood that Mrs. Tatum's name would be published only with her permission. Otherwise, the Georgia Rape Shield Statute would be violated.[9]

Ultimately, the Georgia Supreme Court ruled for the Macon Telegraph, saying:[10]

> * * *[W]e hold that Tatum, who committed a homicide, however justified, lost her right to keep her name private. When she Hill, Tatum became the object of a legitimate public interest and the newspaper had the right under the Federal and State constitution to accurately report the facts regarding incident, including her name.

Patti Bowman, Rape Charges, and Privacy

Stir together salacious details in allegations of sexual misconduct, charges of victimization, and the name of America's most

[8] Macon Telegraph v. Tatum, 208 Ga.App. 111, 430 S.E.2d 18 (1993), 21 Med. L.Rptr. 1116, 1117, overturned at 263 Ga. 678, 436 S.E.2d 655 (1993), 22 Med. L.Rptr. 1126; OCGA § 16–6–23.

[9] Ibid., 112, 1117.

[10] Macon Telegraph Publishing Co. v. Tatum, 263 Ga. 678, 436 S.E.2d 655, 658 (1993), 22 Med.L.Rptr. 1126, 1127.

famous political family: that's tabloid heaven and pure hell for ethical journalism. A case in 1991 involved the televised trial of rape charges against William Kennedy Smith, nephew of Massachusetts Senator Edward Kennedy and of the late President John F. Kennedy. The 30–year-old woman who brought the rape charges was identified by name in a grocery store tabloid paper . Then, in a lowest-common-denominator approach to journalist values, some establishment news media including NBC News and The New York Times also identified the complainant as Patti Bowman.

When Ms. Bowman testified as the plaintiff during the rape trial in a Florida courtroom, her face was obscured by an electronically generated blue blur. Although William Kennedy Smith was acquitted quickly by a six-person jury, the trial generated nationwide distaste and raised the question whether women would henceforth be more reluctant to endure the legal process in order to pursue rape charges.[11]

Lurid media coverage of William Kennedy Smith's trial and acquittal resulted in charges against a tabloid newspaper, The Globe, for violation of Florid Statute § 794.03. That statute specifies criminal sanctions against anyone revealing the identity of the victim of a sexual offense "in any instrument of mass communication." Even though William Kennedy Smith was not convicted of rape, Patti Bowman brought charges against The Globe under the Florida Statute mentioned above. Eventually, both a Florida trial court and a Florida District Court of Appeal held that the Florida statute specifying penalties for identifying victims of sexual offenses "violates free speech and free press provisions of the Constitutions of Florida and the United States ...," is overbroad, and is an unconstitutional prior restraint.[12]

Time Lapse: Sidis v. F–R Publishing Corp. (1940)

Time lapse—the passage of years between an event putting a person in the news and republication of embarrassing facts—has been an occasional issue in privacy cases. How much time must pass before a person recovers from unwanted publicity, loses his or her newsworthiness, and again can be said to have regained anonymity?

In general, courts have said once in the news, always in the news.[13]

[11] See David Margolick, "Smith Acquitted of Rape Charge After Brief Deliberation by Jury," The New York Times, Dec. 12, 1991., p.A1.

[12] Florida v. Globe Communications Corp., 622 So.2d 1066, 1067 (Fla.App., 4th Dist.1993), 21 Med.L.Rptr. 2129.

[13] See Sidis v. F–R Publishing Corep., 113 F.2d 806 (2d Cir.1940); Underwood v. First National Bank (Minn. Dist. Ct. 1982), 8 Med.L.Rptr. 1278 (publication of account of decades-old murder conviction), and Roshto v. Hebert, 439 So.2d 428, 429

Take the case of William James Sidis, a person who was found by publicity. Back in 1910, Sidis was an 11–year-old mathematical prodigy who lectured to famed mathematicians. He was graduated from Harvard in 1916, receiving much publicity. More than 20 years later, a 1937 issue of New Yorker magazine ran a "Where Are They Now?" feature story about Sidis with an additional caption, "April Fool." The article told how Sidis lived in a "hall bedroom of Boston's shabby south end, working at a routine clerical job, collecting streetcar transfers and studying the history of American Indians." Sidis sued for invasion of privacy, but a U.S. Court of Appeals ultimately held that he could not collect damages.

The court conceded that the New Yorker had published "a ruthless exposure of a once public character, who has since sought an has now been deprived of the seclusion of private life." Even so, the court said:[14]

> At least we would permit limited scrutiny of the "private" life of any person who has achieved, or has had thrust upon him, the questionable and indefinable status of "public figure." * * *
>
> We express no comment on whether or not the life of the matter printed will always constitute a complete defense. Revelations may be so intimate and so unwarranted in view of the victim's position as to outrage the community's notions of decency. But when focused upon public characters, truthful comments upon dress, speech, habits, and the ordinary aspects of personality will usually not transgress this line.

The court implied that the invasion of privacy must be so severe that it would cause more than minor annoyance to an hypothetical "average" person of "ordinary sensibilities." But William James Sidis was an unusually sensitive person. It has been speculated that the New Yorker article was a big factor in his early death.[15]

Briscoe v. Reader's Digest

California courts added an element to privacy law with the suggestion that the existence of a public record did not necessarily serve as a defense to a lawsuit for invasion of privacy. One of the more notorious—and most wrong-headed—cases involved the disclosure of embarrassing private facts from the life of Marvin Briscoe. In 1968, Reader's Digest magazine published an article titled "The Big Business of Hijacking," describing efforts made to stop such thefts. Dates ranging from 1965 to the time of publication

(La.1983), 9 Med.L.Rptr. 2417, 2418 (republication of front page including 20–year-old story of cattle theft).

[14] Sidis v. F–R Publishing Corp., 113 F.2d 806 (2d Cir.1940).

[15] Prosser, "Privacy," California Law Review, Vol. 48 (1960), at p. 397.

were mentioned in the article, but none of the hijackings mentioned had a date attached to it in the text.[16]

One sentence in the article said: " 'Typical of many beginners, Marvin Briscoe and [a confederate] stole a "valuable-looking" truck in Danville, Ky. and then fought a gun battle with the local police, only to learn that they had hijacked four bowling-pin spotters.' " There was nothing in the article to indicate that this hijacking had occurred in 1956, some 11 years before publication of the Reader's Digest article. In the words of the California Supreme Court, "As a result of defendant's [Reader's Digest's] publication, plaintiff's 11–year-old daughter, as well as his friends, for the first time learned of the incident. They thereafter scorned and abandoned him."[17] Briscoe argued that he had "gone straight" and paid his debt to society, becoming entirely rehabilitated and leading an exemplary life, making friends who were not aware of his past.

Briscoe conceded the truth of the Reader's Digest article, but claimed that public disclosure of such private facts humiliated him and exposed him to ridicule. He argued that although the *subject* of the article was "newsworthy," use of his *name* was not, and that Reader's Digest therefore had invaded his privacy.

Writing for a unanimous California Supreme Court, Justice Raymond E. Peters refused to grant the magazine a summary judgment, meaning that the magazine would have to defend itself at trial. In Justice Peters' words:

> Plaintiff is a man whose last offense took place 11 years before, who has paid his debt to society, and who has friends and an 11–year-old daughter who were unaware of his early life—a man who has assumed a position in "respectable society." * * * Yet, as if in some bizarre canyon of echoes, petitioner's past life pursues him through the pages of Reader's Digest, now published in 13 languages and distributed in 100 nations, with a circulation in California alone of almost 2,000,000 copies.

> In a nation built upon the free dissemination of ideas, it is always difficult to declare that something may not be published. * * * But the rights guaranteed by the First Amendment do not require total abrogation of the right to privacy.

In sending the matter back to a lower court for trial, Justice Peters declared that although there was good reason to discuss the crime of truck hijacking in the media, there was not reason to us Briscoe's name. A jury, in the view of the California Supreme

---

[16] Briscoe v. Reader's Digest Association, 4 Cal.3d 529, 93 Cal.Rptr. 866, 868, 483 P.2d 34, 36 (1971).

[17] Ibid.

Court, certainly could find that Mr. Briscoe once again had become an anonymous member of his community.[18]

Despite such sweeping language by the California Supreme Court, Briscoe did not win his lawsuit. The case was removed from the California state courts to the United States District Court, Central District of California, where Judge Lawrence T. Lydick granted summary judgment to Reader's Digest. Judge Lydick concluded that the article about Briscoe was newsworthy and published without actual malice or recklessness. Further, the judge concluded that the article neither disclosed private facts about Briscoe nor invaded his privacy.[19]

In general, common law or statutory declarations giving privilege to reports of public official documents *should* protect the media against liability for factual reports in "time lapse" situations. A California statute, for example, declared that publications are privileged if they are [20]

> * * * a fair and true report in a public journal of (1) a judicial, (2) legislative, or (3) other public official proceeding, or (4) of anything said in the course thereof. . . .

Even so, one Milo Conklin sued a weekly, the *Modoc County Record*, for invading his privacy by publishing—in a "Twenty Years Ago" column—an accurate reference to Conklin's having been charged with murdering his brother-in-law. The published statement was true. Conklin had been tried for, and convicted of, the murder of Louis Blodgett. What the news squib didn't say was that Conklin had served a prison sentence, completed parole, remarried, fathered two children, and rehabilitated himself. Once out of prison, he had returned to the scene of the murder, Cedarville, California, a hamlet of 800 people. It is hard to imagine that a town of 800 would be able to forget that it had a convicted murderer living there, yet the California Court of Appeal nevertheless accepted Conklin's argument that some of his friends shunned him after the publication.[21]

Some of the sting of *Briscoe* was lessened by the California Supreme Court's decision in Forsher v. Bugliosi. Vincent Bugliosi,

---

[18] 4 Cal.3d 529, 93 Cal.Rptr. 866, 875, 483 P.2d 34, 43 (1971).

[19] Briscoe v. Reader's Digest Association. (C.D.Cal.1972), 1 Med.L.Rptr. 1852, 1854. This decision in favor of the magazine, not reported in Federal Supplement, was a kind of "best kept secret." The ruling in the federal district court (evidently unknown other than in Media Law Reporter) was either unnoticed or ignored by courts in deciding Forsher v. Bugliosi, 26 Cal.3d 792, 163 Cal.Rptr. 628, 608 P.2d 716 (1980), and Conklin v. Sloss, 86 Cal.App.3d 241, 150 Cal.Rptr. 121 (3d Dist. 1978), 4 Med.L.Rptr. 1998.

[20] West's Ann. Cal. Civil Code § 47, subs. 4.

[21] Conklin v. Sloss, 86 Cal.App.3d 241, 150 Cal.Rptr. 121 (3d Dist. 1978), 4 Med.L.Rptr. 1998, 1999.

prosecuting attorney in the trial of Charles Manson and his "Family" for the "Tate–LaBianca killings." Bugliosi, author of *Helter-Skelter*, a book purporting to be an inside look at the killings and the trial of Charles Manson. James Forsher, mentioned in the book as being on the fringes of the Manson Family's activities, sued for libel and invasion of privacy. Forsher claimed there was no social value in using his name in connection with retelling of past events. Judge Manual wrote for the Supreme Court of California:[22]

> California courts have refrained from extending the Briscoe rule to other fact situations. * * * *Briscoe* * * * [held] that "where the plaintiff is a past criminal and his name is used in a publication, the mere lapse of time may not provide a basis for an invasion of privacy suit."

SEC. 41.   INTRUSION: AN INTRODUCTION

Invading a person's solitude, including the use of microphones or cameras, has been held to be actionable.

Journalists often are seen as prime invaders of privacy, with intrusive photographers ("paparazzi") and hidden cameras on tabloid TV shows catching a lot of heat. Despite such deviant subgroups who are lumped together in the public eye with *real* journalists, members of the media are not the true experts on intrusiveness. The true expertise in intrusiveness belongs to governmental units, including police and the FBI, and to corporate snoopers including credit bureaus.

Even so, there are many lawsuits against the media for "intrusion" and trespass. Courts and legal scholars frequently turn to the definitions in the Restatement (Second) of Torts, which characterized "intrusion" in this fashion:[23]

> One who intentionally intrudes, physically or otherwise, upon the solitude or seclusion of another or his private affairs or concerns, is subject to liability to the other for invasion of his privacy, if the intrusion would be highly offensive to a reasonable person.

The tort of "intrusion" is discussed at length in the following chapter. It has been placed there because recent developments in the law—discussed in the next chapter—have led to listing intrusion as a "newsgathering tort."

[22] Forsher v. Bugliosi, 26 Cal.3d 792, 810, 163 Cal.Rptr. 628, 638, 608 P.2d 716, 726 (1980).

[23] Restatement (Second) of Torts, § 652(B) (1977).

Chapter 7

NEWSGATHERING TORTS AND
RELATED AREAS OF LAW

Sec.

SEC. 42.   NEWSGATHERING TORTS: AN OVERVIEW

Newsgathering torts—which often are privacy torts in new clothes—were growing concerns for the media in the 1990s.

When Diana, Princess of Wales, died in 1997 in a high-speed auto crash in a tunnel in France, public anger against intrusive photographers and videographers was focused as never before. Never mind that the princess used the media to build her own image and then would try to turn off attention as if it were a spigot. Never mind that the biggest offenders in pursuing "Princess Di" were free-lancers salaciously hoping to capture a visual image of this blonde British aristocrat in a compromising situation. Never mind that the free-lancers sold their visual products to tabloid newspapers in England and the United States and to "tabloid TV" shows too. Public anger from a individuals who don't understand—or don't want to understand—the differences among TV shows such as "Hard Copy," "Entertainment Tonite," "Inside Edition," CBS's "60 Minutes" and CBS News led to calls for stricter laws to "control the media."[1] In an era when jurors in libel and privacy lawsuits showed hostility to generally responsible main-line media units, the ghost of Princess Diana may sit, symbolically, on juries when news media are sued for defamation or invasion of privacy.

This new chapter takes up a variety of legal areas lumped together under the label "newsgathering torts." These will be discussed in this fashion:

---

[1] Geoffrey Robertson, "Privacy Matters," The New Yorker, September 15, 1997, p. 36.

*Intrusion

*Intrusion: Nonconsensual Entry and Refusal to Leave

*Intrusion: Hidden Cameras and Recorders

*Intrusion: Cellular Phones

*Fraud Claims and Undercover Reporting

*Contract Claims and Tortious Interference

The basics of invasion of privacy torts were described in the preceding chapter. As listed previously, on page 306, the fundamental privacy torts were outlined and given a much-followed pattern in a 1960 law review article by Dean William L. Prosser. He included the following under the broad label of "invasion of privacy:"[2]

(1) Intrusion on the plaintiff's physical solitude.

(2) Publication of private matters violating the ordinary decencies.

(3) Putting plaintiff in a false position in the public eye, as by singing that person's name to a letter or petition, attributing to that individual views not held by that person.

(4) Appropriation of some element of plaintiff's personality— his or her name or likeness—for commercial use.

The basics of points (2), (3), and (4), above, are discussed in the preceding chapter.

SEC. 43.   THE PRIVACY TORT OF INTRUSION

Invading a person's solitude, including the use of hidden microphones or cameras, has been held actionable.

Media personnel must look to their ethics as they use modern technology to gather and to broadcast news. Telephoto lenses enable photographers and videographers to intrude upon unwary subjects and "shotgun microphones" can pick up quiet conversations hundreds of feet away. The technology may be modern, but the problem is centuries old. Back in 1765, Sir William Blackstone's *Commentaries* described eavesdroppers as "people who listen under windows, or the eaves of a house, to conversation, from which they frame slanderous and mischievous tales."[3] Now, the tort subdivi-

---

[2] Barbieri v. News–Journal Co., 56 Del. 67, 189 A.2d 773, 774 (1963). The Delaware Supreme Court summarized Dean Prosser's analysis of the kinds of actions to be included in the law of privacy. See Prosser's "Privacy," 49 California Law Review (1960), pp. 383–423, and his Handbook of the Law of Torts, 4th ed. (St. Paul, Minn.: West Publishing Co., 1971), pp. 802–818.

[3] Sir William Blackstone's Commentaries on the Law, ed. by Bernard C. Gavit (Washington, D.C.: Washington Book Co., 1892), p. 823.

sion of intrusion sometimes includes matters from illegal entry onto private property to surreptitious tape recording (in some instances) to use of hidden cameras.

Despite what a public irate against "the media" may think, it is not an invasion of privacy to take someone's photograph in a public place. Here, photographers (and videographers) are protected on the theory that they "stand in" for the public, capturing images anyone could see if they were there. It follows, of course, that photographers should beware of taking photos in private places. When journalists or photographers invade private territory, they and their employers could be in trouble.

Barber v. Time provides a classic example. In 1939, Mrs. Dorothy Barber was a patient in a Kansas City hospital, under treatment for a disease which caused her to eat constantly but still lose weight. A wire service (International News Service) photographer invaded her hospital room and took her picture despite her protests. This resulted about stories about Mrs. Barber's illness in Kansas City newspapers. Time Magazine then purchased the picture from the wire service, publishing it along with a story. Time's headline said "Starving Glutton;" a cutline under the picture said "Insatiable–Eater Barber; She Eats for Ten." Mrs. Barber won $3,000 in damages from Time, Inc.[4]

In the late 1970s, a television crew's intrusion onto private property caused huge legal costs for a CBS-owned station, although it wound up paying a minor damage award of only $1,200. Minor award or not, the case of Le Mistral v. Columbia Broadcasting System underlines the principle that journalists must ask themselves whether they are attempting to report from a private place. In the Le Mistral case, reporter Lucille Rich and a camera crew barged into the famous and fashionable Le Mistral Restaurant in New York City. The reporter-camera team was doing a series on restaurants cited for health-code irregularities. The arrival of the camera crew—with lights on and cameras rolling—caused a scene of confusion which a slapstick comedian would love. (Persons lunching with persons other than their spouses were reported to have slid hastily under tables to try to avoid the camera.) The restaurant's suit for invasion of privacy and trespass resulted in a jury award against CBS of $1,200 in compensatory damages and $250,000 in punitive damages. On appeal, the punitive damages were dropped.[5]

If photographers can see their subject from a public spot, without going through strange gyrations such as climbing tele-

---

[4] Barber v. Time, Inc., 348 Mo. 1199, 1203, 159 S.W.2d 291, 293 (1942).

[5] Le Mistral, Inc. v. Columbia Broadcasting System, 61 A.D.2d 491, 402 N.Y.S.2d 815 (1st Dept.1978); TV Guide, May 3, 1980, p. 6.

phone poles or sneaking onto private property, no liability should result. A Louisiana newspaper was sued for invasion of privacy by Mr. and Mrs. James Jaubert, who were upset that a feature photo of their home was published on the newspaper's front page with this caption:"One of Crowley's stately homes, a bit weatherworn and unkempt, stands in the shadow of a spreading oak." Ultimately, the Jauberts' privacy suit failed. The Louisiana Supreme Court ruled that because the photograph was taken from the middle of a public street in front of the Jaubert house, and because any passers-by could see an identical view, there was no invasion of privacy.[6]

Ethical considerations go hand-in-hand with legal concerns in many privacy cases. In Cape Publications v. Bridges, Hilda Bridges Pate sued for invasion of privacy for a photograph published by a Florida newspaper, Cocoa Today. She had been abducted by her estranged husband, who went to her job and—at gunpoint—forced her to go with him to their former apartment. Police were called and surrounded the apartment. The husband forced her to undress in an effort to prevent her from trying to escape, and then shot himself to death. Police heard the gunshot, stormed the apartment, and rushed a partially clad Ms. Pate to safety across a parking lot as she clutched a dish towel to her body. At the trial, a Florida jury awarded Ms. Pate $1 million in compensatory damages and $9 million in punitive damages.

A Florida appellate court overturned all damage awards, saying: "The published photograph is more a depiction of grief, fright, emotional tension and flight than it is an appeal to sensual appetites." In sort, it was a newsworthy story. Judge Dauksch wrote, "The photograph revealed little more than could be seen had . . . [Ms. Pate] been wearing a bikini, and somewhat less than some bathing suits seen on the beaches." The judge added that courts should be slow to interfere with publication of news in the public interest.[7]

Paparazzi and the Death of Princess Diana: Echoes of the Ron Galella Case

If you can see something in a public place, you can photograph it. However, photographers can go too far even in public places if

[6] Jaubert v. Crowley Post–Signal, Inc., 375 So.2d 1386 (La.1979); 5 Med.L.Rptr. 2084.

[7] Cape Publications, Inc. v. Bridges, 423 So.2d 426 (Fla.App. 5th Dist.1982), 8 Med. L.Rptr. 2535, 2536. In footnote 2, the judge quoted the Restatement (Second) of Torts, § 652D, Comment G, on the definition of news: " 'Authorized publicity, customarily referred to as "news," includes publications concerning crimes, arrests, police raids, suicides, marriages, divorces, accidents, fires, catastrophes of nature, narcotics-related deaths, rare diseases, etc., and many other matters of genuine popular appeal.' "

their behavior becomes annoyingly intrusive. When Princess Diana and her lover, Dodi Fayed, died in a 1997 high-speed auto crash in Paris, the species of photographer known as "paparazzi"—Italian slang for a small, annoying insect—was widely blamed for her death.[8] (Never mind that the death car's driver was intoxicated and also had the anti-depressant Prozac in his system.) Inevitably, calls came for legislation in the United States to bring paparazzi under control, in part to cut off the supply of free-lance photographers intrusive photos to supermarket tabloids such as The National Enquirer and The Star.[9]

There are, in fact, ample laws and court precedents against stalking and against the forms of invasion of privacy listed above at footnote 2. Before the death of Princess Diana, the American poster boy for paparazzi behaving badly was Ron Galella. He proudly called himself a paparazzo, and made a career taking photos of America's own version of royalty, Jacqueline Kennedy Onassis, and her children. Mrs. Onassis, widow of the martyred President John F. Kennedy and also of Greek shipping magnate Aristotle (Ari) Onassis, was hounded so enthusiastically by Galella that U.S. Circuit Judge J. Joseph Smith used him as a defining example of paparazzi. The judge declared that paparazzi "make themselves as visible to the public and obnoxious to their photographic subjects as possible to aid in the advertisement and wide sale of their works."

Galella's fixation on photographing Mrs. Onassis and her children ultimately led to issuance of an injunction against the photographer. A 1975 injunction forbade Galella from approaching within 25 feet of Mrs. Onassis or within 30 feet of her children.[10] A major fear was that Galella's intrusiveness might endanger the Kennedy children, John and Caroline, whom he stalked photographically at their private schools in addition to lurking outside the New York high-rise where Mrs. Onassis and her children lived, following them to the theater, and so forth.

Temptation, however, proved too great for Ron Galella. He disobeyed the injunction on four different occasions in 1981, again getting too close and becoming too obnoxious in his photographic shadowing of Mrs. Onassis and her children. U.S. District Judge Cooper found Galella to be in contempt of the court's 1975 order,

---

[8] James Fallows, "Are Journalists People?" U.S. News & World Report, Sept. 15, 1997, pp. 31–32; Marianne MacDonald, "Hunted down by paparazzi, Diana lived a nightmare," London Observer Service for Scripps Howard News Service, The Knoxville News–Sentinel, Sept. 8, 1997, p. A1.

[9] See the paired editorial page comments in USA Today, Sept. 3, 1997, p. 14A, "Our View: More laws won't stop photographers run amok," and "Opposing View" [by security consultant Gavin de Becker], "Protect privacy with laws."

[10] Galella v. Onassis, 487 F.2d 986 (2d Cir.1973).

subjecting the persistent paparazzo to liability for a heavy fine and/or imprisonment.[11]

Dietemann v. Time, Inc. (1971)

To take the long view, there have been relatively few cases of "intrusion" privacy lawsuits against the news media in the United States, although competition for ratings—especially among "tabloid television" programs in the 1990s, suggested that the lessons of the key precedent set by Dietemann v. Time, Inc. (1971) were being ignored, thanks in part to competitive pressures and the need to present fickle TV channel-surfers with titillating fare.

The Dietemann case caused Life magazine—a Time, Inc., publication—to bite the privacy bullet. A reporter and a photographer from Life, cooperating with the Los Angeles county district attorney and the California State Department of Public Health, did some role-playing to entrap a medical quack. Reporter Jackie Metcalf and photographer William Ray went to the home of journeyman plumber A.A. Dietemann, a man suspected of performing medical services without a diploma or state license. They rang a bell at the front gate of Dietemann's home in order to get to his door, and then got inside his house after Mrs. Metcalf claimed that she had been sent by (pardon the expression) the plumber's friends.

Mrs. Metcalf complained to Dietemann that she had a lump in her breast and while Dietemann conducted his "examination" of her, Ray secretly was taking pictures. Life later published pictures from Dietemann's home, and also reported on his "diagnosis." The plumber/medical practitioner told Mrs. Metcalf that her difficulty was caused by eating rancid butter 11 years, 9 months, and 7 days prior to her visit to his home.[12]

Mrs. Metcalf, meanwhile, had a transmitter in her purse and was relaying her conversations with Dietemann to a receiver/tape recorder in an auto parked nearby. That auto contained the following eavesdroppers: another Life reporter, a representative of the DA's office, and an investigator from the California State Department of Public Health. This detective work resulted in convicting Dietemann for practicing medicine without a license. The plumber, however, sued Time, Inc. for $300,000 for invasion of privacy. A jury, recognizing that Dietemann (legally speaking) did not come into court with clean hands, awarded the plumber only $1,000 for invasion of privacy.

Life magazine's attorneys had argued strenuously that concealed electronic instruments and cameras are "indispensable tools of investigative reporting." In a scathing decision written by Judge

[11] 533 F.Supp. 1076, 1108 (S.D.N.Y.1982), 8 Med.L.Rptr. 1321, 1325.

[12] Dietemann v. Time, Inc., 449 F.2d 245, 246 (9th Cir.1971).

Shirley Hufstedler, a United States Court of Appeals upheld the damage award in words quoted ever since when newsgathering becomes overly intrusive. Judge Hufstedler wrote:[13]

> Investigative reporting is an ancient art; its successful practice long antecedes the invention of miniature cameras and electronic devices. The First Amendment has never been construed to accord newsmen immunity from torts or crimes committed during the course of newsgathering.

Florida Publishing Co. v. Fletcher (1972)

Seventeen-year-old Cindy Fletcher was alone one afternoon at her Jacksonville, Fla., home when a fire of undetermined origin broke out. She died in the blaze. When the fire marshal and a police sergeant arrived, they followed their standard practice of inviting reporters and photographers to join them.

The fire marshal wanted a clear picture of the "silhouette" left on the floor after the removal of Cindy Fletcher's body to show that the body was already on the floor before the fire's heat damaged the room. The marshal ran out of film, and asked a photographer from the Florida Times–Union to take the silhouette picture. That photo was made part of the official investigation files of both the fire and police departments.

That picture also was published in the Florida Times–Union, along with other photos from the fire scene. Cindy's mother, Mrs. Klenna Ann Fletcher, first learned of the facts surrounding her daughter's death by reading the newspaper story and seeing the published photographs.

Mrs. Fletcher sued the newspaper for " '(1) trespass . . . , (2) invasion of privacy, and (3) wrongful intentional infliction of emotional distress—seeking punitive damages.' " The trial court dismissed the second count and granted summary judgments to the newspaper on counts 1 and 3. On the issue of trespass, the trial judge said:[14]

> "The question raised is whether the trespass alleged in Count I of the complaint was consented to by the doctrine of common custom and usage.
>
> "The law is well settled in Florida that there is no unlawful trespass when peaceable entry is made, without objection, under common custom and usage."

Numerous affidavits had been filed by news media saying that "common custom and usage" permitted the news media to enter

---

[13] Ibid., at p. 249. Emphasis added by author.

[14] Florida Pub. Co. v. Fletcher, 340 So.2d 914, 915–916 (Fla.1976).

the scene of a disaster.[15]

Mrs. Fletcher appealed, but the Florida Supreme Court held that no actionable invasion of privacy had occurred. That court quoted approvingly from a Florida appeals court judge's opinion:[16]

> "It is my view that the entry in this case was by implied consent. * * * Implied consent would, of course, vanish if one were informed not to enter at that time by the owner or possessor or by their direction. But here there was not only no objection to the entry, but *there was an invitation to enter by the officers investigating the fire.*"

Although the Fletcher case has been enthusiastically cited by media attorneys, it is no magic bullet to keep away trespass lawsuits, especially when officials of a facility or residents of a property say "do not enter."

SEC. 44.   INTRUSION: NONCONSENSUAL ENTRY, REFUSAL TO LEAVE

Photographers and journalists enter private property at their legal peril if they do not have appropriate permission. Official permission may not be enough if owners or tenants of private property object to the presence of media employees.

When a member of the media does not have permission to be on private property, that's trespass. Consider Oklahoma v. Bernstein, decided by the Oklahoma District Court, Rogers County. Benjamin Bernstein and many other reporters were arrested for trespass after they followed anti-nuke demonstrators onto the construction site of a Public Service of Oklahoma (PSO) nuclear power plant, Black Fox Station.

Despite showings of extensive government support for Black Fox Station (e.g. use of eminent domain to acquire part of the site for PSO, government-guaranteed loans, close supervision by the Nuclear Regulatory Commission), the Black Fox site was held to be "private property." Although the Oklahoma court conceded that protests at the construction site were newsworthy, and although PSO was trying to minimize news coverage of an important public controversy, the reporters were found guilty of trespass.[17]

---

[15] Ibid. Affidavits were filed in"friend of the court" briefs by media including the Chicago Tribune, ABC–TV News, the Associated Press, the Miami Herald, the Milwaukee Journal, and the Washington Post.

[16] Ibid., 918–919.

[17] Oklahoma v. Bernstein (Okl.D.C., Rogers County, 1980), 5 Med.L.Rptr. 2313, 2323–2324. Confirmed in 665 P.2d 839 (Okla.Crim.App.1983).

Access to Disaster Scenes: City of Oak
Creek v. Peter Ah King (1989)

When airplanes fall from the sky or industrial plants explode, that is news. Reporters, photographers, and videographers need to get to the news scene to report. In response, police officials and rescue workers argue that they don't need the news media getting in the way or exposing themselves or others to danger.

A 1985 plane crash case provided a case in point. Midwest Airlines Flight 105 crashed in the City of Oak Creek just after taking off from Milwaukee's General Mitchell Field. Just after the crash, the officer in charge of airport security ordered the crash scene secured. Only emergency personnel and equipment were allowed near the crash site. Roadblocks were set up.

An unmarked sedan carrying four employees of Milwaukee station WTMJ–TV rolled through the roadblock, following an emergency vehicle down the only road providing access to the crash site. A detective left the roadblock and chased the sedan. When he caught up, the WTMJ–TV employees were getting cameras out of the auto. The detective told the four news people that they would have to leave. One individual asked if three of the TV news employees—excluding the driver—could walk back along the road to the non-restricted area and began to do so.[18]

Cameraman Peter Ah King then left the others, jumped a fence bearing "No Trespassing" signs, and ran to a low hill where he took pictures of the crash site. The detective then ordered Ah King to leave; Ah King replied that he would not leave unless he was arrested. Ah King was arrested on suspicion of disorderly conduct, and later charged under a statute which says:

> *Disorderly conduct.* Whoever, in a public or private place, engages in violent, abusive, profane, boisterous, unreasonably loud or otherwise disorderly conduct under circumstances in which the conduct tends to cause or provoke a disturbance is guilty of a Class B misdemeanor.

Because Ah King's conduct was not of the kind listed specifically by the statute, one question in appellate review of the case was whether the catch-all phrase "otherwise disorderly conduct" would sustain conviction of the cameraman.

It did. Writing for the Wisconsin Supreme Court, Justice Louis J. Ceci declared:[19]

[18] City of Oak Creek v. Peter Ah King, 148 Wis.2d 532, 436 N.W.2d 285, 286–287 (1989).

[19] Ibid., pp. 292, quoting Branzburg v. Hayes, 408 U.S. 665, 684–685, 92 S.Ct. 2646, 2658–2659 (1972).

Newsmen have no constitutional right of access to the scenes of crime or disaster when the general public is excluded. * * * . Despite the fact that newsgathering may be hampered, the press is regularly excluded from grand jury proceedings, our own [the Wisconsin Supreme Court's] conferences, the meetings of other official bodies gathered in executive session, and meetings of private organizations. * * * The appellant does not have a first amendment right to access, solely because he is a news gatherer, to the scene of an airplane crash when the public reasonably has been excluded.

The crash occurred at 3:30 p.m., and at 4:30 p.m., the airport director held a briefing, then taking media representatives to the site to photograph or film the scene. Justice Ceci used caustic language to underscore his holding that the disorderly conduct ordinance was not unconstitutionally vague as applied to cameraman Peter Ah King. Further, Justice Ceci declared that[20]

* * * the needs and rights of the injured and dying should be recognized by this court as having preference over newly created "rights" that the dissenting justices would give to a "news gatherer" who is simply trying to beat out his competition and make his employer's deadline.

In dissent, Wisconsin Supreme Court Justice Shirley Abrahamson wrote that Peter Ah King did not interfere with or obstruct emergency personnel. That said, she concluded, "[T]he court can and should take into consideration the media's role as the 'eyes and ears' of the public at large."[21]

Invited by Officials: Baugh v. CBS (1993)

Given heightened concerns over privacy—including the anti-media howling occasioned by the death of Princess Diana of Wales discussed at the outset of this chapter—journalists probably should not assume that permission from an official to enter a property will override a "stay out!" command from a tenant or one otherwise in control of property. The 1993 case of Baugh v. CBS hung up another caution flag for broadcasters. CBS's "Street Stories" public affairs magazine program broadcast an episode titled "Stand By Me." The broadcast covered the Alameda County [CA] Mobile Crisis Intervention Team, and focused on the work of Elaine Lopes in helping victims through crises, giving emotional support and information on how to deal with the legal system.

---

[20] Ibid., pp. 293–294.

[21] Ibid., p. 297. Her dissent was joined by Justices Nathan A. Heffernan and William A. Bablitch.

CBS correspondent Bob McKeown's broadcast included videotape of Mrs. Yolanda Baugh talking with Ms. Lopes, describing how her husband "started beating on me and kicking on me and hitting me in the face."[22]

About two months later, Mrs. Baugh said, she learned from social worker Elaine Lopes that her story would be broadcast, and Mrs. Baugh objected that she didn't want to be on television. More than two weeks before CBS aired the episode of "Street Stories" containing footage of Mrs. Baugh, she talked to a producer at CBS who told her that he might be able to obscure her face on the screen. Mrs. Baugh told him that was not sufficient, but her plea got nowhere. Mrs. Baugh said:[23]

> " ...about a week later, I was contacted on the phone by a
> man who identified himself as a CBS lawyer in New York.
> In a rude, uncaring and arrogant manner, he told me that
> I had no case against CBS and there is nothing I could do."

Mrs. Baugh failed in her claim of trespass or intrusion because in this context, "no trespass can be found if actual consent to entry was given," even if the consent was given by police who should not have given it. Ominously for the media, the court refused to dismiss Mrs. Baugh's claim for intentional infliction of mental distress.[24]

Invited by Officials: Ayeni v. CBS (1994)

Whatever comfort intrusive journalists might have found in Baugh v. CBS, a 1994 U.S. district court decision in Ayeni v. CBS held that federal agents' permission for TV journalists to attend a search of a home was insufficient for the journalists to avoid liability. Tawa Ayeni, wife of a man suspected of involvement in a credit card fraud ring, was home with her son Kayode, a minor, when a U.S. Treasury Department agent carried out a search warrant. Six federal agents—four from the Secret Service and two postal inspectors—went to the Ayeni's residence about 6 p.m. Mrs. Ayeni, clad in her dressing gown, opened her door only slightly, but the agents pushed their way into her home.

About 8:15 p.m., Treasury Agent James Mottola entered the Ayeni apartment with a CBS news crew from "Street Stories." Mrs. Ayeni complained that the crew members were not identified as CBS employees, saying that she thought the CBS camera crew and

---

[22] Baugh v. CBS, Inc., 828 F.Supp. 745, 750 (N.D.Cal.1993), 21 Med.L.Rptr. 2065, 2067.

[23] Ibid., 2068.

[24] Ibid. at 758, 2072–2073, citing Miller v. NBC, 187 Cal.App.3d 1463, 1480–1481, 232 Cal.Rptr. 668 (1986).

producer Meade Jorgensen were " 'part of the team executing the warrant.' "[25]

CBS and "Street Stories" producer Jorgensen both claimed a qualified immunity because "they were acting with the permission of government agents ... [and] should be entitled to the qualified immunity enjoyed by government officials."[26] This audacious claim was slapped down by the court. The court held that the CBS employees had been invited into the residence by a U.S. agent "so they could titillate and entertain others was beyond the scope of what was lawfully authorized by the warrant." Concluding that the Ayeni lawsuit against CBS should not be dismissed, Judge Weinstein declared:[27]

> CBS had no greater right than that of a thief to be in the home, to take pictures, and to remove the photographic record.
> * * *
>
> The images, though created by the camera, are a part of the household; they cannot be removed without permission or official right. The television tape was seizure of information for non government-purposes.

Stalking by Media: Wolfson v. Lewis (1996)

What seemed to be egregious misconduct—trespass plus stalking of a family—led to issuance of a temporary injunction against broadcast journalists in Wolfson v. Lewis (1996).

Paul Lewis and Steve Wilson were award-winning journalists employed by the syndicated television news show "Inside Edition." Wilson was in charge of an investigative story being done on U.S. Healthcare. Their investigation led them to seek interviews with officials of U.S. Healthcare, including Richard Wolfson, son-in-law of U.S. Healthcare board chairman and principal executive Leonard

---

[25] Ayeni v. CBS, Inc., 848 F.Supp. 362, 364 (E.D.N.Y.1994), 22 Med.L.Rptr 1466, 1467.

[26] Ibid., p. 367, p. 1469.

[27] Ibid, p. 368, p. 1470. Also, a U.S. Court of Appeals ruled that Treasury Agent Mottola violated the Fourth Amendment protections against unreasonable search and seizure by allowing the CBS crew into the Ayeni home. Mottola was held personally liable for damages for permitting the videotaping intrusion. See Ayeni v. Mottola, 35 F.3d 680 (2d Cir.1994), 22 Med.L.Rptr. 2225. In a similar case, police officers who allowed a TV crew to accompany them as they searched a home were not held liable for invasion of privacy, being immune from suit under 42 USC § 1983. The TV crew members the police allowed to enter the home, however, could be held liable for intrusion because their action was not state action. Parker v. Boyer, 93 F.3d 445 (8th Cir.1996), 24 Med.L.Rptr. 2307. See also Anderson v. WROC–TV, 109 Misc.2d 904, 441 N.Y.S.2d 220 (1981), 7 Med.L.Rptr. 1987, 1988, where a humane society investigator invited TV station personnel into a private residence as he served a warrant. Employees of the TV station ignored a tenant's request to leave the residence, taking some footage and later broadcasting it. The station was held liable for intrusion.

Abramson. Wolfson directs pharmacy and dental operations for U.S. Healthcare; his wife, Nancy Abramson Wolfson, directs the firm's health education department.

Board chairman Leonard Abramson received anonymous threats to himself and his family in February, 1996, and U.S. Healthcare then hired full-time security guards to protect Mr. and Mrs. Abramson, their children, and their grandchildren.

According to the court issuing the injunction against the Inside Edition journalists, those individuals—after being refused a request for an on-camera interview:[28]

*Drove alongside the Wolfsons' autos on public roads in a van with tinted windows.

*Sent a camera and sound crew to do "ambush interviews" at the Abramson and Wolfson homes and places of business.

*Alarmed a security guard with vehicles shadowing the Wolfson car while driving Mrs. Wolfson and her three-year-old daughter to a nursery school. The guard then placed his semi-automatic weapon on his lap, frightening Mrs. Wolfson (who was pregnant). It was learned later that the following vehicles had been rented by the Inside Edition journalists.

*Refused another request for an interview, the Wolfsons were told that surveillance would continue. Inside Edition journalists were told that Mrs. Wolfson was pregnant and pleaded with them to stop frightening the family, but the family was told by journalists that this was "legal newsgathering."

*The Wolfson family then left for an Abramson home in Florida, located on the Intercoastal Waterway. Inside Edition rented a boat, anchoring it 50 yards from the residence. Journalists zeroed in on the residence with telephoto lenses and with "shotgun microphones."

The Wolfson family sought an injunction against being harassed by Inside Edition, and a preliminary injunction was granted. The court held that under both Pennsylvania and Florida law, the Wolfsons showed a reasonable probability of success for a lawsuit for intrusion. The federal district court characterized Inside Edition's conduct as "apparently designed to hound, harass, intimidate, and frighten ..."[29] Further, use of a shotgun microphone in Florida was found actionable, since both Florida and Pennsylvania have statutes prohibiting interception of oral communications.[30]

28 Wolfson v. Lewis, 924 F.Supp. 1413 (E.D.Pa.1996), 24 Med.L.Rptr. 1609.

29 Wolfson v. Lewis, 924 F.Supp. 1413, 1432 (E.D.Pa.1996), 24 Med.L.Rptr. 1617, 1122.

30 Fla. Stat.Ann. ch. 934ff, 18 Pa.C.S. § 5701ff, cited in Wolfson v. Lewis, 924 F.Supp. 1413 (E.D.Pa.1996), 24 Med.L.Rptr. 1609, 1626. See also 168 F.R.D. 530

Competition for viewers and readers has led to more and more strident pursuit of news sources and photo/video targets. Small wonder that citizens seated on juries are not friendly to even the most establishment of the media. However the Wolfson case turns out in the courts after appeals, conduct such as that by Inside Edition and other tabloid TV shows spur loathing of the news media, loathing leading to calls for more restrictive laws and, often, to unfavorable jury verdicts.

Defenses to Intrusion and Trespass

If a journalist or photographer commits an illegal act in pursuit of a story—trespass or stalking are two examples—the only possible defense would seem to be a plea of overriding newsworthiness in the public interest. But that defense is not likely to be of much use, given the basic rule as spelled out by Judge Hufstedler in Dietemann v. Time, Inc., discussed earlier in this chapter at footnote 13:[31] "The First Amendment has never been construed to accord newsmen immunity from torts or crimes committed during the course of newsgathering."

SEC. 45. PROBLEMS WITH HIDDEN CAMERAS AND RECORDERS

The Dietemann case should inspire journalists to think carefully about their use of cameras, and that also applies to tape recorders and electronic listening or transmitting gear. Professor Kent R. Middleton, writing on the *legality* of journalists' use of tape recorders, generalized: "Reporters may record or transmit conversations they overhear, they participate in, or they record with permission of one party."[32] That may be the general rule, but there are exceptions in 10 states where recording of telephone conversations are concerned.[33] In Shevin v. Sunbeam Television Corp. (1977), the Florida Supreme Court ruled that a Florida statute forbidding interception of telephone messages without consent of all parties did not violate a reporter's First Amendment rights.[34]

(E.D.Pa.1996), 25 Med.L.Rptr. 1016, where plaintiffs amended their complaint to add five defendants for invasion of privacy to their claim for violations of the federal [18 U.S.C. § 2511] and Florida wiretap statutes.

[31] Dietemann v. Time, Inc., 449 F.2d at 249.

[32] Kent R. Middleton, "Journalists and Tape Recorders: Does Participant Monitoring Invade Privacy?," 2 COMM/ENT Law Journal (1980), at pp. 299–300.

[33] See Victor A. Kovner, Suznne L. Telsey, and Gianna M. McCarthy, "Newsgathering, Invasion of Privacy, and Related Torts," in James C. Goodale, Chair, Communications Law 1996, Vol. 1 (New York: Practising Law Institute, 1996), p.567. States listed with statutes against such recording are California, Florida, Illinois, Maryland, Massachusetts, Montana, New Hampshire, Oregon, Pennsylvania, and Washington.

[34] Shevin v. Sunbeam Television Corp., 351 So.2d 723 (Fla.1977).

Recording with the permission of one party is "consensual monitoring" in legal jargon. Even where this is legal, is it *ethical*? And does one-party consent sound confusing, or merely silly? What would one-party consent do to the law of burglary? (If I consent to steal from you, would that make it okay?) What "consensual monitoring" actually does as a legal concept is forbid an unauthorized third party from intercepting a conversation, as in the case of an illegal (not authorized by a court) tap on a telephone line that allows an uninvited third party to listen to two other parties.

Many reporters routinely record telephone conversations without telling the party on the other end of the line. This kind of surreptitious recording may not violate state law, but it is forbidden by telephone company tariffs, as Middleton has written. If a person is somehow caught while secretly recording phone conversations to which she is a party, the telephone company could cut off her phone service. This, however, seems a rather remote possibility.[35]

The Federal Wiretap Statute

In addition to state provisions and telephone company "tariffs" [rules] overseen by the Federal Communications Commission (FCC), there also is the Federal Wiretap Statute.[36] That statute makes it a crime to intercept "any wire or oral communication," and assigns penalties of up to a $10,000 fine and up to five years imprisonment.

There is, however, a "participant monitoring" provision in this statute allowing a party to a telephone call or conversation to make a recording. The "one-party consent" provision of the statute says:[37]

It shall not be unlawful under this chapter for a person not acting under color of law [e.g., a private citizen without a court order] to intercept a wire or oral communication where such person is a party to the communication or where one of the parties to the communication has given prior consent to such interception ...

That provision, however, is quickly followed by a huge exception which says, in effect, that a the message interception may not be for the purpose of committing a crime or a tort.[38] That evidently means that a journalist can make a one-party consent recording to make an accurate record of a conversation or for self-protection.[39]

---

35 Middleton, pp. 3304–309, 319–320.

36 See 18 U.S.C.A. §§ 2510–2520, especially § 2511.

37 18 U.S.C.A. § 2511(2)(d).

38 Ibid.

39 See C. Thomas Dienes, Lee Levine, and Robert C. Lind, Newsgathering and the Law (Charlottesville, VA: Michie, 1997), § 13–7(a)(2)(A)(iii), "The Qualified One–Party Consent Exception."

Cassidy v. ABC

Although people dislike hidden tape recorders, they may be even more hostile to hidden video cameras. Sometimes, as Chicago policeman Arlyn Cassidy learned, you can be on TV at an inopportune moment. Cassidy was working as un undercover vice squad agent assigned to investigate a massage parlor.

Policeman Cassidy testified that he had paid a $30 admission fee to see "de-luxe" lingerie modeling. He was then taken to a small cubicle by one of the models, and noticed "camera lights" each side of the bed. He told the model the lights made the room warm, and then reclined on the bed and watched he model change her lingerie several times. As an Illinois judge described the scene, Cassidy made several suggestive remarks to the model and then arrested her for solicitation after she had "established 'sufficient' physical contact." Three other vice squad officers then joined Officer Cassidy, asking if anyone was in the adjoining room.[40]

At that moment, someone rushed out of Room No. 2, yelling "Channel 7 News." That's right, a camera crew from Chicago's ABC Network affiliate had been in the adjacent room, filming Officer Cassidy and the model through a two-way mirror. The TV station personnel testified that they were filming the proceedings because they earlier had received complaints from the massage parlor manager that his establishment was the object of police harassment.

The whole television situation rubbed Officer Cassidy the wrong way. He sued, complaining that the camera crew's activities violated the Illinois anti-eavesdropping statute and that his common-law right to privacy was violated.[41] The Illinois Appellate Court had difficulty in seeing a television camera as an "eavesdropping device," the more so because the noise of a 1970s-model TV camera drowned out sounds from the other room. Furthermore, Cassidy had noticed the lights and had asked the model whether they were "on TV." She replied, "Sure, we're making movies." Under such circumstances, Officer Cassidy was believed by the court not to have much an expectation of privacy.

In addition, Cassidy's effort to assert a cause of action under the "intrusion" theory of privacy failed, on grounds that he was a public official on duty at the time he heard those stirring words, "Channel 7 News."[42]

Desnick v. American Broadcasting Companies (1995)

PrimeTime Live, an ABC network program, was sued by Dr. J.H. Desnick and associates of the Desnick Eye Center for trespass,

[40] Cassidy v. ABC, 60 Ill.App.3d 831, 17 Ill.Dec. 936, 377 N.E.2d 126 (1978).

[41] Cassidy v. ABC, 60 Ill.App.3d 831, 17 Ill.Dec. 936, 377 N.E.2d 126, 127 (1978).

[42] Ibid., at 833, 128.

defamation, and violation of Federal and state . The PrimeTime
Live broadcast was anchored by Sam Donaldson. After assurances
from a PrimeTime Live producer that this would be a fair, balanced
report with no undercover surveillance or ambush interviews, Desnick Eye Center allowed videotaping of a cataract operation in the
clinic's Chicago office. Desnick also consented to interviews with
doctors and patients.

Unknown to Desnick, the ABC producer also sent persons with
hidden cameras into Desnick Eye Center locations in Wisconsin and
Indiana. These persons, posing as patients, asked for eye exams,
and two doctors were secretly videotaped while examining these
"test patients."

When the PrimeTime Live broadcast was made, Donaldson
introduced the segment on Desnick Eye Centers with these words:[43]

> "We begin tonight with the story of a so-called 'big cutter,'
> Dr. James Desnick. . . . [I]n our undercover investigation
> of the big cutter you'll meet tonight, we turned up evi-
> dence that he may also be a big charger, doing unnecessary
> cataract surgery for the money."

And, despite the producer's promise, there was an ambush
interview. Sam Donaldson accosted Dr. James H. Desnick at
O'Hare Airport, crying:[44]

> "Is it true, Doctor, that you've changed medical records to
> show less vision than your patients actually have? We've
> been told, Doctor, that you've changed the glare machine
> so we have a different reading? Is that correct? Doctor,
> why won't you respond to the questions?"

This broadcast also asserted that of the seven "test patients,"
two were under 65 and thus ineligible for Medicare reimbursement.
They were told they did not need cataract surgery. Four of the
other five patients were told they did.[45]

Not surprisingly, Desnick Eye Services sued for a variety of
torts, including defamation, trespass, and fraud. The Court of
Appeals declined to dismiss the defamation part of Desnick's lawsuit, saying that charges of tampering with equipment [to give false
readings indicating need for cataract surgery] and Medicare fraud
needed further investigation through a pre-trial discovery process.[46]

---

43 Desnick v. American Broadcasting Companies, 44 F.3d 1345 (7th Cir.1995), 23
Med.L.Rptr. 1161, 1162.

44 Ibid., at 1348, 1162–1163. Persons with cataracts see badly in bright light;
equipment here termed a "glare machine" is used by ophthalmologists to see
whether cataract surgery is indicated.

45 Ibid., at 1348, 1164.

46 Ibid., at 1348, 1164.

This left questions of *how* PrimeTime Live gathered information: claims by Desnick of trespass, fraud, and violating federal and state statutes regulating electronic surveillance. The Court of Appeals (Seventh Circuit) held:[47]

> There was no invasion in the present case of any of the specific interests that the tort of trespass seeks to protect. The test patients entered offices that were open to anyone expressing a desire for ophthalmic services and videotaped physicians engaged in professional, not personal, communications with strangers (the testers themselves). The activities in the offices were not disrupted. * * * Nor was there any "invasion of a person's private space."

> * * *

> The federal and state wiretapping statutes that the plaintiffs invoke allow one party to a conversation to record the conversation unless his purpose in doing so is to commit a crime or a tort. * * * The defendants did not order the camera-armed testers into the Desnick Eye Center's premises in order to commit a crime or a tort.

> * * *

> Last is the charge of fraud in the defendants' gaining entry to the Chicago office and being permitted while there to interview staff and film a cataract operation ... The alleged fraud consists of a series of false promises by the defendants—that the broadcast segment would be fair and balanced and that the defendants would not use "ambush" interviews or undercover surveillance tactics in making the segment. Since the promises were given in exchange for Desnick's permission to do things calculated to enhance the value of the broadcast segment, they were, one might have thought, supported by consideration and thus a basis for a breach of contract suit. That we need not decide. The plaintiffs had a claim for breach of contract...but they voluntarily dismissed the claim so there would be a final judgment from which they could appeal. The only issue before us is fraud.

> * * *

The Court of Appeals concluded that the fraud alleged by Desnick Eye Centers was not actionable, adopting a kind of "journalists will be journalists" stance comforting to media lawyers and troubling to ethicists:[48]

[47] Ibid., at 1352, 1165–1167.

[48] Ibid., at 1354–1355, 1168.

Investigative journalists well known for ruthlessness promise wear kid gloves. They break their promise to , as any person of normal sophistication would expect. If that is "fraud," it is the kind against which potential victims can arm themselves by maintaining a minimum of skepticism about journalistic goals and methods. Desnick, needless to say, was no tyro, or child, or otherwise a member of a vulnerable group. He is a successful professional and entrepreneur.

Thus, Desnick was not able to win the suit against ABC and PrimeTime Live for fraud based on newsgathering practices.

Juror Dislike for "Hidden Camera" Reporting

Although appellate courts seem quite protective of the news media—even when hidden cameras are involved—because of the great cost of defending against privacy lawsuits, the media really "lose" even though cases often have a favorable outcome. Two cases in point are a Nevada Supreme Court decision, People for the Ethical Treatment of Animals [PETA] v. Berosini (1995),[49] and a California Court of Appeals decision in Sanders v. American Broadcasting Companies (1997).[50]

In the PETA case, animal trainer Bobby Berosini won a $4.2 million jury verdict for defamation and invasion of privacy. Animal rights activists took backstage videotape before a Las Vegas show—without Berosini's knowledge or consent—of Berosini "shaking and punching his trained orangutans and hitting them with some kind of rod." The videotapes later were distributed and shown to the public, and the animal rights advocates also stated that "Berosini regularly abuses his orangutans."

Berosini also sued the individuals responsible for videotaping him—including a Stardust Hotel dancer, Ottavio Gesmundo, who actually accomplished the videotaping—for intrusion and appropriation. Other defendants PAWS, the acronym for Performing Animal Welfare Society. The Nevada Supreme Court, however, overturned the jury award. First, the Nevada Supreme Court held that the defense of truth covered the videotapes. Second, the court ruled that Gesmundo's taping was not conduct of the kind that would be highly offensive to a reasonable person. The court observed that Gesmundo and his camera did not violate Berosini's expectation of privacy, with stagehands and others—including Gesmundo—who

---

[49] People for the Ethical Treatment of Animals v. Bobby Berosini, Ltd.,111 Nev. 615, 895 P.2d 1269 (1995), 23 Med.L.Rptr. 1961.

[50] Sanders v. American Broadcasting Companies, 52 Cal.App.4th 543, 60 Cal. Rptr.2d 595 (2d Dist.1997), 25 Med.L.Rptr. 1343.

had permission to be backstage as part of their jobs. Further, Gesmundo[51]

> ... caused no ... interference. Neither Berosini nor his animals were aware of the camera's presence. If Gesmundo had surprised Berosini and his animals with a film crew and caused a great commotion, we might view this factor differently.

The Nevada Supreme Court also found that what Gesmundo and the animal rights activists had done did not amount to actionable "appropriation," thus reversing all damages awarded by the trial court.

In Sanders v. ABC (1997), tele-psychic Mark Sanders sued ABC because of conversations which ABC reporter Stacy Lescht secretly recorded. Six seconds of that videotape were used as part of a "PrimeTime Live" broadcast. Ms. Lescht answered an ad for a business providing telephone psychic advice to callers for $3.95 a minute. Even though she made clear that she had no relevant experience or training for such a business, she was hired.

Using a tiny camera concealed on her person, Lescht—videotaped two conversations with Sanders. After the PrimeTime Live broadcast, Sanders sued for invasion of privacy and was awarded $1.2 million by a jury. Before the trial in a California Superior Court, the judge had dismissed most of Sanders' complaints, finding that the broadcast was both true and newsworthy. Nevertheless, the trial judge—on his own volition—instructed the jury that it could find ABC liable for a "sub-tort" of violating "the right to be free of photographic invasion."[52]

The $1.2 damage award was overturned, with the California appeals court saying:[53]

> We sympathize with the trial court's concern about the proliferation of secret recording, with its implications for loss of privacy. However ...we decline to extend tort protection under an invasion of privacy, as opposed to a trespass or fraud cause of action, to those secretly photographed who lack an objectively reasonable expectation of privacy ... We leave it to the Legislature to debate the wisdom of any such protection.

SEC. 46.   CELLULAR TELEPHONES AND PRIVACY

Drivers threatened by veering motorists paying more attention to their conversations than to the roadway have inspired the

---

[51] PETA v. Berosini, 111 Nev. 615, 634, 895 P.2d 1269, 1280 (1995), 23 Med. L.Rptr. 1961, 1973.

[52] Sanders v. ABC, 52 Cal.App.4th 543, 60 Cal.Rptr.2d 595, 596 (2d Dist.1997), 25 Med.L.Rptr. 1343.

[53] 60 Cal.Rptr.2d 595, 598, 25 Med.L.Rptr. 1343, 1346.

bumper sticker, "Hang Up and Drive!" Cellular phones were in the news in the mid–1990s for privacy considerations, too: what expectation of privacy can there be when one is using a cellular phone? As a practical matter, not much.

Speaker of the House Newt Gingrich (R–Georgia) was embarrassed early in 1997 by publication of excerpts from a December,21, 1996, conference call among Republican leaders. The call occurred just after Gingrich had admitted to the House Ethics Committee that he had brought discredit on the House of Representatives. He confessed to providing the Ethics Committee with untrue information about the way he used money from tax-exempt foundations for college courses he taught and for town meetings, both with political overtones. Because Gingrich publicly admitted such missteps, he thus avoided an even more humiliating full-bore public trial. But also, an agreement had been reached that in return for avoiding the full-dress hearing, Gingrich would not lead a Republican counterattack against the committee's charges.

At 9:45 a.m. on December 21, 1996, a telephone conference call was organized, including Gingrich and House majority leader Dick Armey of Texas and Representative Bill Paxon of New York. Also participating in the call were Gingrich's lawyer, Ed Bethune, and Ed Gillespie, Communications Director of the Republican National Committee. The technological joker in the deck was held by Representative John A. Boehner, who participated in the conference call from Florida while using a cellular phone. As these men discussed strategies to minimize political fallout for Newt Gingrich, they were oblivious to a couple, John and Alice Martin, out for Christmas-shopping drive near Jacksonville. The Martins were entertaining themselves with a scanner in their car, trying to pick up conversations. Representative Boehner told The New York Times that he believed that the Martins heard the conversation by intercepting the signal from his cellular phone.[54]

Mr. and Mrs. Martin, once they recognized some voices in the conversation, tape-recorded it, saying they wanted to create an historical document to give to their grandchild. They later informed Representative Karen L. Thurman (D–FL) about the tape; she urged them to give it to the House Ethics Committee. Not surprisingly, both The New York Times and the Atlanta Constitution (Newt Gingrich is from Georgia, after all) got copies of the tape recording. Neither newspaper identified the source or sources of their tape copies.[55]

[54] Adam Clymer, "Gingrich Is Heard Urging Tactics in Ethics Case," The New York Times, January 10, 1997, p. A1; Neil A. Lewis, "What the Law Says on Using Scanning Devices," The New York Times, January 16, 1997, p. A13.

[55] Neil A. Lewis, op. cit.

Democrats and Republicans then traded counter-charges. The Democrats claimed Speaker Gingrich had broken his promise to the ethics committee not to drum up a response to the committee's findings. Republicans asserted that laws were broken in intercepting the conversation. Mr. and Mrs. Martin expressed dismay that they "might have broken state and Federal laws both in intercepting the conversation and in distributing a recording of it."[56]

The Federal Wiretap Statute, amended in 1986 to try to deal with the hurricanes of technological change, provides fines of up to $5,000 and imprisonment for up to five years for interception of electronically carried messages. The broadened language of the statute forbids interception of " ...any transfer of signs, signals, writing, images, sounds, data or intelligence of any nature transmitted in whole or in part by a wire, radio, electromagnetic, photoelectronic or photo-optical system."[57]

SEC. 47.   FRAUD CLAIMS AND UNDERCOVER REPORTING

Although only *individuals* are supposed to be able to sue for invasion of privacy, something very like a concept of corporate privacy underlies a 1997 court defeat for ABC–TV news. The depth of public dislike against news media may be gauged somewhat in a startling jury award of $5.545 million in punitive damages early in 1997 against ABC–TV and in favor of the Food Lion grocery chain. The punitive damage award followed a federal court jury finding $1,400 in actual damages for trespassing and fraud involving a "PrimeTime Live" segment on food handling. If there was any good news for ABC–TV, it was that on appeal, after this bruising legal battle, the U.S. district court trial judge reduced the punitive damages to $315,000.[58] But given the original jury verdict, it is likely that undercover reporting with hidden may be "chilled" for some time to come, at least where the false-identity, hidden-camera-and-microphone kind of fact-gathering is concerned. The temptation go the edge with sensational reporting during TV "sweeps" ratings periods may now be muted. One thing sure to happen is closer scrutiny earlier in the reporting process by the legal departments of media corporations. And, as Lyle Denniston of the *Baltimore Sun* has suggested, it may be more dangerous to press freedom to have a lawyer in a newsroom giving advice than it is to have an editor or reporter in jail.

[56] Ibid.

[57] 18 U.S.C.A. § 2510(12).

[58] Food Lion v. Capital Cities/ABC, Inc., 984 F.Supp. 923 (M.D.N.C.1997), 25 Med.L.Rptr. 2185.

The jury made the huge award in Greensboro, N.C. in response to a November 5, 1992, PrimeTime Live segment accusing the supermarket of unsanitary food handling and of rewrapping and changing dates on out-dated meat and fish. And PrimeTime Live seemed to have the good on a Food Lion market, with damaging, surreptitiously made video and audio recordings that were edited into a compelling and highly accusatory report.

Ms. Linne Litt (Dale), working undercover for PrimeTime Live, had made false statements on a job application in order to get hired by Food Lion. She actually worked for a Food Lion store from May 4 to May 14, 1992, using tiny "jacketcam" or "lipstick" hidden cameras and recorders to gather information.[59]

In response to the PrimeTime Live broadcast, Food Lion brought a "scattergun strategy" lawsuit against ABC–TV, alleging defamation, mail and wire fraud, and trespass, claiming a huge decrease in revenue plus a drop inn the price of Food Lion's publicly traded stock, all as a result of the ABC–TV broadcast. The court ruled, however, that Food Lion could not collect damages for defamation unless it could show falsity plus "actual malice"—the publication of knowing falsity or publication made in reckless disregard of the truth.

Since Food Lion did not pursue the libel path, what was at stake was not the truthfulness of the PrimeTime Live report, but the *manner* in which the information was gathered. Indeed, the district court noted that it was understood that Food Lion was avoiding the strict falsity requirements of the defamation tort while nevertheless seeking damages for harm to reputation.[60]

In fact, the Greensboro jury never saw the PrimeTime Live coverage causing the litigation, but was told by Judge Carlton S. Tilley to regard the TV report as accurate. After six days of deliberation, the jury agreed to the $5.545 million punitive damage amount. ABCs New President Roone Arledge promptly announced that the network would appeal.[61]

The mail and wire fraud claims stemmed from ABC employees using the mails and interstate wire facilities to create false identities in order to get hired by Food Lion. Also, the jury learned that some of the video and audio reporting done in non-public food-handling areas of a store—labeled trespass and fraud by the plain-

[59] Barry Meier, "Jury Says ABC Owes Damages of $5.5 Million," The New York Times, January 23, 1997, p. A1. Ms. Litt's name changed to Dale during the course of the litigation.

[60] Food Lion v. Capital Cities/ABC, Inc., 887 F.Supp. 811 (M.D.N.C.1995), 23 Med.L.Rptr. 1673, 1682.

[61] Meier, op. cit.

tiff—was at variance with the ABC News Policy Manual, which says:[62]

> "In the course of investigative work, reporters should not disguise their identity or pose as someone with another occupation without prior approval of ABC News Management. * * * [N]ews gathering of whatever sort does not include any license to violate the law."

Food Lion's trespass complaint was persuasive to the federal district court, which studied the U.S. Supreme Court's promissory estoppel decision in Cohen v. Cowles Media (1991). The Food Lion district court held that, as in the *Cohen* decision, "[l]ike promissory estoppel, the laws governing.... [trespass, etc.] are laws of general applicability which do not [unconstitutionally] target or single out the press. Cohen, 501 U.S. at 670."[63]

Evidently because Food Lion did not pursue the defamation claim—which would have brought truth into play as a defense— rules of evidence were applied in such a fashion that jurors never got to see the PrimeTime Live broadcast. The New York Times quoted a juror who said that she favored undercover investigations, "[b]ut if you're going to do them, just do them legal."[64]

There remains a public stake in clean food, especially with the backdrop of illness and death caused by undercooked, tainted hamburger at a Seattle Jack-in-the-Box restaurant during the early 1990s. If the Food Lion jury verdict, as predicted, really discourages investigative reporting in areas where government can not or will not act to protect citizens, what then of "the public interest?"[65]

Opinions about the Food Lion decision varied among lawyers and journalists. Jane Kirtley of The Reporters Committee for Freedom of the Press argued that punishing an accurate story for newsgathering methods used to get key information "will have a chilling effect on investigative journalists." Other journalists, however, criticized concealing identities or using hidden cameras on private property in order to get a story.[66]

Society of Professional Journalists President Steve Geimann asked whether ends of newsgathering may be used to justify the means. He quoted the SPJ Code of Ethics: " 'Avoid undercover or

---

[62] Food Lion v. Capital Cities/ABC Inc., 887 F.Supp. 811, 814 (M.D.N.C.1995), 23 Med.L.Rptr. 1673, 1682.

[63] Ibid. See discussion of Cohen v. Cowles Media (1991) at pages 557–561 in chapter 10.

[64] Meier, op. cit.,; see also Estes Thompson, "Food Lion to Get $5.5 Million from ABC," Associated Press Dispatch, January 22, 1997, 1:15 p.m. EST.

[65] See John Seigenthaler and David Hudson, "Going Undercover: The public's need to know should be more important," Quill, March 1997, p. 17.

[66] Scott Andron, "Food Lion v. ABC," Quill, March, 1997, p. 15.

other surreptitious methods of gathering information except when traditional open methods will not yield information vital to the public. Use of such methods should be explained as part of the story.' "[67]

Freedom Forum First Amendment Center Ombudsman Paul McMasters contended that ABC–TV got in trouble because it did not exhaust traditional open reporting methods. Before going underground, he wrote, PrimeTime Live staffers could have protected the network by thoroughly checking food inspection records of federal, state, and local agencies, and by purchasing food and having it lab-tested. After that kind of digging, the PrimeTime Live might have had a better explanation for undercover reporting to present to a jury.

On the other hand, as McMasters noted, sometimes hidden cameras and microphones are the only way important news can be gathered to protect the public.[68]

SEC. 48. EMOTIONAL DISTRESS AND INCITEMENT

Accompanying libel's damage to reputation and invasion of privacy's reputation to feelings is a newer tort: emotional distress. Sometimes referred to as "intentional," sometimes termed "negligent," causing emotional distress can refer to the power of words or pictures to carry psychological harm. A tort separate from defamation in many states, it exists in others as part of the law of defamation. Thus Justice Powell, in discussing harmful components of defamation in the 1974 *Gertz* case, said that among them are "personal humiliation, and mental anguish and suffering."[69] The famous case of comedy star Carol Burnett, in which she won damages in a libel suit against National Enquirer, turned almost entirely upon emotional distress over the magazine's portrayal of her as "drunk, rude, uncaring and abusive" at a restaurant.[70]

Hustler Magazine v. Falwell (1988)

In the mid–1980s, the emerging separate tort of infliction of mental injury was a major threat to the media. But in 1988, that threat was lessened somewhat by the U.S. Supreme Court's unanimous decision in Hustler v. Falwell. The Court held that the First Amendment protects parodies—even Hustler magazine's mock ad which said Rev. Jerry Falwell's first sexual experience was in an outhouse, with his mother, while she was drunk.

[67] Steve Geimann, "It's fair to ask whether the ends justify the means," Quill, March, 1997, p. 43.

[68] Paul McMasters, "It didn't have to come to this," Quill, March, 1997, p. 18.

[69] Gertz v. Robert Welch, Inc., 418 U.S. 323, 349–350, 94 S.Ct. 2997 (1974).

[70] Burnett v. National Enquirer (Cal.Sup.1981), 7 Med.L.Rptr. 1321.

Following the scattergun tort approach, Rev. Falwell sued Hustler and its publisher, Larry Flynt, for libel *plus* invasion of privacy *plus* intentional infliction of emotional distress.

Not surprisingly, even though the fine print said "ad parody—not to be taken seriously"—a U.S. district court jury was sympathetic to Rev. Falwell. (After all, Flynt had declared, while giving a pre-trial deposition, that his intent in publishing the parody was to "assassinate" the minister's reputation.)[71] Sympathetic or not, the jury did not believe that Falwell had been libeled: "no reasonable person would believe that the parody was describing actual facts about Falwell." The jury also declined to find that his privacy had been invaded. Jurors, however, seized upon the idea of infliction of mental injury and awarded Falwell $200,000: $100,000 in compensatory damages, plus $50,000 in punitive damages against Flynt and $50,000 against his magazine.

The Court of Appeals, Fourth Circuit—like the trial court—concluded that Falwell was public figure.[72] That public figure status meant that defendants Flynt and Hustler magazine were entitled to "the same level of first amendment protection in an action for intentional infliction of mental distress that they would receive in an action for libel." Even so, the Court of Appeals found the ad parody so obnoxious that it affirmed the trial court's ruling.[73]

The Supreme Court of the United States disagreed. Chief Justice William H. Rehnquist defined the issue as whether the First Amendment limits a state's authority to protect its citizens from intentional infliction of mental distress. He wrote, "We must decide whether a public figure may recover damages for emotional harm caused to him by an ad parody offensive to him and doubtless gross and repugnant in the eyes of most."[74]

To the surprise of many, Chief Justice Rehnquist set out on a sweeping reaffirmation of First Amendment principles—principles which he has questioned in other cases.[75] He wrote approvingly of the free flow of ideas and opinions on matters of public interest as being at the heart of the First Amendment. " '[T]he freedom to speak one's mind is not only an aspect of individual liberty—and

[71] David Margolick, "Some See Threat in Non–Libel Verdict of Falwell," The New York Times, Dec. 10, 1986, p. 6.

[72] Hustler Magazine v. Falwell, 485 U.S. 46, 108 S.Ct. 876 (1988), 14 Med.L.Rptr. 2281, 2282.

[73] Falwell v. Flynt, 797 F.2d 1270, 1274 (4th Cir.1986), 13 Med.L.Rptr. 1145.

[74] 485 U.S. at 50, 108 S.Ct. at 879 (1988), 14 Med.L.Rptr. at 2283.

[75] See the Rehnquist opinion in Wolston v. Reader's Digest Ass'n, 443 U.S. 157, 99 S.Ct. 2701 (1979), rejecting the argument that a person who engages in criminal conduct automatically becomes a limited-purpose public figure. See also his opinion in Time, Inc. v. Firestone, 424 U.S. 448, 96 S.Ct. 958 (1976).

thus a good unto itself—but also is essential to the common quest for truth and the vitality of society as a whole.' "[76]

He declared that under the First Amendment robust political debate will result in speech critical of public officials or public figures who are " 'intimately involved in the resolution of important questions, or by reason of their fame, shape events in areas of concern to society at large.' "[77]

Rehnquist did not treat freedom of expression as an absolute: The First Amendment does not mean that "...any speech about public figures is immune from sanction in the form of damages. Although unknowingly false statements will be protected to insure breathing space needed for open debate, knowingly or recklessly false statements have no value and are not protected."

The Chief Justice wrote that the law does not regard an intent to inflict emotional harm with much solicitude. He termed it understandable that most jurisdictions have created civil liability when such conduct is sufficiently outrageous. But Rev. Falwell, a powerful individual and sometime candidate for President, was a public figure involved "...in the world of debate about public affairs, [where] many things done with motives that are less than admirable are protected by the First Amendment." [78]

Rehnquist declared that any system of civil damages that might teach Flynt a lesson also would endanger a long and valued tradition of caustic American political caricatures—verbal and visual—and political cartoons. He pointed to the prominent role in political debate played by satire and political cartoons, and to the impact of images over the years: Lincoln's gangly frame, Teddy Roosevelt's glasses and teeth, Franklin D. Roosevelt's cigarette holder and jutting jaw.

Even though Falwell argued that the Hustler magazine parody was so outrageous that it lacked First Amendment protection, the Court disagreed. True, wrote Chief Justice Rehnquist, "*Hustler* is at best a distant cousin of ...political cartoons ...and a rather poor relation at that." The Chief Justice expressed doubts that a sufficiently precise standard could be found safely to distinguish Flynt's publication from political cartoons in general.[79]

The Falwell case is important. University of Texas law professor David A. Anderson termed it a tremendous victory because it " ' ...cuts off the main avenues of the emotional distress claim'

---

[76] 485 U.S. at 50, 108 S.Ct. at 879 (1988).

[77] Ibid., at 53, 880, quoting Associated Press v. Walker, 388 U.S. 130, 164, 87 S.Ct. 1975, 1996 (1967).

[78] Ibid.

[79] Ibid., 55, 881.

and ' . . . because it is such a ringing affirmation of the principles of New York Times v. Sullivan.' "[80]

Two other respected communications lawyers, Robert D. Sack and Sandra S. Baron, have asserted that for there to be a successful emotional distress claim, the conduct must be "extreme and outrageous, must cause severe emotional distress, and must be made with conscious disregard of a high degree of probability that severe emotional distress will result." [81]

Kolegas v. Heftel Broadcasting Corp. (1992)

Emotional distress cases causing trouble for the media of share characteristics of extreme and juror-offending conduct by media employees. When jurors perceive a powerful, arrogant mass medium "kicking around" individual citizens, is it any wonder that jury verdicts unfavorable to the media may result?

Consider the case of Kolegas v. Heftel Broadcasting Corp., a confrontation arising when two Chicago radio show hosts did a telephone interview with Anthony N. Kolegas. Mr. Kolegas had called station WLUP to promote a cartoon festival he had organized, with some proceeds to support works of the Neurofibromatosis Foundation (NF). That foundation works to assist persons suffering from the condition commonly called Elephant Man's Disease.

While talking to the hosts, Kolegas mentioned that both his wife and his son suffered from NF. The radio show hosts expressed disbelief that there was such a cartoon festival, and one said that Kolegas was "scamming" them. One host then said:[82]

> "Why would someone marry a woman if she had Elephant Man disease? It's not like he couldn't tell—unless it was a shotgun wedding. * * * If he is producing it [the cartoon festival], he's only producing it part-time. The rest of the time he's too busy picking out their wardrobe . . . to make sure they have large hats to cover their big heads . . ."

In their lawsuit, Mr. and Mrs. Kolegas said they had not had a "shotgun wedding," nor did Mrs. Kolegas or their son have abnormally large heads. The Illinois Supreme Court held that there was sufficient evidence of conduct not protected by the First Amendment to take this emotional distress case to trial against station WLUP–Chicago.

[80] Margaret G. Carter, "Press Breathes Sigh of Relief after the Falwell Decision," Presstime, April, 1988, p. 34.

[81] Robert D. Sack and Sandra S. Baron, Libel, Slander, and Related Problems, 2nd ed. (New York: Practising Law Institute, 1994), pp. 676–677.

[82] Kolegas v. Heftel Broadcasting Corp., 154 Ill.2d 1, 180 Ill.Dec. 307, 607 N.E.2d 201 (1992), 20 Med.L.Rptr. 2105, 2106.

Incitement

The concept of "incitement" or "outrage" was discussed near the outset of Chapter 3, in Section 11. "Incitement" cases not only raise basic issues of human decency and test the boundaries of First Amendment protection, they also can be "newsgathering torts." An agonizing example of such a fact situation exists in Risenhoover v. England,[83] a wrongful injury/wrongful death case growing out of the 1993 raid on the Branch Davidian religious cult's compound near Waco, Texas. In this case, the lawsuit was brought in behalf of agents of the Bureau of Alcohol, Tobacco and Firearms (ATF) killed or injured in the abortive raid on February 28, 1993. A major thing found objectionable by the district judge who ruled against summary judgments against a TV station, using a negligence theory was going to a location where news was expected to happen.

Background: David Koresh, formerly known as Vernon Howell, had clawed his way to leadership of the Davidians by the late 1980s.[84] Koresh's apocalyptic mentality and preaching led to reconstructing the ramshackle Mount Carmel buildings into a fort-like complex, including living quarters, a gymnasium, look-out towers, and an armory. Koresh said believed the end of the world was near "and would be brought about by 'the Beast' or 'the Babylonians,' " which he identified as agents of the Government, particularly the ATF (the Bureau of Alcohol, Tobacco, and Firearms). Reports of child-abuse by Koresh spurred official interest. Koresh, as the self-appointed "messiah," provided himself exclusive access to all women in the cult, and that included "marrying" girls as young as twelve years old. The ATF began investigating the cult in 1992 to check out reports that the cult was stockpiling illegal weapons.

In December, 1992, the ATF began planning to serve an arrest warrant on Koresh and a search warrant at the Mount Carmel Center. Meanwhile, the daily Waco Tribune–Herald was starting work on a series of articles on Koresh for publication. The series, to be titled "The Sinful Messiah," was written by Mark England and Darlene McCormick. At this point, the newspaper feared violent retaliation from the Davidians; it had learned what ATF already knew: the Davidians had stockpiled a number of semi-automatic rifles (with "hell-fire" switches to allow rapid firing) plus .50 caliber guns and, some said, perhaps, fully automatic weapons.[85]

---

[83] Risenhoover v. England, 936 F.Supp. 392 (W.D.Tex.1996), 24 Med.L.Rptr. 1705. This "emotional distress" fact situation is rightly categorized as an "incitement claim" by Victor A. Kovner, Suzanne L. Telsey, and Gianna M. McCarthy, in James C. Goodale, chairman, Communications Law 1996, Vol. I (New York: Practising Law Institute, 1996), at pp. 528–529.

[84] 936 F.Supp. 392 (W.D.Tex.1996), 24 Med.L.Rptr. at p. 1706.

[85] 936 F.Supp. 392, 398, 24 Med.L.Rptr. at pp. 1706–1707.

On February 1, 1993, ATF officials met with Barbara Elmore, managing editor of the Waco Tribune–Herald, asking that the newspaper delay publication of its series on Koresh because of plans to conduct a criminal investigation and to execute a search warrant at the Branch Davidian compound.[86] A search warrant was obtained secretly, under seal, and unknown to the newspaper, on February 25. The newspaper did not begin publishing its series on Koresh until Saturday, February 27, 1993, and even then, did so in spite of the ATF request that publication be delayed until after the raid.

Meanwhile, rumors had been flying. A reporter with the newspaper and a cameraman with KWTX–TV heard, first, that the search warrant would be served on March 1, and then that the execution of the warrant had been moved up to Sunday, February 28. Journalists were able to make informed guesses about when the raid might occur by talking to employees of an ambulance firm, American Medical Transport (the firm was doing business as "AMT" but was owned by Rural Metro of New Mexico–Texas). Also, after learning of the Waco Tribune–Herald's decision to begin publishing its "Sinful Messiah" series on February 27, ATF moved up the date of its raid from March 1 to Sunday, February 28. Both the newspaper and the television station made plans for reporters and photographers to be on duty near the Mount Carmel Center that Sunday morning.[87]

On the morning of Sunday, February 28, KWTX–TV cameraman Jim Peeler, driving a white Bronco with no identifying marks (although sporting several noticeable antennas), was sent to cover a roadblock at the intersection of country roads not far from Mount Carmel. Finding no roadblock, Peeler stopped to check a map, and a mailman stopped, asking if Peeler were lost. Peeler, wearing a jacket with a KWTX–TV logo, told the postman he was a cameraman with KWTX. Asked if something were about to happen, Peeler told the mailman, " 'it might.' * * * The mailman turned out to be David Jones, . . . brother of Koresh's legal wife. Jones left Peeler and drove directly to the compound." Information soon reached Koresh, who said that the ATF and the National Guard were coming, adding: " 'They got me once, they'll never get me again.' "[88]

In the raid on the morning of February 28, 1993, cattle trailers containing ATF agents stopped in front of the Mount Carmel Compound, and helicopters from the Texas National Guard Arrived. David Koresh opened the front door and yelled, "What's

[86] 936 F.Supp. 392, 398 (W.D.Tex.1996), 24 Med.L.Rptr. at p. 1708.

[87] 936 F.Supp. 392, 401, 24 Med.L.Rptr. at p. 1709.

[88] 936 F.Supp. 392, 402, 24 Med.L.Rptr. at pp. 1710–1711.

going on?" ATF agents identified themselves, said they had a warrant, and yelled "Police" and "Lay Down," but Koresh slammed the door before ATF agents could reach it. Gunfire erupted from the Compound, and was returned. When the shooting ceased, four ATF agents were dead, many others had received wounds, and many Branch Davidians were killed. Others, including Koresh, were wounded. Then followed a siege lasting until April 19, 1993, when the FBI decided to launch an assault on the Compound, ending when the building and almost all of its inhabitants died in a fire set by the Davidians.

Lawsuit Damage Claims: The wrongful death and injury suit in behalf of John T. Risenhoover and other ATF agents claimed negligence, breach of contract, conspiracy, intentional infliction of emotional distress, and interference with law enforcement officers in the course of their official duties. After most claims were discarded by the court, negligence remained.

The defendants included Mark England, a reporter with the Waco Tribune–Herald, the newspaper itself and its owner, Cox Enterprises, KWTX–TV, Waco, and Rural/Metro Corporation of New Mexico–Texas, doing business in the Waco area as American Medical Transport.

The plaintiffs claimed that the defendants, either directly or indirectly, " . . . caused their injuries by alerting the inhabitants of Mount Carmel of the impending raid."[89] And once alerted, the Branch Davidians greeted ATF agents trying to serve their warrants with a hail of bullets.

Even though evidence showed that law enforcement officials had set up no road blocks to keep media vehicles away, some media representatives nevertheless had acted in a negligent manner. Relying on Cohen v. Cowles Media (1991), a U.S. Supreme Court decision discussed in Chapter 10 at pages 557 to 561, the U.S. District Court held that because Texas negligence law is a law of general applicability. Therefore, because Texas negligence law does not unfairly target the press, it could be brought to bear in plaintiffs behalf in this action for damages. The district court declared: "As Plaintiffs note, it would be ludicrous to assume that the First Amendment would protect a reporter who negligently ran over a pedestrian while speeding merely because the reporter was on the way to cover a news story."[90]

Ultimately, the district court granted summary judgments on all claims to newspaper reporter Mark England, and to Cox Enterprises/Cox Texas Publications, Inc., owners of the Waco Tribune–Herald *except* in terms of negligence in alerting the Branch Davidi-

[89] 936 F.Supp. 392, 396, 24 Med.L.Rptr. at 1705.
[90] 936 F.Supp. 392, 404, 24 Med.L.Rptr. 1705, 1714.

ans to the impending ATF raid. The district court, however, denied summary judgment motions for KWTX Broadcasting Company and for the ambulance company.

This added up to a troubling use of negligence law to enable a jury to find liability for rather common newsgathering practices—including using sources to find out when something newsworthy is to happen—and weighing that behavior down with the possibility of being found negligent. As noted above, ATF or police officials did not set up road blocks to keep reporters and photographers out of sight from the Branch Davidian Compound.

Even so, U.S. District Court Judge Walter S. Smith declared that the media knew of the need for secrecy and the danger of compromising the raid:[91]

> The media Defendants equally appreciated the risk of compromising the secrecy of the raid, and that the likelihood that agents would be injured if that secrecy were compromised. They were aware that a raid was going to be conducted, and that the timing of the raid could not be disclosed. * * * Knowing of the violent nature of the Davidians, and the ATF's desire for secrecy, it was entirely foreseeable that a breach of that secrecy would increase the danger attendant upon serving the warrants upon the Davidians. The members of the media recognized that the officers could be harmed if secrecy were not maintained.

* * *

> In this case, the balancing of factors clearly establishes that the media defendants owed a duty to the Plaintiffs not to warn the Davidians, either intentionally or negligently, of the impending raid.

The district court's language should be taken as a warning by the news media. There was no appellate review, however, of the legal claims discussed above: the litigation was ended via settlement.[92]

SEC. 49.   CONTRACT CLAIMS AND TORTIOUS INTERFERENCE

It is often hard to get news out of government. Often, government officials don't put much stock in journalists' (and members of the public's) arguments about a "a public right to know." But government business, much of the time, is the public's business,

---

[91] 936 F.Supp. 392, 407, 24 Med.L.Rptr. 1705, 1716.

[92] C. Thomas Dienes, Lee Levine, and Robert C. Lind, Newsgathering and the Law (Charlottesville, VA.: Michie, 1997), p. 566.

and there are tools to help get access to information, including state and federal "FOIAs"—Freedom of Information Acts. FOIAs can help get access to records, and various "Sunshine" statutes—as open meetings laws are called—also can help to get access.

The private sector—business and industry—can be far harder to report. As William Glaberson asked in 1995 in a "Media" column in The New York Times, "Do journalists really know what is going on?" Mr. Glaberson was writing about an effort by Brown & Williamson Tobacco to silence (temporarily, it turned out) a former tobacco scientist who had revealed damaging secrets about the tobacco industry to the CBS "60 Minutes" program and correspondent Mike Wallace.[93]

About November 8, 1996, CBS lawyers ordered "60 Minutes" not to broadcast an interview with a former tobacco company scientist and executive. It turned out that the source formerly worked for Brown & Williamson. Ironically, Mike Wallace, the CBS correspondent working on the interview with the former tobacco executive, also had reported on ABC–TV's $15 million out-of-court settlement to get out of a $10 billion libel suit brought by Philip Morris. Wallace said that ABC–TV's settling that enormous lawsuit did not chill journalists. "It did chill the [CBS] lawyers, who . . . had to say, 'We don't want to . . . risk putting the company out of business.' "[94]

Bill Carter reported in The New York Times that CBS lawyers did not fear a libel suit from Brown & Williamson. The concern was that CBS could be sued for *tortious interference with contractual relations* because of tobacco company secrecy agreement with its former executive.[95]

The New York Times roundly criticized the self-censorship at CBS for the uncommon reason of inducing a former corporate employee to violate a secrecy contract. The Times' editorial said, "many legal scholars argue that liability in such cases can be overridden when a public good is served."[96]

But P. Cameron DeVore, a leading First Amendment attorney, objected in a letter to The Times that although the Supreme Court

---

[93] William Glaberson, "Media" column, "Corporate Veils of Secrecy Limit Access to Important Stories," The New York Times, Nov. 27, 1995, p. C7. See also Glaberson, " '60 Minutes' Case Illustrates a Trend Born of Corporate Pressures, Some Analysts Say," The New York Times, November 17, 1995, p. A18.

[94] Bill Carter, " '60 Minutes' Ordered to Pull Interview in Tobacco Report," The New York Times, Nov. 9, 1995, p. A1. See also Lawrence K. Grossman, "CBS, 60 Minutes, and the Unseen Interview," Columbia Journalism Review, Jan./Feb. 1996, pp. 39ff.

[95] Carter, op. cit.

[96] "Self–Censorship at CBS," editorial in The New York Times, November 12, 1996, Sec. 4, p. 14.

provides First Amendment protection for "reputational torts, it has not recently provided any First Amendment protection for news gathering." In any case, the commission of torts in gathering of news—including contract breaches—could cause liability.[97]

On the other hand, an equally prominent First Amendment lawyer—James C. Goodale—said the CBS lawyers' explanation "doesn't wash." He added, "As far as I know, no news organization has ever been sued for what it published solely on a claim of inducing breach of contract." He argued that if a publication is in the public interest in revealing a danger to the public, " . . . publishers and broadcasters would win virtually any case in which a whistleblower provides important information." [Author's note: That comment may seem over-optimistic in light of the Food Lion fraud/trespass decision against ABC–TV, discussed earlier in this chapter at page 364.] Mr. Goodale doubtless was correct in charging that CBS's retreat would encourage other corporations to demand secrecy agreements from their employees, agreements enforceable even after employees have gone on to other jobs or retired.[98]

Most infuriating to The Times was that the decision to block the broadcast was made by CBS executives and lawyers, not by news executives. Meanwhile, "60 Minutes" regulars Mike Wallace and Morley Safer got into an argument after they both had appeared on the Charlie Rose PBS interview program. There, Safer had complained about CBS yielding to pressure and canceling the interview.

Later, Safer wrote an apology to Charlie Rose, circulating it to 60–Minutes staffers, saying that key facts had been withheld from Safer and at least indirectly blaming Wallace for not letting him know that CBS had paid its inside source. Paying sources may be legal; it is not regarded as ethical behavior in most instances. Also, the notion of indemnifying a source as an inducement to get a person to violate a secrecy agreement with an employer has both ethical and legal sharp edges. The tobacco company source had been paid $12,000 in consulting fees, and also had been promised indemnification against lawsuits plus the power to order CBS not to broadcast the interview.[99]

[97] P. Cameron DeVore, letter to the editor, "In CBS Tobacco Case, Contract Came Before First Amendment," The New York Times, November 17, 1995, p. A22. See also the discussion at pages 557 to 561 of Cohen v. Cowles Media, 501 U.S. 663, 111 S.Ct. 2513 (1991), 18 Med.L.Rptr. 4773, where a publication was held liable for $200,000 for violation of promised source confidentiality.

[98] James C. Goodale, "CBS Must Clear the Air," op-ed column in The New York Times, December 6, 1996, p. A23.

[99] Peter Johnson, "Inside TV" column headlined "Is Safer–Wallace blowup part of bigger problem?" USA Today, November 290, 1995, p. 3D; Peter Johnson and Alan Bash, "CBS fee under fire," USA Today, loc. cit. See also Bill Carter, " '60 Minutes' Insiders Feud on Interview," The New York Times, November 18, 1995, p. 7. A

As criticism mounted against CBS, bitter remarks surfaced. Lowell Bergman, who produced the interview, told Newsweek magazine that he had been ordered not to talk about the controversy. By November 20, 1995, Newsweek was reporting that the interview was with a former senior scientist for Brown & Williamson. Newsweek suggested that tobacco companies' "no prisoners" approach to litigation was daunting. David A. Kaplan wrote that tobacco companies are "the rabid raccoons of corporate litigation. Nobody's better at it." He noted that ABC–TV's settlement of the $10 billion lawsuit brought by Philip Morris (with copycat litigation from R.J. Reynolds), and also mentioned a $3 million libel loss in 1987 to Brown & Williamson by the CBS-owned Chicago TV station.[1]

By late November, 1995, the name of the subject of the "60 Minutes" interviews—Dr. Jeffrey Wigand—was out in the open. For one thing he was being sued by Brown & Williamson for theft, fraud, and breach of contract. The CBS Network said, however, that it would indemnify Dr. Wigand. Then, the tobacco company got a temporary restraining order to stop Dr. Wigand from making any more statements about Brown & Williamson. While the scientist's attorney said the secrecy agreements were extorted from Dr. Wigand and thus invalid, a Brown & Williamson lawyer called Dr. Wigand a "master of deceit."[2]

Late in November, 1995, Dr. Wigand was subpoenaed to testify in Mississippi in a Medicaid reimbursement lawsuit brought by that state's attorney general, Mike Moore. Documents Dr. Wigand brought with him—plus more Brown & Williamson inside reports on tobacco and health were then put on the World Wide Web by a West Coast medical school—promised that the matter would not die quietly.[3]

Finally, doubtless relieved that some of Dr. Wigand's testimony had been given in that deposition in Mississippi, CBS decided to broadcast the interview. Parts of Dr. Wigand's sworn testimony, although sealed, already had been published in The Wall Street Journal and closely matched what Dr. Wigand said in his broadcast interview, aired on CBS on January 28, 1996. Dr. Wigand's remarks included the charge that Dr. Thomas Sandefur, former Brown & Williamson chairman, committed perjury before a Congressional

similar report citing problems of payment to a source and a promise to indemnify the source against suit by his former employer was broadcast November 15, 1995 on the "NBC Nightly News With Tom Brokaw."

[1] David A. Kaplan, "Smoke Gets In CBS's Eye," Newsweek, November 20, 1995, p. 96, mentioning Brown & Williamson Tobacco Corp. v. Walter Jacobson and CBS, 827 F.2d 1119 (7th Cir.1987).

[2] Bill Carter, "Tobacco Company Sues Subject of Interview That CBS Canceled," The New York Times, November 22, 1995, p,. A9.

[3] Barnaby J. Feder, "Former Tobacco Official Begins Giving Deposition," The New York Times, November 30, 1995, p. A10.

committee when he swore that he did not believe that nicotine is addictive.[4]

Clearly wounded by these events, Brown & Williamson spent much money and effort trying to "get the goods" on Dr. Wigand. The Wall Street Journal reported that it had been offered a 500–page file produced by private investigators who had checked his resumes for misstatements and even checked his dissertation looking for plagiarism. The file, titled "The Misconduct of Jeffrey S. Wigand Available in the Public Record," contained subheads such as "Wigand's Lies Under Oath" and "Other Lies by Wigand." The Wall Street Journal's check of the voluminous file suggested that most of its serious claims were backed by "scanty evidence."[5]

[4] Elizabeth Jensen and Suein L. Hwang, "CBS Airs Some of Wigand's Interview Accusing Tobacco Firm, Its Ex–Chief," The Wall Street Journal, January 29, 1996, p. B10.

[5] Suein L. Hwang and Milo Geyelin, "Brown & Williamson Has 500–Page Dossier Attacking Chief Critic," The Wall Street Journal, January 29, 1996, p. B10.

Part III

ACCESS TO GOVERNMENT INFORMATION

Chapter 8

REPORTING THE LEGISLATIVE AND EXECUTIVE BRANCHES

SEC. 50. THE PROBLEM OF SECRECY IN GOVERNMENT

Following World War II, obtaining access to information at various levels of government became an acute problem in American journalism.

A democracy is a political system in which the people dictate the course of their government. But making choices about policies or endorsing official actions requires information. Without that information, the claims that a republic is a democracy become a mockery and a farce. But openness, even in democratic governments, is not easily accomplished. The pressures to keep information from the people are many and compelling, especially when they are rationalized by saying that the greater good requires confidentiality. It is easier to do one's job without intrusive examination by outsiders. Not only is there an increase in efficiency without losing the time spent accounting for one's actions, job performance, as self reported, rises. For example, students spend long hours in lecture and readings for classes. At various times during the school term, they must stop learning new information to cover territory they have already gone through. The reason? Testing. How much more efficient would it be to spend the full term engaged in learning new material? Rather than subjecting students to periodic testing, requiring them to disclose what they have learned in an accountability exercise, why not have the students report their own assessments of their performance? The result would be an increase in the grades and the self reporting would likely show most, if not all, students performing in the A range. The only question left would be to ask if one would want one of these students to be his accountant, airline pilot or surgeon. Governments carry out critical functions that are the equivalents to those jobs. A review of government conduct and misconduct shows the government engaged in activities directly affecting the continued prosperity, health and lives of people.

Information about government must be available to all concerned in order to allow for the existence of self-government. It may or may not be channeled through the mass media. Some critics have suggested that the media, owned by an increasingly smaller number of conglomerates, are spending a correspondingly smaller amount of their energies looking at societal problems. Norman L. Rosenberg and others have suggested that "the media's attention to social problems in the 1950s and 1960s [and arguably into the 1990s] primarily ebbed and flowed in relationship to nonlegal pressures within the communications industry itself ... and to the complex links between the Fourth Estate and other powerful institutions.... "[1]

If such a state of affairs exists, what have journalists been doing about it? Not enough, if one believes Robert M. Entman's gloomy contentions:[2]

> Restricted by the limited tastes of the audience and reliant upon political elites for most information, journalists participate in an interdependent news system, not a free market of ideas. In practice ... the news media fall far short of the ideal version of a free press as civic educator and guardian of democracy.

Access to information about government therefore must exist independent of media pressures, although the media have the capacity to focus attention on the issue. Instead, a commitment to openness allows individuals to examine and criticize government conduct on their own. The Internet and World Wide Web have recreated that time when anyone could become a pamphleteer and freely publish his views. In addition, while giant conglomerates have been absorbing traditional media outlets, new channels have been opening and the traditional mass audience has been splintering. Instead of the Big Three networks that dominated the television market, the growth of cable and satellite television delivery

[1] Norman L. Rosenberg, Protecting the Best Men (Chapel Hill: Univ. of North Carolina Press, 1986), p. 265; for a discussion of problems of access to information about great concentrations of wealth and power involving stock market scandals, see James B. Stewart, Den of Thieves (New York: Simon and Schuster, 1991).

[2] Robert M. Entman, Democracy Without Citizens: Media and the Decay of American Politics (New York: Oxford University Press, 1989) p. 8.

has increased channels by a hundredfold. All have the potential of adding to public understanding and control of its institutions of government and society.

The late Ithiel de Sola Pool, a most important communication theorist, expressed the hope that as new communications networks emerge, they will do so under "guidelines that recognize the preferred position of freedom of discourse."[3] Pool also saw that the First Amendment must apply "to the function of communication, not just to the media that existed in the eighteenth century."[4]

Government information covers more than the activities of civil servants. Government is tied to both public and private concerns and as such is a valuable resource in keeping track of the excesses of the corporate power. On its own, the news media can do only so much in reporting on the private sector. Much news—especially news which is not favorable to corporate America—comes to reporters via reports from federal, state and local regulatory agencies. Since 1980, especially, the federal government has pruned regulatory activities over business, so that less is learned about private concentrations of power until too late for the news media to serve as an effective sentinel. Then, when a scandal such as the estimated $500 billion savings and loan debacle occurs, disaster strikes, showing government regulators and the news media too often impotent and irrelevant. With newspapers, broadcasting stations and cable TV companies generally owned by corporate conglomerates, it is not only the conspiracy buff who wonders whether news media have sufficient independence.

Even with independence, meaningful communication requires that the First Amendment now be given expanded meaning where access to government information is concerned. Growth of governmental power has coincided with expanding government secrecy at all levels and with the rapid changeover to computerized records rather than the more easily accessible paper files. The need for computer-literate reporters and citizens is increasingly important as records once freely available in file drawers now require the intervention of a government gatekeeper. Computer searches for information—and finding patterns in that information—can be far more informative to society than yesterday's paper-chases, but only if citizen access is protected under the Constitution and under supporting statutes.[5] As is discussed in Section 51 of this chapter, the Supreme Court of the United States has viewed the Constitu-

[3] Ithiel de Sola Pool, Technologies of Freedom (Cambridge, MA: Belknap Press of Harvard University, 1983) p. 244.

[4] Ibid., p. 246.

[5] See generally, Sissela Bok, Secrets: On the Ethics of Concealment and Revelation (New York: Pantheon, 1983); for a discussion of computerized aids to reporting, see Elliot G. Jaspin, "Just do it!," ASNE Bulletin, Dec. 1991, p. 4ff.

tion and the First Amendment as something apart from the concept of "a public's right to know" or a "citizen's right to gather information." In that context, as government grows more powerful and the news media increasingly embrace corporate values, greater efforts are needed to prevent the First Amendment from becoming obsolete.

No defined segment of the American public has been more concerned about tendencies to secrecy in government than journalists. Some feel secrecy is the central threat to freedom of expression in Twentieth Century America. Accepting, during World War II, the need for extensive secrecy for an enormous war machine in a government bureaucracy grown gigantic, journalists after the war soon detected a broad pattern of continued secrecy in government operations. Access to meetings was denied; reports, papers, documents at all levels of government seemed less available than before officialdom's habits of secrecy developed in the passion for security during World War II. An intense, insistent campaign for access to government information was launched in the 1950's by editors, publishers, reporters, and news organizations. It went under a banner labeled "Freedom of Information," and under the claim that the press was fighting for the "people's right to know."[6]

To combat what they viewed as a severe increase in denial of access to the public's business, journalists took organized action. "Freedom of Information" committees were established by the American Society of Newspaper Editors (ASNE) and by the Society of Professional Journalists—Sigma Delta Chi. The ASNE commissioned newspaper attorney Harold L. Cross to perform a major study on the law of access to government activity. His book, *The People's Right to Know,* was published in 1953 and served as a central source of information. State and local chapters of professional groups worked for the adoption of state access laws. In 1958, a Freedom of Information Center was opened at the University of Missouri School of Journalism, as a clearing house and research facility for those concerned with the subject. Meanwhile, an early and vigorous ally was found in the House Subcommittee on Government Information under Rep. John E. Moss of California, created to investigate charges of excessive secrecy in the Executive branch of government.[7]

Journalism had powerful allies also in the scientific community. It found that the advance of knowledge in vast areas of government-sponsored science was being slowed, sometimes crippled for

[6] See Annual Reports, Sigma Delta Chi Advancement of Freedom of Information Committee (Chicago, Sigma Delta Chi).

[7] Rep. John E. Moss, Preface to Replies from Federal Agencies to Questionnaire Submitted by the Special Subcommittee on Government Information of the Committee on Government Operations, 84 Cong. 1 Sess. (Nov. 1, 1955), p. iii.

years, in the blockage of the flow of research information between and even within agencies of the federal government. Fear of "leakage" of secrets important to defense in the Cold War with the Soviet Union brought administrative orders that were contrary to the tenets of scientists and researchers. One apocryphal story circulated during this period dealt with a scientist at a government research facility. The scientist, engaged in sensitive research, took a vacation. On his return, he discovered that his laboratory notebooks were missing. He reported the disappearance to the head of security to learn, to his apparent relief, that the notebooks had been placed in a secured area. The scientist's relief was short-lived because he then was told that his security clearance would not allow him access to the area. Stories about roadblocks in research and a too-real snarl of regulations, rules and red tape prevented scientists from sharing their findings with others. Their concern about the damage to the advance of knowledge in science paralleled journalists' alarm about damage to the democratic assumption that free institutions rest on an informed public.[8]

Public understanding of the dangers of official secrecy broadened in the exposé of the Executive's abuse of power in the Watergate episode of the mid–1970's. Earl Warren, retired Chief Justice of the United States, crediting the news media with a share in exposing the fraud and deceit, said if we are to learn from "the debacle we are in, we should first strike at secrecy in government wherever it exists, because it is the incubator for corruption."[9] New recruits entered the battle against official secrecy—Common Cause, the Center for National Security Studies, and Ralph Nader among them. Groups of concerned citizens in states joined to promote openness in their state and local governments and coalitions formed to work to ensure the rights of the people to know what their governments were doing. The National Freedom of Information Coalition came into being to foster cooperation among state access groups and help bring into being organizations in states where none existed.

But even with such grass-roots and journalistic activity, openness continues to be imperiled. Access and openness laws are not self-executing. Bureaucracies and politicians have managed to ignore or circumvent attempts to find out what they really do. In his April, 1987 presidential address to the American Society of Newspaper Editors, Michael Gartner laid out a dirty laundry list of information that is not freely obtainable. Just a few of the many items Gartner listed as being unavailable:

[8] Science, Education and Communications, 12 Bulletin of Atomic Scientists, 333 (Nov.1956); Walter Gellhorn, Security, Loyalty, and Science (Ithaca: Cornell Univ. Press, 1950).

[9] Governmental Secrecy: Corruption's Ally, 60 ABA Journal 550 (May, 1974).

— Information that the government keeps secret for purposes of national defense or foreign policy.

— Information on sources or methods of the Central Intelligence Agency.

— Information concerning virtually anything about the National Security Agency.

— Much of the information at the Consumer Product Safety Commission.

— Information on pre-sentencing investigations and parole reports.

The key to reporting of the legislative and executive branches is persistence: stubbornness in asking questions and virtually endless patience that is often needed in filing and re-filing FOIA (Freedom of Information Act) requests. It took a dozen years of struggle, including three lawsuits, to open the first 1.5 million pages of documents from the Administration of President Nixon, and those pages were mostly trivia and represented less than 4 per cent of the total body of papers. From beyond the grave, Nixon seemed determined to thwart public knowledge about the inner workings of his presidency. The New York Times reported in 1994 that the Nixon's heirs were continuing the late President's two-decade fight "to control more than 3,000 hours of White House tapes and 150,000 pages of Presidential papers."

But Professor Stanley Kutler, a University of Wisconsin historian, who sued to get access to the papers, won several significant victories to gain acceptance, including the release of more than 200 hours of recordings labeled the "Abuse of Government Power" recordings. Kutler published a book on the Nixon tapes, "Abuse of Power: The New Nixon Tapes." The New York Times reported that "The tapes show one of the century's most skilled politicians in a prolonged act of self-destruction, lying to the public, to his political allies, to his closest aides and advisers, and finally to himself. They depict him as eloquent and profane, charming and chilling, brilliant and hapless, powerful and helpless."[10]

It was the New York Times' report on the Pentagon Papers that led to Watergate, the newspaper reported. Former National Security Council aide Daniel Ellsberg had given the New York Times a copy of a 47–volume study of U.S. involvement in Vietnam. Nixon and his staff created a special covert team to stop leaks of classified information. That team was called the Plumbers. As one tape excerpt made clear, Nixon intended to stop any and all threats.

[10] Tim Weiner, "Transcripts of Nixon Tapes Show the Path to Watergate," The New York Times, Oct. 31, 1997, p. A1.

" 'We're up against an enemy, a conspiracy,' Mr. Nixon told his chief of staff, H.R. Haldeman, on July 1, 1971. 'They're using any means. *We are going to use any means.* Is that clear?' "[11] According to the tapes, the conspiracy included anti-war activists, former aides, the Kennedy family, "rich Jews" at the Internal Revenue Service and Ford Foundation and others. In the last tape made before the public learned of Nixon's taping system, he spoke with Henry Kissinger, then Secretary of State, about Nixon's defiance of Senator Sam Ervin, chairman of the Senate Watergate Committee. Ervin sought access to White House files related to the break-in and cover-up.

> Nixon: Let him sue. Christ, they ... If the Supreme Court wants to decide in its wisdom to help destroy the Presidency, the Supreme Court destroys it.... The hell with them [the Senate committee]. I'll sit on those papers, if I have to burn them, I'll burn every goddamned paper in this house. You realize that? Every paper in this house before I'll hand them over to that committee.... So we'll have a Constitutional crisis. If we do it'll be a goddamn ding-dong battle and we might, if we lose, I'll burn the papers. 'Cause I got 'em. That's the point, 'cause I would never turn those papers over to a court. Never give them over to a committee.[12]

The disclosure of the secret taping system led to another fight, this time over the tapes themselves.

President Nixon and the Watergate Tapes

A head-on confrontation emerged in the Watergate investigations, as Nixon refused to turn over to a grand jury, tape recordings of conversations with his White House aides. Federal Judge John J. Sirica ruled that the tapes must be submitted to him for *in camera* scrutiny and possible forwarding to the grand jury. The President refused, asserting executive privilege, and said he was protecting "the right of himself and his successors to preserve the confidentiality of discussions in which they participate in the course of their constitutional duties." Special prosecutor Archibald Cox argued it was intolerable that "the President would invoke executive privilege to keep the tape recordings from the grand jury but permit his aides to testify fully as to their recollections of the same conversations." The President fired Cox, and the Attorney General resigned and his deputy was fired before the President yielded the tapes (which of course were to prove central to the discrediting of him and his aides) amid a public cry for his impeachment.[13]

---

[11] Ibid.

[12] Ibid.

[13] New York Times, Sept. 11, 1973, p. 36; Oct. 24, 1973, p. 1.

The Supreme Court ruled that executive privilege is not absolute, but qualified. The *in camera* court inspection of the tapes that Sirica ordered, it said, would be a minimal intrusion on the President's confidential communications. The President's claim was not based on grounds of national security—that military or diplomatic secrets were threatened—but only on the ground of his "generalized interest in confidentiality." That could not prevail over "the fundamental demands of due process of law in the fair administration of justice." It would have to yield to the "demonstrated, specific need for evidence in a pending criminal trial."[14]

Subsequent assertions of executive privilege by Nixon involved his post-resignation claim to custody of presidential papers from his term in office—millions of pages of documents and almost 900 tapes—and also his denial of the rights of record companies and networks to copy, sell, and broadcast tapes that had been played at one of the trials arising from Watergate. The Supreme Court ruled in one case that the government should have custody of all but Nixon's private and personal papers,[15] and in the other it granted Nixon's plea to deny networks and record companies the right to copy, sell, or broadcast the tapes.[16]

On July 24, 1979, a U.S. District Court ruled that Nixon's dictabelt "diaries" were not personal and would not be screened for use by archivists. Also, the court ruled that the public should have access to the actual tapes, instead of synopses or transcripts.[17] Usage of the tapes is restricted: no more than 24 persons may listen at a time, for 45 to 90 minutes depending on the length of the tape played; and listeners are forbidden to make their own recordings of the tapes.[18]

Additional tapes were released later. Archivists estimated that the process of transcribing will take an extended period because of the poor audio quality. Interfering noise picked up by the microphones in the Nixon taping system have made transcription a laborious process with one estimate that it would take about 100 hours of work to transcribe one hour of tape.

Recent disclosures have provided the public with access to tapes made during the Kennedy and Johnson administrations. The Kennedy tapes provide insight into White House discussions sur-

[14] United States v. Nixon, 418 U.S. 683, 684–685, 713, 94 S.Ct. 3090, 3095–3096, 3110 (1974).

[15] Nixon v. General Services Administrator, 433 U.S. 425, 97 S.Ct. 2777 (1977).

[16] Nixon v. Warner Communications, Inc., News Media and the Law, 1:1 (Oct. 1977), p. 14. Anon., "High Court Bars Networks' Right To Nixon Tapes," New York Times, April 19, 1978, p. 1.

[17] "Nixon Documents Litigation Reaches Court Settlement," News Media & The Law, March–April 1980, 4:2, p. 50.

[18] Ibid.

rounding the Cuban Missile Crisis. The Johnson tapes show him deciding to continue a commitment to employing U.S. forces in Vietnam for fear that Republican presidential candidate Barry Goldwater would use a pullout as a political club showing Johnson's weakness in the face of Communist aggression.

SEC. 51. ACCESS AND THE CONSTITUTION

Courts have given little support to the position that the First Amendment includes a right of access to government information.

In many journalists' view, freedom of speech and press and the First Amendment encompass a right to gather government information as much as they embrace the right to publish and distribute it. Constitutional protection against denial of access seems to them only reasonable. The legal scholar Harold Cross argued that "Freedom of information is the very foundation for all those freedoms that the First Amendment of our Constitution was intended to guarantee."[19]

Famed First Amendment legal scholar Thomas I. Emerson held that "we ought to consider the right to know as an integral part of the system of freedom of expression, embodied in the first amendment and entitled to support by legislation or other affirmative government action." He found the argument for "starting from this point * * * overwhelming," and further, that the Supreme Court has in some respects recognized a constitutional right to know.[20]

A Right of Access?

But while an occasional lower court or dissenting judge has found reason for the First Amendment to protect a right of access to government information,[21] the Supreme Court of the United States has done so only in the setting of public, criminal trials.[22] Justice Potter Stewart delivered a rationale for the denial of a constitutional right of access to government in a famous 1975 speech:[23]

[19] Harold L. Cross, The People's Right to Know (Morningside Heights: Columbia Univ. Press, 1953), pp. xiii–xiv.

[20] Legal Foundations of the Right To Know, 1976 Wash.U.L.Quar. 1–3. See also Jacob Scher, "Access to Information: Recent Legal Problems," Journalism Quarterly, 37:1 (1960), p. 41.

[21] Providence Journal Co. et al. v. McCoy et al., 94 F.Supp. 186 (D.R.I.1950); In re Mack, 386 Pa. 251, 126 A.2d 679, 689 (1956); Lyles v. Oklahoma, 330 P.2d 734 (Okl.Crim.1958).

[22] Richmond Newspapers v. Virginia, 448 U.S. 555, 100 S.Ct. 2814 (1980).

[23] Potter Stewart, "Or of the Press," 26 Hastings L.J. (1975).

So far as the Constitution goes, the autonomous press may publish what it knows, and may seek to learn what it can.

But this autonomy cuts both ways. The press is free to do battle against secrecy and deception in government. But the press cannot expect from the Constitution any guarantee that it will succeed. There is no constitutional right to have access to particular government information, or to require openness from the bureaucracy. The public's interest in knowing about its government is protected by the guarantee of a Free Press, but the protection is indirect. The Constitution itself is neither a Freedom of Information Act nor an Official Secrets Act.

The Constitution, in other words, establishes the contest, not its resolution. Congress may provide a resolution, at least in some instances, through carefully drawn legislation. For the rest, we must rely, as so often in our system we must, on the tug and pull of the political forces in American society.

Justice Stewart's words ring true. The courts have provided scant acknowledgment of a "right of access" under the First Amendment, except for access to public, criminal court trials, declared open as a First Amendment right in a major case of 1980, Richmond Newspapers v. Virginia (detailed in Chap. 9, below). As noted in Chapter 9, the *Richmond Newspapers'* language suggests that there may be a greater right of access than that articulated by Justice Stewart. The decision refers to maintaining openness in government operations and forums that traditionally were open. The problem with applying that reasoning is that so much of government is relatively new and little traditionally has been open to the public. While it operates in the context of criminal trials, *Richmond Newspapers* has not yet proven its effectiveness in other areas of government.

A Right to Travel?

Unlike citizens of many other nations, Americans have long been blessed by taking for granted a right to travel freely from state to state without having to show an "identity card." And for the most part, Americans think they can travel anywhere they wish, but reporter William Worthy was thwarted in his attempt—in the 1950s period of the Cold War tensions with the Soviet Union and other Communist states—to travel to China to report. Worthy, of the *Baltimore Afro–American,* in 1956 ignored an order by Secretary of State John Foster Dulles barring American reporters from going to "Red China" to report. When Worthy returned to the United States, the State Department revoked his passport and refused to give him another. Worthy went to court to attempt to regain it. The trial court held, without elaborating, that Dulles' refusal to issue the passport did not violate Worthy's rights to travel under the First Amendment. Worthy appealed, but his argument for First Amendment protection failed, the Court of Appeals holding:[24]

> The right to travel is a part of the right to liberty, and a newspaperman's right to travel is a part of freedom of the press. But these valid generalizations do not support unrestrained conclusions. * * *

> Freedom of the press bears restrictions * * *. Merely because a newsman has a right to travel does not mean he can go anywhere he wishes. He cannot attend conferences of the Supreme Court, or meetings of the President's Cabinet or executive sessions of the Committees of Congress.

In a 1965 case, Louis Zemel argued that a State Department travel ban was a direct interference with the First Amendment rights of citizens to inform themselves at first hand of events abroad.[25] In making his request to the State Department for the needed validation of his passport to travel to Cuba, Zemel explained that the purpose of his trip was "to satisfy my curiosity about the state of affairs in Cuba and to make me a better informed citizen."[26] The United States Supreme Court agreed that the Secretary of State's denial rendered "less than wholly free the flow of information concerning that country," but denied that a First Amendment right was involved. "The right to speak and publish does not carry with it the unrestrained right to gather information,"[27] the Court said.

On occasion, the U.S. State Department may deny a passport to a person whose foreign travel is thought to create "substantial likelihood of 'serious damage' to national security or foreign policy." The Supreme Court upheld such a passport revocation involving Philip Agee, a dissident former Central Intelligence agent accused of working to expose the cover and sources of CIA employees.[28]

Pell v. Procunier (1974)

Saxbe v. Washington Post Co. (1974)

From restrictions on foreign travel, turn to the question of whether there is a "right" to report on prisoners in American

---

[24] Worthy v. Herter, 270 F.2d 905 (D.C.Cir.1959), certiorari denied 361 U.S. 918, 80 S.Ct. 255 (1959).

[25] Zemel v. Rusk, 381 U.S. 1, 85 S.Ct. 1271 (1965).

[26] Ibid. At 3, 1274.

[27] Ibid. At 17–18, 1281 (1965). See also Trimble v. Johnston, 173 F.Supp. 651 (D.D.C.1959); In re Mack, 386 Pa. 251, 126 A.2d 679 (1956).

[28] Haig v. Agee, 453 U.S. 280, 287, 288, 101 S.Ct. 2766, 2771, 2772 (1981).

prisons. This is not a minor question; to protect freedom, journalists and other citizens need to be able to inquire into the health of the criminal justice system, from beginning to end. That is, the system needs surveillance: from arrest to arraignment, to preliminary hearings, to plea bargains, or trials, to appeals, to sentencing of convicted criminals, to incarceration on through parole. Are all persons caught up in the criminal justice system treated alike, or are members of minority groups treated more harshly than other people? To gather some of this information may require interviews with specific persons who are in prison.

Pell v. Procunier arose when journalists Eve Pell, Betty Segal, and Paul Jacobs challenged a California prison regulation which barred media interviews with specific, individual inmates.[29] Denied their requests to interview prison inmates Apsin, Bly and Guild, they asserted that the rule limited their news-gathering activity and thus infringed freedom of the press under the First and Fourteenth Amendments. They lost in district court and appealed to the U.S. Supreme Court. Stewart wrote for the majority that the press and public are afforded full opportunities to observe minimum security sections of prisons, to speak about any subject to any inmates they might encounter, to interview inmates selected at random by the corrections officials, to sit in on group meetings of inmates. "The sole limitation on news-gathering in California prisons is the prohibition in [regulation] #415.071 of interviews with individual inmates specifically designated by representatives of the press."[30]

Before the regulation was adopted, Stewart continued, unrestrained press access to individual prisoners resulted in concentration of press attention on a few inmates, who became virtual "public figures" in prison society and gained great influence. One inmate who advocated non-cooperation with prison regulations had extensive press attention, encouraged other inmates in his purpose, and eroded the institution's ability to deal effectively with inmates in general. San Quentin prison authorities concluded that an escape attempt there, resulting in deaths of three staff members and two inmates, flowed in part from an unrestricted press access policy, and regulation #415.071 was adopted as a result. Stewart wrote: "The Constitution does not * * * require government to accord the press special access to information not shared by members of the public generally."[31]

Dissenting in this case and in a companion case, Saxbe v.

[29] 417 U.S. 817, 94 S.Ct. 2800 (1974).

[30] Pell v. Procunier, 417 U.S. 817, 94 S.Ct. 2800, 2808 (1974).

[31] Ibid., at 834, 94 S.Ct. at 2810.

Washington Post Co.[32] which involved an unsuccessful challenge to a Federal Bureau of Prisons rule similar to California's, was Justice Powell. He said that "sweeping prohibition of prisoner-press interviews substantially impairs a core value of the First Amendment." In these cases, he argued, society's interest "in preserving free public discussion of governmental affairs" was great and was the value at stake. Since the public is unable to know most news at first hand, "In seeking out the news the press * * * acts as an agent of the public at large. * * * By enabling the public to assert meaningful control over the political process, the press performs a critical function in effecting the societal purpose of the First Amendment."

Houchins v. KQED Inc. (1978)

Much more restrictive access to a jail was at issue when Sheriff Houchins of Alameda Co., Calif., was ordered by injunction to open up his facility to reporters and their cameras and recorders. The controversy arose over conditions in a part of the jail complex, Little Greystone. A judge had ruled previously that conditions in Little Greystone constituted cruel and unusual punishment. One suicide had occurred there and a psychiatrist said that inmates who were his patients were deteriorating in the facility. Television station KQED and the NAACP sued to gain access to the jail. Shortly after the suit was filed, Sheriff Houchins announced the creation of a monthly tour. His rules had limited tours to 25 persons and did not visit Little Greystone. No cameras or recorders were allowed, nor was access to a part of the jail where violence had reportedly broken out earlier. KQED, which made a practice of covering prisons in the area and wanted access to shoot film and interview prisoners, took Houchins to court, saying its journalistic usefulness was reduced by his tour rules. The sheriff objected that the access sought would infringe the privacy of inmates, create jail "celebrities" and cause attendant difficulties, and disrupt jail operations. He told of other forms of access by which information about the jail could reach the public. The district court agreed with KQED's contentions, and enjoined the sheriff from further blocking of media access "at reasonable times," cameras and recorders included.[33] The California Court of Appeals upheld the injunction, saying that the U.S. Supreme Court's *Pell* and *Saxbe* decisions were not controlling.

Houchins appealed to the Supreme Court, and it reversed the lower courts, Chief Justice Warren Burger writing that neither of the earlier cases, nor indeed Branzburg v. Hayes (Chapter 10,

[32] 417 U.S. 843, 94 S.Ct. 2811 (1974). Powell's statements are at 860–874, 94 S.Ct. at 2820–2826.

[33] Houchins v. KQED, Inc., 438 U.S. 1, 98 S.Ct. 2588 (1978), 3 Med.L.Rptr. 2521.

above), provided a constitutional right to gather news, or a constitutional right of access to government.[34] He agreed that news of prisons is important for the public to have, and that media serve as "eyes and ears" for the public. He said, however, that the Supreme Court had never held that the First Amendment compels anyone, private or public, to supply information. He discussed various ways in which information about prisons reaches the public, and said the legislative branch was free to pass laws opening penal institutions if it wished. But the press, Burger said, enjoys no special privilege of access beyond that which officials grant to the public in general. *Pell* and *Saxbe* would hold, and Houchins' access rules also. Separately, Justice Stewart joined in the decision, differing only to the extent of saying that reporters on tour with the public should be allowed to carry and use their tools of the trade, including cameras and recorders.

Justice Powell, who as we have seen had dissented in *Pell* and *Saxbe,* joined two others in dissenting again, on similar grounds. He and the other dissenters in *Pell* had totaled four, the greatest support that the Supreme Court has furnished for "access to government" as a constitutionally protected principle outside the judicial branch.[35]

The government continues to rely on *Pell* and *Saxbe* in responding to subsequent claims for access to both locations and information.

SEC. 52. RECORDS AND MEETINGS OF FEDERAL GOVERNMENT

Access to records and meetings of federal executive and administrative agencies is provided under the "Freedom of Information" and the "Sunshine in Government" Acts; the Privacy Act provides for secrecy of records.

The Freedom of Information Act

On July 4, 1966, Pres. Lyndon B. Johnson signed the Federal Public Records Law, shortly to be known as the federal Freedom of Information (FOI) Act.[36] Providing for the public availability of

---

[34] Ibid., at 11, 2595.

[35] Richmond Newspapers v. Virginia, 448 U.S. 555, 100 S.Ct. 2814 (1980), 6 Med.L.Rptr. 1833. For a view that sees the approach of a broad constitutional right of access to government, see Roy V. Leeper, "Richmond Newspapers, Inc. v. Virginia and the Emerging Right of Access," 61 Journ.Quar. 615 (Autumn 1984).

[36] 5 U.S.C.A. § 552, amended by Pub.Law 93–502, 88 Stat. 1561–1564. For history, text, and extensive judicial interpretation of this act, and information on the federal Privacy Act, see Allan Adler and Halperin, M.H., Litigation under the Federal Freedom of Information Act and Privacy Act, 1984 (Washington, 1983).

records of executive and administrative agencies of the government, it sprang, President Johnson said, "from one of our most essential principles: a democracy works best when the people have all the information that the security of the Nation permits." He expressed a "deep sense of pride that the United States is an open society in which the people's right to know is cherished and guarded."[37]

The FOI Act replaced section 3 of the Administrative Procedure Act of 1946, which had permitted secrecy if it was required in the public interest or for "good cause."[38] The new law expressed neither this limitation nor another which had said disclosure was necessary only to "persons properly and directly concerned" with the subject at hand. In the words of Attorney General Ramsey Clark, the FOI Act.[39]

> imposes on the executive branch an affirmative obligation to adopt new standards and practices for publication and availability of information. It leaves no doubt that disclosure is a transcendent goal, yielding only to such compelling considerations as those provided for in the exemptions of the act.

Every federal executive branch agency is required under the FOI Act to publish in the Federal Register its organization plan, and the agency personnel and methods through which the public can get information. Every agency's procedural rules and general policies are to be published. Every agency's manuals and instructions are to be made available for public inspection and copying, as are final opinions in adjudicated cases. Current indexes are to be made available to the public. If records are improperly withheld, the U.S. district court can enjoin the agency from the withholding and order disclosure. And if agency officials fail to comply with the court order, they may be punished for contempt.

Exceptions to that which must be made public are called "exemptions." There are nine of them:[40]

1. Records "specifically authorized under criteria established by an Executive order to be kept secret in the interest of national defense or foreign policy" and which are properly classified.

[37] Public Papers of the Presidents, Lyndon B. Johnson, 1966 II, p. 699.

[38] 5 U.S.C.A. § 1002 (1946).

[39] Foreword, Attorney General's Memorandum on the Public Information Section of the Administrative Procedure Act (1967).

[40] Some of the exemptions were tightened against abuse by agencies after a three-year congressional study which brought about amendments effective Feb. 19, 1975. On the other hand, as reported later (near the end of this section), the FOI Reform Act of 1986 made it more difficult to get information about businesses and about investigatory records of some law enforcement agencies.

2. Matters related only to "internal personnel rules and practices" of an agency.

3. Matters exempt from disclosure by statute.

4. Trade secrets and commercial or financial information obtained from a person and that are privileged or confidential.

5. Inter-agency or intra-agency communications, such as memoranda showing how policy-makers within an agency feel about various policy options.

6. Personnel, medical and similar files which could not be disclosed without a "clearly unwarranted invasion" of someone's privacy.

7. Investigatory files compiled for law enforcement purposes, if the production of such records would interfere with law enforcement, deprive one of a fair trial, constitute an unwarranted invasion of personal privacy, disclose the identity of a confidential source, disclose investigative techniques, or endanger the life or safety of law enforcement personnel.

8. Reports prepared by or for an agency responsible for the regulation or supervision of financial institutions.

9. Geological and geophysical information and data, including maps, concerning wells—particularly explorations by gas and oil companies.

Openness Is Not Self–Executing

No open records or open meetings victory is ever likely to be won, once and for all. It is simply a fact of life that government officials, especially when under pressure or embarrassed because of mistakes within their agencies, tend to "stonewall" when citizens—including members of the news media—come around asking questions.

Although the Freedom of Information Act, as amended, has been useful in opening government files, any skimming of the American Civil Liberties Union's annual compendium, Litigation Under the Freedom of Information Act and Privacy Act, will indicate that the federal commitment to open records is flawed. To a mind-boggling degree, federal courts have supported federal bureaucracies in keeping secret materials which the public ought to have available.[41] Consider the following "parade of issues," looking at some litigation situations which arose under a number of the

---

[41] See the valuable compendium edited by Allan Robert Adler, ed., Litigation Under the Federal Freedom of Information and Privacy Act, 18th edition (Washington, D.C.: ACLU Foundation, 1993).

Exemptions to the federal FOIA. Federal agencies tried to withhold information under the exemptions for a variety of reasons (some far-fetched), and were quite often supported in such withholding decisions by federal courts.

Exemption 1—National Security Information. As outlined by the ACLU's guidebook, Litigation Under the Freedom of Information and Privacy Act, it may be seen that "national security" is an almost magical incantation. For example, the Central Intelligence Agency (CIA) is allowed, under a 1984 amendment to the National Security Act of 1947, to exempt "operational" files from the search and review requirements of the FOIA.[42] When will the records be available? (When the operation is "over.") When will the operation be declared "over?" (That's a matter for CIA discretion.) The CIA hangs onto secrets: In some cases, the CIA may turn aside a request for information with the response that for national security reasons, it can neither confirm nor deny the existence of the requested records.[43] For an example of the U.S. Supreme Court's deference to the CIA even in the face of massive wrongdoing by that agency, see the discussion of CIA v. Sims (1985) later in this chapter.[44]

The CIA—one of the United States' spy agencies—has blundered egregiously and tragically for a good many years. In 1994, while the CIA guarded its warehouses full of secrets in the name of national security, it was revealed that Aldrich H. Ames, a CIA career operative, had sold out his country for money provided by Russian agents. Even though he lived well beyond his CIA paycheck for a decade, he was not apprehended until years after the Russians "turned" him and after he had compromised 20 CIA operations. Because of Ames, 10 agents were executed, and presumably were tortured before they died.[45]

Yet even after the end of the Cold War and the fall of the Soviet Union, surveillance is still big business. The budget for U.S. spy agents had been an open secret—it was not published by Congress, but comments in The New York Times and elsewhere estimated the annual budget for 1994 at about $28 billion. Facing a federal lawsuit filed by the Federation of American Scientists, the CIA revealed its budget was $26.6 billion.[46] And although the CIA has now made its disclosure, the even more secretive National Security Agency (NSA), which specializes in electronic spying/satel-

[42] Ibid., p. 42.

[43] Ibid., p. 39, citing Phillippi v. CIA, 546 F.2d 1009, 1012–1013 (D.C.Cir.1976).

[44] CIA v. Sims, 471 U.S. 159, 105 S.Ct. 1881 (1985).

[45] "Deadly Mole," Newsweek, March 7, 1994, pp. 24ff.

[46] "Prying Open the Spy Budget," The New York Times, Oct. 17, 1997, A34.

lite intelligence activities, reportedly has a larger budget than the CIA.[47]

And then there's the National Reconnaissance Office (NRO), an organization run jointly by the CIA and the Pentagon, with a budget estimated at $6 billion, or three times that of the U.S. State Department. In the summer of 1994, a furious Senate Intelligence Committee—which oversees American intelligence activities—was grilling CIA officials. How had the NRO managed to have construction well along on a $350 million spy satellite headquarters building outside of Washington, D.C., without the Senate Intelligence Committee knowing the size, location, and cost of the NRO complex? Some intelligence committee Senators seemed to be startled that the project was underway, but then, the existence of the National Reconnaissance Office was a state secret until 1992. As Senate Intelligence Committee member Howard Metzenbaum (D–Ohio) said: "This project is a good example of what happens when * * * the Government does business in the dark."[48]

As the description suggests, Exemption 1 was crafted to preserve the national security and defense interests of the United States. During the Reagan presidency, administration officials noted that the Soviet KGB was a frequent FOI requestor. Challenges to refusals made under Exemption 1 are subject to judicial review as are all exemptions. The courts may not just accept the word of the federal government in every case. FOI case law holds that courts can examine documents in camera (in chambers) to determine the propriety of the exemption claim.[49]

Exemption 2—Internal Agency Rules. For example, the Internal Revenue Service (IRS) attempted to withhold its auditing manual, on grounds that this was merely of internal concern. A federal court, however, held—sensibly enough—that the auditing rules used by the IRS should be available to public inspection.[50]

Exemption 3—Information Exempted by Other Statutes. Obviously, there are many such statutes which exclude information from disclosure. Tax returns and completed census forms fall into this category. The label on this exemption may sound harmless, but this exemption has been used to defend failures to release information which the public clearly ought to know.

[47] For an account of the NSA, see James Bamford, The Puzzle Palace: Inside the NSA, America's Most Secret Intelligence Agency (New York: Viking Penguin, 1983).

[48] Tim Weiner, "New CIA Office Draws Heavy Fire," The New York Times, Aug. 9, 1994, p. A1.

[49] Stein v. Department of Justice & Federal Bureau of Investigation, 662 F.2d 1245 (7th Cir.1981).

[50] Hawkes v. Internal Revenue Service, 467 F.2d 787, 789 (6th Cir.1972).

For example, air-worthiness and crash-worthiness of commercial airliners seems to be, simply and obviously, of public interest. Parties interested in comparative air safety records sued the Federal Aeronautics Authority in the 1970s to get access to "Systems Worthiness Analysis Reports." The FAA refused to release the reports, evidently on grounds that disclosing information would be bad for some air carriers' reputations and thus would not be in the public interest. The U.S. Supreme Court upheld this exercise of FAA "discretion,"[51] although Congress later amended Exemption 3 to restrict administrators' loopholes and to allow a bit more information in the public interest.[52]

For an example of a Supreme Court decision upholding the Central Intelligence Agency's refusal to reveal names of universities and scientists who had dosed unsuspecting "subjects" with LSD (in the name of national security during the 1950s and 1960s), see CIA v. Sims (1985), discussed in more detail later in this Section. The CIA did not have to reveal identities of operatives or informants or employees under a section of the National Security Act, and thus found refuge in Exemption 3—Information Exempted by Other Statutes.[53]

Similarly, horror stories about experimenting on humans with nuclear radiation—information long held secret under Atomic Secrets legislation—finally surfaced late in 1993. Energy Secretary Hazel O'Leary, saying she was " 'appalled, shocked and deeply saddened,' "helped disclose experiments such as injecting plutonium into unsuspecting human "guinea pigs." Mrs. O'Leary helped bring about this disclosure when she ordered declassifying of millions of pages of documents at Department of Energy sites around the nation.[54] More on this in the section on FOIA successes below.

Exemption 4—Trade Secrets, Commercial/Financial Information. David Vladeck and Allan Adler have written that this exemption is often criticized for its lack of clarity. Trade secrets or commercial and financial information about businesses in possession of the federal government are supposed to be privileged or confidential, and definitions of those terms vary somewhat among courts.[55] This exemption came about because of concerns raised by the private sector. A company will spend, sometimes, millions of dollars to develop a new process for manufacturing its products. It

[51] Administrator, Federal Aviation Administration v. Robertson, 422 U.S. 255, 95 S.Ct. 2140 (1975).

[52] Adler, op. cit., p. 59.

[53] CIA v. Sims, 471 U.S. 159, 105 S.Ct. 1881 (1985); see also Adler, op. cit., p.65.

[54] Keith Schneider, "Disclosing Radiation Tests Puts Official in Limelight," The New York Times, Jan. 6, 1994, p. A1; "Nuclear Guinea Pigs," editorial in The New York Times, Jan. 5, 1994, p. A10.

[55] See Adler, op. cit., p.77.

also will have to file reports to government agencies on these processes for safety, environmental and other legitimate government concerns. Companies became concerned that competitors could avoid the expense of research and development by waiting for companies to file their government-required reports and then getting the information through FOIA. The result was a revolt in the private sector and threats to refuse to comply with government reporting requirements unless protections for trade secrets were put into place.

Exemption 5—Inter–and Intra–Agency Memoranda. Allan Adler and co-authors claim this is the most unclear exemption in terms of its definition. It protects "predecisional documents" (presumably, "working papers") from discovery processes. Also, if a government investigation is stalled and no action is taken, the papers attached to that process would be "predecisional."[56]

This exemption was expanded by the U.S. Supreme Court in Federal Open Market Committee of the Federal Reserve Board v. Merrill (1979). There, the Supreme Court upheld an agency's refusal to release monthly policy directives if they contained sensitive information not otherwise available, and if release of the directives would significantly harm the government's monetary functions or commercial interests.[57]

Exemption 6—The "Privacy Exemption." (Personnel, medical, and similar records which could not be disclosed without a "clearly unwarranted invasion" of privacy.) Privacy is an important value in the United States, both sociologically and legally. As important as privacy is, there are countervailing—and sometimes more important—virtues in openness.

The phrase "similar records" in this exemption has taken material exempted from disclosure well beyond personnel or medical files. For example, in U.S. Department of State v. Washington Post, the newspaper sought to confirm information that officials of Iran's revolutionary government held U.S. passports/visas. The Department of State denied this information on grounds that its release might endanger the Iranians, and the Supreme Court upheld the refusal to release this information.[58]

In New York Times Co. v. NASA, the newspaper asked for a duplicate of the tape recording of the voices of astronauts aboard

---

[56] See Adler, op. cit., p. 105, citing case involving Inspector General's evaluation of evidence against two military officers; evidence not released because it was "predecisional;" see Providence Journal v. U.S. Department of the Army, 981 F.2d 552 (1st Cir.1992).

[57] Madens, op. cit., p. 155; Federal Open Market Committee of the Federal Reserve System v. Merrill, 443 U.S. 340, 99 S.Ct. 2800 (1979).

[58] U.S. Department of State v. Washington Post, 456 U.S. 595, 102 S.Ct. 1957 (1982).

the Challenger space shuttle at the time of its explosion on January 28, 1986. The National Aeronautics and Space Administration declined to release a copy of the tape, which had been recovered from the ocean floor. The New York Times then filed suit under the FOIA, but the Court of Appeals found that the tape might be a "similar record" to a medical or personnel file, and remanded the case to a district court.[59] The district court then asserted that "[e]xposure to the voice of a beloved family member immediately prior to that family member's death is what would cause the Challenger families pain." The district court held that the families' privacy interest " * * *outweighs the public interest such that release of the tape would constitute a clearly unwarranted invasion of the families' personal privacy."[60]

Exemption 7—Investigatory files compiled for law enforcement purposes. This exemption is quoted at length, because it provides so many loopholes for federal investigatory agencies—most notably the Federal Bureau of Investigation—to withhold information. Exemption 7 says that the FOIA does not apply to information or records

> * * * compiled for law enforcement purposes, but only to the extent that the production of such law enforcement records or information (A) could reasonably be expected to interfere with enforcement proceedings, (B) would deprive a person of a fair trial or a right to an impartial adjudication, (C) could reasonably be expected to constitute an unwarranted invasion of personal privacy, (D) could reasonably be expected to disclose the identity of a confidential source, including a state, local or foreign agency or authority or any private institution which furnished information on a confidential basis * * * or information compiled by a criminal law enforcement authority * * * or by an agency conducting a lawful national security intelligence investigation, information furnished by a confidential source, (E) would disclose techniques or procedures for law enforcement investigations or prosecutions * * *, or (F) could reasonably be expected to endanger the life or physical safety of any individual.

A key case showing the slipperiness of this exemption for those seeking records access is Federal Bureau of Investigation v. Abramson (1982). Journalist Howard Abramson was investigating President Richard Nixon's use of the FBI to collect information on persons he considered his political "enemies," the better to harass

---

[59] New York Times Co. v. NASA, 920 F.2d 1002 (D.C.Cir.1990), 18 Med.L.Rptr. 1465.

[60] New York Times Co. v. NASA, 782 F.Supp. 628, 631, 633 (D.D.C.1991), 19 Med.L.Rptr. 1688, 1691, 1693.

them. Abramson asked for the files on such "enemies" under the FOIA. The FBI rejected the request, calling release of the information an "unwarranted invasion of privacy" under Exemption 7(C) (quoted above), and also under Exemption 6, which also deals with privacy.

In United States v. Landano (1993), however, the Supreme Court may have put a crimp in the FBI blanket use of Exemption 7(D), records or information compiled for law enforcement purposes that could reasonably be expected to disclose the identity of a confidential source.

Convicted cop-killer Vincent Landano argued that his claims of innocence were thwarted because the FBI refused to release sufficiently complete records that could cast doubt on his guilt. The FBI had interpreted Exemption 7(D) as giving it virtually unlimited authority to protect from disclosure confidential sources or the material they provide.[61]

Writing for a unanimous court, Justice Sandra Day O'Connor declared it is unreasonable to assume that all FBI investigative sources are confidential.[62]

> We think this more particularized approach is consistent with Congress' intent to provide " 'workable rules' " of FOIA disclosure. Department of Justice v. Reporters Committee, 489 U.S. at 779; 16 Med.L.Rptr. 1545, quoting FTC v. Grolier, 462 U.S. 19, 27, 103 S.Ct. 2209 (1983); see also EPA v. Mink, 410 U.S. 73, 80, 93 S.Ct. 827 (1973), 1 Med.L.Rptr. 2448. The government does not deny that, when a document is requested, it generally will be possible to establish factors such as the nature of the crime that was investigated and the source's relation to it. Armed with this information, the requester will have a more realistic opportunity to develop an argument that the circumstances do not support an inference of confidentiality.

Long delays, high costs for searching and copying documents, and widespread agency reluctance to comply with the original act's provisions characterized its early history.[63] Not only were several exemptions tightened by the amendments; also, rules were passed

---

[61] U.S. Department of Justice v. Landano, 508 U.S. 165, 171, 113 S.Ct. 2014, 2019, 2023 (1993); Linda Greenhouse, "Court Limits Shielding F.B.I. Sources," The New York Times, May 25, 1994, p.A7.

[62] Ibid., pp. 2023–2024.

[63] Wallis McClain, "Implementing the Amended FOI Act," Freedom of Information Center Report No. 343, Sept. 1975, p. 1; U.S. Congress, Freedom of Information Act and Amendments of 1974 (P.L. 93–502) Source Book: Legislative History, Texts, and Other Documents. Joint Committee Print (94th Cong., 1 Sess.), Washington: U.S. Government Printing Office, March 1975.

requiring agencies to inform persons making requests for information within ten days whether or not access would be granted, and to decide upon requests for appeals within 20 days. Uniform schedules of fees—limited to reasonable standard charges for document search and copying—were also mandated in the amendments.[64]

The amendments brought a flood of requests for information, primarily from persons who asked the FBI, the CIA, and the IRS, whether files were kept on them, and, if so, what the files contained. The Justice Department was receiving 2,000 requests per month by August 1975.[65] Media requests mounted under the amendments. One study found more than 400 between 1972 and 1984, but said that was far fewer than the actual total. Another study found that almost 50% of its list came from "public interest" groups, and about one-fourth from media.[66]

Court cases decided under the Act as of mid–1976 totaled 295, half of them less than two years old.[67] The increase suggested the impact of the 1975 amendments. Actions concerning investigatory files (Exemption 7) outstripped the pre-amendments leaders, agency memoranda and trade secrets (Exemptions 5 and 4). One important change provided for *in camera* review by judges of documents which the Executive Branch might refuse to open on grounds of national defense or foreign policy (Exemption 1). Under the original FOI Act, Congress had not provided this, but rather, said Justice Stewart in an acid concurring opinion, had simply chosen "to decree blind acceptance of Executive fiat" that secrecy was called for.[68]

From government's side of the desk, the FOI Act takes too much time and money. A Congressional study in 1985 showed that in a year's time, the Federal FOI Act drew 248,000 total requests. Although some agencies approved over 90 percent of the FOI requests, the study did not control for delays in providing information or in fee waivers granted. The Department of State granted less than 30 per cent of its more than 3,000 requests for informa

[64] Anon., "FOI Act Amendments Summarized," FOI Digest, 17:1, Jan.-Feb. 1975, p. 5.

[65] Anon., "FOI Act: Access Increases, Some Nagging Problems Remain," FOI Digest, 17:4, July-Aug. 1975, p. 5, citing Wall Street Journal, June 27, 1975; John A. Jenkins, "Ask, and You Shall Receive," Quill, July–Aug. 1975, pp. 22, 24.

[66] Ibid., quoting Attorney Ronald Plesser, 22; Anon., Media Use of FOIA Documented in New Study, 10 Med.L.Rptr. #34, 8/21/84, News Notes, quoting a study done for the House Subcommittee on Government Information, Justice, and Agriculture; Sam Archibald, Use of the FOIA, Freedom of Information Report #457, May 1982, 3 (Univ. of Mo.).

[67] Anon., "Justice Dept. Indexes Decided FOIA Cases," FOI Digest, 18:5, Sept.-Oct. 1976, p. 5, citing Congressional Record, Senate, Aug. 2, 1976, p. S13028.

[68] Environmental Protection Agency v. Mink, 410 U.S. 73, 95, 93 S.Ct. 827, 840 (1973).

tion, according to the House Subcommittee on Government Information.

With the deluge of requests for information came growing complaints from government agencies that it was too costly and too time-consuming to process FOI Act requests. Costs to the Treasury Department in 1978 alone totaled more than $6 million,[69] and CIA Director William Casey said that FOIA and Privacy Act (below) requests of the agency required 257,420 man-hours of service at a cost of about $2 million. Agencies complained that the act was used by law firms and commercial competitors to learn trade secrets and government enforcement policies, by foreign agents to gain national security information, and by organized crime to discover and thwart criminal investigations.[70]

Congressional efforts to restrict access to various agencies by amending the FOI Act never stop. The 1980s saw several. With President Ronald Reagan's support, the Central Intelligence Agency was authorized by law in 1984 to exempt its operational files on sources and methods from disclosure. In 1983, the 97th Congress passed six measures authorizing withholding by agencies that deal with trade, consumer product safety, income tax, energy, and health.[71]

The FOI Reform Act of 1986

Efforts to "improve" or "reform" the Freedom of Information Act mean different things to different people. The "Freedom of Information Reform Act of 1986" had some good news and some bad news for reporters. Apparently to the good, the Act required the Office of Management and Budget (OMB) to allow up to 100 pages of document copying free to journalists, and to make charges only for duplication on lengthier requests. Also helpful is allowing FOI requests of demonstrable importance to the public—e.g. reporters investigating an environmental hazard—to get speeded-up treatment for such requests.

On the other hand, journalists or citizens seeking information about businesses could face tougher slogging. Under the Reform Act, in order to protect proprietary information for businesses, the businesses named in information requests are to be notified. Then, they have 35 days to oppose disclosure. At the same time, Sen.

---

[69] "Diverse Legislative Efforts To Amend the FOIA Increase," FOI Digest, Jan.-Feb. 1980, 22:1, p. 5. Rod Perlmutter, Proposed FOIA Amendments—2, Freedom of Information Report #451, Jan. 1982 (Univ. of Mo.).

[70] "Congress, Courts Mutilate FOI Act," News Media & The Law, Aug.-Sept. 1980, 4:3, p. 16.

[71] Anon., CIA Exemption Bill Passed, News Media & the Law, Nov./Dec. 1984; 8 Med.L.Rptr. #46, 1/25/83, News Notes; Anon., Note, Developments under the Freedom of Information Act 1983, 1984 Duke Law J. 377, 382; News Media & the Law, Sept./Oct. 1983, 24.

Orrin Hatch (R–Utah) successfully sponsored an amendment to a drug control bill which provided broader FOI exemptions for investigatory records of law enforcement agencies.[72]

The Electronic Freedom of Information Act

A significant change in the FOI Act came in September 1996 when Congress passed the Electronic Freedom of Information Act. The Act, sponsored in some form since 1991 by Sen. Patrick Leahy (D–Vt.), brings FOIA into the electronic age by widening the definition of records and requiring on-line access to them.[73] The definition of a record now includes information stored electronically. That change addressed concerns about agencies storing vast quantities of information in databases and then refusing to create software to retrieve particular records.

The changes also require that records created on or after Nov. 1, 1996 be made available for inspection or copying on-line as well as in hard copy form. If an agency does not maintain on-line capabilities, the information must be made available through some other electronic means such as diskette or on CD–ROM. Agencies were to have complied with this in November 1997. Agencies also must make reasonable efforts to conduct database searches, except where such searches would significantly interfere with their operations. Requesters also may specify the format and form they want to receive the record it, provided the information can readily be produced in that format.

Agencies also benefitted from the changes. Starting in November 1997, agencies had 20 working days to decide whether to grant or deny a request. This is not as significant a change as it might seem. Under the old Act, agencies had 10 working days, but in practice the 10–working-day rule was ineffective. Requesters often referred to the Freedom of Information Act as the Freedom to Delay Information Act. Agencies could extend their processing time if they could show "unusual circumstances." Heavy work loads and short staffs combined to make the unusual the norm. A story in Media Daily in June of 1996 showed the FBI with 15,000 requests awaiting action. A Bureau spokesman reportedly said that the average turnaround time was 923 days, more than two years.

President Clinton's 1994 Memo: Reversing the Reagan–Bush "Culture of Secrecy?"

William Jefferson Clinton's first two years in the White House might optimistically be called "embattled." First Lady Hillary Rod-

[72] Public L. No. 99–570; see also News Media & the Law, Fall, 1986, pp. 28–29, and Spring, 1987, pp. 31–32.

[73] " 'EFOIA' Opened Electronic Data, Speeds Access," The News Media and The Law, Fall 1996, p. 14.

ham Clinton took heat for her reluctance to make certain meetings and records open while chairing the President's Task Force on Health Care Reform. In fact, a federal district court told Mrs. Clinton that under the Federal Advisory Committee Act (FACA) that she must open information-gathering sessions of the Task Force to the public.[74]

The Clintons already were on the political defensive over charges of covering up their involvement in an Arkansas land development called Whitewater. Also involved were loans from a now-defunct savings and loan. The Clintons' 1994 reluctance to make information as freely available as their critics demanded was disruptive to the Administration.[75]

Despite such travails, President Clinton issued an October, 1993, Memorandum on Open Government, countermanding President Ronald Reagan's restrictive 1981 Executive Order. That Reagan Executive Order also had flourished under President George H.W. Bush, and in effect declared that whenever and wherever possible, federal agency records were presumed to be closed.[76]

In what was called the first major step of the Clinton Administration toward greater disclosure, the President and Attorney General Janet Reno demanded a new policy of openness.[77] In his memo, President Clinton urged that federal agencies handle information requests in a "customer-friendly manner," saying that the "existence of unnecessary bureaucratic hurdles" has no place in the implementation of the Freedom of Information Act (FOIA). He called for reduction of information request backlogs, and that federal agencies conform to new guidelines issued in 1994 by Attorney General Reno.

Attorney General Reno's memorandum specifically rescinded the Department of Justice's 1981 guidelines [issued pursuant to President Reagan's 1981 Executive Order]. She stated that the Department of Justice

> * * *will no longer defend an agency's withholding of information merely because there is a "substantial legal

[74] Association of American Physicians and Surgeons, Inc. v. Clinton, 813 F.Supp. 82 (D.D.C.1993), 21 Med.L.Rptr. 1225, also holding that the Task Force could hold secret meetings while forming policy recommendations to go to the President. See also Robert Pear, "Court Rules That the First Lady is a 'De Facto' Federal Official," The New York Times, June 23, 1993, p. A1.

[75] See, e.g., "Whitewater Torture," Newsweek, March 14, 1994, pp. 20ff.

[76] Tim Weiner, "U.S. Plans Secrecy Overhaul to Open Millions of Records," The New York Times, March 18, 1994, p. A1.

[77] "Clinton Memorandum on Administration of the Freedom of Information Act," and the Attorney General's "Memorandum for Heads of Departments and Agencies," Oct. 4, 1993, available from the White House, Office of Press Secretary, (202) 456–2100, or from records available via Internet. Thanks to Professor Dorothy Bowles, University of Tennessee, for capturing this and other key documents.

basis" for doing so. Rather, in determining whether or not to defend a nondisclosure decision, we will apply a "presumption of disclosure."

Such words had a welcome sound to journalists or other citizens who seek access to federal government information via the FOIA. As a practical matter, however, the Clinton Administration (or its successors) seem to have limited ability to make changes in the federal culture of closure. As Harry Hammitt of Access Reports pointed out in the I R E Journal [Investigative Reporters and Editors], application of exemptions to openness in the Freedom of Information Act (FOIA) no longer is as discretionary as once it was. Hammitt wrote that although some discretion remains,[78]

> * * *that discretion is circumscribed by case law. The case law in the 1980s and 1990s has tilted considerably in favor of the government. What this means in a practical sense is that the parameters of agency discretion to release become narrower.

One example of such narrowing emphasized by Hammitt is the 1989 decision of the U.S. Supreme Court in U.S. Department of Justice v. Reporters Committee for Freedom of the Press.[79] In that case, the Reporters Committee's efforts to get criminal history records ran afoul of the Federal Privacy Act. That effort to get FBI criminal identification records—"rap sheets"—was halted by the Court's unanimous[80] decision that releasing such records would violate the FOIA's Exemption 6, constituting a "clearly unwarranted invasion of privacy."

As Hammitt noted, that Supreme Court decision has closed a great deal of information, because the Court made it easier for an agency to refuse to release personnel information or other government files. No longer did the agency have to bear the burden of showing that the files would amount to a "clearly unwarranted invasion of privacy." Instead, because the 1989 decision reversed the standard of proof, the requester received the burden of trying to prove that a record containing personal information ought to be released.[81]

Exemption 1, the national security exemption, temporarily was clarified in an executive order by President Jimmy Carter, effective in 1978, which imposed stricter minimum standards on classification of material. If the disclosure "reasonably could be expected to

---

[78] Harry Hammitt, "Open Government under the Clinton Administration: What can we expect?", The I R E Journal, Jan.-Feb. 1994, p. 6.

[79] Ibid., p. 7; U.S. Department of Justice v. Reporters Committee for Freedom of the Press, 489 U.S. 749, 109 S.Ct. 1468 (1989), 16 Med.L.Rptr. 1545.

[80] 489 U.S. 749, 109 S.Ct. 1468 (1989), 16 Med.L.Rptr. 1545. Justice Stevens delivered the opinion of the Court, with Blackmun, with whom Brennan joined, concurring.

[81] Ibid.; see also Hammitt, p. 7.

cause *identifiable* damage to national security," the information was confidential. However, any reasonable doubt should be resolved in favor of declassification, if the public interest in disclosure outweighed the damage to national security that "might be reasonably expected from disclosure."[82] This presumption favoring disclosure was changed by a March, 1981, Executive Order by President Ronald Reagan, in effect telling federal agencies, in effect, to move from President Carter's presumption of openness to a presumption of disclosure.

Exemption 1 was also the target of suits involving the definition of "possession" of records. In Forsham v. Harris, a 1980 Supreme Court decision, Justice Rehnquist stated that written data held by a private research firm receiving federal grant money from HEW were not "agency records" if the agency providing the funds had not yet obtained possession of the data. The FOI Act provided no direct access to such data; therefore, HEW had not improperly "withheld" the data. The Act applied not to records that could exist, but only to records that did exist.[83]

In Kissinger v. Reporters Committee for Freedom of the Press, the Supreme Court held that the State Department had not "withheld" records of former Secretary of State Henry Kissinger's phone calls by failing to file a lawsuit to recover documents which Kissinger had improperly donated to the Library of Congress, and which would be unavailable to the public for 25 years.[84] A Justice Department suit was considered, and Kissinger later agreed to a new review of documents to determine whether they are needed for departmental files.[85]

In other developments related to national security, a federal district court judge ruled in Hayden v. National Security Agency/Central Security Service that disclosure of the existence of particular records, obtained through NSA monitoring of foreign electromagnetic signals, could be withheld, since the existence of such records might be more sensitive than their substance

Using the FOIA

The FOI Service Center, a project of the Reporters Committee on Freedom of the Press, periodically issues updated booklets titled "How to Use the FOI Act." This useful guide summarizes the uses

---

[82] Alan S. Madens, "Developments Under the Freedom of Information Act—1979," 1980 Duke L.J. 139, 146–147.

[83] "The Supreme Court 1979 Term," 94 Harv.L.Rev. 1, 232–237 (1980); Forsham v. Harris, 445 U.S. 169, 100 S.Ct. 977 (1980).

[84] "The Supreme Court 1979 Term," Harv.L.Rev. 1, 232–235; Kissinger v. Reporters Committee for Freedom of the Press, 445 U.S. 136, 100 S.Ct. 960 (1980), 6 Med.L.Rptr. 1001.

[85] "Nixon Tapes Available to Public: Archives Requests More Materials," FOI Digest, May–June 1980, 22:3, p. 1.

of the FOIA as a news-gathering tool, and also provides thumbnail sketches of the Act's disclosure exemptions. This is truly a "do-it-yourself" guide, and even includes sample FOI Act request letters—and, if needed—sample appeal letters. This material is available from The Reporters Committee, 1101 Wilson Blvd., Suite 1910, Arlington, VA 22209.

Essentially, a requester identifies a likely agency to have the records, files a request and then waits for the agency to make a decision about release. Choosing the right agency is sometimes easy and sometimes difficult. If you lived near an Air Force base where nuclear-equipped bombers were stationed, where would you send your request? It seems logical to say the Air Force or the Department of Defense. The proper agency, though, is the Department of Energy. Thermonuclear devices fall under the Energy Department.

Once the agency has the request, it has 20 working days to make its decision. As mentioned earlier on, this probably will not be the case. Backlogs, time needed for research and labor shortages all add up to increased delays. If the agency decided to give you the information, everything ends. If the agency declines to give you the information, it must write to you explaining the exemption it claims. You have the option of appealing administratively to the agency or going to federal court. Administrative appeals take another "20 working days" and the agency can either change its mind or stick with its denial.

If you decide to sue, you have a choice of filing in the federal court district where you live, the district where the records are kept or the District of Columbia (home to all executive agencies). The court will look at what you are requesting and the reasons the government offers for claiming its exemption. Whoever wins faces the possibility of an appeal to the next higher level by the losing side. The Supreme Court is the last court of appeal for FOIA cases.

Investigating the Death of Karen Silkwood

Attempts by media to open records through court cases commonly run afoul of Exemptions 7 and 5—investigatory files and agency memoranda—source materials which are often expected by media to be relevant to criminal activity. National Public Radio, for example, sought disclosure of records compiled by the Justice Department and the FBI about the perplexing death of Karen Silkwood. An employee of a manufacturer of plutonium and uranium fuels for nuclear reactors, Silkwood was reportedly driving to attend a meeting with a union official and a newspaper reporter when she was killed in an auto crash. Uncertain evidence suggested that her car might have been driven off the road by another car, and that a file of documents she was supposedly carrying was not recovered. NPR also sought the record of the agency's investigation of the contamination of Silkwood by plutonium.

The Justice Department furnished NPR with some of the requested materials, but refused others. The parts of the death investigation file withheld were the "closing memoranda"—agency materials prepared during its final deliberations—and about 15 pages of notes and working papers of Justice Department attorneys. The Justice Department said that exemption 5 of the FOI Act— intra-agency memoranda or letters—protected these materials from disclosure. The Federal district court agreed,[86] saying the agency memoranda are protected as "papers which reflect the agency's group thinking in the process of working out its policy and determining what its law shall be."[87] The court rejected NPR's argument that the memoranda were "final" opinions, which under the Supreme Court's interpretation of the FOI Act would have been subject to disclosure.[88]

As for Exemption 7 of the FOI Act, protecting from disclosure matters which are "investigatory records compiled for law enforcement purposes" whose release would "interfere with enforcement proceedings * * *.": This applied to the Justice Department investigation of Silkwood's contamination by plutonium, and the court said that the records of the case suggested law-violation in materials-handling by personnel. It said that Congress' intent in writing Exemption 7 was plainly to prevent harm to a "concrete prospective law enforcement proceeding" that might result from disclosure of information. And though the department's leads in the investigation had currently run out, and want of finances for the moment precluded assignment of an investigator to the case, the case was "active." Disclosure would present "the very real possibility of a criminal learning in alarming detail of the government's investigation of his crime before the government has had the opportunity to bring him to justice," said the court in rejecting NPR's request.[89]

"Reverse FOIA Suits"

The recorded word, in literally billions of pages of government documents, is the focus of the FOI Act, dedicated to dissemination

---

[86] National Public Radio et al. v. Bell, 431 F.Supp. 509 (D.D.C.1977), 2 Med. L.Rptr. 1808.

[87] Ibid.

[88] N.L.R.B. v. Sears, Roebuck & Co., 421 U.S. 132, 95 S.Ct. 1504 (1975).

[89] National Public Radio et al. v. Bell, 431 F.Supp. 509 (D.D.C.1977). The investigatory exemption was tightened in lower court cases. Records must be both investigatory *and* compiled for law enforcement purposes: Pope v. United States, 599 F.2d 1383 (5th Cir.1979). The information must be originally gathered for law enforcement purposes: Gregory v. Federal Deposit Insurance Corp., 470 F.Supp. 1329 (D.D.C.1979), reversed in part 631 F.2d 896 (D.C.Cir.1980). Courts have given mixed reactions to records for "improper" investigations. See Lamont v. Department of Justice, 475 F.Supp. 761 (S.D.N.Y.1979), and Irons v. Bell, 596 F.2d 468 (1st Cir.1979). See also Madens, op. cit., at 162–163.

of this record. But developments during 1979 and 1980 included two Supreme Court decisions involving "reverse-FOI Act" suits, in which persons or organizations submitting information to a federal agency sought to prevent disclosure in response to FOI Act requests. In Chrysler Corp. v. Brown, the Court banned such suits under the FOI Act, stating that while exempt records could be withheld, the Act did not *require* nondisclosure.[90] However, in GTE Sylvania, Inc. v. Consumers Union, the Consumer Product Safety Act was used successfully to exempt information from release unless its accuracy is verified first.[91]

FOIA Successes

While the case reporters have many cases where government agencies have managed to thwart inquiries into their activities, FOIA and the genuine interest on the part of some public servants have allowed us to pierce the veil of secrecy of government. In many cases, the veil covered up horrendous conduct.

The U.S. Army conducted biological warfare tests around Washington, D.C., in the 1960s. Operatives sprayed travelers at a bus station with bacillus subtilis, a common bacteria, believed at the time to be harmless. Scientists later discovered that concentrated exposure could interfere with the immune systems of the elderly or those with debilitating diseases.[92] In all, disclosures by the government showed that the Army conducted 239 secret tests of germ warfare in American cities. The Army also sprayed a chemical, later determined to be potentially cancer-causing, over Minneapolis in 1953.[93]

An FOI request revealed that a U.S. Air Force bomber accidentally dropped a hydrogen bomb near Albuquerque, New Mexico. The bomb, a 10–megaton bomb, fell from a B–36 bomber returning to base after practice maneuvers. Although the conventional explosives in the bomb detonated, the safety devices prevented a thermonuclear explosion.[94]

90 Madens, op. cit., pp. 141–142. See also Chrysler Corp. v. Brown, 441 U.S. 281, 99 S.Ct. 1705 (1979).

91 "Safety Data Release Depends On Who Reaches Courtroom First," News Media & The Law, Feb.–March 1981, 5:1, p. 49; GTE Sylvania, Inc. v. Consumers Union, 445 U.S. 375, 100 S.Ct. 1194 (1980); Consumer Product Safety Commission v. GTE Sylvania, Inc., 447 U.S. 102, 100 S.Ct. 2051 (1980).

92 "Army Germ Experiments Reported," Facts of File Digest, De. 21, 1984. Disclosures about another secret biological warfare test, this one off the West Coast near San Francisco, led to a lawsuit by the family of a man who believe exposure to the bacteria used caused his death.

93 "Toxic Test by Army in '53 Taints Minneapolis' Past," The Orlando Sentinel, June 12, 1994, A–22.

94 "U.S. Air Force Reveals Hydrogen Bomb Dropped Accidentally," Reuters News Service, Aug. 28, 1986.

Other disclosures showed that the FBI's COINTELPRO program had been used to spy on and harass Vietnam War protestors, that the FBI had the contents of a briefcase stolen from the 1968 Socialist Workers Party candidate for the presidency, that the CIA tried to get the gall bladder and other poisonous parts of a Tanganyikan crocodile and the services of a witch doctor to show them how to make poison from the parts.[95]

FOIA disclosures led to the indictments and convictions of meat processors who had processed cows that died before making it to the slaughterhouse, revealed that plumbing valves purchased for $11 were being sold to the government for $140 apiece, uncovered evidence that defense contractors were charging the government to pay for their Washington lobbyists and that the Nixon administration tried to set up a drug bust on Beatle John Lennon in order to be able to deport him.[96]

Seth Rosenfeld sued the Department of Justice and the Federal Bureau of Investigation under FOIA. A journalist, Rosenfeld sought information about FBI investigations of a number of individuals and protests at the University of California, Berkeley, during the 1960s.

Patiently, Rosenfeld filed open records requests with the FBI from late 1981 through early 1984, asking for FBI documents on investigations of people and organizations active in the Free Speech Movement (FSM) at Berkeley. The FBI found 8,432 documents relevant to Rosenfeld's requests, releasing 1,795 pages, plus another 4,985 in "redacted" form. The FBI withheld 1,652 pages in their entirety.

After lengthy litigation over documents in nine FBI files, the government appealed against release orders. But the appeal only dealt with three files. Those files contained information on the Free Speech Movement, US–Berkeley's then-president Clark Kerr, and journalist Marguerite Higgins. In 1991, the U.S. District Court for the Northern District of California ordered the release of all of the FSM documents generated after June 19, 1965, because none of the documents fell into the FOIA exemption for documents compiled for law enforcement purposes. The court also ordered the FBI files on Chancellor Kerr released as well.

The FBI appealed to the Ninth Circuit Court of Appeals.[97] The appellate court considered the governments reasons for wanting to keep the information from being disclosed. The government said

---

[95] Sid Moody, "Workings and Controversies of the Freedom of Information Act," The Associated Press, Jan. 11, 1985.

[96] Ibid.

[97] Rosenfeld v. U.S. Department of Justice, 57 F.3d 803 (9th Cir.1995), 23 Med.L.Rptr. 2102.

that it should withhold the documents because they were related to national security, were compiled for law enforcement purposes and, under that exemption, would disclose investigatory techniques, disclose confidential information and invade the privacy of the persons the FBI investigated.

The appellate court found that there was little to support a claim that the records would jeopardize national security. In the one instance where that occurred, the district court had allowed the government to delete information that would identify a confidential informant. The court also found that some documents were not really law enforcement documents because the investigations of the subjects were not carried out for purposes of law enforcement.

> Rosenfeld introduced evidence showing that the FBI waged a concerted effort in the late 1950s and 1960s to have Kerr fired from the presidency of UC–Berkeley. * * * We will not recite all of the documentation for this campaign to fire Kerr, but we will describe some of the highlights. FBI agents counted the number of Regents on Berkeley's Board of Regents who would support or oppose an attempt to have Kerr removed as President. One agent made a recommendation to the file in 1965 that Kerr be fired for his "lack of administration" during student protests. Last, then FBI–Director J. Edgar Hoover made a notation on the margin of one report that he knew "Kerr is no good."

> These documents all support a conclusion that these reports were compiled with no rational nexus to a plausible law enforcement purpose—that any asserted purpose for compiling these documents was pretextual. The later documents all strongly support the suspicion that the FBI was investigating Kerr to have him removed from the UC administration, because FBI officials disagreed with his politics or his handling of administrative matters. Conspicuously absent from these documents is any connection to any possible criminal liability by Kerr. [98]

The court also disposed of some of the privacy issues raised by the government saying that it was necessary to have the names of the persons investigated in order to be able to review the government's conduct. "The public interest in this case is knowing whether and to what extent the FBI investigated individuals for participating in political protests, not federal criminal activity. Disclosing the names of the investigation subjects would make it possible to compare the FBI's investigations to a roster of the FSM's leader-

[98] Ibid. At 809.

ship. Therefore, disclosing the names of investigation subjects promotes the public interest of this FOIA request."[99]

The Ninth Circuit upheld most of the district court's order, remanding parts of the order for some of the documents so that the district court could re-examine some privacy concerns for some of the persons identified in some of the documents.

Executive Privilege

A power of withholding has always been asserted by the President and his Executive Department heads. This is the power exercised under the doctrine of "executive privilege." President George Washington was asked by Congress to make available documents relating to General St. Clair's defeat by Indians. He responded that "the Executive ought to communicate such papers as the public good would permit, and ought to refuse those, the disclosure of which would injure the public * * *."[100] In this case the records were made available to Congress, but many Presidents since have refused to yield records, as have the heads of executive departments. Their power to do so was upheld early in the nation's history by the United States Supreme Court. The famous decision written by Chief Justice John Marshall was delivered in 1803 in Marbury v. Madison, where Marshall said that the Attorney General (a presidential appointee) did not have to reveal matters which had been communicated to him in confidence.[1]

> By the Constitution of the United States, the President is invested with certain important political powers, in the exercise of which he is to use his own discretion, and is accountable only to the country in his political character and to his own conscience.

Justice Marshall elaborated the principle in the trial of Aaron Burr, accused of treason, saying that "The propriety of withholding * * * must be decided by [the President] himself, not by another for him. Of the weight of the reasons for and against producing it he himself is the judge."[2]

Executive privilege came to be asserted and used increasingly during the government's efforts to maintain security in the cold war with the U.S.S.R. following World War II. Presidents Truman and Eisenhower used the power to issue orders detailing what might and might not be released from the executive departments;

[99] Ibid. At 812.

[100] Francis E. Rourke, Secrecy and Publicity (Baltimore: Johns Hopkins Press, 1961), p. 65. And see Ibid., pp. 64–69, for general discussion of executive privilege.

[1] 5 U.S. (1 Cranch) 137 (1803).

[2] 1 Burr's Trial 182.

both came under heavy attack from Congress and the news media.[3] President Nixon's Executive Order No. 11–652 of March 8, 1972, replaced and modified rules set by President Eisenhower.

One of the most far-reaching directives of this period was issued by President Eisenhower in 1954. A senate subcommittee was investigating a controversy between the Army and Senator Joseph McCarthy of Wisconsin. President Eisenhower sent to Secretary of the Army Robert Stevens a message telling him that his departmental employees were to say nothing about internal communications of the Department.[4]

> Because it is essential to efficient and effective administration that employees of the executive branch be in a position to be completely candid in advising with each other on official matters, and because it is not in the public interest that any of their conversations or communications, or any documents or reproductions, concerning such advice be disclosed, you will instruct employees of your Department that in all of their appearances before the subcommittee of the Senate Committee on Government Operations regarding the inquiry now before it they are not to testify to any such conversations or communications or to produce any such documents or reproductions.

While the directive was aimed at a single situation and a single Executive Department, it soon became used by many other executive and administrative agencies as justification for their own withholding of records concerning internal affairs.[5] While journalists protested the spread of the practice, and while Congressional allies joined them, there was not much legal recourse then apparent.

The President's powers to restrict access are substantial, used extensively by some and little by others. Journalists have widely asserted that President Ronald Reagan employed these powers more vigorously than his predecessors of many terms. In fact, one of President Reagan's directives placed a "lifelong" nondisclosure restriction on many government employees, although it was partially withdrawn. In his 1982 Executive Order 12,356, he tightened declassification rules set by President Jimmy Carter, permitting permanent exemption from disclosure of documents in the realm of national security and foreign policy. In 1981, he submitted proposals to the Senate to give the Attorney General power to exempt

---

[3] Rourke, pp. 75–83.

[4] House Report, No. 2947, 84 Cong., 2 Sess., July 27, 1956. "Availability of Information from Federal Departments and Agencies," Dwight D. Eisenhower to Sec. of Defense, May 17, 1954, pp. 64–65.

[5] Rourke, p. 74.

some kinds of intelligence files from disclosure. In 1983, the Justice Department, with his support, notably tightened the rules for waiving fees charged to those who seek information from government agencies. Under him as Commander in Chief, journalists were kept uninformed and were excluded from the armed forces' invasion of the Caribbean island of Grenada. Journalists found him and his administration much less accessible than his predecessor, and expert at frustrating reporters, one analyst declaring that "bureaucrats have largely succeeded in undermining the FOI Act at will."[6]

Access to federal officials' papers and claims of executive privilege were active issues during the latter half of the seventies. The Nixon papers cases and the Kissinger "phone calls" case both involved dispute about ownership of executive papers. President Carter signed the Presidential Records Act of 1978, effective January 1981, which clarified ownership of executive branch papers. The National Archives assumes control of presidential papers at the end of a president's last term. Records related to defense and foreign policy, plus presidential appointment records involving trade secrets, may be restricted for 12 years. Papers not restricted become available to the public under the FOI Act as soon as the Archives processes them.[7]

White House e-mail

The Presidential Records Act came into play at the end of the Reagan presidency when administration officials sought to erase e-mail communications in the White House computer system. Included in the e-mail were references to a number of projects, including the Iran–Contra affair. Journalist Scott Armstrong filed suit to prevent Reagan administration officials from sweeping the system. The judge in the case ruled that the government could not simply erase the records. First, it would have to set up a system to determine how to decide which records to keep and which to destroy. The result was the creation of an e-mail protocol. Under the rules, which went into effect in 1995, agencies will have to either automatically store business e-mail electronically or make print outs for delivery to the National Archives.

[6] Floyd Abrams, The New Effort to Control Information, New York Times Magazine, Sept. 25, 1983, 23; Government Shuts Up, Columbia Journalism Rev., July/Aug. 1982, 31; Executive Order No. 12356 on National Security Information, April 2, 1982, 8 Med.L.Rptr. 1306; 1984 Duke L.Journ. 377, 387, op. cit.; Anon., Reagan Signs New Secrecy Order to Seal More Public Documents, News Media & the Law, June/July 1982, 22; 8 Med.L.Rptr. #46, 1/25/83, News Notes; Anon., Coverage Efforts Thwarted, News Media & the Law, Jan.-Feb. 1984, 6; Carl Stepp, Grenada Skirmish over Access Goes On, SPJ/SDX, Freedom of Information 84–'85, Report, 5; Steve Weinberg, Trashing the FOIA, Columbia Journalism Rev., Jan./Feb. 1985, 21, 22; Donna A. Demac, Keeping America Uninformed (N.Y., 1984).

[7] Robert Schwaller, "Access to Federal Officials' Papers," FOI Center Report No. 411, October 1979, pp. 7, 8.

Armstrong also sued the Clinton Administration over records created and held by the National Security Council. Armstrong argued that the NSC should classify records held in its computers as either records subject to the Presidential Records Act or the Federal Records Act. Clinton declared the NSC was not an agency and therefore not subject to the FOIA. The District Court for the District of Columbia, noting the NSC's treatment as an agency in previous administrations, ruled that the NSC was, in fact, an agency. It would then have to comply with FOIA and the Federal Records Act for classifying and storing records. But Armstrong lost in the District of Columbia Court of Appeals, which ruled that the NSC was not an agency because it did not meet the test for agency classification. Instead, the majority concluded, the NSC was more like a presidential staff. Under that analysis, the NSC was not bound by the FOIA or Federal Records Act. The Supreme Court declined to take the case.

Privacy Act of 1974

"After long years of debate, a comprehensive federal privacy law passed the Congress * * * as a solid legislative decision in favor of individual privacy and the 'right to be let alone'," writes attorney James T. O'Reilly.[8] It is a statute shaped to deal with the federal government's gargantuan systems of secret dossiers on citizens, to give citizens access to the content of files that may be kept on them, and to provide citizens with a means for correcting inaccurate content of these files. If agencies are not responsive in making changes, civil suits may be brought against them. A crucial element in the law is that no file may be transferred from one agency to another without the individual's consent, except where the purpose squares with the purpose for which the information was collected.

Under the law, a supposedly exhaustive index to all federal government "data banks" or personal information systems on individuals has been published. Also published in the Federal Register are the categories of individuals on whom records are maintained, and where one can learn whether a particular government agency has information about him.[9] No citizen who inquires about himself need give any reason for a request to examine the record, and may obtain a copy. Some exceptions to citizen access are provided, mostly dealing with law enforcement agencies' rec-

---

[8] "The Privacy Act of 1974," Freedom of Information Report No. 342, Sept. 1975, p. 1.

[9] Anon., "Citizens' Guide to Privacy Act Available," FOI Digest, 18:2 (March–April 1976), p. 2. For an editor's struggle of more than a year to get a file kept on him by the FBI, see John Seigenthaler, "Publisher Finally Gets His FBI Files, or Some of Them," (Memphis) Tennessean, July 10, 1977. False accusations, the FBI said after finally releasing contents of the file, would be purged.

ords, and including, notably, the CIA and the Secret Service.[10] However, foreign nationals working for the government have no access rights to personnel records about themselves under either the FOI Act or the Privacy Act, according to a U.S. Court of Appeals.[11]

Privacy issues intensified during the 1970s and 1980s, as individuals made greater use of the Privacy Act to see records maintained about them and to amend those records or correct inaccuracies.[12] States also were active in protecting privacy of financial, medical, and criminal records.[13]

Recall that privacy issues also are part of the FOIA; as noted at earlier, Exemptions 6 (personnel or medical files) and 7 (law enforcement investigatory files) both list privacy. In U.S. Department of Justice v. Reporters Committee for Freedom of the Press, the U.S. Supreme Court held—in part for privacy reasons—that FBI "rap sheets"—records of a person's arrests, charges, and jailings. Release of such criminal identification records was held to be a "clearly unwarranted invasion of privacy" under the terms of the FOIA.[14] Most states—all but Wisconsin, Florida, and Oklahoma—follow the federal lead in withholding rap sheets from public inspection.[15]

The additional emphasis on secrecy brought about by the Privacy Act concerns some journalists about loss of inside sources of information in the federal government, and the possibility of tracing "leaks" through the agencies' records of who got access to various files.[16]

Government in the Sunshine Act

As the FOI Act is to federal government records, so the "Sunshine Act"[17] is to federal government meetings. The Act

[10] Anon., "Government Information and the Rights of Citizens," 73 Mich.L.Rev. 971, 1317. This study of more than 370 pages describes, analyzes, and criticizes the FOI Act, state open records and meetings laws, and the Privacy Act of 1974.

[11] Raven v. Panama Canal Co., 583 F.2d 169 (5th Cir.1978), certiorari denied 440 U.S. 980, 99 S.Ct. 1787 (1979). See also, "Allows Personnel Files to be Kept From Alien," News Media & The Law, March–April 1980, 4:2, p. 31.

[12] In 1977, of 1,417,214 requests, 1,355,515 were granted either entirely or in part: "Privacy Roundup: Report Shows Increasing Use of Privacy Act by Individuals," FOI Digest, July–Aug. 1978, 20:4, p. 2.

[13] "Poll Shows Privacy Concerns Rising," FOI Digest, May–June 1979, 21:3, p. 2.

[14] U.S. Department of Justice v. Reporters Committee on Freedom of the Press, 489 U.S. 749, 109 S.Ct. 1468 (1989), 16 Med.L.Rptr. 1545.

[15] Ibid., 489 U.S. at 750, 109 S.Ct. at 1470, 16 Med.L.Rptr. at 1547.

[16] Lyle Denniston, "A Citizen's Right to Privacy," Quill, 63:4, April 1975, p. 16. See also Editor & Publisher, Jan. 31, 1976, p. 9.

[17] 5 U.S.C.A. § 552b. The FOI Act and the Privacy Act of 1974 are in the federal statutes under the same number, as 5 U.S.C.A. § 552a and 5 U.S.C.A. § 552c respectively.

mandates open meetings for regular sessions and quorum gatherings of approximately 50 agencies—all those headed by boards of two or more persons named by the President and confirmed by the Senate. Included are the major regulatory agencies such as the Securities Exchange Commission and the Interstate Commerce Commission—whose meetings always had been secret—and such little-known entities as the National Council on Educational Research and the National Homeownership Foundation board of directors.[18]

All meetings of the named agencies are to be open—with at least one week's public notice—unless agendas take up matters in 10 categories which permit closed sessions. Either a verbatim transcript or detailed minutes of all matters covered in closed sessions is to be kept. And as for the record of open meetings, it is to be kept as minutes and made available to the public at minimal copying cost.

Closed-to-the-public meetings will hardly be rare, whatever strength the Sunshine Act may prove to generate. The ten categories of subject-matter whose discussion warrants closed doors for meetings of the boards and commissions are much like the exemptions to disclosure under the FOI Act. Abbreviated, the ten are:

1. National defense or foreign policy matters which are properly classified;

2. Internal agency personnel matters;

3. Matters expressly required by law to be held confidential;

4. Confidential commercial or financial information, and trade secrets;

5. Accusations of criminal activity, or of censure, against a person;

6. Matters which if disclosed would be clearly unwarranted invasions of a person's privacy;

7. Law enforcement and criminal investigatory records, subject to the same categories as FOI Act exemption (b)(7);

8. Bank examiners' records;

9. Matters which if disclosed would generate financial speculation (included to protect the Federal Reserve Board Open Market Committee) or which would frustrate agency action which has not been announced;

---

[18] Editor & Publisher, Feb. 26, 1977, p. 32. This account's details of the Sunshine Act are taken largely from James T. O'Reilly, "Government in the Sunshine," Freedom of Information Center Report 366, Jan. 1977; O'Reilly, p. 2.

10. Matters which involve the agency's issuance of a subpoena or participation in hearings or other adjudication-related proceedings.

It may prove significant that the ten exemptions of the Sunshine Act apply to the some 1,300 Advisory Committees spread throughout the Executive Branch of government. These committees of private citizens contribute expertise, advice, and recommendations to government policy making. The members tend to be prominent persons from industries which deal with the agencies they advise.

Ways exist for attacking illegal secrecy under the Sunshine Act. One may seek an injunction in advance to force a pending meeting to be open, and having found one illegal closing of an agency, a court may enjoin the agency from further illegal closings. One may sue, within 60 days after the secret meeting, to require that a transcript be furnished. No financial penalty for illegal meetings may be levied against members themselves, but courts may assign costs or fees against the United States—or against a plaintiff whose suit is found to be "dilatory or frivolous." The range of possibilities for future secrecy or openness is large, and the crystal balls of various observers offer varied forecasts of cheer and gloom.

Attorneys General

Attorneys general have been called on to interpret meetings and records laws in many states. As for meetings, it is occasionally feasible for a reporter to seek "instant action" in the form of an attorney general's opinion, perhaps by placing a phone call even while an illegal secret meeting is in session. Through such maneuvers, enterprising reporters have, on occasion, forced meetings open.

More likely, however, before an opinion can be had, the meeting will have adjourned. Nevertheless, either a formal opinion delivered at the request of a state government agency, or an informal one delivered at the request of a non-official person or entity—such as a reporter or a newspaper—can have a future impact on the behavior of the secretive group or agency. Reporters, of course, should read up on the open-records, open-meetings opinions of attorneys general. The attorney general interprets the law of a state; an "AG's opinion" does not have the force of a court opinion, but it is authoritative until a court has ruled on a particular question.[19]

---

[19] William Thompson, "FOI and State Attorneys General," Freedom of Information Center Report No. 307, July, 1973, University of Missouri.

SEC. 53. ACCESS TO "SECURITY" INFORMATION, COVERING WARS

As discussed elsewhere in this text, traditions of openness run afoul of restrictive executive orders, statutes and court decisions in areas where claims of "national security" are raised.

Access in the "Surveillance State"

It is likely that the crucial battle to preserve what journalists have come to see as the central meaning of the First Amendment will be fought in the arena of access to government information. What is talked about here goes beyond the traditional tugging and hauling between reporters and government. Resistance to access by government officials is to be expected: human nature, of course, dictates an unwillingness to look foolish, and government officials—like all of us—dislike revealing mistakes.

Extrapolating from the words of First Amendment historian Norman L. Rosenberg suggests a scary phrase, the "surveillance state." He wrote, "The central free-speech issue of the post-World War II era involved the expansion of a vast surveillance apparatus, the growing power of an increasingly monopolistic communications industry, and the problems of its ties to other private and public centers of power."[20]

Journalists—and all citizens and public officials—would do well to keep the phrase "surveillance state" in mind, for it conjures up a vision of a society where government watches the people but the people see only what government wants them to see. A surveillance state, in sum, is an old map of hell.

Anyone paying even scant attention to news reports during the late 1980s saw the phrase "national security" often used as a reason why documents could not be released—or used in a federal court—to try Lt. Col. Oliver North on criminal conspiracy charges coming out of the Iran–Contra affair. (North, along with retired Admiral John M. Poindexter, the former National Security Adviser to President Reagan, was the subject of criminal charges relating to illegal sale of arms to Iran and diversion of the proceeds to fund the Nicaraguan Contras.) With those classified documents unavailable, the main charges against North were dropped early in 1989. The Central Intelligence Agency, itself so clandestine that its budget is secret, opposed release of security-classified documents needed to bring North to trial.[21]

[20] Norman L. Rosenberg, Protecting the Best Men: An Interpretive History of Libel (Chapel Hill: University of North Carolina Press, 1986) p. 266.

[21] Marianne Means, "Dr. Strangelove's super-CIA scheme," column in Austin American–Statesman, July 18, 1987, p. A14; Stephen Engelberg, "Data Disclosure in Contra Case Fought by U.S.," The New York Times, June 4, 1988 (Nat'l. Ed.), p. 9;

The task for reporters or other citizens who try to keep tabs on what government has done or is doing is monumental. In 1988, fourteen years after President Richard M. Nixon resigned in the wake of the Watergate scandal, historian Dan T. Carter complained about difficulties in access to the Nixon Papers as he worked on a biography of former Alabama Governor George Wallace, pursuing tantalizing bits of evidence that Nixon's Republican White House had involved itself strangely in Wallace's Democratic and Third Party political campaigns in the early 1970s.

After Nixon left the White House, he claimed, through his lawyers, that the President had a right to bottle up or even get rid of materials relating to the Presidency. Congress then passed the 1974 Presidential Records Act, declaring Presidential records to be government property and ordering the National Archives to catalog the records, to cull them for national security and privacy-sensitive areas, and to release those records as soon as practicable.

The historian Carter wrote to The New York Times:[22]

Mr. Nixon's lawyers ... sent several representatives-untrained in historical study—or archival management—to conduct their own examination of the 1.5 million documents. In April 1987, less than a month before the scheduled opening of the first batch of papers, Mr. Nixon's lawyers demanded that an additional 150,000 documents be withheld.

It should be obvious that the existence of federal and state freedom of information acts does not mean that information is freely available. Ask any knowledgeable investigative reporter, and you will get a litany of complaints about problems in getting access. For example, James Derk of the Evansville (Ind.) Courier used the federal Freedom of Information Act (FOIA) to report on a regional airline.

Although, as described earlier in this chapter, there are—on paper—just nine broad exemptions to the Federal FOIA, Derk wrote: "I usually run into the unofficial 10th Exemption, known as the 'forget it' exemption." He noted that he received letters saying his requests had been denied for various reasons, or, at times, never got answers at all. "I've been waiting," Derk wrote late in 1988, "for more than two years for a response from the Department of Justice." He added:[23]

"House Sets Secret Sum for Intelligence Groups," A.P. story in The New York Times, June 10, 1987, p. 13.

[22] Dan T. Carter, "The Nixon Cover–Up Goes On," letter to The New York Times, July 25, 1988, p. 23.

[23] James Derk, "It takes a lot of persistence to make the Freedom of Information Act pay off," ASNE Bulletin, November, 1988, pp. 10–11.

When I get answers, often they are not the answers I sought.

* * *

In September, I received 1,150 pages of documents from the U.S. Environmental Protection Agency that I had requested in July. The documents were riddled with deletions and I ended up paying 15 cents a page for 118 blank pages, the contents of which were deemed too sensitive for public eyes.

Road-blocks to information often do seem excessive. John Weiner, a history professor reporting the life of former Beatle John Lennon, reported in 1988 that 14–year–old CIA and FBI files about the singer's anti-Vietnam War activities and his work against President Nixon's reelection were withheld. Professor Weiner asked, " 'How can 14–year–old documents on the peaceful activity of a dead rock singer jeopardize national security?' "[24]

Freedom of information requests, however frustrating they may be, can turn up useful results if persistence is maintained. Late in 1988, for example, it was reported by the Durham (N.C.) Morning Herald—which had received more than 2,000 pages in an FOIA request—that the Federal Bureau of Investigation had kept a confidential file on the Supreme Court of the United States from 1932 until at least 1985. That file included evidence that the FBI had wiretapped (evidently without warrants!) or monitored conversations involving four men on the Court, Chief Justice Earl Warren and Justices Abe Fortas, Potter Stewart, and William O. Douglas.[25]

CIA v. Sims (1985)

A case which provides a disturbing symbol of the power of claimed national security exemptions to shield federal agencies from scrutiny is CIA v. Sims (1985). This Orwellian nightmare of a case concerned a Freedom of Information Act lawsuit to get records on the Central Intelligence Agency's research project code-named MKULTRA. This project, started in 1953 when Richard Helms was CIA deputy director for planning, was to counter Chinese and Soviet advances in brainwashing and interrogation. From 1953 to 1965, the CIA contracted with numerous universities to test the efficacy of certain biological and chemical materials in altering human behavior.[26]

[24] "Educators Assailing Curbs on Data," The New York Times (Nat'l. Ed.), Sept. 14, 1988, p. 26.

[25] "FBI Kept Secret File on the Supreme Court," The New York Times, August 21, 1988, p. 13.

[26] CIA v. Sims, 471 U.S. 159, 161, 105 S.Ct. 1881, 1884 (1985), 11 Med.L.Rptr. 2017.

Sims and others sued in 1977 to discover which universities and individuals had taken part in this secret research, but were unsuccessful. The Supreme Court of the United States upheld lower court rulings saying that Exemption 3 of the FOIA Act, in concert with the National Security Act of 1947, allowed the Director of the CIA to decide what should or should not be released—in the national interest—to protect intelligence sources and methods from unauthorized disclosure.[27]

Hidden in that judicial/bureaucratic verbiage is a dangerous dilemma for a society which would be self-governing. If CIA v. Sims is put in human terms, it boils down to this: can a society which would be self-governing adopt the methods of totalitarianism (surreptitious administration of drugs such as LSD to unwitting "subjects?") And, when some aspects of those CIA research projects went terribly wrong—including death of at least two persons and the likelihood of impaired health for other "subjects"—the CIA attempted to cover its tracks.[28]

Because CIA budgetary records are secret, there is no way of tracking down the financial costs. But the MKULTRA project was massive: it consisted of some 149 subprojects which the CIA contracted out to various universities and research foundations. At least 80 institutions—including, apparently, major universities in the U.S. and even in Canada—and 185 private researchers took part in MKULTRA.[29]

But try to keep this in human terms: shouldn't the universities participating—and the researchers who took part in these bizarre and dangerous experiments—be identified? Or if you had a relative who had committed suicide after being dosed with LSD without his permission, in an MKULTRA "research project" might not you want to find out more, to confront those responsible?

According to the Supreme Court decision in CIA v. Sims, you'll get that information only if the Director of the CIA decides that its release would not be harmful to national security interests. And because the CIA had promised the researchers and their institutions—including universities—anonymity, the Director of the CIA could "properly" conclude that such information could not be released, in order to protect "intelligence sources."

The Supreme Court, in upholding the CIA Director's authority to withhold information, said:[30]

[27] 471 U.S. at 159, 164, 105 S.Ct. at 1882, 1885 (1985).

[28] 471 U.S. 159, 162n, 105 S.Ct. 1881, 1884n (1985).

[29] 471 U.S. at 162, 105 S.Ct. at 1884 (1985).

[30] Ibid., 471 U.S. at 181, 106 S.Ct. at 1894 (1985).

We hold that the Director of the Central Intelligence properly invoked § 102(d)(3) of the National Security Act of 1947 to withhold disclosure of the identities of the individual MKULTRA researchers as protected "intelligence sources." We also hold that the FOIA does not require the Director to disclose the institutional affiliations of the exempt researchers in light of the record which supports the Agency's determination of that such disclosure would lead to an unacceptable risk of disclosing the source's identities.

The lesson of CIA v. Sims, is that the Supreme Court gives an enormous benefit of the doubt to government agencies which can claim some kind of "national security" exemption. The MKULTRA project, which brings to mind certain "research" which led to War Crimes trials in the aftermath of World War II, should never be repeated. After it came to light, a Presidential Executive Order forbade that kind of research.[31]

But it should be kept in mind that MKULTRA—hardly the CIA's finest hour—became known despite a determined effort to erase all evidence that it had ever existed. When Richard Helms—who had himself suggested the project as a CIA functionary in 1953—became President Nixon's CIA director in the 1970s, he ordered all evidence of the project wiped out. But some of the financial records of the project "inadvertently survived" and came to the attention of Admiral Stansfield Turner, CIA Director under President Carter. Turner turned the information over to the Senate Select Committee on Intelligence, resulting in a major Congressional investigation. But even there, the CIA request to treat the names of the MKULTRA researchers as confidential was honored.[32]

Other instances point to government agencies and officials deliberately placing American citizens and servicemen in harm's way. The revelations by Secretary of Energy Hazel O'Leary led to the discovery of a number of persons who had been exposed to harmful radiation in government experiments to see how people would react. The New York Times reported the chilling stories of five of victims of not only the radiation experiments, but also government secrecy.

Anthony Guarisco was a sailor, assigned as a lifeguard on the officers' beach at Bikini Atoll. Following the detonation of two atomic bombs near some 90 unoccupied warships, Guarisco and other sailors were sent to the ships. Ostensibly, they were there to check radiation levels and try to decontaminate the ships by scrub-

[31] Exec. Order No. 12333, § 2,103 CFR 213 (1982).

[32] Ibid., 471 U.S. at 160, 105 S.Ct. at 1883. See also Stansfield Turner, Secrecy and Democracy: The CIA in Transition (Boston: Houghton Mifflin, 1985).

bing them. The real purpose of the experiment, in the words of one document was to see, "how much radiation a man can take."[33] In addition to a degenerative condition of his spine, Guarisco said his situation and that of others like him has been harmed by the government's secrecy. "A lot of us in this work have something like post-traumatic stress disorder," the article quotes Guarisco saying. "But it is made a lot worse when no one believes you."

Guarisco uncovered a letter written by an Army scientist urging human experimentation in radiation research. The letter, which turned up in 1982, warned of the public relations risks, comparing them to reactions to Nazi experiments. "Those concerned in the Atomic Energy Commission would be subject to considerable criticism, as admittedly this would have a little of the Buchenwald touch," the letter said.[34]

Frederick Boyce was fed radioactive oatmeal in a study of the body's absorption of different minerals. The researchers recruited Boyce and 23 other boys at the Fernald School in Boston by telling them they were joining a science club. Parents were told the boys would benefit from the activities and were promised their children would get "a quart of milk daily."

Elmer Allen went to a San Francisco hospital with a knee injury. Doctors said he would have to have an amputation and three days before performing the operation, injected him with plutonium. The researchers knew at the time that plutonium could cause cancer. Years later Allen developed a bone disease linked to radiation but the researchers who discovered the disease did not tell him.

In another instance of government abuse and secrecy, federal researchers studied 400 black men who had contracted syphilis. The researchers withheld treatment from the men even though effective treatments were then available. For four decades the researchers charted the progression of the disease. In 1972 after a former epidemiologist went public, the media reported on the Tuskegee Study of "Untreated Syphilis in the Negro Male." In the spring of 1997, President Clinton delivered a public apology for the experiments.[35]

The Case of Samuel L. Morison

National security concerns present real dilemmas for the United States. Government secrets and secrecy—in large part a legacy

---

[33] Michael D'Antonio, "Atomic Guinea Pigs," The New York Times, Sunday Magazine, Aug. 31, 1997, p 38.

[34] Ibid.

[35] Jeff Stryker, "Tuskeegee's Long Arms Still Touches a Nerve," The New York Times, April 13, 1997, p. E–4.

of Cold War tensions between the United States and Communist-bloc countries in the 1950s through the 1980s—now take on a somewhat different glow in the aftermath of the 1991 collapse of the Soviet Union.

Journalists have long complained about excessive secrecy in the United States' defense and intelligence establishments. One way in which journalists were able to combat secrecy, at least to some extent, was by the "leak," where reporters get tipped off to "inside" or confidential information. In 1988, however, the espionage conviction of Samuel Loring Morison worried some journalists lest that conviction might make it more difficult to get news of wrongdoing out of the Pentagon and the defense industry.

Morison was a civilian employee of the U.S. Navy, and also did some "moonlighting" as a freelance correspondent for a weapons industry journal published in Britain, Jane's Fighting Ships. Morison saw some photos stamped "Secret" on a co-worker's desk, photos taken from a U.S. KH–11 spy satellite. The photos showed construction work on a Russian nuclear aircraft carrier.

Morison, violating a Navy security pledge he had signed, sent the photos to another publication, Jane's Defence Weekly, which published them. The photos were republished in the U.S. in some newspapers. Morison, arguing unconvincingly that he had leaked the pictures to alert the world to a growing Soviet threat,[36] was prosecuted and convicted under an Espionage Statute.[37] Early in 1988, a three-judge panel of the Court of Appeals, Fourth Circuit, upheld Morison's conviction.[38] Thirty-one media organizations joined in a friend-of-the-court brief, arguing that if Morison's conviction stood, the flow of needed information to the public would be impeded. The media groups' amicus brief said: " '[F]or the first time, the court has applied the espionage statute to the dissemination of information to press and public.' "[39]

Court of Appeals Judge Donald Stuart Russell took a hard line in announcing the judgment against Morison. This intelligence department employee had taken secret intelligence from government files and had "wilfully transmitted or given it to one 'not entitled to receive it.' "As such, Morison was "not entitled to invoke the First Amendment as a shield to immunize his act of thievery."[40]

---

[36] Stuart Taylor, Jr., "Court Ruling on Leaks Could Make it a Crime to Talk to the Press," The New York Times, Sec. 4, P. 7, April 10, 1987. On leaks, generally, see Stephen Hess, The Government/Press Connection: Press Officers and Their Offices (Washington, D.C.: Brookings Institution, 1984, pp. 75–79, 92–94).

[37] 18 U.S.C.A. §§ 641, 793(d) and (e).

[38] United States v. Morison, 844 F.2d 1057 (4th Cir.1988).

[39] News Notes, in flyleaves of 14 Med.L.Rptr. No. 22 (Nov. 3, 1987).

[40] United States v. Morison, 844 F.2d 1057, 1069 (4th Cir.1988), 15 Med.L.Rptr. 1369, 1378.

The Court of Appeals ruling was allowed to stand by the U.S. Supreme Court, and Morison began serving a jail term in the fall of 1988.[41] This outcome confirmed fears of some media advocates who argued that the Morison case will discourage government employees from providing information—even evidence of wrongdoing—if that information might be construed as falling under the espionage laws. Further, reporters may face subpoenas to reveal sources if their stories show that they have turned up information (from whatever sources) that the government believes to be classified.

Access to News of Military Operations

One of the true tests of how free a nation is comes when that nation's government is at war. Some of the givens of wartime include:

— There can be prior restraint when safety of military forces or civilians is at stake.

— Prior restraint can be imposed over dispatches sent or broadcast from a battle zone.

— Correspondents in a war zone may have both their mobility and their access to channels of communication curtailed.

"The Uncensored War" is the title Daniel C. Hallin chose for his study of the media and the war in Vietnam. A myth has grown up, Hallin contends, that because the media were allowed, quite freely, to send home images of war in 'Nam, that the U.S. media somehow "lost the war."

The late President Richard M. Nixon blamed television for demoralization at home during the latter stages of the Vietnam conflict. Such views of media—particularly, TV—coverage have affected policy. As Hallin noted,[42]

[I]t was the example of Vietnam, for instance, that motivated the British government to impose tight controls on news coverage of the Falklands crisis [of 1982]. Back at home, the Reagan administration, with Vietnam in mind, excluded the media from the opening phase of the invasion of Grenada.

The excessive secrecy of the 1983 Grenada invasion led to earnest press protests, and to some rueful admissions from military officials that they may have gone too far with their controls.

As a result, "press pools" were organized. A small number of journalists representing largely establishment publications and

[41] Taylor, loc. cit.

[42] Daniel C. Hallin, "The Uncensored War:" The Media and Vietnam (Berkeley: University of California Press, 1986), p. 4; Tom Wicker, "Ghosts of Vietnam," in The New York Times, Jan. 26, 1991, p. 19.

broadcast operations were selected to keep their bags packed, to be "at the ready" should the United States embark on another military action. This arrangement meant that the small number of journalists selected for the pool would share their stories with the far larger number of correspondents and media outlets not selected. When the United States invaded Panama on December 20, 1989, pool correspondents belatedly were put into place to cover actions involving 25,000 highly trained U.S. troops, plus a large assortment of military hardware—tanks, jet fighters, helicopter gunships and Stealth bombers, all to try to capture and arrest General Manuel Noriega. It turned out that the Panama pool was not the solution; it was part of the problem.

From the standpoint of the news media, there was only one thing wrong with the Panama pool arrangement: It didn't work. As Editor & Publisher reported, Secretary of Defense Dick Cheney and his press assistant, Pete Williams, were blamed for the inability of the "National Press Pool" to cover the invasion of Panama effectively.[43]

Fred Hoffman, a former Associated Press reporter who also had served as a Pentagon spokesperson, evaluated the Panama pool experience harshly. It should be noted that Hoffman's evaluative report had been requested by Pete Williams himself.

The Hoffman report complained that Cheney was excessively concerned with secrecy, and concluded that was the reason the pool did not get to the scene until the fighting was nearly over. The press pool—16 reporters—Editor & Publisher quoted from the Hoffman report, which said that in practice sessions during the National Press Pool's five-year history and in covering sea and air battles in the Persian Gulf in 1986–87,[44]

> " * * * reporters demonstrated they could be trusted to respect essential ground rules, including operational security * * *
>
> "Unless the Defense Department's leaders are prepared to extend that trust in hot-war situations, the pool probably will be of little value."

Long after the Panama invasion, many questions remained. How many civilians were killed? On December 20, 1990—exactly a year after the U.S. invasion—U.S. Representative Charles Rangel (D–NY) published his views in The New York Times. He wrote:[45]

[43] George Garneau, "Panning the Pentagon," Editor & Publisher, March 31, 1990, p. 11.

[44] Quoted in Ibid.

[45] Charles B. Rangel, "The Pentagon Pictures," The New York Times (Nat'l.Ed.), Dec. 20, 1990, p. A19.

* * * General Manuel Antonio Noriega sits idly in a Miami jail cell, his trial on charges of drug trafficking delayed by the Government's tape recording of his telephone conversations. But few people know that for the past year Government has been withholding another set of tapes—Government-recorded videotapes of the Panama invasion.

The videotapes of the invasion were taken by highly sophisticated gun cameras aboard Apache attack helicopters. What might those tapes show? They could well suggest that far more civilians died than the U.S. count of 202. (Human rights leaders and some Panamanians have charged that thousands died.) Also, Rangel wrote, as many as 60 percent of the 347 American casualties may have been caused by "friendly fire."[46]

Covering the Persian Gulf War

When President George Bush said that the Persian Gulf war was not to be "another Vietnam," he seemed to refer to his determination to bring enough military resources into play to assure a swift victory. The desire to avoid the "Vietnam syndrome" obviously had fallout for press coverage of the war in the Persian Gulf. Although camera operators on rooftops got spectacular footage of Nintendo-like displays of rockets and tracer bullets, the result of warfare—corpses—was little seen.

In the main, the American press acquiesced in the pooling arrangements. Daniel Hallin's comments on American news media in Vietnam are worth pondering in light of media's coverage of Persian Gulf warfare. Just how independent are the media? Hallin wrote:[47]

> Structurally the American news media are both highly autonomous from direct political control and, through the routines of the news-gathering process, deeply intertwined in the actual operation of government.

Hallin argued that news people combine suspicion of power with a respect for established order, institutions, and authority. Given this anomalous status, small wonder the press—watched most carefully by suspicious military officials—had severe problems in the Persian Gulf. The distinguished military correspondent Malcolm W. Browne, long known for his steadiness and balanced coverage, wrote in January, 1991, that many[48]

[46] Ibid.

[47] Hallin, p. 8.

[48] Malcolm W. Browne, "Conflicting Censorship Upsets Many Journalists," The New York Times, Jan. 21, 1991, p. A8.

* * * news correspondents covering the war with Iraq are bridling under a system of conflicting rules and confusing censorship.

For the first time since World War II, correspondents must submit to near-total military supervision of their work.

Military escorts tagged along with reporters, making it highly unlikely that servicemen and women who were interviewed would speak frankly. At times, escorts interrupted interviews, objecting to questions. When an enlisted man told a reporter how he continued to practice his Christian faith in a country where anything but Muslin rites are not legal, a military "information officer" cut off the interview. The reason? "Military ground rules forbid questions about 'things that we don't know about necessarily.' "[49]

Carol Rosenberg of the Miami Herald and Susan Sachs of Newsday were excluded from covering the First Marine Division in the Persian Gulf because they were thought to have asked "rude questions" of Marine officers.[50]

Uneven application of rules seemed particularly frustrating. Officers in the field would clear a dispatch, only to have it held up somewhere up the line. On the other hand, reporters could understand why a battlefield commander would request that the location of an action not be given, only to have the information withheld in the war zone made public by the Pentagon.

Top brass showed fondness for the spotlight. Malcolm Browne observed that "[t]he Pentagon is clearly eager to be the first to report the most newsworthy information."[51] Later in the war, the Pentagon itself was upstaged by briefings given from Saudi Arabia by General "Stormin Norman" Schwarzkopf.

Despite the grumbling by the press, it surrendered quite meekly to what amounted to military rule, with Cable News Network's Peter Arnett's reports from Baghdad being the most obvious nose-thumbing at pooled journalism. The establishmentarian nature of most American news operations may be seen, perhaps, in the scant coverage given to a lawsuit by Pulitzer Prize-winner Sydney Schanberg, a lawsuit challenging the ground rules for covering Operation Desert Shield (which became "Desert Storm" once the fighting started).

In that lawsuit, nine publications and four journalists sued Secretary of Defense Cheney and Assistant Secretary of Defense for

---

[49] Clarence Page, "Gulf between military, media is so wide that truth has been put in choke hold," Milwaukee Sentinel, Jan. 22, 1991, p. 8, Part 1.

[50] Ibid.

[51] Browne, op. cit.

Public Affairs Pete Williams (among others), seeking an injunction against what were characterized as unfair policies. One press rule, issued January 9, 1991, decreed that media reports from combat pools had to be reviewed by an on-site military public affairs officer before transmission, an obvious cause of delay (or worse).[52]

Despite the pro-Administration-cheerleading-for-the-Persian Gulf war attitudes permeating most of America's news media, the military evidently viewed reporters with less than enthusiasm, if not suspicion or outright hostility. The military controlled its own image during the Persian Gulf war.

SEC. 54. RECORDS AND MEETINGS IN THE STATES

The extent of access in the states varies under statutes providing what shall be open and what closed in the meetings and records of executive, administrative, and legislative agencies.

All states have laws declaring that public policy demands substantial if not maximum disclosure of official business, both meetings and records. Rarely, however, is it conceded that every act or document of officialdom must be open to public scrutiny. Every branch of government in the United States conducts some of its work or maintains some of its records in secret. There are situations in the states as in the federal government's domain which favor secrecy as protection for the individual's private rights and for government's carrying out its work. But the principle of disclosure and openness is as important to the democratic spirit at the state and local levels as it is at the federal level. Thanks to open government efforts pushed by the press and by public spirited citizens in the 1960s and 1970s, by mid–1974 48 states had open-meetings laws.[53]

The great diversity among state open meetings and open records statutes defies easy generalization or detailed discussion here.[54] Citizens who need to know how to get information out of

[52] The journalists bringing the suit were Schanberg (Newsday), novelists E.L. Doctorow and William Styron, and Michael Klare (Nation magazine). The New York Times, the Washington Post, and the Associated Press were not involved in the suit, nor were any of the four big broadcast networks. Plaintiff publications included Harper's, The Nation, Mother Jones, Progressive Magazine, In These Times, and The Village Voice.

[53] All except Miss. and W.Va. by 1974. See John B. Adams, "State Open Meetings Laws: An Overview," Freedom of Information Foundation Series No. 3, July 1974. For another historical treatment, see William R. Henrick, "Public Inspection of State and Municipal Executive Documents," 45 Fordham L.Rev. 1105 (1977). See also "Gaining Access '84," section of the 1985 Freedom of Information Report, Society of Professional Journalists, Sigma Delta Chi.

[54] Of special usefulness is the series Tapping Officials' Secrets: A State Open Government Compendium, a state-by-state project of the Reporters Committee for Freedom of the Press.

particular governmental units—including reporters—need to brief themselves on the special provisions of each state's access laws. Ignorance of such provisions leaves the citizen or reporter at the mercy of officials who choose not to live up to open records or open meetings statutes.

Efforts are made periodically to generalize across state openness statutes, and even to "rank" state statutes in terms of "more open" or "less open." If one learns one is in a state with a highly rated statute, however, do not relax. Openness statutes—or court decisions, for that matter—tend to be rather like airline tickets— good for this time and purpose only. Keeping records and meetings open takes real diligence on the part of the news media and concerned citizens' groups.

To begin with records kept by government offices, just because many records are generically termed "public" does not necessarily mean "open to inspection by the public or press." The old common law (judge-made) definition of public record is something like this: A written memorial by an authorized public officer in discharge of a legal duty to make a record of something written, said, or done.[55]

So, the word "public" does not imply a general right of inspection. In the statutes, furthermore, various qualifications in the public's right to inspect "public records" exist:[56]

> Some documents which constitute public records un- der * * * an open records statute have been exempted from disclosure. There may be available to specified individuals [e.g. licensing examination data available only to the individual examined, or reports of mental examinations of school children available only to their parents.] * * * Not all state-affiliated organizations will meet the definition of "agency" within an open records act [e.g., consulting firms and quasi-public corporations are frequently outside the terms of an open records act.]

All the states have certain statutes specifically providing for secrecy. One example is a provision in income tax laws mandating that individual income tax returns be protected from disclosure. Frequent exemptions appearing in state open records laws have much the same character as the exemptions in the Federal Freedom of Information Act (discussed earlier at page 632), including personnel or medical information, intra-or inter-agency memoranda, preliminary draft documents, and trade secrets. Most if not all states also exempt from disclosure a variety of health department records,

[55] Amos v. Gunn, 84 Fla. 285, 94 So. 615, 616 (1922).

[56] Henrick, p. 1112. A qualified right of inspection does exist under common law. Harold L. Cross, The Public's Right to Know (New York: Columbia University Press, 1953), pp. xiii–xiv.

juvenile and adoption records, licensing examination data, and public assistance or welfare records.

Modern statute-based open records law contains a major improvement over the old common-law right of inspection. At common law, the right to inspect public records ordinarily depended upon a citizen's having a proper purpose in seeing or copying the record. Relatively few statutes include such a provision. Some states—e.g. Louisiana, Tennessee, Texas—have statutes providing that record custodians may not inquire into a record applicant's motives.[57]

Opening the Records

Most state open records laws provide legal instruments for the record-seeker to use in trying to overcome denial of access. Usually, the record-seeker may apply to a court for an order to disclose (which may take several forms, such as an injunction against secrecy or a writ of mandamus ordering disclosure). In a number of states, denial of access to a record may be appealed to a state's attorney general, and, in Connecticut and New York, to a special, statutorily established, freedom of information review group. Penalties for illegal denial of access are provided in many statutes, ranging from the rare removal from office or impeachment to the more common fine and/or imprisonment.[58]

Personnel information is often difficult to obtain, and that difficulty is often linked to claims of "privacy." Even when such claims to privacy are not well-founded, smoking out newsworthy records may take major effort and expenditure. For example, a New York court at first upheld Monroe County in denying a Gannett Company newspaper's request for personnel information. Gannett had asked for the names, titles and salaries of 276 Monroe County employees laid off because of budget cuts. The county's regulations provided that each of its agencies should make such information on every officer or employee available to the news media.

In upholding denial of the request, a court held that the 276 fired individuals were no longer public employees but had become private citizens, and that disclosure of information about them would invade their privacy in a damaging way. A New York appellate court, however, approved Gannett's request for information, saying that the information about the laid off employees was not of a personal nature and that any hardship from disclosure had not been documented.[59]

[57] Ibid., p. 1131, 1163–1196. See also Anon., "Government Information and the Rights of Citizens," 73 Mich.L.Rev. 971, at 1179 (1975).

[58] Ibid., pp. 1135–36.

[59] Gannett Co. v. Monroe County, 59 A.D.2d 309, 399 N.Y.S.2d 534, at 536 (1977), overruling 90 Misc.2d 76, 393 N.Y.S.2d 676 (1977).

A recent trend in state records requests has been for states to try to charge journalists commercial fees for records. These fees can run into the millions of dollars, effectively pricing information out of the reach of news organizations. For example, the Houston Chronicle sought records from the Texas Department of Public Safety related to arrests of motorists. The Chronicle wanted to see if minority were being singled out and ticketed when they drove through white neighborhoods. "The department initially asked for $75 million, and when the paper objected, offered the lower the price to $60 million."[60] A friendly state lawmaker made it possible for the Chronicle to analyze the data for free. The paper then printed a story showing that minorities were twice as likely to be ticketed in certain white communities.

The Texas story is an example of state agencies trying to turn profits from the sale of public records. The idea has merit, as companies make money by mining records for saleable information. Commercial users can identify consumers and find out about their lifestyles by using the information in government databases. States, always strapped for cash, increasingly at their records as a low-or no-cost resource that can be used to generate income. The problem is that news and public interest organizations are caught up in the money-making schemes.

The Belleville News–Democrat in Belleville, Ill., wanted to investigate voter fraud. One of the ways it could look at who was voting was to check state driver's license records. Illinois asked for $37.5 million for the records. The Providence Journal–Bulletin sought motor vehicle records to investigate ticket fixing. Rhode Island asked for $9.7 million.[61] Some media organizations have asked for waivers of the fees, citing their public service use of the records. Others have simply refused to pay and forced agencies into public showdowns. In the case of the Providence Journal–Bulletin, the paper filed a lawsuit.

Police Records

Police records are among the most important in all of government, yet rules of states and municipalities about disclosing such records vary tremendously. If citizens and reporters cannot get access to the "blotter" (the police calls log) and the arrest ("booking") log and the jail log on a constant and continuous basis, the possibility of abuse of citizens' rights may tend to become a probability. According to yet another useful survey by the Reporters Committee on Freedom of the Press, most states have laws

[60] Iver Peterson, "Public Information, Business Rates," The New York Times, July 14, 1997, C–1.

[61] Ibid.

allowing sealing of investigatory files.[62] And in some states—as in Alabama, Georgia, Mississippi, Montana and New Mexico (among others)—state statutes are silent about access to law enforcement records.[63]

Just because a state does not spell out access to law enforcement records in statutory form, that does not mean that reporters or citizens are without remedy. Sometimes getting access to law enforcement records will take a willingness to sue under an open records statute—or, on a common law basis if no such statute applies—to try to get the records. Practical reporters will tell you, however, that developing a good working relationship with police probably is as valuable an avenue to access to their records as is reliance on statutes or courts to enforce access.

Access to Campus Police Records

Many colleges and universities in the United States, said to be educating the young for democracy, have unfortunate histories where openness of campus police records is concerned. Part of the problem, in recent years, has been the United States Department of Education, which was threatening universities with loss of federal funding if they violated student privacy by releasing "educational records." Strangely, the Department of Education functionaries argued that campus police incident reports were "educational records" under the Family Educational Rights and Privacy Act ("FER-PA").

The issue gained national notoriety in 1989 when Traci Bauer, a campus newspaper editor at Southwest Missouri State University (SMSU) claimed that she was entitled to SMSU Security Office incident reports.

Ultimately, Ms. Bauer sued Paul Kincaid, SMSU's director of university relations, seeking release of SMSU security office records. Triggering the controversy was Ms. Bauer's request to see an incident report about a rape involving a student athlete.[64]

In July, 1989, Kincaid had distributed a policy statement ordering the withholding of SMSU Security Office records, including the verbatim "incident" reports. The SMSU campus is located within the jurisdiction of the Springfield, Mo., police force.

Ms. Bauer's suit claimed that she was entitled to the SMSU incident reports, and that those reports—which were to be filed

---

[62] A Guide to Police Records, News Media & the Law, following page 20, Summer, 1987.

[63] Ibid. See also Justin D. Franklin and Robert E. Bouchard, Guide to the Freedom of Information and Privacy Acts, 2nd ed. (New York: Clark Boardman, updated 1990). Contains texts of state open records laws.

[64] Bauer v. Kincaid, 759 F.Supp. 575 (W.D.Mo.1991).

with the Springfield police by the campus Security Office—were sometimes delayed. She charged that this meant that the Springfield police thus were unable, at times, to investigate on-campus crime promptly. She sought access to the SMSU records under the Missouri Open Records or "Sunshine" Act.

SMSU Officials, whether using the Department of Education edict as an excuse or a reason, expressed fear of losing federal funding if the "incident reports" were released to the public and press contrary to the U.S. Department of Education's (DOE) understanding of FERPA. The DOE had urged campus officials to keep confidential police incident reports as "educational records," all in the name of privacy.[65]

U.S. District Judge Russell G. Clark, however, found that there was credible testimony that " * * * in the past SMSU has concealed or destroyed evidence of contraband and failed or refused to release selected criminal investigation and incident reports concerning sex offenses, student athletes, and university personnel."[66] In addition, Judge Clark noted credible testimony from Mark Goodman, President of the Student Press Law Center, that no federal funds actually had been withheld as the result of disclosure of police information or incident reports.

The judge noted, however, that the U.S. Department of Education had issued warnings to some schools, and that all schools that had been issued warnings voluntarily fell into compliance with the DOE's interpretation of FERPA.

In sum, Judge Clark ruled that campus crime records were not "educational records," and thus could not be withheld under FERPA.[67]

> [T]his Court concludes that defendants' actions in withholding the criminal investigation and incident reports which contain names and other personally identifiable information, is unconstitutional under the equal protection. Judge Clark concluded that the criminal investigation and incident reports of SMSU are not exempt from disclosure under Missouri's Sunshine Law.

Evidently intent on making FERPA into a campus secrets act, the U.S. Department of Education was slow to comply with Judge Clark's ruling. As a result, the SPLC and student editors from the University of Tennessee and the University of Colorado sought—and were granted—an injunction to prevent the Department of

---

[65] Ibid., p. 584; Sec. 610.25 of the Missouri Revised Statutes.

[66] Ibid., p. 580.

[67] Ibid., p. 594.

Education from interfering with the release of campus crime reports.[68]

But obviously, it is the most troublesome or "sensitive" incidents (e.g. rape allegations against a star athlete, sexual harassment by professors, or some breach of law by an administrator) that tend to stir the human impulse to conceal damaging information. The trouble with "just a little secrecy"—whether on campus or elsewhere—is that what is hidden is likely to be precisely what society needs most to know.

In one telling example of that need and the risks that can result from secrecy, consider what happened at one Midwestern school. A master key disappeared from a dormitory office. It was promptly reported to university police but the information was not made public.

Over the course of the next several weeks, students in the dormitory began to report thefts of personal belongings. Campus police officers came out and took reports but declined to list them as burglaries or thefts. The reason: there was no sign of forced entry to any of the dormitory rooms. Prompt reporting of the disappearance of the key in the first place might have let students take additional precautions to protect their belongings. Students may consider themselves lucky, though. Although their property was taken, no one was harmed in the series of incidents.

At another campus, two students reported being attacked while walking from a remote parking area to the main campus. The student newspaper learned of the attacks and sought campus police reports about them. During the battle over the university's refusal to release the reports, a third student was attacked while walking through the same area. This time, the student was raped. While universities may profit from the preservation of their images as safe places for parents to send their children, students run risks when they are not able to take measures to protect themselves.

Access to Campus Disciplinary Records

Universities spend a good deal of time and effort promoting themselves as wholesome places where young people engage in the search for knowledge, guided by learned professors and aided by helpful staffs. Occasionally, students will depart from this quest and get into trouble. Just as universities have fought efforts to reveal risks of crime on their campuses, they likewise have tried to keep the lid on student disciplinary issues.

[68] "Judge Orders Release of Campus Crime Reports," The New York Times, March 15, 1991, p. B9, on decision in Student Press Law Center, Lyn D. Schrotgerber (CO), Sam G. Cristy and James C. Brewer, Jr. (TN) v. Lamar Alexander, U.S. Sec. of Education.

Student editors at the University of Georgia won a significant victory for access in the Red & Black case in 1993 when the Georgia Supreme Court held that records of student disciplinary hearings fell outside the category of records made confidential by the Buckley Amendment. Further, the court said that the proceedings were subject to Georgia's open meetings law.

The controversy arose over hazing charges filed against two fraternities. The student editors of The Red & Black student newspaper sent reporters to both hearings but the reporters were barred from both proceedings. The newspaper sued and won a partial victory at the trial court level.

Superior Court Judge Frank Hall rejected the position that the Buckley Amendment applied to the student disciplinary hearing records. But he also refused to grant the newspaper access to the records, saying that the school's judicial board did not fall under the state's open meetings law. It was not a covered body.

But the Georgia Supreme Court disagreed, siding with the newspaper's attorney who argued that openness was proper because it would allow the newspaper to monitor the hearing process.[69] It declared that "the policy of the state is that the public's business must be open, not only to protect against public abuse, but to maintain the public's confidence in its officials."[70]

Even so, the battle for access to student records is by no means resolved. The Student Press Law Center reported in 1995 that the Mercer Cluster faced censure proceedings after reporting that a student athlete at Mercer University had been arrested and brought up on disciplinary charges.[71]

The controversy arose after a member of the women's basketball team was arrested on a charge of driving under the influence of alcohol. There was an additional charge related to leaving the scene of the accident. The newspaper obtained the arrest information from records at a local police station and published its story. The story might have ended there, but the newspaper also published information about the time and location of the judicial board that was to hear the women's case.

The judicial board reacted with a contempt charge against the newspaper, citing internal rules against the publication of the names of students facing disciplinary actions. The board also cited

[69] The Red & Black Publishing Co. v. Board of Regents of the University System of Georgia, 427 S.E.2d 257 (Ga. 1993); "Public Justice, Georgia Supreme Court opens campus proceedings: the ruling may be the start of a national trend," Student Press Law Report, Spring, 1993, p. 4.

[70] Ibid.

[71] "Student newspaper triumphs over charges, Dean reverses earlier censure over reporting of student's arrest," Student Press Law Report, Fall, 1995, p. 13.

the Buckley Amendment, claiming that the federal rule made the information confidential. The judicial board could not make the contempt charge stick because of insufficient evidence, but it found the newspaper guilty of "disorderly conduct." That finding subjected the newspaper to a statement of censure.

But the board's ruling was reversed by the dean of students who explained that, shortly after the ruling, the school received letters from the Department of Education that the Buckley Amendment does not apply to student publications. Even so, the dean maintained that the judicial board still had authority over the newspaper.

A Louisiana State University student and the Shreveport chapter of the Louisiana Society of Professional Journalists lost a bid to force the opening of student disciplinary records at LSU in 1995.[72] The case arose over a disciplinary hearing for two students who admitted taking money from a book exchange operated by the student government. While the trial court found that the student disciplinary records sought by the student and the SPJ chapter fell under the Louisiana Public Records Act, it also concluded that the release of those records was pre-empted by the Buckley Amendment. As a result, the records did not have to be released.

The Shreveport chapter appealed but later dropped the lawsuit. Even with the withdrawal, the head of the Shreveport chapter said that the suit had achieved some results. "The pursuit of this information brought tremendous statewide and some national attention to the issues of crime on campus and university judicial systems," Frank May said.[73]

Access to DMV Records

One of the problems in access is balancing competing interests of the public's right to know against the government's desire to keep things under wraps, often with the intent of protecting individuals' privacy rights of some other rationale that serves "the good of the people."

A prime example of this is the Driver's Privacy Protection Act, a part of the Omnibus Crime Bill of 1994.[75] The Act was prompted by a murder. A high school dropout from Tucson, Ariz., Robert John Bardo, was fixated on television actress Rebecca Schaeffer of the situation comedy "My Sister Sam." He wrote fan letters to her and even traveled from Arizona to California to watch a taping of the show. He received replies and a publicity photo but could not arrange a meeting with Schaeffer.

[72] "SPJ chapter drops appeal," Student Press Law Report, Fall, 1995, p. 15.

[73] Ibid.

[75] Pub.L.No. 103–322, 18 U.S.C. §§ 2721–2725 (1994).

Finally, Bardo went to a Tucson private investigative agency. He took the letters and photos and convinced the staff there that he was an old friend of Schaeffer's who was trying to get in touch with her. Using a number of databases, including one from the California Department of Motor Vehicles, the investigators located Schaeffer's neighborhood. Bardo went there and, by showing his photos of Schaeffer to passers by, found her apartment. But his fixation had turned into something else by the time he got to her apartment. When she answered her door, Bardo shot and killed her.[76]

In 1993, Sen. Barbara Boxer, (D–Calif.) tried to enact a federal law to restrict the release of DMV information. It failed. But in 1994, Boxer and Rep. Jim Moran (D–Va.) reintroduced the measure. It became part of the Omnibus Crime Bill and took effect on Sept. 13, 1997.

The law is intended to shield personal and identifying information about licensed drivers, ostensibly to protect them from being stalked or otherwise identified and located by criminals. The information covered includes driver names, photographs, addresses, telephone numbers, and Social Security numbers. The law pertains to motor vehicle records created and held by the states and subjects the states to fines of $5,000 a day if their departments of motor vehicles do not create systems to keep the information confidential. States may set up systems for release of information if they also have an "opt-out" program whereby individuals may elect to keep their information secret.

The law also provides fines for individuals who obtain or disclose motor vehicle information and even created a private cause of action with minimum liquidated damages of $2,500 for persons who willfully or recklessly obtains or discloses the information.

Although the law was subjected to one First Amendment challenge,[77] it was a different constitutional protection that has led to its being declared unconstitutional in two states. South Carolina and Oklahoma both successfully challenged the law in federal court in 1997. The states asserted their 10th Amendment rights in the challenges, claiming that the federal government was impermissibly intruding into an area of states' rights with the law. The states and not the federal government set up and operate their motor vehicle departments. There is not federal interest in such records and forcing states to make records secret exceeds federal authority under the Constitution.

[76] Stephen Braun and Charisse Jones, "Victim, Suspect, from Different Worlds; Actress' Bright Success Collided With Obsession," Los Angeles Times, July 23, 1989, p. A–1.

[77] The challenge was filed by author Bill Loving in U.S. District Court in the Western District of Oklahoma.

"The power that Congress sought to exercise by dictating when and how States may disclose personal information from driver's license records is a power 'not delegated to the United States by the Constitution, nor prohibited by it to the States, [and such power is therefore] reserved to the States.' U.S. Const. Amend. X. Accordingly, the Act is unconstitutional." [78]

No court has taken up the issue of whether the Driver's Privacy Protection Act is unconstitutional under a First Amendment analysis. If the Tenth Amendment claims are supported by the appellate courts, that issue will never be adjudicated.

[78] State of Oklahoma v. United States of America, CIV–97–1423.

Chapter 9

LEGAL PROBLEMS IN REPORTING COURTS

SEC. 55. ACCESS TO JUDICIAL PROCEEDINGS

In a free society, judicial processes remain open to public view.

Football hero, actor and television sports broadcaster O.J. Simpson's spectacular fall from grace happened mostly on television. Accused in mid–1994 of the savage knife-slash murders of his ex-wife Nicole Brown Simpson and an acquaintance, Ron Goldman, Simpson was acquitted of murder charges on Oct. 3, 1995. But the resoundingly controversial jury verdict—coming after only three hours of deliberation following nine months of trial, by no means ended the legal gauntlet of O.J. Simpson. The criminal jury's finding of "not guilty" brought Simpson little peace. By late 1996, he was back in court, this time defending himself—unsuccessfully, as it turned out—against wrongful death suits brought by the families of Nicole Brown Simpson and Ron Goldman. Early in 1997, the civil jury found against Simpson and decided he should pay a multi-million-dollar judgment that exceeded his net worth and ammunition for those who believed that he escaped justice in his earlier trial.

The Simpson cases are significant because they focused public attention on both the criminal and civil justice systems in a way unprecedented in American media and legal history. All through the criminal trial, the public was subjected to saturation coverage of the case with updates, analysis and commentary from cable, national and local broadcast stations. Judge Lance Ito's decision to permit a camera in the courtroom provided an often-unflattering look at the process of trial. Alternately fascinated and appalled, TV viewers saw a trial in which a jury—sequestered for the longest period in

American history—endured delays and rambling presentations of evidence that seemed to go on forever. This added up to a portrait of the criminal justice system as one in which lawyers spent their days in court grandstanding, making speeches and generally getting in the way of justice.

The prosecution, which seemingly had a strong case bolstered by DNA evidence, appeared to be at cross purposes with itself without a unifying theme to support its theory of the case. The defense, which appeared to many to be blessed with talent and even more cursed with ego, focused on the Los Angeles Police Department and played the race card, even though Simpson's lifestyle enjoyed more in common with the white establishment than the minority community. The jury, alternately lionized and vilified depending on who you talked to, came away with the conclusion that the prosecution had not met its burden of proving beyond a reasonable doubt that Simpson committed the murders. The media, which had the "story of the century," appeared to engage in a feeding frenzy over both the significant and the inconsequential.

When the verdict was in and the initial shock settled, the analysis began. The prosecution had put on a case that was mind-numbingly long and too complicated. The defense had latched onto the position that the investigating officers were racists and could not be trusted. The jury was blamed for voting for reasons of race rather than the evidence. The media were excoriated for having caused all of the participants to behave the ways they did.

Professor Neil Cohen of the University of Tennessee College of Law made a careful study of the criminal case. As was the case with many observers, Professor Cohen's views underwent changes. As the trial began in January of 1995, he predicted a hung jury because the defense team could well instill a reasonable doubt in the minds of some jurors. In May, he characterized news coverage of the trial as "outstanding and educational."

But by June, Professor Cohen—a specialist in criminal law—had changed his mind about the coverage. He declared that the Simpson trial had put the courts "in a very unfavorable light, in the sense that it seems to be an unending quest for something other than the truth." Although the public could learn much about the criminal justice system, Cohen concluded that the television coverage had slowed the proceedings, diminished the likelihood of a fair trial and added to "jury pollution."[1]

The Simpson case came to stand as an example of the clash between the rights guaranteed under the First Amendment and

[1] News releases from the University of Tennessee–Knoxville News Center, Jan. 23, May 3, and June 7, 1995.

those protected under the Sixth Amendment. That amendment says, in part:

> In all criminal prosecutions, the accused shall enjoy the right to a speedy and public trial, by an impartial jury of the State and district wherein the crime shall have been committed . . .

The Criminal Case: The Trial Setting

A number of trials have been called "The Trial of the Century." The outrageously publicized 1995 O.J. Simpson murder trial seemed to be the real deal. Consider the following details, familiar to and endlessly discussed by millions of Americans:[2]

• On Sunday, June 12, the bodies of Nicole Simpson and Ronald Goldman were found outside her condominium in the Brentwood area of Los Angeles. O.J. Simpson, having flown to Chicago the night of the murders, was called back to Los Angeles by police. Although under suspicion for the murders, he attended his wife's funeral, walking hand-in-hand with their children. Simpson, called by Time magazine "the most famous double-murder suspect in history," remained out of custody because he had promised to turn himself in to authorities. Despite being under obvious suspicion, his fame clearly kept him free while others would have been in custody. Why? Many replied, "We never thought he would run."

• Simpson's superstar attorney Robert Shapiro told authorities he was at Simpson's home the morning of Friday, June 17, with Simpson and his boyhood friend, Al Cowlings, when police called to say they were coming to arrest Simpson. O.J. and Cowlings then disappeared. Simpson's arrest on suspicion of murder was accomplished only after a surreal Friday evening (June 17) low-speed "chase" seen nation-wide thanks to video images provided from hovering helicopters. This two-hour ride covered 50 miles of the Los Angeles freeway system, with perhaps a dozen police vehicles, lights flashing, providing an escort while much of the nation watched. Simpson's friend, former teammate Cowlings, was at the wheel of his white Ford Bronco, pleading with police to stay back while a presumably suicidal Simpson crouched low in the back of the truck,

---

[2] See, e.g., "He Could Run . . . But He Couldn't Hide," Newsweek, June 27, 1994, pp. 15–26; Nancy Gibbs, "End of the Run," Time, June 27, 1994, pp. 29–35 (This issue featured a retouched cover photo making Simpson look darker and more ominous, drawing protests from civil rights groups and an apology from the magazine.); Associated Press coverage for June 18, 1994, as in The Knoxville News–Sentinel, "O.J. Simpson leads police on dramatic journey home," pp. A1, A8; Walter Goodman, "Television, Meet Life, Meet TV," The New York Times, Sunday, June 19, 1994, Sec. 4, pp. 1, 6; Mike Jensen, reporting on NBC's Today Show, Sept. 30, 1994; Gale Holland and Haya El Nasser, "Bedlam at Camp O.J.," USA TODAY, Sept. 27, 1994, p. 3A., and Kenneth Noble, "Victim's Sister Denounces Halloween Masks," The New York Times, Oct. 18, 1994, p. A13.

clutching a telephone, a large amount of cash, a pistol, and pictures of his children.

• Simpson was the cover-story for both Newsweek and Time on June 27, and clearly was the biggest story of 1994, getting far more ink and air time than the invasion/occupation of Haiti.

• High-profile attorneys involved in the prosecution and defense and the youthful Judge Lance Ito all became national and international media celebrities. Judge Ito struggled with torrents of leaks and rumors, threatening to end TV coverage of the hearings, then relenting.

• The context became increasingly garish. By September, 1994, paperback books selling hundreds of thousands of copies showed up in supermarkets nationwide. O.J. Simpson crime wristwatches were being sold, and NBC's Mike Jensen reported that his name had been registered as a trademark—after the killings of Nicole Simpson and Ronald Goldman. Playboy was peddling an O.J. Simpson exercise video which it had rushed into production. CNN advertised CD–ROMS on the Simpson case for those who needed even more details. And Denise Brown, sister of Nicole Brown Simpson, complained bitterly about profiteers selling Halloween masks depicting both O.J. and Nicole Simpson.

• At least 75 news organizations had employees attending-or trying to get into pre-trial hearings, and scaffolding of wood and steel rose four and five stories in a parking lot across from the court-house to provide perches for TV cameras and reporters. A 45-foot tower carried the banner, "Brokaw's Butte:" NBC anchor Tom Brokaw would do part of the evening news from that aerie. And the cluttered parking lot? It came to be known as "Camp O.J."[3]

A Detective "On Trial;" A Verdict for "O.J."

During preliminary hearings in the case, television relayed pictures of a confident, articulate Caucasian detective, Mark Furhman, testifying about finding a bloody glove behind Simpson's house. Lawyer Robert Deutsch telephoned Shapiro to tell him that detective Furhman "once applied for a stress disability pension and told psychiatrists that he had tortured suspects and hated 'niggers.' "[4]

The revelations about Fuhrman's attitudes were, in large measure, the mark of how many viewed the investigation and the trial.

[3] Gale Holland & Haya El Nasser, "Bedlam at Camp O.J.," USA Today, Sept. 27, 1994, p. 3a, and Kenneth Noble, "Victim's Sister Denounces Halloween Masks," The New York Times, Oct. 18, 1994, p. A13.

[4] Fox Butterfield, "A Portrait of the Detective in the 'O.J. Whirlpool,' " The New York Times, March 2, 1996, p. 1; David Margolick, "Jurors Will Hear 2 Taped Epithets," The New York Times, Sept. 1, 1995, p. A1.

From the beginning, the defense had attacked the Los Angeles Police Department suggesting that it had badly bungled the investigation through sloppy handling of the evidence and charging that investigators had concluded from the start of the case that Simpson was guilty and doing what they could to see him convicted. Time and again, the defense team hammered away at the investigating officers, suggesting that they had planted evidence pointing to Simpson. Some, including a number of persons in the minority community, found the idea of racially motivated police engaged in misconduct a credible notion. Coming on the heels of the Rodney King assault and criticisms of racially insensitive leadership for the department, the defense claims were all too credible for some.

The prosecution committed what has been called the fatal mistake in the presentation of its case when a prosecutor had Simpson try on the blood-stained gloves found on his property. Television cameras and the jury watched as Simpson tried to fit his hands into the gloves. They appeared to be too small and, a vital piece of physical evidence that the jury could see before them undercut the prosecution's case. Unlike the DNA evidence which required extensive explanations and exhibits that obscure and confusing, the gloves were direct physical evidence. In final arguments the glove played a pivotal role. Defense attorney Johnnie Cochrane also hammered away at the race issue in his summation.

After having endured nine months of testimony, waiting for days while the attorneys and judge wrangled over issues relating to the admissibility of evidence and compelling witnesses to testify, and seeing their numbers dwindle as jury members were removed for different reasons, the jury went out. They came back a few hours later and delivered a "not guilty" verdict. Reactions to the verdict, shock on the faces of predominately white and cheers from predominately black viewers proved a graphic reminder of the racial divisions that still remain in the United States, especially where the justice system is concerned.

Columnist Maureen Dowd wrote after the verdict, "that we are still two separate societies, that whites cannot fathom the distrust that blacks feel given their day-to-day experiences, an accumulated rage that can counter rational arguments."[5]

Another New York Times columnist—Frank Rich—wrote that the verdict enraged him; he had been told by Vincent Bugliosi—who prosecuted the Charles Manson cult successfully—that there was more physical evidence linking Simpson to the murders of Nicole Brown Simpson and Goldman than there had been in the case of the "Manson Family" murders. Upon reflection, however,

[5] Maureen Dowd, "O.J. as Metaphor," The New York Times, Oct. 5, 1995, p. A19.

he placed blame on the Los Angeles Police Department environment that tolerated a Mark Fuhrman in its ranks.[6]

O.J. Simpson: The Civil Trial

Simpson had been found not guilty. He had escaped possible life imprisonment. But he was not free of the justice system. The Goldman and Brown families sued him over the wrongful deaths of the two. The civil trial was virtually the opposite of the criminal case. Simpson could be and was required to testify; the plaintiff presented a clear, cogent and short case that simply told a story about the killings, and the presiding judge, Superior Court Judge Hiroshi Fujisaki kept tight control of his courtroom and excluded cameras. Denied a television feed from the courtroom, one program offered re-creations of the testimony and other news media reported daily on the testimony. But the interest was muted compared with the criminal trial coverage even when Simpson took the stand to deny the killings.

Legal Lessons from the Simpson Trials?

As Frank Rich of the New York Times suggested, there was "ancillary debate about the value of TV cameras in court—as if TV was the message rather than the messenger." It cannot be denied, though, that the criminal trial was a TV trial; Judge Lance Ito even delayed announcing the verdict, reached in mid-afternoon on Oct. 2 until the following day. That ensured that people in the earlier time zones would get the news in a timely fashion. Coverage of the verdict was massive and on the day the verdict was announced the volume of trading on the New York Stock Exchange was down by two-thirds during the time the verdict was being announced. Public relations practitioners were telling their clients to hold major announcements for several days, unless they wanted to "bury" a story.[7]

In the aftermath of the trial and verdict, Time magazine suggested that Judge Ito's inability to control the trial could mean that "TV may cease to be a fixture in American courtrooms." The judge in the re-trial of Erik and Lyle Menendez, who were accused of murdering their parents, excluded cameras from his courtroom. Even during the trial, other judges decided against allowing cameras in their courts. The cases of Susan Smith, found guilty of murdering her sons by drowning them, and the kidnaping murder case of Polly Klaas, were conducted without courtroom cameras.

[6] Frank Rich, "The L.A. Shock Treatment," The New York Times, Oct. 4, 1995, p. A19.

[7] Wall Street Journal News Roundup, "Little Work Got Done Yesterday at 1 p.m.," The Wall Street Journal, Oct. 4, 1995, p. B1.

Even so, Fred Goldman, the father of Ronald Goldman, later argued for cameras in the courtroom. Goldman was quoted in the San Francisco Examiner saying, "I'm glad cameras were there so that everyone could have a chance to see what can actually take place inside a courtroom." Many blamed Ito's failure to control his courtroom on the presence of the camera. But Goldman said that the camera showed what took place in the trial. "Here is the one place in our country where the principles of justice and fairness are supposed to be paramount and everyone could see for themselves how quickly that dishonesty and deceit can take the upper hand. I think it disturbed everyone in the country."[8]

But cameras continue to take the public into courtrooms. In 1997, two nations, the United States and England, were transfixed by the trial of Louise Woodward, the 19–year-old British au pair being tried in the death of the baby left in her care. The trial was carried by Court TV which also broadcasts calls from viewers. O.J. Simpson reportedly called in to express his sympathy for Woodward.[9] Cameras are only a part of the concerns raised when balancing the rights guaranteed under the First and Sixth amendments. Publicity may taint proceedings and deny defendants their right to have their cases decided on the evidence. On the other hand, opening trials to the public serves the functions of trying to preserve fairness as the conduct of the government is laid out for the people to see, helping to ensure that the whole truth is brought out,[10] and serving as a catharsis for the community as it deals with the trauma of crime.

Given the bloody English heritage of secret Star Chamber trials, secret court proceedings are very much against the American grain. The English tradition of public trials was transplanted to American shores during the colonial period. That English tradition arose as did the English Common Law, built upon the history and practices of the people and government which lives today.

> A man can only be accused of a civil or criminal
> offence which is clearly defined and known to the law. The
> judge is an umpire. He adjudicates on such evidence as the

[8] Craig Marine, "Goldman Lashes Out at Ito Blasts Most of the Players of Criminal Trial in His Book," San Francisco Examiner, Feb. 26, 1997.

[9] Cary Goldberg, "Nanny, on the Stand, Denies Killing Baby," The New York Times, Oct. 24, 1997, p. A8. Mrs. Woodward was convicted of manslaughter.

[10] Daniel Petrocelli, the attorney who won the civil case against Simpson, credited media coverage with a major part of his case. The evidence indicated that the bloody shoeprints tied to the crime were made by Bruno Magli shoes. Simpson testified that the Bruno Magli shoes were "ugly-ass" footwear and said that he would never wear such shoes. Press coverage of that part of Simpson's testimony led two photographers to provide pictures of Simpson wearing Bruno Maglis. Petrocelli also reported that the media were instrumental in locating several witnesses. M.L. Stein, "Thanks for the Help (lawyer Daniel Petrocelli Thanks Media)," Editor & Publisher, May 10, 1997.

parties choose to produce. Witnesses must testify in public and on oath. They are examined and cross-examined, not by the judge, but by the litigants themselves or their legally qualified representatives. The truth of their testimony is weighed not by the judge but by twelve good men and true, and it is only when this jury has determined the facts that the judge is empowered to impose sentence, punishment, or penalty according to law.[11]

But compare that to the Civil Code approach, employed by most European countries. Louisiana has the Civil Code as part of its legacy from French colonization. The Civil Code, otherwise known as Roman Law was derived from the Justinian Code. Winston Churchill described the differences between the two in the excerpt above and the unflattering description below.

Under Roman law, and systems derived from it, a trial in those turbulent centuries, and in some countries even to-day, is often an inquisition. The judge makes his own investigation into the civil wrong or the public crime, and such investigation is largely uncontrolled. The suspect can be interrogated in private. He must answer all questions put to him. His right to be represented by a legal adviser is restricted. Witnesses against him can testify in secret and in his absence. And only when these processes have been accomplished is the accusation or charge against him formulated and published.[12]

Advocates of Civil Code point to the service of justice through a professional judiciary that makes the pursuit of truth more efficient and less prone to distortion from advocates who serve a particular party rather than the truth. Advocates of the Common law approach point to the protections of individual rights from abuses by government authority. The clash of advocates will more likely lead to the discovery of the truth rather than relying on a disinterested judiciary. And so, in the United States, we continue to rely on judges and juries to reach the truth. The issue for professional communicators is the extent to which we have access to those legal proceedings in order to report them to the public.

As recently as 1979, the Supreme Court of the United States— with an eye to protecting the rights of defendants in criminal trials—touched off a firestorm of protests from journalists and civil libertarians by suggesting that in some instances, pre-trial hearings (and even trials themselves) could be shut away from public view. That this case was largely shot down by the Supreme Court a year

[11] Winston S. Churchill, The Birth of Britain, A History of the English Speaking Peoples, (New York, Barnes & Noble, 1993) p. 222.
[12] Ibid.

later is of some consolation, true.[13] Even so, it is astonishing that the nation's highest court—as recently as 1979—could in effect call into question the basic right to see and report on the criminal justice process.

SEC. 56.   FREE PRESS *VERSUS* FAIR TRIAL

Attorneys, judges and members of the press continue to try to settle long-standing issues in the "free press—fair trial" dispute.

Back in the 1960s, "trial by newspaper" or "trial by mass media" were phrases which were often heard as the bar-press controversy steamed up. Some attorneys blamed the mass media for many of the shortcomings of the American court system.[14] In reply, many journalists went to great lengths in trying to justify questionable actions of the news media in covering criminal trials.[15]

Many of the lawyers' arguments contained the assertion that the media were destroying the rights of defendants by publicizing cases before they got to court.[16] Such publicity, it was said, prejudiced potential jurors to such an extent that a fair trial was not possible. Editors and publishers—and some attorneys, too—retorted that the media were not harmful, and contended with passion if not historical accuracy that the First Amendment's free press guarantees took precedence over other Constitutional provisions, including the Sixth Amendment.[17] For some critics, the media coverage was to "blame" for Simpson's acquittal.[18]

But what about the traditional concern about prejudicing jurors by media accounts? More than 100 years ago, Mark Twain questioned whether an impartial—in the sense of know-nothing— jury was not a perversion of justice. He wrote that the first 26 graves in Virginia City, Nevada, were occupied by murdered men, and their murderers were never punished.

Twain asserted that when Alfred the Great invented trial by jury, news could not travel fast. Therefore, he could easily find a

13 See Richmond Newspapers v. Virginia, 448 U.S. 555, 100 S.Ct. 2814 (1980).

14 See, e.g., Advisory Committee on Fair Trial and Free Press, Standards Relating to Fair Trial and Free Press (New York, 1966); see also draft approved Feb. 19, 1968, by delegates to the American Bar Association convention as published in March, 1968.

15 See, e.g., American Newspaper Publishers Association, Free Press and Fair Trial (New York): American Newspaper Publishers Association, 1967, p. 1 and passim.

16 See footnotes 22, 23 and 27, below.

17 American Newspaper Publishers Association, op. cit., p. 1.

18 Doug Ferguson, "Speakers Clash on Cameras in Court," The Daily Oklahoman, Sept. 22, 1995.

jury of honest, intelligent men who had not heard of the case they were to try. Mark Twain swore that with newspapers and the telegraph, the jury system "compels us to swear in juries composed of fools and rascals, because the system rigidly excludes honest men and men of brains."[19]

Actually, Mark Twain had the history of the jury system wrong. The jury began in 11th Century England, utilizing a defendant's neighbors who were called to serve both as witnesses and as arbiters of fact. It was not until several centuries later that juries stopped serving as witnesses and served only as triers of fact. In addition, Twain's 19th Century exaggeration does not apply to jury selection procedures in the last quarter of the 20th Century. Jurors need not be absolutely ignorant of—or completely unbiased about—a case which is to go to trial. If jurors can set aside their prejudices and biases, and keep an open mind, that is sufficient.[20]

During the past four decades, the free press-fair trial controversy took place against a backdrop of several sensational, nationally publicized trials and the assassinations of President John F. Kennedy in 1963 and Senator Robert Kennedy and Martin Luther King in 1968. Resultant disputes arrayed the media's right to report against defendants' rights to a fair trial, generated new law in the form of several important Supreme Court decisions, and brought forth efforts to make rules to regularize dealings between the media and law enforcement officials.[21]

The assassination of President Kennedy brought problems of "trial by mass media" dramatically to public consciousness. That fact was underscored by the report of a Presidential Commission headed by Chief Justice Earl Warren. The Warren Commission was intensely critical of both the Dallas police and the news media for the reports of the news of that event. The accused assassin, Lee Harvey Oswald, never lived to stand trial, because he himself was assassinated by Jack Ruby in a hallway of Dallas police headquarters. The hallway was a scene of confusion, clogged with reporters, cameramen, and the curious.[22]

The month after Kennedy's slaying, the American Bar Association charged that "widespread publicizing of Lee Harvey Oswald's

[19] Mark Twain, Roughing It (New York: New American Library, Signet Paperback, 1962) pp. 256–257.

[20] Rita J. Simon, The Jury: Its Role in American Society (Lexington, Mass. D.C. Health and Company, 1980), p. 5; Murphy v. Florida, 421 U.S. 794, 95 S.Ct. 2031 (1975).

[21] See Advisory Committee on Fair Trial and Free Press, op. cit., passim; see also Irvin v. Dowd, 366 U.S. 717, 81 S.Ct. 1639 (1961); Rideau v. Louisiana, 373 U.S. 723, 83 S.Ct. 1417 (1963); Sheppard v. Maxwell, 384 U.S. 333, 86 S.Ct. 1507 (1966).

[22] Report of the President's Commission on the Assassination of President John F. Kennedy (Washington: Government Printing Office, 1964), p. 241.

alleged guilt, involving statements by officials and public disclosures of the details of 'evidence' would have made it extremely difficult to impanel an unprejudiced jury and afford the accused a fair trial."[23] Indeed, had Oswald survived to stand trial, he might not have been convicted. This was so even though the Warren Commission—after the fact—declared that Oswald was in all likelihood Kennedy's killer. Under American judicial procedures, it seems possible that Oswald could not have received a fair and unprejudiced trial, and that any conviction of him might have been upset on appeal.[24]

The Warren Commission placed first blame on police and prosecutors, but additionally criticized the media for their part in the events following the President's death. The Commission said that "part of the responsibility for the unfortunate circumstances following the President's death must be borne by the news media * * *." Journalists were excoriated by Commission members for showing a lack of self-discipline, and a code of professional conduct was called for as evidence that the press was willing to support the Sixth Amendment right to a fair and impartial trial as well as the right of the public to be informed.[25]

If the reporters behaved badly in Dallas, so did the Dallas law enforcement officials, who displayed "evidence" in crowded corridors and released statements about other evidence. Conduct of police and other law enforcement officials, however, has by no means been the only source of prejudicial materials which later appeared in the press to the detriment of defendants' rights. All too often, both defense and prosecution attorneys have released statements to reporters which were clearly at odds with the American Bar Association's Canons of Professional Ethics. Canon 20, adopted more than 50 years earlier, advised lawyers to avoid statements to the press which might prejudice the administration of justice or interfere with a fair trial. In any case, lawyers were not to go beyond quotation from the records and papers on file in courts in making statements about litigation.[26]

Canon 20, in theory, could be used as a weapon to punish lawyers who released statements to the press which harmed a defendant's chances for a fair trial. Although this Canon was adopted by the bar associations of most states, there was rarely a

---

[23] William A. Hachten, The Supreme Court on Freedom of the Press: Decisions and Dissents (Ames, Iowa: Iowa State University Press, 1968), p. 106.

[24] Ibid.

[25] Report of the President's Commission on the Assassination of President John F. Kennedy, p. 241.

[26] Canons of Professional and Judicial Ethics of the American Bar Association, Canon 20.

case brought to disbar or discipline an attorney or judge who made prejudicial remarks to the press.[27]

The ABA's Code of Professional Responsibility—which superseded the old ABA Canons—outlined standards of trial conduct for attorneys. Disciplinary Rule DR 7–107 dealt with "Trial Publicity." It says that lawyers who are involved in a criminal matter shall not make "extra-judicial statements" to the news media which go beyond unadorned factual statements.

In 1991, however, the ABA adopted new Standards for Criminal Justice dealing with out-of-court statements by attorneys. If a state or a court jurisdiction accepts these new standards, they will become mandatory in that region.

Lawyers, again, are allowed to make general statements outside of court about "the general nature of the charges against the accused." This approach is new, according to The News Media & The Law, in that it makes it possible for defense lawyers to try to counterbalance harmful pre-trial publicity against their clients. Lawyers, however, must refrain from making statements which are substantially likely to prejudice a criminal proceeding.

Other language of the ABA's 1991 Fair Trial–Free Press rules may have the potential to make it easier to close pre-trial proceedings, changing the suggested standard for closure to "substantial likelihood of harm" from the harder to demonstrate "clear and present danger." Also, the ABA weakened its previous strictures against using the contempt power to punish lawyers who violate a judge's restrictive order by talking to the press.[28]

Reporters are not the only offenders in disrupting trials. A quick skimming of the General Index of a legal encyclopedia, *American Jurisprudence,* adds support for such a generalization. The General Index of "Amjur" contains nearly 1,000 categories under the topic, "New Trial." New trials may be granted because something went awry in the original trial, somehow depriving a defendant of the right to a fair trial under the Sixth Amendment. These categories include such things as persons fainting in the courtroom, hissing, technical mistakes by attorneys, prejudice of judges, and misconduct by jurors: Jurors who read newspapers.[29]

Findings of social scientists lend modest support to assumptions about jurors being prejudiced by the mass media.[30] Much

[27] Donald M. Gillmor, Free Press and Fair Trial (Washington, D.C., Public Affairs Press, 1966) p. 110.

[28] American Bar Association, Code of Professional Responsibility and Code of Judicial Conduct (Chicago, ABA, 1976) p. 37C, ABA 1991 Fair Trial–Free Press Rules; see News Media & The Law, Spring, 1991, p. 22.

[29] 3 American Jurisprudence, Gen.Index, New Trial.

[30] See, e.g., Mary Dee Tans and Steven H. Chaffee, "Pretrial Publicity and Juror Prejudice," Journalism Quarterly Vol. 43:4 (Winter, 1966) pp. 647–654, and a list of

more research, however, remains to be done before assertions can be made confidently that what a juror reads or learns from the mass media will affect the juror's subsequent behavior. On the other hand, it has been argued that lawyers, before casting aspersions at the press, might consider the question of whether their own legal house is in order. Consider what psychologists can tell lawyers about a fair trial. Consider the rules of procedure in a criminal trial in many states as attorneys make their final arguments to a jury. First, the prosecution sums up its case. Then the defense attorney makes the final argument. And last, the prosecuting attorney makes the final statement to the jury. For years, psychologists have been arguing about order of presentation in persuasion. Some evidence has been found that having the first say is most persuasive; there is other evidence that having the last word might be best.[31] But in many jurisdictions, who gets neither the first say nor the last word during the final arguments before a jury? The defendant.[32]

Whatever the results, the impact of community sentiment on juries can best be explained by the *voir dire* examination of a prospective juror in the murder case that led to Patton v. Yount. The wife of a local minister, called as part of the pool of prospective jurors, known as the veniremen, was asked about talk in her community about the case.

Q. Would your presence in serving as a juror create a difficulty in your parish?

A. Why yes—when people heard my name on for this—countless people of the church have come to me and said they hoped I would take—the stand I would take in case I was called. I have had a prejudice built up from the people in the church.

Q. Is this prejudice, has it been adverse to Mr. Yount?

A. Yes it was. They all say he had a fair trial and he got a fair sentence. He's lucky he didn't get the chair.

* * *

[T]he church people—I haven't asked for any of this but they discuss it in every group—but they say now since

juror prejudice studies on p. 647, notes 4, 5 and 6. But see Don R. Pember, "Does Pretrial Publicity Really Hurt?" Columbia Journalism Review, Sept./Oct. 1984, p. 16.

31 See, e.g., Carl I. Hovland, et al., The Order of Presentation in Persuasion, (New Haven: Yale, 1957) passim.

32 The authors are grateful to Professors Jack M. McLeod and Steven H. Chaffee, of the University of Wisconsin Mass Communications Research Center and Stanford University, respectively for this insight.

you are chosen and you will be there we expect you to follow through.

Q.   Notwithstanding what the Court would tell you, you feel you would be subject to the retributions or retaliations of these people—

A.   I think I would hear about it.[33]

SEC. 57.   PRE–TRIAL PUBLICITY

Pre-trial publicity which makes it difficult—if not impossible—for a defendant to receive a fair trial was summed up in the Supreme Court cases of Irvin v. Dowd (1961) and Rideau v. Louisiana (1963).

"Pre-trial publicity" is a phrase which is a kind of shorthand expression meaning strain between the press and the courts. The kind of publicity which "tries" a defendant in print or over the air before the real courthouse trial starts—that's the issue here. This section discusses two classic instances of pre-trial publicity, instances in which the news media did not cover themselves with glory: Irvin v. Dowd and Rideau v. Louisiana. It also takes up the Supreme Court's subsequent treatment of the issue in Murphy v. Florida and Patton v. Yount.

Irvin v. Dowd (1961)

The Irvin case represents the first time that the Supreme Court overturned a state criminal conviction because publicity before the trial had prevented a fair trial before an impartial jury.[34]

The defendant in this murder case, Leslie Irvin, was subjected to a barrage of prejudicial news items in the hysterical wake of six murders which had been committed in the vicinity of Evansville, Indiana. Two of the murders were committed in December, 1954, and four in March, 1955. These crimes were covered extensively by news media in the locality, and created great agitation in Vanderburgh County, where Evansville is located, and in adjoining Gibson County.[35]

Leslie Irvin, a parolee, was arrested in April, 1955, on suspicion of burglary and writing bad checks. Within a few days, the Evansville police and the Vanderburgh County prosecutor issued press releases asserting that "Mad Dog Irvin" had confessed to all six murders, including three members of one family. The news media had what can conservatively be described as a field day with the

---

[33] Patton v. Yount, 467 U.S. 1025, 1044, 104 S.Ct. 2885, 2895 (1984).

[34] Gillmor, op. cit., pp. 116–117.

[35] Irvin v. Dowd, 366 U.S. 717, 719, 81 S.Ct. 1639, 1641 (1961).

Irvin case, and were aided in this by law enforcement officials. Many of the accounts published or broadcast before Irvin's trial referred to him as the "confessed slayer of six." Irvin's court-appointed attorney was quoted as saying he had received much criticism for representing Irvin. The media, by way of excusing the attorney, noted that he faced disbarment if he refused to represent the suspect.[36]

Irvin was soon indicted by the Vanderburgh County Grand Jury for one of the six murders. Irvin's court-appointed counsel sought—and was granted—a change of venue. However, the venue change, under Indiana law, was made only from Vanderburgh County to adjoining Gibson County, which had received similar prejudicial accounts about "Mad Dog Irvin" from the news media in the Evansville vicinity.[37]

The trial began in November of 1955. Of 430 prospective jurors examined by the prosecution and defense attorneys, 370—nearly 90 per cent—had formed some opinion about Irvin's guilt. These opinions ranged from mere suspicion to absolute certainty.[38] Irvin's attorney had used up all of his 20 peremptory challenges. When 12 jurors were finally seated by the court, the attorney then unsuccessfully challenged all jurors on grounds that they were biased. He complained bitterly that four of the seated jurors had stated that Irvin was guilty.[39] Even so, the trial was held, Irvin was found guilty, and the jury sentenced him to death. Irvin's conviction was upheld by the Indiana Supreme Court, which denied his motions for a new trial.[40] Lengthy appeals brought Irvin's case to the Supreme Court of the United States twice,[41] but his case was not decided on its merits by the nation's highest court until 1961.

Then, in 1961, all nine members of the Supreme Court agreed that Irvin had not received a fair trial. The upshot of this was that Irvin received a new trial, although he was ultimately convicted. This time, however, his sentence was set at life imprisonment.[42]

---

[36] 366 U.S. 717, 725–726, 81 S.Ct. 1639, 1641, 1645 (1961); Gillmor, op. cit., p. 11.

[37] 366 U.S. 717, 720, 81 S.Ct. 1639, 1641 (1961).

[38] 366 U.S. 717, 727, 81 S.Ct. 1639, 1645 (1961).

[39] 359 U.S. 394, 398, 79 S.Ct. 825, 828 (1959).

[40] Irvin v. State, 236 Ind. 384, 139 N.E.2d 898 (1957).

[41] Irvin's appeal for a writ of *habeas corpus* to a Federal District Court was denied on the basis that he had not exhausted his opportunities to appeal through the Indiana courts. 153 F.Supp. 531 (N.D.Ind.1957). A United States Court of Appeals affirmed the dismissal of the writ, 251 F.2d 548 (7th Cir.1958). In a 5–4 decision in 1959, the Supreme Court of the United States sent Irvin's case back to the Federal Court of Appeals for reconsideration. 359 U.S. 394, 79 S.Ct. 825 (1959). The Court of Appeals again refused to grant a writ of *habeas corpus* to Irvin, 271 F.2d 552 (7th Cir.1959). Irvin's case was then appealed to the Supreme Court for the second time.

[42] Gillmor, op. cit., pp. 11–12.

In his majority opinion, Justice Tom C. Clark—a former attorney general of the United States—concentrated on the effect of prejudicial publicity on a defendant's rights. Clark noted that courts do not require that jurors be totally ignorant of the facts and issues involved in a criminal trial. It is sufficient if a juror can render a verdict based on the evidence presented in court.[43]

Justice Clark then considered the publicity Irvin had received, and concluded: "Here the build-up of prejudice is clear and convincing." He noted that arguments for Irvin presented evidence that "a barrage of newspaper headlines, articles, cartoons and pictures was unleashed against him during the six or seven months before his trial" in Gibson County, Indiana. Furthermore, "Evansville radio and TV stations, which likewise blanketed the county, also carried extensive newscasts covering the same incidents."[44]

In a concurring opinion, Justice Frankfurter unleashed a bitter denunciation of "trial by newspapers instead of trial in court before a jury." He stated that the Irvin case was not an isolated incident or an atypical miscarriage of justice. Frankfurter wrote:[45]

> Not a term passes without this Court being importuned to review convictions, had in States throughout the country, in which substantial claims are made that a jury trial has been distorted because of inflammatory newspaper accounts—too often, as in this case, with the prosecutor's collaboration—exerting pressures upon potential jurors before trial and even during the course of trial * * *.

Trial by Television: Rideau v. Louisiana (1963)

If Leslie Irvin was mistreated primarily by newspapers during the period before his trial, Wilbert Rideau found that television was the major offender in interfering with his right to a fair trial. Early in 1961, a Lake Charles, La., bank was robbed. The robber kidnaped three of the bank's employees and killed one of them. Several hours later, Wilbert Rideau was arrested by police and held in the Calcasieu Parish jail in Lake Charles. The next morning, a moving picture—complete with a sound track—was made of a 20-minute "interview" between Rideau and the Sheriff of Calcasieu Parish. The Sheriff interrogated the prisoner and elicited admissions that Rideau had committed the bank robbery, the kidnaping, and the murder. Later in the day, this filmed interview was broadcast over television station KLPC in Lake Charles. Over three days' time, the film was televised on three occasions to an estimated total audience

[43] Irvin v. Dowd, 366 U.S. 717, 723, 81 S.Ct. 1639, 1642–1643 (1961).
[44] 366 U.S. 717, 725, 81 S.Ct. 1639, 1644 (1961).
[45] 366 U.S. 717, 730, 81 S.Ct. 1639, 1646–1647 (1961).

of 97,000 persons, as compared to the approximately 150,000 persons then living in Calcasieu Parish.[46]

Rideau's attorneys subsequently sought a change of venue away from Calcasieu Parish. It was argued that it would take away Rideau's right to a fair trial if he were tried there after the three television broadcasts of Rideau's "interview" with the sheriff. The motion for change of venue was denied, and Rideau was convicted and sentenced to death on the murder charge in the Calcasieu Parish trial court. The conviction was affirmed by the Louisiana Supreme Court,[47] but the Supreme Court of the United States granted *certiorari*.[48]

Justice Potter Stewart's majority opinion noted that three of the 12 jurors had stated during *voir dire* examination before the trial that they had seen and heard Rideau's "interview" with the Sheriff. Also, two members of the jury were Calcasieu Parish deputy sheriffs. Although Rideau's attorney challenged the deputies, asking that they be removed "for cause," the trial judge denied this request. Since Rideau's lawyers had exhausted his "peremptory challenges"—those for which no reason need be given—the deputies remained on the jury.[49]

Justice Stewart noted that the *Rideau* case did not involve physical brutality. However, he declared that the "kangaroo court proceedings in this case involved a more subtle but no less real deprivation of due process of law." Justice Stewart added:[50]

> ... In this case the people of Calcasieu Parish saw and heard, not once but three times, a "trial" of Rideau in a jail, presided over by a sheriff, where there was no lawyer to advise Rideau of his right to stand mute.

Rideau's conviction was reversed, and a new trial was ordered by the Supreme Court. He was convicted again, sentenced to life imprisonment, and became well known again, this time as a journalist writing about prison conditions from inside the walls.

The Supreme Court Takes Another Look

There is no denying that prejudicial pre-trial publicity may deny a defendant a fair trial and provide a constitutional reason to reverse his conviction. But in 1975 and 1984, the Supreme Court took a step back in its consideration of pre-trial publicity. In Murphy v. Florida,[51] the Court was called on to consider the

46 Rideau v. Louisiana, 373 U.S. 723, 724, 83 S.Ct. 1417, 1419 (1963).

47 242 La. 431, 137 So.2d 283 (1962).

48 371 U.S. 919, 83 S.Ct. 294 (1962).

49 373 U.S. 723, 725, 83 S.Ct. 1417, 1418 (1963).

50 373 U.S. 723, 727, 83 S.Ct. 1417, 1419 (1963).

51 421 U.S. 794, 95 S.Ct. 2031(1975), 1 Med.L.Rptr. 1232.

conviction of Jack Roland Murphy for robbery. Murphy argued that the jury that tried him had been prejudiced by news coverage that included references to his prior felony convictions and details of the crime he was being put on trial for.

Jack Murphy was already well known. Murphy, known as "Murph the Surf," had been involved in the 1964 theft of the Star of India sapphire from a New York Museum. His lifestyle, described by the Court as "flamboyant" had made him a popular media subject. Murphy had been charged with the robbery of a Miami Beach home. Before going on trial, he was indicted on two counts of murder. He also was indicted by a federal grand jury on a charge of conspiring to transport stolen securities in interstate commerce. Jury selection began with the summoning of 78 prospective jurors. Thirty were excused for various personal reasons, 20 were dismissed on peremptory challenges by prosecution and defense, and 20 more were excused by the court for have prejudged Murphy's guilt. The remaining eight served as the jury and two alternates.

Murphy tried to have the jury dismissed because it was aware of his connection with the Star of India theft and or the murder charges. When his motion was denied, Murphy refused to put on a defense. He did not testify and he did not cross examine any of the state's witnesses. He was convicted.

The Supreme Court, in an opinion by Thurgood Marshall, denied Murphy's contention that the jurors' knowledge of his prior crime and criminal charges denied him a fair trial. Acknowledging that the Constitution required a panel of "impartial" and "indifferent" jurors, Marshall wrote, "Qualified jurors need not, however, be totally ignorant of the facts and issues involved."[52] Marshall quoted from the opinion in *Dowd*:

> "To hold that the mere existence of any preconceived notion as to the guilt or innocence of an accused, without more, is sufficient to rebut the presumption of a prospective juror's impartiality would be to establish an impossible standard. It is sufficient if the juror can lay aside his impression or opinion and render a verdict based on the evidence presented in court."[53]

The Court looked at the *voir dire* process of questioning the prospective jurors and found no evidence that any member of the seated jury held a prejudiced view of Murphy's guilt. "Some of the jurors had a vague recollection of the robbery with which the petitioner was charged and each had some knowledge of petitioner's past crimes, but none betrayed any belief in the relevance of

[52] Ibid. At 799–800, 95 S.Ct. at 2036.
[53] Irvin v. Dowd, 366 U.S. 717, 723, 81 S.Ct. 1639, 1643–1644.

petitioner's past to the present crime."[54] This was radically different from *Dowd* in which 90 percent of the prospective jurors said they believed Dowd was guilty. Only 20 of the 78 called to the jury pool indicated enough prejudice to be excused, a little more than 25 percent. Chief Justice Burger noted the failure of the trial court to protect jurors from media coverage but still concurred in the result. Justice Brennan dissented.

In 1984, the Court was called on to consider once again the amount of information and bias that individual jurors could bear and still serve. In Patton v. Yount,[55] the Court was faced with a challenge to a conviction for rape and murder. Jon E. Yount was convicted of the rape and murder of 18–year-old Pamela Rimer. Yount, who had been Rimer's math teacher, turned himself in and gave police and oral and written confession. At his trial, Yount claimed temporary insanity but was convicted. Because Yount had not been advised of his Miranda rights, the Pennsylvania Supreme Court ordered a new trial. The trial judge ordered Yount's confession suppressed and the district attorney dismissed the rape charge.

The court then conducted extensive *voir dire*, interviewing 292 prospective jurors before seating a jury panel. Yount's attorneys sought a change of venue arguing that the widespread publicity the case and its predecessor would make it impossible for jurors to forget what they knew and decide the case on its own merits. The court denied the motion and said that the publicity surrounding the case was made up of stories that "merely reported events without editorial comment."[56] Yount was convicted again and appealed.

The Third Circuit Court of Appeals reversed his conviction saying that the pre-trial publicity had made it impossible for Yount to get a fair trial in Clearfield County. The Third Circuit noted that all but 163 of the prospective jurors questioned had heard of Yount's prior confession, plea of insanity and conviction (Most of the other jurors had been excused before individual questioning began. Four had been dismissed for cause before being questioned.). Of the 163 jurors questioned, 126, or 77 percent, "admitted they would carry an opinion into the jury box."[57] The court noted that one juror, a Mr. Hrin, and both alternates indicated in their responses to *voir dire* that they would have required evidence to overcome their beliefs about Yount's guilt. The Third Circuit opinion referred extensively to *Dowd*.

[54] Murphy v. Florida, 421 U.S. 794, 800, 95 S.Ct. 2031, 2036 (1975).

[55] 467 U.S. 1025, 104 S.Ct. 2885 (1984).

[56] Ibid. At 1027–1028, 104 S.Ct. at 2887.

[57] Ibid.

The case then came before the Supreme Court which reversed the Third Circuit and upheld Yount's conviction.[58] First, the Court looked to the pre-trial publicity and found that there had been an average of less than one article a month in the two Clearview County newspapers in the 18 months between the reversal of Yount's first conviction and his second trial. The stories, the Court said, were not inflammatory and did not promote public passions against Yount. The passage of time had softened the prospective jurors' memories of the crime and previous case, the Court said.

Having disposed of the media's influence on the case, the Court in Justice Powell's opinion, turned to the Third Circuit's review of juror opinions.

> "The Court of Appeals below thought that the fact that the great majority of veniremen 'remembered the case' showed that time had not served to 'erase highly unfavorable publicity from the memory of [the] community.' 710 F.2d at 969. This conclusion, without more, is essentially irrelevant. The relevant question is not whether the community remembered the case, but whether the jurors at Yount's trial had such fixed opinions that they could not judge impartially the guilt of the defendant."[59]

Justice Powell pointed to the presumption of the impartiality of juries that attached to the *Yount* case. In part, that impartiality sprang from the *voir dire* process which has been used to determine the views of prospective jurors. Powell read the voir dire transcripts of the questioning of Hrin and the alternates and found no evidence of excludable bias. Powell explained that the juror, like all jurors was not familiar with the court system and could not be expected to express themselves with care or consistency. Hrin may have been ambiguous in his early testimony, but he declared his ability to judge the case in a later answer, the Court said.

> In response to a question whether Hrin could set his opinion aside before entering the jury box or would need evidence to change his mind, the juror forthrightly stated: 'I think I could enter it [the jury box] with a very open mind. I think I could ... very easily. To say this is a requirement for some of the things you have to do every day.' App. 89a. After this categorical answer, defense counsel did not review their challenge for cause. Similarly, in the case of alternate juror Pyott, we cannot fault the trial judge for crediting her earliest testimony, in which she said that she could put her opinion aside '[i]f [she] had to,' rather than the later testimony in which defense counsel

[58] Justice Marshall did not take part in the case.

[59] Ibid. At 1035, 2890.

persuaded her that logically she would need evidence to discard any evidence she might have. * * * Alternate juror Chincharick's testimony is the most ambiguous, as he appears simply to have answered 'yes' to almost any question put to him. It is here that the federal court's deference must operate, for while the cold record arouses some concern, only the trial judge could tell which of these answers was said with the greatest comprehension and certainty.[60]

Justice Stevens dissent, joined by Justice Brennan, picked away at Justice Powell's selective use of Hrin's testimony, providing an excerpt of his own.

"Q. Did I understand Mr. Hrin you would require some—you would ... require evidence or something before you could change your opinion you now have?

A. Definitely. If the facts show a difference from what I had originally—had been led to believe, I would definitely change my mind.

Q. But until you're shown those facts, you would not change your mind—is that your position?

A. Well—I have nothing else to go on.

Q. I understand. Then the answer is yes—you would not change your mind until you were presented facts?

A. Right, but I would enter it with an open mind."[61]

Even with Hrin's declaration that he would have "an open mind," his testimony saying he would require that Yount disprove the allegations was, for Justices Stevens and Brennan, enough to show "manifest error" in the seating of the jury. Other observers questioned Justice Powell's picking and choosing which parts of the prospective jurors' testimony to give credit to in sustaining Yount's conviction. Still, the Court's decision stood and provides guidance in later cases. Without a showing of "manifest error" in the selection of the jury, the appellate courts could not find that a defendant's fair trial rights were denied by pre-trial publicity.

The issue of pre-trial publicity played a significant part in the decision of Playboy magazine to publish it story about Timothy McVeigh's statement to his lawyers about his part in the bombing of the Murrah Federal Building in Oklahoma City. Reporter Ben Fenwick, who had covered the aftermath of the bombing for the Reuters News Service and others, gained access to a number of documents prepared by the defense, including a chronology of the

[60] Ibid. At 1039–1040, 2893.
[61] Ibid. At 1049, 2898.

events leading to the bombing itself. The documents included McVeigh's telling of his part in the attack that killed 168 men, women, and children.

But Fenwick was concerned about the effect the publication might have on McVeigh's chances of a fair trial. He worried that a conviction might be overturned if the appellate courts determined that the case had received too much prejudicial publicity. He also realized that because of the nature of the document he held, that the presiding judge could impose a prior restraint on the story. Fenwick developed his story and held onto it even though it meant a delay of months in publication.

After confidential consultations, he decided that it would be best to wait until presiding Judge Richard Matsch sequestered the jury before publishing. Once the jury was locked away, they would be shielded from any prejudicial effects of the story. But Matsch chose not to sequester the jury and he announced that well before the trial began. Matsch did order the prospective jurors not to read or watch anything about the case and so provided at least some protection. Then, on Feb. 28, 1997, The Dallas Morning News, working with similar documents, published an exclusive story on its Web site about McVeigh's purported admission to the bombing. With the news out, Fenwick and Playboy published his article, first on the Web and then in the pages of the magazine. Matsch's warning appeared to work. Only one juror was luckless enough to admit to having read something about the case. The woman told Matsch that she did not think she would be called and that was why she read a brief story about problems with the FBI crime lab. Matsch responded sternly, asking, "How can we trust you to comply with the court's instructions when you have already violated them?" Matsch told the woman, "You'll be hearing from me."[62]

SEC. 58.   PUBLICITY DURING TRIAL: CAMERAS IN THE COURTROOM

The notorious Lindbergh kidnaping trial of the 1930s and the Estes case of 1965 severely limited still and television cameras in the courtroom. Cameras have returned in many states under the Supreme Court's 1981 decision in Chandler v. Florida.

"The Lindbergh Case" and "the trial of Bruno Hauptmann" are phrases heard whenever the free press—fair trial debate heats up. These phrases, of course, refer to the kidnaping in 1932 of the 19–month-old son of the aviator famed for the first solo crossing of

---

[62] Jo Thomas, "Questioning of Jury Prospects in Oklahoma Bombing Trial Ends," The New York Times, April, 22, 1997, p. A12.

the Atlantic. The child's kidnaping was front-page news for weeks, long after the child's body was found in a shallow grave not far from the Lindbergh home in New Jersey.

More than two years later, in September, 1934, Bruno Richard Hauptmann was arrested. His trial for the kidnap-murder of the Lindbergh child did not begin until January, 1935. The courtroom where Hauptmann was tried had a press section jammed with 150 reporters. During the Hauptmann trial, which lasted more than a month, there were sometimes more than 700 newsmen in Flemington, N.J., the site of the trial.[63]

Much of the publicity of the Hauptmann trial was prejudicial, and lawyers and newsmen authored statements which were clearly inflammatory. Hauptmann was described in the press, for example, as a "thing lacking in human characteristics."[64] After the trial— and after Hauptmann's execution—a Special Committee on Cooperation Between the Press, Radio, and Bar was established to search for "standards of publicity in judicial proceedings and methods of obtaining an observance of them." In a grim report issued in 1937, the 18–man committee—including lawyers, editors, and publishers—termed Hauptmann's trial "the most spectacular and depressing example of improper publicity and professional misconduct ever presented to the people of the United States in a criminal trial."[65]

One result of the committee's investigation of the Hauptmann trial was the American Bar Association's adoption in 1937 of Canon 35 of its Canons of Professional Ethics. Canon 35 forbade taking photographs in the courtroom, including both actual court sessions and recesses. As updated, Canon 35 declared that broadcasting or televising court proceedings "detract from the essential dignity of the proceedings, distract the participants and witnesses in giving testimony, and create misconceptions * * * and should not be permitted." This was replaced by ABA Canon of Judicial Conduct 3(7):[66]

> A judge should prohibit broadcasting, televising, recording, or taking photographs in the courtroom and areas immediately thereto during sessions of court or recesses between sessions * * * The only exceptions involved situa-

[63] John Lofton, Justice and the Press (Boston: Beacon Press, 1966), pp. 103–104.

[64] Lofton, op. cit., p. 124.

[65] American Bar Association, "Report of Special Committee on Cooperation between Press, Radio and Bar," Annual Report, Volume 62, pp. 851–866 (1937), at p. 861. See, also, New Jersey v. Hauptmann, 115 N.J.L. 412, 180 A. 809 (Err. & App.1935), certiorari denied 296 U.S. 649, 56 S.Ct. 310 (1935).

[66] American Bar Association, Code of Professional Responsibility and Code of Judicial Conduct, p. 59C. For Canon 35, see ABA, Annual Report, Vol. 62, at p. 1134; see it as updated by Justice John Marshall Harlan in his concurring opinion in Estes v. Texas, 381 U.S. 532, 601 n., 85 S.Ct. 1628, 1669 n. (1965).

tions when the judge had given permission, or the filming was to be used only for ceremonial or instructional purposes.

Estes v. Texas

Excesses in televising a trial in Texas during the 1960s meant the end of televising virtually all criminal trials for a period of more than a decade. As is discussed later in this section, however, developments in the late 1970s—capped by the January, 1981 decision of the Supreme Court of the United States in Chandler v. Florida[67]—have seen a substantial movement toward getting both television and still cameras back into state courtrooms. At this writing, however, federal courtrooms are still off limits.

The crucial case of the 1960s involved the swindling trial of flamboyant Texas financier Billie Sol Estes. Estes was ultimately convicted, but not until he had received a new trial as a result of the manner in which a judge allowed his original trial to be photographed and televised. Fallout from the U.S. Supreme Court decision which granted Estes a new trial seemed to rule out cameras in the courtroom.[68]

Estes came before a judicial hearing in Smith County, Texas, in 1962, after a change of venue from Reeves County, some 500 miles west. The courtroom was packed and about 30 persons stood in the aisles. A New York Times story described the setting for the pre-trial hearing in this way:[69]

> A television motor van, big as an intercontinental bus, was parked outside the courthouse and the second-floor courtroom was a forest of equipment. Two television cameras have been set up inside the bar and four more marked cameras were aligned just outside the gates.
>
> * * *
>
> Cables and wires snaked over the floor.

With photographers roaming unchecked about the courtroom, Estes' attorney moved that all cameras be excluded from the courtroom. As the attorney spoke, a cameraman walked behind the judge's bench and took a picture.[70]

After the two-day hearing was completed on September 25, 1962, the judge granted a continuance (delay) to the defense, with

---

[67] Chandler v. Florida, 449 U.S. 560, 101 S.Ct. 802 (1981).

[68] Estes v. Texas, 381 U.S. 532, 85 S.Ct. 1628 (1965).

[69] Estes v. Texas, 381 U.S. 532, 553, 85 S.Ct. 1628, 1638 (1965), from Chief Justice Warren's concurring opinion, with which Justices Douglas and Goldberg concurred.

[70] 381 U.S. 532, 553, 85 S.Ct. 1628, 1638 (1965). From concurring opinion by Chief Justice Warren.

the trial to begin on October 22. Meanwhile, the judge established ground rules for television and still photographers. Televising of the trial was allowed, with the exception of live coverage of the interrogation of prospective jurors or the testimony of witnesses. The major television networks, CBS, NBC, and ABC, plus local television station KLTV were each allowed to install one television camera (without sound recording equipment) and film was made available to other television stations on a pooled basis. In addition, through another pool arrangement, only still photographers for the Associated Press, United Press, and from the local newspaper would be permitted in the courtroom.

At its own expense, and with the permission of the court, KLTV built a booth at the back of the courtroom, painted the same color as the courtroom. An opening in the booth permitted all four television cameras to view the proceedings. However, in this small courtroom, the cameras were visible to all.[71]

Despite these limitations the judge placed on television and still photographers, a majority of the Supreme Court held that Estes had been deprived of a fair trial in violation of the due process clause of the Fourteenth Amendment. Chief Justice Warren and Justices Douglas, Goldberg, and Clark asserted that a fair trial could not be had when television is allowed in any criminal trial. Justice Harlan, the fifth member of the majority in this 5–4 decision, voted to overturn Estes' conviction because the case was one of "great notoriety." Even so, it should be noted that Harlan reserved judgment on the televising of more routine cases.

In delivering the opinion of the Court, Mr. Justice Clark wrote:[72]

> We start with the proposition that it is a "public trial"
> that the Sixth Amendment guarantees to the "accused."
> The purpose of the requirement of a public trial was to
> guarantee that the accused would be fairly dealt with and
> not unjustly condemned. * * *.

Justice Clark then took aim on an assertion that if courts exclude television cameras or microphones, they are discriminating in favor of the print media. Clark retorted, "[t]he news reporter is not permitted to bring his typewriter or printing press." Clark did concede that technical advances might someday make television equipment and cameras quieter and less obtrusive.[73]

[71] 381 U.S. 532, 554–555, 85 S.Ct. 1628, 1638–1639 (1965), from Chief Justice Warren's concurring opinion.

[72] 381 U.S. 532, 538–539, 85 S.Ct. 1628, 1631 (1965).

[73] 381 U.S. 532, 540, 85 S.Ct. 1628, 1631 (1965).

In a strongly worded dissent, Justices Stewart, Black, Brennan and White raised constitutional arguments in objecting to the ban on television from courtrooms, at least at that stage of television's development. Justice Stewart expressed doubt that Estes had been deprived of a fair trial by the limited televising of it.[74]

Brennan argued that the *Estes* decision was "*not* a blanket constitutional prohibition against the televising of state criminal trials."[75] Television, said Brennan, was barred by the majority side of *Estes* only from "notorious trials." Nevertheless, from 1965 to 1975, cameras—including television cameras—were kept out of virtually *all* courtrooms.

Cameras in the Courtroom

After 1975, cautious efforts to get cameras back in the courtroom became evident in a number of states. In 1977, the Associated Press Managing Editors Association published a report titled "Cameras in the Courtroom: How to Get 'Em There." The report noted that if "you're going to get your Nikon into that courtroom you've got to have more tools than just a camera. For one thing, you've got to have the clout of your State Supreme Court."

The report described a process, beginning with work with a bench-bar-press committee, through demonstrations and carefully regulated experimental photo and TV coverage of either mock or actual trials. Then, a demonstration videotape should be made for use before a hearing to be conducted by the state's supreme court. The final step is writing guidelines for court coverage for adoption by the state supreme court.[76]

Tentatively, a number of states began to allow television, radio and photographic coverage of judicial proceedings. Modern cameras, available-light photography, smaller and quieter television and camera gear: technological advances have helped get cameras back into many courtrooms. More important, however, has been intelligent negotiation by thoughtful members of bench, bar and press who realize that photography in the courtroom, properly used, can be a valuable tool for educating and informing the public.

By 1979, six states allowed some form of television, radio or photographic coverage on a permanent basis. By mid–1994, such coverage was allowed in 47 states—all but Indiana, Mississippi, and South Dakota. Also, camera coverage was not allowed in the District of Columbia.[77]

[74] 381 U.S. 532, 601–602, 85 S.Ct. 1628, 1669 (1965).

[75] 381 U.S. 532, 617, 85 S.Ct. 1628, 1678 (1965).

[76] Freedom of Information Committee, APME, "Cameras in the Courtroom: How to Get 'Em There," 1977 Freedom of Information Report, p. 2.

[77] Petition of Post–Newsweek Stations, Florida, Inc., 370 So.2d 764 (Fla.1979), Appendix 2; Cameras in the Courts, 1994 study by the RTNDA, summarized in The News Media and the Law, Summer, 1994, p. 62.

Chandler v. Florida: The Lower Courts

A key case testing admission of cameras to courtrooms is *Chandler v. Florida.*[78] It raised the issue of whether admitting television cameras to a courtroom, over the objection of a participant in a criminal case, made a fair trial impossible.[79]

The *Chandler* case stated the issue in rather extreme form, because in jurisdictions where coverage is permitted, consent of parties is required in most instances.[80] The Supreme Court of the United States held early in 1981 that television coverage had not denied Chandler a fair trial.[81]

Chandler v. Florida also is important because of its interrelationship with another Florida matter, In re Petition of Post–Newsweek Stations, Florida, Inc., for Change in Code of Judicial Conduct.[82] In that proceeding, the Supreme Court of Florida ruled that electronic media coverage of courtroom proceedings is not in itself a denial of due process of law. However, the court also held that the First and Sixth Amendments do not mandate the electronic media be allowed to cover courtroom proceedings. The Florida Supreme Court then issued a rule to amend 3A(7) of Florida's Code of Judicial Conduct to allow still photography and electronic media coverage of public judicial proceedings in the appellate and trial courts, subject at all times to the authority of the presiding judge.[83]

The *Post-Newsweek Stations* ruling, with its lengthy appendices spelling out the deployment of equipment and personnel, the kind of equipment to be used, and pooling arrangements for coverage to cut down on in court distractions, has been used elsewhere as a primer for drafting petitions to seek changes in state judicial rules.

Chandler v. Florida: The Trial

Chandler v. Florida involved the burglary trial of two Miami Beach policemen, Noel Chandler and Robert Granger. During their trial, the defendants raised various objections to Florida's [then] Experimental Canon 3A(7). Under that canon, despite requests from the defendants that live television coverage be excluded, cameras were allowed to televise parts of the trial.[84]

[78] Chandler v. State, 366 So.2d 64 (Fla.App.1978), certiorari denied 376 So.2d 1157 (1979), probable juris. noted 446 U.S. 907, 100 S.Ct. 1832 (1980).

[79] 366 So.2d 64, 69 (Fla.App.1978).

[80] See Appendix 2, "Television in the Courtroom—Recent Developments," National Center for State Courts, quoted in entirety in Petition of Post–Newsweek Stations, Florida, Inc., 370 So.2d 764 (Fla.1979).

[81] 449 U.S. 560, 101 S.Ct. 802 (1981).

[82] 370 So.2d 764 (Fla.1979), 5 Med.L.Rptr. 1039.

[83] Ibid., p. 781.

[84] Chandler v. State, 366 So.2d 64, 69 (Fla.App.1978).

The Supreme Court of Florida denied a petition for a writ of certiorari, asserting a lack of jurisdiction. That court said, "No conflict has been demonstrated, and the question of great public interest has been rendered moot by the decisions in Petition of Post–Newsweek Stations, Florida, Inc., 370 So.2d 764 (Fla.1979)."

The Supreme Court of the United States, however, noted probable jurisdiction in Chandler v. Florida in 1980.[85]

Chandler v. Florida: The Supreme Court

In 1981, the Supreme Court of the United States decided *Chandler* by an 8–0 vote, thus upholding the conviction of two Miami Beach police officers for burglarizing Piccolo's Restaurant. This case—regardless of its outcome—would have been memorable for its fact situation. Officers Noel Chandler and Robert Grander had been chatting with each other via walkie-talkies as they broke into the restaurant; they were overheard by an insomniac ham radio operator who recorded their conversations.[86]

Writing for that unanimous Court, Chief Justice Burger based his decision on the principle of federalism. States may work out their own approaches to allowing photographic and broadcast coverage of trials, as long as the Constitution of the United States is not violated.

Chandler and Granger had argued that the very presence of television cameras violated their rights to a fair trial because cameras were psychologically disruptive.[87] Chief Justice Burger wrote for the Court:[88]

> An absolute Constitutional ban on broadcast coverage of trials cannot be justified simply because there is a danger in some cases that prejudicial broadcast accounts of pretrial and trial proceedings may impair the ability of jurors to decide the issue of guilt or innocence. * * * [T]he risk of juror prejudice does not warrant an absolute Constitutional ban on all broadcast coverage. * * *

After the U.S. Supreme Court decision in *Chandler,* states increasingly experimented with cameras in courtrooms. The ABA model code's Section 3A(7) opposing cameras never was mandatory in any state unless adopted formally by a state's highest court. But in 1990, the ABA abandoned Canon 3A(7) completely, removing it from the ABA's model code of judicial conduct.[89] The reason? The

---

[85] 446 U.S. 907, 100 S.Ct. 1832 (1980).

[86] Chandler v. Florida, 449 U.S. 560, 101 S.Ct. 802 (1981).

[87] The News Media & The Law, 5:1 (Feb./Mar.1981) p. 5.

[88] Chandler v. Florida, 449 U.S. 560, 575, 101 S.Ct. 802, 810 (1981).

[89] Kate Aschenbrenner Pate, "Restricting Electronic Media Coverage of Child–Witnesses: A Proposed Rule," University of Chicago Legal Forum 1993, pp. 352–353.

American Bar Association backed off on grounds that the canon did not deal with judicial ethics but was more properly an issue to be governed by separate court rules.[90] Note, that states do not have to admit cameras or broadcast equipment: they *may* do so according to their own rules. Further, any judge who finds cameras disruptive may exclude them.

As the Court said in *Chandler*,[91]

> Dangers lurk in this, as in most, experiments, but unless we are to conclude that television coverage under all conditions is prohibited by the Constitution, the states must be free to experiment. * * * The risk of prejudice to particular defendants is ever present and must be examined carefully as cases arise.

The Federal Cameras in Courts Experiment

Even though remarkable gains have been made in getting television and still cameras into state courtrooms, the federal court picture remained unchanged for many years: No cameras in federal courts. With the camera-despising Chief Justice Warren Burger's retirement—and his replacement as "The Chief" by William Rehnquist—a modest experiment in coverage of federal courts began in July, 1991.

Even so, Rule 53 of the Federal Rules of Criminal Procedure (1953) continued in force, and it forbids photographing or making radio broadcasts during a criminal trial. As the Radio–Television News Directors Association (RTNDA) has pointed out, Rule 53 did not explicitly prohibit TV broadcasts, but it might as well, because that's the way courts interpret it.[92]

With mounting pressure from the news media, the U.S. Judicial Conference approved a three-year experiment with microphones and cameras in federal courtrooms, to run from July 1, 1991 to June 30, 1994. The experiment dealt with substantial media coverage of civil trials and appeals in selected courts, with coverage of criminal trials and appeals forbidden in this experiment.[93]

The TV camera experiment began with civil trials in six (of 94) Federal District Courts and two (of 13) Federal Courts of Appeals. Reports that these experiments were quite trouble-free led journal-

[90] Ibid., p. 353, citing Lisa L. Milord, The Development of The ABA Judicial Code, p. 22 (ABA, 1992).

[91] 449 U.S. 560, 581, 101 S.Ct. 802, 813 (1981).

[92] RTNDA, News Media Coverage of Judicial Proceedings With Cameras and Microphones: A Survey ... (Washington, D.C.: RTNDA, 1994).

[93] RTNDA, News Media Coverage of Judicial Proceedings With Cameras and Microphones: A Survey ... (Washington, D.C., RTNDA, 1991), pp. 9–10. This experimental civil coverage was to occur in six federal district courts and in the U.S. Courts of Appeal for the Second and Ninth Circuits.

ists to hope for cameras in federal courts. Traditions die hard, however, and the U.S. Judicial Conference—perhaps alarmed by sensational media coverage of the early maneuvers in the O.J. Simpson murder case—voted in September, 1994, to end its civil trial coverage experiment.[94]

But in March, 1995, the Judicial Conference reversed itself, deciding to allow further experimentation with coverage of *civil* trials in federal courts. The format for such experimentation was not specified.[95] As Linda Greenhouse explained, the 27–member Judicial Conference—which meets in secret—is made up of chief judges of each federal circuit plus district judges from each circuit, and is chaired by the Chief Justice of the United States. The Judicial Conference has the authority to declare trials open to TV cameras in federal civil cases. However, the more controversial matter of TV coverage of criminal trials is governed by the Federal Rules of Criminal Procedure, which can be changed only with permission from the Supreme Court of the United States and from Congress. Perhaps camera coverage of both criminal and civil trials can help to dilute the harm done by supermarket tabloids, which had a field day sensationalizing the O.J. Simpson trial.[96]

SEC. 59. NOTORIOUS CASES: THE SHADOW OF SHEPPARD

The long ordeal of Dr. Samuel Sheppard ended with the reversal of his murder conviction on grounds that pretrial and during-trial publicity had impaired his ability to get a fair trial.

The Trial of Dr. Sam Sheppard

When the free press—fair trial controversy is raised, the case most likely to be mentioned is that *cause celebre* of American jurisprudence, Sheppard v. Maxwell.[97] This case was one of the most notorious—and most sensationally reported—trials in American history. With perhaps the exception of the Lindbergh kidnaping case of the 1930s, the ordeal of Dr. Sam Sheppard may well have been the most notorious case of the Twentieth Century. His case continued to attract attention more than 40 years after the murder.

This case began in the early morning hours of July 4, 1954, when Dr. Sheppard's pregnant wife, Marilyn, was found dead in the

[94] Linda Greenhouse, "U.S. Judges Vote Down TV in Courts," The New York Times, Sept. 21, 1995, p. A11.

[95] Greenhouse, "Judicial Conference Rejects More Secrecy in Civil Court: Plan to Make Records Easier to Seal Dies," The New York Times, March 15, 1995, p. A12.

[96] See Greenhouse, note 72, above; "Federal Courts, Back in the Dark," The New York Times, Sept. 22, 1994, p. A18.

[97] 384 U.S. 333, 86 S.Ct. 1507 (1966).

upstairs bedroom of their home. She had been beaten to death. Dr. Sheppard, who told authorities he had found his wife dead, called a neighbor, Bay Village Mayor Spence Houk. Dr. Sheppard appeared to have been injured, suffering from severe neck pains, a swollen eye, and shock.

Dr. Sheppard, a Bay Village, Ohio, osteopath, told a rambling and unconvincing story to officials: that he had dozed off on a downstairs couch after his wife had gone upstairs to bed. He said that he heard his wife cry out and ran upstairs. In the dim light from the hall, he saw a "form" which he later described as a bushy haired man standing next to his wife's bed. Sheppard said he grappled with the man and was knocked unconscious by a blow to the back of his neck.

He said he then went to his young son's room, and found him unharmed. Hearing a noise, Sheppard then ran downstairs. He saw a "form" leaving the house and chased it to the lake shore. Dr. Sheppard declared that he had grappled with the intruder on the beach, and had been again knocked unconscious.[98]

From the outset, Dr. Sheppard was treated as the prime suspect in the case. The coroner was reported to have told his men, " 'Well, it is evident the doctor did this, so let's go get the confession out of him.' "Sheppard, meanwhile, had been removed to a nearby clinic operated by his family. While under sedation, Sheppard was interrogated in his hospital room by the coroner. Later, on the afternoon of July 4, he was also questioned by Bay Village police, with one policeman telling Sheppard that lie detector tests were "infallible." This same policeman told Dr. Sheppard, " 'I think you killed your wife.' "Later that same afternoon, a physician sent by the coroner was permitted to make a careful examination of Sheppard.[99]

As early as July 7—the date of Marilyn Sheppard's funeral—a newspaper story appeared quoting a prosecuting attorney's criticism of the Sheppard family for refusing to permit his immediate questioning. On July 9, Sheppard re-enacted his recollection of the crime at his home at the request of the coroner. This re-enactment was covered by a group of newsmen which had apparently been invited by the coroner. Sheppard's performance was reported at length by the news media, including photographs. Front-page headlines also emphasized Sheppard's refusal to take a lie-detector test.[100]

On July 20, 1954, newspapers began a campaign of front-page editorials. One such editorial charged that someone was "getting

[98] 384 U.S. 333, 335–336, 86 S.Ct. 1507, 1508–1509 (1966).
[99] 384 U.S. 333, 337–338, 86 S.Ct. 1507, 1509–1510 (1966).
[100] 384 U.S. 333, 338, 86 S.Ct. 1507, 1510 (1966).

away with murder." The next day, another front-page editorial asked, "Why No Inquest?" A coroner's inquest was indeed held on that day in a school gymnasium. The inquest was attended by many newsmen and photographers, and was broadcast with live microphones stationed at the coroner's chair and at the witness stand. Sheppard had attorneys present during the three-day inquest, but they were not permitted to participate.[1]

The news media also quoted authorities' versions of the evidence before trial. Some of this "evidence"—such as a detective's assertion that " 'the killer washed off a trail of blood from the murder bedroom to the downstairs section' "—was never produced at the trial. Such a story, of course, contradicted Sheppard's version of what had happened in the early morning hours of July 4, 1954.[2] A newspaper published a front-page picture of Marilyn Sheppard's blood-stained pillow. The picture had been altered to show the apparent imprint of a medical instrument.

The news media's activities also included playing up stories about Sheppard's extramarital love life, suggesting that these affairs were a motive for the murder of his wife. Although the news media repeatedly mentioned his relationship with a number of women, testimony taken at Sheppard's trial never showed that Sheppard had any affairs except the one with Susan Hayes.[3]

The Supreme Court of the United States, in Justice Tom C. Clark's majority opinion in the Sheppard case in 1966, summed up the news accounts in this way:[4]

> The publicity then grew in intensity until his indictment on August 17. Typical of the coverage during this period is a front-page interview entitled: "Dr. Sam: 'I Wish There Was Something I Could Get Off My Chest—but There Isn't.' " Unfavorable publicity included items such as a cartoon of the body of a sphinx with Sheppard's head and the legend below: " 'I Will Do Everything In My Power to Help Solve This Terrible Murder.'—Dr. Sam Sheppard." Headlines announced, *inter alia* [among other things], that: "Doctor Evidence is Ready for Jury," "Corrigan Tactics Stall Quizzing," "Sheppard 'Gay Set' Is Revealed by [Bay Village Mayor Spence] Houk," "Blood Is Found in Garage," "New Murder Evidence Is Found, Police Claim," "Dr. Sam Faces Quiz At Jail on Marilyn's Fear Of Him."

Although the record of Sheppard's trial included no excerpts from radio and television broadcasts, the Court assumed that

[1] 384 U.S. 333, 339, 86 S.Ct. 1507, 1510 (1966).

[2] 384 U.S. 333, 340, 86 S.Ct. 1507, 1511 (1966).

[3] 384 U.S. 333, 340–341, 86 S.Ct. 1507, 1511 (1966).

[4] 384 U.S. 333, 341–342, 86 S.Ct. 1507, 1511–1512 (1966).

coverage by the electronic media was equally extensive since space was reserved in the courtroom for representatives of those media.

Justice Clark also noted that the chief prosecutor of Sheppard was a candidate for common pleas judge and that the trial judge, Herbert Blythin, was a candidate for re-election. Furthermore, when 75 persons were called as prospective jurors, all three Cleveland newspapers published their names and addresses. All of the prospective jurors received anonymous letters and telephone calls, plus calls from friends, about the impending Sheppard trial.[5]

During the trial, pictures of the jury appeared more than 40 times in the Cleveland newspapers. And the day before the jury rendered its verdict of guilty against Dr. Sam Sheppard, while the jurors were at lunch in the company of two bailiffs, the jury was separated into two groups to pose for pictures which were published in the newspapers. The jurors, unlike those in the Estes case, were not sequestered ["locked up" under the close supervision of bailiffs]. Instead, the jurors were allowed to do what they pleased outside the courtroom while not taking part in the proceedings.[6]

The intense publicity given the Sheppard case in the news media continued unabated while the trial was actually in progress. Sheppard's attorneys took a "random poll" of persons of the streets asking their opinion about the osteopath's guilt or innocence in an effort to gain evidence for a change of venue. This poll was denounced in one newspaper editorial as smacking of "mass jury tampering" and stated that the bar association should do something about it.

A debate among newspaper reporters broadcast over radio station WHK in Cleveland contained assertions that Sheppard had admitted his guilt by hiring a prominent criminal lawyer. In another broadcast heard over WHK, columnist and radio-TV personality Robert Considine likened Sheppard to a perjurer. When Sheppard's attorneys asked Judge Blythin to question the jurors as to how many had heard the broadcast, Judge Blythin refused to do this. And when the trial was in its seventh week, a Walter Winchell broadcast available in Cleveland over both radio and television asserted that a woman under arrest in New York City for robbery had stated that she had been Sam Sheppard's mistress and had borne him a child. Two jurors admitted in open court that they had heard the broadcast. However, Judge Blythin merely accepted the jurors' statements that the broadcast would have no effect on their judgment and the judge accepted the replies as sufficient.[7]

5 384 U.S. 333, 342, 86 S.Ct. 1507, 1512 (1966).
6 384 U.S. 333, 345, 353, 86 S.Ct. 1507, 1513, 1517 (1966).
7 384 U.S. 333, 346, 348, 86 S.Ct. 1507, 1514–1515 (1966).

When the case was submitted to the jury, the jurors were sequestered for their deliberations, which took five days and four nights. But this "sequestration" was not complete. The jurors had been allowed to call their homes every day while they stayed at a hotel during their deliberations. Telephones had been removed from the jurors' hotel rooms, but they were allowed to use phones in the bailiffs' rooms. The calls were placed by the jurors themselves, and no record was kept of the jurors who made calls or of the telephone numbers or of the persons called. The bailiffs could hear only the jurors' end of the telephone conversations.[8]

When Sheppard's case was decided by the Supreme Court of the United States in 1966, Justice Tom C. Clark's majority opinion included this ringing statement of the importance of the news media to the administration of justice.[9]

> The principle that justice cannot survive behind walls of silence has long been reflected in the "Anglo–American distrust for secret trials." A responsible press has always been regarded as the handmaiden of effective judicial administration, especially in the criminal field. Its function in this regard is documented by an impressive record of service over several centuries. The press does not simply publish information about trials but guards against the miscarriage of justice by subjecting the police, prosecutors, and judicial processes to extensive public scrutiny and criticism.

Implicit in some of Justice Clark's other statements in his opinion was deep disapproval of the news media's conduct before and during the Sheppard trial. But the news media were by no means the only culprits who made it impossible for Sheppard to get a fair trial. There was more than enough blame to go around, and Justice Clark distributed that blame among the deserving: news media, police, the coroner, and the trial court. The trial judge, Herbert Blythin, had died in 1960, but Justice Clark nevertheless spelled out what Judge Blythin should have done to protect the defendant.

At the outset of Sheppard's trial, Judge Blythin stated that he did not have the power to control publicity about the trial. Justice Clark declared that Judge Blythin's arrangements with the news media "caused Sheppard to be deprived of that 'judicial serenity and calm to which [he] was entitled.' "Justice Clark added that "bedlam reigned at the courthouse during the trial and newsmen took over practically the entire courtroom hounding most of the

[8] 384 U.S. 333, 349, 86 S.Ct. 1507, 1515 (1966).
[9] 384 U.S. 333, 349–350, 86 S.Ct. 1507, 1515–1516 (1966).

participants in the trial, especially Sheppard."[10] Justice Clark asserted:

> The carnival atmosphere at trial could easily have been avoided since the courtroom and courthouse premises are subject to the control of the court. As we stressed in *Estes*, the presence of the press at judicial proceedings must be limited when it is apparent that the accused might otherwise be prejudiced or disadvantaged. Bearing in mind the massive pre-trial publicity, the judge should have adopted stricter rules governing the use of the courtroom by newsmen, as Sheppard's counsel requested. The number of reporters in the courtroom itself could have been limited at the first sign that their presence would disrupt the trial. They certainly should have not been placed inside the bar. Furthermore, the judge should have more closely regulated the conduct of newsmen in the courtroom. For instance, the judge belatedly asked them not to handle and photograph trial exhibits lying on the counsel table during recesses.

In addition, the trial judge should have insulated the jurors and witnesses from the news media, and "should have made some effort to control the release of leads, information, and gossip to the press by police officers, witnesses, and the counsel for both sides."[11] Justice Clark asserted that the trial's "carnival atmosphere" could have been avoided because the judge controls the courtroom and the courthouse. This control could have included "limiting the presence of the press" and more closely regulating reporters' conduct, such as keeping them outside the bar of the courtroom and preventing reporters from handling exhibits.[12]

The Sheppard case drew national attention on Oct. 30, 1997, when an Indianapolis forensic scientist reported he could prove a second man was in the Sheppard home the night Marilyn Sheppard was murdered.[13] Mohammad A Tahir, a senior forensic scientist and DNA expert, said that samples taken from the Cuyahoga County coroner's office show that Marilyn Sheppard had sex with two men the night she died. During testing to isolate Marilyn Sheppard's own DNA, Tahir examined slides containing dried fluids gathered from her body in the autopsy. Tahir reported that he found traces of semen from two sources. The new evidence con-

---

10 384 U.S. 333, 358, 86 S.Ct. 1507, 1520 (1966).

11 384 U.S. 333, 359, 361, 86 S.Ct. 1507, 1521–1522 (1966).

12 384 U.S. 333, 358, 86 S.Ct. 1507, 1520 (1966).

13 R. Joseph Gelarden, "DNA Evidence Uncovered in Dr. Sheppard Murder Case," The Indianapolis Star, Oct. 20, 1997.

firmed the presence of another man and was a significant development in Sam Reese Sheppard's attempts to clear his father's name.

Following the revelation about the DNA evidence, Sheppard said his next objective would be to identify that other man. Sheppard had previously identified a convicted killer, Richard Eberling, who operated a window washing service and had worked at the Sheppard home. A judge ordered Eberling to provide a blood sample for additional testing. Dr. Sheppard's body was exhumed to allow for DNA analysis of his blood. Investigators found a trail of blood running from the Sheppard's bedroom out of the house. Tahir has determined the blood did not come from Marilyn Sheppard. Investigators now believe Marilyn Sheppard bit her murderer. The DNA samples from the two men would help identify the source of the blood. Police examined Sheppard when he was arrested but found no fresh wounds.

Tahir announced his findings March 6, 1998, declaring that the blood found in the Sheppard bedroom did not come from Sam Sheppard and pointed to Eberling. The Cuyahoga County prosecutor's office announced in a news conference an hour later that it would not reopen the case.[14]

The Judge's Role

The decision in the Sheppard case left its mark in the recommendations of the American Bar Association's "Reardon Report" discussed later in this chapter. The cases discussed in this chapter—*Irvin, Rideau, Estes,* and *Sheppard*—generated new law and suggested strongly that American courts may insist more and more on tighter controls over the information released to the news media in criminal trials by police, prosecution and defense attorneys, and by other employees under the control of the courts. The primary responsibility, however, for seeing to it that a defendant receives a fair trial, rests with the courts. Judges are expected to remain in control of trials in their courts.

A judge with great respect for the press, Frank W. Wilson of a U.S. District Court in Nashville, Tenn., wrote: "Certain it is that the press coverage of crimes and criminal proceedings make more difficult the job that a judge has of assuring a fair trial. But no one has yet shown that it renders the job impossible. In fact, no one has yet shown, to the satisfaction of any court, an identifiable instance of miscarriage of justice due to press coverage of a trial where the error was not remedied."[15] Note that Judge Wilson said that it is the *judge's* job to assure a fair trial. Judge Wilson declared, "show

---

[14] "Despite DNA Results, 'Fugitive' Case Closed," Chicago Tribune, March 6, 1998.

[15] Frank A. Wilson, "A Fair Trial and a Free Press," presented at 33rd Annual convention of the Ohio Newspaper Association, Columbus, Ohio, Feb. 11, 1966.

me an unfair trial that goes uncorrected and I will show you a judge who has failed in his duty."[16]

Judge Wilson thus placed great—some would argue *too* great—[17]reliance upon the remedies which a judge can use to attempt to set things right for the defendant once he has received what the judge considers to be an undue amount of prejudicial publicity. Some of the most important of these trial-level "remedies" are outlined below:

(1) *Change of venue,* moving the trial to another area in hopes that jurors not prejudiced by mass media publicity or outraged community sentiment can be found. This "remedy," however, requires that a defendant give up his Sixth Amendment right to a trial in the "State and *district* wherein the crime shall have been committed * * *."[18]

(2) *Continuance or postponement.* This is simply a matter of postponing a trial until the publicity or public clamor abates. A problem with this "remedy" is that there is no guarantee that the publicity will not begin anew. It might be well to remember the axiom, "justice delayed is justice denied." A continuance in a case involving a major crime might mean that a defendant—even an innocent defendant—might thus be imprisoned for a lengthy time before his trial. A continuance means that a defendant gives up his Sixth amendment right to a *speedy* trial.

(3) *Voir dire* examination of potential jurors. This refers to the procedure by which each potential juror is questioned by opposing attorneys and may be dismissed "for cause" if the juror is shown to be prejudiced. (In addition, attorneys have a limited number of "peremptory challenges" which they can use to remove jurors who may appear troublesome to one side or the other.) Professor Don R. Pember of the University of Washington says that the voir dire examination is an effective tool and one of the best available trial-level remedies.

(4) *Sequestration,* or "locking up" the jury. Judges have the power to isolate a jury, to make sure that community prejudices—either published or broadcast in the mass media or of the person-to-person variety—do not infect a jury

---

[16] Ibid.

[17] Don R. Pember, Pretrial Newspaper Publicity in Criminal Proceedings: A Case Study (unpublished M.A. thesis, Michigan State University, East Lansing, Mich.) pp. 12–16.

[18] Constitution, Sixth Amendment, emphasis added; Lawrence E. Edenhofer, "The Impartial Jury—Twentieth Century Dilemma: Some Solutions to the Conflict Between Free Press and Fair Trial," Cornell Law Quarterly Vol. 51 (Winter, 1966) pp. 306, 314.

with information during trial which might harm a defendant's chances for a fair trial by an impartial jury. As Professor Pember has said, judges are reluctant to do this today because of the complexities in the life of the average person.[19]

(5) *Contempt of Court.* This punitive "remedy" is discussed at length in Chapter 10. Courts have the power to cite for contempt those actions—either in court or out of court—which interfere with the orderly administration of justice. American courts—until the "gag order" controversies of recent years—have been reluctant to use the contempt remedy to punish pre-trial or during-trial publications. (See Section 61 of this chapter, on "restrictive" or "gag" orders.) Some critics of the American mass media would go even further: they would like to see the British system imported. That would mean using contempt of court citations as a weapon to halt media coverage of ongoing or pending criminal cases.

The British system of contempt citations to regulate media activities has worked well, according to some observers. The British press—knowing that the threat of a contempt citation hangs over it for a misstep—cannot quote from a confession (or even reveal its existence); nor can the British publish material—including previous criminal records—which would not be admissible evidence. One of the things about the British system which is most offensive to American journalists is the prohibition of a newspaper's making its own investigation and printing the results of it. After the trial is concluded, *then* British newspapers can cover the trial.[20]

The *New York Times'* Anthony Lewis has suggested that the British system of using contempt citations to preclude virtually all comment on criminal cases simply could not work in the United States. While some criminal trials in the United States drag on for years, even trials involving major crimes—including appeals—are usually completed in Britain in less than two months' time.[21] Anthony Lewis has also argued that Britain is a small, more homogeneous nation where police or judicial corruption is virtually unknown. America has not been so fortunate: occasionally, corrupt policemen or judges are discovered, and perhaps the media's watch-

---

[19] Another trial-level remedy which is more infrequently used is the blue-ribbon jury. When a case has received massive prejudicial publicity, a court may empower either the prosecution or the defense to impanel a special, so-called "blue ribbon" jury. Intelligent jurors are selected through the use of questionnaires and interviews, under the assumption that a more intelligent jury will be more likely to withstand pressures and remain impartial.

[20] Harold W. Sullivan, Trial by Newspaper (Hyannis, Mass., Patriot Press, 1961).

[21] New York Times, June 20, 1965.

dog function is more needed in reporting on police and courts in this nation than it is in Britain.[22]

SEC. 60.   EXTERNAL GUIDELINES AND SELF–REGULATORY EFFORTS

An external regulatory threat—the fair trial reporting guidelines of the "Reardon Committee"—led to press-bar-bench efforts to agree to rules for covering the criminal justice process.

During the middle 1960s, the American Bar Association again got into the act in attempting to regulate prejudicial publicity.[23] As should be evident from preceding sections, there was plenty of pressure on the ABA to do something. First, as noted earlier in Section 87, the Warren Commission investigating the assassination of President Kennedy had some harsh things to say about media coverage of the arrest of suspect Lee Harvey Oswald.[24] Then, there had been a chain of cases involving prejudicial publicity—Irvin v. Dowd (1961),[25] Rideau v. Louisiana (1963),[26] Estes v. Texas (1965)[27] and Sheppard v. Maxwell (1966).[28] Although the [Attorney General Nicholas DeB.] Katzenbach Guidelines for federal courts and law enforcement officers had met with considerable approval, the ABA's concern continued. Early in 1968, the ABA Convention meeting in Chicago approved the "Standards Relating to Fair Trial and Free Press" recommended by the Advisory Committee headed by Massachusetts Supreme Court Justice Paul C. Reardon.[29] The "Reardon Report," as the document came to be known, was greeted with outraged concern by a large segment of the American media.[30] This report dealt primarily with things that attorneys and judges were *not* to say lest the rights of defendants be prejudiced. For example, if a defendant in a murder case had confessed before trial, that

---

[22] Ibid.

[23] Advisory Committee on Fair Trial and Free Press, Standards Relating to Fair Trial and Free Press (New York, 1966); see also draft approved Feb. 19, 1968, by delegates to the ABA Convention as published in March, 1968. For earlier ABA involvement in trying to come to terms with prejudicial publicity see ABA, "Report of Special Committee on Cooperation Between [sic] Press, Radio and Bar," Annual Report, Volume 62, pp. 851–866 (1937).

[24] Report of the President's Commission on the Association of President John F. Kennedy (Washington: Government Printing Office, 1964) p. 241.

[25] 366 U.S. 717, 81 S.Ct. 1639 (1961).

[26] 373 U.S. 723, 83 S.Ct. 1417 (1963).

[27] 381 U.S. 532, 85 S.Ct. 1628 (1965).

[28] 384 U.S. 333, 86 S.Ct. 1507 (1966).

[29] Advisory Committee on Fair Trial and Free Press (of the ABA), Approved Draft, op. cit.

[30] See, e.g., American Newspaper Publishers Association, Free Press and Fair Trial (New York: ANPA, 1967) p. 1 and passim.

confession should not be revealed until duly submitted as evidence during an actual trial. Most frightening to the media, however, were suggestions that contempt powers be used against the media if they were to publish statements which could affect the outcome of a trial.

The Reardon Report touched off many press-bar meetings, seeking to reach voluntary guidelines on coverage of the criminal arrest, arraignment, hearing and trial process.[31] More than two dozen states adopted voluntary agreements based on conferences among judges, lawyers, and members of the media. States with such guidelines include Colorado, Kentucky, Massachusetts, Minnesota, New York, Oregon, Texas, Washington, and Wisconsin.

In such a setting—in the aftermath of the Warren Commission Report on the Kennedy assassination (which called for curtailment of pretrial news)—the *Sheppard* case came along to illustrate once again just how wretchedly prejudicial news coverage of a criminal trial could become. In that setting, the ABA Advisory Committee on Fair Trial—Free Press (Reardon Committee) was formed.

In many places, a press-bar agreement occurred, leading to construction, by joint press-bar committees in roughly half of the states, of guidelines for the coverage of criminal trials.

Wisconsin Fair Trial and Free Press Principles and Guidelines

In Wisconsin, for example, informal rules titled "Wisconsin Fair Trial and Free Press Principles and Guidelines were drafted by a committee of lawyers and journalists in 1969. These guidelines were reworked and reissued in 1979 and in 1987 in response to changes brought about my cases such as Nebraska Press Association Stuart (1976) and pre–1987 free press-fair trial cases discussed earlier in this chapter."

These are *recommended* principles, for voluntary compliance, and the 1987 version emphasized that they are not binding on anyone. Further, and doubtless in some response to a Washington case which would have made voluntary guidelines mandatory as a condition for covering a trial, Wisconsin's 1987 guidelines specify that they are "not to be applied or used against anyone."[32]

The Wisconsin Guidelines, similarly to those of other states, ask for protection of criminal defendants' presumption of innocence

[31] Advisory Committee on Fair Trial and Free Press, op. cit., 1966 and 1968; "Bar Votes to Strengthen Code on Crime Publicity," Editor & Publisher, Vol. 101 (Feb.24, 1968) p. 9.

[32] See Wisconsin News Reporter's Legal Handbook, 2nd ed. (1987), prepared by the Media–Law Relations Committee, State Bar of Wisconsin, in cooperation with the Wisconsin Broadcasters Assn. and the Wisconsin Newspaper Assn. The Washington case is Federated Publications v. Swedberg. See below at footnote 15.

as a shared responsibility among the judiciary, attorneys, news media, and law enforcement agencies. Both access to news of court proceedings and defendants' rights to a fair, unprejudiced trial are recognized as vital rights to be protected. The news media, which have a constitutional and statutory right to report on courts (subject to rare exceptions), and should strive for accuracy, balance, fairness and objectivity.

As to release of information in criminal trials, the guidelines say there should be no restraint on making available to the public, in criminal investigations, the following:

— Information in a public record.

— Information indicating that an investigation is in progress.

— Information on the general scope of an investigation, including a description of the offense.

Non-prejudicial information—such as the defendant's name, age, residence, and place of employment—may also be given, and the circumstances of the arrest may be described.

However, prejudicial information such as the existence of a purported confession or a defendant's performance on tests related to a crime should not be reported.

Federated Publications v. Swedberg (1981)

Voluntary guidelines may become a two-edged sword. In fact, some states reworked their guidelines after the harsh lesson of Federated Publications v. Swedberg as decided by the Supreme Court of the State of Washington. Reworkings of the state guidelines were to re-emphasize their VOLUNTARY nature.

Judge Byron L. Swedberg presided over a trial involving charges of attempted murder. The case, in Whatcom County, north of Seattle, had great notoriety. It involved Veronica Lynn Compton, a woman reputedly the girlfriend of Kenneth Bianchi. Bianchi was known regionally and even nationally as the "Hillside Strangler."

Judge Swedberg refused to grant a defense motion in the case of State v. Compton which would have closed a pretrial hearing to the public. However, the judge conditioned media attendance at the trial upon reporters' signing an agreement to abide by the Washington Bench–Bar–Press Guidelines. Federated Publications, publishers of the Bellingham Herald, challenged Judge Swedberg's order.

The Washington guidelines were created as a voluntary document and had no legal force until Judge Swedberg incorporated them in his order. In that situation, the guidelines—if enforced— would, for example, have stopped the media from reporting on the defendant's previous criminal record or on the existence of a pre-trial confession. In most cases, journalists will agree that pre-trial confessions should not be reported until officially accepted as evidence in court. However, situations could conceivably arise where the best judgment of journalists would be to include information about the existence of such a confession in pre-trial stories. As journalist Tony Mauro said in a Society of Professional Journalists Freedom of Information report in 1982,

> * * * [I]n a single stroke, Swedberg made suspect all the guidelines, developed in many instances only after years of delicate negotiations. Editors who were wary in the first place of sitting down with judges and lawyers were given new reasons to be suspicious—if we agree to talk about guidelines, the thinking went, someday they'll be used against us, as with Swedberg.

In upholding Judge Swedberg's ruling that members of the press must agree to abide by the Washington guidelines if so ordered by a judge, Justice Rosellini of the State of Washington's Supreme Court concluded that Swedberg's limitation was "reasonable." He compared the Swedberg situation to the Washington Supreme Court's holding in Federated Publications v. Kurtz. In the Kurtz case, the court held that the public has a right under the state and federal constitutions to have access to judicial proceedings, including pretrial hearings.

Justice Rosellini listed alternatives to closing a courtroom (see discussion of a similar list elsewhere this Chapter: Continuance (delay), change of venue, change of venire, voir dire, and so forth). Those alternatives, Justice Rosellini wrote, "all involved some compromise of a right or interest of the accused or the State. None of the suggested alternatives involved the exercise of some restraint on the part of the media." He concluded that since his court had the power to exclude all of the public, including the media, he also had the power to impose reasonable conditions upon the media's attendance at a trial.[33]

SEC. 61. RESTRICTIVE ORDERS AND REPORTING THE JUDICIAL PROCESS

After "gag orders" became a nationwide problem, Nebraska Press Association v. Stuart (1976) halted such prior restraints on the news media.

Bar-press guidelines such as those disclosed in the preceding sections tried to honor both the public's right to know about the

---

[33] Federated Publications, Inc. v. Swedberg, 96 Wash.2d 13, 633 P.2d 74, 75 (1981), 7 Med.L.Rptr. 1865, 1871, citing Federated Publications, Inc. v. Kurtz, 94 Wash.2d 51, 615 P.2d 440 (1980), 6 Med.L.Rptr. 1577. See also Tony Mauro, "Bench-media misunderstanding threatens press access to courts," FOI '82: A Report from the Society of Professional Journalists, p. 3.

judicial process and a defendant's right to a fair trial. Not all was well, however, despite the various meeting-of-minds between press and bar. Another disturbing counter-current was perceived during the late 1960s, starting mainly in California and involving judges issuing "restrictive" or "gag" orders in some cases.[34] In a Los Angeles County Superior Court in 1966, for example, a judge ordered the attorneys in a case, the defendants, the sheriff, chief of police, and members of the Board of Police Commissioners not to talk to the news media about the case in question. The order forbade "[r]eleasing or authorizing the release of any extrajudicial statements for dissemination by any means of public communication relating to the alleged charge or the Accused."

All that could be reported under such an order were the facts and circumstances of the arrest, the substance of the charge against the defendant, and the defendant's name, age, residence, occupation, and family status. If such an arrangement were to be worked out on a voluntary basis between press and bar, that might be one thing. However, the fact of a judge's *order*—a "gag rule"—worried some legal scholars, and with good reason.

In a New York case during 1971, Manhattan Supreme Court Justice George Postel, concerned about possibly prejudicial news accounts, called reporters into his chambers and laid down what he called "Postel's Law." The trial involved Carmine J. Persico, who had been charged with extortion, coercion, criminal usury ("loan sharking") and conspiracy. Justice Postel admonished the reporters not to use Persico's nickname ("The Snake") in their accounts and not to mention Persico's supposed connections with Joseph A. Columbo, Sr., a person said to be a leader of organized crime. The reporters, irked by Postel's declarations, reported what the judge had told them, including references to "The Snake" and to Columbo.

Persico's defense attorney then asked that the trial be closed to the press and to the public, and Judge Postel so ordered. However, the prosecutor—Assistant District Attorney Samuel Yasgur—complained that the order would set an unfortunate and dangerous precedent. For one thing, Yasgur declared, the absence of press coverage might mean that possible witnesses who could become aware of the trial through the media would remain ignorant of the trial and thus could not come forward to testify. Prosecutor Yasgur added:[35]

---

[34] Robert S. Warren and Jeffrey M. Abell, "Free Press—Fair Trial: The 'Gag Order,' A California Aberration," *Southern California Law Review* 45:1 (Winter, 1972) pp. 51–99, at pp. 52–53.

[35] "Trial of Persico Closed to Public," The New York Times, Nov. 16, 1971, p. 1, 40.

But most importantly, Your Honor, as the Court has noted, the purpose of having press and the public allowed and present during the trial of a criminal case is to insure that defendants do receive an honest and a fair trial.

Newsmen appealed Judge Postel's order closing the trial to New York's highest court, the Court of Appeals. Chief Judge Stanley H. Fuld then ruled that the trial should not have been closed.[36]

"Because of the vital function served by the news media in guarding against the miscarriage of justice by subjecting the police, prosecutors, and the judicial processes to extensive public scrutiny and criticism," the Supreme Court has emphasized that it has been "unwilling to place any direct limitations on the freedom traditionally exercised by the news media for '[w]hat transpires in the court room is public property.'"

Chief Judge Fuld added that courts should meet problems of prejudicial publicity not by declaring mistrials, but by taking careful preventive steps to protect their courts from outside interferences. In most cases, Judge Fuld suggested, a judge's cautioning jurors to avoid exposure to prejudicial publicity, or to disregard prejudicial material they had already seen or heard, would be effective. In extreme situations, he said, a court might find it necessary to sequester ("lock up") a jury for the duration of a trial.[37]

Although reporters were ultimately vindicated in the *Postel* case, a Louisiana case went against the press. This case, United States v. Dickinson, arose when reporters Larry Dickinson and Gibbs Adams of the Baton Rouge *Star Times* and the *Morning Advocate* tried to report on a U.S. District Court hearing involving a VISTA worker who had been indicted by a Louisiana state grand jury on suspicion of conspiring to murder a state official. The District Court hearing was to ascertain whether the state's prosecution was legitimate. In the course of this hearing, District Court Judge E. Gordon West issued this order:

"And, at this time,–I do want to enter an order in the case, and that is in accordance with this Court's rule in connection with Fair Trial—Free Press provisions, the Rules of this Court.

[36] Oliver v. Postel, 30 N.Y.2d 171, 331 N.Y.S.2d 407, 414, 282 N.E.2d 306, 311 (1972).

[37] U.S. v. Dickinson, 465 F.2d 496 (5th Cir.1972). See, also, People of the State of New York v. Holder, 70 Misc.2d 31, 332 N.Y.S.2d 933 (1972).

"It is ordered that no * * * report of the testimony
taken in this case today shall be made in any newspaper or
by radio or television, or by any other news media."

Reporters Dickinson and Adams ignored that order, and wrote
articles for their newspapers summarizing the day's testimony in
detail. After a hearing, Dickinson and Adams were found guilty of
criminal contempt and were sentenced to pay fines of $300 each.
Appealing to the Court of Appeals for the Fifth Circuit, the reporters were told that the District Court judge's gag order was unconstitutional.[38] They were not in the clear, however. The Court of
Appeals sent their case back to the District Court so that the judge
could reconsider the $300 fines. The judge again fined the reporters
$300 apiece, and they again appealed to the Court of Appeals. This
time, the contempt fines were upheld. The Fifth Circuit Court
declared that the reporters could have asked for a rehearing or
appealed against the judge's order not to publish. Once the appeal
was decided in their favor, the court evidently reasoned, *then* they
could publish.[39]

Attorney James C. Goodale—then vice president of the *New
York Times*—was indignant.

It doesn't take much analysis to see that what the
Court has sanctioned is the right of prior restraint subject
to later appeal. * * * What this case means, in effect, is
that when a judge is disposed to order a newspaper not to
report matters that are transpiring in public he may do so,
and a newsman's only remedy is to appeal or decide to pay
the contempt penalty, be it a fine or imprisonment.

In the fall of 1973, the Supreme Court—evidently not seeing a
major issue requiring its attention—refused to grant certiorari,
thereby allowing the lower court decision to stand.[40] By 1976,
however, the gag issue was an obvious problem. Attorney Jack C.
Landau, Supreme Court reporter for the Newhouse News Service
and a trustee of the Reporters Committee for Freedom of the Press,
came up with some agonizing statistics. From 1966 to 1976, hundreds of restrictive orders were issued by courts against the news
media.[41]

[38] United States v. Dickinson, 465 F.2d 496, 514 (5th Cir.1972).

[39] 476 F.2d 373, 374 (5th Cir.1973); 349 F.Supp. 227 (M.D.La.1972). See also
James C. Goodale's "The Press 'Gag' Order Epidemic," Columbia Journalism
Review, Sept./Oct. 1973, pp. 49–50.

[40] 414 U.S. 979, 94 S.Ct. 270 (1973), refusing certiorari in 465 F.2d 496 (5th
Cir.1972).

[41] Jack C. Landau, "The Challenge of the Communications Media," 62 American
Bar Association Journal 55 (January, 1976).

Nebraska Press Ass'n v. Stuart (1976)

Although the Supreme Court refused to hear the reporters' appeal in the Dickinson case[42]—thus allowing contempt fines against two reporters to stand—a virtual nationwide epidemic of restrictive orders quickly showed that the Baton Rouge case was no rarity.[43] A ghastly 1976 multiple-murder case in the hamlet of Sutherland, Neb. (population 840) was reported avidly by the mass media. This provided the Supreme Court with the factual setting which led to the Court's clamping down on the indiscriminate issuance of gag orders. The issue was stated succinctly by E. Barrett Prettyman, the attorney who represented the news media in Nebraska Press Association v. Stuart.[44]

> The basic question before the Court is whether it is permissible under the First Amendment for a court to issue direct prior restraint against the press, prohibiting in advance of publication the reporting of information revealed in public court proceedings, in public court records, and from other sources about pending judicial proceedings.

The nightmarish Nebraska case involved the murder of six members of one family, and necrophilia was involved. Police released the description of a suspect, 29–year-old Erwin Charles Simants, an unemployed handyman, to reporters who arrived at the scene of the crime. After a night of hiding, Simants walked into the house where he lived—next door to the residence where six had been slain—and was arrested.

Three days after the crime, the prosecuting attorney and Simants' attorney jointly asked the Lincoln County Court to enter a restrictive order. On October 22, 1975, the County Court granted a sweeping order prohibiting the release or publication of any "testimony given or evidence adduced * * * ".[45] On October 23, Simants' preliminary hearing was open to the public, but the press was subject to the restrictive order. On that same day, the Nebraska Press Association intervened in the District Court of Lincoln County and asked Judge Hugh Stuart to set aside the County Court's restrictive order. Judge Stuart conducted a hearing and on October 27 issued his own restrictive order, prohibiting the Nebraska Press Association and other organizations and reporters from reporting on five subjects:[46]

[42] 414 U.S. 979, 94 S.Ct. 270 (1973).

[43] Landau, p. 57.

[44] "Excerpts from the Gag Order Arguments," Editor & Publisher, May 1, 1976, p. 46A.

[45] 427 U.S. 539, 542, 96 S.Ct. 2791, 2795 (1976).

[46] 427 U.S. 539, 543–544, 96 S.Ct. 2791, 2795 (1976).

(1) the existence or contents of a confession Simants had made to law enforcement officers, which has been introduced in open court at arraignment; (2) the fact or nature of statements Simants had made to other persons; (3) the contents of a note he had written the night of the crime; (4) certain aspects of the medical testimony at the preliminary hearing; (5) the identity of the victims of the alleged sexual assault and the nature of the assault.

This order also prohibited reporting the exact nature of the restrictive order itself, and—like the County Court's order—incorporated the Nebraska Bar–Press Guidelines.[47]

The Nebraska Press Association and its co-petitioners on October 31 asked the District Court to suspend its restrictive order and also asked that the Nebraska Supreme Court stop the gag order. Early in December, the state's Supreme Court issued a modification of the restrictive order "to accommodate the defendant's right to a fair trial and the petitioners' [i.e., the Nebraska Press Association, other press associations, and individual journalists'] interest in reporting pretrial events." This modified order prohibited reporting of three matters:[48]

(a) the existence and nature of any confessions or admissions made by the defendant to law enforcement officers; (b) any confessions or admissions made to any third parties, except members of the press, and (c) other facts "strongly implicative" of the accused.

The Nebraska Supreme Court did not rely on the Nebraska Bar–Press Guidelines. After interpreting state law to permit closing of court proceedings to reporters in certain circumstances, the Nebraska Supreme Court sent the case back to District Judge Hugh Stuart for reconsideration of whether pretrial hearings in the Simants case should be closed to the press and public. The Supreme Court of the United States granted certiorari.[49]

Writing for a unanimous Supreme Court, Chief Justice Burger reviewed free press-fair trial cases and prior restraint cases. He wrote: "None of our decided cases on prior restraint involved restrictive orders entered to protect a defendant's right to a fair and impartial jury, but the opinions on prior restraint have a common thread relevant to this case." The Chief Justice then quoted from Organization for a Better Austin v. Keefe:[50]

[47] 427 U.S. 539, 544, 96 S.Ct. 2791, 2796 (1976).

[48] 427 U.S. 539, 545, 96 S.Ct. 2791, 2796 (1976).

[49] 423 U.S. 1027, 96 S.Ct. 557 (1975).

[50] 402 U.S. 415, 91 S.Ct. 1575 (1971).

"Any prior restraint on expression comes to this Court with a 'heavy presumption' against its constitutional validity. * * * Respondent [Keefe] thus carries a heavy burden of showing justification for the imposition of such a restraint. He has not met that burden. * * * "

Chief Justice Burger noted that the restrictive order at issue in the Simants case did not prohibit publication but only postponed it. Some news, he said, can be delayed and often is when responsible editors call for more fact-checking. "But such delays," he added, "are normally slight and they are self-imposed. Delays imposed by governmental authority are a different matter."[51]

The Court then turned to an examination of whether the threat to a fair trial for Simants was so severe as to overcome the presumption of unconstitutionality which prior restraints carry with them. The Chief Justice borrowed Judge Learned Hand's language (oft criticized by libertarians) from a case involving the trial of Communists in 1950: whether the "gravity of the evil," discounted by its improbability, justifies such invasion of free speech as is necessary to avoid the danger.[52] The Court's review of the pretrial record in the Simants case indicated that Judge Stuart was justified in concluding that there would be intense and pervasive pretrial publicity. The judge could have concluded reasonably that the publicity might endanger Simants' right to a fair trial.

Even so, the restrictive order by the trial court judge was not justified in the view of the Supreme Court of the United States. Alternatives to prior restraint were not tried by the Nebraska trial court. Those alternatives included a change of venue; postponement of the trial to allow public furor to subside, and searching questioning of prospective jurors to screen out those who had already made up their minds about Simants' guilt or innocence. Sequestration ("locking up") of jurors would insulate jurors from prejudicial publicity only after they were sworn, but that measure "enhances the likelihood of dissipating the impact of pretrial publicity and emphasizes the elements of the jurors' oaths." The Chief Justice wrote:[53]

* * * [P]retrial publicity, even if pervasive and concentrated, cannot be regarded as leading automatically and in every kind of criminal case to an unfair trial.

* * *

We reaffirm that the guarantees of freedom of expression are not an absolute prohibition under all circum-

[51] 427 U.S. 539, 560, 96 S.Ct. 2791, 2803 (1976).
[52] 427 U.S. 539, 562, 96 S.Ct. 2791, 2804 (1976).
[53] 427 U.S. 539, 565, 570, 96 S.Ct. 2791, 2804, 2806 (1976).

stances, but the barriers to prior restraint remain high and the presumption against its use continues intact. We hold that, with respect to the order entered in this case prohibiting reporting or commentary on judicial proceedings held in public, the barriers have not been overcome; to the extent that this order restrained publication of such material, it is clearly invalid. To the extent that it prohibited publication based on information gained from other sources, we conclude that the heavy burden imposed as a condition to securing prior restraint was not met and the judgment of the Nebraska Supreme Court is therefore *reversed.*

Nebraska Press Association v. Stuart was hailed as a sizable victory for the news media. Nevertheless, some scholars were fretful about that decision's ultimate impact. Benno C. Schmidt, then a Columbia University law professor, found some "disturbing undertones." He expressed the fear that the[54]

> * * * Court may have invited severe controls on the press's access to information about criminal proceedings from principals, witnesses, lawyers, the police, and others; it is even possible that some legal proceedings may be closed completely to the press and public as an indirect result of *Nebraska.*

He also worried that the Supreme Court's decision might encourage trial judges to place increasing reliance on stipulations that parties in a trial—lawyers, witnesses, police, etc.—not provide information in the press.

Schmidt was correct in his gloomy assessment of the Simants case; the so-called victory of the press in Nebraska Press Association was hollow. As former Washington Star editor Newbold Noyes has observed:[55]

> It was Star Chamber, not publicity, that the founding fathers worried about. Defendants were guaranteed a public trial, not a cleared courtroom. The whole thrust of these amendments was—and must remain—that what happens in the courts happens out in the open, in full view of the citizenry, and that therein lies the individual's protection against the possible tyranny of government. There is no possible conflict between this idea and the idea of a free press.

[54] Schmidt, "The Nebraska Decision," Columbia Journalism Review, November/December, 1976, p. 51.

[55] Speech at the University of Oregon, Ruhl Symposium Lectures, November 21, 1975, reprinted in "The Responsibilities of Power," School of Journalism, University of Oregon, June, 1976, pp. 16–17.

Gagging Everybody But the Press?

Back in 1978, a trend then was discernible: gag news sources related to a judicial proceeding while leaving the press alone. The net result, of course, was much the same: a diminished flow of information about the judicial process. As trial courts close various courtroom proceedings, seal certain records, and decree that witnesses, attorneys and participants in trials do not speak to reporters, all that can be done is for the news media to fight back by going to court themselves. Noted First Amendment attorneys Dan Paul, Richard Ovelmen, James Spaniolo and Steven Kamp wrote late in 1984: "The most troubling trend in the cases decided during the last twelve months has been the use of gag orders on litigants and trial participants in order to block at the source public access to information concerning judicial proceedings."[56] The leading case? Seattle Times v. Rhinehart.[57]

Seattle Times v. Rhinehart (1984)

Keith Milton Rhinehart was the leader of a religious group, the Aquarian Foundation. The Seattle Times had published a number of stories about Rhinehart and the Foundation, a group with fewer than 1,000 members, believers in life after death and the ability to communicate with the dead. Rhinehart was the group's chief spiritual medium.[58] As Justice Powell described articles about Rhinehart in the Seattle Times and the Walla Walla Union–Bulletin:[59]

> One article referred to Rhinehart's conviction, later vacated, for sodomy. The four articles that appeared in 1978 concentrated on an "extravaganza" sponsored by Rhinehart at the Walla Walla State Penitentiary. The articles stated that he had treated 1,100 inmates to a 6–hour-long show, during which he gave away between $35,000 and $50,000 in cash and prizes. One article described a "chorus line of girls [who] shed their gowns and bikinis and sang * * * "The two articles that appeared in 1959 referred to a purported connection between Rhinehart and Lou Ferrigno, star of the popular television program, "The Incredible Hulk."

Rhinehart and five of the female members of the Aquarian Society who had taken part in the presentation at the penitentiary sued for libel and invasion of privacy, claiming that the stories were

[56] Dan Paul, et al., op. cit., pp. 57–58.

[57] Seattle Times Co. v. Rhinehart, 467 U.S. 20, 104 S.Ct. 2199 (1984), 10 Med. L.Rptr. 1705.

[58] 467 U.S. 20, 22, 104 S.Ct. 2199, 2202 (1984), 10 Med.L.Rptr. 1705, 1706.

[59] Ibid.

" 'fictional and untrue.' "They asked damages totaling $14.1 million.

As part of the pre-trial discovery proceedings, the defendant newspapers asked for information about the financial affairs of The Aquarian Foundation, including information on donors. The trial court judge issued a protective order [called a "gag order" by journalists] forbidding the Seattle Times from publishing pre-trial discovery information about the Aquarian Foundation's donors, members, and finances.[60]

A unanimous Supreme Court of the United States upheld the gag order preventing release and publication of deposition material. Writing for the Court, Justice Powell said:[61]

> * * * [I]t is necessary to consider whether the "practice in question [furthers] an important or substantial governmental interest unrelated to the suppression of expression" and whether "the limitation of First Amendment freedoms [is] no greater than necessary or essential to the protection of the particular governmental interest involved." Procunier v. Martinez, 416 U.S. 396, 413, 94 S.Ct. 1800, 1811 (1974) * * *.
>
>   * * *
>
> A litigant has no First Amendment right of access to information made available only for purposes of trying his suit. * * * Moreover, pretrial depositions and interrogatories are not public components of a civil trial.

Attorney Dan Paul and co-authors were unconvinced by that reasoning. They wrote:[62]

> None of these reasons is persuasive. First Amendment cases have uniformly recognized that once the press has information in hand, by whatever lawful means, any prohibition on publication is a prior restraint.

Prior Restraint Revisited: CNN and the Noriega Tapes

The prosecution of Panamanian dictator Manuel Antonio Noriega during 1991 showed that judicial prior restraint still could occur. Although Nebraska Press Association v. Stuart (see text, above) still is regarded as a major bulwark against prior censorship by judges, the bizarre Noriega Tapes case showed that courts, on occasion, still can crack the prior restraint whip.

[60] 467 U.S. 20, 27, 104 S.Ct. 2199, 2204 (1984), 10 Med.L.Rptr. at 1707.

[61] 467 U.S. 20, 32, 104 S.Ct. 2199, 2207 (1984), 10 Med.L.Rptr. at 1711.

[62] Dan Paul et al., op. cit., p. 59.

General Noriega, of course, was a most unusual suspect. Taken into custody after a massive U.S. deployment of armed forces, Noriega took sanctuary in a Vatican consulate. After several days of listening to American rock music played by troops surrounding the Vatican property, General Noriega surrendered. He was then spirited away to a well-appointed jail cell in Florida (outfitted with TV, telephone, and even a paper shredder). (Concerns about a fair trial for a foreign head of state who surrendered after a potent military attack seemed strained: Could a U.S. court *really* find a jury of his peers?)

Suspicion grew that the last thing the U.S. government wanted after Noriega survived the attack on Panama was to get the ex-dictator on the stand where he could sing about his former chums at the Central Intelligence Agency (CIA). In any event, someone got hold of tape recordings of Noriega's Florida jail-cell calls to the office of his attorney, Frank Rubino. The tapes, which Rubino claimed were evidence of a government plot to spy on Noriega's legal defense plans, were given to the Cable News Network (CNN).[63]

After CNN announced that it had the tapes, U.S. District Judge William Hoeveler, on November 8, 1990, granted defense attorneys' request for an injunction to prevent CNN's broadcast of the tapes. Although CNN broadcast no taped excerpts of conversations between the general and his attorneys, excerpts of Noriega's calls to others were broadcast.

Judge Hoeveler evidently saw CNN's eagerness to use the tapes as raising two Sixth Amendment questions: Violation of the attorney-client privilege and the possibility of revealing information harmful to Noriega's defense. Even though Judge Hoeveler noted that prior restraints are "presumptively unconstitutional," he held that the barrier laid down by a three-part test in Nebraska Press Association v. Stuart was not insurmountable. The *Nebraska Press* test for justifying prior restraint to prevent prejudicial publicity requires that:[64]

1. Publicity must impair the right to a fair trial.

2. No less restrictive alternative to prior restraint is available or practicable to mitigate effects of the publicity, and

3. A prior restraint would effectively prevent the harm to defendant's rights.

[63] "Tales of the Tape," Newsweek, Dec. 17, 1990, p. 29; "Eavesdropping on Noriega," Newsweek, Nov. 19, 1990.

[64] United States v. Noriega, 752 F.Supp. 1032, 1033 (S.D.Fla.1990), 18 Med. L.Rptr. 1348, 1349.

Judge Hoeveler found that in this instance, prior restraint was justifiable, and ordered a temporary injunction against CNN's broadcast of the tapes until the court could review the tapes in CNN's possession. The following day—Nov. 9, 1990—after an emergency appeal by CNN to the Eleventh Circuit Court of Appeals, Judge Hoeveler limited the temporary injunction to ten days. He complained about CNN's refusal to turn over the tapes to him, putting him in the position of having to make rulings without having heard them.

The next day—Nov. 10, 1990—the Court of Appeals ruled that the temporary restraining order should remain in effect. The appellate court upheld Judge Hoeveler's injunction against CNN and his demand for production of the tapes.[65] Meanwhile, CNN indeed had been defiant, for it repeatedly broadcast—on Nov. 9—a taped conversation said to be an interchange between Noriega and a legal secretary working for his attorneys. Noriega's attorneys asked for dismissal of the charges against their client and that CNN be fined $300,000 each time it played one of the tapes.[66]

CNN then withdrew a bit, agreeing on Nov. 12 to halt playing the tapes until the U.S. Supreme Court could rule. Noriega contended that he was being railroaded and was powerless before an unjust legal system.[67]

On Nov. 18, 1990, moving swiftly only eight days after the Court of Appeals ruling against CNN, the U.S. Supreme Court allowed the injunction to stand, denying CNN's petition for a writ of certiorari.[68]

After this defeat, CNN handed over the Noriega tapes to a federal magistrate who reported his evaluation of the tapes to U.S. District Judge Hoeveler. Anticlimactically, Judge Hoeveler ruled that CNN could broadcast the taped conversations. CNN, however, decided not to put the tapes on the air ... at least, not immediately.[69] The New York Times confessed to being puzzled by CNN's behavior: Challenging a U.S. district judge, ultimately getting his permission to run the tapes, and then not doing so. A *Times* editorial said:[70]

[65] In re Cable News Network, Inc., 917 F.2d 1543, 1547 (11th Cir.1990), 18 Med.L.Rptr. 1352, 1358.

[66] "CNN to Delay Playing of Noriega Tapes," The New York Times, Nov. 13, 1990, p. A12.

[67] Ibid.; see also David Johnston, "Noriega Tells Judge He's at Mercy of an Unfair and Unjust System," The New York Times, Nov. 17, 1990, p. 1.

[68] Cable News Network, Inc. v. Noriega, 498 U.S. 976, 111 S.Ct. 451 (1990), 18 Med.L.Rptr. 1358, 1359.

[69] David Johnston, "Judge Lifts Ban on Noriega Tapes; No Broadcast is Planned," The New York Times, Nov. 29, 1990, p. A14.

[70] "Odd Behavior in the Noriega Case," The New York Times, Dec. 1, 1990, p. 14.

The network's actions and news judgments obscure the important feature of its own story. The existence, not the airing, of some tapes requires explanation from the [U.S.] Justice Department. What safeguards [for defendant Noriega] were in place at Miami's Metropolitan Correction Center and how were they violated?

On March 30, 1994, long after CNN's broadcast excerpts of the "Noriega tapes," CNN was charged with criminal contempt for " 'knowingly and wilfully' " disobeying Judge Hoeveler's November, 1990, injunction. Lawyers for CNN attended the arraignment proceeding, pleading not guilty before Judge Hoeveler in the cable network's behalf.[71]

In September, 1994, Judge Hoeveler began a non-jury trial, after offering to assign the case to another judge and to empanel and advisory jury to try questions of fact. Neither the Department of Justice, prosecuting, nor CNN, the defendant, accepted those offers.[72]

On November 1, 1994, Judge Hoeveler found CNN guilty as charged of criminal contempt of court, setting the hearing on sanctions to be levied against CNN for December 9, 1994. Judge Hoeveler acknowledged the press's First Amendment responsibility to provide news of government misconduct, and then wrote:[73]

> * * * CNN, however, had already revealed the potential government misconduct. The intense pressure to play the tapes was actually coming from other news organizations, challenging CNN to show them the tapes or "where's the beef?" * * * [Such circumstances] do not justify the action taken by defendant. The 11th Circuit has held that even when a court's order is ultimately deemed to be invalid, the collateral bar rule requires parties to follow that order.

* * *

The thin bright line between anarchy and order—the delicate balance which ultimately is the vital protection of the individual and the public generally—is the rampart which litigants and the public have for the law and the orders issued by the courts. Defiance of court orders and,

[71] Associated Press, "CNN charged in airing tape of Noriega's talks to lawyers," The Knoxville News–Sentinel, March 31, 1994, p. A12; Larry Rohter, "CNN Charged With Ignoring Court Order on Noriega Tapes," The New York Times, March 31, 1994, p.A7.

[72] District Judge William M. Hoeveler's decision in United States v. Cable News Network, Inc., 865 F.Supp. 1549 (S.D.Fla.1994).

[73] Ibid., p. 1564, 23 Med.L.Rptr. 1033.

even more so, public display of such defiance cannot be justified or permitted.

Late in December, 1994, CNN complied with an order from Judge Hoeveler, ending the dispute by broadcasting an apology and paying $85,000 to reimburse the special prosecutor's costs.

SEC. 62.   ACCESS TO CRIMINAL TRIALS AND CIVIL MATTERS

Gannett v. DePasquale (1979) declared that *pre-trial* matters could be closed to press and public; Richmond Newspapers v. Virginia (1980) held that there is a First Amendment right to attend *trials*.

The Supreme Court had some good news for the press in 1978, and it came in the decision in Landmark Communications, Inc. v. Virginia. The Virginian Pilot, a daily newspaper owned by Landmark, late in 1975 published an accurate article reporting on a pending investigation by the Virginia Judicial Inquiry and Review Commission. The article named a state judge whose conduct was being investigated. Because such proceedings were required to be confidential by the Constitution of Virginia and by related enabling statutes, a grand jury indicted Landmark for violating Virginia law.

The newspaper's managing editor, Joseph W. Dunn, Jr., testified that he had chosen to publish material about the Judicial Inquiry and Review Commission because he believed the subject was a matter of public importance. Dunn stated that although he knew it was a misdemeanor for participants in such an action to divulge information from that Commission's proceedings, he did not think that the statute applied to newspaper reports.[74]

Chief Justice Burger, writing for a unanimous Court, said the issue was whether the First Amendment allows criminal punishment of third persons—including news media representatives—who publish truthful information about proceedings of the Judicial Inquiry and Review Commission. The Court concluded that "the publication Virginia seeks to punish under its statute lies near the core of the First Amendment, and the Commonwealth's interests advanced by the imposition of criminal sanctions are insufficient to justify the actual and potential encroachments on freedom of speech and of the press."

Although the Commission was entitled to meet in secret, and could preserve confidentiality of its proceedings and working papers, the press could not be punished for publication of such information once it has obtained it.[75]

---

[74] Landmark Communications, Inc. v. Virginia, 435 U.S. 829, 98 S.Ct. 1535 (1978).

[75] 435 U.S. 829, 838, 98 S.Ct. 1535, 1541 (1978).

Obtaining information about judicial proceedings, of course, implies access by public and press to those proceedings. And then, after the "good news" of *Landmark Communications* (1978), along came one of the Supreme Court's unpleasant surprises for the press: Gannett v. DePasquale.

Gannett v. DePasquale (1979)

Journalists are taught that government should never be given the power of secret arrest, secret confinement, or secret trial. With its decision in Gannett v. DePasquale, the Supreme Court of the United States said, in effect, that two out of three aren't bad. In a badly fragmented 5–4 vote, with a total of five opinions written, the Court held that the public—including the press—has no right to attend pretrial hearings. The issue in *DePasquale* was narrow: the Gannett Company was seeking to overturn a ruling barring its reporter from a pretrial hearing and forbidding the immediate release of a transcript of a secret hearing.

The Court's majority, however, did not restrict itself to pretrial hearings. Justice Potter Stewart's majority opinion also declared that the rights guaranteed by the Sixth Amendment did not extend to the public or to the press. Instead, those rights "are personal to the accused. * * * We hold that members of the public [and thus the press] have no constitutional right to attend criminal trials." Joining Justice Stewart in that view were Justices William Rehnquist and John Paul Stevens.

Chief Justice Warren E. Burger joined the opinion of the Court, but argued that by definition, a " * * *; hearing on a motion before trial is not a *trial:* it is a *pre*-trial hearing." Mr. Justice Lewis Powell, like the Chief Justice, concurred separately. Justice Powell expressed the belief that the reporter had an interest protected by the First Amendment to attend the pretrial hearing. However, he added that this right of access to courtroom proceedings is not absolute and must be balanced against a defendant's Sixth Amendment fair trial rights. In his concurring opinion, Justice William Rehnquist said that so far as the Constitution is concerned, it is up to the lower courts, "by accommodating competing interests in a judicious manner," to decide whether to open or close a court proceeding.

In a 44–page dissent joined by Justices William Brennan, Byron White, and Thurgood Marshall, Justice Harry Blackmun contended that the Sixth Amendment guarantees the public's right to attend hearings and trials. Justice Blackmun wrote that the Court's majority overreacted to "placid, routine, and innocuous" coverage of a criminal prosecution.

Gannett v. DePasquale arose when 42–year-old former police-man Wayne Clapp did not return from a July, 1976, fishing trip on upstate New York's Lake Seneca. He had been fishing with two men, aged 16 and 21, and those men returned in the boat without Clapp and drove away in Clapp's pickup truck. They were later arrested in Michigan after Clapp's disappearance had been reported and after bullet holes were found in Clapp's boat.

Gannett newspapers, the morning *Democrat & Chronicle* and the evening *Times-Union,* published stories about Clapp's disappearance and reported on police speculations that Clapp had been shot on his own boat and his body dumped overboard. In one story, the *Democrat & Chronicle* reported that the 16–year-old suspect, Kyle Greathouse, had led Michigan police to a place where he had buried Clapp's .357 magnum revolver. Defense attorneys then began taking steps to try to suppress statements made to police, claiming that those statements had been given involuntarily. The defense also tried to suppress evidence turned up in relation to the allegedly involuntary confessions, including the pistol.

During a pretrial hearing, when defense attorneys requested that press and public be excluded, Justice Daniel DePasquale granted the motion, evidently fearing that reporting on the hearing might prejudice defendants' rights in a later trial. Neither the prosecution nor reporter Carol Ritter of the *Democrat & Chronicle* objected to the clearing of the courtroom. On the next day, however-er, Ritter wrote Judge DePasquale, asserting a right to cover the hearing and asking to be given access to the transcript. The judge, refused to rescind his exclusion order or to grant the press or public immediate access to a transcript of the pre-trial hearing. Judge DePasquale's orders were overturned by an intermediate-level New York appeals court, but were upheld by the state's highest court, the Court of Appeals.[76] The Supreme Court of the United States subsequently granted certiorari.[77]

Although the issue of covering a pretrial hearing on suppression of evidence is technically narrow, it is important. As James C. Goodale, former vice president of *The New York Times,* has written:[78]

> Only a fraction of the criminal cases brought ever go to trial. The real courtroom for most criminal trials in the United States is the pre-trial hearing, where proceedings of a vital public concern often take place. * * * [A] successful

[76] Gannett Co., Inc. v. De Pasquale, 43 N.Y.2d 370, 401 N.Y.S.2d 756, 372 N.E.2d 544 (1977), reversing the Supreme Court of the State of New York, Appellate Division, Fourth Department's decision in 55 A.D.2d 107, 389 N.Y.S.2d 719 (1976).

[77] 443 U.S. 368, 99 S.Ct. 2898 (1979).

[78] James C. Goodale, "Open Justice: The Threat of *Gannett,*" Communications and the Law, Vol. 1, No. 1 (Winter, 1979) pp. 12–13.

suppression motion will probably mean that an account of the improper methods the police have used to extract a certain confession will be brought out only at the pretrial hearing, and nowhere else. * * * [T]his is information which the public needs to have if its public officers are to be held accountable. Without multiplying examples, we need only remember the shocking trials of Ginzburg and Scharansky behind closed doors in Russia in the summer of 1978 to realize that criminal trials in this country must remain open.

Other constitutional scholars and a variety of publications expressed both shock and outrage at the Supreme Court's decision in *De Pasquale*. Fear of secret trials is in the American grain. Even though England's despised secret Court of the Star Chamber was abolished in 1641, it has been remembered as a symbol of persecution ever since. The assumption by both public and press has long been that open trials are needed to make sure that justice is done. Harvard Law Professor Lawrence Tribe, a leading scholar, said after *De Pasquale* was decided that there " ' * * * will be no need to gag the press if stories can be choked off at the source.' " Allen Neuharth, chairman of The Gannett Co., Inc., declared that " ' * * * those judges who share the philosophy of secret trials can now run Star Chamber justice.' "[79] In any event, the *De Pasquale* holding was far removed from Justice William O. Douglas's words in a 1947 contempt of court case, Craig v. Harney: "[w]hat transpires in the court room is public property."[80]

Justice Potter Stewart wrote for the Court:[81]

* * *

Publicity concerning pretrial suppression hearings such as the one involved in the present case poses special risks of unfairness. The whole purpose of such hearings is to screen out unreliable or illegally obtained evidence and insure that this evidence does not become known to the jury. Cf. Jackson v. Denno, 378 U.S. 368, 84 S.Ct. 1774 (1964). Publicity concerning the proceedings at a pretrial hearing, however, could influence public opinion against a defendant and inform potential jurors of inculpatory information wholly inadmissible at the actual trial.

* * *

[79] "Slamming the Courtroom Doors," Time, July 16, 1979, p. 66.

[80] Craig v. Harney, 331 U.S. 367, 374, 67 S.Ct. 1249, 1254 (1947).

[81] Gannett Co., Inc. v. DePasquale, 443 U.S. 368, 378–381, 99 S.Ct. 2898, 2905–2906 (1979).

The Sixth Amendment, applicable to the States through the Fourteenth, surrounds a criminal trial with guarantees such as the rights to notice, confrontation, and compulsory process that have as their overriding purpose the protection of the accused from prosecutorial and judicial abuses. Among the guarantees that the Amendment provides to a person charged with the commission of a criminal offense, and to him alone, is the "right to a speedy and public trial, by an impartial jury." The Constitution nowhere mentioned any right of access to a criminal trial on the part of the public; its guarantee, like the others enumerated, is personal to the accused. See Faretta v. California, 422 U.S. 806, 846, 95 S.Ct. 2525, 2546 (1975) ("[T]he specific guarantees of the Sixth Amendment are personal to the accused.") (Blackmun, J., dissenting).

Our cases have uniformly recognized the public trial guarantee as one created for the benefit of the defendant.

Chief Justice Burger's concurring opinion simply maintained that by definition, a hearing on a motion before trial to suppress evidence is not a *trial,* it is a *pre-trial* hearing. Trials should be open, but pre-trial proceedings are "private to the litigants" and could be closed.

Justice Powell's concurrence argued that the reporter had an interest protected by the First and Fourteenth Amendments in being present at the pretrial suppression hearing. He added:[82]

As I have argued in Saxbe v. Washington Post Co., 417 U.S. 843, 850, 94 S.Ct. 2811, 2815 (1974) (Powell, J., dissenting), this constitutional protection derives, not from any special status of members of the press as such, but rather because "[i]n seeking out the news the press * * * acts as an agent of the public at large," each individual member of which cannot obtain for himself "the information needed for the intelligent discharge of his political responsibilities." Id., at 863, 94 S.Ct., at 2821.

Justice Powell then swung into his balancing act, stating that the right of access to courtroom proceedings is not absolute. It is limited by both the right of defendants to a fair trial and by needs of governments to obtain convictions and to maintain the confidentiality of sensitive information and of the identity of informants. In his view, representatives of the public and the press must be given an opportunity to protest closure motions. Then it would be the defendant's burden to offer evidence that the fairness of his trial would be jeopardized by public and press access to the proceedings. On the other hand, the press and public should have to show that

[82] 443 U.S. 368, 397–398, 99 S.Ct. 2898, 2914 (1979).

alternative procedures are available which would take away dangers to the defendant's chances of receiving a fair trial.[83]

Justice Rehnquist's concurring opinion scoffed that Justice Powell was advancing the idea " * * * that the First Amendment is some sort of constitutional 'sunshine law' that requires notice, an opportunity to be heard and substantial reasons before a governmental proceeding may be closed to public and press."[84]

Justice Blackmun's lengthy dissent was joined by Justices Brennan, White, and Marshall. Blackmun termed the news coverage of this case "placid, routine, and innocuous" and, indeed, relatively infrequent. After a long review of Anglo–American historical and constitutional underpinnings for public trials, he pointed to dangers he saw in closing court proceedings.[85]

> I, for one, am unwilling to allow trials and suppression hearings to be closed with no way to ensure that the public interest is protected. Unlike the other provisions of the Sixth Amendment, the public trial interest cannot adequately be protected by the prosecutor and judge in conjunction, or connivance, with the defendant. The specter of a trial or suppression hearing where a defendant of the same political party as the prosecutor and the judge—both of whom are elected officials perhaps beholden to the very defendant they are to try—obtains closure of the proceeding without any consideration for the substantial public interest at stake is sufficiently real to cause me to reject the Court's suggestion that the parties be given complete discretion to dispose of the public's interest as they see fit. The decision of the parties to close a proceeding in such a circumstance, followed by suppression of vital evidence or acquittal by the bench, destroys the appearance of justice and undermines confidence in the judicial system in a way no subsequent provision of a transcript might remedy.
> * * *

III

* * *

It has been said that publicity "is the soul of justice." J. Bentham, A Treatise on Judicial Evidence, 67 (1825). And in many ways it is: open judicial processes, especially in the criminal field, protect against judicial, prosecutorial, and police abuse; provide a means for citizens to obtain

[83] 443 U.S. 368, 398–399, 99 S.Ct. 2898, 2915 (1979).
[84] 443 U.S. 368, 405, 99 S.Ct. 2898, 2918 (1979).
[85] 443 U.S. 368, 438–439, 448, 99 S.Ct. 2898, 2935–2936, 2940 (1979).

information about the criminal justice system and the performance of public officials; and safeguard the integrity of the courts. Publicity is essential to the preservation of public confidence in the rule of law and in the operation of courts.

Richmond Newspapers v. Virginia (1980)

On July 2, 1980—exactly one year after the Supreme Court of the United States ruled in Gannett Co., Inc. v. DePasquale[86] that pretrial hearings could be closed—the Court held 7–1 that the public and the press have a First Amendment right to attend criminal trials. The 1980 case, Richmond Newspapers, Inc. v. Virginia, brought joyous responses from the press.

Anthony Lewis of *The New York Times* wrote, "For once a Supreme Court decision deserves that overworked adjective, historic."[87] His newspaper editorialized: "Now the Supreme Court has reasserted the obvious, at least as it pertains to trials. 'A presumption of openness inheres in the very nature of a criminal trial under our system of justice.' "[88] Even though *Richmond Newspapers* did not overrule *Gannett* where pretrial matters are concerned, the Court's 1980 reliance on the First Amendment—and not on the Sixth Amendment as in *Gannett*—gave hope to journalists.

Justice John Paul Stevens' concurring opinion likewise saw *Richmond Newspapers* as remarkable: "This is a watershed case." He continued,[89]

> Until today the Court has accorded virtually absolute protection to the dissemination of information or ideas, but never before has it squarely held that the acquisition of newsworthy matter is entitled to any constitutional protection whatsoever.

Lewis said " * * * the Court today established for the first time that the Constitution gives the public a right to learn how public institutions function: a crucial right in a democracy."[90] Attorney James Goodale said the Richmond case would help reporters to see " 'prisons, small-town meetings, the police blotter' " and other places and documents often closed to the news media in the past.

[86] Richmond Nsprs. v. Virginia, 448 U.S. 555, 100 S.Ct. 2814 (1980).

[87] Anthony Lewis, "A Right To Be Informed," The New York Times, July 3, 1980, p. A–19.

[88] Editorial, "Wiping the Graffiti Off the Courtroom," The New York Times, July 3, 1980, p. A–18.

[89] Opinion of Mr. Justice Stevens, 448 U.S. 555, 581, 100 S.Ct. 2814, 2830 (1980).

[90] Lewis, loc. cit.

Years ago, Judge Learned Hand described his career on the bench as "shoveling smoke." In 1979, the Supreme Court unlimbered its smoke generator in the infamous *Gannett* case, ruling by a 5–4 margin that the public and the press did not have a right to attend pre-trial proceedings in criminal cases. Some of the Justices' language billowed beyond pre-trial matters. As noted, Justice Potter Stewart's plurality opinion announcing the Court's judgment in *Gannett* declared that rights guaranteed by the Sixth Amendment did not reach to the public or to the press. Those rights, said Stewart, " * * * are personal to the accused. * * * We hold that members of the public [and thus the press] have no constitutional right to attend criminal trials."[91]

Four members of the Court later made public statements professing shock about the way *Gannett* had been "misinterpreted," and that wholesale closings had not been endorsed by a majority of the Court. Howls of protest arose from the media. Goodale, then executive vice president of *The New York Times,* wrote in 1979 that only a small fraction—perhaps 10 per cent—of all criminal cases reach the trial stage. The real courtroom for most criminal proceedings is the pre-trial hearing.[92]

In the wake of *Gannett,* many pretrial *and* trial proceedings were closed. As a study by The Reporters Committee for Freedom of the Press showed, in the 10 months between the *Gannett* decision of July 2, 1979 and April 30, 1980, there were at least 220 attempts to close criminal justice proceedings. More than half were successful. Jack C. Landau, director of The Reporters Committee, wrote that "[j]udges are closing pre-indictment, trial, and post-trial proceedings, in addition to pre-trial proceedings."[93] *Newsweek* reported that in the year after *Gannett,* 155 proceedings were closed, including 30 actual trials. Four hundred attempts were made to close courtrooms between July, 1979, and May, 1981.[94]

The Richmond case arose when Baltimore resident John Paul Stevenson was convicted of second-degree murder in the slaying of a Hanover County, Virginia, motel manager. In late 1977, however, the Virginia Supreme Court reversed Stevenson's conviction, concluding that a bloodstained shirt belonging to Stevenson had been admitted improperly as evidence.[95] Subsequently, two additional jury trials of Stevenson ended in mistrials, one when a juror had to be excused and the other because a prospective juror may have read

[91] Gannett Co., Inc. v. DePasquale, 443 U.S. 368, 99 S.Ct. 2898 (1979).

[92] Goodale, loc. cit.

[93] The Reporters Committee for Freedom of the Press, Court Watch Summary, May, 1980; Southern Newspaper Publishers Association Bulletin, Aug. 10, 1981.

[94] Newsweek, July 14, 1980, p. 24.

[95] Stevenson v. Commonwealth, 218 Va. 462, 237 S.E.2d 779 (1977).

about the defendant's previous trials and may have told other jurors about the case before the retrial began.

On September 11, 1978, the same court—for the fourth time—attempted to try Stevenson. Reporters Tim Wheeler of the *Richmond Times–Dispatch* and Kevin McCarthy of the *Richmond News–Leader,* along with all other members of the public, were barred from the courtroom by Hanover County Circuit Court Judge Richard H.C. Taylor, after defense counsel said:[96]

> "[T]here was this woman that was with the family of the deceased when we were here before. She had sat in the Courtroom. I would like to ask that everybody be excluded from the Courtroom because I don't want any information being shuffled back and forth when we have a recess as to what—who testified to what."

Trial Judge Taylor had presided after two of the previous three trials of Stevenson. After hearing that the prosecution had no objection to the closure, excluded all parties from the trial except witnesses when they testified.[97] Since no one—including reporters Wheeler and McCarthy—had objected to closure, the order was made. Later that same day, however, the Richmond newspapers and their reporters asked for a hearing on a motion to vacate the closure order. Reporters were not allowed to attend the hearing on that order, however, since Judge Taylor ruled that it was a part of the trial. The closure order remained in force.

On the trial's second day, Judge Taylor—after excusing the jury—declared that Stevenson was not guilty of murder, and the defendant was allowed to leave. The Richmond Newspapers then appealed the court closing, unsuccessfully petitioning the Virginia Supreme Court for writs of mandamus and prohibition. The Supreme Court of the United States granted certiorari.

Chief Justice Burger's Opinion

Chief Justice Warren Burger reiterated his view, as stated in Gannett v. DePasquale, that while pre-trial hearings need not be open, trials should be open. In this case, he did not take the Sixth Amendment (right to fair trial) route of the majority in *DePasquale.*[98] Instead, he emphasized that the question in *Richmond Newspapers*[99] was whether the First and Fourteenth Amendments guarantee a right of the public (including the press) to attend trials.

[96] Opinion of Chief Justice Burger, Richmond Newspapers, Inc. v. Virginia, 448 U.S. 555, 559, 100 S.Ct. 2814, 2818 (1980).

[97] Virginia Code § 19.2–2.66, which provided that courts may, in their discretion, exclude any persons from the trial whose presence would impair the trial's conduct, provided that the right of an accused to a fair trial shall not be violated.

[98] Gannett Co., Inc. v. DePasquale, 443 U.S. 368, 99 S.Ct. 2898 (1979).

[99] Richmond Newspapers, Inc. v. Virginia, 448 U.S. 555, 564, 100 S.Ct. 2814, 2821 (1980).

He said that in prior cases, the Court has dealt with questions involving conflicts between publicity and defendants' rights to a fair trial, including Nebraska Press Association v. Stuart,[100] Sheppard v. Maxwell,[1] and Estes v. Texas.[2] But this case, in his view, was a "first:" the Court was asked to decide whether a criminal trial itself may be closed to the public on the defendant's request alone, with no showing that closure is required to protect the right to a fair trial.

After having thus stated the issue, the Chief Justice traced Anglo–American judicial history back to the days before the Norman Conquest and forward through the American colonial experience.[3] In addition to this historical ammunition, Burger quoted Dean Wigmore, who wrote long ago that " '[t]he publicity of a judicial proceeding is a requirement of much broader bearing than its mere effect on the quality of testimony.' "The Chief Justice also found a "significant community therapeutic value" in public trials. He then became expansive about the role of the press as a stand-in for the public, a role often claimed by the press but one which had received little judicial support.[4]

> Looking back, we see that when the ancient "town meeting" form of trial became too cumbersome, twelve members of the community were delegated to act as surrogates, but the community did not surrender its right to observe the conduct of trials. The people retained a "right of visitation" which enabled them to satisfy themselves that justice was in fact being done.

> People in an open society do not demand infallibility from their institutions, but it is difficult for them to accept what they are prohibited from observing.

* * *

> In earlier times, both in England and America, attendance at court was a common mode of "passing the time." * * * With the press, cinema and electronic media now supplying the representations of reality of the real life drama once available only in the courtroom, attendance at court is no longer a widespread pastime. * * * Instead of acquiring information about trials by firsthand observation

---

[100] 427 U.S. 539, 96 S.Ct. 2791 (1976).

[1] 384 U.S. 333, 86 S.Ct. 1507 (1966).

[2] 381 U.S. 532, 85 S.Ct. 1628 (1965). The Chief Justice also cited Murphy v. Florida, 421 U.S. 794, 95 S.Ct. 2031 (1975), in which Jack (Murph the Surf) Murphy, unsuccessfully pleaded that prejudicial pre-trial publicity had deprived him of a fair day in court.

[3] Richmond Newspapers, Inc. v. Virginia, 448 U.S. 555, 100 S.Ct. 2814 (1980).

[4] 448 U.S. 555, 572, 100 S.Ct. 2814, 2825 (1980).

or by word of mouth from those who attended, people now acquire it chiefly through the print and electronic media. In a sense, this validates the media claim of functioning as surrogates for the public. While media representatives enjoy the same right of access as the public, they often are provided special seating and priority of entry so that they may report what people in attendance have seen and heard. This "contribute[s] to public understanding of the rule of law and to comprehension of the functioning of the entire criminal justice system. * * * " Nebraska Press Ass'n v. Stuart, 427 U.S. 539, 587, 96 S.Ct. 2791, 2816 (1976) (Brennan, J., concurring).

Burger than disposed of the State of Virginia's arguments that neither the constitution nor the Bill of Rights contains guarantees of a public right to attend trials. He responded that the Court has recognized that "certain unarticulated rights" are implicit in the Bill of Rights, including the rights of association, privacy, and the right to attend criminal trials. He then inserted footnote 17, which may become important in the future: "Whether the public has a right to attend trials of civil cases is a question not by this case, but we note that historically *both civil and criminal trials* have been presumptively open."[5]

Despite the sweep of Burger's words, he was not saying that all criminal trials must be open to the press and public. Instead, he criticized the conduct of the court in the murder trial of John Paul Stevenson. There, despite its being the fourth trial of the defendant, the judge " * * * made no findings to support closure; no inquiry was made as to whether alternative solutions [such as sequestration of the jury] would have met the need to insure fairness; there was no recognition of any right under the Constitution for the public or press to attend the trial." He concluded: "Absent an overriding interest articulated in findings, the trial of a criminal case must be open to the public. Accordingly, the judgment under review is reversed."[6]

Note that Justice Powell took no part in the consideration or decision of this case. And remember that Powell declared, concurring in Gannett v. DePasquale, that reporters had a *limited* First Amendment right to attend pre-trial hearings. And Justices Blackmun, Brennan, White, and Marshall all agreed that public and press had a right, either under the First or the Sixth Amendment, to attend both pre-trial hearings and trials. Thus, although the First Amendment is not an absolute, it appears that the breadth of

[5] 448 U.S. 555, 581, 100 S.Ct. 2814, 2829 (1980), at footnote 17. Emphasis added.

[6] 448 U.S. 555, 581, 100 S.Ct. 2814, 2830 (1980).

the language in *Richmond Newspapers* about *trials* has once again made attendance at *pre-trial* proceedings an open question.

In his concurring opinion, Justice Stevens said:[7]

> * * * I agree that the First Amendment protects the public and the press from abridgment of their rights of access to information about the operation of their government, including the judicial branch; given the total absence of any record justification for the closure order entered in this case, that order violated the First Amendment.

Justice Brennan, joined by Justice Marshall, presented a marvelously complex concurrence, speaking of the structural value of public access in various circumstances. "But the First Amendment embodies more than a commitment to free expression and communicative interchange for their own sakes; it has a *structural* role to play in securing and fostering our republican form of self-government." He added:[8]

> Open trials assure the public that procedural rights are respected, and that justice is afforded equally. Closed trials breed suspicion of prejudice and arbitrariness, which in turn spawns disrespect for the law. Public access is essential, therefore, if trial adjudication is to achieve the objective of maintaining public confidence in the administration of justice.

Note also that Justice Rehnquist, seeming unconcerned by possible threats of secret judicial proceedings to society, was the only member of the court in both the *Gannett* and *Richmond* cases who could find no support for a right of public and press to attend judicial proceedings under either a Sixth Amendment or First Amendment rationale.[9]

Access Rights Need Defense

Although *Richmond Newspapers* has a much nicer ring than Gannett v. DePasquale, it did leave unanswered questions about the right to cover pre-trial matters, the matters which make up the bulk of our criminal justice process. During the dark days of 1979 and '80, after Gannett v. DePasquale was decided, reporters covering the judicial process began carrying their "Gannett cards." Various organizations made up statements for reporters to read in court when they were about to be ousted from pre-trial or trial proceedings. In fact, a Gannett card—literally from the Gannett organization—said:[10]

---

[7] 448 U.S. 555, 584, 100 S.Ct. 2814, 2829 (1980).

[8] 448 U.S. 555, 595, 100 S.Ct. 2814, 2833, 2837 (1980).

[9] 448 U.S. 555, 606, 100 S.Ct. 2814, 2843 (1980).

[10] Other news organizations, such as Knight–Ridder, had similar cards made for their reporters.

"Your honor, I am _____, a reporter for _____, and I would like to object on behalf of my employer and the public to this proposed closing. Our attorney is prepared to make a number of arguments against closings such as this one, and we respectfully ask the Court for a hearing on those issues. I believe our attorney can be here relatively quickly for the Court's convenience and he will be able to demonstrate that closure in this case will violate the First Amendment, and possibly state statutory and constitutional provisions as well. I cannot make the arguments myself, but our attorney can point out several issues for your consideration. If it pleases the Court, we request the opportunity to be heard through counsel."

Reporters, then, should hang on to their "Gannett Cards" and be ready to read them should a judge decide—on application from counsel—to give them the heave-ho from a judicial (including pre-trial) proceedings. After all, as attorney James C. Goodale has written, even the *Gannett* case required three conditions before closure of a pre-trial hearing:[11]

(1) there would be irreparable damage to the defendant's fair trial rights,

(2) there were no alternative means to deal with the publicity and

(3) the closure would be effective, i.e. no leaks.

If judicial proceedings are to remain open, reporters will have to stand ready to speak up, to protest closures. And their employers, obviously, will have to stand ready to go to court—to expend the money and energy to try to keep court proceedings open. Without protests and court tests, closures will simply occur. And when contested, closures can often be reversed. Reporters in courts—whether they like it or not—must sometimes be a first line of defense against secret court proceedings.[12]

Access to Courts after *Richmond Newspapers*

During the first few years after Richmond Newspapers v. Virginia (1980), the Supreme Court of the United States filled in some of that decision's promising outlines where coverage of the judicial process is concerned. Four key cases are:[13]

[11] James C. Goodale, "The Three–Part Open Door Test in Richmond Newspapers Case," The National Law Journal, Sept. 22, 1980, p. 26.

[12] See James D. Spaniolo, Dan Paul, Parker D. Thomson and Richard Ovemlen, "Access After *Richmond Newspapers*," in James C. Goodale, chairman, Communications Law 1980 (New York: Practising Law Institute, 1980), pp. 385–648, for an intensive discussion of and listing of recent cases involving access to judicial proceedings. See especially pp. 452–456, dealing with access to judicial records.

[13] Globe Newspaper Co. v. Superior Court for Norfolk County, 457 U.S. 596, 102 S.Ct. 2613 (1982), 8 Med.L.Rptr. 1689; Press–Enterprise Co. v. Superior Court of

1. Globe Newspaper Co. v. Superior Court (1982).

2. Press–Enterprise Co. v. Superior Court (1984). ("Press Enterprise I")

3. Waller v. Georgia (1984).

4. "Press–Enterprise II (1986)."

Globe Newspaper Co. v. Superior Court (1982)

The Boston Globe challenged the constitutionality of a Massachusetts statute providing for the exclusion of the public from trials of certain sex offenses involving victims under the age of 18. Globe reporters had tried unsuccessfully to get access to a rape trial in the Superior Court for the County of Norfolk, Massachusetts. Charges against the defendant in the trial involved forcible rape and forced unnatural rape of three girls who were minors at the time of the trial—two were 16 and one was 17. Writing for the Court, Justice Brennan held that the Massachusetts statute providing for mandatory closure of such cases violated the First Amendment of access to criminal trials. He said:[14]

> The Court's recent decision in Richmond Newspapers firmly established for the first time that the press and the general public have a constitutional right of access to criminal trials. Although there was no opinion of the Court in that case, seven Justices recognized that this right of access is embodied in the First Amendment, and applied to the States through the Fourteenth Amendment.
>
>   * * *
>
> * * * [T]he right of access to criminal trials plays a particularly significant role in the functioning of the judicial process and the government as a whole. Public scrutiny of a criminal trial enhances the quality and safeguards the integrity of the factfinding process, with benefits to both the defendant and to society as a whole.
>
>   * * *
>
> We agree * * * that the first interest—safeguarding the physical and psychological well being of a minor is a compelling one. But as compelling as that is, it does not justify a mandatory closure rule, for it is clear that the circumstances of the particular case may affect the significance of the interest. A trial court can determine on a case-

California, 464 U.S. 501, 104 S.Ct. 819 (1984), 10 Med.L.Rptr. 1161; Waller v. Georgia, 467 U.S. 39, 104 S.Ct. 2210 (1984), 10 Med.L.Rptr. 1714.

[14] Globe Newspaper Co. v. Superior Court for Norfolk County, 457 U.S. 596, 603–607, 102 S.Ct. 2613, 2618–2620 (1982), 8 Med.L.Rptr. 1689, 1692–1694.

by-case basis whether closure is necessary to protect the welfare of a minor victim.

Chief Justice Burger and Justice Rehnquist dissented, complaining that Justice Brennan had ignored " * * * a long history of exclusion of the public from trials involving sexual assaults, particularly those against minors."[15]

Press-Enterprise v. Superior Court (1984)

The Riverside (California) Press–Enterprise was trying to cover a rape trial, and wanted its reporters present during the *voir dire* proceedings, the in-depth questioning of prospective jurors. The newspaper moved that the *voir dire* be open to public and press. The State of California opposed the motion, arguing that with the public and press present, jurors' responses would not be candid, and that this would endanger the entire trial.

Writing for a unanimous Supreme Court, Chief Justice Burger wrote that the roots of open trials reach back to the days before the Norman Conquest in England, and related to that was a "presumptive openness" in the jury selection process.[16] He added:

> No right ranks higher than the right of the accused to a fair trial. But the primacy of the accused's right is difficult to separate; from the right of everyone in the community to attend the *voir dire* which promotes fairness.

This fact situation was made harsher by the trial judge's keeping six weeks of the *voir dire* proceedings closed (although three days were open). Media requests for transcripts of the *voir dire* were refused; the California court argued that Sixth Amendment (defendant's right to a fair trial) and juror privacy rights coalesced to support closure of the proceeding. The Supreme Court disagreed. Chief Justice Burger wrote:[17]

> The judge at this trial closed an incredible six weeks of *voir dire* without considering alternatives to closure. Later the court declined to release a transcript of the voir dire even while stating that most of the material in the transcript was "dull and boring." * * * Those parts of the transcript reasonably entitled to privacy could have been sealed without such a sweeping order; a trial judge should explain why the material is entitled to privacy.

Waller v. Georgia (1984)

Waller was a defendant charged with violation of Georgia's Racketeer Influenced and Corrupt Organizations (RICO) Act. A

---

15 457 U.S. 596, 614, 102 S.Ct. 2613, 2624 (1982), 8 Med.L.Rptr. at 1697.

16 Press–Enterprise Co. v. Superior Court of California, 464 U.S. 501, 104 S.Ct. 819, 823 (1984), 10 Med.L.Rptr. 1161, 1164.

17 464 U.S. 501, 513, 104 S.Ct. 819, 825 (1984), 10 Med.L.Rptr. 1161, 1166.

pre-trial suppression hearing was held, in which Waller and other defendants asked that wiretap evidence and evidence seized during searches be suppressed—that is, disallowed or declared inadmissible.

The prosecuting attorney asked that the suppression hearing be closed, contending that if the evidence were presented in open court and published, it might become "tainted" and therefore unusable, especially in future prosecutions. The court ordered the suppression hearing closed to all persons except witnesses, the defendants, and lawyers and court personnel. Defendant Waller, however, wanted the hearings to be open.

Writing for the Court, Justice Lewis Powell cited Press Enterprise I approvingly, noting that even though the suppression hearing had been closed for its entire seven days, there was less than two and one-half hours worth of wiretap evidence tapes played in the court.[18]

"Press–Enterprise II" [Press–Enterprise v. Riverside County Superior Court (1986)]

In 1986, the Supreme Court of the United States continued to back away from its much-criticized decision in Gannett v. DePasquale (1979), which held that pre-trial hearings could be closed to press and public. *De Pasquale*, decided under the Sixth (fair trial) amendment, now seems to have been overruled by "Press Enterprise II, decided under the First Amendment."

In that case, Robert Diaz—a nurse suspected of murdering a dozen hospital patients by lethal injections of huge amounts of the heart drug lidocaine—was to have a hearing to see whether there was probable cause to hold him for trial. The magistrate excluded the press from the hearing, which dragged on for 41 days. The magistrate ordered a trial for Diaz.[19]

The California Supreme Court upheld the exclusion order, on the ground that there is no general First Amendment right of access to preliminary hearings, not if a judge found there was "a reasonable likelihood of substantial prejudice."[20]

The U.S. Supreme Court overturned that view, stating that the California rule called for a lesser burden of proof than is required under the First Amendment: there should be a "substantial probability" of prejudice before closure could be allowed.[21]

[18] Waller v. Georgia, 467 U.S. 39, 42, 104 S.Ct. 2210, 2213 (1984).

[19] 478 U.S. 1, 106 S.Ct. 2735 (1986).

[20] Press–Enterprise Company v. Superior Court, 478 U.S. 1, 5, 106 S.Ct. 2735, 2739 (1986).

[21] 478 U.S. 1, 14, 106 S.Ct. 2735, 2743 (1986).

Chief Justice Burger, writing for a total of seven Justices (Stevens and Rehnquist dissented), declared that the interest of free press and of fair trial are not necessarily inconsistent. He added, "[O]ne of the important means of assuring a fair trial is that the process is open to neutral observers." Finally:[22]

> The considerations that led the Court to apply the First Amendment right of access to criminal trials in *Richmond Newspapers* and the selection of jurors in *Press–Enterprise I* lead us to conclude that the right of access applies to preliminary hearings as conducted in California.

Access to Civil Matters

Coverage of the justice system overwhelmingly focuses on criminal cases. A person who has "seemed pretty quiet and never bothered anybody" is charged with multiple murders. The case immediately involves the defendant, victims and the families and acquaintances of all concerned. But apart from Timothy McVeigh, how many defendants have been involved in the deaths or injuries of hundreds? Yet the scale of manufacturing and marketing means that a single product injected into the stream of commerce has the ability to affect hundreds or thousands of lives with sometimes deadly results.

Although civil trial coverage may not appear as important or sexy as criminal trials to journalists and civil libertarians, all of the judicial process—criminal or civil, or in law or equity—needs to be open to the public. Public funds pay for the courts and judges, whether the cases involved be criminal or civil. Furthermore, when the judicial process is closed or otherwise hidden from public view, the likelihood is great that private rather than public welfare is being served.

Ford became known as the American automaker that made dangerously defective automobiles in the 1970s when the media focused on the Pinto and its rear-mounted gas tank. What most Americans did not know, was that General Motors had a similar design that was responsible for a number of fires and explosions.

> * * * General Motors built cars with designs similar to Ford's and GM cars were involved in numerous accidents in which persons were severely injured or killed because of gas-tank fires and explosions.

> The difference between the publicity the two received lay in General Motors' savvy use of the court system to throw up a shield of secrecy over its legal problems * * *[23]

[22] 478 U.S. 1, 10, 106 S.Ct. 2735, 2741 (1986).

[23] Bill Loving, "Media Access to Civil Court Records," paper presented to the Law Division, Association for Education in Journalism and Mass Communication, Boston, MA, Aug. 1991, p.1.

In a series published in 1988, the Washington Post reported on GM's strategies in keeping its name out of the press. "Over the last five years, in defending itself against scores of lawsuits filed by victims of fiery car crashes, General Motors Corp. has used court secrecy procedures throughout the nation to keep closely held and controversial documents about auto safety from becoming public."[24]

GM had good reason to keep its secrets. While Ford was losing major lawsuits and suffered declining sales linked to the news about the Pinto, GM's reputation was largely intact despite the similarities between the companies' car-making techniques and safety analyses.

In 1970, GM officials were told of risks associated with the rear placement of its gas tanks. In 1971, GM considered moving its gas tanks from behind the axle where they were vulnerable, to a position in front of the rear axle where they would be more protected. To do so would result in the loss of some trunk space and cost between $8.59 and $11.59 per car. GM decided not to make the change. Two years later, the company considered the risks from the rear gas tank placement. A June 29, 1973 memo, titled "Value Analysis," looked at the problem, the Washington Post reported.

"A GM engineer, Edward C. Ivey, assigned a $200,000 value to each human life and assumed that a maximum of 500 people died annually in GM cars 'where the bodies were burnt.'

Then, in a two-stage calculation relating to new GM cars, Ivey determined what level of expenditure could be justified to try to avoid fiery deaths in the 5 million cars GM was producing annually. "This analysis indicates that for GM it would be worth approximately $2.20 per new auto to prevent a fuel fed fire in all accidents."[25]

Ford did not keep information about its suits or its documents secret. Ford had allowed a similar Ford analysis to become public. That document also placed a value of $200,000 per human life lost in a fiery accident. In February of 1978, Ford lost a California case involving a Pinto. The jury awarded the plaintiffs $128.5 million. A few days later, GM lost one of the few fuel tank cases it was forced to go to trial on. GM lost and the plaintiffs were awarded $2.5 million. GM appealed saying the jury had been influenced by the publicity about the Pinto. GM settled the case for less than the amount of the judgment and entered into a confidentiality agreement with the plaintiffs.

[24] "Court Secrecy Masks Safety Issues," The Washington Post, Oct. 21, 1988, p. A1–22.

[25] Ibid.

Other instances of secrecy involving products include defective mechanical heart valves, children's playground equipment, prescription painkillers, cigarette lighters while other cases involve claims of medical and legal malpractice. The common thread is the use of settlements and confidentiality orders to keep news of the injuries and suits out of the public eye. The means of achieving this secrecy include:

Protective Orders: This in effect gags persons who receive information from the defendant, thus keeping information damaging to the defendant away from the public, the press, or other litigants.

Confidentiality Agreements: Defendants and plaintiffs often agree to keep details of the lawsuit, including causes of injuries or amounts of settlements, secret.

Sealed Files: When a lawsuit is settled out of court, sealing the files will keep everyone else—the public, environmental health officials, the news media—from knowing just what kind of deal has been cut.

In an adversarial system with opposing counsel and the supervision of a judge, how can corporations manage to keep things quiet? It is a combination of factors in which all the participants can find themselves working together for the purpose of limiting publicity. Lawyers, parties and the courts take their parts in this.

Lawyers are required to serve their clients with the utmost devotion. The Canons of Professional Ethics, Canon 15, states:

> "The lawyer owes 'entire devotion to the interests of
> his client, warm zeal to the maintenance and defense of his
> rights and the exertion of his utmost learning and ability'
> to the end that nothing be taken or withheld from him,
> save by the rules of law, legally applied."

That means defense lawyers must serve their clients and if that means keeping things confidential, so be it. Confidentiality is an important consideration. For example, a person buys a widget from the Widget Co. She is severely injured because of a design and manufacture defect. The person may attribute her injury to bad luck or some other external factor. Without publicity about the defective widget, the injured party may not even realize that she has a claim to pursue. If a lawyer can prevent a lawsuit from being filed, he has saved his client great expense. If an injured party does suspect a design and manufacturing defect, the defense lawyer has the job of trying to eliminate the suit before it can generate publicity and put other injured persons on notice that their injuries might have been caused by the Widget Co. thus generating more suits. That can mean offers of settlement that include extra money in return for confidentiality agreements.

Plaintiff's attorneys likewise have strong pressures to go along with secrecy. Just like defense lawyers, plaintiff's attorneys have a duty to their clients. They are required to inform their clients about settlement offers even when those offers may seem to be against the greater public good. James Gilbert, an attorney in Arvada, Colo. told Newsday that he settled a case involving a "dangerous vehicle." But because of the settlement agreement's secrecy terms, Gilbert, "can't say whether the vehicle is a car or truck. I can't say who makes it. I can't even say which part of the vehicle is involved. And it bothers me because that vehicle is still on the road."[26]

If the client wants to take the settlement offer and sign a secrecy agreement, the lawyer must comply. Defendants may pay more than the injury is worth to avoid dangerous publicity. Sometimes, though the plaintiff's attorney will see a compelling need for confidentiality. Premature disclosure of a suit could lead to hundreds more being filed by other, similar victims. A flood of suits could bankrupt the defendant and prevent recovery for anyone. That was the case for the A.H. Robins Co., the company that produced the Dalkon Shield I.U.D. "Hundreds of women who filed claims against the company went unpaid after the company sought bankruptcy protection in the face of the legal onslaught."[27] Secrecy therefore protects the plaintiff and her lawyer must see to that need first.

Judges are caught in the middle. The courts are clogged with cases and any settlement means one less case that needs to be tried. If lawyers for both sides come to chambers with a signed settlement agreement, judges are likely to approve. After all, the opposing sides are in agreement so why should the court object. Many times the settlement agreements are brought during court recesses, on lunch breaks, or get squeezed into spaces between appointments. The Washington Post learned that some judges who sign settlement and confidentiality agreements have little idea of what they are approving. There are simply too many pages in too many controversies for the judge to examine all of the details. Judges who oppose secrecy face problems from savvy litigators. In one case, GM attorneys sought a confidentiality order on all of the documents the car maker was turning over to the plaintiff's attorney. When Judge David Peeples expressed his reluctance to grant a sweeping order, the GM attorney said he would ask for a hearing on each document.

[26] "System Thwarts Sharing Data on Unsafe Products," Newsday, April 24, 1988, p. 24.

[27] "Legal Merry–Go–Round," Newsday, June 5, 1988.

There were 15,000 documents. Judge Peeples granted the GM request.[28]

Paul McMasters, Freedom of Information chair for the Society of Professional Journalists in 1990, put the issue of civil litigation secrecy in sharp focus:[29]

> "We're not talking about irrelevant facts left in the files of the litigants. We're talking about documents and decisions involving unsafe products, dangerous drugs, toxic wastes, all with potentially devastating effects on people unaware of that danger."

Such records secrecy in civil litigation has long been routine in most jurisdictions. In Texas, however, Justice Lloyd Doggett of the Texas Supreme Court led the fight which resulted in a new standard in that state for sealing court records, saying explicitly that records may not be removed from (civil) court files except as allowed by statute or court rule. Such records are presumed open, and may be closed only upon a showing of a substantial interest outweighing the presumption of openness and any probable adverse effect that sealing records might have on public health or safety. This presumption of openness in Texas does include settlement agreements "that seek to restrict disclosure of information concerning matters that have a probable adverse effect upon general public health or safety * * *."[30]

Similarly, in 1990, Florida passed its Sunshine in Litigation statute which demands that courts not enter secrecy orders or seal records which would prevent the public from being informed about hazardous products or public hazards in general. Nationwide attention is needed to provide public knowledge of all trials; information embedded in civil trials can be at least as important to the public as knowledge of criminal trials.

GM was not able to forestall publicity about another fuel-tank problem that arose in the early part of the 1990s. A Georgia family sued GM over the death of their son, who was killed in a GM pickup truck. Shannon Moseley's family sued, claiming that GM had defectively designed and manufactured trucks with side-saddle gas tanks, gas tanks placed outside of the rails of the frame. The Moseley family would not settle the case. They wanted their day in court. The controversy over the GM trucks also led to the NBC Dateline debacle in which Dateline ran a story about the GM trucks

[28] Even so, GM lost in the Texas Supreme Court where the plaintiff's attorney fought the broad protective order.

[29] Quoted at Bill Loving, "Media Access to Civil Court Records," paper presented to the Law Division, Association for Education in Journalism and Mass Communication, Boston, MA, Aug. 1991, p.1.

[30] Quoted in Ibid.

and illustrated the story with a crash test that included an over-filled gas tank, a wrong gas cap and toy rocket engines that were to ensure ignition of the gas. That video cost NBC a great deal of credibility and led to an on-air apology. If NBC had done its job differently it might have gotten a copy of GM's own crash testing showing the dangers of the fuel tanks.[31]

James Butler, Jr., was the Moseley's attorney. He had researched the GM truck and learned about secret crash tests, company memos and other evidence that pointed to GM's knowledge of the risks of the fuel-tank design. Shannon Moseley was 16 when his parents bought him the 1985 GMC Sierra pickup truck. The family had been loyal GM drivers and bought the truck because they believed it to be safe. On Oct. 21, 1989, Shannon Moseley's truck was struck on the side by another truck driven by a drunk driver. Moseley's truck skidded 150 feet. The fire started before the truck came to a halt. Moseley was not visibly injured. The autopsy concluded that he survived the crash and then burned to death.[32]

Butler found a disaffected, retired GM engineer who blew open the case for him. Ronald Elwell was, at one time, one of GM's star testifying experts. He explained fuel systems in GM cars for juries and was considered "an integral part of GM's product liability team."[33] One of Butler's partners, Bob Cheeley, tracked Elwell down and told him the story of Shannon Moseley. Elwell opened up and began talking about GM including the story that low-level engineers had expressed doubts about the fuel tank design but had been overruled by management.

> "Perhaps most important, Elwell told Cheeley about a highly sensitive series of 22 truck crash tests that GM had staged in the early '80s but had failed to disclose to any of the more than 100 plaintiffs who had sued the company over post-collision fuel-fed truck fires. Elwell said he had been in the dark about the tests until September 1983."[34]

Elwell said that he discovered the tests when the head of GM's engineering analysis division told him to check on some safety research at GM's facility in Milford, Mich.

> "At the proving grounds, he later testified, he saw a row of pickup trucks that had been crash-tested, obviously

---

[31] It turns out that the danger resulted not from the placement of the fuel tanks outside the rails of the frame, but rather from the use of metal straps to hold the tanks in place. The straps caused the fuel tank failures when they pierced the metal of the gas tanks.

[32] Terence Moran, "How GM Burned Itself," Automotive News, May 3, 1993.

[33] Ibid.

[34] Ibid.

for the purpose of exploring the performance of the outside-the-frame-rail fuel tanks. Virtually all the fuel systems had failed. ('They were badly smashed,' Elwell to the jury in Atlanta. 'There were holes in them as big as melons. They were split open.' ")[35]

Elwell's deposition revealed GM strategies for dealing with discovery. Where tests supported GM claims, the company would produce many documents. If the tests reflected poorly on GM vehicles, the discovery requests were carefully parsed.

" 'It was very, very constricted,' he said. 'So that if you had to give anything, you gave only one test, or maybe you would say that none (existed) because none (of the vehicles in the test) were painted red with white sidewalls (like the vehicle described in the request.' ")[36]

The jury returned a $105 million award against GM. GM settled with the Moseleys in 1995 for an undisclosed amount.

[35] Ibid.
[36] Ibid.

Chapter 10

SHIELDING INFORMATION
FROM DISCLOSURE

SEC. 63. THE GOVERNMENT CONTEMPT POWER

Persons who disobey the orders of courts may be cited, tried and convicted for contempt of court, the coercive power that underlies the courts' authority. The legislative branch has similar power. Journalists most often have come in conflict with the contempt power when they have refused court orders to disclose confidential information.

The common law has long provided that relationships between certain people are so personal that their confidences deserve protection against legally compelled disclosure. The clergyman and penitent, the physician and patient, the attorney and client, the husband and wife all share information that in some circumstances warrants unbroken confidentiality. The law has resisted expanding the protection to other interpersonal relationships, and even in the few listed above it has carefully avoided establishing any never-failing or absolute protection against the general rule. When government requires a citizen's testimony in furthering its legitimate ends such as ensuring fair judicial process or making laws, it is the citizen's duty to appear and testify.[1]

Printers of the American colonial period universally provided many contributors with anonymity, and occasionally resisted demands of the legislative branch to reveal their names. Early in nationhood, journalists continued to refuse demands of Congress and legislatures to break confidences, and as the Nineteenth Century progressed, sought expansion of the common law's protection to their own setting. They argued that journalistic ethics and their own professional livelihood required that they keep confidences. Especially in reporting corruption in government, they added, the

---

[1] 8 J. Wigmore, Evidence, 2286, 2290, 2394 (J. McNaughton Rev.Ed.1961).

public interest required that the news be told and that sometimes the news could be told only if they promised their source confidentiality. Their success was modest indeed, but by the end of the century, a start was made toward legal protection when the State of Maryland passed the nation's first "shield law" for journalists—a law that recognized a journalist's privilege to not reveal confidential sources. Within the next three or four decades, a few more states joined Maryland in establishing journalists' privilege by statute.[2] Broad protection, however, did not emerge until the 1970s, when some expansive readings of the First Amendment, increased numbers of state statutes, and the federal common law were brought to bear on problems of confidentiality.

The authority of government to compel testimony and to respond to persons'—including journalists'—refusal to break confidences is its contempt power. Government may declare that refusals to testify are contempt of authority, and may punish the person in contempt with imprisonment. It was a student journalist in Oregon who showed professional journalists that contests over compelled testimony is a real issue that should concern them.

Annette Buchanan wrote a story for her college newspaper, the University of Oregon *Daily Emerald,* about the use of marijuana among students at the University. She said that seven students, whom she did not name, gave her information. And when the district attorney asked her to name the sources of information to a grand jury that was investigating drug use, and subsequently a judge directed her to do so, she refused. A reporter should be privileged not to reveal her sources, she said, and not to break confidences. To betray a pledge of secrecy to a source, Buchanan added, would be a signal to many sources to "dry up." The judge, and upon appeal the Oregon Supreme Court, found her in contempt of court for refusing to obey the judge's order, and she was sentenced to a brief jail term.[3]

Buchanan's situation was a case of "direct" contempt. It took place in the presence of the judge. Goss, a television personality, was not within shouting distance of the court when on his program he attacked witnesses in a divorce case in which he was accused of adultery with the wife. For his attempt to prevent witnesses from giving testimony unfavorable to him by vilifying them, he was convicted of contempt which takes place away from the court, by

[2] The history of journalists' privilege not to reveal information is best told by A. David Gordon, "Protection of News Sources: the History and Legal Status of the Newsman's Privilege," Ph.D. dissertation, unpublished (Univ. of Wis., 1970). See also Thomas H. Kaminski, "Congress, Correspondents and Confidentiality in the 19th Century: a Preliminary Study," Journalism History, 4:3, Autumn 1977, pp. 83–87. For a recent overview, see The News Media & The Law, Fall, 1989.

[3] State v. Buchanan, 250 Or. 244, 436 P.2d 729 (1968), certiorari denied 392 U.S. 905, 88 S.Ct. 2055 (1968).

publication, called indirect or "constructive" contempt.[4] On appeal, his conviction was overruled, the court holding that his broadcasts were no real danger to justice because while the targets might have been angered by his words, they had no reason to feel threatened in their testimony by them.[5]

In the *Goss* case of contempt by publication as in the *Buchanan* case of direct contempt, a judge ruled initially that the reporter's acts interfered with the administration of justice—that the acts were contemptuous of court. In each case, the judge convicted the reporter under a judge's inherent power to punish for the interference, punishment for contempt being the basis of all legal procedure and the means of courts' enforcing their judgments and orders.[6]

The cases diverged in their results, Buchanan failing in her appeal, Goss succeeding in his. Indeed, the outcomes illustrate the varying fortunes of reporters in recent years in similar circumstances. Direct contempt is a current, serious problem for the press. Indirect or "constructive" contempt has almost vanished, as we saw in Chapter 2, Sec. 10, and needs no further treatment in this chapter.

"Summary" procedure is the ordinary procedure in contempt. In a summary proceeding, a judge accuses, tries, and sentences in his or her own case without resort to trial by jury. It is often justified by reference to the British legal writer of the 18th Century, Sir William Blackstone, who declared that rude or "contumelious" [insolent] behavior in front of a judge, or lying, or "any wilful disturbance whatever" in court could be grounds for punishment for contempt. Also punishable, to Blackstone, were:[7]

> disobeying or treating with disrespect the king's writ, or the rules of process of the court; by perverting such writ or process to the purposes of private malice, extortion, or injustice * * *
>
> The process of attachment for these and the like contempts must necessarily be as ancient as the laws themselves * * *.

In the United States, an act establishing the law of contempt in the federal courts, passed in 1831, is the basis of contempt proceedings before federal judges. State courts likewise possess the power to punish for contempt, under authority of a judicially proclaimed

---

[4] People v. Goss, 10 Ill.2d 533, 141 N.E.2d 385, 390 (1957).

[5] Goss v. State of Illinois, 204 F.Supp. 268 (N.D.Ill.1962), reversed on other grounds 312 F.2d 257 (7th Cir.1963).

[6] Sir John C. Fox, History of Contempt of Court (Oxford, 1927), p. 1.

[7] Blackstone, pp. 284, 285.

inherent power, by a statute, or both.[8] State courts have ignored or denied acts by state legislatures to limit this power.[9] For example, in State v. Morrill (1855) an Arkansas court was faced with a state statute limiting contempt proceedings to specified acts not including out-of-court publications. The court ruled that the statute was not binding upon the judiciary, for it must have power to enforce its own process, and the contempt power which provides this springs into existence upon the creation of the courts.[10] Without this authority, courts would be powerless to enforce their orders.

Attempts by Congress and state legislatures to limit contempt to certain specific classifications have not been universally successful. The legislative and judicial branches of government are equal in importance under the "separation of powers" doctrine that gives each branch of government autonomy. While the legislative branch of any governmental unit has the power to make the law, the judicial branch has inherent rights to enforce its orders, rules, writs, or decrees. Even in states where there is a strict definition of what constitutes contempt, under special circumstances there is precedent for courts' to consider their own inherent power as superior to a legislative enactment.[11]

Some headway has been made by those who pose a more general challenge to the contempt power of courts, and who assert that jury trials should be substituted for a judge's summary proceeding. It is sometimes objected by these that American traditions are violated where a judge may sit as accuser, prosecutor, and judge in his own or a fellow judge's case: "It is abhorrent to Anglo–Saxon justice as applied in this country that one man, however lofty his station * * *, should have the power of taking another man's liberty from him."[12] There are flaws in the Blackstonian position that summary procedure is an "immemorial power" of judges in all contempt cases.[13] The United States Supreme Court addressed itself to that flawed argument in 1968 and said that the old rule did not justify denying defendants a jury trial in serious contempt cases. The Court ruled in Bloom v. Illinois that "If the right to a jury trial is a fundamental matter in other criminal cases, * * * it must also be extended to criminal contempt cases." Bloom's jail

---

[8] Act of Mar. 2, 1831, c. 99, 4 Stat. 487.

[9] State v. Morrill, 16 Ark. 384 (1855) is an influential case mimicked by courts elsewhere to protect their "inherent" contempt powers from legislative limitations.

[10] Ibid., 384, 407.

[11] Farr v. Superior Court of Los Angeles County, 22 Cal.App.3d 60, 69, 99 Cal.Rptr. 342, 348 (1971) 1 Med.L.Rptr. 2545.

[12] Ballantyne v. United States, 237 F.2d 657, 667 (5th Cir.1956); J. Edward Gerald, The Press and the Constitution, pp. 30–31.

[13] Walter Nelles and Carol Weiss King, "Contempt by Publication in the United States," 28 Columbia L.Rev. 408 (1928).

sentence for contempt was two years, which the Court found to be a "serious" penalty.[14]

Legislative Contempt and the Press

In addition to courts, legislative bodies are protective of their power to cite for contempt. Congressional and state legislative investigating committees sometimes seek the testimony of reporters who have special knowledge about subjects under the committees' official inquiry. Citations for contempt have occurred when reporters have refused to answer lawmakers' questions, and occasionally, over the last two centuries, journalists have been convicted.

The legislative power to cite for contempt derives its force from the power possessed by the English Parliament, on which both the legislatures and the Congress were modeled.[15] No limitations are imposed upon Congress in its punishment for either disorderly conduct or contempt, but in Marshall v. Gordon,[16] it was held that the punishment imposed could not be extended beyond the session in which the contempt occurs.

The Supreme Court has conceded to Congress the power to punish nonmembers for contempt when there occurs "either physical obstruction of the legislative body in the discharge of its duties, or physical assault upon its members, for action taken or words spoken in the body, or obstruction of its officers in the performance of their official duties, or the prevention of members from attending so that their duties might be performed, or finally, for refusing with contumacy to obey orders, to produce documents or to give testimony which there was a right to compel."[17]

Seldom has a reporter gone to jail for refusing to reveal a source of information to Congress. One of the cases involved Z.L. White and Hiram J. Ramsdell, Washington correspondents of the *New York Tribune*. They published what they claimed was the "Treaty of Washington," a document being studied by the Senate in a closed session. They refused to say from whom they got the copy, were tried and convicted of contempt by the Senate, and were committed to the custody of the Sergeant at Arms until the end of the Session.[18]

[14] Bloom v. Illinois, 391 U.S. 194, 208, 88 S.Ct. 1477, 1485 (1968).

[15] Max Radin, Anglo American Legal History, pp. 63, 64.

[16] 243 U.S. 521, 37 S.Ct. 448, L.R.A.1917F, 279, Ann.Cas.1918B, 371 (1917).

[17] Ibid.

[18] U.S. Senate, Subcommittee on Administrative Practice and Procedure of Committee on the Judiciary, The Newsman's Privilege, 89 Cong., 2 Sess., Oct. 1966, pp. 57–61. Nineteenth century investigations of news media and reporters were not rare according to Kaminski, op.cit., p. 85.

Congress has not in many decades chosen to try and convict for contempt. Instead, it has cited for contempt and certified the persons cited to the district attorney of the District of Columbia for prosecution under a law that gives the courts power to try such cases.[19]

It is uncertain how far the principles of freedom of the press protect a reporter from contempt charges if he refuses to answer the questions of a Congressional committee. Journalists have argued that the First Amendment sharply limits Congress in questioning and investigating the press: Congress may investigate only the matters on which it may legislate, they point out, and the First Amendment says that "Congress shall make no law * * * abridging freedom of * * * the press."

"The Selling of the Pentagon"

In 1971, a prize-winning television documentary by CBS, "The Selling of the Pentagon," raised a storm of protest against alleged bias in the film's portrayal of the American military's public information programs. Selective editing for the documentary, the military charged, distorted the intent, management and messages of the military. The House of Representatives Commerce Committee, under its chairman Rep. Harley O. Staggers, undertook an investigation of the matter, and CBS president Frank Stanton refused to furnish the committee parts of film edited out of the final version. In response to the subpoena ordering him to appear with the materials, he appeared but declared that furnishing materials would amount to a violation of freedom of the press. The Committee voted 25 to 13 to recommend to Congress a contempt citation. The House, however, turned down the recommendation, Rep. Emanuel Celler declaring that "The First Amendment towers over these proceedings like a colossus. No tenderness of one member for another should cause us to topple over this monument to our liberties."[20]

Daniel Schorr and Congress

In the 1970s, newsman Daniel Schorr, then of CBS, came under protracted investigation by Congress, and heavy fire from a segment of the media, for his refusal to testify. Schorr had obtained a copy of the Pike Committee (House Intelligence Committee) report on operations of the Central Intelligence Agency, which the House of Representatives had voted should be kept secret after heavy pressure not to disclose it from the federal administration. National security, the administration said, was at stake. Schorr broadcast some of the contents; passed the report to the *Village*

---

[19] 2 U.S.C.A. §§ 192, 194.

[20] Congressional Record, 117:107, July 13, 1971, p. 6643.

Voice which published much of it; was investigated for several months during which he was suspended by CBS; and finally came before the House Ethics Committee.[21] Under a congressman's solemn admonition against publishers' taking it "upon themselves to publish secret and classified information against the will of Congress and the people,"[22] Schorr illuminated the rationale for a journalist's refusing to reveal sources, saying in part:[23]

> For a journalist, the most crucial kind of confidence is the identity of a source of information. To betray a confidential source would mean to dry up many future sources for many future reporters. The reporter and the news organization would be the immediate losers. The ultimate losers would be the American people and their free institutions.

> But, beyond all that, to betray a source would be to betray myself, my career, and my life. It is not as simple as saying that I refuse to do it. I cannot do it.

Unlike the committee that recommended on Stanton, the Ethics Committee did not recommend to the full House that Schorr be cited for contempt. He was released from subpoena without revealing his source.

The courts have not decided contempt of Congress cases on First Amendment grounds, one of them saying, "We shrink from this awesome task" of drawing lines between the investigative power of Congress and the First Amendment rights of a member of the press. Instead, the courts have found other reasons for reversing convictions of newsmen—such as faulty indictments—who were found in contempt of Congress for refusing to answer questions.[24]

Deja vu set in early in 1992, when reporters Nina Totenberg (National Public Radio) and Timothy Phelps (Newsday) balked at answering Senate questions. They faced subpoenas to reveal the sources of their reports of Professor Anita Hill's charges of sexual harassment against Supreme Court nominee—and ultimately Supreme Court Justice—Clarence Thomas.[25] The Senate soon dropped the inquiry.

[21] See Daniel Schorr, Clearing the Air (New York: Houghton Mifflin, 1977), passim; "The Daniel Schorr Investigation," Freedom of Information Center Report, #361, Oct. 1976.

[22] Anthony Lewis, "Congress Shall Make No Law * * *," New York Times, Sept. 16, 1976, p. 39.

[23] I. William Hill, "Schorr Sticks to His Refusal to Name Source," Editor & Publisher, Sept. 25, 1976, p. 14.

[24] Shelton v. United States, 117 U.S.App.D.C. 155, 327 F.2d 601 (1963); 89 Editor & Publisher 12, July 7, 1956. Russell v. United States, 369 U.S. 749, 767, 82 S.Ct. 1038, 1049 (1962).

[25] Neil A. Lewis, "Constitutional Test Is Seen in Inquiry in Leak to Press," The New York Times, Feb. 3, 1992, p. A9.

SEC. 64.   REFUSING TO TESTIFY ABOUT
SOURCES AND INFORMATION

Journalists' clashes with courts for refusing to testify as to sources and information were infrequent until the 1970s when the incidence multiplied manyfold. Protection has developed under the First Amendment, the common law, and state statutes.

Reporters' refusal to testify before grand juries and courts about confidential sources has become a familiar phenomenon since the 1970s. Subpoenas to appear and testify were for decades only an occasional problem for journalists whose stories suggested to officials that the reporters had information of use to government. There were probably fewer than 40 reported contempt cases before 1965 for refusal to testify when subpoenaed. But in 1969 and 1970 the sometime trickle of subpoenas changed to a flood, and across the nation hundreds of reporters faced demands that they appear and testify. No one was able to track down every subpoena issued during the early 1970s. But in a 2½ year segment of this period, 121 subpoenas for news material were said to have gone to CBS and NBC alone, and in three years, more than 30 to Field Enterprises newspapers.[26]

In particular demand were reporters who had been reporting widespread social and political turmoil of the 1970s. Grand juries wanted these journalists to reveal their confidential sources as well as to surrender their unpublished notes and records, unused photographs, tape recordings and television film "outtakes." To much of this, reporters responded "no" with intensity and solidarity.[27] Their unwritten code of ethics stood in the way of breaking confidences, they said. Even more important, if they broke confidences they would become known as untrustworthy and their sources would dry up, thereby harming or destroying their usefulness as news gatherers for the public, and their own status as professionals would be damaged. Moreover, some argued, compelling them to disclose their news sources was tantamount to making them agents of government investigation.

As for turning over unused film, files, photos and notes, some media adopted the policy of early destruction of unpublished mate-

[26] House of Rep. Committee on the Judiciary, Subcommittee No. 3, 92 Cong., 2d sess., "Newsmen's Privilege," Hearings, Oct. 4, 1972, p. 204; Sept. 27, 1972, p. 134.

[27] S.Res. 3552, 91 Cong., 2d Sess., 116 Cong.Rec. 4123–31, 1970; Noyes & Newbold, "The Subpoena Problem Today," Am.Soc. Newspaper Editors Bull., Sept. 1970, pp. 7–8; Editor & Publisher, Feb. 7, 1970, p. 12. For several journalists' positions, see U.S. Congress, Senate, Committee on the Judiciary, Newsmen's Privilege Hearings Before the Subcommittee on Constitutional Rights, 93rd Cong., 1st Sess., 1973, passim.

rials after *Time, Life, Newsweek,* the *Chicago Sun–Times,* CBS, NBC and others were called by subpoena, or in the name of cooperation with government, to deliver large quantities of news materials.[28] According to Attorney General John Mitchell, who served under President Nixon, journalists' willingness to accept contempt convictions and jail terms rather than reveal confidences, along with their unyielding protests to government, made the controversy "one of the most difficult issues I have faced * * *."[29] The storm of objection to subpoenas issuing from the Department of Justice led attorneys general to issue "Guidelines for Subpoenas to the News Media"—a set of instructions to Justice Department attorneys across the nation—that sought to resolve testimonial questions with reporters through negotiating rather than through subpoenas except in the last resort.[30]

From the mid–1970s through the 1980s, there was growing protection shielding journalists from being compelled to testify about sources or otherwise to reveal confidences. The pattern was by no means uniform nationally, however, and there were indications in the 1990s that those hard-won, if spotty, protections are being whittled away.

The Constitutional Protection

Journalists who assumed or asserted that the First Amendment guarantee of freedom of the press has protected the craft historically against compelling testimony did not understand the course of court decisions. Privilege cases were adjudicated for most of a century under the common law or state statutes without the Constitution even entering the picture. Not until 1958, in Garland v. Torre,[31] was the first claim to First Amendment protection an issue in the reported cases.

Marie Torre, columnist for the *New York Herald Tribune,* attributed to an unnamed executive of a broadcasting company, certain statements which actress Judy Garland said libeled her. In the libel suit, Torre refused to name the executive, asserting privilege under the First Amendment. She was cited for contempt and convicted, and the appeals court upheld the conviction. "The concept that it is the duty of a witness to testify in a court of law," the Second Circuit Court of Appeals said, "has roots fully as deep in our history as does the guarantee of a free press." It added that if freedom of the press was involved here, "we do not hesitate to

[28] Columbia Journalism Rev., Spring 1970, pp. 2–3.

[29] Editor & Publisher, Aug. 15, 1970, pp. 9–10.

[30] Department of Justice, Memo No. 692, Sept. 2, 1970. The guidelines were adjusted and developed by subsequent attorneys general. See "Guidelines on News Media Subpoenas," 6 Med.L.Rptr. 2153 (11/5/80) for more recent guidelines.

[31] 259 F.2d 545 (2d Cir.1958), certiorari denied 358 U.S. 910, 79 S.Ct. 237 (1958).

conclude that it too must give place under the Constitution to a paramount public interest in the fair administration of justice."[32] Subsequent claims to constitutional protection also were denied in other cases.[33]

The Branzburg Case (1972)

The United States Supreme Court in 1972 ruled for the first time on whether the First Amendment protects journalists from testifying about their confidential sources and information. The cases of three newsmen who had refused to testify before grand juries during 1970 and 1971 were decided together in Branzburg v. Hayes.[34] Paul Branzburg, a reporter for the *Louisville Courier-Journal,* had observed two people synthesizing hashish from marijuana and written about that and drug use, and had refused to answer the grand jury's questions about the matters. Paul Pappas, a television reporter of New Bedford, Mass., had visited Black Panther headquarters during civil turmoil in July 1970, and refused to tell a grand jury what he had seen there. Earl Caldwell, a black reporter for the *New York Times* in San Francisco, who had covered Black Panther activities regularly for some years, was called by a federal grand jury and had refused to appear or testify.

Only Caldwell received protection from the lower courts. The federal district court of California and the Ninth Circuit Court of Appeals ruled that the First Amendment provided a qualified privilege to newsmen and that it applied to Caldwell.[35] The Kentucky Court of Appeals refused Branzburg protection under either the Kentucky privilege statute, or the First Amendment interpretation of the Caldwell case.[36] And the Supreme Judicial Court of Massachusetts, where no privilege statute existed, rejected the idea of a First Amendment privilege.[37]

The Supreme Court of the United States found that none of the three men warranted First Amendment protection. It reversed the Caldwell decision of the lower federal court and upheld the Kentucky and Massachusetts decisions, in a 5–4 decision.[38] It said that the First Amendment would protect a reporter if grand jury

[32] Ibid., at 548–549.

[33] In re Goodfader's Appeal, 45 Haw. 317, 367 P.2d 472 (1961); In re Taylor, 412 Pa. 32, 193 A.2d 181 (1963); State v. Buchanan, 250 Or. 244, 436 P.2d 729 (1968), certiorari denied 392 U.S. 905, 88 S.Ct. 2055 (1968).

[34] Branzburg v. Hayes, 408 U.S. 665, 92 S.Ct. 2646 (1972), 1 Med.L.Rptr. 2617.

[35] Application of Caldwell, 311 F.Supp. 358 (N.D.Cal.1970); Caldwell v. United States, 434 F.2d 1081 (9th Cir.1970).

[36] Branzburg v. Pound, 461 S.W.2d 345 (Ky.1970); Branzburg v. Hayes, 408 U.S. 665, 92 S.Ct. 2646 (1972).

[37] In re Pappas, 358 Mass. 604, 266 N.E.2d 297 (1971).

[38] Branzburg v. Hayes, 408 U.S. 665, 92 S.Ct. 2646 (1972).

investigations were not conducted in good faith, or if there were harassment of the press by officials who sought to disrupt a reporter's relationship with his news sources.[39] But it found neither of these conditions present here. The journalist's obligation is to respond to grand jury subpoenas as other citizens do and to answer questions relevant to commission of crime, it said.

The Caldwell decisions in lower courts had focused on the need of recognition for First Amendment protection for the news gathering process; the Supreme Court said "It has generally been held that the first Amendment does not guarantee the press a constitutional right of special access to information not available to the public generally * * *," and "Despite the fact that news gathering may be hampered, the press is regularly excluded from grand jury proceedings, our own conferences, the meetings of other official bodies gathered in executive session * * *."[40]

The reporters had asserted that the First Amendment should take precedence over the grand jury's power of inquiry. The Supreme Court said that at common law, courts consistently refused to recognize a privilege in journalists to refuse to reveal confidential information, and that the First Amendment claim to privilege had been turned down uniformly in earlier cases, the courts having concluded "that the First Amendment interest asserted by the newsman was outweighed by the general obligation of a citizen to appear before a grand jury or at trial, pursuant to a subpoena, and give what information he possesses."[41] It said that the only constitutional privilege for unofficial witnesses before grand juries is the Fifth Amendment privilege against compelled self-incrimination, and the Court declined to create another.

The reporters argued that the flow of news would be diminished by compelling testimony from them. The Supreme Court said it was unconvinced, and "the evidence fails to demonstrate that there would be a significant constriction of the flow of news to the public if the Court reaffirms the prior common law and constitutional rule regarding the testimonial obligations of newsmen."[42]

The reporters said the freedom of the press would be undermined. The Court said this is not the lesson that history teaches, for the press had operated and thrived without common law or constitutional privilege since the beginning of the nation.[43]

The Supreme Court said that while the Constitution did not provide the privilege sought, Congress and the state legislatures

[39] Ibid., at 706–709, 92 S.Ct. at 2669–2670.

[40] Ibid., at 682, 684, 92 S.Ct. at 2657, 2658.

[41] Ibid., at 684, 686, 92 S.Ct. at 2658, 2659.

[42] Ibid., at 692, 92 S.Ct. at 2663.

[43] Ibid., at 698, 92 S.Ct. at 2665.

were free to fashion standards and rules protecting journalists from testifying by passing legislation.

Concurring, Justice Lewis F. Powell, Jr., expanded, in general terms, the possibilities for first Amendment protection for journalists subpoenaed to testify. "The Court," he said, "does not hold that newsmen * * * are without constitutional rights with respect to the gathering of news or in safe-guarding their sources. * * * the courts will be available to newsmen under circumstances where legitimate First Amendment interests require protection." And where they claim protection, Powell said, "The asserted claim to privilege should be judged on its facts by the striking of a proper balance between freedom of the press and the obligation of all citizens to give relevant testimony * * *."[44] His opinion was to become central to many subsequent cases.

The dissenting justices wrote two opinions. One was that of Justice William O. Douglas, who said that a reporter's immunity from testifying is "quite complete" under the First Amendment and a journalist "has an absolute right not to appear before a grand jury * * *."[45]

Concurring for himself and two others, Justice Potter Stewart argued for a qualified privilege. He called the majority's opinion a "crabbed view of the First Amendment" that reflected a disturbing insensitivity to the critical role of an independent press. And he said that in denying the protection, "The Court * * * invites state and federal authorities to undermine the historic independence of the press by attempting to annex the journalistic profession as an investigative arm of government." Justice Stewart said the protection was essential, not "for the purely private interests of the newsman or his informant, nor even, at bottom, for the First Amendment interests of either partner in the news-gathering relationship."[46]

> Rather it functions to insure nothing less than democratic decisionmaking through the free flow of information to the public, and it serves, thereby, to honor the "profound national commitment to the principle that debate on public issues should be uninhibited, robust, and wide-open."

Stewart indicated what he felt the government should be required to do in overriding a constitutional privilege for the reporter:[47]

---

[44] Ibid., at 708, 710, 92 S.Ct. at 2670, 2671.

[45] United States v. Caldwell, 408 U.S. 665, 712, 92 S.Ct. 2686, 2691 (1972).

[46] Branzburg v. Hayes, 408 U.S. 665, 737, 92 S.Ct. 2646, 2678 (1972).

[47] Ibid., at 739–742, 92 S.Ct. at 2679–2680.

* * * it is an essential prerequisite to the validity of an investigation which intrudes into the area of constitutionally protected rights of speech, press, association and petition that the State *show a substantial relation between the information sought and a subject of overriding and compelling state interest.*

* * *

Government officials must, therefore, demonstrate that the information sought is *clearly* relevant to a *precisely* defined subject of governmental inquiry. * * * They must demonstrate that it is reasonable to think the witness in question has that information. * * * And they must show that there is not any means of obtaining the information less destructive of First Amendment liberties.

These were essentially the requirements placed upon government by the lower courts in holding that Caldwell had been protected by the First Amendment, and Stewart endorsed that decision. He would have upheld the protection for Caldwell, and vacated and remanded the Branzburg and Pappas judgments.

Largely innocent of the history of the shield, reporters and editors expressed shock and dismay that the First Amendment did not protect the reporters in the Supreme Court's *Branzburg* decision.[48] A few years later, William H. Hornby wrote that the decision had "beclouded what American newsmen had come to assume was a traditional privilege—to refuse to testify either as to the source or the content of information received under confidential circumstances."[49]

After the *Branzburg* decision, many journalists predicted doom for press freedom. Those predictions were premature: buried within *Branzburg* were statements which said the First Amendment was still around and could be used in confidentiality cases. There was Justice White's plurality opinion, which said that journalists would be protected against the harassment of bad-faith investigations. Justice Powell's concurrence said that courts would protect journalists "where legitimate First Amendment interests require protection." And Justice Stewart's dissent, as matters turned out, contained concepts that courts quickly came to use in subsequent cases to protect journalists. (See discussion on following pages.)

Then only months after *Branzburg* was decided, the U.S. Court of Appeals, Second Circuit, gave the doom-predictors a most wel-

[48] See generally Columbia Journalism Review, 10:3, Sept.–Oct. 1972, for articles by Norman E. Isaacs, Benno C. Schmidt, Jr., and Fred W. Friendly. The only extensive history of journalists' privilege is Gordon, op.cit.

[49] William H. Hornby, "Journalists Split in Shield Law Imbroglio," IPI Report, 25:3, March 1976, p. 8.

come surprise. That court said that journalist Alfred Balk was *protected* by the First Amendment in his refusal to name a source. Balk had once written an article on discriminatory real estate practices—"block busting" for the Saturday Evening Post. Civil rights advocates, in a court action, sought to have Balk reveal the identity of one of his confidential sources ("Vitchek," a pseudo-nym). Balk refused, on grounds that Vitchek gave him the informa-tion in confidence. The trial court ruled in Balk's favor, and the appeals court affirmed. The decision stood because the Supreme Court of the United States—for whatever reason—refused to grant certiorari.[50]

The court found that the identity of Vitchek did not go to the heart of the appellants' case, and that, anyway, there were other available sources that the appellants could have tried to reach and that might have disclosed Vitchek's identity (*vide* Stewart, dissent in *Branzburg*). It said that the majority in *Branzburg* had applied traditional First Amendment doctrine, which teaches that First Amendment rights cannot be infringed absent a "compelling" or "paramount" state interest (once more, Stewart).[51] Even though the *Branzburg* majority emphasized public interest in grand jury investigation of crimes, this case found that

> "there are circumstances, at the very least in civil cases, in which the public interest in non-disclosure of a journalist's confidential sources outweighs the public and private in-terest in compelled testimony. The case before us is one where the First Amendment protection does not yield."

Here was a line of reasoning (one which took its departure from the widely damned *Branzburg* decision) that was to prove a protection for the journalist in the court-room face up in which his testimony was being demanded with increasing and truly disturb-ing frequency. In civil cases, the public's interest was likely to weigh with the journalist's refusal to name his sources, and thus the journalist's position would outweigh the private litigant's de-mand for disclosure. It was the start of courts' using *Branzburg* in both civil and criminal cases to establish a qualified privilege under the First Amendment for journalists who claimed protection not to reveal sources.

Quickly other courts brought the privilege into play.[52] In a case decided in 1973, the District Court for the District of Columbia ruled on a demand of the Committee for the Re–Election of the

[50] Baker v. F and F Investment, 470 F.2d 778 (2d Cir.1972), certiorari denied 411 U.S. 966, 93 S.Ct. 2147 (1973).

[51] Ibid., 783–785. See also United States v. Orsini, 424 F.Supp. 229 (E.D.N.Y. 1976).

[52] See Press Censorship Newsletter, IX, April–May 1976, pp. 46, 48–9; Loadholtz v. Fields, 389 F.Supp. 1299 (M.D.Fla.1975).

President (Nixon) for news materials.[53] The Committee was party to civil actions arising out of the break-in at the Watergate offices of the Democratic National Committee. It had obtained subpoenas for reporters or management of the *New York Times,* the *Washington Post,* the *Washington Star–News,* and *Time* magazine to appear and bring all papers and documents they had relating to the break-in. The media asked the court to quash the subpoenas.

Judge Richey defined the issue: Were the subpoenas valid under the First Amendment? He distinguished this case from *Branzburg,* noting that the re-election committee was not involved in criminal cases, but civil contempts. He declared, furthermore, that the cases were of staggering import: " * * * unprecedented in the annals of legal history." "What is ultimately involved in these cases * * * is the very integrity of the judicial and executive branches of our Government and our political processes in this country."[54]

Not only did the civil nature of the cases involving the re-election committee weigh for the media in Richey's opinion. He saw a chilling effect in the enforcement of the subpoenas upon the flow of information about Watergate to the press and thus to the public:[55]

> This court stands convinced that if it allows the discouragement of investigative reporting into the highest levels of Government no amount of legal theorizing could allay the public suspicions engendered by its actions and by the matters alleged in these lawsuits.

Then Richey tried to balance competing interests. As Justice Powell had instructed in *Branzburg,* a reporter's claim to privilege should be judged " * * * 'on its facts by the striking of a proper balance between freedom of the press and the obligation of all citizens to give relevant testimony.' " Richey said that here, "The scales are heavily weighted in the ... [media's] favor." For the Committee for the Re–Election of the President had made no showing that "alternative sources of information have been exhausted or even approached. Nor has there been any positive showing of the materiality of the documents and other materials sought by the subpoenas [i.e., that the materials sought 'go to the heart of the claim']."[56]

[53] Democratic National Committee v. McCord, 356 F.Supp. 1394 (D.D.C.1973).

[54] Ibid., 1395–1397.

[55] Ibid., 1397.

[56] Ibid., 1398. On exhausting the sources of information, see also Connecticut State Board of Labor Relations v. Fagin, 33 Conn.Sup. 204, 370 A.2d 1095, 1097 (1976), 2 Med.L.Rptr. 1765, 1766; Altemose Const. Co. v. Building Trades Council of Philadelphia and Vicinity, 443 F.Supp. 489 (E.D.Pa.1977), 2 Med.L.Rptr. 1878.

Even the legal proceeding which the lead opinion in *Branzburg* was so concerned to elevate above reporter's privilege—namely, the grand jury investigation—could in some circumstances give way to the journalist's claim.

This happened in the case of Lucy Ware Morgan, who for three years fought a 90–day contempt sentence for refusing to disclose her source, and finally won.[57] Her story in the St. Petersburg, Fla., *Times* brought two actions against her to compel her to say who told her of a grand jury's secret criticism of Police Chief Nixon. The Florida Supreme Court found the story innocuous. It overruled the lower court which had found that the mere preservation of secrecy in grand jury proceedings outweighed any First Amendment considerations. The high state court said "A nonspecific interest, even in keeping the inner workings of the Pentagon secret, has been held insufficient to override certain First Amendment values."[58] It found further that the proceedings against Morgan had an improper purpose—namely, "to force a newspaper reporter to disclose the source of published information, so that the authorities could silence the source." Then it called on the leading case in precedent:[59]

> The present case falls squarely within this language in the *Branzburg* plurality opinion: "Official harassment of the press undertaken not for purposes of law enforcement but to disrupt a reporter's relationship with his news sources would have no justification."

Thus with *Branzburg* supporting, First Amendment protection for the reporter's shield was being discovered.[60] No court conceded that the privilege under the First Amendment was an "absolute" protective shield for the journalist in all conceivable circumstances. In applying the First Amendment, courts widely started with Justice Powell's instruction in *Branzburg* ("striking a proper balance between freedom of the press and the obligation of all citizens to give relevant testimony"), and then used criteria such as those advocated by Justice Stewart in his *Branzburg* dissent (whether the testimony sought from reporters was clearly relevant, whether the subject was one of overriding state interest, whether all other means of obtaining the sought-after information had first been

[57] Morgan v. State, 337 So.2d 951 (Fla.1976).

[58] Ibid., 955.

[59] Ibid., 956.

[60] Gora, p. 28. Gora's handbook, prepared for the American Civil Liberties Union, despite being dated, should be available to every reporter and editor. It covers true-to-life, practical problems in several fields of law that involve journalists, using a "Q" and "A" approach.

exhausted). In most cases in which the First Amendment was employed, the procedure worked out to provide protection.[61]

But the First Amendment shield sometimes dropped. For one thing, in balancing the journalist's right to a shield against the need of the state or a plaintiff, as Powell instructed, courts sometimes found that the hurdles such as Stewart's criteria were surmounted by those seeking testimony, and the balance tipped against the journalist. This could happen at trial, or in pre-trial discovery procedure (see Chap. 4, Sec. 26) in which plaintiffs were attempting to obtain from journalists certain facts that would help them establish their cases. Also, some courts interpreted *Branzburg* to deny a First Amendment shield of any kind.

First, consider the hurdles which the state in criminal cases, or the plaintiff in civil cases, would have to clear before overcoming the journalist's First Amendment qualified privilege. These have been expressed in several ways. The most-used rules[62] are that the party seeking the information from the journalist must show:

• That the information sought can be obtained from no other source or by means less destructive of First Amendment interests:

• That the information is centrally relevant to the party's case ("goes to the heart of the claim," or is information for which the party has a "compelling need").

• That the subject is one of "overriding and compelling state interest."

As we saw on the preceding pages, the journalist won because the plaintiffs failed to show that the materials sought "went to the heart of their claim," or that the information might not be available from an alternative source, other parties seeking information have been more successful in piercing the shield of the First Amendment. That was the case in Winegard v. Oxberger,[63] decided by the Iowa Supreme Court in 1977.

---

[61] United States v. Hubbard, 493 F.Supp. 202, 206, 209 (D.D.C.1979), 5 Med. L.Rptr. 1719; Montezuma Realty Corp. v. Occidental Petroleum Corp., 494 F.Supp. 780 (S.D.N.Y.1980), 6 Med.L.Rptr. 1571; Application of Consumers Union of United States, Inc., 495 F.Supp. 582 (S.D.N.Y.1980), 6 Med.L.Rptr. 1681; Hart v. Playboy Enterprises (D.Kan.1978), 4 Med.L.Rptr. 1616; United States v. DePalma, 466 F.Supp. 917 (S.D.N.Y.1979), 4 Med.L.Rptr. 2499; Zelenka v. State, 83 Wis.2d 601, 266 N.W.2d 279 (1978).

[62] Others have included: Plaintiff must show that the information "is necessary to prevent a miscarriage of justice" Florida v. Taylor (Fla.Cir.Ct.1982), 9 Med.L.Rptr. 1551; there is "reasonable possibility that information sought would affect the verdict" State v. Rinaldo, 36 Wash.App. 86, 673 P.2d 614 (1983), 9 Med.L.Rptr. 1419; the action is not "facially frivolous or patently without merit" Winegard v. Oxberger, 258 N.W.2d 847, 852 (Iowa 1977).

[63] 258 N.W.2d 847 (Iowa 1977), certiorari denied 436 U.S. 905, 98 S.Ct. 2234 (1978), 3 Med.L.Rptr. 2409. See also Goldfeld v. Post Pub. Co. (Conn.Sup.1978), 4 Med.L.Rptr. 1167; In re Powers (Vt.Dist.1978), 4 Med.L.Rptr. 1600.

Winegard v. Oxberger (1977)

Diane Graham, a reporter for the *Des Moines Register,* wrote articles about legal proceedings brought by Sally Ann Winegard to dissolve her claimed common-law marriage to John Winegard. The articles quoted Sally's attorney extensively. John, who denied that there had been a marriage, brought a libel suit and invasion of privacy action against the attorney, who had told John that he had spoken with reporter Graham, but who denied saying the alleged libel. Then John sought, through discovery proceedings before the trial, to obtain from Graham or the Register any information they had in connection with the preparation of the articles.

Graham was subpoenaed, and refused to answer questions about conversations with her sources or their identity, and about preparation and editing of the articles. She said that the First Amendment and the Iowa Constitution protected her. She and the Register applied to the court for an order quashing the subpoena; John Winegard moved to compel discovery; and Judge Oxberger ruled for Graham and the Register, saying that a qualified privilege under the First Amendment protected Graham.

Winegard appealed to the Iowa Supreme Court, which reversed the trial court and said that Judge Oxberger had erred in denying John's motion to compel discovery by reporter Graham. The Supreme Court said that a First Amendment qualified privilege existed, but was lost to Graham upon the application of the Court's "three-pronged standard."[64]

First, it said that John's basic discovery objective "is necessary and critical to his cause of action" against the attorney; John "needs to know what was said to Graham and by whom." Second, the Court said, John's questioning of Sally's attorney resulted in the attorney's denying "having made statements attributed to him by Graham's articles. Under these circumstances we find Winegard did reasonably exercise and exhaust other plausible avenues of information," and that "Graham is apparently the only remaining person who could conceivably provide the information essential to Winegard's invasion of privacy and defamation action." And as for the last of the "three-prong standard," the Court said there was nothing in the record to suggest that John's action against the attorney was frivolous or without merit. For good measure, the unanimous opinion said that the Court found no cause to hold that John was abusing judicial process to force a "wholesale disclosure of a newspaper's confidential sources of news," nor that John was embarked upon a course "designed to annoy," embarrass or oppress Graham.[65] John won the case for compelled disclosure.

[64] Winegard v. Oxberger, 258 N.W.2d 847, 852 (Iowa 1977).

[65] The Iowa Court relied directly on the first of the shield cases in which a reporter claimed a First Amendment protection—Garland v. Torre, 259 F.2d 545 (2d

Some courts have denied or doubted that any First Amendment protection exists. The Massachusetts Supreme Judicial Court did so in the case of Paul Pappas,[66] and reaffirmed that position in 1982.[67] A Connecticut Superior Court has said that the First Amendment gives no greater protection to the electronic media "than the same action by any other citizen," nor "any privilege to refuse to reveal information solely because the writers deem it confidential."[68] Idaho's Supreme Court once read Branzburg v. Hayes, the leading case,[69] to mean that "no newsman's privilege against disclosure of confidential sources exists * * *."[70] In 1985, however, the Idaho Supreme Court recognized a reporter's right to protect source confidentiality in both criminal and civil cases.[71]

For journalists, the best defense against subpoenas probably is a "good offense." That is, if a news organization is known to judges and prosecuting attorneys as one willing to fight against subpoenas—even to the point of having reporters and editors go to jail to resist yielding up confidential sources or information—chances of subpoenas being served doubtless are lessened.

In re Farber (1978)

A shield case which arose in New Jersey cost its media principals more than any other in the 1970s. It was the famous case called In re Farber.[72] Before it had run its course, in fines alone it had cost the *New York Times* approximately $285,000, at the rate of $5,000 per day in civil contempts plus a flat $101,000 in criminal contempts. Reporter Myron Farber was jailed for 40 days. Farber had written lengthy articles about deaths at a New Jersey hospital,

Cir.1958), which continues to carry weight with courts in frequent citations. An example is Silkwood v. Kerr–McGee Corp., 563 F.2d 433 (10th Cir.1977), 3 Med. L.Rptr. 1087, 1091.

[66] In the Matter of Pappas, 358 Mass. 604, 266 N.E.2d 297 (1971).

[67] Corsetti v. Massachusetts, 458 U.S. 1306, 103 S.Ct. 3 (1982), 8 Med.L.Rptr. 2117 and reporter's jail term for contempt commuted in 1982, 8 Med.L.Rptr. #28, 9/14/82, News Notes. In 1984, the Massachusetts Supreme Judicial Court was asked by a governor's task force to promulgate rules about journalists' privilege, and recommended details for protection of journalists asserting such, the Court having denied until then any recognition of privilege: 10 Med.L.Rptr. #41, 10/16/84, News Notes.

[68] Rubera v. Post–Newsweek (1982), 8 Med.L.Rptr. 2293, 2295.

[69] 408 U.S. 665, 92 S.Ct. 2646 (1972), 1 Med.L.Rptr. 2617.

[70] Caldero v. Tribune Pub. Co., 98 Idaho 288, 562 P.2d 791 (1977), 2 Med.L.Rptr. 1490, 1495.

[71] In re Contempt of Wright, 108 Idaho 418, 700 P.2d 40 (1985).

[72] In re Farber, 78 N.J. 259, 394 A.2d 330, 345 (1978), 4 Med.L.Rptr. 1360, 1362; see also Anon., "Lets Stand Contempts Against New York Times," News Media & the Law, Jan. 1979, 4–5. For a step-by-step account of the complex process applied to the Times and Farber, see Anon., "Reporter Jailed; N.Y.Times Fined," Ibid., Oct. 1978, 2–4. Farber and the Times were ultimately pardoned of the criminal contempt conviction by the Governor of New Jersey, and the $101,000 criminal contempt fine was returned: 7 Med.L.Rptr. #42, 2/2/82, News Notes.

and their possible connection with drugs. A grand jury probe of the matter resulted in the indictment of Dr. Mario Jascalevich for murder, and after he went to trial, Farber and the Times were subpoenaed to bring thousands of documents to the court for *in camera* inspection. The Times and Farber demanded a hearing before turning over materials. But the trial judge refused a hearing, saying he would have to examine the documents before deciding whether the shield law would protect them against disclosure to Jascalevich. Facing contempt citations, the Times and Farber appealed unsuccessfully; the contempt findings went into effect, with jail for Farber and the $5,000–a-day fine against the Times pending its bringing forth the materials.

Appealing once more, the newspaper and reporter reached the New Jersey Supreme Court. That court denied that the First Amendment provided any privilege to remain silent, interpreting Branzburg v. Hayes to be a flat rejection of that notion. In response to the journalists' claim to privilege, the New Jersey court said that U.S. Supreme Court Justice White, had "stated the issue and gave the Court's answer in the first paragraph of his opinion":[73]

> "The issue in these cases is whether requiring newsmen to appear and testify before state or federal grand juries abridges the freedom of speech and press guaranteed by the First Amendment. We hold that it does not."

* * *

> Our conclusion that appellants cannot derive the protection they seek from the First Amendment rests upon the fact that the ruling in *Branzburg* is binding upon us and we interpret it as applicable to, and clearly including, the particular issue framed here. It follows that the obligation to appear at a criminal trial on behalf of a defendant who is enforcing his Sixth Amendment rights is at least as compelling as the duty to appear before a grand jury.

Having settled the First Amendment issue for New Jersey, the court went on to say that the Times and Farber of course deserved a hearing such as they sought, but that they had aborted it by refusing to submit the material subpoenaed for the court to examine in private—and that such an examination is no invasion of the New Jersey shield statute. "Rather, it is a preliminary step to determine whether, and if so to what extent, the statutory privilege must yield to the defendant's constitutional rights."

[73] In re Farber, 78 N.J. 259, 266, 394 A.2d 330, 333 (1978), 4 Med.L.Rptr. 1360, 1362.

It added, however, that in future similar cases there should be a preliminary determination before being compelled to submit materials to a trial judge—in which the party seeking the materials would show the relevancy of them to his defense, and that the information could not be obtained from any less intrusive source. This, it said, did not stem from any First Amendment right, but rather, it would seem necessary from the legislature's "very positively expressed" intent, in passing the shield law, to protect confidentiality of media sources.

Farber was released from jail in October 1978, following the acquittal of Jascalevich by a jury at the end of an eight-month trial. The New Jersey legislature began work on a bill to prevent a recurrence of the Farber incident, and on Feb. 28, 1981, Governor Byrne signed a law saying that a criminal defendant would have to prove at a subpoenaed journalist's hearing that the material sought was relevant and unavailable elsewhere, and that the hearing would be held before the start of the criminal trial.[74]

It should be clear that despite the language of shield laws or of court precedent erecting some sort of a "shield" for journalists, such shields often turn out to be of little help at crunch time. First Amendment attorney James C. Goodale, for example, looked at the Farber case and exclaimed about the persistent ineffectiveness of New Jersey's shield statute. He complained that Farber had been shipped off to jail without a hearing, even though there was a statute stating that Farber was totally protected against requests for confidential sources and even though there are scores of decisions upholding claims of privilege even in states where there is no shield statute.

Journalists need to keep up with the kaleidoscopically shifting patterns of shield protection. One way of managing this is to subscribe to The News Media & the Law, published four times a year by the Reporters Committee for Freedom of the Press, and which puts out periodic guides on the status of shield laws from jurisdiction to jurisdiction.[75]

Confidentiality Under the Federal Common Law

Even as journalists' successes in asserting a First Amendment privilege not to testify were proving about as frequent as were their failures, in 1979 the United States Third Circuit Court of Appeals

[74] New York Times, Feb. 28, 1981, p. 25. Maressa v. New Jersey Monthly, 89 N.J. 176, 445 A.2d 376 (1982), 8 Med.L.Rptr. 1473, 1475–1476.

[75] "Reporters Have Rights, Too," The Nation, Nov. 3, 1979, pp. 435–436; The Reporters Committee for Freedom of the Press, Suite 504, 1735 Eye Street, N.W., Washington, D.C. 20006. The Reporters Committee has an all-day, every-day libel and freedom of information hotline, including emergency legal aid on subpoena questions: Toll free 800–F–FOI–AID. In Washington, D.C., area, (202) 466–6313.

discovered and applied an added basis of privilege for journalists to rely on in refusing to divulge sources: the federal common law. In 1979, Judge Sloviter wrote that the Court of Appeals, Third Circuit, had concluded "that journalists have a federal common law privilege, albeit qualified, to refuse to divulge their sources."

Riley v. Chester (1979)

That case began when Policeman Riley of Chester, Pa., a candidate for mayor, alleged that Mayor Battle and Police Chief Owens had violated his constitutional right to freedom to conduct his campaign, by surveillance of his activity, by conducting investigations of his performance as a policeman, and by public announcements of the investigations. He sought a preliminary injunction from federal court to restrain them from continued activities of this kind. Reporter Geraldine Oliver was called as a witness concerning her news story which reported that Riley had been suspended as a policeman, docked, and officially reprimanded, and that he had been investigated on several occasions during his 13 years as a policeman. She refused to give the source of her information and under an order by the trial judge was cited for civil contempt. She appealed, and the Third Circuit Court reversed the contempt citation.[76]

The Court found that Riley had not first exhausted other sources of information that might have "leaked," including other reporters, Battle, and Owens. Nor had Riley shown that the information sought to be disclosed was more than marginally relevant to his case—a matter "of most significance." Criteria such as these were applicable to the case of anyone seeking disclosure, the Court said, under any standard. And with that, it applied the standard of the federal common law, emerging from Rule 501 of the Federal Rules of Evidence and the legislative history of the Rule. The importance of the decision for journalists' privilege emerges not so much in the finding for Oliver as for the general matter of journalists' privilege.[77]

The Court then added:

> The strong public policy which supports the unfettered communication to the public of information, comment and opinion and the Constitutional dimension of that policy, expressly recognized in Branzburg v. Hayes, lead us to conclude that journalists have a federal common law privilege, albeit qualified, to refuse to divulge their sources.

[76] Riley v. Chester, 612 F.2d 708 (3d Cir.1979). For a state decision bottomed explicitly on common law as providing privilege, see Senear v. Daily Journal–American, 97 Wash.2d 148, 641 P.2d 1180 (1982), 8 Med.L.Rptr. 1151, 1152.

[77] Ibid., 713, 714.

In two later federal common law cases in the Third Circuit, the reporter's shield was denied. One, concerning a newspaper reporter's refusal to say whether she had conversations with a U.S. attorney in the "Abscam" prosecutions, ruled that the information was crucial to the defendant's case and that it could be obtained only from the reporter. The court followed standard judicial procedure in choosing to decide the case on common law instead of a First Amendment standard: " ' ... [W]e ought not to pass on questions of constitutionality * * * unless such adjudication is unavoidable * * *.' "[78]

In the other case, a television network was ordered by a court to submit to a pre-trial, *in camera* [in private, in the judge's chambers] proceeding. In that proceeding film, audio tapes, and written transcripts were to be revealed concerning persons whom the government intended to call as witnesses in a trial. The TV network refused and appealed the order. But the order was upheld so far as it applied to the named persons whom the government intended to call, but was overturned as to other people, whose testimony was not relevant.[79]

Confidentiality Under State Statutes and in State Courts

The mixed results for confidentiality under the First Amendment and the federal common law, meanwhile, were characteristic of developments under state shield statutes and state court decisions. Media Attorney Robert Sack has said that shield laws are like insurance policies, in that "they cover absolutely everything except what happens to you."[80] If, as attorney Joel Gora had said in the journalistic climate of discouragement under *Branzburg*, "the situation is far from bleak," there were nonetheless more than enough jailings to warrant confusion and anger among journalists. Probably more reporters were going to jail in the 1970s for refusal to reveal sources, than for any offense since 1798–1800 and the Alien and Sedition Acts.[81] The interpretations of the legitimacy of journalists' privilege under state laws and rulings contributed heavily to this unlovely fact. Yet it was plain by the 1980s that the large majority of state (and federal) jurisdictions had recognized qualified shield protection. Further, the number of actions by the mid 1980s was declining; media Attorney James C. Goodale found state shield laws increasingly effective.[82] Into the mid–1990s, however, it appeared that subpoenas again were on the increase.

---

[78] United States v. Criden, 633 F.2d 346, 353 (3d Cir.1980).

[79] United States v. Cuthbertson, 630 F.2d 139 (3d Cir.1980), 6 Med.L.Rptr. 1545.

[80] 9 Med.L.Rptr. #7, 3/15/83, News Notes.

[81] Quill, 61:1, Jan. 1973, p. 28.

[82] Note, "Developments in the News Media Privilege: the Qualified Constitutional Approach Becoming Common Law," 33 Maine L.Rev. 372, 441 (1981); 10 Med. L.Rptr. #47, 11/27/84, News Notes.

State Shield Laws

The Supreme Court in *Branzburg* made it plain that either Congress or the states or both might pass laws providing a shield. Attempts in state legislatures to adopt shield laws (15 preceded *Branzburg*) were sometimes successful in following years, the total of old and new reaching 28—27 states plus the District of Columbia by 1990. In addition, 16 other states' courts had adopted a qualified privilege in case decisions by that year, while a few rejected the privilege.[83] Some statutes provided a privilege that appeared "absolute," while others qualified the protection in various ways. Alabama's, passed in 1935 and amended in 1949, was one of those that, on the surface, seemed absolute—as long as a person could claim to be with a journalistic organization:[84]

> No person engaged in, connected with, or employed on any newspaper, or radio broadcasting station or television station, while engaged in a news gathering capacity shall be compelled to disclose in any legal proceeding or trial, before any court or before a grand jury of any court, before the presiding officer of any tribunal or his agent or agents or before any committee of the legislature or elsewhere the sources of any information procured or obtained by him and published in the newspaper, broadcast by any broadcasting station or televised by any television station on which he is engaged, connected with or employed.

Among states that hedged the privilege, Illinois, for example, said that a person seeking the reporter's information could apply for an order divesting the reporter of the privilege. The application would have to state the specific information sought, its relevancy to the proceedings, and a specific public interest which would be adversely affected if the information sought were not disclosed. And the court would have to find, before taking away the privilege, that all other available sources of information had been exhausted and that disclosure of the information was essential to the protection of the public interest involved.[85]

But absolute or qualified, state laws might contain loopholes through which under certain conditions, journalists could lose the

---

[83] The News Media & the Law, Fall 1987, special section on source confidentiality; see also Henry R. Kaufman, ed., LDRC (Libel Defense Resource Center), 50–State Survey 1994–95 (New York: LDRC, 1988), *passim*. See also "Confidential Sources and Information," 1990 guide for reporters, The Reporters Committee for Freedom of the Press, and Appendix 3, pp. 867–901 in Robert D. Sack and Sandra S. Baron, Libel, Slander and Related Problems, 2nd ed. (New York: Practising Law Institute, 1994).

[84] Ala.Code § 12–21–142 (Cum.Supp.1988). See Jacqueline L. Jackson, "Shield Laws Vary Widely," Presstime, May 1981, p. 14; See also New Jersey's, Maressa v. New Jersey Monthly, 89 N.J. 176, 445 A.2d 376 (1982), 8 Med.L.Rptr. 1473.

[85] Ill.Legis.H.Bill 1756, 1971, Gen. Assembly.

privilege. Branzburg, before seeking constitutional protection, had failed to receive protection under Kentucky's statute. The statute gave him a firm shield, as a newspaper employee, against disclosing before a court or grand jury, the source of information procured by him and published in a newspaper. But the Kentucky court held that he himself was the source of information for a story reporting his observation of the manufacture of hashish by others. He would have to give the identity of the manufacturer—to identify those whom he saw breaking the law. It was contempt for him to refuse to do so.[86]

New York's shield law is termed "absolute" in its protection, and even protects a journalist against testifying before a grand jury.[87] But it applies only to information obtained under the "cloak of confidentiality," and did not protect CBS against producing, under subpoena, video and audio takes and outtakes not made under promises of confidentiality.[88] California's constitution immunizes against contempt convictions for refusing to testify, but not against various other sanctions[89] nor does it protect certain free-lance authors. California's shield statute protects unpublished or "out-take" materials.[90] Ohio's shield law protects against disclosure only of the source of the information, not against disclosure of information in notes, tapes, and records from the source.[91] Under Tennessee's statute, both confidential and nonconfidential information is protected, which has the effect of shielding notes, tapes, or video out-takes from courts or grand juries.[92]

The William Farr Case

A case whose permutations enmeshed a reporter for eight years was that of William Farr, reporter for the *Los Angeles Herald*

[86] Branzburg v. Pound, 461 S.W.2d 345 (Ky.1970). For a similar position under New York's statute, see People v. Dupree, 88 Misc.2d 791, 388 N.Y.S.2d 1000 (1976); for Texas, Ex parte Grothe, 687 S.W.2d 736 (Tex.Cr.App.1984), .10 Med.L.Rptr. 2009.

[87] Beach v. Shanley, 62 N.Y.2d 241, 476 N.Y.S.2d 765, 465 N.E.2d 304 (1984), 10 Med.L.Rptr. 1753.

[88] People v. Korkala, 99 A.D.2d 161, 472 N.Y.S.2d 310 (1984), 10 Med.L.Rptr. 1355; see also Knight–Ridder Broadcasting, Inc. v. Greenberg, 70 N.Y.2d 151, 518 N.Y.S.2d 595, 511 N.E.2d 1116 (1987), 14 Med.L.Rptr. 1299.

[89] KSDO v. Superior Court Riverside County, 136 Cal.App.3d 375, 186 Cal.Rptr. 211 (1982), 8 Med.L.Rptr. 2360. Also New York: Oak Beach Inn Corp. v. Babylon Beacon, 62 N.Y.2d 158, 476 N.Y.S.2d 269, 464 N.E.2d 967 (1984), 10 Med.L.Rptr. 1761; see Calif. Constitution Art. I, § 2, subd. (b).

[90] In re Van Ness (Cal.Super.1982), 8 Med.L.Rptr. 2563; Evidence Code of Calif. (§ 1070).

[91] Ohio v. Geis, 2 Ohio App.3d 258, 441 N.E.2d 803 (1981), 7 Med.L.Rptr. 1675.

[92] Dorothy A. Bowles, Media Law in Tennessee (Stillwater, OK: New Forums Press, 1993), at pp. 106–107, discussing Tennessee Code Ann. 24–1–208, and Austin v. Memphis Pub. Co., 655 S.W.2d 146 (Tenn.1983), and State ex rel. Gerbitz v. Curriden, 738 S.W.2d 192 (Tenn.1987).

Examiner and later the *Los Angeles Times*. Reporting the murder trial of Charles Manson, Farr learned that a Mrs. Virginia Graham had given a statement to a district attorney in the case, claiming that a Manson "family" member, Susan Atkins, had confessed taking part in the multiple crimes and told of the group's plans for other murders. The judge in the case had ordered attorneys, witnesses and court employees not to release for public dissemination, any content or nature of testimony that might be given at the trial; but Farr obtained copies of the Graham statement, according to him from two attorneys in the case. The court learned that he had the statement. Farr refused to tell the court the names of the sources, and published a story carrying sensational details. Later, he identified a group of six attorneys as including the two. The judge queried them, and all denied being the source. Once more the court asked Farr for his sources, and he continued to refuse under the California reporters' privilege law.[93] The court denied him protection under the statute and he appealed.

The appeals court upheld the conviction for contempt, essentially under the doctrine of the "inherent power" of courts to regulate judicial proceedings without interference from other government branches—a principle, as we have seen, reaching far back in the history of contempt. It said that courts' power of contempt is inherent in their constitutional status, and no legislative act could declare that certain acts do not constitute a contempt. If Farr were immunized from liability, it would violate the principle of separation of powers among the three branches of government; it would mean that the legislative branch could interfere with the judicial branch's power to control its own officers:[94]

Farr served 46 days in jail before he was released pending a further appeal, and in his uncertain freedom lived with the possibility of indeterminate, unlimited imprisonment if his appeal failed and he persisted in refusing to reveal his sources. That "coercive" sentence was later ruled by the courts to have no further purpose, as there was no likelihood that continuing it would induce Farr to testify. It was still possible, however, that he might have to serve a further "punitive" sentence for his contempt. Five years after the opening of the case against Farr—on Dec. 6, 1976—he was finally freed from the latter possibility by ruling of the California Court of Appeal, Second District.[95] He had served the longest jail term on

[93] West's Ann.Cal.Evidence Code § 1070 (1966).

[94] Farr v. Superior Court of Los Angeles County, 22 Cal.App.3d 60, 99 Cal.Rptr. 342, 348 (1971). New Mexico's Supreme Court ruled similarly that that state's shield law was without effect where testimony before courts was concerned: Ammerman v. Hubbard Broadcasting, Inc., 89 N.M. 307, 551 P.2d 1354 (1976).

[95] In re Farr, 64 Cal.App.3d 605, 134 Cal.Rptr. 595 (1976); Milwaukee Journal, Dec. 7, 1976.

record in the United States for refusing to reveal news sources, and his case had lasted longer than any other.

But his ordeal was not over. Two of the six attorneys whom he had identified brought a libel suit for $24 million against him. The trial court and the California Appellate Court ruled that the shield law did not protect him from answering questions in the case.[96] The long contest ended in April 1979. The libel plaintiffs had missed the five-year statute of limitations for bringing an action, and Farr's attorney convinced the trial court that their failure was a result of insufficient effort to bring the case to trial. At long last, the judge dismissed the suit.[97]

Sixteen months later, Californians voted to elevate the state's shield for journalists to a better-fortified position than that of a statute; they passed Proposition 5, which placed the shield directly into the State Constitution.[98]

In 1982, one test demonstrating the limitation of the new California shield came when Riverside (Calif.) policemen brought a libel suit against KSDO radio and its reporter, Hal Brown, for a story that implicated police in drug traffic. They demanded Brown's notes and memoranda.[99] And while the journalists won in their refusal to yield the material, they did so under *First Amendment* protection, said the court of appeal: the police had failed to show that the information was not available from any other source, or that the desired material went to the heart of their case.[100]

But so far as California's constitutional shield was concerned, said the court, decades of assumptions about its protective reach were mistaken: All it does is protect a journalist from contempt conviction. It does not stop courts from taking other actions in a libel case, as here, where journalists themselves are defendants: Their refusal to testify about information needed by the plaintiff could result in the court's striking their defense, or even awarding the plaintiff a default judgment. The court said that the shield law[1]

> * * * does not create a privilege for newspeople, rather, it provides an immunity from being adjudged in contempt. This rather basic distinction has been misstated

[96] 64 Cal.App.3d 605, 134 Cal.Rptr. 595 (1976). See also Quill, Nov. 1977, p. 14.

[97] Anon., "William Farr's Seven [sic] Year Fight to Protect Sources Is Victorious," News Media & the Law, Aug./Sept. 1979, 22.

[98] Anon., "Californians Vote to Include a Newsmen's Shield in the State Constitution," Quill, July/August 1980, 9; Calif.Const. § 2, subd. (b).

[99] KSDO v. Superior Court of Riverside County, 136 Cal.App.3d 375, 186 Cal.Rptr. 211 (1982), 8 Med.L.Rptr. 2360.

[100] Ibid., at 217, 8 Med.L.Rptr. at 2366.

[1] Ibid., at 213, 8 Med.L.Rptr. at 2362.

and apparently misunderstood by members of the news media and our courts as well.

Though vulnerable under any law journalists occasionally got more protection from their states' courts than the statutes suggested might be available. One loophole in several "absolute" statutes was the lack of provision protecting the reporter from revealing *information* that he had gathered, even though it protected him from revealing the *source* of that information. Robert L. Taylor, president and general manager, and Earl Selby, city editor of the *Philadelphia Bulletin*, were convicted of contempt of court for refusing to produce documents in a grand jury investigation of possible corruption in city government. Both were fined $1,000 and given five-day prison terms. They appealed, relying on the Pennsylvania statute stating that no newsman could be "required to disclose the source of any information" that he had obtained. "Source" they said, means "documents" as well as "personal informants." The Pennsylvania Supreme Court, reversing the conviction, agreed. The court said that the legislature, in passing the act, declared the gathering of news and protection of the source of news as of greater importance to the public interest than the disclosure of the alleged crime or criminal.[2]

Shield Laws and Libel

Finally, there is the frequent case of whether a shield against testifying is justified where a newspaper and reporter are sued for libel. If a reporter refuses to reveal an unnamed source who had allegedly libeled the plaintiff, may the plaintiff be foreclosed from discovering and confronting his accuser? Who, besides the reporter, can identify the accuser? Conversely, if the sources must be revealed, then is it not possible "for someone to file a libel suit as a pretext to discover the reporters' sources and subject them to harassment"?[3] This line of actions, of course, produced the suit which, perhaps more than any other, alerted the news world to the possibilities of danger in required testimony—Garland v. Torre, of 1958. As Marie Torre in that case, most other reporters since then who have been sued for libel have argued fruitlessly that they should not be required to name the source.

Shield statutes of Oregon, Rhode Island, Oklahoma and Tennessee provide expressly that the privilege is not available to persons sued for libel.[4] Supreme Courts of Massachusetts[5] and

---

[2] In re Taylor, 412 Pa. 32, 193 A.2d 181, 185 (1963). The Reporters Committee 1990 Guide, "Confidential Sources of Information," lists "absolute" and "qualified privilege" states as to both confidential sources *and* information.

[3] Gora, p. 40.

[4] Gora, p. 247. See Kaufman, op. cit., at footnote 84, above, *passim*, for comments on state shield statutes.

Idaho, which have no shield statutes, reject reporters' claims that there is an alternative First Amendment protection against the requiring of testimony—including testimony about sources of alleged libel. An Idaho decision, in which certiorari was denied by the United States Supreme Court, confirmed a 30–day jail sentence for reporter-editor Jay Shelledy.[6] He had quoted a "police expert" as criticizing state narcotics agent Michael Caldero who had been involved in a shooting incident. He was sued for libel by the agent, and, refusing to reveal the name of the expert, was held in contempt. The trial judge decided not to press the contempt citation, however, finding that another course of action would be more helpful to Caldero: The court would treat Shelledy's failure to identify the police expert "as an admission by the defendant Shelledy that no such 'police expert' exists, and the jury shall be so instructed."[7] The trial proceeded; the jury was instructed, and in place of the shield that his now-spent effort had hoped to raise, the jury served as armor: It brought in the verdict that Shelledy's article was not libelous.

The Caldero trial judge's ruling that Shelledy "had no source" was unusual but not unique. Only months before, one case in precedent had used the move—a decision by the New Hampshire Supreme Court. A former police chief sued for libel after a newspaper cast doubt on his truthfulness, alleging that he had failed polygraph tests. Its staff refused to reveal the sources of the accusation. The court, after determining that the sought-after testimony was "essential to the material issue in dispute," and "not available from any source other than the press," granted the chief's motion to compel disclosure. The newspaper appealed, and the New Hampshire Supreme Court felt that there was a better way to enforce the trial court's order than by holding the newspaper in contempt.[8]

> We are aware * * * that most media personnel have refused to obey court orders to disclose, electing to go to jail instead. Confining newsmen to jail in no way aids the plaintiff in proving his case. Although we do not say that contempt power should not be exercised, we do say that

[5] Dow Jones & Co., Inc. v. Superior Court, 364 Mass. 317, 303 N.E.2d 847 (1973).

[6] Caldero v. Tribune Pub. Co., 98 Idaho 288, 562 P.2d 791 (1977), certiorari denied 434 U.S. 930, 98 S.Ct. 418 (1977).

[7] Anon., "Lewiston reporter Wins Jury Verdict in Libel Case," News Media & the Law, Oct./Nov.1980, 10–11, Downing v. Monitor Pub. Co. Inc., 120 N.H. 383, 415 A.2d 683 (1980), 6 Med.L.Rptr. 1193.

[8] Downing v. Monitor Pub. Co. Inc., 120 N.H. 383, 415 A.2d 683, 686 (1980), 6 Med.L.Rptr. 1193, 1195; see also Sprague v. Walter, 518 Pa. 425, 543 A.2d 1078, 1086 (1988), in which the Pennsylvania Supreme Court held that a reporter-defendant in a libel case could invoke the state's shield law to protect the identity of sources. And the jury was to draw "*no inference either favorable or adverse*" from the invoking of the shield law as to the reliability of an unidentified source.

something more is required to protect the rights of a libel plaintiff. Therefore, we hold that when a defendant in a libel action, brought by a plaintiff who is required to prove actual malice under *New York Times,* refuses to disclose his sources of information upon a valid order of the court, there shall arise a presumption that the defendant had no source. The presumption may be removed by a disclosure of the sources a reasonable time before trial.

See also DeRoburt v. Gannett[9] and Miller v. Transamerican Press[10] for additional case law holding for the plaintiff's right to uncover confidential sources. In *Miller,* the 5th Circuit holding that disclosure can be compelled when the plaintiff has no other means to establish actual malice.

Successful Shield Claims

Nonetheless, the frequent success of the claim to the shield (usually where plaintiffs fail to show necessity, relevancy, and unavailability of the information) occasionally can extend to the libel situation, where the reporter is so likely to be vulnerable because he is the only source of the information sought. Before Marie Torre ever pleaded for protection in a libel case, a decision under the shield law of Alabama had furnished it to a reporter who refused to reveal sources of a story on prison conditions.[11] New York, New Jersey, and Pennsylvania protect, in varying degree, confidentiality in libel cases.[12]

Even in Idaho (which has no shield law and whose Supreme Court has interpreted *Branzburg* to provide no First Amendment protection), the appeal process has brought relief to journalists who fruitlessly sought a shield in discovery proceedings in a libel case. Sierra Life Insurance Co. demanded the names of confidential sources for a series of stories about the firm's financial difficulties, written by reporters for the *Twin Falls Times–News.*[13] Through complex legal processes, the reporters and the newspaper alleged

[9] 507 F.Supp. 880 (D.Hawai'i 1981).

[10] 621 F.2d 721 (5th Cir.1980).

[11] Ex parte Sparrow, 14 F.R.D. 351 (N.D.Ala.1953). Federal courts have provided protection in some libel cases also: Mize v. McGraw–Hill, Inc., 82 F.R.D. 475 (S.D.Tex.1979), 5 Med.L.Rptr. 1156; Bruno & Stillman, Inc. v. Globe Newspaper Co., 633 F.2d 583 (1st Cir.1980), 6 Med.L.Rptr. 2057.

[12] Respectively, Oak Beach Inn Corp. v. Babylon Beacon, Inc., 62 N.Y.2d 158, 476 N.Y.S.2d 269, 464 N.E.2d 967 (1984), 10 Med.L.Rptr. 1761; Maressa v. New Jersey Monthly, 89 N.J. 176, 445 A.2d 376 (1982), 8 Med.L.Rptr. 1473; D'Alfonso v. A.S. Abell Co., 765 F.2d 138 (4th Cir.1985), 11 Med.L.Rptr. 2117; and Hatchard v. Westinghouse Broadcasting Co., 516 Pa. 184, 532 A.2d 346 (1987): Reporters have to yield up evidence in a libel suit when it does not reveal identify of sources of confidential information.

[13] Sierra Life Insurance Co. v. Magic Valley Newspapers, Inc., 101 Idaho 795, 623 P.2d 103, (1980), 6 Med.L.Rptr. 1769.

that their stories were true and refused to name sources. In response, the trial judge ruled that Idaho provided no protection for them, struck all their defenses, and entered a "default" judgment against them for $1.9 million.

But the Idaho Supreme Court reversed the trial court. It did not feel that the refusal to testify should stand in the way of the newspaper's employing defenses—truth and lack of a connection between the stories and the damages suffered. Striking defenses in this case, it agreed, amounted to unwarranted punishment of the newspaper. And it said that Sierra had failed to show that its inability to discover the sources damaged its ability to prove the news stories false, which would be necessary to its case. It remanded the case, with "guidance" to the trial judge which included the Supreme Court's suggestion that the confidential sources' identity might not be relevant.[14]

Summarizing Issues in Confidentiality

The *Branzburg* decision having hedged the constitutional protection that the news world sought, the media turned to lobbying for statutes at the state and federal levels, and to strengthening existing state statutes. The number of states with statutes reached 28 by 1990,[15] about half of them passed during the 1960s and 1970s.

At the federal level, the major news organizations tried periodically for passage of a federal shield law, with—as of early 1989—no success. They found strong support and strong opposition among congressmen. It was estimated back in 1973 that more than 50 bills offering a shield had been introduced,[16] and more appeared in subsequent years. Whatever the level of government, the issues were similar.

(1) What are the competing social values in granting or denying journalists an immunity from testifying? The reporter's ethic of not betraying sources, and his property right in not losing his effectiveness and value as a reporter through losing his sources, had long been asserted unsuccessfully in cases under the common law. Now he was grounding his claim in society's loss of his service if he lost his sources through betraying them.

Earl Caldwell was one of a tiny number of reporters who had gained the confidence of the Black Panthers at a time when society had a real need to know about this alienated group. The Ninth Circuit Court of Appeals accepted Caldwell's argument that he

[14] Ibid., at 109, 6 Med.L.Rptr. at 1773.

[15] Reporters Committee 1990 guide, "Confidential Sources of Information."

[16] Thomas Collins, "Congress Grapples with Press Bill," Milwaukee Journal, March 25, 1973, p. 16.

would lose the Panthers' confidence if he even entered the secret grand jury chambers, for this extremely sensitive group would not know what he might say under the compulsion of the legal agency.[17] And if Caldwell could not report the Panthers, society was the real loser. This situation illustrated the difference between the values served in the case of privilege for the journalist and that for the doctor, lawyer, or clergyman:[18]

> " * * * the doctor-patient privilege is there to make it possible for patients to get better medical care. A journalist's privilege should be there not only to make it possible for a journalist to get better stories, but to contribute to the public's right to know. So in that sense it is a more critical privilege than some of these other privileges, which are based primarily on the relationship between two people."

Asserting an equal service in the cause of the "public's right to know" was the position that in many circumstances, government-as-the-public sought information from reporters vital to the public welfare. In State v. Knops,[19] an "underground" newspaper editor refused to tell a grand jury the names of people to whom he had talked about the bombing of a university building that killed a researcher, and about alleged arson of another university building. "[T]he appellant's information could lead to the apprehension and conviction of the person or persons who committed a major criminal offense resulting in the death of an innocent person," said the Wisconsin Supreme Court in denying privilege to editor Mark Knops.[20] Here government was saying that the journalist was practicing secrecy similar to that which he so often criticized in government, and that government was trying to serve the public's right to know about a major crime.

The Janet Cooke Debacle

A few reporters, meanwhile, rejected the notion that the privilege was either needed by or appropriate to the journalist. They said that most journalists of the nation had done their work for decades without a shield. And they worried about unethical reporters using a shield law to hide behind in dishonest reporting. Keeping in mind the respect, or lack of respect with which journalists are held from the chapters on defamation, unethical activities

---

[17] Caldwell v. United States, 434 F.2d 1081, 1088 (9th Cir.1970).

[18] House of Rep. Committee on the Judiciary, Subcommittee No. 3, 92 Cong., 2d Sess., "Newsmen's Privilege," Hearings, Testimony of Victor Navasky, Oct. 5, 1972, p. 236.

[19] State v. Knops, 49 Wis.2d 647, 183 N.W.2d 93 (1971).

[20] Ibid., at 99.

only serve to reinforce positions holding that a privilege is undeserved.

Directly on point was the episode—dismaying to journalists everywhere—of the fabricated story of rookie reporter Janet Cooke of the *Washington Post* in 1981. Her account of an unnamed eight-year-old heroin addict, whose identity she refused to disclose to her editors out of alleged fear of death from the child's "supplier," was awarded a Pulitzer Prize. But the award was scarcely announced when a standing challenge to the story's accuracy by city officials (resisted by Post editors who had insisted on shielding their reporter from disclosure of her sources), took strength from the revelation that Cooke had falsified her biographical resumé in applying for a position at the Post. Faced with the dual challenge, she confessed that she had made up the story and resigned. The Post returned the Pulitzer Award with agonized apologies to readers, the city, and the field of journalism. No law court, no threat of contempt was involved, but the parallels were too close for comfort. The integrity of a shield claimed by a reporter and afforded by editors had been shattered; and so, too, in some measure, had that of a great newspaper, and the fact-gathering principle of special treatment—privilege—for the journalist.[21]

(2) Can the news gathering function be protected by a qualified immunity, or must it be absolute? Hard positions for absolute shields were taken by many journalists and their organizations including the directors of the American Newspaper Publishers Association and those of the American Society of Newspaper Editors.[22]

Yet "absolute" protection was an illusion, as we have seen in the previous section.[23] And a federal statute of any kind became a more and more remote possibility as years of drafting, committee work, and lobbying failed.[24]

(3) Also at issue was the question: Who deserves the shield? and following that: Would not defining "reporter" in effect be to license journalists and thus bring them under state control? The United States Supreme Court in denying Paul Branzburg protection summarized the question and found that deciding it would bring practical and conceptual difficulties of a high order:[25]

[21] Jerry Chaney, "Level With Us, Just How Sacred Is Your Source?", Quill, March 1979, 28; Quill, 61:4, April 1973, 38. Paul Magnusson, "Reporter's Lies Undermine Paper, Profession," Wisconsin State Journal, April 19, 1981, Sec. 4, p. 6; Robert H. Spiegel, "Notes from Pulitzer Juror," Wisconsin State Journal, April 21, 1981, Sec. 1, p. 6.

[22] Quill, 61:1, Jan. 1973, 29.

[23] AP Log, Sept. 3–9, 1973, pp. 1, 4.

[24] Press Censorship Newsletter No. IX, April–May 1976, p. 53.

[25] Branzburg v. Hayes, 408 U.S. 665, 702, 92 S.Ct. 2646, 2668 (1972).

Sooner or later, it would be necessary to define those categories of newsmen who qualified for the privilege, a questionable procedure in light of the traditional doctrine that liberty of the press is the right of the lonely pamphleteer who uses carbon paper or a mimeograph just as much as of the large metropolitan publisher who utilizes the latest photo-composition methods.... Freedom of the press is a "fundamental personal right" which "is not confined to newspapers and periodicals." It necessarily embraces pamphlets and leaflets.... Almost any author may quite accurately assert that he is contributing to the flow of information to the public, that he relies on confidential sources of information, and that these sources will be silenced if he is forced to make disclosures before a grand jury.

Troubling as the question was, it did not deter states as they adopted statutes from 1970 onward. New York's 1970 law defined "professional journalist" and "newscaster" in its law that protected only those agencies normally considered "mass media"—newspaper, magazine, news agency, press association, wire service, radio or television transmission station or network.[26] Illinois, in its 1971 statute, defined "reporter" as one who worked for similar media.[27] Neither included books among the media immunized; neither included scholars and researchers among the persons immunized. In two cases, courts have ruled that state statutes which gave protection specifically to newspapers did not protect magazines.[28] But in late 1977, the U.S. Court of Appeals, Tenth Circuit, ruled that Arthur (Buzz) Hirsch, a film maker engaged in preparing a documentary on Karen Silkwood who had died mysteriously in a puzzling auto accident in Oklahoma, was indeed protected by the First Amendment in refusing to disclose confidential information concerning his investigation. This was the case despite the fact that the Oklahoma shield law gave protection only to those "regularly engaged in obtaining, writing, reviewing, editing or otherwise preparing news."[29]

The Second Circuit reached a different conclusion with respect to a reluctant witness in the civil case of von Bulow v. von Bulow[30]

---

[26] McKinney's N.Y.Civ.Rights Law § 79–h (Supp.1971). In People v. LeGrand, 67 A.D.2d 446, 415 N.Y.S.2d 252 (1979), 4 Med.L.Rptr. 2524, the law was held not to apply to a book author, because the law specifies that only professional journalists and newscasters are shielded.

[27] Ill.Legis.H.Bill 1756, 1971 Gen.Assembly.

[28] Cepeda v. Cohane, 233 F.Supp. 465 (S.D.N.Y.1964); Deltec, Inc. v. Dun & Bradstreet, Inc., 187 F.Supp. 788 (N.D.Ohio 1960).

[29] Silkwood v. Kerr–McGee, see "Court Protects Film Maker's Sources," News Media & the Law, 1:1 (Oct.1977), p. 26.

[30] 811 F.2d 136 (2d Cir. 1987), see also von Bulow v. von Bulow, 634 F.Supp. 1284 (S.D.N.Y.1986).

The children of Martha "Sunny" von Bulow sued Claus von Bulow alleging that Claus von Bulow put Sunny von Bulow into a permanent coma with a surreptitious injection of insulin. In the course of discovery, the plaintiffs sought notes taken by Andrea Reynolds, an intimate friend of von Bulow. Reynolds was his companion in his trial on charges of assault to murder his wife. The plaintiffs also sought investigative reports into the von Bulow matter that Reynolds had commissioned and a manuscript of an unpublished book that Reynolds described as "the manuscript of my story of the von Bulow affair."[31]

Reynolds submitted the notes and investigative reports but kept her manuscript. The district court ruled that all the materials were discoverable and ordered them turned over. Reynolds asserted a journalist's privilege and refused to comply[32] The district court found her in contempt and Reynolds appealed. The issue for the Second Circuit was whether Reynolds deserved to assert the privilege. (It should be noted that Reynolds' conduct during this controversy did little to help her position.) She failed to comply with the first subpoena, denied the existence of any of the subpoenaed documents other than her manuscript and in her deposition without benefit of counsel claimed the journalist's privilege as well as "any other privilege that exists under the sun."[33]

The district court looked to Reynolds' journalistic pedigree. Reynolds offered the court a press card from Polish Radio and Television that had been issued in 1979. She also said she had "drafted" an article about von Bulow for the German magazine Stern, had an agreement with a German publishing agency for serialization of her completed work, and said she had a press pass for the von Bulow trial from the New York Post along with a letter from a Post editor asking her to cover the trial.

That list might appear to justify a claim to being a journalist, but the district court looked further into her materials. It found that Reynolds never published anything herself, that she had not managed to come to an agreement with the Post for coverage, that the Post had never published any by Reynolds, that the article in Stern magazine she claimed credit for had been carried her husband's name on the byline. She also said that the manuscript she was working on had not been prepared under contractual obligation to any publisher and "that her relationship with the publisher of her proposed book 'has nothing to do with my privileges as a journalist.' "[34] The district court found Reynolds did not qualify for

---

[31] 811 F.2d 136, 139 (2d Cir.1987).

[32] Reynolds later asserted an attorney-client privilege saying that she was a "paralegal" for the defense team during the trial. That issue is not dealt with here.

[33] 811 F.2d 136, 139 (2d Cir.1987).

[34] Ibid.

the journalist's privilege because persons who claim the privilege must be actively involved in the gathering and dissemination of news to do so.

In its review of the district court's findings, the Second Circuit panel laid out the requirements for asserting the journalist's privilege.

> First, the process of newsgathering is a protected right under the First Amendment, albeit a qualified one. This qualified right, which results in the journalist's privilege, emanates from the strong public policy supporting the unfettered communication of information by the journalist to the public. Second, whether a person is a journalist, and thus protected by the privilege, must be determined by the person's intent at the inception of the information-gathering process. Third, an individual successfully may assert the journalist's privilege if he is involved in activities traditionally associated with the gathering and dissemination of news, even though he may not ordinarily be a member of the institutionalized press. Fourth, the relationship between the journalist and his source may be confidential or nonconfidential for purposes of the privilege. Fifth, unpublished resource material likewise may be protected.[35]

The court then examined the New York shield law which, in a previous case, did not serve to protect the author of a book because the author was found to fall outside the definition of a "professional journalist" as laid out in the statute.[36] Finding the state law and the federal approach to be similar because of their similar interests in protecting the press, the court then applied its standard to Reynolds' case. "We hold that the individual claiming the privilege must demonstrate, through competent evidence, the intent to use material—sought, gathered or received—to disseminate information to the public and that such intent existed at the inception of the newsgathering process."[37] Such a test, the court said, would require the district court to look into the intent element. The Second Circuit did not put limits on how the "journalist" would have to disseminate his news. The court said it could be through every sort of medium. The court also said that while prior journalistic experience would be helpful, it was not going to require that every person asserting the privilege to have had such a background.

[35] Ibid. at 142.

[36] People v. LeGrand, 67 A.D.2d 446, 415 N.Y.S.2d 252 (2d Dep't 1979), although the case left the door open for such a finding with a future author under different facts.

[37] 811 F.2d 136, 144.

The court looked at Reynolds' claim and the testimony she provided explaining how and why she engaged in her information gathering. The investigative reports focused on Sunny von Bulow's children to check on their credibility and for her primary concern of vindicating Claus von Bulow. Reynolds said her notes from the case were "worthless doodles." Her manuscript contained either material in the public domain or the notes and investigative reports. The public domain information was already known and the court concluded that the notes and reports were not the result of any journalistic endeavor when they were created. As such, the court affirmed the contempt order.

The Reynolds court may seem troubling with the finding by the court that she was not entitled to assert the journalist's privilege. But the court's analysis makes clear that it intended to prevent a misuse of the label journalist. The court noted the Tenth Circuit's decision regarding Silkwood film maker Arthur "Buzz" Hirsch.[38] The Second Circuit found a journalistic intent in that case that agreed with its own test. The Second Circuit explicitly said that even authors who have not published or are just beginning could assert the privilege if the requisite intent existed and was proven. "The burden indeed may be sustained by one who is a novice in the field."[39]

9th Circuit Provides Investigative Authors With a Qualified Shield

A wealthy family's internal struggles for control over the U–Haul Co. are part of the background for a defamation/author's privilege action known as Shoen v. Shoen. Leonard Shoen, a major owner of U–Haul, cooperated with investigative author Ronald Watkins, helping him to write a book titled *Birthright*. This book dealt with members of the family jousting for control of the company.

In 1990, the wife of Shoen's oldest son, Sam, was the victim of an unsolved murder. In interviews with the news media, Leonard Shoen said he suspected two other sons, Mark and Edward Shoen, of having some indirect ties to the murder.[40]

Mark and Edward Shoen sued their father for defamation. Seeking information for their lawsuit, they subpoenaed book author Watkins to give a deposition and to produce any information he had about the murdered woman, Eva Berg Shoen. District Court Judge Roger C. Strand refused Watkins' order for a protective order to

[38] Silkwood v. Kerr–McGee Corp., 563 F.2d 433 (10th Cir.1977).

[39] 811 F.2d 136, 144.

[40] Shoen v. Shoen, 5 F.3d 1289 (9th Cir.1993), 21 Med.L.Rptr. 1961; News Media & the Law, Fall, 1993, pp. 28–29.

protect him from a subpoena on grounds that a state court had interpreted Arizona's state law as excluding book authors.[41]

Held in contempt for refusing to testify, Watkins appealed to the U.S. Court of Appeals for the Ninth Circuit. Watkins contended that a First Amendment privilege should be available to protect not only regularly employed establishment journalists but also independent authors such as himself. He also argued that if forced to testify, that would discourage his sources from providing information. Perhaps most telling, the point was made that the persons subpoenaing Watkins had not exhausted other sources.[42]

The Ninth Circuit held that Watkins, as an investigative journalist, could invoke the shield privilege: "The journalist's privilege is designed to protect investigative reporting, regardless of the medium used to report news to the public.* * * What makes journalism is not its format but its content." Further, even if Watkins did not gain access to his material under a confidentiality agreement, the shield privilege still should protect him.

Shoen v. Shoen (1995): Round Two

The Ninth Circuit's 1993 remanding of the case to the district court was not the end of the Watkins' problems with subpoenas. The district court again found Watkins in contempt for refusing to obey a discovery subpoena, and Watkins again appealed.[43]

In a 2–1 decision, the Ninth Circuit again found in Watkins' favor. The court held that the plaintiffs had not made a sufficient showing to overcome Watkins' assertion of the journalist's qualified privilege. Writing for the majority, Court of Appeals Judge Farris showed substantial concern for protecting that privilege. The court held that when a civil litigant's discovery efforts run into a valid assertion of journalist's privilege by a non-party (in this case a writer who was no directly involved in the matter as a litigant), substantial deference should be given to that privilege. The Ninth Circuit held that in a civil suit, a litigant could overcome the journalist's privilege:

> * * * only on a showing that the requested material is: (1) unavailable despite exhaustion of all reasonable alternative sources; (2) non-cumulative; and (3) clearly relevant to an important issue in the case. We note that there must be a showing of actual relevance; a showing of potential relevance will not suffice.[44]

[41] News Media & The Law, Fall, 1993, p. 28.

[42] Shoen v. Shoen, 5 F.3d 1289 (9th Cir.1993), 21 Med.L.Rptr. p. 1961.

[43] Shoen II (Shoen v. Shoen), 48 F.3d 412 (9th Cir.1995), 23 Med.L.Rptr. 1522; Shoen I (Shoen v. Shoen), 5 F.3d 1289 (9th Cir.1993), 21 Med.L.Rptr. 1961.

[44] Shoen v. Shoen, 48 F.3d 412 (9th Cir.1995), 23 Med.L.Rptr. 1522, 1525.

The Ninth Circuit held that the plaintiffs had not made the necessary showing to overcome the journalist's privilege. Notes or tapes Watkins had compiled in interviewing the father, Leonard Shoen, appeared to the Ninth Circuit to be superfluous. The elder Shoen's plaintiff sons' defamation suit against their father already contained substantial evidence of the father's ill will toward them. In fact, in a deposition the elder Shoen referred repeatedly to one of his sons as "Hitler" and said he believed his sons were sociopaths.

As a result of the conclusion that the plaintiffs had not made out a case for demanding discovery of author Watkins, the Ninth Circuit reversed the contempt order and again remanded the case to the district court.

These issues and questions run deep. They are not likely to be resolved for all sides soon. For the journalists who will live with them and who may find them coming to bear personally in their professional work, a veteran investigative reporter—the late Clark R. Mollenhoff, a Pulitzer Prize-winner, had a key piece of advice: "You'd better know what you're getting into."[45] In other words, journalists should be reluctant to pledge confidentiality. They may find that if they wish to stay "on the record," sources often will talk to them anyhow. And if confidentiality is pledged, for how long? Until the moon no longer shines? Or for some lesser period? Promises of confidentiality are not to be entered lightly.

Is a Reporter's Confidentiality Pledge a Contract?
Cohen v. Cowles Media (1991)

Ethically, if a reporter promises to protect the identity of a source, that sounds relatively simple. Unless the journalist is released from that pledge by the source, then the journalist—if ordered to testify before a grand jury or in court—must choose between ethically keeping the confidence or refusing to testify and being fined or jailed for contempt. That is a hard choice, to be sure, but the rules seem understandable.

But matters are not that simple. Refer back to unfortunate Janet Cooke, discussed earlier in this chapter at page 550. She turned in a brilliant story to the Washington Post about an 8-year-old heroin addict, and said that her source was confidential. The Washington Post backed her, and—perhaps due to its own success with "confidentially sourced" stories by Bob Woodward and Carl Bernstein[46]—did not learn who her source was.

Ever since 1981, when it was seen that Ms. Cooke had made up the entire story and had caused the mortified Washington Post to hand back a Pulitzer Prize, most editors have insisted upon know-

---

[45] Quill, March 1979, p. 27, for Mollenhoff's rules.

[46] Cf. Woodward and Bernstein's All the President's Men (New York: Simon & Schuster, 1974).

ing the source's identity. This makes sense because if a paper (or broadcaster) is going to stake its reputation on a story, it is essential to have a good idea of the source's veracity and reliability. With some editors, also, it is an additional protection for a reporter. As John Seigenthaler of the Nashville Tennessean instructed his staff before his retirement in 1991, he insisted on knowing the identity of a confidential source so he could evaluate both source and information. (Then, if a judge wants to put a reporter in jail for not testifying, the judge may also have to jail the editor).[47]

The case of Cohen v. Cowles Media illustrates a situation in which editors decided—over the reporters' objections—that a confidential source's identity should be edited into a story. Its lesson—as handed down by the Supreme Court of the United States in June of 1991—is that a reporter's oral promise of source confidentiality amounts to a contract. Breaking such a contract may expose the reporter's employing organization to financial liability.

Dan Cohen, a former Minneapolis alderman, had been working as a political consultant to a Republican candidate for governor. Cohen found his candidate trailing badly in the polls late in October of 1982, only weeks before the election. Cohen arranged meetings with reporters from Twin Cities news organizations, including the Minneapolis Star and Tribune, the St. Paul Pioneer Press, and WCCO–TV.

Cohen offered to provide information that a candidate for state-wide election had been convicted of a misdemeanor. (The candidate involved was Marlene Johnson, the Democratic–Farmer–Labor [DFL] candidate for lieutenant governor; the DFL was then far ahead of Republicans in the governor's race. The misdemeanor was for shop-lifting merchandise worth $6 a dozen years earlier.)[48]

Reporters for both the Star Tribune and the Pioneer Press promised to keep Cohen's identity anonymous, and Cohen then gave the reporters two court documents showing that Marlene Johnson had been "charged in 1969 with three counts of unlawful assembly, and the second that she had been convicted in 1970 of petty theft." (The unlawful assembly charges stemmed from Ms. Johnson engaging in a protest against claimed failure to hire minority workers in city construction, and those charges were dismissed. The shoplifting conviction involved leaving a store without paying for $6 worth of sewing materials. That incident apparently happened, the Supreme Court noted, at a time when Ms. Johnson was emotionally distraught, "and the conviction was later vacated.")

[47] Seigenthaler comments on July 26, 1988, edition of MacNeil–Lehrer News Hour.

[48] Cohen v. Cowles Media Co. (1987), 14 Med.L.Rptr. 1460; News Media & the Law, Summer, 1988, p. 349; Andrew Radolf, "Anonymous Sources," Editor & Publisher, Aug. 27, 1988.

Evidently not liking being caught by Dan Cohen's political dirty trick, reporters for the newspapers interviewed Marlene Johnson to get her comments. Both the Minneapolis and the St. Paul newspapers decided independently to use Dan Cohen's name as the source of their last-minute-before-the-election stories about Johnson.[49]

> In their stories, both papers identified Cohen as the source of the court records, indicated his connection with the Whitney [Republican candidate for governor] campaign, and included denials by Whitney campaign officials of any role in the matter. The same day the stories appeared, Cohen was fired by his employer.

(At least one newsman, David Nimmer of WCCO–TV, listened to Cohen's proposition and refused to use the information. It was "no story," Nimmer said: "A conviction when she was 18 years old for shoplifting needles and thread.")[50]

Tim McGuire, managing editor of the Star Tribune, said that " * * * disclosure of an 11th–hour dirty trick [in the political campaign] was at least as important as the 12–year–old shoplifting record which Cohen was revealing."[51]

The trial court rejected the newspapers' contentions that the First Amendment erected a barrier to Dan Cohen's lawsuit alleging fraudulent misrepresentation and breach of contract. By a 5–1 margin, a jury awarded Cohen $200,000 in compensatory damages and $500,000 in punitive damages.[52] In a split decision, however, the Minnesota Court of Appeals overturned the punitive damages award after concluding that Cohen had not established a fraud claim which would support a punitive damage award. That court, however, left standing the $200,000 compensatory damages award.[53]

The Supreme Court of the United States held that the First Amendment does not prohibit a plaintiff from collecting damages for a newspaper's breaking of a promise of confidentiality in exchange for information. Liability could be assessed under Minnesota's "doctrine of promissory estoppel."[54] Justice Byron White wrote for the Court's 5–member majority:

[49] Cohen v. Cowles Media Co., 501 U.S. 663, 670, 111 S.Ct. 2513, 2516 (1991), 18 Med.L.Rptr. 2273, 2274.

[50] MacNeil–Lehrer News Hour, July 26, 1988.

[51] "Verdict on news sources distresses journalists," Associated Press report in Milwaukee Journal, July 23, 1988.

[52] News Media & the Law, Summer, 1988, p. 49.

[53] Ibid., at 50, 18 Med.L.Rptr. at 2276.

[54] Ibid. Black's Law Dictionary says: "*Estoppel.* A man's own act or acceptance stops or closes his mouth to allege or plead the truth." With *promissory estoppel,*

* * * "[G]enerally applicable laws do not offend the First Amendment simply because their enforcement against the press has incidental effects on its ability to gather and report the news. * * * [T]ruthful information sought to be published must have been lawfully acquired. The press may not with impunity break and enter an office or dwelling to gather news."

The U.S. Supreme Court declared that the Minnesota Supreme Court's "incorrect conclusion that the First Amendment barred Cohen's claim may well have truncated its consideration of whether a promissory estoppel claim had otherwise been established under Minnesota law and whether Cohen's claim could be upheld on a promissory estoppel basis."[55] Or, Justice White wrote, perhaps the Minnesota Constitution might be construed to protect the press from such a promissory estoppel action.

In dissent, Justice Blackmun (joined by Justices Marshall and Souter) argued that a damage claim for promissory estoppel should not be used to punish reporting of truthful information about a political campaign.[56] Justice Souter's dissenting opinion (joined by Marshall, Blackmun, and O'Connor) took the tack that the higher value to be served is an informed public, not a promise kept by a newspaper:[57]

> The importance of this public interest [the information provided by the press necessary to self-government] is integral to the balance that should be struck in this case. There can be no doubt that the fact of Cohen's identity expanded the universe of information relevant to the choice faced by Minnesota voters in that State's 1982 gubernatorial election, the publication of which was thus of the sort quintessentially subject to strict First Amendment protection.

Justice Souter summarized his dissent, arguing that "the State's interest in enforcing a newspaper's promise of confidentiality [is] insufficient to outweigh the interest in unfettered publication of the information revealed in this case * * *."

Whatever else Cohen v. Cowles Media means, the way it was argued by the newspapers ought to be a tremendous embarrassment to the journalistic world. Journalists have long argued that because they serve the public, they are somehow special and do not have to testify—like ordinary mortals—about the sources of their

---

"* * * such promise is binding if injustice can be avoided only by enforcement of [the] promise."

55 Ibid., 670–673, 111 S.Ct. at 2519–2520, 18 Med.L.Rptr. at 2277.

56 Ibid., 673, 111 S.Ct. at 2520, 18 Med.L.Rptr. at 2279.

57 Ibid., 678, 111 S.Ct. at 2523, 18 Med.L.Rptr. at 2280.

information. "We gave our word to protect our confidential sources, and courts should respect that." But in the Cohen case, the newspapers wanted it both ways; they wound up appearing to want to be free to give promises to get information, and also to have the luxury of reneging on promises when convenient.

But what of Dan Cohen? This political operative wanted to be a paid political consultant—anonymously—while lobbing bricks over a wall at an opposition candidate. But was he harmed $200,000 worth (the amount of compensatory damages left standing by the Minnesota Supreme Court)? Cohen, who lost a $35,000–a–year job in public relations in 1982 the day the story was published, by 1987 had his own PR firm and earned $97,000.[58]

Ironically, the Minneapolis Star Tribune was twice burned in 1988 on the issue of confidential sources. A second controversy over naming a source resulted in the newspaper halting circulation of its Sunday magazine for July 24, 1988. The New York Times reported that the Star Tribune could not ascertain whether a story to appear in its magazine had breached a secrecy agreement between a source (who is a lawyer) and the author, a freelance journalist.[59] That magazine issue was withheld.

Ruzicka v. Conde–Nast and Claudia Dreyfus (1992)

This case raises the legal question about how precise a journalist's promise needs to be to incur liability when broken. (Ethical concerns here might take up the question of making sure journalists and their sources understand each other's ground rules about confidentiality, etc.)

A 1988 issue of Glamour magazine contained an article by Claudia Dreyfus on sexual abuse by therapists. In researching the article, Ms. Dreyfus interviewed Jill Ruzicka, who told of being victimized by a psychiatrist. Ms. Ruzicka contended in her lawsuit against the magazine that she agreed to the interview only on condition that she not be identified. Ms. Dreyfus, on the other hand, recalled only that Ms. Ruzicka had casually asked for "some kind of masking."

The article used the first name "Jill" but did use a fictitious last name. But Ms. Ruzicka argued that the article identified her in other ways. (The article said "Jill" had filed a complaint against the therapist with the state medical examiners, had filed suit against him, and had gone to law school, become an attorney, and

---

[58] "2 Newspapers Lose Suit for Disclosing a Source," Associated Press story in New York Times, July 23, 1988. Early in 1992, the State's Supreme Court upheld the $200,000 jury award. The News Media & The Law, Winter, 1992, p. 2.

[59] Charles J. Lewis, Trading News for Anonymity, The Bulletin of the American Society of Newspaper Editors, April 1988, p. 3.

served on a state task force on sexual abuse by therapists—all accomplishments of the real-life Ms. Ruzicka.) She sued Conde–Nast and Ms. Dreyfus for breach of contract (promissory estoppel), fraudulent misrepresentation, invasion of privacy, intentional infliction of emotional distress, and unjust enrichment.[60]

A federal district court in Minnesota granted summary judgment to the defendants on all claims, and the Eighth Circuit Court of Appeals affirmed the summary judgments but sent the case back to the district court to consider the promissory estoppel issue as involved in Cohen v. Cowles media, discussed above. (Promissory estoppel is a doctrine which holds that if a person relies on a clear, unambiguous promise to his or her detriment, he or she may ask compensation for harm caused by the broken promise.)[61]

The federal district court held that Ms. Ruzicka's promissory estoppel claim failed because media coverage of her lawsuit against the psychiatrist before the magazine article appeared had increased the possibility that she would be identifiable from the magazine article. Second, the district court distinguished Ms. Ruzicka's lawsuit from the Cohen case because in her case, neither the promise nor the breach was clear. In the Cohen situation, the defendants simply decided to break a promise not to name him; in the Ruzicka case, defendants made an effort (however unsuccessful) to mask her identity.[62]

Some Ethical Concerns on Attribution

These problems surfaced in a time when journalists were worrying about their ethical standards. Charles J. Lewis, Washington bureau chief of the Associated Press, expressed concern about misuse of confidential sources eroding media credibility.

How can readers evaluate stories when sources are not known? For example, news from the State Department tends to follow certain rules: "on the record" means use names and information, but much news called "background" means that information can be used, but only vaguely attributed, as to "U.S. Officials" or "State Department sources." "Deep Background" means no specific attribution, and "off the record" means reporters can't use what they're told except for background.

Bureau Chief Lewis noted that the Associated Press has developed a three-part test which has helped to cut down the number of unattributed stories sent by the wire service.[63]

---

[60] Ruzicka v. Conde–Nast Publications, 794 F.Supp. 303, 304–305 (D.Minn.1992), 20 Med.L.Rptr. 1233, 1234.

[61] 794 F.Supp. at 308, 20 Med.L.Rptr. at 1236.

[62] 794 F.Supp. at 312, 20 Med.L.Rptr. at 1240.

[63] Charles J. Lewis, "Trading News for Anonymity," ASNE Bulletin, April, 1988, p. 5.

(1) The information should be newsworthy.

(2) We couldn't get the information elsewhere with attribution.

(3) The information is arguably factual rather than opinion or judgmental.

Beyond that, some sources discover that they have been quoted after they thought they had an agreement that their names would not be used.[64] Sometimes, releasing a source's name is necessary, as when the source has lied. For example, Lt. Colonel Oliver North complained about "leaks" which had led to a story in Newsweek about interception of an Egyptian plane carrying hijackers. Understandably, Newsweek published the rejoinder that the Colonel had failed to mention that he was the source of the leaks.

The Wall Street Journal distinguishes "anonymous sources" from "confidential sources." A memo circulated by managing editor Norman Pearlstine says that anonymous sources are those whose names the Journal has agreed to leave out of the paper but whose identity may later be disclosed, as in defending against a libel suit. A confidential source, on the other hand, is one whose identity the paper has promised to keep secret, even it means losing a lawsuit or going to jail.[65]

Source confidentiality, then, is serious business. Secrecy agreements with sources are not to be entered lightly. Especially worrisome are situations in which reporters' pledges are broken, either by reporters themselves or by their editors.

The basic question is whether the press is to be trusted and credible. Editors wishing to avoid difficulties would do well to emulate John Seigenthaler, former editor of the Nashville Tennessean: He says the only conceivable time to name a source pledged confidentiality would be if it turns out that the source has provided false information.[66]

SEC. 65. PROTECTING NEWSROOMS FROM SEARCH AND TELEPHONE RECORDS FROM DISCLOSURE

Courts have not granted First Amendment protection against officials' searches of newsrooms, but Congress and several states have passed laws providing protection. Confidentiality of journalists' telephone-call records that are on file at telephone companies has not been recognized.

[64] Monica Langley and Lee Levine, Broken Promises, Columbia Journalism Review July/August 1986, p. 21.

[65] Ibid., p. 23.

[66] MacNeil–Lehrer News Hour, July 26, 1988. In 1991, Mr. Seigenthaler became chairman of the Freedom Forum First Amendment Center at Vanderbilt University.

When the United States Supreme Court rejects a claim to First Amendment protection, Congress and state legislatures may be able to furnish protection by passing laws. The news world's drive for a statutory privilege against revealing sources—after the Supreme Court in Branzburg v. Hayes seemed to journalists to restrict protection under the First Amendment to a shadow—succeeded in a few states by dint of long, hard work, and failed in others. The effort to get a law through Congress ground to a frustrated halt in 1976 and 1977 as we saw above.

But another aspect of confidentiality denied First Amendment protection by the Supreme Court—shielding news rooms and offices against official searches and seizures of news material—got an early remedy in the form of state legislation and a national law—the Privacy Protection Act of 1980.[67] It was passed less than three years after a Supreme Court decision of May 1978 sent the news media into a reaction of alarm and denunciation; the very security of their news rooms and files was at stake. Journalists' outrage over the decision was widespread at what they saw as the Court's approval of a "right to rummage" in their offices, a breach of custom and understanding.

By a 5–3 margin, the Court said in 1978's Zurcher v. Stanford Daily that newspapers (and all citizens, for that matter) may be the subjects of unannounced searches as long as those searches are approved beforehand by a court's issuance of a search warrant.[68] They need not be suspected of any crime themselves; but as "third parties" who may hold information helpful to law enforcement, their property may be searched. A particular issue in this case was a question of how to interpret the words of the Fourth Amendment to the Constitution. That amendment says:

> The right of the people to be secure in their persons, houses, papers, and effects, against unreasonable searches and seizures, shall not be violated, and no Warrants shall issue, but upon probable cause, supported by Oath or affirmation, and particularly describing the place to be searched, and the persons or things to be seized.

The *Zurcher* case arose during violent demonstrations at Stanford University on April 9, 1971. Two days later, the *Stanford Daily* carried articles and photographs about the clash between demonstrators and police. It appeared to authorities from that coverage that a Daily photographer had been in a position to photograph

---

[67] Pub.Law #96–440, 94 Stat. 1879, approved Oct. 13, 1980, 6 Med.L.Rptr. 2255. For summary and discussion of the law and the state actions, see Anon., "Newsroom Searches," News Media & the Law, Oct./Nov. 1980, 3–5.

[68] 436 U.S. 547, 98 S.Ct. 1970 (1978) 3 Med.L.Rptr. 2377.

fighting between students and police. As a result, a search warrant was secured from a municipal court. The warrant was issued[69]

> on a finding of "just, probable and reasonable cause for believing that: Negatives and photographs and films, evidence material and relevant to the identification of the perpetrators of felonies, to wit, Battery on a Peace Officer, and Assault with a Deadly Weapon, will be located [on the premises of the Daily]."

Later that day, the newspaper office was searched by four police officers, with some newspaper staffers present. The search turned up only the photographs already published in the Daily, so no materials were removed from the newspaper's office. In May of 1971, the Daily and some of its staffers sued James Zurcher, the Palo Alto chief of police, the officers who conducted the search, and the county's district attorney.

A federal district court held that the search was illegal. It declared that the Fourth and Fourteenth Amendments forbade the issuance of a warrant to search for materials in possession of a person not suspected of a crime unless there was probable cause to believe, based on a sworn affidavit, that a subpoena *duces tecum* would be impractical.

Some translation is needed here. As *New York Times* reporter Warren Weaver, Jr. noted, a subpoena *duces tecum* (that's Latin for "bring it with you") "can be enforced by a judge only after a hearing in which the holder of the evidence has the opportunity to present arguments why the material should not be given to the government." That process means, of course, that the holder of the documents sought would have some warning and perhaps even a chance to "clean up" files. (But if one does tamper with evidence under subpoena—and if that tampering is revealed, it is surely punishable as contempt.) If investigators have a search warrant, on the other hand, the holder of the documents "has no more warning than a knock on the door."[70] In finding in favor of the Stanford Daily, District Judge Robert F. Peckham wrote:[71]

> It should be apparent that means less drastic than a search warrant do exist for obtaining materials from a third party. A subpoena duces tecum, obviously, is much less intrusive than a search warrant: the police do not go rummaging through one's house, office, or desk armed only with a subpoena. And, perhaps equally important, there is no opportunity to challenge the search warrant

[69] Ibid., at 551, 98 S.Ct. at 1974.

[70] Warren Weaver, Jr., "High Court Bars Newspaper Plea Against Search," New York Times, June 1, 1978, pp. Al ff, at p. B6.

[71] Stanford Daily v. Zurcher, 353 F.Supp. 124, 130 (N.D.Cal.1972).

prior to the intrusion, whereas one can always move to quash the subpoena before producing the sought-after materials. * * * In view of the difference in degree of intrusion and the opportunity to challenge possible mistakes, the subpoena should always be preferred to the search warrant, for non-suspects.

The Daily's lawsuit thus was upheld by a U.S. district court and, five years later, by a U.S. Court of Appeals.[72] The Supreme Court of the United States, however, in a decision announced by Justice White, declared that newspapers are subject to such unannounced "third party" searches as the one involving the *Stanford Daily*. Justice White's majority opinion said:[73]

It is an understatement to say that there is no direct authority in this or any other federal court for the District Court's sweeping revision of the Fourth Amendment. Under existing law, valid warrants may be issued to search *any* property, whether or not occupied by a third party, at which there is probable reason to believe that fruits, instrumentalities, or evidence of a crime will be found.

* * *

The critical element in a reasonable search is not that the owner of the property is suspected of a crime but that there is reasonable cause to believe that the specific "things" to be searched for and seized are located on the property to which entry is sought.

The Court enumerated—and rejected—the following arguments that additional First Amendment factors would forbid use of search warrants and permit only the subpoena *duces tecum*— arguments which held that searches of newspaper offices for evidence of crime would threaten the ability of the press to do its job.[74]

This is said to be true for several reasons: first, searches will be physically disruptive to such an extent that timely publication will be impeded. Second, confidential sources of information will dry up, and the press will also lose opportunities to cover various events because of fears of the participants that press files will be readily available to the authorities. Third, reporters will be deterred from recording and preserving their recollections for future use if such information is subject to seizure. Fourth, the processing of news and its dissemination will be chilled

[72] 550 F.2d 464 (9th Cir.1977).

[73] Zurcher v. Stanford Daily, 436 U.S. 547, 554–556, 98 S.Ct. 1970, 1975–1977 (1978).

[74] Ibid., at 561–566, 98 S.Ct. at 1977–1982.

by the prospects that searches will disclose internal editorial deliberations. Fifth, the press will resort to self-censorship to conceal its possession of information of potential interest to the police.

Justice White's majority opinion brushed aside such arguments and expressed confidence that judges could guard against searches which would be so intrusive as to interfere with publishing newspapers.

Justice Potter Stewart, joined by Justice Thurgood Marshall, dissented, arguing that in place of the unannounced "knock-on-the-door" intrusion, "a subpoena would afford the newspaper itself an opportunity to locate whatever material might be requested and produce it." Then, as did his dissent in Branzburg v. Hayes, his argument hammered at society's need for confidentiality of the journalist's information, and for its constitutional protection.[75]

> Perhaps as a matter of abstract policy a newspaper office should receive no more protection from unannounced police searches than, say, the office of a doctor or the office of a bank. But we are here to uphold a Constitution. And our Constitution does not explicitly protect the practice of medicine or the business of banking from all abridgment by government. It does explicitly protect the freedom of the press.

Justice John Paul Stevens' dissent focused not on First Amendment matters, but on the justification needed to issue a search warrant without running afoul of the Fourth Amendment. Stevens wrote that every private citizen—not only the media—should be protected.[76]

Students of the problem questioned Justice White's reliance on "neutral magistrates" to protect media from harassment, and to issue warrants only upon reasonable requests whose propriety they could gauge on the basis of probable cause to believe that evidence would be found on the premises to be searched. For one thing, between the 1971 raid on the *Stanford Daily* offices and the Supreme Court decision in 1978, there were at least 14 other searches of media properties. And in addition:[77]

> Journalists should perhaps be forgiven if they regard the protection of "neutral magistrates" as illusory. First, most, if not all, journalists tend to believe the folklore item about police walking around with fill-in-the-blank search

[75] Ibid., at 572, 576, 98 S.Ct. at 1985, 1987.

[76] Ibid., at 581–583, 98 S.Ct. at 1990–1991.

[77] Dwight L. Teeter and Singer, S.Griffin, Search Warrants in Newsrooms, 67 Ky.L.Journ. 847, 858 (1978–79).

warrants already signed by a complacent magistrate. Even if that is rankest slander of the judiciary, statistics on the issuance of search warrants compel the belief that the preconditions for warrant issuance are often improperly administered. "From 1969 through 1976, police sought 5,563 applications for search warrants under the 1968 Omnibus Crime Control Act. Only 15 of these applications were denied." Bluntly, the general rule seems to be that a search warrant sought equals a search warrant granted.

The legislation that Congress passed in 1980 in reaction to the *Zurcher* decision took effect in 1981. It provides a subpoena procedure, and a hearing for those subpoenaed. It prohibits "knock-on-the-door," search-warrant raids of news media offices and those of authors and researchers, by federal, state, and local law enforcement agencies, except in three unusual circumstances. These are: where there is cause to believe that the reporter himself is involved in a crime, where the information sought relates to the national defense or classified information, or where there is reason to believe that immediate action through search warrant is needed to prevent bodily harm or death to a human being.[78] *News Media & the Law* found that at least nine states had adopted their own laws along the same lines, some extending the protection to all private citizens, not only those in the field of writing. While the federal law avoids that reach, it requires the Justice Department to work out guidelines for federal searches that will take into account personal privacy interests of the person to be searched.[79]

The Privacy Protection Act was amended in 1996 to allow law enforcement personnel to conduct searches of newsroom for additional types of materials. The law, sponsored by Sen. Orrin Hatch (R–Utah), allows searches for materials linked to child pornography and other child exploitation offenses. Hatch said the amendment was needed to protect law enforcement officers from being sued over searches conducted in connection with child pornography cases.[80]

Journalists' Telephone Records

Searches of newsrooms slowed after adoption of the Privacy Protection Act of 1980, but—as discussed at the end of this chapter—occasional police or FBI searches (of dubious legality) may

[78] Pub.Law 96–440, 94 Stat. 1879; 6 Med.L.Rptr. 2255, 2256 (1981). And see "Carter Signs Newsroom Raid Ban," News Media & the Law, Oct./Nov. 1980, 3–5.

[79] Attorney General's Guidelines for Litigation to Enforce Obligations to Submit Materials for Predissemination Review, 6 Med.L.Rptr. 2261 (1981), dated 12/9/80, and published 1/2/81.

[80] "Amendments to Privacy Protection Act Become Law," News Media and the Law, Fall 1996.

occur.[81] And there are other intrusions. In 1976, the Reporters Committee for Freedom of the Press and other journalists lost a case in federal district court to compel AT & T to inform media when government subpoenas were issued for media phone records. The court of appeals also turned down the media, saying that no right of privacy under the First Amendment existed because the records belonged to the telephone company and not the media.[82] In an unsuccessful appeal to the United States Supreme Court to review the decision, the journalists stated the heart of their case for protection of their telephone records:[83]

> The impact of the ruling below cannot be minimized * * *. When government investigators obtain a reporter's toll records * * * they learn the identity of (his) sources. And they also learn * * * much about the pattern of his investigative activities—whom he called, when and in what order he makes calls to develop his leads, what subjects he is looking into and how actively he is exploring these subjects.

In the fall of 1980, it was reported that phone records of the Atlanta bureau of the *New York Times,* as well as those of its bureau chief, Howell Raines, had been subpoenaed in June by the Justice Department. The telephone company had waited 90 days, at the request of the Justice Department, before telling the Times. Shortly thereafter, attorney General Benjamin Civiletti announced new rules for issuing subpoenas for phone records—essentially, that no subpoena is to be issued to media people for their toll phone records without "express authorization" of the Attorney General.[84] This was the extent of protection that the media found.

Thus in one more setting, journalists were asserting that secrecy—anathema when employed by the government—was essential to the highest performance of their own craft. And once again, it was clear that deep values in the journalist's work—the "watch dogging" of government and other powerful institutions, and informing the members of an open society about their world—would be overshadowed in some contests where other values sometimes would take precedence.

Reporters Committee was criticized in the Eleventh Circuit in a case involving a subpoena of brokerage firm records pertaining to a

---

[81] "Police Raid Newspaper Printing Office," News Media & the Law, Aug./Sept. 1980, 25.

[82] Reporters Committee for Freedom of Press v. American Tel. & Tel. Co., 593 F.2d 1030 (D.C.Cir.1978), certiorari denied 440 U.S. 949, 99 S.Ct. 1431 (1979), 4 Med.L.Rptr. 2536.

[83] News Media & the Law, Oct./Nov. 1980, p. 6.

[84] New York Times, Nov. 13, 1980, A30; 28 C.F.R. § 50.10.

separate organization under investigation.[85] In rejecting the application of that precedent in the Eleventh Circuit, the court said that Judge Wilkey's contention that "the First Amendment affords no additional privacy protections beyond those created by the Fourth and Fifth amendments" enjoyed little support in either the circuit courts of appeal or the Supreme Court. The Eleventh Circuit pointed to cases in the Second, Ninth and Tenth circuits rejecting Judge Wilkey's position and offered a countering case, Pollard v. Roberts[86]

> "In Pollard, the three-judge district court, including then-Circuit Judge Blackmun, concluded that the enforcement of a subpoena duces tecum directed to the First National Bank of Little Rock, requiring the production of records that would identify contributors to the Arkansas Republican Party, would violate the contributors' and the Party's freedom of association. * * * The Supreme Court summarily affirmed the judgment of the three-judge district court. * * * The summary affirmance of Pollard v. Roberts applied the fact that the relevant records were held by the bank, not the party or its contributors. We must conclude, therefore, that appellants can invoke the protection of the First Amendment freedom of association to challenge the subpoena in Roberts."

We must wait for the Supreme Court to grant certiorari in some similar case to finally resolve the extent of First Amendment protection for records about journalists that are held by others.

Newsroom Confidentiality: A Continuing Struggle

Despite passage of the federal Privacy Act of 1980, aimed at protecting newsrooms from searches under most circumstances,[87] the late 1980s saw a number of efforts to search newsrooms. The searches showed that law is not self-executing, and that reporters need a working understanding of the law—with preparation from knowledgeable attorneys—when a search is attempted. Searches became sufficiently bothersome in 1988 that the National Association of Broadcasters (NAB) issued a memo urging broadcast sta-

[85] In re Grand Jury Proceeding, 842 F.2d 1229 (11th Cir.1988).

[86] 283 F.Supp. 248 (E.D.Ark.1968) *aff'd mem.*, 393 U.S. 14, 89 S.Ct. 47, 21 L.Ed.2d 14 (1968).

[87] See discussion at footnote 58, above. Those limited occasions in which a federal or state judge may issue a warrant for a newsroom search include a reasonable showing that newsroom personnel are involved in commission of a crime, in possession of contraband or classified or national defense information, or where there is reason to believe that information in a newsroom is needed by authorities to protect human life.

tions to review procedures with their attorneys for fending off a search.[88]

When a police department or sheriff asks a judge for a search warrant, there is some likelihood that the judge won't know that the Privacy Protection Act of 1980 forbids searches of newsrooms except in limited situations as noted above, at footnote 78. Despite this statute and despite similar legislation in at least nine states, occasional searches have continued. The News Media & The Law reported in the fall of 1988 that four newsroom searches had taken place between December, 1986, and mid-August of 1988, in Minneapolis and Golden Valley, Minnesota, and in Palm Springs and Los Angeles, California.

The News Media & The Law emphasized that the Privacy Protection Act of 1980 made it illegal for the seizure of either the "work product" or "documentary materials" from persons who are creating newspapers, books or broadcasts.[89] That magazine recommends:

First, journalists in the newsroom should object to the search and, if possible, should stall long enough for the company's lawyer and upper-level management to arrive.

Second, journalists should not interfere with the search, but they do not have to assist in it. The search should be limited by the terms of the warrant to certain areas and to specific materials.

Third, News Media & The Law recommends that a videotape or photographic record be made if the search proceeds.

Finally, once a search has taken place, a lawyer should be consulted about the possibility of suing the governmental agency carrying out the search. If the search is deemed found illegal under the terms of the Privacy Protection Act of 1980, the journalist whose office was searched can collect $1,000 in damages (plus reimbursement for any actual harm done in the search) plus lawyer's fees.[90] It should be apparent that most search warrants issued against newsrooms are illegal and invalid, and journalists should be prepared to fight back. Lawsuits are not the only weapons, however. Publicity about governmental units acting illegally may be the media's strongest weapon in protecting newsrooms from searches.

Obviously, journalists must remain vigilant, ready to contend— by all lawful means—against newsroom subpoenas or searches. While the threat of searches may have abated considerably, news-

[88] Jane E. Kirtley, Counsel Memo: "Dealing With Newsroom Searches," N.A.B. Info–Pak, October/November, 1988.

[89] News Media & The Law, Fall, 1988, pp. 4–5.

[90] Ibid., p. 6; See also Kirtley, op. cit.

room subpoenas seem to be alive and well. In 1991, for example, the Reporters Committee on Freedom of the Press released a study of 4,400 subpoenas asking for notes, tapes, or testimony served on 1,042 news operations during 1989. Significant details included:[91]

— Television stations are far more likely than newspapers to be subpoenaed, and are more likely to comply with subpoenas.

— Responding news organizations (about half of the 2,127 surveyed) indicated that only about 8 percent of the subpoenas were challenged in court. But nearly half of the subpoenas sought material that had actually been published or broadcast.

— News organizations' courtroom challenges to subpoenas were successful more than 75 percent of the time.

[91] Anna America, "News Media Under Legal Siege," Presstime, March, 1991, page 34.

Part IV

MASS COMMUNICATIONS AND GOVERNMENT

Chapter 11

THE FIRST AMENDMENT AND ELECTRONIC MEDIA

The constitutional history of American broadcasting is neither as impressive nor as extensive as that of the American press. Yet nothing in the language of the Constitution itself denies to broadcasting any of those free speech rights now being exercised by the press. Why, then, should American broadcasting have its own distinctive and less expansive body of constitutional law? What prevents a broadcaster from simply claiming that full legacy of First Amendment protections already won for American mass media by the press?

The answers to these questions can be found in the earliest days of radio regulation in the United States, when the federal government began to draw those legal distinctions that would isolate broadcasting from all other forms of American mass communication, restricting it to a much narrower range of constitutionally protected free speech rights.

SEC. 66. FROM RADIOTELEGRAPHY TO BROADCASTING

Broadcasting began in the United States as a service regulated by laws designed for an entirely different form of communication.

It all began with Guglielmo Marconi, who never wanted to be known as the "father of radio" and in reality—wasn't. Marconi was interested only in discovering some way to transmit telegraphic code through space, so he could offer the owners of the world's

573

great merchant fleets a global communications system capable of delivering messages directly to their ships at sea.[1] In 1901, Marconi demonstrated the effectiveness of his new "radiotelegraphy" device, and immediately began building "wireless" stations to relay telegraphic messages to vessels following every major trade route of the world.

Marconi expected to profit from his invention by selling or leasing the equipment he manufactured to all the large shipping companies of Europe and North America. It soon became apparent, however, that in freeing the telegraph from the constraints of its wire, he had created a *public* communications network, accessible to anyone possessing a transmitter or receiver obtained from any source. To discourage ship owners from building their own wireless devices or buying them from a growing number of competitors, Marconi instructed his own operators not to acknowledge or relay any radio message from a vessel known to be using non-Marconi radiotelegraphy equipment.

International reaction to Marconi's decision was both prompt and hostile. What might have been viewed as a sensible business policy for a land-based communications service seemed brutal and barbaric at sea, where refusal to relay a distress signal could easily imperil the lives of innocent ship passengers and crews.

The first radio law enacted in the United States, "The Wireless Ship Act of 1910,"[2] dealt only with this single issue in the field of maritime radiotelegraphy, requiring every large ocean-going vessel leaving an American port to have a wireless transmitter and receiver aboard, and making it unlawful for any ship wireless operator to refuse to acknowledge or to relay a wireless message from any other radiotelegraphy operator on sea or shore.

As the number of radio-equipped vessels increased with each passing year, interference caused by the growing volume of ship-to-shore transmissions became a serious problem. International maritime radiotelegraphy conferences were held in Berlin in 1903 and 1906, and in London in 1912 to negotiate treaty arrangements for the supervision of these radio communications that each country would be expected to enforce though its own national laws.[3]

---

[1] Because Marconi attempted to design a "closed" communication system, not intended for the general public but only those using his equipment, he could be described more accurately as the father of "narrowcasting," forerunner of modern pay–TV services, rather than broadcasting.

[2] Public Law 262, 61st Congress June 24, 1910. This requirement was imposed only on vessels carrying 50 or more people, and traveling more than 200 miles between ports.

[3] These international negotiations took on a special urgency after the sinking of the Titanic in April 1912. The ship rammed an iceberg in the north Atlantic, and sank three hours later. Some 700 of her 2,200 passengers and crew were saved, but a nearby ship that might have been able to save many more lives failed to respond to

The United States complied with these international obligations by enacting the "Radio Act of 1912," [4] requiring all wireless companies operating within the United States to transmit only on those frequencies approved for their use by the Commerce Department. This law authorized stations engaged in maritime communication to select and use two separate channels of radio frequencies, while all other operators were restricted to a single channel. In addition, those not engaged in either business or maritime radio communication message delivery service were relegated to a less effective frequency band, and were limited to a maximum of one kilowatt of transmission power.

American radio experimenters who attempted to "broadcast" to anyone who might be listening, rather than directing their messages to a specific receiver, were placed in this miscellaneous category of communication service by the Radio Act.

Reginald Fessenden, an early radio experimenter, designed the first wireless equipment capable of transmitting the sound of the human voice in 1906. But Fessenden, as Marconi, had no interest in "broadcasting" to the general public. His "radiotelephone", as the name suggests, was developed only to allow voice as well as telegraph messages to be delivered by wireless transmission anywhere in the world.[5]

In reality, of course, there was no American broadcast audience of any size to serve in 1906, because the complicated and expensive radio receivers of this era were still being designed and produced only for business use, while the inexpensive "crystal" detector receiver that had recently been developed was still crude and unreliable and required some degree of skill to assemble and operate.

From 1906 through 1917, the only broadcast service available anywhere in the United States was being provided by a rather small band of amateur radio operators in various parts of the country who enjoyed spending an evening or two each week transmitting a blend of recorded music and commentary to an equally small group of amateur radio enthusiasts who had assembled the reception equipment necessary to hear their broadcasts.

During this same period, the continuing expansion in the volume of private radio communications began to overcrowd that band of frequencies that had originally been allocated in 1912 to

her distress call because no wireless operator was on duty during the early morning hours when the Titanic was sinking.

[4] Public Law 264, 62nd Congress, August 13, 1912.

[5] For a more complete account of this early history of broadcasting, see Christopher H. Sterling and John M. Kittross, Stay Tuned: A Concise History of American Broadcasting (Belmont, CA: Wadsworth Publishing, 1977), pp. 16–46.

maritime and business service. But although the Department of Commerce was urged by several radio industry leaders to reclaim for business radio those spectrum assignments that had been made to amateur broadcast operators, the Department refused to do so, deciding that such experimentation would continue to be tolerated as long as it did not interfere in any way with the more important and useful communication functions of private radio.

That era of toleration ended in 1917, when the United States entered World War I, and the only important radio communication function suddenly became support of the nation's war effort. In April 1917 all radio transmission equipment not under government control was ordered dismantled, and the United States Navy was granted emergency power to develop the most effective radio equipment possible by requiring all American radio manufacturers to pool their existing radio patents and to cooperate in future research efforts.

The immediate effect of this wartime control was to transform radio equipment manufacturing in the United States into a growth industry. The U.S. Navy alone had purchased 10 million dollars of radio equipment from these suppliers by the end of 1917, and the government imposed "patent pool" stimulated more technological advances during two years it remained in effect than the industry itself had been able to achieve during the previous decade of fierce competition.

But then, with the American radio equipment manufacturers producing transmitters and receivers at a record pace, the war came to an end in November 1918, ending at the same time the massive military market for radio equipment. Soon afterward the Navy announced its intention to abandon its program protecting radio manufacturers from patent infringement claims, setting off an incredibly complex series of mergers and cross-licensing agreements to maintain those conditions that had permitted the industry to develop so rapidly during the war-time era.

By June 1921 these corporate maneuvers created a patent pooling, cross-licensing combination among General Electric, Westinghouse, the newly formed Radio Corporation of America (RCA) and American Telegraph and Telephone (AT & T) that made them the dominant force in the field of American radio equipment manufacturing and marketing.[6] At the same time, these corporate giants entered into a formal agreement granting to General Electric and Westinghouse exclusive rights to manufacture radio receivers that RCA would market as sales agent for the two companies.

[6] For a much more detailed discussion of these corporate negotiations, including a description of AT & T's important role in this trade combination, see Sterling–Kittross, op.cit, pp. 53–58.

RCA, General Electric and Westinghouse each realized that to create public demand for their radio receivers, they would have to provide regular broadcast service themselves. By the end of 1920, KDKA, a Westinghouse station, was providing such a service and in 1921 the Department of Commerce began to issue licenses to broadcast applicants.

Yet, even before the first of these new stations went on the air, this two-decade history had already begun to determine the future status of broadcasting as a mass medium in the United States. The Radio Act of 1912 had been designed for communication common carriers; services that did not communicate themselves, but merely served as channels to deliver the messages of others.[7] As a very secondary service within this regulatory scheme, broadcasting was tolerated but never recognized as having any unique rights of its own as a communications medium.

The Act made access to the electromagnetic spectrum a privilege, subject to governmental approval. Those private radio services regulated under its provisions had no legal basis for challenging this type of federal control because as common carriers, they were already subject to other similar regulatory constraints on their operations.[8] Since experimental broadcasting was authorized under the same law, it was simply assumed that its privilege of operation was also dependent upon government approval, an assumption that no small and disorganized band of radio amateurs was in a position to challenge.

Thus, as the radio era was beginning in the United States, a precedent had already been established for making the broadcaster's right to communicate a conditional one, dependent on the willingness of government to grant the applicant a license. At this point, however, the decision of whether or not to issue such a

---

[7] This vital distinction between the rights and obligations of *communication common carriers*, such as telephone and telegraph companies on one hand, and broadcasters on the other, would not be drawn until 1927, when the Federal Radio Commission was granted authority to regulate *broadcasting*, while the Department of Commerce continued to regulate common carriers under an entirely different set of standards. Today, the Federal Communications Commission regulates both types of communication services, but under those distinctly different standards established for each in 1927.

[8] A "communications common carrier" at law is one who provides message delivery facilities for public use. Because most carriers, such as local telephone companies, exercise at least limited monopoly power over the service they offer, they are subject to regulation to ensure that they furnish this public access in a non-discriminatory manner, provide all necessary services, and establish reasonable rates for those services. In contrast, a broadcaster has no general obligation to provide either free or paid public access to the station's facilities. Instead, the broadcast licensee has complete editorial control over the content of each message transmitted and is legally responsible for the content of every message delivered to the public. These distinctions are reflected in the Communications Act of 1934, at Sections 153(b) and 153(h) that declare "a person engaged in radio communication shall not ... be deemed to be a common carrier."

license was still being made solely on the basis of engineering criteria; determining in each case whether the broadcast license requested could be approved without creating an unacceptable level of interference with other existing radio services in the area in which it would operate. This single criterion for licensing did not pose any threat to the free speech rights of the broadcaster, but the precedent of licensing itself would soon serve as the basis for a much broader range of government controls.

SEC. 67.   SPECTRUM SPACE: FROM CRISIS TO CONTROL

Unprepared for rapid growth of broadcasting, Congress was forced to react with regulatory legislation outdated by the time it was enacted.

RCA, Westinghouse and General Electric each applied for broadcast licenses in 1921, as did a number of other smaller radio manufacturers and retailers. By 1923, nearly half (46%) of the radio stations on the air were being operated by radio manufacturers, dealers, or department stores selling radio receivers.[9] Except for its promotional value in marketing radio receivers, there was as yet no other financial incentive for providing broadcast service, because at the time it was still considered to be improper and unethical to use the broadcast spectrum to transmit advertising messages.

As Secretary of Commerce Herbert Hoover told industry representative at the Third National Radio Conference in 1924,

> I believe that the quickest way to kill broadcasting would be to use it for direct advertising. The reader of the newspaper has an option whether he will read an ad or not, but if a speech by the President is to be used as the meat in a sandwich of two patent medicine advertisements, there will be no radio left.[10]

By 1926, however, this opposition had become less intense and stations were permitted to begin broadcasting commercials; although they were still discouraged from accepting advertising that detailed the qualities of a specific product or mentioned its selling price.

During this same period, another significant change was taking place in American broadcasting. When radio began in 1921, there were an estimated 60,000 radio receivers in the United States, or approximately one radio for every 500 American households. This

[9] Sydney W. Head, Broadcasting in America, 2nd ed. New York, Houghton Mifflin, 1972, p. 137.

[10] Herbert Hoover at the Third National Radio Conference, October 6–10, 1924 as quoted in Sterling–Kittross, op. cit, p. 49.

broadcast audience of 1921 was still primarily one of radio experimenters, testing the sensitivity of their homemade receivers each evening by attempting to "pull in" as many different static-laden signals as possible from stations in distant states. By 1926, the typical household radio came encased in a handsome wooden cabinet for display and use in the family living-room. The set's storage battery had been replaced by a convenient wall plug, and its speaker allowed the entire family to enjoy its favorite radio programs together every evening. By this time there were already 4.5 million radio households and by 1928, eight million, or more than 25% of all homes in the United States.[11]

Unfortunately, as the number of new American broadcast stations increased proportionately during this same era, it soon became impossible to prevent one station's transmissions from interfering with those of other radio stations using the same or an adjacent frequency channel. When the Secretary of Commerce began issuing broadcast licenses in 1921, only two different frequency channels were assigned to be used by every broadcast station in the nation.[12]

In 1922, the Department of Commerce hurriedly added a third channel for broadcast service, and the following year, developed a far more comprehensive frequency allocation plan that set aside 73 new frequency channels exclusively for broadcast use. Yet, even though this new license assignment plan seemed well designed from an engineering standpoint to protect against future broadcast band interference, the Commerce Department's power to enforce its plan was dependent upon that very narrow base of regulatory authority it had been granted by the Radio Act of 1912.

Although the 30 radio stations using the broadcast spectrum in 1921 had swelled to 530 stations by 1924, Congress continued to disregard annual requests of the Secretary of Commerce to provide him with that broader authority he needed to deal with this ever increasing problem of broadcast interference. As one scholar in this field suggests, Congress may have been reluctant to act because

> the nature of broadcasting had not yet been clearly defined, and it was difficult to pass a law to regulate an unknown quantity.[13]

Whatever the reason for this reluctance, the failure of Congress to revise the antiquated radiotelegraphy legislation soon placed the Commerce Department in a difficult position. When the Secretary

[11] Sterling and Kittross, op.cit., p. 533.

[12] In September 1921, 833.3 Khz was the frequency to be used for all regular news and entertainment broadcast stations, while 618.6 Khz was set aside for broadcast of special government weather or crop information reports.

[13] Head, op.cit, p. 158.

of Commerce tried to enforce the Department's new broadcast frequency allocation plan by denying a license on the grounds of insufficient spectrum space to accommodate it, a federal court could find nothing in the Radio Act of 1912 that gave him the right to make such a regulatory judgment.[14]

Despite the fact that this decision suggested quite clearly that the Department's license assignment plan was not legally enforceable, most major broadcast organizations continued to comply voluntarily with its provisions, realizing that it was in their best interests to do so. As Commerce Secretary Hoover pointed out to industry leaders at each of the National Radio Conferences held between 1921 and 1925, broadcasting could continue to avoid direct governmental control only as long as self-regulation maintained an orderly, interference free broadcast service.

Unfortunately, self-regulation gave the radio industry no legal authority to compel any of its more than 500 licensed broadcasters to comply with Commerce Department directives, as Congress had given the Department no legal power to punish such noncompliance. As a result, the entire broadcast licensing and frequency assignment structure during this period had to rest upon the fragile hope that no broadcaster would ever force the Commerce Department to rely upon the Radio Act of 1912 again to enforce those regulatory policies the Department had adopted to solve the industry's interference problems.

That hope ended in 1926, and the voluntary licensing plan collapsed within a matter of months. Zenith Radio Corporation, a receiver manufacturer, had grown dissatisfied with the two hours a week it was authorized to broadcast on a frequency channel it was compelled to share with several other stations in the Chicago area. Believing that it deserved the same type of broadcast license privileges that Westinghouse, General Electric, RCA and other radio industry competitors had been granted, Zenith ignored the Commerce Department's refusal to grant it another channel and began to transmit its programs on that channel without authorization. Although Secretary Hoover was reluctant to have the Commerce Department's licensing authority tested in federal court, this challenge left him no alternative. The frequencies Zenith was using without permission had been reserved for Canadian stations by international agreement, an agreement that legally obligated the Department to protect these Canadian interests. In addition, after Zenith had defied the Commerce Department in this way, other stations soon announced their intention to follow its example.

As expected, when the Commerce Department tried to enforce its frequency assignment decision in federal court, the court found

14 Hoover v. Intercity Radio Company, 52 App.D.C. 339, 286 Fed. 1003 (1923).

nothing in the Radio Act of 1912 that authorized its enforcement, or that permitted the Secretary of Commerce to do anything more than issue broadcast licenses upon request.[15] Required from this point onward simply to grant each broadcast application as it was received, the Department was forced to issue more than 200 new licenses during the remainder of 1926, creating an even more intolerable level of broadcast interference in urban areas throughout the United States.

Realizing that radio service under these conditions could not survive for long, leaders of broadcast industry themselves began demanding that broadcasting be regulated by the federal government. As the year 1926 was ending, even President Calvin Coolidge, never an ardent supporter of government control, was urging Congress to enact legislation to regulate broadcasting, justifying his position by pointing out that

> ... many more stations have been operating than can be accommodated within the limited number of wave lengths available; further stations are now in the process of construction; many stations have departed from the scheme of allocation set down by the Commerce Department and the whole service of this most important public function has drifted into such chaos as seems likely, if not remedied, to destroy its great value.[16]

In March of the following year, Congress passed the Radio Act of 1927.[17] A new agency, the Federal Radio Commission, was created to administer the Act. Having failed in the past to provide the Commerce Department with the authority needed to protect the technical quality of broadcast transmissions, Congress now seemed to lurch in the opposite direction, granting the new Commission power not only over the engineering aspects of radio, but over the "public interest" qualities of broadcast programming as well. As the one of the co-authors of the new Radio Act declared at the time:

> We have reached the definite conclusion that the rights of our people to enjoy this means of communication can be preserved only by the repudiation of the idea underlying the 1912 law that anyone who will may transmit and by the assertion in its stead of the doctrine that the right of the public is superior to the right of any individual to use the airwaves.[18]

[15] United States v. Zenith Radio Corporation, 12 F.2d 614 (N.D.Ill.1926).

[16] As quoted in Frank J. Kahn (ed.) Documents of American Broadcasting (3d ed.) Englewood Cliffs, NJ; Prentice Hall, 1978, pp. 15–17.

[17] Public Law 632, 69th Congress.

[18] Senator Wallace H. White, as quoted by Commissioner Robert T. Bartley in FCC mimeo. 1336 (January 29, 1934).

Although the Act expressly prohibited censorship of broadcasting, it did officially empower an agency of the federal government to grant or revoke the right to communicate by radio on the basis of the quality of that communication.[19] While not as severe a constraint upon freedom of expression as actual censorship, this unique degree of governmental influence authorized over broadcast free speech during the past seven decades has resulted in electronic mass media being relegated to a less privileged status in terms of constitutional protections, unable to assert that full range of First and Fourteenth Amendment rights recognized by the courts as properly belonging to the American press.

In the last analysis, broadcast self-regulation had failed primarily because Congress itself had failed to sense the growing popularity and importance of the broadcast medium until the problem of chaotic interference compelled immediate legislative action. If Congress had simply revised the obsolete Radio Act of 1912 to give the Secretary of Commerce the broadcast licensing authority he had requested, it seems quite likely that the interference crisis of 1926 could have been averted.

In that sense, then, self-regulation actually may have worked too well, because in cooperating as effectively as it did with the Department of Commerce's licensing plan to reduce the degree of broadcast interference through the years, the radio industry permitted Congress to postpone and delay consideration of the federal government's proper role in the field of broadcast communication until it was too late for such a profound and complex question to be raised, much less answered.

SEC. 68.   RATIONALIZING GOVERNMENT REGULATION

Although a number of arguments have been advanced to justify federal broadcast regulation, the judiciary has relied upon only one in affirming this right of government control, the rationale of spectrum scarcity.

The Federal Radio Commission began with the assumption that Congress had provided it with sufficient legal authority to regulate broadcast programming. As the agency declared in one of its first annual reports to Congress,

> The radio act specifies that the commission shall exercise no censorship over programs. Nevertheless, the kind of

---

[19] Section 29 of the Radio Act of 1927 stated in part, "Nothing in this Act shall be understood or construed to give the licensing authority the power of censorship over the radio communication or signals transmitted by any radio station, and no regulation or condition shall be promulgated or fixed by the licensing authority which shall interfere with the right of free speech by means of radio communication." This statutory provision was incorporated as Sec. 326 of the current broadcast law, The Communications Act of 1934.

service rendered by a station must be a means of appraising its relative standing and must be considered by the commission in making assignments.[20]

In 1930 the Commission decided for the first time to refuse to renew a broadcast license solely on the basis of what it deemed to be programming not in the public interest. The broadcaster appealed, contending that permitting a federal agency to determine what was proper or permissible broadcast program content constituted a form of censorship clearly prohibited by the Radio Act.

The federal court disagreed, upholding the Commission's action by observing,

> There has been no attempt on the part of the commission to subject any part of appellant's broadcasting matter to scrutiny prior to its release. In considering the question whether the public interest, convenience or necessity will be served by a renewal of the applicant's license, the commission has merely exercised its undoubted right to take note of appellant's past conduct, which is not censorship.[21]

A second FRC denial of license renewal based primarily on inadequate broadcast programming performance was also sustained by a federal court the following year. In appealing the agency's action, the broadcaster invoked First Amendment as well as the non-censorship provision of the Radio Act, arguing that even if a federal licensing decision based upon the quality of broadcast communication was not "censorship" as defined by the Act, it was at least an unconstitutional abridgement of a broadcaster's right of freedom of expression.

Once again the court disagreed, upholding the agency's right to consider a broadcaster's past programming efforts in deciding whether to renew a broadcast license, and declaring that such a review of program content was

> ... neither censorship nor prior restraint, nor is it a whittling away of the rights guaranteed by the First Amendment, or an impairment of their free exercise.[22]

In each of these cases, the Federal Radio Commission's position may have been strengthened by the fact that the broadcasters involved were rather notorious characters with long and well documented histories of using their stations for their own personal

[20] Federal Radio Commission, Third Annual Report (Washington: Government Printing Office, 1929) p. 3.

[21] KFKB Broadcasting Ass'n v. Federal Radio Commission, 47 F.2d 670 (D.C.Cir. 1931).

[22] Trinity Methodist Church, South v. Federal Radio Commission, 62 F.2d 850, 853 (D.C.Cir.1932).

benefit. "Doc" Brinkley, owner of KFKB, was a diploma-mill physician who used the airwaves to sell his patent medicines and fabulous "goat gland" operation, guaranteed to rejuvenate the lagging sexual powers of older men, while Reverend Shuler, whose church owned the Trinity Methodist station, seemed to specialize in defaming public officials. Describing Shuler's conduct while on the air, the federal court said:[23]

> On one occasion he announced over the radio that he had certain damaging information against a prominent unnamed man which, unless a contribution (presumably to the church) of a hundred dollars was forthcoming, he would disclose. As a result he received contributions from several persons ... He alluded slightingly to Jews as a race, and made frequent and bitter attacks on the Roman Catholic religion ...

The FRC also may have been benefitted to some extent in gaining judicial approval of its authority over broadcast program content from its special relationship with the federal court that reviewed its actions. The Court of Appeals for the District of Columbia was designated by statute to be the court to hear all appeals from FRC actions and during this period it seemed particularly willing to apply the doctrine of "judicial forbearance;" that is, not to substitute its own judgment for that of the regulatory agency unless that agency decision was obviously in error.[24]

It's important to note, however, that during this entire FRC era, the United States Supreme Court had never considered, much less affirmed, the authority of the government agency to evaluate the quality of broadcast programming in deciding whether an applicant would be granted the right to communicate with a broadcast audience.[25] In 1934, Congress replaced the FRC with the Federal Communications Commission, consolidating regulation of both broadcast and communication common carrier services in the same agency, but controlling each separately under different provisions of the Communications Act of 1934.[26]

In 1937, the FCC launched an investigation of broadcast networks to determine whether the virtual monopoly control they exercised over the production and distribution of popular evening radio programming in the United States was in the public interest.

---

[23] Ibid., at 852.

[24] See Don Le Duc, Thomas McCain, "The Federal Regulatory Commission in Federal Court: Origins of Broadcast Doctrines," Journal of Broadcasting, Fall 1970, pp. 393–410.

[25] The Trinity Methodist decision had been appealed, but the Supreme Court declined to review the lower court decision. 288 U.S. 599, 53 S.Ct. 317, 77 L.Ed. 975 (1933).

[26] Public Law 416, 73rd Congress, 1934.

In the FCC's view, these networks were using their programming power to force stations seeking to affiliate with them to delegate to the networks too much authority over each station's broadcast scheduling decisions.

In order to protect station owners from these network pressure tactics, the FCC adopted rules in 1941 that limited the amount of network broadcast time that any affiliate station could carry, and authorized the agency to revoke the license of any broadcast station that exceeded this limit.[27]

The networks challenged the Commission's new rule, alleging among other things that by establishing limitations in advance upon the amount of time a broadcast station could devote to any specific type of programming, the federal government was encroaching upon the First Amendment protected free speech rights of the broadcaster. Justice Felix Frankfurter, speaking for a unanimous Supreme Court, furnished the first clear expression of the court's willingness to allow the federal government to establish and enforce programming standards in the field of broadcast speech.[28] Frankfurter wrote:[29]

> The question here is simply whether the Commission, by announcing that it will refuse licenses to persons who engage in specified network practices ... is thereby denying such persons the constitutional right of free speech ... The licensing system established by Congress in the Communications Act of 1934 was a proper exercise of its power over commerce. The standard it provided for the licensing of stations was the "public interest, convenience or necessity." Denial of a station license on that ground, if valid under the Act, is not a denial of free speech.

The underlying rationale for this position, Frankfurter explained, was that unlike other mass media, being allowed by government to broadcast was a privilege, not a right because,[30]

> ... its facilities are limited; they are not available to all who may wish to use them; the radio spectrum simply is not large enough to accommodate everybody.

[27] CFR 47 §§ 3.101–3.108. The FCC was forced to impose these rules upon individual radio stations because the networks used telephone circuits rather than spectrum space to distribute their programming to affiliated stations, and therefore did not require a FCC issued broadcast license to operate.

[28] Although the decision was unanimous, Justices Black and Rutledge took no part in the consideration of this case.

[29] National Broadcasting et al. v. United States et al., 319 U.S. 190, 226–227, 63 S.Ct. 997, 1014 (1943).

[30] Ibid., at 213, 63 S.Ct. at 1008.

In essence, then, the court held that by accepting the privilege of using the limited and valuable public resource of spectrum space, each broadcast licensee also assumed an obligation to exercise this privilege for the benefit of the public; an obligation the FCC had the authority to enforce on behalf of the public.

The Supreme Court did not return to this specific broadcast free speech question again for more than a quarter of a century, but when it finally did so in 1969, Justice White, speaking once more for a unanimous court, explained its "spectrum scarcity" justification for broadcast content control even more clearly and forcefully than it had been described in the earlier Supreme Court decision.[31]

> Although broadcasting is clearly a medium afforded First Amendment interest, differences in the characteristics of new media justify differences in the First Amendment standards applied to them ... When there are substantially more individuals who want to broadcast than there are frequencies to allocate, it is idle to posit an unabridgeable First Amendment right to broadcast comparable to the right of every individual to speak, write or publish ... the people as a whole retain their interest in free speech by radio and their collective right to have the medium function consistently with the ends and purposes of the First Amendment. It is the right of the viewers and listeners, not the right of the broadcasters, which is paramount.

Scarcity of broadcast spectrum space remains the only legal justification for federal regulation of broadcast programming in the United States. Following the sensible judicial practice of phrasing exceptions to general legal rules as narrowly as possible, the federal courts have been unwilling to adopt any broader rationalization for this governmental role in media free speech than absolutely necessary, fearing that expanding the basis for media content control might encourage this uniquely threatening power to extend beyond its intended range.[32]

As long as broadcasting remained the dominant electronic mass medium in the United States, there was nothing particularly unfair about all regulatory authority being based upon the legal concept of scarcity of spectrum space. Broadcasters might complain about

[31] Red Lion Broadcasting Co. v. FCC, 395 U.S. 367, 386–390, 89 S.Ct. 1794, 1805–1806 (1969).

[32] A number of other rationales have been suggested through the years for imposing content controls on broadcasting, while protecting other media from similar governmental constraints, including broadcasting's unique pervasiveness and influence upon our society, its unique accessibility to children in the home, and its status as the only medium operating under government license.

their "second class" mass communications status in comparison to the press, but at least all FCC regulations applied equally to every station competing for the same broadcast audience.

All this changed, however, when cable TV began for the first time to pose a serious competitive challenge to broadcasting in the late 1970s. Unlike broadcasting, cable TV systems did not require broadcast spectrum channels to deliver their programming, and so the FCC had no constitutional basis for imposing the same type of regulatory controls on a cable system as it imposed on its broadcast competitor. Now, the issue was no longer simply whether broadcasters should enjoy the same degree of freedom of expression as the American press, but whether within the field of electronic media itself, radio and television should be singled out by law as being the only forms of mass communication that remain subject to government content control.

SEC. 69.   SPECTRUM SCARCITY AND EXPANDING NEW MEDIA CHANNELS

The federal government has moved toward deregulation largely because it seems inequitable to impose regulation upon certain forms of electronic media that cannot legally be imposed upon others.

Although the FCC never attempted to license cable TV operators, the agency did use its regulatory authority over those microwave systems cable TV required to import their television signals to dictate cable TV programming policies. The Commission's technique was simply to adopt rules prohibiting the use of microwave relay services by cable systems not conforming to the agency's programming standards. Since virtually every cable system needed those additional television channels from distant markets to attract subscribers, this indirect regulatory influence upon cable programming worked quite effectively.

In 1968 the Supreme Court was asked for the first time to consider whether the FCC could exert this type of influence over a communications medium Congress had not granted it legal authority to regulate directly. The Court affirmed this authority, but suggested quite clearly that its scope was limited.[33]

> There is no need here to determine in detail the limits of the Commission's authority to regulate CATV. It is enough to emphasize that the authority we recognize today ... is restricted to that reasonably ancillary to the effective performance of the Commission's various responsibilities for the regulation of television broadcasting.

[33] United States v. Southwestern Cable Co., 392 U.S. 157, 88 S.Ct. 1994 (1968).

Four years later, in reviewing a FCC rule that required all major cable TV systems to originate one channel of television programming themselves, the Supreme Court, in a 5–4 decision, again affirmed the Commission, but with Chief Justice Burger warning that such a cable programming requirement,[34]

> strains the outer limits of even the open-ended and pervasive jurisdiction that has evolved by decisions of the Commission and the Courts.

That limit of judicial toleration was finally reached in 1979, when the Supreme Court reviewed FCC regulations requiring cable TV systems serving more than 3,500 subscribers to set aside certain cable channels for public access programming. The cable operator in this case had argued that by denying the system the right to decide who should be allowed access to these channels, or how these channels should be programmed, the FCC had deprived cable TV of constitutionally protected editorial control over the nature of its programming services.

The Court agreed with this argument, but chose to overturn the cable TV access rules without considering their First Amendment implications. Instead, the Court found the rules to be unenforceable because they treated cable TV systems as communication "common carriers," required to provide access to all, and Congress had not authorized the FCC to impose this type of communication obligation upon either broadcasting or cable.[35]

In 1977, a federal appeals court struck down FCC rules attempting to protect broadcasters from the competitive threat of cable delivered pay–TV services. In Home Box Office, Inc. v. Federal Communications Commission[36], the court found that Commission restrictions imposed upon the type of programming pay–TV could provide were not within the regulatory powers granted the agency by Congress. Although this finding in itself determined the outcome of the case, the court also discussed the broader First Amendment implications of such federal cable TV program regulation.

In essence, it pointed out that while incidental constraints upon cable TV free speech might be permissible to achieve some broader electronic media policy objective, there was no reasonable justification for believing in this situation that pay–TV would siphon away the most popular programs from traditional broadcast services. As the court observed, "where the First Amendment is

---

[34] United States v. Midwest Video Corp., 406 U.S. 649, 92 S.Ct. 1860 (1972).

[35] Federal Communications Commission v. Midwest Video Corp., 440 U.S. 689, 99 S.Ct. 1435 (1979). A communications "common carrier" is an organization such as a telephone or telegraph company in the business of conveying messages that others pay to have delivered.

[36] Home Box Office, Inc., v. FCC, 567 F.2d 9 (D.C.Cir.1977).

concerned, creation of such a rebuttable presumption of siphoning without clear record support is simply impermissible."

As the 1980s began, it was apparent that the federal courts were no longer sympathetic with FCC efforts to impose content controls of any kind upon cable TV systems. While the courts still chose to overturn Commission cable policies on the basis of these regulations exceeding the authority granted the agency by Congress, it was doubtful that any cable programming legislation Congress might adopt could actually withstand First Amendment challenge in the courts.

At this point, then, the FCC began moving in the opposite regulatory direction. Although as an agency of Congress, the Commission was compelled to continue to enforce all requirements imposed upon broadcasters by the Communications Act of 1934, the FCC started rescinding every radio and television rule of its own that no longer seemed justified by the less active regulatory role in broadcasting it intended to play in the future.

At the same time, the Commission began actively to encourage the development of other new electronic media, authorizing direct broadcast satellite (DBS), low power TV (LPTV) and multi-point, multi-channel distribution systems (MMDS) under standards much less stringent than those traditionally imposed upon broadcast license applicants.[37]

The underlying policy objective of both deregulation and new media system authorization has been to create such a vast electronic media marketplace of viewing and listening alternatives for American audiences that there will be no need for any further intervention on the part of the federal government to protect public interests in electronic mass communication. The Supreme Court has already acknowledged the impact such an electronic marketplace of ideas could have upon the traditional spectrum scarcity justification for broadcast regulation observation. Justice Brennan observed, in a footnote comment, that,[38]

> The prevailing rationale for broadcast regulation based upon spectrum scarcity has come under increasing criticism in recent years. Critics ... charge that with advent of cable and satellite technology, communities now have access to such a wide variety of stations that the scarcity doctrine is obsolete ... We are not prepared, however, to reconsider our long standing approach without some signal from Congress or the FCC that technological

[37] These systems and their regulation will be discussed in more detail in Chapter 10.

[38] Note 11, FCC v. League of Women Voters of California, 468 U.S. 364, 104 S.Ct. 3106 (1984).

developments have advanced so far that some revision of the system of broadcast regulation may be required.

Is the time approaching, then, when all legal distinctions between broadcasting and the press will be abolished? Will the rights of the "fourth" and "fifth" estates eventually merge, creating a single body of constitutionally protected mass communication freedom of expression? Until the rise of the Internet as a medium of effective mass communication took place, broadcast and print convergence seemed the likeliest route for development. The relative ease of creating an Internet presence without intrusive government regulation has led many newspapers to reconsider a turn to broadcasting. Still, many others have chosen to use cable.

Chapter 12

OBLIGATIONS ON BROADCASTING
AND CABLE

SEC. 70.   LICENSING BROADCASTERS

The licensing process has provided both the legal authority and the procedures essential for the regulation of broadcast service in the United States.

The Radio Act of 1927 marked both the beginning of broadcast regulation in the United States and the end of that era when use of the airwaves was an inherent right of every citizen, limited only by the availability of spectrum space.[1] Section 11 of the Radio Act diminished this *right* to the status of a *privilege*, to be granted by the Federal Radio Commission (FRC) only in circumstances where the agency found that issuing or renewing a broadcast license would serve the "public interest".[2] This same regulatory approach was followed by the Communications Act of 1934 that created the Federal Communications Commission (FCC) to replace the FRC.[3]

Because these governmental bodies were viewed as bestowing a *privilege* upon those they permitted to broadcast, the United States Supreme Court upheld their authority as regulatory agencies to impose conditions on the private use of this public resource of broadcast spectrum space, including a requirement that broadcast

---

[1] Section 2 of the Radio Act of 1912 required the Secretary of Commerce to issue licenses upon request, allowing conditions to be imposed upon a license only in instances where its operation might interfere with those of other licensed stations.

[2] Section 11, Radio Act of 1927, "If upon examination of any application for a station license or for the renewal or modification of a station license the licensing authority shall determine that public interest, convenience or necessity would be served by the granting thereof, it shall authorize the issuance, renewal or modification thereof in accordance with such finding."

[3] Communications Act of 1934, Public Law 416, 73d Congress, Secs. 307–309.

programming serve the interests of the public.[4] As a later Supreme Court decision would declare in even stronger terms, such government program standards were viewed as enhancing, rather than repressing broadcast freedom of expression because,

> When there are substantially more individuals who want to broadcast than there are frequencies to allocate, it is idle to posit an unabridgeable First Amendment right to broadcast comparable to the right of individuals to speak, write or publish ... the people as a whole retain their interest in free speech and their collective right to have the medium function consistently with the ends and purposes of the First Amendment.[5]

It is this broadcast licensing power, then, that has furnished the federal government with both the legal authority essential to regulate American broadcast service and that administrative process necessary to enforce its regulatory policies during the past seven decades.

The licensing process itself has always been more a matter of form than of substance. Applications for a construction permit, a broadcast license or renewal of a license each require the completion of countless forms, all filed in multiple copies with the Commission in Washington. There a small desk-bound staff of less than two dozen civil servants processes this paperwork to determine whether each application should be approved.[6]

The forms themselves are generally prepared for the broadcaster by one of the major communication law firms in Washington that specializes in dealings with the FCC. These attorneys, often former FCC employees, are in daily contact with the Commission staff to resolve any problems that might arise from their clients' broadcast filings. In nearly all cases, the end result of the process is that the application for the permit, license or license renewal is eventually granted.[7]

However, in that very small percentage of cases where a broadcast license application cannot be approved because, "a substantial and material question of fact is presented, or the Commis-

---

[4] National Broadcasting Company, et al. v. United States, et al., 319 U.S. 190, 63 S.Ct. 997 (1943). See also, chapter 3, Sec. 14 of this text for a more extensive discussion of this decision.

[5] Red Lion Broadcasting Co. v. FCC, 395 U.S. 367, 89 S.Ct. 1794 (1969).

[6] For an excellent description of this administrative process, see Barry Cole and Mal Oettinger, Reluctant Regulators: The FCC and the Broadcast Audience (Reading, MA: Addison–Wesley, 1978).

[7] In 1976, for example, the FCC processed 2,995 applications for renewal of broadcast licenses of which just 23 were designated for hearing, and only 8 ultimately denied. In other words, 99.2% of all renewal applicants were approved without hearing and only $\frac{3}{10}$ of 1% were eventually denied. Cole, Oettinger, op. cit., p. 147.

sion for any reason is unable to make the finding specified," the applicant is notified of the Commission's intention to hold a hearing before deciding what action should be taken.[8]

In most instances, a broadcaster unsuccessful at the informal hearing level still has the right to have this administrative finding reviewed both within the FCC itself and then by the Court of Appeals for the District of Columbia before being forced to accept an adverse Commission decision.[9]

The FCC does not monitor broadcast transmissions and so at time of renewal, it has always had to rely upon the records or "logs" of programming maintained by each station in determining whether the broadcaster has complied with the program proposals the station filed with the Commission when the license was last renewed.[10] During the 1980s the agency reduced this level of supervision even further, releasing broadcasters from the obligation to submit program logs to the Commission at the time of a station's license renewal.[11]

In 1991, however, the Commission decided to begin enforcing certain basic broadcast rules more aggressively, using its forfeiture power to impose monetary fines on licensees violating these rules. This tactic allowed the FCC to react to these violations much more quickly and efficiently than if it threatened a broadcaster's license, because many of the procedural safeguards of the licensing process did not apply in cases where the Commission sought only a monetary penalty.

After adopting a comprehensive *Table of Forfeitures* which for the first time specified the specific monetary amount that would be levied for each type of rule violation, the agency started almost

[8] U.S.C.A. Title 47, § 309(e). Recently, one of the few comparative standards the FCC had been using in deciding among competing candidates for a broadcast license was overturned by the court in Bechtel v. FCC, 957 F.2d 873 (D.C.Cir.1992). The court questioned the validity of the "integrated ownership" standard the Commission claimed to have been following since 1965, asking the FCC to produce one case during those years in which an applicant who received a license after pledging to personally manage a station had actually done so. Rather than respond to this challenge, the agency decided in April 1992 to review its entire comparative licensing process. See Reexamination of the Policy Statement on Comparative Broadcast Hearings, 7 FCC Rcd 2664 (1992); see also, Anchor Broadcasting, 72 R.R. 2d 98 (1993).

[9] U.S.C.A. Title 47, § 402(b). Although a broadcaster may also seek U.S. Supreme Court review of an adverse Court of Appeals decision, the Supreme Court agrees to review, or accept certiorari only in a very limited number of appeal situations each year.

[10] For a more detailed description of this license renewal process and its flaws, see Don R. Le Duc, Beyond Broadcasting: Patterns in Policy and Law (White Plains, NY: Longman, 1987) pp. 43–56.

[11] Revision of Applications of Renewals of License of Commercial and Non–Commercial AM, and Television Licensees, 50 R.R. 2d 704 (1981).

immediately to invoke its new sanctions.[12] During 1993 alone the Commission imposed fines totally more than one million dollars on some 140 different broadcasters for violations ranging from technical offenses such as inadequate tower lighting or failure to maintain public files to more serious charges of inadequate compliance with EEO requirements, improper political advertising practices or violation of the Commission's indecency standards.[13]

For the most part, though, broadcasters have tended to conform to Commission regulatory policies not because of any fear of forfeiture, or concern about what the licensing process might reveal about their programming practices, but rather because even the slightest threat to a station's license is a risk worth avoiding at virtually any cost.

This type of indirect rule worked particularly well during an era when the Commission could decide for itself when its understaffed Broadcast Bureau was capable of using the license renewal process to enforce certain specific FCC regulatory standards. Until the mid 1960s, only a competing broadcaster could compel the FCC to conduct a comparative hearing before awarding or renewing a broadcast license of another station in that market, and then only if the evidence clearly indicated that the award could cause intolerable transmission interference or severe economic injury to the complaining broadcaster.[14]

In all other situations, the Commission had sole authority to decide whether the public interest demanded that it conduct an elaborate and time consuming hearing before renewing a broadcast license. Not surprisingly, it rarely did.

In 1966, however, a federal court found that the FCC had been wrong in assuming that because the Commission was created to protect the interests of the public, members of the public themselves had no right to become involved in a broadcast licensing proceeding.[15] This decision, authorizing members of a community

---

[12] In re Standards for Assessing Forfeitures, 69 R.R. 2d 823 (1991), affirmed on reconsideration 70 R.R. 2d 11206 (1992). In July 1994, the U.S. Court of Appeals for the D.C. District upheld a U.S. Telephone Association challenge of this new uniform forfeiture schedule, holding that the FCC had failed to give those broadcasters, cable operators and telephone company licensees it affected adequate opportunity to comment on the new schedule before it was adopted. The Court did not find the concept of uniform fines to be unacceptable in itself but did question the equity of this particular schedule of fines that seemed to be overly severe in punishing telephone company regulatory violations.

[13] "Informal Listing of FCC Forfeiture Proceedings 1993", Mass Media Bureau, 1994. (mimeo). However, in U.S. Telephone Assn. v. FCC, 28 F.3d 1232 (D.C.Cir. 1994) a federal court overturned the Commission's uniform schedule, holding that the penalties it had established for telephone carrier violations were excessively high.

[14] Title 47, U.S.C.A. § 316(b).

[15] Office of Communication of the United Church of Christ v. FCC, 359 F.2d 994 (D.C.Cir.1966).

to challenge in federal court any license renewal granted by the Commission without adequate evidence of the local station's effective past performance, set off such a massive barrage of "citizen group" license challenges that the entire structure of American broadcast regulation seemed imperiled for a time.

Licensing has become an even more important issue with the rise in the number of station licenses that any one entity may own.

Renewing the Broadcast License

Recognizing the right of citizen groups to challenge the renewal of a broadcast license created new constraints upon broadcast freedom of expression.

During the period from 1970 to 1977, the FCC received a total of 447 citizen petitions or objections involving the licenses of 936 broadcast stations; almost 10 percent of all the commercial broadcasters then being licensed by the Commission.[16] Many in the broadcast industry felt that they had been betrayed by the courts, and abandoned by a Commission no longer capable of protecting them from private pressures. After complying with FCC rules for almost a half century with the understanding that the agency posed the only threat to their licenses, they were now suddenly being forced to defend themselves from citizen challenges as well, attacks upon an unprotected flank that left them vulnerable to interest group demands.

The FCC tried to end this siege of license renewal challenges in 1970 by proposing rules that made it virtually impossible to deny license renewal to an existing broadcast station, but a federal court refused to allow these rules to be adopted.[17] As the 1970s drew to a close, this "citizen group" movement lost its momentum, frustrated by the Commission's skilled use of procedural delay to deny them the hearings they sought. But this chaotic era of widespread license challenge had convinced the broadcast industry that it could no longer rely upon the FCC or the Communications Act of 1934 to protect their broadcast licenses from challenge.

Instead, the primary political objective for broadcasters during the 1980s became convincing Congress to adopt new legislation capable of sheltering existing broadcast station licenses from citizen group attack much more effectively at time of renewal. In 1981, Congress did act to reduce the dimensions of the license renewal

---

[16] Comptroller General, Report to the Congress, "Selected FCC Regulatory Policies and Consequences for Commercial Radio and Television," CED 79–62, 4 June 1979, p. 17.

[17] The FCC rules were proposed in "Policy Statement Concerning Comparative Hearings Involving Regular Renewal Applicants," 22 FCC2d 424 (1970). The rules were rescinded when challenged by a public service law firm in Citizens Communication Center v. FCC, 447 F.2d 1201 (D.C.Cir.1971).

problem to some extent by increasing the length of each television station license from three years to five, and lengthening each radio license period from three years to seven.[18] However, Congress has refused thus far to grant the industry the broad license renewal protection it has been seeking, forcing the FCC to try to provide these safeguards under the more restrictive language of the Communications Act of 1934.[19]

The Commission's decision to attempt to protect broadcasters from citizen organized license challenges is based upon the belief that such private pressure can pose a greater, if more subtle threat to broadcast freedom of expression that any federal regulatory policy may have posed in the past. Although the First Amendment shields broadcasting from government censorship, it provides no legal protection against private pressure. In addition, while government regulation is a public process, open for all to observe, interest group negotiations typically are conducted in secret, with concessions being granted without public knowledge or consent.

Ironically, then, the same FCC that was once viewed by the industry as the enemy of broadcast free speech is now the industry's only ally in the struggle to safeguard those free speech rights from the influence of self-styled "citizen groups."

But why should broadcast industry be so susceptible to such private pressure, particularly since any "citizen group" license challenge will ultimately be brought to the FCC for resolution? Those who champion the First Amendment rights of broadcasting are often critical of stations or networks willing to negotiate their programming practices with these interest groups, arguing that such broadcast organizations have the financial resources to protect, rather than bargain away their precious freedom of expression.

What these critics fail to realize is that while a media organization may have such resources, the decision to fight rather than negotiate a license challenge must be made by some highly paid executive within this organization, generally the station manager, whose dependence upon that generous salary to meet monthly mortgage payments and other financial obligations makes this employee far more vulnerable to such private pressure than any abstract concept of broadcast free speech would suggest.

Continuing controversy over station programming practices tends to disrupt normal business operations, is likely to damage a station's public image in the area it serves, and is almost certain to

18 Omnibus Reconciliation Act of 1981, 95 Stat. 736–37, as amended by Public Law 97–259.

19 See, for example, "FCC: Time to Modernize Comparative Renewal," Broadcasting, June 27, 1988, p. 35.

be viewed with alarm and displeasure at the corporate headquarters of the station's group owner. In addition, even a successful defense of a station's license may result in uncompensated legal expenses ranging from $100,000 to $500,000.[20] With these facts in mind, then, it may be easier to understand why a number of broadcast stations have yielded to the programming demands of well organized, politically sophisticated pressure groups, and why both the industry and the FCC view such privately negotiated programming concessions with such concern.

The FCC was finally able to adopt a revised set of license renewal rules in 1989, designed to discourage the challenging of a broadcast license merely to profit from a subsequent payment by the licensee to withdraw the challenge.[21] The new rules require that the Commission approve in advance all negotiated settlements between the license holder and a challenger or competing applicant. No settlement will be approved if payments to the challenger exceed what the FCC finds to be the "legitimate and prudent" expenses actually incurred by the challenger during the proceeding.

In addition, other forms of indirect compensation are now also presumed to violate the agency's settlement standards, such as an agreement by the station to hire or retain any member of the challenging organization, or to schedule specific programming produced or provided by that organization.

A survey of renewal proceedings conducted soon after the new rules were adopted disclosed a significant decrease in the number of challenges being filed, suggesting that these new procedural safeguards were achieving their desired policy objectives. Encouraged by these results, the FCC decided in May 1990 to impose similar settlement payment restrictions on all future comparative hearings involving new broadcast license applications as well.

After two decades of rulemaking and litigation, the Commission finally appears to have developed renewal standards capable of discouraging the filing of improperly motivated license challenges, while at the same time continuing to permit legitimate challenges to be evaluated fairly and impartially. Although the broadcast industry might have hoped for an even more elaborate set of regulatory safeguards to shelter licensees from the threat of other types of unjustified challenges, this appears to be the most exten-

[20] For example, WBBM–TV Chicago viewed it as a "victory" when they were able to settle a license challenge brought by Center City for *only* $187,000; reimbursement of Center City's legal expenses in filing the challenge. See "Settlement Reached in WBBM–TV Chicago Challenge", Broadcasting, July 18, 1988, p. 33.

[21] Broadcast Renewal Process, 66 RR2d 708 (1989); petition for reconsideration denied, 67 RR2d 1515 (1990) also see 67 RR2d 1526 (1990) for the adoption of similar standards for citizen petitions to deny applications for new stations, license modifications and transfer applications.

sive protection of a broadcaster licensee's renewal rights that the FCC, as an agency of Congress, has the legal authority to provide.

There are some things to keep in mind regarding renewal. If a station is sold, the renewal process will only concern itself with the performance of the current licensee. This can be a benefit or a detriment. To the good, a new licensee will not be saddled with the poor performance of the predecessor and to the bad the new licensee will have little time to create a record sufficient to withstand a challenge.

In addition to complying with general public service requirements, television stations also need to show evidence of compliance with the Children's Television Act. The Act requires stations to broadcast three hours of educational programming for children 16 years old and younger. The programing must advance their cognitive, social and emotional development. That tosses out broadcasts of "The Jetsons," "The Flintstones," and "G.I. Joe." In the early years of the Children's Television Act, broadcasters had tried to argue that "The Jetsons" prepared children for life in the 21st century, "The Flintstones" taught children about prehistoric times (apparently the failure of hominids and dinosaur co-existence from that time is a valuable lesson that children need to learn for present co-existence with endangered species), and "G.I.Joe" provided the much needed lesson that good or evil can live together as long as they keep missing each other as they blow up each other's stuff.

New, much stricter rules went into effect Sept. 1, 1997. Broadcasters will not have to label their educational and information shows. The programming must be shown between 7 a.m. and 10 p.m., though broadcasters may show additional hours of children's programming at other times. The new requirements mean that broadcasters must identify their qualifying programming and designate a station employee to serve as a liaison and file annual reports with the FCC. Failure to comply will be a consideration in license renewal.

Ownership Rules

The Telecommunications Act of 1996 provided for major changes in the rules governing station ownership. These changes reflect the changing market in which fewer media conglomerates own more media outlets. Ownership in radio is now subject only to limits related to markets themselves. Where there are 45 or more commercial stations in a particular market, an entity may own a maximum of eight stations. Of those eight stations, a maximum of five are permitted in either service. That is to say that an owner could own five FM stations at most. The rest would have to be AM stations, or vice versa. If the market had between 30 and 44 commercial stations, ownership would be limited to seven with a maximum of four in one service. In markets of 15 to 29 stations, the limit is six with a maximum of four in one service. Where there are fewer than 15 stations, the limits are governed by two rules: owners may own up to five stations, but if owning five would constitute more than 50 percent of the stations in the market, that number would be reduced. No single owner can own more than 50 percent of a market's stations. Owners are limited to three stations in one service for this smallest category.[22]

Television ownership rules also changed. As with radio there is no limit as to the number of television stations that one entity can own. The limitation deals with coverage. No single entity can own an aggregate of stations that reaches more than 35 percent of the national audience (The previous limit was 25 percent.). The Telecommunication Act of 1996 retained the television duopoly rule that limited entities to owning a single television station per market. But the Act also granted the FCC the power to waive the duopoly rule where the agency finds compelling circumstances. This waiver provision applies to the top 50 markets.[23]

The Act also permits common ownership of broadcast networks and cable systems. It also allows cross ownership of cable and wireless cable services, subject to the requirement that the cable operator continues to exist in a competitive environment. A 1975 rule, the Broadcast–Newspaper Cross Ownership rule, remains in effect. It means that an entity may not own both a broadcast license and a newspaper in the same community.

A portion of the ownership rules bars ownership of an American broadcast license by a foreign government or alien. This extends to both direct station ownership and ownership through a parent corporation. Section 310 (a) and (b) says that aliens may not own more than 20 percent of an individual station and no more than 25 percent of a corporation that holds a license. In 1995, Australian-born, media magnate Rupert Murdoch won permission to retain his ownership of six television stations that helped form the Fox Network. Although Murdoch himself became an American citizen to comply with the law, his holding company was based in Australia. That holding company put up nearly all the money to pay for the stations. In granting Murdoch permission to keep the stations, the FCC said it would not serve the public interest to punish his company .. Murdoch acted in the public interest by

[22] Peter D. O'Connell, "Summary of FCC Multiple Ownership Rules and Policies," presented to American Bar Association Forum on Communications Law, Representing Your Local Broadcaster, April 6, 1997, Las Vegas, Nev.

[23] Leon T. Knauer, Ronald K. Machtley, and Thomas Lynch, Telecommunications Act Handbook (Rockville, Md., Government Institutes Inc., 1996, p. 63.)

creating the Fox Network, a competitor for the three major networks, the FCC said.[24]

Digital and High Definition TV (HDTV) broadcasting have raised issues of spectrum ownership. Although satellite direct broadcast services have transmitted their programming in digital form, over-the-air stations are still working on both digital and HDTV. Because HDTV/Digital signals can't be picked up by current analog television sets, broadcasters will simulcast both types of signals during a transition period when older, analog sets wear out and are replaced by newer technology. The government gave stations additional spectrum to add the new broadcast signals. One question that arose after the award of the new spectrum was the ultimate fate of the analog signal spectrum. Stations announced plans to use the frequencies to sell information services and lawmakers responded with threats to take back the spectrum that the stations had gotten for free. A special commission was created in the fall of 1997 to consider what obligations stations would have in return for the spectrum grant.

SEC. 71.   CONTROLLING CABLE

In truth, the emergence of cable TV was simply an historical accident, caused by a noble but flawed policy effort of the FCC to design a system of "community oriented" local television in the United States.

The FCC television allocation plan of 1952 provided for more than 2000 television stations to serve some 1300 different communities throughout the nation.[25] The engineering staff of the Commission had based its television service projections on just such a fully operational system. Unfortunately, only 530 of these 2000 stations were actually in operation at the end of that decade, even though nearly 85 percent of all American homes already were television households.[26]

What the FCC planners had failed to foresee was that no one would apply for a television license in any of those communities too small to generate enough advertising revenues to interest a television network in providing the station with programming. As a result, instead of establishing a nationwide system of local television stations, the Commission succeeded only in creating conditions

---

[24] "U.S. Allows Murdoch to Keep TV Stations," The Wall Street Journal, July 31, 1995.

[25] 6th Report and Order, 17 Reg. 3905–4100 (May 2, 1952) allocated 2,053 television stations to 1,291 different communities in the United States, many with populations of less than 50,000.

[26] U.S. Congress, Senate, Committee on Interstate and Foreign Commerce, Television Inquiry: Television Allocations 86th Cong. 2nd sess. 1960, p. 4587.

that would allow a new, more effective system of television program distribution to develop.

Community Antennas

Originally "community antennas," as cable systems were then called, were exactly that; shared master antenna hookups that allowed a cluster of homes located just beyond the coverage area of the nearest television station to receive a marginally acceptable picture.[27] During the early 1950s these primitive aerials were viewed as being nothing more than a temporary solution to an immediate problem, destined to disappear in time as newly licensed stations began filling in each of the many gaps remaining in national network television coverage.

Within a few years, however, it became clear the Commission would not abandon its original television station allocation policy despite the plan's obvious limitations. As late as 1958, some 34 percent of America's television households still could receive only one television channel.[28] Located in less populous markets without an audience base large enough to support additional affiliate television stations, these viewers had access to only one of those three sources of network fare they were eager to watch each evening.

During this era an enterprising community antenna operator asked the FCC's Common Carrier Bureau for permission to use a microwave system to deliver to his system the network programming not available in his area from nearby network affiliate stations.[29] Because communication common carrier regulation at that time involved nothing more than a review of the reasonableness of the charges for service, his request was routinely granted.[30]

The CATV Era

Microwave relays opened an entirely new domain for CATV operators, allowing them for the first time to enter larger communi-

[27] As in the early days of radio, many of these first community antenna operators were actually appliance stores, trying to stimulate demand for the TV receivers they wanted to sell by providing television reception to households that otherwise would have been unable to receive a broadcast television signal.

[28] U.S. Congress, Senate, Committee on Interstate and Foreign Commerce, "VHF Boosters and Community Antenna Legislation"; Hearings on S. 1739 ... 86th Congress, 1st sess. 1959, p. 455.

[29] FCC 54–58; In the Matter of J.E. Belnap. For a discussion of the impact this decision had upon cable TV development and regulation in the 1950s and 1960s, see Don R. Le Duc, Cable Television and the FCC (Philadelphia):(Temple University Press, 1973) pp. 74–77.

[30] In a 1961 case, Federal Power Com'n v. Transcontinental Gas P.L. Corp., 365 U.S. 1, 81 S.Ct. 435, the Supreme Court approved the common carrier regulatory approach of looking beyond simple authorization of a service to determine whether the ultimate result of its use would be in the public interest. It was this decision that gave the FCC authority to begin denying cable TV its microwave relay requests in Carter Mountain Transmission Corp. v. FCC, 321 F.2d 359 (D.C.Cir.1963).

ties where some television service was already available. Until this time, a cable system could only improve the quality of existing over-the-air television service.

Now, however, cable TV could attract far more subscribers by offering them channels of network programs they were unable to receive over-the-air. Although those affiliate stations whose network programs were being exported by CATV systems without payment or permission were the first to complain about this usage, they really sustained no economic injury through this unauthorized carriage of their signals.[31] Few of the programs being exported by CATV were actually owned by these stations, and the wider circulation each station's advertising messages gained through cable dissemination actually increased rather than diminished their potential to earn revenues.

Instead, the damage was being inflicted upon small market television stations located in those communities where the CATV systems were operating. Until this time, station managers had generally been pleased with the community antenna systems that sprang up along the edges of their coverage contours, for they extended a station's effective transmission range at no cost to the broadcaster.

Now, however, these CATV systems were providing competing television channels to subscribers in the broadcaster's own market, substantially reducing the number of viewers watching the local station's programs. What had been a symbiotic relationship between the station and community antenna had been transformed into a parasitic one, for CATV was preying on small one station markets in the weakest financial condition. Yet, ironically, it was the marginal nature of these markets that sheltered CATV from immediate federal regulatory reaction.

Because the networks and the major stations instrumental in shaping industry policies saw little need to protect the economic welfare of stations in markets that cumulatively represented less than one percent of the total television audience, they made no effort to convince the FCC to intervene to prevent this damaging competition.[32]

In 1960, at the urging of several members of Congress whose small market television broadcasters faced such CATV competition, a Congressional committee considered legislation that would place the cable industry under FCC's regulatory jurisdiction. The FCC vigorously opposed the legislation, declaring that it did not believe

[31] Intermountain Broadcasting & Television Corp. v. Idaho Microwave, Inc., 196 F.Supp. 315 (D.Idaho 1961).

[32] For a more complete discussion of this era of cable TV growth, see Le Duc, Op.Cit. pp. 82–113.

the cable threat to be severe enough to justify the heavy administrative burden its supervision would impose upon the agency.[33] Ultimately the bill died in committee and because Congress would not adopt any cable TV legislation during the next 20 years, the FCC was compelled to operate continually at the very edge of its legal authority when dealing with cable, uncertain when the federal courts might find the agency had exceeded the boundaries of its Congressionally delegated power over cable TV.

Local Cable TV Controls

Because the federal government had not claimed exclusive control over cable TV, local governments began to exert their own legal authority to impose program service obligations upon cable operators who wanted to construct cable systems in their communities. They were able to do this without unconstitutionally abridging the free speech rights of the cable operator because of one special characteristic of cable TV operation.

It was virtually impossible to construct a cable system without first obtaining a public *easement*, the property right a cable operator needed from local government to permit the system's cable to be strung across the municipality's streets and other public rights-of-way. Within a short time, however, local governments began to realize if a cable operator expected to benefit from this use of public property, the citizens of the community to be served also had a right to benefit from this use of their land.

The contract that local governments offered an operator interested in providing cable TV service became known as the *franchise agreement*, offering the operator the privilege of a "public easement" to construct the cable system in return for an annual lease payment, called the *franchise fee,* and other regulatory requirements imposed on the system for the benefit of the citizens of that community who were the rightful owners of this municipal property.

As large corporations began buying groups of small CATV systems in the early 1960s, they started to exert strong influence upon the industry's trade group, the National Cable Television Association (NCTA), to *support*, rather than oppose federal regulation of cable TV. These new corporate cable owners found it extremely inconvenient to manage cable systems operating under vastly different local franchise agreements, and so they favored the

---

[33] "In the Matter of Inquiring into the Impact of CATV ... upon the Orderly Development of Television Broadcasting." Docket 12443, 18 RR2d 1573 (1959). The FCC realized that without constitutional authority to license each cable system, the agency would have no power to prevent the damaging impact CATV competition had upon broadcast stations, and yet would be held responsible for such damage because of being given this responsibility for cable supervision.

broadest possible federal preemption of cable control to reduce the degree of diversity among these local cable laws.

The NAB and NCTA tried to draft a jointly sponsored cable TV bill to submit to Congress that would grant the FCC at least some type of regulatory authority over cable TV. However, by 1964, bitter factional clashes between the new pro-regulatory and the old anti-regulatory groups within NCTA had become too intense to allow for any hope of future agreement on the "industry consensus" legislation Congress had requested.

As these industry negotiations were ending in failure, several of the larger, corporate owned CATV systems were preparing to enter a number of the "top 100," or largest 100 American broadcast markets, where 90 percent of the nation's television homes were located. Suddenly cable's competitive threat was no longer viewed as a minor one by broadcast industry leaders, and the FCC now shared this viewpoint.

Federal Cable Microwave Constraints

Although the FCC had no legal authority to regulate cable, it did have such authority over the microwave relay services essential to deliver the additional television signals cable TV needed to attract subscribers in major markets.[34] In 1963, the Commission had actually begun, on a case-by-case basis, to decide whether approving an application for a particular cable microwave relay would lessen the financial capacity of local television stations in the cable system's area to provide effective broadcast service.

When the FCC began to deny microwave applications on this basis, a federal court upheld the agency's right to use this power to protect the public's interest in maintaining the quality of broadcast television.[35] Then in 1965 the FCC declared that it would no longer authorize *any* applications to microwave television programs into a "top 100" broadcast market until the agency was able to adopt permanent cable microwave rules.[36] In the end, this "temporary" freeze on microwave applications would actually remain in force for

---

[34] To attract paying subscribers in major markets, cable TV had to offer viewers more service than those three network channels virtually all households in urban area could already receive with a simple antenna. This meant that programming from non-network stations in distant markets had to be imported as well, offering different film packages, syndicated programs and sports than local stations provided. Until 1975, when the first communication satellites began operation, there was no other means for delivering television signals from one market to another except by microwave network.

[35] Carter Mountain Transmission Corp. v. FCC, 321 F.2d 359 (D.C.Cir.1963), cert. denied 375 U.S. 951, 84 S.Ct. 442 (1963).

[36] "Proposed Rulemaking in Docket 15971", 1 FCC2d 463 (1965). By making this an interim or temporary rule, the FCC protected it from being challenged in federal court, because the court, except in an exceptional case, will not hear an appeal from an order until the action is final.

more than seven years, effectively denying the cable TV industry any growth opportunities in the nation's most profitable broadcast markets from 1965 to 1972.

Although the Commission has been widely criticized for suppressing cable industry expansion during this extended period of time, it is only fair to point out that Congress was at least equally to blame for the agency's conduct. The FCC was convinced that it would not be in the public interest to allow the cable industry to undermine the economic stability of television stations, while at the same time offering the public virtually no programming of its own and contributing nothing to the production costs of those television programs it carried.

Cable TV was free to take and distribute whatever broadcast programming it wanted without permission or payment simply because the only legally recognized property rights in these programs were defined by the Copyright Act of 1909, a law adopted before the birth of radio broadcasting. Because it had been written in the era of vaudeville and the musical hall, the Act of 1909 protected copyrighted material from infringement only if it was being "performed" without permission. In 1968, the Supreme Court affirmed earlier decisions by several lower federal courts that mere delivery of a television program by a cable TV system was not a "performance" of that program, and therefore that television programming was not protected by the Copyright Act of 1909 from unauthorized cable TV usage.[37]

Congress had begun efforts to revise the copyright law to include cable TV carriage of broadcast programming in 1965, but it took more than a decade to accomplish this task and cable TV would not actually come under the provisions of the new Copyright Act of 1976 until January 1, 1978.[38] During this entire era, the FCC stood as the broadcast industry's only legal defense again cable TV's unauthorized use of television programming.

In 1968 the Supreme Court affirmed for the first time the Commission's use of its microwave relay authority to discourage cable TV from entering major broadcast markets.[39] At that point the FCC announced its intention to launch a series of full scale hearings to develop rules and long range policy for the development

[37] Fortnightly Corp. v. United Artists Television, Inc., 392 U.S. 390, 88 S.Ct. 2084 (1968).

[38] Title 17, United States Code, "Copyright Act of 1909" was rescinded and replaced by the new Title 17, as enacted by Public Law No. 94–553, 94th Stat. 2541 (1976).

[39] United States v. Southwestern Cable Co., 392 U.S. 157, 88 S.Ct. 1994 (1968), in which the high court affirmed the FCC's authority to regulate cable TV's use of television signals as being a reasonable ancillary of its power to regulate broadcasting in the public interest.

of cable TV service in the United States. Four years later the agency completed these deliberations, and in March 1972, it issued these new rules, declaring that the era of modern cable TV service in the United States had finally begun.[40]

In reality, the FCC would continue to make it virtually impossible for cable TV systems to serve the 50 largest broadcast markets, where 75 percent of the television audience was located, until the Copyright Act of 1976 came into force. However, from 1972 onward, the cable TV industry would at least be regulated by rules designed for its systems, rather than solely for the protection of its broadcast industry competitor.

Cable TV had sprung up like a weed in a carefully cultivated garden. In attempting to create favorable conditions for the growth of locally oriented television service, the FCC had succeeded only in providing fertile opportunities for a rival distribution system to take root.

In this environment cable TV was the intruder, the electronic medium to be restrained in order to encourage more useful growth. Viewed from this perspective, it is easier to understand why the FCC simply suppressed cable TV, rather than trying to incorporate its systems within plans to provide more effective distribution of the nation's television services. Unfortunately, the damage caused by this repression would become all too apparent in the near future, when the cable industry did not have the financial capacity necessary to fulfill the promises it made to citizens in a number of American cities.

Federal Cable TV Regulation

The 1972 FCC cable rules required every new system being constructed in one of the largest 100 broadcast markets to provide its subscribers with a minimum of 20 channels, and to set aside specific channels for educational, governmental, leased and public access programming. While the FCC denied local governments any regulatory authority over cable TV's television signal carriage or program origination practices, it permitted municipal or state cable regulators to continue to establish franchise boundaries, select cable operators, determine terms of service and decide upon the amount to be collected as a franchise fee, although each of these powers now had to be exercised within standards set by the federal government.

It was difficult for the Commission to regulate cable TV effectively, because the agency had no constitutional authority to deny these non-spectrum communication systems permission to operate. Instead, the agency could only deny those cable systems in violation

---

[40] "Third Report and Order on Docket 18397", 24 RR2d 1501 (1972).

of its rules the right to carry broadcast signals, and if necessary, to enforce this denial through a federal court order. However, since the effect of this order would be to prevent the system's subscribers from receiving those services for which they were willing to pay, it was an action the Commission was obviously reluctant to take.

Initially, the FCC imposed an extremely elaborate system of restrictions upon the importation of television signals to major market cable systems, but after the Copyright Act of 1976 established a system compensating broadcasters and program suppliers for cable TV carriage, the Commission rescinded most of these restraints. By 1983, the only major FCC rule remaining in this field was "must carry", requiring cable TV systems to provide channel space for all local television stations their subscribers could receive over-the-air.

Even though the new copyright law did require cable TV systems to begin paying for the television programming they were importing, the terms and conditions of payment reflected a clear legislative victory for the cable industry. Cable was granted a *compulsory license* by the Copyright Act, compelling television stations and program suppliers to allow cable TV to carry their programs in return for a program use fee to be determined by a government body, the Copyright Royalty Tribunal. The Tribunal was empowered by the Act to collect from each cable system a percentage of that system's gross subscriber revenues to be used to compensate these television program suppliers.[41]

In gaining the "compulsory license," the cable industry was able to avoid having to pay the marketplace value for the programs it used. When the first distribution was made from this cable copyright pool, program suppliers complained bitterly that payments they received from the Tribunal were not only far less than the actual value of these programs, but even less than the financial damage they sustained because of this cable TV usage.[42]

In 1982 the Tribunal instituted new proceedings to adjust the amount of subscriber revenues each system would be required to pay into the copyright revenue pool. Until that time, cable systems paid only 0.625 percent of their annual revenues to import one distant television signal, and another 0.425 percent for each additional distant signal imported. Program suppliers urged the Tribunal to increase this fee substantially, because by bringing major

[41] This "secondary transmission" cable copyright payment procedure is described in Title 17, U.S.C.A. §§ 801–810.

[42] The Tribunal collected $15 million from cable systems during 1978, the first year this system was in operation. The distribution formula granted 75% of this money to program and movie syndicators, 12% to sports organizations and only 3.5% to television stations. This allocation was approved by the courts in National Ass'n of Broadcasters v. Copyright Royalty Tribunal, 675 F.2d 367 (D.C.Cir.1982).

feature films packages and popular series programming into areas where they had not yet been sold to local stations, cable TV was significantly diminishing the value, and thus the price of these features as "first run" attractions for television stations in that market where the cable system was located.[43]

After lengthy deliberations the Tribunal finally decided upon new rates for cable systems to pay for each distant television signal imported, almost 10 times higher than the base percentages established only four years before.[44] Although the cable industry complained bitterly about this massive increase in its copyright fee payments, the actual economic impact of these higher copyright rates upon cable systems was not very severe, simply because cable operators were by this time far less dependent upon broadcast stations for cable system programming.[45]

Cable Satellite Networks

Between 1975 and 1980, satellite delivered pay-TV services, superstations, and advertising supported cable networks not only reduced cable TV's dependence on the broadcast industry for programming, but also furnished cable systems with new sources of revenue. Home Box Office (HBO) launched the first cable pay-TV service in 1975, offering system owners the opportunity to earn profits from a vacant channel by devoting it to the delivery of the HBO service.

In 1977, USA, the first advertising supported cable TV network, began operation. It sought, at least initially, to cover its costs and generate profits solely on the basis of the commercials it could place in its programming. Although cable operators receive no payment from these advertising supported channels, and in most cases are now charged a monthly per subscriber fee for the privilege of carriage, systems can earn money from placing local advertising in network time slots provided, and are likely to attract a greater number of subscribers because of offering these additional channels of programming.

[43] This problem became more severe in 1980 when the FCC rescinded its "syndicated exclusivity" rules, that until this time had forced cable TV to "black out" programs on those channels it imported that local stations held exclusive rights to broadcast in that market.

[44] CRT 1982 "Distribution Proceeding and Partial Distribution of Fees" 48 Fed.Reg. 46412 (Oct. 12, 1983). This determination was sustained by the courts in National Cable Television Ass'n v. Copyright Royalty Tribunal, 689 F.2d 1077 (D.C.Cir.1982).

[45] In December 1993, Congress abolished the Copyright Royalty Tribunal, replacing this tax-supported agency with ad hoc arbitration panels chosen by the Librarian of Congress and working in consultation with the Register of Copyrights. Copyright owners will now be required to provide the funding for these panels that will decide how to allocate the compulsory license payments that cable systems and juke box owners make annually to those who own the programs and music they use.

So-called "superstation" cable service began in 1976, when Ted Turner, owner of a small UHF station in Atlanta, started delivering his station's programming by satellite to cable systems throughout the nation. Turner, whose ownership of the Atlanta Braves and part-ownership of the Atlanta Hawks allowed him to offer professional sports as well as the usual assortment of older syndicated series programs, generated his revenues through the higher advertising rates he could charge sponsors for his vastly expanded national cable viewing audience. By the mid–1980s, his service was already reaching more than 12.5 million American homes, or roughly one-sixth of all television households in the United States.

By 1980, cable TV system operators could choose among five competing pay-TV services, six "superstations" and more than 40 advertising supported cable networks, such as Entertainment and Sports Network (ESPN), Cable Satellite Public Affairs Network (C–SPAN), Cable News Network (CNN) and a host of other general and specialized program services to fill their systems' channels.

Ironically, this explosive growth in new satellite delivered services that transformed cable TV from a passive relay system for broadcast services into a truly unique and independent electronic medium was also the unanticipated by-product of an FCC major policy decision involving a different form of communication.

When the FCC authorized domestic communication satellite service in 1972, no one could foresee how its competitive "open skies" satellite policy would affect future cable TV service in the United States.[46] Until this time AT & T had held a virtual monopoly over the national distribution of television programming. Broadcast networks were charged a relatively low rate to deliver their programs to affiliate stations, because they were willing to pay for 24 hour a day usage of special AT & T television circuits set aside specifically for this purpose. When other television distributors tried to lease similar circuits from AT & T on an occasional use basis, however, the charge for this service was prohibitively high, because AT & T was forced to reroute thousands of telephone circuits to find the space necessary to deliver a full-sized television channel.

The Commission's policy decision to encourage competition by opening the communication satellite field to any organization meeting basic qualifications standards was not designed with the intention of ending this AT & T monopoly over national television delivery, but rather in the hope of reducing AT & T's domination over nationwide distribution of telephonic, telegraphic and other personal and business messages.[47] However, when Western Union's

[46] "Domestic Communication Satellite Facilities," 35 FCC2d 844 (1972).

[47] The FCC Common Carrier Bureau had begun this policy effort to reduce the AT & T–Bell domination of American personal and business communication services in 1959 by allowing carriers other than AT & T to operate microwave relay networks.

Westar I and RCA's Americom were finally launched in the mid–1970s, these new satellite system owners were eager to lease their unused delivery channels to video program organizations at rates far lower than AT & T had been charging.

The other factor that had inhibited the growth of new nation-wide television services had been the absence of local outlets to distribute these programs. Most broadcast markets had only three television stations, each already affiliated with a major network. As cable TV began to expand during the mid–1970s, however, with the 20 channel system capacity required by the FCC rules, virtually all operators had vacant channels available to serve as those local outlets that national satellite delivered program services required.

Thus, through another fortunate historical accident, the emergence of privately owned, competitively priced national domestic satellite system service happened to coincide with the growing demand of urban multi-channeled cable systems for additional programming to result in the establishment of a much more independent and prosperous cable industry.

The Urban Cable System Era

Unfortunately, though, extensive campaigns launched by each of the major cable ownership groups to capture as many urban cable franchises as possible once the FCC signal importation restrictions had been lifted, left most of these multiple system owners (MSOs) in a very precarious financial position as the 1980s began. In their eagerness to win franchise agreements from major city governments, each applicant tried to outbid all other competitors by offering an impressive range of communication services without carefully considering the operational costs involved. Adding to their difficulties was the fact that as many of these urban systems were being built in 1978 and 1979, interest rates on the substantial investment needed for cable construction soared to more than 20 percent.[48]

If the cable industry had been allowed by the FCC to expand gradually in urban markets through the years, it seems reasonable to assume that this period of frantic franchise speculation would have been avoided. Instead, the net result of all this destructive bidding was simply a trail of broken cable franchise promises, denying subscribers those benefits that had earned the MSO its franchise.

During the late 1970s, cable growth came to a virtual halt as financially overextended MSOs sought the additional funding essential to complete those systems they were already committed to

---

[48] For a detailed summary of many of these urban market problems, see "Cable Franchising Update," *Broadcasting* July 12, 1982, p. 37.

build. The timing couldn't have been more unfortunate for the cable industry, because, ironically, that very satellite delivered programming that could have made cable TV successful in major television markets was now seen by direct broadcast satellite (DBS), multi-channel, multi-point, distribution system (MMDS) and low power television (LPTV) promoters as being the program services that would allow them to invade these markets and claim that urban audience cable TV was still struggling to reach.[49]

Cable TV had been the first of the "new media." What made cable TV different from broadcasting was its program delivery function. Each radio or television station must depend upon a single channel of communication to entertain and inform its audience and earn its advertising revenues. In contrast, a cable system serves as a broadcast spectrum for its subscribers, allowing them to select from among those various channels of programming it provides.

This difference gave cable TV a tremendous competitive advantage over the individual television station. The cable system did not have to displace a popular, profitable program in order to provide more specialized features for particular segments of the audience. Instead, popular and specialized programs could be distributed simultaneously, attracting as paying subscribers not only those seeking mass appeal features, but also viewers especially interested in sports, politics, religion, culture, news or any of the many other cable delivered services. In fact, cable systems soon began packaging groups of these program channels in various priced "tiers" of subscriber fees, allowing operators to profit to an even greater extent from the diversity of services the system offered.

Yet, although cable TV was able to exploit this multi-channel distribution system advantage when competing with broadcasting, its massively expensive coaxial distribution system made it vulnerable to challenge from newer multi-channeled systems far less expensive to build, and capable of beginning service much more rapidly than cable.

Until this point, the cable industry had been totally committed to the principle of free competition in a marketplace environment to determine which form of electronic media service should prevail. During the 1980s, that commitment became somewhat less than total.

---

[49] As late as 1981, more than 60% of all American cable TV systems still had no more than a 12 channel delivery capacity, a capacity reduced even further by franchise and FCC signal carriage rules. Sydney Head and Christopher Sterling, Broadcasting in America 4th ed. (Boston: Houghton Mifflin, 1982) p. 296.

SEC. 72.   CONTENT CONTROL

Broadcast program requirements have always been stated in general terms to avoid encroaching unnecessarily upon the free speech rights of the broadcast licensee. But both broadcast and cable must comply with certain minimum standards regarding their content.

In 1929, only two years after it began regulating broadcast service in the United States, the FRC issued its first comprehensive description of federal broadcast program policy. Beginning a regulatory tradition that would endure until the 1980s, the agency pointed out in this earliest public programming statement that it would not establish any list of *preferred* program categories. Instead, the FRC simply directed each station to offer its audience a balanced schedule of different types of programs capable of serving the needs of every segment of the station's audience. The Commission described its program policy objectives in this way:

> The tastes, needs and desires of all substantial groups among the public should be met, in fair proportion, by a well-rounded program schedule, in which entertainment, religion, education and instruction, important public events, discussions of public questions, weather, market reports, news and matters of interest to all members of the family find a place.[50]

Network Program Control

The FRC soon discovered, however, that it was difficult to achieve even these rather basic and generalized programming goals because stations had begun to rely upon national broadcast networks to provide a substantial portion of their daily program schedule. Network broadcasting had existed since 1924, but it was not until 1929 that NBC and the newly formed CBS became the dominant national programming and advertising forces in American radio.[51]

Stations were eager to affiliate with one of the major broadcast networks because they offered the type of popular, professionally produced entertainment shows no local station could hope to duplicate. To become a network affiliate, however, a station had to agree to carry a substantial number of network programs each week, and to reserve other portions of its broadcast schedule to be used for whatever programs the network chose to provide.

[50] In the matter of the application of Great Lakes Broadcasting, 3 FRC Annual Reports 32 (1929).

[51] NBC actually operated two separate radio networks until 1941, the "Red" network which it retained, and the "Blue" network sold in 1941 and renamed the American Broadcasting Company in 1945.

Both the FRC and the FCC saw the networks as distorting that balance in the various forms of programming these regulatory bodies had sought to encourage; furnishing affiliate stations with a vast array of light entertainment shows while offering virtually no public affairs, educational or children's' programming.

Yet neither agency had authority to regulate the networks *directly*, because networks did not use the broadcast spectrum to distribute their programs, delivering them instead to their affiliated stations through privately leased telephone lines. Since the networks required no broadcast license to operate these non-spectrum programming services, there was no legal basis for imposing any public interest standards upon the shows they provided their affiliate stations.[52]

Unable to regulate network program practices directly, the FCC began during the late 1930s to use its licensing authority instead to force the network affiliate stations themselves to reclaim from their national network the right to program a larger proportion of their own daily broadcast schedule. In 1940, the Commission adopted rules that established severe restrictions on the amount of broadcast time any station could devote to network programming, including an enforcement provision that allowed the Commission to revoke the broadcast license of any station exceeding these network time limitations.[53]

In 1970, the Commission tried a somewhat similar tactic in television, restricting network affiliate television stations in major markets to only three hours of network supplied prime-time programming each evening.[54] This "Prime Time Access Rule", modified and amended several times to make it more effective, was designed to stimulate local station production during the most popular viewing period of the day, or at the very least to provide non-network program suppliers with access to major market television audiences.

Neither of these efforts was particularly successful. The Commission's vision of a locally oriented broadcast service, offering a broad and balanced assortment of public affairs, educational and other programs overlooked those powerful economic incentives that propelled the broadcast industry towards nationwide delivery of popular entertainment financed by national advertising.

[52] Each network did own and operate broadcast stations itself, (O & O stations) but the tactic of trying to influence national network program practices through regulations imposed upon these network owned stations never worked successfully.

[53] FCC rules CFR § 47. 3.101–3.108. The NBC v. US Supreme Court opinion that approved these rules is discussed in chapter 3, Sec. 14.

[54] 23 FCC2d 282 (1970); modified by 44 FCC2d 1081, and further modified by 46 FCC2d 829.

Through the years, however, the FCC and the broadcast networks managed to develop a rather close working relationship on most regulatory issues. The FCC was useful to the networks, because by regulating broadcasting, it shielded the industry from other, more powerful political pressures, and furnished broadcasting with a stable and predictable legal environment in which the networks could prosper. On the other hand, the FCC had to rely upon the networks to carry out programming reforms the Commission did not have the legal authority to achieve on its own.[55]

Abolishing Format Requirements

Although the Commission was constantly involved in efforts to improve the quality of network broadcast service, it was generally reluctant to interfere in any way with the programming practices of individual broadcast stations. As long as stations were not violating any specific FCC programming rule, the agency was willing to allow broadcasters the widest possible discretion in selecting their own format or schedule.

Thus, in 1970, when a classical music station was being sold to investors who intended to change its musical format, the Commission routinely approved the sale, even though a citizens' group had petitioned the FCC to deny the license transfer. Upon appeal, the court reversed the Commission decision, ordering the FCC to conduct a hearing to determine whether the sale would result in depriving the audience in that broadcast market of its only source of this type of programming.[56] In response to the FCC's argument that it was not authorized to act as a "national arbiter of taste," the court declared,

> The Commission is not dictating tastes when it seeks to discover what they presently are, and to consider what assignment of channels is feasible and fair in terms of their gratification.[57]

Four years later the Commission was faced with another sale of a classical music station to a group eager to convert it into a "top 40" outlet, and once again the agency approved the sale without permitting the local citizens' group the hearing they had requested to oppose the license transfer and change of format. The court again reversed the FCC decision, this time with the observation that,

[55] For one example of such close FCC–network cooperation, see the "Family Viewing" opinion in Writers Guild of America West, Inc. v. FCC, 423 F.Supp. 1064 (C.D.Cal.1976).

[56] Citizens Committee to Preserve the Voice of Arts in Atlanta v. FCC, 436 F.2d 263 (D.C.Cir.1970).

[57] Ibid., 272 n. 7.

We think it axiomatic that preservation of a format that would otherwise disappear; although economically and technologically viable and preferred by a significant number of listeners, is generally in the public interest.[58]

At this point the Commission decided to conduct a public policy hearing to determine what its future role in such program format controversies should be. At the conclusion of these deliberations, the FCC adopted the rather daring stance that despite any instructions it had received from the federal court of appeals, it would no longer allow itself to be involved in any regulation of broadcast station formats because, as the Commission explained it,

> Our reflection ... has fortified our conviction that our regulation of entertainment formats as an aspect of the public interest would produce an unnecessary and menacing entanglement in matters that Congress meant to leave to private discretion.[59]

A citizens' group immediately appealed this FCC policy decision, but after it had been reversed at the Court of Appeals level, the Supreme Court decided to consider this format regulation issue itself for the first time. In Federal Communications Commission v. WNCN Listeners Guild[60] the Commission's position was upheld by the court, on the basis that the FCC's format policy reflected a reasonable balance between, "promoting diversity in programming and ... avoiding unnecessary restrictions upon licensee discretion."

Must Carry

In 1997, the Supreme Court became involved in a content-related case that tested the ability of the federal government to force cable operators to support over-the-air television. In Turner Broadcasting System v. F.C.C.,[61] cable operators sued claiming that the "Must Carry" provisions of the Cable Television Consumer Protection and Competition Act were unconstitutional.

In the Cable Act of 1992, television broadcasters were given a choice in their treatment by cable operators. The TV broadcasters could choose to negotiate for payment for the carriage of their signals on cable systems under the "Retransmission Consent" agreement or they could require cable operators to include them in their service under the "Must Carry" rules. As part of the "Must Carry" provision, the Cable Act required cable operators with more

[58] Citizens Committee to Save WEFM v. FCC, 506 F.2d 246 (D.C.Cir.1973).

[59] "Changes in the Entertainment Formats of Broadcast Stations," 37 RR2d 1679, 1976.

[60] 450 U.S. 582, 101 S.Ct. 1266 (1981).

[61] 117 S.Ct. 1174 (1997), 25 Media L. Rep. 1449.

than 12 channels to set aside one-third of their channel capacity for local broadcasters.

The cable industry challenged the "Must Carry" provisions and in a series of lawsuits and appeals reached the Supreme Court twice. In the first Supreme Court appearance, the case was remanded to the lower courts for additional fact-finding. After 18 months of fact gathering, the district court found for the government. When the case returned in 1997, the Court ruled by a 5–4 margin that the "Must Carry" provisions were constitutional. The provisions were the government's way to ensure the continued existence of speakers, here local television stations.

Delivering the majority opinion for the Court, Justice Kennedy found that the "Must Carry" provisions served three interconnected and important government interests: "preserving benefits of free, over-the-air local broadcast television; promoting widespread dissemination of information from multiplicity of sources; and promoting fair competition in market for television programming."[62]

Kennedy said that the government had a legitimate interest in protecting the broadcast station that would rely on "Must Carry" to reach the audiences they needed to remain viable. Kennedy said that Congress could constitutionally conclude there was a need to protect local broadcasters. There was a substantial body of evidence that

> "[A] broadcast station's viability depends to a material extent on its ability to secure cable carriage and thereby to increase its audience size and revenues; broadcast stations had fallen into bankruptcy, curtailed their operations, and suffered serious reductions in operating revenues as a result of adverse carriage decisions by cable systems; stations without carriage encountered severe difficulties obtaining financing for operations; and the potentially adverse impact of losing carriage was increasing as the growth of 'clustering'—i.e., the acquisition of as many cable systems in a given market as possible—gave multiple system operators centralized control over more local markets."[63]

The need to preserve the over-the-air stations was important because some 40 percent of U.S. households still relied on broadcast stations for their television programming. In his analysis of the relationship between broadcast stations and cable operators, Justice Kennedy pointed to legislative findings of Congress as it developed the Cable Act. Included were data showing that cable operators

[62] Ibid.
[63] Ibid. At 1182.

enjoyed monopolies in the communities they served. Only 1 percent of communities were served by more than one cable operation. Congress also found that cable operators had economic incentives, through relationships with programmers, to favor those affiliated programming services over broadcasters. Further, cable operators were in direct competition with broadcasters because the incentive to subscribe to cable is lower in markets with many over-the-air viewing options. If broadcasters failed, cable operators were more likely to get more subscribers.

Justice Kennedy also took into consideration the serious problems encountered by over-the-air broadcasters when they were dropped from cable service or not picked up at all by cable operators.

"Documents produced on remand reflect that internal cable studies 'clearly establish the importance of cable television to broadcast television stations. Because viewership equals ratings and in turn ratings equate to revenues, it is unlikely that broadcast stations could afford to be off the cable system's line-up for an extended period of time.' "[64]

Justice Kennedy found further support for his position with an FCC-sponsored study showing a denial of carriage for broadcast stations when a previous "Must Carry" requirement was struck by a lower court. In that study, 280 out of 912 stations responding to the survey reported they had been denied carriage. The "Must Carry" rules meant that broadcast stations would be preserved with little impact on cable operators.

> "[S]ignificant evidence adduced on remand indicates the vast majority of cable operators have not been affected in a significant manner. This includes evidence that: such operators have satisfied their Must Carry obligations 87 percent of the time using previously unused channel capacity; 94.5 percent of the cable systems nationwide have not had to drop any programming; the remaining 5.5 percent have had to drop an average of only 1.22 services from their programming; operators nationwide carry 99.8 percent of the programming they carried before Must Carry; and broadcast stations gained carriage on only 5,880 cable channels as a result of Must Carry. The burden imposed by Must Carry is congruent to the benefits it affords because, as appellants concede, most of those 5,880 stations would be dropped in its absence. Must Carry therefore is narrowly tailored to preserve a multiplicity of broadcast stations

[64] Quoting, "Memorandum from F. Lopez to T. Baxter re: Adlink's Presentations on Retransmission Consent," dated June 14, 1993, (App. 2118), in *Turner*, at 1196.

for the 40 percent of American households without cable."[65]

The dissent, led by Justice O'Connor, focused on the standard of review applied by the majority, an "intermediate scrutiny" approach. The proper standard, Justice O'Connor argued, was a "strict scrutiny" analysis because the case dealt with the content of speech and as such, should have to pass a more demanding test. Justice O'Connor was not persuaded by the findings that Justice Kennedy cited as he explained his conclusion. The fact that some broadcast stations would fail without the "Must Carry" rule was not enough to justify the imposition of the requirement on cable operators because of their anti-competitive pressures.

"I fully agree that promoting fair competition is a legitimate and substantial Government goal. But the Court nowhere examines whether the breadth of the 'Must Carry' provisions comports with a goal of preventing anti-competitive harms."[66] Instead, Justice O'Connor argued, the majority simply assumed that broadcasters would be harmed by the cable operators decisions not to carry them.

"The Court provides some raw data on adverse carriage decisions, but it never connects that data to markets and viewership. Instead, the Court proceeds from the assumption that adverse carriage decisions nationwide will affect broadcast markets in proportion to their size; and that all broadcast programming is watched by all viewers. Neither assumption is logical or has any factual basis in the record."[67]

Indecent Programming

Yet, even though the Commission has been reluctant to become involved in most phases of local station programming, one specific type of programming has been singled out recently by the FCC for close supervision. Both the Radio Act of 1927 and the Communications Act of 1934 contained regulatory provisions authorizing the imposition of fines and possible revocation of the license of any station broadcasting obscene, indecent or profane language.[68]

As discussed at pages 618 to 622, punishing "indecent" broadcast language presented no constitutional problem for either federal

[65] Ibid. At 1182.

[66] Ibid. At 1206–1207.

[67] Ibid. At 1207.

[68] In 1948, Congress transferred these statutory provisions to the U.S. Criminal Code, Title 18, U.S.C.A. § 1464, because they also contained criminal penalties (imprisonment of up to 5 years) that could be enforced more effectively by the U.S. Justice Department. However, the FCC was granted continuing authority to penalize broadcasters under the new code section.

regulatory agency, because speech or conduct found to be obscene is not recognized by American law as meriting First Amendment protection.[69] "Indecent" or "profane" speech, on the other hand, is constitutionally protected, and so regulatory efforts to discourage such utterances or to penalize stations for scheduling an "indecent" or "profane" program impose greater constraints upon the broadcast medium than upon any other form of American mass communication.

In reality, though, the broadcast networks and their industry association, the National Association of Broadcasters (NAB), were able to shield the FRC and FCC from the problem of tasteless broadcast content until the early 1970s. Each of the networks demanded that their affiliated stations follow NAB program standards far more restrictive in areas of public taste than any regulatory agency could have required, and while independent stations were not bound by these agreements, they hesitated to isolate themselves in this way from the protection of the NAB.

As the 1970s began, however, a number of smaller, typically urban market FM stations saw an opportunity to attract a larger audience with a new format called "topless radio," featuring sexually oriented talk shows to capitalize upon the so-called new morality of that era. By 1973, stations adopting the "topless" format had become top-rated during their sex talk segments in several major markets, as letters of complaint from outraged listeners began flooding the FCC.[70]

In that same year the FCC imposed a $2,000 fine upon a station that had presented a particularly explicit discussion of oral sex techniques, pointing out,

> We are emphatically not saying that sex per se is a forbidden subject on the broadcast medium ... sex and obscenity are not the same things.[71]

but holding that because the program had been broadcast at a time when a substantial number of children could be presumed to be listening, the station had disregarded its public interest responsibilities towards that special segment of its audience.

A citizens' group petitioned for a hearing to challenge the Commission's decision, but a federal appeals court upheld both the FCC action and its right to reject such a petition.[72]

[69] See FCC v. Pacifica Foundation, 438 U.S. 726, 98 S.Ct. 3026 (1978).

[70] The FCC received more than 2,000 letters from listeners complaining about these programs in 1972; in 1974, they received more than 20,000 letters of complaint. "Programming of Violent, Indecent or Obscene Material", Broadcast Management/Engineering, June 1975, pp. 22–24.

[71] Sonderling Broadcasting, 27 RR2d 285 (1973).

[72] Illinois Citizens Committee for Broadcasting v. FCC, 515 F.2d 397 (D.C.Cir. 1974).

In that same year, another station, in a mid-afternoon program, featured an excerpt from a comedy album of George Carlin, his "Filthy Words" routine, discussing in detail the nuances of several of the seven four-letter words he said couldn't be mentioned on radio or television. The FCC issued a declaratory ruling against the station, this time defining its position on indecency with even greater clarity. According to the Commission, "indecent" programming was that which,

> ... describes, in terms patently offensive as measured by contemporary community standards for the broadcast medium, sexual or excretory activities and organs, at times of the day where there is reasonable risk that children may be in the audience.[73]

The FCC's newly established indecency standard was overturned almost immediately by a federal appeals court, but at that point the Supreme Court intervened to consider whether more stringent restrictions could legally be imposed upon broadcast free speech than other forms of media expression.

A majority of the Justices affirmed the Commission's position, basing their affirmation of the FCC's right to hold broadcasting to a higher standard of care in this area of speech on two special characteristics of the medium, its pervasiveness and its unique accessibility to children.[74] In addition, the crucial factor in the view of the court was that the FCC was not attempting to ban the broadcasting of indecent programs, but only to require that such programs be scheduled at times when they were not likely to reach a large youthful audience.

Although a divided Court had affirmed the right of the Commission to treat indecent programming as a nuisance, "channeling" it away from younger viewers or listeners, the new "marketplace" oriented FCC of the 1980s seemed reluctant to exercise this power. Despite complaints from various citizen groups about the explicit nature of certain new "shock" radio formats, the agency decided initially to restrict its definition of "indecent" only to broadcasts containing one or more of those famous seven words George Carlin had uttered in the monologue that led to the *Pacifica* action.[75]

In 1987, however, the Commission, under pressure from Congress, began to assert that authority the Supreme Court had

[73] Pacifica Foundation, 56 FCC2d 94 (1975).

[74] FCC v. Pacifica Foundation, 438 U.S. 726, 98 S.Ct. 3026 (1978). It's important to note, however, that the FCC's indecency definition was upheld by a narrow 5–4 vote, suggesting quite clearly that its authority to enforce this type of content control would be narrowly construed.

[75] The "shock" radio format goes one step beyond "topless," trying to offend the sensibilities of as many different groups in our society as possible by using racial jokes, ethnic slurs and other forms of base humor to attract an audience.

authorized almost a decade earlier. The FCC sent public notices to two broadcast stations the agency found to be in violation of the rule, and declared its intention to adopt rules reestablishing the broader definition of indecency it had followed during the 1970s.

Channeling Indecency to a Safe Harbor

Following the "channeling" approach the Supreme Court had approved in *Pacifica,* the FCC declared that indecent programming would be punished only if were scheduled at a time when there was "reasonable risk that children might be in the audience."[76] Originally the Commission had stated that programs scheduled after 10 p.m. could be aired without concern for their accessibility to children. However, when audience research revealed that a substantial number of children were still listening or viewing at 10 p.m. each evening, the FCC narrowed its "safe harbor;" making the period from midnight to 6 a.m. the only appropriate time for such "adult" programming.

This new campaign by the Commission to shield young viewers and listeners from indecent broadcast programming was immediately attacked by a coalition of public interest and trade organizations.[77] Upon review, the D.C. Court of Appeals affirmed the fundamental right of the FCC to restrict indecent programming to those hours of the day when children were least likely to be present in the broadcast audience. In this instance, however, the Court held that the Commission had not adequately documented its claim that the midnight to 6 AM period it selected as a "safe harbor" for such programming was actually the most narrowly drawn one capable of realizing this policy objective.

As the FCC was preparing to justify its six hour indecency "harbor" as being the least extensive time period required to achieve its goal, Congress acted to make the agency's already difficult legal position virtually impossible to defend. In October 1988 Congress passed legislation that compelled the Commission to enforce an absolute *ban* on indecent broadcast programming on a

[76] New Indecency Enforcement Standards, 62 RR2d 1218 (1987).

[77] Action for Children's Television v. FCC, 852 F.2d 1332 (D.C.Cir.1988). It is interesting to note that this legal challenge was spearheaded by the nation's largest and most influential advocacy group for the broadcast programming rights of young viewers and listeners. Through the years ACT has constantly campaigned for more extensive government restrictions on broadcast commercials to protect American youth from the damaging effects of advertising, but its leaders apparently saw no similar need to protect young viewers from the damaging effects of indecent programming, defined by the FCC as "describing or depicting sexual or excretory activities in a patently offensive manner." ACT has explained that it opposes any governmental restrictions on "indecent" broadcasts because indecency is expression protected by the First Amendment. The only problem with that explanation is that commercial speech is also expression protected by the First Amendment.

24 hour a day basis.[78] The FCC had no choice but to comply with this Congressional directive, even though it meant that the agency would now be required to *prohibit* a constitutionally protected form of expression it had sought only to channel within a "safe harbor" of time.

When the Commission announced its intention to begin enforcing a total ban on indecent programming in January 1989, the same coalition of media and public interest groups was able to obtain an order from the D.C. Court of Appeals preventing the Commission from implementing this new rule until its validity could be determined by the Court. In doing so, however, the Court granted the FCC permission to continue the enforcement of its indecency standards on a provisional basis in order to gather further documentation relating to the nature of this indecent programming it could submit when the case was ultimately heard by the Court.

After completing its review in July 1990, the Commission voted unanimously to adopt a report supporting a 24 hour a day ban of both indecent radio and television program content, arguing that because at least some portion of the broadcast audience was likely to be composed of children at all times of the day and night, anything less than a total ban of such programming would not achieve the objectives of the regulation.[79]

In April 1991 the U.S. Court of Appeals struck down the 24 hour a day ban of indecent broadcast programming, but directed the FCC to consider once again the possibility of establishing a reasonable defined "safe harbor" for indecent content capable of channeling such programs away from children without unduly restricting adult access to them.[80]

Freed by the Court of its Congressionally imposed burden to *ban* indecent broadcasting from the airwaves, the FCC tried initial-

---

[78] Public Law 100–459, § 608 (1988). Two months later the FCC adopted an order enforcing this ban. See 67 RR2d 1714.

[79] 67 RR2d 1714 (1990). To understand more clearly the type of content that triggered the FCC action, and that had motivated the more than 6,000 indecency complaints the FCC had been receiving annually since the mid 1980s, here are a few excerpts from some of those programs broadcast during a time of day when a substantial number of children could be expected to be in the broadcast audience: WLUP Chicago, " * * * went down on that other woman and oh God, you had your tongue in her vagina. It was fabulous * * * "; KSJO, San Jose, "I'd love to lick the matzo balls right off your butt * * * I'd like to have a smorgasbord in your butt. I'd like to have matzos in there with borscht, everything. I'd just have a buffet * * * "; WLLZ Detroit, "He puts Penthouse on his desk/he's got big muscles in his wrist/he holds his organ in his fist/He gives his pink dolphin a mighty twist * * * All the girls in the office they say, 'Hard-on, hard-on, beg my pardon.' Walk with an erection"; WMCA New York, "When you can't call welfare people 'sluts' and 'whores,' 'cocksuckers' or 'freeloaders,' then our English language serves no purpose."

[80] ACT v. FCC, 932 F.2d 1504 (D.C.Cir.1991) cert. denied 503 U.S. 913, 112 S.Ct. 1281 (1992).

ly to enlarge its "safe harbor" from six to ten hours a day, permitting such programs to be aired at any time between 8 P.M. and 6 A.M. But when Congress attached a 12 P.M. to 6 A.M. "safe harbor" provision to the Public Broadcasting funding bill of 1992, the FCC was forced to revert to a uniform midnight to 6 A.M. "harbor" for all its licensees, aware that it could not justify punishing one group of broadcasters for scheduling indecent program material during a time period when another group was free to schedule such programming without penalty.[81]

The Public Telecommunications Act of 1992 contained a provision requiring the FCC to adopt new (30b) regulations prohibiting the transmission of indecent programming between the hours of 6 a.m. and midnight, thereby restricting such programs to a midnight to 6 a.m. "safe harbor." However, the same legislation allowed public broadcast stations that signed off before midnight to air such programming after 10 p.m.[82]

The rules adopted by the FCC in response to this Congressional directive faced their customary challenges from Action for Children's Television (ACT), perennial champion of the right of children to have access to a wide spectrum of programming on a 24-hour-a-day basis. A three-judge panel of the Court of Appeals for the District of Columbia upheld the ACT challenge and the court voted the hear the case, *en banc*.[83]

In a 7–4 decision, the full court affirmed the FCC's legal authority to adopt such indecency regulations, although it expanded the agency's indecency "safe harbor" to an eight-hour period from 10 p.m. to 6 a.m. to avoid what the full court found to be an unjustifiably different set of standards on commercial and public stations.

In what is now known as the "ACT III" decision, the majority found that the government did have a compelling interest in protecting children under 18 years of age from indecent program content, and that the channeling of such programs to a period of time when minors were least likely to have access to them did not unduly burden the First Amendment rights of broadcasters or the public.

Writing for the majority, Judge Buckley described this compelling interest as being a dual obligation on the part of the government to protect the well-being of children and to support parental efforts to supervise the viewing and listening choices of their children. In terms of "least restrictive means," Judge Buckley

[81] Public Telecommunications Act of 1992, Pub. Law 102–356. § 16(a), 106 Stat. 949, 954.

[82] Pub. L. 102–356, § 16(a)., 106 Stat. 949, 954.

[83] ACT v. FCC, 11 F.3d 170 (D.C.Cir.1993).

deferred to the judgment of Congress. He declared that the judiciary should not reject a Congressional decision involving the particular period of time that would best serve its policy objective as long as there was sufficient evidence to support that legislative determination.

In his dissent, Chief Judge Edwards argued that the government had not demonstrated any compelling need for such restrictive regulation. He wrote that even if some form of constraint were required, less sweeping alternatives such as scrambling devices or blocking chips could achieve the same objective without infringing on the free speech rights of broadcasters.[84] In a separate dissent, joined by Judges Rogers and Tatel, Judge Wald attacked the majority's decision as granting government virtually unharnessed power to censor. She wrote that the majority ruling permitted a government agency to suppress free speech without offering a scintilla of evidence to establish the degree of potential harm involved to the children its regulations claimed to be protecting.

In July, 1995, the FCC won another victory in this area when the D.C. Court of Appeals—in what is called the "ACT IV" decision—found that the Commission was properly administering its own indecency policy.[85] The court, responding to ACT's appeal against several indecency forfeitures previously imposed by the FCC, held that the Commission had not infringed on the rights of broadcasters, even though some indecency cases had remained unresolved for as long as seven years.[86]

In January, 1996, the Supreme Court refused to review the D.C. Court of Appeals' "ACT III" decision. That allowed the FCC to continue enforcing its current indecency policy with a 10 p.m. to 6 a.m. "safe harbor." The following week, the Supreme Court also refused to review the "ACT IV" case, making the FCC's victory in the field of broadcast indecency complete.

The FCC and Cable Indecency

The Telecommunications Act provides guidelines for cable operators in the area of indecent and obscene communications. The Act provides for fines of up to $100,000 for transmitting obscene material over cable TV; requires, at the subscriber's request, the scrambling or blockage of audio and video of programming a subscriber has chosen not to buy; and to block the audio and video content of sexually explicit channels so that subscribers who do not buy them do not see them.

[84] Action for Children's Television v. FCC, 58 F.3d 654 (D.C. Cir. *en banc* 1995).

[85] Action for Children's Television v. FCC, 59 F.3d 1249 (D.C. Cir. *en banc.* 1995).

[86] "High Court Stands by Indecency Ban," Variety, Jan. 15, 1995, p. 43.

In 1997, the Supreme Court upheld a lower court's ruling on a portion of the Act requiring blockage of signals of sexually explicit channels. The Playboy and Spice channels had sued over that portion of the Act when cable operators decided to black out the two channels' programming from 6 a.m. to 10 p.m. The cable operators took that action because of a technical problem in blocking channel signals. A phenomenon called "signal bleed" allowed some distorted and undistorted signal to be picked up by nonsubscribers. Cable operators had the option of installing expensive scrambling or blocking technologies or simply dropping the adult programming until late night hours. They chose the less expensive black-out option. A lower federal court ruled against Playboy and Spice and the Supreme Court, without commenting, issued an order upholding the lower court decision.[87]

Government regulation of adult cable content was limited in *Denver Area Educational Telecommunications Consortium v. FCC.*[88] In *Denver*, providers of content on public, educational and governmental (PEG) channels challenged a portion of federal regulation requiring cable operators to block "patently offensive" programming offered on leased channels or to place all indecent programs on a single channel and block it at subscribers' requests. In a highly splintered ruling, the Court allowed cable operators to decline to show such material on leased channels. But the Court upheld protections for PEG channels. Opponents of the regulation said it could serve to ban programs on AIDS, abortion or human reproduction.[89]

The V–Chip and Television Ratings

One of the provisions of the Telecommunications Act of 1996 was the inclusion of a requirement that all television sets produced after a particular date have an additional piece of technology called the "V–Chip." The V–Chip was the creation of Canadian Tim Collings[90] and would allow set owners to decide the level of violence, language and sex they watched. Explained most simply, broadcasters would send a signal out along with their programs. The signal would carry three separate indicators for violence, language and sex. When any one of the indicators reached the maximum amount determined by the viewer, the V–Chip would block the television broadcast and leave the viewer with a dark and

---

[87] Lyle Denniston, "Cable TV's Adult Fare May Be Limited," The Baltimore Sun, March 25, 1997.

[88] 518 U.S. 727, 116 S.Ct. 2374, 135 L.Ed.2d 888 (1996).

[89] "Justices Overturn Cable TV Smut Law," The Capital Times, June 28, 1996.

[90] Collings stepped into the pages of media law history when he said at the press conference announcing the V–Chip, "In Canada, Thank God, there is no First Amendment."

silent screen. The V–Chip is adjustable and would let viewers choose to see more violence and less sex and rough language or more sex and less violence and language.

The FCC announced its technical standards for the V–Chip in the fall of 1997. The Commission said it expects that all television sets with screens at least 13 inches, manufactured starting in July of 1999. to have the chip.[91] In order for the V–Chip to work, broadcasters will have to employ ratings codes for their program that will continuously monitor the targeted categories. The categories released by the FCC are: S for sex, V for violence, L for foul language, D for suggestive dialogue and FV for fantasy violence for use on children's shows.[92] Networks took a big step in compliance when they adopted a set of ratings for their shows in October of 1997. The two exceptions were NBC and the Black Entertainment Network which said they were drawing the line at the age-based guidance ratings they had adopted. Lawmakers, including Rep. Edward Markey (D–Mass.) and Sen. Joseph Lieberman (D–Conn.) pressed NBC's affiliates asking them to adopt the new system. NBC said it would not go further in the rating system.

> "NBC West Coast President Don Ohlmeyer, the network's point man in this dispute, noted that the process started with the V–Chip to curb violence. The networks meekly acquiesced and this evolved into the V-and S–Chips. When the politicians and activists again encountered no resistance, they moved for the age-based ratings. Within hours of the networks capitulating to this system, there were demands for the letters (the current V, S, L and D). This is where NBC drew the line.

* * *

> [Ohlmeyer's] position is that this campaign will not stop until it achieves its ultimate goal: full control of program content. It's not hard to see a flaw in his reasoning. Sen Joseph Lieberman (D–Conn.), one of the ringleaders in the anti-TV crusade, has acknowledged that the letter ratings can serve as a starting point to rid the air of objectionable shows."[93]

[91] Bloomberg News, "FCC Releases its Plan for Phasing in Television V–Chip Broadcasting," The Los Angeles Times, Sept. 26, 1997.

[92] Ibid.

[93] Tom Jicha, "NBC Stands Alone Against Arrogance," Fort Lauderdale Sun–Sentinel, Oct. 11, 1997. Bill Loving, one of the authors, was present at the International Radio and Television Society's annual program in New York in 1996 when Rep. Markey and Sen. Lieberman announced the ratings plan. "The V used to stand for violence. But now the V stands for values," Lieberman said to college and university faculty on hand for the program.

Lawmakers have leveled veiled and not-so-veiled threats at NBC suggesting that the networks intransigency will be a factor when individual station licenses come up for renewal.

Broadcast Hoaxes

From 1938 onward, when Orson Welles's *Mercury Theater* adaptation of H.G. Well's *War of the Worlds* caused panic among thousands of Americans who were convinced by the broadcast program that Mars had attacked the United States, the FCC has never been amused by any effort, however clever or humorous, to tease or frighten a broadcast audience.[94]

In 1992 the Commission reacted to complaints about a series of broadcast hoaxes that had aired during the previous two years by adopting new rules authorizing it to fine stations a maximum of $25,000 for knowingly broadcasting

> ... information or other material it knows to be false if it is foreseeable that broadcast of the information could cause substantial public harm, and if the broadcast of the information does in fact directly cause substantial public harm.[95]

Recent hoax broadcasts have included a news report asserting that the United States was under nuclear attack, another claiming that a popular radio personality had just been shot and a third involving a talk show host who had arranged for a caller to confess falsely on air to having just committed a murder.[96]

The agency will consider such harm to be "foreseeable" if the broadcaster could reasonably expect that public harm will occur. In this context, the FCC pointed out that an April Fools Day newscast claiming that a local football team had just traded one of its stars would not come under this rule, because while it might distress some fans, it would not create that degree of harm or damage contemplated by the rule.

SEC. 73.   POLITICAL ACCESS RULES

Despite deregulation, Congress still requires the FCC to enforce all equal access broadcast requirements.

The "equal time", or more accurately the "equal opportunities" requirement for political candidates has been an obligation

---

[94] For a vivid description of some of the public hysteria caused by this broadcast, see "Radio Listens in Panic, Taking War Drama As Fact", New York Times, October 31, 1938, p. 1.

[95] Amendment of Part 73 Regarding Broadcast Hoaxes.

[96] Nuclear attack; Emmis Broadcasting, KSHE–FM, 69 R.R. 2d 195 (1991); false report of a shooting, Letter to Frank Battaglia, President, North American Broadcasting Co. 70 R.R. 2d 1329 (1992); false report of a murder; General Manager, Radio Station KROQ–FM, 6 F.C.C. R. 7262 (1991).

imposed upon broadcasting since the Radio Act of 1927 was adopted. Section 18 of the Radio Act became the well known Section 315 of the Communications Act of 1934, stating,

> If any licensee shall permit any person who is a legally qualified candidate for any political office to use a broadcasting station, he shall afford equal opportunities to all other such candidates for that office in the use of such broadcasting station ...

This section also denied the broadcaster any authority to censor political candidates exercising their rights of access under the terms of Section 315.

In 1959, a political candidate used this access to make defamatory remarks about his opponent. The opponent sued the broadcast station for airing these defamatory statements, but in Farmers Educational & Cooperative Union of America v. WDAY, Inc.,[97] the Supreme Court held that in establishing the terms and conditions for such political broadcast access, Congress had preempted state defamation law and created an absolute privilege that shielded the broadcast station from legal liability for statements made by such candidates.

During this same era, television news coverage of public events began raising a question Congress had no reason to consider when Section 315 was adopted. If a political candidate could be seen by viewers in film clips of a news event broadcast by a television station, was such an appearance a "use" of broadcast facilities requiring the station to offer all opponents of that candidate equal access to television time?

The Commission decided in 1959 that such an appearance did constitute a "use" under the Act, even though broadcast journalists had pointed out that if each televised glimpse of a candidate triggered an obligation by a station to make free time available to all opponents, it would be virtually impossible for a television station to provide its viewers with adequate local news coverage during an election campaign.[98]

Congress reacted promptly by amending Section 315 to exempt from its equal opportunities requirement any appearance by a legally qualified candidate on a

(1) bona fide newscast

(2) bona fide news interview

---

[97] Farmers Educ. & Coop. Union v. WDAY, 360 U.S. 525, 79 S.Ct. 1302 (1959).

[98] Columbia Broadcasting System, 26 FCC2d 715 (1959).

(3) bona fide documentary (if the appearance of the candidate is incidental to the presentation of the subject or subjects covered by the news documentary), or

(4) on-the-spot coverage of bona fide news events (including but not limited to political conventions and activities incidental thereto) . . .

This amendment offered broadcast journalists the protection from equal access obligations necessary to cover most news events, but in special situations not fitting neatly into one of these four exempted categories of coverage, the FCC has been reluctant to extend the scope of such exemptions. In 1960, for example, Congress was forced to suspend the application of Section 315 to presidential candidates to permit the three television networks to broadcast the famous Kennedy–Nixon debates without being required to provide an equal amount of free network broadcast time to all minor party presidential candidates.

In 1975, however, the Commission reversed its earlier position that neither broadcast coverage of political candidate debates nor candidate press conferences came within the exemption Congress had granted for on-the-spot coverage of bona fide news events.[99] It now held that debates were exempt from Section 315 requirements if they were controlled by someone other than the candidates or the broadcaster, and also exempted coverage of press conferences if they were "newsworthy and subject to on-the-spot coverage."[100]

The League of Women Voters acted as the independent host of these presidential debates for the television networks in 1976 and 1980. Since 1984, however, the Commission no longer has required the presence of an outside sponsoring organization in order to exempt political debates from 315 requirements, finding no basis for its previous belief that such an independent group was needed to insure impartial coverage of such debates.[1]

In 1991 the Commission relaxed its equal access requirements still further, expanding the "spot news" exemption of Section 315 to permit the broadcasting of candidate-prepared campaign state-

[99] Petition of Aspen Institute and CBS, 35 RR2d 49 (1975). In Petition of Henry Geller, et al., 54 RR2d 1246 (1983) the FCC relaxed its political candidates' debates rules still further, allowing broadcasters themselves to sponsor debates between political candidates without being required by Section 315 to extend this right of debate to all candidates for the office in question.

[100] This change in FCC policy was sustained by the court of appeals in Chisholm v. FCC, 538 F.2d 349 (D.C.Cir.1976), cert. denied 429 U.S. 890, 97 S.Ct. 247 (1976). Senator Kennedy challenged the new press conference exemption, claiming that President Carter had used such a conference to attack Kennedy, then a competing presidential candidate. The FCC's position was upheld in Kennedy for President Committee v. FCC, 636 F.2d 432 (D.C.Cir.1980).

[1] The FCC's position was affirmed in League of Women Voters Educ. Fund v. FCC, 731 F.2d 995 (D.C.Cir.1984).

ments and interviews limited to the two major presidential candidates without obligating a station to offer lesser candidates equal access.[2]

Through the years the FCC has also extended its category of broadcast programs exempted from political access requirements to include entertainment shows that provide news or current event coverage as regularly scheduled segments of the program. In this way, not only "Today", "Good Morning America" and "This Morning" but even "Donahue", "Entertainment Tonight" and "Entertainment This Week" have been able to invite political candidates to discuss public issues without exposing the network or station carrying them to "equal time" demands by rival candidates.[3]

On the other hand, the Commission has held rigidly to its position that any "use" of station time by a political candidate not expressly exempted by Section 315 creates an obligation for equal access. For example, the FCC declared that any station broadcasting a Ronald Reagan film during any campaign period in which he was a political candidate would obligate that station to offer all his legally qualified opponents the same degree of access to its audience.[4]

In 1991 the agency did modify this policy significantly, declaring that an appearance by a political candidate would be considered a "use" only when the candidate's voice or picture was authorized or sponsored by the candidate or the candidate's campaign committee.[5] Recognizing the increasingly common practice in negative campaign commercials to include audio clips or video footage of a candidate's opponent, the FCC wanted to clarify its position that

[2] Request of King Broadcasting Company Licensee of KING–TV, Seattle, Washington for a Declaratory Ruling. 69 R.R. 2d 1017 (1991). However, in reversing earlier decisions denying these exemptions in Request for Declaratory Ruling by WEBE, 108 Radio Co. 63 R.R. 2d 1748 (1987) rev'd and remanded sub nom., King Broadcasting Co. v. FCC, 860 F.2d 465 (D.C.Cir.1988), the Commission did caution broadcasters that failure to include a major third-party presidential candidate in their news coverage might risk the loss of the spot news exemption the agency had authorized.

[3] Although the Donahue exemption was originally denied by the FCC, it was subsequently granted in 1984 despite the show's rather sporadic commitment to coverage of significant political events or issues. See Multimedia Entertainment 56 RR2d 143 (1984). In justifying its exemption for show business promotional programs such as "Entertainment Tonight," the FCC observed that the news exemption to Section 315 is not based on "the subject matter reported" but only on whether a program "reports news of some area of current events". In addition, the agency pointed out that if it began deciding in each case whether the information provided by a particular program was sufficiently important or significant to justify an exemption, it could be involving itself more deeply in the evaluation of broadcast program content than the First Amendment would permit. Request for Declaratory Ruling by Paramount Pictures Corp. (1988).

[4] In re Adrian Weiss, 36 RR2d 292 (1976). See also In re Pat Paulsen, 23 RR2d 861 (1972), affirmed 491 F.2d 887 (9th Cir.1974).

[5] Codification of the Commission's Political Programming Policies, 70 R.R. 2d 239 (1991).

unauthorized use of a political opponent's voice or image would not then entitle the candidate who produced such ads to claim air time on the basis of this "appearance" by the opponent.

Under this new standard, then, the broadcast of an old feature film of a candidate such as Ronald Reagan would no longer provide his political opponents with a right of equal access unless Reagan or his campaign committee had actually approved or authorized the scheduling of the film.

At the same time, though, the Commission refused to alter its policy regarding typical broadcast employees, a policy that still effectively denies any broadcast performer the right to run for political office. The FCC has defined "use" of broadcast facilities to include virtually any type of on-air performance, including working under an assumed name as the radio host of a weekly dance show.[6] Under this strict interpretation of the rules, as soon as a broadcast performer becomes a political candidate, each subsequent on-air performance obligates the station to provide a similar amount of free air time to each of the employee's political opponents.

In one recent case, station management estimated that it would be required to provide more than 33 hours of free broadcast response time if a television reporter went ahead with his plans to become a candidate for a town council position.[7] Not surprisingly, the reporter was ordered by the station to make an immediate choice between a career in politics and one in broadcasting.

Yet, it would be unfair to blame the FCC too severely for this unfortunate result, because Congress has allowed the Commission virtually no discretion in the enforcement of this broadcast "use" standard. Despite the fact that both the NAB and the Radio Television News Directors Association (RTNDA) have on several occasions urged that Congress amend Section 315 to allow broadcast employees to exercise this basic right of citizenship, Congressional leaders have seemed content to continue treating broadcasting as a less legally privileged medium.

Nowhere is that attitude of Congress more clearly reflected than in legislation it enacted in 1971 to take advantage of broadcasting's status as a federally regulated medium. In that year the Communications Act was amended by Congress to compel each broadcast station to provide candidates for federal office a reasonable amount of broadcast time, and to furnish time for purchase by federal candidates at the lowest rate charged regular advertisers for that same time period.[8] In essence, members of Congress had

---

[6] See Letter to WUGN, 40 FCC 2d 293 (1958).

[7] Branch v. FCC, 824 F.2d 37 (D.C.Cir.1987), 14 Med.L.Rptr. 1465.

[8] The "reasonable access" amendment created section 312(a)(7) of the Communications Act, and the "lowest rate" provision became section 315(b).

decided to combat the rising costs of federal election campaigns by imposing upon broadcasting, the only medium controlled by government, requirements designed to reduce their own campaign costs at the broadcast industry's expense.

The first major test of this new legislation occurred in 1980, when the Carter–Mondale Committee sought to purchase a half hour of prime time from each network to present a documentary portraying President Carter's first term accomplishments just after Carter's formal announcement of his intention to seek a second term. When none of the networks were willing to provide the full 30 minutes of time the Committee demanded, the group filed a complaint with the FCC.[9] The Commission found the networks in violation of the "reasonable access" rule, and on appeal, the Supreme Court, in a five to four decision, narrowly affirmed this finding.[10]

In 1990, an extensive FCC audit revealed that more than two-thirds of the 30 radio and televisions stations the agency had investigated were not charging political candidates the lowest advertising rates required by federal law.[11] The Commission also discovered that a substantial number of these stations had not fully informed candidates of the availability of lower priced packages of advertising for which they qualified. As a result of this audit the FCC adopted new rules requiring stations to make full disclosure to political candidates of all advertising unit rates offered to any of the station's regular commercial accounts.[12]

However, when several politicians who had been candidates during the 1990 election campaign sued broadcast stations to recover what they claimed were excessive charges for political commercials, the FCC quickly intervened to shield broadcasters from such litigation, asserting that the Commission had sole authority to decide when a station was in violation of federal political broadcast advertising laws.[13] Instead of permitting such controversies to be decided by the courts, the agency offered candidates two options for resolving future broadcast advertising rate disputes; either to submit them to a neutral arbitrator for a binding decision,

[9] Networks were reluctant to sell a large block of prime time for a political program during a non-election year, aware that inserting such a political documentary into a regular evening lineup of shows would substantially reduce the audience for all programs following the political program the evening it was scheduled. CBS offered a 5 minute prime time segment, and ABC a full 30 minute prime time slot during a non-rating period in January, but the Committee refused these offers.

[10] CBS, Inc. v. FCC, 453 U.S. 367, 101 S.Ct. 2813 (1981).

[11] Political Program Audit, 68 R.R. 2d 113 (1990).

[12] Codification of the Commission's Political Programming Policies, 70 R.R. 2d 219 (1991).

[13] Exclusive Jurisdiction with Respect to Potential Violations of the Lowest Unit Charge Requirements of Section 315 (b), Communications Act, 70 R.R. 2d 1 (1991).

or to ask the Commission to determine the proper charges through the agency's complaint process.

Considering the advantages that politicians currently obtain from the "equal opportunities," "lowest advertising rate" and "reasonable access" provisions of the Communications Act of 1934, it seems highly unlikely that Congress will ever be eager to release broadcasting from the constraints of regulation so long as these benefits continue to result from such control.[14]

The Content of Political Ads

The Federal Communications Commission does not engage in censorship of political broadcasts, in most cases. Section 315, which provides candidates with equal access at lowest rates, also denies stations from censoring the "use" of political advertising time by a bona fide candidate. This doctrine has led to some painful decisions by the FCC and the courts when dealing with political language and messages that are shocking.

In Re Complaint by Julian Bond,[15] the FCC ruled that it could not ban the use of the word, "nigger" by a legally qualified candidate for the governorship of Georgia. J.B. Stoner, running for the Georgia governorship had used the offending word in his radio and television spots. The FCC replied that "in light of Section 315, we may not prevent a candidate from utilizing that word during his 'use' of a licensee's broadcast facilities."[16] Bond and the Atlanta NAACP sought in the alternative to have the word declared obscene or indecent and added to the list of proscribed words from *Pacifica*. The FCC declined saying that the word did not fall into the narrow category of words from *Pacifica*, words that were patently offensive and dealing with sex or excretion.

The issue arose again in the 1980 presidential race when Citizens Party candidates used the word "bullshit" in a political ad transmitted by NBC.[17] NBC initially rejected the ad but relented, although it preceded the transmission of the ad to its affiliates with an advisory about "offensive language." The FCC ruled that the

---

[14] Congress has always favored the "equal opportunities" provision of Section 315, because while virtually every incumbent can gain constant broadcast access to constituents between elections through news items most local stations are eager to carry, any challenger is restricted by § 315 during the campaign period to access under the same terms and conditions as the incumbent, thus protecting the incumbent's pre-election advantage.

[15] 69 F.C.C.2d 943 (1978).

[16] Ibid.

[17] In Re Complaint of Barry Commoner and LaDonna Harris, 87 F.C.C.2d 1 (1980). The ad contained the following lines:

    Man: Bullshit.

    Woman: What?

    Man: Carter, Reagan and Anderson. It's all such bullshit.

advisory to the NBC affiliates, many of which did not run the ad with the offending words, did not constitute censorship, although it said, "[t]he initial reactions of the NBC staff in rejecting the spot and urging its modification were clearly in error. NBC needs to take additional steps to assure that its staff is fully aware of the no-censorship requirements of the law, and we expect it to take such steps."[18]

It took Larry Flynt to make the FCC take a step back from its expansive protection of political ads. The FCC ruled in 1984 that stations were not required to broadcast obscene or indecent material as part of a political advertisement. The issue arose when Flynt, publisher of Hustler Magazine, showed some ads from his 1984 bid for the presidency. Flynt intended to use clips from adult movies to illustrate his campaign ads. Lawmakers sprang into action and sought a ruling from the FCC. Then FCC Chairman Mark Fowler wrote to Rep. Thomas Luken (D–Ohio) to tell him that the anti-censorship provision of Section 315 had not been tested against a situation in which a candidate aired obscene materials. But an FCC staffer said that laws should not be read to lead to unreasonable results.

> "Because the purpose of fostering political debate is untainted by subjecting broadcasters to the prohibitions against obscenity and indecency (which by definition lack serious political value), it is concluded that it would be unreasonable to exempt broadcasters from (the law's) criminal prohibitions," Fowler wrote to Luken.[19]

Flynt left the issue unresolved when he withdrew from the race for the Republican nomination. The question of content arose again when a congressional candidate sought protection for his political ads that featured graphic images of aborted fetuses. The FCC had granted stations permission to review Becker's ads and channel them to "safe harbor" because of their intense and graphic nature. But in Becker v. FCC,[20] the D.C. Circuit Court of Appeals ruled that the FCC's order violated the rule against censorship of political advertising.

As the court noted, "the 1992 election campaign witnessed the advent of political advertisements depicting the aftermath of abortions. * * * At 7:58 p.m. on July 19, Station WAGA–TV aired, at Mr. Becker's request, a campaign advertisement that included

---

[18] Ibid.

[19] "Stations Needn't Show Political Ads with Obscenities," The Wall Street Journal, Jan. 25, 1984.

[20] 95 F.3d 75 (D.C.Cir.1996).

photographs of aborted fetuses. WAGA–TV received numerous complaints from viewers who saw the advertisement."[21]

Anticipating that Becker would want to repeat his commercials, WAGA, an Atlanta station, sought a ruling from the FCC that would permit the station to channel Becker's ads to a "safe harbor." A number of other broadcasters also sought a ruling from the Commission that they would not have to air political advertisements that presented, "graphic depictions or descriptions of aborted fetuses or any other similar graphic depictions of excised or bloody fetal tissue, where there is ... the good-faith judgment of the licensee, a reasonable risk that children may be in the audience."[22] The stations asked the FCC to declare such advertisements indecent. The FCC viewed the ads and concluded they were not indecent. The FCC viewed the ads and concluded they were not indecent and said that the station could not censor them.

Becker returned to the station and tried to buy time for a 30–minute political commercial, "Abortion in America: The Real Story," which he wanted to air after a televised professional football game. The station refused claiming the program would violate the indecency rules. The FCC then issued a notice saying that until it ruled, stations could decline to broadcast material they believed were indecent. The FCC later ruled that while Becker's ads were not indecent, they posed a threat of psychological damage to children who saw them. The Commission ruled, "that nothing in 312(a)(7)[23] precludes a broadcaster's exercise of some discretion with respect to placement of political advertisements so as to protect children * * * and channeling would not violate the no-censorship of section 315(a)."[24]

But the D.C. Circuit Court of Appeals ruled that the FCC's order violated Becker's rights under the reasonable access rules. The court also said that in issuing its order, the FCC was giving permission for broadcasters to discriminate against political advertisers on the basis of content, which violated the no censorship and equal opportunity sections of the Telecommunications Act.

> "As we explain below, by permitting a licensee to channel political advertisements that it believes may harm children, the Declaratory Ruling frustrates what the Commission itself has identified as Congress's primary purpose in enacting Section 312(a) (7); namely to ensure 'candidate access to the time periods with the greatest audience

[21] Ibid. At 76–77.

[22] Ibid.

[23] Section 312 provides that a station license may be revoked for willful or repeated failure to allow reasonable access by qualified political candidates.

[24] 95 F.3d 75, 78 (D.C.Cir.1996).

potential ...' Licensee Responsibility, 47 F.C.C.2d at 517"[25]

The court said that it would be impossible for the FCC to meet that responsibility and also channel the advertisement to a safe harbor where no children might be harmed. It acknowledged the conflicting interests of protecting children from "images that are not indecent but may nevertheless prove harmful," and the candidate's interest in reaching the largest audience he can. If the FCC were permitted to grant discretion to stations, the risk would be that candidates would lose access to potential supporters. Merely requiring that the station's judgment be "reasonable" would open the door to questionable decisions that might mean the difference in an election.

> "These are slippery standards, and it is of small solace to a losing candidate that an appellate court might eventually find the Commission's approval of a licensee's channeling decision was an abuse of discretion or contrary to law. Moreover, the acceptance of a subjective standard renders it impossible to determine whether it was the advertisement's message rather than its images that the licensee found too shocking for tender minds."[26]

For some messages, like that of the abortion opponents, the message is inextricably entwined with image, the court said. Candidates might well tone down their ads for fear of being denied carriage and so result in self-censorship. If a candidate did not change an ad, a station might channel it to "safe harbor" while continuing to show an opponent's ads in prime time. If a station chose to be fair and channel both candidates' ads, the second and non-offensive candidate would suffer for the excesses of another and be denied the fair access guaranteed under the law.

The court did not address Becker's First Amendment claim because it had disposed of the case based on the Telecommunications Act.

SEC. 74. FAIRNESS DOCTRINE OBLIGATIONS

Although the FCC has repealed the Fairness Doctrine, it has never been declared unconstitutional by the courts, and could be reinstituted by Congress or the Commission.

In contrast, the "fairness doctrine", the other major public issue oriented principle of broadcast regulation, has never been as

---

[25] 95 F.3d 75, 80.

[26] Ibid. At 81.

directly related to Congressional self-interest. In fact, Congress never bothered to formally codify the doctrine, simply declaring when amending the "equal opportunities" provision of Section 315 in 1959 that it had no intention of relieving broadcasters,

> ... from the obligations imposed upon them under this Act to operate in the public interest and to afford reasonable opportunity for the discussion of conflicting views on issues of public importance.[27]

The concept of broadcast "fairness" emerged instead from years of specific decisions made by the FRC and FCC in determining the exact extent of a licensee's obligation to provide the public with balanced coverage of controversial matters of public importance. In 1949, the FCC issued the first formal description of this doctrine, declaring,

> One of the most vital questions of mass communications in a democracy is the development of an informed public opinion through the public dissemination of news and ideas concerning the vital public issues of the day.[28]

Elaborating on this concept, the Commission established a twofold obligation for every broadcaster; to devote a reasonable amount of time to the coverage of important public issues, and to provide this coverage in a fair and balanced manner.

In 1969, the Supreme Court had its first opportunity to consider the First Amendment issues raised by the fairness doctrine. Although only one narrow portion of the doctrine, its personal attack rule, was truly at issue, the consolidation of this case with an action brought by a group of broadcast news directors allowed the court to consider the broader constitutional implications of this Commission policy.

Justice White, speaking for a unanimous court, declared in affirming the doctrine that the federal government did have the constitutional authority to require broadcasters to furnish their audiences with balanced coverage of controversial issues of public importance because,

> It is the purpose of the First Amendment to preserve an uninhibited marketplace of ideas in which truth will ultimately prevail, rather than to countenance monopolization of that market, whether it be by the Government itself or a private licensee.... It is the right of the viewers and listeners, not the right of the broadcasters, which is paramount.[29]

[27] Public Law No. 274, 86th Congress 1959.

[28] Editorializing by Broadcast Licensees, 13 FCC 1246 (1949).

[29] Red Lion Broadcasting Co. v. FCC, 395 U.S. 367, 89 S.Ct. 1794 (1969).

In 1967 the Commission had taken the position that in accepting cigarette advertising, a station obligated itself under the fairness doctrine to present programming or public service announcements balancing the advocacy of smoking with information describing the threat that cigarette smoking posed to health.[30] By establishing this precedent, the FCC soon found itself under pressure from a wide range of interest groups demanding that this "counter advertising" broadcast obligation be extended to require informational messages criticizing virtually every product advertised on television or radio.

Expanding the scope of the fairness doctrine in this way would have made it extremely difficult for broadcasters to continue to compete with newspapers or magazines for advertising revenues, since few advertisers would be likely to use a medium that was obligated by law to provide free air time to those who wished to criticize the products they had paid to promote. As a result, when the Federal Trade Commission (FTC) filed a brief with the FCC in 1972 that urged the Commission adopt broadcast counter advertising rules as a "suitable approach to some of the present failings of advertising which are beyond the FTC's capacity," the FCC realized that it was being maneuvered into a regulatory position that would undercut the financial base of the entire broadcast industry.[31]

In 1974 the Commission rejected this FTC proposal and issued a policy statement effectively removing all product advertising from the requirements of the fairness doctrine, except in situations where the advertising itself expressly raised a controversial issue of public importance.[32] In this same policy statement the FCC also tried to clarify basic broadcast obligations under the doctrine, concluding that broadcasters needed only to devote a reasonable amount of time to the coverage of public issues, and through this coverage, to provide opportunities for the presentation of contrasting points of view relating to these issues.

Citizen groups viewed this effort at clarification as an attempt to retreat from regulatory guidelines that in the past had been construed by the agency itself as requiring broadcasters actively to seek out controversial issues of public importance and to assume primary responsibility for providing balanced coverage of these issues. Eventually, however, the FCC's new, more limited definition of broadcast fairness doctrine obligations was sustained by the courts.[33]

[30] Banzhaf v. FCC, 405 F.2d 1082 (D.C.Cir.1968).

[31] FTC Docket 19.260.

[32] In the Matter of Handling of Public Issues under the Fairness Doctrine, 48 FCC 2d 1 (1974).

[33] National Citizens Committee for Broadcasting v. FCC, 567 F.2d 1095 (D.C.Cir. 1977), cert. denied 436 U.S. 926, 98 S.Ct. 2820 (1978).

As the 1980s began, even this more narrowly defined set of fairness obligations soon appeared too repressive of free speech for an FCC now fully committed to a policy of deregulation. In 1981, the Commission asked Congress to repeal the fairness doctrine, pointing to what it felt was an ever increasing inequity between the programming requirements broadcasters had to accept, and the much less extensive programming obligations the agency could legally impose upon all other forms of competing electronic media service.[34]

When Congress failed to respond to the FCC's request, the agency launched its own extensive investigation of the doctrine's effects on broadcast free speech. In 1985, the Commission released its report based on this investigation, concluding the fairness doctrine no longer served the public interest.[35] This was true, according to the report, because a rapid expansion in the number of information services available to American audiences made them far less dependent upon broadcasting to be informed than they had been when the doctrine was adopted. In the absence of such continuing dependence, further intrusion by government in this area of broadcast free speech was not only unwarranted, in the Commission's view, but also dangerous, because it provided too many opportunities for political pressure to affect broadcast coverage of public issues.

Congress reacted to this FCC report by ordering the agency *not* to alter any of its existing fairness doctrine enforcement policies for a two year period ending in August 1987. Instead, the Commission was directed to complete, within this two year period, a detailed assessment of various alternative methods the agency might recommend for continuing to protect the public's interest in balanced treatment of controversial issues without unnecessarily infringing upon a broadcaster's editorial discretion.

During the preparation of its 1985 Fairness Doctrine report, the FCC had actually enforced its provisions for the first time in nearly a decade. In 1984 the Commission found that *Meredith Broadcasting*, owner of a television station in Syracuse, New York violated the doctrine's provisions by refusing to balance editorial advertisements supporting the building of a nuclear power plant with anti-nuclear energy public service announcements pointing out the drawbacks of this source of energy.[36]

Perhaps it was only coincidental that the Commission had decided to begin enforcing the doctrine again at this particular

[34] FCC Report No. 5068, Setting Forth Proposals for Amending the Communications Act (Sept. 17, 1981).

[35] Fairness Report, 102 FCC 2d 143 (1985).

[36] In re Syracuse Peace Council, 57 RR2d 519 (1984).

time, but there certainly was a clear tactical advantage in doing so. As long as Congress remained unwilling to relieve the FCC of its statutory obligation to enforce the fairness doctrine, the only avenue open for the Commission to escape this responsibility was to give the D.C. Court of Appeals the opportunity to declare its efforts to punish an alleged fairness doctrine violator to be unconstitutional and therefore unenforceable; exactly the situation that the *Meredith* case just happened to present.

But whatever the FCC's intentions, the Court of Appeals acted instead in Telecommunications Research and Action Center (TRAC) v. FCC to free the Commission from its legal obligation to enforce the fairness doctrine without considering the constitutionality of the doctrine itself.[37] In this relatively obscure case decided just prior to *Meredith,* the Court held that the FCC was not obligated to make broadcast teletext services conform to fairness doctrine standards because, contrary to the prevailing view, the attempt of Congress in 1959 to incorporate the doctrine into the Communication Act had not been clear or specific enough to actually *codify* it into law.

As a result, when the Court returned the *Meredith* case to the Commission, it instructed the FCC to resolve the controversy simply on the basis of whether the agency *itself* believed the fairness doctrine served the public interest, because in its *TRAC* decision the Court had already released the Commission from any Congressional imposed obligation to enforce the doctrine.[38]

As the year 1987 began, members of Congress who wanted to preserve the doctrine realized that they would soon have to add a new, more clearly stated "fairness" clause to the Communications Act in order to prevent the FCC from exercising the freedom the Appeals Court had just given it to rescind the doctrine on its own. Congressional leaders succeeded in marshaling new "fairness" legislation through both houses of Congress during the spring of 1987 and a bill codifying the doctrine was presented to President Reagan by mid-June.[39]

During this period of feverish legislative activity, the NAB decided not to oppose this attempt to codify the fairness doctrine, fearing that such opposition might antagonize members of Con-

---

[37] 801 F.2d 501 (D.C.Cir.1986).

[38] Meredith Corp. v. FCC, 809 F.2d 863 (D.C.Cir.1987). Because the Supreme Court had found that the fairness doctrine did not infringe upon broadcaster First Amendment rights in the *Red Lion* case, the lower court obviously preferred to avoid basing its decision on constitutional grounds.

[39] S. 742 was passed by the Senate on April 21 and H.R. 1934 was passed by the House in May. The reconciled bill was vetoed by President Reagan on June 19, 1987, and unable to override the veto, the legislation was returned to committee without action.

gress whose support was needed for more important comparative renewal legislation.[40] Yet, even though the broadcast industry had been unwilling to campaign publicly to extend its right of freedom of expression under these circumstances, President Reagan decided on his own to veto the bill, a veto Congress lacked the votes to override.

After this veto, the FCC stood alone in the political spotlight. The Court of Appeals had found no language in the Communications Act compelling the Commission to continue to enforce the doctrine, and Congress had failed in its efforts to insert a new fairness doctrine provision in the Act.

At the time the agency was still bound by instructions from Congress not to abandon its enforcement of the doctrine prior to August 1987, when it was to provide Congress with a list of alternative methods for achieving the same objectives of balance in the broadcast coverage of controversial issues. On August 4, 1987, it issued this study Congress had requested.[41] At the same time, however, the agency released its decision in the *Meredith* case, rescinding all broadcast fairness doctrine requirements, except those rules relating to "personal attack" and "political editorializing".[42]

Supporters of the doctrine in Congress reacted angrily to the Commission's action, drafting new fairness legislation while seeking some approach that could shelter it from presidential veto. But despite their best efforts, this second attempt to make the fairness doctrine part of the Communications Act also failed to survive President Reagan's veto in December 1987.

On review, the FCC's decision to rescind the Fairness Doctrine was upheld by a divided three-judge panel.[43] The Court found that the Commission had not acted in an arbitrary or capricious manner in abolishing both of the Doctrine's requirements; to seek out controversial issues of public importance and to cover them in a balanced, impartial fashion. In essence, the majority decision accepted the FCC's conclusions that the Fairness Doctrine tended to discourage broadcast coverage of controversial public issues and also tended to encourage too great a degree of governmental interference in areas of broadcast freedom of expression.

[40] "CBS's Bob McConnell and the Story Behind the Veto", Broadcasting, July 6, 1987, p. 33.

[41] Fairness Alternatives, 63 RR2d 488 (1987).

[42] In re Complaint of Syracuse Peace Council Against WVTH, Memorandum Opinion and Order, 63 RR2d 542 (1987). See also "The Decline and Fall of the Fairness Doctrine: Fairness Held Unfair," Broadcasting, Aug. 19, 1987, p. 27.

[43] Syracuse Peace Council v. FCC, 867 F.2d 654 (D.C.Cir.1989). See also the FCC reconsideration of its Meredith Broadcasting decision that formed the basis for this appeal in Syracuse Peace Council, 64 RR2d 1073 (1988).

Each judge wrote a separate opinion. Judge Starr, while concurring in the result, argued that the constitutionality of the Doctrine itself was so closely interwoven into the Commission's action that its validity under the First Amendment needed to be considered independently by the court before reaching its decision. On the other hand, Judge Wald in his dissent contended that although no independent consideration of First Amendment issues was necessary, the FCC had not adequately demonstrated the need to repeal the "first prong" of the Doctrine, the requirement "to seek out controversial issues" when finding that the second or "balance" prong no longer serves the public interest.

At this point, then, the Commission's decision to repeal the basic requirements of the Fairness Doctrine has been sustained by the D.C. Court of Appeals, but because of the Court's refusal to base its decision on constitutional grounds, Congress has not been precluded from adopting legislation in the future that would once again require the FCC to enforce its requirements.

In the meantime the FCC continues to reduce the range of its fairness doctrine obligations, deciding by a 3–2 vote in 1992 that it will no longer enforce one of the doctrine's corollaries, the requirement of fairness in broadcast coverage of elections or ballot issues.[44] In a 7–5 vote affirming the Commission's decision, a federal appeals court agreed that the agency was not obligated to enforce any element of the doctrine unless Congress enacted legislation that required it to do so.[45]

SEC. 75.   PERSONAL ATTACKS AND POLITICAL EDITORIALS

When a broadcast attacks the integrity or character of a person or group, or an editorial supports or opposes a political candidate, the station must promptly notify the person attacked or opposed, furnishing that person with the content of the attack, and offering air time to respond.

An attack upon the character, honesty, or integrity of a person or group during a broadcast of a controversial issue of public importance is one situation still governed by the rules of the fairness doctrine. The other occurs when a station broadcasts an editorial supporting or opposing a political candidate.

The Commission has justified its reluctance to rescind either of these rather specialized fairness rules until it has considered them more carefully by explaining that neither of these corollaries ap-

---

[44] Arkansas AFL–CIO v. KARK–TV, 70 R.R. 2d 369 (1992).

[45] Arkansas AFL–CIO v. FCC, 980 F.2d 1190 (8th Cir.1992).

pears to infringe significantly upon the editorial judgment of broadcasters.[46]

These Commission rules require that the broadcaster must notify the target of the attack promptly, and furnish this person with a transcript, tape or summary of the attack. Also, an offer of time to reply must be given. Where the licensee has broadcast an editorial endorsing or opposing a political candidate, the opposing candidates are to be notified within 24 hours after the endorsement or attack, and furnished with the transcript and an offer of time.[47]

Personal attacks occurring during bona fide newscasts, news interviews and commentaries are *exempted* from these fairness requirements.[48] This leaves station editorials and documentaries among the types of programs that do impose these special responsibilities upon broadcasters.

While the FCC contends that notification requirements such as those imposed by personal attack and political editorial rules do not exert the same degree of "chilling effect" on broadcast freedom of expression as regulations directly affecting program content, there are those who disagree with this assessment. It has been argued, for example, that personal attack rules do not serve the claimed FCC objective of airing crucial public issues.

Instead, according to these critics, it is only when issues retreat and name-calling comes to the fore that the personal attack rules require reply opportunity. "To a large extent, the personal attack rules generate name calling exercises, allowing those parties whose personalities are criticized to rebut the charges without requiring rebuttal opportunities on the more substantive issues."[49]

There is no way of being able to determine at this point whether the personal attack and political editorializing rules have been preserved to achieve some long term policy objective of the Commission, or have only been spared until the agency can find a valid justification for their recision. In either case, they now represent the last remaining regulatory vestiges of that once broad and powerful doctrine that shaped the programming policies of broadcast stations and networks throughout the United States.

---

[46] Another reason for being somewhat reluctant to repeal the "personal attack" rule could be that it was this specific rule the Supreme Court found to be constitutional in the *Red Lion* decision. See Syracuse Peace Council, 64 RR 2d 1873 (1988).

[47] 32 Fed.Reg. 10303–ff (1967).

[48] 32 Fed.Reg. 11531 (1967).

[49] Steven J. Simmons, "The FCC Personal Attack and Political Editorializing Rules Reconsidered," Pennsylvania Law Review (Fall 1977) p. 990.

SEC. 76. PUBLIC BROADCASTING

Created to offer an alternative to commercial radio and television, public broadcasting has been sheltered from direct FCC control by a separate set of regulations.

Unlike most other Western industrial nations, no special provisions were made for non-commercial broadcasting when broadcast regulation began in the United States. Those college and university radio stations that had already received a broadcast license from the Commerce Department during the early 1920s were permitted to remain on the air, but no spectrum space was specifically set aside by either the Radio Act of 1927 or the Communications Act of 1934 to encourage the development of a nationwide educational or cultural broadcasting service.[50]

In 1945, as part of its revised approach to broadcast frequency assignments, the FCC allotted some 10 percent of the new FM service spectrum space to non-commercial applicants and in 1952, following the same approach, it allotted a similar percentage of the television spectrum for non-commercial stations.[51] However, this belated recognition of non-commercial broadcast service did little to stimulate the growth of educational broadcasting in the United States. By 1960, for example, there were only 162 educational FM stations in operation throughout the nation, and only 44 educational television stations.

What these educational television stations lacked in particular was any major source of funding capable of underwriting the massive production costs demanded by even a relatively modest television program schedule. In 1962 the federal government passed

[50] Many of the earliest radio stations had been experimental projects of some college physics or engineering department. Yet as late as 1927, when the FRC began issuing broadcast licenses, most of the more than 200 noncommercial stations it licensed were still operated by educational institutions. Within the decade however, their number had dwindled to less than 30, victims of both a Depression era economy and the absence of any clearly defined educational broadcasting objectives. Most were purchased by commercial broadcasters, eager to obtain their valuable frequency assignments. Section 307(C) of the Act of 1934 did require the FCC to report to Congress on the advisability of allocated fixed percentages of radio broadcasting facilities to various types of non-commercial broadcasters but the Commission reported back to Congress in 1935 that existing commercial stations were providing sufficient cultural and education programming to make any special non-commercial allocations unnecessary.

[51] The first FCC attempt to reserve space for non-commercial FM broadcasting actually occurred in 1940, but World War II suspended efforts to implement this allocation plan and it was substantially modified when reintroduced in 1945. Radio broadcast licenses have always been issued nationwide on a first-come, first-serve basis, only conditioned on an applicant being able to establish that transmission on the frequencies assigned will not interfere with other existing radio broadcast signals. In contrast, the FCC's FM and TV license allocation programs have assigned each specific authorized FM or TV channel to a particular locality in the United States, and designed a specified segment of the FM band and a specific proportion of all TV channels for non-commercial use.

the first significant piece of legislation offering financial support for educational television, the Educational Television Facilities Act.

Five years later an extremely influential report issued by the Carnegie Commission on Educational Television resulted in Congress enacting the Public Broadcasting Act of 1967. This Act created the Corporation for Public Broadcasting (CPB), a non-profit, non-governmental organization charged with funding all forms of educational broadcasting in the United States.[52]

To protect this new non-commercial service from being dominated by a centralized bureaucracy in Washington, CPB was denied the right to provide any type of broadcast service of its own to the general public. Instead, it was directed to work with existing public broadcast stations to develop new forms of culturally or educationally oriented radio and television programming.

In 1970 CPB and a coalition of public broadcast stations formed the Public Broadcast Service (PBS) and National Public Radio (NPR), organizations established to distribute public radio and television programs to member stations. Four years later CPB and its member television stations created the Station Program Cooperative (SPC) plan, further decentralizing public television operation by making local stations primarily responsible for deciding which specific proposed television series productions will be funded.

When Congress established the Corporation for Public Broadcasting in 1967, it inserted new regulatory language in the Communications Act of 1934 specially designed to govern its functions.[53] The question soon arose whether by creating a separate set of regulatory requirements for public broadcasting, Congress had thereby exempted these stations from all other obligations imposed on broadcasters by the Communications Act.

In Accuracy in Media, Inc. v. FCC a federal court found that because Congress had included specific language in the Act of 1967 requiring public broadcasters to provide balanced and objective programming, it was Congress rather than the FCC that should be primarily responsible for supervising compliance with its directive.[54]

[52] The Carnegie Commission had recommended the term "public" rather than "educational" to describe the new non-commercial broadcast services it proposed, contended that to label them as "educational" would unduly restrict their role as alternatives to commercial broadcasting.

[53] Statutory provisions of the Communications Act of 1934 that relate to CPB and public broadcasting are found in Section 390–399 of the Act of 1934.

[54] 521 F.2d 288 (D.C.Cir.1975), cert. denied 425 U.S. 934, 96 S.Ct. 1664 (1976). The court was particularly impressed by the argument that Congress had sought to shelter public broadcasting as much as possible from federal interference, and FCC regulation in the area of program content would operate to undercut that objective.

This special regulatory language governing non-commercial broadcasting had also denied those stations receiving funding from CPB the right to editorialize. In a 5–4 decision, the U.S. Supreme Court struck down this ban as an unconstitutional abridgement of broadcast free speech.[55]

In Muir v. Alabama Educational Television Commission, a majority of the huge en banc panel of 22 federal judges held that public broadcast stations had the same degree of editorial freedom in selecting and scheduling their programming as all other broadcasters.[56] Viewers challenging the refusal of two public broadcast stations to carry a controversial PBS documentary had argued that their tax supported status transformed them into "public forums" with less discretion to ignore the demands of the citizens who provided their funding, but the majority opinion rejected this distinction between commercial and non-commercial public interest standards.

Although most non-commercial licenses in the United States are held by public broadcast stations operated by state or local governments, universities, or school districts, other non-profit organizations are also licensed to broadcast by the FCC. Religious groups or institutions do not qualify for a reserved educational broadcast channel unless the primary emphasis of their programming is on education, but they as well as other community supported broadcasters such as "Pacifica" are authorized to receive a non-commercial broadcast license.

Periodic campaigns have been waged to deny religious broadcasters spectrum space because their opponents contend they are too narrowly oriented to serve the interests of the general public.[57] The FCC has never accepted this argument, however, maintaining that religious and other non-commercial broadcasters perform a useful service by enhancing that degree of diversity available to American broadcast audiences.

[55] FCC v. League of Women Voters of California, 468 U.S. 364, 104 S.Ct. 3106 (1984). In this instance, the station editorializing was not a public broadcaster but rather a non-commercial station that had accepted funding from CPB and therefore came under the federal statute.

[56] 688 F.2d 1033 (5th Cir.1982). The large panel of judges resulted from the consolidation of appeals from two conflicting lower court actions resulting from the refusal of two public broadcast stations to carry the controversial documentary "Death of a Princess" that portrayed Saudi Arabian society as being primitive and barbaric.

[57] See Multiple and Religious Ownership of Educational Stations, 34 RR2d 1217 (1975). The Commission rejected this argument, but does employ the "fair break" principle first described in Noe v. FCC, 260 F.2d 739 (D.C.Cir.1958), requiring a broadcast licensee to give all listeners reasonable access to views opposing those held by the broadcaster.

Chapter 13

NEW MEDIA AND REGULATION

SEC. 77. MASS MEDIA AND THE COMMON CARRIER CONNECTION

Common carriers have played a crucial role in the development of mass communications in the United States.

It was the telegraph that transformed the provincial gazette of the early 1800s into the modern newspaper capable of providing comprehensive coverage of national and world events. The steam-driven rotary press may have launched the era of mass news in the 1830s, but not until telegraph lines of the newly formed Western Union spanned the continent from coast to coast in 1861 did reports of major events occurring in San Francisco, New Orleans or Atlanta begin reaching newsrooms in the Northeast in a matter of seconds rather than days or weeks.

Associated Press, the first American wire service, was formed in 1848, and by the end of the Civil War this cooperative newspooling venture of the nation's largest newspapers provided its member publishers with immediate coverage of events anywhere in the United States through telegraphed news dispatches from local AP reporters at the scene.[1]

Less than a decade later, as the first trans-Atlantic submarine cable began operation, this channel of telegraphed dispatches linked American publishers not only with Europe, but through the British news agency Reuters and the French news agency Havas, with

[1] During the 1850s, several of the privately owned telegraph companies tried to form their own news organizations in competition with AP. When many of these companies merged to form Western Union in 1861, AP offered to give the new nationwide telegraph company the exclusive right to carry its news dispatches, in return for priority handling of these dispatches. Western Union agreed, and by 1880, these AP transmissions constituted 11 percent of Western Union's total message traffic. By 1880, the volume in telegraphed news traffic was so heavy that Western Union began dedicating private leased lines solely to AP news dispatches. See Robert Thompson, Wiring A Continent (Princeton: Princeton University Press, 1947). The AP organized in 1848 was later supplanted by the Western AP, which survived when the earlier AP went out of business in 1892.

647

colonial offices of these agencies located throughout the Middle East, Africa and Asia.

Thus, in less than a half century, the telegraph and those wire services formed to take advantage of this new technology allowed local newspapers in the United States to begin covering the world for their readers. The daily newspaper was no longer isolated from distant events by days or weeks of mail delivery, but connected directly by reports traveling at the speed of light through the wires of the Western Union.

During the late 1920s, it was AT & T, another communications common carrier, whose long distance lines transformed a weak, locally oriented collection of radio stations into a national broadcast medium. In its original license allocation plan, the Federal Radio Commission had established an elaborate system of local and regional broadcast services, but had made no provision for simultaneous nationwide distribution of broadcast programming.

A small group of radio stations had begun to use AT & T lines as early as 1923 to pool programs, but it was not until the late 1920s that NBC's two national networks (its second network would later become ABC) and the newly formed CBS leased AT & T's recently completed nationwide broadcast lines to emerge as the dominant forces in American broadcasting. By using AT & T's lines to distribute programs *directly* to each of its affiliate stations, networks were able avoid the elaborate FRC local licensing system to offer their audiences a nationwide service of polished and professional entertainment that no other medium could rival.

Then, when the FCC attempted to establish a system of community oriented television stations in the early 1950s, it was AT & T's long line systems, now augmented by microwave relays, that once again allowed the networks to by-pass the agency's spectrum licensing regulations to establish *national* programming channels where only local services had been envisioned by government planners.

In a very real sense, then, it is entirely possible that if AT & T and its Bell Systems had not established their nationwide system of telephone networks before broadcasting emerged as a mass medium in the United States during the 1920s, our radio and television services of today might be as provincial in nature as our local newspapers were before the advent of the telegraph.

Then, during the mid–1950s, when "community antenna systems" were simply enhancing the quality of the television picture from one or two nearby television stations, it was AT & T's microwave relay systems that allowed cable TV operators to begin importing from distant markets the programs of television networks with no local affiliates. In time, the FCC began restricting this microwave signal importation to preserve its broadcast market system, but not before the cable TV industry was firmly established in the United States.[2] Without this AT & T microwave network, it is quite likely that "community antenna," dependent solely on local television signals, would have withered away as predicted when more television stations began broadcast service during the late 1950s. In that event, of course, there would have been no cable TV industry to emerge during the 1980s with dozens of new program channels, and viewers in the United States today would still have to be content with only a handful of viewing alternatives.

In 1972, when the FCC announced its "Open Skies" communication satellite policy, no government planner could have foreseen how encouraging new operators to provide nationwide satellite common carrier services in competition with AT & T would alter the competitive relationship between broadcasting and cable TV in the United States, or erode the strength of the American television networks. It was this decision by the Commission that eventually allowed cable TV to become a medium in its own right, able because of lower nationwide video distribution costs, to launch its own unique cable networks.

In addition, these lower video distribution costs also enabled television stations affiliated with a network to become more independent of that network in making their own programming decisions, because they now had the option of using satellites to obtain their own programs directly from feature film, sports or series program syndicators.

In each of these past situations, the communications common carrier has only played a supporting role to the mass medium it has served, providing the distribution function essential for its growth and expansion. But what if a carrier should attempt to take over the medium and become the mass communicator itself?

Until 1982 this would have been an idle question, because federal law prohibited a communications common carrier from offering any service other than its traditional distribution of communication messages. In that year, however, a *consent decree,* negotiated without any serious consideration of its possible implications for mass media, offered AT & T and its former Bell Systems the promise of eventual freedom to move beyond basic telephone service and into the field of mass communications.

SEC. 78.   THE TELEPHONE NETWORK COMPETITOR

When local and national telephone networks are released from legal constraints, they could radically transform the existing structure of mass media service in the United States.

[2] For a more detailed account of this era, see Don R. Le Duc, Cable TV v. the FCC: A Crisis in Media Control (Temple University Press: Philadelphia, 1973).

In 1974 the Justice Department launched a massive antitrust action against AT & T, its manufacturing subsidiary, Western Electric and Bell Laboratory, the research and development facility it owned jointly with its Bell Systems. The suit charged AT & T and its subsidiaries with using their dominant position in the telecommunications market to inhibit competition.

The government wanted AT & T to divest itself of one or more of these subsidiaries to prevent the possibility of the company using revenues from its regulated monopoly telephone networks to subsidize its development and promotion of specialized services in competitive areas of the telecommunications marketplace. In addition, the Justice Department believed that breaking up the AT & T–Bell System would deny AT & T any opportunity to use its monopoly control over its telephone networks in the United States either to discourage the use of non-AT & T equipment on its lines, or block the carriage of rival telecommunication services.

In January 1982 AT & T agreed to the terms of the Justice Department settlement requiring it to divest itself of its 22 Bell Systems, Bell Laboratory and Western Electric in return for the right to enter markets previously denied it because of its regulated common carrier monopoly status. In August of that same year, Federal District Judge Harold Greene indicated he would approve the agreement if certain additional conditions were added. Judge Greene insisted that the agreement prohibit AT & T from offering "electronic publishing"[3] through its own facilities for a minimum period of seven years, and allow the new and independent Regional Bell Operating Companies (RBOCs) formed from the old Bell Systems to produce, publish and distribute telephone directory "yellow pages."

On August 24, 1982, Judge Greene gave final approval to the AT & T divestiture plan.[4] During the next year AT & T spun off its 22 Bell Systems; systems that then reorganized themselves into seven separate Regional Bell Operating Companies.[5]

---

[3] Judge Greene defined "electronic publishing" in legal context as including "the provision of any information which AT & T or its affiliates has, or has caused to be originated, authored, compiled, collected or edited, or in which it has a direct or indirect financial or proprietary interest and which is disseminated to an unaffiliated person through some electronic means."

[4] United States v. AT & T, 552 F.Supp. 131 (D.D.C.1982), affirmed sub nom. Maryland v. U.S., 460 U.S. 1001, 103 S.Ct. 1240 (1983). Thirteen state regulatory commissions contested the consent agreement on various grounds but since only three Supreme Court Justices voted to accept an appeal from the consent agreement (4 are needed to grant review), no further legal challenge was possible.

[5] These newly formed Regional Bell Operating Companies (RBOCs) were Ameritech, Atlantic, Nynex, Bell South, Pacific Telesis, Southwestern Bell and US West.

In 1984 Greene approved a proposed order filed by the Justice Department to permit these newly formed RBOCs to engage in non-telephonic businesses as long as the estimated net revenues of these activities would not exceed 10 percent of the company's telephone service net revenues. Under this standard, the Justice Department allowed several RBOCs to enter a wide variety of businesses from equipment leasing and real estate management to retail sales and international consulting.[6]

Judge Greene retained authority to approve or disapprove each new non-telephone venture, and to review the agreement every three years to determine whether conditions had changed sufficiently to authorize RBOCs to engage in an even broader range of these activities. However, under the terms of the modified final judgment (MFJ) entered in 1987, he continued to prohibit the RBOCs from providing "information services"—a broad category of activities Judge Greene defined as including everything from video-text to the operation of a cable TV system.

The non-telephone business revenues of these RBOCs increased from a 1986 total of $4.3 billion to $7 billion in 1987, nearly doubling within a single year as their telephone earnings remained relatively stable at $70 billion.[7] To put these industry revenues in perspective, as the seven BOCs were earning this $77 billion in 1987, the entire newspaper industry, including some 1,640 papers, generated combined earnings of $40 billion; some 15,000 broadcast stations earned a total of $24.4 billion, and the nation's 8,800 cable TV systems were sharing revenues of $14 billion.[8]

And none of these RBOC revenues had been generated by those non-telephonic activities that the companies could perform the most effectively; distributing public information, electronic publishing and video services through their telecommunication networks.

At the time of the consent agreement in 1982, the American Newspapers Publishing Association proposed what it called a "diversity principle" to guide future judicial supervision of the RBOCs under the terms of the agreement. To ensure the greatest degree of diversity, the press association urged that telephone companies controlling transmission facilities be prevented from acquiring any

Although they are often called "Baby Bells," each of them actually commands sufficient corporate wealth to be listed among the Fortune magazine's largest 500 American corporations.

[6] "Broadening Business Horizons for BOCs," Telecommunications, December 1984, p. 42.

[7] "Putting Out Lines in All Directions," Time, May 5, 1986, p. 49. "Baby Bells Prospering," Telecommunications, March 1988, p. 12.

[8] "Broadcasting versus the Telco Monster," Broadcasting, May 8, 1989, p. 44. In 1987, the combined revenues of just two BOCs, Nytex and Bell South in itself exceeded the combined revenues of the entire cable TV industry.

interest in or control over the information content flowing through their facilities.

Although Judge Greene did allow the RBOCs to begin offering their customers access to information services in 1987, he did so in a manner consistent with this principle, limiting the companies to the role of a *conduit*, simply furnishing subscribers data bases supplied by others. But in 1991 the D.C. Court of Appeals overturned this decree, directing Judge Greene either to permit RBOCs to provide their own information services, or to make a finding of fact that allowing RBOC entry into this information market would significantly lessen competition in this field.[9] Lacking the evidence required for such a finding, Judge Greene was forced to lift the ban he had imposed.[10]

At this time, though, this right of the Bell Companies to deliver their own information services to their customers has been overshadowed by another right these companies were granted in 1992.

Telco Video Services

In July 1992 the FCC authorized the seven major regional Bell companies to begin providing *video dial tone* services.[11] The decision allowed these telephone carriers to deliver a full range of television programming to their customers, as long as the phone company did not own or exercise editorial control over the programming it distributed.[12]

Chesapeake & Potomac Telephone, a subsidiary of Bell Atlantic and US West each challenged the FCC's authority to prevent them from owning or controlling the video services they provided. In both cases a federal district judge agreed with the telephone carrier position. In the US West case, a federal district judge found the ban to be "unnecessarily severe" and in violation of US West's first amendment rights, while in the Chesapeake and Potomac case, the judge described the ban as directly abridging the telephone carrier's

[9] For Judge Greene's initial review holding see, United States v. Western Electric Co., 673 F.Supp. 525 (D.D.C.1987) and 714 F.Supp. 1 (D.D.C.1988). Reversal by the U.S. Court of Appeals, directing Greene to apply a broader range of criteria than those used in his original decision can be found at United States v. Western Electric Co., 900 F.2d 283 (D.C.Cir.1990).

[10] Unable to do so, Greene was forced to vacate his original decision in United States v. Western Electric, 767 F.Supp. 308 (D.D.C. 1991); review denied sub nom. American Newspaper Publishers Association v. U.S., 502 U.S. 932, 112 S.Ct. 366 (1991).

[11] Further Proceedings on Cable Cross–Ownership Rules, 69 RR2d 1613 (1992).

[12] In 1984, Congress had prohibited telephone carriers from operating as cable TV systems in section 533(b)(1) of the Cable Policy section of the Communications Act of 1934. Because of this Congressional ban, the FCC had no choice but to limit the role of these BOCs to that of a passive video delivery system.

"right to express ideas by means of a particular and significant mode of communication-video programming."[13]

However, even though these decisions may strengthen the legal position of telephone carriers challenging federal video program ownership restrictions in other regions of the nation, they apply at the moment *only* to telco video operations in communities within the jurisdiction of these two district courts. As a result, pending further litigation or an affirming decision by a federal appeals court, the impact of these decisions remains limited to those areas surrounding Alexandria, Virginia and Seattle, Washington.

In July 1994, the FCC approved the first of more than 20 telephone carrier applications it had already received, authorizing Bell Atlantic to build a "video dialtone" network to compete directly with local cable TV systems.[14]

Today's telephone network, unlike the modern cable TV system, is all-switched, virtually all-digital and is rapidly becoming all fiber optic. A *switched* system is one that is totally interactive, permitting each subscriber select any signal or channel available from its switching center, ordering and being charged for that order at the same instant the specific channel chosen is being sent directly to that subscriber. Thus, unlike even the most advanced cable TV system, the telephone switching center is already capable of responding directly and individually to each subscriber request for any type of communication service from pay-per-view (PPV) feature films to international banking transactions, billing the customer automatically as the service is being provided.[15]

All electronic media are attempting to convert from analog to digital transmission as rapidly as possible, because delivering audio or visual information by binary code rather than in a continuous wave of signals reduces distortion significantly while at the same time allowing the transmission to be compressed into a much narrower band of frequencies. What may eventually provide the telephone industry with a distinct advantage in this area of new

[13] Chesapeake & Potomac Telephone v. United States, 830 F.Supp. 909 (E.D.Va. 1993); U.S. West v. United States, 855 F.Supp. 1184 (W.D.Wash.1994).

[14] Kate Fitzgerald and David Wallace, "The First Baby Bell Gets Green Light," Advertising Age, July 18, 1994, p. 23. See also, Christopher Stern, "Hundt Has Dialtone on Fast Track," Broadcasting, April 18, 1994, p. 6. These local cable TV systems in the areas Bell Atlantic plans to serve have reason to fear this competitive challenge, because this single RBOC posted earnings of more than $12 billion in 1993, revenues ⅔ the size of those earned by the entire cable TV industry.

[15] One example of the impressive service capacity of an all-switched network is provided by the "Video-on-Demand" channels developed for the telephone carrier operated test project in Cerritos, California. "Video-on-Demand" not only allows a subscriber to select any movie offered by the system at any time, but also to control the delivery of the movie by being able to "fast forward," "reverse" or stop the movie to view a still frame whenever desired. This is only possible because of the completely interactive qualities of the telephone "switched network."

technology is its continuing commitment to developing *Integrated Service Digital Networks* (ISDN), special broadband communications channels capable of distributing a broad array of different types of communication services simultaneously within a single network channel.[16]

But the most impressive advantage the telephone carriers appear to have over the cable TV industry is that 1.5 million miles of fiber optic trunk lines that are already in service delivering telephone company voice and data transmissions.[17] A fiber optic circuit is a hair-thin, flexible glass filament that guides pulses of message-delivering light along the length of the narrow fiber. Typical fiber systems carry data at a rate of more than a billion digital bits of information per second, and can transport this data for 20 miles without need of amplification.[18] In contrast, the coaxial cable used by cable TV systems can deliver data at a rate of only 1.5 million bits per second and requires amplification at least once every mile.[19]

Studies indicate that fiber optic circuits have the potential to be at least 30 times more cost effective than coaxial circuits, when operating at full capacity and delivering digital signals. At the moment, though, this potential can't be realized because "full capacity" would require a payload of 500 separate video-sized communication channels during an era when those 50 to 60 video channels now available have access only to analog produced programs.[20]

[16] The primary barrier in the path of ISDN development has been international politics, with various regions of the world clashing over the one universal set of standards that should be adopted for ISDN operation, so that worldwide ISDN service will be possible. Currently, some telcos have been experimenting with ASDL (asymmetrical digital subscriber line), a technique that can use existing copper wire system trunk lines to deliver video programming, but this approach is considered too expensive and ultimately too inefficient to ever be more than a stop-gap approach to video distribution.

[17] In contrast, at the end of 1990, cable TV systems had installed only 1,000 miles of fiber optic trunk lines. "Fiber Optics and the Future of Television," NVR Reports, Winter 1991, p. 4.

[18] In addition, fiber optic performance continues improving. In 1990, for example, each fiber optic filament was capable of delivering 100 times the amount of data it could carry in 1980, as the price of the fiber dropped from $3 dollars to 15 cents a yard. Karen Wright, "The Road to the Global Village," Scientific American, March 1990, p. 92.

[19] Because each time a signal is amplified, distortion is introduced by the amplifier, the fact that fiber optic delivered signal can travel 20 times as far as coaxial cable delivered signal without need of amplification not only significantly reduces equipment, installation and maintenance costs, but also substantially diminishes signal distortion.

[20] Technology already being developed for HDTV and cable TV channel compression will be capable of converting video productions for digital transmission easily and inexpensively, but with the huge channel capacity already available to it, this is unlikely to increase fiber optic cost effectiveness in the foreseeable future. The

In other words, today's fiber optic networks are still much faster, larger and more efficient than necessary to carry those video services available for them to deliver. At this point, then, using an optic network to deliver cable TV service would be much like buying a Concorde jet to travel to work each morning. And, engineers must still solve the "last mile" problem of fiber optic networks, finding some way of reducing the cost of connecting individual homes to the network. Adding subscribers to a coaxial cable system can be accomplished for less than $150 per household, but because there has been no economic inducement as yet to provide fiber optic service to the home, the cost for each hookup is still estimated to be in the range of $1,500–$2,000.[21]

New Federal Regulatory Policies

In 1990, the Bush administration launched the first major federal effort to break down the traditional regulatory barriers that separated broadcast, cable and communication common carrier services. Although Congress rejected each of the administration's legislative proposals, the FCC during this era drew upon all the regulatory authority it could muster to undercut those barriers Congress had erected.

In addition to its video dialtone decision, the Commission, guided by chairman Alfred Sikes, also allocated spectrum space for personal communication service (PCS), a new form of wireless phone and computer terminal network the cable industry is eager to develop.[22] These low-cost PCS systems will enable cable operators to compete directly with existing telephone companies, providing an alternative system for the delivery of point-to-point messages. In essence, then, the FCC was seeking to encourage cable operators to offer telephone services, as it encouraged telephone companies to offer video services, intending to let the marketplace determine which combination of services each could provide most cost-effectively.

Underlying these decisions was the philosophy that rival communication delivery services should be permitted to compete or combine in whatever form they believed they could function most efficiently, with government playing the most limited role possible in deciding how various video, audio or information services actually reach the home. As Sikes once explained it, whether by telephone

greater problem for the BOCs is that most of these channels are owned by cable MSOs unlikely to permit fiber optic carriage of their programming.

[21] "Sikes Says Telcos Are Revaluating Fiber to Home," Broadcasting, February 12, 1990, p. 15.

[22] "FCC Releases PCS Spectrum Allocations," Broadcasting September 21, 1992, p. 6. Major cable organizations such as Time Warner, Continental Cablevision, Tele–Communications Inc., and Viacom International, among others, have already received experimental licenses for PCS development.

fiber optic, coaxial cable, satellite or some hybrid combination of the three, the actual distribution system should be *transparent* to the message being delivered, a "seamless" universe of communication channels in which the specific method of dissemination is irrelevant as long as the entire system functions in the most effective manner possible.[23]

Soon after the Clinton administration assumed power, Vice President Gore launched a policy initiative designed to eliminate every outdated federal regulatory restriction that prevented direct competition among the various telecommunication service providers.[24] This proposal envisioned the development of national fiber optic networks capable of providing a full range of communication services, a concept that soon became known as the *information superhighway*.

In 1994, the House passed two telecommunications bills designed to achieve some of these objectives; legislation to repeal the telco-cable cross-ownership ban, to permit telephone carriers to distribute video programming, to allow cable TV to offer phone services and to authorize regional Bell systems, subject to Justice Department and FCC approval, to provide long distance service and sell telephone equipment.[25]

In the Senate, however, Commerce Committee Chairman Hollings slowed the progress of this RBOC legislation, questioning the need to free RBOCs from all Congressional control and expressing serious concern about the ability of either the FCC or the Justice Department to supervise this radical transformation of American telecommunications policy.[26] As a result, complete regulatory freedom for telephone carriers seems unlikely in the near future as each industry group continues to pressure its own coalition of politicians to obtain the greatest benefits from every proposal under consideration.

[23] "Subject to Change," Broadcasting, Jan. 28, 1991, p. 82.

[24] Kim McAvoy, "Al Gore: Directing Traffic onto the Superhighway," Broadcasting, January 10, 1994, p. 10.

[25] The Brooks–Dingell bill (H.R. 3626) would have authorized the RBOCs to compete with AT & T and others in the long-distance telephone service market and to manufacture and sell their own telephone equipment. The Markey–Fields bill (H.R. 3636) would have repeal the Congressionally imposed telco-cable cross-ownership ban and would have pre-empted state regulation in order to permit cable operators to provide telephone service everywhere in the United States, despite any State or local law to the contrary. Both bills were passed by an overwhelming margin in the House; H.R. 3626 by a vote of 423 to 5 and H.R. 3636 by a vote of 423 to 4.

[26] Hollings own bill, S.1822, would bar RBOCs from entering long distance service field until they could clearly establish that they no longer monopolized local phone service in their own area and that their entry would create a more competitive telecommunications service market. The bill also provides strict standards the FCC and Justice Department must follow in determining when these conditions have been met.

It is far easier, of course, to proclaim a visionary policy than it is to achieve it. Whatever long range benefits might be gained from a merging of separate and overlapping broadcast, satellite, cable TV and telephone distribution services, it is the short term effects of this policy that will decide how each rival medium will react to it; an impact almost certain to threaten many of each media industry's most fundamental and cherished economic interests.

Yet, even if this particular legislative initiative should fail, the trend towards an ever greater degree of consolidation among previously independent video, audio, informational and personal distribution systems seems destined to continue, simply because every media industry will be able to realize substantial savings from combining with others to permit its messages to be delivered through a single network, rather than continuing to maintain and operate its own distribution facilities.

As all previous "revolutions" in the history of American mass communications, this trend towards consolidation among media delivery systems is likely to occur so gradually and sporadically during this decade and the next that it will again be difficult in the future to point to any specific date when the final form of the new multi-media delivery network was actually determined. But even at this point it is possible to begin considering what effects this tendency is likely to have upon future broadcast, cable TV and newspaper service in the United States and those First Amendment rights now accorded to each of these media by American law.

SEC. 79. COMMUNICATION LAW AND THE CHALLENGE OF CHANGE

Changing the way mass media are distributed in the United States could have a profound effect on those legal rights each medium can now assert.

From Copper Wire to Digital Broadcast

The nation's telephone carriers appear to be in the best position to emerge as the dominant partners in future media merger ventures. In addition to their greater economic power and more advanced distribution systems, the phone companies also have a significant advantage in being able to underwrite the costs of network operation through their capacity to offer and bill their customers for a far broader range of telecommunications related services than any of their media competitors.[27]

---

[27] In 1990, for example, telephone carrier local exchange billings in themselves were reported to be in excess of $20 billion, thereby generating 50% of the revenues of the entire newspaper industry, and virtually equaling the earnings of the entire broadcasting industry.

And, the 500 video channel capacity of their fiber optic networks that now seems so totally unnecessary could actually be their most significant competitive advantage of all.[28] This vast channel space not only permits each fiber optic network to carry a large number of "high definition television" (HDTV) channels without reducing its other services, but also makes it an ideal distribution system for "pay-per-view" feature films and other special events.

But that raises fundamental issues about what will be carried and whose standards of transmission will be used. Recall the question of video recorder formats. Sony developed its beta system while Matsushita, JVC and Hitachi turned out VHS format VCRs. Even though the beta machines were praised for their technical superiority, beta machines disappeared from the American market as the longer recording and playing time of the VHS machines proved more compatible with American lifestyles.[29]

In television, from the mid–1990s, the question became which of the different transmission systems would become the new VHS and which systems and manufacturers would suffer Sony's fate. The base for the new television (and in a few years students will treat this section much like they do the preceding passages about telegraphy) will be digital television. Digital television, unlike the current standard of analog television, converts the data (picture and sound) into digital form. The use of digital or binary language allows for the acquisition of much greater amounts of data, much like a CD ROM contains more data than the LP record. The broadcasters will be able to compress the digital information allowing the greater signal quality.

Broadcasters can use this greater data capacity to broadcast High Definition TV (HDTV) which has about six times the clarity of current analog television. But the changeover will take time and the FCC rules and statute provide for a staged phase-in of digital television through 2006.[30] The FCC has granted stations additional spectrum to provide both digital and analog television signals. But the ability to broadcast HDTV does not mean that stations would and some broadcasters suggested in 1997 that they were considering using the signal capacity to multicast, that is, to offer six channels of current broadcast quality in order to sell packages of

[28] The cable industry is planning to increase dramatically the number of video channels their systems can carry through digital compression of each video signal. In reality, however, this will not increase the coaxial cable actual frequency capacity, but only allow more signals to be delivered within the same space constraints.

[29] James Lardner, "Fast Foreward Hollywood, the Japanese and the VCR Wars," (New York, W.W. Norton & Co., 1987).

[30] Mike Snyder, "Television's Next Wave," USA Today, Nov. 17, 1997, p. E1.

programming. That drew a quick and negative response from Washington and broadcasters quickly retreated.[31]

Content also is an issue in the shift to digital television. The National Law Journal reported in March of 1997 that broadcast regulators and the White House were eager to see broadcasters give something back in return for the use of the second digital channels.[32] They suggested that broadcasters might be required to provide free air time to political candidates. That would reduce some of the fund-raising pressures on candidates and serve as a substantial and real public service by broadcasters.

In addition to content regulation, broadcasters face problems with gearing up for digital television. Stations must spend between $2 million to $14 million to broadcast the new signal. Part of that will go to transmitter and tower expenses. Other expenses will come in the purchase of equipment to broadcast syndicated programs in the digital mode and to create their own in-house digital broadcasts for news, local programming and commercials. Towers must be modified or built to transmit the signals. Local governments and activists have already signaled their unwillingness to allow additional towers to be built in their communities. FCC power may, however, eliminate such opposition by the use of federal preemption over local government.

"Must-carry" also is implicated in the changeover to digital television. Cable operators can use digital cable casting equipment to improve the quality of the signals they carry to individual homes. Cable's delivery systems mean that one cable channel could carry two HDTV shows or six standard-definition shows or as many as 16 reduced-resolution programs. Under the "must-carry" rules, local stations must be given places in a cable company's lineup. A refusal of a cable company to carry the digital broadcast signal will mean that broadcasters will have spent the money on digital only to see a lower-resolution signal on the home television set.

The Internet as Democracy, Bureaucracy and Trade

On June 26, 1997, the Supreme Court ruled 9–0 that the Communications Decency Act (CDA), which would make it a crime to make "indecent" material available to minors on line, was unconstitutional.[33] In his opinion for the court, Justice John Paul Stevens held that Internet speech was entitled to the fullest protection of the First Amendment.[34]

[31] David Lieberman, "An Expensive Proposition," USA Today, Nov. 17, 1997, E4.

[32] Marianne Lavelle, "Give Free Time to Pols?" The National Law Journal, March 31, 1997, p. A1.

[33] Linda Greenhouse, "Court, 9–0 Upholds State Laws Prohibiting Assisted Suicide; Protects Speech on Internet," The New York Times, June 27, 1997, p. A1.

[34] Reno v. ACLU, ___ U.S. ___, 117 S.Ct. 2329 (1997), 25 Med.L.Rptr 1833.

The CDA had been a late addition to the Telecommunications Act of 1996. There were no hearings on the CDA and questions arose from the beginning about its constitutionality. The sponsors of the CDA agreed to special provisions for quick Supreme Court review. A coalition of communications entities, libraries and librarians, free speech activists, Internet programmers and service providers led by the ACLU filed suit in federal court in Philadelphia. A three-judge panel undertook to learn about the Internet and computers as they considered the arguments advanced by the government and the opponents of the CDA. They wrote a 147–page ruling that held that the CDA was unconstitutional. The Supreme Court relied extensively on that ruling and the opinions of judges Stewart Dalzell, Dolores K. Sloviter and Ronald L. Buckwalter.

The government had argued that the Internet could properly be regulated as it was most like broadcasting and broadcasters were subject to restrictions on indecency arising from the case of FCC v. Pacifica Foundation.[35] The regulations also were intended to protect children from harmful adult materials.[36] Opponents countered that the CDA would deprive them of their First Amendment rights. The CDA's failure to define indecency would mean that Internet service providers and content creators could be prosecuted without

[35] 438 U.S. 726, 98 S.Ct. 3026 (1978).

[36] The Communications Decency Act of 1996 (CDA), codified at 47 U.S.C. § 223(a) to (h).

§ 223(a)(1)(B) provides:

(a) Whoever—

(1) in interstate or foreign communications—

(B) by means of a telecommunications device knowingly—

(I) makes, creates, or solicits, and

(ii) initiates the transmission of, any comment, request, suggestion, proposal, image, or other communication which is obscene or indecent, knowing that the recipient of the communication is under 18 years of age, regardless of whether the maker of such communication placed the call or initiated the communication;

§ 223(d) provides:

(d) Whoever—

(1) in interstate or foreign communications knowingly—

(A) uses an interactive computer service to send to a specific person or persons under 18 years of age, or

(B) uses any interactive computer service to display in a manner available to a person under 18 years of age, any comment, request, suggestion, proposal, image, or other communication that, in context, depicts or describes, in terms patently offensive as measured by contemporary community standards, sexual or excretory activities or organs, regardless of whether the user of such service placed the call or initiated the communication; or

(2) knowingly permits any telecommunications facility under such person's control to be used for an activity prohibited by paragraph (1) with the intent that it be used for such activity, shall be fined under Title 18 United States Code, or imprisoned not more than two years, or both.

their knowing beforehand that they were breaking the law. That would mean that even if they attempted to censor their own content, they still might be punished for their speech. Fears of prosecution also would prompt their on-line carriers to censor content in their own self interest. Finally, the CDA would prevent people from speaking out on important public issues.

Justice Stevens, writing for seven members of the unanimous Court,[37] said that the CDA's provisions were not constitutional. "Notwithstanding the legitimacy and importance of the congressional goal of protecting children from harmful materials, we agree with the three-judge District Court that the statute abridges 'the freedom of speech' protected by the First Amendment."[38]

While acknowledging Congressional intent to protect minors, the Court said that the First Amendment required freer discourse. Referring Sable Communications of California, Inc. v. FCC,[39] a case in which federal restrictions on "dial-a-porn" telephone services were found unconstitutional with respect to indecent content, Justice Stevens said that invoking the important purpose of protecting children would not foreclose an examination of the constitutionality of the statute. In both *Sable* and the case of *Reno v. ACLU*, Stevens said, protection of minors could not justify the restriction of all speech. " '[R]egardless of the strength of the government's interest' in protecting children, '[t]he level of discourse reaching a mailbox simply cannot be limited to that which would be suitable for a sandbox.' Bolger v. Youngs Drug Products Corp., 463 U.S. 60, 74–75, 103 S.Ct. 2875, 2884–2885, 77 L.Ed.2d 469 (1983)."[40]

The provision of the CDA which made it a crime to engage in "indecent" speech when a minor was part of the audience would allow critics to shut off all such speech they did not agree with, Stevens said: "It would confer broad powers of censorship, in the form of a 'heckler's veto,' upon any opponent of indecent speech who might simply log on and inform the would-be discoursers that his 17–year-old child—a 'specific person ... under 18 years of age,' * * * would be present."[41] To allow the CDA to stand as constitutional would be to reduce the adult population to the level of children in what they could access on the Internet and the Court had ruled previously that that was not constitutional.

The Internet allows for the freest possible discourse through the nature of its elemental parts. "Through the use of chat rooms,

---

[37] Justice O'Connor wrote a separate concurring opinion also signed by Chief Justice Rehnquist.

[38] Reno v. ACLU, ___ U.S. ___, ___, 117 S.Ct. 2329, 2334 (1997).

[39] 492 U.S. 115, 126, 109 S.Ct. 2829, 2836–37, 106 L.Ed.2d 93 (1989).

[40] Reno v. ACLU, ___ U.S. ___, ___, 117 S.Ct. 2329, 2346 (1997).

[41] Ibid. At 2349.

any person with a phone line can become a town crier with a voice that resonates further than it could from any soapbox. Through the use of Web pages, mail exploders, and newsgroups, the same individual can become a pamphleteer. As the District Court found, 'the content on the Internet is as diverse as human thought.' "[42]

Based on the failure of the government to show how it could both protect minors and the speech of adults and the vagueness of the indecency provisions, the Court struck down the CDA. The Clinton administration backed off on plans to re-institute content restrictions on the Internet in the weeks following the decision.

Adult content is not the only regulatory issue facing the Internet. Privacy and commerce issues continue to develop. How binding are contracts completed exclusively through the Internet without benefit of human signatures on contract forms? Should advertisers be able to track visitors to their Web sites and sell that marketing information to others? Do users of e-mail enjoy the same privacy rights that the senders and recipients of "snail mail (letters carried by postal employees)?"

In the area of contracts, the questions are governed by statutes in the various states that control the enforcement of contracts. The electronic contract and Internet allow parties, who are separated by great distances, to conduct business as easily as next-door-neighbors. But how enforceable are those contracts? While several states, including California, Texas, Minnesota, Utah and Washington have laws that allow the use of digital signatures on electronic contracts, most states still require that a contract be signed by the party against whom it is sought to be enforced.[43]

The Uniform Commercial Code, the guideline for commercial transactions,[44] is undergoing revision to guide states in their treatment of electronic commerce. In addition, the National Conference of Commissioners on Uniform State Laws, also is examining electronic contracts to cover the areas not encompassed by the U.C.C.

Until then, the basic issue that stands in the way of the greater adoption of electronic contracts is the reliability of the contract. Electronic forgery appears to be a greater risk than paper fraud and the risks of entering into fraudulent contracts stands in the way of this electronic commerce. Other problems with electronic transactions include the difficulty involved in being able to sue to enforce contracts and a failure of parties to truly understand essential elements of the agreements. That difficulty was illustrated by a

[42] Ibid. At 2344.

[43] Geanne Rosenberg, "Legal Uncertainty Clouds Status of Contracts on Internet," The New York Times, July 7, 1997, p. C3.

[44] The U.C.C. governs sales, commercial paper, secured transactions and bank deposits. The U.C.C. has been adopted by virtually all states.

dispute between a trading card dealer in Florida and a teenager in New Jersey. Bob Deak, the Florida dealer, entered into a contract with 14–year-old Ted Clark for a card collection for $1,200. When he received the collection, Deak concluded that the cards were not in the "near mint" condition they had been represented as being. He canceled part of the payment. Clark sought to enforce his electronic contract and, after negotiations, persuaded Deak to pay the total.[45]

But even though Clark realized his desired goal, other electronic transactions could as easily fail to be resolved. The key issue is the ability of a party seeking to enforce a contract to prove that it was entered into by the other party. Keystrokes are anonymous and codes and passwords can be discovered and misused. Without the surety of enforceability, commerce on the Internet will be restricted to small-scale transactions, the electronic version of mail order, rather than major deals.

Another issue involving the Internet is the tracking of Web site visitation. Unlike window shopping, where consumers remain anonymous as they browse, the Internet allows for close scrutiny of every move that a consumer will make.

"When you belong to a frequent buyer club at the bookstore, they probably keep a record of the books you buy," said Christine Varney, a member of the Federal Trade Commission. "But no one follows you around the store and keeps track of what you looked at and how long you looked before you bought."[46] Electronic tags, known as "cookies," record the sites that Internet travelers visit. The electronic trail is a valuable tool for marketers who want to know more about consumer habits. But these records also implicate consumer privacy rights. Consumers, already in rebellion about the use of government records by mass marketers, are concerned about the uses of these records by those engaged in commerce.

Another privacy issue attached to electronic communication deals with e-mail. In one of the few cases to deal with e-mail privacy, the federal court found that in a private-company context, that employees did not have a reasonable expectation of privacy and that the company could read and take action based on the content of the employee's e-mail. In Smyth v. The Pillsbury Co.,[47] Michael Smyth was a regional operations manager for the Pillsbury Co. Pillsbury operated an e-mail system that it used for internal corporate communications. Pillsbury told its employees "that all e-mail

45 Geanne Rosenberg, "Legal Uncertainty Clouds Status of Contracts on Internet," The New York Times, July 7, 1997. p. C3.

46 John M. Broder, "Making America Safe for Electronic Commerce," The New York Times, June 22, 1997, p. E4.

47 914 F.Supp. 97 (E.D.Pa.1996).

communications would remain confidential and privileged."[48] Pillsbury also said that e-mail could not be intercepted or used for termination or as grounds for reprimands. In October of 1994, Smyth received an e-mail at his home from his supervisor. He responded. On Jan. 17, 1995, Pillsbury fired Smyth for sending what the company called inappropriate and unprofessional comments.[49]

Smyth filed suit against Pillsbury claiming that the company's interception of his e-mail and termination violated public policy as a violation of his privacy rights. Pillsbury moved to dismiss the case arguing that Smyth had failed to state a claim on which he could recover. Smyth argued that his dismission violated "public policy which precludes an employer from terminating an employee in violation of the employee's right to PRIVACY as embodied in Pennsylvania common law."[50]

But the district court found that Smyth did not have a reasonable expectation of privacy in his e-mail communication.

> "In the first instance, unlike urinalysis and personal property searches, we do not find a reasonable expectation of PRIVACY in E–MAIL communications voluntarily made by an employee to his supervisor over the company E–MAIL system notwithstanding any assurances that such communications would not be intercepted by management. Once plaintiff communicated the alleged unprofessional comments to a second person (his supervisor) over an E–MAIL system which was apparently utilized by the entire company, any reasonable expectation of PRIVACY was lost. Significantly, the defendant did not require plaintiff, as in the case of an urinalysis or personal property search to disclose any personal information about himself. Rather, plaintiff voluntarily communicated the alleged unprofessional comments over the company E–MAIL system. We find no PRIVACY interests in such communications."[51]

Finally, the Internet poses questions relating to its reliability. In the spring of 1997, the Internet carried stories about Kurt Vonnegut's commencement address to the Massachusetts Institute of Technology. The commencement address was, for the type of speech, remarkably brief and humorous. It began, "Ladies and gentleman of the class of 1997: Wear sunscreen."

---

[48] Ibid. At 98.

[49] Defendant alleges in its motion to dismiss that the E–MAILS concerned sales management and contained threats to "kill the backstabbing bastards" and referred to the planned Holiday party as the "Jim Jones Koolaid affair." Ibid. At 99.

[50] Ibid. at 100.

[51] Ibid. at 101.

But the commencement address never took place. The speech was, in fact, a column written by Mary Schmich, a columnist for The Chicago Tribune.[52] But the story gained widespread acceptance as fact and proved the power of the Internet to make history. Other examples include chain e-mail. People logging onto the Internet found e-mail messages that told of the story of Jessica Mydek. Jessica was only 7 years old and dying of cancer. Her e-mail urged people to live their lives fully and told recipients that for every e-mail message they forwarded the American Cancer Society and other corporations would contribute 3 cents to cancer research.[53]

Like the Vonnegut address, the e-mail was phony. The return address was a fake. The use of phony e-mails provide marketers with specific e-mail addresses and allow them to sell lists to advertisers for direct e-mail solicitation. While Postal regulations prohibit e-mail that seeks money (under private lottery laws), e-mail that seeks only to gain return addresses is, as yet, lawful.

The continuing growth of electronic communication provides novel questions of law and regulation. In some cases, the new questions may be answered by application of existing law such as the protection of intellectual property on the Internet under long-established copyright rules. For other issues, the courts and regulators will have to educate themselves and create new policies.

[52] Ian Fisher, "What Vonnegut Never Said Is All the Talk on the Internet," The New York Times, Aug. 6, 1997, p. A16.

[53] Iver Peterson, "Chain E–Mail: Heartrending Pleas, But Sometimes Counterfeit," The New York Times, July 14, 1997, p. C5.

Chapter 14

REGULATION OF ADVERTISING

SEC. 80. FROM *CAVEAT EMPTOR* TO CONSUMER PROTECTION

The history of advertising in the United States has seen a gradual change away from the motto of *caveat emptor* ("let the buyer beware").

It is hardly news that advertising is both a necessity and a nuisance in American society. It encourages and advances the nation's economy by providing information to the public about goods and services. Although its economic role in supporting the news media has been criticized, advertising has paid the bills for most of the news and vicarious entertainment which we receive. Historically, we owe advertising another debt. The rise of advertising in the 19th Century did much to free the press from excessive reliance on political parties or government printing contracts— which tended to color news columns with their bias.

Despite advertising's undeniably worthwhile contributions, this chapter unavoidably must emphasize the seamy side of American salesmanship. It will concentrate to a great extent upon issues raised by cheats and rascals. There can be little question that all too much advertising has been—and is—inexact, if not spurious and deceitful. Better units of the communications media now operate their advertising as a business with a definite obligation to the public. The realization evidently has dawned on some advertisers that unless there messages are both truthful and useful, the public may react unfavorably.

Advertising in the United States has a colorful if sometimes sordid past. From the first days of the nation throughout the Nineteenth Century, the philosophy motivating advertising was largely *laissez faire*. Too much advertising, in spirit if not to the letter, resembled this 1777 plug for "Dr. RYAN's *incomparable* WORM *destroying* SUGAR PLUMBS, *Necessary to be kept in all* FAMILIES:"[1]

> The plumb is a great diuretic, cleaning the veins of slime; it expels wind, and is a sovereign medicine in the cholic and griping of the guts. It allays and carries off vapours which occasion many disorders of the head. It opens all obstructions in the stomach, lungs, liver, veins, and bladder; causes a good appetite, and helps digestion.

Such exploitation of the *laissez faire* philosophy went unpunished for more than a century of this nation's existence. There was little or no regulation; what would be termed unreliable or even fraudulent advertising was published by some of the most respectable newspapers and periodicals. The general principle seemed to be that advertising columns were an open business forum with space for sale to all who applied.

Before 1900, advertising had little established ethical basis. The liar and the cheat capitalized on glorious claims for dishonest, shoddy merchandise. The faker lured the ill and suffering to build hopes on pills and tonics of questionable composition. Cures were promised by the bottle. Fortunes were painted for those who invested in mining companies of dubious reliability. Foods often were adulterated.

Exposés of frauds and fraud promoters who were using advertising to ensnare new prospects were important early in the Twentieth Century. Mark Sullivan exposed medical fakes and frauds in the *Ladies Home Journal* in 1904. Upton Sinclair's novel, *The Jungle,* revolted readers with its description of filthy conditions in meat-packing plants. Spurred by such exposés, Congress passed the Pure Food and Drug Act in 1906. Despite being a truth-in-labeling measure the 1906 statute did nothing to insure truth in advertising.[2]

Campaigning against advertising chicanery, many magazines and newspapers exposed fraudulent practices.[3] Some newspapers of this period, including the Cleveland Press and other Scripps–McRae League papers, monitored advertisements, refusing those which appeared to be fraudulent or misleading. A Scripps–McRae official

[1] Pennsylvania Gazette, March 12, 1777.

[2] Ibid.

[3] H.J. Kenner, The Fight for Truth in Advertising (1936) pp. 13–14; Alfred McClung Lee, The Daily Newspaper in America (1937), p. 328.

asserted that the newspaper group turned away approximately $500,000 in advertising revenue in one year by rejecting advertisements.

Such self-regulation has grown considerably over the years, and legal restraints have grown, too. People working in advertising come under all the laws which affect other branches of mass communications, including libel, invasion of privacy, copyright infringement, and obscenity. In addition, there are batteries of statutes and regulatory powers aimed at advertising *in addition to* the laws which affect, for example, the editorial side of a newspaper. There's the Food and Drug Administration (FDA), the Securities Exchange Commission (SEC), the Federal Communications Commission (FCC), and quite an alphabet soup of other federal agencies which gets into the advertising regulation act. Beyond that, there is increasing activity at the state level to attempt to control false or deceptive advertising. This chapter, then, can be only a sparse survey of advertising regulatory structures.

SEC. 81.   FEDERAL ADMINISTRATIVE CONTROLS: THE FEDERAL TRADE COMMISSION

The most important federal government controls over advertising have been exercised by the Federal Trade Commission, which has experienced considerable controversy.

The Federal Trade Commission

During the 20th Century, the Federal Trade Commission became more important than other official controls over advertising. The FTC Act was passed in 1914 to supplement sanctions against unfair competition which had been provided by the Sherman Anti–Trust Act of 1890 and by the Clayton Act of 1914.[4] Gradually, the FTC grew in power and assumed an increasingly important place in regulating advertising.

The Federal Trade Commission is an example of administrative rule and law-making authority delegated by Congress. Five Federal Trade Commissioners are appointed by the President and confirmed by the Senate for five-year terms. No more than three of the five commissioners may be from the same political party. The strength of the FTC as a regulatory agency has varied greatly over the years, changing with the level of Congressional support and with the variable political attitudes toward the effectiveness of government efforts to control unfair competition.

---

[4] Sherman Act, 26 Stat. 209 (1890), 15 U.S.C.A. § 1; Clayton Act, 38 Stat. 730 (1914), 15 U.S.C.A. § 12.

The FTC machinery—which is described later at some length—is set up to enforce Section 5 of the Federal Trade Commission Act, which says: "Unfair methods of competition in commerce, and unfair or deceptive practices in commerce, are declared unlawful."[5]

Early FTC cases which came before the courts cast doubt on the Commission's powers over advertising.[6] And when the FTC tried to stop an underwear manufacturer from mislabeling with terms such as "Natural Merino" or "Australian Wool," a U.S. Court of Appeals held that the FTC was powerless to prevent misleading labels.[7] The Supreme Court of the United States, however, upheld the FTC in language broad enough to support the Commission's power to control false labeling and advertising as unfair methods of competition. That was the emphasis: harm to competitors, *not* harm to consumers, although Justice Brandeis at least mentioned consumers. Speaking for the Court, Justice Brandeis declared that the FTC was justified in regarding misbranded goods as a fraud diverting customers from the producers of truthfully marked goods.[8]

Despite the efforts of the Federal Trade Commission, the idea of consumer protection had little support from the courts well into the Twentieth Century.[9]

The FTC's authority over advertising grew slowly. As late as 1936—when the FTC had existed for 22 years—the famed Judge Learned Hand of a U.S. Circuit Court decided a case against the FTC and in favor of an advertising scheme for encyclopedias which involved a false representation that free volumes would be given away.[10] "Such trivial niceties are too impalpable for practical affairs, they are will-o'-the-wisps, which divert attention from substantial evils," Judge Hand declared.

When this case reached the Supreme Court, Justice Hugo L. Black reacted indignantly, saying the sales method used to peddle

---

[5] 5 U.S.C.A. § 45(a)(1).

[6] Federal Trade Commission v. Gratz, 253 U.S. 421, 40 S.Ct. 572 (1920); L.B. Silver Co. v. Federal Trade Commission of America, 289 Fed. 985 (6th Cir.1923).

[7] Winsted Hosiery Company v. Federal Trade Commission, 272 Fed. 957 (2d Cir.1921).

[8] Federal Trade Commission v. Winsted Hosiery Co., 258 U.S. 483, 493–494, 42 S.Ct. 384, 385–386 (1922).

[9] See Federal Trade Commission v. Raladam Co., 283 U.S. 643, 51 S.Ct. 587 (1931). The Supreme Court of the United States held that Section 5 of the FTC Act did not forbid deceiving customers unless it could be shown that deceptive advertising injured competing businesses. Raladam Co. was unscrupulously selling an "obesity cure" made of "dessicated thyroid" as safe and effective when it doubtless was extremely dangerous to health when ingested.

[10] Federal Trade Commission v. Standard Educ. Society, 302 U.S. 112, 116, 58 S.Ct. 113, 115 (1937), quoting Judge Hand's opinion in the same case in the Circuit Court, 86 F.2d 692, 695 (2d Cir.1936).

the encyclopedia "successfully deceived and deluded its victims."[11] In overturning Judge Hand's "let the buyer beware" ruling in the lower court, Justice Black added:[12]

> The fact that a false statement may be obviously false to those who are trained and experienced does not change its character, nor take away its power to deceive others less experienced. There is no duty resting upon a citizen to suspect the honesty of those with whom he transacts business. Laws are made to protect the trusting as well as the suspicious.

In 1938, the year after the Supreme Court endorsed the concept of consumer protection from advertising excesses, Congress acted to give the FTC greater authority over deceptive advertising. The 1938 Wheeler–Lea Amendment changed Section 5 of the Federal Trade Commission Act to read: "Unfair methods of competition *in commerce,* and unfair or deceptive acts or practices in commerce, are hereby declared unlawful."[13] Note the italicized phrase. These words were added by the Wheeler–Lea Amendment, and this seemingly minor change in phrasing proved to be of great importance. No longer would the FTC have to prove that a misleading advertisement harmed a competing business. Now, if an advertisement deceived consumers, the FTC's enforcement powers could be put into effect.[14]

Aiming at false advertising, the Wheeler–Lea Amendment also inserted Sections 12 and 15(a) into the Federal Trade Commission Act. Section 12 provides:[15]

> It shall be unlawful for any person, partnership, or corporation to disseminate, or cause to be disseminated, any false advertisement—(1) by United States mails, or in [interstate] commerce by any means, for the purpose of inducing, or which is likely to induce, directly or indirectly, the purchase in commerce of food, drugs, devices or cosmetics.

Section 15(a) of the FTC Act says:

> The term "false advertising" means an advertisement, other than labeling, which is misleading in a material respect; and in determining whether any advertisement is misleading, there shall be taken into account (among other

11 302 U.S. 112, 117, 58 S.Ct. 113, 115 (1937).

12 302 U.S. 112, 116, 58 S.Ct. 113, 115 (1937).

13 52 Stat. 111 (1938); 15 U.S.C.A. § 45. Italics added.

14 Ibid.; Earl W. Kintner, "Federal Trade Commission Regulation of Advertising," Michigan Law Review Vol. 64:7 (May, 1966) pp. 1269–1284, at pp. 1275–1276, 1276n.

15 Section 12, 52 Stat. 114 (1938), 15 U.S.C.A. § 52; Section 15(a), 52 Stat. 114 (1938), 15 U.S.C.A. § 55(a).

things) not only representations made or suggested by statement, word, design, device, sound, or any combination thereof, but also the extent to which the advertisement fails to reveal facts material in the light of such representations or material with respect to consequences which may result from the use of the commodity * * *.

Such statutory changes gave the FTC some of the power it sought to protect consumers. As FTC Commissioners Everette MacIntyre and Paul Rand Dixon wrote in the 1960s, the Wheeler-Lea "amendment put the consumer on a par with the businessman from the standpoint of deceptive practices."[16]

Even so, this commission was often called "toothless" and other less flattering things. The delays which have dogged FTC enforcement procedures—especially those involving lengthy court battles—became legendary. An often cited example was the famed "Carter's Little Liver Pills" case. In 1943, the FTC decided that the word "liver" was misleading, and a classic and lengthy battle was on. Carter's Little Liver Pills had been a well known laxative product for 75 years. It took the FTC a total of 16 years—from 1943 to 1959—to win its point before the courts and get "liver" deleted.[17]

In addition, the FTC could not hope to regulate all advertising in (or affecting) interstate commerce—it could merely regulate by example, by pursuing a relatively small number of advertisers who appeared to operate in a deceptive fashion, in hopes that this would encourage others to tone down their advertising claims. It has been objected that during most of the FTC's history, it had tended to go after "little guys" or unimportant issues, too often ignoring misdeeds by big and powerful corporations which tied into important issues.

Strengthening the FTC: The 1970s

Strengthening of the FTC's regulatory powers came in 1973 in a sneaky fashion. While an energy crisis had the attention of Congress in 1973, a rider to the Trans–Alaska Pipeline Act gave the FTC powers it had sought for many years.[18] Thanks to that rider, the FTC was given the power to go to a federal court and seek an injunction against an advertisement which the FTC believes to be

[16] Everette MacIntyre and Paul Rand Dixon, "The Federal Trade Commission After 50 Years," Federal Bar Journal Vol.24:4 (Fall,1964) pp. 377–424, at p. 416.

[17] Carter Products, Inc. v. Federal Trade Commission, 268 F.2d 461 (9th Cir. 1959), certiorari denied 361 U.S. 884, 80 S.Ct. 155 (1959).

[18] 15 U.S.C.A. § 53. See Note, " 'Corrective Advertising' Orders of the Federal Trade Commission," 85 Harvard Law Review (Dec., 1971), pp. 485–486. The FTC has injunctive powers to deal with advertising for products which could pose an immediate health threat to consumers, including foods, drugs, cosmetics, and medical devices.

clearly in violation of federal law prohibiting false and misleading advertising. This injunctive sanction is little used because it is drastic. However, an injunction could, in critical instances, put a stop to ads which might otherwise continue to run through their campaign cycle—be it three months or six months or longer—before the FTC could take action.

The FTC was further strengthened in 1975 with what is commonly called the Moss–Magnuson Act, signed into law by President Gerald R. Ford.[19] Before the Moss–Magnuson Act, jurisdiction of the FTC was limited to advertising in **interstate commerce**, but under Moss–Magnuson, the FTC was given the power to regulate advertising **affecting** commerce. A small change, on the surface, but not in actuality. This wording change gave the FTC the power, in effect, to say that **all** commerce affects interstate commerce, and therefore is under FTC jurisdiction.[20]

Also, the Moss–Magnuson Act gave the FTC power to get beyond "regulation by example." That is, the FTC no longer had to be content with issuing a "cease and desist" order against a shave cream manufacturer using a misleading advertising campaign. Moss–Magnuson gave the FTC the ability to issue Trade Regulation Rules with the force of law. Fines for violation of a Trade Regulation Rule through misleading advertising can draw fines of up to $10,000 [check amount!] a day, so the FTC was given the clout to make advertisers pay attention.

Weakening the FTC: The 1980s

Although the Magnuson–Moss Act strengthened FTC powers, the activist stance of the FTC during the late 1970s brought a counter-attack from business plus legislation to weaken the FTC. Although the Great Sugar Controversy—an abortive FTC rulemaking to regulate e sugar in cereals heavily advertised to children—was by not means the only source of the FTC's troubles in the 1980s, it is an example of Commission behavior that drew fire from business and industry. In 1977 and 1978,[21]

> [t]he FTC staff proposed rules that would have resulted in a ban of most children's television advertising. The FTC primarily premised its far-reaching rulemaking proceeding on "unfairness," a standard with few legal precedents, rather than on

[19] Pub.L. 93–637, 88 Stat. 2183 (1975). The official title of the statute was the Consumer Product Warranties and Federal Trade Commission Improvements Act, providing disclosure standards for written consumer product warranties.

[20] The Moss–Magnuson Act overcame a 1941 Supreme Court decision which held that an Illinois company limiting its sales only to wholesalers in that state was not in interstate commerce, and therefore was beyond FTC control. See Federal Trade Commission v. Bunte Bros., 312 U.S. 349, 61 S.Ct. 580 (1941).

[21] Foote and Mnookin, op. cit., p. 90.

"deception," a well-established standard with more confining limits.

Issues involving regulation of children's advertising—including an FTC hearing on whether some sugary foods should be banned—resulted in strenuous attacks on the commission. FTC Michael Pertschuk, in particular, was accused of unfairness and asked by the Kellogg Company and by the Association of National Advertisers to disqualify himself from any hearing on sugary cereals. Pertschuk had incurred wrath by saying, among other things, that " 'Advertisers seize on the child's trust and exploit it as a weakness for their gain. * * * Cumulatively, commercials directed at children tend to distort the role of food.' "[22]

The FTC Improvements Act of 1980

Under severe political leverage and with millions of dollars in campaign contributions at stake, Congress folded like a $2 umbrella. Congress passed the ironically named Federal Trade Commission Improvements Act of 1980.[23] This legislation removed "unfairness" as a basis for regulation of commercial advertising. Instead of being to forbid "unfair" ads, the FTC had to show out-and-out deception, which is harder to prove. Also, the 1980 act removed FTC powers to make rules on children's advertising and on the funeral industry, another target of FTC activism for preying on the grief-stricken. In addition, the so-called "FTC Improvements Act" gave the FTC the problem of having Congress breathing down its neck. A 90–day review period was established by Congress for any proposed FTC Trade Regulation Rules. If both Houses of Congress pass a resolution objecting to an FTC rulemaking the rule is overturned. This was sometimes called the "two-House legislative veto."[24]

"Unfairness" in the 1990s

Remember that the key provision of the Federal Trade Commission Act is Section 5, which reads: "Unfair methods of competition in commerce, and unfair or deceptive practices in commerce, are declared unlawful." In 1994, Congress again tinkered with the operational meaning of "unfairness" as that term is to be interpret-

---

[22] The News Media & the Law, Vol. 3: No. 2 (May/June, 1979), p.18. The Court of Appeals for the D.C. Circuit ruled that Chairman Pertschuk's mind was not unalterably closed during the proceeding on children's advertising, refusing to disqualify him. Association of National Advertisers v. FTC, 627 F.2d 1151 (D.C.Cir. 1979). Even so, Pertschuk withdrew from that administrative rulemaking procedure.

[23] Pub.L.No. 96–252, 94 State. 374 (1980); Foote and Mnookin, op. cit., pp. 90–91.

[24] Pub.L.No.96–252, 94 Stat. 374 (1980), § 21, discussed in Earl W. Kintner, Christopher Smith, and David B. Goldston, "The Effect of the Federal Trade Commission Improvements Act of 1980 on the FTC's Rulemaking and Enforcement Authority," 58 Washington University Law Quarterly No. 4 (Winter, 19809), pp. 847–859, at 853.

ed by the FTC. The 1994 amendment to Section 5 added this language: Before an act can be found unlawful by the FTC on grounds of "unfairness," the Commission must show that "the act or practice causes or is likely to cause substantial injury to consumers which is not reasonably avoidable by consumers themselves and not outweighed by countervailing benefits to consumers or to competition."[25]

In other words, the FTC can't assume harm to consumers. The Commission must show, at the least, a likelihood that an advertisement will cause "substantial injury." At best, this can be a set of minor procedural hurdles for the FTC. At worst, Section 5, as amended, could stifle efforts to head off real harm to consumers.

FTC Organization and Advertising Regulation

The Federal Trade Commission looks formidable on a table of organization. Then, one realizes that the FTC's **entire** budget for handling **both** antitrust matters **and** protecting consumers (including regulation of advertising) was roughly $80 million annually in the mid 1990s. Even if $40 million were available exclusively to regulate advertising, keep in mind that the FTC's ad regulation resources are dwarfed by the size of the U.S. advertising industry: more than $150 billion per annum in 1998.

This is a classic overmatch. It is on the scale of a little league baseball team taking on the Cleveland Indians.

The FTC has three Bureaus, two of which do not deal directly with advertising regulation:

* The Bureau of Competition, the FTC's antitrust arm.

* The Bureau of Economics, which aids the FTC in predicting the economic consequences of its actions.

* The Bureau of Consumer Protection, which has a broad mandate to protect consumers against unfair, fraudulent or deceptive practices.

The Bureau of Consumer Protection has five divisions all having some relationship to advertising regulation. These divisions are:[26]

1) **The Division of Advertising Practices.** This unit will be discussed at some length, below.

2) The Division of Credit Practices.

3) The Division of Marketing Practices, which concentrates its enforcement activities on matters including fraudulent telemarketing schemes and "900" number telephone programs.

---

[25] Section 5 of the FTC Act, 15 U.S.C. § 45ff.

[26] A Guide to the Federal Trade Commission, 1992, ed., pp. 6–18.

4) The Division of Service Industry Practices, which includes enforcement activates on consumer fraud in sales of investments, art, precious metals, gems and rare coins. Also within this division's concerns are fraud or deception in advertising and sale of health care services, plus claims relating to cures and remedies and deceptive marketing of health care programs.

5) The Division of Enforcement checks on compliance with FTC cease and desist orders and enforces a number of laws and trade regulation rules, including requirements that companies ship purchases when promised.

The Division of Advertising Practices

FTC literature summarizes the scope of the Division of Advertising Practices' law enforcement activities in this fashion:[27]

* Tobacco and alcohol advertising, including monitoring for unfair practices or deceptive claims, and reporting to Congress on cigarette and smokeless tobacco labeling, advertising, and promotion.

* Advertising claims for food and over-the-counter drugs, particularly those relating to nutritional or health benefits of foods and safety and effectiveness of drugs or medical devices.

* Performance and energy-savings claims made for energy–related household and automotive products.

* Environmental performance claims made for consumer products, including claims that products are environmentally safe, ozone-friendly, or biodegradable.

* Infomercials, long-form (30–minute) advertising, to ensure that both the format and the content of programs are non-deceptive.

* General advertising at the national and regional level, particularly advertising making claims that are difficult for customers to evaluate.

"Weapons" of the FTC

The FTC has several weapons to use against misleading advertising; "getting the FTC's attention" is accomplished in a variety of ways. Letters from consumers or businesses, inquiries from Congress, or articles on consumer issues all may trigger FTC actions:[28]

---

[27] A Guide to the Federal Trade Commission, 1992 ed., pp. 6–7.

[28] Federal Trade Commission, "A Guide to the Federal Trade Commission," 1992 pamphlet, p. 19.

(1) **"Voluntary Compliance" (Consent Orders):** When the FTC suspects that a violation of law occurred, it will begin an investigation. Typically, such investigations are nonpublic, the FTC says, "in order to protect both the investigation and the company" being investigated. One mechanism available to the Commission is to try to get what is termed "voluntary compliance" by negotiating a "consent order" with the company. "A company that signs a consent order need not admit that it violated the law, but must agree to stop the disputed practices ..." as outlined by the FTC in a complaint.

(2) Administrative Complaints: If a consent agreement is not reached, the FTC may issue an administrative complaint. As the "Guide to the Federal Trade Commission" says, "If an administrative complaint is issued, a formal proceeding before an administrative law judge begins that is much like a court trial: evidence is submitted; testimony is heard; and witnesses are examined and cross-examined. If a law violation is found, a cease and desist order ... may be issued. Initial decisions by administrative law judges [Civil Service employees independent of the FTC] may be appealed to the full Commission." If the finding of a law violation is the FTC may issue a **cease and desist order**. Appeals from a final FTC decision may be made to a U.S. Court of Appeals and, ultimately, to the U.S. Supreme Court. Violation of such an order is punishable by a civil penalty of $10,000 a day for each offense.[29]

(3) Other FTC Sanctions: In situations where substantial harm to consumers, as in cases of suspected fraud, "the FTC can go directly to court to obtain an injunction, civil penalties, or consumer redress.... 'By going directly to court, the FTC can stop the fraud' ... to try to minimize the number of consumers injured."

(4) Publicity: The FTC publicizes complaints and cease and desist orders which it promulgates. News releases on such subjects are issued regularly to the media, and publicity has proven to be one of the strongest weapons at the FTC's disposal.[30]

As seen in the foregoing list, the FTC is not dependent solely on harsh actions such as cease-and-desist orders or court procedures. The Commission also takes positive steps to attempt to clarify its view of fair advertising practices. The Commission has three major programs which provide guidance to competitors and consumers. These are:

[29] Ibid.; Rosden & Rosden, op. cit., Vol. II, § 25.06.
[30] Federal Trade Commission, Your FTC: What It Is and What It Does, p. 19.

1. INDUSTRY GUIDES. This program involved issuing interpretations of the rules of the Commission to its staff. These
guides are made available to the public, and are aimed at
certain significant practices of a particular industry, especially
those involved in advertising and labeling. The guides can be
issued by the Commission as its interpretation of the law
without a conference or hearings, and, therefore, in a minimum
of time.

2. ADVISORY OPINIONS. In 1962, the FTC began giving
advisory opinions in response to industry questions about the
legality of a proposed industry action. Advisory opinions generally predict the FTC's response, although the Commission
reserves the right to reconsider its advice if the public interest
so requires.[31]

3. TRADE REGULATION RULES. The FTC publishes a notice
   before issuing a Trade Regulation Rule on a specific practice.
   Industry representatives may then comment on the proposed
   Trade Regulation before the rule is adopted and put into
   effect.[32]

Over the years, the FTC became much more active in challenging nutritional claims made for various food products in our health-
obsessed society. The Commission has developed standards to be
used to determine when a processed food can be called "lite" or
"light", and has challenged the right of those marketing products
with a substantial amount of saturated fat from claiming they are
"cholesterol free."

The Federal Trade Commission established guidelines in 1992
requiring documentation of advertising claims that use of a particular product benefits the environment. The FTC standards allow an
advertiser to claim that a product is "ozone safe," "biodegradable"
or "compostable" only if the manufacturer can produce evidence
that the ecological benefits of the product are substantial.

SEC. 82.   DECEPTIVENESS: THE FTC'S DEFINITION

**Even literally true statements may cause an advertiser diffi-
culty if those statements are part of a deceptive advertisement.**

Since the mid–1980s, the Federal Trade Commission has defined deceptive advertising as "a material representation, omission,
or practice that is likely to mislead a consumer acting reasonably
under the circumstances." Taking this definition apart, "material

[31] Rosden and Rosden, Law of Advertising, III, § 32.04.
[32] Ibid., § 32.05.

representation" may be taken to mean an important or decision-influencing statement in an advertisement. Also, the consumer who is to be protected is not naive or foolish, but a reasonable person who is acting sensibly. This is some distance from the old, avaricious slogan of caveat emptor ("let the buyer beware"), but it will not protect persons who do not protect themselves by "acting reasonably under the circumstances."[33]

Note that the definition does not refer to "false advertising." As noted advertising law scholar Ivan L. Preston has noted, many people will say regulators regulate "false advertising." He cautions:[34]

> That's fine for ordinary usage, but technically it's better to use the term deceptive advertising. By strict definition, false means only claims that are explicitly, literally false. However, ads also make claims [often by omission of key facts] that are explicitly true but produce false meanings.

Deception by Omission

In some advertisements, what is not said may be more important—and deceptive—than what is said. Omitted material, in other words, may make an implied claim which is misleading. The case of Bristol–Myers v. FTC (1984) involved various Young & Rubicam advertising campaigns for Bufferin, the well known pain reliever. For a time, Bufferin ads claimed that "doctors recommended Bufferin more than any other 'leading brand' of OTC [over-the-counter] internal analgesic." The FTC found it was true that from 1967 through 1971, Bufferin was recommended by doctors more often than Bayer, Excedrin, and Anacin—all, like Bufferin, aspirin-based pain relievers. Upholding an FTC finding of deceptiveness against Bristol–Myers, the Second Circuit stated:[35]

> ...[T]he Commission found that the ads conveyed the message that physicians recommend Bufferin more than any other OTC internal analgesic, and not just the three other leading brands of aspirin-based products. Since in fact doctors recommend Tylenol, Ascriptin and generic aspirin more often than Bufferin, the FTC found the message conveyed by the ads false and misleading.

Similarly, an over-reaching claim in an advertisement can cause difficulties for the advertiser. In the 1973 case of Firestone Tire & Rubber Co. v. FTC, the Commission took exception to ads with the slogan, " 'When you buy a Firestone tire—no matter how

---

[33] AMREP Corporation v. FTC, 768 F.2d 1171, 1177 (10th Cir.1985).

[34] Ivan L. Preston, The Tangled Web They Weave: Truth, Falsity and Advertisers (Madison: University of Wisconsin Press, 1994), p. 9.

[35] Bristol–Myers Company v. FTC, 738 F.2d 554, 563 (2d Cir.1984).

much or how little you pay—you get a safe tire.' "Note that the advertisement made no overt claim that all Firestone tires are safe, but the FTC ruled that the ad's language contained an implied message that all Firestone tires are absolutely safe. A U.S. Court of Appeals upheld the FTC's cease-and-desist order against Firestone.[36]

Television Ad Mock–Ups

To what extent can "reality" be suspended during the filming of a television commercial without producing an ad that improperly misleads the public? Products such as butter and ice cream that would melt under the hot studio lights of yesteryear had to be adulterated in some fashion in order to be filmed. New cars are parked under powerful floodlights to accentuate the sheen of their finishes, and the complexions of many of those breathtakingly beautiful models shown in cosmetic ads have been artfully retouched in the photo lab. Do such common practices actually deceive consumers and cause them to buy goods they would otherwise refuse to purchase?

The FTC attempted to establish a standard of non-deception in this field of television advertising during the early 1960s that is not likely to be recorded in the annals of history as one of bureaucracy's finest hours. The FTC's great "sandpaper caper" dragged on for five years at substantial expense to the American taxpayer and only minimal benefit to the American consumer.[37]

An aerosol shaving cream client, Rapid Shave, had commissioned the Ted Bates advertising agency to produce a series of television commercials dramatizing the superior qualities of that product. Realizing that all shaving creams were pretty much alike, some creative genius at the agency came up with the idea of demonstrating on camera that Rapid Shave could not only soften tough beards but even soften the roughest type of sandpaper. But when the agency tried to film the commercial, the shaving cream dampened the sandpaper, causing it to rip as it was being shaved. Rather than abandon the idea, the agency decided instead to coat a piece of plastic with sand to make it look like sandpaper, and use this plastic replica in its Rapid Shave campaign.

As the "sandpaper" was shown being shaved in the commercial, an announcer intoned, "To prove RAPID SHAVE'S super-moisturizing power, we put it right from the can onto this tough

[36] Firestone Tire & Rubber Co. v. FTC, 481 F.2d 246, 249 (6th Cir.1973), cert. denied 414 U.S. 1112, 94 S.Ct. 841 (1973).

[37] Federal Trade Commission v. Colgate–Palmolive Co., 380 U.S. 374, 85 S.Ct. 1035 (1965). For an amusing account of this case, see Daniel Seligman, "The Great Sandpaper Shave: A Real–Life Story of Truth in Advertising," Fortune (Dec.1964) pp. 131–133ff.

dry sandpaper. It was applied * * * soak * * * and off in a stroke."[38]

One hopes that few consumers rushed out to buy Rapid Shave to see whether they could shave sandpaper. Colgate–Palmolive, the manufacturer of Rapid Shave, may well have been startled when the FTC issued a complaint contending that this ad constituted a deceptive advertising practice. However, when an FTC hearing examiner discovered that sandpaper actually could be shaved with Rapid Shave after it had soaked to the paper for an hour or so, he dismissed the complaint.[39]

Unwilling to allow the public to be led astray by this sandpaper hoax, the FTC reversed the hearing examiner's finding and issued a cease and desist order declaring that all depictions in advertisements that were not "accurate representations were illegal."

But a Circuit Court of Appeals concluded that the FTC was going too far in declaring all mock-ups illegal. The court declared, "where the only untruth is that the substance [the viewer] sees on the screen is artificial, and the visual appearance is otherwise a correct and accurate representation of the product itself, he is not injured."[40]

In May, 1963, the Commission issued its final order that Colgate and Bates cease and desist from:[41]

> Unfairly or deceptively advertising any * * * product by presenting a test, experiment or demonstration that (1) is represented to the public as actual proof of a claim made for the product which is material to inducing a sale, and (2) is not in fact a genuine test, experiment or demonstration being conducted as represented and does not in fact constitute actual proof of the claim * * *.

Although Colgate and Bates also challenged the 1963 FTC order, the Supreme Court of the United States made the order stick. Note that the use of *all* mock-ups in televised commercials was not forbidden as deceptive. The Court found that "the undisclosed use of plexiglas" instead of sandpaper in the Rapid Shave commercials was "a material deceptive practice."

[38] 380 U.S. 374, 376, 85 S.Ct. 1035, 1038 (1965).

[39] 380 U.S. 374, 376–377, 85 S.Ct. 1035, 1038 (1965).

[40] 380 U.S. 374, 381, 85 S.Ct. 1035, 1040 (1965), quoting 310 F.2d 89, 94 (1st Cir.1962).

[41] 380 U.S. 374, 382, 85 S.Ct. 1035, 1041 (1965), quoting Colgate Palmolive Co., No. 7736, FTC May 7, 1963. This clause was added by the FTC for the benefit of Ted Bates & Co., because advertising agencies do not always have all the information about a product that a manufacturer has. The clause said, " 'provided, however, that respondent [Bates] neither knew nor had reason to know that the product, article or substance used in the test, experiment, or demonstration was a mock-up or a prop.' "

Marbles in the Soup

The Campbell Soup Company, however, slipped over the fine line between "demonstration" and "deception," at least in the eyes of the Federal Trade Commission. Campbell Soup consented to stop the practice of putting marbles in bowls of soup to force solid chunks of meat and vegetables to the surface, making them visible to viewers of television ads.[42]

SEC. 83. CORRECTIVE ADVERTISING ORDERS OF THE FTC

The Federal Trade Commission has attempted to enforce truth in advertising by requiring some advertisers to correct past misstatements.

An old FTC action against Standard Oil Company of California illustrates how the Commission has made "corrective advertising" work. In the late 1960s, the oil company's advertising claimed that its Chevron gasoline, thanks to an additive called F–310, could significantly decrease harmful substances in auto exhaust emissions, thus helping to reduce air pollution. This sort of "we're good for the environment" advertising has been termed "Eco–Porn" by cynical critics of advertising.

The FTC issued a cease and desist order to halt allegedly misleading F–310 advertising claims, but the matter did not end there. The FTC also demanded that the Standard Oil Company run "corrective" ads for a year, adding another FTC sanction to use against deceptive advertising in addition to a cease-and-desist order. In the Chevron F–310 case, the Standard Oil Company of California had to disclose that its earlier advertising campaign had included false and deceptive statements. The Commission said that 25 per cent of the advertising for Chevron—either published space or broadcast time—should be devoted to making "affirmative disclosures" about the earlier advertising.[43] Ultimately, the U.S. Court of Appeals for the Ninth Circuit held that the FTC was correct in concluding that the F–310 commercials had a tendency to mislead consumers. However, the FTC was held to have erred in having issued an order against Standard Oil Company asking the company to refrain from making certain representations about F–310 "or

---

[42] Campbell Soup Co., 3 Trade Reg.Rep. Para. 19,261 (FTC, 1970); the Campbell Soup Co. consented to stop the practice of putting marbles in soup bowls to force solid chunks of meat and vegetables to the surface of the soup so as to be visible to viewers of television ads.

[43] 3 Trade Reg.Rep.Para. 19,420 (FTC Complaint issued, Dec. 29, 1970). See also William F. Lemke, Jr., "Souped Up Affirmative Disclosure Orders of the Federal Trade Commission," 4 University of Michigan Journal of Law Reform (Winter, 1970) pp. 180–181; Note, " 'Corrective Advertising' Orders of the Federal Trade Commission," 85 Harvard Law Review (December, 1971) pp. 477–478.

any other product in commerce" unless every statement is true and completely substantiated. The court said that order was too broad, and had to be narrowed to deal only with gasoline additive F–310.[44]

Other corporate defendants in cases where the FTC has sought to obtain corrective advertising include Coca Cola, for claims made about nutrient and vitamin content of its Hi–C fruit drinks,[45] and ITT Continental Baking Company, for ads implying that eating Profile Bread could help people to lose weight. The FTC charged that Profile was different from other bread only in being more thinly sliced, meaning that there were seven fewer calories per slice. ITT Continental Baking Company consented to a cease and desist order which does two things: first, it prohibits all further claims of weight-reducing attributes for Profile Bread, and second, the company has to devote 25 per cent of its Profile advertising for one year to disclosing that the bread is not effective for weight reduction.[46]

Similarly, the FTC ordered in 1972 that Warner–Lambert make this disclosure in its advertisements for some months: "Contrary to prior advertising, Listerine will not help prevent colds or sore throats or lessen their severity." Hearing the case on appeal, the Court of Appeals for the Fifth Circuit affirmed the order, but dropped the phrase "Contrary to Prior Advertising."[47] Writing for the court in 1977, Circuit Judge J. Skelly Wright found persuasive scientific testimony that gargling Listerine could not help a sore throat because its active ingredients could not penetrate tissue cells to reach viruses.[48] In this case the Warner–Lambert Company was not playing for small monetary stakes. The FTC required the corrective advertising statement to appear in Listerine advertising until about $10 million had been spent on touting the mouthwash.

The Court of Appeals thus approved the Commission's standard for imposing corrective advertising. The FTC standard said if a deceptive advertisement played a substantial role in creating or reinforcing "in the public's mind a false and material belief which lives on after the false advertising ceases," then there is clear harm to competitors and to the consuming public. Since merely ceasing the ad cannot avert injury to the public, the FTC said it could require corrective ads: "affirmative action designed to terminate the otherwise continuing ill effects of the advertisement."[49]

[44] Standard Oil Co. of California v. FTC, 577 F.2d 653, 658 (9th Cir.1978).

[45] 3 Trade Reg.Rep. Para. 19,351 (FTC, 1970).

[46] 3 Trade Reg.Rep. Para. 19,780 (FTC, Aug. 17, 1971); Note, " 'Corrective Advertising' Orders of the Federal Trade Commission," 85 Harvard Law Review (December, 1971), p. 478.

[47] Warner–Lambert Co. v. FTC, 562 F.2d 749, 762 (D.C.Cir.1977).

[48] Ibid., p. 754.

[49] Ibid., p. 762.

Comparative Advertising

People reading or viewing advertising sometimes see claims made that Product A is "better," "more effective," etc. than Product B. This is what is known as "comparative advertising" and has been encouraged by the Federal Trade Commission in the belief that this will assist consumers in getting more needed information about products. This comparative advertising, however, must be susceptible of substantiation; false and misleading comparative statements will draw legal consequences.

For example, consider American Home Products [makers of Anacin] v. Johnson and Johnson [makers of Tylenol]. Anacin ads based on the theme "Your Body Knows" contended that Anacin was superior to Tylenol, that it was more effective in reducing inflammation, and that it worked faster than Tylenol. Johnson and Johnson [Tylenol] complained to the three television networks that the Anacin advertising was deceptive and misleading. American Home Products [Anacin] countered by suing Johnson and Johnson, claiming that the makers of Tylenol violated the Lanham Trademark Act by disparaging a competitor's product,[50] seeking an injunction against Tylenol advertising.[51]

This lawsuit backfired, however, because a federal district court dismissed the American Home Products [Anacin] suit and instead slapped a permanent injunction on American Home Products forbidding publishing of a misleading advertisement.[52]

The Lanham Act (Sec. 43a) & Deceptive Advertising

The Lanham Trademark Act is another lever to be used with the FTC Act to discourage deceptive advertising or promotional activities. Section 43(a) of the Lanham Act, as amended in 1989, makes it possible for persons who believe they are injured by deceptive advertising to sue for damages. P. Cameron DeVore and Robert D. Sack have written that the present Section 43(a) is intended to operate as a commercial defamation act. That portion of the Lanham Act says that individuals who misrepresent "the nature, characteristics, qualities or geographical origins of his or her or another person's goods, services, or commercial activities shall be liable in a civil action [brought] by any person who believes that he or she is likely to be damaged by such act."[53]

[50] Lanham Trademark Act, 44 Fed.Reg. 4738 § 43(a).

[51] American Home Products Corp. v. Johnson and Johnson, 436 F.Supp. 785 (S.D.N.Y.1977), affirmed 577 F.2d 160 (2d Cir.1978).

[52] Ibid.

[53] P. Cameron DeVore and Robert D. Sack, "Advertising and Commercial Speech," in James C. Goodale, chairman, Communications Law 1993 (New York: Practising Law Institute, 1993), p. 175, see Lanham Act as amended in 1987, Sec. 43(a), 15 U.S.C.A. Sec. 1125(a) (1988).

And the Lanham Act can be used to protect against unauthorized use of trademarks. The gigantic brewing firm of Anheuser–Busch sued Balducci Publications because its magazine—"Snicker"—had run a fictitious parody ad for "Michelob Oily," using the beer manufacturer's familiar trademarks as part of the effort at humor. The brewer won what it sought: a ruling that "Snicker" magazine's use of Anheuser–Busch's virtually unaltered trademarks could create an unfavorable impression of Michelob with readers. Anheuser–Busch won $1 in damages plus an injunction against further unauthorized use of the trademark by the magazine.[54]

Another part of Section 43(a) of the Lanham Act allows an individual or company to sue for damages for confusion created by an advertisement misrepresenting a product. That is precisely what singer Tom Waits did when a singer imitating Waits was used in a Frito–Lay commercial to tout a new product. Holding that Waits has a recognizable product (his voice), the Court of Appeals for the Second 9th Circuit upheld a $2.375 million judgment for Waits for linking his identity to a commercial product without his permission.[55]

Comparative advertising cases can involve both ad regulation and copyright law. Triangle Publications—when publishers of *TV Guide*—sued Knight–Ridder Newspapers, publishers of *The Miami Herald*. The newspaper had started a television program guide as a Sunday supplement.

The *TV Guide* complaint stemmed from the newspaper's use of a copyrighted cover in a promotional ad. Ultimately, it was held that *The Herald*'s use of the *TV Guide* cover in the context of a truthful comparative advertisement was indeed a "fair use".[56] (See Copyright, Chap. 15, on the defense of "fair use.")

Advertising Substantiation

Since the early 1970s, the FTC has set down requirements that advertisers make available proof—"substantiation," in FTC terminology—to back up their claims. At the start of its substantiation efforts, the Commission demanded of entire industries—e.g. soap and detergents, air conditioners, deodorant manufacturers—that they come forward to back up their claims. An early case in the substantiation area was the FTC proceeding, In re Pfizer, Inc., decided in 1972. Pfizer, a chemical/drug manufacturing concern,

---

[54] Anheuser–Busch v. Balducci Publications, 28 F.3d 769 (8th Cir.1994), 22 Med. L.Rptr. 2001.

[55] Waits v. Frito–Lay, Inc., 978 F.2d 1093, 1101–1105 (9th Cir.1992).

[56] Triangle Publications, Inc. v. Knight–Ridder Newspapers, Inc., 626 F.2d 1171 (5th Cir.1980), affirming 445 F.Supp. 875 (S.D.Fla.1978), 3 Med.L.Rptr. 2086; see also DeVore and Sack, op. cit., p. 476.

had advertised its "Un–Burn" product with claims that its application would stop the discomfort of sunburn by tuning out nerve endings. The FTC told Pfizer that unless it could prove such a claim, that would be considered an unfair (and therefore illegal) trade practice. That meant an advertiser should have "a reasonable basis [for its claims] before disseminating an ad."[57] As FTC Associate Director for Advertising Practices Wallace S. Snyder wrote in 1984, " * * * ads for objective claims imply that the advertiser has a prior reasonable basis for making the claim. In light of the implied representation of substantiation, therefore, a performance claim that lacks a reasonable basis is deceptive."[58]

State Regulation of Advertising

In the 1980s, a time in which "deregulation" was a major theme of the Reagan Administration, one effect was a continued scaling back of the aggressiveness of the nation's prime governmental regulator of advertising, the Federal Trade Commission. But from the mid–1980s on, occasional comments were heard from leaders in the advertising business to the effect that deregulation had its problems, too. Although "getting government off the back of business and the public" was good for political mileage, when FTC regulation diminished, regulatory efforts in some states to some extent moved into the void. Perhaps it might be said that regulators, like nature, abhor a vacuum.

Advertising executives had reason to worry as state ad regulation became more insistent. Whatever their feelings about the FTC, state-to-state regulatory differences in the 1980s threatened to assemble a crazy-quilt pattern of regulations.

Part of the rise of more aggressive state regulation of advertising may be found in the National Association of Attorneys' General. In February, 1988, Daniel Oliver, then chairman of the Federal Trade Commission, expressed some doubts about the states' consumer-protection, saying the state attorneys general were exceeding their authority. Oliver added, "Obviously, deregulation gives the opportunity for the most restrictive of attorneys general to bring cases that will have national effect, and that's not what the American consumer needs."[59]

[57] Wallace S. Snyder, "Advertising Substantiation Program," in Christopher Smith and Christian S. White, chairmen, The FTC 1984 (New York: Practising Law Institute, 1984), p. 121; In re Pfizer, Inc., 81 FTC 23 (1972).

[58] Snyder, loc. cit., citing General Dynamics Corp., 82 FTC 488 (1973), and also Firestone Tire & Rubber Co., 81 FTC 398 (1972), affirmed 481 F.2d 246 (6th Cir.1973), certiorari denied 414 U.S. 1112, 94 S.Ct. 841 (1973).

[59] M.D. Hinds, "States Are Taking Lead on Consumer Protection," The New York Times, Feb. 8, 1988, p. 12.

In the late 1980s, The New York Times reported that attorneys general of New York, Texas, California, Missouri, Kansas, Illinois, Minnesota and Wisconsin created a study group to look into consumer complaints about airline fares. "The group reported . . . that airline advertising was deceptive and that it amounted to a 'bait-and-switch' practice," and later distributed enforcement guidelines on false advertising. One consumer advocate even told The New York Times in 1988 that many activists were working with state attorneys general, getting action to resolve complaints also filed—evidently with little result—with Federal agencies.[60]

In 1992, however, the U.S. Supreme Court held 5–3 that the Airline Deregulation Act of 1978 denies a State the right to enforce any law relating to air carrier rates, routes or services and also denies it the right to regulate advertising pertaining to those matters. Dan Morales, former attorney general of Texas, had sued Trans World Airlines for failing to follow advertising disclosure requirements relating to "frequent flyer" programs established by the National Association of Attorneys General.

Speaking for the Supreme Court's majority, Justice Antonin Scalia found that the state requirements imposed unnecessarily heavy financial burdens on airlines. He held requiring airlines to create different ads to conform to the laws of various states did not benefit consumers to the extent necessary to justify such a burden.[61]

In the late 1980s, under FTC Commission Chair Janet Steiger, the Commission to a considerable extent repaired relations with the National Association of [State] Attorneys General (NAAG). (One wit speculated that NAAG might also stand for National Association of Aspiring Governors.) State Attorneys General, whose concern for consumers seemed on some occasions to be fueled by high-profile cases useful to the politically ambitious, had been free-lancing on national problems. Thus, an advertisement might be acceptable (or at least not challenged) in many states but might be unacceptable "bait and switch" advertising to the Attorney General of, say, the New York. The result was that one state could cause restructuring of a national advertising campaign.

The National Association of Attorneys General (NAAG): Enlisting in the "Tobacco Wars" of the Late 1990s

During the 1990s the organization of state attorneys general became even more active. The issue: regulation of sales and advertising tobacco. By mid–1997, Big Tobacco—Philip Morris, RJR Nabisco Holdings Corp., B.A.T. Industries, Brown & Williamson

---

[60] Ibid.

[61] Morales v. Trans World Airlines, 504 U.S. 374, 112 S.Ct. 2031 (1992).

and Loew's Corp's. Lorillard—was ready to compromise with regulators and critics. There had been a drumfire of criticism from Dr. David Kessler, Commissioner of the Food and Drug Administration and from former Surgeon General C. Everett Koop, and they sang along in a chorus with public health organizations including the American Cancer Society and the American Heart Association. This common-sense chorus was assisted by scores of lawsuits filed by cancer victims or their survivors, and by lawsuits filed by state attorneys general seeking billings in damages to reimburse states for healthcare costs caused by smoking. Those lawsuits, not incidentally, smoked out documents giving the lie to tobacco executives' claims that they had doubts that tobacco was a carcinogen or that nicotine was addictive.

The $50 billion-a-year tobacco industry reached a settlement agreement on June 27, 1997, reaching agreement with the attorneys general of two-thirds of the states. This agreement called for the tobacco industry to cough up $368.5 billion over a 25-year period, to submit to FDA regulation, including giving the FDA power to regulate tar and nicotine levels and even to ban nicotine from cigarettes by the year 2009.

The tobacco industry agreed to huge changes in its marketing and advertising. All human images or cartoon characters—notably the Marlboro Man and Joe Camel—were to be banned. Tobacco billboards and even store signs facing the outside would be outlawed. Advertisements would be in black and white text with no illustrations, except in adult establishments and publications. Showing off tobacco labels in movies would be halted, as would distribution of merchandise with brand names and logos of tobacco products.[62]

The big compromise with Big Tobacco, however, was torpedoed when President Clinton would not endorse it. The President wanted a freer hand for the FDA to regulate nicotine as an addictive drug, to get rid of a proposed $50 billion tax break for tobacco manufacturers, and to provide some compensation tobacco farmers for lost income.[63] Without President Clinton's vigorous support, the deal would not go through—and it might not be accepted by Congress, in any case, given the political clout of tobacco-state legislators. As of late 1997, the agreement seemed to have a long way to go in clearing Congress. Would Congress act responsibly? Consider the words of historian Richard Kluger: "If government

[62] See, e.g., Jill Smolowe, "Big Tobacco Takes a Hit," Time, June 30, 1997, pp. 25–28; Matthew Cooper, "Ifs, Ands and Butts," Newsweek, June 30, 1997, pp. 30–34.

[63] Barry Meier, "White House's Bottom Line Is Reported in Tobacco Deal," The New York Times, September 8, 1997, p. A9; New York Times News Service, "President to reject nationwide tobacco deal," The Knoxville News–Sentinel, September 17, 1997, p. A10.

will not act effectively to protect the public health, how can its very existence be justified?" Death, after all, is relentlessly nonpartisan.[64]

SEC. 84.   OTHER FEDERAL ADMINISTRATIVE CONTROLS

In addition to the Federal Trade Commission, many other federal agencies—including the Food and Drug Administration, the Federal Communications Commission, and the United States Postal Service—exert controls over advertising in interstate commerce.

Although of paramount importance as an advertising regulator, the FTC does not stand alone among federal agencies in its fight against suspect advertising. Federal agencies which have powers over advertising include:

(1) The Food and Drug Administration

(2) The United States Postal Service

(3) The Securities and Exchange Commission

(4) The Alcohol and Tobacco Tax Division of the Internal Revenue Service

Such a list by no means exhausts the number of federal agencies which, tangentially at least, can exert some form of control over advertising. Bodies such as the Federal Aeronautics Administration and the Interstate Commerce Commission and the Federal Power Commission have power to curtail advertising abuses connected with matters under each agency's jurisdiction.[65]

1.   The Food and Drug Administration and Tobacco Smoke

The Food and Drug Administration's (FDA) activities in controlling labelling and misbranding overlap the powers of the FTC to a considerable degree. The Pure Food and Drug Act gives the FDA jurisdiction over misbranding and mislabeling of foods, drugs, and cosmetics.[66] The FTC, however, was likewise given jurisdiction over foods, drugs, and cosmetics by the Wheeler–Lea Amendment.[67] It

---

[64] Richard Kluger, "Is It Really a Good Deal?" Time, June 39, 1997, at p. 32. Kluger won the 1997 Pulitzer Prize for his book, Ashes to Ashes: America's Hundred-year Cigarette War, the Public Health, and the Unabashed Triumph of Philip Morris.

[65] See Note, "The Regulation of Advertising," Columbia Law Review Vol. 56:7 (Nov. 1956) pp. 1019–1111, at p. 1054, citing 24 Stat. 378 (1887), 49 U.S.C.A. § 1 (ICC); 41 Stat. 1063 (1920), 16 U.S.C.A. § 791(a) (FTC); 52 Stat. 1003 (1938), as amended, 49 U.S.C.A. § 491.

[66] 52 Stat. 1040 (1938), 21 U.S.C.A. § 301.

[67] See "The Wheeler Lea Amendment" to the Federal Trade Commission Act, 52 Stat. 111 (1938), as amended, 15 U.S.C.A. § 45(a)(1).

used to be said that the FTC and the FDA have agreed upon a division of labor whereby FTC concentrates on false advertising and the FDA focuses attention on false labelling.[68] However, this division of labor is quite inexact. Pamphlets or literature distributed with a product have been held to be "labels" for purposes of FDA enforcement.[69]

Unlike the five-commissioner FTC—with no more than three individuals from one political party—the FDA is headed by one individual. That can add up to more aggressive approaches to high-profile controversies by the FDA than the FTC will take on. The high-energy Dr. David Kessler, a physician and a lawyer, became FDA Commissioner in 1991, resigning in 1997. In the early to mid-1990s, the FDA was handed increased responsibility for blood safety and drugs from aspirin to AIDS medications. As science writer Herbert Burkholz wrote, "25 cents out of every dollar spent by the American consumer goes for products regulated by the FDA."

The FDA also has responsibility for inspection of fish and meat and food products, under the 1938 Federal Food, Drug, and Cosmetic Act. Dr. Kessler faced daunting challenges, but set about streamlining FDA investigations and enforcement, and was much in the headlines in 1994 as he took on tobacco industry claims that nicotine is not addictive. Among Dr. Kessler's suggestions to Congress was the possibility of regulating nicotine as a drug (to be sold by prescriptions at pharmacies?) and restricting cigarette advertising to protect children from intentional or unintentional encouragement to smoke.[70] As the FDA confronted the tobacco industry, the FTC decided not to take on the "Joe Camel" billboards and magazine ads criticized on the theory they were aimed at making cigarette smoking attractive to children. The crusading Dr. Kessler, however, resigned from the FDA in 1997.

2. The U.S. Postal Service

Postal controls over advertising can be severe. Congress was provided with lawmaking power to operate the postal system under Article I, Section 8 of the Constitution. This power was long delegated by Congress to a Postmaster General and his Post Office Department. It has long been established that the mails could not be used to carry things which, in the judgment of Congress, were

[68] See, for example, 2 CCH Trade Reg.Rep. (10th ed.), Paragraph 8540, p. 17,081 (1954).

[69] See United States v. Kordel, 164 F.2d 913 (7th Cir.1947); United States v. Article of Device Labeled in Part "110 V Vapozone," 194 F.Supp. 332 (N.D.Cal. 1961).

[70] Philip J. Hilts, "Ban on Cigarettes Could be Avoided, FDA Chief Says," The New York Times, June 29, 1994, pp. A1, A10.

socially harmful.[71] The Postmaster General had the power to exclude articles or substances which Congress has proscribed as nonmailable. With the passage of the Postal Reorganization Act of 1970, the Post Office Department was abolished as a Cabinet-level agency, and was replaced by the United States Postal Service, a subdivision of the Executive branch.[72]

Perhaps the Postal Service's greatest deterrent to false advertising is contained in the power to halt delivery of materials suspected of being designed to defraud mail recipients.[73] The Postal Service can order nondelivery of mail, and can impound suspected mail matter.[74]

The administrative fraud order is not the only kind of mail fraud action available to the Postal Service. Instead of administrative procedure through the Service, a *criminal* mail fraud case may be started. Criminal cases are prosecuted by a U.S. attorney in a United States District Court. Conviction under the federal mail fraud statute can result in a fine of up to $1,000, imprisonment for up to 5 years, or both.[75] Criminal fraud orders are used when the U.S. Postal Service wishes to operate in a punitive fashion. The administrative fraud orders, on the other hand, are more preventive in nature.

3. The Securities and Exchange Commission

Securities markets are attractive to fast-buck artists, so the sale and publicizing of securities are kept under a watchful governmental eye. Most states have "Blue Sky" laws which enable a state agency to halt the circulation of false or misleading information about the sale of stocks, bonds or the like.[76] The work of the Securities and Exchange Commission, however, is far more important in protecting the public.

After the stock market debacle of 1929, strong regulations were instituted at the federal level to prevent deceptive statements about securities. Taken together, the Securities Act of 1933[77] and the Securities Exchange Act of 1934[78] gave the S.E.C. great power over the sale and issuance of securities.

---

[71] See, for example, early federal tax laws on obscenity discussed in Chapter 11, or see Public Clearing House v. Coyne, 194 U.S. 497, 24 S.Ct. 789 (1904).

[72] 39 U.S.C.A. § 3003.

[73] Ibid., III, § 50.02.

[74] Ibid., Rosden & Rosden II, § 18.02, n. 17.

[75] 18 U.S.C.A. § 1341; Ague, ibid., p. 61.

[76] See Note, "The Regulation of Advertising," Columbia Law Review op. cit. p. 1065.

[77] 48 Stat. 74 (1933), 15 U.S.C.A. § 77.

[78] 48 Stat. 881 (1934), as amended, 15 U.S.C.A. §§ 78(a)–78(jj).

Sale of securities to investors cannot proceed until complete and accurate information has been given, registering the certificates with the S.E.C.[79] A briefer version of the registration statement is used in the "prospectus" circulated among prospective investors before the stock or bond can be offered for sale.[80] If misleading statements have been made about a security "in any material respect" in either registration documents or in the prospectus, the Commission may issue a "stop order" which removes the right to sell the security.[81] Furthermore, unless a security is properly registered and its prospectus accurate, it is a criminal offense to use the mails to sell it or to advertise it for sale.[82]

An unscrupulous seller of securities has more to fear than just the S.E.C. Under a provision of the United States Code, a person who has lost money because he was tricked by a misleading prospectus may sue a number of individuals, including persons who signed the S.E.C. registration statement and every director, officer, or partner in the firm issuing the security.[83]

4. The Alcohol and Tobacco Tax Division, Internal Revenue Service

Ever since this nation's unsuccessful experiment with prohibition, the federal government has kept a close eye on liquor advertising. The responsible agency is the Alcohol and Tobacco Tax Division of the Internal Revenue Service.[84] Liquor advertising may not include false or misleading statements, and may not disparage competing products. False statements may include misrepresenting the age of a liquor, or claiming that its alcoholic content is higher than it is in reality.[85]

The Alcohol and Tobacco Tax Division has harsh sanctions at its disposal. If an advertiser violates a regulation of the Division, he is subject to a fine, and could even be put out of business if his federal liquor license is revoked.[86]

The FTC and other federal agencies by no means provide the whole picture of controls over advertising. There are many state regulations affecting political advertising and legal advertising by government bodies, but they cannot be treated here. States also

[79] 48 Stat. 77 (1933), as amended, 15 U.S.C.A. § 77(f).

[80] 48 Stat. 78 (1933), 15 U.S.C.A. § 77(j).

[81] 48 Stat. 79 (1933), as amended, 15 U.S.C.A. § 77(h)(b) and (d). For an example of litigation charging false statements in the sale of corporate bonds, see Escott v. BarChris Construction, 283 F.Supp. 643 (S.D.N.Y.1968).

[82] 48 Stat. 84 (1933), as amended, 15 U.S.C.A. § 77(e).

[83] 48 Stat. 82 (1933), 15 U.S.C.A. § 77(k).

[84] 27 U.S.C.A. § 205.

[85] Ibid.

[86] Ibid.

regulate the size and location of billboards, but space does not permit discussion of these statutes. We now turn to consideration of some of the ways in which states have regulated commercial advertising in the mass media.

SEC. 85. THE PRINTERS' INK STATUTE

Most states have adopted some version of the model statute which makes fraudulent and misleading advertising a misdemeanor.

One of the best known restraints upon advertising exists at the state level in the various forms of the Printers' Ink statute adopted in 48 states. *Printer's Ink* magazine, in 1911, advocated that states adopt a model statute which would make false advertising a misdemeanor. Leaders in the advertising and publishing world realized the difficulty in securing prosecutions for false advertising under the usual state fraud statutes. Considerable initiative in gaining state enactment of Printers' Ink statutes was generated through the Better Business Bureau and through various advertising clubs and associations.

All but two states—Delaware and New Mexico—have some version of the Printers' Ink statute on their books.[87] Although the Printers' Ink statute is famous, its fame is greater than its present-day usefulness as a control over advertising. Relatively few relevant cases exist which indicate that the statute has seen little use in bringing cheating advertisers to court. The Printers' Ink statute may still be useful as a guideline, or in providing a sanction which local Better Business Bureaus may threaten to invoke even if they seldom do so.[88]

The Printers' Ink statute is aimed and enforced primarily against advertisers rather than against units of the mass media which may have no knowledge that an ad is false or misleading.[89] This statute was widely adopted, apparently because the common law simply did not provide adequate remedies against false advertising, especially in an economy which has grown so explosively.

SEC. 86. LOTTERIES

Federal and state prohibitions on advertising or publicizing of lotteries are changing as many states have started lotteries as revenue measures.

[87] "Basis for State Laws on Truth in Publishing—The Printers' Ink Model Statute," Reprint, Printers' Ink Publishing Corp., 1959. Note, "Developments in the Law—Deceptive Advertising," Harvard Law Review, op. cit., p. 1122.

[88] Note, "The Regulation of Advertising," op. cit. p. 1057.

[89] Ibid., pp. 1059–1060; State v. Beacon Pub. Co., 141 Kan. 734, 42 P.2d 960 (1935).

The theory of laws forbidding advertising or publicizing lotteries is that the public needed to protected from gambling.[90] In recent years, however, the desperate search for revenues led to creation of government-run lotteries in many states, making federal efforts to silence advertising or publicity hopelessly outdated.

What then, is a lottery? There are three elements:

(1) *Consideration*—This usually means money paid to purchase a lottery ticket or a chance on an auto or some other item which a service organization is offering to raise money. But in some states, consideration need not be money paid. Just the effort required to enter a contest, as going to a store to get an entry blank or having to mail a product label, at times has been termed "consideration."[91]

(2) *Prize*—A prize in a lottery is something of value, and generally of greater worth than the consideration invested.

(3) *Chance*—The element of chance—the gambling element—is what led Victorian–era Congressmen to pass the first federal statutes against lotteries in 1890. There can, however, be an element of certainty accompanying the buying of chances in a lottery. For example, if a woman buys a newspaper subscription she is certain to receive the newspaper which includes a chance in a prize contest, but— many years ago—one court termed that promotion a lottery.[92]

In May 1990, a new federal law, the "Charity Games Clarification Act," went into effect, permitting print or broadcast promotion and advertising of lotteries conducted by non-profit organizations and of all official state lotteries in any state conducting such lotteries.[93] The new law also allows commercial corporations to advertise occasional lotteries as long as such a promotional activity is not related to the corporation's usual course of business.

Originally, Congressional lottery legislation was aimed at helping states to control that form of gambling. In general, federal law made broadcasting of a lottery advertisement a crime. However, an exception was made to allow broadcasters to carry ads for state-run lotteries on those stations licensed in states which themselves have lotteries.[94]

[90] 18 U.S.C.A. § 1304 forbade ads or information about lotteries, and 39 U.S.C.A. § 3005 prohibited mailing information giving publicity to lotteries.

[91] Brooklyn Daily Eagle v. Voorhies, 181 Fed. 579 (C.C.E.D.N.Y.1910).

[92] Brooklyn Daily Eagle v. Voorhies, 181 Fed. 579 (C.C.E.D.N.Y.1910).

[93] Public Law 100–667, 132, amending Sec. 43(a) Title 15 USC 1125(a).

[94] 18 U.S.C.A. § 1307.

Radio and television broadcasts, however, don't stop at state lines. This was the underlying problem confronting the U.S. Supreme Court involving a North Carolina radio station owned by Edge Broadcasting Co. That broadcaster is located in the non-lottery state of North Carolina. The radio station, however, is only three miles from the Virginia state line, and Virginia does have a state lottery. More than 90 percent of the radio station's audience lives in Virginia.

The radio station challenged the federal ban on broadcasting lottery ads, and a federal district court and a U.S. Court of Appeals held that the ban was unconstitutional. The Court of Appeals held 2–1 that there was no reasonable fit between the goal of protecting North Carolina listeners and the means chosen to achieve it. The reason? About 10 percent of the listeners in North Carolina could get the same lottery information from Virginia media.[95]

The U.S. Supreme Court, however, reversed the appellate court by a margin of 7–2. Writing for the Court, Justice Byron White found that despite its minimal impact in this case, the federal statute was sufficiently effective in advancing a state's legitimate governmental aim of restricting dissemination of gambling ads. This upheld the constitutionality of the federal ban on advertising lotteries over stations which are not physically located in states having state lotteries.[96]

SEC. 87.   SELF-REGULATION

Leading communications companies have developed standards to govern their acceptance or rejection of advertising.

Publishers and broadcasters must know the legal status of advertising. If it can be proved that they knew that an advertisement is fraudulent, they may be held responsible for that ad along with the person or company who placed it in the publication. Advertising departments on many newspapers, moreover, often serve as a kind of advertising agency. In this capacity, the advertising staff must be able to give knowledgeable counsel and technical advice to advertisers.

In general, publishers are not liable to the individual consumer for advertising which causes financial loss or other damage unless the publisher or his employees knew that such advertising was fraudulent or misleading. The absence of liability for damage,

[95] Edge Broadcasting Co. v. United States, 956 F.2d 263 (4th Cir.1992).

[96] United States v. Edge Broadcasting Co., 509 U.S. 418, 113 S.Ct. 2696 (1993), 21 Med.L.Rptr. 1577.

however, does not mean that there is an absence of responsibility to the public generally and to individual readers of a publication.

The newspaper or broadcast station which permits dishonest or fraudulent advertising hurts its standing with both its readers and its advertisers. Publishers and broadcasters, who perceive psychological and economic advantages in refusing dishonest advertising, also appear to be becoming more cognizant that they have a moral duty to protect the public.

Responsible media units go to great lengths to ensure that advertising which they publish or broadcast is honest. Some newspapers' advertising acceptance statements, such as the one used by the Dallas Morning News, are very specific, spelling out advertisements which will not be accepted for publication. For example, the Dallas Morning News says it will not accept "bait and switch" ads: "Advertisements describing goods not available and not intended to be sold on request, but used as 'bait' to lure customers." Other newspapers provide long lists of ads that are not acceptable; some include fortune tellers, palm readers, and faith healers, along with forbidding publication of ads for illegal or harmful activities or substances.[97]

The National Advertising Division/National Advertising Review Board

In Addition to self-regulation by individual media units, a broader voluntary alternative exists in the National Advertising Division of the Council of Better Business Bureau and the National Advertising Review Board (NAD/NARB). These organizations serve as unofficial channels to try to resolve advertising disputes. Established in the 1970s by the Council of Better Business Bureaus and major advertising associations,[98] the NAD receives questions and complaints about national advertising, and conducts preliminary discussions with advertisers. Its purview is strictly national advertising which is suspected of deception. The NAD takes complaints from individuals and companies and also generates some of its own "cases" by monitoring national advertising in print and electronic mass media. During 1991, NAD Case Reports closed 88 cases, with challenges competitors making up 71% of the total; 14% came from NAD's own activities, 6% came from customer complaints, and 2% from local Better Business Bureaus.[99]

If an advertiser and the NAD cannot agree after initial discussions, NAD publishes a report outlining the issues for referral to

[97] Advertising Standards of Acceptability in the Dallas Morning News, pamphlet dated August, 1983.

[98] The American Advertising Federation, the American Association of Advertising Agencies, and the Association of National Advertisers.

[99] NAD Case Reports, Sample Issue, 1992.

the NARB.[1] Later, the NARB will produce its own report on the specific controversy. For example, the NAD in 1992 investigated Norelco's 950 RX electric razor, in response to an inquiry about how accurately a TV animation depicted "the action of the lift and cut system." After Norelco produced copies of six United States patents plus microphotography showing the lift and cut system actually in operation, the NAD concluded that the animated claim in the TV ad was substantiated. Findings such as these—including some which are adverse to advertisers and then referred to the NARB for further review—are published in NAD Reports. The reports contain the disclaimer that if an advertisement is changed or stopped, that "is not be taken as an admission of impropriety on any advertiser's part."

Nevertheless, some advertisers who face NAD questions do discontinue or modify ads, or provide substantiation before running the ads again. Take the case of a consumer who complained that the U.S. Postal Service had not lived up to its TV ads claiming "Two, Two, Two, Two–Day Priority Mail. Two. That's delivery in just two days of up to two pounds for just $2.90." The ad did have a disclaimer, "Some restrictions Apply." In fact, a consumer who mailed documents from Michigan to Connecticut discovered that his shipment took 10 days, not two. This NAD inquiry resulted in the Postal Service agreeing to add a statement telling customers to consult their local post office for details.[2]

SEC. 88.   THE RIGHT TO REFUSE SERVICE

A newspaper or magazine is not a public utility and, in general, may choose those with whom it cares to do business. The right, however, is not absolute when media use advertising refusal as an unfair competitive weapon.

The general rule: A newspaper or magazine is a private enterprise and may carry on business transactions with whom it pleases. An old but important case decided in 1931 declared:[3]

> If a newspaper were required to accept an advertisement, it could be compelled to publish a news item. If some good lady gave a tea, and submitted to the newspaper a proper account of the tea, and the editor of the newspaper refused to publish it ...she, it seems to us, would have as much right to compel the newspaper to publish the account as would a person engaged in

[1] NAD Case Reports, Feb. 17, 1992.

[2] NAD Case Reports, Feb. 17, 1992.

[3] Shuck v. Carroll Daily Herald, 215 Iowa 1276, 1281, 247 N.W. 813, 815 (1933). See also Miami Herald Pub. Co. v. Tornillo, 418 U.S. 241, 94 S.Ct. 2831 (1974).

business to compel a newspaper to publish an advertisement. . . .

Thus, as a newspaper is strictly a private enterprise, the publishers thereof have a right to publish whatever advertisements they desire and to refuse to publish whatever advertisements they do not desire to publish.

The Resident Participation Case

One of the most eloquent pleas for forced access to advertising space was seen in an air pollution dispute in Denver, Colorado. The setting in Denver should be idyllic—a city ringed by the magnificent Rocky Mountains. But not all was well in the late 1960s. On some days, Denver residents suffered from eyeburning smog

When news arrived that Pepcol, Inc., a subsidiary of the giant conglomerate Beatrice Foods, was going to build a rendering plant within the Denver city limits, protests resulted. A citizens group calling itself Resident Participation of Denver, spurred by visions of a smelly plant processing "dead animals, guts, and blood" and producing "disgusting garbage,"[4] attempted to place advertisements in Denver's competing dailies, the Denver Post and the Rocky Mountain News. The newspapers rejected the ads on the ground that the proposed wording called for a boycott of Beatrice Foods products, and boycott advertising was forbidden by Colorado statute.[5]

The Resident Participation group then re-worded its advertising without reference to boycott, but listed Beatrice Foods products such as Meadow Gold milk, cheese, and ice cream. The ad, as rewritten, included suggested letters. Readers were asked to clip out, sign, and mail the letters, protesting the rendering plant project to city and state officials. Both newspapers again refused to print the advertisements.[6]

Resident Participation then sought a court order under the First Amendment to force the newspapers to publish the advertisements. The newspapers countered with arguments that the First Amendment forbids only government abridgements of free speech, not private rejections, and this was an argument the ecology group could not overcome. Nevertheless, Resident Participation argued to have newspapers declared to be official or state action, on grounds that the newspapers "enjoy monopoly control in a vital area of

---

[4] Plaintiffs Exhibit "A," Resident Participation, Inc. Newsletter quoted in brief of Resident Participation of Denver, Inc. v. Love, 322 F.Supp. 1100 (D.Colo.1971). Thanks to Thomas A. Stacey for his help.

[5] Colo.Rev.Stat.Ann. § 80–11–12.

[6] Resident Participation of Denver, Inc. v. Love, 322 F.Supp. 1100, 1101 (D.Colo. 1971).

public concern" and because Colorado statutes required publication of legal notices in newspapers of general circulation.[7] Other provisions said to make newspapers a public entities included a statute exempting editors and reporters form jury service and a Denver ordinance allowing newspaper vending machines on public property, including sidewalks.[8]

A three-judge federal district court rejected these arguments, saying it could find noting "remotely suggesting that these measures are sufficient to justify labeling the newspapers' conduct state action."[9]

Other Allowable Advertising Refusals

In California (naturally), Times–Mirror Co.—publishers of the Los Angeles Times—was sued by the Adult Film Association of America, distributors of sex films. The film producers and distributors claimed that refusals to publish their ads created a business tort. A California court disagreed, saying that a newspaper's advertisements, like a newspaper's editorial policy, fix the newspaper's image in readers' minds. The newspaper, in other words, had a right to protect itself from public disfavor by *not* accepting some ads.[10]

The Milwaukee Journal, which had published a series of articles critical of nursing homes, was sued by the Wisconsin Association of Nursing Homes after the newspaper refused to carry an advertisement responding to the newspaper's reporting. A Wisconsin appellate court held that under the First Amendment, the newspaper's executives had the discretion to refuse such advertising.[11]

Financial Interests May Limit Ad Refusals

If a publication has a financial conflict of interest with a would-be advertiser, that can put a dent in the otherwise sweeping right to refuse advertisements. A United States Court of Appeals case— Home Placement Company v. Providence Journal (1982)[12]—gives an illustration of that scenario. After the newspaper refused classi-

[7] Ibid., 1102.

[8] Colo.Rev.Stat.Ann. § 7801.3 (1963); Denver Municipal Code, §§ 339G, 334.1–2.

[9] 322 F.Supp. 1100, 1103 (D.C.Colo.1971).

[10] Adult Film Association of America v. Times Mirror Co., 3 Med.L.Rpt. 2291 (Cal.Super.Ct.1978), affirmed 97 Cal.App.3d 77, 158 Cal.Rptr. 547 (1979), 5 Med. L.Rptr. 1865.

[11] Wisconsin Association of Nursing Homes v. Journal Co., 92 Wis.2d 709, 285 N.W.2d 891 (App.1979).

[12] Home Placement Service v. Providence Journal, 682 F.2d 274, 8 Med.L.Rptr. 1881 (1st Cir.1982), cert. denied 460 U.S. 1028, 103 S.Ct. 1279 (1983).

fied advertising from a rental referral company, this was held to run afoul of federal antitrust law.

The court noted that the Providence Journal not only had monopoly power as the only metropolitan daily in its area, it also was competing with Home Placement Company for real estate advertisements. This refusal to run advertising was viewed as an illegally anticompetitive refusal to do business under the Sherman Antitrust Act.[13] Thus, under unusual circumstances where a media unit has a financial conflict, advice from an antitrust law specialist could make good sense before rejecting an ad which is somehow in competition with the media unit itself.

One other situation where an ad refusal could bring legal trouble involves contract law. If a newspaper, for example, has entered into a contract to carry advertising and then refuses to do so, that could be a problem. That's the message from a 1982 Indiana case, Herald Telephone v. Fatouros. That case involved a political ad which was accepted by a newspaper—as was payment for the ad—then the message was refused because it might be "inflammatory." The Indiana Court of Appeals, Fourth District, said:[14]

> * * * we agree ... that a newspaper has a right to publish or reject advertising as its judgment dictates. However, once a newspaper forms a contract to publish an advertisement, it has given up the right to publish nor not publish ...

In usual situations, however, the media are free to refuse ads, as in Person v. New York Post Corp. (1977). The plaintiff asked a court order to prevent a newspaper from refusing to carry a "tombstone" ad on a financial matter. Instead, the federal district court declared that it is a newspaper's prerogative to accept or to reject advertisements as it sees fit.[15]

"State Action" Limits Right of Ad Refusal

Non-private entities such as transit authorities or state-owned publications can not refuse advertising with impunity. Back during the troubled 1960s, a California case involved a group called Women for Peace. That group sought to place advertising placards in buses owned by the Alameda–Contra Costa Transit District. The placards said:[16]

---

[13] Ibid., finding that §§ 1 and 2 of the Sherman Antitrust Act, 15 U.S.C §§ 1, 2 were violated.

[14] Herald–Telephone v. Fatouros, 431 N.E.2d 171 (Ind.App. 4th Dist.1982), 8 Med.L.Rptr. 1230, 1231.

[15] Person v. New York Post Corporation, 427 F.Sup. 1297 (E.D.N.Y.1977), affirmed 573 F.2d 1294 (2d Cir.1977).

[16] Wirta v. Alameda–Contra Costa Transit District, 68 Cal.2d 51, 64 Cal.Rptr. 430, 432, 434 P.2d 982, 984.

"Mankind must put an end to war or war will put an end to mankind." President John F. Kennedy.

"Write to President Johnson: Negotiate Vietnam. Women for Peace, P.O. Box 944, Berkeley."

The private advertising agency which managed advertising for the transit district rejected the placards. It was declared that "political advertising and advertising on controversial subjects are not acceptable unless approved by the [transit] district, and that advertising objectionable to the district shall be removed . . ." After a trial and two appeals, Women for Peace won their case before the California Supreme Court. The court said that thee ad was protected under the First Amendment and that once a public facility is opened for use of the general public, arbitrary conditions cannot be imposed upon the use of that facility.[17]

The theme of state action also ruled the outcome of a number of other cases in which courts held that publications must accept advertisements. When the official campus newspaper at Wisconsin State University–Whitewater refused to accept "editorial advertisements," ads expressing political views. U.S. District Court Judge James Doyle ruled that the newspaper's restrictive advertising policy—"enforced under color of state law—is a denial of free speech and expression."[18]

Advertising Boycotts and Antitrust Law

At times, anger against a media units becomes so extreme that an advertising boycott results. Under certain circumstances, that may bring antitrust law—either federal or state—into play on the side of a publisher or broadcaster. P. Cameron DeVore and Robert D. Sack cited Mims v. Kemp (1977), a case in which a jury, under federal antitrust law, awarded treble damages to a newspaper suffering losses from an advertising boycott.[19]

Newspaper Liability for Allegedly Discriminatory Ads?

Sometimes, despite the quest for revenue, newspapers might be better off if they would refuse some advertisements. Ragin v. New York Times[20] and Housing Opportunities Made Equal v. Cincinnati

---

[17] 68 Cal.2d 51, 64 Cal.Rptr. 430, 433, 434 P.2d 982, 985 (1967).

[18] Lee v. Board of Regents of State Colleges, 306 F.Supp. 1097, 1101 (W.D.Wis. 1969).

[19] P. Cameron DeVore and Robert D. Sack, "Advertising and Commercial Speech," in James C. Goodale, chairman, Communications Law 1996, Vol. III (New York: Practising Law Institute), p. 534, citing Mims v. Kemp, No. 72–627 (D.S.C. 1977). They added, however, that if the ad boycott is political rather than economic, it may be protected. See Environmental Planning & Information Council v. Superior Court, 36 Cal.3d 188, 203 Cal.Rptr. 127, 680 P.2d 1086 (1984), 10 Med.L.Rptr. 2055.

[20] Ragin v. New York Times, 923 F.2d 995 (2d Cir.1991).

Enquirer[21] both addressed the question of whether a newspaper is liable for publishing advertising that may violate the standards of the Federal Fair Housing Act. Based on conflicting outcomes, the answer seemed to depend on the federal circuit where the newspaper is located.

The New York Times was sued by a group of African Americans who asserted that the newspaper's real estate ad section over two decades rarely displayed pictures of blacks as prospective home owners or renters, an omission constituting a racial preference in violation of federal law. The Second Federal Circuit refused to dismiss the action, holding that a jury might reasonably conclude that such a pattern over a long period of time was not protected commercial speech because it would be an illegal activity.[22]

On the other hand, the Sixth Federal Circuit Court of Appeals dismissed similar allegations brought against the Cincinnati Enquirer, finding that a series of housing ads depicting only whites constituted legally protected commercial free speech. Further, the Sixth Circuit held that the newspaper should not be reburied to serve as an arm of government reviewing all housing advertisements it accepted to make sure that they reflected a proper mixture of races.[23]

Is An Advertising Offer a Contract?

American courts traditionally have not wanted to get into the business of governing business, especially when dealing with the area of offers and promises and contracts that arise under advertising.

An old case—Craft v. Elder & Johnston Co. (1941)—still states the law as it is in most jurisdictions. Craft looked in a newspaper one day and saw and advertisement by the Elder & Johnston Co., offering for sale an "all-electric sewing machine" for the sum of $26 as a "Thursday Only Special." Ms. Craft went to the store that Thursday and tried to pay $26 for the sewing machine. The store refused to sell.

She sued for the normal value of the machine $149 (less the $26 she would have paid). The trial court dismissed her case saying the ad was not an offer which could be accepted to form a contract. Her case went to an Ohio Court of Appeals, which said, "It is clear that in the absence of special circumstances an ordinary newspaper

[21] Housing Opportunities Made Equal v. Cincinnati Enquirer, 943 F.2d 644 (6th Cir.1991).

[22] Ragin v. New York Times, 923 F.2d 995 (2d Cir.1991), cert. denied 502 U.S. 821, 112 S.Ct. 81 (1991).

[23] Housing Opportunities Made Equal v. Cincinnati Enquirer, 943 F.2d 644 (6th Cir.1991).

advertisement is not an offer, but is an offer to negotiate—an offer to receive offers ..."[24]

The court gave an example:[25]

"A clothing merchant advertises coats of a certain kind for sale at $50. This is not an offer but an invitation to the public to come and purchase.

"Thus, if goods are advertised for sale at a certain price, it is not an offer and no contract is formed by the statement of an intending purchaser that he will take a specified quantity of goods at that price.

"[Advertisements] are merely invitations to all persons who may read them that the advertiser is ready to receive offers for the goods at the price stated."

Consumer advocates learned from cases such as this that they could not use contract law to force businesses to live up to the ads they had published. So, they instead turned to rules regulating advertising. In Geismar v. Abraham & Strauss (1981), a New York case,a consumer sued a department store. The store had advertised china that normally sold for $280 for only $39.95. Judith Geismar went to the store and tried to pay $39.95, but the store wouldn't take the money. She sued for breach of contract but lost under the principles of the Craft v. Elder & Johnston Co. case discussed above.

Ms. Geismar didn't walk away completely empty-handed, because the court allowed recovery under a New York statute providing that if anyone is injured by a misleading ad, they can collect up to $50. However, a cost-benefit analysis for consumers might suggest that suing over misleading ads—especially when major corporations are involved—is a situation of diminishing returns. Major corporations, of course, have legal departments that can tie the single plaintiff in knots.[26]

SEC. 89.   BROADCAST ADVERTISING

Broadcasters also have the right to refuse to accept advertising messages, except for federal political candidate ads during an election period.

In Columbia Broadcasting System Inc. v. Democratic National Committee, the Supreme Court held that radio and television

[24] Craft v. Elder & Johnston Co., 38 N.E.2d 416, 419   (Oh.Ct.App.2d Dist. Montgomery County 1941).

[25] Ibid.

[26] Geismar v. Abraham & Strauss, 439 N.Y.S.2d 1005, 109 Misc.2d 495, 439 N.Y.S.2d 1005 (Dist.Ct., Suffolk County, 1981).

stations are not legally required to broadcast any advertisements they do not want to accept.[27] By a 7–2 vote, the Court recognized a right for broadcasting similar to the print media's "right to refuse service".

This case dealt with the efforts of a political party and an anti-war group to get airtime for their respective viewpoints. Business Executives' Move for a Vietnam Peace (BEM) was the anti-war group that filed a complaint with the Federal Communications Commission alleging that a radio station in Washington D.C., WTOP had violated the fairness doctrine by refusing to sell the group time to broadcast a series of one-minute spot announcements against the Vietnam conflict. (The fairness doctrine, which held that broadcasters should make reasonable time available for differing sides of public issues, was repealed by the FCC in 1987.)[28] WTOP refused, saying it already had presented full and fair coverage of all important viewpoints concerning U.S. policy in Southeast Asia.

A few months later, the Democratic National Committee (DNC) sought a declaratory ruling from the FCC on this statement:

> That under the First Amendment ... and the Communications Act, a broadcaster may not, as a general policy, refuse to sell time to responsible entities ... for comment on public issues.

The Commission rejected the demands of both DNC and BEM, but the Court of Appeals reversed the FCC, declaring that a flat ban on paid public-issue announcements was "in violation of the First Amendment, at least when other types of paid announcements are accepted."[29]

The Supreme Court, however, upheld the FCC's decision by a margin of 7 to 2. Chief Justice Burger's plurality opinion—he was joined by Justices Rehnquist and Stewart—concluded that broadcast licensees were not common carriers.

He compared a newspaper's right of editorial judgment with that of a broadcast licensee, finding that the broadcaster's degree of freedom was somewhat less extensive than that of the newspaper publisher. Broadcasters are supervised—and periodically licensed—by the FCC which must "oversee without censoring."[30] Even so, the

[27] CBS, Inc. v. Democratic Nat. Committee, 412 U.S. 94, 93 S.Ct. 2080 (1973).

[28] The fairness doctrine, although not in force through the 1990s, could be reinstated if both Congress and the President agreed that it is good policy. The fairness doctrine was upheld as constitutional by the Supreme Court of the United States in Red Lion Broadcasting Co. v. FCC, 395 U.S. 367, 89 S.Ct. 1794 (1969).

[29] Business Executives' Move for Vietnam Peace v. FCC, Democratic National Committee v. FCC, 450 F.2d 642 (D.C.Cir.1971) overturning Business Executives, 24 FCC2d 242 (1970) and Democratic National Committee, 25 FCC2d 216 (1970).

[30] 412 U.S. 94, 93 S.Ct. 2080 (1973).

opinion declared, government control over broadcast licensees is not broad enough to transform their stations into "common carriers" or "public utilities", compelled to accept and deliver whatever message any individual might be willing to pay to have transmitted.

Based upon this decision, then, a broadcaster has the judicially recognized right to refuse to sell commercial time to anyone except those within that one specific category guaranteed advertising access by Congress: legally qualified candidates for federal elective offices.[31]

Advertising and Children

Action for Children's Television (ACT), a citizens' group, had been pressuring the FCC since the early 1970s to reduce the amount of commercialism in television programs produced for children. In 1986, the Commission eliminated the commercial guidelines it had established for television broadcast licensees, including limitations on the number of commercial minutes per hour of programs designed for children.[32] ACT challenged this FCC action, and the Court of Appeals, D.C. Circuit, sustained the challenge, declaring that the Commission had not presented adequate justification for its assumption that the marketplace would operate to prevent over-commercialization of children's programs.[33]

In October 1988, a consensus children's television advertising bill, reflecting the compromise agreement the NAB had negotiated with various interest groups, was enacted by Congress but vetoed by President Reagan.[34]

Two years later Congress passed new legislation with many of the same provisions contained in the earlier compromise agreement. This time, however, President Bush's failure to veto the "Children's Television Act" allowed it to become law in October

[31] Title 47 Section 312(a)(7) provides that station licenses may be revoked for refusing to allow reasonable access or to allow the purchase of reasonable amounts of time by legally qualified candidates for federal elective offices. For a more detailed discussion of this requirement, see chapter 12.

[32] Programming Commercialization Policies, 60 RR2d 526 (1986).

[33] Action for Children's Television v. FCC, 821 F.2d 741 (D.C.Cir.1987). For more than a half century, the National Association of Broadcasters had been actively involved in limiting the amount of commercialization in programs designed for children, working with the networks to voluntarily limit the number of commercial minutes per hour. In 1982, however, the Justice Department decided to bring an antitrust action against the NAB, charging that its commercial codes were in constraint of trade. At that point, the NAB was forced to enter into a consent agreement to abandon all efforts to negotiate for further limitations upon broadcast advertising. See United States v. National Association of Broadcasters, 536 F.Supp. 149 (D.D.C.1982). As a result, the FCC's rescission of its commercial time limitations in 1986 left broadcasters free of any regulatory or self regulatory constraints upon commercialization.

[34] "Congress, in Overtime, Passes TVRO, Children's Ad bills," Broadcasting, October 24, 1988, p. 27.

1990.[35] The Act limited advertising contained in weekday television or cable TV programs intended for children to 10½ minutes per hour, while allowing 12 minutes per hour on the weekend.

In addition, the law also requires broadcasters to meet the educational needs of children or face possible license revocation by the FCC, and established a federal endowment to fund the production of educational programs for children. At the insistence of Action for Children's Television, the bill also directed the FCC to determine whether certain "super-hero" cartoon strips based on toy characters merchandised by the advertiser constitute "program-length" commercials, and therefore automatically violate the law by exceeding maximum advertising time standards for such programs.

In January, 1992, the FCC began an audit of broadcast stations to determine the degree of compliance with the rules the Commission adopted to enforce the Children's Television Act of 1990. The audit revealed seven stations and three cable systems in apparent violation of one or more provisions of the Act. Only one of the stations cited by the FCC was able to provide a satisfactory explanation of its programming practices. The others were either fined or admonished. One TV station, KWHE, Honolulu, was fined $20,000 for its violations and two other stations, WFTS Tampa and WTTA St. Petersburg were each fined $10,000.[36]

Continuing its effort to get compliance with the Act, the FCC decided in February, 1993, to delay renewing the licenses of seven TV stations in Ohio and Michigan until the stations demonstrated they were meeting the educational needs of children.[37]

The Commission also issued a notice of inquiry to determine whether it was proper for broadcasters to log entertainment shows for children as programs meeting their informational needs, and whether short "educational" inserts could properly be considered as fulfilling broadcasters' obligations to children.[38]

Although the National Association of Broadcasters supported the legislation, its constitutionality was challenged by the Radio–Television News Directors Association. The RTNDA claimed the bill violated the First Amendment rights of broadcasters by requir-

[35] Children's TV Act of 1990, PL 101–437, 47 U.S.C.A. §§ 303a, 303b, 394. Implemented by the FCC, In the Matter of Policies and Rules Concerning Children's Television Programming, 68 RR2d 1615 (1991). See also, "President's Pocket Unveto Allows Children's Bill to Become Law," Broadcasting, October 22, 1990, p. 35.

[36] Harry Jessell, "Six TV's Hit for Violating Kids TV Rules," Broadcasting, Jan. 18, 1993, p. 95.

[37] "FCC Means Business," Broadcasting, Feb. 1, 1993, p. 36.

[38] Policies and Rules Concerning Children's Television Programming, 58 Fed. Reg. 14367 (1993).

ing them, "to provide programming and supporting advertising material as the federal government demands."[39]

Even if such legislation is upheld as constitutionally valid, its value in protecting children from the hazards of over-commercialization may turn out to be less significant than hoped. Studies of children's viewing behavior in the early 1990s revealed a continuing downward trend in the amount of time spent watching broadcast television each day.[40] These studies do not suggest that children are actually viewing less video entertainment each year, but rather that they were spending more of their time watching rented cassettes on the family VCRs where they can expose themselves to program-length commercials like "The Care Bears Battle the Freeze Machine", "Transformers: The Ultimate Doom" or "Mutant Ninja Turtles" to their hearts' content without interference from any well-intentioned adult interest group.

SEC. 90. ADVERTISING AND THE CONSTITUTION

Beginning in 1975, some commercial advertising began to receive protection under the First Amendment.

Commercial speech often is referred to as a stepchild of the First Amendment. Over the years, commercial speech—or advertising, to use an everyday term—was denied freedoms of speech and press granted to unconventional religious minorities,[41] to persons accused of blasphemy,[42] to free-love advocates,[43] and to persons sued for defaming public officials or public figures.[44] During the 1970s and 1980s, the Supreme Court—however grudgingly and qualifiedly—held that just because a message is disseminated as paid-for advertising does not wipe out all First Amendment protection for that message.[45] By the late 1990s, however, Supreme Court backing for constitutional support for advertising evidently was wobbling.[46]

[39] "Media Groups Challenge Kidvid Bill Constitutionality," *Variety* January 28, 1991, p. 44.

[40] See, for example, Nielsen 1990, Report on Television.

[41] Minersville School Dist. v. Gobitis, 310 U.S. 586, 60 S.Ct. 1010 (1940).

[42] Joseph Burstyn, Inc. v. Wilson, 343 U.S. 495, 72 S.Ct. 777 (1952).

[43] Kingsley Intern. Pictures Corp. v. Regents of N.Y.U., 360 U.S. 684, 688–689, 79 S.Ct. 1362, 1365 (1959).

[44] See New York Times Co. v. Sullivan, 376 U.S. 254, 84 S.Ct. 710 (1964) and later cases, including Rosenblatt v. Baer, 383 U.S. 75, 86 S.Ct. 669 (1966); Curtis Pub. Co. v. Butts, Associated Press v. Walker, 388 U.S. 130, 87 S.Ct. 1975 (1967), and St. Amant v. Thompson, 390 U.S. 727, 88 S.Ct. 1323 (1968).

[45] Bigelow v. Virginia, 421 U.S. 809, 95 S.Ct. 2222 (1975); Virginia State Board of Pharmacy v. Virginia Citizens Consumer Council, 425 U.S. 748, 96 S.Ct. 1817 (1976).

[46] See Posadas de Puerto Rico v. Tourism Co., 478 U.S. 328, 106 S.Ct. 2968 (1986); Board of Trustees of the State University of New York v. Fox, 492 U.S. 469, 109

Back in 1942, evidently with little reflection or receiving of evidence, the Supreme Court of the United States denied advertising First Amendment protection in Valentine v. Chrestensen.[47] In 1940, F.J. Chrestensen owned a World War I submarine moored at an East River pier in New York City. As World War II threatened to engulf the U.S., Chrestensen was trying to make money by charging for tours of a "U–Boat." New York City officials, however, ordered him not to distribute handbills advertising the submarine. Chrestensen's handbill listed an admission fee. New York City Police Commissioner Lewis J. Valentine said that the city's Sanitary Code forbade distributing commercial advertising matter in the streets.[48]

Chrestensen changed his handbill. One side then consisted of a notice about the submarine, but reference to the admission fee was deleted. The other side of the redone handbill was used to protest against city policies he disliked. Police officials then told Chrestensen he could distribute a handbill criticizing the city, but that invitation to visit the submarine was a commercial ad and was not permitted. In 1942, the Supreme Court held unanimously that although streets may be used to communicate information and disseminate opinion, the Constitution does not restrain government from controlling "purely commercial advertising," and that it is not entitled to First Amendment protection.[49]

The 1942 Valentine v. Chrestensen decision stated the law for some years to come. In 1959, in a now-famous concurring opinion in Cammarano v. United States, Justice William O. Douglas complained that the Chrestensen decision was "casual, almost offhand. And it has not survived reflection." Cammarano, a beer distributor, had tried to deduct, as a business expense, a contribution to a fund used to buy political ads to oppose a ballot measure which would have turned all wine and beer sales over to a state agency. Although he concurred in the decision denying Cammarano the IRS deduction, Justice Douglas wrote: " * * * I find it impossible to say that the owners of the * * * business who were fighting for their lives in opposing these initiative [ballot] measures were not exercising First Amendment rights."[50]

N.Y. Times v. Sullivan (1964) and Advertising

Ironically, the "breakthrough" case in protecting advertising under the Constitution is little thought of as a "commercial speech

S.Ct. 3028 (1989), and Austin v. Michigan Chamber of Commerce, 494 U.S. 652, 110 S.Ct. 1391 (1990).

[47] 316 U.S. 52, 62 S.Ct. 920 (1942).

[48] Valentine v. Chrestensen, 316 U.S. 52, 54, 62 S.Ct. 920, 921 (1942).

[49] Ibid.

[50] 358 U.S. 498, 79 S.Ct. 524 (1959).

case." In part, however, that's exactly what the landmark 1964 libel decision of New York Times v. Sullivan was. In *Sullivan*, the Supreme Court granted First Amendment protection for advertisements which deal with important political or social matters.

The Supreme Court held that such a reliance on *Chrestensen* to deny First Amendment protection to all advertising was "wholly misplaced." Writing for the *Sullivan* majority, Justice William J. Brennan, Jr. declared:[51]

> The publication here [in Times v. Sullivan] was not a "commercial" advertisement in the sense in which the word was used in *Chrestensen*. It communicated information, expressed opinion, recited grievances, protested claimed abuses, and sought financial support on behalf of a [civil rights] movement whose existence and objectives are matters of the highest public concern. * * * That the Times was paid for publishing the advertisement is as immaterial in this connection as is the fact that newspapers and books are sold.

What advertising, then, was protected by the First Amendment after New York Times v. Sullivan (1964)? Not all advertising—and especially, not advertising for an illegal activity—the Supreme Court said in Pittsburgh Press Co. v. Pittsburgh Commission on Human Relations (1973). A Pittsburgh ordinance empowered the city's human relations commission to issue cease and desist orders against discriminatory hiring practices. The Pittsburgh Press ran "Help Wanted" ads in columns labeled "Jobs—Male Interest," and "Jobs—Female Interest." The city commission sought—and won—a cease and desist order against the Pittsburgh Press to prevent it from publishing illegal advertisements.[52]

Writing for the Court's five-member majority, Justice Lewis Powell disagreed: Discrimination in employment is illegal commercial activity under the city's ordinance. "We have no doubt that a newspaper constitutionally could be forbidden to publish a want ad proposing a sale of narcotics or soliciting prostitutes."[53]

Bigelow v. Virginia (1975)

It should be emphasized that the Court, in New York Times v. Sullivan, drew a distinction between "commercial advertising" which attempted to sell products or services and other kinds of expression. This distinction, however, was too simple. Some products or services—by their very nature—are matters of public debate

[51] Ibid.

[52] Pittsburgh Press Co. v. Pittsburgh Commission on Human Relations, 413 U.S. 376, 377, 93 S.Ct. 2553, 2555 (1973).

[53] 413 U.S. 376, 387, 93 S.Ct. 2553, 2560 (1973).

or controversy, and advertisements for those products or services may have the characteristics and importance of political speech. A 1975 Virginia case involving advertising about the availability and legality of abortions in New York—the case called Bigelow v. Virginia—showed that "commercial speech" can have some degree of constitutional protection.

Early in 1971, an advertisement for a New York-based abortion service—saying only that there were no residency requirements and offering to provide information and counseling—was published in The Virginia Weekly, a newspaper focusing its coverage on the University of Virginia. Jeffrey C. Bigelow was managing editor and a director of the newspaper when it published the ad.[54]

A Virginia court convicted Bigelow of violating a section of the Virginia Code: "If any person, by publication, lecture, advertisement, or by the sale or circulation of any publication, or in any other manner, shall encourage or prompt the procuring of an abortion or miscarriage, he shall be guilty of a misdemeanor."[55] The Virginia Supreme Court affirmed Bigelow's conviction, declaring that because the ad involved was a "commercial advertisement," Bigelow's First Amendment claim was not valid. Such an advertisement, said the Virginia Supreme Court, " 'may be constitutionally prohibited by the state, particularly where, as here, the advertising relates to the medical-health field.' "[56]

The Supreme Court overruled the Virginia Supreme Court. Writing for a 7–2 majority, Justice Harry Blackmun concluded that Virginia courts erred in assuming that advertising is not entitled to First Amendment protection. Justice Blackmun distinguished the Virginia case from *Chrestensen.* He wrote that the handbill ad involved in *Chrestensen* did no more than propose a purely commercial transaction, while The Virginia Weekly's advertisement about abortions "contained factual material of clear 'public interest.' "[57]

A State, Justice Blackmun wrote, "may not * * * bar a citizen of another State from disseminating information about an activity that is legal in another State." Although advertising "may be subject to reasonable regulation that serves a legitimate public interest," some commercial speech is still worthy of constitutional protection. "The relationship of speech to the marketplace of products or services does not make it valueless in the marketplace of ideas."[58]

[54] Bigelow v. Virginia, 421 U.S. 809, 95 S.Ct. 2222 (1975).

[55] Bigelow v. Virginia, 421 U.S. 809, 813, 95 S.Ct. 2222, 2228 (1975).

[56] Bigelow v. Virginia, 421 U.S. 809, 814, 95 S.Ct. 2222, 2229 (1975), quoting Bigelow v. Commonwealth, 213 Va. 191, 193–195, 191 S.E.2d 173, 174–176 (1972).

[57] Bigelow v. Virginia, 421 U.S. 809, 819, 95 S.Ct. 2222, 2231 (1975).

[58] Bigelow v. Virginia, 421 U.S. 809, 826, 95 S.Ct. 2222, 2235 (1975).

Virginia State Board of Pharmacy v. Virginia Citizens Consumer Council, Inc. (1976)

What the Supreme Court started in 1975 with the *Bigelow* case continued the next year with the decision in the Virginia State Board of Pharmacy case. In fact, an excellent study of advertising law emphasized—as of 1991—that VSBP represented the decision in which the Supreme Court gave broadest First Amendment protection for commercial advertising.[59]

The Virginia State Board of Pharmacy case was not directly about a political or social issue. Instead, it dealt with a matter of price advertising. It arose because a Virginia statute forbade "the advertising of the price for any prescription drug." This statute was challenged in a lawsuit by two consumer organizations and by a Virginia citizen who had to take prescription drugs on a daily basis. The plaintiffs claimed that the First Amendment entitled users of prescription drugs to receive information from pharmacists—through advertisements or other promotional means—about the price of those drugs.[60]

By a 7–1 vote expressed via Justice Blackmun's majority opinion in *Virginia State Board of Pharmacy,* the Court overturned the state's ban on advertising of prescription drug prices.[61] The Supreme Court declared that the consumer had a great interest in the free flow of commercial information—perhaps a greater interest than in the day's most important political debate. The individuals hardest hit by the suppression of prescription price information, wrote Justice Blackmun, were the poor, the sick and the old.[62]

Subsequent cases indicated that commercial speech could receive constitutional protection in a variety of areas. Later in 1976, for example, the Horner–Rausch Optical Co. case, decided by a Tennessee court, declared an administrative regulation against price ads for eyeglasses to be unconstitutional.[63] And in 1977, the U.S. Supreme Court decided the now famous "lawyer ad case," Bates v. State Bar of Arizona.[64] By a 5–4 margin, the Court held

[59] For an excellent discussion of the Virginia Board of Pharmacy case and, indeed, of the key cases involving advertising and the First Amendment to 1991, see Richard T. Kaplar, Advertising Rights, The Neglected Freedom: Toward a New Doctrine of Commercial Speech (Washington, D.C.: The Media Institute, 1991).

[60] Virginia State Board of Pharmacy v. Virginia Citizens Consumer Council, Inc., 425 U.S. 748, 96 S.Ct. 1817 (1976) 1 Med.L.Rptr. 1930.

[61] Virginia State Board of Pharmacy v. Virginia Citizens Consumer Council, Inc., 425 U.S. 748, 759–761, 96 S.Ct. 1817, 1824–1825 (1976).

[62] Virginia State Board of Pharmacy v. Virginia Citizens Consumer Council, Inc., 425 U.S. 748, 763, 96 S.Ct. 1817, 1826 (1976).

[63] Horner–Rausch Optical Co. v. Ashley, 547 S.W.2d 577 (Tenn.App.1976).

[64] Bates v. State Bar of Arizona, 433 U.S. 350, 97 S.Ct. 2691 (1977).

that lawyers have a constitutional right to advertise their prices for their various services.

Justice Blackmun's majority opinion in *Bates* said, "[I]t is entirely possible that advertising will serve to reduce, not to advance, the cost of legal services to the consumer." In this case, the consumer's need for information about the cost of legal services was held to outweigh the legal profession's interest in having a regulated self-restraint against virtually all kinds of advertising by attorneys. The majority opinion added that the time, place and manner of advertising may be regulated, and that false or misleading advertising by lawyers may be forbidden.[65]

The Bellotti Case (1978): Protecting Corporate Speech

If abortion clinics, pharmacists, and lawyers have some First Amendment protection for their ads, what about corporations right to exercise political speech? In First National Bank of Boston v. Bellotti (1978),[66] the U.S. Supreme Court invalidated a Massachusetts statute forbidding business corporations from making contributions or expenditures " 'for the purpose of * * * influencing or affecting the vote on any question submitted to the voters, other than one materially affecting the property, business, or assets of the corporation.' " That statute provided that a corporation violating its provisions could be fined $50,000 and that its officers could be fined up to $10,000, imprisoned for up to one year, or both.

The U.S. Supreme Court, however, found the Massachusetts statute unconstitutional. Writing for the Court, Justice Lewis Powell declared that the political argument the bank wished to make "is at the heart of the First Amendment's protection." He added, "[t]he question in this case, simply put, is whether the corporate identity of the speaker deprives the proposed speech of what otherwise would be its clear entitlement to protection."[67]

Justice Powell cited the Court's 1970s commercial speech cases—including *Virginia State Board of Pharmacy*—as illustrating "that the First Amendment goes beyond protection of the press and the self-expression of individuals to prohibit government from limiting the stock of information from which members of the public

[65] Bates v. State Bar of Arizona, 433 U.S. 350, 383, 384, 97 S.Ct. 2691, 706, 2708, 2709 (1977). Advertising by attorneys can go too far, however, when it includes a lawyer's visiting the family of a person injured in an auto accident, and even visiting with the driver herself in her hospital room. Personal solicitation of that nature (bedpan chasing?) is unreasonable. See Ohralik v. Ohio State Bar Ass'n, 436 U.S. 447, 98 S.Ct. 1912 (1978). If lawyer advertising is fundamentally misleading, it will not be tolerated: See Peel v. Attorney Registration and Disciplinary Com'n of Illinois, 496 U.S. 91, 110 S.Ct. 2281 (1990).

[66] First National Bank of Boston v. Bellotti, 435 U.S. 765, 98 S.Ct. 1407 (1978).

[67] First National Bank of Boston v. Bellotti, 435 U.S. 765, 778, 98 S.Ct. 1407, 1416 (1978).

may draw." Thus corporations' political speech was entitled to First Amendment protection.[68]

Central Hudson (1980) and the Four–Part Test

In 1980, the Supreme Court of the United States created an important test to try to outline just when advertising might be deemed worthy of constitutional protection. This case, Central Hudson Gas & Electric Corp. v. Public Service Commission of New York, involved a commission order that the utility stop promoting consumption of electricity. This order was promulgated during an energy shortage, under the assumption that cutting Central Hudson's "buy appliances" advertising might assist in energy conservation. The U.S. Supreme Court, however, invalidated New York's ban on promotional advertising by electric utilities. Justice Powell, writing for an 8–1 Court, laid out a four-part test:[69]

> In commercial speech cases, then, a four-part analysis has developed. At the outset, we must determine [1] whether the expression is protected by the First Amendment. For commercial speech to come within that provision, it at least must concern lawful activity and not be misleading. [2] Next, we ask whether the asserted governmental interest is substantial. If both inquiries yield positive answers, we must determine [3] whether the regulation directly advances the governmental interest asserted, and [4] whether it is not more extensive than necessary to serve that interest.

Because advertising promoting use of electricity was seen as protected by the First Amendment, and because the ad was neither misleading nor "unlawful," the New York regulation was overturned as unconstitutional. Although the state had a substantial interest in energy conservation, the state's regulation was more extensive than necessary. No demonstration was made that the state's interest in energy conservation could not have been served adequately by a more limited restriction on the content of promotional advertisements.[70]

[68] First National Bank of Boston v. Bellotti, 435 U.S. 765, 783, 98 S.Ct. 1407, 1409 (1978).

[69] Central Hudson Gas & Electric Corp. v. Public Service Com'n of New York, 447 U.S. 557, 100 S.Ct. 2343 (1980).

[70] Central Hudson Gas & Elec. Corp. v. Public Service Com'n, 447 U.S. 557, 100 S.Ct. 2343 (1980). See also a related case, Consolidated Edison Co. of New York, Inc. v. Public Service Commission of New York, 447 U.S. 530, 100 S.Ct. 2326 (1980), 6 Med.L.Rptr. 1518. There, the Court struck down an order forbidding the utility's including in mailings statements of "Con Ed's" views on public policy controversies. Powell, quoting First National Bank of Boston v. Bellotti, 435 U.S. 765, 98 S.Ct. 1407 (1978), wrote for the Court that the Commission's censorship attempt "strikes at the heart of the freedom to speak."

Narrowing Constitutional Protection: Posadas de Puerto Rico v. Tourism Company (1986)

For eleven years after deciding the abortion advertising case of Bigelow v. Virginia (1975),[71] the U.S. Supreme Court held that if a product or service was legal and was the subject of public or corporate interest, truthful ads for that product or service had First Amendment protection.[72] As noted earlier in this Section, this protection covered ads for abortion referral services, prices of prescription drugs, eyeglasses, lawyers, banks' political stances, promotions by a public utility, even during an energy shortage.

This expansiveness came to a halt in 1986, when the Supreme Court ruled that government may forbid truthful ads for some products or services, even though they are legal for sale. Not surprisingly, this decision—involving Puerto Rico's regulations against *local* ads promoting gambling in Puerto Rico's legal casinos—alarmed the tobacco and liquor industries in the United States.[73]

When a hotel-casino challenged the advertising regulations as unconstitutional, it did seem to have plenty to complain about. The regulations were sweepingly broad. For example, consider this Tourism Company memo:[74]

> "This prohibition includes the use of the word 'casino' in matchbooks, lighters, envelopes, inter-office and/or external correspondence, invoices, napkins, brochures, menus, elevators, glasses, plates, lobbies, banners, flyers, paper holders, pencils, telephone books, directories, bulletin boards or in any hotel dependency or object which may be accessible to the public in Puerto Rico."

When the case reached the U.S. Supreme Court, Justice (subsequently Chief Justice) William H. Rehnquist wrote for the Court's five member majority. He said the issue was whether the Puerto Rico statute and regulations "impermissibly suppressed commercial speech in violation of the First Amendment and the equal protection and due process guarantees of the United States Constitution."[75]

Justice Rehnquist said that this case involved " * * * the restriction of pure commercial speech which does 'no more than

---

[71] 421 U.S. 809, 95 S.Ct. 2222 (1975).

[72] See also New York Times Co. v. Sullivan, 376 U.S. 254, 84 S.Ct. 710 (1964), the pivotal libel case extending First Amendment protection to ads dealing with major social or political concerns.

[73] Stuart Taylor, Jr., "High Court, 5–4, Sharply Limits Constitutional Protection for Ads," The New York Times, July 2, 1986, p. 2 (National Edition).

[74] 478 U.S. at 333, 106 S.Ct. at 2873, 13 Med.L.Rptr. at 1035.

[75] 478 U.S. at 328, 106 S.Ct. at 2971, 13 Med.L.Rptr. at 1034.

propose a commercial transaction.' "[76] That meant, he wrote, that First Amendment discussion of this case was controlled by the four-part analysis set forth in the Central Hudson Gas & Electric Corp. case discussed earlier in this Section.

The Court's majority opinion concluded that advertising of casino gambling in Puerto Rico "concerns a lawful activity and is not misleading or fraudulent, at least in the abstract."[77] Even so, Justice Rehnquist's majority opinion deferred to Puerto Rico's legislative judgment: It was not an unreasonable policy choice to believe that excessive casino gambling by Puerto Rico's residents would produce great harm to citizens welfare. The Court's majority concluded that the hotel/casino's First Amendment claims had been rejected properly.

He wrote acidly that even though products or activities including cigarettes, alcoholic beverages, and prostitution had been legalized for sale in some jurisdictions did not mean that their advertising could not be limited.[78]

The Posadas decision promised to make it more difficult to overturn State laws that constrain commercial free speech. The Central Hudson test Justice Rehnquist claimed to be applying in the Posadas case had permitted States to use only the "least restrictive means" available in regulating advertising messages. In fact, however, *Posadas* simply required a State to demonstrate that any advertising laws it adopts are "reasonable" ones, in effect diluting the four-part test from *Central Hudson* and making First Amendment protection for advertising seem less secure.[79]

Rethinking *Posadas*: *Edenfield v. Fane* (1993), *Rubin v. Coors* (1995), and *Florida Bar v. Went For It Inc.* (1995)

As noted on page 717 of this textbook, the four-part test from Central Hudson Gas & Electric Corp. v. Public Service Commission of New York (1980) laid out a routine for determining whether commercial speech qualified for First Amendment protection.[80] Following that four-part test, and until Posadas de Puerto Rico v. Tourism Commission (1986), it seemed that if advertising was not

---

[76] 8 U.S. at 340, 106 S.Ct. at 2976, 13 Med.L.Rptr. at 1038–1039.

[77] 478 U.S. at 340–341, 106 S.Ct. at 2975, 13 Med.L.Rptr. at 1039.

[78] 478 U.S. at 346, 106 S.Ct. at 2977.

[79] See Denise M. Trauth and John L. Huffman, "The Commercial Speech Doctrine: Posadas Revisionism," Communication and the Law (Feb. 1988), pp. 43–56. For an example of a case strengthening state regulation of advertising, see Board of Trustees of State University of New York v. Fox, 492 U.S. 469, 109 S.Ct. 3028 (1989).

[80] Central Hudson Gas & Electric Corp. v. Public Service Comm'n of New York, 447 U.S. 557, 100 S.Ct. 2343 (1980).

misleading and was about a lawful service or product, it had First Amendment protection. In *Posadas*, however the Supreme Court of the United States upheld efforts to protect Puerto Ricans from the lure of *legalized* casino gambling through sweeping local advertising regulations.[81]

Back in 1986, *Posadas* was seen as shrinking hard-won gains for constitutional protection for advertising. This decision made it more difficult to overturn state laws constraining commercial speech. The *Central Hudson* test Justice Rehnquist claimed to be applying in *Posadas* had permitted states to use only the "least restrictive means" in regulating advertising. In fact, however, *Posadas* simply required a State to demonstrate that any advertising laws it adopted were "reasonable." In 1993, however, the judicial pendulum moved a bit toward reestablishing protections eroded by the *Posadas* decision in a decision about regulating advertising by accountants.

Edenfield v. Fane (1993)

Scott Fane, a certified public accountant (CPA) licensed in Florida, sued the Florida Board of Accountancy to prevent the Board from enforcing one of its rules. That rule prohibited CPAs from " 'direct, in-person, uninvited solicitation' " to get new clients. A U.S. district court enjoined the rule's enforcement, and the Court of Appeals, 11th Circuit, upheld the injunction. Writing for an 8–1 Supreme Court, Justice Kennedy ruled that as applied to CPA advertising, "Florida's prohibition is inconsistent with the free-speech guarantees of the First and Fourteenth Amendments." Using language far more supportive of commercial speech than that used in *Posadas*, Justice Kennedy wrote for the Court:[82]

> The commercial marketplace . . . provides a forum where ideas and information flourish. Some of these ideas and information are vital, some of slight worth. But the general rule is that the speaker and the audience, not the government, assess the value of the information presented. Thus even a communication that does no more than propose a commercial transaction is entitled to the coverage of the First Amendment.

Rubin v. Coors (1995)

If *Edenfield* sounded supportive of commercial speech, consider the U.S. Supreme Court's specific downplaying of *Posadas* and reaffirmation of the *Central Hudson* test in Rubin, Secretary of the Treasury v. Coors Brewing Company (1995). Coors brought an

---

[81] Posadas de Puerto Rico v. Tourism Company of Puerto Rico, 478 U.S. 328, 333, 106 S.Ct. 2968, 2973 (1986).

[82] 507 U.S. 761, 761, 113 S.Ct. 1792, 1798 (1993), 21 Med.L.Rptr. 1321.

action for a declaratory judgment that the Federal Alchohol Administration Act (FAAA) section forbidding use of beer labels listing alcohol content violated the First Amendment. Upholding a Tenth Circuit ruling, the U.S. Supreme Court agreed 9–0 that the FAAA had overstepped itself in trying to control brewers "strength war" advertising.

Writing for the unanimous court, Justice Clarence Thomas agreed with the Tenth Circuit's conclusion that no relationship had been shown between factual information about alcohol content and competition based on that information. Justice Thomas relied on language from *Central Hudson* asking " 'whether the regulation advances the governmental interest asserted, and whether it is not more extensive than is necessary to serve that interest.' "[83] The court relied on federalism, a faith in state powers, holding that states have sufficient authority to ban the disclosure of alcohol content if they chose to do so. Then, citing *Edenfield*, Justice Thomas concluded that the FAA Act " ...would not withstand First Amendment scrutiny because the Government's regulation of speech is not sufficiently tailored to its goal."[84] Therefore, the Court found that the statute section forbidding advertising of alcohol strength on malt beverage labels flunked the *Central Hudson* test.

Relying on federalism, a faith in state powers, Justice Thomas concluded that the federal government's interest in preserving its authority in the alcohol labeling area is not exclusive. "...[O]ne state's decision to permit brewers to disclose alcohol content will not preclude neighboring States from effectively banning such disclosure of information within their borders."[85]

Florida Bar v. Went For It, Inc. (1995)

First Amendment lawyers found the outcome of *Rubin*, discussed above, to be a welcome return to heightened protection for commercial speech. However, in the *Went For It* decision, the U.S. Supreme Court—by a vote of 5–4—found it could bend the *Central Hudson* test to uphold a Florida State Bar rule forbidding lawyers from sending direct mail solicitations to disaster victims for 30 days after harm had befallen them or their loved ones.[86]

---

[83] Rubin, Secretary of the Treasury v. Coors Brewing Company, 514 U.S. 476, 486, 115 S.Ct. 1585, 1591 (1995). The FAAA subsection under scrutiny was § 5 (3) 2.

[84] Ibid., pp. 1591–1592.

[85] Ibid., p. 1591. Here, Justice Thomas distinguished *Rubin* from United States v. Edge Broadcasting Co., 509 U.S. 418, 113 S.Ct. 2696 (1993). In *Edge*, the U.S. Supreme Court upheld a federal law prohibiting lottery advertising on broadcast stations located in states that did not operate lotteries.

[86] Florida Bar v. Went For It, Inc., 515 U.S. 618, 622, 115 S.Ct. 2371, 2375 (1995), 23 Med.L.Rptr. at 1801–1802.

Writing for the Court, Justice Sandra Day O'Connor paid specific attention to a survey done by the Florida Bar, showing substantial public opposition to direct mail from attorneys. Again, commercial speech had lesser standing in the majority opinion's phrasing about " 'its limited measure of protection, commensurate with its subordinate protection in the scale of First Amendment values.' "[87]

Curiously, the four-part *Central Hudson* test discussed earlier was here termed a "three-part test "by the Court. The first part of the *Central Hudson* test—that the commercial speech must be neither false nor misleading and must be for a legal product or activity—was used as a preamble for the rest of the test. As renumbered, that changed the test to:[88]

(1) Does government have a substantial interest in restricting this particular commercial speech?

(2) Does the regulation directly advance that governmental interest?

(3) Is the regulation more extensive than needed to serve that governmental interest?

In her majority opinion, Justice O'Connor that a state's interest in " ' ...protecting the personal privacy and tranquility of personal the home is certainly the highest order in a free and civilized society.' " The also expressed concern about protecting the integrity of the legal profession.[89] The majority also found that the Florida Bar's rule against direct mail solicitation of disaster victims directly advanced an important government interest and was not too extensive in serving that interest.[90]

This led to some acrimony on the Court, with Justice Kennedy (joined by Justices Stevens, Souter, and Ginsburg) arguing in dissent that commercial speech has a higher constitutional value than admitted to by the majority. Justice Kennedy declared that the Court "today undercuts this guaranty in an important class of cases and unsettles leading First Amendment precedents, at the expense of those victims most in need of legal assistance."[91]

But by a margin of one vote, Justice O'Connor and the majority upheld the Florida Bar Rule against direct mail solicitation of disaster victims during their first 30 days after being injured or

[87] Ibid., at 623, 2376, 1803, quoting Board of Trustees of the State University of New York v. Fox, 492 U.S. 469, 477, 109 S.Ct. 3028 (1989) quoting Ohralik v. Ohio State Bar Assn., 436 U.S. 447, 456, 98 S.Ct. 1912, 1918 (1978).

[88] Ibid., at 624, 2376, 1804–1805.

[89] Ibid., at 624, 2381, 1808.

[90] Ibid., at 635, 2381, 1808.

[91] Ibid., at 635-636, 2381, 180, quoting Shapero v. Kentucky Bar Assn., 486 U.S. 466, 108 S.Ct. 1916 (1988).

suffering a loss. It may be that she quoted, in passing a better rule on how to protect free expression and deal with direct mail. In another direct mail case, the Supreme Court advised that the " ' "short, though regular, journey from mail box to trash can . . . is an acceptable burden, at least so far as the Constitution is concerned." ' "[92]

44 Liquormart, Inc. v. Rhode Island (1996)

This decision echoed the Supreme Court's insistence in *Rubin* (see above) that advertising is protected by the First Amendment. The *44 Liquormart* case grew out of Rhode Island's forbidding price advertising for alcoholic beverages. The Court without a dissenting vote—held that the ban on price advertising for a lawful product was not permitted by the First Amendment.[93]

> When a State regulates commercial messages to protect consumers from misleading, deceptive, or aggressive sales practices, or requires the disclosure of beneficial consumer information, the purpose of its regulation is consistent with the consistent with the reasons for according constitutional protection to commercial speech and therefore justifies less than strict review. However, when a State entirely prohibits the dissemination of truthful, nonmisleading commercial messages for reasons unrelated to the preservation of a fair bargaining process, there is far less reason to depart from the rigorous review that the First Amendment generally demands.

Justice Stevens also took pains to renounce the narrower view of First Amendment protection for advertising expressed in *Posadas*.[94]

> [O]n reflection, we are now persuaded that *Posadas* erroneously performed the First Amendment analysis. The casino advertising ban was designed to keep truthful, misleading speech from members of the public for fear that they would be more likely to gamble if they received it. * * *

* * *

> The *Posadas* majority's conclusion cannot be reconciled with the unbroken line of prior cases striking down similarly broad

[92] Ibid., 115 S.Ct. at 2379, 23 Med.L.Rptr. at 1806 (1995), with Justice O'Connor quoting Bolger v. Youngs Drug Products Corp., 463 U.S. 60, 72, 103 S.Ct. 2875, 2883 (1983), quoting Lamont v. Commissioner of Motor Vehicles, 269 F.Supp. 880, 883 (S.D.N.Y.1967), affirmed 386 F.2d 449 (2d Cir.1967).

[93] 44 Liquormart, Inc. v. Rhode Island, 517 U.S. 484, 116 S.Ct. 1495, 1498 (1996). Justice Stevens was joined in this part of his opinion by Justices Ginsburg and Kennedy. *Liquormart*, although decided without a dissenting vote, was more a collection of complementary opinions than a "unanimous" judgment.

[94] Ibid., p. 1498. Justice Stevens was joined by Justices Kennedy, Souter, and Ginsburg in this portion of his opinion.

regulations on truthful, nonmisleading advertising when non-speech alternatives were available. See *Posadas*, 478 U.S. at 350, 106 S.Ct. at 2981–9882 (Brennan, J., dissenting)* * *; Kurland, Posadas de Puerto Rico v. Tourism Company: " 'Twas Strange,' 'Twas Passing Strange;" 'Twas Pitiful,' 'Twas Wondrous Pitiful,' " 1986 S.Ct. Rev. 1, 12–15.)

Finally, *44 Liquormart*—in abandoning the weaker protection for commercial speech as expressed in *Posadas*—breathed new life into the four-part *Central Hudson* test for evaluating the constitutionality of advertising regulations.

Cincinnati v. Discovery Network, Inc. (1993)

A city has an interest in keeping litter off its streets, but can it regulate distribution of free-circulation magazines that get taken from newsracks and thrown about?

Discovery Network, Inc. had permission from Cincinnati to place its newsracks on public property to distribute free-circulation magazines consisting mostly of advertising. In 1990, evidently because of littering around the newsracks, the city revoked permission, stating that the magazines were "commercial handbills." A pre-existing Cincinnati ordinance forbade distribution of commercial handbills.[95]

A U.S. District Court held that although the city may regulate newsracks for safety and esthetics, its regulations had to meet a standard set by the U.S. Supreme Court in State University of New York v. Fox (1989).[96] That standard said the regulation of speech "should be accomplished by a means narrowly tailored to achieve the desired objective." So under that decision, a government entity regulating commercial speech bears the burden of establishing a "reasonable fit" between the ends and the means chosen to achieve those ends.[97]

When this case reached the U.S. Supreme Court, Justice Stevens declared for a 6–3 majority that although the city's interest in preventing litter had some validity, it was not enough to discriminate against the free circulation of these magazines that were predominantly advertising. Justice Stevens wrote:[98]

> In our view, the city's argument attaches more importance
> to the distinction between commercial speech than our

[95] Cincinnati v. Discovery Network, Inc., 507 U.S. 410, 113 S.Ct. 1505 (1993), 21 Med.L.Rptr. 1161, 1162.

[96] Board of Trustees of State University of New York v. Fox, 492 U.S. 469, 109 S.Ct. 3028 (1989).

[97] Cincinnati v. Discovery Network, Inc., 507 U.S. 410, 414, 113 S.Ct. 1505, 1509 (1993), 21 Med.L.Rptr. 1161, 1163.

[98] Ibid., 419, 1151, 1165.

cases warrant and seriously underestimates the value of commercial speech.

Concurring, Justice Blackmun likened unresolved issues remaining form the Central Hudson decision of 1980 (see discussion earlier in this section) to chickens coming home to roost. He wrote: " ... I continue to believe that the commercial speech analysis set forth in Central Hudson and as refined in Fox [Board of Trustees v. State University of New York v. Fox] affords insufficient protection for truthful, non-coercive commercial speech concerning lawful activities."[99]

Dissenting, Chief Justice Rehnquist—joined by Justices White and Thomas—complained that the Cincinnati newsracks decision will "unduly hamper our cities' efforts to come to grips with the unique problems posed by the dissemination of commercial speech."[100]

[99] Ibid., at 431, 1517, 1170.
[100] Ibid., at 445, 1525, 1173.

Chapter 15

COPYRIGHT: PROTECTION AND CONSTRAINT

SEC. 91. THE RATIONALE OF COPYRIGHT LAW

Copyright law provides a financial incentive for creativity while ensuring that the public will eventually gain full access to the copyrighted work.

"Imitation is not the sincerest form of flattery—Money is!"[1]

Copyright is the legal protection for works of creativity. Literally, it is the right to copy. More generally, it is the right to exploit an original work of creativity. After going through chapters on the worth of freedom, the protection of media in reporting and the restrictions on prior restraint, we come to an area of the law that restricts the free use of works. It may seem counterintuitive, but copyright law works to ensure the free flow of creativity that ultimately benefits society.

Suppose that you are a publisher. In order to ensure that you have a continued flow of profitable books, you encourage new authors. You pay advance royalties on a dozen books, most of which do not sell enough to cover the costs of production. Finally, one of your authors comes up with a book that will be a best seller. Your profits from that one book must help cover the cost of doing business for your whole company. You must pay royalties to your new star author. But, a competitor, seeing the potential for profits, buys a copy of your hard-back book. He scans the pages into a computer and produces his own version of the book that he can sell for less. He, after all, is not paying to support 11 other, less successful authors. He is not paying royalties to the author. He undercuts your sales. You fail to make enough profit to remain in business.

---

[1] Author unknown, though believed to have been inspired by Robert Heinlein.

The result of the scenario is the failure of your publishing business and all other publishers who do business in traditional ways. Without publishers to nurture and encourage new authors, no new writing occurs. Authors, robbed of their royalties, will choose other pursuits that will put food on the table. The end result is that society is denied the product of the creativity of artists, composers, writers, film makers—all those creative people who add to the sum and substance of life.

It is for this greater societal good that governments have, for hundreds of years, guaranteed monopolies for those who bring new art into the world. The United States is no exception and has expressly declared:

> The copyright law, like the patent statute, makes reward to the owner a secondary consideration. The sole interest of the United States and the primary objective in conferring the monopoly lies in the general benefits derived by the public from the labors of authors.[2]

That monopoly is of limited duration ensuring that however tightly a copyright owner controls a work, it will eventually pass into the public domain where it may freely be used by all. But during that monopoly period, those who use the creativity of others run the risk of civil suit, the loss of profit, fines and even imprisonment.

This principle is expressed in Article I, Section 8 of the United States Constitution. As you will note, copyright and patent protection were written into the body of the Constitution while protections for speech and press had to rely on an amendment.

> The Congress shall have power * * * to promote the Progress of Science and useful Arts by securing for limited Times to Authors and Inventors the exclusive Right to their respective Writings and Discoveries.

Passage of the first federal copyright statute as early as 1790 indicates that America's Revolutionary generation had a lively concern about the need for copyright protection. Additional copyright statutes were enacted during the 19th century[3] and the copyright statute was rewritten during this century.

History of Copyright

Underlying the words of Article I, Section 8 of the Constitution was the principle of copyright, which had been recognized by law for several centuries. It is known, for example, that the Republic of

---

[2] United States v. Paramount Pictures, 334 U.S. 131, 158, 68 S.Ct. 915 (1948) quoting Fox Film Corp. v. Doyal, 286 U.S. 123, 127, 52 S.Ct. 546, 547 (1932).

[3] Thorvald Solberg, Copyright Enactments of the United States, 1783–1906. Washington, 1906.

Venice in 1469 granted John of Speyer the exclusive right to print the letters of Pliny and Cicero for a period of five years.[4]

The development of printing increased the need for some form of copyright. Although printing from movable type began in 1451 and was introduced in England by 1476, the first copyright law was not passed in England until 1790 in the "Statute of 8 Anne." Before this time, the printing business was influenced in two distinct ways.

First, printing gave royalty and government in England the opportunity to reward favored individuals with exclusive printing monopolies. Second, those in power recognized that printing, unless strictly controlled, tended to endanger their rule.

Hoping to control the output of the printing presses, Queen Mary I granted a charter to the Stationers Company in 1556. This guild of printers was thus given a monopoly over book printing in England. Simultaneously these printers were given the authority to burn prohibited books and to jail the persons who published them.[5] The Stationers Company acted zealously against printers of unauthorized works, making use of terrifying powers of search and seizure. Tactics paralleling those of the Inquisition were used defending the doctrines of the Catholic Church against the burgeoning Reformation movement.[6]

The Stationers Company remained powerful into the seventeenth century, with its authority augmented by licensing statutes. The Act of 1662, for example, confined printing to 59 master printer members of the Stationers Company then practicing in London, and to the printers at Oxford and Cambridge Universities. The privileged position of the Stationers Company in England during the sixteenth and seventeenth centuries underlies the development of the law of copyright of more recent times. Printers who were officially sanctioned to print by virtue of membership in the Stationers Company complained when their works were issued in pirated editions by unauthorized printers.[7]

In time, the guild printers who belonged to the Stationers Company began to recognize a principle now known as "common law copyright." They began to assume that there was a common law right, *in perpetuity,* to literary property. That is, if a man printed a book, duly approved by government authority, the right

---

[4] R.C. DeWolf, Outline of Copyright Law (Boston: John W. Luce, 1925) p. 2.

[5] Philip Wittenberg, The Law of Literary Property (New York: World Publishing Co., 1957), pp. 25–26; Fredrick S. Siebert, Freedom of the Press in England, 1476–1776 (Urbana: University of Illinois Press, 1952) pp. 22, 65, 249.

[6] Siebert, op. cit., pp. 82–86; Mrs. Edward S. Lazowska, "Photocopying, Copyright, and the Librarian," American Documentation (April, 1968) pp. 123–130.

[7] Siebert, pp. 74–77, 239.

to profit from its distribution remained with that man, or his heirs, forever.[8]

Authors, like England's printers, came to believe that they also had some rights to profit from their works. Authors joined printers in the latter half of the seventeenth century in seeking Parliamentary legislation to establish the existence of copyright. In 1709, Parliament passed the *Statute of 8 Anne,* believed to have been drafted, in part, by two famed authors of that period, Joseph Addison and Jonathan Swift. This statute recognized the authors' rights, giving them—or their heirs or persons to whom they might sell their rights—exclusive powers to publish the book for 14 years after its first printing. If the author were still alive after those 14 years, that person could renew copyright for an additional 14 years.[9]

This limitation of copyright to a total of 28 years displeased both authors and printers. They complained for many years that they should have copyright in perpetuity under the common law. In 1774, the House of Lords, acting in its capacity of a court of the highest appeal, decided the case of Donaldson v. Beckett.

Common Law and Statutory Copyright

This 1774 decision was of enormous importance to the history of American law, because it outlined the two categories of copyrights, *statutory copyright* and *common law copyright.* The House of Lords ruled that the Statute of 8 Anne, providing a limited 28 year term of copyright protection, had superseded the common law protection for *published* works. Only *unpublished* works, therefore, could receive common law copyright protection in perpetuity. An author was to have automatic, limitless common law copyright protection for his creations only as long as they remained unpublished.

But once publication occurred, the author or publisher could have exclusive right to publish and profit from his works for only a limited period of time as decreed by legislative authority. The Statute 8 Anne, as upheld by the House of Lords in Donaldson v. Beckett, is the ancestor of modern copyright legislation in the United States.[10]

When the first federal copyright statute was adopted in the United States in 1790, implementing Article I, Section 8 of the Constitution, it gave the federal government *statutory* authority to administer copyrights. Since there was no general common law authority for federal courts, questions involving *common law* copy-

---

[8] Wittenberg, op. cit., pp. 45–46.

[9] Siebert, op. cit., p. 249; Wittenberg, Ibid., pp. 47–48.

[10] Burr. 2408 (1774); Lazowska, op. cit., p. 124.

right remained to be adjudicated in state courts.[11] In the 1834 case of Wheaton v. Peters, the Supreme Court of the United States enunciated the doctrine of common law copyright in America:[12]

> That an author at common law has a property right in his manuscript, and may obtain redress against any one who endeavors to realize a profit by its publication, cannot be doubted; but this is a very different right from that which asserts a perpetual and exclusive property in the future publication of the work, after the author shall have published it to the world.

Congress tried to do away with state authority over common law copyrights, phasing them out of existence with Sec. 301 of the Copyright Act of 1976. Of course, there would have to be a transitional period: Sec. 301 specifically preserved common law copyrights which were in effect before January 1, 1978—the effective date of the 1976 Copyright Act. The 1976 Act also worked to preempt much of state law regarding copyright. Today, copyright issues are litigated almost exclusively under the federal statute.

Common law copyright had both advantages and disadvantages. Its advantages were that it was automatic and perpetual so long as a manuscript or creation was not published. An author could circulate a manuscript among friends, could use it in class for experimental teaching materials, or, perhaps, could send it to several publishing houses without publication in the technical, legal sense. In general, as long as the manuscript was not offered to the general public, common law copyright protection remained intact.

Published works, however, had to have a copyright notice—for example, © John Steinbeck, 1941—in a specified place on a book or manuscript or other copyrightable item or the work would fall into the public domain. Once "in the public domain" a work no longer has copyright protection, and may be freely republished by others for their own profit.[13]

The Nature of Copyright

Copyright is an exclusive, legally recognizable claim to literary or pictorial property. It is a right, extended by federal statute, to entitle originators to ownership of the literary or artistic products of their minds. Before launching into more detailed discussion of provisions of the copyright statute now in force, consider the following five principles:

[11] Wheaton v. Peters, 33 U.S. (8 Pet.) 591 (1834); W.W. Willoughby, Constitutional Law of the United States, p. 446.

[12] 33 U.S. (8 Pet.) 591 (1834); Hirsch v. Twentieth Century–Fox Film Corp., 207 Misc. 750, 144 N.Y.S.2d 38, 105 U.S.P.Q. 253 (1955).

[13] 17 U.S.C.A. § 102.

(1) *Copyright applies to original works of creativity.* Copyright is separate from protections for useful articles like fuel injectors, video monitors and cellular telephones. Those items are protected by patent laws. Copyright also does not apply to those symbols that represent corporations or businesses. Those marks are protected by trademark laws. Instead, copyright protects original creativity expressed in an artistic manner. As such, it applies to the literary style of an article, news story, book, or other intellectual creation. It does *not* apply to the themes, ideas, or facts contained in the copyrighted material. Anyone may write about any subject. Copyright's protection extends only to the particular manner or style of expression. What is "copyrightable" in the print media, for example, is the order and selection of words, phrases, clauses, sentences, and the arrangement of paragraphs.[14]

(2) *Copyright is both a protection for and a restriction of the communications media.* Copyright protects the media by preventing the wholesale taking of the form of materials, without permission, from one person or unit of the media for publication by another person or unit of the media. Despite the guaranty of freedom of the press, newspapers and other communications media must acquire permission to publish material that is protected by copyright.[15]

(3) *As a form of literary property, copyright belongs to that class of personal property including patents, trade-marks, trade names, trade secrets, good will, unpublished lectures, musical compositions, and letters.*

(4) *Copyright, it must be emphasized, is quite different from creativity.* Copyright is created at the moment that an original work of creativity is fixed in tangible form. The creator has the copyright from the act of creation, generally. But, unlike the artistic spark of creativity, copyright can be held by someone other than the creator. If sold or otherwise transferred, the copyright will belong to someone else. If the work is a work for hire (a term of legal art), then the copyright will belong to the hiring party even at the moment of fixation in tangible form.

(5) *Copyright is distinct from the tangible thing created.* A letter, for example, may be copyrighted. The recipient of the letter is said to own the physical letter—the ink and paper—but the copyright remains with the author. The author has the exclusive right to decide whether or how to exploit what was said in the letter.[16] If you buy a painting, unless you have pur-

[14] Kaeser & Blair v. Merchants' Ass'n, 64 F.2d 575, 577 (6th Cir.1933); Eisenschiml v. Fawcett Publications, Inc., 246 F.2d 598 (7th Cir.1957).

[15] Cf. Chicago Record–Herald Co. v. Tribune Ass'n, 275 Fed. 797 (7th Cir.1921).

[16] Baker v. Libbie, 210 Mass. 599, 97 N.E. 109 (1912); Ipswich Mills v. Dillon, 260 Mass. 453, 157 N.E. 604 (1927). See also Alan Lee Zegas, "Personal Letters: A Dilemma for Copyright and Privacy Law," 33 Rutgers Law Review (1980) pp. 134–

chased the copyright, you do not have the right to make and sell lithographic copies.

SEC. 92.   SECURING A COPYRIGHT

Essentials in acquiring a copyright include notice of copyright, application, deposit of copies in the Library of Congress, and payment of the required fee.

What May Be Copyrighted

Reflecting awareness that new technologies will emerge and that human ingenuity will devise new forms of expression, the language of the new copyright statute is sweeping in defining what may be copyrighted. Section 102 says:[17]

(a) Copyright protection subsists * * * in original works of authorship fixed in any tangible medium of expression, now known or later developed, from which they can be perceived, reproduced, or otherwise communicated, either directly or with the aid of a machine or device. Works of authorship include the following categories:

 (1) literary works;

 (2) musical works, including any accompanying words;

 (3) dramatic works, including any accompanying music;

 (4) pantomimes and choreographic works;

 (5) pictorial, graphic, and sculptural works;

 (6) motion pictures and other audiovisual works; and

 (7) sound recordings.

(b) In no case does copyright protection for an original work of authorship extend to any idea, procedure, process, system, method of operation, concept, principle, or discovery, regardless of the form in which it is described, explained, illustrated, or embodied in such work.

The Copyright Notice

Under the 1976 statute, once something has been published the omission of a copyright notice or an error in that notice does not destroy the author or creator's protection.[18] Section 405 gives a copyright owner up to five years to register a work with the Register of Copyrights, Library of Congress, Washington, D.C., even

---

164. Writers who seek relief for unauthorized publication may sue for recovery under both copyright and privacy theories, although the author suggests that those areas of law offer writers inadequate protection.

[17] 17 U.S.C.A. § 102.

[18] 17 U.S.C.A. §§ 405, 406.

if that work has been published without notice.[19] In 1989, when the United States joined the Berne Copyright Union, this provision was further liberalized to provide full protection beyond this five year period to a copyrighted work without a proper notice.[20]

Section 401 makes the following general requirement about placing copyright notices on "visually perceptible copies."[21]

> Whenever a work protected under this title [Title 17, United States Code, the copyright statute] is published in the United States or elsewhere by authority of the copyright owner, a notice of copyright in this section shall be placed on all publicly distributed copies from which the work can be visually perceived, either directly or with the aid of a machine or device.

The copyright notice shall consist of these three elements:[22]

(1) the symbol © (the letter C in a circle), or the word "Copyright" or the abbreviation "Copr."; and

(2) the year of first publication of the work; in the case of compilations or derivative works incorporating previously published material, the year date of the first publication of the compilation or derivative work is sufficient. The year date may be omitted where a pictorial, graphic, or sculptural work, with accompanying text matter, if any, is reproduced in or on greeting cards, postcards, stationery, jewelry, dolls, toys, or any useful articles; and

(3) the name of the owner of copyright abbreviation by which the name can be recognized or a generally known alternative designation of the owner.

If a sound recording is being copyrighted, the notice takes a different form. The notice shall consist of the following three elements:[23]

(1) The symbol CIRP (the letter P in a circle); and

(2) the year of first publication of the sound recording; and

(3) the name of the owner of copyright in the sound recording, or an abbreviation by which the name can be recognized, or a generally known alternative designation of the owner; if

---

[19] Formerly, under the 1909 statute, publication without notice could mean that the authors lost any copyrights in their works if a defective notice—or no notice at all—appeared on the work. Leon H. Amdur, Copyright Law and Practice (New York: Clark Boardman Co., 1936), pp. 64–65; Holmes v. Hurst, 174 U.S. 82, 19 S.Ct. 606 (1899).

[20] U.S.C.A. ¶ 405

[21] 17 U.S.C.A. § 401(a).

[22] 17 U.S.C.A. § 401(b).

[23] 17 U.S.C.A. § 402(b), (c).

the producer of the sound recording is named on the phono record labels or containers, and if no other name appears in conjunction with the notice, the producer's name shall be considered a part of the notice.

The copyright statute adopts one of the former law's basic principles: in the case of works made for hire, the employer is considered the author of the work (and therefore the initial copyright owner) unless there has been an agreement to the contrary. The statute requires that any agreement under which the employee will own rights be in writing and signed by both the employee and the employer.[24]

The copyright notice shall be placed on the copies "in such manner and location as to give reasonable notice of the claim of copyright." Special methods of this "affixation" of the copyright notice and positions for notices on various kinds of works will be prescribed by regulations to be issued by the Register of Copyrights.[25]

Even though the lack of a proper copyright notice no longer bars a claim for copyright infringement, it is still extremely important to provide proper notice in order to prevent someone who has used a copyrighted work without permission from escaping statutory penalties by claiming to be unaware that the work was copyrighted.

Duration of Copyright

A most welcome change under the Act of 1976 set copyright duration at the life of the owner plus 50 years. This replaced the fouled-up and complicated system of the 1909 statute of an initial period of 28 years plus a renewal period of another 28 years. Copyright case law has any number of cautionary tales about the complexity of renewal, stories of valuable works whose copyrights were lost to their owners because of simple mistakes. One such case involved the movie "It's a Wonderful Life." In 1973, Republic Pictures, which had owned the copyright, failed to file the needed renewal papers and the movie fell into the public domain. That led to dozens of showings of the Frank Capra holiday classic by television stations that no longer had to get permission or pay royalties.[26]

---

[24] 17 U.S.C.A. § 201(b); see discussion of this section in House of Representatives Report No. 94–1476, "Copyright Law Revision."

[25] 17 U.S.C.A. § 401(c).

[26] Republic need not be pitied for too long. It managed to regain control of the film by acquiring the rights to the music. It already held the rights to the underlying short story. Republic's savvy move is discussed in the section on derivative works.

Under the old Act, renewals had to be applied for, and if unwary copyright owners waited a full 28 years to apply for their second term, they had waited too long and their works became part of the public domain—everybody's property. Also, the U.S. system was badly out of step with a great majority of the world's nations which had adopted a copyright term of the author's life plus 50 years. As noted in the legislative commentary accompanying the 1976 statute,[27]

> * * * American authors are frequently protected long-er in foreign countries than in the United States ... [This] disparity in the duration of copyright has provoked * * * some proposals of retaliatory legislation. * * * The need to conform the duration of U.S. copyright to that prevalent throughout the rest of the world is increasingly pressing in order to provide certainty and simplicity in international business dealings. Even more important, a change in the basis of our copyright term would place the United States in the forefront of the international copyright community. Without this change, the possibility of future United States adherence to the Berne Copyright Union would evaporate, but with it would come a great and immediate improve-ment in our copyright relations.

Existing works already under statutory copyright protection at the time of passage of the new copyright statute have had their copyright duration increased to 75 years. Works now in their first 28–year copyright under the old system must be renewed if they are in their 28th year, but the second term will be expanded to 47 years to provide a total of 75 years' protection. For copyrighted works in their renewal term, 19 years will be added so that copyright on such works will exist for a total of 75 years.[28] Congress repeatedly extended the terms of expiring copyrights from 1964 to 1975, in anticipation of the enactment of copyright revision.[29]

So works created today will have copyright durations that will vary from work to work as they are arise from creator to creator. The chief difference: the life span of the artistic creator. The term is not drawn from the life of the copyright holder, which can be different from the author or creator. If the copyright duration was decided by the life of the copyright holder, one could make copy-right perpetual by assigning the copyright to an infant every 70 or 80 years.

When a work is the result of collaboration, it is considered a joint work and the duration of copyright is the life of the last

[27] H.R. Report No. 94–1476, p. 135, discussing 17 U.S.C.A. § 302.

[28] 17 U.S.C.A. § 304.

[29] See H.R. Report No. 94–1476, p. 140.

surviving author plus 50 years. Can you extend the duration of copyright by attaching the names of several newborns to a copyright registration form? You can, but if challenged, it might be hard to explain how an infant contributed to the work. Another problem is that any of the joint authors can exploit the work meaning that the infant joint authors could make use of the work in ways the first author did not like. The only restriction on the joint author's use is that the profits must be accounted for with the other joint authors. Anonymous or pseudonymous works have copyrights of 75 years from the date of first publication. If the work is not published when created, the duration of the copyright is 100 years from the date of creation or 75 years from first publication, whichever comes first.

What about works for hire? Under the works-for-hire definition, the work is copyrighted in the hands of the person who has hired the author or artist. Should the duration of the copyright be measured in the employer or the actual creator? Under the 1976 statute, the duration is 75 years from the date of first publication or 100 years from the date of creation, whichever comes first. That avoids problems when the hiring party is young or the creator is old.

Copyright Registration and Deposit

Copyright registration is accomplished by filling out a form obtainable from:

> Register of Copyrights
> Library of Congress
> Washington, D.C. 20559

In addition, corresponding with the Publications Division of the Copyright Office can yield much helpful information. Information Package 109 contains sample forms, and Copyright Office Packet R–1, "Copyright Basics," provides a clear, concise description of the Act and its major provisions. The Copyright Office information service—as of 1998—was available by calling (202) 707–3000 weekdays between 8:30 a.m. and 5 p.m. A copyright hotline is provided for ordering specific forms: (202) 707–9100.

The Register of Copyrights will require (with some exceptions specified by the Copyright Office), that material deposited for registration shall include two complete copies of the best edition.[30] These copies are to be deposited within three months after publication, along with a completed form as prescribed by the Register of

---

[30] 17 U.S.C.A. § 407. Other useful circulars available in 1989 from the Publications Division of the Copyright include Circular Ric, Copyright Registration Procedures; Circular R22, How to Investigate the Copyright Status of a Work, and Circular R21, Reproduction of Copyrighted Works by Educators and Librarians.

Copyrights.[31] In 1998, a fee of $20 was set for most items being copyrighted.[32] It should be noted that registration is required before any action for copyright infringement can be started.[33]

Under the 1909 Act, a failure to properly give notice of the copyright meant a loss of the copyright. The 1976 Act provides that such a failure does not invalidate the copyright provided the omission was on a limited number of copies or if a reasonable attempt was made to fix the omission within five years or if the omission was a mistake on the part of the distributor where the copyright holder had expressly called for the distributor to put the proper notice on the works.

If an individual attempts a "bluff copyright"—that is, places a copyright notice on a work at the time of publication without bothering to register it and deposit copies as outlined above, that person could have some real difficulties with the Register of Copyrights. The Register of Copyrights may demand deposit of such unregistered works. Unless deposit is made within three months, an individual may be liable to pay a fine of up to $250. If a person "willfully or repeatedly" refuses to comply with such demand, a fine of $2,500 may be imposed.[34]

Copyright Ownership and Transfer

Copyright comes into being at the moment of fixation in tangible form and belongs to the copyright holder. In most cases that will be the creative person who has put words or music on paper, paint to canvas, chisel to stone, light to photographic emulsion or photosensitive electronic. Sometimes, it will be to the person who has hired the creative personality under the concept of "work for hire." Once in existence, copyright may be disposed of like other forms of property under the special rules of copyright law and practice.

Works for Hire

Section 101 of the 1976 Act defines a "work made for hire" as: (1) a work prepared by an employee within the scope of his or her employment; or (2) a work specially ordered or commissioned for use as a contribution to a collective work, as part of a motion picture or other audiovisual work, as a translation, as a supplementary work, as a compilation, as an instructional text, as a test, as answer material for a test, or as an atlas, if the parties expressly agree in a written instrument signed by them that the work shall be considered a "work made for hire."

[31] 17 U.S.C.A. § 407.

[32] Payment of fees is specified by 17 U.S.C.A. § 708.

[33] 17 U.S.C.A. § 411; see also 17 U.S.C.A. § 205.

[34] 17 U.S.C.A. § 407(d).

It is relatively easy to dispose of questions of copyright owner-ship under (2) of the definition. In order for someone other than the artist herself to claim the copyright ownership, there must be an express written agreement signed by the parties. Any agree-ments must be made at the time the work is being created. Once the work has been fixed in tangible form, the copyright has already been created and vested in the artist. Any agreement covering ownership after fixation would be a transfer and not a definition of rights under the "work made for hire" provision of the Act. Where there is no agreement, the artist retains the copyright. For (2) to apply, the work must fall into one of the categories laid out in the definition. But what about (1)? When is an artist considered an employee and what creative activity falls within the "scope of his or her employment?" Does anyone lose her copyright just because she is employed by someone else?

The Supreme Court took up the issue in Community for Creative Non–Violence v. Reid.[35] The case arose over a dispute between the Community for Creative Non–Violence (CCNV), a group dedicated to aiding the homeless, and a sculptor. The home-less group asked Reid to create a sculpture to show the plight of the homeless. "[I]n lieu of the traditional Holy Family, the two adult figures and the infant would appear as contemporary homeless people huddled on a street side steam grate" with the legend, "and still there is no room at the inn."[36] It was to be shown during the 1985 Christmas pageant in Washington.

On several occasions during the creation of the work, members of CCNV visited Reid to both check on his progress and make preparations for the construction of the base of the sculpture which CCNV was to make. The CCNV visitors commented and, as the Court reported in its syllabus of the case, "Reid accepted most of CCNV's suggestions and directions as to the sculpture's configura-tion and appearance."[37] Once the project was completed and paid for, CCNV and Reid installed the sculpture on the base and put it on display. Then, a dispute developed over CCNV's plans to take the sculpture on tour. Reid, who had possession of the sculpture, and CCNV then independently filed for copyright. The district court ruled that CCNV owned the copyright because it was a "work made for hire." The court of appeals reversed saying that the work did not fall under "work for hire" because Reid was not an employee. He was, instead, an independent contractor. Because sculpture was not on the list of "commissioned or specially or-

[35] Community for Creative Non-Violence v. Reid, 490 U.S. 730, 109 S.Ct. 2166 (1989).

[36] Ibid. at 733, 109 S.Ct. at 2169.

[37] Ibid. at 730, 109 S.Ct. at 2167.

dered" works, it could not be considered a work for hire, especially since there was no written agreement making it a work for hire.

The Supreme Court agreed with the appellate court that the sculpture did not fit into the list of works under § 101(2) that would qualify it as a work for hire. The Court then turned to the question of whether Reid was an employee under § 101(1). The justices had little direct guidance from the Copyright Act. Unlike many other terms, it does not define employee or scope of employment and the lower courts had come up with several different and conflicting approaches. One approach looked at the degree of actual control exercised over the creative person. A second test rested on whether the hiring party retained the right to control regardless of whether the hiring party actually exercised that control. A third approach would limit "employee" status only to those people who were "formal, salaried employees."

The Supreme Court rejected those approaches and settled on a straightforward approach that relied on traditional ways to defining who is what. "In the past when Congress has used the term 'employee' without defining it, we have concluded that Congress intended to describe the conventional master-servant relationship as understood by common-law agency doctrine ... "[38]The Court then laid out the rule that would apply to determine when a work belonged to the hiring party or the actual creator.

> In determining whether a hired party is an employee under the general common law of agency, we consider the hiring party's right to control the manner and means by which the product is accomplished. Among the other factors relevant to this inquiry are the skill required; the source of the instrumentalities and tools; the location of the work; the duration of the relationship between the parties; whether the hiring party has the right to assign additional projects to the hiring party; the extent of the hired party's discretion over when and how long to work; the method of payment; the hired party's role in hiring and paying assistants; whether the hiring party is in business; the provision of employee benefits; and the tax treatment of the hired party. * * * No one of these factors is determinative.[39]

In *Reid*, the Court determined that consideration of these factors led to a conclusion that Reid was not an employee and that his work was not a work for hire. Among other things, Reid was a highly skilled artist, he supplied his own tools, worked for CCNV for a brief period, made his own decisions in hiring his assistants,

---

[38] Ibid. at 739–740, 109 S.Ct. at 2172.
[39] Ibid. at 751, 109 S.Ct. at 2178–2179.

he was paid in a manner consistent with independent contractors and did not have Social Security or payroll taxes paid by CCNV. Therefore, CCNV was not the copyright owner under "work for hire." However, the Court did not make Reid the copyright owner either. Because of the contributions that CCNV made in the process of creating the sculpture, a lower court had raised the issue of whether it was a joint work. The Supreme Court sent the case back down to the lower courts for a disposition of the issue.

Reporters employed by periodicals and broadcast operations will be treated as employees when they are reporting the news. Free-lance journalists will most likely sell the copyrights to their works. Students working in the classroom may be considered under the direction of their schools.

Joint Works

Section 101 of the Copyright Act defines a "joint work" as "a work prepared by two or more authors with the intention that their contributions be merged into inseparable or interdependent parts of a unitary whole." Joint work can create problems if the language is read literally. An editor will make contributions to an article or book and those contributions are intended to be merged into the work as a whole. A research assistant will prepare a summary of the materials found which may be included verbatim in the final research project. A songwriter, looking for just the right word to complete a lyric may ask an acquaintance for help. Does the editing, research summary or single word turn the work into a joint work? This can be particularly troubling when dealing with works that have many contributors, such as team projects. Joint works are valuable to the copyright owners. Each may exploit the work, with or without the consent of the other owner, and is only required to account for the profits to the other owner.

A case from the Second Circuit Court of Appeal has helped refine the concept. In Childress v. Taylor[40] the Second Circuit dealt with a case arising over conflicting copyright claims by a playwright and actress. *Childress* arose over a play about the life of the legendary comedienne Jackie "Moms" Mabley. Actress Clarice Taylor had portrayed "Moms" Mabley in an off-Broadway production in the 1980s. After the experience, Taylor began collecting material about the comedienne and interviewing friends and family. In 1985, Taylor contacted Alice Childress, an award-winning playwright about writing a play based on "Moms" Mabley.

After an initial rejection, Childress agreed to take on the project, although the two did not enter into any firm arrangements about the play at the time. The theater chosen for the production required that the work be completed in six weeks. Taylor turned

---

[40] Childress v. Taylor, 945 F.2d 500 (2d Cir.1991).

her research material over to Childress and conducted additional research at Childress' request. Childress was the author, though Taylor provided insights into the character of "Moms" Mabley, suggested scenes and proposed the inclusion of additional characters. In all, Childress identified eight major contributions to the play made by Taylor. As the court wrote, "Essentially, Taylor contributed facts and details about "Moms" Mabley's life and discussed some of them with Childress. However, Childress was responsible for the actual structure of the play and the dialogue."[41]

Childress finished the play in time for the production. Taylor paid her $2,500 and produced the work. Childress filed for and received the copyright in the play. Taylor then prepared for a second production. In the course of the writing of the play and during the two productions, Taylor sought to establish through her agent that both she and Childress would own the play together. Childress responded through her agent that she was "claiming originality for her words only in said script." The two exchanged draft contracts but could not come to terms. Eventually Childress sued Taylor for copyright infringement. Taylor responded that she was a joint author and had an equal right to the play.

The district court granted summary judgment to Childress saying that the facts were clear enough that Childress, who had written the play, was the sole owner that trial was not necessary. Taylor appealed and the court of appeals took over from there dealing with the issues of copyrightability as a requirement of co-authorship and the intent question. At the time, a significant issue in joint authorship was whether the contribution of the second author had to be copyrightable itself. Various lower courts had reasoned that if the contribution could not stand alone as a copyrightable work, it could not lead to a joint copyright. The appellate court criticized the copyrightability test.

> The Act surely does not say that each contribution to a joint work must be copyrightable, and the specification that there be "authors" does not necessarily require a copyrightable contribution. "Author" is not defined in the Act and appears to be used only in its ordinary sense of an originator. The "author" of an uncopyrightable idea is nonetheless its author even though, for perfectly valid reasons, the law properly denies him a copyright on the result of his creativity. * * * It has not been supposed that the statutory grant of "authorship" status to the employer of a work for hire exceeds the Constitution, through the

[41] 945 F.2d 500, 502 (2d Cir.1991).

employer has shown skill only in selecting employees, not in creating protectable expression.[42]

But even though it voiced the criticism the appellate court decided to adopt the copyrightability test. It may seem counterintuitive that it did, but the court explained that to decline to require that the claimed contribution be copyrightable would be to open the doors to false claims by people who could not point to a concrete contribution, but who nonetheless could still say they had inspired or in some other way helped along the way. The court said that the copyrightability requirement struck a balance between the provinces of copyright and contract law. Where two or more authors contribute copyrightable material, copyright protects relative interests. Where one party hires an author, contract law will establish the relationship and the "work for hire" rules will assign the copyright where it belongs. Where a contributor does not have a copyrightable contribution, a contract can set out the rights of the parties even down to an assignment of part of the copyright. "It seems more consistent with the spirit of copyright law to oblige all joint authors to make copyrightable contributions, leaving those with non-copyrightable contributions to protect their rights through contract."[43]

The Second Circuit then turned to the intent test for joint works. The intent test that the Second Circuit focuses on goes beyond the simple "intention that their contributions be merged into inseparable or interdependent parts of a unitary whole" laid out in the Act. The Second Circuit concludes that a simple application of that intent test would create unintended and unwanted consequences.

> For example, a writer frequently works with an editor who makes numerous useful revisions to the first draft, some of which will consist of additions of copyrightable expressions. Both intend their contributions to be merged into inseparable parts of a unitary whole, yet few editors and even fewer writers would expect the editor to be accorded the status of joint author, enjoying an undivided half interest in the copyright in the published work. Similarly, research assistants may on occasion contribute to an author some material as would be entitled to copyright, yet not be entitled to be regarded as a joint author of the work in which the contributed material appears. What distinguishes the writer-editor and the writer-researcher from the true joint author relationship is the lack of intent of

[42] Ibid. At 506.
[43] Ibid. At 507.

both participants in the venture to regard themselves as joint authors.[44]

In *Childress*, the Second Circuit noted that the trial court found no such intent on Childress' part. "As Judge Haight observed, whatever thought of co-authorship might have existed in Taylor's mind 'was emphatically not shared by the purported co-author.' There is no evidence that Childress ever contemplated, much less would have accepted, crediting the play as 'written by Alice Childress and Clarice Taylor.' "[45]

Contributors who wish to preserve their rights then must make sure that what they bring to a project first qualifies as copyrightable material and then firmly establish that joint authorship is what all contributing authors had in mind. Evidence can take the form of declarations of the authors *at the time the work is created*, jointly approved promotional material or solicitations that clearly state the co-authorship relationship and representations, by the author who later claims sole authorship, of his intent at the time, to be involved in a joint work.

Transfer of Rights

As with many work of creativity, the truest test of admiration of a work is the willingness of someone else to part with cash for it. In copyright, the value of a work may be tested by a buyer's willingness to pay for the right to exploit the work. In this segment, we talk about the process of transferring the various rights of the copyright bundle to buyers.

The rights that accrue to the copyright holder are laid out in the segment on "The Bundle of Rights." In this segment we deal with the ways a copyright holder can transfer some or all of her rights in the copyrighted work. During the term of the copyright, addressed in the section on duration, the copyright holder has the right to transfer all or part of her rights. On her death, if the rights have not been transferred, they may pass by descent to her heirs who then have the right to transfer the rights until the remainder of the copyright term expires.

Under the 1909 statute, a *single* legal title was held by a "proprietor" to any writing or artistic creation. Typically if an author sold the right to publish a work, it meant that *all* rights then belonged to the purchaser.[46] Under the revised statute, authors can sell *some* rights or *all* rights as they wish. Section 201(d)(2) says that, "Any of the exclusive rights comprised in a

---

44 Ibid. At 507.

45 Ibid. At 509.

46 Harry G. Henn, "Ownership of Copyright, Transfer of Ownership," in James C. Goodale, chairman, Communications Law 1979 (New York: Practising Law Institute, 1979), pp. 709–711.

copyright, including any subdivision of any of the rights specified by section 106 may be transferred and owned separately." In that way, a writer may sell "one-time rights"—for use of the work only once—and then will keep other rights to re-sell the same work. For example, a magazine article—such as "The Urban Cowboy," published in *Esquire Magazine*—became the basis for a smash motion picture of the same name. Under § 201 of the revised copyright act, an author retains ownership in anything that author has written unless those rights are *expressly* granted to a publisher.[47]

The Copyright Act defines transfers as "an assignment, mortgage, exclusive license, or any other conveyance, alienation, or hypothecation of a copyright or of any of the exclusive rights comprised in a copyright, whether or not it is limited in time or place of effect, but not including a nonexclusive license."[48] In plain English, this means that there are any number of ways to move the rights from the original copyright holder to someone else. When authors are beginning their careers, they often start out in weak bargaining positions and when publishers take a chance on them, they may ask for an assignment of all rights. That means that if the work is a success, the publisher will be able to recoup the expenses of developing new authors. Periodicals may seek the exclusive rights for North American publication, becoming the party able to control publication in that geographical area. Other times, parties may seek to purchase serialization rights, the right to publish in a series of articles. Movie rights are the grail for many new writers. Movie production companies may seek to purchase all rights to a work. They may also seek, for substantially less money, a license for a period of time in which to develop a movie. If the movie is made the license will continue, if not the license will expire and the writer is free to seek new producers.

Copyright holders should take care to protect the bundle of rights and to sell only what they want to sell at a particular time. One of the ways to help protect copyright holders come in the requirement that copyright transfers be in writing and signed by the owner. That formality makes the transfer one that is not lightly undertaking. Transfers may be recorded with the Register of Copyrights and that will provide the transferee with a constructive (understood rather than actual) notice of his rights.

The Bundle of Rights

A copyright grants to its holder certain exclusive rights that involve the exploitation of the work. They are:

1. reproduction of the work in copies or phono records;

---

[47] 17 U.S.C.A. § 201.
[48] Ibid.

2. preparation of derivative works based on the work itself;

3. distribution by rent, lease, loan, sale or other transfer of ownership of copies or phono records of the copyrighted work;

4. public performance of literary, musical, dramatic, choreographic works, pantomimes, motion pictures and other audiovisual work;

5. public display of pictorial, graphic, sculptural, literary, musical, dramatic, choreographic works, pantomimes, and individual images of motion pictures and other audiovisual works; and

6. public performance of sound recordings by means of digital audio transmission.[49]

There are limitations to these exclusive rights that will be taken up in this chapter. Of special importance is the "fair use" provision of the copyright statute that permits some uses without the consent of the copyright holder. Authors, artists, movie makers, multimedia producers need to know what is included in these rights in order to more effectively protect their interests and to avoid costly litigation in infringement actions.

1. The right to reproduce is just that—making copies. The copyright holder (and here we will presume that the copyright holder is also the author), having given birth through the creative process, has the right to decide when or even if his creativity will be copied. This is the most basic of the rights regarding the exploitation of creative works. In NBC v. Sonneborn[50] a federal district court found that a firm that made and sold reprints of audiovisual works had infringed NBC's copyright to a kinescope (precursor of today's videotape) of "Peter Pan," shown by the network on Dec. 8, 1960. The network lost track of several of the kinescopes after its broadcast. One of the copies apparently made it to the East Brunswick, New Jersey, library. In 1979 Joel Sonneborn, president of Reel Images, was told by someone at the library that the library had a copy of the "Peter Pan" kinescope. Sonneborn offered to repair the kinescope, which was damaged, in return for being able to copy and sell videotaped copies of "Peter Pan." In 1980, NBC applied for copyright registration for "Peter Pan" and obtained an injunction against Sonneborn. As mentioned above, NBC had to go through the formalities of registration before it could go to court. The district court found that once it had the valid copyright registration, NBC could exercise its rights under § 106(1) to prevent Sonneborn from making copies.

2. Preparation of derivative works goes to the adaptation of a work. Take a novel. A play based on the novel will be derived from

---

[49] 17 U.S.C.A. § 106.

[50] NBC v. Sonneborn, 630 F.Supp. 524 (D.Conn.1985).

that literary work. A movie made of the play will be derived from the play and the novel both. A multimedia presentation made from the movie will be derived from the movie, play and novel. As long as a work is taken from the creative expression of a previous work, it is considered a derivative. This right is particularly valuable as movie rights can command impressive sums.

An interesting point about derivative rights is that each subsequent version of the original work will have copyrights all their own. Ricordi & Co. v. Paramount Pictures[51] illustrates the point. The case deals with the rights of the original author of the novel "Madame Butterfly," the author of a stage play made from the novel and the authors of an opera made from play and novel. John Luther Long, the author of the novel, wrote his work in 1897. In 1900, David Belasco wrote his play with Long's permission. In 1904, Ricordi obtained the rights to make a libretto for an opera based on Belasco's play, which was based on Long's novel. In 1932, the administrator of Long's estate granted Paramount the right to make a movie based on the novel. Both sides claimed the rights to make the movie—Ricordi, because it owned the rights to libretto; Paramount, because it had obtained the movie rights to the novel. Each side asserted its right to what it owned. The result was a standoff. Paramount could not make a movie without the dramatic elements from the opera. Ricordi could not make a movie without the underlying story (The court ended its work with the finding of the respective rights. It was then up to the parties to resolve the issue.).[52]

The issue of derivative rights came into play over the Frank Capra movie, "It's a Wonderful Life." Republic Pictures owned the copyright to the 1947 movie. In 1973, Republic failed to file the necessary papers to renew its copyright (This was under the 1909 Act which created an initial copyright term and a second renewal term). The movie fell into the public domain and anyone and everyone could exploit it without getting permission from or paying fees to Republic. But a 1990 case involving another movie that ran afoul of the complexities of the renewal process gave Republic a means of reasserting control.

The case, Stewart v. Abend[53] dealt with the movie "Rear Window." "Rear Window" was based on a short story, "It Had to Be Murder" written by Cornell Woolrich. Woolrich sold the movie

---

[51] Ricordi v. Paramount, 189 F.2d 469 (2d Cir.1951).

[52] Ibid. At the risk of making this even more complicated, Belasco did not renew his copyright in his play and it passed into the public domain, which meant that anyone could use it, that is the elements he added to the novel. The copyright in the novel was renewed so the elements of the novel incorporated into the play could not be used without permission.

[53] Stewart v. Abend, 495 U.S. 207, 110 S.Ct. 1750 (1990).

rights to "It Had to Be Murder" and five other stories. He agreed to renew those rights when he renewed his copyright. But Woolrich died before he could do that. He had renewed his copyright in the story and that went into his estate. Abend bought the rights from the executor of Woolrich's estate for $650 plus 10 percent of the proceeds he generated from the story. The Supreme Court held that Abend had the rights to the underlying work and those rights controlled the uses of the derivative work movie.

Republic owned the rights to the story. It obtained the rights to the music used in the picture and then announced a crackdown on the unauthorized display, distribution and sales of "It's a Wonderful Life."[54] In addition to halting the multiple showings of the movie, Republic's actions also served to take out of circulation unauthorized colorized versions of the movie. Executive vice president of Republic Pictures Steven Beeks said that Republic had taken steps to ensure the quality of the copies of the movie available to the public. "People have hacked it up ... people have these scratched up negatives ... the picture isn't given its due."[55]

Derivative rights include other media and works as well. In Mirage Editions v. Albuquerque A.R.T.[56] the courts dealt with a company that was taking artworks and creating ceramic decorative tiles out of them. Albuquerque A.R.T. had taken a commemorative book of the artwork of Patrick Nagel, removed selected pages and mounted them on ceramic tiles which it then sold. The trial court found that the transformation from book form to decorative tile amounted to the creation of derivative works and that Albuquerque did not have permission from the copyright holder to do so. The district court granted summary judgment to Mirage and the 9th Circuit affirmed.

In a broadcasting case, Lone Ranger Television, Inc. v. Program Radio Corp.[57], the owner of radio program scripts and tapes sued two distributors in an infringement action. Lone Ranger had obtained copyrights in 15 scripts about the Lone Ranger. It recorded the scripts and broadcast the programs in 1953 and 1954. In 1979, a former radio personality Jim Lewis started leasing Lone Ranger episodes through his two distribution companies. He had taken the old broadcast tapes and re-mixed them, recording them on cartridges for broadcasters. It was this re-mixing that constituted the creation of derivative works. The derivative work is more than simply copying. It is taking the copyrighted work and adding

[54] Chris Koseluk Entertainment News Service, "Not a 'Wonderful' Year Now We'll Discover What Life is Like Without George Bailey," Chicago Tribune, Dec. 1993.

[55] Ibid.

[56] 856 F.2d 1341 (9th Cir.1988).

[57] Lone Ranger Television v. Program Radio, 740 F.2d 718 (9th Cir.1984).

to it to exploit it in a new market. "The Lone Ranger tapes meet this test: the contribution of independent expression by the actors, together with the contribution of independent expression by the special production methods of taping and editing for radio, effectively created a new work for a market different from both the market for printed scripts and the market for live dramas."[58]

Persons engaged in multimedia production should take note of derivative works rights for two reasons: (1) the use of a copyrighted work in a multimedia production may infringe a copyright holder's exclusive right to make derivative works, and (2) multimedia producers may not be protected even if they obtain a right from a single party to use a derivative work, such as a movie, because that license may not cover all potential plaintiffs.

> The copyright holder in an original literary work turned into a motion picture holds the underlying copyright. The screenwriter can hold a derivative copyright in the photo play for those elements she has added to the original. The songwriter holds the copyright in the music for the score, the choreographer can hold the copyright in the choreography and the motion picture company holds the copyright for the work as a whole.[59]

3. Distribution of copies through sale, lease, loan, etc., to the public encompasses a large part of the economic heart of copyright. Best sellers mean high volume sales and each sale generates income for the copyright holder. In most cases, though, the creator of the work will have transferred the bundle of copyrights to a publisher who will exploit the work and reap the income.

In Columbia Pictures, et al., v. Landa,[60] thirteen movie and video production companies took three owners of video rental stores to court over their copying and distribution of more than 200 movies. An undercover investigator for the Motion Picture Association of America (MPAA) swore by affidavit that he purchased or rented 35 illegally duplicated videocassettes from the three stores between May 14 and June 14 of 1996. The investigator also said that he and other MPAA investigators saw Domingo Landa, one of the defendants, transporting videocassettes from the home of co-defendant Jason Frank to Landa's video store. Deputy U.S. Marshals, on orders of the court, seized more than 4,000 videocassettes from the defendants' stores and seven duplicating machines and supplies to make copies from Frank's home. In granting summary judgment to the plaintiffs, the court noted that the movie compa-

---

[58] Ibid. At 721.

[59] Bill Loving, "Teaching Multimedia in the Law Class," Feedback, Volume 37, Number 4, Fall 1996.

[60] Columbia Pictures v. Landa, 974 F.Supp. 1 (C.D.Ill.1997).

nies had not granted copying or distribution rights to Landa and the other defendants, that Frank admitted copying and distribution and that the videocassettes themselves failed to show the marks that would prove they were authorized copies. That meant that Landa and his co-defendants were liable for infringement two ways:

> [T]he uncontradicted evidence reveals that Defendant Landa, without proper authorization, illegally distributed to the public copyrighted material owned by Plaintiff. Thus, whether the Court draws the inference that Landa copied the protected material or finds that Landa distributed illegally duplicated videocassettes, does not change the result; Landa is liable for copyright infringement pursuant to 17 U.S.C. § 106.[61]

4. Public performance of works covers the economic exploitation through the process of letting the people come see the work as expressed by performers. Friday and Saturday nights we see this in action as people line up at the CineOmniPlexOdeon to watch the latest Hollywood blockbuster. It also covers concerts, stage plays and even night clubs. The genesis of the public performance right began in the mid to late 1800s when the right of public performance was granted to the copyright owners of dramatic and musical works. Things were relatively quiet on that front until the composer Victor Herbert sued the Shanley Company over the performance of one of Herbert's songs in the dining room of the Vanderbilt Hotel.

At the time composers benefitted from their copyrighted compositions through royalties they earned on the sale of their sheet music. Herbert, though, believed that others were gaining an advantage by being able to play his compositions. He wanted to be compensated for this exploitation and he brought suit. The district court agreed with Herbert and decided he should be paid for this public performance. The circuit court of appeals reversed, saying that the Shanley Company's performance in the hotel dining room was not a performance for profit. Herbert would be entitled to compensation if the hotel were selling tickets to a concert, the circuit court said. "We construed the language of the act giving to the copyright proprietor the exclusive right 'to perform the copyrighted work publicly for profit, if it be a musical composition,' to be limited to performances where an admission fee or some direct pecuniary charge is made."[62] That set the stage for the Supreme Court to rule. Justice Holmes delivered the opinion of the court in which he concluded that the 2nd Circuit's analysis was incorrect.

---

[61] Ibid. at 13.

[62] Herbert v. Shanley, 229 Fed. 340 (2d Cir.1916).

If the rights under the copyright are infringed only by a performance where money is taken at the door, they are very imperfectly protected.

* * *

The defendants' performances are not eleemosynary. They are part of a total for which the public pays, and the fact that the price of the whole is attributed to a particular item which those present are expected to order is not important. It is true that the music is not the sole object, but neither is the food, which probably could be got cheaper elsewhere. The object is a repast in surroundings that to people having limited powers of conversation, or disliking rival noise, give a luxurious pleasure not to be had from eating a silent meal. If music did not pay, it would be given up.[63]

The principle in *Herbert* applies today to businesses that install sound systems to create a more pleasing atmosphere for their customers. It also requires that television stations, radio stations, movie companies pay royalties to the copyright owners of musical compositions. As it is difficult for the individual to promote, distribute and oversee the use of her works, this right will often be sold to a corporation that specializes in public entertainment or a voluntary association that will represent all its member copyright holders for purposes of negotiation and collection of their just due (Broadcast Music Licensing Rights are dealt with later in this chapter.).

With the advent of commercial radio broadcasts, the courts and later Congress had to deal with the treatment of music played in commercial establishments through radio receivers. In Buck v. Jewell–La Salle Realty,[64] the Supreme Court concluded that a hotel that had wired its guests' room with radio speakers was publicly performing the works and had to compensate the copyright holders.[65]

The issues posed by the case were both clarified and muddied in Twentieth Century Music Corp. v. Aiken[66]. In *Aiken* the court was faced with a case in which a business was playing the plaintiff's copyrighted works through four speakers connected to a radio receiver. George Aiken owned George Aiken's Chicken, a small fast-food restaurant in Pittsburgh, Pa. It was a small restaurant and

---

[63] Herbert v. Shanley, 242 U.S. 591, 594–595, 37 S.Ct. 232, 233 (1917).

[64] 283 U.S. 191, 51 S.Ct. 410 (1931).

[65] In this case, the radio station had failed to secure a permission to publicly perform the songs as well. The station also was forced to make payments. The case left open the question of whether the hotel would have had to pay if the radio station had already obtained permission to publicly perform the works. That would be answered in the next case.

[66] Twentieth Century v. Aiken, 422 U.S. 151, 95 S.Ct. 2040 (1975).

much of the business was carry-out trade. The evidence suggested that the primary benefit of having the radio and speakers was to keep the restaurant staff entertained on the job. The few patrons who ate at Aiken's Chicken did so quickly and left without whiling away the time listening to the radio. The plaintiff sued Aiken alleging that his radio reception of a Pittsburgh radio station amounted to public performance. The Supreme Court disagreed saying that it would be impossible to keep track of all the small businesses that keep radios on their premises. Further, the Court said, holding that tuning in to a radio broadcast amounted to public performance would mean that small business owners would have to monitor the songs to be sure that only those compositions for which they had licenses were heard. Finally, the Court said, giving copyright holders the right to force listeners to pay would exceed the logic of the system of copyright protections.

[T]o hold that all in Aiken's position "performed" these musical compositions would be to authorize the sale of an untold number of licenses for what is basically a single public rendition of a copyrighted work. The exaction of such multiple tribute would go far beyond what is required for the economic protection of copyright owners * * *[67]

When Congress wrote the 1976 Copyright Act, it looked at *Aiken*. The House committee sponsoring the Act referred to the case and said that *Aiken* represented the "outer limit" of the exemption to the public performance right. That exemption allowed small businesses with unsophisticated sound systems to receive radio broadcasts. The committee said that larger establishments and better sound systems could be equated to commercial music services. In 1981, the federal courts had the opportunity to apply that to a case involving copyright holders and the business community.

In Sailor Music v. Gap,[68] a federal district court dealt with the public performance rights in music played through radio broadcasts used in a retail setting. A group of music companies sued The Gap Stores for playing their copyrighted songs over sound systems in two Gap stores in New York City. One Gap store encompassed 2,769 square feet of customer space and the second had 4,690 square feet. That compared with Aiken's Chicken's 620 square feet. The smaller Gap store had four speakers mounted in the ceiling and the larger had seven, all placed to provide music in the customer areas. Aiken's had four located in the kitchen area. The Gap sought the protection of Section 110 (5)[69] which lays out

---

[67] Ibid. At 162–163, 95 S.Ct. at 2047.

[68] 516 F.Supp. 923 (S.D.N.Y.1981), *affirmed* 668 F.2d 84 (2d Cir.1981) *cert. denied* 456 U.S. 945, 102 S.Ct. 2012 (1982).

[69] 17 U.S.C. § 110(5).

exemptions to the exclusive rights granted under Section 106. Subsection 5 provides that it is not an infringement to communicate a radio broadcast provided that the broadcast is received on a single receiver "of a kind commonly used in private homes." But even if the broadcasts are relayed through such a receiver it still can be an infringement if: "(A) a direct charge is made to see or hear the transmission; or (B) the transmission received is further transmitted to the public,"[70]

The presiding judge explained that the exemption would serve those "small commercial establishments whose proprietors merely bring onto their premises small standard radio or television equipment and turn it on for their customers' enjoyment * * * "[71] But the Gap store sound systems went beyond the simple home systems that were intended to be protected by Section 110(5), the judge said. The Gap's set up amounted to a retransmission of the copyrighted songs to the public through its use of its loudspeaker music system which carried the radio broadcasts.

The public performance issue became a public relations hot potato from 1995 through 1997 when the American Society of Composers, Authors and Publishers (ASCAP) approached the American Camping Association in 1995 and said it wanted to settle the matter of public performance fees.[72] Campers were singing songs covered by copyrights held by ASCAP members and their singing, "where a substantial number of persons outside of a normal circle of a family and its social acquaintances is gathered."[73] ASCAP offered to discount its site fees and the camping association agreed. But later in 1995, the camping group sent a newsletter to its members warning that ASCAP could charge for singing around the campfire. ASCAP was dealing with an attack on the public performance fees it collected under the Copyright Act.[74] Small businesses and religious groups were in front of Congress seeking an exemption from the fees. Bloomberg Business News reported that the Girls Scouts were facing fees for singing around the campfire and the national media seized the story with both hands culminating in a scene in which a group of Elves, Girls Scout helpers, danced the Macarena in silence for reporters. ASCAP eventually reached an agreement with the camping association in which the association would pay $1 per camp per year for the right to publicly perform ASCAP-licensed music.

[70] Ibid.

[71] Sailor Music v. Gap, 516 F.Supp. 923, 925 (S.D.N.Y.1981).

[72] Elisabeth Bumiller, New York Times News Service, "Campfire Royalties Burn ASCAP," Cleveland Plain Dealer, Dec. 22, 1996.

[73] 17 U.S.C. § 101.

[74] Lou Carlozo, "The Sound of Money," Chicago Tribune, Aug. 12, 1996.

5. The right of public display covers those works that generally are considered to be in the fine arts. It also applies to individual images from movies or other audiovisual works. Persons familiar with college campuses will note that bands often create promotional material by using still photos from movies. Such uses can run afoul of Section 106(5).

6. Section 106(6) deals with the rights of copyright holders when their works are transmitted by means of digital audio transmission. Simply put, this covers the field of specialized music services, including interactive "music on demand" services that have arisen as technology has provided the means to offer personalized information, data and entertainment services.

The division of the copyright into these six areas came with the implementation of the 1976 Copyright Act. This bundle of rights has benefitted copyright holders by allowing them to sell or license them individually and thus more effectively exploit the works. As Professor Kent R. Middleton has pointed out, authors' ownership of rights under the old statute was precarious indeed. "One change," Middleton wrote, "which makes copyright divisible, gives the author greater flexibility in selling his work to different media. The other, vesting initial ownership with the creator of a work, makes the author's title more secure."[75]

Technology has added complexity to the issue of sale of rights and royalties. In 1993, Jonathon Tasini and nine other free-lance writers sued the New York Times, Time, the Atlantic, Mead Data Central and University Microfilms.[76] Tasini and his co-plaintiffs sued over the defendants' use of their articles in electronic databases and CD ROMs. The writers had sold their articles to the periodicals for publication. The periodicals, after printing the articles on paper, then published them on their web sites, databases and CD–ROMs. The case was significant because many of the contracts used by publishers did not mention electronic publishing. The district court ruled that the publishers were entitled to publish in both paper and electronic forms without having to get additional permissions from the free-lance writers.[77]

The court concluded that the publishers had the right to include the articles in electronic form under the terms of § 201© "Copyright in each separate contribution to a collective work is distinct from copyright in the collective work as a whole, and vests initially in the author of the contribution. In the absence of an express transfer of the copyright or any rights under it, the owner

[75] Kent R. Middleton, "Copyright and the Journalist: New Powers for the Free–Lancer," Journalism Quarterly 56:1 (Spring, 1979), p. 39.

[76] Tasini v. New York Times, 972 F.Supp. 804 (S.D.N.Y.1997).

[77] Tasini v. New York Times, 972 F.Supp. 804 (S.D.N.Y.1997).

of copyright in the collective work is presumed to have acquired only the privilege of reproducing and distributing the contribution as part of that collective work, *any revision of that collective work* (emphasis added), and any later collective work in the same series."

The plaintiffs advanced a number of reasons why their works could not be used, including the fact that they had not expressly transferred electronic rights to their articles, that the revision clause of § 201© only applied to changes made in the same medium (here paper periodicals), that the defendants were engaged in "display" and that the plaintiffs had not granted those rights. But the court rejected those arguments, saying that the use of the articles in the electronic revisions of the periodicals did not amount to the creation or taking of electronic rights and that publication in a revision, even though in electronic form, was not "display" under the terms of the Copyright Act.

The court spends a great deal of the opinion examining the "revision" question. As the articles were published under the titles of the periodicals, they remained a part of the work. The form, then would be the key issue. The court concludes that there is ample evidence in the Copyright Act to show that an electronic version could be considered to be yet another form of the same publication and therefore protected under the "revision" clause of § 201(c). "As defendants emphasize, the 1976 Act was plainly crafted with the goal of media neutrality in mind. * * * Equally telling none of the provisions of the Act limit copyright protection to existing technologies. * * * In sum, it is unwarranted simply to assume * * * that Congress intended for the terms 'reproduction' and 'revision' to announce a radical departure from the media neutrality otherwise characterizing the Copyright Act of 1976."[78] The court declared, "Indeed, Section 201© contains no express limitation upon the medium in which a revision can be created. To the contrary, 'any revision' of a collective work is permissible provided it is a revision of 'that collective work.' "[79] The result was the publishers could include the free-lance work in their electronic versions without having to bargain for, and pay the writers, for that additional use.

What result if Time, one of the defendants, had put together an "Encyclopedia of the 20th Century" and included articles written by the plaintiffs for the magazine? There the question would turn on whether an encyclopedia would be considered a revision of the individual issue of the magazine itself. Under those circumstances, and without an agreement covering that additional use, the plaintiff writers would have been in a better position.

[78] Ibid. At 818–819.

[79] Ibid. At 817–818.

SEC. 93. ORIGINALITY

The concept of originality means that authors or artists have done their own work, and that their work is not copied from or grossly imitative of others' literary or artistic property.

Originality is a fundamental principle of copyright; originality implies that the author or artist created the work through his own skill, labor, and judgment.[80] The concept of originality means that the particular work must be firsthand, pristine; not copied or imitated. Originality, however, does not mean that the work must be necessarily novel or unique, or that it have any value as literature or art. What constitutes originality was explained in an old but frequently quoted case, Emerson v. Davies. The famed Justice Joseph Story of Massachusetts wrote in 1845:[81]

> In truth, in literature, in science and in art, there are, and can be, few, if any, things, which, in an abstract sense, are strictly new and original throughout. Every book in literature, science, and art, borrows, and must necessarily borrow, and use much which was well known and used before.

The question of originality seems clear in concept but this quality of composition is not always easy to separate and identify in particular cases. This is true especially when different authors have conceived like expressions or based their compositions upon commonly accepted ideas, terms, or descriptions in sequence. It must be borne in mind that *an idea* as such cannot be the subject of copyright; to be eligible for copyright, ideas must have particular physical expressions, as signs, symbols, or words. As was stated in Kaeser & Blair, Inc. v. Merchants' Association, Inc., "copyright law does not afford protection against the use of an idea, but only as to the means by which the idea is expressed."[82]

The originality requirement will even protect similar expression, that is, when that similar expression is the product of independent creation. In this way, copyright is unlike patent, which gives the patent holder all rights against similar or identical devices no matter how they came into being. Therefore, a work might be identical but protectable if an original and uncopied work. As Judge Learned Hand explained in Sheldon v. Metro–Goldwyn Pictures,[83]

---

[80] American Code Co. v. Bensinger, et al., 282 Fed. 829 (2d Cir.1922).

[81] 8 Fed.Cas. 615, No. 4,436 (C.C.Mass.1845).

[82] Kaeser v. Blair, 64 F.2d 575, 577 (6th Cir.1933). See also, Holmes v. Hurst, 174 U.S. 82, 19 S.Ct. 606 (1899); Eisenschiml v. Fawcett Publications, Inc., 246 F.2d 598, 114 U.S.P.Q. 199 (7th Cir.1957).

[83] 81 F.2d 49 (2d Cir.1936), *aff'd*, 309 U.S. 390, 60 S.Ct. 681 (1940).

an infringement case involving the unauthorized copying of a stage play in move form, while the law of copyright does not protect the copier, it will stand for the person who, however coincidentally, creates the same expression. "Borrowed the work indeed not be, for a plagiarist is not himself pro tanto an 'author'; but if by some magic a man who had never known it were to compose Keats's Ode on a Grecian Urn, he would be an 'author,' and, if he copyrighted it, others might not copy that poem, though they might of course copy Keats's."[84]

We can look to two important Supreme Court cases to understand the concept of originality as applied to works other than in mere words. Burrow–Giles Lithographic Co. v. Sarony[85] and Bleistein v. Donaldson Lithographing Co.[86] provide insight into the analysis of originality. *Sarony* dealt with the, then, relatively new issue of whether photographs were works of sufficient originality to qualify for copyright. *Bleistein* dealt with the concept of protection of drawings and engravings that were made of actual persons.

Napoleon Sarony, a photographer, sued Burrow–Giles Lithographic over copying of a photograph of Oscar Wilde. Burrow–Giles had obtained a copy of the photograph and made 85,000 copies. Burrow–Giles argued that while it had made the copies, it had not violated Sarony's copyright because photographs were not capable of copyrightability. Photographs, the lithographer argued, were mere reproductions of the exact features of objects or persons. As such, they did not amount to works of creativity. Further, photographs were not listed in the sorts of works protected by copyright when the statute was created. The Supreme Court disposed of this argument by simply noting that the Constitution could stretch to cover photographs "as far as they are representatives of original intellectual conceptions of the author."[87]

The Court then turned to the question of the originality of photographs. Engravings, prints and paintings were original works of creativity because they represented the creativity of their creators with all the novelty, invention and originality that involved. Photographs, on the other hand, were mechanical and chemical reproductions of the physical features of objects or people. They were the result of the reaction of chemicals to light allowed to strike the photographic plate. Development and printing are mere steps in a mechanical process. But the Court looked beyond that recitation of the process of photography and noted the findings of the lower court that the picture was "a new, harmonious, charac-

[84] Ibid. at 54.
[85] Burrow–Giles v. Sarony, 111 U.S. 53, 4 S.Ct. 279 (1884).
[86] Bleisten v. Donaldson, 188 U.S. 239, 23 S.Ct. 298 (1903).
[87] 111 U.S. 53, 58, 4 S.Ct. 279, 281, (1884).

teristic, and graceful picture, and that said plaintiff made the same * * * entirely from his own original mental conception, to which he gave visible form by posing the said Oscar Wilde in front of the camera, selecting and arranging the costume, draperies, and other various accessories in said photograph, arranging the subject so as to present graceful outlines, arranging and disposing the light and shade, suggesting and evoking the desired expression * * * "[88] For those reasons, the Supreme Court concluded that Sarony's photograph was a work of original creativity that deserved copyright protection.

In *Bleistein*, the Supreme Court dealt with a copyright claim arising over the preparation of advertising posters for a circus. The posters featured portraits that purported to represent drawings of the circus performers engaged in their acts. "One of the designs was of an ordinary ballet, one of a number of men and women, described as the Stirk family performing on bicycles, and one groups of men and women whitened to represent statues."[89] Bleistein and his company, the Courier Lithographic Co., had made the chromolithographs (colored lithographs) which Donaldson Lithographing had used to make the advertising posters.

The trial court ruled that the lithographs did not deserve the protection of the copyright law and the court of appeals sustained the verdict. The Supreme Court reversed. Justice Holmes took up and quickly disposed of the issue of the subject matter of the lithographs. They appeared to be representations of actual performers engaged in performance.

> [T]he plaintiff's case is not affected by the fact, if it be one, that the pictures represent actual groups—visible things. They seem from the testimony to have been composed from hints or description, not from sight of a performance. But even if they had been drawn from life, that fact would not deprive them of protection. The opposite proposition would mean that a portrait by Velasquez or Whistler was common property because others might try their hand on the same face.[90]

Holmes then turned to an issue raised by the trial court that the degree of artistic accomplishment as an actual depiction or "copy" of the actual performers and the use of the work in an advertisement meant it did not deserve copyright protection. The trial court reserved copyright protection to the fine arts and not to such works as this. "That the picture which represents a dozen or more figures of women in tights, with bare arms, and with much of

88 Ibid. At 54, 4 S.Ct. at 279.

89 188 U.S. 239, 248, 23 S.Ct. 298, 299 (1903).

90 Ibid. At 249, 23 S.Ct. at 299.

the shoulder displayed, and by means of which it is designed to lure men to a circus, is in any sense a work of the fine arts or a pictorial illustration in the sense of the statute, I do not believe."[91]

Holmes replies that the test is not the degree of sophistication of the work or its usefulness in trade. "A picture is none the less a picture, and none the less a subject of copyright, that it is used for an advertisement."[92]

On the other hand, the Supreme Court decision has held that no amount of "sweat of the brow" labor ever merits copyright protection in itself unless accompanied by some degree of originality.[93] Rural Telephone, a small Kansas phone company, had invested a substantial amount of time compiling a directory that listed the names and addresses of its subscribers in several different communities.

When Feist Publications sought to publish a regional phone directory, Rural refused to give Feist permission to include Rural's copyrighted white pages in this directory. Feist proceeded to incorporate the Rural listings in its regional telephone directory without permission, altering some of the information to conform to its own directory format, but publishing many of the listings exactly as they appeared in the Rural telephone directory.

Justice O'Connor, speaking for the Court, explained that although both the Copyright Act of 1909 and 1976 recognized the right of a compiler to claim copyright protection for a collection of facts, a subsequent compiler was free to use those same facts in preparing a competing work so long as the new work did not follow exactly the same selection and arrangement of those facts.

Here the Court found that although Rural had devoted sufficient effort to make its white pages useful, it had not done so in a sufficiently creative way to make the work original. As the Court itself had explained this crucial distinction between effort and originality almost a century ago,

> The right secured by copyright is not the right to forbid the use of certain words or facts or ideas by others; it is a right to that arrangement of words which the author has selected to express his ideas which the law protects.[94]

[91] Bleistein v. Donaldson Lithographing Co., 98 Fed. 608 (C.C.D.Ky.1899).

[92] 188 U.S. 239, 251, 23 S.Ct. 298, 300 (1903).

[93] Feist Publications, Inc. v. Rural Telephone Service Co., Inc., 499 U.S. 340, 111 S.Ct. 1282 (1991).

[94] Holmes v. Hurst, 174 U.S. 82, 19 S.Ct. 606 (1899); Van Rensselaer v. General Motors Corp., 324 F.2d 354 (6th Cir.1963).

SEC. 94. INFRINGEMENT AND REMEDIES

Violation of copyright includes such use or copying of an author's work that his possibility of profit is lessened.

Anyone who violates any of the exclusive rights spelled out by Sections 106 through 108 of the copyright statute is an infringer. As such, infringers bear liability to the copyright holder for lost profits, actual losses and the damage created by the taking.

In order to win a lawsuit for copyright infringement, a plaintiff must establish two separate facts, as the late Circuit Judge Jerome N. Frank wrote some years ago: "(a) that the alleged infringer copied from plaintiff's work, and (b) that, if copying is proved, it was so 'material' or substantial as to constitute unlawful appropriation."[95]

Even so, the material copied need not be extensive or "lengthy" in order to be infringement. "In an appropriate case," Judge Frank noted, "copyright infringement might be demonstrated, with no proof or weak proof of access, by showing that a simple brief phrase, contained in both pieces, was so idiosyncratic in its treatment as to preclude coincidence."[96] Judge Frank also noted that even a great, famous author or artist might be found guilty of copyright infringement. He wrote, "we do not accept the aphorism, when a great composer steals, he is 'influenced'; when an unknown steals, he is 'infringing'."[97]

Infringement cases will rest on the parties' abilities to prove that the original work was protected by copyright, that the defendant had access to the work, and that the defendant took from the original. It may seem easy enough, but in case after case, defendants have won by showing that they came up with the work themselves through independent creation of a work of their own originality. Recall Judge Learned Hand's explanation in *Sheldon* about the possibility of independent creation.

That principle, which forms the basis for the requirement that the plaintiff in a copyright case show both similarity and access, came into play in Selle v. Gibb,[98] an infringement case brought by a Chicago musician against the brothers Gibb, otherwise known as the Bee Gees. Selle had written a song, "Let It End," in the fall of 1975. He obtained copyright the same fall. He played the song several times with his band in the Chicago area and then send a demo tape and sheet music of the song to 11 different recording and publishing companies. Eight companies returned the materials and three did not. Other than that, Selle did not publicize his song. In

[95] Heim v. Universal Pictures Co., 154 F.2d 480, 487 (2d Cir.1946).
[96] Ibid., p. 488.
[97] Ibid.
[98] Selle v. Gibb, 741 F.2d 896 (7th Cir.1984).

1978, Selle heard the Bee Gees' song, "How Deep Is Your Love, "and recognized it as his own "Let It End." Selle sued for infringement. Time Magazine write Michael Walsh described the case in an essay on musical infringement: "For Selle's suit against the Bee Gees, four bars of the two scores were blown up to display a suspiciously exact correspondence of notes; on the witness stand, even Bee Gees Maurice Gibb couldn't tell the two songs apart."[99]

The Bee Gees, their manager and two musicians testified about the creation of "How Deep Is Your Love?" in a recording studio near Paris in 1977. They introduced a work tape that showed how the song came into being. The court of appeals described the creative process, saying that "[a]lthough the tape does not seem to preserve the very beginning of the process of creation, it does depict the process by which ideas, notes, lyrics and bits of the tune were gradually put together."[100] Only one expert witness testified, a professor of music at Northwestern University, who analyzed the two songs and said, "the two songs had such striking similarities that they could not have been written independent of one another."[1] Even the Time reporter noted the similarities, writing, "The similarities between the Bee Gees' hit from Saturday Night Fever and the unpublished Let It End are amusing; it seems to defy chance that two composers could have hit upon the same ugly tune."[2] The jury agreed and found for Selle.

But the judge overruled the jury , granting the Gibb brothers a judgment notwithstanding the verdict (the judge here substituted his own decision for that of the jury). The judge focused on the fact that Selle had not established that the Gibbs had had access to his song and had failed to refute the testimony regarding the Gibbs' independent creation of the work. The 7th Circuit affirmed the district court, rejecting Selle's contention that the jury could infer access by the striking degree of similarity between the two songs. But the court rejected that saying that access was an essential element. "Proof of copying is crucial to any claim of copyright infringement because no matter how similar the two works may be (even to the point of identity), if the defendant did not copy the accused work, there is no infringement."[3]

Other cases have turned on the defendant's ability to show that what he copied was not the plaintiff's work, but rather another work altogether, one that already has fallen into the public domain and thus can be used by anyone. In these cases, it is up to the

---

[99] Michael Walsh, "Has Somebody Stolen Their Song?" Time, Oct. 19, 1987, p. 86.

[100] 741 F.2d 896, 899 (7th Cir.1984).

[1] Ibid. Quoting trial transcript.

[2] Michael Walsh, "Has Somebody Stolen Their Song?" Time, Oct. 19, 1987, p. 86.

[3] 741 F.2d 896, 901 (7th Cir.1984).

plaintiff to prove that the defendant copied his original and not someone else's. Sometimes, the defendant can prove that the material in question is not copyrightable, such as a collection of facts incorporated into a copyrighted work.

The U.S. Court of Appeals, Second Circuit ruled that A.A. Hoehling could not collect damages from Universal City Studios in a dispute involving the motion picture, *The Hindenburg*. Back in 1962, Hoehling—after substantial research—published a copyrighted book, *Who Destroyed the Hindenburg?* That book advanced the theory that a disgruntled crew member of The Graf Zeppelin had planted a crude bomb in one of its gas cells.

Ten years later, after consulting Hoehling's book plus many other sources, Michael MacDonald Mooney published his own book, *The Hindenburg*. Mooney's book put forward a similar cause for the airship's destruction, but there was also evidence that other authors before Hoehling had suggested the same cause for the explosion. Circuit Judge Kaufman said for the court:[4]

> All of Hoehling's allegations of copying, therefore, encompass material that is non-copyrightable as a matter of law * * *.
>
> * * *
>
> * * * in granting * * * summary judgment for defendants, courts should assure themselves that the works before them are not virtually identical. In this case, it is clear that all three authors relate the story of the Hindenburg differently.
>
> In works devoted to historical subjects, it is our view that a second author may make significant use of prior work, so long as he does not bodily appropriate the expression of another. *Rosemont Enterprises, Inc.*, 366 F.2d at 310. This principle is justified by the fundamental policy undergirding the copyright laws—the encouragement of contributions to recorded knowledge * * * Knowledge is expanded as well, by granting new authors of historical works a relatively free hand to build upon the work of their predecessors.

Alex Haley, author of the best-seller *Roots,* was sued for both copyright infringement and unfair competition by Margaret Walker Alexander. Ms. Alexander claimed that Haley's book, published in 1976, was drawn substantially from her novel, *Jubilee,* published in 1966, and a pamphlet, *How I Wrote Jubilee,* published in 1972. A

---

[4] Hoehling v. Universal City Studios, Inc., 618 F.2d 972, 979–980 (2d Cir.1980), 6 Med.L.Rptr. 1053, 1057–1058.

federal district court granted Haley a summary judgment, finding that no copyright infringement had occurred. The court said:[5]

> Many of the claimed similarities are based on matters of historical or contemporary fact. No claim of copyright protection can arise from the fact that plaintiff has written about such historical and factual items, even if we were to assume that Haley was alerted to the facts in question by reading *Jubilee.* * * *
>
> Another major category of items consists of material traceable to common sources, the public domain, or folk custom. Thus, a number of claimed infringements are embodiments of the cultural history of black Americans, or of both black and white Americans planning out the cruel tragedy of white-imposed slavery. Where common sources exist for the alleged similarities, or the material that is similar is otherwise not original with the plaintiff, there is no infringement. * * * This group of asserted infringements can no more be the subject of copyright protection than the cause of a date or the name of a president or a more conventional piece of historical information.

There are numerous cases where copyright claims have failed because the plaintiff cannot show that his work was reproduced in the allegedly infringing work. The similarity test has been a tough obstacle for many who believe that their creations have been pirated.

In Litchfield v. Spielberg, the U.S. Court of Appeals for the Ninth Circuit decided in 1984 that a copyright infringement/unfair competition lawsuit involving the movie *E.T.—The Extraterrestrial* was—if not out of this world—at least legally insupportable. Lisa Litchfield claimed that her copyrighted one-act musical play, Lokey from Maldemar, had been infringed upon by *E.T.,* the box-office smash hit. As the appeals court put it, the issue, in addition to that of infringement, was whether the lower court had acted properly in granting defendants a summary judgment.[6]

> After independently reviewing the facts, the Court of Appeals held:[7]
>
> There is no substantial similarity * * * between the sequences of events, mood, dialogue and characters of the two works. Any similarities in plot exist only at the general

[5] Alexander v. Haley, 460 F.Supp. 40, 44–45 (S.D.N.Y.1978).

[6] Litchfield v. Spielberg; MCA, Inc., Universal City Studios, Inc., Extra–Terrestrial Productions, Kennedy, Tanen, and Mathison, 736 F.2d 1352 (9th Cir.1984) 10 Med.L.Rptr. 2101, 2102–2103.

[7] 736 F.2d 1352, 1355 (9th Cir.1984), 10 Med.L.Rptr. 2102, at 2105–2106.

level for which plaintiff cannot claim copyright protection.
* * *

* * *

As is too often the case, Litchfield's action was premised "partly upon a wholly erroneous understanding of the extent of copyright protection; and partly upon that obsessive conviction, so common among authors and composers, that all similarities between their works and any others to appear later must be ascribed to plagiarism." Dellar v. Samuel Goldwyn, Inc., 150 F.2d 612 (2d Cir.1945).

A similar result occurred in Beal v. Paramount Pictures[8] over the movie, "Coming to America." Alveda King Beal had written a novel, "The Arab Heart," which she described as a story or romance and adventure. The novel featured a protagonist, Sharaf Ammar Hakim Riad, a prince and heir to the fictional sheikdom of Whada. As the novel begins, Sharaf has been sent to Georgia Tech to learn more about oil production. Sharaf, who desires to live as an ordinary student, meets two women and considers marrying both. Plots against the sheikdom require Sharaf's return to support his grandfather, the sheik. Sharaf returns to Georgia, marries one of the women, and returns to the sheikdom where conflicting customs create tensions in his marriage. A violent attempt to overthrow Sharaf's grandfather end in the deaths of the grandfather, the usurper and Sharaf's ascendency to the leadership of the country.

"Coming to America" is a romantic comedy about Akeem, Prince of Zamunda, who travels to America to find a wife and avoid an arranged marriage. Akeem decides to go to Queens to find his queen but is determined that he will find a woman who wants to be his wife for himself and not for his position of wealth. He conceals his identity, has his belongings stolen and finds a home in a run-down tenement. He encounters Lisa McDowell, a community activist and daughter of a fast food restaurateur. Akeem takes a menial job in the restaurant to get to know McDowell. Eventually Akeem woos and wins McDowell. A surprise visit by Akeem's parents destroys his deception and McDowell rebuffs him. Akeem returns to Zamunda to enter the prearranged marriage. When he lifts his bride's veil, he discovers McDowell and the movie ends at that point.

In affirming the grant of summary judgment for Paramount, the 11th Circuit noted the differences between the book and the movie. Acknowledging that the idea of royalty from another country coming to America and finding true love might be similar from work to work, the expression is dissimilar. "[A] basic premise of

---

8 Beal v. Paramount, 20 F.3d 454 (11th Cir.1994).

copyright is that, while expression is protected, ideas are not the proper subject of copyright. 17 U.S.C. § 102(b); Baker v. Selden, 101 U.S. 99, 103 (1880). Therefore, copyright infringement exists only if protected expression is wrongfully appropriated."[9]

Copyright cases involving music have proved to be difficult. The evidence in such cases is largely circumstantial, resting upon similarities between songs. The issue in such a case, as one court expressed it, is whether "so much of what is pleasing to the ears of lay listeners, who comprise the audience for whom such popular music is composed, that defendant wrongfully appropriated something which belongs to the plaintiff."[10]

More than "lay listeners" often get involved in such cases, however. Expert witnesses sometimes testify in copyright infringement cases involving music. But it can happen that the plaintiff who feels that his musical composition has been stolen, and the defendant as well, will *both* bring their own expert witnesses into court, where these witnesses expertly disagree with each other.[11]

In proving a case of copyright infringement—and not just for those cases dealing with music—it is often useful if plaintiffs can show that the alleged infringement had "access" to the original work from which the copy was supposed to have been made. Such "access" needs to be proved by the plaintiff, if only by the circumstantial evidence of similarity between two works.

During the 1940s, songwriter Ira B. Arnstein tried to show that the noted composer, Cole Porter, not only had access to his work, but that Porter had taken freely from Arnstein. The courts declared that Porter had not infringed upon any common law or statutory copyrights held by Arnstein. Porter's victory in the courts was hard-won, however.

Arnstein began a copyright infringement lawsuit against Cole Porter in a federal district court. Arnstein charged that Porter's "Begin the Beguine" was a plagiarism from Arnstein's "the Lord is My Shepherd" and "A Mother's Prayer." He also claimed that Porter's "My Heart Belongs to Daddy" had been lifted from Arnstein's "A Mother's Prayer."

On the question of access, plaintiff Arnstein testified that his apartment had been burglarized and accused Porter of receiving the stolen manuscripts from the burglars. Arnstein declared that Porter's "Night and Day" had been stolen from Arnstein's "I Love You Madly," which had never been published but which had been

[9] Ibid. At 458.

[10] Arnstein v. Porter, 154 F.2d 464, 473 (2d Cir.1946).

[11] Ibid.

performed once over the radio. Technically, this meant that Arnstein's "I Love You Madly" had never been published.

In reply, Porter swore that he had never seen or heard any of Arnstein's compositions, and that he did not know the persons said to have stolen them. Even so, Arnstein's lawsuit asked for a judgment against Porter of "at least one million dollars out of the millions this defendant has earned and is earning out of all the plagiarism."[12]

At the original trial, the district court directed the jury to bring in a summary verdict in favor of Porter. Arnstein then appealed to a U.S. Circuit Court of Appeals, where Judge Jerome Frank explained what the appellate court had done. The Circuit Court of Appeals had listened to phonograph records of Cole Porter's songs and compared them to records of Arnstein's songs. As he sent the case back to a district court jury, Judge Frank wrote:

> * * * we find similarities, but we hold that unquestionably, standing alone, they do not compel the conclusion, or permit the inference, that defendant copied. The similarities, however, are sufficient so that, if there is enough evidence of access to permit the case to go to the jury, the jury may properly infer that the similarities did not result from coincidence.

The jury then found that Cole Porter's "Begin the Beguine" had indeed been written by Cole Porter.

Stephen King found himself in similar straits after publication of his book, "Misery." King was named in a copyright infringement case by a New Jersey woman who complained that King had stolen the work from her in two ways. The woman claimed that King had burglarized her home and taken poems that he used as the basis for "Misery." The National Law Journal reported on Nov. 16, 1992, that, "[t]he same woman, Anne Hiltner, had previously claimed that Mr. King had eavesdropped on her while flying in an airplane over her home. Ms. Hiltner's 1991 copyright infringement and conspiracy suit, filed in federal court in Washington, D.C., named several federal officials as co-defendants, in addition to Mr. King. Among these were Senate Majority leader George Mitchell, Speaker of the House Tom Foley and then-vice chairman of the Senate Intelligence Committee, Sen. William Cohen."[13] Ms. Hiltner reportedly claimed that the defendants placed her under surveillance in order that she might serve as the "living character" of King's novel. The suit was dismissed.

[12] Ibid., 474.

[13] Stan Soocher, "His Tales of Horror," National Law Journal, Nov. 16, 1992, p. 1.

As noted earlier in this chapter, facts or ideas are not copyrightable, only the style in which they are expressed. An additional gloss was put on this by a 1978 case, Miller v. Universal City Studios, which raised the question whether the research effort put into gathering facts is copyrightable.

Pulitzer Prize-winning reporter Gene Miller of The Miami Herald collaborated on writing a book with Barbara Mackle about her ordeal in a famous kidnaping incident. Ms. Mackle was held for ransom while literally buried alive in a box with seven days' life-sustaining capacity. She was rescued from the box on the fifth day. Miller worked an estimated 2500 hours in researching and writing this book.

A Universal Studios executive, William Frye, then offered Miller $15,000 for rights to use the Miller–Mackle account in a television "docudrama." Miller refused, asking for $200,000. At this point, negotiations between Miller and the studio collapsed, but the studio proceeded to produce and air a docudrama titled "The Longest Night." This production had obvious similarities to the Miller–Mackle book, and Miller sued for copyright infringement.[14]

The script writer had proceeded to write "The Longest Night" on the assumption that his studios had closed a deal with Miller for rights to the book and that he could proceed to write the script on that basis. Even so, Universal City Studios argued that no matter how hard Miller had worked to research the facts in the Mackle kidnaping case, he "may not monopolize those facts because they are historical facts and everyone has the right to write about them and communicate them to the public." The court disagreed with Universal City Studios' argument, saying:[15]

> To this court it doesn't square with reason or common sense to believe that Gene Miller would have undertaken the research involved in writing of *83 Hours Till Dawn* (or to cite a more famous example, that Truman Capote would have undertaken the research required to write *In Cold Blood*) if the author thought that upon completion of the book a movie producer or television network could simply come along and take the profits of the books and his research from him.

On appeal, however, Universal City Studios won a reversal of the judgment. The U.S. Court of Appeals, Fifth Circuit, ruled that Universal should have a new trial " * * * because the case was presented and argued to the jury on a false premise: that the labor of research by an author is protected by copyright." The Court of Appeals added that its decision was difficult to reach because there

[14] Miller v. Universal City Studios, Inc., 460 F.Supp. 984, 985–986 (S.D.Fla.1978).
[15] Ibid., p. 987 n. 988.

was " * * * sufficient evidence to support a finding of infringement * * * under correct theories of copyright law." In sum, the Court of Appeals did not believe that *research* itself is copyrightable, only the manner in which it is *presented.* "It is well settled that copyright protection extends only to an author's expression of facts and not to the facts themselves."[16]

Infringement occurs even though an unauthorized user does not profit directly from the copyrighted material he is using. The ruling case here is Herbert v. Shanley Co. (1917), where a restaurant owned by the defendant Shanley employed musicians to play at mealtimes. Victor Herbert's song "Sweethearts," was performed, but no arrangement had been made with Herbert or his representatives to use the song. Defendant Shanley argued that he had not infringed upon Herbert's copyright because he did not charge customers for the music they heard. The Supreme Court of the United States disagreed, finding that Shanley had benefitted at least indirectly from the music he provided because it attracted diners to his place of business .[17]

As under the former statute, a court may, in its discretion, award full court costs plus a "reasonable attorney's fee" to the winning party in a copyright lawsuit.[18] A plaintiff in an infringement suit also may opt to ask for "statutory damages" rather than actual damage and profits:[19]

(1) * * * the copyright owner may elect, at any time before final judgment is rendered, to recover, instead of actual damages and profits, an award of statutory damages for all infringements involved in the action, with respect to any one work, for which any one infringer is liable individually, or for which any two or more infringers are liable jointly and severally, in a sum of not less than $250 or more than $10,000 as the court considers just. * * *

(2) In a case where the copyright owner sustains the burden of proving, and the court finds, that infringement was committed willfully, the court in its discretion may increase the award of statutory damages to a sum of not more than $50,000. In a case where the infringer sustains the burden of proving, and the court finds, that such infringer was not aware and had no reason to believe that his acts constituted an infringement of copyright, the court in its discretion may reduce the award of statutory damages to a sum of not less than $100.

[16] Miller v. Universal City Studios, Inc., 650 F.2d 1365, 1368 (5th Cir.1981).

[17] 242 U.S. 591, 37 S.Ct. 232 (1917).

[18] 17 U.S.C.A. § 505.

[19] 17 U.S.C.A. § 504(c)(1), (2).

If you own a copyright and it is infringed upon, you have an impressive arsenal of remedies or weapons under the 1976 copyright statute.

For openers, if you know that someone is infringing on your copyright or you can prove is about to do so, a federal court has the power to issue temporary and final injunctions "on such terms as it may deem reasonable to prevent or restrain injunctions."[20] Furthermore, this injunction may be served on the suspected copyright infringer anywhere in the United States.[21] That's a form, in other words, of prior restraint at the disposal of an affronted copyright owner.

A copyright owner may also apply to a federal court to get an order to impound "on such terms as it may deem reasonable, * * * all copies or phono records claimed to have been made or used in violation of the copyright owner's exclusive rights."[22] And, if a court orders it as part of a final judgment or decree, the articles made in violation of the copyright owner's exclusive rights may be destroyed or otherwise disposed of.[23]

A copyright infringer, generally speaking, is liable for either of two things: (1) the copyright owner's actual damages and any additional profits of the infringer * * * or (2) statutory damages.[24]

Actual Damages and Profits

Consider the statute's language on "actual damages and profits".[25]

> The copyright owner is entitled to recover the actual damages suffered by him or her as a result of the infringement, and any profits of the infringer that are attributable to the infringement and are not taken into account in computing actual damages. In establishing the infringer's profits, the copyright owner is required to present proof only of the infringer's gross revenue, and the infringer is required to prove his or her deductible expenses and the elements of profit attributable to factors other than the copyrighted work.

[20] 17 U.S.C.A. § 502(a). For an example of an unsuccessful attempt to get an injunction, see Belushi v. Woodward, 598 F.Supp. 36 (D.D.C.1984), 10 Med.L.Rptr. 1870. The case involved widow of actor John Belushi asking that author Bob Woodward and publisher Simon & Schuster be enjoined from publishing book because of allegedly unauthorized use of her copyrighted photo.

[21] 17 U.S.C.A. § 502(b).

[22] 17 U.S.C.A. § 503(a).

[23] 17 U.S.C.A. § 503(b).

[24] 17 U.S.C.A. § 504(a).

[25] 17 U.S.C.A. § 504(b).

"Damages are awarded to compensate the copyright owner for losses from the infringement, and profits are awarded to prevent the infringer from unfairly benefitting from a wrongful act."[26]

In seeking to recover profits from a copyright infringer, the burden of proof falls upon the plaintiff to show the gross sales or profits arising from the infringement. The copyright infringer is permitted to deduct any legitimate costs or expenses which he can prove were incurred during publication of the stolen work. The winner of a suit to recover profits under copyright law can receive only the *net profits* resulting from an infringement. As the Supreme Court of the United States has declared,"The infringer is liable for actual, not for possible, gains."[27]

Net profits can run to a great deal of money, especially when the work is a commercial success as a book or motion picture. Edward Sheldon sued Metro–Goldwyn Pictures Corp. and others for infringing on his play, "Dishonored Lady" through the production of the Metro–Goldwyn film, "Letty Lynton." A federal district court, after an accounting had been ordered, found that Metro–Goldwyn had received net profits of $585,604.37 from their exhibitions of the motion picture.[28]

Mr. Sheldon did not get *all* of Metro–Goldwyn's net profits from the movie, however. On appeal, it was held that Sheldon should not benefit from the profits that motion picture stars had made for the picture by their talent and box-office appeal. Sheldon, after his case had been heard by both a United States Court of Appeals and the Supreme Court of the United States, came out with only 20 per cent of the net profits, or roughly $118,000. It still would have been much cheaper for Metro–Goldwyn simply to have bought Sheldon's script. Negotiations with Sheldon for his play had been started by Metro–Goldwyn, but were never completed. The asking price for movie rights to the Sheldon play was evidently to be about $30,000, or slightly more than one-fourth of the amount the courts awarded to the playwright.[29]

Sometimes, in dealing with a major Hollywood film studio, establishing infringement is actually less difficult than forcing the studio to make an honest disclosure of a film's earnings. Although it is not a copyright case, it does show the difficulties in finding out how much an infringer has profited. Humorist Art Buchwald sold a screen *treatment* (a story outline) to Paramount in 1983 for a movie

[26] H.R.Rep. No. 94–1476 (Sept. 3, 1976), "Copyright Law Revision," p. 161.

[27] Sheldon v. Metro–Goldwyn Pictures Corp., 309 U.S. 390, 400–401, 60 S.Ct. 681, 683 (1940); Golding v. R.K.O. Pictures, 35 Cal.2d 690, 221 P.2d 95 (1950).

[28] Sheldon v. Metro–Goldwyn Pictures Corp., 26 F.Supp. 134, 136 (S.D.N.Y.1938), 81 F.2d 49 (2d Cir.1936), 106 F.2d 45 (2d Cir.1939).

[29] 309 U.S. 390, 398, 407, 60 S.Ct. 681, 683, 687 (1940); see Nimmer, op. cit., § 14.03 fn. 30 (1988).

featuring Eddie Murphy. Paramount subsequently made the movie, "Coming To America" that followed the general plot line of Buchwald's treatment, but refused to honor its contract to pay Buchwald the $250,000 and 19% of the film's net profits specified by the agreement.

Although Paramount contended that the Buchwald screen treatment was only one of several the studio had used in preparing a shooting script, and that three other writers were claiming similar rights in the picture, the Court found that a substantial number of obvious parallels between Buchwald's treatment and the actual screen play justified a holding that the movie was based primarily upon his work and that the contract had been fulfilled.[30]

However, when Buchwald sought to claim his share of the film's profits, Paramount's accountants maintained that even though the film had grossed more than $125 million in all media sales worldwide, there were no profits to share with him because the studio's account books still showed a net loss for the film of $18 million.[31] The judge was not impressed by studio bookkeeping that appeared to be far more creative than the film itself, and insisted on an independent analysis of the accounting procedures employed by Paramount before making his final award to Buchwald. On the basis of that analysis, the Court awarded Buchwald and his partner a $900,000 judgment.[32]

Criminal Penalties

There can be *criminal* penalties for copyright infringement. The new statute ups the ante where phono record or movie pirates are concerned. Section 506 provides:[33]

> (a) CRIMINAL INFRINGEMENT.—Any person who infringes a copyright willfully and for purposes of commercial advantage or private financial gain shall be fined not more than $10,000 or imprisoned for not more than one year, or both: *Provided, however,* That any person who infringes willfully and for purposes of commercial advantage or private financial gain the copyright in a sound recording shall be fined not more than $25,000 or imprisoned for not more than one year, or both, for the first such offense and shall be fined not more than $50,000 or imprisoned for not more than two years, or both, for any subsequent offense.

[30] Buchwald v. Paramount Pictures Corp. (Cal.1990), 17 Med.L.Rptr. 1257.

[31] "Par to Buchwald; We're $18–Mil in Hole," Variety February 28, 1990, p. 5.

[32] Dan Cox, "Paramount Finally Files Buchwald Appeal," Variety, April 11, 1994, p. 32.

[33] 17 U.S.C.A. § 506. See also § 507, which orders a three-year statute of limitations for both criminal prosecutions and civil proceedings under the Copyright Statute.

Criminal penalties—fines of up to $2,500—await any person who, "with fraudulent intent," places on any article a notice of copyright that is known to be false. Similar fines may be levied against individuals who fraudulently remove a copyright notice, or who knowingly make misstatements in copyright applications or related written statements.[34]

SEC. 95.   COPYRIGHT, UNFAIR COMPETITION, AND THE NEWS

The news element of a story is not subject to copyright, although the style in which an individual story is written may be protected from infringement. Reporters, in short, should do their own reporting.

Any unauthorized and unfair use of a copyrighted news story constitutes an infringement which will support either lawsuits for damages or an action in equity to get an injunction against further publication. Although a news story—or even an entire issue of a newspaper—may be copyrighted, the *news element* in a newspaper story is not subject to copyright. News is *publici juris*—the history of the day—as was well said by Justice Mahlon Pitney in the important 1918 case of International News Service v. Associated Press. Justice Pitney wrote:[35]

> A News article, as a literary production, is the subject of copyright. But the news element—the information respecting current events in the literary production, is not the creation of the writer, but is a report of matters that ordinarily are publici juris; it is the history of the day. It is not to be supposed that the framers of the Constitution, when they empowered Congress to promote the progress of science and useful arts, by securing for limited times to authors and inventors the exclusive rights to their respective writings and discoveries (Const. Art. 1, § 8, par. 8), intended to confer upon one who might happen to be first to report an historic event the exclusive right for any period to spread the knowledge of it.

The Associated Press had complained of news pirating by a rival news-gathering agency, International News Service. The Supreme Court granted the Associated Press an injunction against the appropriation, by INS, of non-copyrighted AP stories while the news was still fresh enough to be salable. This was true even though in that era, and until the Copyright Act of 1976, material was not copyrighted unless it carried the © symbol and notice at

---

[34] 17 U.S.C.A. § 506(c), (d) and (e).

[35] INS v. AP, 248 U.S. 215, 234, 39 S.Ct. 68, 71 (1918).

the time of publication. "The peculiar value of news," Justice Pitney declared, "is in the spreading of it while it is fresh; and it is evident that a valuable property interest in the news, as news, cannot be maintained by keeping it secret."

Justice Pitney also denounced the taking, by INS, of AP stories, either by quoting or paraphrasing. Justice Pitney wrote that INS, "in appropriating * * * news and selling it as its own is endeavoring to reap where it has not sown, and by disposing of it to newspapers that are competitors * * * of AP members is appropriating to itself the harvest of those who have sown."[36]

What, then, can a newspaper or other communications medium do when it has been "beaten" to a story by its competition? It must be emphasized that the historic case of International News Service v. Associated Press did *not* say that the "beaten" news medium must sit idly by. "Pirating" news, of course, is to be avoided: pirating has been defined as "the bodily appropriation of a statement of fact or a news article, with or without rewriting, but without independent investigation or expense."[37]

However, first-published news items may be used as "tips." When one newspaper discovers an event, such as the arrest of a kidnaper, its particular news presentation of the facts may be protected by copyright. Even so, such a first story may serve as a tip for other newspapers or press associations. After the first edition by the copyrighting news organization, other organizations may independently investigate and present their own stories about the arrest of the kidnaper. In such a case, the time element between the appearance of the first edition of the copyrighting newspaper and the appearance of a second or third edition by a competing newspaper might be negligible as far as the general public is concerned; only a few hours. If other newspapers or press associations make their own investigations and obtain their own stories, they do not violate copyright.

But, to copy a copyrighted news story—or to copy or paraphrase substantially from the original story—may lead to court action, as shown in the 1921 case of Chicago Record–Herald Co. v. Tribune Association. This case arose when the *New York Tribune* copyrighted a special news story on Germany's reliance upon submarines. This story, printed in the *New York Tribune* on Feb. 3, 1917, was offered for sale for exclusive publication in the *Chicago Herald*. The *Herald* declined this opportunity, and the *Chicago Daily News* then purchased the Chicago rights to the story.

With full knowledge that the *Tribune's* story on the German submarine campaign was copyrighted, the *Herald* nevertheless ran

---

[36] 248 U.S. 215, 239–240, 39 S.Ct. 68, 71–72 (1918).

[37] 248 U.S. 215, 243, 39 S.Ct. 68, 74 (1918).

a version of the same story featuring identical paragraph after identical paragraph on the morning of Feb. 3.

The *Chicago Daily News* then refused to publish the story or to pay the *New York Tribune* for it. The *Daily News,* having agreed to purchase an exclusive story, had the right to refuse a story already published in its market. The publishers of the *New York Tribune* successfully sued the *Chicago Herald* for infringement.

The judge declared that the *New York Tribune's* original story "involves authorship and literary quality and style, apart from the bare recital of the facts or statement of news." So, although facts are not copyrightable, the style in which they are expressed is protected by law.

As noted in International News Service v. Associated Press (1918), the AP won its case despite the fact that the news stories it telegraphed to its members were not copyrighted. There, the Supreme Court of the United States held that the AP had a "quasi property" right in the news stories it produced, even after their publication. Once the Supreme Court found that such a "quasi property" right existed, it then declared that appropriation of such stories by INS amounted to unfair competition and could be stopped by a court-issued injunction against INS.[38]

More recently, a newspaper—the Pottstown, Pa., *Mercury*— won an unfair competition suit against a Pottstown radio station, WPAZ, getting an injunction which prevented WPAZ, "from any further appropriation of the newspaper's local news without its permission or authorization."[39]

Adopting the rather cynical view that news coverage was simply a function newspapers and broadcasters employed to attract advertisers, the Pennsylvania Supreme Court held that the radio station had unfairly competed with the *Mercury* for these advertisers through its unauthorized taking of the newspaper's new stories. The court said:[40]

> * * * for the purpose of an action of unfair competition the specialized treatment of news items as a service the newspaper provides for advertisers gives the News Company [publishers of the Pottstown *Mercury*]a limited property right which the law will guard and protect against wrongful invasion by a competitor * * *

[38] See reference to this case at footnote 82, above. The case of International News Service v. Associated Press was cited as important by the more recent case of Pottstown Daily News Pub. Co. v. Pottstown Broadcasting Co., 411 Pa. 383, 192 A.2d 657, 662 (1963).

[39] Ibid.

[40] 411 Pa. 383, 192 A.2d 657, 663–664 (1963).

The limited property right in news is to some extent waived by member organizations of the Associated Press. All A.P. members are entitled to all *spontaneous* news from areas served by other A.P. member newspapers or broadcasting stations. Membership in the Associated Press includes agreement to follow this condition as stated in Article VII of the A.P. bylaws:

> Sec. 3. Each member shall promptly furnish to the [A.P.] Corporation all the news of such member's district, the area of which shall be determined by the Board of Directors. No news furnished to the Corporation by a member shall be furnished by the Corporation to any other member within such member's district.

> Sec. 4. The news which a member shall furnish to the Corporation shall be all news that is spontaneous in origin, but shall not include news that is not spontaneous in its origin, or which has originated through deliberate and individual enterprise on the part of such member.

A.P. member newspapers or broadcasting stations are expected to furnish spontaneous or "spot" news stories to the Associated Press for dissemination to other members throughout the nation. However, Section 3 of the A.P. By–Laws (above) will protect the news medium originating such a story within its district.

Even if a newspaper copyrights a spot news story, other A.P. members could use the story despite the copyright. By signing the A.P. By–Laws, the originating newspaper has given its consent in advance for all A.P. members to use news stories of *spontaneous* origin. On the other hand, if a newspaper copyrights a story based on that newspaper's individual enterprise and initiative, the other A.P. members could not use the story without permission from the copyrighting newspaper.

Roy Export Company v. CBS

Eagerness to present the news as effectively as possible in pressure situations may sometimes lead to disregard of ownership rights. Evident lack of concern about such rights cost the Columbia Broadcasting System $717,000[41] in copyright and unfair competition damages for missteps making a documentary on the occasion of the death of film legend Charlie Chaplin.

In 1977, CBS broadcast a film biography of Chaplin, including film clips from six Chaplin-motion pictures. Exclusive rights in

---

[41] Roy Export Co. Establishment of Vaduz, Liechtenstein v. CBS, 672 F.2d 1095, 1097 (2d Cir.1982), 8 Med.L.Rptr. 1637, 1639. See footnote 6: "Of the compensatory total, $7,280 was for statutory copyright infringement, $1 was for common-law copyright infringement, and $300,000 was for unfair competition. The punitive damages were divided between the common-law claims: $300,000 for common-law copyright infringement and $110,000 for unfair competition."

those films were held by several parties, including the first-named plaintiff in this case, Roy Export Company Establishment of Vaduz, Liechtenstein.[42]

The events leading to this lawsuit are traceable to 1972, when the Academy of Motion Picture Arts and Sciences (AMPAS) arranged to have a film tribute made from highlights of Chaplin's films. This tribute was broadcast by NBC–TV in connection with an appearance by Chaplin at the 1972 Academy Awards ceremonies. It was understood that excerpts compiled in that tribute were to be used only on that one occasion.[43]

In 1973, CBS started work on a retrospective of Chaplin's life, to be used as a broadcast obituary when Chaplin died. CBS made repeated requests for permission to use excerpts from Chaplin's films, but was rebuffed. CBS was told that the copyright owners were involved in producing their own film biography of Chaplin titled "The Gentleman Tramp." That production used some of the same footage used in the Academy Awards show compilation, but did not use that compilation itself. CBS, meanwhile, made a "rough cut" of a Chaplin obituary/biography. The network was offered a chance to purchase rights to show "The Gentleman Tramp" in 1976 and 1977, but did not do so.

Chaplin died on Christmas day, 1977. CBS had its "rough cut" biography ready to use, but instead used a copy of the 1972 Academy Award show compilation which CBS had obtained from NBC. CBS put together a new biography, depending heavily "on what CBS knew to be copyrighted material." This hastily assembled new biography was broadcast on December 26, 1977.[44]

Roy Export Company and other copyright owners of Chaplin films then sued CBS for copyright infringement and for unfair competition. The latter claim said the CBS broadcast competed unfairly with the copyright owners' own Chaplin retrospective, "The Gentleman Tramp." A jury trial in a U.S. district court found CBS liable to the plaintiffs for $307,281 compensatory and $410,000 punitive damages.

In its appeal, CBS asserted that the First Amendment provides a general privilege to report newsworthy events such as Chaplin's death, and that this privilege shielded the network from liability.

[42] 672 F.2d 1095 (2d Cir.1982), 8 Med.L.Rptr. 1637, cert. denied 459 U.S. 826, 103 S.Ct. 60 (1982). This case was complicated, Circuit Judge Newman said, by troublesome questions coming from pre–1978 common law protection for intellectual property, plus challenges to statutory copyrights, "on the ground that the work lost its common copyright prior to January 1, 1978, entered the public domain, and therefore was not eligible for statutory copyright." Judge Newman cited M. Nimmer, Nimmer on Copyright, Sec. 4.01 [B].

[43] 672 F.2d at 1098 (2d Cir.1982), 10 Med.L.Rptr. at 1639.

[44] Ibid.

CBS claimed that the main reason for Chaplin's fame was his films, and that it would be meaningless to try to provide a full account of his life without making use of his films. Circuit Judge Newman summed up the network's First Amendment argument:[45]

> In CBS's view, the 1972 Academy Awards ceremony, at which the Compilation received its single public showing, was an "irreducible single news event" to which the showing of the Compilation was integral. The significance of the ceremony, CBS contends, was not simply that Chaplin appeared after a twenty-year exile provoked by Senator [Joseph] McCarthy's investigations, but that a collection of his work was shown, thereby bringing home to the American people both what they had been deprived of by McCarthyism and how ludicrous had been the attempt to find subversion and political innuendo in Chaplin's films. CBS concludes that the plaintiff's claims for infringement of the copyright in the films and the compilation must give way to an asserted First Amendment news-reporting privilege.

The Court of Appeals found CBS's First Amendment arguments "unpersuasive," resting on a theory that someday, some way, there might be an inseparability of news value and copyrighted work to the extent that copyright would have to yield. Judge Newman wrote, however: "No Circuit that has considered the question * * * has ever held that the First Amendment provides a privilege in the copyright field distinct from the accommodation embodied in the 'fair use' doctrine." And in a footnote he added,[46]

> Fair use balances the public interest in the free flow of ideas and information with the copyright holder's interest in exclusive proprietary control of his work. It permits use of the copyrighted matter 'in a reasonable manner without [the copyright owner's] consent, notwithstanding the monopoly granted to the owner.' Rosemont Enterprises, Inc. v. Random House, Inc., 366 F.2d 303 (2d Cir.1966), cert. denied 385 U.S. 1009, 87 S.Ct. 714 * * * (1967) * * *.

The Roy Export Case and Unfair Competition

CBS also argued that the plaintiffs could not maintain a claim that the network's December 26, 1977, broadcast unfairly competed with the plaintiffs' rights in "The Gentleman Tramp." CBS asserted the unfair competition claim rested on "misappropriation" of films under New York state law, " * * * and that a state law claim

---

[45] 672 F.2d 1095, 1099 (2d Cir.1982), 8 Med.L.Rptr. 1637, 1640.

[46] 672 F.2d 1095, 1099 (2d Cir.1982), 8 Med.L.Rptr. 1637, 1640.

based on misappropriation of federally copyrighted materials is pre-empted * * * "[47] The Court of Appeals replied:

> An unfair competition claim involving misappropria-tion usually concerns the taking and use of the plaintiff's property to compete against the plaintiff's use of the same property, e.g. International News Service v. Associated Press * * * [248 U.S. 215, 39 S.Ct. 68 (1918)]. By con-trast, in this case the Compilation was taken and used to compete unfairly with a different property, "The Gentle-man Tramp." Despite the unusual facts, we are satisfied that the plaintiffs have established an unfair competition tort under New York law.

> * * *

> CBS unquestionably appropriated the "skill, expenditures and labor" of the plaintiffs to its own commercial advan-tage. Its actions, in apparent violation of its own and the industry's guidelines, were arguably a form of "commercial immorality." We are confident that the New York courts would call that conduct unfair competition.

The Court of Appeals ruled that the damages of more than $700,000 against CBS should stand, including the punitive damage awards totaling $410,000. Judge Newman wrote, "The deterrent potential of an award of $410,000 must be measured by its likely effect on a national television network with 1977 earnings of some $217,000,000 * * * ".[48]

Special Technology Concerns

The spread of computer technology has raised a number of copyright issues that require the courts to apply long-established legal doctrines to novel situations. In many instances, common sense and a comparison between old issues and new settings will provide the answers. For example, how will the courts decide the treatment of the pirating of images. Scanners that digitize images allow for mass reproduction and the Internet provide for world-wide distribution. What rights will copyright holders be able to assert and, as important, how will they be able to establish the proof of the elements of infringement.

In many cases, the proof will be as plain as the picture on the computer screen. If it is the same picture as was published with copyright protection by a magazine, it will be easy enough to show infringement of the picture. But how does a periodical that pub-lishes hundreds of pictures a year and has a library of tens of

[47] 697 F.2d at 1104–1105 (2d Cir.1982), 10 Med.L.Rptr. at 1644–1645.

[48] 697 F.2d at 1107 (2d Cir.1982), 10 Med.L.Rptr. at 1646.

thousands of pictures keep track of any one image? Playboy entered into an agreement with Digimarc Corp.,[49] a company that has developed a system for inserting a digital "watermark" into pictures.[50] The "watermark" that Digimarc has developed will do more than indicate the genuineness of the photograph. It will work to help protect Playboy's copyrights in its pictures. Playboy has been involved in an number of copyright complaints against persons for taking its pictures and putting them on the Internet and World Wide Web either in edited or unaltered form. Federal marshals, acting on a copyright infringement complaint, seized CD–ROMS and computer equipment from a California site that was charging subscribers for access to Playboy pictures.

The watermark replaces an older identification system that placed a string of identifying code on the top of an image file. That code string could be removed without difficulty. The new "watermark" will be encoded into the digital information that makes up the photograph itself making it difficult, if not impossible to remove. The new system has two benefits for its users: informing users of the photographs that they are using someone else's copyrighted work, and, allowing the copyright holder to track down web sites that are displaying works without permission. The coding in the "watermark" causes a copyright symbol to appear when a user calls the photograph up on an editing program. By clicking on the symbol, the user would have information about the copyright holder and be able to try to get copyright permission to use the image. If the user does not do that, he runs the risk of being found out and subjected to an infringement action if he puts the image on the Web. Digimarc has a search engine that looks at Web sites for images containing the "watermark." Once the search program finds a site, it makes a notation which is placed in a database that copyright holders who use the Digimarc service can access. A quick check of sites using the images with a list of sites that have permission to use them will identify the lawful and unlawful users. A warning or copyright infringement lawsuit will then follow.[51]

Another copyright issue deals with taking of music through sampling. There are any number of myths about copyright and what people freely can take. Some believe that taking 30 seconds of any song is permitted while other believe that eight bars falls within the rights of the public. There is no such rule and court

---

[49] Roger R. Crockett, "Playboy Wants Digimarc Expertise," Portland Oregonian, July 1, 1997.

[50] Watermarks are designs or symbols that can be seen when a piece of paper is held up to light. It indicates the origin of the paper or its genuineness. Counterfeits will not have the mark. Currency carries watermarks.

[51] John Burgess, "Making Their Watermark On the World; Digital IDs Put Stamp of Authority on Works," The Washington Post, Sept. 29, 1997.

rulings make clear that even small snippets of songs can be protectable.

In one of the first cases to deal with sampling, a federal district court in New York declared quite simply, "Thou shalt not steal." In Grand Upright Music v. Warner Brothers Records,[52] the court was faced with a case involving the taking of three words from a copyrighted song. The case was relatively simple. Rap artist Biz Markie was recording a song for Cold Chillin' Records called "Alone Again." That song took portions of the previously recorded and copyrighted song "Alone Again Naturally," written by Gilbert O'Sullivan. After the song was recorded, but before it was released, Markie and his recording company sought permission to use the song. They were denied but decided to go ahead with the release, as part of the album "I Need a Haircut."

The copyright holders learned of the action and went to federal court to prevent the release of the album. The court agreed. The portion taken from the O'Sullivan song were three words and a portion of the music. That was enough to constitute unlawful use of the recording. The court focused on the record company's attempt to sell the record without the required license for use of the song. In the analysis, the court is critical of the record company's conduct and motivation. "From all the evidence produced at the hearing, it is clear that the defendants knew that they were violating the plaintiff's rights as well as the rights of others. Their only aim was to sell thousands upon thousands of records. This callous disregard for the law and for the rights of others requires not only the preliminary injunction sought by the plaintiff but also sterner measures."[53]

In a later case, Jarvis v. A & M Records,[54] a federal district court looked to the use of "ooh," "moves," and "free your body" in terms of copyright infringement. In that case, the defendants had sampled portions of a previous work written by Boyd Jarvis. A significant issue was whether the taking of the words and phrase would constitute infringement. Other cases have held that where the copying is of material does not rise to the level of copyrightability, there is no infringement. The material must be sufficiently original and novel to get copyright protection. If it is not, there is no infringement. In this case, the court held that the use of the words and music riff were significant.

> "There is no question that the combined phrase 'ooh ooh ooh ooh ... move ... free your body' is an expression of an idea that was copyrightable. Moreover, the keyboard

[52] 780 F.Supp. 182 (S.D.N.Y.1991).

[53] Ibid. At 185.

[54] Jarvis v. A & M Records, 827 F.Supp. 282 (D.N.J.1993).

line that was copied represents a distinctive melo-dy/rhythm that sets it far apart from the ordinary cliched phrases held not copyrightable. It, too, is and idea, and is capable of being infringed."[55]

The conclusion then is that multimedia or song artists must think twice about "borrowing" bits and pieces of existing works. It may be that the material taken will support an infringement claim. It is mostly a matter of common sense. If a piece is taken because it appeals to the user, its theft shows its distinctiveness and value to the infringer.

SEC. 96. THE DEFENSE OF FAIR USE

The fair use doctrine—invented by courts to allow some use of others' works—was made explicit by the Copyright Act of 1976. Major cases—such as *Sony* and *The Nation* magazine—continue to add to the definition of fair use in a piecemeal fashion.

The copyright law phrase "fair use" made a good deal of news during the mid–1980s. Its growth in importance is quite remarka-ble, stemming as it does from judicial wriggling many years ago. Its growth may be understood as being fueled, in a major way, by onrushing technological changes. Recent examples of important fair use cases decided by the Supreme Court—and which are taken up later in this Section—are Sony Corporation of America v. Universal City Studios, Inc.,[56] and Harper & Row Publishers, Inc. v. Nation Enterprises.[57]

The old 1909 copyright statute gave each copyright holder an exclusive right to "print, reprint, publish, copy and vend the copyrighted * * *." As stated in that Act, it was an *absolute* right; the wording was put in terms so absolute that even pencil-and-paper copying was a violation of the U.S. Copyright Act.[58] Because the 1909 statute's terms were so stringent, if enforced to the letter, it could have prevented anyone except the copyright holder from making any copy of any copyrighted work.

Such a statute was clearly against public policy favoring dis-semination of information and knowledge and was plainly unen-forceable. As a result, courts responded by developing the doctrine called "fair use."

[55] Ibid. At 292.

[56] 464 U.S. 417, 104 S.Ct. 774 (1984).

[57] 471 U.S. 539, 105 S.Ct. 2218 (1985).

[58] See 17 U.S.C.A. § 10 of the statute which preceded the Copyright Statute of 1976: Verner W. Clapp, "Library Photocopying and Copyright: Recent Develop-ments," Law Library Journal 55:1 (Feb., 1962) p. 12.

American courts assumed—in creating a judge-made exception to the absolute language of the 1909 copyright statute—that "the law implies the consent of the copyright owner to a fair use of his publication for the advancement of science or art."[59] The fair use doctrine, although a rather elastic yardstick, was a needed improvement. The 1976 copyright statute has distilled the old common law copyright doctrine into some statutory guidelines. Factors to be considered by courts in determining whether the use made of a work in any particular case is a fair use include:[60]

(1) the purpose and character of the use, including whether such use is of a commercial nature or is for nonprofit educational purposes;

(2) the nature of the copyrighted work;

(3) the amount and substantiality of the portion used in relation to the copyrighted work as a whole; and

(4) the effect of the use upon the potential market for or value of the copyrighted work.

What, then, is fair use? In 1964, one expert asserted that fair use of someone's copyrightable materials exists "somewhere in the hinterlands between the broad avenue of independent creation and the jungle of unmitigated plagiarism."[61] No easy or automatic formula can be presented which will draw a safe line between fair use and infringement. Fifty words taken from a magazine article might be held to be fair use, while taking one line from a short poem might be labeled infringement by a court. The House of Representatives Committee on the Judiciary said this in its report on the 1976 copyright statute:[62]

General intention behind the provision

The statement of the fair use doctrine in section 107 offers some guidance to users in determining when the principles of the doctrine apply. However, the endless variety of situations and combinations of circumstances that can rise in particular cases precludes the formulation of exact rules in the statute. The bill endorses the purpose and general scope of the judicial doctrine of fair use, but there is no disposition to freeze the doctrine in the statute, especially during a period of rapid technological change. Beyond a very broad statutory explanation of what fair use

[59] Wittenberg, op. cit., p. 148, offers a good non-technical description of fair use before it was expanded in 1967.

[60] U.S.C.A. § 107.

[61] Arthur N. Bishop, "Fair Use of Copyrighted Books," Houston Law Review, 2:2 (Fall, 1964) at p. 207.

[62] H.R. Report No. 94–1476, discussing the fair use provisions of 17 U.S.C.A. § 107.

is and some of the criteria applicable to it, the courts must be free to adapt the doctrine to particular situations on a case-by-case basis. Section 107 is intended to restate the present judicial doctrine of fair use, not to change, narrow, or enlarge it in any way.

Generally speaking, courts have been quite lenient with quotations used in scholarly works or critical reviews. However, courts have been less friendly toward use of copyrighted materials for commercial purposes, or in works which compete with the original copyrighted piece.[63] The problems surrounding the phrase "fair use" have often arisen in connection with scientific, legal, or scholarly materials. With such works, it is to be expected that there will be similar treatment given to similar subject matters.[64] A crucial question, obviously, is whether the writer makes use of an earlier writer's work without doing substantial independent work.

Wholesale copying is *not* fair use.[65] Even if a writer had no intention of making unfair use of someone else's work, that writer still could be found liable for copyright infringement.[66] The idea of independent investigation is of great importance here. Copyrighted materials may be used as a *guide* for the purpose of gathering information, provided that the researcher then performs an original investigation and expresses the results of such work in the researcher's own language.[67]

Fair Use and Public Interest

Although many earlier cases expressed a narrow, restrictive view of the doctrine of fair use, some important decisions since the mid–1960s have emphasized the idea of *public* interest. This changed approach is of great importance to journalists and scholars, for where there are matters which are newsworthy or otherwise of interest to the public, courts will consider such factors in determining whether a fair use was made of copyrighted materials.

A key case here is the 1967 decision known as Rosemont Enterprises, Inc. v. Random House, Inc. and John Keats. This case arose because Howard Hughes, a giant in America's aviation, oil and motion picture industries had a passionate desire to remain

[63] Eisenschiml v. Fawcett Publications, Inc., 246 F.2d 598 (7th Cir.1957); Benny v. Loew's Inc., 239 F.2d 532 (9th Cir.1956), affirmed 356 U.S. 43, 78 S.Ct. 667 (1958), rehearing denied 356 U.S. 934, 78 S.Ct. 770 (1958); Pilpel and Zavin, op. cit., pp. 160–161.

[64] Eisenschiml v. Fawcett Publications, Inc., 246 F.2d 598 (7th Cir.1957), certiorari denied 355 U.S. 907, 78 S.Ct. 334 (1957).

[65] Benny v. Loew's Inc., 239 F.2d 532 (9th Cir.1956), affirmed 356 U.S. 43, 78 S.Ct. 667 (1958), rehearing denied 356 U.S. 934, 78 S.Ct. 770 (1958).

[66] Wihtol v. Crow, 309 F.2d 777 (8th Cir.1962).

[67] Jeweler's Circular Pub. Co. v. Keystone Pub. Co., 281 Fed. 83 (2d Cir.1922), certiorari denied 259 U.S. 581, 42 S.Ct. 464 (1922).

anonymously out of the public eye. A brief chronology will illustrate how this copyright infringement action came about:

• January and February, 1954: *Look* magazine, owned by Cowles Communications, Inc., published a series of three articles by Stanley White, titled "The Howard Hughes Story."

• In 1962, Random House, Inc., hired Thomas Thompson, a journalist employed by *Life* magazine, to prepare a book-length biography of Hughes. Later, either Hughes or his attorneys learned of the forthcoming Random House book. An attorney employed by Hughes warned Random House that Hughes did not want this biography and "would make trouble if the book was published." Thompson resigned from the project, and Random House then hired John Keats to complete the biography.

• Rosemont Enterprises, Inc., was organized in September, 1965 by Hughes' attorney and by two officers of his wholly-owned Hughes Tool Company.

• On May 20, 1966, Rosemont Enterprises purchased copyrights to the *Look* articles, advised Random House of this, and five days later brought a copyright infringement suit in New York. Attorneys for Rosemont somehow had gained possession of Random House galley proofs of the Random House biography of Hughes then being published: "Howard Hughes: a Biography by John Keats."[68]

Rosemont Enterprises sought an injunction to restrain Random House from selling, publishing, or distributing copies of its biography of Hughes because the book amounted to a prima facie case of copyright infringement. With his five-day-old ownership of the copyrights for the 1954 Look magazine articles, Hughes was indeed in a position to "cause trouble" for Random House.

The trial court agreed with the Rosemont Enterprises argument that infringement had occurred, and granted the injunction against Random House, holding up distribution of the book. The trial court rejected Random House's claims of fair use of the Look articles, saying that the privilege of fair use was confined to "materials used for purposes of criticism or comment or in scholarly works of scientific or educational value." This district court took the view that if something was published "for commercial purposes"—that is, if it was designed for the popular market—the doctrine of fair use could not be employed to lessen the severity of the copyright law.[69] The district court found that the Hughes

68 Rosemont Enterprises, Inc. v. Random House, Inc. and John Keats, 366 F.2d 303, 304–305 (2d Cir.1966).

69 Ibid., p. 304, citing the trial court, 256 F.Supp. 55 (S.D.N.Y.1966).

biography by Keats was for the popular market and therefore the fair use privilege could not be invoked by Random House.[70]

Circuit Judge Leonard P. Moore, speaking for the Circuit Court of Appeals, took another view. First of all, he noted that the three *Look* articles, taken together, totaled only 13,500 words, or between 35 and 39 pages if published in book form. Keats' 1966 biography on the other hand, had 166,000 words, or 304 pages in book form. Furthermore, Judge Moore stated that the *Look* articles did not purport to be a biography, but were merely accounts of a number of interesting incidents in Hughes' life. Judge Moore declared:[71]

> * * * there can be little doubt that portions of the *Look* article were copied. Two direct quotations and one eight-line paraphrase were attributed to Stephen White, the author of the articles. A mere reading of the *Look* articles, however, indicates that there is considerable doubt as to whether the copied and paraphrased matter constitutes a material and substantial portion of those articles.
>
> Furthermore, while the mode of expression employed by White is entitled to copyright protection, he could not acquire by copyright a monopoly in the narration of historical events.

In any case, the Keats book should fall within the doctrine of fair use. Quoting a treatise on copyright, Judge Moore stated: "Fair use is a privilege in others than the owner of a copyright to use the copyrighted material in a reasonable manner without his consent, notwithstanding the monopoly granted to the owner * * *."[72]

Judge Moore demanded that public interest considerations—the public's interest in knowing about prominent and powerful men—be taken into account. He wrote that "public interest should prevail over possible damage to the copyright owner." He complained that the district court's preliminary injunction against Random House deprived the public of the opportunity to become acquainted with the life of a man of extraordinary talents in a number of fields: "A narration of Hughes' initiative, ingenuity, determination and tireless work to achieve his concept of perfection in whatever he did ought to be available to a reading public."[73]

---

[70] Ibid.

[71] Ibid., pp. 306–307, certiorari denied 385 U.S. 1009, 87 S.Ct. 714 (1967).

[72] Ibid., p. 306, quoting Ball, Copyright and Literary Property, p. 260 (1944).

[73] Ibid., p. 309. And, at p. 311, Judge Moore discussed Rosemont's claim that it was planning to publish a book: "One can only speculate when, if ever, Rosemont will produce Hughes' authorized biography."

The Zapruder Case

A stunning event—the assassination of President John F. Kennedy—gave rise to a copyright case which added luster to the defense of fair use in infringement actions. On November 22, 1963, dress manufacturer Abraham Zapruder of Dallas stationed himself along the route of the President's motorcade, planning to take home movie pictures with his 8 millimeter camera. As the procession came into sight, Zapruder started his camera. Seconds later, the assassin's shots fatally wounded the President and Zapruder's color film caught the reactions of those in the President's car.

On that same day, Zapruder had his film developed and three color copies were made from the original film. He turned over two copies to the Secret Service, stipulating that these were strictly for governmental use and not to be shown to newspapers or magazines because Zapruder expected to sell the film.

Three days later, Zapruder negotiated a written agreement with *Life* magazine, which bought the original and all three copies of the film (including the two in possession of the Secret Service). Under that agreement, Zapruder was to be paid $150,000, in yearly installments of $25,000. *Life,* in its November 29, 1963, issue then featured thirty of Zapruder's frames. *Life* subsequently ran more of the Zapruder pictures. *Life* gave the Commission appointed by President Lyndon B. Johnson to investigate the killing of President Kennedy permission to use the Zapruder film and to reproduce it in the report.[74]

In May of 1967, *Life* registered the entire Zapruder film in the Copyright office as an unpublished "motion picture other than a photo play." Three issues of *Life* magazine in which the Zapruder frames had been published had earlier been registered in the Copyright office as periodicals.[75] This meant that *Life* had a valid copyright in the Zapruder pictures when Bernard Geis Associates sought permission from *Life* magazine to publish the pictures in Josiah Thompson's book, *Six Seconds in Dallas,* a serious, thoughtful study of the assassination. The firm of Bernard Geis Associates offered to pay *Life* a royalty equal to the profits from publication of the book in return for permission to use specified Zapruder frames in the book. *Life* refused this offer.

Having failed to secure permission from *Life* to use the Zapruder pictures, author Josiah Thompson and his publisher decided to copy certain frames anyway. They did not reproduce the Zapruder

---

[74] Time Inc. v. Bernard Geis Associates, 293 F.Supp. 130, 131–134 (S.D.N.Y.1968). Although the Commission received permission from Time, Inc. to reproduce the photos, the Commission was told that it was expected to give the usual copyright notice. That proviso evidently was disregarded by the Commission.

[75] Ibid., p. 137.

frames photographically, but instead paid an artist $1,550 to make charcoal sketch copies. Thompson's book was then published, relying heavily on the sketches, in mid-November of 1967. Significant parts of 22 copyrighted frames were reproduced in the book.[76]

The court ruled that *Life* had a valid copyright in the Zapruder film, and added that "the so-called 'sketches' in the book are in fact copies of the copyrighted film. That they were done by an 'artist' is of no moment." The Court then quoted copyright expert Melville B. Nimmer:[77]

> "It is of course, fundamental, that copyright in a work protects against unauthorized copying not only in the original medium in which the work was produced, but also in any other medium as well. Thus copyright in a photograph will preclude unauthorized copying by drawing or in any other form, as well as by photographic reproduction."

The court then ruled that the use of the photos in Thompson's book was a copyright infringement, "unless the use of the copyrighted material in the Book is a 'fair use' outside the limits of copyright protection."[78] This led the court to a consideration of fair use, the issue which is " 'the most troublesome in the whole law of copyright.' "[79]The court then found in favor of Bernard Geis Associates and author Thompson, holding that the utilization of the Zapruder pictures was a "fair use."[80] The court said:

> There is an initial reluctance to find any fair use by defendants because of the conduct of Thompson in making his copies and because of the deliberate appropriation in the Book, in defiance of the copyright owner. Fair use presupposes "good faith and fair dealing." * * * On the other hand, it was not the nighttime activities of Thompson which enabled defendants to reproduce copies of Zapruder frames in the Book. They could have secured such frames from the National Archives, or they could have used the reproductions in the Warren Report [on the assassination of President Kennedy] or in the issues of *Life* itself. Moreover, while hope by a defendant for commercial gain is not a significant factor in this Circuit, there is a strong point for defendants in their offer to surrender to *Life* all profits of Associates from the Book as royalty payment for a license to use the copyrighted Zapruder

[76] Ibid., pp. 138–139.

[77] Ibid., p. 144, citing Nimmer on Copyright, p. 98.

[78] Ibid., p. 144.

[79] Ibid., quoting from Dellar v. Samuel Goldwyn, Inc., 104 F.2d 661 (2d Cir.1939).

[80] Ibid., p. 146.

frames. It is also a fair inference from the facts that defendants acted with the advice of counsel.

In determining the issue of fair use, the balance seems to be in favor of defendants.

There is a public interest in having the fullest information available on the murder of President Kennedy. Thompson did serious work on the subject and has a theory entitled to public consideration. While doubtless the theory could be explained with sketches * * * [not copied from copyrighted pictures] * * * the explanation actually made in the Book with copies [of the Zapruder pictures] is easier to understand. The Book is not bought because it contained the Zapruder pictures; the Book is bought because of the theory of Thompson and its explanation, supported by the Zapruder pictures.

There seems little, if any, injury to plaintiff, the copyright owner. There is no competition between plaintiff and defendants. Plaintiff does not sell the Zapruder pictures as such and no market for the copyrighted work appears to be affected. Defendants do not publish a magazine. There are projects for use by plaintiff of the film in the future as a motion picture or in books, but the effect of the use of certain frames in the Book on such projects is speculative. It seems more reasonable to speculate that the Book would, if anything, enhance the value of the copyrighted work; it is difficult to see any decrease in its value.

Harper & Row v. Nation Enterprises (1985)

The defense of fair use, often helpful in fending off lawsuits for copyright infringement, can be pushed too far. The Supreme Court of the United States served notice in 1985 that the fair use doctrine at times may not prevent liability for unauthorized publishing, even if the material involved is highly newsworthy.

Nation Magazine—reputedly America's longest continuously published weekly magazine—in 1979 received an unauthorized copy of former President Gerald R. Ford's memoirs. Nation Editor Victor Navasky received the draft from an undisclosed source; this writing was the result of a collaboration between Ford and Trevor Armbrister, a senior editor of Reader's Digest.[81]

Nation Magazine carried an article developed by Navasky from the unauthorized copy, published in its issue of April 3, 1979, and was just over 2,000 words long. Harper & Row and The Reader's

---

[81] Harper & Row Publishers, Inc. and Reader's Digest Ass'n, Inc. v. Nation Enterprises and Nation Associates, 557 F.Supp. 1067, 1069 (S.D.N.Y.1983), 9 Med. L.Rptr. 1229.

Digest Association, Inc., sued for copyright infringement. At the trial court level, U.S. District Judge Owen found that Navasky knew that the memoirs were soon to be published in book form by Harper & Row and Reader's Digest, with some advance publication rights assigned to Time Magazine. Judge Owen wrote:[82]

> However, believing that the draft contained "a real hot news story" concerning Ford's pardon of President Nixon .* * * Navasky spent overnight or perhaps the next twenty-four hour period quoting and paraphrasing from a number of sections of the memoirs. Navasky added no comment of his own. He did not check the material. As he later testified, "I wasn't reporting on the truth or falsity of the account; I was reporting the fact that Ford reported this * * *." Part of Navasky's rush apparently was caused by the fact that he had to get the draft back to his "source" with some speed.

The Nation's article was about 2,250 words long, of which 300 to 400 words were taken from the Ford memoirs manuscript. Nation's publication may be said to have skimmed some of the more newsworthy aspects from the manuscript, which Harper & Row and Reader's Digest Association, as copyright holders, were preparing to market. For one thing, the copyright owners had negotiated a pre-publication agreement in which Time Magazine agreed to pay $25,000 ($12,500 in advance and the balance at the time of publication) for rights to excerpt 7,500 words from Mr. Ford's story of his pardon of President Nixon.

The Supreme Court of the United States said that The Nation had timed its publication to "scoop" Time Magazine's planned article. As a result of Nation's publication, Time canceled its article and refused to pay the remaining $12,500 to Harper & Row and to Reader's Digest Association.[83] Writing for the Court, Justice Sandra Day O'Connor found that Nation's publication was not covered by the fair use defense:[84]

> * * * The Nation has admitted to lifting verbatim quotes of the author's original language totaling between 300 and 400 words and constituting some 13% of The Nation article. In using generous verbatim excerpts of Mr. Ford's unpublished manuscript to lend authenticity to its account of the forthcoming memoirs, The Nation effectively arrogated to itself the right of first publication, an important marketable subsidiary right. * * * [W]e find that use of

[82] Ibid.

[83] Harper & Row Publishers, Inc. v. Nation Enterprises, 471 U.S. 539, 105 S.Ct. 2218 (1985), 11 Med.L.Rptr. 1969, 1971.

[84] 471 U.S. 539, 549, 105 S.Ct. 2218, 2225 (1985), 11 Med.L.Rptr. 1969, 1973.

the copyrighted manuscript, even stripped to the verbatim quotes conceded by The Nation to be copyrightable expression, was not a fair use within the meaning of the Copyright Act.

Justice O'Connor examined the tension between racing to publish news first and copyright:[85]

> In our haste to disseminate news, it should not be forgotten that the Framers intended copyright itself to be the engine of free expression. By establishing a marketable right to the use of one's expression, copyright supplies the economic incentive to create and disseminate ideas.

Further, she held that a writer's public figure status did not create a waiver of the copyright laws:[86]

> In view of the First Amendment protections already embodied in the Copyright Act's distinction between copyrightable expression and uncopyrightable facts and ideas, and the latitude for scholarship and comment traditionally afforded by fair use, we see no warrant for expanding the doctrine of fair use to create what amounts to a public figure exception to copyright. Whether verbatim copying from a public figure's manuscript in a given case is or is not fair must be judged according to the traditional equities of fair use.

The Court's majority opinion marched through the Copyright Statute's list of four factors to be considered in determining whether a use is "fair":

(1) *The Nature and Purpose of the Use*—Justice O'Connor said the general purpose of The Nation's use was "general reporting." Part of this, however, was The Nation's stated purpose of scooping the forthcoming hardcover books and the excerpts to be published in Time Magazine. This, Justice O'Connor said, had " * * * the intended purpose of supplanting the copyright holder's commercially valuable right of first publication."[87]

(2) *Nature of the Copyrighted Work*—Justice O'Connor wrote that President Ford's narrative, "A Time to Heal" was "an unpublished historical narrative or autobiography." She said the unpublished nature of the work was critical to considering whether use of it by The Nation was fair. Although substantial quotes might qualify as fair use in a

---

[85] 471 U.S. 539, 559, 105 S.Ct. 2218, 2230 (1985), 11 Med.L.Rptr. 1969, 1978.

[86] 471 U.S. 539, 559–560, 105 S.Ct. 2218, 2230–2231 (1985), 11 Med.L.Rptr. 1969, 1978.

[87] 471 U.S. 539, 563, 105 S.Ct. 2218, 2232 (1985), 11 Med.L.Rptr. 1969, 1978.

review or discussion of a published work, "the author's right to control the first public appearance of his expression weighs against such use of the work before its release."[88]

(3) *Amount and Substantiality of the Copying*—"Stripped of the verbatim quotes, the direct takings from the unpublished manuscript constitute at least 13% of the infringing article. * * * The Nation article is structured around the quoted excerpts which serve as its dramatic focal points."

(4) *Effect on the Market*—Noting that Time Magazine had canceled its projected serialization of the Ford memoirs and had refused to pay $12,500, Justice O'Connor said those occurrences were direct results from the infringement. "Rarely will a case of copyright infringement present such clear cut evidence of damage."[89]

Thus a six-member majority concluded that The Nation's use of the Ford memoirs was not a fair use. This meant that a Court of Appeals finding that The Nation's publication was overturned, and that The Nation was liable to pay the $12,500 in damages, matching the amount which Time Magazine had refused to pay the copyright holders after the unauthorized publication.

Justice William J. Brennan, Jr.—who was joined by Justices Byron White and Thurgood Marshall—dissented. "The Court holds that The Nation's quotation of 300 words from the unpublished 200,000–word manuscript of President Gerald R. Ford infringed the copyright," wrote Brennan. He said the Court's majority reached this finding even though the quotations related to a historical event of undoubted significance—the resignation and pardon of President Richard M. Nixon. Brennan added that "this zealous defense of the copyright owner's prerogative will, I fear, stifle the broad dissemination of ideas and information copyright is intended to nurture."[90]

Brennan concluded,[91]

The Court's exceedingly narrow approach to fair use permits Harper & Row to monopolize information. This holding "effect[s] an important extension of property rights and a corresponding curtailment in the free use of knowledge and of ideas." International News Service v. Associated Press, 248 U.S. at 263 (Brandeis, J., dissenting). The Court has perhaps advanced the ability of the historian—or at least the public official who has recently left

[88] 471 U.S. 539, 563, 105 S.Ct. 2218, 2232 (1985), 11 Med.L.Rptr. 1969, 1980.

[89] 471 U.S. 539, 564, 105 S.Ct. 2218, 2233 (1985), 11 Med.L.Rptr. 1969, 1981.

[90] 471 U.S. 539, 578, 105 S.Ct. 2218, 2240 (1985), 11 Med.L.Rptr. 1969, 1983.

[91] 471 U.S. 539, 604, 105 S.Ct. 2218, 2254 (1985), 11 Med.L.Rptr. 1969, 1994–1995.

office—to capture the full economic value of information in his or her possession. But the Court does so only by "risking the robust debate of public issues * * *."

Publication of Another's Private
Letters Held Not a "Fair Use."

J.D. Salinger is a highly regarded novelist and short story writer, best known for his novel, "The Catcher in the Rye". His last work was published in 1965, and since that time he has been trying to avoid any publicity about himself, refusing to grant interviews or to respond to any inquiries about his private life. Ian Hamilton, a respected literary critic for *The London Sunday Times,* contacted the reclusive author in 1983 to tell him that he intended to write a biography about Salinger to be published by Random House. Although Salinger responded that he did not want to have his biography written during his lifetime, Hamilton spent the next three years completing the work, titled "J.D. Salinger: A Writing Life."

Lacking any cooperation from Salinger himself, Hamilton relied heavily upon information contained in letters Salinger had written to various friends during his early years as a writer. These letters had been donated by their recipients to several university libraries, but Salinger was apparently unaware that they would be available to Hamilton.

When Salinger read the galley proofs of the book Random House planned to publish, he notified the publisher that he would attempt to block its publication unless all direct quotations from these private letters he had written his friends were deleted.

Responding to these objections, Hamilton revised his work, omitting most of the direct quotations from Salinger's letters, but still paraphrasing very closely some 59 passages from this correspondence. As Random House was about to publish this revised version of the biography, Salinger sued to prevent publication, claiming among other things that such extensive reliance upon passages from his unpublished letters exceeded the reasonable bounds of fair use.

After originally granting Salinger's request for a preliminary injunction, a lower federal court had decided to lift the injunction and allow publication when a U.S. Court of Appeals intervened, ordering that this ban on publication be made permanent.[92] In its

[92] Salinger v. Random House, 811 F.2d 90 (2d Cir.1987), 13 Med.L.Rptr. 1954. The Supreme Court has declined to review this decision, so the ban on the publication of the book remains permanent. "Supreme Court Refuses to Review Salinger Ruling," New York Times, October 6, 1987, p. 11. On the other hand, in Maheu v. CBS, 201 Cal.App.3d 662, 247 Cal.Rptr. 304 (1988), 15 Med.L.Rptr. 1548, a California court

attempt to follow the Supreme Court's concept of fair use as defined in the Harper & Row case, this Court of Appeals decision placed special emphasis upon the fact these letters of Salinger's were unpublished.

That Supreme Court opinion had declared that "the scope of fair use is narrower with respect to unpublished works." Following this argument, the court found that because an author's privilege to incorporate unpublished material of another in his own work was a relatively limited one, and because Hamilton had relied so heavily upon the unpublished letters of Salinger in his biography, he had clearly exceeded the reasonable boundaries of permissible fair use.

In essence, then, the "nature of the copyrighted work" and "the amount and substantiality of the portion used" were the two elements of the Harper & Row decision that this court emphasized in finding that Hamilton's biography of Salinger had abused this legal privilege.

In Craft v. Kobler, the material to be used was from several copyrighted works but the result was exactly the same.[93] In this case an author completing a biography of Igor Stravinsky sought to include in his manuscript passages from the copyrighted works of the composer's personal assistant. Here again the problem was one of excessive usage of the work of others, because the passages to be taken from these copyrighted works of the plaintiff represented nearly three percent of the total biography, and included many richly descriptive paragraphs about Stravinsky based upon the assistant's special knowledge of him.

Technology and Fair Use: The Sony "Betamax" Decision (1984)

When videocassette recorders became available to the general public in the early 1980s, it was clear that technology was once again moving beyond the scope of existing copyright law. The public had rejected RCA's efforts to market a videodisc player with no ability to record video programs, but was eager to buy Sony's new Betamax machines that allowed them to record and duplicate those broadcast programs and films that copyright owners had only expected them to view off-air.[94]

refused to allow an action for copyright infringement by an assistant of Howard Hughes for the unauthorized use of correspondence he received from Hughes because of his failure to obtain copyright protection for this unpublished correspondence that was copyrightable.

[93] Craft v. Kobler, 667 F.Supp. 120 (S.D.N.Y.1987), 14 Med.L.Rptr. 1617.

[94] For a concise description of both RCA's marketing failure and Sony's marketing success, see,"RCA Calls It Quits With Videodisks," Broadcasting, April 4, 1984, p. 39. By the time the Supreme Court decided the Sony case in 1984, more than 13

Because Congress proved itself incapable of amending the Copyright Act of 1976 to establish what rights copyright owners had to prevent such unauthorized copying of their works, the courts were soon forced to interpret an already out-dated Act in some manner that would bring this new form of usage within its provisions.

In January, 1984, the Supreme Court decided 5–4 that video recorders are legal for sale and home use under the Copyright Statute and the doctrine of fair use.[95] This case arose when Universal City Studios and Walt Disney productions sued Sony, claiming that use of Sony Betamax VCRs in homes by private individuals constituted copyright infringement.

In 1979, a federal district court held off-the-air copying for private, non-commercial use to be a "fair use." Plaintiffs had not proved to the court's satisfaction that harm to copyrighted properties was being done by such taping.[96] But in 1981, the United States Court of Appeals for the Ninth Circuit overturned that ruling, holding that makers and distributors of home video recorders were liable for damages if the machines were used to tape programs broadcast over-the-air.[97]

The Supreme Court, after granting certiorari, agreed in mid–1982 to hear Sony's appeal from the Court of Appeals holding. The Court, however, held the case over into a second term, and had it argued a second time in October, 1983.[98] Writing for a five-Justice majority, Justice John Paul Stevens said that most people use a VCR principally to record a program they cannot see as it is being telecast, and then use the home recording to watch the program at another time. This "time-shifting" practice, Justice Stevens said, enlarges the viewing audience:[99]

> * * * [A] significant amount of television programming may be used in this manner without objection from the owners of the copyrights on the programs. For the same reason, even the two respondents in this case, who do assert objections to time-shifting * * * were unable to

million VCRs had already been sold. "3–d Quarter VCR U.S. Population Pegged at 13 Mil," Variety, October 23, 1984, p. 1.

[95] Sony Corporation of America v. Universal City Studios, Inc., 464 U.S. 417, 104 S.Ct. 774 (1984). Ironically, although Sony had won this legal battle, its "Beta" format lost out in the marketing war to its "VHS" format competitors. By 1988 Sony was abandoning "Beta" and producing its own VHS format VCRs. See, "Sony Adds VHS to VCR Format," Variety, January 12, 1988, p. 1.

[96] 480 F.Supp. 429, 452–453 (D.Cal.1979).

[97] 659 F.2d 963 (9th Cir.1981).

[98] 464 U.S. 417, 418, 104 S.Ct. 774, 777 (1984); Wermeil, loc. cit.

[99] 464 U.S. 417, 421, 104 S.Ct. 774, 778 (1984).

prove that the practice has impaired the commercial value of their copyrights * * *

Justice Stevens noted that Universal and Disney studios were not seeking damages from individual Betamax users whom they claimed infringed their copyrights. Instead, they charged Sony with "contributory infringement." To prevail, this required them to prove that Sony encouraged those who purchased its Betamax machines to unlawfully copy feature films produced by studios such as Universal and Disney.[100] Justice Stevens added,[1]

> If vicarious liability is to be imposed on * * * [Sony] * * *, it must rest on the fact that they have sold equipment with constructive knowledge of the fact that their consumers may use that equipment to make unauthorized copies of copyrighted material. There is no precedent in the law of copyright for the imposition of vicarious liability on such a theory.

The Betamax decision was limited to noncommercial home uses. "If the Betamax were used to make copies for a commercial or profit-making purpose, such use would be presumptively unfair," Justice Stevens said.[2] Thus the Sony case is clearly distinguishable from a situation where off-the-air taping is being done for commercial reasons.[3]

Importantly, Justice Stevens concluded that the home use of VCRs for noncommercial purposes was a fair use.[4]

> * * * [To] the extent that time-shifting expands public access to freely broadcast television programs, it yields societal benefits. Earlier this year, in Community Television of Southern California v. Gottfried, 103 S.Ct. 885, 891–892, 74 L.Ed.2d 705 (1983), we acknowledged the public interest in making television broadcasting more available. Conceitedly, that interest is not unlimited. But it supports an interpretation of the concept of "fair use" that requires the copyright holder to demonstrate some likelihood of harm before he may condemn a private act of time-shifting as a violation of federal law.

---

[100] 464 U.S. 417, 434, 104 S.Ct. 774, 785 (1984).

[1] 464 U.S. 417, 438, 104 S.Ct. 774, 787 (1984).

[2] 464 U.S. 417, 449, 104 S.Ct. 774, 792 (1984).

[3] Melville B. Nimmer, Nimmer on Copyright, Vol. 3, § 13.5[F] (New York: Matthew Bender, 1963, 1980), citing Elektra Records Co. v. Gem Electronic Distributors, Inc., 360 F.Supp. 821 (E.D.N.Y.1973) (taping of copyrighted records for commercial redistribution ruled infringing) and Walt Disney Productions v. Alaska Television Network, Inc., 310 F.Supp. 1073 (W.D.Wash.1969) (videotaping for commercial use).

[4] 464 U.S. 417, 454, 104 S.Ct. 774, 795 (1984).

Justice Stevens concluded the opinion of the Court with a summary of findings and with an invitation to Congress to provide legislative guidance in this case:[5]

In summary, the record and findings of the District Court lead us to two conclusions. First, Sony demonstrated a significant likelihood that substantial numbers of copyright holders who license their works for broadcast on free television would not object to having their broadcasts time-shifted by private viewers. And second, respondents failed to demonstrate that time-shifting would cause any likelihood of nominal harm to the potential market for, or the value of, their copyrighted works. The Betamax is, therefore, capable of substantial noninfringing uses. Sony's sale of such equipment to the general public does not constitute contributory infringement of respondent's copyrights.

* * *

One may search the copyright act in vain for any sign that the elected representatives of the millions of people who watch television every day have made it unlawful to copy a program for later viewing at home, or have enacted a flat prohibition against the sale of machines that make such copying possible.

It may well be that Congress will take a fresh look at this new technology, just as it so often has examined other innovations in the past. But it is not our job to apply laws that have not yet been written. Applying the copyright statute, as it now reads, to the facts as they have been developed in this case, the judgment of the Court of Appeals must be reversed.

Justice Blackmun, joined by Justices Marshall, Powell, and Rehnquist, dissented.[6]

It is apparent from the record and from the findings of the District Court that time-shifting does have a substantial adverse effect upon the "potential market for" the Studios' copyrighted works. Accordingly, even under the formulation of the fair use doctrine advanced by Sony, time-shifting cannot be deemed a fair use.

Justice Blackmun added that the case should have been sent back to District Court for additional findings of fact on the matter of infringement and contributory infringement.[7]

[5] 464 U.S. 417, 456, 104 S.Ct. 774, 796 (1984).
[6] 464 U.S. 417, 485, 104 S.Ct. 774, 811 (1984).
[7] 464 U.S. 417, 493, 104 S.Ct. 774, 815 (1984).

Parody and Fair Use

Can a parody be fair use? The "Saturday Night Live" television program did a skit poking fun at New York City's public relations campaign and its theme song. In this four-minute skit, the town fathers of Sodom discussed a plan to improve their city's image. This satire ended with the singing of "I Love Sodom" to the tune of "I Love New York." In a per curiam opinion, the U.S. Court of Appeals, Second Circuit rejected the complaint of Elsmere Record Co., owner of copyright to "I Love New York." "Believing that, in today's world of often unrelieved solemnity, copyright law should be hospitable to the humor of parody," the Court of Appeals approved District Judge Goettel's decision granting the defendant National Broadcasting Company a summary judgment on ground that the parody was a fair use.[8]

Judge Goettel's opinion said, in words useful for understanding both the concept of fair use and its application to parodies charged with copyright infringement:[9]

> In its entirety, the original song "I Love New York" is composed of a 45 word lyric and 100 measures. Of this only four notes, D C D E (in that sequence), and the words "I Love" were taken in the Saturday Night Live sketch (although they were repeated 3 or 4 times). As a result, the defendant now argues that the use it made was insufficient to constitute copyright infringement.

> This court does not agree. Although it is clear that, on its face, the taking involved in this action is relatively slight, on closer examination it becomes apparent that this portion of the piece, the musical phrase that the lyrics "I Love New York" accompanies, is the heart of the composition. * * * Accordingly, such taking is capable of rising to the level of a copyright infringement.

> Having so determined, the Court must next address the question of whether the defendant's copying of the plaintiff's jingle constituted a fair use which would exempt it from liability under the Copyright Act. Fair use has been defined as a "privilege in others than the owner of the copyright to use the copyrighted material in a reasonable manner without his consent, notwithstanding the monopoly granted to the owner of the copyright".

Judge Goettel then reviewed the four criteria set out by the 1976 copyright revision, 17 U.S.C.A. § 107 [quoted at the beginning

[8] Elsmere Music, Inc. v. NBC, 623 F.2d 252 (2d Cir.1980), 6 Med.L.Rptr. 1457.

[9] Elsmere Music, Inc. v. NBC, 482 F.Supp. 741, 742 (S.D.N.Y.1980), 5 Med.L.Rptr. 2455, 2456.

of this Section], and compared those criteria to relevant cases on the fair use doctrine. He quoted copyright specialist Melville B. Nimmer, who has said, "short of * * * [a] complete identity of content, the disparity of functions between a serious work and a satire based upon it, may justify the defense of fair use even where substantial similarity exists."[10]

Plaintiff Elsmere Records argued that "I Love Sodom" was not a valid parody of "I Love New York." Elsmere pointed to two raunchy cases in which copyright infringement was found because use of copyrighted material was not parodying the material itself, but was instead using someone's intellectual property, without permission, to make statements essentially irrelevant to the original work.[11] Elsmere Records cited MCA, Inc. v. Wilson, in which the song "Cunnilingus Champion of Company C" was held to infringe the copyright of "Boogie Woogie Bugle Boy of Company B."[12] And in Walt Disney Productions v. Mature Pictures Corporation, the court held that using the copyrighted "Mickey Mouse March" as background for a teen-age group sex scene in a "Happy Hooker" movie was not fair use.[13]

However, Judge Goettel found that the Saturday Night Live sketch validly parodied the plaintiff's jingle and the "I Love New York" ad campaign. Also, he ruled that the parody did not interfere with the marketability of a copyrighted work. Therefore, he held that the sketch was a fair use, and that no copyright violation had occurred.

Campbell a.k.a. Skyywalker v. Acuff–Rose Music, Inc.

In 1992 Acuff–Rose Music, Inc. sued 2 Live Crew, contending that the Crew's song "Pretty Woman" infringed the Acuff–Rose copyright of Roy Orbison's rock ballad, "Oh Pretty Woman." The District Court granted summary judgement for 2 Live Crew, holding that its song was a parody that made *fair use* of the original ballad.[14]

The Court of Appeals overturned the lower court decision, deciding that the parody's commercial nature, coupled with what the court found as a matter of law to be its too extensive use of the

---

[10] Nimmer on Copyright, § 13.05[C], at 13–60–61 (1979), quoted by Judge Goettel at 482 F.Supp. 741 at 745 (S.D.N.Y.1980), 5 Med.L.Rptr. 2455, 2457.

[11] 482 F.Supp. 741, 745 (S.D.N.Y.1980), 5 Med.L.Rptr. 2455, 2457.

[12] MCA, Inc. v. Wilson, 425 F.Supp. 443 (S.D.N.Y.1976).

[13] 389 F.Supp. 1397 (S.D.N.Y.1975). Similarly, in Fisher v. Dees, 794 F.2d 432 (9th Cir.1986), 13 Med.L.Rptr. 1167, a U.S. Court of Appeals Court found that a parody of the plaintiff composers' song "When Sunny Gets Blue," performed as "When Sunny Sniffs Glue," took no more from the copyrighted song than was necessary to reasonably accomplish its purpose. It was neither obscene nor immoral in nature, and was parody entitled to fair use protection.

[14] Acuff–Rose Music, Inc. v. Campbell, 754 F.Supp. 1150 (M.D.Tenn.1991).

original song in the parody, presented issues that could result in a finding of copyright infringement against 2 Live Crew.[15]

A unanimous Supreme Court reversed the Court of Appeals.[16] Justice Souter, speaking for the Court, stated that the key in determining whether the parody of a copyrighted work infringes on the original is not its commercial or non-commercial nature, but the extent it alters the original through new expression, message or meaning. Thus, as Souter expressed it, the more "transformative" the parody, the less significant the other factors—(the commercial/non-commercial nature of the use; the amount used; its impact on the market value of the original).

The Court of Appeals had erred, according to Souter, both in finding the borrowing from the original to be too extensive, and in presuming without adequate evidence that market harm would result from the parody.

In essence, then, this decision indicates that the Supreme Court, in cases of parody of copyrighted materials, will place greatest emphasis on the first of the four elements of the fair use defense, not in terms of whether the parody is commercial or non-commercial, but whether it alters substantially the message or meaning of the original. The more "original" the parody, then, the less likely it is to be found to have infringed the copyrighted work.

SEC. 97.   BROADCAST MUSIC LICENSING RIGHTS

Electronic media must obtain copyright clearance for the music they use through private agreements with organizations that represent the composers and publishers of this music.

In 1923 the National Association of Broadcasters (NAB) was founded primarily to negotiate an agreement with the American Society of Composers and Publishers (ASCAP) to allow radio stations to broadcast the copyrighted music of the society's composers and music publishers.

ASCAP had been formed in 1914 as a performing rights, copyright licensing agency for a group of music publishers and their composers whose works were being performed in music halls and in Vaudeville theaters without permission or payment.[17] When radio

---

[15] Acuff–Rose Music, Inc. v. Campbell, a.k.a. Skyywalker, 972 F.2d 1429 (6th Cir.1992).

[16] Campbell v. Acuff–Rose Music, Inc., 510 U.S. 569, 114 S.Ct. 1164 (1994).

[17] During this era, sheet music was still the primary source of income for the music industry. Publishing companies would either hire composers and lyricists to write the songs that would be published and sold to the public or purchase songs from established composers. Today a music publisher simply promotes and produces musical recordings.

stations began broadcasting recorded music of ASCAP's composers and publishers during the early 1920s, the organization demanded copyright royalties for this program use.

During this pioneering era of broadcasting, stations were not yet permitted to sell commercial time and so until the early 1930s these radio station music licensing payments were little more than token contributions. By 1932, however, as radio was emerging as one of the few profitable industries during the Great Depression, ASCAP suddenly demanded a 300 percent increase in its broadcast music licensing fees.

For a time the NAB was able to convince its member stations to fill their schedules with the few public domain compositions they had on record, but when ASCAP offered a lower rate to newspaper owned stations, opposition collapsed and broadcasters agreed to this massive rate hike.

In 1937 the broadcast industry attempted to dilute ASCAP's absolute power over broadcast music rights by encouraging the formation of a rival group, Broadcast Music Incorporated (BMI), hoping that competition for broadcast business would force ASCAP to reduce its fees. The tactic worked for a short time, but soon BMI began bargaining as aggressively as ASCAP during each renegotiation of its licensing agreements.

When television began to emerge during the 1950s as the dominant electronic medium in the United States, the "blanket license" approach that both ASCAP and BMI used to grant broadcast use of their music was challenged by the television industry. Most radio stations had been willing to accept this type of license that granted them full broadcast use of music from ASCAP and BMI composers in return for a payment of less than one percent of their annual advertising revenues. For television stations, however, with their far larger advertising revenues, and their far less extensive use of music, neither the blanket license nor the per-use alternative offered by ASCAP or BMI seemed reasonably related to the actual value a station owner received from such music usage.

Beginning in 1950, the All–Industry Television Station Music License Committee, negotiating on behalf of its member stations, sought some other type of arrangement with the music licensing groups that would reflect more accurately the minimal benefits the blanket license offered television stations. Although each new round of negotiations resulted in a further reduction of the percentage of advertising revenues to be charged during the subsequent license period, neither ASCAP nor BMI was willing to abandon a licensing structure that by 1970 was providing an estimated 20–25 percent of their annual music rights revenue.[18]

After failing to reach agreement with the music licensing organizations on a satisfactory alternative to the blanket license, CBS, acting on behalf of the television networks, began an antitrust action against ASCAP and BMI in 1969. CBS alleged that these organizations had acted in concert to prevent the composers and publishers they represented from dealing directly with the television networks or its producers who sought to purchase broadcast music rights from the parties who held title to them, in restraint of trade and in direct violation of section 1 of the Sherman Antitrust Laws.[19]

In 1981, the U.S. Supreme Court held that the blanket license was not a per se violation of the Act, and on remand the Court of Appeals then dismissed the action.[20] In 1978 a group of local television stations began their own antitrust action against ASCAP and BMI, alleging the same type of anticompetitive practices. Unlike CBS, however, these local stations were successful in convincing a lower court that the blanket music licensing agreements did constitute an illegal restraint of trade.[21]

According to the opinion, what made the conduct of ASCAP and BMI anti-competitive was their concerted effort to discourage program producers from obtaining directly from composers complete copyright clearance for broadcast usage of the programs they produced. The court found that, unlike the television networks, individual stations did not have sufficient bargaining power to force music licensing organizations to alter their practices, and therefore they required the protection the law provided in order to be capable of bargaining with ASCAP and BMI on equal footing.

ASCAP and BMI challenged this federal trial court decision, and a federal appeals court reversed the lower court holding, finding that the difference in the degree of bargaining power exercised by the stations and the networks was not substantial enough to require a finding that the music licensing organizations were acting in restraint of trade.[22]

When the U.S. Supreme Court refused to review this appellate court decision, broadcasting turned immediately to Congress to obtain through legislation what it had been unable to gain through litigation. During recent years the NAB has been attempting during each session of Congress to obtain passage of a law that would legally obligate every television producer to acquire full musical

---

[18] "Broadcasters Press On Against ASCAP, BMI," Variety January 8, 1986, p. 209.

[19] CBS v. ASCAP, 620 F.2d 930 (2d Cir.1980).

[20] BMI v. CBS, 441 U.S. 1, 99 S.Ct. 1551 (1979).

[21] Buffalo Broadcasting Co. v. ASCAP, 546 F.Supp. 274 (S.D.N.Y.1982).

[22] Buffalo Broadcasting Co. v. ASCAP, 744 F.2d 917 (2d Cir.1984).

broadcast performance rights to all programs to be distributed for television broadcast. Although none of these "source licensing" bills have been adopted by Congress, the NAB continues in its lobbying efforts because it believes that such "source licensing" would clear at least 90 percent of the musical content now broadcast by television stations throughout the United States, making it possible for networks and most television stations to avoid the need of a "blanket" music license from ASCAP or BMI.

In 1990, the cable industry charged these music licensing organizations with anti-competitive practices under the Sherman antitrust act, challenging the refusal of these groups to offer cable TV networks a blanket music license. The industry eventually prevailed, obtaining agreements from both organizations to accept license payments from each cable network and a single annual fee from each cable system.[23]

Because payment arrangements for electronic media usage of copyrighted music are not established by the statutory provisions of the Copyright Act, all terms and conditions of usage must be negotiated between the music licensing organizations and representatives of electronic media. Considering the amount of money involved, it is not surprising that so many of these efforts have ended up in litigation, requiring the courts to define for the parties the reasonable value of the music rights involved.

Recently, pay-TV organizations have begun to have their day in court. Early in 1991, HBO negotiated an interim settlement with BMI, agreeing to pay the broadcast music performing rights organization a monthly fee for use of BMI music until a federal court determines whether BMI can rightfully demand music rights payments both from a pay-TV service that is providing programming and each cable system that is distributing it.[24] One week later ASCAP, the other major broadcast music licensing organization, negotiated a similar interim settlement with Showtime.[25]

This entire electronic media music performing rights controversy is yet another illustration of technology complicating the process of effectively compensating the creative artist for the use of that individual's intellectual property. Paying some arbitrarily determined amount of money to a licensing organization to be divided in almost as arbitrarily a fashion among that group of artists it

[23] National Cable Television Assn. v. Broadcast Music Inc., 772 F.Supp. 614 (D.D.C.1991). U.S. v. American Society of Composers, Authors and Publishers (ASCAP), 782 F.Supp. 778 (S.D.N.Y.1991) affirmed per curiam 956 F.2d 21 (2d Cir.1992), cert. denied 504 U.S. 914, 112 S.Ct. 1950 (1992).

[24] "BMI Makes Deal with HBO; Lawsuit Dropped," Variety, January 14, 1991, p. 121.

[25] "ASCAP, Showtime Settle on Fees," Variety, January 21, 1991, p. 90.

represents is certainly far less efficient or cost effective than direct negotiations between the purchaser and the artist.[26]

Unfortunately, though, such direct negotiations for the use of music are seldom possible in this modern era. At the beginning of the twentieth century a vaudeville or music hall producer could purchase from a publisher the performing rights to a complete musical score for a stage show that might run for several years. Today, however, it would be virtually impossible for the typical radio station to negotiate for the rights to each of fifteen to twenty different musical compositions it schedules on each hour's Playlist.

---

[26] Cable TV's compulsory license to allow it to pay a percentage of its subscriber revenues into a pool to compensate those who own the TV programs the system has imported from a distant broadcast market operates in basically the same fashion as the broadcast music licensing agreement, but in cable TV's situation the pooling arrangement is created by federal law.

Chapter 16

MEDIA OWNERSHIP: CONSOLIDATION
AND GLOBALIZATION

SEC. 98. INTERNATIONAL DIMENSIONS
OF MEDIA OWNERSHIP

Foreign commerce considerations have begun shaping American media ownership policies.

As long as the United States remained preeminent in the arena of world trade, the federal government firmly opposed mergers among major media organizations. Diversity of opinion was the key principle supporting this policy position; to protect the American marketplace of ideas from domination by a small group of giant mass media corporations.

But as this nation's foreign trade deficits began to mount, federal media ownership policy began to change as well. During the past 20 years, the mass media industries have become one of a very few areas of international commerce still providing the United States with a favorable foreign trade balance.[1]

This fact has not gone unnoticed by other powerful industrial nations. Since the mid–1980s, foreign interests have acquired three of America's six major film studios, and two of the nation's three largest music organizations.[2] Only three of the world's ten largest

---

[1] The annual U.S. foreign trade deficit increased from $20 billion in 1980 to nearly $150 billion in 1993. During that same time, our trade *surplus* from foreign sales of U.S. feature films, television programs, music and video cassettes increased from less than $2 billion in 1980 to more than $7 billion in 1993.

[2] In little more than a decade Rupert Murdoch's News Corporation acquired the film studio 20th Century Fox and Metromedia Broadcasting; Sony purchased Columbia Pictures and Matsushita took over MCA, owner of Universal Studios. Technically, Murdoch's acquisition is no longer "foreign," since he is now an American citizen but the organization he controls is still a global conglomerate. In the field of music, Bertelsmann, a German media conglomerate, bought RCA Music and Sony acquired CBS Records. Disney and the newly conglomerated Time–Warner and Viacom–Paramount are the only remaining American owned film studios, and Warner is also

798

mass media conglomerates are now American-owned, and several of the European and Japanese media groups have been expanding at a more rapid pace than their American competitors.[3]

Because of growing concern that many other American mass media corporations might be tempting foreign takeover targets, mergers to strengthen the financial position of domestic mass media properties and enhance their capacity to compete in a global media marketplace are now viewed with much greater sympathy in Washington.

If anyone had expected this policy would be reversed by a Democratic administration, that hope was dashed in January 1994 when the Clinton Justice Department stood aside as Viacom and Paramount merged to become one of the largest media conglomerates in the United States. With the $10 billion Viacom and its partner Blockbuster paid to acquire Paramount, the new media giant will own nine TV stations, 800 motion picture theaters, five cable TV networks, a library of 890 feature films, an 8,500 title syndication library, 3,500 video rental stores, a major television and film production center as well as five regional theme parks, a major wholesale and retail interactive game distribution system and five publishers.[4]

Yet all this attention being given to foreign trade implications of media ownership in the United States should not obscure the fact that permitting domestic mass media organizations to merge reduces the number of mass cultural options available to the American public, diminishing that level of competition essential for a marketplace of ideas to flourish. So, while it is important to understand why our federal government appears at this point to be permitting and even encouraging national media mergers and consolidations, it is at least equally important to understand what adverse effects this policy could have upon the quality of future media service in the United States.

the only remaining major music distributor in the United States. Although foreign corporations have been somewhat less interested in acquiring American publishing interests, five of the largest book publishers in the United States are now foreign owned, as well as over 100 magazines, including TV Guide, McCalls, Family Circle and two of America's largest mass media trade magazines, Variety and Broadcasting.

[3] Since its recent merger, Time–Warner has become the largest media conglomerate in the world, generating global annual entertainment revenues of $9 billion. Bertelsmann, the German media conglomerate that also owns RCA Music, Doubleday Publishing, Bantam Books and Dell is in second place, and closing rapidly on Time–Warner. In third place is Berlusconi's Italian media organization Fininvest, with an American entity, Capital Cities/ABC in fourth place. Thomson, the Canadian publisher, is the world's fifth largest media corporation while Rupert Murdoch's News Corporation, owner of the Fox Network, TV Guide and Harper & Row, among other American magazines and book publishers, trails Thompson by a small margin.

[4] Adam Sandler, "The Merged Paramount–Viacom Duo", Variety Jan 27, 1994, p. 185.

Clear patterns in national media conglomeration have emerged. At this point then, there are two significant questions to raise and consider. First, why has the federal government been so firmly opposed to such consolidation in the past, and secondly, are those fears that prompted that opposition still justified today?

SEC. 99. THE TREND TOWARD MEDIA CONCENTRATION

The natural tendency of media organizations has been to combine and thereby reduce competition, a trend that has become more pronounced during the past two decades.

The disappearance of many daily newspapers—particularly independent, locally owned newspapers—is part of the story. Phrases frequently heard include "concentration of newspaper ownership," "problems of bigness and fewness," and "fewer voices in the marketplace of ideas."[5]

But this threat to the daily newspaper is by no means the only area of concern. Professor Bagdikian of the University of California—one of the best-known media critics—is an important voice pointing out that media power is political, and that only a small group of corporations has real opportunities to control most of "what America sees, hears, and reads." Bagdikian wrote that finance capitalism and new technologies have forged[6]

> * * * a new kind of central authority over information—the national and multinational corporation. By the 1980s, the majority of all major American media—newspapers, magazines, radio, television, books, and movies—were controlled by fifty giant corporations. These corporations were interlocked in common financial interest with other massive industries and with a few dominant banks.

Microsoft Brings New Concerns

Before the 1980s ended, the 50 giant corporations Bagdikian had described in 1982 had already merged into 26 much larger and more powerful media conglomerates.[7] Despite the enormous power of media conglomerates, patterns had emerged by late 1997 sug-

[5] Toby J. McIntosh, "Why the Government Can't Stop Press Mergers," Columbia Journalism Review, December, 1980, pp. 48–50; "America's Press: Too Much Power for Too Few?," U.S. News & World Report, Aug. 15, 1977, pp. 27ff; Kevin Phillips, "Busting the Media Trusts," Harper's Magazine, July 1977, pp. 23ff, and Neil Hickey, "Can the Networks Survive," TV Guide, March 21, 1981, pp. 7ff.

[6] Ben H. Bagdikian, The Media Monopoly (Boston: Beacon Press, 1983), book jacket copy, plus quote from p. xv.

[7] Ben Bagdikian, "The 26 Corporations That Own Our Media," Extra, June 1987, p. 1.

gesting that old behemoths were in some decline. For example, the combined prime-time viewership share of the three old-line broadcast networks—ABC, CBS, and NBC—had sagged to only 50 percent of the viewing audience, an all-time low. Cable TV, of course, cut into network market shares, but increasingly, time spent with personal computers and on-line services increasingly took a toll from television viewing.[8]

In the late 1990s, antitrust/ownership pattern talk increasingly focused on Microsoft and its wealthiest-man-in-the-United States guru/leader, Bill Gates. Software from microsoft, after all, was the dominant supplier of computer operating system software, which gave Microsoft/Gates a net worth estimated at $70 billion in 1996. Microsoft turned its attention from dominating operating systems to becoming a bigger player in the Internet. Microsoft moved into browser programs on the World Wide Web, distributing its Internet Explorer at no charge. Further, Microsoft invested billions of dollars in Internet companies including UUNET, the top provider of Internet services. Furthermore, on-line advertisements and stores and programming in competition with traditional media are playing for high stakes: By the year 2000, it was predicted that there would be 39 million online households in North America.[9]

Changing Regulatory Patterns

Until deregulation became the policy of choice in Washington during the late 1970s, such a clear pattern of media consolidation would almost certainly have triggered federal antitrust investigations by the Justice Department. In the late 1990s, however, federal media antitrust actions—the focus of this chapter—are not politically in vogue. Yet, since fads and fashions change in politics as they do in the real world, it's important to be aware of basic concepts in an area of law that may soon become fashionable once more if the trend towards media consolidation should continue at its present pace.

So what is "antitrust?" Black's Law Dictionary says:[10]

> Antitrust acts. Federal and state statutes to protect trade and commerce from unlawful restraints, price discriminations, price fixing, and monopolies. Most states have mini-antitrust acts patterned on the federal acts. The principal federal antitrust acts are: Sherman Act (1890);

[8] Ellen Graham, "Where Have All the Viewers Gone?", The Wall Street Journal, June 27, 1997, p. R1.

[9] Joshua Cooper Ramo, "Winner Take All," Time, September 16, 1996, pp. 55–64; Peter McGrath, "The Web: Infotopia or Marketplace?", Newsweek, January 27, 1997, pp. 82–84.

[10] Black's Law Dictionary, Fifth Edition (St. Paul, West Pub. Co., Minn., 1979) p. 86.

Clayton Act (1914); Federal Trade Commission Act (1914); Robinson–Patman Act (1936). See Boycott; Combination in restraint of trade; Price fixing; Restraint of trade; * * *

Antitrust law is a term which from time to time causes considerable concern among publishers and broadcasters. For example, the Federal Communications Commission (FCC) proposed in 1970 that broadcast station owners who also owned a newspaper in their coverage area should be forced to sell either their station or their newspaper property. That FCC "proposed rulemaking" was enough to cause a substantial number of cross-ownerships to be split up by their owners.

The FCC backed down from its proposal in 1975, issuing a ruling which "grandfathered"—left in effect—most existing local cross-ownerships of broadcast and newspaper properties. A group calling itself The National Citizens Commission for Broadcasting sued the FCC, demanding that such cross-ownerships be broken up unless positive showings could be made that such patterns served the public interest.[11] In 1978, the Supreme Court held that it was within the FCC's authority to decide that existing cross-media ownerships were in the public interest. That upheld the FCC's grandfathering of existing ownership patterns.[12] The FCC, however, made clear it would approve no new local cross-media ownerships.

In certain circumstances, the power of antitrust law over the media can be awesome. The shock wave generated by the *RKO General* case provides one example. The Federal Communications Commission (FCC), claiming (among other things) antitrust law violations by RKO General and its parent company—General Tire and Rubber Company—refused to renew broadcast licenses of three television stations owned by RKO General. With that decision, the FCC tried to take away the license of WNAC–TV, Boston; WOR–TV, New York City, and KHJ–TV, Los Angeles.

RKO General appealed the FCC's decision, setting off lengthy court battles. The antitrust/trade practices complaints were only part of the FCC's proceedings against RKO General. Even though an FCC administrative law judge had found in 1987 that RKO was unfit to hold a broadcast license, the Commission decided against immediate revocation, giving RKO the opportunity to sell its broadcast properties and transfer the station licenses to purchasers the agency had approved.[13]

[11] National Citizens Committee for Broadcasting v. FCC, 555 F.2d 938 (D.C.Cir. 1977).

[12] FCC v. National Citizens Committee for Broadcasting, 436 U.S. 775, 98 S.Ct. 2096 (1978).

[13] RKO General, 63 RR 2d 866 (1987). See also, "FCC Gives RKO Green Light to Sell Stations," Broadcasting July 25, 1988, p. 33.

Also, it should be kept in mind that antitrust law is not exclusively a federal matter. Although this chapter concentrates on federal antitrust activity, State antitrust laws are a formidable thicket. Under the laws of several States, convictions for antitrust violations can result in the forfeiture of a corporation's charter. This would mean that a media corporation could lose the right to operate not only in the State in which it is chartered, but also in any other State which permits it to conduct business as a "foreign" (out of State) corporation.[14]

This chapter will not consider in any detail the entire range of antitrust activity affecting the media. It is aimed, instead, at the increasingly interrelated question of newspaper and broadcast/cable ownership situations. It does not take up such matters as exclusive syndication or newspaper distribution problems, nor does it treat important related questions of ownership of magazines, community newspapers and billboards.[15]

Because of the structure of the newspaper industry, the Antitrust Division of the Department of Justice has been unable to make much of an impact on large publishing chains continually acquiring additional newspapers throughout the United States. As long as the expansion of these publishing empires does not diminish the level of *local* newspaper competition, the federal government has generally refused to intervene to prevent such purchases.

The communications media are businesses, and as such, are ringed about by federal and state laws which regulate businesses. Congress has enacted several statutes—most commonly called antitrust laws—which attempt to preserve competition. The most important statements of national antitrust policy are found in the *Sherman*[16] and *Clayton*[17] *Acts*.

The *Sherman Act of 1890* begins: "Every contract, combination in the form of a trust or otherwise, or conspiracy, in restraint of trade or commerce among the several states, or with foreign nations, is hereby declared to be illegal."[18] Every person who acts to restrain trade, as mentioned generally above, is guilty of a crime.[19]

[14] Conrad M. Shumadine and Michael S. Ives, "Selected Antitrust Issues of Interest to the Media," in James C. Goodale, editor, Communications Law 1980, Vol. 2 (New York: Practising Law Institute, 1980) pp. 296–298.

[15] Exclusive syndication problems involve features such as columns or comic strips. Such features are offered to major newspapers under an agreement that no other newspapers within a certain region can publish those particular features. For a discussion of territorial exclusivity problems and distribution problems involving newspapers, see Marc A. Franklin, et al., The First Amendment and the Fourth Estate (Mineola, N.Y.; Foundation Press, 1977 and later editions).

[16] 26 Stat. 209, 15 U.S.C.A. §§ 1–7; P.L. No. 190, 51st Congress (1890).

[17] 38 Stat. 730, 15 U.S.C.A. § 12ff; P.L. No. 201, 63rd Congress (1914).

[18] 15 U.S.C.A. § 1.

[19] 15 U.S.C.A. § 20.

The Sherman Act prohibits "contracts, combinations * * * or conspiracies in restraint of trade or commerce" and makes it illegal to "monopolize, or attempt to monopolize, or combine or conspire * * * to monopolize * * * trade or commerce."[20]

Criminal prosecution—with penalties of fines, imprisonment, or both—is provided for in the Sherman Act. Fines may reach a maximum amount of $100,000 per individual, and imprisonment for up to three years may also be imposed. A corporation may be fined up to $1 million for violating the Sherman Act. The Act also enables the government to seek injunctions against violators of the statute to stop anti-competitive practices. Also, a business that has suffered damages because a competitor has violated the Sherman Act may sue the competitor for *treble damages.*

Treble damages lawsuits work in this way: suppose that the Daily Tribune newspaper has violated the Sherman Act. The United States Department of Justice takes the Daily Tribune to court and gets an order to make it stop monopolistic or trade-restraining practices. An interested spectator, meanwhile, is the Tribune's competitor, the Evening Post. The Post then begins a treble damage antitrust suit, and is able to prove in court that the Daily Tribune's illegal business practices cost the Post $100,000 in business. However, since this would be a *treble damage* lawsuit, the Post would actually collect $300,000 from the competing Tribune company.

The *Clayton Act of 1914* added to the government's antitrust enforcement powers, enumerating many acts as illegal when "they tend to lessen competition or to create a monopoly in any line of commerce."[21] Section 7 of the Clayton Act—more commonly called the Celler–Kefauver Act of 1950—is the most important section of the Clayton Act where the media are concerned.[22] The "Celler–Kefauver Act" forbids corporations to acquire stock or assets of a competing corporation "where * * * the effect * * * may be substantially to lessen competition, or tend to create a monopoly."

Upon such vaguely worded provisions of the Sherman and Clayton Acts is built federal antitrust policy. The vagueness of the statutory provisions make antitrust one of the most perplexing branches of public law, especially where newspapers and other units of the communications media are involved.

Increasingly and perhaps inevitably, the business of media is more prominent—and often seems more highly valued—than the socio-political roles of the media. Unfortunately, media theorists who talk about a free press or competition in the marketplace of

[20] 15 U.S.C.A. §§ 1, 4.

[21] 15 U.S.C.A. § 18.

[22] 64 Stat. 1125, 15 U.S.C.A. § 18; P.L. 899, 81st Congress (1950).

ideas seem more and more out-of-date. But it is commonly accepted—or at least given lip-service—that freedom of speech and press are essential; that they are needed for a meaningful "marketplace of ideas" necessary for self-government. This is one key reason why the press is shielded by the First Amendment, so that citizens might be informed about government and speak out as necessary. Those are the kinds of assumptions ringed about the First Amendment.

Now, however, despite hopes for the Internet as a citizens' medium, there is room for skepticism about the First Amendment as a citizens' right. Increasingly, it demands enormously large amounts of capital to own a newspaper or broadcast station, on the one hand, or to defend oneself against a libel or privacy lawsuit, on the other. And as the pace of media mergers accelerates, the number of different voices able to exercise this right continues to diminish with each passing year.

Government Policies Favor Merger Activity

In April 1985, the FCC relaxed its broadcast station ownership restrictions, increasing the number of radio, FM and television properties a licensee could own from 7 to 12 of each type of station.[23] This action set off a massive surge of broadcast industry acquisitions and mergers, resulting in a record-breaking total of $30 billion in broadcast and allied media industry sales transactions occurring before the year ended.[24]

During the late 1980s there were more than 100 separate media purchases that each exceeded $10 million. Of special note was the acquisition of RCA–NBC by General Electric for $6.3 billion; the purchase of ABC by Capital Cities Broadcasting for $3.5 billion, and Australian media baron Rupert Murdoch's takeover of Metromedia for $2 billion captured the great amounts of public attention. Through acquiring the Metromedia stations, Murdoch's new Fox Network obtained virtually the same amount of network-owned television station audience coverage as his three major network competitors.[25] More than 1,300 broadcast stations were sold in the year 1987 alone, at a value of $7.5 billion.[26]

[23] The following FCC rules were amended for the three broadcast services 47 CFR 73.35(a); 47 CFR 43.240(a) 1; 47 CFR 73.636(a) 1–2; and 47 CFR 76.501. Bowing to Congressional pressure, the FCC did limit to 25% the maximum size of the national television audience that any 12 group owned stations could serve.

[24] "Fifth Estate's $30 Billion-plus Year," Broadcasting, December 30, 1985, p. 35.

[25] ABC's owned and operated TV stations reach 24.5% of all American TV households; NBC's O & O stations reach 22.4%; CBS reaches 19.46% and Fox, through its Metromedia holdings, now serves 19.39% of the total TV population. "Television's Top 20," Broadcasting, August 31, 1987, p. 33.

[26] "Broadcasting–$7.5 Billion, Cable–$6 Billion," Broadcasting February 6, 1988, p. 61.

Small wonder that Newsweek Magazine termed this wave of acquisitiveness a "feeding frenzy." Newsweek added:[27]

> For the American news media, accustomed to thinking of themselves as a Fourth Estate, it has been something of a shock to be treated as Wall Street darlings instead. The pell-mell quest for media properties has bid up their sale prices to heady levels.

Many journalists (except for business writers, Wall Street Journal types, and the like) have long had the reputation for being financial illiterates. But when the media became such attractive properties in the 1980s, self-interest began to impel journalists to learn some new terms, such as:

"Leveraged Buyout"—This is a deal in which money is borrowed to buy a corporation. Then, the cash flow from the purchased company is put to work to pay off the interest and principal of the loan.

> The purchase of the ABC Network by Capital Cities is a startling example of a leveraged buyout. A Nebraska financier—Warren Buffett—bought Capital Cities stock to provide $517.5 million of the $3.5 billion "Cap Cities" spent to get control of ABC. Note that Cap Cities was much smaller than ABC—its 1984 revenues amounted to $950 million, compared to $3.7 billion for ABC. "It's a little like the canary eating the cat," said Roone Arledge, president of ABC News and Sports.[28]

> But then, with media companies, cash flow can be so great that enormous loans can be paid off. Alex S. Jones reported in The New York Times that "well-run television stations in major markets can generate pre-tax operating income of over 50 percent * * * cash flow can be 60 percent or more of revenues." Further, cash flow for the more profitable newspapers can range as high as 40 percent or more.[29]

"Friendly Takeover"—As the term implies, it is an amicable merger between two corporations. The Capital Cities Communications–ABC merger again provides a good example. ABC's architect and Chairman, 79–year-old Leonard Goldenson, had for some years been the subject of speculation: who would replace him at the 214–station network? Cap Cities Chairman Thomas Murphy talked with the ABC Executive Vice President, and they agreed that if the FCC

[27] Ibid.

[28] Peter W. Kaplan, "Takeover's Impact Is Uncertain," The New York Times, March 19, 1985, p. 54.

[29] See Geraldine Fabrikant, "3 TV Stations High Margins," The New York Times, July 1, 1985, p. 25.

ever liberalized its "7–7–7 rule" to permit one corporation to own a larger number of television stations, the two companies would be a "natural fit." After the FCC changed to its "12–12–12" rule on April 1, 1985, the merger took place.[30]

Similarly, General Electric's purchase of NBC in December of 1985 for $6.3 billion was also a friendly merger. The management of NBC's parent company RCA, had taken defensive measures against a hostile take-over, but was still concerned about its long term vulnerability. The merger, creating the second largest industrial corporation in the nation (excluding the auto industry) provided NBC with a massive infusion of capital, while GE gained re-entry into a field with the strong profit base the company saw as being essential to support its worldwide manufacturing and marketing activities.[31]

"Hostile Takeover"—There had been rumors that ABC was being stalked for a hostile takeover—a situation in which entrepreneurs buy up a controlling interest in a company's stock, thus gaining effective ownership. The rumors mentioned potential take-over bidders as the Bass brothers of Fort Worth, Texas, and Ted Turner, the feisty and aggressive owner of Atlanta "super-station" WTBS, Cable News Network, the Atlanta Braves baseball team, and so on. But ABC Board Chairman Goldenson said that the network had found no evidence of investors buying up huge blocs of ABC stock, and added that the sale to Capital Cities was not put together to prevent someone less desirable from gaining control of the network.[32]

"Junk Bonds"—A failed hostile takeover, especially one financed with "junk bonds", can sometimes be as damaging for media organizations as a successful takeover. In 1985, Ted Turner, the cable TV magnate, decided he wanted to own CBS. Turner tried, unsuccessfully, to purchase the 67 percent of CBS's common stock required under New York to gain control of the corporation. Since he lacked the $5.4 billion needed to acquire the stock, he attempted to float more than $5 billion of the purchase price in "junk bonds," trying to persuade stockholders to support him by promising them an annual dividend some seven times their current dividend rate.[33]

[30] Newsweek, April 1, 1985, p. 54.

[31] "RCA + GE: Marriage Made in Takeover Heaven," Broadcasting, December 16, 1985 p. 43. At the time of the merger, GE did own one television property, KCNC–TV Denver that NBC had previously tried to acquire. With the purchase, it became the 6th NBC owned and operated TV station.

[32] Ibid., p. 53; "Network Blockbuster," Time, April 1, 1985, p. 60.

[33] The term "junk bond" is slang for a bond issued by a company that is too poor a credit risk to borrow money in a conventional manner. These bonds can often be

Although Turner failed in his campaign to take over CBS, the massive expenses the network incurred in fighting off his attack weakened its financial structure, making it much more vulnerable to the next takeover effort by another corporate giant. For a time it seemed that giant might be Coca–Cola, but while CBS executives were guarding their corporate flanks from attack, the actual takeover of CBS was occurring right behind their backs.

"Inside Takeover"—When Lawrence Tisch used the 24.9% of CBS stock he had recently acquired through his Loews Corporation to become acting chief executive officer (CEO) of CBS in September 1986, the FCC accepted the network's argument that Tisch's stock purchase and CEO appointment did not require Commission review because there had been no actual change in the ownership or control of CBS.[34] Before the year 1986 had ended, however, the 500 network employees he had already fired were among those who had reason to question the FCC's determination that Tisch was not in charge of CBS.

For a few brief weeks, Tisch was viewed as a hero at the network, because he had saved CBS from the rumored take-over move by Coca–Cola. But, as *Time* magazine described it, as Tisch continued to direct a "rapid and ruthless austerity program,"

> The September mood of euphoria at CBS suffered accordingly. Says one mid-level executive: "Half the people here curse Tisch." A television producer ... describes employee morale as "pulverized with fear." Staffers soon coined a bitter name for the layoffs; to be fired was to be "tisched".[35]

When that 1980s merger activity is considered—and there was far more of it than a short summary can include—it's clear that the pace of media consolidation in the United States accelerated significantly during that decade. The 50 major media organizations of

purchased for far less than their stated value (e.g. $10,000 face value worth of bonds for $100) because the chance that the company issuing them will ever being able to pay them off is so slight. What usually happens after "junk bonds" have financed the purchase of corporate stock is that the new owner then plunders the assets of the corporate acquired to pay the high rates of return demanded by the bonds tendered to purchase it.

34 "FCC on CBS: No Change in Control," Broadcasting, October 20, 1986, p. 28. The FCC's concern was not about ownership of the network per se, but about control of those licensed broadcast stations owned by CBS, because the Commission is required by Sec. 310(d) of the Communications Act to determine whether the transfer of control over a broadcast license is in the public interest before authorizing any change in ownership or control.

35 "A Cut Above the Ordinary," Time, December 22, 1986, p. 53.

1982 that had become only 26 media giants of 1988 are almost certain to continue merging and combining until perhaps only a dozen of them will be dominating every form of American mass culture by early years of the Twenty–First Century.

More Merger Mania in the 1990s: Disney, ABC/Capital Cities, Knight Ridder

In 1995, corporate mergers int he United States surged 51% to a record $866 billion, propelled by record stock prices and low interest rates. One week in August, 1995, accounted for $25 billion of this merger activity, as Disney offered $18.5 billion to buy ABC/Capital Cities and Westinghouse Broadcasting made a $5.4 billion bid for CBS.[36]

Disney's purchase of ABC/Capital Cities, completed with Department of Justice approval in February, 1996, was prompted by the repeal of the Financial Interest Rules by the Federal Communications Commission. That repeal allowed Disney to use ABC's network of stations as a major television distributor of its own programming.[37] Disney's decision to offer the second-highest price ever paid for a U.S. company (at that time topped only by the $25 billion paid for RJR Nabisco in 1989) was based on its belief that Disney would have ideal outlets for its products. Disney gained ABC's 11 network stations, and network contracts brought along more than 200 affiliated TV stations. With these acquisitions, Disney would have ideal outlets for feature films produced by Disney's own studio or by its other production organizations, Touchstone Pictures, Miramax Films, Caravan Films, and Hollywood Films.

In addition, Disney also consolidated its cable network holdings in ESPN, Lifetime Network, an the A & E Channel. It was not surprising that neither the FCC nor the Department of Justice used antitrust concerns to derail that purchase. The merger created great economies of scale allowing a new megamedia giant to compete more effectively and efficiently in the global media market than either Disney or ABC/Capital Cities might do on its own.

Not all aspects of this corporate marriage-made-in-Heaven, however, were enduring. Walt Disney Company announced early in 1997 that it was selling the publishing entities it had received in 1995 as part of the deal to acquire ABC/Capital Cities. The publishing properties, including seven newspapers, a dozen business publications and more than two dozen agricultural publications simply

---

[36] "A Record Year for Mergers," Milwaukee Journal–Sentinel, January 4, 1996, p. 1H; Don West, "The Dawning of Megamedia: Broadcasting's $25 Billion Week," Broadcasting & Cable, August 7, 1995, p. 4.

[37] West, Ibid.

were seen as outside Disney's main focus.[38] The publishing enterprises, including two major dailies—the Kansas City Star and the Fort Worth Star–Telegram—were sold to Knight Ridder later in 1997.

Westinghouse Purchases CBS (1995)

In 1995, the day after Disney announced plans to acquire ABC/Capital Cities, Westinghouse offered to buy CBS for $5.4 billion.[39] Media mogul Ted Turner had been pursuing CBS vigorously, but Westinghouse successfully maneuvered to get some needed waivers from the Federal Communications Commission to allow the proposed merger to be okayed.

Westinghouse needed a waiver from the FCC because acquiring CBS would mean that the combination of Westinghouse and CBS would then have 15 stations reaching 33 percent of the national TV audience. Under the rules prevailing before the Telecommunications Act of 1996, that was three more stations than permitted in 1995 and 8 per cent more total TV audience than FCC regulations then allowed. Sensing vulnerability of Westinghouse/CBS at that point, interest groups seeking more programming for children sought to convince the FCC that any waiver granted Westinghouse should be conditioned on willingness of the network's new owner to increase its commitment to such programming.[40]

The FCC made no formal demand on Westinghouse concerning changes in programming. In December, 1995, however, when granting the waivers, the Commission acknowledged its appreciation of Westinghouse's "voluntary promise" to provide more children's programming each week, with a commitment to increase this to three additional hours a week over several years.[41]

While reduced competition may mean greater prosperity for the American media conglomerates themselves, it will certainly continue to diminish the vigor of public discourse and discussion totally dependent upon competition for its vitality.

SEC. 100. NEWSPAPER ANTITRUST LAW

Antitrust statutes, as applied to the press, are not in violation of the First Amendment guarantee of freedom of the press.

[38] Geraldine Fabrikant, "Disney to Sell Capital Cities Publications," The New York Times, January 29, 1997, p. C1.

[39] West, op. cit.

[40] Charles McConnell, "FCC Smiles on Disney, Westinghouse," Broadcasting & Cable, August 7, 1995, p. 45.

[41] Chris McConnell, "FCC Gives Green Light to Westinghouse/CBS," Broadcasting & Cable, November 27, 1995, p. 10.

Until the late 1970s, national rather than international mass media competition was the primary concern of the federal government. During this era the Justice Department was deeply committed to preventing anti-competitive trade practices in the newspaper industry.

Although decided just after the end of World War II, the decision of the Supreme Court of the United States in Associated Press v. United States[42] still ranks as a leading case in antitrust law affecting the media. The Justice Department had brought suit under the Sherman Act[43] to get an injunction preventing the AP from continuing to operate under a restrictive clause in its by-laws.

The Associated Press is a cooperative news-gathering organization. Its by-laws forbade AP member newspapers or broadcast stations from selling news to non-members. Other by-law provisions also gave a newspaper which had an AP membership virtual veto power over competing newspapers' attempts to gain AP membership.[44]

Associated Press v. United States (1945)

One of several cases combined under the case name of Associated Press v. United States involved Chicago publisher Marshall Field's efforts to get an AP membership for his Chicago Sun, a new newspaper trying to compete with crusty Col. Robert R. McCormick's Chicago Tribune. The Chicago Tribune protested against the upstart Chicago Sun's AP membership application, trying to prevent the competition from gaining the benefit of the premier news wire service.

Once such a protest was made, the AP by-laws then required a majority vote of ALL members of the Associated Press before the new applicant could be admitted to the club.[45] That majority vote—from publisher members of AP, many of whom enjoyed exclusive use of that wire service in their own publication areas—was most unlikely to occur. Thus Marshall Field's Chicago Sun could not join the AP without Col. McCormick's consent, unless the federal government intervened—in the public interest, of course—to use antitrust laws to force a change in the AP bylaws.

In 1943, the Justice Department charged that the conduct of the AP and the Chicago Tribune constituted "(1) a combination

[42] 326 U.S. 1, 65 S.Ct. 1416 (1945).

[43] See discussion of the Sherman Act, Section 93, supra, at footnote 15.

[44] Chafee, op. cit., pp. 542–543; Associated Press v. United States, 326 U.S. 1, 9–10, 65 S.Ct. 1416, 1419 (1945).

[45] Chafee, p. 543; Associated Press v. United States, loc. cit. Another newspaper which like the Chicago Sun had applied for AP membership and had been turned down by a 2–1 vote margin of AP members, was the Washington Times–Herald.

and conspiracy of restraint of trade and commerce in news among the states, and (2) an attempt to monopolize a part of that trade."[46] The Associated Press and the Chicago Tribune fought against the Justice Department charges, arguing that the application of the Sherman Act in this case would violate freedom of the press guaranteed by the First Amendment. A majority of the Supreme Court was not impressed by this argument. Writing for the Court, Justice Hugo L. Black said:[47]

> * * * All are alike covered by the Sherman Act. The fact that the publisher handles news while others handle goods does not, as we shall later point out, afford the publisher a peculiar constitutional sanctuary in which he can with impunity violate laws regulating his business practices.

Finally, Justice Black answered the assertion that the Sherman Act's application to the Associated Press abridged the AP's First Amendment freedom. He declared that it would be strange if the concern for press freedom underlying the First Amendment should be read "as a command that the government was without power to protect that freedom." Black continued,[48]

> Freedom to publish means freedom for all and not for some. Freedom to publish is guaranteed by the Commission, but freedom to combine to keep others from publishing is not. Freedom of the press from governmental interference under the First Amendment does not sanction repression of that freedom by private interests. The First Amendment affords not the slightest support for the contention that a combination to restrain trade in news and views has any constitutional immunity.

Justice Frankfurter added other arguments in favor of government action under the Sherman Act to attempt to control media activities which tended to restrain trade. To Frankfurter, the press was a business, but it was also much more: "in addition to being a commercial enterprise, it [the press] has a relation to the public interest unlike that of any other enterprise pursued for profit." Following this premise, Justice Frankfurter then quoted words written by America's most famous United States District Court judge. The oft-quoted words below came from Judge Learned Hand's lower-court opinion in this same case of Associated Press v. United States,[49]

46 326 U.S. 1, 4, 65 S.Ct. 1416, 1417 (1945).

47 326 U.S. 1, 6, 65 S.Ct. 1416, 1418 (1945).

48 326 U.S. 1, 20, 65 S.Ct. 1416, 1425 (1945).

49 326 U.S. 1, 28, 65 S.Ct. 1416, 1428 (1945), quoting Judge Hand, United States v. Associated Press, 52 F.Supp. 362, 372 (S.D.N.Y.1943).

* * * that [the newspaper] industry serves one of the most vital of all general interests: the dissemination of news from as many different sources, and with as many different facets and colors as is possible. That interest is closely akin to, if indeed it is not the same as, the interest protected by the First Amendment; it presupposes that right conclusions are more likely to be gathered out of a multitude of tongues than through any kind of authoritative selection. To many this is, and always will be, folly; but we have staked upon it our all.

To Frankfurter, the By–Laws of the Associated Press were a clear restriction of commerce. Such a restriction was unreasonable because it subverted the function of a constitutionally guaranteed free press.

Dissents from Justices Owen J. Roberts and Frank Murphy took a traditional libertarian view: In general, government should leave the press alone.[50]

A series of Supreme Court decisions following Associated Press v. United States illustrated the Court's determination to hold newspapers to accepted legal standards of competitive behavior. Anticompetitive behavior would not be shielded by the protections of the First Amendment.

Lorain Journal Company v. United States (1951)

Media can violate antitrust laws in one of two general ways. The first is by attempting through acquisition, merger or some other type of corporate restructuring to reduce the level of media competition in an unlawful manner. The second is to engage is some form of anti-competitive media business practice. The Lorain Journal case presented a clear illustration of the type of anti-competitive practices antitrust law has been designed to prevent.[51]

The paper had tried and failed to obtain a broadcast license to operate a radio station in the city in which it was located, Lorain, Ohio.[52] Soon afterward, the FCC issued a radio license to an applicant whose station was located in Elyria, Ohio, just eight miles from Lorain.

In an effort to force this competitor out of business, the paper adopted a strict policy of refusing to accept advertising from any

---

[50] 326 U.S. 1, 29, 49, 65 S.Ct. 1416, 1428, 1438 (1945).

[51] Lorain Journal Co. v. United States, 342 U.S. 143, 72 S.Ct. 181 (1951).

[52] See 92 F.Supp. 794 (N.D.Ohio 1950). See also Mansfield Journal Co. v. FCC, 180 F.2d 28 (D.C.Cir.1950). This refusal of the FCC to grant the license application was based in part on allegations of similar past anti-competitive behavior of the Mansfield Journal, jointly owned with the Lorain Journal, in its advertising practices and its refusal to print the schedules of competing radio stations in its area.

local merchants who also purchased any advertising time from the radio station. Because the Lorain Journal reached 99 percent of the area's households, local advertisers had little choice but to avoid buying commercial time from the radio station.

The Justice Department brought a civil antitrust suit against the Journal, charging the paper with attempting to monopolize commerce under the Sherman Act. The newspaper responded by claiming that this government action infringed not only on its constitutionally protected right of free speech, but also its right to accept or refuse advertisements from whomever it pleased.

A federal district court found that Lorain Journal had indeed been attempting to illegally monopolize commerce, and issued an injunction to prevent the paper from continuing its anticompetitive trade practices. The Journal appealed to the Supreme Court but to no avail. In a 7–0 decision, the Court upheld the lower court decision and the injunction that issued from it.

The Court, through Mr. Justice Harold Burton, declared that the newspaper's "bold, relentless and predatory commercial behavior" was not sheltered by the First Amendment.[53]

Because the findings of fact in a civil or criminal antitrust action brought by the government may be used in a lawsuit for treble damages by the injured party, the radio station was later able to sue the Journal and recover three times the damages it actually sustained for advertising revenues lost because of the newspaper's anticompetitive behavior.[54]

Times–Picayune Pub. Co. v. United States (1953)

In this case, the publisher of a morning (Times–Picayune) and an afternoon newspaper (States) in New Orleans would not accept advertising unless a merchant purchased advertising space in both of its newspapers, but did not refuse ads from those who also advertised in a competing afternoon paper (The Item). The Justice Department challenged this advertising practice, claiming that it constituted an anticompetitive "tying agreement"—that is, forcing a customer to buy an unwanted product in order to obtain the one desired.

The government contended that most advertisers desired to place their ads in the morning Times–Picayune, with a circulation of 188,000, but were forced by its unit-buying rule to purchase space in its sister afternoon paper, the States, with a circulation of only 105,000.[55] This, of course, would operate to divert potential

[53] Lorain Journal Co. v. United States, 342 U.S. 143, 155, 72 S.Ct. 181, 187 (1951).

[54] Elyria–Lorain Broadcasting Co. v. Lorain Journal Co., 298 F.2d 356 (6th Cir.1961).

[55] Times–Picayune v. U.S., 345 U.S. 594, 73 S.Ct. 872 (1953).

advertising revenues away from the independent New Orleans afternoon paper, the Item.

In a 5–4 decision, the Supreme Court disagreed with the Justice Department, finding that there had been no unlawful "tying" because the government had not established that the publisher's morning paper was in fact the desired or "dominant" product or that its afternoon paper the unwanted or "inferior" product for newspaper advertisers. Instead, Justice Tom C. Clark's majority opinion held that the two newspapers—owned by one publisher—were selling identical products: advertising space in a newspaper. But did competition survive? The name of the afternoon paper—after a 1958 merger—is the States–Item.

United States v. Kansas City Star (1957)

In Kansas City, the morning Times and afternoon and Sunday Star were owned by the same publisher, who also owned a local radio and television station. The Kansas City Post, the Star's only former competitor had gone bankrupt and ceased publication.

Readers were forced to subscribe to all three papers, the Times, and both the afternoon and Sunday Star in order to receive service. Advertisers were also forced to place their ads in all three papers, and there was evidence that merchants who did not advertise in the newspaper were not permitted to buy radio or television commercial time from the newspaper's stations.

In prosecuting its case, the government was able to show that the Star's dominant media position in the Kansas City area gave it the power to exclude competition. The government also assembled evidence to demonstrate that this power had been exercised in a ruthless fashion to coerce both readers and advertisers in a manner that would not have been possible in a truly competitive environment.

The Star was found guilty of criminal violations of antitrust law, as the jury rejected the publisher's argument that the morning and afternoon papers were separate entities in competition with one another. Eventually, after a federal appeals court affirmed the conviction, the Star agreed to a consent decree, ending a companion civil suit brought by the government.

This decree, like other consent decrees between an antitrust defendant and the government, was a negotiated settlement. By it terms, the Star agreed, in return for the government ending its civil action, to sell its radio and television stations and never again attempt to purchase any broadcast properties without the prior consent of the government. The decree also prohibited the newspapers from forcing advertisers to buy advertising space in both the Star and the Times in order to have their ads accepted.

Even the consent decree did not end the Star's legal problems. The criminal antitrust conviction was used repeatedly as evidence by would-be competitors who brought treble-damage antitrust suits against the paper. Defending against such lawsuits was an expensive proposition, and a number of such actions were settled out of court.[56]

United States v. Times–Mirror (1967)

The *Times Mirror* case was an attempt to reduce competition through merger activity.[57] The Times–Mirror Corporation had purchased the San Bernardino (California) Sun, a profitable daily newspaper located about 40 miles from Los Angeles for $15 million. The Pulitzer Corporation of St. Louis had offered to pay the same amount for the Sun, but the Sun's owner decided to accept the Times–Mirror offer instead.

Acquisition of the Sun by the Times–Mirror Corporation was challenged by the Antitrust Division of the Justice Department. The government complained that the merger meant that the publisher of California's largest daily newspaper, the Times, had now gained control of the largest independent daily newspaper in Southern California.

The federal trial judge found that the three San Bernardino County newspapers published by the Sun Corporation constituted the only major advertising competition faced by the Times–Mirror in the area and its primary competitor for subscribers in that region of the state.

Based on these findings, the Court ruled that the purchase of the Sun Company by Times–Mirror violated the anti-merger provisions of Section 7 of the Clayton Act. As a result, the Times–Mirror was forced to divest itself of Sun Company stock and present a plan for divestiture that provided for the continuation of the Sun Company as a strong and viable organization.

The Antitrust Division of the Department of Justice viewed its victory in the Times–Mirror case as significant. In 1968, leading antitrust lawyer Charles D. Mahaffie, Jr. wrote that the Antitrust Division was "and will continue to be particularly concerned with mergers which may eliminate the actual and potential competition afforded by the suburban, small-city and community papers."[58]

[56] See e.g. Goodfriend and Levinson v. Kansas City Star Co., 158 F.Supp. 531 (W.D.Mo.1958); Duff v. Kansas City Star Co., 299 F.2d 320 (8th Cir.1962) and Siegfried v. Kansas City Star Co., 193 F.Supp. 427 (W.D.Mo.1961).

[57] United States v. Times Mirror Co., 274 F.Supp. 606 (C.D.Cal.1967), affirmed by the U.S. Supreme Court without opinion 390 U.S. 712, 88 S.Ct. 1411 (1968).

[58] Charles D. Mahaffie, Jr., "Mergers and Diversification in the Newspaper, Broadcasting and Information Industries," The Antitrust Bulletin Vol. 13 (Fall 1968) pp. 927–935, at p. 928.

Underlying this statement was a basic philosophy of communication and freedom of expression protected through antitrust law. The idea is that many voices in the marketplace of information and opinion—"diversified, quarrelsome, and competitive"—are; in the public interest.[59]

However, although the Justice Department had been able to prevent the Times–Mirror from acquiring the San Bernardino Sun, the Sun newspapers were eventually acquired by the nation's largest newspaper group, The Gannett Company.

And after one last action during the Reagan administration to block the Orlando Sentinel's acquisition of five competing weekly suburban papers, the Justice Department has stood by passively as major daily newspapers throughout the United States have continued to absorb their suburban competitors.[60]

United States v. Citizen Publishing Co. (1968) and the "Newspaper Preservation Act" of 1970

In 1969, the Supreme Court of the United States decided a case of great importance to the daily newspaper industry: United States v. Citizen Publishing Company, often called "The Tucson Case." That decision declared *joint operating agreements* to be illegal. Such agreements were and are important to the profit margins if not to the very survival of competing newspapers in about two-dozen cities.[61]

The Supreme Court's judgment that joint operating agreements were illegal didn't last long. The ruling brought a wave of protests from publishers whose newspapers are involved in joint operating agreements. On March 12, 1969, just two days after the Court's Tucson decision, a number of bills were offered in both the U.S. House of Representatives and the Senate to legalize joint operating agreements between two newspapers. Those bills tied in with lengthy hearings held by the preceding Congress on the so-called "Failing Newspaper Act."[62]

[59] See the classic statement by Judge Learned Hand in United States v. Associated Press, 52 F.Supp. 362, 372 (S.D.N.Y.1943), quoted at 326 U.S. 1, 28, 65 S.Ct. 1416, 1428 (1945), and printed in the text to footnote 52 earlier in this chapter.

[60] In 1989, for example, the Columbus Dispatch, owner of a radio and television station in Columbus, Ohio, bought a chain of five suburban weeklies and three shoppers; in 1990, the Orange County Register, the Los Angeles Times, the Chicago Sun–Times and the Seattle Times each acquired competing suburban papers and in 1992 the Mason City Globe–Gazette purchased its competing Mason City Shopper, all without attracting the attention of the Justice Department.

[61] Editor & Publisher, Jan. 18, 1969, p. 9. Such cities include Tucson; San Francisco; Madison, Wisconsin; El Paso, Texas, and Honolulu.

[62] See Subcommittee on Antitrust and Monopoly of the Committee on the Judiciary, United States Senate, 90th Congress, First Session, on S. 1312, The Failing Newspaper Act, Part 1, July 12–14, 18–19, 25–26, 1967, at p. 2.

After the Supreme Court's decision in the Tucson Case, the "Failing Newspaper Act" was given the euphemistic label "Newspaper Preservation Act" and was passed by both houses of Congress.[63] President Nixon signed the bill into law on July 24, 1970.

Joint operating agreements work in this fashion. Two competing newspapers in one town combine their printing, advertising, circulation and business operations. The news and editorial operations of the two newspapers, however, retain their separate identities. Then, the two newspapers—one published in the morning and the other in the afternoon—can use the same publishing, business and distribution facilities, resulting in substantial economies in operation.

To say that the Tucson Case obviously worried a number of publishers would be a major understatement. Arguments filed before the Supreme Court in the Tucson Case early in 1969 included an amicus curiae brief filed on behalf of newspaper publishers in 16 cities. In that brief, attorney Robert L. Stern asserted that "a joint operating plant is the only feasible way to preserve competition in cities which cannot support two completely separate newspapers."[64]

The Antitrust Division of the Department of Justice, however, disagreed with the line of thinking argued by attorney Stern. So did a Federal district court, in deciding that the Tucson joint operating agreement was illegal.[65] That joint operating agreement had been in existence since 1940. Then, Citizen Publishing Company (publishers of The Tucson Daily Citizen, an evening paper) and The Star Publishing Company (publishers of The Arizona Daily Star, a morning and Sunday paper) joined forces to form a third corporation: Tucson Newspapers, Inc. Tucson Newspapers, Inc. took over all departments of the two newspapers except news/editorial.

This joint operating agreement was started because the publishers of the two newspapers later said they believed there could not be successful operation of two competing dailies in a city with a population of less than 100,000.

In the district court decision, Chief Justice James A. Walsh found that the joint operating agreement amounted to illegal "price fixing, profit pooling, and market allocations by the parties to the agreement," a violation of the Sherman Act.

In arguments to the Supreme Court of the United States, the Tucson newspapers contended that joint operating agreements

[63] 15 U.S.C.A. §§ 1801–1804.

[64] Editor & Publisher, Dec. 21, 1968, p. 9.

[65] United States v. Citizen Pub. Co., Tucson Newspapers, Inc., Arden Pub. Co. and William A. Small, Jr., 280 F.Supp. 978 (D.Ariz.1968).

were necessary in a number of cities to allow newspapers to survive while maintaining competing news and editorial voices. There were 22 cities with a total of 44 newspapers involved in joint operating agreements similar to the Tucson situation in the mid–1960s. Thus, it was feared that the Justice Department, should it succeed in the Tucson case, would begin antitrust actions against other newspapers' joint operating agreements. That would mean, to use the example of Arizona, that Tucson Newspapers, Inc., could no longer operate single advertising and circulation departments serving both newspapers.[66]

In March of 1969, the Supreme Court of the United States indeed did find the Tucson joint operating agreement illegal. Writing for the Court, Mr. Justice Douglas ruled that the agreement was for the purpose of ending competition between the two newspapers.

> The Supreme Court thus affirmed the orders issued by the U.S. District Court in the Tucson case. This meant that the Tucson newspapers must "submit a plan for divestiture and re-establishment of the Star as an independent competitor and for modification of the joint operating agreement so as to eliminate the price-fixing, market control, and profit pooling provisions."[67] The Supreme Court, as Justice Douglas put it, found that "beyond peradventure of doubt" the joint operating agreement between Tucson's two daily newspapers violated antitrust laws.

The Newspaper Preservation Act

As noted earlier, the Supreme Court's decision in the Citizen Publishing Company case was promptly legislated out of existence by the Newspaper Preservation Act.[68] This act's purpose was stated to be maintaining—in the public interest—"a newspaper press editorially and reportorially competitive in all parts of the United States" by legalizing such joint operating agreements.

In one sense, this legislation might be viewed as "too little, too late" because by 1969 there were not many cities left with competing, independently owned daily newspapers. In another sense, there is also room for doubt about how truly "independent" newspapers that are bound together by common financial and business inter-

[66] Ibid. See also Editor & Publisher, Jan. 18, 1969, p. 9.

[67] 394 U.S. 131, 89 S.Ct. 927 (1969); United States Law Week, Vol. 37, pp. 4208–4212 (March 11, 1969); Barry Schweid, "Newspapers Want Congress to Legalize Joint Operation," Associated Press dispatch in Madison, Wis., Capital Times, March 11, 1969; "Publishers seek relief in Congress," Editor & Publisher, March 15, 1969, p. 9ff. See also International Shoe Co. v. Federal Trade Commission, 280 U.S. 291, 302, 50 S.Ct. 89, 93 (1930).

[68] 15 U.S.C.A. §§ 1801–1804.

ests will be when a choice has to be made between serving the public interest and serving economic self-interest.[69]

The Newspaper Preservation Act of 1970 approved all 22 joint operating agreements then in existence, involving 44 daily papers.[70]

The Act was passed despite strenuous objections from the Antitrust Division of the Department of Justice. The government's attorneys expressed fear that if profit pooling or price fixing laws were relaxed to aid newspapers, "many publishers will opt for that way [joint operating agreements] even though they might be capable of remaining fully independent, or of finding other solutions to the difficulties which preserve competition."[71] Weekly newspapers, small dailies, and the American Newspaper Guild also strongly and repeatedly urged against passage of the Act, complaining that joint advertising rates provide newspapers in a joint operation situation with a competitive advantage that other newspapers in the area simply could not overcome.[72]

The Newspaper Preservation Act authorizes the creation of a joint operating agreement only when at least one of the two newspapers is "failing," or "in probable danger of financial failure." In addition, the Act requires that any *new* joint operating agreements must receive written approval in advance from the Attorney General of the United States. The Act also specifies that the Attorney General cannot approve the agreement without first making a formal determination that at least one of the newspapers applying for joint operation is "failing" or "in probable danger of financial failure."

Despite its initial opposition to the Newspaper Preservation Act, the Justice Department eventually approved each of the seven additional newspaper joint operating agreements (JOA) it reviewed during the next 20 years.[73] The most controversial of these approv-

[69] See Ben H. Bagdikian, The Media Monopoly (Boston: Beacon Press, 1983), pp. 98–103.

[70] Cities with daily newspapers in JOA in 1970 included: Albuquerque, N.M.; Bristol, Tenn.; Charleston, W.Va.; Columbus, Ohio; El Paso, Texas; Evansville, Ind.; Fort Wayne, Ind.; Franklin–Oil City, Pa.; Honolulu; Knoxville, Tenn.; Lincoln, Neb.; Madison, Wis.; Miami, Fla.; Nashville, Tenn.; Pittsburgh, Pa.; Saint Louis, Mo.; Salt Lake City; San Francisco; Shreveport, La.; Tucson, and Tulsa. Since then, Birmingham, Ala.; Cincinnati, Oh.; Chattanooga, Tenn., and Seattle, Washington, have gone into JOAs. Dailies in Anchorage, Alaska, dissolved a JOA after a brief period, and The Derrick, Oil City, Pa., ended its JOA in 1985 by buying its partner, the Franklin News–Herald. The Knoxville, TN, News–Sentinel and the Journal ended their JOA at the end of 1991.

[71] Statement of Donald F. Turner, assistant attorney general, Antitrust Division, Department of Justice, before the Senate Judiciary Committee, Subcommittee on Antitrust and Monopoly, on S. 1312, April 1968, p. 18.

[72] See, e.g., The Guild Reporter, Sept. 8, 1967, p. 8; "Failing Newspaper Bill Assailed," Associated Press dispatch in Wisconsin State Journal, Madison, Sec. 1, p. 8, April 17, 1968.

[73] The seven new joint operating agreements were in the cities of Anchorage (1974), Cincinnati (1979), Chattanooga (1980), Seattle (1982), Detroit (1988), York, Pennsylvania (1990) and Las Vegas (1990).

als occurred in 1988, when then Attorney General Edwin Meese overruled his own Antitrust Division lawyers to permit a JOA between Knight–Ridder's Detroit Free Press and Gannett's Detroit News.

Several local citizen groups formed a coalition, "Michigan Citizens for a Free Press" to challenge the Justice Department decision in federal court. They argued that both newspapers had intentionally adopted short-term practices designed to reduce their revenues, creating artificial losses to justify their application for the JOA. A divided federal court of appeals upheld the JOA but admitted:

> We can envision a perfectly rational different policy, one that would require a showing that the weaker paper was more bloodied before approving a JOA and therefore *might* discourage the sort of competition we saw in Detroit. Congress, however, delegated to the Attorney General and not to us the delicate and troubling responsibility of putting content into the ambiguous phrase "probable danger of financial failure."[74]

Rehearing en banc was denied 5–4. The Supreme Court affirmed without a written opinion, 4–4, Justice White not participating.[75]

Yet, although these two wealthy newspaper chains had managed by the narrowest of margins to claim the benefits of a JOA, their success soon led to disappointment. Instead of achieving the massive increase in profits they anticipated, the consolidation left them instead with diminished advertising revenues and a weakened publishing empire.

In reality, though, the Detroit experience merely confirmed what many other newspaper publishers were already beginning to realize; that JOA arrangements were no longer as financially beneficial as they once might have been. In fact, the major trend among JOA operations during the past 1980s and 1990s has been for the stronger local newspaper to absorb its weaker competitor; exactly the result the Newspaper Preservation Act was enacted to prevent.[76] And one expert recently predicted that as many as seven of the remaining 18 cities in which these agreements still remain in

[74] Michigan Citizens for an Independent Press v. Thornburgh, 868 F.2d 1285 (D.C.Cir.1989).

[75] 493 U.S. 38, 110 S.Ct. 398 (1989).

[76] This trend began in St. Louis in 1983, when Newhouse, operating under a JOA, closed the Globe–Dispatch. Since that time JOAs have ended in six other cities: Columbus, Ohio; Shreveport, Louisiana; Knoxville, Tennessee; Tulsa, Oklahoma; Miami, Florida; and Pittsburgh, Pennsylvania, leaving each with only one dominant newspaper.

effect are likely to lose their second newspaper within the next few years.[77]

SEC. 101. ELECTRONIC MEDIA OWNERSHIP POLICIES

Traditional electronic media ownership policies have been altered substantially by greater government reliance on deregulation as the policy of choice.

The FCC's primary broadcast ownership policy, as that of the FRC that preceded it, has often been described as favoring the licensing of locally owned stations to provide broadcast audiences with locally produced, community oriented programming. Yet as most government "policies," local ownership was not a specific objective that either regulatory agency worked systematically to attain, but rather only a vague statement of intention appearing periodically in various regulatory pronouncements.[78]

The FCC's efforts to prevent broadcast networks from exerting too much influence upon local station program decisions have been discussed in Chapter 9 of this text. In addition, the Commission adopted rules that prevented any licensee from owning more than one station in a single broadcast market.[79] Later, when television and FM services emerged, the FCC prohibited joint ownership of television and either an AM or FM facility in a single market, but "grandfathered" those already owning such broadcast facilities.[80]

In contested license proceedings, the Commission has attempted to broaden the base of broadcast ownership by favoring the candidate without other media holdings. For example, as discussed earlier in this Chapter, the FCC decided in 1975 to adopt rules that

[77] Stephen R. Barnett, "Anything Goes," American Journalism Review October 1993, p. 39. Barnett believes the cities most likely to lose their second newspaper are San Francisco, Nashville, Tucson, Birmingham, Cincinnati, Detroit and Evansville, Indiana.

[78] As the President's Task Force on Telecommunications: Final Report (Govt. Printing Office, Wash. D.C.1969) pointed out, the concept of a nationwide system of local stations, "produced a relatively large number of individual stations, but relatively few accessible broadcast signals for the individual listener." Chapter 7, p. 12–13. The industry itself evolved towards national network services popular with broadcast audiences, and federal policy was powerless to impose upon this national system the local orientation Congress had once envisioned.

[79] 47 CFR § 73.35. It was this rule that lead to the famous NBC case, 319 U.S. 190, 63 S.Ct. 997 (1943) discussed in Chapter 7 of this text.

[80] CFR § 73.240 and CFR § 73.636. To "grandfather" is to enforce a rule only prospectively, allowing those currently in violation of its terms to continue their existing practices without penalty. From an equitable standpoint, grandfathering avoids punishing those who were acting in good faith at a time when their actions were not in violation of law. The greatest drawback of grandfathering, however, is that it creates a privileged class of individuals who are thereafter able to do what all others are prohibited from doing. From a practical point, agencies like the FCC prefer to "grandfather" whenever possible, because in this way they can avoid legal challenges from those who otherwise would be adversely affected by their new rules.

prohibited newspaper ownership of any broadcast station within the paper's main service area.[81] However, in adopting this rule, the FCC managed to avoid antagonizing powerful publishers by "grandfathering" all existing newspaper owned stations except those controlling the only radio or television station in their market.[82]

FCC Minority Ownership Policies

From 1978 onward the Commission began to retreat from vigorous enforcement of its broadcast ownership policies, relying more heavily on a deregulated marketplace to decide how broadcast licenses should be acquired or transferred.[83] During the same period though, the FCC also developed new licensing policies to encourage more widespread minority ownership of broadcast stations.

In 1978 the Commission adopted a policy statement offering tax certificates to those selling their broadcast stations to minority owners. These certificates allowed sellers to defer the capital gains tax that otherwise would be imposed on any profits made from the sale. At the same time the agency also authorized anyone whose license renewal had been designated for hearing to avoid possible loss of license by disposing of the broadcast property to a minority owner for a price not in excess of 75% of its fair market value.[84]

In addition, after having been instructed by the D.C. Court of Appeals in the TV 9 v. FCC case that, "when the minority ownership is likely to increase diversity of content, especially on opinion and viewpoint, merit should be awarded," the agency began granting "enhancement" points to minority applicants in comparative license hearing cases, thus improving their prospects of being awarded the license.[85]

In 1995, however, Congress voted to abolish the tax certificate program that had encouraged sale of broadcast and cable TV properties to minority buyers. This program had given sellers of such properties a tax break by deferring capital gains tax the seller otherwise would have had to pay at the time of sale.[86] This recision

[81] 50 FCC 2d 1046, amended on rehearing by 53 FCC 2d 589 (1975).

[82] This decision to grandfather all other newspaper owners of broadcast stations was sustained by the U.S. Supreme Court in FCC v. National Citizens Committee for Broadcasting, 436 U.S. 775, 98 S.Ct. 2096 (1978).

[83] At the FCC's urging, Congress has even authorized the agency to award licenses by chance through use of a lottery, rather than by hearing, Omnibus Reconciliation Act of 1981, 95 Stat. 736–37, but the Commission has used a lottery only to award LPTV, MMDS and other specialized spectrum services to this point.

[84] Minority Ownership of Broadcast Facilities, 44 RR 2d 1051 (1978).

[85] 495 F.2d 929 (D.C.Cir.1973), cert. denied 419 U.S. 986, 95 S.Ct. 245 (1974).

[86] PL 104–7 (1995).

was made retroactive to January, 1995, in order to prevent Viacome, one of the nation's larger media conglomerates, from receiving a $620 million tax break from the sale of its cable systems to a minority purchaser. However, abolishing the program also penalized 18 other broadcasters who had applied for similar tax relief, as well as those minority groups that were negotiating for the purchase of those broadcast and cable properties.[87]

Adarand Case Weakens FCC Minority Ownership Policies

Shortly after Congress ended the tax certificate program discussed above, minority ownership of broadcast properties received another serious blow from the Supreme Court.

The constitutional basis for FCC policies seeking to increase minority ownership of broadcast and cable properties was eroded by the decision in Adarand Constructors Inc. v. Pena. That decision overturned a federal program designed to provide highway contracts to companies owned by minorities.[88]In *Adarand,*the Court specifically questioned the continuing validity of the *Metro Broadcasting* decision affirming preferences the FCC accorded to minority broadcast applicants.[89]

The majority declared that minority preference classifications would be constitutional "only if they are narrowly tailored measures to further compelling governmental interests." The Court then declared, "To the extent that Metro Broadcasting is inconsistent with this holding, it is overruled."[90]

The FCC's pre-*Adarand* efforts to extend the same rights to women as a minority group was struck down by the Court in Steele v. FCC,[91] because Congress had not authorized women to be classified as a minority in awarding these license preferences. When the *Steele* case was remanded to the Commission for further consideration, the agency indicated that it was no longer certain that granting any minority preferences served the public interest.[92]

[87] "Congress Closes Tax Loophole for Viacom, Others," Broadcasting & Cable, April 3, 1995, p. 10.

[88] Adarand Constructors Inc. v. Pena, 515 U.S. 200, 115 S.Ct. 2097 (1995).

[89] Metro Broadcasting Co. v. FCC, 497 U.S. 547, 110 S.Ct. 2997 (1990).

[90] Adarand Constructors Inc. v. Pena, 515 U.S. 200, 115 S.Ct. 2097 (1995).

[91] Steele v. FCC, 770 F.2d 1192 (D.C.Cir.1985).

[92] The FCC had originally launched its regulatory programs to expand minority ownership of broadcast properties because studies indicated that less than 2 percent of all broadcast stations were owned by minorities in the mid 1970s. When the Supreme Court in Wygant v. Jackson Board of Education, 476 U.S. 267, 106 S.Ct. 1842 (1986) held that mere numerical evidence of minimal minority presence in a particular activity is not sufficient in itself to justify government intervention to rectify racial imbalance in the absence of actual evidence of prior discrimination, this holding undercut the entire basis for the Commission's position, because there was no documentation of any discrimination in the issuance or sale of broadcast licenses.

Alarmed by this apparent change in regulatory attitude, Congress included in its Omnibus Spending Bill of 1987 a provision preventing the agency from repealing or even continuing to reconsider its minority preference policies.[93]

In 1983, Alan Shurberg had filed a license application for television channel 18 in Hartford, Connecticut. Shurberg's application was rejected by the Commission because the current licensee of channel 18, Faith Center, was facing a license revocation hearing. Before the hearing was completed, Faith Center took advantage of the FCC's "distress sale" policy to sell the station to Astroline Communications, an Hispanic partnership qualifying as a minority-owned organization under FCC rules.

Shurberg, a white applicant, challenged this minority preference policy, and in a 2–1 decision, one panel of D.C. Court of Appeals judges upheld the challenge, deciding that this FCC minority ownership program was "not narrowly tailored to remedy past discriminations or to promote program diversity. Specifically, the program unduly burdens Shurberg, an innocent non-minority, and is not reasonably related to the interest it seeks to vindicate."[94]

Three weeks later a different three judge D.C. Court of Appeals panel in another 2–1 decision upheld the Commission's policy of awarding minority enhancements in comparative hearing situations.[95] In this case Winter Park Communications with 20 percent black ownership and non-minority owned Metro Broadcasting both challenged the FCC's awarding of a new television license in Orlando, Florida to Hispanic-owned Rainbow Broadcasting. In affirming the Commission's decision to grant the license to the Hispanic group the court declared, "the Commission's award of minority enhancements is not a grant of any number of permits to minorities or a denial to qualified non-minorities of the ability freely to compete for permits."

Because the D.C. Court of Appeals was unable to resolve these two conflicting decisions, the Supreme Court agreed to hear both cases, and in June 1990 it rendered its decision.

The Court affirmed, by a 5–4 vote, the constitutionality of both the FCC distress sale and its minority preference policies. The decision to uphold these two Commission affirmative action pro-

[93] Pub.L. 100–202 (1987). However, in January 1991, while still serving on the D.C. Court of Appeals, now Supreme Court Justice Clarence Thomas wrote the majority opinion for a divided three-judge panel in Lamprecht v. FCC that overturned the FCC female ownership preference policy on the grounds that Congress had not demonstrated previous discrimination against women who sought to acquire broadcast properties. Harry A. Jessell, "Court Overturns FCC Gender Preference," Broadcasting, February 24, 1992, p. 16.

[94] Shurberg Broadcasting of Hartford, Inc. v. FCC, 876 F.2d 902 (D.C.Cir.1989).

[95] Winter Park Communications, Inc. v. FCC, 873 F.2d 347 (D.C.Cir.1989).

grams surprised many communication lawyers who had expected only three Justices; Brennan, Marshall and Blackmun to support these measures.[96] This assumption become even more widespread after oral arguments before the Court in which all parties seemed to agree that changing the racial characteristics of broadcast ownership would be unlikely to have any significant effect on the nature of broadcast programming, because programming decisions tended to be dictated primarily by marketplace considerations.

In the end, however, Justices White and Stevens joined the three strongest proponents of minority preference, influenced perhaps by the special circumstances of this particular type of affirmative action. Justice Brennan, writing for the majority, placed great emphasis on broadcasting's status as a unique institution, legitimately subject to a far wider range of Congressional controls than any other medium simply because a scarcity of spectrum space has required the federal government to regulate the privilege of spectrum access.

Under such circumstances, according to Brennan, Congressional intent must be given special recognition, and as he observed, these particular FCC policies, "have been specifically approved—indeed, mandated—by Congress," through riders attached to FCC appropriation bills in 1988, 1989 and 1990, preventing the FCC from spending any portion of its funding to reconsider the validity of its minority preference policies.

Quoting Justice White's *Red Lion* opinion with approval, Brennan pointed out that since no one has a First Amendment right to broadcast, no applicant has the right to expect that a broadcast license will be granted without consideration of such significant public interest factors such as minority ownership.

In essence, then, the majority opinion affirmed those specific FCC ownership preference programs under review because in this particular instance there was clear evidence of Congressional support for such programs to serve the public interest through encouraging broader minority participation in a field where federal authority is paramount. (The issue of broadcast ownership preferences for women was not considered by the court because it was not involved in FCC actions being appealed.)

Justice O'Connor wrote a scathing 30 page dissent, in which Justices Rehnquist, Scalia and Kennedy joined. She charged the FCC with using "race as a proxy for whatever views it believes to be underrepresented in the broadcast spectrum," adding, "The reflexive or unthinking use of a suspect classification is the hallmark of an unconstitutional policy."

[96] Metro Broadcasting v. FCC, 497 U.S. 547, 110 S.Ct. 2997 (1990).

Justice Kennedy also wrote a separate dissent, in which Justice Scalia joined. Kennedy said that he could not accept the argument of the majority that, "the Constitution permits the government to discriminate among its citizens on the basis of race in order to serve interests so trivial as 'broadcast diversity' ".

If this case had been considered by the Court just a few months later, after Justice Brennan had retired, those minority broadcast ownership policies it affirmed might well have been rejected, quite possibly by the 6–3 margin the experts had been predicting before Brennan began working both on his opinion and his colleagues.

Antitrust and Electronic Media Ownership Practices

In National Broadcasting Company v. United States[97], the Supreme Court had affirmed the power of the FCC to consider federal antitrust implications of broadcast practices in determining whether broadcast licensees were operating in the public interest. In his opinion, Justice Frankfurter quoted with approval the justification the Commission had advanced for adopting regulations designed to prevent this type of abuse of the broadcast license privilege:

> While many of the network practices raise serious questions under the antitrust law, our jurisdiction does not depend on a showing that they do in fact constitute a violation of the antitrust laws. It is not our function to apply the antitrust laws as such. It is our duty, however, to refuse licenses or renewals to any person who engages or proposes to engage in practices which will prevent either himself or other licensees or both from making the fullest use of radio facilities. This is the standard of public interest ... which we must apply to all applications for licenses and renewals.[98]

One casualty of the FCC's decade-long policy of deregulation seems to have been this traditional concern for anti-trust implications of broadcast ownership. As discussed earlier in this chapter, during the 1980s the FCC increased the number of TV, AM and FM stations each licensee could own from 7–7–7 to 12–12–12. In 1992, the Commission raised its ownership limits once again, this time permitting each licensee to own as many as 20 AM and 20 FM stations.[99]

[97] National Broadcasting Co. v. United States, 319 U.S. 190, 222–223, 63 S.Ct. 997, 1012–1013 (1943).

[98] Ibid., at 222, 63 S.Ct. at 1013.

[99] Revision of Radio Rules and Policies, 71 R.R. 2d 227 (1992). The Commission established the ownership limit at 18 AM and 18 FM stations per owner in 1992 with the proviso that this number would increase to 20 AM and 20 FM stations in

In the same proceeding, however, the agency made another and even more controversial decision, authorizing the creation of local AM and FM *duopolies* by permitting a single licensee to own *two* separate FM or AM stations in markets with less than 15 radio stations; and *two FM and two AM stations* in markets with more than 15 radio outlets. Thus, for the first time in American broadcast regulatory history, one owner may now operate as many as *four* different stations in the same community.

In 1992 the FCC also relaxed its 22 year ban on television network ownership of cable TV systems, permitting each network to acquire cable systems serving a maximum of 10 percent of all cable homes nationwide and no more than 50 percent of the cable homes in a single market.[1] [For a discussion of ownership rules as updated under the Telecommunications Act of 1996, see Section 70 of Chapter 12, above.]

It is the Justice Department, rather than the FCC, that has primary responsibility for enforcing federal antitrust laws in the field of broadcasting, as in every other area of American commerce.[2] However, the courts have given the FCC far greater latitude than the Justice Department to prevent media practices that are not illegal in terms of anti-trust law, but that might tend to constrain "the development of diverse and antagonistic sources of program service."[3]

During the 1980s and into the 1990s, the Commission contended that broadcast ownership restrictions are no longer as necessary to protect this diversity in service, because electronic media audiences have such a wide range of viewing and listening alternatives today that no combination of conglomerates could possibly deny them their free choice of programming.

This view of electronic mass communication operation completely overlooks the anti-competitive influences that electronic media conglomerates are capable of exerting on those entertainment and information services seeking to reach their audiences. From the beginning, broadcasting has acted primarily as a distribution system for the programming of others, and today, all electronic media remain dependent upon the film and music industries for their most popular features.

Radio began this pattern of dependency, as local stations delegated popular "prime time" programming responsibility to a net-

September 1994, unless the agency decided prior to that time not permit this increase to occur.

[1] Common Ownership of Cable Television Systems and National Television Networks, 70 R.R. 2d 1531 (1992).

[2] United States v. RCA, 358 U.S. 334, 79 S.Ct. 457 (1959).

[3] Mount Mansfield Television, Inc. v. FCC, 442 F.2d 470, 480 (2d Cir.1971).

work that in turn relied upon advertising agencies to produce its shows.[4] When television program production became too expensive to be underwritten by advertising agency sponsors in the mid 1950s, the network turned to Hollywood film studios to produce their series programs.

Financial Interest Rules

With film audiences dwindling because of television competition, these Hollywood producers were only too eager to accept this new type of financial support. The problem these film producers faced in dealing with the networks, however, was that they were sellers in a market with only three potential buyers who often seemed less interested in obtaining the best program quality than in obtaining the most favorable ownership terms for the programs they agreed to schedule.

When the Justice Department began an anti-trust action against the three networks in 1972, alleging that they used their dominant position in the field of television program distribution to obtain financial advantages from program producers, the FCC enacted *financial interest rules* denying the networks the right to benefit financially from the distribution of any programs they had not produced themselves.[5] Not satisfied either by the scope of these rules or the Commission's commitment to enforce them, the Justice Department continued its anti-trust action until each of the three networks eventually entered into consent agreements to alter their program procurement practices.[6]

In enacting its financial interest rules, the FCC explained quite clearly why it believed these network practices were not only damaging to independent producers, but to the interests of the public as well. As the Commission pointed out, selecting network programs on the basis of price rather than quality artificially deprived television audiences of their best possible viewing opportunities while encouraging those who produced these shows to be more concerned with production costs than production values.

[4] American newspapers tried to prevent radio stations from using press wire services for their newscasts, but after a short period of constraint, broadcasting became as dependent upon the newsgathering capacity of the American press during the 1930s as it was dependent upon the music and entertainment industries for its popular programming. The short-term agreement between the press and broadcasting specifying how wire service stories could be handled on radio is published as "The Biltmore Agreement" in Frank J. Kahn, Documents of American Broadcasting 4th ed. (Englewood Cliffs NY: Prentice Hall 1984) p. 101.

[5] 47 CFR 73.658(j). The Justice Department action was United States v. CBS, Civ.Action #74–5399 (C.D.Cal.1974).

[6] For details of these settlements, see "NBC Breaks Ranks: Settles with Justice," Broadcasting, November 22, 1976, p. 21; "CBS Settles with Justice," Broadcasting, May 12, 1980, p. 29; "It's Settled; ABC, Justice Come to Terms," Broadcasting, August 25, 1980.

In 1982 the FCC attempted to rescind these rules, but pulled back when program producers rallied enough support in Congress to discourage this effort.[7] During this same period, the Justice Department had indicated its willingness to release the networks from the terms of their consent agreements if the Commission repealed its rules.[8]

In 1988, the networks began a new campaign to be released from these program ownership restraints.[9] As might be expected, they based their plea for release upon the FCC's own argument that there is now such a competitive electronic media environment that marketplace alone should determine how programs are to be financed and distributed.

In January 1990, Fox Broadcasting petitioned the FCC for permission to provide its stations more than 15 hours of weekly programming without thereby becoming a "network" subject to the agency's financial interest rules.[10] Fox contended that granting it an 18 month waiver would allow it to take advantage of its ownership of 20th Century Fox film studios to produce programming during this period that would increase its audience and enable it to compete more effectively with the three major television networks.

Instead of responding directly to the Fox petition, the FCC tried to avoid getting caught in the middle of this controversy by directing the television networks and Hollywood film producers to work out some compromise agreement the Commission could then adopt as its new rules. By June 1990, however, it was clear that no compromise agreement could be reached and the FCC was forced to begin its own deliberations to determine whether the rules should be retained, modified or rescinded.

Hollywood producers claimed that the networks had not been bargaining in good faith, because they were confident that the administration would not be sympathetic to a continuation of restrictions on the marketplace behavior of the television networks. That suspicion seemed to be confirmed when the U.S. Justice

[7] 54 RR2d 457 (1983). The Hollywood producers were even successful in enlisting the help of former Actors Guild President Reagan to stop this recision effort. For a more detailed account of this entire financial interest issue, see Don R. Le Duc, Beyond Broadcasting: Patterns in Policy and Law (White Plains NY: Longman, 1987) chapter 5.

[8] "Consent Decree Held Hostage: Justice Department Backs FCC," Variety, February 2, 1983, p. 84.

[9] "Fin–Syn Phoenix Out of the Ashes," Broadcasting July 4, 1988, p. 30.

[10] "Fox Waiver Petition May Be Open Sesame for Fin–Syn Revision." Broadcasting Jan. 29, 1990, p. 19. FCC rules defined a television "network" as an organization that distributed 15 hours or more hours of weekly programs to its affiliated stations. Fox was distributing less than 15 hours a week to its stations to avoid becoming a "network" subject to the Commission's financial interest rules.

Department, the Federal Trade Commission and the President's Chief of Staff all urged the Commission to repeal the rules.[11]

The networks argued that to continue to deny them the right to share in the off-network domestic and international sales revenues of those programs they scheduled unfairly reduced their capacity to survive in the much more competitive electronic media environment of the 1990s.

On the other hand, producers contended that because the networks pay only 75–80 percent of the production costs of those programs they schedule, they have no right to demand a share of those domestic and international syndication revenues producers need to recoup their costs and profit from their own productions. In addition, these producers pointed out that without the protection of the rules, networks would be able to coerce them into granting the networks ownership or monetary concessions because only a very limited number of programs are able to obtain network exposure, and each network can exert a significant influence on a show's popularity by determining where it will be positioned in its schedule, and how heavily it will be promoted.[12]

Obviously, there was no simple, sensible solution to this extremely complex problem and so in April 1991, by a 3–2 vote, a sharply divided Commission adopted new financial syndication rules that as everyone had expected, pleased none of the parties.[13]

The one major benefit these new rules would have offered the networks was immediate entry to the international television program sales market. Limited by the old rules to the sale of only those programs the networks themselves produced, network international program sales had never exceeded $175 million, less than 8 percent of the $2.3 billion earned annually from foreign sales of American television programs.[14] However, counterbalancing this benefit was the restriction the new rules continued to impose on network program ownership, limiting each network to the prime-time scheduling of no more than 40 percent of its own productions.

In November 1992, a federal court overturned these new *financial interest* rules, finding no justification for continuing to impose

[11] "Justice Dept. Urges Fin–Syn Repeal in FCC Filing Flood," Variety, June 20, 1990, pg. 47; "White House Sends Loud and Clear Fin–Syn Signal," Broadcasting, Feb. 18, 1991, pg. 27.

[12] The ratings success of a program is vitally important to the TV producer, because the amount of money a producer will earn from the $5.7 billion domestic syndication market and $2.3 billion foreign syndication market is largely dependent on the program's popularity during its network run.

[13] 69 RR2d 341 (1991). This 30 day waiting period has been provided in the rules to give a TV producer who has been coerced by the network into granting it syndication rights adequate opportunity to revoke this permission before the network exercises its right.

[14] "MIP Hip to Net's New Game", Variety, April 22, 1991, p. 1.

any program ownership restrictions on television networks.[15] Soon afterward the court agreed to delay issuing its vacating order for 120 days to give the Commission sufficient time to revise its findings in a manner that would satisfy the court.

As the deadline approached, acting FCC chairman Quello managed to obtain from a deeply divided Commission the approval he needed for a revised report that phased out virtually all limitations on network ownership and syndication of television programming by November 1995.[16] Until that time, the new FCC policy permits networks to acquire financial interests and syndication rights in any programs they air, but does not allow them to domestically syndicate *prime time or first-run* programs, or to withhold any of their own programs from syndication.[17]

In July 1994 the federal court approved these revised Commission financial interest rules, praising the agency for its decision to authorize immediate entry by the three networks into the program syndication business.[18] At this point then, all remaining restrictions are set to expire in November 1995 unless independent program producers are able to convince the Commission before this date that existing restrictions on network domestic program syndication are still essential to protect these producers from unfair competitive practices by the networks.

Ironically, the three major networks could end up losing far more than they gain from the repeal of the financial interest rules. Until now, the Fox network has been providing its affiliate stations less than 15 hours of programming a week to avoid being classified by FCC rules as a *television network* and thereby subject to network financial interest restrictions. When these restraints end in November 1995, Fox will be free to expand its program offerings in order to compete more effectively with ABC, CBS and NBC.

Two other major media powers, Warner and Paramount, both major television program producers, have also been waiting for the financial interest rules to be repealed in order to be able to achieve the greatest financial benefit from the new television networks they are both in the process of creating. So the net result of this victory for the three major networks is likely to be a significant increase in the level of economic competition these networks will be forced to face.

[15] Schurz Communications v. FCC, 982 F.2d 1043 (7th Cir.1992).

[16] Financial Interest Rules, 72 RR2d 1044 (1993); affirmed on reconsideration, 73 RR2d 1452 (1993).

[17] The primary constraints imposed on the three major television networks by the consent decrees they had entered into in the mid 1970s were vacated by a federal district court in United States v. NBC, 74 RR2d 986 (C.D.Cal.1993).

[18] Capital Cities/ABC v. FCC, 29 F.3d 309 (7th Cir.1994).

Prime Time Access Rules Repealed

In an allied development, First Media Corporation, owner of a CBS affiliate station in Orlando, Florida, petitioned the FCC in 1990 to rescind the agency's "Prime Time Access Rule." The current version of the rule, adopted in 1975, requires network affiliate television stations in the nation's largest 50 broadcast markets to set aside one hour of their primetime schedules each evening for non-network programming.[19] First Media argued that such sweeping interference in the programming choices of urban television stations no longer was justified by electronic media marketplace conditions, and therefore improperly infringed upon the First Amendment rights of those broadcasters.

The Commission initially appeared ready to ignore the First Media petition, with FCC Chairman Sikes declaring that a review of PTAR was, "certainly not on the front burner." As *Broadcasting* magazine noted editorially,[20]

> If anything remains sacrosanct in this day and age, it is that no one in his right mind will suggest laying a glove on PTAR. It is that most peculiar of regulations: one that apparently benefits everyone. Creation of PTAR cut back the network inventories and made ABC a competitive third network. It almost singlehandedly created a viable syndication industry * * * and it improved the position of the top 50 independents remarkably.

However, after Disney, Bonneville International and a large coalition of ABC and CBS affiliates joined First Media in asking that the rule be re-examined, the FCC came under increasing pressure to hold hearings to evaluate the continuing validity of this 15 year old policy.[21] Those opposing the rule point out that television producers of those "first-run" game and tabloid news programs that now dominate the first hour of affiliate station primetime schedules no longer need to be guaranteed major market exposure to survive economically, because the vast number of new cable TV networks that have emerged since 1975 now furnish such non-network producers a broad range of purchasers for their shows.

In addition, these PTAR opponents argued that the rule unfairly discriminates against producers of network programs, because it denies them the opportunity to recoup their production expenses through subsequent syndication of these shows in major markets during one of the most lucrative periods of the broadcast day.

---

[19] 47 CFR § 73.658(k) 1.

[20] "No Larger Than A Man's Hand," Broadcasting, Dec. 10, 1990, p. 138.

[21] "Bonneville Calls for PTAR Relaxation," Broadcasting, Jan. 21, 1991, p. 44.

In 1995, the FCC completed its review of the Prime Time Access Rules and decided that the rules no longer served the public interest.[22] The Commission found that the rules artificially deprived the three largest networks and their affiliates of the opportunity to take advantage of network efficiencies to offer audiences popular, well-produced network shows during the first hour of "prime time" viewing each evening. These rules went into effect on August 30, 1996.

Program Standards, Violence and Anticompetitive Practices

Although program producers constantly claimed during the 1980s that television networks were engaging in anticompetitive practice, the only broadcast-related antitrust action launched by the Justice Department during the decade was against the National Association of Broadcasters' Radio and Television Codes. These Codes the NAB had developed to prevent over-commercialization and encourage good taste in broadcast programs were challenged by the Justice Department in 1981 as being anticompetitive in nature.[23]

Smaller corporations claimed they could not purchase network television advertising time because the NAB Code specified that each commercial should be no less than 30 seconds in length to avoid cluttering each two minute commercial break with too many different messages. The Codes had no legal effect, but the three networks complied with them voluntarily to enhance the image and reputation of the industry. Because of this compliance, these advertisers contended that the networks refused to sell them the less expensive 10–15 seconds segments of network commercial time they could afford.

Charging that the networks and their affiliate stations were acting in concert to prevent these advertisers from being able to place their ads on television, the Justice Department forced the NAB to agree to a consent decree, pledging to abandon all efforts to negotiate further restrictions on broadcast advertising.

This "victory" of the Justice Department over those who dared to try to limit the number of commercials on American television also had another unintended consequence. When the NAB was forced by the government to end its "program practices" activities in 1981, it provided the industry with a perfect excuse for avoiding any further responsibility for the quality of television programming.

[22] Review of the Prime Time Access Rule, Sec. 73.658 of the Commission Rules, 78 $$2d 1076 (1995).

[23] United States v. NAB, 536 F.Supp. 149 (D.D.C.1982).

From that time onward, industry representatives could simply explain even though they were eager to cooperate with one another in efforts to improve the overall quality of the programs they broadcast, the Justice Department could once again find such a cooperative industry effort to be anticompetitive in nature.

In November 1990, Congress gave the broadcast and the cable industry the protection they had claimed to be so eager to receive, granting both industries a three year exemption from antitrust laws in order to develop program standards capable of reducing the amount of violence and improper sexual behavior portrayed in the shows they distributed.[24] The anti-trust exemption granted by Congress in 1990 for "any joint discussion, consideration, review, action or agreement by or among persons in the television industry for the purpose of, and limited to, developing and disseminating voluntary guidelines designed to alleviate the negative impact of violence in telecast material" was to end on December 1, 1993.

However, the Justice Department agreed at the last minute to extend that deadline for an additional two months to provide time for the networks to set up some process for monitoring and controlling the amount of violence portrayed on network TV.[25] When the networks tried to stand united against what they saw as unwarranted Congressional pressure, the cable industry moved in for a public relations victory, offering to have an independent panel rate each cable program for violence and then encode them so that the "V-chip" proposed by Congressman Markey, a circuit that could be activated by concerned parent, would prevent children from viewing any program with an unacceptable level of violence.[26]

Isolated and exposed to political pressure by this maneuver, television networks are expected to agree eventually to establishing a similar violence monitoring plan.

Although it has been the programming practices of the broadcast networks that have attracted most regulatory attention in the past, some of the competitive tactics of the nation's major cable TV MSOs would seem to deserve similar attention.

In 1980, for example, ATC Home Box Office was the only pay TV service offered by 87 percent of all ATC-owned cable-TV systems. Warner's "The Movie Channel" was the sole pay-TV service available to 80 percent of Warner's cable system subscribers and

[24] Pub.L. 101–650 (1990). Also see "TV Violence Bill Passed by Congress in 11th Hour," Broadcasting, November 5, 1990, p. 90.

[25] "Justice Dept. Comes Through at 11th Hour", Broadcasting, December 6, 1993, p. 90.

[26] Dennis Wharton, "Cable Tries on a White Hat", Variety, February 7, 1994, p. 30.

Teleprompter's jointly owned "Showtime" was the only pay service provided by 78 percent of Teleprompter's cable systems.[27]

Although market demand forced most systems to add other pay-TV services during the 1980s, the recent example of Manhattan Cable TV suggests quite clearly that the tendency to base program carriage decisions upon participation in the service's profits still exists today, always ready to dictate program choices under the right conditions.[28]

Recently, a disturbing new trend has begun to surface in the cable TV programming field. From 1986 onward, MSO ownership and profit participation in new satellite delivered programming services has become the quid pro quo for choosing one service instead of others in competitive contests to fill the last remaining cable channels in many group owned systems.[29] Here, as in the pay TV field of a decade ago, cable conglomerates are using their dominant power over electronic media distribution to obtain economic advantages from those program channels they agree to deliver, and allowing those financial considerations to dictate which particular communication options they will offer the subscribers they serve.

And yet, while such influence over entertainment programming is unfortunate, an even greater threat to the interests of the public may be posed by the cable industry's control over those information services cable systems are likely to be distributing in the near future. As a recent Congressional report points out, although cable in the United States is still primarily involved in the dissemination of entertainment services, the 1990s are likely to see a significant expansion in cable's role as a distributor of a wide range of information services as well.[30] Its broadband capacity, providing the ability to handle high volumes of electronic traffic, makes cable the ideal network for computer data, electronic mail, videotext, security monitoring, home banking and other interactive services.

[27] Paul Kagan Associates, The Pay TV Census, December 31, 1980. The same survey revealed that only 4% of all ATC systems, and 5% of all Teleprompter and Warner systems offered any competing non-owned pay TV services at the time, and no system offered only the pay TV service of a competing MSO.

[28] In December 1987, Manhattan Cable, owned by ATC, entered into a settlement with a local citizens group, agreeing to add to its ATC owned HBO and Cinemax pay TV services a group of non-owned pay TV channels. See "MCTV Forced to Offer Channels Not Affiliated with HBO or Time," Variety December 9, 1987, p. 34.

[29] For a description of this trend, see "Vertical Integration: The Business Behind the Boom in Cable Programming," Broadcasting November 23, 1987, p. 40. Increasing cable system capacity by compressing the size of each channel may lessen the impact of this vertical integration, but it is more likely that this additional channel space will be used for data and pay-per-view services.

[30] U.S. Congress, Office of Technology Assessment, "Science, Technology and the First Amendment," Special Report. (Washington D.C., GPO 1988) See particularly chapter 3.

Although such "blue sky" claims have been made for cable during the past two decades, a number of recent studies predict that both a saturation point in terms of increased demand for cable delivered entertainment and the competitive challenge posed by telephone companies will motivate major MSOs to become more deeply involved in developing their own cable-distributed information services during the next few years.[31]

Based upon their past performance, there is every reason to believe that during such a "new information age," cable MSOs will continue to follow their old strategy of denying carriage to any videotext, home banking or other interactive service in which they have no ownership interest. Once again, then, the public as well as the supplier of each communication service will be at the mercy of a media distributor who has the power to demand tribute for the privilege of delivery, and who is free to offer the public only those services for which this tribute has been paid.

It's difficult to believe that this is that "media marketplace" to which the FCC has delegated responsibility for all public entertainment or information programming decisions, or that this is the competitive environment the Justice Department will continue to rely upon to protect the interests of the public in these vital areas of mass communication.

And yet, as media mergers continue to consolidate control in the hands of an ever smaller group of media conglomerates, their power to determine what communication services the public will receive solely on the basis of their own financial interest in these services will increase with each passing year.

SEC. 102. THE GLOBALIZATION OF AMERICAN MEDIA

An expanding international market for film and television productions and mergers to prevent foreign acquisitions of American media could both have a significant impact on future media service in the United States.

Foreign corporations currently are not interested in trying to acquire an American television network because the Communications Act prohibits granting a broadcast license to an alien or any corporation organized under the laws of a foreign government.[32]

[31] See, for example, Yankee Group, "Cable and the Telcos: From Confrontation to Detente," (Cambridge, MA: Yankee Group, 1983) or Walter S. Baer, "Telephone and Cable Companies: Rivals or Partners," in Eli Noam (ed.) Video Media Competition (New York: Columbia University Press 1985) p. 187.

[32] Title 47, U.S.C.A. § 310(b)1–2. Virtually every nation in the world has a similar citizenship requirement. Rupert Murdoch was not allowed to receive the licenses to those Metromedia television group stations that form the backbone of his Fox television network until he applied for and received American citizenship.

Because the most valuable assets of each of the three major networks are those television stations they own and operate in the nation's largest television markets, a foreign purchaser would be prevented by law from realizing the greatest benefits of such an acquisition.

Recently, however, because tighter credit controls and declining advertising revenues have resulted in a sluggish market for broadcast station sales, lobbying efforts have begun to convince Congress to rescind this section of the Act so that foreign investors will be able to acquire broadcast properties in the United States.[33] If Congress yields to this pressure, particularly now that the networks have been released from virtually all program ownership restrictions of the old "Financial Interest" rules, it is quite likely that several of the world's largest media conglomerates would be in the market for an American television network.

An even more likely scenario is that one or more of these networks will eventually merge with or be taken over by a Hollywood studio.[34] NBC's General Electric is known to be dissatisfied with its broadcast earnings, and CBS continues to struggle financially. It is reasonable to expect that General Electric eventually will sell its marginally profitable television network to an entertainment conglomerate better equipped to produce and promote its programming, and that Westinghouse—1995 purchaser of CBS— may turn its operations over to a media giant with financial assets necessary to allow CBS to stay competitive in a global market beset by constantly escalating production costs.

One question that should concern the American public if one or more of the major networks are taken over either by a foreign or domestic mass entertainment conglomerate is how supportive the new owners will be of that vital national and international broadcast journalism service provided by that network it acquires? Although it is true that the present network owners have pared their news department budgets down substantially during the past few years, it is difficult to believe that entertainment giants such as Warner, Disney, Bertelsmann or Berlusconi will be even as committed as the current owners are to a service that informs rather than entertains, and does so without increasing a conglomerate's bottom line.

But broadcast journalism isn't the only type of American television programming that may be affected by changing patterns in mass media commerce. As broadcast and satellite services contin-

[33] See, for example, the arguments advanced in "Monday Memo," Broadcasting, April 22, 1991, p. 16.

[34] See, for example. Paul Noglows, "Mergers That Might Be," Variety, July 18, 1994, p. 1 and Jim Benson, "TV's Traumatic Times, "Variety, July 18, 1994, p. 1.

ue to expand in Europe, American television producers have become increasingly unwilling to produce programs for the networks that are too "American" in orientation to attract foreign audiences as well. Because these producers depend on sales to foreign broadcast organizations to recoup a significant portion of production costs not covered by network license payments, they have become more reluctant with each passing year to produce dramas or situation comedies reflecting values that are alien to other cultures.[35]

Foreign television audiences find it much easier to understand and enjoy simple and superficial series such as "Baywatch" or "Melrose Place" rather than dialogue-driven, American context shows such as "Murphy Brown." Similarly, Hollywood studios have begun to analyze foreign audience preferences as carefully as domestic audience interests when deciding which major feature films to produce. For example, Warner studio made the third, fourth and fifth sequels to "Police Academy" even though box office revenues in the United States didn't justify their production, simply because of their continued popularity in foreign nations. On the other hand, several major studios rejected the opportunity to produce the 1989 Oscar winning film, "Driving Miss Daisy" because they doubted that foreign film audiences would be attracted to a story about an elderly Jewish Southern woman and her Afro–American driver.

In addition, the growing involvement of American television networks in hundreds of European and Japanese co-productions projects also tends to result in the creation of generalized, somewhat simplistic action-oriented television films and series, rather than drama reflecting any particular American issues or values.[36]

This increasing desire of the American mass entertainment industry to produce feature films and television series capable of satisfying the tastes of global television and film audiences will not result in these producers totally ignoring the interests of the largest and most prosperous domestic audience in the world. It will, however, cause them to be more cautious in the future about producing films or television series reflecting uniquely American

[35] With the explosive growth of newly authorized private commercial broadcast networks and satellite services, the number of Western European television channels is likely to increase from 74 in 1989 to 97 in 1995, with the 484,000 hours of broadcast time increasing to 602,285 by the end of that period. This should result in Europe alone providing a $2 billion market for US programs, constituting 25% of their total broadcast schedules. See, "Euro TV Boom Seems a Steady Thing," Variety, April 15, 1991, M–2 and "U.S. TV Exports to Rise, Study Says", Variety, February 4, 1991, p. 70. At the same time, 43 percent of the $3.13 billion American film rentals came from foreign countries in 1990, up from only 33 percent in 1985.

[36] For example, CBS now is co-producing films and television series with Antenna 2 (France), ORF (Austria), RAI (Italy) ZDF (Germany), as well as film and broadcast organizations in Switzerland, Spain and the United Kingdom. None of its current co-production projects in production—"Eurocops," "Eureka" and "S.O.S. Disparus" is set in the United States.

social issues or concerns. In this way then, that global dominance of our mass entertainment industry that some feared would result in shaping foreign mass cultures in America's image may in the end have shaped American mass culture far more significantly than their own.

In the late 1990s, Federal policy was so preoccupied with reducing the foreign trade deficit and encouraging economic growth that those mass cultural issues raised by media mergers or international film and television trade practices have been virtually ignored. Yet, are American mass media just another domestic industry, whose value to this society is determined solely by the revenues it generates for the United States in international trade? Arguably, a vigorous marketplace of ideas is more vital to the welfare of any nation than a prosperous marketplace for consumer goods.

Reducing media competition through mergers and conglomerations may offer tangible domestic and international trade benefits, but at what cost in diminishing those reading, listening, and viewing options that provide the American public with access to diverse thoughts and ideas?[37] There are no longer any simple answers to these complex media ownership issues in an era when the globalization of media operations extends the scope of policy considerations far beyond national borders. Yet it is important to keep in mind that many of those concerns of the past about media conglomeration and its tendency to concentrate too much influence over our society in the hands of too few still seem equally valid today.

[37] Media industry representatives are quick to claim that with technology providing a continuous expansion in the number of electronic channels available for distributing entertainment and information services, there is no need for concern about reduced media competition through mergers. This is about as reassuring as a government promising to increase commerce simply by expanding its network of roads. The critical mass of funds available to produce mass entertainment and news is relatively fixed, and increasing the number of channels through which it can be distributed does not operate to increase significantly the amount of content produced. See Le Duc, Beyond Broadcasting: Patterns in Policy and Law, chapter 7.

Appendix A

ABBREVIATIONS

A.	Atlantic Reporter.
A.2d	Atlantic Reporter, Second Series.
A.C.	Appeal Cases.
A.L.R.	American Law Reports.
Aff.	Affirmed; affirming.
Ala.	Alabama;—Alabama Supreme Court Reports.
Am.Dec.	American Decisions.
Am.Jur.	American Jurisprudence, a legal encyclopedia.
Am.Rep.	American Reports.
Am.St.Rep.	American State Reports.
Ann.Cas.	American Annotated Cases.
App.D.C.	Court of Appeals, District of Columbia.
App.Div.	New York Supreme Court, Appellate Divisions, Reports.
Ariz.	Arizona; Arizona Supreme Court Reports.
Ark.	Arkansas; Arkansas Supreme Court Reports.
Bing.	Bingham, New Cases, Common Pleas (England).
C.D.	Copyright Decision.
C.J.	Corpus Juris, a legal encyclopedia.
C.J.S.	Corpus Juris Secundum, a legal encyclopedia.
Cal.	California; California Supreme Court Reports.
Can.Sup.Ct.	Canada Supreme Court Reports.
Cert.	Certiorari, a legal writ by which a cause is removed from an inferior to a superior court.
C.F.R.	Code of Federal Regulations.
Colo.	Colorado; Colorado Supreme Court Reports.
Conn.	Connecticut; Connecticut Supreme Court of Errors Reports.
Cranch	Cranch, United States Supreme Court Reports; United States Circuit Court Reports.
Cush.	Cushing (Massachusetts).
D.C.App.	District of Columbia Court of Appeals Reports.
Dall, Dal.	Dallas, United States Supreme Court Reports; Pennsylvania Reports.
Del.	Delaware; Delaware Supreme Court Reports.
Edw.	Edward; refers to a particular king of England; which king of that name is indicated by the date; used to identify an act of Parliament.
Eng.Rep.	English Reports (reprint).
F.	Federal Reporter.
F.2d	Federal Reporter, Second Series.
F.C.C.	Federal Communications Commission Reports.
F.R.D.	Federal Rules Decisions.
F.Supp.	Federal Supplement.
Fed.Cas. or F.Cas.	Reports of United States Circuit and District Courts, 1789–1879.
Fla.	Florida; Florida Supreme Court Reports.
Ga.	Georgia; Georgia Supreme Court Reports.
Ga.App.	Georgia Appeals Reports.

How.St.Tr.	Howell's State Trials.
Hun	Hun, New York Supreme Court Reports.
Ibid.	Ibidem, the same, in the same volume, or on the same page.
Ill.	Illinois; Illinois Supreme Court Reports.
Ill.App.	Illinois Appellate Court Reports.
Ind.	Indiana; Indiana Supreme Court Reports.
Ind.App.	Indiana Appellate Court Reports.
Johns.Cas.	Johnson's Cases (New York).
K.B.	King's Bench Reports (England).
Kan.	Kansas; Kansas Supreme Court Reports.
Ky.	Kentucky; Kentucky Court of Appeals Reports.
L.J.	Law Journal (England).
L.R.Q.B.	Law Reports, Queen's Bench (England).
L.R.A.	Lawyers Reports Annotated.
L.R.A.,N.S.,	Lawyers Reports Annotated, New Series.
L.R.Ex.	Law Reports, Exchequer (England).
L.T.	The Law Times (England).
La.	Louisiana; Louisiana Supreme Court Reports.
La.Ann.	Louisiana Annual Reports.
Mass.	Massachusetts; Massachusetts Supreme Judicial Court Reports.
Md.	Maryland; Maryland Court of Appeals Reports.
Me.	Maine; Maine Supreme Judicial Court Reports.
Mich.	Michigan; Michigan Supreme Court Reports.
Minn.	Minnesota; Minnesota Supreme Court Reports.
Miss.	Mississippi; Mississippi Supreme Court Reports.
Mo.	Missouri; Missouri Supreme Court Reports.
Mo.App.	Missouri Appeals Reports.
Mont.	Montana; Montana Supreme Court Reports.
N.C.	North Carolina; North Carolina Supreme Court Reports.
N.D.	North Dakota; North Dakota Supreme Court Reports.
N.E.	Northeastern Reporter.
N.E.2d	Northeastern Reporter, Second Series.
N.H.	New Hampshire; New Hampshire Supreme Court Reports.
N.J.	New Jersey; New Jersey Court of Errors and Appeals Reports.
N.J.L.	New Jersey Law Reports.
N.M.	New Mexico; New Mexico Supreme Court Reports.
N.W.	Northwestern Reporter.
N.W.2d	Northwestern Reporter, Second Series.
N.Y.	New York; New York Court of Appeals Reports.
N.Y.S.	New York Supplement Reports.
Neb.	Nebraska; Nebraska Supreme Court Reports.
Nev.	Nevada; Nevada Supreme Court Reports.
Ohio App.	Ohio Appeals Reports.
Ohio St.	Ohio State Reports.
Okl.	Oklahoma; Oklahoma Supreme Court Reports.
Ops.	Opinions, as of Attorney General of the United States, or a state.
Or., Ore., Oreg.	Oregon; Oregon Supreme Court Reports.
P.	Pacific Reporter.
P.2d	Pacific Reporter, Second Series.
P.L. & R.	Postal Laws and Regulations (1948 ed.).
Pa.	Pennsylvania District and County Court Reports.
Pa.D. & C.	Pennsylvania District and County Court Reports.

Pa.Super.	Pennsylvania Superior Court Reports.
Paige	Paige, New York Chancery Reports.
Phila. (Pa).	Philadelphia Reports.
Pick.	Pickering, Massachusetts Reports.
Q.B.	Queen's Bench.
R.	Rex king; regina, queen.
R.C.L.	Ruling Case Law.
R.C.P.	Rules of Civil Procedure.
R.I.	Rhode Island; Rhode Island Supreme Court Reports.
R.R.	Pike & Fisher Radio Regulations.
S.C.	South Carolina; South Carolina Supreme Court Reports.
S.D.	South Dakota; South Dakota Supreme Court Reports.
S.E.	Southeastern Reporter.
S.E.2d	Southeastern Reporter, Second Series.
S.W.	Southwestern Reporter.
S.W.2d	Southwestern Reporter, Second Series.
Sandf.	Sandford, New York Superior Court Reports.
Sec.	Section.
So.	Southern Reporter.
So.2d	Southern Reporter, Second Series.
Stark.	Starkie, English Reports.
S.Ct.	Supreme Court Reporter.
T.L.R.	Times Law Reports (England).
Tenn.	Tennessee; Tennessee Supreme Court Reports.
Tex.	Texas; Texas Supreme Court (and the Commission of Appeals) Reports.
Tex.Civ.App.	Texas Civil Appeals Reports.
Tex.Cr.R.	Texas Court of Criminal Appeals Reports.
U.S.C.	United States Code.
U.S.C.A.	United States Code Annotated.
U.S.P.Q.	United States Patents Quarterly.
V.	Volume.
Va.	Virginia; Virginia Supreme Court of Appeals Reports.
Vt.	Vermont; Vermont Supreme Court Reports.
W.Va.	West Virginia; West Virginia Supreme Court of Appeals Reports.
Wash.	Washington; Washington Supreme Court Reports.
Wash.L.Rep.	Washington Law Reporter, Washington, D.C.
Whart.	Wharton (Pa.).
Wheat.	Wheaton (U.S.).
Wis.	Wisconsin; Wisconsin Supreme Court Reports.
Wyo.	Wyoming; Wyoming Supreme Court Reports.

Appendix B

SELECTED COURT AND PLEADING TERMS

Action

A formal legal demand of one's rights made in a court of law.

Actionable per quod

Words not actionable in themselves may be defamatory when special damages are proved.

Actionable per se

Words that need no explanation in order to determine their defamatory effect.

Amicus curiae

A friend of the court or one who interposes and volunteers information upon some matter of law.

Answer

The pleading of a defendant against whom a complaint has been filed.

Appeal

An application by an appellant to a higher court to change the order or judgment of the court below.

Appellant

The person or party appealing a decision or judgment to a higher court.

Appellee

The party against whom an appeal is taken.

Bind over

To hold on bail for trial.

Brief

A written or printed document prepared by counsel to file in court, normally providing both facts and law in support of the case.

Cause of action

The particular facts on which an action is based.

844

Certiorari

A writ commanding judges of a lower court to transfer to a higher court records of a case so that judicial review may take place.

Change of venue

Removing a civil suit or criminal action from one county or district to another county or district for trial.

Civil action (suit, trial)

Court action brought to enforce, redress, or protect private rights, as distinguished from a Criminal action (q.v.).

Code

A compilation or system of laws, arranged into chapters, and promulgated by legislative authority.

Common law

The law of the decided cases, derived from the judgments and decrees of courts. Also called "case law." Originally, meant law which derived its authority from the ancient usages or customs of England.

Complaint

The initial proceeding by a complainant, or plaintiff, in a civil action.

Contempt of court

Any act calculated to embarrass, hinder, or obstruct a court in the administration of justice, or calculated to lessen its dignity or authority.

Courts of record

Those whose proceedings are permanently recorded, and which have the power to fine or imprison for contempt. Courts not of record are those of lesser authority whose proceedings are not permanently recorded.

Criminal action (trial)

An action undertaken to punish a violation of criminal laws, as distinguished from a Civil action (q.v.).

Damages

Monetary compensation which may be recovered in court by a person who has suffered loss, detriment, or injury to his person, property, rights, or business, through the unlawful or negligent act of another person or party.

De novo

Anew, afresh. A trial de novo is a retrial of a case.

Dictum (pl. Dicta; also, Obiter Dictum)

An observation made by a judge, in an opinion on a case, that does not go to the main issue—a saying "by the way".

Discovery

A party's pre-trial devices used, in preparation for trial, to obtain facts from the other party.

Due process

Law in its regular course of administration through the courts of justice. The guarantee of due process requires that every person have the protection of a fair trial.

En banc

A session where the entire membership of a court, instead of one or a few, participates in the decision of an important case. ("Banc" means the judge's "bench" or place to sit.)

Equity

That system of jurisprudence which gives relief when there is no full, complete and adequate remedy at law; based originally upon the custom of appealing to the King or chancellor when the formality of the common law did not give means for relief.

Estoppel

An admission which prevents a person from using evidence which proves or tends to prove the contrary.

Executive session

A meeting of a board or governmental body that is closed to the public.

Ex parte

By or concerning only one party. This implies an examination in the presence of one party in a proceeding and the absence of the opposing party.

Ex post facto

After the fact.

Habeas corpus

Latin for "you have the body." A writ issued to an officer holding a person in detention or under arrest to bring that person before a court to determine the legality of the detention.

In camera

In the judge's private chambers or in a courtroom from which all spectators have been excluded.

Indictment

A written accusation of a crime prepared by a prosecuting attorney and presented for the consideration of a grand jury.

Information

A formal, written accusation of a crime prepared by a competent law officer of the government, such as a district or prosecuting attorney.

Injunction

A judicial order in equity directed against a person or organization directing that an act be performed or that the person or organization refrain from doing a particular act.

Judgment

The decision of a court of law.

Jury

A group of a certain number of persons, selected according to law and sworn to inquire into certain matters of fact, and to declare the truth from evidence brought before them. A *grand jury* hears complaints and accusations in criminal cases, and issues bills of indictment in cases where the jurors believe that there is enough evidence to bring a case to trial. A *petit jury* consists of 12 (or fewer) persons who hear the trial of a civil or criminal case.

Mandamus

An extraordinary legal writ issued from a court to a corporation or its officers, to a public official, or to an inferior court commanding the doing of an act which the person, corporation, or lower court is under a duty to perform.

Motion to dismiss

A formal application by a litigant or his counsel addressed to the court for an order to dismiss the case.

Nol pros, nolle prosequi

A formal notification of unwillingness to prosecute which is entered upon the court record.

N.O.V. ("non obstante veredicto")

A judgment by the court in favor of one party notwithstanding a verdict that has been given to the other party.

Per se

In itself or by itself, as in libelous *per se*.

Plaintiff

The person (including an organization or business) who initiates a legal action.

Pleading

The process in which parties to a lawsuit or legal action alternately file with a court written statements of their contentions. By this process of statement and counterstatement, legal issues are framed and narrowed. These statements are often termed "pleadings."

Preliminary hearing, preliminary examination

A person charged with a crime is given a preliminary examination or hearing before a magistrate or judge to determine whether there is sufficient evidence to hold that person for trial.

Prima facie (pron.: prī ma fā shē)

"At first sight" or "on the face of it." So far as can be judged from the first disclosure.

Reply

The pleading of plaintiff in response to the "answer" of the defendant.

Res adjudicata or res judicata

A thing decided.

Respondent

A party who gives an answer to a bill in equity; also, one who opposes a party who has taken a case to a higher court.

Stare decisis

To stand by the decisions, or to maintain precedent. This legal doctrine holds that settled points of law will not be disturbed.

Subpoena

A command to appear at a place and time and to give testimony. "Subpoena-duces tecum" is a command to produce some document or paper at a trial.

Summary

Connoting "without a full trial." A summary judgment is a judge's rule that one party in a lawsuit wins before the conclusion of a full trial.

Venue

The particular county, city, or geographical area in which a court with jurisdiction may hear and decide a case.

Verdict

The decision of a jury as reported to the court.

Voir dire

Denotes the preliminary examination which the court may make of one presented as a witness or juror, where his competency or interest is objected to.

Writ

A legal instrument in the judicial process to enforce compliance with orders and sentences of a court.

Appendix C

SOME NOTES ON THE LEGAL PROCESS

During the first chapter of this book you were introduced rather rapidly to a wide assortment of legal terms. At that point, you probably did nothing more than to try to memorize as many of these terms as possible, expecting to find one or more of them lurking somewhere on your mid-term exam.

In reality, though, the most effective way of understanding what each of these legal terms actually means is to see how it operates in an actual case situation. Here, for example, are how the terms "criminal", "civil", "common" and "constitutional" law apply to various elements of a case discussed in Chapter 7 of this text. Although the right of the press to publish public information has been extended to some extent since Cox Broadcasting v. Cohn[1] was decided in 1975, the case still serves as a useful illustration of how the legal process operates.

A. Criminal, Civil and Common Law

In Cox Broadcasting v. Cohn a reporter disclosed the name of a rape victim during a television broadcast. The State of Georgia, where the broadcast originated, had enacted a provision in its criminal code that made it a crime for,

> any news media or other person to print, publish, broadcast, televise or disseminate through any other medium ... the name or identity of any female who may have been raped.

If that official responsible for prosecuting those in that locality violating Georgia's "criminal law", (generally called the "District Attorney") believed that a reporter had violated this statute and thus committed a crime as defined by the criminal code of Georgia, the District Attorney would file a complaint describing the nature of the crime and charging the reporter with having committed it.[2] If the reporter entered a plea of "guilty" to this charge, the criminal

---

[1] 420 U.S. 469 (1975). This protection was extended to include information gathered from a police report in Florida Star v. B.J.F., 491 U.S. 524 (1989). Also see Smith v. Daily Mail, 443 U.S. 97 (1979).

[2] Criminal law in most states classifies each crime as being either a "misdemeanor" or a "felony". A misdemeanor is a less serious crime, generally providing for a maximum jail term of less than one year, while a felony is a more serious crime, carrying a prison sentence in excess of one year. In this instance, disclosing the name of a rape victim was classified as being a misdemeanor crime.

court judge would then have the authority to impose any penalties provided by the law for this offense. However, if the reporter should enter a plea of "not guilty", the state would be required to prove "beyond a reasonable doubt" that *each* element of the crime had occurred—in this case that (1) that the defendant reporter had knowingly disclosed the name of a woman (2) who may in fact have been a rape victim (3) and that the reporter's disclosure was disseminated by broadcasting or some other communications medium to the general public. Unless the state can establish beyond a reasonable doubt that each element of the criminal charge has taken place, the defendant reporter must be found "not guilty".

Here, for instance, if the District Attorney could not prove that this disclosure had actually been broadcast or disseminated to the public through some other medium, the charge against the defendant would have had to be dismissed "with prejudice", meaning that the State could not try this reporter again for this same offense.

But even if the reporter had been tried and found not guilty of any criminal offense, he could still be required by "civil law" to compensate anyone damaged because of the disclosure. In other words, even though not guilty of violating a criminal law designed to protect society in general, a reporter could still be required by civil law to pay money damages to any specific individual actually injured by this same act.

Civil law actions can be based either upon statutory rights granted individuals by State legislation or upon traditional rights granted by Anglo Saxon "common law". In the *Cox* case the father of the deceased rape victim used a "common law" right of "invasion of privacy" as the basis for a legal action claiming damages from the reporter and his television station employer.[3] Although the state of Georgia had not enacted a law granting an individual the right to sue for invasion of privacy, the Georgia courts did recognize a historic right of privacy developed by past judicial decisions that allowed those damaged by public disclosure of private information to be compensated for their embarrassment or humiliation.[4]

As this civil action to recover damages for invasion of privacy was about to begin, however, an issue of "constitutional law" was raised, delaying the trial until this question could be resolved.

[3] Even though the reporter may have been the one primarily responsible for any damages the father of the deceased rape victim sustained, law suits of this type always attempt to include the media organization as a co-defendant, because juries tend to be far more generous in awarding damages when they are taking them from a giant corporation, rather than an individual.

[4] At common law, this type of right is called a "tort", meaning that the law allows a party injured by the act of another to recover damages caused by that act.

The defendant broadcast station claimed that the rape victim's name had already been revealed to the public before it was disclosed during the television news program, because she had been identified by name in the criminal proceedings used to charge her assailants. Under these circumstances, the defendant argued that to compel a broadcast station to pay damages for disclosing a fact that any member of the public could have discovered in the files of the local courthouse improperly penalized a communications medium for exercising its free speech right to disseminate public information.

In essence then, the defendant broadcast station was claiming that no matter how much anguish or embarrassment it might have caused, there should be no civil trial to determine what monetary compensation it should pay for these damages. Instead, the defendant demanded that the case be dismissed immediately without awarding any damages, because to punish a station for reporting information already a matter of public record would improperly inhibit its right of freedom of expression protected by the First and Fourteenth Amendments.

B. The Judicial Process

The Supreme Court of Georgia rejected this constitutional argument, finding nothing in either the Georgia state constitution or the federal constitution that guaranteed a broadcaster an absolute right to reveal the identity of an individual whose privacy was expressly protected by Georgia law. This decision meant that the civil action to decide whether the defendants were actually liable for damages caused by their news report could now begin.

Here, however, the Supreme Court of the United States intervened to grant *certiorari*, meaning that it would review the Georgia court's decision to determine if the State court had correctly interpreted the constitutionally protected free speech rights of the broadcast medium under these circumstances. Once again, then, the trial had to be postponed until the Supreme Court was able to decide whether the defendant broadcast station could be held liable for invasion of privacy damages without illegally infringing upon its right of freedom of expression.

Eventually, as you may recall, a majority of the Supreme Court Justices joined in a decision that shielded the broadcast defendant from civil liability for any damages caused by the disclosure of information already a matter of public record, finding that to allow a communications medium to be penalized for disseminating facts available to every citizen would "invite timidity and self-censorship and very likely lead to the suppression of many items ... that should be made available to the public".[5]

Thus in *Cox*, as in many of the other cases discussed in this book, there was never any exciting conflict in open court; no trial with its fascinating array of witnesses, caustic cross examinations, angry objections or eloquent closing statements. Instead, clashes between attorneys representing the embittered family of the rape victim and those protecting the free speech rights of the broadcasters occurred in the hushed atmosphere of an appeals court, defined by carefully researched legal arguments in written documents called "briefs", and explained by these attorneys in polite, precisely reasoned statements to the court.

After considering these briefs and arguments, an appeals court determines how to resolve the issue or issues of law raised by the appeal, writing an opinion to explain the legal basis for this decision, and to point out to those lower trial courts under its authority how they should resolve the same legal issue if it should arise again during any legal proceeding in the future.

But what if the trial in the *Cox* case had already taken place before the defense attorneys raised any questions about its constitutionality, and the jury had found that this news broadcast did invade the privacy of the plaintiff, entering a verdict granting the injured party a massive award of monetary damages? In that case, the attorneys for the defendants would have the right to appeal this verdict, asking the court with review authority over the trial judge to consider any material legal issues the appealing attorney claims were not considered, or were decided erroneously at during the trial, resulting in the appealing party losing the case.

In our *Cox* case example, the reviewing court judge would then accept briefs and hear arguments on only that single issue raised on appeal, determining whether the free speech safeguards of the First and Fourteenth amendments protect a broadcast station from being held liable for monetary damages caused by disclosure of information already a matter of public record.

This appeals court generally has three options available to it after considering the legal issues it has reviewed. The first option is to *affirm* the lower court decision, indicating that the lower court was correct in its interpretation of the legal issue raised on appeal. The second option is to *reverse and remand* with instructions, finding the lower court to be in error and sending the case back for a new trial or "retrial" in which the judge will follow the guidance of the review court to avoid those errors that caused the first trial to be invalid. In this situation, the third option would be to *vacate* the judgement, declaring that law suit should not have been tried

---

[5] Cox Broadcasting v. Cohn, 420 U.S. 469 (1975).

in the first place because the plaintiff had no legal right to bring the action.

Unfortunately, this is seldom the end of the litigation process. The party losing at this appeal court level generally has the right to seek a review of the appeal court decision by a higher level appellate court or the state Supreme Court, and if as in the *Cox* case, an important federal issue has been raised by the litigation, the entire matter can be removed to federal court, where the proceedings begins anew.

A process this slow, expensive and risky is one that provides every incentive for out-of-court settlements and explains why one legal scholar described litigation as being the "pathology" of the law. In reality, then, those appeal court opinions published and discussed in this book can be understood most accurately not as typical cases in communication law, but rather the unusual ones that were considered so important by the parties involved that they were willing to accept the delays, costs and risks of litigation in order to establish that point of law described in the opinion.

C. Administrative Law and the Courts

The FCC is an administrative agency, created by Congress to enforce the provisions of the Communications Act of 1934. As a regulatory body, the Commission has been granted authority by Congress to adopt "administrative law" rules to define more clearly those generalized broadcast public interest standards contained in the Communications Act. In addition, the FCC has been empowered by Congress to hold hearings to determine whether a broadcast licensee may have violated Commission rules, or the provisions of the Communications Act, and to impose penalties upon those licensees not conforming to these regulatory standards.

At the same time, Congress has established the Court of Appeals for the District of Columbia as the federal court responsible for reviewing FCC decisions. In a case such as CBS v. FCC, described in chapter 12 of your text, an administrative law judge held a hearing to determine whether the refusal of CBS to provide air time for the broadcast of a political documentary represented a violation of the reasonable access requirements of section 312(a) of the Communications Act.

As administrative law has been structured by Congress, this hearing is considered to be a "trial court" proceeding, establishing a legal record for the decision that can later be reviewed on appeal by the Court of Appeals for the District of Columbia, and ultimately by the United States Supreme Court if it should decide to accept certiorari.

The finding of the administrative law judge that CBS had violated the access requirements of section 312(a) was reviewed initially within the FCC by review board created expressly for this purpose. When this decision was affirmed by the board, and finally approved by a 4–3 vote of the FCC Commissioners, the network petitioned the D.C. Court of Appeals to review those errors in law alleged to have caused the Commission to improperly interpret the legal requirements of this section of the Act.

As in the *Cox* case, the Court of Appeals had the option of affirming the Commission decision, remanding it for a new hearing on issues it overlooked or improperly decided at the original hearing, or vacating the decision if the appeals court could find no legal basis for the FCC's determination.

In this example, after the appeals court affirmed the FCC decision, the Supreme Court agreed to review the case and eventually also affirmed the Commission's decision by a 6–3 margin, with Justice Burger writing the majority opinion explaining that such a reasonable political access requirement did not improperly infringe upon the free speech rights of the broadcaster because there was "nothing in the First Amendment which prevents Government from requiring a licensee to share his frequency with others ..."[6]

Understanding these basic legal terms in the context of that system of law in which they operate should help you to become more fully aware of the actual legal effects of those communication law decisions contained in this book. But if you'd be interested in finding and actually reading these or other important communication law opinions on your own, no area of study is organized more logically or indexed more effectively than the field of American law.

D. Locating Judicial Source Material

All decisions of the United States Supreme Court are published officially in a series called *US Reports*, and by two commercial publishers in series called *Supreme Court Reporter* (West Publishing) and another called *U.S. Supreme Court Reports, Lawyer's Edition* (Lawyers' Cooperative Publishing Company). Each of these series contains every opinion of the Supreme Court, but West and Lawyers' Cooperative provide additional reference and indexing material as part of their total system of legal publications for lawyers.

Decisions of the federal Courts of Appeal are published in the *Federal Reporter*, and most federal District Court decisions are found in the *Federal Supplement*, both West Publishing series. All reported decisions of state courts are contained in West Publishing's National Reporter System, divided geographically into seven

---

[6] CBS v. FCC, 453 U.S. 367 (1981).

different regional series; the *Atlantic, Pacific, Southern, Southwestern, Southeastern, Northwestern* and *Northeastern*. To locate a particular judicial opinion, all you need to do is to follow the instructions provided by its citation. For example, to find the famous United Church of Christ v. FCC case, cited as 359 F.2d 994, that recognized the right of citizen groups to challenge the renewal of a broadcast license, you would open the 359th volume of the *Federal Reporter*, 2nd series, and turn to page 994 where the opinion begins.

If your university library doesn't have these legal publications among its holdings, they can all be found in the library of your nearest county courthouse. In addition, you should find a service called *Shepard's Citators* there that allows you, by using its various judicial indexing books, to discover whether any later decisions have had any effect upon those legal principles defined by that judicial opinion you've just been reading.

This brief survey of communication law research literature is not intended to do anything more than illustrate how simple the process of legal research can really be. There is no reason to provide a elaborate description of a wide variety of communication law research techniques here, because there are so many excellent books and studies already covering every aspect of this topic in great detail. For further guidance, any of the following books and articles are highly recommended:

1. Cohen, M.L. *How to Find the Law* St. Paul, Minn., West Publishing. (often updated with new editions)

2. Cohen, M.L. *Legal Research in a Nutshell* St. Paul, Minn., West Publishing, (frequently updated).

3. Foley, J.M. "Broadcast Regulation Research: A Primer for Non–Lawyers," *Journal of Broadcasting* 17/2 (Summer 1973) pp. 147–159.

4. Goehlert, R. *Congress and Law Making: Researching the Legislative Process* Santa Barbara, CA Clio Books, 1979.

5. Honigsburg, P.J. *Cluing Into Legal Research* Berkeley, CA Golden Rain Press, 1979.

6. Jacobstein J.M. and R. M. Mersky, *Fundamentals of Legal Research* Mineola, NY Foundation Press, 1992.

7. Le Duc, D.R. "Broadcast Legal Documentation: A Four–Dimensional Guide," *Journal of Broadcasting* 17/2 (Summer 1973) pp. 131–146.

8. Pauwels, C.K, in J.R. Bittner, *Broadcast Law and Regulation* Englewood Cliffs NJ Prentice Hall 1982 pp. 397–411.

9. Price, M.O. and H. Bittner, *Effective Legal Research* Boston Little Brown (1979).

Appendix D

BIBLIOGRAPHY

American Law Institute, Restatement of the Law: Torts. 2d ed. St. Paul, 1977.

Adler, Allan Robert, Litigation Under the Federal Open Government Act, 18th ed., Washington, D.C., 1993.

Adler, Renata, Reckless Disregard, New York, 1986.

Angoff, Charles, Handbook of Libel. New York, 1946.

Bagdikian, Ben, The Media Monopoly. Boston, 1993.

Baker, C. Edwin, Human Liberty & Freedom of Speech. New York, 1989.

Barnouw, Erik, A History of Broadcasting in the United States, 3 vols. (N.Y., 1966–1972).

Barron, Jerome, Freedom of the Press for Whom? Bloomington, Ind., 1973.

Berns, Walter, The First Amendment and the Future of American Democracy. New York, 1976.

Bezanson, Randall P., Gilbert Cranberg, and John Soloski, Libel Law and The Press: Myth and Reality, New York, 1987.

Black's Law Dictionary.

Blackstone, William, Commentaries on the Law of England, IV, adapted by Robert Malcom Kerr, Boston, 1952.

Blasi, Vincent, The Checking Value in First Amendment Theory, American Bar Foundation Research Journal, 1977, #3.

Bok, Sissela, Secrets. New York, 1983.

Brant, Irving, The Bill of Rights: Its Origin and Meaning. New York, 1965.

Brenner, Daniel L. and William L. Rivers, Free But Regulated: Conflicting Traditions in Media Law. Ames, Iowa, 1982.

Canavan, Francis, Freedom of Expression: Purpose as Limit. Durham, N.C., 1984.

Chafee, Zechariah, Jr., Free Speech in the United States. Boston, 1941.

_____, Government and Mass Communications, 2 vols. Chicago, 1947.

Churchill, Winston S., A History of the English–Speaking Peoples. New York, 1963.

Bittner, John R., Law and Regulation of Electronic Media (2nd ed.) New Jersey, 1994.

Chamberlin, Bill F., and Charlene Brown, The First Amendment Reconsidered. Chapel Hill, 1981.

Cline, Victor (ed.), Where Do You Draw the Line? Provo, UT, 1974.

Cooley, Thomas M., Constitutional Limitations. (8th ed.). Boston, 1927.

Cooper, Thomas, The Law of Libel and the Liberty of the Press. New York, 1830.

Cross, Harold L., The People's Right to Know. New York, 1953.

Denniston, Lyle, The Reporter and the Law. New York, 1980.

Devol, Kenneth S., Mass Media and the Supreme Court, 2d ed. New York, 1976.

Dienes, C. Thomas, Lee Levine, and Robert C. Lind, Newsgathering and the Law, Charlottesville, Virginia, 1997.

Duniway, Clyde A., The Development of Freedom of the Press in Massachusetts. Cambridge, 1906.

Emerson, Thomas I., The System of Freedom of Expression. New York, 1970.

Emery, Walter B., Broadcasting and Government: Responsibilities and Regulations. East Lansing, Mich., 1961.

Fueroghne, Dean K., Law & Advertising: Current Legal Issues for Agencies, Advertisers and Attorneys. Chicago, 1995.

Folkerts, Jean and Dwight L. Teeter, Voices of a Nation: A History of the Mass Media in the United States, 3rd ed., New York, 1998.

Fox, Sir John C., The History of Contempt of Court. Oxford, 1927.

Friendly, Fred, Minnesota Rag. New York, 1981.

Gellhorn, Walter, Security, Loyalty, and Science. Ithca, New York, 1950.

Gerald, J. Edward, The Press and the Constitution, 1931–1947. Minneapolis, 1948.

Gillmor, Donald M., Free Press and Fair Trial. Washington, D.C., 1966.

Goldfarb, Ronald L., The Contempt Power. New York, 1963.

Goodale, James, C., chairman, Communications Law 1996, 3 vols. New York, 1984.

Goodman, Mark, Law of the Student Press (2nd ed.) Washington, D.C., SPLC, 1994.

Gora, Joel M., The Rights of Reporters. New York, 1974.

Griswold, Erwin, The First Amendment Today. Cambridge, 1955.

Hachten, William A., The Supreme Court on Freedom of the Press: Decisions and Dissents. Ames, Iowa, 1968.

Haight, Anne Lyon, Banned Books (rev. 2d ed.). New York, 1955.

Hallin, Daniel C., "The Uncensored War:" The Media and Vietnam. Berkeley, 1986.

Havick, John J., Communications Policy and the Political Process. Westport, Conn., 1983.

Head, Sydney W. and Christopher Sterling, Broadcasting in America. (5th ed.). Boston, 1987.

Hentoff, Nat, History of Freedom of the Press in America. New York, 1980.

Hocking, William E., Freedom of the Press. Chicago, 1947.

Holmes, Oliver Wendell Jr., The Common Law. Boston, 1881.

Hopkins, W. Wat, Mr. Justice Brennan and Freedom of Expression. New York, 1991.

Hurst, James Willard, Law and Conditions of Freedom. New York, 1962.

Jolliffe, John, The Constitutional History of Medieval England (2d ed.). London, 1947.

Jones, William, Cases and Materials on Electronic Mass Media. Mineola, N.Y., 1977.

Kahn, F.J., ed., Documents of American Broadcasting, 4th ed. New York, 1984.

Katz, Stanley Nider, A Brief Narrative of the Case and Trial of John Peter Zenger. Cambridge, Mass., 1963,

Kaufman, Henry R., ed., LDRC 50–State Survey 1984, III. New York, 1984.

Kinsley, Philip, Liberty and the Press. Chicago, 1944.

Konvitz, Milton R., First Amendment Freedoms. Ithaca, 1963.

Le Duc, Don R., Beyond Broadcasting: Patterns in Policy and Law. (New York, 1987).

Levin, Harvey J., Fact and Fancy in Television Regulation. New York, 1980.

Levy, Leonard W., Emergence of a Free Press. New York, 1985.

————, ed., Freedom of the Press from Zenger to Jefferson. Indianapolis, 1966.

————, Legacy of Suppression: Freedom of Speech and Press in Early American History. Cambridge, 1960.

Lewis, Anthony, Make No Law: The Sullivan Case and the First Amendment. New York, 1991.

Lockhart, William B., and Robert C. McClure, Censorship of Obscenity: the Developing Constitutional Standards, 45 Minnesota Law Review 5 (Nov. 1960).

————, Literature, the Law of Obscenity, and the Constitution, 38 Minnesota Law Review (March 1954).

Lofton, John, The Press as a Defender of the First Amendment. Columbia, S.C., 1980.

Main, Jackson Turner, The Antifederalists: Critics of the Constitution. Chapel Hill, 1961.

McCormick, Robert R., The Freedom of the Press. New York, 1936.

Meiklejohn, Alexander, Free Speech and Its Relation to Self Government. New York, 1948.

Miller, Arthur, The Assault on Privacy. Ann Arbor, 1971.

Miller, Charles, The Supreme Court and the Uses of History. Cambridge, Mass., 1969.

Murphy, Paul, World War I and the Origins of Civil Liberties in the United States. New York, 1979.

Nelson, Harold L., ed., Freedom of the Press from Hamilton to the Warren Court. Indianapolis, 1967.

Nimmer, Melville B., Nimmer on Copyright, 4 vols. New York, 1963–1988.

Nye, Russel Blaine, Fettered Freedom. East Lansing, Mich., 1951.

Odgers, W. Blake, A Digest of the Law of Libel and Slander (6th ed.). London, 1929.

Owen, Bruce M., Economics and Freedom of Expression. Cambridge, 1975.

Parsons, Patrick, Cable Television and the First Amendment. Lexington, MA, 1987.

Paterson, James, Liberty of Press, Speech and Public Worship. London, 1880.

Patterson, Giles J., Free Speech and a Free Press. Boston, 1939.

Paul, James C.N., and Murray L. Schwartz, Federal Censorship: Obscenity in the Mail. New York, 1961.

Pember, Don R., Privacy and the Press. Seattle, 1972.

Peterson, H.C., and Gilbert C. Fite, Opponents of War, 1917–1918. Madison, 1957.

Phelps, Robert H. and E. Douglas Hamilton, Libel: Rights, Risks, Responsibilities. New York, 1966.

Pilpel, Harriet, and Theodora Zavin, Rights and Writers. New York, 1960.

Plucknett, Theodore F.T., A Concise History of the Common Law. London, 1948.

Pool, Ithiel de Sola, Technologies of Freedom. Cambridge, Mass., 1983.

Powe, Lucas A., Jr., American Broadcasting and the First Amendment, Berkeley, 1987.

————, The Fourth Estate and the Constitution. Berkeley, 1991.

Preston, Ivan, The Tangled Web They Weave: Truth, Falsity and Advertisers. Madison, 1994.

Preston, William, Jr., Aliens and Dissenters. Cambridge, 1963.

Prosser, William L., The Law of Torts. 4th ed. St. Paul, 1971.

Rosden, George Eric and Peter Eric, The Law of Advertising, 4 vols. (New York, 1963—present).

Rosenberg, Norman L., Protecting the Best Men: An Interpretive History of Libel, Chapel Hill, 1986.

Rourke, Francis E., Secrecy and Publicity. Baltimore, 1961.

Sack, Robert D., and Sandra S. Baron, Libel, Slander, and Related Problems, 2nd ed. New York, 1994.

Sanford, Bruce, The Law of Libel and the Right of Privacy. New York, 1984.

Schmidt, Benno C., Jr., Freedom of the Press vs. Public Access. New York, 1976.

Schlesinger, Arthur M., Prelude to Independence: The Newspaper War on Britain, 1763–1776. New York, 1958.

Seldes, George, Freedom of the Press. Cleveland, 1935.

Shapiro, Martin, Freedom of Speech: The Supreme Court and Judicial Review. Englewood Cliffs, N.J., 1966.

Siebert, Fredrick S., Freedom of the Press in England, 1476–1776. Urbana, 1952.

Simmons, Steven J., The Fairness Doctrine and the Media. Berkeley, 1978.

Simon, Morton J., Public Relations Law. New York, 1969.

Smith, James Morton, Freedom's Fetters: the Alien and Sedition Laws and American Civil Liberties. Ithaca, 1956.

Smolla, Rodney, Jerry Falwell v. Larry Flynt. Urbana, 1988.

————, Law of Defamation.

————, Suing the Press. New York, 1986.

Stansbury, Arthur J., Report of the Trial of James H. Peck. Boston, 1833.

Starkie, Thomas, The Law of Slander, Libel, Scandalum Magnatum and False Rumors, with the Practise and Pleadings. London, 1813; 4th ed. by Henry C. Folkard, with notes and references to American Cases by Horace G. Wood. New York, 1877.

Sterling, Christopher, and John Michael Kittross, Stay Tuned: An Informal History of American Broadcasting. Belmont, CA, 1978.

Sullivan, Harold W., Contempts by Publication. New Haven, 1940.

————, Trial by Newspaper. Hyannis, Mass., 1961.

Warren, Samuel D., and Louis D. Brandeis, The Right to Privacy, 4 Harvard Law Review 193 (1890).

Westin, Alan, Privacy and Freedom. New York, 1967.

Winfield, Richard N., New York Times v. Sullivan, the Next Twenty Years (New York, Practising Law Institute, 1984).

Wolff, Robert Paul, Barrington Moore and Herbert Marcuse, A Critique of Pure Tolerance. Boston, 1965.

Wortman, Tunis, Treatise Concerning Political Enquiry, and the Liberty of the Press. New York, 1800.

Yudof, Mark G., When Government Speaks. Berkeley, 1983.

Additional Resources

American Digest System, Decennial Digests, valuable for lists of cases and points adjudicated.

American Jurisprudence, a legal encyclopedia.

Annotated Report System, selected reports and annotations, with summaries of arguments of counsel.

Compilations of Laws Affecting Publications, particularly those put out by various states. Consult managers of various state press associations.

Corpus Juris Secundum, a legal encyclopedia.

Freedom of Information Center, University of Missouri, issues frequent Reports, the FOI Digest (bi-monthly newsletter), and occasional studies covering a wide variety of media-and-law-subjects. Invaluable for state laws on meetings and records.

Law Dictionaries, including Black's, Ballentine's, and Bouvier's.

Law Reviews. Among the outstanding law reviews published under the direction of law schools are Columbia Law Review, Cornell Law Quarterly, Harvard Law Review, Illinois Law Review, Michigan Law Review, Texas Law Review, Wisconsin Law Review, and Yale Law Journal.

Libel Defense Resource Center, LDRC 50–State Survey 1996–97: Media Libel Law (New York, 1996) *and* LDRC 50–State Survey 1996–97: Media Libel Law (New York, 1996).

Media Law Reporter. Bureau of National Affairs, Inc., Washington, D.C. This looseleaf service provides up-to-date coverage of court decisions (full texts) and news notes in communication law, beginning in 1976.

National Reporter System, giving texts of appellate court decisions in various jurisdictions of the nation.

News Media and the Law, publication of the Reporters Committee for Freedom of the Press (formerly Press Censorship Newsletter). Washington, D.C.

WestLaw, a computerized search and reference service.

Words and Phrases, a legal encyclopedia based on definitions of terms as used in statutes and by the courts.

Appendix E

THE SOCIETY OF PROFESSIONAL JOURNALISTS AND ASNE CODES OF ETHICS

THE SOCIETY OF PROFESSIONAL JOURNALISTS CODE OF ETHICS

Preamble

Members of the Society of Professional Journalists believe that public enlightenment is the forerunner of justice and the foundation of democracy. The duty of the journalist is to further those ends by seeking truth and providing a fair and comprehensive account of events and issues. Conscientious journalists from all media and specialties strive to serve the public with thoroughness and honesty. Professional integrity is the cornerstone of a journalist's credibility.

Member of the Society share a dedication to ethical behavior and adopt this code to declare the Society's principles and standards of practice.

SEEK TRUTH AND REPORT IT

Journalists should be honest, fair and courageous in gathering, reporting and interpreting information.

Journalists should:

> Test the accuracy of information from all sources and exercise care to avoid inadvertent error. Deliberate distortion is never permissible.

> Diligently seek out subjects of news stories to give them the opportunity to respond to allegations of wrongdoing.

> Identify sources whenever feasible. The public is entitled to as much information as possible on sources' reliability.

> Always question sources' motives before promising anonymity. Clarify conditions attached to any promise made in exchange for information. Keep promises.

> Make certain that headlines, news teases, and promotional material, photos, video, audio, graphics sound bites and quotations do not misrepresent. They should not oversimplify or highlight incidents out of context.

864

> Never distort the content of news photos or video. Image enhancement for technical clarity is always permissible. Label montages and photo-illustrations.

> Avoid misleading re-enactments or staged news events. If reenactment is necessary to tell a story, label it.

> Avoid undercover or other surreptitious methods of gathering information except when traditional open methods will not yield information vital to the public. Use of such methods should be explained as part of the story.

> Never plagiarize.

> Tell the story of the diversity and magnitude of the human experience boldly, even when it is unpopular to do so.

> Examine their own cultural values and avoid imposing those values on others.

> Avoid stereotyping by race, gender, age, religion, ethnicity, geography, sexual orientation, disability, physical appearance or social status.

> Support the open exchange of views, even views they find repugnant.

> Give voice to the voiceless; official and unofficial sources of information can be equally valid.

> Distinguish between advocacy and news reporting. Analysis and commentary should be labeled and not misrepresent fact or context.

> Distinguish news from advertising and shun hybrids that blur the lines between the two.

> Recognize a special obligation to ensure that the public's business is conducted in the open and that government records are open to inspection.

MINIMIZE HARM

Ethical journalists treat sources, subjects and colleagues as human beings deserving of respect.

Journalists should:

> Show compassion for those who may be adversely affected by news coverage. Use special sensitivity when dealing with children or inexperience sources or subjects.

> Be sensitive when seeking or using interviews or photographs of those affected by tragedy or grief.

> Recognize that gathering and reporting information may cause harm or discomfort. Pursuit of the news is not a license for arrogance.

> Recognize that private people have a greater right to control information about themselves than do public officials and others who seek power, influence or attention. Only an overriding public need can justify intrusion into anyone's privacy.

> Show good taste. Avoid pandering to lurid curiosity.

> Be cautious about identifying juveniles or victims of sex crimes.

> Be judicious about naming criminal suspects before the formal filing of charges.

> Balance a criminal suspects fair trial rights with the public's right to be informed.

ACT INDEPENDENTLY

Journalists should be free of obligation to any interest other than the public's right to know.

Journalists should:

> Avoid conflicts of interest, real or perceived.

> Remain free of associations and activities that may compromise integrity or damage credibility.

> Refuse gifts, favors, fees, free travel and special treatment, and shun secondary employment, political involvement, public office, and service in community organizations if they compromise journalistic integrity.

> Disclose unavoidable conflicts.

> Be vigilant and courageous about holding those with power accountable.

> Deny favored treatment to advertisers and special interests and resist their efforts to influence news coverage.

> Be wary of sources offering information for favors or money; avoid bidding for news.

BE ACCOUNTABLE

Journalists are accountable to their readers, listeners, viewers and each other.

Journalists should:

> Clarify and explain news coverage and invite dialogue with the public over journalistic conduct.

> Encourage the public to voice grievances against the news media.

> Admit mistakes and correct them promptly.

> Expose unethical practices of journalists and the news media.

> Abide by the same high standards to which they hold others.

ETHICS HOTLINE

Struggling with a dilemma or just want to talk about a tough call you had to make? Call SPJ's Ethics Hotline at (317) 653–2070 ext. 208. The hotline is monitored daily by members of the national Ethics Committee.

ASNE STATEMENT OF PRINCIPLES

PREAMBLE

The First Amendment, protecting freedom of expression from abridgment by any law, guarantees to the people through their press a constitutional right, and thereby places on newspaper people a particular responsibility.

Thus journalism demands of its practitioners not only industry and knowledge but also the pursuit of a standard of integrity proportionate to the journalist's singular obligation.

To this end the American Society of Newspaper Editors sets forth this Statement of Principles as a standard encouraging the highest ethical and professional performance.

ARTICLE I: RESPONSIBILITY

The primary purpose of gathering and distributing news and opinion is to serve the general welfare by informing the people and enabling them to make judgments on the issues of the time. Newspapermen and women who abuse the power of their professional role for selfish motives or unworthy purposes are faithless to that public trust.

The American press was made free not just to inform or just to serve as a forum for debate but also to bring an independent scrutiny to bear on the forces of power in the society, including the conduct of official power at all levels of government.

ARTICLE II: FREEDOM OF THE PRESS

Freedom of the press belongs to the people. It must be defended against encroachment or assault from any quarter, public or private.

Journalists must be constantly alert to see that the public's business is conducted in public. They must be vigilant against all who would exploit the press for selfish purposes.

ARTICLE III: INDEPENDENCE

Journalists must avoid impropriety and the appearance of impropriety as well as any conflict of interest or the appearance of conflict. They should neither accept anything nor pursue any activity that might compromise or seem to compromise their integrity.

ARTICLE IV: TRUTH AND ACCURACY

Good faith with the reader is the foundation of good journalism. Every effort must be made to assure that the news content is accurate, free from bias and in context, and that all sides are presented fairly. Editorials, analytical articles and commentary should be held to the same standards of accuracy with respect to facts as news reports.

Significant errors of fact, as well as errors of omission, should be corrected promptly and prominently.

ARTICLE V: IMPARTIALITY

To be impartial does not require the press to be unquestioning or to refrain from editorial expression. Sound practice, however, demands a clear distinction for the reader between news reports and opinion. Articles that contain opinion or personal interpretation should be clearly identified.

ARTICLE VI: FAIR PLAY

Journalists should respect the rights of people involved in the news, observe the common standards of decency and stand accountable to the public for the fairness and accuracy of their news reports.

Persons publicly accused should be given the earliest opportunity to respond.

Pledges of confidentiality to news sources must be honored at all costs, and therefore should not be given lightly. Unless there is clear and pressing need to maintain confidences, sources of information should be identified.

These principles are intended to preserve, protect and strengthen the bond of trust and respect between American journalists and the American people, a bond that is essential to sustain the grant of freedom entrusted to both by the nation's founders.

Originally adopted in 1922 by the ASNE as the Canons of Journalism, it was revised and renamed the Statement of Principles in October, 1975.

TABLE OF CASES

INDEX

References are to Pages

1–56662–602–1

90000

9 781566 626026